Nineteenth-Century Literature Criticism

Guide to Gale Literary Criticism Series

For criticism on	Consult these Gale series
Authors now living or who died after December 31, 1959	*CONTEMPORARY LITERARY CRITICISM (CLC)*
Authors who died between 1900 and 1959	*TWENTIETH-CENTURY LITERARY CRITICISM (TCLC)*
Authors who died between 1800 and 1899	*NINETEENTH-CENTURY LITERATURE CRITICISM (NCLC)*
Authors who died between 1400 and 1799	*LITERATURE CRITICISM FROM 1400 TO 1800 (LC)* *SHAKESPEAREAN CRITICISM (SC)*
Authors who died before 1400	*CLASSICAL AND MEDIEVAL LITERATURE CRITICISM (CMLC)*
Authors of books for children and young adults	*CHILDREN'S LITERATURE REVIEW (CLR)*
Dramatists	*DRAMA CRITICISM (DC)*
Poets	*POETRY CRITICISM (PC)*
Short story writers	*SHORT STORY CRITICISM (SSC)*
Black writers of the past two hundred years	*BLACK LITERATURE CRITICISM (BLC)*
Hispanic writers of the late nineteenth and twentieth centuries	*HISPANIC LITERATURE CRITICISM (HLC)*
Native North American writers and orators of the eighteenth, nineteenth, and twentieth centuries	*NATIVE NORTH AMERICAN LITERATURE (NNAL)*
Major authors from the Renaissance to the present	*WORLD LITERATURE CRITICISM, 1500 TO THE PRESENT (WLC)*

Rosalía de Castro

1837-1885

Spanish poet and novelist. For additional information on Castro's life and career, see *NCLC,* Volume 3.

INTRODUCTION

Castro is counted among the outstanding Spanish poets of the nineteenth century. She composed verse chiefly in the vernacular of her native Galicia (a dialect similar to Portuguese) and incorporated the folk themes, political ideology, and longings of the Galician people into her poetry. To these she added her own deep nostalgia, love of nature, and pervasive melancholy. Her poetry, while simple in form, is mystical, religious, and highly symbolic in content. As an examination of the human soul it offers universality, despite its regional concerns. As for her prose fiction, Castro wrote five novels and a few shorter works in Castilian, which have only in the latter half of the twentieth century been considered for their merit as social criticism. Overall, contemporary reassessment of Castro's works has shown her to be a major figure in Spanish letters, influential as a versifier and as a progenitor of the Galician cultural renaissance in nineteenth-century Spain.

Biographical Information

Born on 25 February, 1837, in the Galician town of Santiago de Compostela, Castro was the illegitimate daughter of a Spanish noblewoman, Teresa Castro, and a priest, José Martínez Viojo. Raised by her aunt until Castro reached age eleven, she received her education at the Liceo de San Agustín and Sociedad Económica de los Amigos del País in Santiago, where she was educated in languages and the arts. Demonstrating an early talent in music, art, and writing, Castro composed her first poem at the age of twelve. Castro's early life was characterized by deepening sadness, thought by some critics to have been brought on by her illegitimacy, which forced her separation from her mother. In 1856 she moved to Madrid, where her involvement in literary circles led to the publication of her first small book of poems, *La flor* (1857). The following year, she married Manuel Martinez Murguía, a historian and champion of the Galician literary renaissance. Although their marriage was troubled by financial difficulties, ill health, and the deaths of two of their seven children, Marguía's encouragement prompted Castro to publish *Cantares gallegos* (1863; *Galician Songs*), the verses that brought her first acclaim as a poet. In the years that followed, Castro produced another collection of Galician poems, *Follas novas* (1880; *New Leaves*), and

a series of controversial novels. It was not until the publication of *En las orillas del Sar* (1884; *Beside the River Sar*), however, that Castro won national attention as a poet. She died of cancer on 15 July, 1885 in Padrón, Galicia.

Major Works

Castro's first collection of verse, *La flor,* contains conventional love poetry, and is thought by critics to be of little consequence. *A mi madre* (1863) is, like *La flor,* a small book of Castilian poems. Its title piece, written in response to the death of Castro's mother, celebrates a woman's sacrifices for her daughter. In the larger *Cantares gallegos* Castro employed the language of the Galician peasantry for the first time to evoke the traditions and people of her homeland. Among its subjects are the cultural beliefs of Galicia, the natural beauty of its countryside, and the struggles of its poor. The unadorned Galician verses of *Follas novas* continue in the vein of *Cantares gallegos* by portraying Castro's passion for Galicia and her defense of its people and way of life. Castro's final collection of poetry, *En las orillas del Sar,* offers a somewhat darker tone than her previous works and a return to the Castilian dialect. It includes a variety of political verses in support of Galician culture, as well as poems suffused with a deep sense of loneliness and the desolation of love. Castro's five novels—*La hija del mar* (1859), *Flavio* (1861), *Ruinas* (1866), *El caballero de las botas azules* (1867), and *El primer loco* (1881)—contain elements of romantic fantasy blended with social criticism and Castro's incipient feminism. Each is generally focused on the struggles of women in paternalistic society. Having never known her parents, Esperanza, the persecuted heroine of *La hija del mar,* ends her desperate life by casting herself into the ocean. In *El caballero de las botas azules,* Castro presents a satire of the dominant literature of Spain and explores its degrading effects on women.

Critical Reception

Due in large part to perceptions of her as a regionalist poet, Castro failed to achieve substantial literary esteem for most of her lifetime. An ongoing critical reassessment of her work begun in the twentieth century, however, has demonstrated the enduring significance of Castro's poetry and, to a lesser degree, opened her prose works to serious critical consideration. Scholars have since acknowledged that while her contemporaries adhered to a rigid poetic structure in their works, Castro sought a fluid metrical style. Her simple, musical prosody, emotional themes, and natural symbols and motifs have been seen as influences on the writing of such modern poets as Rubén Dario, Amado Nervo, and Federico García Lorca. Additionally, the publication of Castro's *Cantares gallegos* in 1863 is now thought to mark the inauguration of the Galician literary revival in Spain. Most recently, scholars have begun to look beyond the ostensible regionalism of Castro's works and her marginalization as a female writer, to acclaim the universal import of her poetic achievements. Summarizing this view of Castro, Gerald Brenan has stated: "Had she written in Castilian rather than in her native Galician dialect, she would, I feel sure, be recognized as the greatest woman poet of modern times."

PRINCIPAL WORKS

La flor (poetry) 1857
La hija del mar (novel) 1859
Flavio (novel) 1861
A mi madre (poetry) 1863
Cantares gallegos [*Galician Songs*] (poetry) 1863
Ruinas (novel) 1866

El caballero de las botas azules (novel) 1867
Follas novas [*New Leaves*] (poetry) 1880
El primer loco (novel) 1881
En las orillas del Sar [*Beside the River Sar*] (poetry) 1884
Obras completas (poetry, novels, and prose) 1952
Poems: Rosalía de Castro (poetry) 1964

CRITICISM

Kathleen K. Kulp (essay date 1968)

SOURCE: "Reality and the Poet," in *Manner and Mood in Rosalía de Castro: A Study of Themes and Style,* Ediciones José Porrúa Turanzas, 1968, pp. 63-132.

[*In the following excerpt, Kulp considers style, technique, and theme in Castro's* Follas novas, *comparing this collection of Galician poetry with an earlier work,* Cantares gallegos.]

FOLLAS NOVAS

Everyday reality and popular tradition

Some of the touches of realism which characterize **Cantares** are continued in **Follas novas,** but in the second book Rosalía tends to concentrate on the more tragic manifestations of life around her. A few poems are filled with realistic details and local color and employ colloquial expressions: **"Vamos bebendo"** (p. 460) [All page citations are taken from Rosalía de Castro, *Obras completas.*], **"Miña casiña"** (pp. 501-03), **"Soberba"** (pp. 503-04), **"Xan"** (pp. 512-13), **"Tanto e tanto nos odiamos"** (pp. 519-22), and others. A note of humor is sometimes discernible, but it is always diluted with irony, manifesting a keen observation of human nature which is comical in its pathos. The comic always borders very closely on the tragic. The long narrative poem "¡ **A probiña qu'está xorda . . . !**" (pp. 504-12) is one of the most extensive, animated and colorful of Rosalía's production, Nevertheless it contains a strong tone of sobriety. The courageous and clever old woman (sister to the loquacious *vella* in **Cantares,** III), is nonetheless a pathetic figure as she wanders through the night. The gaiety of the feast and the musicians, the generosity of the wealthy hostess, and the brief warmth of the fire do not alter the fact that there is poverty in the midst of plenty and that, after one night of food and warmth, the old woman will once more wander through the night, precariously maintaining the breath of life and the spark of human dignity[12].

The supernatural beings and superstitious beliefs of the people also appear as motifs in **Follas.** The poem **"Soberba"** re-enacts the fear of simple folk during a storm, which penetrates them with a sort of atavistic guilt and the fear of divine punishment. There is not, however, the same conviction in the use of these motifs as in **Cantares.** The poet's own attitude asserts itself and she reveals in various places the real significance of the folk symbols in her work. They do not have a literal significance, as they have for the people, but become symbols for abstract concepts in the more rational mind of the poet. The dramatic narration of tragic love, "N'hay peor meiga que un-ha gran pena" (pp. 455-59) implies that the mysterious wasting away of Marianiña, attributed by her mother to the malevolent power of a *meiga,* is the result of emotional and psychological causes. An explicit statement of the use of mythological motifs appears in the poem "**Xigantescos olmos**" (pp. 462-63), which creates a mysterious and somber mood through the description of the dark forest where "a nai de toda-las meigas" lives, who represents to Rosalía a kind of fictitious scapegoat:

> *Y estes mals que nos afrixen*
> *din que todos veñen d'ela;*
> *¡mais socede n'esta vida*
> *que os que tên culpa n'a levan!*

> (p. 463).

The enchantment which one feels in his own land is personified by the fantastic creatures with which the collective imagination has populated nature:

> *¡Hay n'as ribeiras verdes, hay n'as risoñas*
> *prayas*
> *e n'os penedos ásperos d'o noso inmenso*
> *mar,*
> *fadas d'extraño nome, d'encantos non sabidos*
> *que sô con nós comparten seu prácido folgar!*

> *Hay antr'a sombr'amante d'as nosas*
> *carbelleiras;*
> *e d'as curtiñas frescas no vívido esprendor,*
> *e n'ô romor d'as fontes espritos cariñosos*
> *que sô ôs qu'aquí naceron lles dan falas*
> *d'amor*

> (pp. 500-01).

Color

While **Cantares** is a book of vivid visual impressions where the colors of nature and of peasant dress sparkle in its pages, the palette of **Follas** is less rich. Colors tend to be diluted, barely suggested, and objects are seen in tones of light and dark. Color, so important in the outer world, does not belong to the shadowy realm of the soul. Sometimes the objects themselves seem to be neutral, and the changing play of light and shadow passes over them:

> *Tal com'as nubes*
> *que lleva ò vento,*
> *y agora asombran, y agora alegran*
> *os espaços inmensos d'o ceo,*
> *así as ideas*
> *loucas qu'eu teño,*
> *as imaxes de múltiples formas*
> *d'extrañas feituras, de cores incertos,*
> *agora asombran,*
> *agora acraran,*
> *o fondo sin fondo d'o meu pensamento*

> (pp. 421-22).

Darkness is an indication of the prevailing doubt and mystery of the poetry of **Follas:**

> *Y-a péndola no-máis xorda batento*
> *cal bate un corazón qu'hinchan as penas,*
> *resóa pavorosa*
> *n'a escuridade espesa.*
> *En vano a vista con temor n'o escuro*
> *sin parada vaguea.*
> *Uns tras d'outros istantes silenciosos*
> *pasando van, e silenciosos chegan*
> *outros detrás, n'a eternidá caendo*
> *cal cai ò grau n'a moedora pedra,*
> *sin qu'ò porvir velado ôs mortais ollos*
> *rompan as pesadas brétemas*

> (p. 446).

Interiors are much more prevalent in **Follas** than in **Cantares** reflecting the movement from exterior to interior worlds. This mysterious inner world is often represented by the Cathedral, which is a world full of illusions and hallucinations, apart from the harsh light of reality:

> *Mais xa n'os vidros d'a grand'araña*
> *cai ò postreiro*
> *rayo tranquilo qu'ò sol d'a tarde*
> *pousa sereno;*
> *e en cada prancha d'a araña hermosa*
> *vivos refrexos,*
> *cintileando com'as estrelas,*
> *pintan mil cores no chan caendo,*
> *e fan qu'a tola d'a fantesía,*
> *soñe milagres, finxa portentos.*
> *Mais de repente veñen as sombras,*
> *tod'é negrura, tod'é misterio,*
> *adiós alxofres, e maravillas . . .*
> *Tras d'o Pedreso púxese Febo*

> (pp. 433-34).

The poet is nonetheless aware of the colors of the external world, but she excludes them from the shadowy inner regions of the soul:

N'ò ceo, azul crarísimo;
n'ò chan; verdor intenso;
n'ò fondo d'a alma miña
todo sombriso e negro

(p. 444).

The colors of the outer world fade or darken in consonance with her mood:

¡Qué bonitas eran
n'outro tempo as rosas
que n'aqueles campos
medran e s'esfollan!
Mais muchas estonces
s'amostraban todas.
Y ò sol cal á lúa
en noite de brétema,
brilaba tembrando
por antr'as vimbieiras,
tan descolorido
com'a mesma cera
   Y ò ferir as ondas
revoltas e oscuras,
víanse n'ò espeso
d'a negra fondura
as herbas marinas
e longas que a surcan

(pp. 551-52).

Colors, when they do occur, are soft, vague, barely suggested: "lua descolorida", "transparentes cores", "un máis ou menos azul", "cores de brilo soave, de transparencia húmida,/de vaguedad'incerta . . ." (p. 501).

Sinesthesia

Sinesthesia, so much a part of the poetic language of the twentieth century, is not a main feature of Rosalía's poetry, but certain of her characteristic images cross the boundaries of the senses and apply qualities from one sensory realm to that of another. These instances are not so daring as those to appear in later poets, but indicate another direction which Rosalía takes to characterize the intangible subjects with which she deals. In speaking of her poetry, words, ideas, sound and light all fuse;

Diredes d'estos versos, y é verdade,
que tên extraña insólita armonía,
que n'eles as ideas brilan pálidas
   cal errantes múxicas
     qu'estalan por istantes
que desparecen xiña . . .

(p. 422).

Black and white are often applied to ideas and sentiments and represent corresponding spiritual values: "brancas

ilusiós", "negra melancolía", "negra tentazón", "negro olvido", "negro desengaño".

Sound

The world of sound has also become more muted in **Follas novas.** Direct imitation of sounds with onomatopoeic words occurs in the more realistic pieces, which continue the tendency of **Cantares.** "*A probiña qu'está xorda . . .*" is a vividly dramatized sketch full of visual and auditory effects:

"¡Viv'a cega! ¡Viv'o cego! . . ."
De cand'en cando lle berran,
y-el di, berrando máis forte:
"¡Vivan eles! . . . ¡Vivan elas! . . .
Y a máis bonita de todas
que veña a darm'un-ha prenda."
"¡Ju-ju-ru-ju!" Y aturuxa
hastra ensordecel-as pedras,
y a cega dall ô pandeiro
y ò cego toca n'as tecras
y ô compás d'o "zongue, zongue",
de novo bailan as nenas . . .

(p. 508).

The tendency more prevalent in **Follas,** however, is that of harkening to an interior music, whose echoes are faint and indistinct. These sounds can only be suggested, leaving the reader the task of perceiving them with his mind's ear. Rosalía has said of the poetry of **Follas** that it has an "extraña insólita armonía" as opposed to the lilting, audible music of **Cantares:**

Diredes d'estos versos, y é verdade,
que tên extraña insólita armonía,
que n'eles as ideas brilan pálidas
   cal errantes múxicas
     qu'estalan por istantes
      que desparecen xiña,
que s'asomellan â parruma incerta
que voltexa n'ò fondo d'as curtiñas,
y ò susurro monótono d'os pinos
   d'a veira-mar bravía.

Eu direivos tan sô qu'os meus cantares
así sân en confuso d'alma miña,
como sai d'as profundas carballeiras,
   ô comezar d'o día,
     romor que non se sabe
     s'é rebuldar d'as brisas,
     si son beixos d'as frores,
s'agrestes, misteriosas armonías
     que n'este mundo triste
o camiño d'o ceu buscan perdidas

(p. 422).

The effect of sounds often arises from the language itself, so rich in words suggesting the sound they represent:

> *Y ô fin soya quedéi, pero tan soya,*
> *qu'oyo d'a mosca ò inquieto revoar,*
> *d'o ratiño o roer terco e costante*
> *e d'o lume ò "chis chas",*
> *cando d'a verde ponla*
> *o fresco zugo devorando vai . . .*
>
> (p. 427).

> *¡Tas-tis!, ¡Tas-tis!, n'a silenciosa noite*
> *con siniestro compás repite a péndola . . .*
>
> (p. 445).

The alliteration of *s* in the poem **"N'a catredal"** gives the effect of whispered prayers; and the [k] sound echoes the clash of the organ and the dissonant notes of the chorus:

> *Com'algún día pól-os corrunchos*
> *d'o vasto tempro*
> *vellos e vellas, mentras monean*
> *silban as salves y os padrenuestros,*
> *y os arcebispos n'os seus sepulcros*
> *reises y reinas con gran sosego*
> *n'a paz d'os mármores tranquilos dormen*
> *mentras n'ò coro cantan os cregos.*
> *O órgano lanza tristes cramores*
> *os d'as campanas responden lexos,*
> *y a santa imaxen d'o Redentore*
> *parés que suda sangre n'ò Huerto*
>
> (p. 432).

As in **Cantares,** music and bells have a magic power of enchantment. They are a stimulus for recollection or a means of communication with the unseen powers of nature and with those of her own soul:

> *D'a catredal campana*
> *grave, triste'e sonora,*
> *cand'ô rayar d'o día*
> *o toque d'alba tocas,*
> *n'ò espaço silencioso*
> *soando malencólica,*
> *as tus bataladas*
> *non sei qué despertares me recordan*
>
> (p. 440).

> *De tempos remotos,*
> *d'edades leixanas,*
> *de noites sereas,*
> *pra sempre acabadas,*
> *aquel cantar tróuxome*
> *non sei qué lembranzas,*

> *non mortas . . . , dormentas,*
> *¡quén sab'en qué campas!*
>
> (p. 493).

In her perception of sounds and constant recourse to musical terms to express sensations and sentiments, Rosalía approaches the symbolists. Music and familiar sounds make up an intangible but affective presence which belongs to other worlds and to other times and can recreate them in the present. They suggest the non-material, the spiritual values which cannot be described or stated, and serve as a language without words, heard only by the soul. Even in descriptive passages, sound always makes up a part of the background and the voices of man and nature are a part of every scene:

> *Sô se sinte ò piar d'o paxariño,*
> *o marmurar d'as auguas,*
> *en n'a cima d'o monte ô cantar triste*
> *d'un-ha muller que pasa,*
> *mentras c'o seu marmurio ò manso rego*
> *n'aquel ritmo monótono á acompaña*
>
> (p. 557).

Silence

Silence plays a much more important part in **Follas.** Silence is indicative of the infinite mystery, of the profound inner world of the poet, or of the void of nothingness which surrounds her. When the emotion or the mystery cannot be expressed, even by the vaguest and most provocative suggestion, the poet stands speechless in the face of the ineffable. Silence is the only adequate means to indicate the inexpressible intensity of her feeling. In this she is similar to another introspective poet, Antonio Machado, to whom Rosalía is often compared: "Rosalía y Machado son poetas insinuantes, de *auténticos silencios*"[13]. The shades of the dead or the images of the past which she sees in her mind are silent:

> *Un a un desfilaron silenciosos*
> *por aquí, por alá,*
> *tal como cando as contas d'un rosario*
> *s'espallan pol-o chán:*
> *y ò romor d'os seus pasos, mentras s'iñán*
> *de tal modo hastra min veu resoar,*
> *que non máis tristemente*
> *resoará quisáis*
> *n'fondo d'os sepulcros*
> *ò último adiós qu'un vivo ôs mortos dá*
>
> (p. 427).

The passage of time is silent:

> *¡Tas-tis!, ¡Tas-tis!, n'a silenciosa noite*
> *con siniestro compás repite a péndola, . . .*

. . . . .

Y-a péndola no-máis xorda batendo
cal bate un corazón qu'hinchan as penas,
resóa pavorosa
n'a escuridade espesa.
En vano a vista con temor n'o escuro
sin parada vaguea.
Uns tras d'outros istantes silenciosos
pasando van, e silenciosos chegan
outros detrás, n'a eternidá caendo
cal cai ò grau n'a moedora pedra,
sin qu'ò porvir velado ôs mortais ollos
rompan as pesadas brétemas.
¡Qué triste é a noite, y-o relox qué triste,
s'inquieto ò corpo y-a concencia velan!

(pp. 445-46).

Death and the dead are silent;

Todo é silencio mudo,
soidá, pavor,
ond'outro tempo a dicha
sola reinou . . .

(p. 450).

Silence represents the mysterious and the sinister:

Tod'está negro, as sombras envolven a
vereda,
e nin ó ceu ten ollos, nin ò pinar ten lengua

(p. 461).

Dramatic mode

The poetry of *Follas* delves into the innermost regions of Rosalía's soul, exposing the most intimate experiences and probing the most painful secrets of her life. She was as revealing in *La flor,* but in a much less restrained manner, pouring forth her anguish in overwrought, painfully emotional lines. In *Follas* there is a reticence and a delicacy which is maintained by a screen of dramatic presentation, by means of which she can objectify her feelings, directing the reader's attention away from herself and to the emotion expressed, which is attributed to a symbolical figure or to one of her *dramatis personae.* Thus she maintains the illusion of esthetic distance, even though the content of the poems is largely subjective. A few of the poems in *Follas,* like those of *Cantares,* have well-defined characters, but for the most part the *personae* are vague "tú", "él", "ella", "a estranxeira", etc. Through the dialogues or monologues of the speakers, feelings and concepts are made corporeal; the reenactment of the inner events makes them tangible and actual, with the vividness of words and gestures. The dramatic scenes of *Follas* are thus no longer a "mirror held up to nature" as those of *Cantares,* to reenact reality vividly, but rather a symbolic projection of inner experience, a means of exteriorizing the non-material world of the spirit.

Drama implies conflict, hence the dramatic form is well-suited to the poetry of *Follas novas,* the fruit of the poet's years of conflict the conflict of mind and heart, of body and soul, of passion and reason. In the poems where she is more objective, it is the tragic drama of others she portrays; that of the emigrant who leaves his beloved Galicia to eke out a living in foreign lands and, more particularly, that of the woman who remains behind, a widow, of the living or of the dead. Rosalía wrote no theatrical works, yet her sense of the dramatic and of the tragic is revealed in a variety of manners in *Follas.* There are no extensive dramatic works, but rather brief scenes, with no exposition and no conclusión, but which nonetheless contain the germ of a whole tragedy. Or they may be allegorical representations of spiritual conflicts.

In some of the dramatic compositions, Rosalía follows the folk heritage of the *cantigas de amigo* and the *romances.* Her predecessor and alleged master, Antonio de Trueba, as well as other early nineteenth-century poets revived these forms and effectively used the techniques of dialogue and dramatic narration. Among the poems employing dramatic technique in *Follas,* the ones in the traditional manner most closely resemble the poetry of *Cantares gallegos* and are more objective in the treatment of the themes. One senses, however, that Rosalía identifies herself to a greater extent with the personages, whose conflicts often coincide with her own. At times we can discern the poet's own voice speaking through the mask of her characters.

There are brief scenes resembling the *cantigas de amigo* where the girl speaks to her absent lover, to her mother or to another interlocutor. These continue, in outwardly simple and ingenuous scenes, the constant themes of disappointed love, exile and *saudades* of which so many haunting examples are to be encountered in *Cantares.* The tragic implications in *Follas,* however, tend to be much greater:

Cand'era tempo d'inverno
pensaba en dond'estarías;
cand'era tempo de sol
pensaba en dond'andarías,
¡Agora . . . tan soyo penso,
meu ben, si m'olvidarías!

(p. 428).

The dialogue may be held with an object of nature, personified and addressed by the speaker. This device is really a form of internal monologue, an exteriorization of thoughts, feelings and meditations by means of an imagined conversation with a silent companion. The device, of course, dates back to medieval times in the *cantigas* and *romances.* The Galicians, like the Celts, have always felt a particular affinity for nature and have tended to animate all of its manifestations. Romanticism reaffirmed the tendency with its propensity to communicate with nature. Rosalía, heir of both tendencies, achieves an exquisite empathy with nature:

> *Fermoso campo de Cornes,*
> *cando te crobes de lirios*
> *tamén se me cobre á yalma*
> *de pensamentos sombrisos.*
> *De Cornes lindo lugare*
> *que cruzan tantos camiños,*
> *anque cuberto de rosas,*
> *as rosas tamén fan guizos*
>
> (p. 522).

Personification of the inanimate is extended to abstract concepts such as thoughts, feelings and her own poetry:

> *"¡Follas novas!" risa dame*
> *ese nome que levás,*
> *cal s'a un-ha moura ben moura*
> *branca ll'oise chamar*
>
> (p. 422).

> *¿Por qué, miña almiña,*
> *por q'hora non queres*
> *o que antes querías?*
>
> (p. 439).

Longer narratives, in the manner of *romances,* interweave popular refrains and employ dramatic action and dialogue interspersed with vivid narration. Character development, exposition and dramatic intensity are conveyed with brief, incisive gestures and words. An example of this is the long composition **"N'hay peor meiga qu'un-ha gran pena"**, which incorporates many popular themes—the girl "enchanted" or "bewitched" by a fatal passion; her projection of her troubled mind on all of nature so that all seems ominous:

> *—Que onte â mañán n'a debesa*
> *a yagua se tornóu roxa*
> *cando me fun lavar n'ela;*
> *qu'en baixo d'os meus peiños;*
> *íñanse muchand'as herbas . . .*
>
> (p. 455).

There is also the frenzy of the devoted but superstitious mother who attributes the girl's illness to a supernatural power. The tragic "mal d'amores" and "honra enferma" of traditional Spanish literature also figure in this poem.

We can detect Rosalía's own emphasis on the themes of fatal, unrequited love and secret guilt, of persecution by the "mala boca" of society. The count is honorable, as is the lover of the poem **"Cantan os galos"** (IV) in *Cantares,* but in **"N'hay peor meiga"** all ends tragically for both lovers. The dramatic intensity is conveyed by the dialogue in which a few precise details reveal character and the emotional tone of the situation—the confident reason of the man accustomed to commanding all situations and the fearfulness of the old woman filled with dreadful terror. The leit-motifs of the cawing of crows and of tolling of bells, with all their symbolic implications, heighten the dramatic effect:

> *—Meu señor . . . , ¿n'oís os corvos?*
> *Veñen camiño d'á aldea . . .*
> *Mirá cal baten as alas . . .*
> *Cal baten as alas negras.*
> *—Deixa que as batan, qu'é cousa*
> *d'os corvos facer tal moestra*
>
> (p. 458).

The tragic denouement is a masterpiece of dramatic understatement, starkly simple in its utterance, yet conveying the intense pathos of the final recognition scene:

> *Morréu, morréu Mariana;*
> *o conde viun'antr'as velas,*
> *mais ela non veu a él,*
> *qu'antes de chegar morrera*
>
> (p. 459).

Rosalía in *Follas* also uses dramatic technique for vivid portrayal of characters and customs, achieving a direct and animated realism like that of *Cantares,* employing onomatopoeic words, popular expressions, sensory images of taste and smell and rapid action and dialogue. These homely genre scenes contain a sharp penetration of human nature and depict the preoccupations of the simple life and humble tragedy of the people, relieved at times with a note of humor. **"A probiña qu'está xorda"**, who is very much like the old woman of III of *Cantares,* is one of Rosalía's most vivid characters, a mixture of courage and humble wisdom as well as expert opportunism:

> *"Alá enriba d'a montaña*
> *sai fume d'as chamineas . . .*
> *Valor, meu corpiño vello,*
> *levaim'aló miñas pernas.*
> *Paseniño, paseniño,*
> *aquí para, alí te sentas,*
> *irás chegando Xuana,*
> *adond'as casas fomegan.*
> *¡Dios diante! a Virxe che valla,*
> *qu'hoxe, seica . . . , seica . . . , seica . . . ,*
> *has de comer sete cuncas*

de bon caldo, c'o a da cea,
e máis compango de porco
ou de sardiñas salpresas,
qu'os montañeses son homes
que cando dan, dan de veras.
Dempois, quentaráste a un lume
grande com'un-ha fogueira,
e cando xa estés ben quente,
¡a dormir . . . e qu'amaneza!"

(pp. 504-05)[14]

In **Follas** there appear brief, dramatic scenes in the manner of the *doloras* of Campoamor, who dominated the contemporary literary scene and had made of poetry something rational and conceptual. He developed for this purpose a dramatic form, with which he hoped to "hacer de toda poesía un drama, procurando basar este drama sobre una idea que sea trascendental y que puede universalizarse"[15]. Cossío calls these forms "verdaderos monólogos representables"[16]. Some of Rosalía's short dialogues and monologues resemble Campoamor, but, as with all her forms, from whatever source they derive, they become the vehicle for a passionately felt content. The calculated, detached and intentionally prosaic tone of Campoamor, designed to "escribir poesía cuyas ideas y cuyas palabras fueran o pareciesen ser pensadas y escritas por todo el mundo"[17] is replaced in Rosalía by the palpitating and naked suffering of the human heart. Among the poems in this category is: "Como venden a carne n'o mercado" (pp. 537-38), in which a more worldly speaker berates a girl who has been betrayed for her continued devotion to her faithless lover. Other disinterested persons enter and comment on the incident, "Un incrédulo", "Un-ha vella", "Outro", and "Un bon"—only the latter evincing any compassion and comprehension. The theme is a perennial one of Rosalía—an abandoned girl whose love remains true. If the form is Campoamoresque, the content is Rosalía. In **"N'é de morte"** (pp. 541-42), a story of love grown cold, the indifferent, cynical attitude on the part of the man is demonstrated:

—¿Ti que me pides, rapaza, cando
desmemoriado son coma un deño?
E ademáis, Rosa, direicho todo
pra que non volvas a pensar n'esto:
Bebín con outras n'aquela fonte,
pouséi con outras n'aquel portelo,
¡ay, e con tantas â luz d'á lúa
n'o mes d'agosto toméi o fresco! . . .

(p. 542).

In another instance, "Pois, consólate, Rosa", the speaker's advice to a rejected girl becomes the vehicle for the exposition of Rosalía's theories on love:

Pois consólate, Rosa,
que moito ten que padecer n'a vida

quen moito d'ela goza,
e olvidada ha de ser quen foi querida;
o que a ti che pasou, pásalle a todos
d'esa maneira ou de distintos modos.

. . . . .

Mais des que ó amor quere voar ña prenda,
e que lle cai á venda,
forza é deixalo ire,
que n'hay virtude sin poder que o prenda,
y o que antes nos mirou tras de un-ha nube
ou trasparente gasa,
des que á gasa se rompe e á nube pasa,
Rosa, val moito más que no-nos mire

(pp. 555-57).

A series of these brief dramatic scenes enacts the insistent theme of fatal love and seduction, followed by guilt and remorse. These are rapid and schematic, with only a hint of a backdrop. They are usually nocturnal, which casts a note of lugubrious foreboding on the action.

Rosalía's predilection for this theme and the intensity with which it is expressed would suggest autobiographical content. Perhaps Rosalía sees herself as the protagonist and the incidents represent an actual experience transformed by the theatrical illusion into an objective reality. Rosalía may not necessarily be portraying herself at all times, however, but other instances of tragic love with which she strongly sympathizes:

—¡Valor!, qu'anqu'eres como branda cera
aquí en perigro estamos,
e n'outro lado á libertá che espera
qu'aquí ninguén che dera,
—Vamos, señor, a donde queiras . . .
¡Vamos!

—Tan nobre eres, neu ben,
com'esforzada,
mais, ¡tembras com'a cerva acorralada,
hora que xuntos por ventura estamos
para fuxir, ña prenda namorada!
—¡Pois fuxamos . . . , fuxamos!
—¿Tés medo, miña vida,
a seres nos meus brazos sorprendida
e a que xuntos amándonos morramos?
—¡Ay!, nos qu'a dicha así fora comprida . . . ;
mais partamos . . . , partamos . . .
¡E adiós, paz e virtú sempre querida!

(pp. 471-72)[18]

The recurrent theme of fleeing from one's self or from the condemning eyes of others is dramatized as a lone woman hastening through the night, pursued by unseen mockers and concerned about her innocent children whom she has left behind to set out on a wild escapade:

> Ladraban contra min, que camiñaba
> casi-que sin alento,
> sin poder c'o meu fondo pensamento
> y a pezoña mortal qu'en min levaba.
> Y a xente que topaba
> ollándome a mantenta
> d'o meu dôr sin igual y a miña afrenta
> traidora se mofaba.
> Y eso que nada máis qu'a adiviñaba.
> Si á souperan. ¡Dios mío!,
> penséi tembrando, contra min volvera
> a corrente d'o río,
>
> Buscand'ò obrigo d'os máis altos muros,
> n'os camiños desertos,
> ensangrentando os pes nos seixos duros,
> fun chegando ô lugar d'os meus cariños
> maxinando espantada: "Os meus meniños,
> ¿estarán xa despertos?
> ¡Ay, qu'ô verme chegar tan maltratada,
> chorosa, sin alento e ensangrentada,
> darán en s'afrixir . . . , mal pocadiños,
> por sua nay mal fadada!"
>
> Pouco a pouco fun indo
> y as escaleiras con temor subindo,
> c'o triste corazón sobresaltado:
> ¡Escoitei! . . . Nin as moscas rebulían
> no berce ind'os meus ánxeles dormían
> c'a Virxen ô seu lado.

(pp. 438-39)[19]

The harsh landscape seems to symbolize the tribulations of the poet's life, her anguish in an alien world. The safety and serenity of the children affirms the existence of innocence and security in spite of her own unhappy destiny. The desperate woman is the configuration of the pilgrimage of her soul as it passes through its inner sufferings.

The theme of Galicia appears in **Follas** in its more tragic aspects in dramatic form. Galicia, a small and rugged land, has never been able to support its population and has been forced throughout its history to send its men either to other parts of Spain or to America to earn their sustenance. The necessity of leaving loved ones, the enforced separation from the homeland and the great risk of the venture have marked the soul of the Galician, and consequently his literature, with a perpetual sadness. Exile, widowhood, thwarted love take on the larger dimensions of man's spiritual exile and essential loneliness, his embarcation into the unknown abyss—the sea of death. The little dramas presented in the poems are truly tragic as man faces alone his fatal destiny, evoking the emotions of pity and terror in the reader:

> ¡Van a deixal-a patria! . . .
> Forzoso, mais supremo sacrificio.
> A miseria está negra en torno d'eles,
> ¡ay!, ¡y adiant'está ò abismo!

(p. 528)

At times the scene is visual and kinetic, a pantomime filled with awesome forebodings, as in the poem "O mar castiga bravamente as penas", where, after a description of desolate nature, a slow procession of human figures appears on the beach, going down to the sea:

> De humanos seres á compauta línea
> que brilla ô sol adiántase e retórcese,
> mais preto e lentamente as curvas sigue
> d'o murallón antiguo d'o Parrote.
> O corazón apértese d'angustia,
> óyense risas, xuramentos s'oyen,
> y as blasfemias s'axuntan c'os sospiros . . .
> ¿Onde van esos homes?
> Dentro d'un mes, n'o simiterio imenso
> d'á Habana, ou n'os seus bosques,
> ide a ver que foi deles . . .
> ¡No'o etern'olvido sempre dormen! . . .
> ¡Probes nais que os criaron,
> y as que os agardan amorosas, probes!

(pp. 528-29)

The human element appears at first as an almost insensitive part of the landscape, then slowly approaches the observer, and the sounds of voices are heard in a wordless lament, an outcry of human grief.

Another eloquent presentation of the drama of the men who depart and the women who remain is placed in the mouth of a departing emigrant:

> "¡Animo, compañeiros,
> tod'a terra é d'os homes.
> Aquel que non veu nunca mais que a propia
> a iñoranza o consume.
> ¡Animo! ¡A quen se muda, Dio-l-o axuda!
> ¡E anque hora vamos de Galicia lonxe,
> verés dês que tornemos
> o que medrano os robres!
> Mañan é ò día grande, ¡â mar, amigos!
> ¡Mañan, Dios nos acoche!"
> N'o sembrante á alegría,
> n'o corazón ò esforzo
> y a campana armoniosa d'á esperanza,
> lonxe, tocando a morto.

(p. 529)

As usual, Rosalía's sympathies are primarily with the women. If America provides adventure and escape for the men, the woman must wait and grieve, like Penelope:

Tecín soya a miña tea,
sembréi soya a meu nabal,
soya vou por leña ô monte,
soya a vexo arder n'ó lar.

. . . . .

O meu homiño perdeuse,
ninguén sabe ónde vai . . .
Andariña que pasache
con él las ondas d'o mar,
andariña, voa, voa,
ven a dime en ónd'está.

                              (p. 536)

All the tragedy of Galicia is distilled in these brief but eloquent lines:

Foi a Pascoa enxoita,
choveu en San Xoan,
a Galicia á fame
logo chegará.

Con malenconía
miran para o mar
os que n'outras terras
tên que buscar pan.

                              (p. 538)

Notes

[All page citations are taken from Rosalia de Castro, *obras completas.*]

[12] See alse, "Miña casiña, meu lar", pp. 501-03.

[13] Celestino F. de la Vega, "Campanas de Bastabales" in *7 ensayos sôbre Rosalía* (Vigo: Editorial Galaxia, 1952), 78.

[14] For other portrayals of local types and customs see "Xan", pp. 512-13; "Miña casiña", pp. 501-03; "Soberba", pp. 503-04; "Tanto e tanto nos odiamos", pp. 519-22; and "Vamos bebendo", p. 460.

[15] Quoted by José María de Cossío in *Historia general . . .* , ed. Díaz Plaja, V., 18.

[16] *Ibid.*, p. 22.

[17] *Ibid.*, p. 19.

[18] See also "Espantada, o abismo vexo", pp. 472-73; and "Para a vida, para a morte", p. 473.

[19] See also "A Xusticia pol-a man", pp. 445-45; "O Encanto d'a Pedra Chan", pp. 514-19.

Kessel Schwartz (essay date 1972)

SOURCE: "Rosalía de Castro's *En las orillas del Sar:* A Psychoanalytic Interpretation," in *Symposium*, Vol. XXVI, No. 4, Winter, 1972, pp. 363-75.

[*In the following essay, Schwartz explores the destructive, libidinal, and neurotic themes and imagery of* En las orillas del Sar.]

Poets have always been concerned with death, the world's greatest mystery. With its own special function in an ordered universe, death has been viewed as something of infinite horror yet at the same time as something desired, the final answer to incomprehensible truths, as a new experience, and as a peaceful end to pain. In **En las orillas del Sar** (1884), written over a period of years,[1] Rosalía de Castro elevated death (for her not a conventional metaphor) to a poetic as well as external reality. It represents her most exalted concentration on and contemplation of death. Whether as the result of traumatic events or because of the infinite sadness of everyday life, death and depression are constant notes in her work.[2] Azorín saw in her "sentido difuso de la muerte" (O. C., p. 156), and she approached death "resignada primera, amistosa después, y llamándola con tono desgarrador en su ayuda más tarde."[3] Through her overriding obsession, the poet sees in nature and the world objects which take on a subjective connotation beyond their objective limits, as "la razón se acomoda sobre cimientos de desengaño."[4]

In an attempt to relate biographical material to Rosalía de Castro's poetry, it may well be argued that anyone can see almost anything one wishes through emphasis on certain imagery. Literary psychoanalysis is speculative without specific documents, but in this case it seems obvious that the poet was driven to sum up the emotions boiling within her through subconscious projections. Relieved by occasional patches of hope and love, the poems on the whole reveal, even in their brighter moments, a lining of helpless despair and an over-all pattern of incipient deterioration, a dark sobriety into which psychoanalytical interpretations may give some insight. Superficially, Rosalía de Castro's inferiority feelings, sensitivity, and need for love, easily account for her anxiety attacks and emotional response. Her desperate songs of unsatisfied love, tempered by deep physical pain, also seem to reflect a number of unconscious fantasies. Her revealed conflicts and anxieties may indeed conceal others unexpressed. The difficulty lies in finding the early matrices which foreshadow later more developed states.

Much of the biographical information about the poet is open to question.[5] Her father, possibly a priest or seminarian, could not marry Rosalía's mother.[6] The poet was raised by an aunt, but at about nine years of age joined her mother. Around the age of fourteen or fifteen

Rosalía apparently suffered a serious personality change and an attack of melancholia, intensified by her mother's own depression. Perhaps she learned at that time about her illegitimate birth; perhaps she suffered from the lack of a father surrogate.[7] Coming into the world "endeble y con escasa vitalidad,"[8] Rosalía suffered in her youth from respiratory ailments which included colds and tuberculosis. She almost died from a bad case of the measles. Physical ills, which plagued her all her life, intensified her nervousness and psychic feelings of insecurity.[9] Biographers, in general, do not accept the popular image of the poet as sweet and religious. They talk of her "carácter difícil," her rebellious and passionate nature, and her ambivalent relationship with her husband whom she apparently loved deeply but felt compelled to wound constantly.[10] Her confession of tortured love affairs, apparently known to her husband,[11] reinforces this ambivalence. The death of her mother, a terrible blow, "le causó una larga y grave enfermedad" (O. C., pp. 75-76). Rosalía's husband saw her death of cancer of the uterus at the age of forty-eight as a final rest for a "pobre alma atormentada, tú que has sufrido tanto en este mundo" (O. C., p. 120), although one of her daughters insists "que mi madre [. . .] era alegre, muy alegre, y extremadamente acogedora y simpática [. . .]" (O. C., p. 139).

Rosalía de Castro's thanatophobia, brought on by intrafamilial stress and a very real parental loss, also reveals an unconscious fantasy life. Her anxiety, implemented by her mourning, is a "reliving of the early depressive anxieties."[12] Her ambivalent poetry involves love and hate, hope and despair, polarities which reflect her attempts to compensate through creativity for an inability to lead a satisfying personal life. She disguises and distorts her fantasy world to avoid confronting strong repressions and transmutes unconscious conflicts into a more socially acceptable symbolic form.[13] Her poetry, in part, seems to relate specifically to the psychoanalytical concept of the dream screen. The original blankness of the dreaming infant is considered to be a dreaming of the breast onto which later events and situations seem projected as if it were a cinematic screen. The dream screen involves visually perceived actions in ordinary manifest dream content as taking place on or before it. It also represents the wish to sleep, a bliss obtained after oral satisfaction. Aside from various overwhelming masses and the loss of ego boundaries, images involve dreams of pure white (milky substance), clouds, receding waves, vaporous mists, roses or pinkish color (the aureola of the breast), white and blue contrasts (the breast and veins), and constant implications of thirst related at the same time to concepts of dry, sandy, desert wastes.[14]

One aspect of the invisible and formless but yet directly apprehended breast involves nebulous and ill-defined perceptions, feelings of formless elements, ineffable experiences, not localizable or even nameable. This lost paradise of contentment at the breast is never to be attained again. Though original memories are vague, the need to return to that period and nostalgic attractions to infancy appear to relate specifically to Rosalía de Castro's "negra sombra." Her feeling of never achieving happiness (whatever the concrete pains and sorrows of her life) which she felt she could never have, is constantly and both consciously and unconsciously associated in her own words with "fantasía juvenil [. . .] de contentamiento que casi pudiera decirse infantil." She associates her feelings with the room in which her mother slept and recalls "aquella alegría y aquel éxtasis," which she could never again recapture (O. C., p. 108). This unattainable longing and spiritual intranquility, associated with a sad, indefinable and vague shadow, accompanies her everywhere (O. C., pp. 579, 598, 613, 625). It is a lost happiness, "un eco perdido [. . .] de dorados sueños y santas alegrías" (O. C., p. 569), "fantasma del bien soñado" (O. C., p. 616), and an inexpressable (O. C., p. 618) and veiled mystery (O. C., pp. 647, 651). The poet exclaims:

> Yo no sé lo que busco eternamente
> en la tierra, en el aire y en el cielo;
> yo no sé lo que busco, pero es algo
> que perdí no sé cuando y que no encuentro,
> aun cuando sueñe que invisible habita
> en todo cuanto toco y cuanto veo.
> (O. C., p. 627)

This sense of loss is intimately associated in Rosalía de Castro's poetry with oral aspects of negation and rejection: "La venturosa copa del placer, para siempre rota a mis pies está" (O. C., p. 611); "me destierran del cielo, donde las fuentes brotan/ eternas de la vida" (O. C., p. 580); "siento la sed devoradora/ y jamás apagada que ahoga el sentimiento" (O. C., p. 580); "secóse la fuente [. . .] y a un río profundo de nombre ignorado/ pidióle aguas puras su labio sediento [. . .]/ la sed que atormenta y el hambre que mata" (O. C., p. 593); "ya no mana la fuente, se agotó el manantial" (O. C., p. 605). Lack of satisfaction in the poetic context almost always involves sensations of thirst and a frustration based on sand of beach or desert. Thus the transparent waves of the blue sea on the sandy beach tempt her, kiss her and search her out with their snow-white foam:

> lánzanme, airosas, su nevada espuma,
> y pienso que me llaman, que me atraen
> hacia sus alas húmedas.
> Mas cuando ansiosa, quiero
> seguirlas por la líquida llanura,
> se hunde mi pie en la linfa transparente
> y ellas de mí se burlan.
> Y huyen, abandonándome en la playa
> a la terrena, inacabable lucha,
> como en las tristes playas de la vida
> me abandonó, inconstante, la fortuna.
> (O. C., p. 634)

A mouth-thirst orientation, a repetitive pattern, in addition to sand, fountain, beach, and desert, is also related to forest and wood imagery;[15] frequently the poet makes a conscious association with the breast. Rosalía recalls the beauty of forests and heights where a nameless pleasure awaits like a sweet caress. In a white and desert setting, where once she had hoped to "beber el néctar sano," she would gladly drink the waters of forgetfullness, death's brother. She recalls the sap:

> que extraje de tu seno,
> como el sediento niño el dulce jugo extrae
> del pecho blanco y lleno,
> de mi existencia oscura en el torrente amargo
> [. . .] una visión de armiño, une ilusión
>   querida,
> un suspiro de amor.
> (O. C., pp. 578-80)

Standard associations with dream screen symbols permeate her work and become its *sine qua non:* "Si en ti secó la fuente del consuelo/ secas todas las fuentes has de hallar" (O. C., p. 597); "ya un pinar, ya una fuente aparece/ que brotando en la peña musgosa [. . .] entre un mar de verdura se pierde/ dividiéndose en limpios arroyos" (O. C., p. 598); "secóse la fuente y el árbol nególe" (O. C., p. 593); "Ya no mana la fuente, se agotó el manantial [. . .] El sediento viajero [. . .] humedece los labios en la linfa serena/ del arroyo, que el árbol con sus ramas sombrea,/ y dichoso se olvida de la fuente ya seca" (O. C., p. 605); "su eterna sed es quien le lleva hacia la fuente abrasadora,/ cuanto más bebe, a beber más [. . .]/ la sed del beodo es insaciable, y la del alma lo es aún más" (O. C., p. 615); "Del labio amargado [. . .]/ como de fuente abundosa, fluyó la miel a raudales/ vertiéndose en copas de oro que mi mano orló de rosas" (O. C., p. 638).

Sensations of thirst and satiation are intimately intertwined with those of frustration, dryness, desert wastes, and sand. Thus the fountain, "always serene and pure," contrasts with "vía arenosa y desierta" (O. C., p. 579). If the poet dreams that the sea may be strong enough to quench her thirst, she at the same time compares herself to the thirsty sands of the beach:

> y no lejos las ondas, siempre frescas
> [. . .] Pobres arenas, de mi suerte imagen:
> no sé lo que me pasa al contemplaros,
> pues como yo sufrís, secas y mudas,
> el suplicio sin término de Tántalo.
> (O. C., p. 590)

She relates her intimate memories of satisfaction to "el áspero desierto" (O. C., pp. 646-47); sees in the most profound and dry circumstances that "fresca brotó de súbito una rosa,/ como brota una fuente en el desierto" (O. C., p. 616); and equates these events not only with a lost happiness but also with death "el cauce arenoso de la seca corriente/le recuerda al sediento el horror de la muerte" (O. C., p. 605).

Pleasurable and unpleasurable screen memories combine a wish to sleep and to join the mother. The poet hopes to fuse like "a white cloud in blue space," to be one with the breast, and to lose individual consciousness (in a sense to die). She also consciously refers to another aspect of her relationship with her mother with concomitant guilt feelings:

> Cada vez que recuerdo tanto oprobio,
> cada vez, digo, ¡y lo recuerda siempre!
> Avergonzada su alma,
> quisiera en el no ser desvanecerse,
> como la blanca nube
> en el espacio azul se desvanece.
> (O. C., p. 633)

The adult's unconscious has the same oral needs as that of the child, a pattern which offers the possibility of various fantasies in which the idea of death and dying is related to sleep and indeed a reflection of an anxious transmutation of what was originally pleasurable (satiation at the breast). In her poetry Rosalía de Castro almost always associates death with sleep which in adults repeats an "orally determined infantile situation, and is consciously or unconsciously associated with the idea of being a satiated nursling."[16] The poet's real pain from the cancer which was eating her from within, logically ending in sleep and/ or death and her other losses easily explain her depressive attacks; but they are almost always equated with an oral frustration, hence the omnipresent references to sandy wastes. Although the poet's approaching death must have concentrated her thoughts on her impending demise, her preoccupation with death, from her earliest poetry on, transcends the real sorrows of her life and any Esproncedian romantic longing for lost illusions. In **"La flor,"** written when she was twenty, terrified at the thought of future nothingness, she exclaims: "Padecer y morir: tal era el lema" (O. C,, pp. 220-23). In **En las orillas del Sar** death represents regret (O. C., p. 606), surcease (O. C., p. 592), doubt and terror (O. C., p. 662), and the only inevitable truth (O. C., pp. 645, 660).

Death in a Spanish Catholic framework would have been easier for her had she been able to resolve her doubts about the possibility of a final place in heaven: "No, no puede acabar lo que es eterno (O. C., p. 583); "¿Qué es la muerte?" (O. C., p. 584). She begs God not to let her wander alone in the wasteland of life to contemplate the plains of nothingness. Her thoughts focus on the black abyss which will end all hope, for perhaps no life exists after death (O. C., p. 628). Some critics see in her doubts, not Christianity, but metaphysical preoccupations with existence, "la existencia realizándose a sí misma—que es la zozobra y angustia ante la posible amenazadora nada."[17]

In her ambivalence the poet constantly contrasts happiness and sadness, life and death, love and hate (O. C., pp. 621, 605, 657). She realizes that to live is to be alone, consoled only by illusive hope in the face of death (O. C., pp. 611, 655). The poet compulsively repeats her theme of hope as though through reiteration she might alleviate the fear that man's destiny ends in the tomb: "Siempre el ansia incesante y el mismo anhelo siempre/ que no ha de tener término sino cuando cerrados/ ya duermen nuestros ojos el sueño de la muerte" (O. C., p. 611); "de polvo y fango nacidos, fango y polvo nos tornamos/ ¿por qué, pues, tanto luchamos/ si hemos de caer vencidos?" (O. C., p. 619). In spite of death's certainty she is consoled by the hope that love can happen more than once (O. C., pp. 620 ff), that one can die in peace, "si no dichosa" (O. C., p. 620), and that even in death one may hope for "en los terrones removidos/ verde y pujante crecerá la hierba" (O. C., p. 582). Unable to document her belief in life's harshness, she escapes into dreams and a fantasy world (O. C. pp. 632-33, 640), for "infeliz el que vive sin soñar" (O. C., p. 585).

Since her belief in immortality was less than secure Rosalía de Castro reflects on the temporal to which she gives a kind of spatial quality, re-emphasizing that if death is linked to life it is also linked to a postmortem future.[18] In preparing for the possibility the impulse which drives life forward "aspires to destroy yesterday in order to make way for to-morrow: the autumn leaves must rot on the ground before spring can turn it green with grass. Life cannot encumber itself with the graves of past days."[19] But it is equally true that life maintains its vanished forms, clinging to anything that was once a reality. Thus in Santiago, a "cementerio de vivos" (O. C., p. 628), she recalls the spectres of the past. Individual life seeks constant self-affirmation, longing never to cease to be, but since one must die "the individual clings desperately to anything which may provide him with the illusion of survival."[20]

In *En las orillas del Sar* the poet's emotional recall of both interior and exterior realities favors shade and twilight. Everything reminds her of death and a past life. The sun seems to be dying; leaves wither; with autumn light comes night, pain, and death. Recalling her sad infancy, the death of her son, and her general desolation, she turns to Galicia, its mountains and the sea, as death and nature fuse (O. C., p. 598). She remembers a forest where she once found shade, and nature reminds her constantly of her mortality (O. C., pp. 639-40). The setting sun, the leafless trees, and the very melancholy of afternoons and changing nature make her aware of death (O. C., p. 653), as do church bells which accompany one to the grave (O. C., pp. 578, 624).

These life-death relationships conceal an unconscious identification of the state after death with the feeling that at death we pass along an already traveled road.

Pre-mortal life is easily equated with post-mortal life, and by extension relates to early infancy and the mother. In death we return to the place which gave us birth, and to be born is to be cast from Paradise to which we wish to return.[21] Her constant references to sleep (death) appear to relate to the satisfaction at the breast, an ecstasy achieved in the warmth and softness of the mother, memory traces which determine later semi-mystical emotions. Homer saw sleep (hypnos) and death (thanatos) as twins, and Rosalía de Castro also acknowledges their kinship (O. C., p. 611). One pre-logical aspect of the poet's mystical thought reflects the mental state characteristic of early childhood, a kind of reversion to original innocence beyond good and evil. The poet's sense of unity with God, the strong and soothing presence, the occasional fullness and joy, recall the mother-child relationship as the satiated infant falls asleep, sinking into its mother's warmth and softness, the larger absorbing the smaller. This memory, being pre-verbal, cannot be expressed by the adult. Many mystics describe their experiences as a reversion to original innocence and Rosalía de Castro's view of eternity, a unity between a smallness and a vastness, includes the presence of a strong, hovering being. Ill-defined and nebulous perceptions involving the invisible in the breast situation may be brought into "juncture with God, the invisible, so that He may be perceived in this same way, directly."[22] Her ecstasy in her search for and union with God intensifies the ineffable experiences which are indefinable.

Fleeing pain and sorrow, Rosalía de Castro looks for refuge in both the past and religion, losing herself in a mystic identification with the universe and the immortal. In her poetry dedicated to her mother she exclaims: "En su regazo amoroso/ soñaba [. . .] sueño quimérico/ dejar esta ingrata vida/ al blando son de sus rezos" (O. C., p. 247). In the same way she associates the idea of birth and death with nature in her last volume of poetry (O. C., pp. 587-88, 653). Just as winter presages a happy spring so in life her pain may presage "eterna primavera de mis sueños" (O. C., p. 606). These dreams relate more to the eternal than to life, as the poet views an "inmensidad que asombra,/ aspiración celeste, revelación callada;/ la comprende el espíritu y el labio no la nombra,/ y en sus hondos abismos la mente se anonada" (O. C., p. 618). Here we see all the elements previously mentioned, the swallowing of the smaller by the larger, a search for immortality, and an inability to articulate her feelings. But dreams of future life also inevitably relate to the transmutation of past sorrows and lost illusions, past emotional realities evoked as a counterpart of her thanatophobia. Her narcissistic desire to go on living in spite of everything causes her current external reality to take on the attributes of illusion, no more real than the evanescent past, to be replaced by the timeless world of dream and fantasy (O. C., pp. 651-52), as though she were in a different time and place, "cual si en suelo extranjero me hallase" (O. C., p. 578). Yet nobody can fully escape the unpleasant realities, "algunos aborrecidos recuerdos que se resistían a abandonarme" (O. C., p. 108), any more than one can escape future terrors. Denying the very thing she longs for, the regressively attractive mother symbol, she refuses to lose a single atom of her being (O. C., p. 641), to be devoured. Unlike nature where plants killed by winter will bloom again, she has visions of bursting arteries and broken bones, lamenting the impossibility of resurrection and that "están tejiéndome la mortaja" (O. C., p. 640).

Inevitably, however, the human spirit is inseparably united with "lo eterno," in a "misterioso arcano," and the poet experiences "otro calor más dulce en mi alma penetrando/ me anima y me sustenta con su secreto halago/ y da luz a mis ojos, por el dolor cegados" (O. C., pp. 625-27). Vagueness and the eternal, the presence of an immensity, the union of birth and death, burning thirst assuaged by immortal love, and life beyond death reinforce one another as the principal notes of her poetry: "ni puede tener fin la inmensidad [. . .] en donde nace, vive y al fin muere" (O. C., p. 583); "un amor inmortal los leves átomos/ sin marcharse, en la atmósfera flotaban [. . .] saciará al fin su sed el alma ardiente/ donde beben su amor los serafines!" (O. C., p. 590). "Immortal essence," "immense space," and similar images reinforce the concept of mystic union and life beyond death (O. C., pp. 599, 654, 662). Contemplating this immortality amidst clouds of incense (O. C., p. 578), and feeling herself to be in the presence of a superior being, Rosalía de Castro feels "el sueño del éxtasis," finding her soul stirred by memories of "tiempos más dichosos, reminiscencias largas" (O. C., pp. 631-32). As she reflects on immortality and immortal love, considering herself less than a small atom lost in the universe, she becomes like a child "que reposa [. . .] después de llorar, tranquila" (O. C., pp. 634-35). She can now accept a concept of existence for she is "por el vacío envuelto" (O. C., p. 640).

Her mystic state also involves a kind of adult sexuality and desire, a surrender to a higher power that cannot be resisted, that overwhelms her and compels her. She dwells on her sin which is but the work of an instant but whose terrible expiation will last "mientras dure el Infierno!" She refers to her thirst of love which leaves her "sin honra" and a "pecadora" (O. C., p. 652). If we are to believe some of her biographers, her adult sexuality involved a compulsion which was somehow related to her need for a fatherly love she never had.[23] Beyond this possibility, she exhibits a regression bordering at the very least on neurotic fixation, for her melancholy need for love seems addressed to her own self-punishing ego:

> no lograréis cambiar de la criatura,
> en su esencia, la misma eternamente,
> los instintos innatos.
> (O. C., p. 641)

The postulated love interest may have been a dream of falling in love rather than a reality, a screening of her rivalry for her mother's love for her unknown father which enabled her to avoid a conflict by disguising a primitive transference in an effort to allay guilt.

It must be understood that psychological connotations, whether of previous happiness or pain, may be sought in disguised relationships between symbol and meaning at unconscious levels. Love disappointments during infancy, before the Œdipus complex is resolved, and a repetition of that disappointment in later life can easily cause depression. Ignored and abandoned by her mother during her early years, it was natural that Rosalía should have ambivalent feelings toward her, wishing for her death and at the same time fearing it. The projection of this subconsciously remembered death wish against her mother intensified the fear of her own death as punishment. Losing a loved object makes one wish to restore and recreate it. In her case, apparently, a later conscious manifestation repressed into her unconscious. Rosalía's sense of guilt causes her to idealize the loved object which enables her to shield her hostility toward her mother by an insistence on her love for her, the once loved and now lost object. The poet's excessive love helped her hide from herself her inner destructive attitude. Thus she recalls her life with her mother, "era un tiempo tan hermoso" (O. C., p. 245), as if only in happy childhood memory could she feel alleviation, breathe freely (one may recall in this connection her respiratory ailments), and find relief from her fear of separation. Recalling her mother in her coffin, she conveys her terrible sorrow, repeating constantly that she should have died in place of her mother (O. C., p. 253). Rosalía's real separation from her mother caused intense longing and loneliness and even terror. Deprivation of this kind would establish the groundwork for an unexpressed antagonism displaced to unconscious levels. Substituting a conscious memory of her mother for an earlier experience, she displaces the unconscious memory of early years to a later time and identification with her real mother.

Rosalía de Castro's self-reproaches and depressions were applied more directly to her mother and unknown father than to herself, but by interjecting and incorporating the lost object she identifies herself with it and assumes its guilt. Her own conscience visits on her the anger intended for the mother. Thus her melancholia, a despairing cry for love, is not represented by the physical but rather by a purely internal psychic object, the conscience or superego.[24] Severely damaged by her disappointment in mother love and later reinforced by the lack of a father, her infantile narcissism needed reinforcement. Because of her mother's special situation in the society of her time, Rosalía, as a teenager, was unable to go out as much as other young ladies. Her dread of society intensified, her feelings of hostiity and fear. Anxious and frustrated, she needed reassurance and constant love, which she did not receive. Thus her perpetual vulnerability and need to suffer were intensified.

Because of her apparent death wish against her mother, deeply repressed, she suffered from guilt and a need to be punished. A fantasy punishment for censured impulses may be detached from immediate causes, and the external world may represent internal feelings.[25] By self-recrimination and suffering Rosalía could avoid exterior accusation. Thus consolation is impossible for her, since all fountains will be dry. In heaven stars exist and on the earth flowers, but they are not for her (O. C., p. 597). The poet, in her depression, accuses herself of a *mancha,* a distortion of her own unconscious hostility toward her mother. She repeats over and over that happiness is not for her since she carries "la traición por guiá," contemplating "tu pecado y tu mancha irredimibles" (O. C., p. 622). In this connection her second person address to herself may be of interest. Each time she recalls "tanto oprobio" she is ashamed and wants to die (O. C., p. 633). Her unconscious rage at her mother's betrayal was never resolved, although she exclaims that no stain can be forever without pardon if one is repentant enough (O. C., p. 639).

Since Rosalía de Castro could not easily express her hostility, she usually associates it with shade and darkness: "el execrable anatema llevando en la frente escrito, refugio busque en la sombra para devorar mi afrenta" (O. C., p. 639); "y en tanto el olvido, la duda y la muerte/agrandan las sombras que en torno le cercan" (O. C., p. 593); "son las sombras que envuelven las almas" (O. C., p. 611). A well-known relationship exists between darkness and the mother symbol[26] through whose further association with death we obtain the traumatic key to understanding some of the imagery. Death may be overcome by escape from the relationship between inner emotional reality and the outer world. Destructive and libidinal instincts fuse together, for neurotic dread of death, primarily related to the fear of being devoured,[27] is also equated with love. In Rosalía de Castro's poetry, objects and places change into reflections of her mother's death. The wish to sleep may be to be forever with a deceased love object in eternity, a death perhaps unconsciously brought on by guilt because of the need to punish a lover, husband, or father substitute as a kind of reassurance. This would help explain the love-hate ambivalence of her poetry: "En mi pecho ve juntos el odio y el cariño,/mezcla de gloria y pena" (O. C., p. 581); "me odias, porque te amo; te amo, porque me odias" (O. C., p. 611); "¿Por qué le preguntáis que amores siente/ y no qué odios alientan su venganza?" (O. C., p. 603).

The theme of death became a part of the poet, united with a kind of transfer, from the dark depths of her subconscious, of an inner compulsion of love. Both at times reinforce the feeling of unreality in her poetry, rather than reflecting the tenet that poetry is an instrument for the discovery of the invisible. This effect seems to stem from her inability to handle her aggression toward her family, always related to a love she felt she had never received and which time and again returned her to innocent and symbolic reunion with her mother and an intuitive belief in a mystical new beginning. Combining her subconscious drives and defenses, Rosalía sought surcease in her literary and esthetic sublimation, which without completely displacing or disguising, the latter buttressed an exterior literary belief in Celtic sadness. Today, without attempting dogmatic conclusions about love and death, constants of all great poetry, we may read into her personal vision of experience and inner emotions and communication a deeper significance, seeking those moral and psychological imperatives which constitute their human quality.

Notes

[1] Elvira Martín, *Tres mujeres gallegas del siglo xix* (Barcelona: Editorial Aedos, 1962), p. 140.

[2] Victoriano García Martí, "Rosalía de Castro o el dolor de vivir," in *Obras completas* by Rosalía de Castro (Madrid: Aguilar, 1960), p. 156, believes that "la raza gallega siente como ninguna raza el dolor de vivir." Citations from *Obras completas* are taken from this edition hereafter cited as O. C.

[3] Elvira Martín, p. 98.

[4] José Luis Varela, "Rosalía y sus límites," *Revista de Literatura,* 30 (1966), p. 72.

[5] Aside from those previously mentioned, among the many studies, are Ricardo Carballo Calero, *Historia da literatura galega contemporánea* Vigo: Galaxia, 1962; Kathleen Kulp, *Manner and Mood in Rosalía de Castro,* Madrid: Ediciones José Porrúa Turanzas, 1968; Marina Mayoral, "Sobre el amor en Rosalía de Castro y sobre la destrucción de ciertas cartas," *Cuadernos Hispanoamericanos,* 233 (1969), pp. 486-502; Rosalía de Castro, *Beside the River Sar,* trans. S. Griswold Morley, Berkeley: University of California Press, 1937; Alberto Machado da Rosa, "Rosalía de Castro, poeta incomprendido," *Revista Hispánica Moderna,* 20 (1954), pp. 181-223; and Sister Mary Pierre Tirrell, *La mística de la saudade,* Madrid: Ediciones Jura, 1951.

[6] Carballo Calero, p. 142.

[7] See *Obras completas,* p. 40; Elvira Martín, p. 97. Morley, p. 10, feels that the "knowledge of her illegitimacy must have cast a shadow over her sensitive spirit." Juan Rof Carballo, "Rosalía, ánima galaica," in *Siete ensayos sobre Rosalía de Castro,* Vigo: Galaxia, 1952, pp. 111-49, contends that when her mother first ignored

her, through her education by her father's sister she formed an idealized image of him for which she was eternally searching. Mayoral, p. 487, also cites "la falta de un imago paterno." Alberto Machado da Rosa, p. 200, contends that the change revolved around a sexual problem and her relationship to the poet, Aguirre. Deprived of the love of father and mother, she sought for understanding through other channels.

[8] Martín, p. 94.

[9] Her own husband, Manuel Murguía, exclaimed: "¿ Qué se podía esperar de una mujer delicada de salud, sensible, que cada emoción la hería hondamente?" (O. C., p. 564). For references to her "heridos pulmones" and delicate health see also Rosalía de Castro, *Obra poética,* ed. Augusto Cortina (Madrid: Espasa-Calpe, 1963), p. 15.

[10] Mayoral, p. 489. See also Martín, p. 135, who claims that the poet was "pasional por temperamento y por herencia."

[11] Machado da Rosa, p. 223.

[12] Hanna Segal, "A Psychoanalytic Approach to Aesthetics," *International Journal of Psychoanalysis,* 33 (1952), pp. 197-99.

[13] Sigmund Freud, *The Standard Edition of the Complete Psychological Works of Freud* (London: The Hogarth Press, 1961), XIX, 42; see also Sigmund Freud, "Formulations on the Two Principles of Mental Functioning," *Standard Edition* (1958), XII, 224.

[14] For a complete discussion of the dream screen see Bertram D. Lewin, "Sleep, the Mouth, and the Dream Screen," *The Psychoanalytic Quarterly,* 15 (1946), pp. 419-34, and "Reconsiderations of the Dream Screen," *The Psychoanalytic Quarterly,* 22 (1953), pp. 174-98.

[15] Freud, *The Standard Edition* (1959), XX, 67, states that the forest, like the tree, mythologically has been portrayed as a maternal symbol. See also Freud, *The Basic Writings of Sigmund Freud,* trans. and ed. A. A. Brill, New York: The Modern Library, 1938, p. 372, who states that "wood, generally speaking, seems, in accordance with its linguistic relations, to represent feminine matter."

[16] Lewin, "Sleep, the Mouth and the Dream Screen," p. 420.

[17] Julieta Gómez Paz, "Rubén Darío y Rosalía de Castro," *Asomante,* 23, 2 (1967), p. 47.

[18] Frederick J. Hoffman, "Mortality and Modern Literature," in Herman Feifel, *The Meaning of Death* (New York: McGraw-Hill, 1959), p. 134.

[19] Marie Bonaparte, "A Defense of Biography," *International Journal of Psychoanalysis,* 20 (1939), pp. 232-33.

[20] *Ibid.,* p. 236.

[21] J. C. Flügel, *The Psychoanalytic Study of the Family* (London: The Hogarth Press, 1935), p. 66; also see Patrick Mullahy, *Oedipus, Myth and Complex* (New York: Hermitage Press, 1948), p. 163.

[22] Bertram D. Lewin, *The Psychoanalysis of Elation* (New York: Norton, 1950), p. 111.

[23] Alberto Machado da Rosa, pp. 181-223.

[24] Sandor Rado, "The Problem of Melancholia," *International Journal of Psychoanalysis,* 9 (1928), pp. 420-38.

[25] Milton L. Miller, *Nostalgia* (Boston: Houghton Mifflin, 1956), p. 129.

[26] Karl Abraham, *Selected Papers on Psychoanalysis* (London: The Hogarth Press, 1948), p. 203, relates darkness to womb fantasies. As the symbol of the mother it signifies both birth and death.

[27] Lewin, *The Psychoanalysis of Elation,* p. 104.

Martha LaFollette Miller (essay date 1982)

SOURCE: "Aspects of Perspective in Rosalía de Castro's *En las orillas del Sar,*" in *Kentucky Romance Quarterly,* Vol. 29, No. 3, 1982, pp. 273-82.

[*In the following essay, Miller studies Castro's complex stylistic and thematic use of perspective in the poems of* En las orillas del Sar.]

The poetry of Rosalía de Castro has frequently been characterized as simple, clear, and unadorned.[1] Like Bécquer's, her verse possesses a certain simplicity to which it owes part of its charm. Yet many of her poems, though outwardly uncomplicated in theme and technique, have a strangely complicated effect on their reader, and often this effect is due to her subtle manipulation of perspectives.

Rosalía's use of perspective play is related to what critic Kathleen Kulp terms the "dramatic mode" in her works and defines as the use of dialogue and dramatic presentation. For Kulp, who rightly points out the importance of these techniques in maintaining "esthetic distance" and in creating the illusion of objectivity,[2] the use of the dramatic mode declines in Rosalía's final book, *En las orillas del Sar,* due to that book's more intimate nature and because the poet, having risen above her human vulnerability as she nears death, no longer needs to distance herself from subject and audience in precisely this way.[3] Yet even in the intimate poetry of *En las orillas del Sar,* poetic effect depends at times on sudden changes in point of view, ambiguous perspectives and vague personae. As the analysis of several poems from that book demonstrates, these perspectivist techniques serve not only to underline themes and psychological realities, but also to increase the active involvement of the reader in the process of reading, through forcing him to adjust to shifting and uncertain points of view. Rosalía's handling of perspective, moreover, frequently allows her to universalize emotion and thus to transcend the limits of her own situation; in the process she creates complex poems that are compelling for the present-day reader.[4]

In the seven-stanza poem beginning **"Era apacible el día"**[5] (pp. 576-77), we follow a mother through various stages of grief over the death of her young child. Abrupt shifts in the speaker's perspective, accompanied by changes in rhyme, meter and temporal frame of reference, reflect the conflict and contradiction between human aspirations and the grim impassivity of death. Furthermore, these shifts mirror the turbulence of the protagonist's emotions as she passes through states of greater and lesser distance from the events that give rise to the poem. In Stanza One, in which she recalls in a severely understated way the day when her son lay dying, she reveals a certain objectivity that allows her to view his death as part of a larger pattern. In Stanzas Two and Three, however, she abruptly abolishes the emotional distance she has established as she first implores those at his gravesite to quickly cover the grave and then (perhaps at a later point in time) questions and scolds those who would visit his tomb. A second moment of objectivity, in Stanza Four, is quickly replaced by a lapse back into the irrationality of denial, a less-distanced state that continues through Stanzas Five and Six as she futilely attempts to speak directly to her son in a gesture symbolic of a possible reunion in heaven. Only in the final stanza does she regain enough distance to once again put this death into a larger context. Thus, in Stanzas Two through Seven, she moves through a succession of stages of grief, passing from denial to full realization and acceptance, and gradually working her way back to (and even beyond) the objectivity and broader vision of Stanza One.

As the speaker's perspective on the event recounted in **"Era apacible el día"** vacillates between greater and lesser objectivity and distance, corresponding changes inevitably occur in the extent to which the reader shares her perspective (and by perspective I mean here neither judgment nor emotional involvement—both of which certainly may vary from reader to reader—but rather the angle or point of view on events thrust on the reader by the text as he moves from stanza to stanza). The attempt to understand these shifts and their role in the poem is a process similar to the one Stanley Fish advocates as "an analysis of the developing responses of the reader in relation to the words as they succeed one another in time," in which emphasis is placed on what elements in the poem *do* rather than what they *mean.*[6] As this type of analysis shows, in **"Era apacible el día"** the reader's perspective comes closest to that of the speaker when the latter is at her most objective; divergence between speaker and reader perspective, on the other hand, is greatest when the speaker is least objective and most irrationally immersed in events. This divergence in perspective (which is heightened by the shocking effect of brusque changes in tone from stanza to stanza) creates in turn a certain kind of distance between speaker and reader; this distance, furthermore, itself becomes a bearer of meaning, underlining on the level of reader participation the loss of communication, occasioned by death, that is the ultimate concern of the poem.

A close inspection of each stanza reveals precisely how shifts in the two types of distance mentioned above—between speaker and event and between speaker and reader—function in the poem. The first stanza, which differs from the rest of the poem both in verb tense and in the use of consonant rather than assonant rhyme, in itself form a tightly knit structural whole with a unified point of view:

> Era apacible el día
> y templado el ambiente,
> y llovía, llovía
> callada y mansamente;
> y mientras silenciosa
> lloraba yo y gemía,
> mi niño, tierna rosa,
> durmiendo se moría.
> Al huir de este mundo, ¡qué sosiego en su frente!
> Al verle yo alejarse, ¡qué borrasca en la mía!

Here the use of the imperfect tense creates a certain narrative distance between speaker and event, and this distance is reinforced by the fact that in recalling her own emotions she describes them from the standpoint of their outward manifestations, referring to her inaudible tears and the storm on her forehead as if she were observing herself from the outside. She becomes at once the protagonist whose anguish is internal and the narrator who focuses on the outward signs of that anguish from a certain distance. This distance interposed between speaker in her role as narrator and the event she recalls echoes, on the formal level, the fundamental theme of the poem: the separation brought about by death and time.

The disjunction caused by death is further emphasized by the alienation embodied in the contrast between the world of nature (to which the dying child belongs) and the realm of human emotions. On the one hand, the short lines and consonant rhyme create an effect of harmony and simplicity that parallels the peaceful view of nature suggested by the quiet rain and by the words "apacible" and "mansamente." The child, a "tierna rosa," belongs to this world; his calm expression—"sosiego en la frente"—matches its tranquillity. On the other hand, the mother's fundamental estrangement from such cruel serenity is expressed through the contrast between the quiet rain and her anguished tears and between the calm of nature and her stormy face. Thus the distance between speaker as narrator and speaker as active protagonist parallels that between the latter and her dying son. At the same time, however, in recalling this event, the speaker's narrative distance allows her to view herself as part of a larger picture; she weaves herself and her grief into the pattern of nature through the continuation of the rain image, which she applies to herself in the word "borrasca," and through the structural and semantic parallels between quiet rain and silent tears:

> . . . . .llovía
> callada. . . . .
> . . . . .silenciosa
> lloraba. . . . .

Thus in the first stanza, although an opposition is created between the weeping mother and the world of nature that impassively absorbs her son, this mother becomes at the same time, as participant in the event, part of that larger-than-human natural world, and she is thus distanced from her present perspective as speaker by more than just the imperfect verb tense.

The clear distinction drawn between speaker as participant and speaker as narrator is important largely because of its effect on the reader. Because as narrator she herself is distanced from the event, her perspective is close to that of the reader; because she objectively presents a scene in its appearance and outward signs, the reader can join her in the awareness of the rift between mother and child and even between past and present. Thus at this point in the poem, reader and speaker share a perspective and distance between them is at a minimum.

In the second stanza, the speaker's objectivity is abruptly destroyed, as we progress chronologically from death to burial but move backwards in terms of her distance from the event. Instead of remembering the death of her child from a narrative distance, the speaker here experiences the event directly:

> Tierra sobre el cadáver insepulto
> antes que empiece a corromperse . . . , ¡tierra!
> Ya el hoyo se ha cubierto, sosegaos;
> bien pronto en los terrones removidos
> verde y pujante crecerá la hierba.

The temporal aspects of the stanza—the elliptical command, the urgency of the clause beginning "antes que,"

the shift between the second and the third lines to the present perfect and to a slightly later moment, even the speaker's vision of the immediate future—all emphasize her complete immersion in the action in progress. Furthermore, the lack of temporal distance between speaker and event is matched by her total lack of objectivity; instead of viewing the death of her child in its ultimate significance, she focuses on details that in the larger picture are unimportant, on the burial rather than on the death itself. Her attempts to calm others with the fact that the grave has been covered disclose the deep irrationality of her desire to deny, to see her child buried and all signs of death obliterated.

The reader, in Stanza Two, is suddenly faced with a shift in his relationship to the speaker. Whereas in the first stanza, both he and the speaker share a perspective of distance from the event narrated, here their perspectives diverge; regardless of the sympathy he may feel for the distraught mother, he can not logically share her conviction that covering the grave is cause for relief. Here, therefore, he is aware of her lack of objectivity; recognizing her state as an irrational stage of mourning, he can pity her but he can not actually share her viewpoint as in the first stanza.

In the third stanza, which continues the perspective of the second, grief separates the speaker markedly from those she addresses:

> ¿Qué andáis buscando en torno de las
>   tumbas,
> torvo el mirar, nublado el pensamiento?
> ¡No os ocupéis de lo que al polvo vuelve! . . .
> Jamás el que descansa en el sepulcro
> ha de tornar a amaros ni a ofenderos.

Her continued desire to obliterate outward signs of death and thus to deny its reality is evident in the tone of resentment with which she addresses those whose facial expressions reveal mourning. Her lack of solidarity with other human beings and her identification with her son suggest a desire to be beyond the world of the living with her dead. At the same time, she has come somewhat closer to full recognition of what has happened; even while stating the essential finality of death, however, she directs her attention away from her inner self, avoiding the impact of her own words. Here the reader's perspective is even further distanced from that of the speaker than in Stanza Two. Although again he may be able to understand her behavior and sympathize with her situation, at the same time he recognizes the injustice of her tone towards those she addresses; this identification with them, rather than with her, is furthered, moreover, by the fact that he—as spectator and sympathizer—shares their position and their role.

In Stanza Four, the speaker, suddenly reacting to the words she herself has just uttered, turns to an inner

OBRAS COMPLETAS

DE

ROSALÍA DE CASTRO

I

EN LAS ORILLAS DEL SAR

PRÓLOGO DE

MANUEL MURGUÍA

MADRID

LIBRERÍA DE LOS SUCESORES DE HERNANDO

Calle del Arenal, 11.

—

1909

dialogue in which she considers but quickly rejects the absolute finality of the separation wrought by death:

> ¡Jamás! ¿Es verdad que todo
> para siempre acabó ya?
> No, no puede acabar lo que es eterno,
> ni puede tener fin la inmensidad.

In the fifth and sixth stanzas, which echo and develop the affirmation of the final lines of Stanza Four, she addresses her dead child directly (thus leaving reader and listeners of previous stanzas out of the picture completely):

> Tú te fuiste para siempre; mas mi alma
> te espera aún con amoroso afán,
> y vendrás o iré yo, bien de mi vida,
> allí donde nos hemos de encontrar.
>
> Algo ha quedado tuyo en mis entrañas
> que no morirá jamás,
> y que Dios, porque es justo y porque es bueno,
> a desunir ya nunca volverá.
>
> En el cielo, en la tierra, en lo insondable
> yo te hallaré y me hallarás.
> No, no puede acabar lo que es eterno,
> ni puede tener fin la inmensidad.

Here the speaker's perspective underlines her faith that communication with her son is still possible; yet this faith depends on the goodness and justice of God, both of which are called into question, for the reader, by the situation itself: the untimely death of a child.

In the final stanza, the speaker catches up with the reader's position of doubt, when she poignantly abandons her attempts to address the child directly, shifting from second to third person:

> —Mas . . . es verdad—ha partido,
> para nunca más tornar.

The futility of her attempt to undo the separation wrought by death and the self-delusion inherent in her faith in God's goodness becomes apparent and are underlined by the transformation of the previous stanza's affirmative "a desunir ya nunca volverá" into the more pessimistic, yet semantically similar, "para nunca más tornar."

In the last four lines of the poem, the speaker is able to move from her own blinded grief to a recognition of the finality and universality of death:

> Nada hay eterno para el hombre, huésped
> de un día en este mundo terrenal
> en donde nace, vive y al fin muere,
> cual todo nace, vive y muere acá.

Thus in a sense she returns to the perspective of the first stanza, where the objectivity gained by stepping back from an experience allowed her to see it as part of a larger pattern and permitted the reader to share her point of view. Yet in several important ways she has gone beyond Stanza One; what was merely hinted at there has here become full awareness. As we saw earlier, separation of the speaker's past from her present perspective in Stanza One served to reinforce the theme of the distance and separation brought on by death, and thus even there the lines between the process of death and the processes of life were blurred, with both the child and her own past receding in the flow of time. Furthermore, the lessening of the distinction between the living and the dead continued to develop throughout Stanzas Five and Six, where the speaker denied death's finality by affirming that what she believed eternal was partly within her; thus in Stanza Seven, when she says that nothing is eternal, she has extended the meaning of death to include not only that of her son but also the dissolving of what remains in her of the bond between them. At the end of the poem, therefore, she is talking as much about her own death as about his. Her struggle throughout the poem is now revealed as an attempt to overcome death's inexorable work within herself. Ironically, the oneness with her child that she attempted to find through denial, through rejection of human society and through religious faith comes, finally, in the recognition of death's universality. In reaching Stanza Seven's awareness, furthermore, she has picked up another thread of suggestion from Stanza One: that death is feared only by those who do not accept it as part of them; like her son, whose face revealed only tranquillity as death carried him away, she recovers a certain calm when she can see death as a process in which she is involved.

In the last stanza of the poem, furthermore, reader-speaker distance is suddenly abolished as the conclusions the reader has already reached in witnessing the speaker's struggle come together with her own realizations. The trajectory of union and separation undergone by reader and speaker throughout the poem increases the impact of this stanza. Moreover, although in a sense this coming together represents a return to Stanza One, there is a difference; whereas there the reader, from a distance, witnessed death as a private episodic event, here he himself is included, as part of the totality of humanity to which the speaker alludes, in its universal action. Because the poem has extended the meaning of death to embrace distance of all sorts, furthermore, his changing relationship with the speaker, which parallels the separation she has experienced through death, makes his inclusion at the end meaningful. The process of reading here is thus an experience akin to the one the speaker of the poem undergoes.

It is clear from the above analysis that beneath the disjointed façade of the poem "**Era apacible el día**" lies a unity based upon the speaker's anguished path through denial to resignation. The framework provided by her emotional trajectory allows us to interpret elements of the poem that otherwise would seem maudlin or excessive as manifestations of temporary psychic states.[7] Much of the effect of the poem, furthermore, depends upon the skillful manipulation not only of the speaker's perspective, but also of the changing position of the reader as the poem progresses. The poem is thus more subtle and more complex—as well as more successful—than it appears at first glance.

Another poem in which perspective plays a fundamental role, though in a very different way, is the one beginning **"En los ecos del órgano o en el rumor del viento"** (p. 621). The poem opens with a stanza describing its protagonist's unsatisfied, eternal yearning for a vague and as yet unspecified goal:

> En los ecos del órgano o en el rumor del
> viento,
> en el fulgor de un astro o en la gota de lluvia,
> te adivinaba en todo y en todo te buscaba,
> sin encontrarte nunca.

The longed-for object, which is addressed directly, is just as elusive as the echoes, starlight and evanescent raindrops where it is sought. For the reader, it is clear from the fleeting, intangible nature of all these substances that we are in the presence of an intimate, subjective search, an intensely personal, almost prayer-like longing for the absolute.

Yet in passing from the first to the second stanza, the reader is immediately disoriented and must revise his reading of Stanza One, for what appeared to be a first-person testimony of direct experience now turns out to be a commentary narrated by a speaker other than the searching protagonist; the verbs "adivinaba" and "buscaba" must now be re-read as third person. Our impression of the speaker's total knowledge of the intimate, fleeting perceptions of the protagonist, furthermore, is suddenly destroyed by the conjectural "quizá" that opens the second stanza:

> Quizá después te ha hallado, te ha hallado, y
> . ha perdido
> otra vez, de la vida en la batalla ruda,
> ya que sigue buscándote y te adivina en todo,
> sin encontrarte nunca.

We now realize that in effect the first stanza was a merger of two voices: that of a protagonist who underwent a search, and that of a speaker who witnessed it. In the second stanza, these voices abruptly separate. Although such a separation may be jarring to the reader, it serves to underline the elusive quality of union that in part is the subject of the poem. In these few two stanzas, furthermore, a counterpoint movement is established; where speaker's and protagonist's voices are united, the

protagonist searches without finding; where on the other hand the protagonist finds what he is seeking (line five), his perspective is abruptly separated from the speaker's. Thus human voices are only joined in separation from what is perfect or eternal (much as they are united in their mortality in **"Era apacible el día"**), and conciliation of the fallible human dimension and the perfect divine one is presented as impossible. The relationship between speaker and protagonist, furthermore, mirrors that between the protagonist and what he seeks; it is fragile like the echoes and raindrops of Stanza One.

In the final stanza of the poem, the speaker's voice is basically reunited with that of the protagonist:

> Pero sabe que existes y no eres vano sueño,
> hermosura sin nombre, pero perfecta y única;
> por eso vive triste, porque te busca siempre,
> sin encontrarte nunca.

Here the speaker's ability to address and define the perfection sought—"hermosura sin nombre"—is matched by the protagonist's certainty ("Pero sabe que existes"). Yet this certainty is accompanied by a greater awareness of the impossibility of reaching this beauty (as the counterposition of "siempre" and "nunca," as well as the cumulative effect of the repetition of the final line, suggests); and the poem's final irony becomes clear: the closer one comes to a perfection greater than man, the sadder one must be at the certainty that it is beyond reach. Greater approximation thus means greater sadness.[8]

The interplay of perspectives is thus as important an element here as in **"Era apacible el día,"** both contributing depth and drawing the reader into actively experiencing the poem. In both poems, the reader's reaction to jarring shifts or ambiguities in perspective is an integral part of the poem's functioning. In both cases, a seemingly disjointed poem is unified on the level of the significance of perspective play, which can in no way be separated from the thematic level of the poems.

Perspective play of greater and lesser complexity occurs throughout ***En las orillas del Sar.*** A final example, which I will examine only briefly, is the long poem ***Los tristes.*** Here seven sections (in reality complete poems in themselves) treat from a variety of perspectives different aspects of what for Rosalía was a perennial preoccupation: those unfortunate human beings seemingly predestined, through no fault of their own, to suffer.[9] As in the poems analyzed above, here perspective is linked to theme; thus in Section Three, the breach between these souls and those more fortunate becomes more striking because of the distance created by the presence of a speaker who must intercede on their behalf, thus putting them a step away from those she addresses: "Vosotros, que lograsteis vuestros sueños, / ¿qué entendéis de sus ansias malogradas?" (p. 585). Another kind of distance is created in Section Six:

> Cada vez huye más de los vivos,
> cada vez habla más con los muertos:
> y es que cuando nos rinde el cansancio,
> propicio a la paz y al sueño,
> el cuerpo tiende al reposo,
> el alma tiende a lo eterno. (p. 586)

Here the vagueness of the unnamed protagonist underlines his distance from the world of the living, the speaker's sudden identification with him, through the pronoun "nos" in line three, followed by the reiteration of the concept of separation in the last two lines, suggests the same irony underlying **"Era apacible el día":** that at times men are only united in the universal isolation of mortality.[10]

Through various perspectivist techniques, therefore—shifts, distancing, ambiguity, vagueness—Rosalía universalizes emotion through extending it beyond specific situations and individuals. In dramatizing inner emotions, she dissolves the boundaries of the self, weaving sorrows, suffering and desire into a universal fabric and transcending, in the process, her intensely personal anguish.

Multiplicity and contradiction in perspective have been viewed as comparatively recent developments in art.[11] Although apparently Rosalía was unaware that her manipulation of perspective constituted a technical advance within her poetry,[12] this manipulation has nevertheless caused critics to consider her a precursor of such creators of personae and heteronyms as Fernando Pessoa and Antonio Machado,[13] and certainly aligns her with modern sensibility. Yet perhaps it is neither her self-awareness regarding her use of perspective nor her modernity with which we should concern ourselves, but rather the simple fact that critical approaches and ways of seeing literature that are operative today allow us to read her poems in a new way and thus to discover new depths and complexity within her seemingly uncomplicated poetry.

Notes

[1] See S. Griswold Morley, Preface, *Beside the River Sar: Selected Poems from* En las orillas del Sar *by Rosalía de Castro* (Berkeley: Univ. of Calif. Press, 1937), p. xii; also Marina Mayoral, *La poesía de Rosalía de Castro* (Madrid: Editorial Gredos, 1974), p. 564.

[2] Kathleen K. Kulp, *Manner and Mood in Rosalía de Castro: A Study of Themes and Style* (Madrid: Ediciones José Porrúa Turanzas, 1968), p. 82.

[3] Kulp, p. 126.

[4] Although both Kulp and Mayoral have pointed out the importance of the variety of perspectives found in Rosalía's poetry, neither has shown how the poet manipulates perspective within individual poems, creating a shifting relationship between speaker and reader that forms part of the total experience of the poem and an integral part of its theme.

[5] All quotations from Rosalía's poetry are taken from *Obras completas,* 6th ed. (Madrid: Aguilar, 1966).

[6] "Literature in the Reader: Affective Stylistics," *New Literary History* 2 [1970], 123-62. For a discussion of aesthetic or psychic distance as I will use it here, see also Andrew P. Debicki, *Poetas hispanoamericanos contemporáneos: Punto de vista, perspectiva, experiencia* (Madrid: Gredos, 1976), pp. 161-63, hereafter *Phc.*

[7] An analogous effect has been observed by Andrew Debicki (*Phc,* p. 160) in the poetry of Nicanor Parra. By distancing his speaker from the subject, or his reader from the vision communicated, Parra converts his commentary into vital experience, "evitando el peligro de limitar el poema a un pronunciamiento dogmático."

[8] Although I have viewed this poem as complete in itself, it may be considered as Part I of a two-section poem; it is followed by a ten-line continuation that treats the same subject from a first-person perspective. Considering the two poems as part of one longer poem would not fundamentally alter my reading, but would support the theory that Rosalía was consciously interested in experimenting with the use of different perspectives to achieve different poetic effects.

[9] See Mayoral, p. 61.

[10] Among other poems in which the manipulation of voices and perspectives plays an important role are those beginning "Tú para mí, yo para ti, bien mío" (p. 651), in which the speaker's inner self is first fragmented, then reunited, and "Hora tras hora, día tras día" (p. 655), in which a first-person narrator commits suicide, necessitating a switch to third-person narration.

[11] See Claudio Guillén's discussion of Nietzsche in *Literature as System: Essays toward the Theory of Literary History* (Princeton, N.J.: Princeton Univ. Press, 1971), pp. 331-32.

[12] Mayoral, p. 522.

[13] Xesús Alonso Montero, *Rosalía de Castro* (Madrid: Ediciones Júcar, 1972), p. 41.

Julian Palley (essay date 1984)

SOURCE: "Rosalía de Castro: Two Mourning Dreams," in *Hispanófila,* Vol. 82, September, 1984, pp. 21-27.

[*In the following essay, Palley analyzes Castro's somber, dream-like poems "A mi madre" and "En sueños te di un beso, vida mía."*]

The encounter with a departed beloved person in dream, in the subconscious or pre-conscious mind, in an under - or other-world which resembles both, is a major motif of literature that goes back to Ulysses' meeting with his mother in Book XI of the *Odyssey:* "As my mother spoke, there came to me . . . the one desire, to embrace her spirit, dead though she was. Thrice, in my eagerness to clasp her to me, I started forward with my hands outstretched. Thrice, like a shadow or a dream, she slipped through my arms and left me harrowed by an even sharper pain."[1] Achilles' dream of Patroclus (in book XXIII of the *Iliad*) describes a poignant meeting with the hero's dead friend and companion: "He spake, and reached forth with his hands, but clasped him not; for like a vapour the spirit was gone beneath the earth with a faint shriek."[2] George Devereux defines these dreams as "mourning dreams in which one tries vainly to clasp the dream image of the departed."[3] Devereux devotes a long and complex study to Menelaus' dream of an erotic encounter with the flown (but still alive) Helen.[4] The dream is narrated by the Chorus (Aeschylus, *Agamemnon,* 410-426). One of the best-known mourning dreams in English poetry is Milton's superb sonnet, "Methought I saw my late espoused Saint," his wife who

> Came vested all in white, pure as her mind:
> 　Her face was vail'd, yet to my fancied sight
> 　Love, sweetness, goodness, in her person shined
> So clear, as in no face with more delight.
> 　But O as to embrace me she enclin'd,
> 　I wak'd, she fled, and day brought back my night.

There are few mourning-dream poems in Spanish literature; the reader may recall Antonio Machado's "Soñé que tú me llevabas" which evokes his departed wife Leonor's image in dream.[5] I would like to discuss two such poems by Rosalía de Castro; they are both written in Castilian, although neither is included in her *En las orillas del Sar.* The first occurs as part of her long poem **"A mi madre"**;[6] the second, which begins **"En sueños te di un beso, vida mía,"** is found among the "Poesías varias" collected by García Martí.

Rosalía was not obsessed with dreams, as was her contemporary Bécquer. Things dream occasionally, in the manner of Heine's northern spruce *(Fichtenbaum),* which dreams of a southern palm. Flowers, for example, dream:

> De la noche en el vago silencio
> cuando duermen o sueñan las flores

> (*Obras completas,* p. 618)

The general romantic tendency to see human emotion reflected in nature is reinforced by the pervading pantheism of Galician thought and art.[7] At times the subject is not certain whether he/she has thought, dreamt or otherwise experienced a sensation or idea:

> Mas aun sin alas cree o sueña que cruza el
> 　aire,
> 　　　　los espacios,
> y entre el lodo se ve limpio, cual de la nieve
> 　　el copo blanco.

> (p. 609)

This is the romantic dream of flight or ascension, characteristic of Bécquer and the Germans.[8] The third-person subject is probably Rosalía, since she often creates a distance in this manner, by objectifying herself. Elsewhere the verb *soñar* seems to refer to a waking fantasy or momentary hallucination:

> yo no sé lo que busco, pero es algo
> que perdí no sé cuando y que no encuentro,
> aun cuando sueñe que invisible habita
> en todo cuanto toco y cuanto veo.

> (p. 621)

Why does Rosalía objectify herself in the third person, and even more so, as a masculine subject (as in the poem previously cited)? Or is she really speaking of someone else, perhaps of Aurelio Aguirre, whom she loved passionately before she married Murguía?[9] Criticism has not really come to grips with the problem of the *personae* and subjects of Rosalía's lyrics, especially in the complex and often enigmatic dialogues of *En las orillas del Sar.*

Rosalía was born out of wedlock and possibly did not know her father, who evidently entered the priesthood in Padrón.[10] She spent her early childhood with her aunt and godmother, Teresa Martínez Viojo, and went to live with her mother at about age ten. On the latter's death in 1863, Rosalía, then 26, and only beginning to write her lasting Galician and Castilian lyrics, published privately a long poem of devotion and veneration. **"A mi madre"** has thirteen sections; the final one is a description of a meeting with her parent in dream.

The relations between a child and its parents are always complex, and more so in the case of Rosalía.[11] It is likely that she felt a repressed resentment toward her mother, who did not recognize her during the first ten years of her life, certainly the crucial period of a child's development. A child's love or anger toward its parents are normally diffused between mother and father, moving from one to the other. The fact that Rosalía had no recognized father may explain the passionate attachments she felt toward, and her dependence upon, her husband and other men, substitutes for the lost father. It also complicated her role vis-à-vis her mother, who had to play both parental roles. A girl's ties to her mother are more lasting and deeply rooted than those of a boy to his father, since the mother, who gave physical birth to her, is also rival and model; and she feels herself, for better or worse, becoming like her mother. A male child cannot know all of the complexities of this special attachment. The mixture of love and hate which sometimes characterizes this bond between mother and daughter is portrayed with agonizing clarity in the dream encounter of **"A mi madre."**

Ayer en sueños te vi . . .
¡Qué triste cosa es soñar,
y qué triste es despertar
de un triste sueño . . . ¡ay de mí!

Te vi . . . La triste mirada
lánguida hacia mí volvías,
bañada en lágrimas frías,
hijas de la tumba helada.

. . . . .

Y aunque era mi madre aquella
que en sueños a ver tornaba,
ni yo amante la buscaba
ni me acariciaba ella.

Allí estaba sola y triste,
con su enlutado vestido,
diciendo con manso ruido:
"te he perdido y me perdiste."

. . . . .

Aun en sueños, tan sombría
la contemplé en su ternura,
que el alma con saña dura,
la amaba y la repelía.

. . . . .

¡Aquella a quien dio la vida,
tener miedo de su sombra,
es ingratitud que asombra
la que en el hombre se anida!

(pp. 250, 251)

In these verses, together with the romantic platitudes of tomb imagery and rhetorical lament, we find an uncommon confession of resentment and inability to overcome a real, if suppressed, anger. As in Ulysses' meeting with his mother, the image cannot be embraced, and recedes. But here the poetic speaker is surprised to discover that she made no effort to demonstrate affection, nor did the mother-image seek to initiate it: "Ni yo

amante la buscaba / ni me acariciaba ella." There is a cold silence between the dreaming subject and the image, broken by the latter's ambiguous statement, "Te he perdido y me perdiste." Another level of meaning appears to exist here, beyond the manifest "I lost you (by dying)." The loss here could refer to previous events in their lives, rather than to the results of death. Perhaps the dream was expressing an anger which Rosalia's conscious mind refused to accept, and which she, on waking and reflecting, finds astonishing: "que el alma, con saña dura, / la amaba y la repelía." In fact, she uses the word "asombra" in the final stanza, referring to the ingratitude the speaker observes in the dream-subject's attitude toward her mother: "Tener miedo a su sombra." Kessel Schwartz speaks of the Freudian dream screen in Rosalía (the images of whiteness, vaporous mists, receding waves), which he believes are a regressive memory of the maternal breast, and also alludes to a repressed hostility directed toward her mother.[12] **"A mi madre"** certainly affirms this psychoanalytic interpretation. Note also the recurring motif of "sombra . . . asombra," a paronamasia found in other poems, notably in the Galician sonnet **"Negra sombra."**

Following is poem II from the "Poesías varias" collected by García Martí in his edition of the *Obras completas.* The footnote states: "Reproducida en *Cuadernos de estudios gallegos,* no se registra fecha ni título."

En sueños te di un beso, vida mía,
tan entrañable y largo . . .
¡Ay!, pero en él de amargo
tanto, mi bien, como de dulce había.
    Tu infantil boca cada vez más fría,
dejó mi sangre para siempre helada,
y sobre tu semblante reclinada,
besándote, sentí que me moría.
    Más tarde, y ya despierta,
con singular empeño,
pensando proseguí que estaba muerta
y que en tanto a tus restos abrazada
dormía para siempre el postrer sueño
soñaba tristemente que vivía
aun de ti, por la muerte separada.

(p. 1519)

According to Marina Mayoral and other sources,[13] Rosalía and Manuel Murguía had six children, and a seventh, Valentina, who died in childbirth. The six children were: Alejandra (1859), Aura (1868), Gala and Ovidio (twins) (1871), Amara (1873) and Adriano (1875). Rosalía was 38 at the time of the birth of her sixth child. Mayoral states that " . . . el segundo hijo varón, Adriano, murió siendo muy pequeño, cuando tenía un año y medio, a consecuencia de una caída."[14] The child alluded to in the poem could only have been Adriano, who died in 1877 or 1878. Evidently, the poem was written between that year and Rosalía's death in 1885.

A close examination of this poem reveals that beneath its apparent simplicity lies an extraordinary complexity, syntactic, conceptual and oneiric. The first strophe recalls both the Homeric dream encounters and the poem **"A mi madre,"** with their affective ambiguity; the kiss which the poet relives in dream was a mixture of *amargo* and *dulce*. We may speculate that the subject of the dream was Adriano, and the image here summoned was that of her farewell to her dying child. The dream continues in the second strophe. There is introduced the underlying idea on which the poem is based: that after the child's death, she (the poetic speaker) believed or dreamt that she herself was dead. The death of her last male child may, in fact, have weakened her will to live, and contributed to her fatal illness.

The final strophe embodies a series of paradoxes, of mirror images of waking and dreaming, that, in bewildering succession, seem to be incapable of a final conceptual resolution. Let us try to paraphrase these verses in prose: "Later, awake . . . I went on thinking that I was dead, and, while embracing your (dead) body, I slept the final sleep (of death). I was dreaming that I lived, still separated from you by death." The sequence of states of consciousness are as follows: (a) awake *(despierta)*; (b) dead *(pensando que estaba muerta)*; (c) sleeping *(el postrer sueño)*; and (d) dreaming *(soñaba)*. The structure is circular, since it begins with waking existence, and concludes in dream that she is alive. Is she awake or dreaming in this last strophe? If we take this to be a lucid dream (a dream-within-a-dream) the various states of consciousness would all take place within the dream. In lucid dreams, it is common to dream that we are awake, observing our own dream.[15] Thus (according to this interpretation) Rosalía, while dreaming, becomes awake, sees herself die, and dreams, while dead, that she is alive. This bewildering series is within the endless possibilities of our dream state. Another interpretation would place the series of events (described in the final strophe) in daydream, as passing through her mind in a waking state. Death in life, life in death, dreaming and waking reality are involved in a labyrinthine convolution which, in the last analysis, is an attempt at a metaphoric description of her state of mind, her sorrow at the loss of a child. The entire complex of images and concepts is the vehicle, for which the tenor is her anguished and fragmented state of consciousness. We would have to look to some of Quevedo's baroque sonnets to find a similarly paradoxical statement of the equations life-death, life-dream; but even in Quevedo (as in his "Fue sueño ayer, mañana será tierra") the images seem, by comparison, easy to unravel and define.[16]

The "shades" of the departed that Rosalía sees in dream, in these examples, are yet another variation of the theme of *sombra*, at the core of many of her best lyrics; and they may also be related to the Galician legend or tradition of the *Santa Compaña*,[17] the procession of ghosts that occasionally makes its appearance in the countryside. These two examples therefore belong to a continuum in Rosalía's writings, from the early, romantic **"La flor"**[18] to what is perhaps one of her last lyrics, the tragic dream-vision of the lost child. They are both explicitly acts of mourning for a dead and beloved person, mother and child. They both have the disturbing quality of nightmare, and both appear to be real dreams, dreamt by the poet. In both cases there is a sense of inadequacy, of affective ambiguity. The dream of the mother belongs to a well-known tradition of Western literature; that of the son explores unsuspected areas of our oneiric experience, areas which we are beginning now to understand through research on the lucid dream. The "mourning" expressed by both poems may be looked upon as paradigmatic of the tonality of most of her finest poetry, especially that of **En las orillas del Sar.**

Notes

[1] *The Odyssey,* trans. E. V. Rieu (Middlessex: Penguin Books, 1973), p. 176.

[2] *The Iliad,* trans. A. Lang, W. Leaf, and E. Myers (New York: Modern Library, n.d.), p. 418.

[3] *Dreams in Greek Tragedy: An Ethno-Psycho-Analytical Study* (Berkeley and Los Angeles: Univ. of California Press, 1976), p. xxii.

[4] *Ibid.* Chap. 3, "Menelaeos' Reactive Depression and Dream," pp. 59-145.

[5] Manuel y Antonio Machado, *Obras completas* (Madrid: Editorial Plenitud, 1957), p. 795.

[6] Rosalía de Castro, *Obras completas,* ed. V. García Martí, 6th ed. (Madrid: Aguilar, 1968), pp. 250, 251. Subsequent citations of Rosalía de Castro will refer to this edition.

[7] J. Rof Carballo, "Rosalía, ánima galaica," in *Siete ensayos sobre Rosalía,* ed. L. Pimentel (Vigo: Galaixa, 1952), pp. 112-49, esp. p. 133.

[8] See my article, "Bécquer's Disembodied Soul," to appear soon in the *Hispanic Review.*

[9] See A. Machado da Rosa, "Rosalía, poeta incompreendido," *RHM, 20 (1954), pp. 181-223.*

[10] See Marina Mayoral, "Apéndice biográfico" *La poesía de Rosalía de Castro* (Madrid: Gredos, 1974), pp. 570-85; Ángel Lázaro, *Rosalía de Castro* (Madrid: Compañía Bibliográfica Española, 1966), *passim;* and Jesús Alonso Montero, *Rosalía de Castro* (Madrid: Júcar, 1972), *passim.*

[11] See Rof Carballo, op. cit.

[12] "Rosalía de Castro's *En las orillas del Sar*: A Psychoanalytic Interpretation," *Symposium* 26 (1972), pp. 363-75.

[13] See note 10.

[14] Mayoral, p. 580.

[15] See Patricia Garfield, *Creative Dreaming* (New York: Ballantine Books, 1974), Chap. VI; and Celia Green, *Lucid Dreams* (London: Hamilton, 1968).

[16] Anthropologist William Morgan (quoted in Jackson S. Lincoln, *The Dream in Primitive Cultures*, [New York: Johnson Reprint Corp., 1970] p. 209) points out that such dreams are thought to be prophetic in Navajo culture. " . . . when a Navajo dreams that he is dead, he means that in his dream, he was in the next world with the spirits of the dead . . . To be there and come back is not necessarily a bad dream; but if the dead beckons to the dreamer, or he shakes hands with the dead, it means he is going to die."

[17] On the *Santa Compaña* see, e.g., Antonio Risco, *El demiurgo y su mundo: hacia un nuevo enfoque de la obra de Valle-Inclán* (Madrid: Gredos, 1977), p. 192; and Mayoral, op. cit., Chaps. I and V.

[18] Mayoral, pp. 89, 90.

[19] I should like to express my gratitude to Professor John Kronik of Cornell University for certain recommendations that were incorporated into this essay.

Shelley Stevens (essay date 1986)

SOURCE: "Society, Legend and the Poet," in *Rosalía de Castro and the Galician Revival*, Tamesis Books Limited, 1986, pp. 17-35.

[*In the following excerpt, Stevens surveys Castro's life and criticism of her work, and discusses Castro's association with the nineteenth-century Galician Revival in Spanish literature.*]

1. Biography

Rosalía de Castro was born in Santiago de Compostela on February 24, 1837. She was the illegitimate daughter of María Teresa da Cruz de Castro e Abadía, the descendant of a noble family that had seen better days.[1] Almost nothing is known of Castro's father, José Martínez Viojo, except that he was a priest and native of Ortoño and was born in 1798. According to birth records she was not sent to the orphanage connected with the Hospital Real where she was born. But the confusion about who cared for the child during the first years of her life has been cleared up only recently. Early critics thought that

María Francisca Martínez, who was present at the infant's baptismal ceremony, was a sister of Rosalía's father. Francisca Martínez was, however, a servant of Rosalía de Castro's mother.[2] This confusion arose because Teresa Martínez Viojo—no relation to María Francisca Martínez—, José Martínez Viojo's sister, also cared for her, first in Ortoño and later in Padrón.[3]

It appears then, that the child was handed over, some time after the baptism, to her father's sister: «Foi, pois, a familia paterna a que se encarregóu nos primeiros intres da crianza da picariña. Ista, ao cabo de algún tempo, foi levada a Ortoño, en cuia 'Casa do Castro' vivíu ao coidado de dona Tereixa Martínez Viojo.»[4]

Not only were arrangements made for Rosalía's care within the respective families of her «unknown» parents, we must assume that members of both families were in occasional if not frequent contact from the time of her birth. I agree with Marina Mayoral that Rosalía de Castro's strong attachment to her mother suggests contact between mother and daughter that preceded their actual reunion in Santiago in about 1852, when Castro was fifteen: «No sabemos si doña Teresa vio con frecuencia a su hija mientras ésta vivió con la familia paterna, quizá sí, y quizá también la recogió antes de ese año de 1852 que antes citamos; de otro modo resulta sorprendente el profundo cariño que llegó a inspirar a su hija.»[5] In effect, according to Fermín Bouza Brey, Castro first joined her mother on a permanent basis around 1846 in Padrón when she was eight or nine.[6] We must also keep in mind that members of both families lived in the same geographical area.

But what of the woman whose obscure social position allowed her to assume the care of her brother's illegitimate daughter? We know from a letter written by Castro's daughter to María Josefa Martínez Viojo on April 9, 1884, that Castro had through the years remained close to members of her father's family:

> A no haber estado mamá bastante grave (como acaso V. no ignorara) ya habríamos pasado un día a visitarla [a doña María Josefa Martínez Viojo], pero, aunque la distancia desde aquí a Brión es corta y los deseos que madre tiene de abrazar a doña Josefa grande, no está su saluz [*sic*] para esas caminatas.[7]

This single but important reference to her adoptive family is a valuable piece of biographical evidence totally excluded from the official hagiography. Rosalía de Castro's knowledge of Galician songs in large part comes out of a childhood spent under the guardianship of women whose importance has never been acknowledged and about whom we know almost nothing.

Rosalía de Castro's early childhood, spent in the rural Galician towns of Ortoño and Padrón, was by all accounts a happy one. In biographical passages from one of the poems in **Cantares gallegos, «Como chove miudiño»,** Castro casts a nostalgic glance at the now-deserted Arretén, the house in Iria Flavia where she lived off and on with her mother between the ages of about nine and fifteen.[8] A childhood remembered for songs, laughter, and the tolling of bells contrasts with the desolate silence that now looms over the place:

> ¡Bosques, casa, sepulturas,
> campanarios e campanas
> con sons vagos de dosuras
> que despertan—ai—ternuras
> que en jamáis podrán ser vanas!
>
> . . . . .
>
> Risas, cantos, armonía,
> brandas músicas, contento,
> festas, dansas, alegría,
> se trocóu na triste e fría,
> xorda vos do forte vento.[9]

In 1881 Rosalía de Castro writes in *costumbrista* prose of the happiness of childhood days spent at Torres de Hermida in Lestrove, the home of her mother's (Teresa Castro) sister Josefa and her husband Gregorio:

> En otros días, saltaba yo del lecho toda alborozada al percibir el primer reflejo del día, para ver cómo tras del Miranda se abría paso la luz por entre nubes color de naranja, y hería con sus rayos las gotas de rocío suspendidas en cada cinta de hierba.

In the same article she describes the joy of being with her mother:

> No he vuelto a experimentar en esta habitación, en donde mi madre . . . durmió un día para despertar cada mañana sonriéndome, aquella alegría y aquellos éxtasis, en los cuales, sin yo saberlo, la esperanza, ahora huida, andaba agitando entonces sus luminosas alas.[10]

In his important article on Rosalía de Castro, written shortly before her death, and published as a chapter in *Los precursores* (1885), Manuel Murguía states that the happiness of his wife's childhood was interrupted by the early arrival of puberty when she was eleven:[11]

> Esta vida de dolor empezó pronto para ella, porque física e intelectualmente su precocidad fue grande. Contaba apenas once primaveras cuando compuso sus primeros versos y tuvo que cambiar su traje de niña por el de la mujer . . . ¡Y cuán amargos y tristes para los que, tocando apenas en los límites de la juventud, tienen ya que luchar con la tristísima realidad! . . . Ilevó siempre abierta la herida causada por los primeros desencantos. (LP 175-76)

Common sense suggests that the early misfortunes he alludes to were related to the discovery of who her father was and of her illegitimate birth.

Prevailing prejudices against teaching girls how to write did not prevent Castro from learning, although frequent spelling errors in surviving autograph manuscripts are a poignant reminder that she was deprived of a rigorous primary school education. According to Geraldine Scanlon, until the Revolution of 1868 little had been accomplished to improve the Spanish girl's extremely limited education. Scanlon quotes from a report published in an 1852 edition of the Madrid periodical, *Album de señoritas,* in which a journalist, who visited a girls' school in Madrid, asked the teacher to locate the writing desks, and was told that there were none.[12] The teacher explained that they were unnecessary and caused more harm than benefit. Conditions in Galicia could not have been markedly different from those in Castile. Girls who learned more than the rudiments of reading and writing did so in spite of considerable social and institutional opposition. Rosalía de Castro's talent appears to have been recognized and nurtured by her family (or families) from an early age.

As an adolescent in Santiago, where she lived with her mother, she may have attended classes at the «Sociedad Económica de Amigos del País», where young women were instructed in music and drawing. In 1856 she and her mother lived next door to the building that housed the Society.[13] And during the same period, between 1853 and 1856, Rosalía de Castro frequented the «Liceo de la juventud», taking part in the many literary and cultural activities provided there. In 1854, at the age of seventeen, she played the principal role in *Rosamunda,* a play by Gil y Zárate.[14]

Santiago itself was the center of growing political and cultural life of the region. Castro's contemporaries in the liceum were other writers and political activists: Aurelio Aguirre, Eduardo Pondal, Rodríguez Seoane, and Manuel Murguía, whom she would eventually marry. She, Murguía, and the poet and physician, Pondal, would become in the 1860s and 1870s leading members of the emerging regionalist movement. Rosalía de Castro's association with this society was crucial for her later political and literary development.

Judging from contemporary descriptions of the meagerness of even upper-class education for girls, we must assume that for the most part Rosalía de Castro educated herself. She knew classical Spanish literature and read a great deal of contemporary European literature; an awareness of the latest trends in poetry had a profound effect on her own work.

In 1856 Rosalía de Castro went to Madrid to live with her aunt, María Carmen Luguín y Castro, in whose house it appears she met several literary figures of the day, including Gustavo Adolfo Bécquer. Though commentators have speculated widely about Castro's motives for going to Madrid, a serious young writer's trip to the center of literary activity in her country really does not require a lengthy explanation.

She made this trip at a time of political unrest in the capital when the liberal gains of the 1854 Revolution were reversed by the reinstatement of the *Moderado* order and the nullification of the 1856 Constitution. The further consolidation of the *Moderado* forces in the formation of the Liberal Union with its anti-federalist policies served to further spur regionalist politics, and regionalism became increasingly associated with democracy in Spain.[15] The next eighteen years, the most active of Castro's literary career, are also years of constant political change in Spain.

While residing in Madrid she published in 1857 her first collection of poetry, *La flor.* Manuel Murguía reviewed the book on May 12, in *La Iberia,* a Madrid periodical that had a wide national circulation. There is more than a hint of personal acquaintance in this review, as its praise and advice are aimed directly at the author.[16]

But we have no conclusive proof that they knew one another at the time of this review. Though they both attended the «Liceo de la Juventud», Murguía left for Madrid in 1852 when Castro was only fifteen. He returned to Santiago in the summer of 1856, after Castro had left for Madrid. What seems most likely is that they knew of one another through a mutual friend, the Romantic poet, Aurelio Aguirre. If they coincided in the liceum and knew one another in 1852, or at some time between 1852 and 1856, Manuel Murguía adamantly denied it and Castro never mentioned it. According to Alejandra, the first child of the couple, the occasion of the publication of *La flor* provoked the first contact between her parents.

She and Murguía were married in Madrid on October 10, 1859. The courtship and her marriage to Manuel Murguía is yet another example of the many gaps in Rosalía de Castro's biography. We do know that the marriage was a decisive factor for the history of Galician literature. Without Murguía's encouragement *Cantares gallegos* might never have been written; without his aquaintance with publishers it might never have been printed. Also, his intense interest in Galician history and culture probably led him to recognize in her the logical candidate for the task of reviving the popular songs of rural Galicia.

Rosalía de Castro gave birth to seven children, five of whom survived infancy. Most recent critics agree that the marriage was probably not a happy one for either spouse. Personal frictions were aggravated by long separations and financial need, all made worse by Castro's ill health. Judging from his abundant historical writings,

Manuel Murguía was an energetic and optimistic person, compelled to perceive the world within an idealistic historical framework. Rosalía de Castro's view of the world, by contrast, was markedly disillusioned and skeptical. Where he is hopeful, she is despondent. Common intellectual interests and mutual respect could not remedy problems caused by basic emotional and temperamental differences.

Expressing always a clear and profound appreciation of Castro's poetic talent, he regrets that it deprived her of a quiet and anonymous existence: «Conservándose para su patria, se conservó asimismo para sus grandes infortunios.» Murguía understood the dangers women faced in the public arena and claimed that Rosalía de Castro was especially vulnerable because she was, according to him, more sensitive than most:

> ¿Y si el alma atormentada es la de una mujer? . . . Bien puede decirse entonces que sus sufrimientos no han de tener límite, que las penas se duplican al caer sobre su corazón . . . ¿Quién las conoce? ¿Quién las cuenta? ¿A quién interesan? ¿Quién es ni qué importa, así sea la más ilustre, así la más desconocida? ¿Qué otro camino, si no el de la muerte, ve ante sus ojos? ¿La misma notoriedad no es para ella un peligro? (LP 176)

Remarkably similar observations about nineteenth-century women writers abound. Virginia Woolf, for example, wrote in *A Room of One's Own:*

> It was the relic of the sense of chastity that dictated anonymity to women even as late as the nineteenth century. Currer Bell, George Eliot, George Sand, all the victims of inner strife as their writings prove, sought ineffectively to veil themselves by using the name of a man. Thus they did homage to the convention, which if not implanted by the other sex was liberally encouraged by them (the chief glory of a woman is not to be talked of, said Pericles, himself a much-talked-of man), that publicity in women is detestable.[17]

Manuel Murguía never reconciles his role in promoting Rosalía de Castro's literary career with his ideal of sacred domesticity: «La mujer debe ser sin hechos y sin biografía, pues siempre hay en ella algo a que no debe tocarse. Limitada su acción al círculo de la vida doméstica, todo lo santifica desde que entra en su hogar» (LP 176).

But Rosalía de Castro's life was not limited to the domestic terrain as Murguía himself, resorting to metaphors of warfare, situates Castro squarely in the public arena of the regionalist struggle: «Cada uno escogió su puesto, y nuestra escritora, que, como la mujer gala, seguía a los suyos al combate, conociendo que podía ayudarles, se colocó resueltamente en las primeras filas» (LP 183).

Manuel Murguía closes his essay with a haunting but moving vision of her imminent death: «Todo es igual . . . sólo ella, siendo la misma, es distinta. En sus ojos no se refleja ya otra luz que la del mal que la consume y aniquila» (LP 200).

Although the seeds of the myth of domesticity are clearly planted in Murguía's essay, the much more convincing part emerges when he uses his skills as a historian. In effect, he evaluates her role in the regionalist movement and describes with a great deal of accuracy the importance of **Cantares** and **Follas** within Galicia and beyond its regional boundaries.

2. Criticism

Rosalian criticism can be grouped into three periods reflecting different ideological and intellectual tendencies. The first period emerged after her death and was headed by her husband, Manuel Murguía, his friends and associates. Almost all of them were Galicians and members of the Royal Galician Academy (Real Academia Gallega), where Murguía was a leading figure. These writers treat her as an embodiment of the Galician soul and as a symbol of virtue and saintliness. They mention pain and suffering only in the context of a selfless martyrdom. References to her private life are intentionally avoided. Serious studies of her poetry are non-existent during this period. J. A. Durán correctly assessed the idealization of Rosalía de Castro by these writers as mediated by middle-class values associated especially with Madrid.[18]

Recent critics have pointed an accusing finger at Manuel Murguía for withholding and destroying biographical documents.[19] After Rosalía de Castro's death he insisted that this information was the exclusive property of himself and his immediate family. Furthermore, he and fellow Galicians set out to deny Castro her role as a public figure and to create the «santiña» image wherein she embodies the suffering soul of Galicia, always outside society and politics and always inside a romanticized and sacred home. We see this image delineated most clearly in his 1909 preface to **En las orillas del Sar,**[20] where he quotes Daudet: «'¡Y, es tan buena, tan sencilla y tan poco literata!' Y, por cierto, que si a alguna otra escritora pudiera aplicarse tan breve como envidiable triunfo, a ninguna con mayor justicia que a Rosalía.» He continues:

> Confieso que sería para mí como cosa sagrada hablar con toda extensión de quien en este mundo fue tan buena, tan modesta, y conmigo en conformidad con la desgracia, que ni en sus mayores tribulaciones salió de sus labios una queja, ni le faltó jamás el valor para arrostrar las penas que le devoraban cuerpo y alma.[21]

And he writes concerning Rosalía de Castro's life and the lives of all women:

> Después de todo, la vida de una mujer, por muy ilustre que sea, es siempre bien sencilla. La de Rosalía, como la de cuantos se hallan en su caso, se limita a dos fechas: La de su nacimiento y la de su muerte; lo demás sólo importa a los suyos . . . *Boa te fía quen seus fillos cría,* dice el adagio gallego, y en verdad que nadie podía decirlo como ella, pues todo su amor, todo su cuidado, todos sus afanes puso en la crianza de aquellos hijos de su corazón, quienes no la dejaban momento libre para otra cosa. ¡Santo ministerio, ocupación amorosísima![22]

We must, however, give Manuel Murguía credit for writing in 1885 the article referred to earlier, in which he gives a far from simple portrayal of his wife's life. . . . .in the seventh chapter of *Los precursores,* Murguía attempts to take account of Castro's life in both historical and individual terms. In spite of rhetorical excesses this is an invaluable and substantive essay, written while she was alive and with the idea that she would read it. It also forms one of a series of historical biographies of the forerunners of the Galician cultural revival.

In describing the ceremony involving the transportation of Castro's body from the cemetery in Adina near Padrón to a newly constructed monument in the convent of Santo Domingo in Santiago, five years after her death, Eugenio Carré Aldao, a friend of Murguía's, shows us to what extent she had become much more than a historical figure:

> Ese monumento recordará perdurablemente a propios y extraños que existió en el mundo una santa, venerable y abnegada mujer, personificación de la sublime, heroica e incomparable mujer gallega, que con su inspiración y por sus sentimienos hizo el milagro de resucitar a la vida, dándole alma y corazón, a todo un pueblo.[23]

Other writers in this line include Augusto Cortina, Vitoriano García Martí, Augusto González Besada, Antonio Picón, and Alicia Santaella Murias.[24] García Martí's prologue to the first edition of the **Obras completas,** 1944, «Rosalía de Castro o el dolor de vivir», turns the controversy of her social and political awareness into mystery. Here Castro's role in the provincialist movement is alluded to but quickly dismissed. Whatever the intention of these writers may have been, the result was to deprive her of a personal and social history:

> Por su sensibilidad exquisita sintió los dolores concretos en un momento histórico de su pueblo, pero no se engañe Rosalía: ningún género de bienes habría hecho tampoco la felicidad de su país. Cuando lo hubiera logrado todo, seguiría queriendo algo más. Ese anhelo de otra cosa es la esencia y aristocracia del espíritu gallego, la raíz de su eterna nostalgia, o de su morriña. Rosalía es la personificación de este sentimiento.[25]

Martí tries to rescue Castro from what he sees as the contamination of political involvement by converting the specific social implication of her poetry into a vague and aristocratic nostalgia. How he arrives at «aristocracy of the Galician spirit», from reference to a specific historical moment, he does not explain.

Three writers, Emilia Pardo Bazán, Francisco Blanco García, and César Barja, belong only chronologically to this first group.[26] And Carolina Michaëlis de Vasconcellos made brief but important mention of Rosalía de Castro in *Cancioneiro da Ajuda* where she calls Castro the creator of modern Galician poetry and sees a relationship between Castro's Galician songs and the feminine origins of the *cantares de amigo*.[27] Emilia Pardo Bazán (1885) and Blanco García (1894) write directly about Castro's literary output, and César Barja (1926) was one of the first critics to break with Manuel Murguía and his generation by suggesting that we investigate Castro's private life in order to answer questions that arise from biographical allusions in her lyric poetry.

The next generation of critics, published in *Siete ensayos sobre Rosalía*,[28] reflects a rising interest in the intimate, introspective poetry of Rosalía de Castro: *En las orillas del Sar* and certain poems from *Follas novas*. They view *Cantares* as a masterpiece of its type but with a restricted range of interest. With the publication of *Sar* Castro leaves the picturesque countryside of Galicia to join the world of European lyric poetry. Like Bécquer, she eschews the high-flown rhetoric of Espronceda and other early romantics, while retaining the romantic emphasis on heightened emotional states. Ricardo Carballo Calero, Domingo García Sabell, Celestino F. de la Vega, and Ramón Piñero interpret her spiritual malaise as a state of metaphysical anguish, alienation, and radical loneliness. Her name is associated by these critics with the poets Heine, Novalis, and Holderlin and with the philosopher Heidegger. Carballo Calero is unequivocal in his existentialist reading of Castro:

> Trátase de unha poesía humá, impurísima pol-o tanto, que está sempre ameasando con deixar de ser poesía e aparecer filosofía, con deixar de ser arte e transformarse en vida . . . En *Follas novas* ou *En las orillas del Sar* . . . Rosalía ten acabado unha outura de pensamento e sentimento que a fai portavoz da anguria humá. Pois o seu tema fundamental e a saudade da esistencia humá e n-iste senso é o poeta máis esistencialista que cabe imaxinar. E o poeta esistencialista por escelencia.[29]

The first serious psychological study of Rosalía de Castro, the one by Rof Carballo, is based on Jung's psychic division: masculine, feminine; animus, anima.[30] The circumstance of her birth and childhood created a psychic imbalance that resulted in the overdevelopment of the feminine component and the underdevelopment of the masculine one. Rof Carballo argues that in representing the collective soul of Galicia Castro is overstocked with «feminine» traits of tenderness, vulnerability, and passivity and understocked with «masculine» ones of ambition and emotional distance.

A far more comprehensive view of Rosalía de Castro is that presented by Alberto Machado da Rosa.[31] In his interesting and highly speculative study he seeks through a biographical approach to her subjective poetry to discredit many of the myths that surround this important nineteenth-century poet. While da Rosa broke new ground by questioning the legend and searching for evidence of the person, the disproportionate attention he gives to alleged romantic crises obscures in its own way important areas of Castro's artistic production.

Machado da Rosa, as initiator of the third group of Rosalian critics, prepares the way for detailed psychoanalytic studies of the imagery of *En las orillas del Sar*, and provides the basis for further examination of biographical material.[32] In an article by Marina Mayoral, for example, contrary to what the «santiña» legend would have us believe, we see Rosalía de Castro's personality marked by rebelliousness, resentment, and impatience.[33] Mayoral bases her conclusions on several letters written by Castro.

Two complete studies of Castro's poetry have been published in the last decade by Kathleen Kulp-Hill and Marina Mayoral.[34] Kulp-Hill examines Castro's poetry and prose within the context of her life and times. The first chapters of her work present historical and biographical background and the last half is devoted to the poetry and prose. Kulp-Hill organizes her study around the examination of the sources and themes of Castro's work. Solitude, suffering and the anguish of passing time are among them. She argues that in Castro's prose we can see her as a woman of her times: « . . . an aspect of her identity which alters the usual image of her as the melancholic recluse or dreamer».[35]

Marina Mayoral treats exclusively the poetry, although she brings Castro's prose into the discussion to shed light on psychological themes. Mayoral examines the predominant stylistic and thematic elements in all of Castro's poetry. Although the present study is more concerned specifically with the social background of the Galician poetry and its relation to the interest in Europe and Spain in popular lyric, I am indebted to the comprehensive scope of these two recent works.

3. History

The Romanticism of the late eighteenth century, which flourished first in Germany and sought out a national spirit in the language and customs (folk culture) of the countryside, had clear proponents in Galicia in the first half of the nineteenth century.[36] In an attempt to redefine Galicia within the modern state of Spain, regionalists

saw as part of their task the retrieval of a lost or forgotten history. One of the most important features of
this redefinition was the preoccupation with language.
In the sixteenth century, after the formation of the central bureaucracy, Castilian replaced Galician as the language of official transactions. Also, the prominence of
Galician-Portuguese as the lyric language of the Peninsula was superseded in the fifteenth century by the
«language of the Empire», Castilian.

The recuperation of language was synonymous with the
recovery of history and the first generation of the regionalist movement looked to the rural sector as the
keeper of language and the transmitter of traditional
values. Those associated with this generation, Pastor
Díaz, Manuel Pintos, Francisco Añón, Antolín Faraldo,
and Losada, were all born in the second and third decades of the nineteenth century. They came of age during the last stages of Esproncedan Romanticism and
were very much influenced by the liberal political atmosphere associated with Spain's short-lived constitution of 1812.

In a period of increased political awareness in many
areas of society in the late eighteenth and early nineteenth centuries in Spain, the concern for the rights of
previously unrepresented groups became an important part of the new political climate. As Charles III
(1759-1788) took increased measures to consolidate
national unity, the various regions of Spain reacted
against what they saw as an enfringement upon their
own claims of autonomy and separateness. National
unification became associated by regionalists with
Castilian domination. Thus, the legacy of German Romanticism with its focus on regional culture coincided
with a strong current of regional resistance to increased
central control from Madrid.[37]

In Galicia regionalists became spokesmen for landless
peasants, immigrants, and workers, but had really very
little direct political influence. Unlike the situation in
Catalonia, the economy and politics of Galicia were
controlled from Madrid. Political bosses conducted elec-
tions according to the dictates of the center and Galicia
suffered the subordinate status of a colony in relation to
Madrid. The kind of organized political activity we see
in Catalonia by the second half of the nineteenth century, was practically nonexistent in Galicia.

José Luis Varela, historian of the cultural restoration of
nineteenth-century Galicia, stresses the impossibility of
separating political from cultural considerations in the
region. The affirmation of cultural uniqueness through
the production of a literary Galician was at the same
time an act of independence and political autonomy:

> Durante el siglo XIX, Galicia se hace por vez
> primera problema de sí misma en el artículo, poema
> o discurso; reaparece cuantiosamente el gallego
> como medio expresivo después de muchos años de
> ausencia literaria; ese poema, discurso o artículo,
> trata con cierta frecuencia un tema específicamente
> regionalista: celtismo, centralización, emigración,
> etc.»[38]

Within the larger political picture in Spain regionalism
in Galicia aligned itself with the intermittent successes
of the *Progresista* forces through the September Revolution of 1868. The failure of the parliamentary Monarchy of Macedo, and the first Spanish Republic following the 1868 Revolution, led to the Restoration of the
Bourbon Monarchy in 1875. The struggle for social
change through constitutional channels was no longer a
realistic course of action for democratic or federalist
forces, since by 1879 oligarchic groups representing the
propertied classes had managed to squelch liberal ini-
tiatives from within the government. After the Restoration of 1875, regionalists in Galicia either remained
liberal but detached from effective political action, as
was the case of Manuel Murguía and his generation, or
in the case of Curros Enríquez, they became associated
with radical opposition to the entrenched religious and
economic oligarchy.

But, to return to the early stages of Galician regionalism, *Progresista* and provincialist interests formed a
lively and productive alliance in the early 1840s in Santiago
where the first generation manifested itself in the journal-
istic field. In the pages of *Recreo Compostelano* (1842),
Antolín Faraldo draws the first outlines of regionalist
theory. José Elías de Tejada portrays this incipient regionalism of Faraldo and his contemporaries as a negation of cultural homogeneity while at the same time
reaffirming Spanish unity.[39]

Varela describes the repressive decade (1844-1854)
of Narváez's regency as one of sporadic political and
cultural activities in Galicia. Faraldo himself staged
in 1846 an unsuccessful «pronunciamiento», a local
armed uprising against Narváez and the presence of
his troops in Galicia.[40] At the end of this period, in
1853, Manuel Pintos published the most important book
of poetry to appear in Galician before **Cantares gallegos,
A gaita galega.**

According to Varela, this first generation, while failing
to produce a coherent or representative literary work,
nevertheless paved the way for the successes of the
second generation.[41] Announcing the literary orientation of this generation and following the example of
Catalonia, Eduardo Pondal organized the «Juegos
florales», which took place in La Coruña in 1861. This
competition led to the publication in 1863 of the *Album
de la Caridad,* an anthology including works in Castilian.
The result was an abundant repertory of prose and poetry by Galician writers dating from the beginning of
the nineteenth century. The *Album* included among its
contributors Rosalía de Castro, Eduardo Pondal, and

José Ballesteros, prominent members of the emerging second generation of Galician cultural and political revival.

4. Gender and Literature

Most of the poetry in Galician including **Follas novas** relies heavily on popular forms and an oral tradition. The manner in which it was conceived was very different from **La flor** and **En las orillas del Sar,** which belong to the cultured European tradition of lyric poetry.

In an eagerness to include Castro within the mainstream of European lyric tradition, critics have overlooked her ambivalent position in relation to the male-dominated tradition of European lyric poetry. This ambivalence is a striking feature of the Castilian poetry and the subject of various pieces of prose. That it is missing from most of the Galician poetry and completely from her traditional lyric in that language is highly significant.

That Rosalía de Castro relied on two different artistic worlds—one non-literate, regional and rural, and the other cultured, national and European; one absorbed informally from the time of childhood and the other learned later in a more formal setting—lead to the present exploration of these influences and how her perceptions of them affected her work.

Rosalía de Castro was a master of popular forms and was capable of using them for a variety of purposes. The shift from the popular framework to the straight narrative or to the subjective, confessional mode which depends on rhetorical conventions of the Castilian lyric tradition, can be described as a shift from a feminine mode to a masculine one, from the familiar to the unfamiliar, from the known to the unknown. The important point here is that a woman's access to the dominant male culture was limited but other areas of artistic expression were open to her.

Castro's position among nineteenth-century female poets is unique precisely because the popular tradition she draws on is one which is accessible to women. In the case of the traditional verse she was part of a marginal culture with a long history of female participation. Not only was she familiar with this tradition, she recognized its literary and human qualities and approached with confidence her role as intermediary between a non-literate tradition and a cultured public.

The circumstances of the Galician popular lyric lead logically to a female author; in the case of the introspective lyric she must constantly explain and justify a woman's right and ability to produce this kind of poetry since so few women had done it before.

It is not difficult to surmise, since songs accompanied certain daily tasks, that women had their own repertory. In his study, *The Spanish Traditional Lyric,*[42] J. G.

Cummins explains that a high percentage of lyrics in his book express female emotions and viewpoints since, as he writes:

> The female members of a Spanish rural community sing more than the men; singing is often a group activity, and the women are more commonly gathered in a group in the execution of their daily activities, washing clothes, spinning, etc., while the men's occupations, except at certain seasons, tend to be more solitary.

As an exception to this he mentions the importance of the male singer in the flamenco song of Andalusia. He concludes that a field-researcher

> can always collect more material from the women, and in any social gathering of neighbours the verses of the songs will be sung by one or other of the women, with the rest of the women, and sometimes one or two of the more extrovert of the men, joining in the refrain.[43]

The predominance of women in the composition and performance of traditional songs in rural Galicia captured the attention of observers in the eighteenth and nineteenth centuries in their paradoxical search for an art born of nature. For example, Padre Sarmiento, the historian and philologist to whom later critics referred, states in 1775: «En la mayor parte de las coplas gallegas hablan las mujeres con los hombres, y es porque ellas son las que componen las coplas sin artificio alguno y ellas mismas inventan los tonos o aires a que las han de cantar, sin tener idea del arte músico».[44] Milá y Fontanals reports a similar observation from Manuel Murguía: «No hay acto de la vida vulgar que no tenga sus coplas; las mujeres principalmente parecen haber inventado este medio de dar a conocer a sus sentimientos.»[45]

In direct reference to **Cantares gallegos** and **Follas novas,** the late nineteenth-century literary historian, Francisco Blanco García, echoes Sarmiento and elaborates further on the idea of art free of artifice by claiming that Castro accomplishes a miraculous conversion of «nature» into «culture» while still conserving nature's original qualities, a feat possible in part because she is a woman:

> Por su condición de mujer, por su entrañable cariño al suelo en que nació y por el vínculo secreto que hermanaba su musa con la musa popular, sentíase con vocación para dignificarla, haciendo que aquellas *coplas sin artificio,* de procedencia femenina en gran parte, mencionadas por P. Sarmiento, se convirtiesen en manjar exquisito aun para los más refinados paladares, y se revistieran de nuevos encantos sin perder su nativa ingenuidad.[46]

Blanco García's words deserve special attention since they unwittingly delineate the creative process in its most conscious manifestations. His words define nothing if not the deliberate hand of the artist and the «art» of the popular song: «Poner la mano en esas delicadas y voladoras manifestaciones de la poesía anónima de un pueblo cuyas intimidades psicológicas encierran bajo la envoltura de la concisión y la sencillez más inimitables; parafrasear lo que es perfecto y acabado en su línea.» And while recognizing the difficulties and risks involved in giving written form to anonymous or collective expression, he still cannot fully acknowledge in Castro's Galician poetry the artistic process he alludes to with such pomp and eloquence:

> Ensanchar los moldes de un arte que rechaza toda innovación hija del estudio; asimilarse ideas y sentimientos colectivos no adulterando su esencia ni la forma de expresión tradicional, era empeño tan arriesgado como glorioso para quien consiguiera realizarlo cumplidamente.[47]

The patronizing tendency to view women as ignorant creators rather than as active participants in transcendent processes of culture reflects a universal of human society as analyzed by the anthropologist Sherry Ortner in «Is Female to Male as Nature is to Culture?»[48] Her formulation, supported by convincing arguments and evidence, is that «culture (still equated unambiguously with men) recognizes that women are active participants in its special processes, but at the same time it sees them as being more rooted in, or having more direct affinity with nature». Ortner notes that in every society women «can appear from certain points of view to stand both under and over (but really simply outside of) the sphere of culture's hegemony».[49]

Blanco García sees Rosalía de Castro as an interpreter of nature, preserving its special qualities, while at the same time making it accessible to an educated public. Ortner's metaphor of woman's intermediate position seems appropriate in the context of Rosalía de Castro's perceived role as mediator between nature and culture: «We may envision culture as a small clearing within the forest of the larger natural system. From this point of view, that which is intermediate between culture and nature is located on the continuous periphery of culture's clearing.»[50]

The presumed primitive qualities of the traditional songs were highly valued; the female association with the songs reaffirmed their natural condition and their tenuous relation to conscious creation. But this is perhaps why *Cantares,* while always described as a masterpiece, is never studied as one. *Cantares* is removed twice from the realm of culture, first by its rural and feminine origins and second by the «marginal» language in which it is written.

Nine years before Blanco García published his history, Emilia Pardo Bazán praised *Cantares gallegos* as an

example of the successful convergence of sexual and artistic factors. Pardo Bazán, with characteristic clarity, rather than wrapping this convergence in mystery, simply identifies it as the universal literary process whereby the specific and the quotidian are given metaphoric or symbolic meaning:

> Ese es el principal encanto de Rosalía: haber expresado como poeta lo que entendió como mujer: y no creáis que es cosa tan fácil, después de penetrar en el cerebro de la moza que va a la foliada o lleva la vaca al pasto, interpretar su pensamiento en forma poética, que no parezca al lector artificiosa y falsa . . . cuando nos cautiva es al impregnarse del sentimiento del pueblo, al reproducirlos con sin igual donaire, al aceptar el carácter verdadero de este renacimiento regionalista, donde forzosamente ha de dominar el elemento idílico y rústico, por virtud de la lengua que, desde tanto tiempo hace, sólo vive entre silvanos y ninfas agrarias . . . [51]

In this address to the Liceum of Artisans of La Coruña, given in honor of Rosalía de Castro, less than two months after her death, Pardo Bazán also criticized Castro's subjective poetry, condemning most of the poems in *Follas novas* as «sickly complaints» («enfermizas quejas»); thus, she reveals her impatience with the narrow scope of the intimist poetry of Campoamor and other lesser known writers of the latter half of the nineteenth century. In spite of her blanket judgment of *Follas novas,* she recognized, as no one before or since, Castro's primary creative accomplishment of providing the Galician restoration with a voice whose oral tradition led to powerful written literary expression.

Castro drew mainly from the rhetorical conventions of traditional poetry, but also depended on a rich fund of written literary sources of classical Peninsular lyric. *Follas novas,* while dispensing for the most part with the *cantar,* is nevertheless a literary and political continuation of the first Galician collection, *Cantares gallegos.* The importance of Galician itself as concrete source of poetry and as metaphor of poetry, first suggested in the prologue to *Cantares,* is fully realized in *Follas novas.* The interpenetration of the lyric persona with the peasant's voice is much more complete in this second collection. One might argue that a more sophisticated creative process is carried out there, one more aware of literary possibilities and directions.

The evolution of Rosalía de Castro's Galician poetry is only comprehensible within the context of the avid interest of avant-garde poets in the lyric potential of traditional poetry. Castro's relation to the movement of lyric renovation, whose most famous member is Gustavo Adolfo Bécquer, is essential to an understanding of *Follas novas* and its relation to *Cantares gallegos.* That her contribution to this movement is in Galician rather than Castilian must be considered in light of sexual as well as social circumstances.

With romantic poetry as her model, Rosalía de Castro pursued a strategy of attack and retreat, never fully resolving the contradiction between gender and poetic vocation. . . . This conflict is most visible in relation to the Castilian poetry because her literary models in that language were implicitly removed from her sphere of access. Her freedom as an artist is greatly enhanced when she has recourse to traditional poetic models in the Galician language. For, as we have seen, her precursors were not always men, her tradition not always male-dominated.

Although she was clearly attracted to the introspective mode most dramatically represented by Byron, her strengths as a poet, as she herself realized, lay with the popular poetic forms. Paradoxically it is the work of Castro with its source in the oral traditions of Galicia which transcends regional and temporal boundaries and thus deserves serious attention.

Notes

[1] The fragments of information that make up Castro's biography come primarily from the following sources: Marina Mayoral, apéndice biográfico, *La poesía de Rosalía de Castro* (Madrid: Gredos, 1974), pp. 570-85; Ricardo Carballo Calero, *Historia da literatura galega, 1808-1936* (Vigo: Galaxia, 1962), pp. 142-50; Manuel Murguia, *Los precursores* (La Coruña: Imprenta de la Voz de Galicia, 1865), pp. 171-200; Augusto González Besada, *Rosalía Castro: notas biográficas* (Madrid: Biblioteca Hispania, 1916); Juan Naya Pérez, *Inéditos de Rosalía* (Santiago, Publicaciones del Patronato Rosalía de Castro, 1953); Alberto Machado da Rosa, «Rosalía de Castro, a mulher e o poeta» (Ph.D. dissertation, University of Wisconsin, 1953); and Geraldine Foster, «Nature and Emotion in Rosalía de Castro's *En las orillas del Sar*» (Ph.D. dissertation, University of Wisconsin, 1979), Chapter I.

[2] According to Fermín Bouza Brey, when Rosalía de Castro was living with her mother in Santiago in the 1860s, María Francisca was a member of the household. See «Los *Cantares gallegos* de Rosalía y los suyos entre 1860 y 1863», *Cuadernos de Estudios Gallegos,* XVIII (1963), pp. 236-37.

[3] Ricardo Carballo Calero, *Historia da literatura galega contemporánea,* Vol. I (Vigo: Galaxia, 1963), p. 145.

[4] Ricardo Carballo Calero, *Historia,* p. 145.

[5] Marina Mayoral, ed., *En las orillas del Sar* (Clásicos Castalia, 1976), pp. 11 and 12.

[6] Fermín Bouza Brey, «El solar y mayorazgo de *Arretén* de los antepasados de Rosalía de Castro», *Cuadernos de Estudios Gallegos,* XV (1960), p. 184.

[7] Bouza Brey, «Poesía de Pondal a Rosalía enferma», *Cuadernos de Estudios Gallegos,* V (1950), p. 144.

[8] «Whatever the family reaction had been to the birth of Teresa's child in 1837, not only Teresa but also Rosalía's aunts and uncles later accepted her into the Castro family. During these years [1846-1852] she spent time at the family home of Arretén in Iria Flavia, owned by her Uncle José, and also at Torres de Hermida in Lestrove, the home of Teresa's sister Josefa and her husband Gregorio.» Geraldine Foster, «Nature and Emotion», p. 5.

[9] Rosalía de Castro, *Cantares gallegos,* pp. 168-69 and 171.

[10] Rosalía de Castro, «Padrón y las inundaciones» IV, *La Ilustración Gallega y Asturiana,* March 8, 1881, p. 75, col. 3; p. 76, col. 1. Original cited by Geraldine Foster, «Nature and Emotion», pp. 5 and 6.

[11] According to Murguía the move from Padrón to Santiago also marked a turning point in Castro's life: « . . . hubiera pasado su vida si los primeros contratiempos no la hubiesen obligado a marchar a la triste ciudad en que había nacido y a la cual tornaba para hacer de ella su única patria y la patria de sus hijos. Atrás dejaba los recuerdos de la infancia y sus primeros cielos risueños.» *Los precursores,* pp. 175-76.

[12] *Polémica feminista en la España contemporánea* (Madrid: Siglo Veintiuno de España Editores, 1976), p. 15.

[13] «Se sospecha que frecuentó las aulas de la Sociedad Económica de Amigos del País, donde se estudiaban música y diseño. Rosalía habitó en una casa de la Porta Faxeira, que por el año 1856 llevaba el número 6. Su domicilio estaba, pues, próximo al edificio del colegio de San Clemente, donde se encontraba instalada la Sociedad. Rosalía tenía conocimientos de música y diseño, según acreditan Murguía y González Besada.» Ricardo Carballo Calero, *Historia,* p. 163.

[14] Fermín Bouza Brey, «La joven Rosalía en Compostela (1852-1856)», *Cuadernos de Estudios Gallegos,* X (1955), pp. 201-57.

[15] See Richard Herr, *An Historical Essay on Modern Spain* (Berkeley: University of California, 1974), pp. 99-112.

[16] See Vitoriano García Martí's discussion of this issue in the prologue to *Obras Completas,* «El dolor de vivir», pp. 54-55.

[17] Virginia Woolf, *A Room of One's Own* (New York: Harcourt, Brace, and World, 1957), p. 52.

[18] José A. Durán, *Historia de caciques, bandos e ideologías en la Galicia no urbana* (Madrid: Siglo Veintiuno, 1972), p. 138, note 225.

[19] See for example, Marina Mayoral, «Sobre el amor y sobre la destrucción de ciertas cartas», *Cuadernos Hispanoamericanos,* no. 233 (Madrid: 1969), pp. 486-502.

[20] Manuel Murguía's preface to the 1909 edition of *Orillas del Sar* appears in all subsequent editions.

[21] Castro, *Orillas del Sar,* p. 60.

[22] Castro, p. 61.

[23] Eugenio Carré Aldao, «Estudio bio-bibliográfico crítico acerca de Rosalía de Castro», *Boletín de la Real Academia Gallega,* La Coruña, XVI (1927), XVII (1928), p. 43.

[24] Augusto Cortina, «Rosalía de Castro y su obra poética», in *Obra Poética* (Buenos Aires: Espasa Calpe, 1942); Vitoriano García Martí, «Rosalía de Castro o el dolor de vivir», prologue to *Obras completas,* sexta edición (Madrid: Aguilar, 1968), pp. 9-203; Augusto González Besada, *Rosalía Castro, notas biográficas* (Madrid: Biblioteca Hispania, 1916); Octavio Picón, «Discurso», read before the Real Academia Española, May 7, 1916. Published in A. González Besada, *Rosalía de Castro;* and Alicia Santaella Murias, *Rosalía de Castro. Vida-poética y ambiente* (Buenos Aires: Imprenta López, 1942).

[25] Vitoriano García Martí, Prologue to *Obras completas,* 6th ed. (Madrid: Aguilar, 1968), p. 12.

[26] Emilia Pardo Bazán, *De mi tierra, Obras completas,* IX (Madrid: Administración, 1892), pp. 3-47; Padre Francisco Blanco García, *Historia de la literatura española en el siglo XIX,* Vol. III (Madrid: Sáenz de Jubera, 1894); César Barja, «En torno al lirismo gallego del siglo xix», *Smith College Studies in Modern Languages* VII, nos. 2 and 3 (January and April 1926), note 12, p. 48.

[27] *Cancioneiro da Ajuda* (Halle: 1904), note 2, p. 790.

[28] *Siete ensayos sobre Rosalía* (Vigo: Galaxia, 1952). Other recent studies on Rosalía de Castro include Jesús Alonso Montero, introduction to his edition of *En las orillas del Sar* (Salamanca: Biblioteca Anaya, 1964), and «Rosalía de Castro: compromiso, denuncia, desamparo y violencia», in *Realismo y conciencia crítica en la literatura gallega* (Madrid: Editorial Ciencia Nueva, 1968); Ricardo Carballo Calero, *Aportaciones a la literatura gallega contemporánea* (Madrid: Gredos, 1955); Javier Costa Clavel, *Rosalía de Castro* (Barcelona: Editorial Plaza-Janes, 1967); and Maria Antonia Nogales de Muñiz, *Irradiación de Rosalía de Castro* (Barcelona: 1966).

[29] *Siete Ensayos,* p. 22.

[30] Rof Carballo, «Rosalía, Anima Galaica», *Siete Ensayos,* pp. 111-49.

[31] Alberto Machado da Rosa, «Rosalía de Castro, poeta incomprendido», *Revista Hispánica Moderna,* XX, no. 3 (July 1954); and «Rosalía de Castro, a mulher e o poeta» (Ph.D. dissertation, University of Wisconsin, 1953).

[32] Two studies are based on Machado da Rosa's premise that serious sexual problems motivate Rosalía's lyric poetry: Kessel Schwartz, «Rosalía de Castro's *En las orillas del Sar.* A Psychoanalytical Interpretation», *Symposium,* XXVI (1972), pp. 363-75; and Robert Havard, «Image and Persona in Rosalía de Castro's *En las orillas del Sar*», *Hispanic Review,* XLII (1974), pp. 393-411.

[33] Mayoral, «Sobre el amor», pp. 486-502.

[34] Kathleen Kulp, *Manner and Mood in Rosalía de Castro: A Study of Theme and Style* (Madrid: Ediciones José Porrúa Turanzas, 1968); and Marina Mayoral, *La poesía de Rosalía de Castro* (Madrid: Gredos, 1974).

[35] Kathleen Kulp-Hill, *Rosalía de Castro* (Boston: Twayne Publishers, 1977), p. 125.

[36] The historical information in this chapter is drawn from the following works: José Luis Varela, *Poesía y restauración cultural de Galicia en el siglo XIX* (Madrid: Gredos, 1958); Raymond Carr, *Spain 1808-1939* (London: Oxford, 1975); Richard Herr, *The Eighteenth Century Revolution in Spain* (Princeton: 1958); and Richard Herr, *An Historical Essay on Modern Spain* (Berkeley: University of California, 1974). Three literary histories treat the problems of culture and politics in nineteenth century Galicia: Francisco Blanco García, *Historia;* Ricardo Carballo Calero, *Historia de la literatura gallega contemporánea,* I (Madrid: Editorial Nacional, 1975); and Guillermo Díaz Plaja, *Historia general de las literaturas hispánicas* (Barcelona: Barna, 1949).

[37] For a history of German influence on Spanish poetry in the nineteenth century, see José Pedro Díaz, *Gustavo Adolfo Bécquer, vida y poesía* (Madrid: Gredos, 1958), pp. 113-90. See also II, pp. 43-44, of this study.

[38] José Luis Varela, *Poesía y restauración cultural,* pp. 83-84.

[39] José Luis Varela, pp. 87-89.

[40] In *Poesía y restauración çultural,* Varela describes the political background of the 1846 rebellion: «Toda revindicación autonómica o de los derechos democráticos

es condenada al silencio por Narváez en la década 1844-1854. Como es sabido, Narváez acentúa la censura de prensa, pone en práctica la abolición de los principios democráticos mediante la constitución del 45, suspende los derechos de reunión y reprime todo conato de rebeldía—como el gallego de 1846—» (p. 89). In note 10 on the same page Varela quotes from the *Manifiesto de la Junta Suprema de Gobierno de Galicia,* edited (published?) so it seems by Faraldo: «Galicia arrastrando hasta aquí una existencia oprobiosa, convertida en una verdadera colonia de la corte, va a levantarse de su humillación y abatimiento . . . Despertando al poderoso sentimiento de provincialismo, y encaminando a un solo objeto los talentos y todos los esfuerzos, llegará a conquistar Galicia la influencia de que es merecedora, colocándose en el alto lugar a que está llamado el antiguo reino de los suevos. Que la espada de Galicia haga inclinar una sola vez a la balanza en que pesan los destinos de España.» *La Revolución,* I (Santiago: April 17, 1846).

[41] José Luis Varela, pp. 30-31.

[42] J. G. Cummins, ed., *The Spanish Traditional Lyric* (Oxford: Pergamon Press, 1977).

[43] Cummins, p. 22.

[44] Padre Sarmiento, *Memorias para la historia de poesía y poetas españoles* (Madrid: D. J. Ibarra, 1775), p. 238. González Besada refers to Sarmiento's words and makes a connection between a woman's role in popular Galician songs and the feminine voice in the thirteenth century *Cancioneros:* «Es digno de notarse y esto bastará para perpetuar su memoria, que en un país fecundo en hombres de ciencia y de saber . . . ; ha sido una mujer el verdadero y genuino intérprete de sus ansias. Sin duda que esta aparente singularidad no puede sorprender a cuantos, impuestos en la historia de la poesía popular gallega, recuerden las afirmaciones del P. Sarmiento . . . y es curioso y digno de consignarse, que en opinión de ilustres críticos, lo más hermoso de los cancioneros arcaicos *(Cancionero de la Vaticana y de Colocci-Brancutti)* son cantares de amigo, precisamente los cantos populares, obra de mujer.» *Discurso leído ante la Real Academia Española* (Madrid: Imprenta Clásica Moderna, 1916), p. 46.

[45] Milá y Fontanals, «De la poesía popular gallega», *Obras completas,* Vol. 5 (Barcelona: Alvaro Verdaguer, 1893), p. 364. Virginia Woolf in *A Room of One's Own* offers a parallel observation: «Indeed I would venture to guess that Anon, who wrote so many poems without signing them, was often a woman. It was a woman Edward Fitzgerald, I think, suggested who made the ballads and the folksongs, crooning them to their children, beguiling her spinning with them, or the length of the winter's night» (p. 51).

[46] Francisco Blanco García, *Historia,* p. 240.

[47] Blanco Garcá, p. 240.

[48] Sherry Ortner, «Is Female to Male as Nature is to Culture?», in *Woman Culture and Society,* ed. Rosaldo & Lamphere (Palo Alto: Stanford, 1975), pages 67-87.

[49] Ortner, pp. 73 and 86.

[50] Ortner, p. 85. For a rejection of Ortner's argument of universal female subordination, see Peggy Reeves Sanday, *Female Power and Male Dominance. On the Origins of Sexual Inequality* (Cambridge: Cambridge University Press, 1981), pp. 4-5; 175 & 176.

[51] Emilia Pardo Bazán, *Obras completas,* IX, p. 29.

Anna-Marie Aldaz and Barbara N. Gantt (essay date 1991)

SOURCE: Introduction to *Poems* by Rosalía de Castro, State University of New York Press, 1991, pp. 1-24.

[*In the following excerpt, Aldaz and Gantt discuss Castro's life, place in Spanish literature, and poetic themes.*]

Her Life

At the time of her death in 1885, Rosalía de Castro was little known outside of her native Galicia, a region in northwestern Spain. Yet this woman poet who wrote more than half of her poems in a regional language and did not follow the poetic conventions of her time is now considered one of the outstanding figures of Spanish literature.

Rosalía was born on February 24, 1837, in the historic city of Santiago de Compostela, now the capital of Galicia.[1] Though her birth certificate calls Rosalía "hija de padres incógnitos [daughter of unknown parentage]," she was actually the illegitimate child of a once-wealthy noblewoman, María Teresa de la Cruz de Castro y Abadía and José Martínez Viojo, a priest.[2]

The maternal grandfather, José de Castro Salgado, did not want his daughter to raise a child born out of wedlock; therefore, Rosalía spent her early years in the country, though it is not certain whether she lived with her godmother or a paternal aunt.[3] From the age of nine to fifteen, Rosalía lived at the Castro family manor of Arretén in Padrón, as well as with her maternal uncle at Torres de Hermida in Lestrove. It is probable that mother and daughter spent time together during those years. However, the official date of their reunion is often given as 1852, when Rosalía joined her mother in Santiago. The deep bond which developed between them continued even after Rosalía moved away. When her mother died in 1862,

Rosalía expressed her grief in a privately printed collection·of elegaic poems titled *A mi madre* [To my Mother].

Although Rosalía's formal education may not have been extensive, she was overly modest when in one of her two autobiographical prologues she described herself as "no habendo deprendido en máis escola que a dos nosos probes aldeáns [having no other education than that of our poor village schools]." In fact, she began writing poetry when she was about twelve, studied French, and enjoyed drawing, singing, and acting, as well as playing guitar and piano. She was familiar with the classic Spanish authors and read the works in translation of such Romantics as Heinrich Heine, Edgar Allen Poe, Lord Byron and E. T. A. Hoffman, all of whom seem to have influenced her own writing.

In 1856 Rosalía moved to Madrid where she published her first volume of poems at age nineteen. This youthful work entitled *La flor* [The Flower] was enthusiastically reviewed a year later by a young Galician critic called Manuel Murguía. Even though Murguía pretended not to know Rosalía, referring to her politely and distantly as "Señorita de Castro," it is probable that they knew each other from the Liceo de la Juventud in Santiago where Rosalía had also met her fellow Galician poets Eduardo Pondal and Aurelio Aguirre. While Rosalía was in Madrid, Aguirre died tragically at the age of twenty-four of an accidental drowning, and some critics, especially Alberto Machado da Rosa, suggest that he was the lost love that Rosalía often recalls in her poetry.[4] Machado's theory is not shared by everyone, though it is generally agreed that Aguirre might have been the model for Flavio, the protagonist of Rosalía's novel by that name.

In October of 1858, a year after the review appeared, Rosalía de Castro and Manuel Murguía were married and moved back to Galicia. Manuel Martínez Murguía (1833-1923), a writer and historian,· is applauded by some biographers for promoting his wife's work, but accused by others of being jealous of her talent and trying to influence her writing. Yet during the thirty-eight years that he survived her, Murguía wrote numerous articles in his wife's praise. His other important contribution was that, as a champion of the Galician literary Renaissance, he encouraged Rosalía to write in her native language, "o galego."

Galicia's language, which resembles Portuguese, has an illustrious history dating back to the Middle Ages. Medieval lyrics, among them those of Alfonso el Sabio, were written in Galician-Portuguese, probably the earliest literary language of the Iberian Peninsula. By the fifteenth century, however, Castilian had become the dominant literary language of Spain, and Galician was relegated to everyday usage, surviving in purely oral form.

In 1863, when Rosalía was twenty-six years old, her first collection of poems written in Galician, *Cantares gallegos* [*Galician Songs*], appeared. The publisher was reluctant to undertake such a risk, and Rosalía apparently had reservations herself since she used a Spanish title. As the first book-length work in Galician after several centuries, the collection greatly advanced the cause of the "Rexurdimento [Restoration]," an attempt by Murguía and a group of Galician intellectuals to reinstate their language for literary purposes and restore it to its former splendor.

In her prologue, Rosalía apologizes for her Galician pointing out that, "sin gramática, sin regras de ningunha clase, o lector topará moitas veces faltas de ortografía, xiros que disoarán ós oídos dun purista [since I had no grammar or rules of any kind, the reader will find many spelling errors or expressions which will offend a purist's ear]." Even though there are certain grammatical inconsistencies and orthographic idiosyncrasies, these short-comings are insignificant in comparison to her unique contributions to Galician identity and culture.

Both the prologue and the poems in *Cantares gallegos* reveal Rosalía's love for her region and her interest in its folklore, customs, and songs. The title of *Cantares gallegos* echoes that of Rosalía's avowed model, *El libro de cantares* [The Book of Songs], by Antonio Trueba, whom she praises in her essay. Her other source, though not mentioned by name, is La Choina, a family servant who taught her "aqueles cantares, aquelas palabras cariñosas e aqueles xiros nunca olvidados que tan docemente resoaron nos meus oídos desde a cuna [those songs, those affectionate words, and those unforgettable phrases that have echoed so sweetly in my ears since I was a child]."

Rosalía's characteristic technique of taking a popular stanza and elaborating it into a ballad is well illustrated by one of the poems in *Cantares,* **"Adiós rios, adiós fontes"** ["Farewell to rivers, farewell to streams"]. This poem, the first she wrote in Galician, exemplifies one of the recurrent motifs in the collection: the plight of the emigrant who is forced to leave his "patria chica [native region]." In her gloss on a popular refrain, Rosalía assumes the persona of a young man who, before having to leave his familiar surroundings, enumerates everything that he will miss. At the time of writing this poem, Rosalía herself lived in dry Castile, and the poem's prevalent water imagery evokes the misty beauties of Galicia with its abundant rivers, fountains, and brooks.

During the years that her husband's job as government historian took them to Simancas (in Valladolid) and to Madrid, Rosalía, who was very attached to her native region, felt uprooted. The nostalgia caused by this internal exile underlies many of her poems. Mingled with her recurrent theme of vague yearning is the more specific grief over the death in infancy of two of her seven children. Furthermore, Rosalía's frequent bouts with illness may explain the numerous references to suffering which pervade her work.

Seventeen years after **Cantares,** which was well received and assured Rosalía de Castro's fame as a regional poet, she published her only other work written in Galician, **Follas novas** [New Leaves]. In her prologue to **Follas,** Rosalía explains the reasons for the notable difference between the present work and the earlier one. She calls **Cantares** a youthful work which exuded a sense of freshness, innocence, and hope in contrast to the present collection whose poems she calls "'probes enxendros da mina tristura' ['poor children of my sadness']" and "fillos cativos das horas de enfermedades e de ausencias [captive children of my hours of sickness and nostalgia]." She also apologizes for the fact that many of the poems in this book

> refrexan, quisáis con demasiada sinceridade, o estado do meu esprito unhas veces; outras, a miña natural disposición (que no en balde son muller) a sentir como propias as penas alleas.

> [reflect, perhaps with too much candor the state of my soul and my natural disposition as a woman to feel other people's sorrow as my own].

As Rosalía points out, the mood in these poems is indeed very different. In addition to her feelings of solidarity with her compatriots, especially the widows, orphans, and beggars, she also explores her own feelings of exile, separation, solitude, and yearning, all expressed by "soidá" (or "soidade"), a word which has no precise English equivalent.

Rosalía continues to illuminate "soidá" in her last set of poems, **En las orillas del Sar** [**Beside the River Sar**], published in 1884, a year before her premature death. Many of the Spanish poems contained in this collection were undoubtedly written at the same time as some of the Galician one in **Follas,** which explains their thematic similarities.

It is in these last two books that Rosalía seems to realize that, for her, "dolor [grief, suffering, anguish, pain, anxiety]" is inevitable. In several poems she tries to define the nature of this affliction which she variously compares to an illness or a "negra sombra [black shadow]," but to which she often refers simply as "something." Actually Rosalía prefers not to resolve the ambiguity, leaving "dolor" as an open-ended symbol.

Rosalía de Castro challenged 19th-century literary standards by writing in both Spanish and Galician. As Claude Poullain has shown, her bilingualism also implies a greater complexity of styles. In a comparison of her Spanish and Galician verse, the critic finds that it varies according to the linguistic audience the poet addresses: the language of her Galician poetry is more specific and popular, while her Spanish poems tend to be more general and abstract. The critic concludes his study with the assertion that, "Todo esto muestra que el bilingüismo, en la obra de Rosalía, es una extraodinaria fuente de riqueza y de variedad. . . . [All this shows that in Rosalía's work, bilingualism is an extraordinary source of richness and variety. . . .]"[5]

Yet it is also probable that this bilingualism, coupled with her being a woman, contributed to the delay in her acceptance. In the words of Gerald Brenan, echoed later by John Frederick Nims, "Had she written in Castilian rather than in her native Galician dialect, she would, I feel sure, be recognized as the greatest woman poet of modern times."[6]

Rosalía de Castro in the Context of Spanish Literature

Contemporary critics regard **Follas novas** and **En las orillas del Sar** as Rosalía's best work, but during her lifetime her fame, which was primarily regional, rested more on **Cantares gallegos.** It is symptomatic that her compatriot and contemporary, the regional novelist Emilia Pardo Bazán, preferred **Cantares,** praising it for skillfully capturing the essence of the Galician spirit and representing, in her words, "lo más sincero de nuestra poesía, lo que mejor refleja la fisionomía tradicional y pintoresca de nuestro país [our sincerest poetry and that which best reflects the traditional and picturesque traits of our country.]"[7]

Perhaps the public reception of **Follas** was less enthusiastic because of the poetry's political dimensions. Here Rosalía depicts not only Galicia's quaint and charming folk customs, but also its oppressive poverty.

Though Rosalía achieved some degree of recognition in Galicia by the time of her death, it is not until the turn of the century that she was rediscovered in the rest of Spain. Today she is thought to be the equal of Gustavo Aldolfo Bécquer who had previously been regarded as the only Spanish post-romantic poet of merit.

It is generally assumed that Rosalía de Castro and Bécquer (1836-70) knew each other, though there is no documentation of their personal acquaintance. In her poetry, as well as in that of Bécquer, there is a personal, intimate, and suggestive lyricism which is imbued with melancholy and yearning.

I. L. McClelland suggests that Rubén Dario was influenced by both Bécquer and Rosalía in his experimentation with unusual line lengths and combinations, and his preference for an unconvoluted and direct style.[8] This same view was voiced much earlier by Manuel Murguía, one of the first to recognize Rosalía's innovative role. Murguía, who even during her lifetime referred to his wife as a "precursora [forerunner]," attributed her experimentations with unusual metric combinations to her innate musical talent. In an essay written after Rosalía's death, Murguía quotes another young writer who praised Rosalía for daring to break the metric rules prevalent during her time:

> Se necesitó que un joven escritor de nuestros días, dolido de la injusticia, se adelantase a quejarse del hecho, proclamándola como *precursora* de la reforma por ella iniciada sencilla, instintivamente, sin ánimo de constituir escuela y sólo porque, como tan gran música, le estaba permitido romper con los viejos moldes, ensanchando los dominios de la métrica castellana.[9]

> [It needed a young writer of our times who, hurt by the injustice, stepped forward to complain about it and to proclaim her as the *forerunner* of the movement which she began simply and instinctively, without any intention of starting a school, simply because, as a great musician, she was allowed to break with the old forms and to enlarge the domain of Spanish metrics.]

This view was also held by another young writer, Azorín, who knew Murguía and this essay. In an essay about Juan Ramón Jímenez, Azorín admonishes his readers not to forget that "antes que Rubén, en 1884, Rosalía de Castro había sido la precursora de la revolución poética realizada en la métrica y en la ideología [before Rubén, in 1884, Rosalía de Castro was a forerunner of the poetic revolution in metrics and ideology]."[10] In "Rosalía de Castro," one of his several essays devoted to her, Azorín complains about the exclusion of her poetry from anthologies and the unmerited critical neglect of her work.[11]

It is largely thanks to Azorín and other members of the Generation of '98 that Rosalía de Castro was rediscovered in Spain. Miguel de Unamuno, Juan Ramón Jiménez, and Antonio Machado all showed their appreciation for Rosalía in their own fashion. Unamuno praised her in his essays on Galicia[12]; Juan Ramón translated some of her Galician poems into Spanish, and he knew much of her poetry by heart; and Machado's poetry offers evidence of his affinity with Rosalía's poems and the influence they exerted upon him. In general, these poets came to regard Rosalía as one of their own, because they found a foreshadowing of their own sense of spiritual dislocation and existential anxiety in Rosalía's poetry.

Several recent critics have studied the affinities between Rosalía and the Generation of '98. In her article "Rosalía de Castro, anticipación del 98," Pilar G. Suelto de Sáenz has shown that Rosalía anticipates many of the themes found in the poetry of the Generation of '98, among them a lyric and personal treatment of nature and landscape.[13] Another critic, Eliana Suárez Rivero, expanding on a brief analysis by Rafael Lapesa which compares Bécquer, Rosalía, and Machado, specifies the following similarities between the latter two: a subjective treatment of nature as a reflection of their mood; a predilection for late afternoon and sunset imagery; and a feeling of solitude. She also remarks that Machado sings the beauties of Castile, Rosalía those of Galicia; Machado identifies with the river Duero, Rosalía with the Sar.[14]

Suárez Rivero comments on several poems that prefigure the verse of the Generation of '98, particularly, Rosalía's "Unha vez tiven un cravo / cravado no corazón [Once a nail pierced my heart]" and Machado's "En el corazón tenía / la espina de una pasión [In my heart I carried / a passion's thorn]." Most likely, Rosalía's poem found resonances in Machado because he shared her ambivalent love / hate relationship with suffering, unable to live either with or without it.

As for the next generation of poets, known as the Generation of '27, three in particular have paid tribute to Rosalía. Luis Cernuda, though he found fault with what he considered her sentimentality, praised Rosalía for her timelessness.[15] Gerardo Diego invoked her name metaphorically in his poetry, and Federico García Lorca paid homage to her by writing "Seis poemas gallegos," among them an elegy dedicated to her, "Canzón de cuna pra Rosalía Castro, morta [Lullaby for the Late Rosalía de Castro]."

Ever since the beginning of this century, the list of articles and books devoted to Rosalía de Castro's work has increased steadily. In 1985, the centennial of her death was commemorated with numerous congresses and symposia world-wide. The published proceedings from the international congress held in Santiago de Compostela constitute an important addition to the growing body of scholarship on Rosalía.[16]

Rosalía de Castro and the English-speaking Reader

Rosalía's work is still largely unknown to non-Spanish audiences. Most of the criticism about her is by Hispanic critics and only available in Spanish publications. As a glance at [a] bibliography shows, little has been written about her in English. Some British critics, such as Aubrey Bell and especially Gerald Brenan, were pioneers in praising her, but in the United States Rosalía has only received critical attention in the last thirty years, mainly as the subject of doctoral dissertations. Two dissertations which have been published in book form are Kathleen Kulp's *Manner and Mood in Rosalía de Castro* and Shelley Stevens' *Rosalía de Castro and the Galician Revival*. The only other full-length book in English devoted to Rosalía is Kathleen Kulp-Hill's *Rosalía de Castro*, which offers an excellent introduction to the poet's life and works.

Recently two critics, Antonio Gómez Costa and Martha LaFollette Miller, studied similarities in the poetry of Rosalía de Castro and that of Emily Dickinson. The Spanish critic emphasizes what he calls these poets' "authenticity" and comments on their shared imagery.[17] Miller points out that both poets were very private persons, who, for the most part, omitted titles to their poems because they did not intend to publish them. The critic stresses that a similar note of intimacy and authenticity is discernible in their poetry. Both poets regarded suffering as unavoidable and they tried to come to terms with their pain, realizing that, for them, it is interrelated with pleasure. Further parallels are the occasional use of modest personae and their intimate, almost loving, relationship with death.[18]

A Thematic Analysis of Rosalía de Castro's Poetry

Since many of Rosalía's thematic and stylistic characteristics are well illustrated in her early poem, **"Adiós ríos, adiós fontes"** [Farewell to rivers, farewell to streams], an analysis of this poem will serve as a starting point for a general discussion of her poetry. **"Adiós ríos, adiós fontes,"** untitled like the majority of her poems, is a gloss on a popular verse. The poem is written in "coplas," stanzas of four lines with eight syllables, one of the most accessible and preferred metric forms in popular Spanish poetry. In keeping with her tendency to experiment with established forms, in stanzas 8 through 11, the poet adds an unorthodox fifth line to the usual quatrains.

The prevalence of diminutives ("casiña," "hortiña," "figueriña," etc.) exemplifies one of Rosalía's characteristics and reflects a common linguistic habit in Spanish which is even more prevalent in Galician. As Amado Alonso has remarked, "el diminutive es una de las más decisivas características de nuestro pueblo [the diminutive is one of the most definitive characteristics of our people]."[19] Another typical trait, her preference for repetition and enumeration of nouns and adjectives, sometimes in incomplete phrases, is apparent in stanzas 3 and 4 which do not include a verb. Rosalía's predilection for anaphora, the repetition of an identical word or group of words, is noticeable in stanzas 6 and 7 "deixo [I leave]," in 12 and 13 "lonxe, máis lonxe [far, far away]" and with the recurrence of "adiós [farewell]" throughout the poem.

The poem also illustrates Rosalía's use of personae, in this case a young man who says good-bye to his homeland and to his beloved. Among the personae she has used in her poetry, one can mention the simple peasant girl in the humorous **"San Antonio bendito"** [Blessed Saint Anthony] who implores the saint of unmarried girls to give her a husband. In a more serious vein, a young Galician girl whose beloved died in Castile vents her hatred of central Spain and its inhabitants in **"Castellanos de Castilla!"** [Castilians of Castile].

Probably one of the most unusual personae occurs in the poem **"Viéndome perseguido por la alondra"** [Chased by a swift skylark] where the speaker is a golden-winged insect that is afraid of being eaten by a bird. In **"En balde"** [Free of charge], the speaker is a poor person who takes mischievous delight in the fact that, though the clergy charge plenty for burial, they are forced to bury the poor for free.

Rosalía identified with the poor and downtrodden. She laments not only the lot of the emigrant, but also that of the beggars, orphans, and other homeless:

> Cuando sopla el Norte duro
> y arde en el hogar el fuego,
> y ellos pasan por mi puerta
> flacos, desnudos y hambrientos,
> el frío hiela mi espíritu
> como debe helar su cuerpo.

> [When the North wind blows cold
> and a fire warms our home,
> they pass by my door—
> thin, naked, and hungry—
> and my spirit becomes frozen
> like their bodies.]

As Gerald Brenan was the first to remark, in her bitter reaction to poverty Rosalía reintroduces a "note that had not been heard in Spanish poetry since the time of the Archpriest of Hita."[20]

The plight of the emigrant, who symbolizes Galicia's poverty, recurs frequently in her later poems. Rosalía mourns both the men who must leave and the women who stay behind. It is to these women that she dedicates a section in *Follas novas* entitled "As viudas dos vivos e as viudas dos mortos" [Widows of the Living and Widows of the Dead]. The mournful dirge **"Este vaise i aquel vaise"** [One after another departs], translated into Spanish by Juan Ramón Jiménez, is a lament for the widows, as well as for Galicia itself.

Another theme which appears in **"Adiós rios"** is that of religion. The conventional sentiment represented here by a prayer to the Virgin is rather typical for much of Rosalía's early poetry. However, in her last two books, she is often tormented by doubts about the existence of God and divine justice. Nevertheless, she implores God to restore her faith which she compares, as in other poems, to a blindfold:

> ¿Es verdad que lo ves? Señor, entonces,
>   piadoso y compasivo
> vuelve a mis ojos la celeste venda
> de la fe bienhechora que he perdido. . . .

> [Is it true that you see it? Lord, then
>   with pity and compassion,

give me back my divine blindfold
of soothing faith which I have lost. . . .]

It is not until the end of her life that Rosalía seems to have regained the traditional faith for which she often longed in vain. In the very last poem in *En las orillas del Sar,* **"Tan solo dudas y terrores siento; / divino Cristo si de ti me aparto"** [Oh, my Christ, when I forget you, / all I feel is doubt and fear], the speaker compares God to a lighthouse that will guide her to a safe harbor.

The detailed description of the natural surroundings in **"Adiós rios"** intimates Rosalía's love of nature. It is quite in keeping with the tradition of post-romantic poetry that most of Rosalía's poems are suffused with nature with which she identifies almost pantheistically. Whether it reflects her state of being or serves as a contrast to her mood, nature is always present as a lovingly and minutely observed backdrop for her emotions. In many poems, Rosalía specifically evokes the Galician landscape with its open fields, valleys, and mountains. She particularly likes the region's lush greenness and is fond of the oaks and pine trees which abound there.

Rosalía is also skillful in depicting the various seasons, though she seems to have an admitted predilection for winter, **"Meses do inverno fríos/ que eu amo a todo amar"** [Cold months of winter/ that I love so much]. Yet the freshness of spring is captured in **"Adivínase el dulce y perfumado/ calor primaveral"** [Sweet fragrance foretells/ the warmth of spring]; the scorching summer is apparent in the poem which follows it, **"Candente está la atmósfera"** [The air is white-hot]; while **"Moría el sol, y las marchitas hojas"** [The sun was dying, and withered oak leaves] is a paen to autumn. In several poems Rosalía identifies with clouds, birds, or flowers. Of special interest are the lyric poems where the poet has an intimate relationship with a personified moon.

Since nature prevails in her poetry, it may be surprising that at the beginning of *Follas novas,* in one of several poems which reflect her artistic creed, Rosalía states that she does not sing of doves and flowers. However, Rosalía is trying to differentiate herself from poets who write about nature in a sentimentalized and mawkish fashion. In explaining why she entitled the collection "follas novas" [new leaves], she makes it clear that she identifies her art with nature's untamed and wild imagery when she compares her verses to a wreath of gorse and brambles:

hirtas como as miñas penas
feras, como a miña dor.
Sin olido, nin frescura,
bravas, magoás e ferís . . .

[unyielding like my sorrow,
wild as my pain.

Without fragrance or freshness,
untamed, crushed, and bruised . . .]

Her description of her painful creative process is equally unsentimentalized as can be seen in this powerful image from "Silencio! [Silence!]":

mollo na propia sangre a dura pruma
rompendo a vena hinchada,
e escribo . . . . .

[I dip a sharp pen in my own blood,
break the swollen vein,
and I write. . . .]

The final stanza of **"Adiós ríos"** contains the word "soidás," suggesting loneliness, homesickness, nostalgia, longing, yearning, and sadness, a key to much of Rosalía's poetry. This same sentiment underlies the poem **"Campanas de Bastabales"** and, on a more abstract level, it is visible in one of her most often anthologized poems, **"En los ecos de los órganos o en el rumor del viento** [In the organ's echo or in the murmuring wind],"** where her longing is for an unknown bliss.

Since it is an early poem, **"Adiós ríos"** captures the wistfulness of "soidá" but does not really touch on the more complex "dolor," Rosalía's spiritual anxiety pervading many of the poems in *Follas* and *En las orillas.* A good example of her fear of an unknown menace can be found in the short poem **"¿ Qué pasa o redor de min?"** [What is this confusion around me?]. Other times she refers to the vague threat which haunts her as a "negra sombra" [black shadow] which she characterizes as "Una sombra tristísima, indefinible y vaga" [A mournful shadow, undefined and vague]. In her famous poem **"Cando penso que te fuches"** [Just when I think you have fled], the emotion is more lyrical and less apprehensive, but the ubiquity of her "negra sombra" is still palpable. Her feelings toward her black shadow are the same mixture of hate and love visible in **"Unha vez tiven un cravo."**

Although her uneasiness is not meant to be analyzed, it can be associated with the closely intertwined elements of time, solitude, memories, and illness. Many of Rosalía's poems deal with the passage of time, most notably **"'Tas-tis, tas-tis' na silenciosa noite"** ['Tick-tock! Tick-tock!' the pendulum repeats] and **"Hora trás hora, día, trás día"** [Hour after hour, day after day]. In these and other poems, the poet comes to the painful conclusion that an experience can only be remembered but never relived again.

Yet the remembrance of the past is also a source of her suffering and that is why the poet asks plaintively,

"¿ **Por qué tan terca/ tan fiel memoria me ha dado el Cielo?**" [Why has Heaven / given me a memory so stubborn and so true?]. She would prefer to bury her memories forever, as becomes obvious in several poems, especially in "**Cava lixeiro, cava**" [Dig swiftly, dig].

At other times Rosalía compares her suffering to an illness, especially a sick heart. Perhaps the most memorable image of her "dolor" appears in one of her best poems, "**Mais ve que o meu corazón**" [But see my heart] where her heart is likened to a hundred-petalled rose, similar to the poetic rose of mystic tradition, where every petal is a sorrow.

Since Rosalía often felt that life was a burden, it is not surprising that in many of her poems death is depicted as a liberation from pain and as a welcome rest. In one poem the speaker asks why it is a sin to take one's life:

> ¿ Por qué, Dios piadoso,
> por qué chaman crime
> ir en busca da morte que tarda, . . .
>
> [Why, merciful God,
> why is it a crime
> to look for death if it tarries, . . .]

In "**Soia**" [Alone], she describes the suicide by drowning of a lonely woman:

> Tomou un día lene
> camiño do areal . . .
>   como naide a esperaba
> ela non tornóu máis.
>
> [One gentle day she walked
> towards the sand dunes . . .
>   since no one ever waited for her,
> she never returned.]

In other poems Rosalía actually imagines her own death:

> Hoxe ou mañán, ¿ quén pode decir cándo?,
>   pero quisáis moi logo,
> viránme a despertar, i en vez dun vivo,
>   atoparán un morto.
> [Perhaps today, perhaps tomorrow, who can
>   say when?
>   but maybe very soon,
> they will come to waken me
>   and find me dead.]

The theme of death is fused with that of love in a lyrical poem where Rosalía compares the sea to a demon lover who invites her with these words:

> "Neste meu leito misterioso e frío
> -dime-ven brandamente a descansar."

["Come softly to rest," he says,
"in my cold and secret bed."]

The emotions of peace and tranquility associated with love in this poem are similar to those described in a poem entitled "**Bos amores**" [Good Loves]. Yet the feelings mentioned in its companion piece, "**Amores cativos**" [Enslaving Loves], more often accompany love in Rosalía's erotic poetry. For Rosalía, love is often linked to a sense of dishonor, shame, and remorse. An example of guilty love can be found in "**Cada vez que recuerda tanto oprobio**" [Every time she recalls that shame] or "**Ladraban contra min**" [They barked at me as I walked].

The sense of persecution expressed in "**Ladraban contra min**," where gossip-mongers are compared to a pack of dogs who bark at her, is also noticeable in "**A xusticia pola man**" [Justice by my Own Hand], one of Rosalía's most interesting and unusual poems. In its fierce tone and content, this poem differs somewhat from her other works, but the underlying feeling is similar. In a shout of protest and rebellion, the speaker compares herself to a wounded and enraged she-wolf that kills those who have offended her with their slander.

It is interesting that, in contrast to most of her poetry where nature is seen as a friend, here it is depicted as inhospitable: the open fields with their gorse and brambles are juxtaposed unfavorably to the shelter and comfort of a home.

On a more general level, the poet indicts justice, both human (the judges mock her) and divine (God does not hear her). The poem is one of a handful which are titled, and the title underlines the strong message: one must take justice into one's own hands. The novelty of this shocking conclusion is emphasized by one of Rosalía's critics, Xesús Alonso Montero, who points out that, "hasta entonces nadie había escrito un poema tan implacable y menos un poema sobre la inevitalibidad de la violencia como respuesta [up until then nobody had written such a relentless poem, much less one about the inevitability of violence as an answer]."[21]

The poem is written in quatrains (except for the last two lines), with alexandrines which all rhyme assonantly with the letter "a." If one looks at Rosalía's own Spanish translation of this poem (one of the few Galician poems she translated into Castilian), it becomes clear that she felt that the harsh and aggressive sound of the end rhyme was essential to the poem. In her translation, she preferred to make minor changes in the content in order to be able to preserve the rhyme scheme.

Rosalía de Castro is a key figure in the transition from Romanticism to Symbolism in Spanish poetry. In contrast to the regular symmetric meter of some 19th-century poets, Rosalía boldly varies her line lengths, experimenting with unusual metric combinations and even free verse. She also differs from her contemporaries in her preference for a natural syntax and a simple, even colloquial, diction. Hence, her poetry is not dramatic or declamatory, but rather intimate and conversational.

Her prologues and the two books of poetry written in Galician reflect her intense love for her native region. In these writings Rosalía captures both the gaiety and melancholy of the Galician spirit. However, her greatest appeal to the modern reader lies in the lyric and personal touch with which she imbues her themes, and, above all, her sensitive explorations of her own emotions.

Notes

[1] In works written in Spanish about Rosalía de Castro, she is usually called "Rosalía," and the body of criticism about her is known as "crítica rosaliana." Some of her English critics have been reluctant to follow this Spanish custom because in Anglo-Saxon literary tradition calling a woman writer by her first name has implied patronization (for example, in the case of Emily Dickinson).

Since in Spanish criticism the use of a first name does not carry any sexist bias (the poet Juan Ramón Jiménez is known as Juan Ramón), we feel that there is no reason not to refer to the poet as Rosalía, the name by which she is best known.

Most sources cite Rosalía's birthdate as February 24, though the inscription on a plaque at "La Matanza" gives the date as February 23.

[2] The godmother's name, mentioned in Rosalía's birth certificate, was María Francisca Martínez. Some biographers also refer to a Teresa Martínez Viojo, who may have been a paternal aunt, but in a recent publication, Avelino Albuín de Tembra wonders whether these two names belong to one and the same person, *Rosalía*. (Santiago: Edicións do Patronato, 1987) 16.

[3] Biographers used to say, as does Benito Varela Jácome in his introduction to *Rosalía de Castro* (Barcelona: Bruguera, 1980), that José Martínez Viojo "cursaba estudios eclesiásticos y fue más tarde capellán de Iria" ["was a student of theology who would later be chaplain in Iria"]. However, according to more recent sources, Rosalía's father, who was thirty-nine at the time of her birth, was already an ordained priest.

[4] Alberto Machado da Rosa, "Rosalía de Castro, poeta incompreendido," *Revista Hispánica Moderna* XX (1954): 181-223.

[5] Claude Poullain, "Poesía gallega y poesía castellana en Rosalía de Castro," *Actas do Congreso internacional*

de estudios sobre Rosalía de Castro e o seu tempo. vol. 2 (Santiago de Compostela: Universidad de Santiago de Compostela, 1985): 413-37.

[6] Quoted by John Frederick Nims in Stanley Burnshaw, ed. *The Poem Itself* (Schocken: New York, 1960) 162 and in "Poetry: Lost in Translation?" *Delos: A Journal on and of Translation* V (1970): 108.

[7] Emilia Pardo Bazán, "De mi tierra," *Obras completas.* Vol. 9. (Madrid: Aguilar, 1947).

[8] McClelland, I. L. "Bécquer, Rubén, Darío and Rosalía Castro," *Bulletin of Spanish Studies* XVI (1939): 63-83.

[9] Manuel Murguía, "Rosalía de Castro," *Obras completas.* 7th edition. (Madrid: Aguilar, 1982) 552. It must be mentioned that many of Rosalía's Galician poems have recently been set to music.

[10] Azorín (José Martínez Ruiz), "Los valores literarios," *Obras completas.* Vol. 2. (Madrid: Aguilar, 1959) 1077.

[11] Azorín, "Clásicos y modernos," *Obras completas.* Vol. 2. (Madrid: Aguilar, 1959) 771-5.

[12] Miguel de Unamuno, "Santiago de Compostela" and "Junto a las rías bajas de Galicia," *Andanzas y visiones españolas.* (Madrid: Renacimiento, 1927).

[13] Pilar G. Suelto de Sáenz, "Rosalía de Castro, Anticipación del '98," *Actas do congreso.* Vol. 2: 453-60.

[14] Eliana Suárez Rivero, "Machado y Rosalía: dos almas gemelas," *Hispania* XLIX (1966): 748-54.

[15] Luis Cernuda, "Rosalía de Castro," *Estudios sobre poesía española contemporánea.* (Madrid: Guadarrama, 1957) 59-69.

[16] *Actas do Congreso internacional de estudios sobre Rosalía de Castro e o seu tempo.* 3 vols. (Santiago de Compostela: Universidad de Santiago de Compostela, 1985).

[17] Antonio Costa Gómez, "Rosalía de Castro e Emily Dickinson," *Grial* 18 (1980): 276-85.

[18] Martha Miller LaFollette, "Aspects of Perspective in Rosalía de Castro's *En las orillas del Sar,*" *Kentucky Romance Quarterly* 29, 3 (1982): 273-82.

[19] Amado Alonso, "Noción, acción, y fantasía en los diminutivos," *Estudios lingüísticos* (Madrid: Gredos, 1951) 37.

[20] Gerald Brenan, "Rosalía de Castro," *The Literature of the Spanish People* (Cambridge: Cambridge U. Press, 1970) 357.

[21] Xesús Alonso Montero, "Rosalía de Castro: compromiso, denuncia, desamparo y violencia," *Realismo y conciencia crítica en la literatura gallega.* (Madrid: Ciencia Nueva, 1968) 79.

Susan Kirkpatrick (essay date 1995)

SOURCE: "Fantasy, Seduction, and the Woman Reader: Rosalía de Castro's Novels," in *Culture and Gender in Nineteenth-Century Spain,* edited by Lou Charnon-Deutsch and Jo Labanyi, Clarendon Press, 1995, pp. 74-95.

[*In the following essay, Kirkpatrick investigates the relationship of Castro's novels* El caballero de las botas azules *and* La hija del mar *to the tradition of seduction fantasy.*]

> Do you think a thriving virgin imagination can gorge itself with impunity on *Martin, the Orphan Boy, A Doctor's Memoirs,* and *The Man of the Three Pantaloons?* . . . Devouring *The Three Musketeers,* [the young girl learns of] Milady's evil deeds, the adulterous love of *Madame Bonacieux,* and the scandalous passion of *Mlle. Lavalliere* for the king, a passion that infiltrates young and naïve hearts the more easily when dressed in a sweetly poetic and sentimental form. . . . [T]ender female readers, when they reach thirteen, follow as best they can in the footsteps of the heroines of their novels.

(Sinués de Marco, 1859)

Nineteenth-century Spaniards defined women's relation to reading and writing as a matter of morality. Debates about women's education—that is, their access to the printed word as either consumers or producers—centred on the question of whether reading/writing would lead women astray, as the traditionalists argued, or would refine their moral sensibility, as reform-minded liberals claimed. At the heart of this debate lay the question of fantasy, of women's desire, for·that was the crucial link between the printed word and feminine behaviour. In particular, the reading of novels was seen as dangerous. By the mid-nineteenth century, when the serial novel began to prove itself an effective means of expanding the market of print consumers, concerns with the genre's impact on women, a growing sector of that market, became widespread. The fear that the novelesque might contaminate the daily lives of women was exacerbated by the seductive strategies through which the serial novel secured buyers for its proliferating instalments: exalted romantic passions, melodramatic dilemmas, sensational plots played upon the erotic fantasies of its readers.

Interestingly enough, the women who now entered the expanding field of print culture as producers seized on the issue of fiction's contaminating influence as a means of justifying their own writing projects. Thus, Cecilia

Böhl de Faber *(Fern án Caballero),* defensive about putting herself forward in public as an author, claimed in 1853 that 'la tendencia de mis obritas es combatir lo novelesco, sutil veneno en la buena y llana senda de la vida real' [the tendency of my little works is to combat the novelesque, a subtle poison in the good, plain path of real life].[1] The strategy of offering one's own writing as an antidote to the poisonous effects of competing fiction became prevalent among women writers of the 1850s. It was central to the influential work cited in the epigraph, *El ángel del hogar* [The Angel in the House], Pilar Sinués's amalgam of fiction and conduct book for women. Already in a second, expanded edition in 1859, this book was re-edited many times in the nineteenth century. While admitting that reading the wrong kind of fiction (the works of Alexandre Dumas *peýe* are singled out as an example) can contaminate girls' hearts with scandalous passions and overheat their imaginations (180), Sinués insists that reading works written by women committed to the domestic ideal of womanhood plays an important part in feminine moral education. She counsels mothers accordingly: 'La mujer que siente, es buena hija, buena esposa y buena madre: y para desarrollar la sensibilidad de vuestras hijas no tenéis que hacer más que enseñarlas a leer, y dirigir con tino sus lecturas' [The woman of feeling is a good daughter, a good wife, and a good mother: and to develop the sensibility of your daughters you need only teach them to read and direct their reading with judgement] (64). Sinués thus deftly transforms the concern about fiction infecting women's imagination into an argument for the positive effects of reading on feminine subjectivity. Women's imaginations can be nurtured and channelled in ways that protect them from the corrupting seductions of melodramatic fiction, her argument goes, if they are absorbed by 'historias dulces, llenas de sentimiento y de verdad' [agreeable stories full of feeling and truth] (188). Truth, *El ángel del hogar* makes clear, consists of women's biological mission as domestic angels, a mission significantly enhanced by certain kinds of reading and writing, that is, those capable of shaping desirable feminine subjectivity.[2] Thus, in accepting the premise of female susceptibility to reading, Sinués makes a case justifying the moral effects of a controlled female exercise of literacy.

Sinués's adept manipulation of the ideological debate on women and literature, however, does not resolve the argument about feminine fantasy and narrative seduction. It merely proposes the replacement of one kind of fiction by another, leaving in place the restrictions on women's activity and their subordination to men. To find an intervention in nineteenth-century Spanish discourse about women's reading that confronts the subordinating effects of all types of fiction on women, we must turn to the fiction of Sinués's contemporary Rosalía de Castro. Boldly identifying herself in her epigraphs and citations as a reader of Soulié, Sand, and Dumas, novelists habitually denounced as pernicious to women,

Castro sidesteps the question of morality and explores in her novels the connected issues of fiction, female fantasy, and women's oppression. What Jessica Benjamin has termed 'the intricate relationship between woman's desire and women's submission' (80) becomes the implicit problem posed in the narratives that Castro situates within or in relation to the genre of romance fiction, or popular Romantic melodrama. In this essay I will discuss at length Rosalía de Castro's engagement with this problem in her fourth novel, **El caballero de las botas azules** [The Knight of the Blue Boots], but first I want briefly to consider her treatment of seduction in her first novel, **La hija del mar** [Daughter of the Sea].

In both novels Castro was concerned with the seductive and powerful male figures that dominated popular fiction because the desire they produced had a subjugating effect on the female psyche. Moral response was not the issue: her texts suggest that, whether the woman protagonist—or reader—gives in or remains virtuous, she remains in a subordinate and disadvantaged position in this kind of narrative since her desire must be passive rather than active—the desire to be desired. Consequently, these novels can be read as attempts not only to represent but also to critique the structures that determine feminine identity in modern Western culture. One of the most basic of these structures is the one that inclines women to choose a father-figure as their love object. In featuring female characters' relationships with powerful male figures, Castro's narratives highlight the seduction scenario identified by psychoanalytic theory as the origin of heterosexual desire in the woman: the father's desire for her is perceived by the daughter as the means of her access to sexuality, to desire and power.[3] By inducing women to channel their sexuality into the wish to please the father or his substitute at all costs, the seduction fantasy subordinates women's desire to the demands of the patriarchal bourgeois family. James Mandrell has observed that the literary incarnation of this fantasy in avatars of the seducer, Don Juan, 'serves to draw the woman into the passion of patriarchy and serves as the paradigm by which desire is articulated in society, as the subtext for relations between men and women, as a literary and social text in which the latter are seduced by the former into fulfilling a specific role' (127-8). Although Castro wrote before the theoretical model of Oedipalization had been formulated, some of her narratives display the process theorized later by Freud, and at the same time resist it through a critique of the woman/reader's tendency to internalize the seduction narrative as the figure of her desire.

The mid-century *folletines* that formed a literary context for Castro's novels had two main strategies for manipulating the seduction fantasy. The first was the drama of seduction and abandonment, in which the dark, Romantic hero with semi-diabolic powers occupies the position of the father in relation to the girl child who becomes his victim. The second strategy was to narrate the redemption of the seductive male by the innocent heroine, a story that was crucial to the image of *el ángel del hogar* promoted by Pilar Sinués and other writers of women's fiction. Following a pattern established by José Zorrilla in his *Don Juan Tenorio,* in these narratives the fascinating reprobate's desire for a virtuous and innocent girl transforms him into a proper bourgeois mate. For James Mandrell, the conjunction of the two scenarios—seduction and redemption—in Zorrilla's drama initiates the bourgeois domestication of the traditional figure of the seducer in nineteenth-century Spanish fiction, a process that adapts the significance of seduction to the shift in social organization from kinship structures to the nuclear family (Mandrell 265-7). The seduction and redemption fantasies coincide in identifying female sexuality with the capacity to arouse desire in the father-figure, and this feminine 'power' is clearly equated with passivity. As Alicia Andreu has shown, the Spanish fiction that incorporates this scenario insists monotonously that passivity, obedience, humility, patience, are the virtues that will arouse redemptive desire in the man (71-91). Identification with the feminine protagonists of such fiction, no matter whether they appeared in the scandalous *folletín* or in the sentimental novellas advocated by Sinués, reproduced in the woman reader a mode of sexuality and fantasy that equated femininity with being the passive object of the male desire, perpetuating in psychic life structures that support bourgeois marriage and its sexual division of labour.

Rosalía de Castro's first novel, **La hija del mar,** responds quite directly to the seduction fantasies incorporated in the popular fiction that Rosalía—only 22 when she wrote the novel—had been reading throughout her adolescence. I have argued elsewhere that while this novel acknowledges the insistent power of the seduction scenarios centred on Byronic male figures like the main male character, Albert Ansot, it also registers the extent to which such fantasies make women victims in the politics of gender relations.[4] The two female protagonists—Teresa, the passionate and powerful adult woman who finds Ansot irresistible though reprehensible, and Esperanza, the girl whom Ansot twice attempts to seduce, not realizing she is his abandoned daughter—exemplify alternative trajectories for feminine subjectivity in relation to patriarchally inscribed desire. The two women also represent two levels of female subjection—the political and the psychological. Both Teresa and Esperanza, the narrator explains, 'permanecían atadas al victorioso carro de su dueño, la una sujeta por los robustos brazos que la oprimían, la otra . . . ¡por su corazón!: cadenas que en aquellos instantes supremos no podían romperse a pesar de todas las violencias de la tierra' [were tied to the victorious chariot of their master, the one subjected by the strong arms of the man who oppressed her, the other . . . by her heart!, a chain that in those supreme moments could not be broken by all the violence on the earth] (117).[5] Teresa, whose position within the novel duplicates that of the female reader conditioned by the *folletín,* demonstrates the psychological form of subjection: despite her active resistance to Ansot's sexual power over her, that patriarchal power is continually regenerated within her—and, by implication, within the woman writer and reader—by a fantasy structured around the father's seduction. Esperanza, on the other hand, is subjected to her father only by his physical and social power, not by the psychological chains of desire. Unlike Teresa, her fantasy is not captured by the seduction scene. Staying back from the brink of seduction and sexuality, she consciously sees Ansot only as a tyrant and enslaver and learns at the end of the novel, with the revelation of her origins, that her desire is really for her mother—for the lost mother of her now unremembered earliest infancy. In Esperanza, then, Castro explores the possibility of a pre-Oedipal desire for reunion with the mother as an alternative to subjection to the sexual law of the father.

As a reading and rewriting of the fantasies projected in the popular fiction of nineteenth-century Spain, *La hija del mar* resists at a number of levels the subjecting effects of the seduction fantasy on women: it treats as tyranny both the political and the psychological power of pulp fiction's seductive father-figures; it debunks the myth of female power to redeem through passivity; and it presents the mother as an alternative object of women's desire. This struggle to transform the meanings of the given narrative materials is very clearly an unresolved process within the text. Esperanza, the 'hope' of an un-Oedipalized feminine subjectivity, can find no place in the social world and throws herself from a cliff into the sea. Her story exposes the painful dilemma of the female reader—and the feminine subject—within modern patriarchal society.

Several years after the publication of her first novel, Rosalía de Castro again addressed the issues of reading, seduction, and desire, but this time in the register of satire and self-reflexive irony rather than that of melodrama. *El caballero de las botas azules* appeared in 1867, on the eve of a revolutionary crisis of the Spanish state. In a period when the serialized novel reigned supreme, Castro's novel attacked the dominant forms of literature in her society, exposing the manipulation of desire that buttressed structures of economic exploitation and political domination. The question of women's desire is not so thematically predominant in this novel as in *La hija del mar,* yet, as I will argue, the underlying strategy of self-reflexive consciousness is directed against women's destructive habits of reading and desiring.

El caballero establishes its self-reflexive strategy by immediately implicating and satirizing its own context of production and consumption. It begins with a dialogue titled 'A Man and a Muse', in which a would-be author, only too aware that the contemporary arena of writing is a competitive market-place, seeks inspiration to create a work so original that it will triumph over all others and win him immortal fame (Castro 1977: 561-2). The ironic and unconventional Muse identifies his problem as the chaotic proliferation of print:

¿[Q]ué hacer en medio de ese desbordamiento inconmensurable en donde nadie hace justicia a nadie, y en el cual los más ignorantes y más necios, los más audaces y pequeños quieren ser los primeros? He aquí por qué me llamaste . . . por qué me buscarás siempre, pues sin mí serás '¡uno de tantos!' y nada más que esto.

What could you do in that measureless deluge in which no one does justice to anyone else, and the most ignorant and foolish, the most audacious and petty want to be number one? That is why you called me . . . why you will always seek me out, because without me you will be 'one of the crowd' and nothing more. (572-3)

This text self-consciously exposes the desire or objective motivating its own generation, as well as the generation of all works flooding the market in which it will be received, thus calling attention to the need of literature published in this context to create a singular desire in its target audience. The prefatory dialogue identifies the achievement of this aim with novelty, a degraded version of the Romantic ambition toward originality produced by the development of modern market structures as the framework of literary production.[6] The Muse reveals that her name is Novelty, and this is the key to the success she promises the Man who accepts her inspiration: 'Te haré el más popular de los hombres, y miles de corazones se estremecerán de curiosidad y emoción a tu paso' [I will make you the most popular of men, and thousands of hearts will tremble with curiosity and emotion when you go by] (579). Sired by doubt and birthed by desire (578), Novelty engenders new desires—or desire for the new—in the hearts of consumers, helping create the necessary conditions of a capitalist economy.

The story that follows this dialogue (a 'strange story' according to its own subtitle) is, to put it in the most reductive terms, the story of how the Muse, transforming the Man into the Knight of the Blue Boots, inspires him to carry out a supremely successful marketing strategy to ensure that his book, the Book of Books, is the only one read in Madrid. The incarnation of novelty with his luminescent blue boots and ambiguous cravat, which sometimes looks like a live eagle, the *Caballero* arouses and focuses on himself the unsatisfied desires of the whole city, then disappears, promising his Book in answer to their expectations. The story closes with the distribution of the Book of Books, whose contents are never revealed. As a satiric commentary on the contemporary situation of the writer, Castro's novel could not be more acerbic: the story of a successful literary inspiration has nothing to do with the textual product, but only with the strategy for marketing it.

Explicit satire on contemporary literature runs throughout the narrative. The indictment probes beneath the question of aesthetic quality in the chaotic proliferation of the printed word, and targets the economic structure of the print industry. Castro characterizes the reigning system of serial publication as exploitative when a poet laments 'la lastimosa popularidad que han llegado a adquirir esas novelas que, para explotar al pobre, se publican por entregas de a dos cuartos' [the unfortunate popularity recently acquired by those novels that, in order to exploit the poor, are published in penny instalments] (647). The exploitation of the female reading public is exposed as a particularly lucrative publishing practice by the parodically self-congratulatory remarks of a publisher commenting on women's fiction:

> ¡Oh! Es un éxito fabuloso el que estas novelas obtienen. Casi todos los maestros y maestras de primera enseñanza, casi todas las obreras de Madrid, se han suscrito, sin contar los directores del Hospicio, de la Inclusa y de otros colegios particulares que las compran para que las niñas, al mismo tiempo que se entretienen los días de fiesta con su amena lectura, se instruyan y aprendan en ellas a ser virtuosas.

> Oh, the success these novels are having is fabulous! Almost all the primary school teachers, almost all the women workers of Madrid have subscribed, not to mention the directors of the Orphanage, of the Home for Foundlings, and of other private schools that buy them so the girls, at the same time as having enjoyable reading for holidays, are taught by them to be virtuous. (799)

The titles Castro invents to characterize this genre provide a succinct ironic summary of the ideological message of the kind of fiction Sinués advocated: *La mujer honrada* [The Honourable Woman], *El amor sacrificado* [Self-Sacrificing Love], and *La pobreza sin mancilla* [Poverty without Stain]. Indeed, the publisher uses some of Sinués's terms when he goes on to say that his novels 'además de estar llenas de escenas tiernas y conmovedoras . . . encierran al mismo tiempo una moral que la misma Inquisición no hubiera reprobado' [besides being full of tender and moving scenes . . . contain at the same time a moral the Inquisition itself wouldn't have disapproved of]. The satiric intent of this passage is underlined by the editor's interlocutor, who remarks ironically that while this fiction may observe good morals, it does not observe good grammar, and the editor replies cynically: '¿Qué importa todo eso? ¡Aprensiones! . . . Las mujeres, que son las que realmente aman y se impresionan con esta clase de libros, no saben gramática en nuestro país' [What does that matter? Idle misgivings! . . . In our country, women,

who are the ones who really love and are impressed by this kind of books, don't know anything about grammar] (799).

The conclusion of *El caballero de las botas azules* enacts Castro's condemnation of contemporary literary production as being not only aesthetically mediocre, but, even worse, shaped by economic and political interests that aim to reinforce the subordination of women and the working classes. As part of the theatrical grand finale that the *Caballero* offers to the astonished eyes of Madrid's élite before he disappears, the city's stock of current publications, which his helper has bought from the booksellers and stored in preparation for this moment, is dumped in a deep well and buried forever. With great fanfare, the *Caballero* shows the guests at his goodbye banquet the pit filled to the brim with modern literature and announces: '¡Señores, la obra está cumplida! La humanidad se ve libre de un peso inútil; . . . ya no leerá artículos distinguidos, ni historias inspiradas, ni versos insípidos, ni novelas extravagantes, ni artículos críticos cuya gracia empalagosa trasciende a necio' [Ladies and gentlemen, my mission is fulfilled! Humanity has been freed from a useless burden; . . . no longer must it read distinguished articles, or inspired stories, or insipid verses, or extravagant novels, or critical articles whose tiresome wit smells of idiocy] (825). Self-reflexive irony is not absent here, for the *Caballero* continues by observing that the field has now been cleared for his own soon-to-appear work, exposing the possibility that he is no better than the self-promoting editors and authors whose books lie buried, only a more successful strategist.

That this satiric put-down of contemporary literature has a connection with the subordination of women is suggested by another *coup de théâtre* at the book-burying. At the beginning of the banquet, the Duke of Glory (as the *Caballero* is known in Madrid) announces that the evening's festivities include the appearance of some slave-women, whom he will with his own hands set free. Indeed, just as the condemned books begin to shoot through the air on their way to the pit, another spectacle greets the eyes of the guests: tunic-clad slave-girls, their bluepainted faces hidden by the long visors of their jockey caps, come tremblingly forward to kiss the Duke's boots. A tumult of indignation arises among those present, who, recognizing the slave-girls as some of Madrid's most wealthy and beautiful noblewomen, ask each other what is going on. That is a question we must ask ourselves, too, at this point. Why is this tableau of feminine subjugation, reminiscent of the image in *La hija del mar* of the two women tied to the chariot of their master, cropping up in this context? What does the Knight of the Blue Boots, Castro's instrument of satire against bad literature, have in common with the abusive and tyrannical Ansot?

To answer this question, we must go back to the activities through which the blue-booted Duke has brought all Madrid under his sway. What I have somewhat crudely characterized as a marketing strategy is, like any such strategy, a campaign to arouse and channel desires. In her perceptive Lacanian reading of this novel, Lou Charnon-Deutsch argues that the Duke's function is to teach others 'the mechanics of desire', by 'repeatedly display[ing] himself and then withdraw[ing]' (81, 85). At the most explicit level, the Duke aims to pique curiosity—the desire to know—through the novelty of his dress and behaviour; thus, his first victim, the Duke of Albuérniga, who has devoted his life to cultivating a Stoic lack of desire, is hooked when curiosity about the *Caballero's* singular appearance overcomes his anger that the other has disturbed his nap (592). What other desires may be veiled beneath Albuérniga's tormented attempts to repress his fascination with the Duke of Glory are never made clear, but in the case of the ladies who find the Duke irresistible, his assumption of a powerfully masculine persona is a central factor, as Charnon-Deutsch argues (85). The Duke's appearance and accoutrements, along with the mystery surrounding his sudden appearance in the capital, are sufficient to arouse the interest of the *madrileñas,* who endeavour to entice him to their soirées and salons and write secretly to arrange private tête-à-têtes.

In fact, the *Caballero's* principal technique of seduction is to occupy the role of the tall, dark stranger, the magnetic male figure of the *folletín,* albeit with a disturbing ironic twist. Here is how he appears to the astonished eyes of the first persons he encounters:

> Era el singularísimo y nunca bien ponderado personaje de elevada talla y arrogante apostura, de negra, crespa y un tanto revuelta, si bien perfumada, caballera. Tenía el semblante tan uniformemente blanco como si fuese hecho de un pedazo de mármol, y la expresión irónica de su mirada y de su boca era tal que turbaba al primer golpe el ánimo más sereno.

> This singular and never adequately praised character was tall of stature and carried himself with arrogance. His hair was black, curly, and somewhat tousled, though well perfumed. His face was as uniformly white as if it were made of marble, and the expression of his eyes and mouth was so ironic it could instantly trouble the serenest mind. (587)

Picking up the cues concerning the fictional genre to which this character corresponds, two of the city's leading society ladies—Laura, the Countess of Pampa, and the noble Casimira—hide their identity under cloaks like countless heroines of adventure novels and roam the streets at night, hoping to encounter the mystery man. When they finally do see him in person at a ball where he confounds Madrid's assembled élite by mocking its frivolity and walking out, the snub inflames their unsatisfied longings. The next day the Duke receives billets-doux from a representative sample of Madrid's

women. Each of the letters, with the exception of the one from the ignorant and innocent Mariquita, which we will take up in a moment, reveals the literary origin of the fantasy that the letter's writer wishes to enact with the Duke. Thus the letter from a Creole poetess refers to the primeval forests of 'la virgen América' [virgin America] and to the 'desgraciado e inmortal Moctezuma' [unfortunate and immortal Montezuma] (668), evoking the Romantic literature that exoticized the New World as a setting for sentimental love stories. The note from the Countess of Pampa requests an interview with the Duke because she wishes to learn from him 'cómo las mujeres de la aristocracia rusa visten de mañana' [about the morning dress of the aristocratic women of Russia] (668), thus identifying the *Caballero* with the country of Lermontov, whose novel *A Hero of our Time* obsesses her, as she has earlier confessed to Casimira. In replying to each woman, the Duke uses language corresponding to the fantasy script she has revealed and he raises the stakes by refusing the specific request made, but proposing the rendezvous secretly desired. Yet when the tête-à-tête occurs, he steps out of the role assigned, forcing the woman concerned to acknowledge the unavowed fantasy that has motivated her actions. The Duke's strategy of arousing, then thwarting, feminine desire is most fully elaborated in the subplots involving Laura and Casimira. Two significant features of these subplots—their self-conscious literariness and their sadomasochistic overtones—are connected, in my reading of the novel, and provide a key to the disturbing scene of female subjugation in the novel's finale. Confusion of life and literature occurs at several levels in this subplot. As their venture incognito into the night-time streets suggests, the two women identify themselves with the heroines of the novels they read. The influence of Romantic melodrama is particularly strong in their concept of themselves as 'las independientes', superior to other women, as free and powerful as men (639), very much along the lines of Stendhal's Mathilde. They affect Romantic ennui: 'Sólo sé que el mundo envejece rápidamente y que todo me parece usado y de mal gusto' [I only know that the world is quickly getting old and everything seems worn out and in bad taste] (639), says Laura, turning to her reading of Lermontov to imagine new thrills in the arms of a son of the Caucasus. Her projection of this fantasy on the Knight of the Blue Boots gives a comic cast to the scene of their encounter. All the Duke need do to send her into a delirium of excitement is to smile 'de la manera que se sonreía Petchorín' [in the same way as Petchorin] (742), the disillusioned hero of Lermontov's *A Hero of our Time.* Nothing will persuade her that the Duke is not the Russian poet in some form (744). Maddened in her desire to receive verification of this fantasy, Laura agrees to kiss the Duke's boots in exchange for learning who he is. Her awakening will occur when the concluding scene demonstrates to what extent her literary fantasies of love have enslaved her.

Casimira seems to seek her thrills in fantasies of domination and surrender. In her note, she offers the Duke a role similar to that of Albert Ansot: '¿Sin duda es [el duque] un tirano que se digna regir a los suyos con mano de hierro? De cualquier modo, yo seré siempre su fiel amiga, seré su sierva, su esclava seré si él lo desea' [Doubtless [the Duke] is a tyrant who deigns to rule his subjects with an iron hand? At any rate, I will always be his faithful friend, I will be his handmaiden, his slave, if he so desires] (677). It is she, then, who has introduced the sadomasochistic script that the Duke develops, both in his reply, which he addresses 'Señora y esclava mía' [My lady and slave] (678), and in his subsequent interview with her. In this encounter, he ironically calls attention to the melodramatic language of her note, letting her know that, far from engaging in the gallant badinage she expects, he intends to play out the metaphor on a more literal level: 'Pero cuando se trata de una sierva . . . de una esclava . . . ¡oh! entonces mi severidad no tiene límites: me vuelvo analítico, meticuloso' [But when dealing with a handmaiden . . . a slave . . . oh, then my severity has no limits: I become analytical, meticulous] (699-700). Playing on Casimira's wish to emulate audacious novelistic heroines who will stop at nothing, the Duke ultimately induces her to promise to play his slave in the public tableau he is planning.

What Casimira hopes to obtain from accepting the subjugated role becomes clear when she states what she expects in return if she does as the Duke demands:

> (ya he dicho que no pretendo ser la amante ni la esposa del señor duque), lo que sí pretendo es que en tal caso me haga su confidenta, la depositaria de sus secretos . . . la fuerte y fiel guardadora de los misterios que nadie sino yo entienda. Sí, señor duque: quiero saber su historia; quiero saber qué significan esa corbata y esas botas.

> (I've already said I don't want to be your lover or wife), what I do want in such a case is for you to make me your confidante, the depository of your secrets . . . your strong and faithful guardian of the mysteries no one understands but me. Yes, Duke, I want to know your story; I want to know what that cravat and those boots signify. (708)

Castro has here revealingly rewritten the seduction scenario that figured so prominently in her first novel. In *La hija del mar* the woman's seduction into heterosexual sexuality was linked directly to a power relationship that subjugated her; here the power relationship of master and slave presents more analytically the underlying exchange operating in the sexual economy of gender difference. Casimira is willing to occupy the subordinated position in the belief that thus she will gain access to the secret source of male power, tantalizingly symbolized in the Duke's cravat and boots. If we find that this revised representation of the seduction scene

seems to prefigure the terms in which psychoanalytic theory would later theorize the feminine relationship to phallic desire, then it should not surprise us that the Duke seems to behave very much like a psychoanalyst in relation to Casimira and the other women he 'treats'. He attracts upon himself the projection of their repressed or barely conscious desires, then, by refusing to play the role assigned him, forces them both to acknowledge their fantasies and to recognize the impossibility or undesirability of satisfying them. The therapeutic intent of the final tableau now becomes clear. In appearing as slave-girls and kissing the Duke's boots, Casimira and Laura act out on a very different level from the one they anticipated their fantasies of seduction in relation to the Duke;[7] they take part in the tableau with full awareness that there is no pleasure for them in the scenario, only humiliation. And the knowledge—that is, the possession of the 'secret'—they expected to obtain eludes them. But they have learnt something about themselves. Once they have performed their part of the bargain, the Duke pronounces them free, declaring 'Esas pobres hijas de la esclavitud aman la libertad como el mayor bien de la vida, pero no han comprendido todavía la manera de alcanzarla' [These poor daughters of slavery love freedom as life's greatest good, but they have not yet understood how to achieve it] (823).

In playing a therapeutic role, a consciousness-raising role, in relation to women, the Duke functions like a text that demands a different kind of reading from the one the female characters are used to. Like an enticing novel, he engages their fantasies, insinuating that his story will provide mysterious satisfactions while repeatedly deferring the desired outcomes and disclosures. Yet, unlike the popular fiction that traded on mysteries and revelations (Eugène Sue's *The Mysteries of Paris* had initiated a whole subgenre of translations and imitations in Spain), the *Caballero* baffles his readers' desire to know his story. Instead of playing out the expectations his feminine admirers have internalized from their reading, he turns these expectations back on themselves to produce uncomfortable self-consciousness rather than satisfaction. This, then, is what unites the two spectacles with which the blue-booted Duke concludes his sojourn in Madrid. His staging of the liberation of the slave-girls while having modern literature cast into the pit implies a connection between the sexual enslavement of women and the reading habits through which women seek pleasure in fiction. The Duke attempts to teach women to be resistant readers, to read critically the fantasies scripted for them.[8]

The idea of the Duke's function as a text that invites women's fantasy projection and then promotes a critical evaluation of that fantasy casts light on the other important subplot of the novel as well, the story of his interaction with Mariquita, an innocent girl of the lower middle class who lives in a village—satirically named Dog Run—outside Madrid. Mariquita has been kept as ignorant as possible, having been brought up in the way considered exemplary for Spanish girls of her class. Castro's indignation is palpable in the description of the systematic deprivation of any form of self-expression or pleasure to which Mariquita is subject; so deprived is she that solitary strolls through the nearby cemetery constitute her only enjoyment. Unfortunately for the matchmaking plans of her aunt and father, they have kept her so rigorously isolated from images and analogues of sexuality that, when presented with the young man intended to be her husband, Mariquita finds him utterly ridiculous and repellent. Following the pattern Castro is exploring in these novels, her desire is instead awakened by a seductive stand-in for the father, when Mariquita observes the Duke one day in the graveyard (like any Romantic ironist worth his salt, he is conversing with the grave-digger). The experience is analogous to that of reading: not only is everything about the *Caballero* as distant from her daily life as pulp fiction, but she is also hooked as passionately as if she had picked up a forbidden novel: 'pudo Mariquita contemplarle a su gusto, desde los pies a la cabeza y desde la cabeza a los pies, sin pestañear siquiera y sin tomar apenas aliento. Sucedíale a la niña que cuanto más le miraba mayor placer y encanto le causaba verle' [Mariquita was able to gaze at him as much as she liked, from head to toe and back again, without even blinking and hardly drawing breath. What was happening to the child was that the more she looked at him, the more pleasure and enchantment she felt from seeing him] (621). Desiring more of this enchanting experience, she dreams obsessively of the *Caballero* and ends up doing exactly what the worldly society ladies do—she writes to him. Unlike the ladies, however, she is direct about her desires: she wishes to be near him again and states that if her father decided to marry her to the Duke, she would be very happy (669). In response to her directness and innocence, the Duke is gentler in teaching her to understand the impossibility of realizing her desire. He makes her see that union with a character like him—powerful and dominating—would bring pain and not pleasure. Essentially, he shows her that a sado-masochistic fantasy is not love, and leaves her grieving for the loss of her dreams, but now emotionally prepared to find another kind of relationship with her intended—an authentic artistic genius whose creations, significantly, have not yet been commercialized.

The gentler treatment accorded to Mariquita and her intended distinguishes them from Madrid's élite, the members of the aristocracy and the urban bourgeoisie relentlessly mocked by the Duke. Castro's critique of women's 'enslavement' does not fail to make it clear that the class structure of society enslaves some women more than others. Indeed, some of the novel's most biting scenes show the aristocratic women's imperious and illogical treatment of their maids, who as feminine subjects also feel the Duke's seductive power but have not their mistresses' freedom to try to enact their fantasies.

There is more to be said about the process the Duke sets in motion within the narrative, however. In eliciting seduction fantasies and then subjecting them to critique, he also registers the instability of the gendered positions within them. Castro develops the possibilities of treating gender as a position or a role rather than a stable identity in a number of ways. Let us return for a moment to the episode involving Casimira, whose interaction with the Duke highlights the reversibility of roles in the sadomasochistic schema that structures their relationship. The Duke interprets the text of her note, which ostensibly offers to be his slave, as a subtextual desire to dominate him, to be the seducer rather than the seduced. 'Historia de José' [Joseph's story], he exclaims after reading her letter and gazing at the portrait sent with it, 'ven a mi pensamiento y sé para mis deseos lo que son los diques para las hirvientes olas del mar. . . . Y tú, Musa o demonio, no te burles de mi flaqueza ni me abandones cuando la serpiente tentadora, atraída por mis botas azules, se me acerca presentándome la dorada manzana para hacerme perder mi paraíso' [come into my thoughts and be to my desires as dykes to the boiling waters of the sea. . . . And you, Muse or demon, don't mock my weakness nor abandon me when the tempting serpent, attracted by my blue boots, approaches, offering me the golden apple to make me lose my Paradise] (677-8). The *Caballero* is here projecting a fantasy of his own—the counter-transference, to extend our earlier analogy with psychoanalysis—in which Casimira becomes Potiphar's wife, the agent rather than object of seduction, or, alternatively, occupies the masculine position as Tempter with the Duke playing the feminine part of Eve.[9] That he does not cast himself as Adam to Casimira's Eve suggests that gender ambiguity is implied in the play with role reversal here. For her part, Casimira clearly seeks the advantageous, active position in her verbal fencing match with the Duke; as we have seen, she is willing to enact servitude only because she believes it will give her access to the secret of the Duke's power.

Just as the narrative shows instability in the positions that the Duke and Casimira occupy in the sado-masochistic fantasy, so too it explores reversals of the active and passive roles related to the textual communication situation. Women, who are generally positioned as readers in this novel—readers of novels and Romantic poetry, readers of the Duke as text—become writers once the Duke has elicited their desires. In a complex and ambiguous passage, Castro introduces the transition from one gendered role to another by the women who write notes to the Duke. Playing on the conservative Spanish assumption that the ability to write leads women into sin, which would be one way of interpreting this episode, the narrator describes this and other hazards women face in writing, not least of which is the danger of revealing their ignorance and lack of education.[10] The narrator then goes on to beg indulgence for real women's imperfections in relation to their literary models, and the critical bite in these comments makes itself felt:

> no debe culpárselas a fe porque cumplan debidamente su misión, haciendo hasta la muerte su papel de mujeres. Cosa es esta digna de la mayor alabanza, cuando hay tantos hombres que ejecutan el suyo de la peor manera . . . puesto que nacieron para vivir modesta y honradamente, haciendo compás, con el martillo o el azadón, al huso con que hilan el blanco lino sus buenas esposas.

> they should not be blamed, surely, for fulfilling their mission as expected, for playing their part as women until they die. This is something worthy of the highest praise, when there are so many men who play their part in the worst way . . . given that they were born to live modestly and honourably, keeping time with their hammer or spade to the wheel on which their good wives spin white linen thread. (667)

Aside from the irony with which Castro suggests that women are scorned for an ignorance that is prescribed as necessary to their social function, what I want to emphasize in this passage is the treatment of gender positions, represented here through highly traditional images, as assigned roles. The Spanish term she uses—'papel' meaning both 'part' and 'paper'—intensifies the theatricality implied by the concept of part as something scripted and assigned by society rather than by nature. And although, tragically, those assigned the part of women seem to have little choice but to play it 'until they die', this narrative suggests that the parts are to some degree transferable, interchangeable, for women can imagine writing their own script, as Casimira seems to do, and men can find themselves slipping into the feminine position, as the Duke does momentarily.

Sliding out of his privileged male position is not the only slippage that threatens the Knight of the Blue Boots in a narrative that shifts playfully among frames without confirming any point of origin or fixed reference. In the key episode we have already examined, as the Duke peruses Casimira's note and portrait, he begins to slip into the character of another story, presumably prior to the story he is tracing with the help of the Muse in the main body of the narrative. He has known Casimira in another time and under another identity: '¡El duque conocía demasiado aquel rostro que en otro tiempo había adorado en vano!' [The duke knew only too well that face, which he had once adored in vain!] (677). The Duke's earlier life, mentioned only in scattered references, cannot be read as his 'real' life, however. The vocabulary and punctuation of these references give this other life the status of pulp fiction, suggesting that the Duke played the same part as victim of *folletín*-inspired fantasies that his female admirers play in the story he is currently developing. The ironic stance he maintains, not without some struggle, is what permits him to free

himself from the seductions of fiction and to teach the women of Madrid to do the same, just as the self-reflexivity of Castro's text transcends her earlier novel's reproduction of the seduction fantasy.

The Duke's mysterious power is not, in fact, the power of phallic privilege, which is elusive and precarious in this novel, but of self-knowledge and self-criticism. He eludes both seduction and attack by laughing at himself, indicting himself as he indicts others: 'Lo conozco: yo merecería el primero ser arrojado en el pozo de la moderna ciencia en compañía de las "historias inspiradas", de los malos versos, de las zarzuelas sublimes y de las novelas que se publican por entrega de a dos cuartos' [I know it: I deserve to be the first one thrown into the pit of modern knowledge along with the 'inspired stories', the bad verses, the sublime *zarzuelas,* and the novels sold by penny instalments] (788). Addressing these words to the Muse, the *Caballero* refers to yet another frame to the main story: the dialogue of the Man and the Muse, the interaction that transformed him into the Duke by teaching him the advantages of irony and ambiguity.

Here the roles, later duplicated in the relation of the Duke and the women, are reversed: the Man seeks from the Muse fulfilment of his 'más ferviente deseo' [most fervent desire] (561), but she does not conform to his expectations, and instead teases and provokes him into jettisoning his fantasies and self-deceptions about writing, fame, and genius. As in the implied story of his previous relations with Casimira, he occupies the position of desirer, but at this level the object is literary glory. The question of gender is foregrounded almost as soon as the Man invokes the Muse: when she refuses to step out of the cloud that veils her, he counters with a misogynist commonplace about women, '¡Hasta las Musas son coquetas!' [Even the Muses are coquettes!], to which she replies, 'Considera que soy Musa pero no dama, y que no debemos perder el tiempo en devaneos' [Bear in mind that I am a Muse but not a lady, and that we shouldn't waste time on idle flirtation] (561).[11] In bringing to the surface of the text and then mocking traditional assumptions about the gendered relation of muse to writer, Castro prepares for the destabilizing ambiguity of the Muse's appearance when she does reveal herself visually: 'Su rostro es largo, ovalado y de una expresión ambigua; tiene los ojos pardos, verdes y azules, y parecen igualmente dispuestos a hacer guiños picarescamente o languidecer de amor. Un fino bozo sombrea el labio superior de su boca, algo abultada' [Her face is long, oval, and has an ambiguous expression; her eyes are grey, green, and blue, and seem equally likely to wink roguishly or to languish with love. A fine moustache shadows the upper lip of her rather thick mouth] (577). The Man reacts emphatically to the gender indeterminacy of a being whom he, along with literary tradition, had cast firmly in the feminine part: 'Conque mi Musa era un marimacho, un ser anfibio de esos que debieran quedar para siempre en el vacío?

¡Qué abominación!' [So my Muse was a man-woman, an amphibious being of the sort that should remain forever in the void? What an abomination!] (577). It is this attitude the Muse must change to make the Man into the Knight of the Blue Boots. It is necessary, she tells him, 'que concluyas por apreciarme en lo que valgo' [that you end up appreciating what I'm worth] (577). And when he finally understands the advantage of ironic double vision and can take pleasure in ambiguity, he is ready to sally forth, a new kind of Quijote, to defeat fantasies through critical self-consciousness.[12]

The indeterminacy of meaning in this text, which has been analysed in semiotic terms by Antonio Risco, was noted by the person who was presumably its first reader, Castro's husband Manuel Murguía.[13] The novel is constructed, he said, in such a way 'que al final se pregunte [el lector], entre dudoso y confiado, si es verdad que lo ha comprendido' [that at the end [the reader] asks himself, hesitating between doubt and confidence, if it is true that he has understood it] (Risco 1982: 193). This uncertainty is intensified by the novel's self-reflexive satire, which uses the technique of *mise en abyme* to subject its own procedure to ridicule. In the final banquet scene, for instance, a critic mocked by the Duke declares that he is reading a novel called *El caballero de las botas azules:* 'Solo puede decirse de tal novela que le falta todo para serlo: argumento, pensamiento, moral . . . en fin, es una simple monstruosidad, lo peor entre lo peor' [All that can be said about it is that it has nothing that makes a novel a novel—plot, ideas, moral judgement . . . in short, it's simply a monstrosity, the worst of the worst] (801). The novel's destabilization of even its own ground of narration, I would argue, is closely connected with its treatment of gender categories. Just as the protagonist, in learning to appreciate the Muse's gender ambiguity, frees himself from the literalness of fixed positions, so too the text teaches its readers to break out of an economy of desire that reinforces women's subordination.

Rosalía de Castro's novels situate themselves in a troubled relationship to the fiction of her time, particularly in regard to how the narratives elicited the reading pleasure of women. Mandrell comments that, as a prototype of women reading seductive texts, Ana Ozores's response to *Don Juan Tenorio* in *La Regenta* shows how 'reading and interpretation, even if loosely construed in terms of watching a drama, draw women more deeply into the web of patriarchy' (149). To combat the effects of texts that acted the role of seducing fathers, leading women's desire along the path that would subject them to patriarchy, Castro attempted to replay the fantasies in new and liberating ways. In *La hija del mar* she exposed as violently oppressive the effects of the seduction fantasy and experimented with attaching women's desire to the maternal object. Later, in *El caballero de las botas azules,* she turned to an attack on the conventional erotics of reading. Peter Brooks has argued that the reader's desire in nineteenth-century narratives follows a pattern of arousal, expectation, and discharge that seems clearly masculine and Oedipal (61, 107-12).[14] Castro's novel certainly does not follow this trajectory. The Duke, functioning as a text within the text, refuses to permit the desire he arouses to follow the phallic pattern described by Brooks, but instead turns his audience's attention to the structure of desire itself. In the same way, this novel, by refusing to resolve its ambiguities into stable meaning, will not allow the reader a satisfactory identification with the subject positions fixed by such resolution. Formally as well as thematically, Castro calls for a new narrative paradigm, and, by implication, a new social organization.[15]

The Muse of Novelty who presides over *El caballero de las botas azules* is the Muse of Mutability, and, as the Muse observes of herself, she has 'su contra y su pro' [her pros and cons] (577). Although Castro seems to symbolize in her the stimulus to capitalism's commodification of culture, this same figure also suggests the possibility of change and transformation. At the end of the novel, on the morning after the Duke's spectacular demonstration of the absurdity of current literature and the oppressiveness of current social forms, Madrid awakes to a sense of agitation and expectancy. ' "¿Hay revolución?" preguntaban algunos con sobresalto' ['Has a revolution started?' asked some with consternation] (829). One passer-by, explaining that no one is sure what is happening, but that all are waiting for the arrival of the Book of Books, adds that he is ready for another kind of fiction: 'Por mi nombre, como ya me canso de tan estupendas mentiras como por ahí se escriben para engañarnos . . . Dicen que va a aparecer ahora un libro cual no se ha visto otro todavía . . . Por ese, por ese aguardo yo' [Upon my honour, I'm getting tired of such stupendous lies as the ones they write around here to deceive us . . . They say that now there's about to appear a book like no other that has yet been seen . . . That's the one I'm waiting for] (830). In 1868, a year after the novel's publication, the long-expected Glorious Revolution occurred and, in its aftermath, a new national novelistic tradition arose. But neither the revolution nor the realist canon incorporated the radical openness of structure that Castro's Muse sought to inspire.

Receiving more critical attention now than in Castro's own time, her novels elicit the desirous readings of late twentieth-century feminist critics, who can find in their complex ambiguities corroboration of their own interest in understanding gender identity as discursively constructed and inherently unstable. Yet at the same time, the fate of the liberatory project these texts embody offers us a salutary warning about the intractable embeddedness of discursive systems in the material relations of human society: it reminds us that too many individuals did, and still do, play their part as women 'until they die'.

Notes

[1] This defence of Böhl's work was published in *La Ilustración* (quoted in Montesinos 35).

[2] Blanco makes a similar point.

[3] See Laplanche and Pontalis 5-34. Jane Gallop discusses the treatment of the father-daughter seduction scenario in the psychoanalytic tradition, along with Luce Irigaray's critique of it: Gallop 70-9.

[4] See Kirkpatrick.

[5] All translations of Castro's texts are mine.

[6] Francisco Rodríguez argues that this and other novels by Castro show the influence of utopian socialism in a subtextual critique of developing capitalist forms (Rodríguez 169-79).

[7] Casimira alludes to these fantasies early in the novel, when she recognizes that Laura harbours the same hopes as she in relation to the Duke: 'Te veo y te comprendo . . . Caminamos a un mismo paso y por un mismo sendero; falta ahora saber quién llegará la primera' [I see what you're up to . . . We're going at the same pace down the same path; we'll see who gets there first] (639).

[8] The foregoing reading of the Duke's relation to the women characters coincides in many respects with that of Charnon-Deutsch. It differs in so far as I am concerned with women as reading subjects, while Charnon-Deutsch is interested in suggesting that the underlying desire the Duke's shenanigans reveal in women is the desire to be a writing or speaking subject: 'What their impossible demands finally reveal is that beyond sexual desire lies the will to know and understand things, that is, to be in possession of the words that would make the unknown familiar' (88). She argues that the freedom mentioned by the Duke as what women regard as the greatest good 'is clearly related to women imagining themselves as writing subjects' (94).

[9] It might be noted here that the psychoanalytical account of primal fantasies like the seduction fantasy implies that the subject is not fixed in any one position. Laplanche and Pontalis stress this in their article.

[10] This is Castro's tactic also in other pronouncements on women writing: she focuses on the negative experiences of women who write, leaving the tacit indictment of the injustice of this situation for the reader to infer. Shelley Stevens analyses this rhetorical strategy in her discussion of 'Las literatas' (1866) and the prologue to *Follas novas* (1880) (Stevens 79-85).

[11] Castro plays simultaneously with gender difference and class difference here: the Muse in effect says, 'I'm not a woman and I'm not an aristocrat.' The Muse's democratic tendencies are suggested in a number of ways throughout the dialogue: her citatoin of the popular French poet Béranger, for exmple (573).

[12] Don Quijote comes up once or twice in the dialogue. When the Man asks the Muse if she wants to make a rascal or a Quijote out of him, she replies that he already is a little of each (580). Several critcs have note the Cervantine references and textual strategies in the novel, among them Germán Gullón (490) and Enrique Miralles (459). It should be pointed out that the *Caballero,* in attacking the fantasies elicited by the serial novel, acts not so much like Don Quijote the character, as like *Don Quijote* the text.

[13] See Risco 1982: 184-97. Risco cites Murguía's commentary on the novel. These comments were, according to F. Rodríguez (206), first published in Murguía's essay 'Rosalia de Castro', *La Voz de Galicia* (La Coruña), 17 July 1885.

[14] Susan Winnett questions the universalization of paradigms of male sexual pleasure to all narratives and representation (505-18).

[15] Many critics consider the demand for a new kind of novel to be a central theme. See articles by Enrique Miralles, Carme Fernández-Pérez Sanjulian, Antonio Risco (1982). Risco (1986), Miralles, and F. Rodríguez (176-9) link Castro's critique of literature with her critique of society.

John C. Wilcox (essay date 1997)

SOURCE: "Rosalía de Castro," in *Women Poets of Spain, 1860-1990: Toward a Gynocentric Vision,* University of Illinois Press, 1997, pp. 43-83.

[*In the following excerpt, Wilcox examines Castro as a marginalized woman poet whose collection* Cantares gallegos—*ostensibly a poetic celebration of her native Galicia—offers an ambivalent feminist vision.*]

Unlike her sisters, Rosalía de Castro has established a secure reputation in Peninsular literature, but such was not the case during her lifetime (1837-85), when she fluctuated between being a "Nobody" (Emily Dickinson's word) and a "santiña" (dear little saint).[1] Few have noted her "monstrous" qualities, to use Gilbert and Gubar's metaphor for a committed woman artist whose subconscious mind is intent on self-determination; but it is the "monstrous" as opposed to "angelic" persona that interests today's students of poetry. Rosalía's "monster" persona can be glimpsed if her poems are read as texts that were generated by a writing subject who was also female. By foregrounding the monster within Rosalía, I believe that more of her poetic originality and influence on poets of this century can be appreciated.

With one or two notable exceptions, the major criticism of Rosalía's work focuses not on female or feminist impulses but on those characteristics her poems share with all poetry: themes, style, symbols, regionalism, personal angst, religious doubt.[2] These studies are empathetic and exhaustive in their careful treatment of the important characteristics of Rosalía's poems, but they focus on features that could be found in any Modern poet, most of whom are males—those very males who established the canonical standards by which poetry by women is traditionally judged. The fact that Rosalía was a woman, though not ignored,[3] is not foregrounded, a perspective that was altered in the early 1980s when Matilde Albert Robatto carefully studied the condition of woman during Rosalía's time as well as the view the poet presents in her prose and poetry of the Galician woman's predicament.[4] Then in 1986, several critics began to focus on Rosalía's female and feminist characteristics[5] and to unearth a feminized infrastructure to her poetry; that is, such studies began to allow postmodern readers to see that on one level Rosalía's work is a covert exploration of experiences that were central to her as a woman. A reader today can therefore make a legitimate attempt to find that on one level Rosalía's poetry was dealing "with central female experiences from a specifically female perspective."[6] Or, to follow Ostriker (*Stealing* 7) but to adapt her words: postmodern readers of Rosalía's poetry should begin to argue that an increasing proportion of her work is explicitly female in the sense that Rosalía chose to explore experiences central to her sex and to find a form and a style appropriate to the exploration of such experiences.

Rosalía de Castro published three principal books of poetry over a period of twenty years:[7] *Cantares gallegos (Galician songs)* appeared in 1863, in Galician; *Follas novas (New Leaves)* in 1880, also in Galician; and *En las orillas del Sar (Beside the River Sar)* in 1884, in Castilian.[8] In general, her first book is known for its regionalistic joie de vivre, while her second and third books are singled out for their resignation, sadness, and homesickness *(saudade)*. Although I agree in general with this poetic trajectory,[9] I think it diminishes her work by making us see it through andromyopic eyes.[10] Hence, in the following remarks I shall focus on Rosalía's marginalization (i.e., "Nobody" status) and foreground her "monstrous"—as opposed to "angelic"—qualities. I study her anger and her negative vision of womanhood, as well as the gynocentric style and vision she selects to undermine patriarchal norms.

Rosalía's marginalization was threefold: political, social, and esthetic. Catherine Davies, the first to research Rosalía's marginalization, has demonstrated that Rosalía and her husband, Manuel de Murguía, as Galician regionalists, identified themselves with liberal and progressive policies which provoked the hostility of the conservative Castilian centralists. The latter's antiregionalist campaign of prolonged hostility, Davies says, "discouraged Rosalía during her lifetime and belittled the reputation of her work after her death in July 1885" ("Rosalía" 610). Davies documents the intense anti-Rosalía campaign initiated by the prestigious novelist Emilia Pardo Bazán.[11] In her fascinating study, Davies concludes: "it was by means of their savage attack on a pluralist society and an autonomous Galicia that Rosalía's enemies, the Church, the oligarchy, and their cultural cliques, managed to keep her out of the main current of Spanish literature for so long" ("Rosalía" 619).[12] This politically based marginalization lasted until around 1912, when, as Davies notes, both Unamuno and Azorín "wrote warmly of Rosalía" (618).[13] Much later, in 1953, Juan Ramón Jiménez acknowledged Rosalía's originality in his lectures on Modernism.[14]

In addition to political marginalization, Rosalía, like all women artists of the nineteenth century, had to deal with pressures of a social—and psychological—nature that dissuaded her from being a writer. Some women writers of the time dealt with this by using their initials rather than their full names; others opted to publish under a male pseudonym.[15] Rosalía de Castro contemplated the latter, as a brief excursus on the extrinsic history of the *Cantares* (1863) will testify.

It was Manuel Murguía, if we are to believe him, who pressured his wife into completing the *Cantares* as well as into writing additional poems and a prologue required for their publication. For a while, Rosalía refused to oblige; she even went to the extreme of telling her husband that it would be better if the poems appeared under his own name.[16] It is quite possible to gloss over these *rapports de fait* as indications of Rosalía's modest nature. However, recent feminist criticism (Gilbert and Gubar, *Madwoman* 554-58) has clearly demonstrated that patriarchal culture conditioned the nineteenth-century woman artist to believe that she possessed neither the talent nor even the humanity to be a creative artist. The woman poet learned quickly that she was "Nobody" as far as "Poetry" with a capital "P" was concerned, and she acted accordingly.

Such an attitude is apparent in Rosalía's concluding poem to the *Cantares,*[17] where she apologizes for what she perceives as her lack of poetic finesse:

> *Yo cantar, cantar, canté,*
> *aunque mi gracia era poca,*
> que nunca (y de ello me pesa)
> fui yo una niña graciosa.
>
> Canté como mal sabía,
> con mil vueltas enredosas,

como hacen los que no saben
directamente una cosa.
Pero después, con cuidado,
y un poco más alto ahora,
fui soltando mis cantigas
como a quien nada le importan.
Mas en verdad bien quisiera,
que fuesen más melodiosas.
Yo bien quisiera que en ellas
bailasen sol y palomas,
con la luz las blandas aguas,
mansos aires con las rosas.
Que en ellas claras se viesen
espumas de verdes ondas,
del cielo blancas estrellas,
de tierra plantas hermosas,
nieblas de color sombrío
que las montañas arropan,
los gritos del triste búho,
y aún las campanas que doblan,
la primavera que ríe,
y las aves voladoras.
Canta que te canta, mientras
el corazón triste llora.
Esto y aún más, bien quisiera
decir con lengua graciosa:
mas donde gracia me falta
el sentimiento me sobra:
aunque éste tampoco basta
para explicar ciertas cosas;
por fuera a veces se canta,
mientras por dentro se llora.
No me expliqué cual quisiera
que soy de palabras corta;
si gracia al cantar no tengo,
el amor patrio me ahoga.
Yo cantar, cantar, canté,
aunque mi gracia era poca.
¡Mas qué he de hacer, desdichada,
si no nací más graciosa!

(**Cantares,** trans. Barja, 298, 300)[18]

(*As for me, I sing and sing, I sang, / even though I had little grace, / for I never was a graceful girl / (which distresses me). / I sang, poor singer that I am, / but with hundreds of intricate trills, / like those who've never known / a thing by heart. / But later, with care, / and now a little higher, / I chirped out my songs, / as if it were all the same to me. / But in truth, I wished / they'd been more melodious. / I really wanted the sun / to dance in them with the doves, / the light with the smooth waters, / the gentle breezes with the roses. / I wanted in their clarity to manifest / the green waves' spray / the sky's white stars, / the earth's lovely plants, / the somber mists / that cover the mountains, / the sad owl's cries, / and even the bells that toll, / the Spring that laughs, / and the birds that fly. / You go on singing, while / your sad heart weeps. / All this and more I really

wanted / to express in gracious speech: / but what I lack in grace, / I make up for in feeling: / but nor is that enough / to explain certain things; / from the outside at times it seems that one's singing, / when inside one's weeping. / I couldn't say what I wanted to / because I'm poor with words; / if I'm graceless when I sing, / it's because I choke on love for my native land. / As for me, I sing and sing, / I sang, even though I had little grace. / But, woe is me, what more could I do / if I wasn't born more graceful.)

This is a *romance* ("ballad") but unlike a traditional *romance* that presents a coherent vision of an aspect of reality, this poem's vision is bifurcated:[19] there is an imaginative response to the wonders of nature (ll. 15-30) which is framed by the speaker's protestations of her inferior talent (ll. 1-14, 31-46). Because of this dichotomy, the poem becomes an intriguing text: is it its frame (lack of talent), or that which it frames (nature)?

The text's frame is certainly an exercise in self-deprecation and, in retrospect, a clear manifestation of the inferiority complex from which Rosalía suffered at the beginning of her poetic career. Despite the fact that she has just given her readers thirty-four original poems, the **Cantares gallegos,** in her concluding piece Rosalía chooses to apologize for the lack of "gracia" (charm and wit [ll. 2, 33, 41, 44]) she perceives in all those songs; she even attributes this to the fact that she herself has never been a "graciosa" (charming woman [ll. 4, 32, 46].[20] The words "gracia" and "graciosa" signify "grace" or "charm," but also something or someone "amusing," "witty," "entertaining."

Is Rosalía begging for her readers' indulgence? Is she saying: this poem is written by a woman, therefore you should not expect linguistic grace and mental wit (e.g., ll. 5, 6, 14, 40), and to compensate for my gauche talents, I offer you my own honest and straightforward feelings (l. 34)—which, of course, tradition allows women poets to display—and my deep-felt love for the region of the country where I was born (l. 42)?

It may well be that Rosalía is playing the modesty game. However, she may also be protesting too much, thereby subconsciously offering a critique of the lack of grace and wit to be found in poetry written by males at that time. Poullain notes that Murguía claimed that Rosalía published the **Cantares** in Galician because she was so disgusted by the poor use of the Galician language she found in the 1861 *Album de la caridad* (Charity album) (*Rosalía Castro* 51 and n. 67).[21] We can therefore assume that in part Rosalía was conscious of the superiority of her own talents.[22] Indeed, today's readers who carefully consider the four stanzas that constitute the body of **"Yo cantar, cantar"** (As for me, I sing and sing [ll. 15-30]) must disagree with the speaker of the poem and conclude that the poet displays both grace and intelligence in the way she represents that ideal world of natural beauty (which she also describes in similar terms but in prose in her prologue [**Obras** 1:67-71]). Rosalía's metaphors (ll. 16, 24) are audacious, her use of bird imagery (ll. 16, 25, 28) apposite, as is her exploitation of chiaroscuro (ll. 17, 21, 23), sound symbolism (ll. 25-26), synaesthesia (ll. 17-18), and the elements (earth, air, water). She writes what we are accustomed to think of as a "modern" poem.

Hence, for today's readers this poem (and all the **Cantares**) is more than just a paean to Galicia from one who was overwhelmed by an intense love for her native region ("amor patrio" [l. 42]). Its double vision can be read on another level as a schizophrenic response to an androcentric culture. It is a text that manifests a psychological split between a voice that claims that it has little talent and a poet who demonstrates no few poetic gifts. This double-voiced text is Rosalía's response to the patriarchal culture of her time, her way of coping with the restrictions placed on women poets in the nineteenth century, when women were conditioned to believe that it was unnatural for them to be poets. What better way of demonstrating real talent than by framing a nature poem with a reflection on one's limitations as a woman poet, by turning one's reputed physical and linguistic drawbacks into an intriguing verbal artifact?

I have been arguing that Rosalía was marginalized as a poet by both the political and social prejudices that prevailed in the latter part of the nineteenth century. There is also a third factor in Rosalía de Castro's marginalization: an esthetic self-marginalization, which derived from the fact that as a fledgling poet she tried to imitate a male model to whom she compared her own talents unfavorably.

In her prologue to the **Cantares,** Rosalía affirms that the inspiration for her poems came from *El libro de los cantares* (The book of songs) by the Galician writer don Antonio de Trueba y de la Quintana (1819-89). Trueba's was a very popular collection of fifty-four poems (*romances* [ballads] and *coplas* [folksongs]) which first appeared in 1851. As Kulp-Hill observes in her remarks on Rosalía's debt to and striking difference from Trueba, *El libro de los cantares* "had eight editions in twenty years" (*Manner and Mood* 34-35) In addition, Poullain (*Rosalía Castro* 56) reminds us that, in his prologue to Ferrán's *La soledad* (Solitude), Bécquer himself praised Trueba highly as a model for "intimist" poetry. However, Varela (*Poesía* 152) sums up the reaction of today's readers to *El libro de los cantares* when he asserts that in comparison to Rosalía, Trueba's verse appears "pale, insipid, trite" ("pálido, soso, simplón"). More recently, Feal Deibe ("Sobre el feminismo" 313 and n. 13) found little human value in Trueba's poems. Indeed, today these fifty-four poems will strike a reader as commonplace, sentimental, jingoistic. They now read as a well-versified collection of

facile tales, ridden with clichés and superficial thoughts. Let me justify these assertions and, by implication, suggest the originality and talent of Rosalía de Castro.

Trueba is both traditional and conservative in his religious views and his political outlook. He presents the perfect mother as one who indoctrinates her children in the religion of the country (no. 10). He praises the queen (Isabel II) not only because she is good but also because she is a woman and a mother (no. 1); he lauds the birth of the princess (no. 32); he glorifies the history of the motherland (no. 27), and he intones the greatness of Spain's newly formed Civil Guard:

> Un grito de regocijo
> resonó en mi dulce patria
> y á la voz de Isabel, fué
> la Guardia civil creada,
> y al verla el pueblo español
> cantó lleno de esperanza:
> —*¡Viva la Guardia civil*
> *porque es la gloria de España!*
>
> (*Libro* 226)

(A cry of joy / rang out in my dear homeland / for the Civil Guard, created / by [Queen] Isabel's voice, / and when they beheld it, the Spanish people / sang out with hope: / *Long live the Civil Guard / for it's the glory of Spain!*)

Likewise, Trueba's vision of womankind is conservative and traditional: a blend of simplistic stereotypes and patriarchal attitudes. In his prologue he refers to "blue-eyed virgins who hold pride of place in my nugatory portraits" ("las vírgenes de ojos azules que ocupan el primer término en mis desaliñados cuadros" [x]), and then asks: "but where is there more purity and feeling than in children and mothers?" ("pero ¿dónde hay mas [*sic*] pureza y sentimiento que en los niños y las madres?" [xii]). In his *cantares,* we find such descriptions as these: "To my eyes, woman / is a weak plant / threatened / by eternal hurricanes, / and hence I endeavour / to be her valiant aide / in this world" ("La mujer á mis ojos / es débil planta / de eternos huracanes / amenazada, / y así procuro / su generoso apoyo / ser en el mundo" [no. 10, 38]); or, "girls are flowers / whom even the wind can depetal" ("las niñas son flores / que hasta las deshoja el viento" [no. 16, 51]). A later poem, "The Glories of Womanhood" ("Glorias de la mujer" [no. 41]), has a refrain—"I say that you have neither the soul / nor the heart of a woman" ("digo que no tienes alma / ni corazón de mujer")—which may well have impressed Rosalía.[23] "Glorias de la mujer" represents the state of motherhood as one of sublime delight and one to which every girl should aspire.[24] In addition to a patriarchal attitude toward the woman, Trueba's poems pretend that a woman's fulfillment consists in finding a loving man (no. 35), and they consistently present women from the male point of view as objects for sensual pleasure (nos. 5, 6, 7, 11, 13, 46):

> ¡Salada, qué hermosa eres!
> ¡Salada, por ti me muero!
> Tienes una cinturita
> que se abarca con dos dedos,
> tu mano y tu pié parecen
> de una niña en lo pequeños.

> (*Libro* 151)

(Darling, how cute you are! / Darling, I die for you! / Your waist's so slender / it's just a few inches wide; / so tiny are your hands and feet, / they look like a child's.)

And finally, if women speak in these poems, it is because they have been seduced (no. 2) or because they are mad (no. 28).

As Trueba expresses so many platitudinous views, it is difficult today to understand why Rosalía thought him so fine a poet.[25] Nevertheless, in the prologue she wrote for the **Cantares,** she lauds the sophistication of "don Antonio," "Antón, el de los *Cantares,*" while introducing herself as "a person of poor talent" ("un pobre ingenio" [trans. Barja 14]), "with little ability, and schooled in no other place than our poor villages" ("débil de fuerzas, y no habiendo aprendido en otra escuela que la de nuestros pobres aldeanos" [trans. Barja 16]):

> Mis fuerzas en verdad quedaron muy por debajo de lo que alcanzaran mis deseos, y por eso, comprendiendo cuánto podría hacer en esto un gran poeta, aún más me dolió mi propia insuficiencia. *El libro de los cantares,* de D. Antonio Trueba, que me inspirara y me diera aliento para llevar a cabo este trabajo, pasa por mi mente como un remordimiento, y casi asoman las lágrimas a mis ojos al pensar cómo se levantaría Galicia hasta el lugar que le corresponde si un poeta como Antón el de los "*Cantares*" fuese el destinado a dar a conocer sus bellezas y sus costumbres. Mas mi patria infeliz, tan desventurada en esto como en lo demás, tiene que contentarse con unas páginas frías e insulsas, que apenas serían dignas de acercarse de lejos a las puertas del Parnaso si no fuera por el noble sentimiento que las creó. ¡Que esto mismo me sirva de disculpa ante quienes justamente critiquen mis faltas, pues pienso que el que se esfuerza por desvanecer los errores que manchan y ofenden injustamente a su patria es acreedor de alguna indulgencia![26]

(My talent was not up to my desire, and hence, realizing just how much a great poet could achieve, I was all the more pained by my own inadequacy. *The Book of Songs,* of don Antonio Trueba, which had inspired me and given me the courage to carry out this work, passes through my mind like a regret, and tears almost come to my eyes when I think how Galicia would be elevated to its due place if a poet like Antón, he of the *Songs,* had been the one destined to make known her beauties and her customs. But my unfortunate native land, as luckless in this as in all else, must be satisfied with a few dull, cold pages that would be most unworthy of approaching the gates of Parnassus from afar, if it were not for the noble feeling that created them. May this itself excuse me before those who justly criticize my faults, for I think that he who struggles to dispel the fallacies that unjustly stain and offend his native land is entitled to some indulgence!)

In her first book of poems, Rosalía sees herself as singing of the beauty and the customs of Galicia, and she feels inferior to the task. Why, when in comparison her poetry is far superior to Trueba's? I suggest that one of the reasons Rosalía fixates on the alleged paucity of her own talent is that she sets out to imitate a model for poetry supplied to her by a man; she sees herself as trying to do what a man has already done (i.e., versify the beauty and customs of a particular region). Rosalía even claims that she made every effort to "make known how some of our poetic customs still retain some primitive and *patriarchal* freshness" ("dar a conocer cómo algunas de nuestras poéticas costumbres todavía conservan cierta frescura *patriarcal* y primitiva" [**Cantares,** trans. Barja 16, italics mine]).

In imitating a male model, Rosalía is trying to succeed at doing what males do, which is to "tell male stories about a male world" (Gilbert and Gubar, *Madwoman* 67). Rosalía is suffering from an "anxiety of authority," which means that she is attempting to imitate a patriarchal literary model, one invented and historically developed by men; the more she employs that model, the more anxious she feels about her lack of talent, the more "diseased and infected by the sentences of patriarchy" she becomes (Gilbert and Gubar, *Madwoman* 71).

Rosalía de Castro's marginalization is therefore a complex web of social, political, and esthetic factors. Some of these—the social and political—she would have been conscious of, while others (psychological and esthetic) she could combat only subconsciously given her time and place.[27] This subconscious combat constitutes her "monstrous" side and gives her work its feminist infrastructure.

I turn now to the poems themselves, to argue that in many texts Rosalía struggles with the "monster" within, with a woman's experiences from a feminist and female perspective—something traditional criticism has ignored. In her **Cantares,** Rosalía is subconsciously subverting the patriarchal order and covertly undermining the androcentric worldview. This struggle is manifested in the fact that she foregrounds numerous and diverse female personae, and that she herself is engaged in a search for her own matrilineal roots. In doing this, she finds her own voice, one that can express her experience—an experience conditioned by the fact that she is a woman.

Is it not monstrous—beyond the bounds of expectation of that time—that the speaker of most of Rosalía's *Cantares* is a woman, and that the dominant experience treated in this book is female, not male? Just how remarkable this is becomes apparent when one notes that fifty-two of the fifty-five poems in Trueba's *El libro de los cantares* are spoken by males and deal with a man's experience from a male perspective.[28] In most of Rosalía's poems, by contrast, the speaker is a woman and most of her *Cantares* do not just deal with a woman's experience but also treat it from a woman's perspective.[29] Stevens, the first to investigate this feature of Rosalía's poetry,[30] concludes her study with the following assertion: "If I were to name one source with which Castro had the most intimate contact and the least ambivalence, it would be the women of rural Galicia whose lives and voices came closer than any others to expressing Castro's own predicament. Although Castro undoubtedly learned about women's emancipation from literate Spanish and European sources, the peasant women of Galicia provided her with the invaluable proof of women's artistic and spiritual achievement against all odds" (*Rosalía* 122).

In the *Cantares* there are women who sing (nos. 1, 32) and women who sin (nos. 3, 12); there are independent women (no. 4), rebellious women (no. 7), unfaithful (no. 10) and faithful women (nos. 26, 30); there are old women who dialogue with young women (nos. 3, 5); simple peasant women (no. 31) and mountain women (no. 18); there are ethereal women (no. 14),[31] seductive women (no. 24), and seduced women (nos. 2, 13, 30); there are love-struck and confused women (nos. 9, 27) and lovelorn and angry women (nos. 13, 28); there are religious women (nos. 11, 33, 37) and superstitious women (no. 16); there are snooty (Castilian) women (no. 23); silly, loquacious women (nos. 13, 27, 29); there are women who suffer from infertility (no. 20) and those who suffer from a profound longing for their native region ("saudade," nos. 17, 18, 19). All of these poems present an image of woman that is diverse, complex, and fascinating—especially in contrast with Trueba's.

But the *Cantares* do not just "present" an image of woman, female personae present themselves by articulating their desires, disappointments, and predicaments; they exchange advice and reveal the untextualized community women have always had; they criticize hypocritical women (no. 21) and the male world. For example, the female speaker of **"Un arrogante gaitero"** ("An Arrogant Bagpiper" [no. 8]) takes a critical look at the arrogant bagpiper and at the stupid girls he seduces in every village:

Ellas loquinas, bailaban,
y a donde estaba corrían,
ciegas . . . , ciegas, no veían
las zarzas que las cercaban;
cual mariposas, buscaban
a luz para irse a quemar,
(trans. Barja 86, **Obras** 1:109)

(Silly girls, they'd dance, / and run to where he was, / blind . . . , blind, and not see / the brambles that encircled them; / like moths, they'd search out / the light to burn themselves up.)

In this poem, a woman finds fault with women. In others, a woman displays her strength of character, as for example in the poem that begins:

—Cantan los gallos al día,
yérguete, mi bien, y parte.
—¿Cómo partir, queridiña,
como partir y dejarte?
(trans. Barja 48, **Obras** 1:88)

(—The cocks are crowing in the day,/rise up, my darling, and take your leave./—How can I take my leave, beloved,/how can I depart and leave you?)

This poem—like the *alboradas* ("dawn songs")—is a dialogue between young lovers who have spent the night together and must part at daybreak. This is a frequent topos in all types of literature, but with Rosalía there is a twist. Carballo Calero notes: "Unlike what happens in the famous scene in Shakespeare's *Romeo and Juliet,* Rosalía, like the song she glosses, presents the man as loathe to leave" ("A diferencia de lo que ocurre en la famosa escena de *Romeo y Julieta,* de Shakespeare, Rosalía, como el cantar que glosa, hace al hombre representante de la actitud de resistencia a la separación" [Castro, *Cantares,* ed. Carballo Calero 56 n. 2]). Unlike Carballo Calero, who focuses his comment on the male's resistance in this poem, I would say that, consciously or not, Rosalía presents a girl who takes the initiative, who pushes the boy out of bed and makes him leave. Rosalía subconsciously undermines—or fails to subscribe to—the androcentric worldview of traditional literature, in which the boy (male) is resolute, decisive, quick to leave after taking his pleasure, while the girl (female) is weak, resists his leaving, and clings desperately to the boy.

Traditional criticism has not foregrounded the predominance of female speakers and of a woman's experience as distinctive features of the *Cantares.* It has not done so, I suggest, because (following Rosalía herself) it sees the book as a depiction of Galician life. However, it is evident that, while imitating poems about men, Rosalía in fact writes poems about women. In subconsciously working through her "anxiety of authority," Rosalía finds her own voice, and this leads her to deal "with central female experiences from a specifically female perspective" (Gilbert and Gubar, *Madwoman* 72).

Cantares also reveals that the poet is involved in a quest for her matrilineal heritage. Gilbert and Gubar interpret nineteenth-century women's interest in idyllic settings as a "pained yearning for a lost, visionary continent," which in turn signifies "their yearnings for motherly or sisterly precursors" (*Madwoman* 100). As the poem **"Yo cantar, cantar"** (As for me, I sing and sing) frames an idyllic, natural setting with expressions of female inadequacy, I want to pursue this line of investigation in another (but earlier) poem from *Cantares.* **"Cómo llovía, suaviño"** (How gently it rained) is an unusually long discursive poem in which Rosalía's struggle to find a style and an original voice is manifested. The poem begins:

> Cómo llovía, suaviño,
> cómo, suaviño, llovía;
> cómo llovía, suaviño
> día y noche por Laíño,
> por Lestrove, noche y día.
> (trans. Barja 270, *Obras* 1:215)[32]

> (How it rained, so gently,/how, ever so gently, it rained;/how it rained, so gently,/day and night on Laíño,/on Lestrove, night and day.)

In this poem, Rosalía musically descends into the depths of her own mind where she follows her thoughts poetically:[33] she muses on the regenerative effects of the rain on the earth, meditates on her recently deceased mother (d. 1862), and reflects on the decaying condition of the mansion and estate ("Casa grande") where she and her mother grew up.[34] This extremely long poem ostensibly deals with Galicia: how the fine rain refreshes the countryside, the sailboats hearten the rivers, and how the old estates lie fallow (because these days there are no decent men ["venerable cabaleiro"] to care for them and for the poor who depended on them for survival).

However, and more importantly, Rosalía's thoughts lead her back in every instance to her mother—to what Sandra Gilbert called "the powerful womb of the matriarchal muse" ("Literary Paternity" 494)—so that the poem evolves into a meditative communion with a kindred female spirit who has been lost and whom the speaker tries to recuperate. The poem's first nine stanzas describe the rain from its first appearance until it dissolves into vapor, and the tenth stanza shifts gears thus:

> Así imagino a la triste
> sombra de mi madre, errando
> en la esfera donde existe;
> que a ir al cielo se resiste,
> por los que quiso aguardando.
> (trans. Barja 272, *Obras* 1:216)

(That's how I imagine / my mother's sad shade, as she wanders / in the sphere where she exists, / reluctant to go to heaven, / while she waits for those she loved.)

As she thinks of her mother's spirit, Rosalía is led to recall their shared experiences of tender and affectionate memories—"ternuras," "memorias cariñosas"—one of which are the songs "cantigas" her mother sang—those very "cantares" she alluded to in the apologetic concluding poem of her *Cantares.*[35] Later she recalls the ringing of the bells and writes:

> Aquéllas, sí, que animadas
> me llamaban mansamente
> en las mañanas doradas,
> con las cantigas amadas
> de mi madre, juntamente.
> (trans. Barja 278, *Obras* 1:219)

> (Yes, those merry bells, / they softly called me / together with my mother's dear songs, / on golden morns.)

In this free association of childhood memories, Rosalía subconsciously connects the "cantares" she is now writing with her mother's "cantigas"—a step she did not take in the final poem of her *Cantares.*[36] She is dreaming "of an archaic language that predates the patronymics of culture . . . gaining strength through fantasies of either an original or an originary linguistic matrilineage, a 'grandmatology' that [is] implicitly set against the patrilineal linguistics of the grammatology that has historically subordinated [women] and their ancestresses" (Gilbert and Gubar, "Ceremonies" 25).

Moreover, as she searches through the past to give meaning to the present, the woman poet in Rosalía settles on a strong precursor, her mother (who loved the "cantigas" she learned as a child). The poem then moves on to meditate on the huge, abandoned house ("casa grande") where her mother was born. However, the text evolves in such an ambiguous way as to imply that the abandoned house is also her mother ("amazona malherida" [badly wounded amazon]),[37] abandoned by Rosalía's father, and maybe even the speaker herself, "abandoned" by her mother who had just died. Hence, although this poem ostensibly treats the parlous state of Galicia, on a very different level it constitutes—as Adrienne Rich might say—a dive into the wreck of the self, from which the woman poet emerges clinging to central bits and pieces of submerged and lost experience.

Ostriker describes such a process when she offers a version of the Demeter/Kore myth as a model for the way women poets cease to be "Nobody" and become "Somebody"—they "retrieve and revive" their mutilated mother. She writes: "Rather than Oedipus and Laius at the crossroads, the model among women writers, critics as well as poets, is Demeter and Kore: except that it is the daughter who descends to Hades, step by step, to retrieve and revive a mother who has been raped, or perhaps seduced, by a powerful male god. For as the mother returns to earth, the daughter expects to blossom" (*Stealing* 16). Ostriker's focus on identity through recuperation and connectedness illuminates what Rosalía achieved in her *Cantares:* her own mother had been seduced by a powerful male (a priest) and had been ostracized by society because of the shame. By incorporating her mother's memory into literature, by textualizing a small piece of the untextualized culture women have always had (e.g., "cantigas"), Rosalía the daughter "blossoms": she retrieves and revives the mother, returns her to earth, and she makes society subsequently see her worth.

Also, Ostriker's focus on identity through recuperation and connectedness suggests that Rosalía subconsciously connected submerged pieces of her female experience, bits and pieces that are dispersed, that have hardly yet found their way into the written culture of (male) hegemonic texts. In this poem, Rosalía enters the "cave of the mind"; she begins to connect the scattered fragments—"revitalize the darkness, retrieve what has been lost, regenerate, reconceive, give birth" (Gilbert and Gubar, *Madwoman* 99), as demonstrated in "Yo cantar, cantar, canté" and "Cómo llovía suaviño."

Despite my rhetorical claims, *Cantares* is not the work of an acknowledged feminist but of a woman who sees herself as conforming to—if constrained by—cultural norms. However, the contradictions in its poetic vision manifest the writer's unconscious thoughts and hint at a feminist infrastructure that underlies the entire work. This feminist vision constitutes one of the woofs or warps of the *Cantares*—one of the subtexts or codes that constitute its total discourse. If such a subtext is read today with the benefit of the novel insights of gynopoetics, Rosalía's latent feminism can be glimpsed.

Cantares, I argue, manifests a split vision: a poet who thinks negatively of her talent writes original poems that reconnect her with her matrilineal roots. A comparable polarity between negative vision and positive achievement characterizes Rosalía's subsequent work, *Follas novas* (1880) and *En las orillas del Sar* (1884), which offer a host of material for a feminist rereading of her work. In these books of poetry, Rosalía is criticizing the condition of nineteenth-century womanhood by presenting us—at times angrily—with negative views on womanhood, marriage, motherhood, and on the condition of the female poet. However, she also rebels creatively against these conditions by initiating an inscription of a strong female self; by selecting gynocentric imagery

and metaphors to develop a female vision and subvert androcratic norms. . .

Notes

[1] Mayoral comments on true and false images of Rosalía in her conclusion (*Poesía* 567-68). She writes of "una dulce y morriñosa mujer gallega que llora y se lamenta continuamente en no menos dulces y suaves versos" ("a sweet and homesick Galician woman who weeps and moans in verses that are just as sweet and smooth"), as opposed to "aquella mujer de espíritu fuerte, tantas veces áspera . . . que [habla] en un tono feroz" ("that strong-spirited woman, often harsh . . . who speaks in ferocious tones").

[2] For instance, Carballo Calero's edition of the *Cantares* and studies by Alonso Montero, Kulp-Hill, Mayoral, and Poullain, and the recent three-volume *Actas do Congreso internacional de estudios sobre Rosalía de Castro e o seu tempo.*

[3] For example, both Mayoral and Kulp-Hill study Rosalía's "Electra" complex—her desire to compete against her mother for her father's affections.

[4] Albert Robatto's *Rosalía de Castro y la condición femenina,* in my estimation, focuses on Rosalía's presentation of the "angel" woman. She writes: "Sintetizaremos esta parte de nuestro estudio reafirmando una vez más que la capacidad de entrega, la ternura y la disposición al trabajo son tres cualidades de la mujer gallega, recurrentemente expresadas en la obra de Rosalía, que nos han ayudado a precisar ese particular feminismo rosaliano" (We would sum up this part of our study reasserting once more that her capacity for giving, her tenderness and her aptitude for work are three qualities of the Galician woman, repeatedly expressed in Rosalía's work, that have helped us specify that particular aspect of Rosalía's feminism [112]).

[5] See especially Stevens, *Rosalía de Castro* (who on pp. 118 and 121 makes the same point I am making here). And in the three-volume *Actas,* see Blanco García ("A problemática"), Briesemeister ("Rosalía de Castro"), Ciplijauskaité ("Cárcel estrecha"), Feal Deibe ("Sobre el feminismo"), March ("Rosalía de Castro"), M. Miller ("Rosalía de Castro"), Noia Campos ("Elementos literarios"), Sánchez Mora ("Rosalía de Castro"), and Stevens ("Apología feminista").

[6] Gilbert and Gubar (*Madwoman* 72) discuss how nineteenth-century women writers grew beyond the permitted bounds of female "modesty" and male mimicry.

[7] I omit *La Flor* and *A mi madre.*

[8] All future references to these books will be abbreviated to *Cantares, Follas,* and *Orillas del Sar* respectively and will be given in Spanish.

[9] However, I do agree with Poullain that a bipartite trajectory does not do justice to Rosalía's complexity. Moreover, an argument could be made that attention needs to be paid to the idea that her "saudade" would have been intensified and aggravated by the fact of her being a woman writer in the nineteenth century.

[10] For example, all poets toward the end of the last century were mournful and somewhat effete (decadent), and hence Rosalía's mournfulness ("saudade") is over-emphasized in all criticism of her work. As early as 1890 Pardo Bazán was implying that Rosalía's poetry was decadent: "repite quejas [de] la enferma poesía lírica" ("repeats the complaints of sick, lyric poetry" [see Davies, "Rosalía" 612; and Stevens, *Rosalía de Castro* 34]).

[11] For example, Davies notes that in 1885 Pardo Bazán "insisted on relegating Rosalía to the role of a minor provincial poet," and in 1891, in "La mujer española" (The Spanish woman), she "praises Avellaneda, Carolina Coronado, and Concepción Arenal" ("Rosalía" 612) but ignores Rosalía. This campaign was sustained by such figures as Núñez de Arce, Juan Valera, Tamayo y Baus, Menéndez Pelayo, and Emilio Castelar: "all [of whom] contributed to the formation of a solid block of intellectuals bound to officialdom which ostracized Rosalía de Castro" (612, 617).

[12] Rosalía's vilification by her nineteenth-century peers is also treated by Cardwell ("Rosalía de Castro" 440-41), who, recognizing his own debt to Davies, notes that Rosalía's early work, which attacks the status quo, helped inspire the self-serving campaign conducted against her after 1874 and continued after her death by Pardo Bazán, Valera, Menéndez Pelayo and others. Criticism of Rosalía and Murguía, Cardwell argues, was directed against the decentralization of Spain and the autonomy of Galicia. Such political emancipation was fiercely attacked by the supporters of the monarchy, restored in 1875, who also marginalized Rosalía's work by arguing that it reflected a decadent culture.

[13] Unamuno in an article collected in *Andanzas y visiones españolas;* Azorín in *Clásicos y modernos* (1912), *El paisaje de España visto por los españoles* (1917), and *Leyendo a los poetas* (1929).

[14] Jiménez told his students that in 1896 Rosalía was one of his favorite poets and that he was reading her at that time in Galician (*El modernismo* 54). Jiménez did translate a few poems from *Follas novas*. Aguirre writes that he translated "Sombra negra que me asombras" and "A [sic] la Habana ("Influencia" 46-47). Sánchez Romeralo says that he translated "Cuando creo que te has ido" and "Esta parte y aquella parte," which is the fifth section of "Hacia la Habana." He also notes that only the former has appeared in print, in Jiménez, *El modernismo* 302 ("Rosalía" 214 and 219).

[15] See for example, Gilbert and Gubar's "Ceremonies" (esp. 26-27).

[16] Alonso Montero (*Rosalía* 49) cites a letter of Murguía's, published in the *Boletín de la Real Academia Gallega* (Dec. 1950, 102-3), in which he claims that unbeknown to Rosalía he took the poems to a publisher friend in Vigo and demanded a prologue from her while they were being printed. For a month Rosalía refused, insisting "en que era mejor saliese el libro con mi nombre" ("that it were best that the book appear under my name," i.e., her husband's). In *Los precursores* (145), Murguía adds that Rosalía was obliged to write the rest of the book once the first printing was complete.

[17] The collection originally ended with this poem. However, the *Obras completas* (hereafter cited as *Obras* with the volume number)—which contain thirty-eight *Cantares*—have a different order. For further analysis of this poem, see Stevens (*Rosalía de Castro* 58-60).

[18] For the Galician original, see *Obras* 1:232-33. I give the Spanish because I assume that few of my readers will follow Galician sufficiently well to grasp poetic nuances.

[19] For a discussion of the traditional "romance," see note 22 to my introduction [in *Rosalía de Castro*]. . . A *romance* has lines of eight syllables, with assonance in alternate lines. In this *romance* the assonance is in o-a.

[20] Critics (e.g., Mayoral) have noted that Rosalía was not physically attractive.

[21] This collection of poetry in Galician, together with the *Juegos Florales de la Coruña,* marked the beginning of the Galician Renaissance. (Nothing had been written in Galician since the sixteenth century.)

[22] The issue of Rosalía's command of Galician is more complex than this; see Stevens (*Rosalía de Castro* 36-48, and esp. 39).

[23] She described her own heart as unfeminine in the opening poem of *Follas* (*Obras* 1:277).

[24] The poem reads: "Bajo ese vínculo santo, / ¿tus ojos, niña, no ven / á la madre cariñosa / que besa con embriaguez / la rosada faz del ángel / desprendido de su ser? / ¿no ves al feliz esposo / sellar con su labio fiel / la mejilla de la esposa / lleno de amor y placer? / ¿no piensas que en estos goces / hay tal encanto y tal bien / que solamente en el cielo / mayores los puede haber? / Pues si nada de esto piensas, / pues si nada de esto ves, / *digo que no tienes alma / ni corazón de mujer*" (In this sacred bond, / do your eyes, girl, not see / the caring mother / who kisses madly / the rosy face of the angel / that sprung from her being? / Don't you see the contented husband / filled with love and pleasure / seal

with his faithful lip / his wife's cheek? Don't you think that in such joy / there's such enchantment and good / that only in heaven / can there be anything better? / Well, if you think nothing like this, / if you see none of this, / *I say that you have neither the heart / nor the soul of a woman* [Trueba, *Libro* 169]).

[25] However, let me note the following parallels—all from *Follas*—as they probably demonstrate her debt to him. "Todo clavo se saca / con otro clavo" (Trueba, *Libro* 78), and "Unha vez tiven un cravo" (*Obras* 1:286). Poem no. 24, "Oros sin triunfo" (Trueba, *Libro* 88) should be compared to "No hai peor meiga que unha gran pena" (*Obras* 1:355), as they concern counts and country girls. Poem no. 44 (Trueba, *Libro* 177) has a woman who kills the man who seduced her; Rosalía in "A xusticia pola man" (*Obras* 1:332) has a woman who kills a family with a scythe.

[26] Trans. Barja 16; for the text in Galician, see *Obras* 1:68.

[27] Additional factors of a psychological nature which would have contributed to Rosalía's marginalization are her illegitimacy and rumored marital infidelities.

[28] Only poems nos. 2, 18, and 21 deal with women and/ or a woman's experience.

[29] To be precise, seven of the thirty-eight poems have male speakers and/or focus predominantly on a male predicament (nos. 14, 15, 22, 23, 24, 35, 38). "A gaita gallega," "Castellanos de Castilla," and "Alborada" each have a female speaker but are not really about a woman's experience.

[30] For Stevens's analysis of *Cantares* in particular see *Rosalía* 36-71.

[31] This ethereal woman, it should be noted, does not lead her man to perdition. Compare Bécquer, *Rimas,* Rima 11 "soy incorpórea" etc., and "Los ojos verdes."

[32] This is the first stanza of a very long poem of 225 lines. In consists of fifty-five "quintillas" in abaab.

[33] As will Machado in "Poema de un día—Meditaciones rurales" [128] of *Campos de Castilla* (for which see Wilcox, "Self-Referentiality"). The resonance of Rosalía in Machado and Jiménez is astounding (and, apart from meriting a detailed study, is another testimony to her greatness).

[34] Rosalía's early years are complicated. Her father, a priest, abandoned her mother. Rosalía was initially brought up by distant relatives, but joined her mother when she was about eight years old.

[35] For "cantigas," see note 22 to my introduction [in *Rosalía de Castro*]. . .

[36] Possibly written under pressure from Murguía and therefore less meditated.

[37] This is an allusion to the medieval "cantiga de amigo," "Malferida iba la garza" (cited in my introduction, n. 22. . .).

FURTHER READING

Bibliography

March, Kathleen N. "Rosalía de Castro (1837-1885)." In *Spanish Women Writers: A Bio-Bibliographical Source Book,* edited by Linda Gould Levine, Ellen Engelson Marson, and Gloria Feiman Waldman, pp. 104-15. Westport, Conn.: Greenwood Press, 1993.

> Bibliography of translations, primary and secondary sources preceded by a biographical and critical introduction.

Criticism

Balbontin, José Antonio. "Rosalía de Castro." In *Three Spanish Poets: Rosalía de Castro, Federico García Lorca, Antonio Machado,* pp. 15-55. London: Alvin Redman, 1961.

> Comprehensive formal and thematic study of Castro's writings.

Courteau, Joanna. *The Poetics of Rosalía de Castro's* Negra Sombra. Lewiston, N. Y.: The Edwin Mellen Press, 1995, 119 p.

> Considers Castro's contribution to Galician language and culture by analyzing her poetic imagery of *sombra* (shadow).

Davies, Catherine. "Rosalía de Castro, Criticism 1950-1980: The Need for a New Approach." *Bulletin of Hispanic Studies* LX, No. 3 (July 1983): 211-20.

> Surveys limitations in modern criticism of Castro's poetry, asserting the need for further socio-historical and ideological evaluation of her work.

—. "Rosalía de Castro's Later Poetry and Anti-Regionalism in Spain." *Modern Language Review* 79, No. 3 (July 1984): 609-19.

> Dicusses poetic protests against the Spanish clergy and dominant Castilian government in Castro's *En las orillas del Sar.*

—. "The Return to Mother Cathedral, A Stranger in No Man's Land: Rosalía de Castro Through Julia Kristeva." *Neophilologus* LXXIX, No. 1 (January 1995): 63-81.

> Views Castro as a "revolutionary and transgressive" poet, interpreting her work in light of Julia Kristeva's conceptions of the semiotic and of rejection.

Dias, Austin. "Rosalía de Castro: A Mother's Lament." In *East Meets West: Homage to Edgar C. Knowlton, Jr.,* edited by Roger L. Hadlich and J. D. Ellsworth, pp. 32-39. Honolulu: University of Hawaii Department of European Languages and Literature, 1988.

Detailed analysis of Castro's late poem of a mother's loss of her child.

McClelland, I. L. "Bécquer, Rubén Darío and Rosalía Castro." *Bulletin of Spanish Studies* XVI, No. 61 (January 1939): 63-83.

Investigates the mutual influence of Gustavo Adolfo Bécquer, Rubén Darío, and Castro.

Miller, Martha LaFollette. "Rosalía de Castro and Her Context." In *Ensayos de literatura europea e hispanoamericana,* edited by Félix Menchacatorre, pp. 325-29. San Sebastián: Universidad del País Vasco, 1990.

Explores Castro's poetic challenges to religious and political tradition, her relation to women's expression, and her ambivalence concerning her role as a writer.

Ghalib

1797-1869

(Pseudonym of Mirza Muhammed Asadullah Beg Khan. Also wrote under pseudonym Asad.) Indian poet, essayist, historian, memoirist, and handbook writer.

For additional information on the life and works of Ghalib, see *NCLC,* Volume 39.

INTRODUCTION

Ghalib is regarded as the most important Urdu-language poet of the nineteenth century. Praised in particular for his artful use of the short lyric form known as the *ghazal,* he also wrote poetry in other forms, numerous volumes of letters, and a compelling account of the Sepoy Rebellion of 1857, an attempt by natives of India to overthrow British colonial rule.

Biographical Information

Ghalib was born into an aristocratic Muslim family in Agra. Orphaned at age five, he was reared with his brother and sister by maternal relatives. Ghalib started writing poetry in both Urdu and Persian as a child. At age thirteen, he married and moved to his wife's home in Delhi, where, except for occasional travel, he resided the rest of his life. In Delhi he made the acquaintance of several prominent and influential poets and wrote both occasional and lyric poetry for patrons at the Mughal court. In 1827, Ghalib made a business trip to Calcutta and met a number of writers and scholars in that city and in Lucknow, gaining him admittance to the literary world outside of Delhi. While in Calcutta, Ghalib observed the material prosperity of British civilization and attributed this wealth to English academic and legal innovations. Thereafter, Ghalib began to challenge Indian institutions, especially the practice of educating Muslims in an Indianized dialect of Persian that varied from the traditional Persian in both vocabulary and grammar; Ghalib argued that Indians should write Persian as native speakers wrote it, and he presented his ideas at a symposium held by the university at Calcutta. Ghalib's audience strongly criticized the unfamiliar style of Persian he was espousing, which prompted Ghalib to condemn his opponents in Calcutta newspapers. His challenge to Indian tradition and his outspokenness provoked animosity among many of Ghalib's colleagues and involved him in a lifelong controversy. However, the quarrel also brought Ghalib greater attention and the resulting correspondence with other

scholars established his reputation as both an innovative writer and an uncompromising scholar.

Major Works

In 1841, Ghalib published his collected Urdu poems, *Divan-i-Ghalib.* His next book did not appear until 1849, when he produced *Panj ahang,* a kind of handbook on the writing of letters and poetry interspersed with samples of his own work; throughout the next decade, he published only sporadically. In 1857, Ghalib was forced to reassess his great admiration for Western culture when the British rulers of India responded to the Sepoy Rebellion with violence, martial law, and the forced exile of Delhi's Muslim and Hindu populations. Eighteen months after the start of the fighting, he published *Dastanbu,* his memoirs of the suffering brought on by the conflict, and sent copies to various British officials, including Queen Victoria, both to plead for moderation in the treatment of Indians and to establish his own innocence in the rebellion. At this time,

motivated by the realization that most of his unpublished manuscripts had been destroyed when the rebels
and British alike looted the libraries of Delhi, Ghalib
attempted to gather his remaining *ghazals* into expanded
editions of his *Divan*. In the loneliness caused by the
deaths and exile of many of his friends, Ghalib began
to write several letters a day for solace; many of these
were collected for publication. Despite rapidly failing
health in his later years, Ghalib helped edit some of
these collections and critiqued poems sent to him by
poets all over India. He died in 1869.

Critical Reception

Although Ghalib wrote in several genres, his *ghazals*
have generally been the best received of his works.
Ghazals usually consist of five to twelve couplets linked
by common meters and rhyme schemes, but not necessarily by subject matter or tone. They were common in both Urdu and Persian, although Persian poetry
generally brought greater prestige. As a young man,
Ghalib preferred to compose in Persian until he noticed a growing taste for Urdu verse among Delhi
poets. From the 1820s onward, he composed increasingly in Urdu and now is remembered chiefly for his
Urdu writings. Critics remark that Ghalib expanded
the range of themes of the *ghazal* genre and utilized
conventional Persian and Urdu poetic devices in new
ways. For example, a nightingale singing in a garden
for love of a rose was a common metaphor for a poet
composing his works through the inspiration of a
beloved, but unresponsive, woman. Ghalib used the
same allusion to suggest his interest in progress and
modernity: "My songs are prompted by delight / In the
heat of my ideas; / I am the nightingale / Of the flower
garden of the future." By identifying his symbolic
beloved as a future age, Ghalib stressed his interest in
change. He broke more strongly with established literary practice in his letters. Educated Indian Muslims
usually wrote letters, as they did poetry, in Persian
rather than in Urdu, while Ghalib wrote increasingly in
Urdu. Moreover, in either language, letter writers customarily employed rhyming sentences and addressed
their correspondents with flattering epithets. In place
of such formality, Ghalib substituted colloquial language and nicknames or terms of endearment like
"brother." His letters proved so popular that they were
adopted as models by subsequent writers of Urdu.

Highly regarded for his contributions to the development of Urdu poetry, Ghalib was virtually unknown
outside of Urdu-speaking communities for decades
following his death. His work, however, came to the
attention of Western readers as a result of the efforts
of Indian and Pakistani scholars in the 1960s, and the
centenary of his death in 1969 was marked by several volumes of English translations of his poems,
with critical notes and biographical essays. Recent

scholars have focused in particular on his handling of
ghazal stylistic conventions and his contribution to
the development of Urdu literature, and they agree that
his extraordinary skill as a lyric poet makes him one of
the most prominent figures in nineteenth-century Indian
literature.

PRINCIPAL WORKS

Divan-i-Ghalib (poetry) 1841; revised editions, 1847,
    1861, 1862, 1863
Kulyāt-i-Nazm fārsī (poetry) 1845, 1863
Panj ahang (poetry and handbook) 1849
Mihr-i-Nīmrōz (history) 1854-55
Dastanbu (memoirs) 1858
Kuliyat-i-nasr (poetry, memoirs, history, and hand-
    book) 1868
Ud-i-Hindi (letters) 1868; revised as *Urdu-i-moalla*
    1869, 1899
Makatib-i-Ghalib (letters) 1937
Khutut-i-Ghalib (letters) 1941; revised edition, 1969
Nadirat-i-Ghalib (letters) 1949
Ghalib ka nadir tahirin (letters) 1961
Dastanbūy: A Diary of the Indian Revolt of 1857
    (memoirs) 1970
Ghazals of Ghalib (poetry) 1971
Urdu Ghazals of Ghalib (poetry) 1977
Urdu Letters of Mirza Asadu'llah Khān Ghālib (let-
    ters) 1987

CRITICISM

N. N. Wig (essay date 1968)

SOURCE: "New Evaluation of Ghalib and His Poetry," in *Indian Literature*, Vol. XI, No. 1, 1968, pp.
36-48.

[*In the following essay, Wig attempts "to study Ghalib's
life from a psychological point of view, in an effort to
understand his complex personality and the way it
influenced his poetry."*]

The first centenary of Ghalib's death will be celebrated
in 1969. Perhaps no other Indian poet in recent times
except Tagore has won so much acclaim. Unfortunately,
in Ghalib's case, most of it came after his death. There
are more than 40 books on his life and works by different authors, apart from numerous articles and special numbers of magazines devoted to him.

The amazing fact about this poetic genius is that
much of his popularity rests on only one slender
volume, **Diwan-i-Ghalib,** in Urdu, containing 185

Ghazals. Perhaps no other poet in history can claim such abiding popularity for such a slender work. This is not surprising; rarely has there been a book in the world literature which contained such breadth and depth of human emotions, from utter despair to the height of ecstasy; such wit and humour; such wisdom and insight expressed in unmatched lyricism and poetry.

What was the personality of this man who has stimulated and delighted countless generations of poetry lovers? Though there is no satisfactory definition of a genius, every individual is essentially a product of hereditary and environmental influences. In this article an attempt is made to study Ghalib's life from a psychological point of view, in an effort to understand his complex personality and the way it influenced his poetry.

Ghalib, whose original name was Asad Ullah Beg Khan, was born in Agra in December, 1797 and had a Turko-Persian ancestry of which he was very proud. His grandfather Mirza Quqan Beg migrated to India in King Mohamed Shah's time and came from a family of warriors. Ghalib's father held minor jobs with various princes and eventually died in a small battle when Ghalib was only about five years old. Ghalib's uncle, Nasar Ullah Beg Khan, took up the burden of bringing up his brother's children, but he too died a few years later when Ghalib was only nine. Nasar Ullah Beg Khan was quite a successful army officer and in appreciation of his services to East India Company he was given a 'Jagir' by the British. After his death, the 'Jagir' was taken over by the Government and a small annuity bestowed upon the bereaved family, including Ghalib. The legal battle over the recovery of the full estate dominated a large part of Ghalib's life.

Ghalib's mother belonged to a rich aristocratic Muslim family of Agra and his father probably lived with his in-laws most of the time. Ghalib, born in his maternal grandfather's house, was the second of three children. The eldest was a sister and the youngest a brother, Yusuf Ali Khan, two years junior to Ghalib. It is recorded that this brother developed mental illness at the age of 29 which persisted till his death in 1857 during the days of Mutiny.

Unfortunately, not much is known about Ghalib's childhood. He was brought up at his mother's place, and by all accounts his early life was spent in luxury. His pet name in childhood, which remained popular among his friends throughout his life, was 'Mirza Nausha' or the Young Bridegroom. Death of father and later of the uncle probably added to the laxity of discipline and soon Ghalib drifted into an easy life of leisure, which was typical of rich aristocracy in the nineteenth-century North India. Spending time in kite-flying, cock-fighting, gambling or in the company of dancing girls was the accepted mode of behaviour among such class, to which Ghalib was no exception. He picked up the habit of drinking quite early, and could never leave it.

Writing verses was also considered fashionable for the leisured class, which is probably how Ghalib's early forays into poetry began. It is possible that had his father not died so soon as he did and had Ghalib not been brought up in such luxurious childhood, he would have followed his father's footsteps. He might have made a moderately good army officer under some native prince, but Urdu language would have lost one of its priceless jewels. This early period certainly coloured whole of Ghalib's life, and in spite of the hardships, the terrible poverty and heavy domestic burdens in his later days, Ghalib remained a Bohemian at heart. The revival of that lost childhood—for him, a golden age—remained his favourite dream, which was reflected in his poetry. This is also what probably made him an incurable optimist.

Not much is known either about his early education. He probably went to some local school and was soon proficient in Urdu and Persian. There were hints of his precocious intellect at a very early age. He wrote his first poem before he was in his teens, and had completed a book of verse before he was twenty. Legend has it that a poem, which Ghalib wrote when he was about eleven, was taken by an admirer and read to the great Mir Taqi Mir in Lucknow who praised it. At about thirteen, he came in contact with a great scholar who was to have a profound influence on his life: Mulla Abdul Samad, an Iranian and a Parsi recently converted to Islam, who met Ghalib during his travels in India. Obviously struck by the young boy's sharp intellect and keen desire to learn, he stayed with him for two years and taught him Persian language and literature and history of Persian civilization and religion. From thereon we perceive a strong influence of Persian culture on Ghalib, who idealised everything Persian and took pride in being the foremost Persian scholar of his day. For a number of years he even considered it as unbecoming to write in Urdu. He preferred to wear a Persian dress and followed the Shia cult which came from Iran, though he originally belonged to a Sunni family.

I think that Ghalib's obsession with Persian civilization can be traced to his subconscious idealization of his missing father, whose vacant place in his mind was at least partially taken by Mulla Abdul Samad. One other interesting speculation would be to guess the impact of his early years in mother's home on his future life. In Indian culture, a son-in-law staying with wife's parents is always a subject of mild ridicule and petty jealousies. To a sensitive mind like Ghalib's such slighting references to his father and talk of their dependence on maternal family would not have gone unnoticed. Especially, the early death of father might have made Ghalib feel more insecure. As an inevitable reaction to similar situations, it is not unusual in children to develop defensive attitudes and secretly day-dream about the father being all powerful and glorious.

Ghalib shifted to Delhi from Agra quite early in life and started living independently. It is not clear why he did it. Perhaps the dissatisfaction with the life in the maternal home played a part. Subsequently, especially after his mother's death, his relations with maternal family seemed to have cooled down. For the first few years, he continued to receive plenty of money from his mother and persisted in his life of easy luxury. As was the custom those days, he got married quite early, at the age of thirteen, with a girl of eleven. By all accounts, including some of his own letters, this did not turn out to be a very happy marriage. She was an average housewife, a thoroughly religious and devout muslim, who could never fully put up with her husband's extravagant habits, drinking, debts and a non-conformist outlook on life. She bore Ghalib seven children, but none survived. Ghalib adopted one of his wife's nephews who died at a young age. In later years, he looked after the two children of his adopted son.

There are some piquant references in his letters to his domestic life. Perhaps the most well-known is the one in a letter to Munshi Har Gopal Tafta in which Ghalib is advising another friend who has lost his second wife and plans to marry again, not to make this mistake. He says:

'On the plight of Umrao Singh, I felt pity for him and envy for myself. Good God, there are those whose chains have been cut twice and here am I, hanging by this noose around my neck for over fifty years. Neither do I die nor does the rope break.'

Little is known of Ghalib's amorous life. In those days it was not unusual for the rich to have dancing girls as companions. In one of Ghalib's letters there is a reference to his deep love for one such girl in his youth. A couple of his early ghazals also seem to have been addressed to some woman he might have loved. Apart from this, nothing much is known about Ghalib's relations with the opposite sex. In spite of an unhappy domestic life, he does not seem to have drifted to extramarital affairs. Perhaps alcohol was his main vice.

The next important event in his life was the case of his pension. This affair dragged on for almost fifteen years and was largely responsible for his mental unhappiness and financial difficulties. As we have noted earlier, after his uncle's death the British Government had fixed a pension for his family. After the death of the trustee, Ghalib filed a case in the court in 1828, claiming that the pension should not have been divided in small parts but all of it should be given to Ghalib's family with

effect from the date of his uncle's death. Ghalib even undertook a journey to Calcutta, the then Capital of British India. The case lingered on for years with many ups and downs. Ghalib took the case to the Governor General's Council, and eventually to the Privy Council, but he lost every time. He even wrote a petition to Queen Victoria. To complicate matters, he had borrowed a large sum of money, his luxurious habits continuing during all this time. The failure of this case came as a staggering blow to him and the rest of his life was a story of unending pecuniary hardship.

However, through all these years his literary stature was growing. He had attracted a small band of intellectual admirers very early in life but by now his fame had spread far and wide. A large number of scholars from different parts of the country accepted him as their mentor in poetry and sent their verses to him for correction. By 1840, he was recognised as one among the two or three top Persian scholars in the country.

Another event which seems to have left a mark on his life was his arrest and imprisonment for three months in 1846 for the offence of using his premises as a gambling club. There are varying versions of this event, but Ghalib probably was guilty, although it is possible that he did not realize the seriousness of the offence nor imagined that a man of his standing in the community could be so treated by the police. The subsequent trial and punishment came as a shocking blow to his pride and reputation. Barring a few close and loyal friends, everyone he knew, including many relatives, forsook him in this predicament, which naturally made him very bitter.

July 1850 marked the beginning of a somewhat happy period in Ghalib's tormented life. Bahadur Shah, the last Mughal Emperor, honoured him with a title and monetary gift. Ghalib was employed to compile a history of the Mughal dynasty in Persian, with a monthly stipend of Rs. 50/- for this work. This brought him in close contact with the exclusive literary circle that existed in the Red Fort. It turned out to be one of the poet's most glorious productive periods, more so because the King was himself a significant poet in Urdu. Zauq, another leading literary figure of Delhi, was his teacher. After Zauq's death in 1854 Bahadur Shah turned to Ghalib for poetical guidance. Ghalib was writing mainly in Persian in those days, but the influence of Bahadur Shah revived his interest in Urdu. Some of his best Ghazals are of this period. His financial condition and social status further improved when the King's eldest son and heir apparent accepted him as his poetry teacher in 1854 with a salary of Rs. 400/- per annum. Probably, Wajid Ali Shah, the last King of Oudh, also started paying him a stipend of Rs. 500/- annually at about the same time.

Ghalib's happiness however was short-lived. The political upheaval of 1857 saw the destruction of all his hopes and dreams. With the deportation of the King, all financial help from the King and the British government ceased. During this period of hardship, some of the poet's more affluent pupils and friends came to his rescue. After the 'mutiny', he was accused by the British of siding with the deposed King, though he had taken no active part in the disturbances. However, the British government agreed to resume his pension within three years and his literary stature was regained. By this time he was the most famous of old Delhi poets. The Nawab of Rampur took him as his teacher and put him on a stipend.

From 1860 onward Ghalib's health deteriorated rapidly and for the last four or five years of his life, he was almost confined to bed. Numerous letters written during this period give details of his illness, of which the main symptoms were repeated abscesses and boils all over his body, especially legs, frequency of micturition, increasing deafness, failing eyesight, tremors in hands, etc. In spite of all this, his mental faculties remained sharp, as his letters of later years amply show. The end came in February 1869 after a paralytic stroke.

The diagnosis of Ghalib's illness has never been properly discussed, but the symptoms point to the strong probability of its being Diabetes Mellitus. Alcoholism might have also contributed to the general poor health, deafness and tremors. The frequency of micturition may on the other hand suggest an enlarged prostate gland. His death was almost certainly due to a cerebro-vascular attack (a blood clot or haemorrhage in the brain vessels) resulting in paralysis and death. These are known to occur more in diabetic patients.

Much has been written about Ghalib's personality, his physical attributes, his love for Persian language and way of life, his liberalism, his religious tolerance, his sparkling wit and humour, his alcoholism, etc. But one striking aspect of his personality has missed the attention of his biographers: the contrast in his moods from utter gloom and despair to the height of elation and ecstasy. Some critics have noted his sharp wit and humour as his poetry's most distinctive feature, while others with equal vehemence have tried to prove that his writing mirrored human suffering and misery. The truth is that Ghalib was both a pessimist and an optimist, depending on his moods. In the following example, one of his famous ghazals, there is almost a classical description of what psychiatrists would call a depressive illness. Medically speaking, depressive illness is recognised in a patient by a mood of hopelessness, pre-occupation with ideas of death, lack of interest in everything, lack of sleep, suicidal thoughts, feeling of undue guilt, etc. Let us now see how the various couplets of the ghazal can be cited as an example to illustrate these points:

'Koi Ummid bar nahin ati'

I see no end to my despair,
As my troubles before me loom;
No ray of hope illumes my breast,
It is a cell of the deepest gloom.

Why can't I go to sleep at night?
Why can't I realize
that death will come when it will come
and not a day too soon . . .

Time was when I could laugh
at the wanton whimsies of my heart
. . . But now my heart has lost all hope
and naught can make me smile.

I am in that far off land where even the
     news of my
own self is rare to obtain.
I know the reward of piety, good thoughts
     and
pious deeds. No more I can solace myself,
     no
more I feel inclined.

What face you will show in Kaaba with all
     your sinful
          past?
Don't you feel ashamed, oh Ghalib, to even
     think such
          things.

(Translation by J.L. Kaul)

I have always thought that this is a masterpiece of a poem which so beautifully records an almost clinical picture of a psychological illness. An occasional sad couplet or ghazal is certainly not unusual in any poet's collection; but here it is not one or two couplets. The mood pervades through the whole poem. The remarkable thing which makes it distinctive is not sadness (other poets may have written about sadder things) but the accuracy of description. There cannot be much doubt that Ghalib had personally experienced such depressed moods of clinical intensity.

Here is another example, also a ghazal, written around 1828-33:

I long to go to a lonely place
     Far, far away from here
No doors, no walls, I'd build me there
     A shelter lone and bare
A way from man's vain company
     And all this petty strife
Unwatched by neighbour's prying eyes
     I'd lead a lonely life

If I fall ill, no fellow-man
    Need minister to me.
And if, perchance, I die, no one
    Need grieve or mourn for me.

(Translation by J.L. Kaul)

The above are only two instances taken from among his various ghazals, reflecting the same mood. As is well known in modern psychology, a person suffering from such depression can also experience at times an absolutely contrary feeling, marked by an undue elation, extraordinary happiness and a sense of extreme confidence and superiority in himself. This type of personality is called cyclic, cyclothymic or manic-depressive. Such persons will suddenly go into a state of gloom for days and weeks on minor provocation and then would swing to the opposite side of complete elation without apparent cause. This was also Ghalib's case as a section of his poetry amply demonstrates. As an example, I am quoting below only the first few lines of a ghazal:

'Bazicha-e-atfal hai'

This world is a children's nursery for me. I
    delight
in the spectacle of creation morning and
    evening.

King Sulaeman's throne is a play-thing of
    children
for me. Christ's miracles hold no wonder for
    me.

Seeing me, the desert covers itself in sand.
The mighty river humbles itself before me
    lying low in
        dust.

Don't bother how I feel in your absence. You
    had
        better watch how you look in my presence.

A lover, yes, but a clever lover am I. When I
    am there
Laila forgets Majnu and belittles him in my
    presence.

Laila and Majnu's love is as sacrosanct as anything can be in Urdu poetry, but here Ghalib in his elated mood feels confident that Laila is ready to deceive Majnu for him.

I have made efforts to trace the dates of writing of various ghazals to see if the varying moods of Ghalib can be correlated with actual events in his life. Dating the ghazals is not easy as there is a lack of agreement among authorities. The ghazal **'Koi Ummid bar nahin ati'** was written probably sometime between 1847-1850. Very few of Ghalib's letters of this period are available. However, a newly published collection of his letters, *Nadirat-e-Ghalib,* has some belonging to this period. I have come across one such letter in the collection which Ghalib wrote to his friend Nabi Bakhsh 'Haqeer' on January 9, 1850 and which I am quoting below:

My dear friend,

I owe you the reply to a letter. But what can I do? I am so grief-stricken and depressed. Further, stay in this city is no longer to my liking. On the other hand, there are so many impediments in my way that I cannot go away from here. My grief and sorrow has reached a point where my only hope lies in death.

One whose only solace is in death.

His disappointment has no bounds.

In this flood of depression and sorrow, I began thinking today of you and your children. It is a long time you have not written anything about yourself or the children either . . . I wish you all well.

Most probably the ghazal **'Koi Ummid bar nahin ati'** was also written during the same period. The similarity of the mood is striking. The period is soon after the imprisonment of Ghalib in the summer of 1847. Some other ghazals reflecting a similar depressive mood might also have been written at about then.

The other ghazal which I have quoted to depict his elated mood, namely, **'Bazicha-e-atfal hai'** can be timed more accurately. In one of his letters, written in July 1854, Ghalib refers to this ghazal and says it was written a year ago. This would put it in the year 1853—a period when he was relatively well off and happily settled in the King's court. Another ghazal depicting also a confident mood, was written a year later, in 1854, which was incidentally the year of the death of Zauq, one of Ghalib's main literary rivals in Delhi.

A cyclothymic or manic-depressive personality is often a victim of heredity. Manic-depressive psychosis, one form of insanity, is closely associated with such personality. Details of Ghalib's brother's mental illness are not available, but possibly he could have suffered from a similar disease. It must, however, be made clear that Ghalib himself never suffered from any insanity or mental illness. Cyclothymic personality is only a variation of normal and is fully compatible with high intelligence and excellence of other faculties.

Other notable features of such a personality are his extrovert nature, gregariousness, love for eating and drinking, etc. All of these were present in Ghalib. It has been suggested that, generally, drinking was a source of inspiration for his poems, which he mostly composed in the evening after his drinks. Much of the mystical quality of his couplets reminds one of alcoholically inspired ecstasy. ·

The contrast in Ghalib's mood and attitude towards life is evident not only in his poetry but in other spheres also. At times we find him supremely self-confident, headstrong and cocky. At other times he is vacillating, apologetic and unsure of himself. Under the façade of self-assurance and self-aggrandizement, there was basically an insecure personality, which can be traced to the childhood events, death of his father and other happenings. In such moods of exaltedness he was quick to offend people. But he was not a good fighter and when pressed hard, would rather compromise than fight. In 1851, for example, he wrote a beautiful 'sehra' for the prince and was so carried away by its poetical excellence that the last two lines of the poem contained a veiled but slighting reference to Zauq who was then King's mentor, as if challenging him or anyone else to write a better 'sehra'. When he heard about the King's displeasure about this reference, he wrote a long poem of apology saying, how could he dare compete with Zauq. His famous literary quarrel in Calcutta in 1828 was also typical. When he read a Persian poem in a private gathering, some people criticized the grammatical use of certain words and phrases and quoted certain authorities in support. Ghalib immediately and arrogantly dismissed those quoted authorities as non-entities with no knowledge of Persian. The result was an uproar, and for weeks following the event, Ghalib was criticised in public and press. Finally, though he was convinced of his literary ground, he decided to issue a letter of apology.

The same pattern we find in the defamation case of *Qati-Burhan* in his later years. During the days of mutiny he had a copy of the Persian dictionary *Burhan-Qati* with him. As he had nothing better to do those days, he went through the book, found it full of mistakes and ended up by writing a new book on its corrections. When it was published, it raised a storm of protest from traditional and conservative exponents of Persian language. Some people went to the extent of sending Ghalib threatening and abusive letters. One of them wrote a book derogatory to Ghalib, full of vulgar and obscene language. Ghalib filed a court suit claiming damages for defamation, but when he found a large number of defence witnesses against him, he ended up by compromising outside the court without pursuing the case.

Similar examples can also be cited from Ghalib's behaviour during the 1857 mutiny, when he first tried to remain on the side of the King and afterwards was as pro-British as any one could be.

It will be naïve to suggest that by analysing certain traits of his personality we can understand the genius of Ghalib or the beauty of his poetry. A genius is beyond analysis. It is a mysterious quality, almost a divine gift. Ghalib was intensely aware of his greatness, his destined place in history. In one Persian poem he predicts how posterity will remember him and how believers and non-believers will both find expositions of their viewpoints in his poetry. Ghalib's tragedy was that of a tormented soul—a genius who is caught in the midst of mediocres who do not know his worth. As he says:

> They have never understood nor will understand what I say. Oh God, give them a new heart if you cannot spare a new tongue for me.

> There are many a poet in this world highly praised and highly talked. But the style of Ghalib is his own, unrivalled and unmatched.

M. Mujeeb (essay date 1969)

SOURCE: "The Personal and the Universal in Ghalib," in *Indian Literature*, Vol. XII, No. 2, 1969, pp. 5-14.

[*In the following excerpt, Mujeeb provides a brief appraisal of Ghalib's career as a poet.*]

Ghalib's biographer finds it difficult to identify any event that could be called significant in his life; it was so much a life of the mind. We cannot be sure even of the external circumstances that could have influenced him. He came of what was then considered a good family, and his own statement could be quoted to prove that he was proud of his family and his aristocratic connections. As against this we have the verse, hitherto overlooked, it seems, of his earlier period:

> I cannot tell you how perverse they are:
> Disgrace itself now shuns the nobly born.

This was written before an overzealous kotwal of Delhi had sent him to jail for gambling and before a desperate liquor merchant had prosecuted him for failure to pay his debts, an event commemorated in his verse:

> 'Tis true I drank on credit, but always knew
>   for sure
> My spendthrift poverty one day my ruin would
>   procure.

If his statement about the nobly born has any biographical significance, it would show what he really felt about the young men among whom he moved as a blithe and charming figure.

He was always in financial difficulties and spent well over fifteen years in fruitless prosecution of his claim to a larger share in the income of the Firozpur Jhirka estate. But would he have really benefited if his claim had been accepted? He was by nature thriftless and incapable of controlling his generous instincts. It is true that poverty and such sensitiveness and imagination as he possessed would make a man more conscious of his humanity, of that dignity of which man is deprived by being too poor to think of anything except what he is to eat and how he is to cover his nakedness. There is a ghazal of Ghalib which begins:

> Stark destitution: beggar's hand outstretched
> For something to erase the crushing lines of
>   want,

but this is a ghazal of his earlier period, written before he was twenty-five years old, and comparatively well off, able to pay for his liquor and to help out his friends. Later verses, where he complains directly or indirectly of his poverty, do reflect an actual condition of utter wretchedness. But it is only in the last ten years of his life that he felt crushed, and then he had given up writing poetry. Lack of means was a limitation on the play of his instincts which he would have felt acutely under any circumstances, and we should not try to establish a too direct connection between his poverty and his poetic lament over it. We must also remember that the resentment and bitterness he feels is not against the social order in which some are affluent and some poor, but against the very conditions of human existence.

Ghalib was pampered in his boyhood by the ladies of his family, and not subjected to any kind of discipline. He was married at the age of about fourteen to a girl of eleven. Neither his elders nor he himself took interest in his education; his literary talent became apparent very early, and it does not seem that lack of systematic study made much difference. He was fond of company, of games, of conversation. We do not know when he began to drink; but though drinking became a habit, he seems generally to have kept within self-imposed limits. Respectable people of his class would have considered his habits and his way of life improper. Ghalib was, however, anxious not to offend. Once, in an angry mood, he wrote:

> I have man's nature, I am born of man
> And proud that I commit the sins I can. . . .
> My worship of the vine I'll ne'er abandon
> In stormy whirlpools I shall always dive,

and we could regard this as a bold statement of a concept of sin which was an integral part of his philosophy of life. But we cannot say that he felt oppressed by adverse public opinion, or that there was any element of retaliation in what he said about piety and the pious. In practice, he never failed to show reverence where it was due.

But Ghalib did not have a pronounced mystical tendency. Certain doctrines, like the unity of existence, had become a part of culture, and Ghalib seems to have taken them for granted. A disparagement of the externals of religion had for centuries been the fashion among Muslim poets and intellectuals, and though this attitude had its origin in sufi thought, it could not, in Ghalib's time, be regarded as an indication of any positive mystical leanings. Ghalib did not follow the Muslim practice of praying. Very late in life he said, 'I am no Muslim if I prayed even once in my life.' He was, no doubt, being flippant, but it is true that his belittling of religious practices was not because of a preference for some other form of religiosity.

The sufi view of life had created certain symbols, around which poetry revolved for centuries. The attraction of these symbols was such that they became the distinctive feature, indeed, the essence of poetry. Love, beloved, lover, wine, tavern, saqi, intoxication, madness, garden, wilderness and other images were the warp and woof of poetry. The symbols were, inevitably, taken from the physical world, but they could also be given a transcendent spiritual quality. However, there always remained an element of intoxicating doubt. The physical and the spiritual, the sacred and the profane could never be clearly distinguished, and the symbols could be interpreted by the spiritual and the sensuous to mean what they wanted them to mean. The quality of poetry would be judged according to the manner in which the two aspects had been blended. An exclusive or a too obvious emphasis on the spiritual or religious aspect would lead to the poetry being classed as religious, and to that extent less of true poetry. A concentration on the gross and physical would be frowned upon as vulgar. The poetic image was a creation of light and shade, and the light did not come from a spiritual beyond, but from the human heart.

The traditional symbols were all used by Ghalib in the composition of his poetic images. They had their basis also in the facts of his life. He admired and was admired by beautiful women, he once fell in love and his love was returned in what seemed to him an excessive and ultimately embarrassing measure. In one of his later verses he says:

> I long for that release from care when I could
>   lose
> Myself in thoughts of my beloved—and no
>   day or night,

but, except in an elegy, love for a woman hardly ever appears as an overpowering passion. Love has, however, another and philosophically and symbolically more significant aspect. The terms Ghalib uses for such love can be translated as ardour, longing, irresistible urge, uncontrollable desire, a power, a daemonic force within man which takes complete possession of his being, which may destroy him or lead him to freedom and ecstasy.

The best starting point for an appraisal of Ghalib would be to begin where he himself began—with the will to live free from care and restraints, guided by an instinct that was itself thoroughly imbued with gentleness and goodwill. His intelligence, sensitivity and the interest and encouragement of some of his elders gradually drew him away from kite-flying and other youthful games to poetry, till he was seized with a passion for it. The kind of poetry that was written and admired in his time did not appeal to him. It was too elementary, too obvious for him, and leaned too heavily on the spoken idiom and play of words. No doubt it was not lacking in sincerity; sometimes there was evidence of deep feeling, but it was intellectually too shallow and reduced the poet, who should be a man and something more, to a lover defeated and mauled as it were by his own love. Ghalib was attracted and impressed most by the poet Bedil, who wrote in Persian and lived about a century before him. Some critics attribute the involved language of the first phase of Ghalib's poetry to a desire to imitate Bedil. Ghalib himself expresses his profound admiration for his predecessor with an astonishing frankness and zeal. Possibly it was Bedil who made Ghalib aware of his own potentialities and induced him to abandon the beaten tracks in order to break new ground in unexplored regions of thought and feeling, or, as Ghalib put it, to create new meaning in old forms.

Ghalib began his career as a poet by forging a medium of his own, a mixture of Urdu and Persian, startling in its terseness and sheer novelty. In the perspective of history, this does not appear as a mere fad or an idiosyncrasy. The Urdu of Ghalib's days was a language in the making. It was following the healthy tendency of refining itself while drawing sustenance from the spoken idiom, but the spoken idiom would by itself have kept expression at a low intellectual level. Something had to be done to increase its capacity. This was ultimately the result of Ghalib's bold experiments because, though he began by disregarding current idiom, he returned later to enrich it with the treasure he had collected during his wanderings. The reason for his disregard was that the current idiom could not take him to the heights he wanted to scale, to a poetry beyond the poetry of his days. He had all the shortcomings of the pioneer, but there is a vigour, a grandeur, even I would say a fascination in his earlier poetry which one misses in his later work.

Ghalib, the man, who demanded of life that it should let him be himself, matured as a creator of poetic images. 'Being himself' had now vastly different implications. The satisfaction of living as he liked was no longer possible because satisfaction itself had come to

have a different meaning. But it is still Ghalib the man who looks at life and who asks why he cannot be himself, whatever the implications of that might be. He is not, like the legendary Dr Faustus, willing to sell his soul in return for an experience of all that the world of mind and matter holds within itself. Ghalib's humanity is not divisible into body and soul; there is nothing he can bargain with, the devil does not enter into the picture because he does not have an independent existence, and God has a way of giving with which Ghalib is not at all satisfied.

It would not perhaps be demonstrably correct to say that Ghalib had a concept of man which can be deduced from his verses. He would have found it irksome to commit himself to any idea that would obstruct the free expression of his mood. He does not seem willing to accept the restraints of belief; he looks at love from all sides, and finds that it brings joy and misery, that it creates and destroys, and though its full realisation is not possible without surrender, man must not only maintain his identity but exercise his right to judge. And so, though the beloved is adorable, Ghalib is a lover who cannot discard his cultivated playfulness, and in any confrontation the lover seems to have the best of it.

Every thoughtful reader will make his own selection of the typical verses representing Ghalib's various moods. Here are a few which, taken together, would make a rough outline of the personality of the poet, and, therefore, indicate his concept of man.

> A song that dwells within the singer's
>   throat,
> An ecstasy that needs no wine:
> Be sinful charm incarnate, and your head
> Before the pious multitude incline.
>
> Like the commotion of the judgement Day I
>   roam
> Across the worlds seeking myself;
> My dust whirls on the other side
> Of non-being's barren waste.
> Shy not at sight of me, you who've imbibed
>   the illusion
> Of streamlined sense and knowledge;
> Dust of the road is all I am, my twists and
>   twirls
> Have no intent, no meaning.
>
> At least once in my life I must
> Let flesh be on its mettle—Ardour of love,
> Give me to drink such wine
> As only a full man can hold!
>
> Walking the common road brought blisters
>   on my feet:
> Now I rejoice the way leads into thorny
>   bushes
> For now I feel there must be a beyond.

I long to break my chains, but then I fear
My madness will but add to my disgrace
Better let prudence be my guide
To ways of momentary, small relief.

If I look out upon the world I see
The common faith blaming all ills on fate;
I think it's better far to let my mind
Create insensibility with the stuff
Of selfishness and cautious circumspection.
But still I would not that my heart became
Cold or inert; much rather should my life
Reflect the image of the futile sigh.
But then I am, O God, from head to heart,
Embodiment of pain that knowledge brings;
Better my world became a dream sea at
   whose shore
I stand in endless wonder.

Ghalib believed too much in his humanity to believe in anything else. There are verses that reveal a degree of religiosity, such as

Shame at unworthiness in my offering God's
   grace to
      win
And claims to pious living dyed a hundred
   times in sin.

In mosque and church and temple I seek only
   the
      Friend:
Wherever my forehead kisses the ground,
   His
      threshold responds to the kiss.

How long, O God, this begging for fulfilment
   of desire?
Grant me the grace to raise my hands aloft in
   prayer
      for all.

Mostly there is a touch of irony or a suspicion of banter when he addresses himself to God. There is an ode which has been surprisingly neglected by literary critics.

The tongue must beg Thee for the power of
   speech,
For silence has its way to catch Thy ear.
In days of gloom the stricken cry to Thee,
For Thine the lamp faint in the morning light.
Thine the despondent autumn flower.
Wondrous and colourful for the sight what
   man
      endures—
Thy work the henna'ed feet of death, in
   blood of
      lovers dipped. . . .

Aside from spell cast by the prayer that's
   granted,
Thou givest piquancy to cry of pain,
And lamentation becomes music for Thy ear.
Meadow on meadow lush within
The mirror of desire is Thine,
And hope lost in delight of gardens yet to
   be.
Our worship is a veil, Thou dost adore
   Thyself—
For Thine the suppliant forehead, Thine
The threshold where it rests.
Resourceful in excuses, Mercy lies in wait
To bring us near to Thee;
To Thee we owe fulfilment and the pain
Of trials by Thee ordained.
         Sad and beyond belief
Asad should be as in a magic cage confined,
When grace of movement, garden, morning
   breeze
Are Thine to give.

Here is an example of mild sarcasm:

More thrilling than wild dreams of pastures
   green
Is resignation to the will of God:
His are the fields thirsting for rain and His
The carefree rain-clouds floating gracefully
   away.

And then there is the impudence of the lover:

The ardour of our love reveals Thy glory;
   Thy world
Would be but a poor mirror for Thy face.

Ghalib's portrayal of lover, love and beloved tends to be rather conventional in the later period, that is, from 1850 to 57, when he had to make allowances for the senile romanticism of his royal patron, Bahadur Shah Zafar, and the taste of his audience. He was more imaginative and original in the earlier phase. Here are a few examples:

I marvel at my musk-anointed wound of love:
   a taper's flame
Clothed with the perfumed darkness of the
   night.

'Tis a scarred evening where I make
A darker shadow; though I'm meeting her
The time will pass too soon, my taper's flame
Already has the blossoming glow of dawn.

She strikes me speechless and yet speech
   expects,
When only silence can reveal the passion in
   my heart.

Awareness should be enemy of sight, sight of the
eye;
Come in such splendour that neither you know it
nor I.

I have deliberately tried to give as few translations as
possible of ghazals or verses for which Ghalib is most
admired, because it is impossible to reproduce the symmetry of the language or the epigrammatic delicacy of
the images. Closer study has also made me partial to
the youthful Ghalib, who tried to squeeze out of language more than it could possibly give. None the less,
it is clear why the later poetry of Ghalib has made such
a wide and profound appeal. It is intensely personal, but
at a level where the intensely personal becomes the universal. The lover, the man of the world, the agitator, the
man of frustrated ambition, the common man whose only
source of intellectual satisfaction is to repeat at an appropriate moment what everyone knows or feels, the
divers after pearls of meaning whose aspiration is to
fathom the deepest waters, all have their separate reasons for looking upon Ghalib as an exalted genius as
well as a kindred spirit. And Ghalib himself can well
ask,

Because of me each particle with longing
overflows,
Whose heart am I that I am so immersed in
heaven
and earth?

Ahmed Ali (essay date 1969)

SOURCE: "Ghalib's Thought and Poetry," in *Perspective,* Vol.
II, Nos. 8 and 9, February-March, 1969, pp. 107-10.

[*In the following essay, Ali provides a short overview
of Ghalib's thought and approach to writing poetry.*]

Ghalib died a hundred years ago in Delhi at the age of
seventy-two, having lost his sense of hearing and all
interest in life which, anyway, had not treated him too
kindly. Not fully appreciated in his own day, he stands
very high today wherever Urdu is read, including the
Soviet Union. This should give us food for thought,
not so much for the sake of Ghalib as that of poetry
and ourselves. Whether we like him or not, whether
we understand him or do not, Ghalib's poetry has a
quality which, in the essence, is for all time, having
been in his own time far in advance of the age, so that
it strikes us as modern and still advancing into the
future. His approach to life is highly individualistic
and his attitude, sophisticated and difficult, expresses
the sum total of cumulative feeling and intellectual
experience based on diverse factors present in the age.

He could not accept the established view of things
and was sceptical of known beliefs. In act, he was in
revolt against many of them which his rational mind
was loath to accept; and though a good deal of his
imagery was based on the conventional one, he in-
verted it to suit his thought, sometimes grotesquely
perverting it:

I know the truth of Paradise:
A futile thought, but comforting.

exposing, at the same time, the emptiness of orthodox
attitudes:

If Paradise he desires,
None else but Adam is heir to Adam.
The brilliance of the preacher's faith
Is dullness of action.

Ghalib saw through hypocrisy:

Deception of the hypocrite,
I'm the illusion of those
Distressed without a cause

and emphasised action:

Men are put to shame
By false courage. Therefore
Produce tears, Asad,
If the sigh has no effect.

He could see both sides of thought at once, the face and
the obverse, the light and the shadow. This is not confined to one facet, but is a characteristic of his mind:

In my construction lies
Concealed a form of ruin;
The lightning's flash that strikes
The grain-filled granary
Is the burning blood
Of the peasantry.

which was certainly written before the publication of
Das Kapital. For the same reason he had a dread of
conventions:

Kohkan could not die unaided by the
pick;
Poor man was slave to conventional
thought and belief.

This is not a mere facade or sophistication. It is a
mental state, a personal realisation of things born of a
realistic approach and the habit of analysis, which is
the basis of Ghalib's contemporaneity and consciousness of movement and change:

Each change of the mirror
Of creation
Brings sorrow in its train:

The cloud sheds its tears
At the departure of Autumn.

He is the perfect example of the intellectual poet, a poet not so much of the nineteenth century as the present, and in the present of the modern age to which both Eliot and Baudelaire belong. But in the positiveness of his vision, the affirmation of faith in humanity, Ghalib stands apart from both Eliot and Baudelaire, his vision and insight penetrating the darkness of the mind:

> Your light is the basis of creation;
> The grain of sand is not formed
>   without
> The glow of the sun.

presenting not the nemesis of an over-ripe civilisation, but a message of hope:

> Wearied, desire invents and seeks
>   refuge
> In temple and mosque, mere reflec-
>   tions in
> The mirror, hope's images multi-
>   plied

Hopeless and weary, humanity has gone on from faith to faith, accepting one, discarding another. And yet each one has proved illusory, a reflection in the glass, not reality. But out of despair hope is born again, and man multiplies illusions, never to become hopeless and lost. The thought recurs in Ghalib time and again. Those interested in Ghalib's thought should turn to my book on Ghalib just published by ISMEO from Rome; and for his style and technique to my published lecture: "The Problem of Style and Technique in Ghalib". Here, for lack of space, I must give a few translations of Ghalib from my book already mentioned:

1. When there was nothing there was God,
    Had nothing been, God would have been.
    My being has brought about my fall,
    Had I not been, what would have been?

2. Burnt has been the heart
    By the hidden heat within,
    Burnt as though it were
    A fire smouldering.

    How long, O thought, the grief
    For warmth of friends' company?
    The heart has been consumed
    By the heat of longing's wounds.

    No longer remains desire
    For union, nor memory
    Of love; such fire raged
    All that there was, was burnt.

How then can I express
The heat of the fire of thought?
I had only thought of despair
When the desert was consumed.
I've no heart or else I would
Have shown the landscape of wounds;
What use this tree of lamps?
Burnt is the source of light.
I am left with only a longing
For sadness, as the heart,
Seeing the ways of the world's
Esteem, was impetuously burnt.

3. The talk was of that lovely one,
    The style was mine, my eloquence;
    That's how my true and trusted friend
    Became my rival then.
    What need had she to drink so deep,
    And in my rival's company?
    And when she had to test me, why
    Today for ignominy?
    I could have built another scene,
    Another landscape on a height,
    If only my home were far away
    Beyond the empyrean.

    I was not versed in any art,
    Nor had I sagacity;
    O Ghalib, why the heavens then
    Became my enemy?

4. Beauty shall be freed

    Of the constant strife of coquetry,
    And perpetrators of cruelty
    Shall be at peace when I am dead.

    As when the candle dies out
    It leaves behind a trail of smoke,
    So will the flame of love put on
    Black clothes of mourning when I am
      dead.
    "Come, who wishes to drink
    The man-effacing wine of love?"
    This question will rise again, again
    To the lips of saki when I am dead.
    I grieve that after me
    None will remain within the world
    To mourn the death of friendship and
    Of love when I am dead.
    I'm moved to tears, O Ghalib,
    To think of the helplessness of love;
    Where will this all-destructive flood
    Go after me when I am dead?

5. My Foolish heart, what is ailing thee?
    What is thy sorrow's remedy?
    Wherefore all this tumult, O Lord,
    When nothing here exists without Thee?

Who are these beguiling ones? What is
This winking, ogling, coquetry?
Wherefore these curls in waving hair?
And why this kohl-bedarkened eye?
Where has the cloud come from? What is
The air, the rose, this greenery?
Devoted to you with all my heart
I know not prayer or piety.

K. N. Sud (essay date 1969)

SOURCE: "Ghalib's Ghazals," in *Eternal Flame: Aspects of Ghalib's Life and Works,* Sterling Publishers Ltd., 1969, pp. 57-77.

[*In the following excerpt, Sud discusses Ghalib's contribution to ghazal writing through an examination of several ghazals, finding him the greatest of all poets of this genre in his originality, subtlety of thought, simplicity, and grace.*]

Hain aur bhi duniya men sukhanwar bahut achhe

Kehte hain ke Ghalib ka hai andaz-i-biyan aur

(In the world are poets good, galore;
But different, they say, is Ghalib's style.)

The ghazal has not only taken pride of place in Urdu poetry but has also overshadowed all forms of versification in other Indian languages. At the *mushairas,* it is the ghazal that draws the longest and loudest applause and leaves the listener in a state of transcendental bliss. Even the Westerners have paid it a compliment by trying to imitate this style of poetry.

What is a ghazal? Briefly stated, it is the medium of expression of a man's love for his beloved. The word ghazal, in Arabic, means talking to women or talking love. The ghazal, as originally composed, was a song consisting of the stray thoughts of a lover, complaining of separation, longing for union and giving expression to sensations of pain and pleasure that characterise the experiences of love.

A ghazal starts with a verse called the *matla,* which contains two lines, the last but one word of which in the first line, known as *qafia,* rhymes with the last but one word in the second line. It closes with a verse called *maqta* in which the poet introduces his name or nom de plume. All the verses from the *matla* to the *maqta* are written in the same metre, and endings of the second line of each verse, known as *radif,* must rhyme together.

The traditional ghazal contains between six and eleven couplets, but nowadays some poets write ghazals containing up to twenty-five verses. Each verse gives full meaning to a thought and can stand by itself.

There are usually three actors who make up the cast of a conventional ghazal: the lover (*aashiq*), the beloved (*mashooq*) and the lover's rival (*raqeeb*). The lover, with whom the ghazal writer identifies himself, is the one who has been sinned against most. He is shown as luckless, restless, grief-stricken, given to drinking, unjustifiably defamed, unmindful of the cruelties of the beloved, and a victim of the intrigues of his rivals. Though he is sick and weak, he is faithful and ever ready to barter away his life for a smile of the beloved.

On the other hand, the beloved, though a paragon of beauty, is boastful, unfaithful, callous of heart, careless of manner and bitter of tongue. She is like an idol who is indifferent towards her worshippers and their sufferings, being also likened to a hangman (*qatil*) and a non-believer (*kafir*).

The rival (*raqeeb*) supposedly gets preferential treatment at the hands of the beloved. He is always plotting to prevent a conciliation between the *aashiq* and the *mashooq.* The former treats him with contempt while the latter shows him consideration, for the most part, to spite the lover.

Shah Wali-ullah, a renowned poet who wielded his pen during the reign of King Mohamed Shah in the early decades of the eighteenth century, was the first man to write an Urdu ghazal. He was a native of Aurangabad, but shifted to Delhi in 1722. Urdu in those days was a curious mixture of Hindi and Persian words and had yet to develop a syntax and grammar of its own. Most Muslim poets wrote verses in Persian. The credit for making Urdu the language of the nobility and giving it the same status as was enjoyed by Persian goes to Wali. He occupies the same place in Urdu as Amir Khusro does in Hindi and Chaucer in English. Wali's verses have a peculiar charm and flow, for example:

Dekhna har suboh tujh rukhsar ka
Hai mutala matla-i-anwar ka
Yad karna har ghari tujh yar ka
Hai wazifa mujh dil-i-beemar ka

(To see your rosy cheeks in the morning is like having a good look at the rising sun. To think of you every minute has become a duty of mine—a lovesick heart).

The next great writer of Urdu ghazals, Mir Mohamed Taqi Mir, was born at Agra in 1700 and lived a life of full one hundred years. He too shifted to Delhi and became so popular that travellers from Delhi used to recite his ghazals before gatherings of men in the cities they visited. When Nawab Asaf-ud-Daula of Oudh heard of Mir's fame, he sent for the poet and granted him a handsome pension. Mir's verses are liked for their spontaneity, facile expression and touching imagery. Mark the following lines:

> Patta patta boota boota haal hamara jane hai
> Jane na jane gul hi na jane bagh to sara
>   jane hai
> Aashiq sa sada to koee na hoga duniya
>   men
> Ji ke zian ko ishq men uske apna wara jane
>   hai

> (Every leaf and every plant knows my condition. The whole garden is familiar with it. If there is one who does not know it, it is the rose. In the whole world, you cannot find a person as trustful as a lover who regards even his death for his beloved as his own gain).

A well-known contemporary of Mir was Mirza Rafi Sauda, who was born at Delhi in 1713. He was the son of an Afghan trader and that perhaps explains why he chose the word "Sauda" (transaction) for his nom de plume. He became so popular in a few days that his ghazals began to be recited in every street and corner of Delhi. The Moghal King, Shah Alam, got his own compositions revised by Sauda.

Sauda's ghazals are marked by elegance and bold expression. He was always on the look-out for new words, but avoided the pedantic style employed by court poets like Mushafi, Insha and Jurrat, whose attachment to the kings and nawabs reduced their poetry to sycophancy and pleasure–songs for their patrons. In the use of poetic symbols, there is none to beat Sauda. For example:

> Barabari ka teri gul ne jab khayal kiya
> Saba ne mar thapera munh uska lal kiya

> (When the rose made a claim of equality with you—the beloved—the morning breeze slapped it so hard that its cheeks turned red).

After Mir and Sauda, further improvements in the ghazal were carried out by Khwaja Mir Dard, Mohamed Mir Soz, Nasikh and Atish, but it was left to Momin, Zauq and the greatest of them all, Ghalib, to introduce new subjects, new motifs and new symbols, and to chisel the language of this poetic medium. During this period, we find Urdu at its best abounding in king's idioms and civilised expressions. All these three poets were born in the last decade of the eighteenth century and wielded their pen through the greater part of the nineteenth century. The names of the lanes (*kuchas*) of Chandni Chowk, in Delhi, where they lived have been immortalised

through association with them. When Zauq received an invitation from the King of Deccan, he declined it by saying:

> Aajkal garche Deccan men hai bari
>   qadr-i-sukhan
> Kaun jae Zauq par Dilli ki galian chhor kar

> (These days there is high appreciation of poetry in Deccan but, O Zauq, who has the heart to leave the bylanes of Delhi?)

Though Ghalib's output of ghazals in Urdu is much smaller than that in Persian, it is his Urdu **Diwan** containing a little over 200 pieces (about 1500 couplets) that has rocketed him into immortal fame. And no other style of verse except the ghazal could have caught aesthetically better the deep emotional tension of his mind and the flights of his imagination of which Iqbal said:

> Fikr-i-insan par teri hasti se ye roshen hua
> Hai par-i-murgh-i-takheyyul ki rasaee ta kuja

> (Your existence has made man realise what heights the wings of imagination can reach).

But to Ghalib even the ghazal did not appear adequate for a full employment of his high-soaring genius. He observes:

> Baqadr-i-shauq nahin sahne tangna-i-ghazal
> Kuchh aur chahiye wusaat mire biyan ke liye

> (The expanse of ghazal is not large enough to fulfil my desires. I need something with bigger dimensions to express my thoughts.)

Ghalib transformed the entire spirit of ghazal writing. He broadened its sphere from a mere love prattle to encompass the whole gamut of man's life and experiences. He began composing verses before he had completed eleven years of his age. When he showed his first poem in Persian to his teacher, Sheikh Muazzam, the latter commented that it had a meaningless *radif*. This silenced the boy. Shortly afterwards, however, Ghalib spotted a verse having the same *radif* in the wellknown poet, Mulla Zahuri's collection of ghazals. He showed the book to the teacher who was taken aback on seeing the particular couplet. He then told the young pupil: "You have God-given aptitude for the Persian language. You must practise verse writing and never mind any criticism."

When Mir Taqi saw the young poet's compositions, he commented: "If this boy gets a competent teacher who sets him on the right road, he will become a peerless poet. Otherwise, he will rattle off meaningless stuff." How prophetic was Mir! He was proved right on both counts. Ghalib did start on a wrong note but since he was gentle and understanding by nature he thought-fully listened to the advice of his teachers and well-wishers and soon came on to the right path. He weeded out from his early compositions such verses as the critics regarded improper and not in good taste. And having finally found his moorings, he never looked back.

What distinguishes Ghalib's ghazals from those of many other poets is that in his case it is the words that follow the thoughts whereas the method generally employed by others is to think of a number of rhyming words for the *qafia* and then to think of suitable ideas for their use. This accounts for the fact that most of Ghalib's ghazals consist of no more than ten or twelve lines. Others who preceded as well as those who followed him wrote lengthy ghazals thinking that by reeling off a large number of verses in the same *radif* and *qafia* they could display their power of versification. Most such verses are nothing but efforts at rhyming. Their claim to literary merit is at best limited.

The thought contained in Ghalib's verses is for the most part expressed in a strikingly original manner. For instance, in his love poems he avoided the line taken by most others, that is, giving expression to the pangs of love by using the metaphor of the beloved causing injury to the lover. A common theme is to describe the kind of dagger used, the force with which it is thrust and the extent and depth of the wound inflicted. Ghalib's way of alluding to the injuries caused by the indifference or heartlessness of the beloved is peculiarly his own. For example:

Nazr lage na kahin unke dast-o-bazoo ko
Ye log kion mere zakhm-i-jigar ko dekhte
    hain

(Why do the people stare at the injuries in my heart? May the strong hand and arm of my beloved not catch the evil eye!)

Nothing else could have described better the intensity of the pain suffered by a lover as a result of the beloved's callousness. By implying that the wounds are such as will show the strength of her arm, Ghalib leaves the whole description of the manner in which they have been caused to the imagination of the reader. Besides, he tells us of his concern for the slightest harm that may be done to the beloved by the evil eye of the beholder. The subtlety of Ghalib's thought can be judged from another verse:

Samajh ke karte hain bazar men wo
    pursash-i-haal
Ke ye kehe ke sar-i-rahguzar hai kya kehiye

(The beloved enquires about my condition only in the bazar knowing full well that, being in

the market place, I won't make a complaint against her indifference.)

What the poet actually wants to say is that there is no sincerity in the beloved's inquiry about his health or wellbeing. She is only feigning concern about it.

When he wants to say that he would rather be killed at the hands of the beloved than die a slow death, he alludes to the excuses made by the latter for not obliging him, like there not being a dagger at hand or the non-availability of a shroud:

Aaj wan tegh o kafan bandhe hue jata hun
    main
Uzr mere qatl karne men wo ab laenge kya

(Today I am going to my beloved armed with the sword and shroud. What excuse will she now offer for refusing to behead me?)

The same sentiment is found in another couplet:

Sar urane ke jo waide ko mukarrar chaha
Hans ke bole tere sar ki qasm hai hamko

(When I requested her to repeat her promise to behead me, she smiled and said: "I swear by your head.")

The beloved's reply has a double meaning: (i) that I swear I shall behead you, and (ii) that your head is so dear to me that I swear by it.

A few more specimens of Ghalib's couplets on the theme of love:

Gada samajh ke wo chup tha meri jo shamat
    aaee
Utha aur uth ke qadam men ne pasban ke liye

(The beloved took me for a beggar and kept silent. But as ill-luck would have it, I made the mistake of falling at the feet of the sentry.)

The idea is that had he (the lover) not requested the sentry for help in letting him in, he might have escaped the wrath of the beloved when he appeared at the latter's door by being mistaken for a beggar.

Is sadagi pe kaun na mar jae ai Asad
Larte hain aur hath men talwar bhi nahin

(Who will not give his life for the beloved's naivety? She has no sword in her hand and yet she fights!)

Ishq mujh ko nahin wehshat hi sahi
Meri wehshat teri shohrat hi sahi

Ham bhi tasleem ki khu dalenge
Beniazi teri aadat hi sahi

(You say I am not in love with you and that it is
only madness on my part. But you can't deny
that my madness is the cause of your fame.
Besides, I shall develop the habit of bowing my
head even though you are habitually indifferent
towards me.)

Jab tak dahn-i-zakhm na paida kare koee
Mushkil tha tujh se rah-i-sukhan kare koee

(Until I took injury on my lips, it was difficult to
establish communion with you).

Chhora na rashk ne ke tere ghar ka nam lun
Harik se poochhta hun ke jaun kidhar ko main

(Envy has made me unfit to think of going to
your house. Hence I ask everybody where I
should go.)

Ham rashk ko apne bhi gavara nahin karte
Marte hain magar unki tamanna nehin karte

(I cannot tolerate even my own envy of her. I am
dying, yet I would not wish for her—lest I should
appear jealous.)

Unke dekhe se jo aajati munh par raunaq
Wo samajhte hain ke beemar ka haal achha
    hai

(When I see the beloved, my face displays rapture,
but she takes it to be a sign of improvement in my
sickness.)

Dekhiye paate hain ushaaq buton se kya
    faiz
Ik Brahmin ne kaha hai ke ye saal achha hai

(Let us see what benefit the lovers get from their
beloveds. A Brahmin has predicted that this is a
hopeful year.)

Ek ek qatre ka mujhe dena para hisab
Khoon-i-jigr wadiyat-i-mizghan-i-yar tha

(I had to account for each drop of blood of my
heart which I held in trust for the eyelashes of my
beloved.)

All the blood in the lover's heart is the property of the
beloved which he is holding in trust. He is returning it
drop by drop through tears of blood.

Ye kahan ki dosti hai ke bane hain dost naseh
Koee charasaz hota koee ghamgusar hota

(It is no friendship if a companion turns a counsellor;
he had better be a healer or a confidant.)

Marne ki ai dil aur hi tadbir kar ke main
Shayaan-i-dast-o-bazoo-i-qatil nahin raha

(O my heart, think of some other manner of death;
I am no longer fit to be beheaded by the beautiful
hand of the assassin—the beloved.)

Dil se mitna teri angusht hinayee ka khayal
Hogaya gosht se nakhun ka juda ho jana

(To erase from mind the thought of your hand's
colour is like detaching the nail from the flesh).

Rone se aur ishq men bebaak ho gae
Dhoe gae ham aise ke bas paak ho gae

(Tears have made me fearless and desperate in love.
They have washed me so much that I can hide my
love no more.)

Badguman hota hai wo kafir na hota kashke
Is qadr zauq-i-nawai murgh-i-bustani mujhe

(My beloved gets diffident when I go to the garden.
I wish I did not love so intensely the voice of the
nightingale.)

The poet says that his beloved gets annoyed when she
sees him go to the garden to hear the nightingale (who
also like the lover sings sad songs) instead of going
into the wilderness as any true lover would do.

De mujh ko shikayat ki ijazat ke sitamgar
Kuchh tujh ko maza bhi mere azaar men aawe

(Give me, O heartless, a cause to complain so that
you derive more pleasure from my discomfiture.)

The lover asks the beloved, who is a tyrant, to make
it possible for him to complain (of her callousness) so
that she becomes more wrathful and consequently inflicts harsher punishment on him. This will, according
to the lover, bring more joy and satisfaction to the
beloved. And that is what he secretly desires.

Maanga karenge ab se du'a hijr-i-yar ki
Akhir to dushmani hai asr ko du'a ke saath

(From now on I shall pray for separation from the
beloved. After all, is not there enmity between the
prayer and effect?)

The lover's wish always has the opposite effect.
He would therefore henceforth pray only for a thing
that he does not really want. The same sentiment
is found in the following verse:

Khoob tha pahle se hote jo ham apne
  badkhuah
Ke bhala chahte hain aur bura hota hai

(I should have been an ill-wisher from the very
beginning as every time I wish something the
opposite happens.)

Dosti ka pardah hai beganagi
Munh chhupana ham se chhora chahiye

(Posing unfamiliarity with the lover will only betray
the beloved. Hence she should give up the habit of
turning away her face.)

Ghalib tells the beloved that the latter should not try to
convince the people that there is nothing between them
by pretending lack of acquaintance with him. This only
betrays their relationship. She should therefore freely
meet him.

Dushmani ne meri khoya ghair ko
Kis qadr dushman hai dekha chahiye

(Her enmity has estranged other men too, See how
hostile she is towards me!)

The beloved is so much cross with the lover that when
other people talk of him, she gets angry with them too!

Bahut dinon men taghaful ne tere paida ki
Wo ik nigah jo bezahir nigah se kam hai

(Your prolonged indifference at least turned into a
half-look, a look that cannot be called a full view).

After remaining unconcerned for a long time, the
beloved shows slight interest in the lover. This
itself, though not adequate, brings great relief to
him.

Kare hai bada tere lab se kasb-i-rang-i-firogh
Khat-i-piala sarasar nigah-i-gulchin hai

(When you drink, the wine acquires colour from
your lips while the cup looks at you with the greedy
eyes of the gardener).

Kion na ho chashmi-butan mehw-i-tughafil
  kion na ho
Yaani is beemar ko nazarra se parhez hai

(Why should not the eyes of the idol be engrossed
in inattention? This patient is forbidden to see
anything.)

The beloved is compared to an idol of stone which
always appears to be too absorbed in thoughts to
look at the admirer.

Diya hai dil agar usko bashr hai kya kehiye
Hua raqeeb to ho namabar hai kya kehiye

(If the go-between has given her his heart, let
him. What can I say? He too is a human being.
If he has turned my rival, let him. After all, he is
my messenger.)

The lover's messenger himself turned a lover the moment he saw the beloved and thus became his rival. But
the poet does not mind it because after all the messenger too is a human being. Moreover, since he has carried his messages to her, it is not fair to reproach him.

Hai mujhe abr-i-bahari ka baras kar khulna
Rote rote gham-i-furqat men fana ho jana

(It is no more than a cloudburst for me to dissolve
myself into tears of separation.)

To annihilate himself by crying his heart out over separation from the beloved is a small matter for the lover—as
small as the burst of a cloud in the rainy season.

Mund gayin kholte hi kholte aankhen Ghalib
Yar lae meri balin pe use par kis waqat

(In vain I looked till the eyes finally shut. They
brought her to my bedstead only when I could
see no more.)

The lover kept his eyes open in the hope of seeing his
beloved one day but when his friends were at last able
to persuade her to visit him, the light had gone out of
his eyes.

Sar phorna wo Ghalib-i-shorida haal ka
Yad aagaya mujhe teri deewar dekh kar

(The sight of your house reminds me of the days
when I used to hit my head against walls like mad.)

Raaz-i-mashooq na ruswa ho jae
Warna mar jane men kuchh bhed nahin

(Were it not for fear of disgracing the beloved, I
would gladly die. There is no secret in death as
such.)

De wo jis qadr zillat ham hansi men talenge
Baare aashna nikla unka pasban apna

(I shall laugh away whatever humiliation she
may heap on me. How nice that her watchman
turned out to be an acquaintance of mine!)

Hamnashin mat keh ke barham kar na
  bazm-i-aish-i-dost
Wan to mere nala ko bhi aitbaar-i-naghma hai

(Do not say I am disrupting the happy assembly of the beloved with my wails because there even my lament is enjoyed like a song.)

Raha bla men bhi main mubtalae afat-i-rashk
Blai jan hai ada teri ik jahan ke liye

(The fact that your blandishments are a source of distress to the whole world has kept me a prisoner of jealousy. How I wish your coquetry was meant only for me!)

Kion jal gaya na taab-i-rukh-i-yar dekh kar
Jalta hun apni taaqat-i-deedar dekh kar

(Why didn't I burn with the radiance of the beloved's face? Now I am burning with anger over my strong eyesight which has withstood her glare.)

Uljhte ho tum agar dekhte ho aeena
Jo tum se shahr men hon ekdo to kionkar ho.

(You get irritated with your reflexion in the mirror. What would happen if there were one or two more like you in the town?)

The beloved becomes jealous even of her own reflexion when she looks into the mirror. What would be the condition of her mind if there were a few more beautiful women like her in the town? She would surely go mad with jealousy.

Kionkar us but se rakhun jan aziz
Kya nahin hai mujhe eeman aziz

(Why should I value life more than the beloved? Don't I hold dear my faith?)

To sacrifice life for the sake of the beloved is the real religion, according to the poet. Therefore, if the lover has any regard for his faith he should not hesitate to die for her.

Khat likhenge garche matlab kuchh na ho
Ham to aashiq hain tumhare nam ke

(I shall continue to write letters even if there is nothing to say because I am a lover of your name.)

Ishq ne Ghalib nikamma kar diya
Warna ham bhi aadmi the kam ke

(Love has left Ghalib unfit for anything; otherwise, he too was a useful man.)

Wo aaen ghar men hamare Khuda ki qudrat hai
Kabhi ham unko kabhi apne ghar ko dekhte hain

(How wonderful that she should have graced my house with a visit! Sometimes I look at her and sometimes at the house!)

The lover is wonderstruck that the beloved should have come to a house like his!

Ghalib had varied experiences of life. He was a genius without wordly luck. But fortunately these things did not cow him down and he did not turn sarcastic like Swift or pessimist like Keats though a feeling of despondency is easily discernible in some of his verses.

Ranj se khugar hua insan to mit jata hai ranj
Mushkalen itni parin mujh par ke aasan ho
    gaeen

(When man gets used to suffering, the suffering disappears. I faced so many troubles that it became easy for me to solve them.)

It is our experience that when we are overwhelmed by difficulties we stop worrying about them any more. This was the case with Ghalib as well. There was no end to his troubles with the result that he became insensitive to them and therein lay their solution.

Karte kis munh se ho ghurbat ki shikayat
    Ghalib
Tumko bemehri-i-yaraan-i-watan yad nahin

(How dare you complain, O Ghalib, against the strangers? Don't you remember the indifference of your own countrymen?)

Mujhko dyar-i-ghair men mara watan se door
Rakh li mere Khuda ne meri bekasi ki sharm

(Death came to me in a stranger's house far away from my country. That way God took care of my helplessness and poverty.)

Nobody wants to die in a foreign land but Ghalib thanks God for giving him such a death (he is only imagining it) because he has no shroud or a tomb and as such can avoid the uncharitable remarks of his countrymen. It is an accusation against the poor return for his labours.

Kehte hain jeete hain umeed pe log
Ham ko jeene ki bhi umeed nahin

(Men, they say, live on hope. As for me, I hope not to live.)

Munhasr marne pe ho jiski umeed
Na-umeedi uski dekha chahiye

(It is worth knowing the extent of the dismay of one whose hope rests on his death.)

Koee weerani si weerani hai
Dasht ko dekh ke ghar yad aya

(What desolation! I am reminded of home when I see the desert.)

The poet thinks that his home is the most desolate place in the world. He is reminded of its solitariness when he sees a desert.

Darya-i-ma'asi tanak aabi se hua khushk
Mera sar-i-daman bhi ahbi tar na hua tha

(The river of sins dried up for want of water while I had not dipped even the fringe of my skirt in it.)

The poet has exhausted the list of all possible sins and yet not even a fraction of his desires has been satisfied.

Ham kahan ke dana the kis hunar men yakta
 the
Besabab hua Ghalib dushman aasman apna

(I was neither learned nor a master of any art. Why then for nothing did the heaven turn against me?)

In aablon se paon ke ghabra gaya tha main
Ji khush hua hai rahko purkhar dekh kar

(My foot sores had scared me but the sight of the thorny path has put my mind at ease.)

Zindgi men to wo mehfil se utha dete the
Dekhun ab mar gaye par kaun uthata hai
 mujhe

(They used to turn me out of the assembly when I was alive. Now that I am about to die let me see who turns me out, i.e. carries my corpse to the grave.)

Aur bazar se le aae agar toot gaya
Jam-i-Jam se ye mera jam-i-safal achha hai

(My cup of mud is better than the cup of Jamshed. If it breaks I can buy a new one from the bazar.)

The allusion is to Ghalib's rich rivals who enjoyed royal patronage and therefore could afford to keep expensive articles. Another couplet on the same subject:

Tum shahr men ho to hamen kya gham jab
 uthenge
Le aaenge bazar se jakar dil-o-jaan aur

(I am not worried if you are in the town, i.e. well off. When I want a heart and life, I shall go to the market and get them.)

Ghalib's verses are full of deep philosophic truths, expressed with remarkable facility in the language of a mystic. For example:

Hai ghaib-i-ghaib jisko samajhte hain ham
 shahud
Hain khwab men hanuz jo jaage hain khwab
 men

(It is the absence of absence which we call manifestation. Those who have awakened in a dream are still dreaming.)

The eternal conflict "to be or not to be" was always there in Ghalib's mind as is evident from this verse:

Na tha kuchh to Khuda tha kuchh na hota to
 Khuda hota
Duboya mujh ko hone ne na hota main to kya
 hota

(When I was not born I was God and had I not been born I would have remained God. My being here has been the cause of my ruin. What would have happened if I were not born?)

Ghalib, while trying to convey succinctly the direct awareness of the mystic that there is no being but God and that God is all, laments that his coming into the world has been the cause of his undoing. He is inspired by an unexpressed faith in God Almighty and he alludes to Him again and again.

Milna tera agar nahin aasan to sehl hai
Dushwar to yahi hai ke dushwar bhi nahin

(Were it impossible to reach you, it would have simplified matters. But the fact is that to find you is also not very difficult.)

The poet would have been content to leave the matter alone if he were convinced that God was beyond his reach. Then there would have been no problem before him. He would as well have given up all effort. But the trouble is that it is not so difficult to find Him. Hence he cannot give up the search and must continue to suffer.

Ishrat-i-qatra hai darya men fana ho jana
Dard ka had se guzrna hai dawa ho jana

(The drop becomes happy when it merges in the Ocean. When pain passes the stage of toleration, it turns into a cure.)

Just as a drop of water loses its significance or individuality by getting lost in the ocean, so also man loses all sense of pain when he dies. In other words, death brings him cure and emancipation.

Qaid-i-hayat-o-band-i-gham asal men dono
    ek hain
Maut se pahle aadmi gham se najat paae
    kion

(Life imprisonment and the sentence of sorrow
are the same thing. Why should then man find
deliverance before death?)

Life and grief go hand in hand and therefore there is
no point in seeking deliverance from the difficulties
of living until death intervenes.

Chalta hun thori door harik tezro ke saath
Pehchanta nahin hun abhi rahbar ko main

(I join everyone whom I see walking fast and
accompany him up to some distance. So far I
have not recognised the right guide.)

A man in search of God is too willing to accompany or follow anybody in whom he sees something unusual or who can perform some miracle.
This process continues in the hope that the seeker
might one day find God but it turns out to be an
illusion and the right person who can really guide
him is seldom found.

Raat din gardish men hain saat aasman
Ho rehega kuchh na kuchh ghabraen kya

(The seven skies are rotating day and night.
Something is bound to happen. Why should I
then worry?)

Harchand subukdast hue butshakni men
Ham hain to abhi rah men hai sang-i-garan
    aur

(What use if I became proficient in breaking idols?
There will always be a heavy stone in my path so
long as I live.)

Life itself is a heavy weight on man and howsoever
hard he may try to push it away, it will always be
there as long as he is alive.

Once the destination is reached, Ghalib has no complaint. He says:

Safeena jabke kinare pe aalaga Ghalib
Khuda se kya sitam-o-jor-i-nakhuda kehiye

(Now that the ship has reached the shore, what
is the use of complaining against the tyranny of
the boatman?)

Although we find Ghalib has devoted much of his time
and energy to writing verses on love and wine, he is

not altogether lacking in valuable moral teachings. The
moralist in him finds expression in couplets like these:

Ibn-i-Mariam hua kare koee
Mere dukh ki dawa kare koee

(How am I concerned with the son of Mary?
There should be someone who can heal *my*
wounds.)

Rok lo gar ghalat chale koee
Baksh do gar khata kare koee

(Check a man if he goes astray; Forgive him if he
makes a mistake.)

Na suno gar bura kahe koee
Na kaho gar bura kare koee

Hear not if someone speaks ill of you; Complain
not if he acts wrongly.)

Kon hai jo nahin hai hajatmand
Kis ki hajat rawa kare koee

(Who is there who is not needy? How can anyone
help him?)

Kya kiya Khizr ne Sikander se
Ab kise rahnuma kare koee

(You know what Khizr did to Alexander. Whom
can we now trust as our guide?)

Jab tawakko hi uth gayee Ghalib
Kion kisi ka gila kare koee

(When we have lost all hope, why should we
complain against anyone?)

Baske mushkil hai har kam ka aasan hona
Aadmi ko bhi muyyasar nahin insan hona

(It is not easy for every task to be easy. Even a man
cannot easily be a man.)

In Urdu *aadmi* and *insan* both stand for man. The first
one is taken from the Persian language and the other from
the Arabic. Idiomatically, however, *insan* has come to
mean all that is good, human and manly in man. The poet
therefore means that it is not easy for a man to be manly.

Ghalib mainly prided himself on his unique and inimi-
table style. Its simplicity and grace rattled his more
affluent rivals and, as if to tease them, he said:

Yarab na wo samjhe hain na samjhenge meri
    baat
De aur dil unko jo na de mujhko zaban aur

(O God, they have neither understood me nor will
they understand. Give them another heart to follow
my poetry rather than giving me another tongue
to explain it to them.)

The allusion is to critics who dubbed Ghalib's verses
as meaningless or beyond comprehension.

Bik jate hain ham aap mata-i-sukhan ke saath
Lekin ayyar-i-taba-i-kharidar dekh kar

(I sell myself also along with my compositions but
only after scrutinizing the crafty nature of the buyer.)

Dekhna taqrir ki lazzat ke jo us ne kaha
Main ne ye jana ke goya ye bhi mere dil men
    hai

(See the charm of his talk. We feel as if what he
said was also in our heart.)

This is quite a common experience. Whenever we are
impressed by someone's speech, we feel as if he has
said just the thing that we wanted to say.

The way Ghalib recited his verses, particularly at
mushairas, had a remarkable effect on the listeners.
Hali writes: "Before the Mutiny when the mushairas
were held in the Hall of Audience at the Red Fort, I
heard him recite a ghazal in the early hours of the
morning. As he got his turn last of all, he remarked,
'Gentlemen, let me also now sing my *bhairavi*'. Then
he recited one Urdu and one Persian ghazal in such a
melancholy voice as would make it appear that he was
complaining against lack of appreciation of his verses
by the audience."

Though Ghalib wrote a large number of *qasidas* and
eulogies (mostly in Persian), the rewards he received
were too small compared to the effort involved. However, he had to resort to writing verses in praise of the
King or some other nobleman whenever he needed
money. But he scrupulously shunned satirising anybody to which many other poets resorted either out of
malice or as blackmail tactics. Ghalib did not write a
single *hijow* (derisive poem).

We do not find in Ghalib's compositions studies of
nature and natural beauty and lengthy and connected
descriptive poems like those written by Wordsworth
and Tennyson. This is because the ideals of poetry
followed in the East and the West until a few decades back were in some respects quite dissimilar.
Ghalib's lot was cast in entirely different surroundings and he did not get opportunities that were available to the Western poets. Had he been born in the
West, he would have perhaps done equally well in
writing poetry of nature. A few Urdu poets like Iqbal,
who came on the scene after Ghalib and who had the
benefit of an intimate touch with the West, wrote
some excellent pieces on the objects of nature.

Evermore poets will compose verses on evermore subjects—subjects that seemed unworthy of treatment to
the greats of the nineteenth century. But the ghazal
and the way Ghalib handled it will continue to rule
supreme in the realm of Urdu letters. A maestro of the
art in the fullest sense of the word, Ghalib lived for
literature and died serving its cause up to the very last
days of his life. Just as there has been no second Kali
Das in Sanskrit or a second Shakespeare in English
though century after century has rolled by, similarly
one cannot visualise a second Ghalib in Urdu in the
centuries to come.

Ish Kumar (essay date 1981?)

SOURCE: "The Poet of Sorrow," in *The Melody of An
Angel: Mirza Ghalib—His Mind and Art*, Publication
Bureau, Panjab University, 1981?, pp. 55-68.

[*In the following excerpt, Kumar discusses how Ghalib
expressed the grief, yearning, and regret in his own
life in his poetry and how his poetry, in turn, helped
him overcome his sorrow.*]

Great art is mostly the product of frustration. Lips begin to sing when they cannot kiss.[1] It is the sick oyster
that is said to bear the pearls. The poets "learn in
suffering what they teach in song."[2] Keats went a step
further:

"None can usurp this shade", returned the
    shade,
"But those to whom the miseries of the world,
Are miseries; and will not let them rest."[3]

Valmiki, the father of Sanskrit poetry and the author of
Ramayana, has narrated how he saw a hunter shoot a
bird while mating and the shock he received, brought
the first ever couplet out of him.[4] "Sorrow became
poetry", he says.[5]

Here is Iqbal on the same theme. *Khãn-i-jigar se
tarbiyat pãtī hai sukhanwarī* [6] (poetry is nurtured by
the bleeding of the heart). Ghalib's testimony, however, should be the most relevant at the moment:

Husn-i-farogh-i-shama' bahut dūr hai Asad,
Pahilē dil-i-gudãkhtah paidã karē koi

(The flame of poetry does not attain its full
    splendour,
Till the heart learns to bleed.)

Elsewhere, *sukhan guftan az haq jigar suftan ast* (writing poetry is in sooth piercing the heart).

Ghalib knew what sorrow was, if any body did. The death of his father and after that his guardian uncle when he was still a child, of his seven children one after another, of his dearly-loved brother, and still more dearly-loved adopted son in young age, the scourge of poverty and constant danger of debtor's jail, non-recognition of merit and vulgar vilification over literary controversies, the torture and disgrace of gambler's prison, the pain and suffering of half a dozen diseases and, above all, bitter domestic life—what could be more miserable for a sensitive mind like Ghalib's. But Ghalib did not succumb to his miseries not in his poetry at any rate. In fact, he turned his grief into poetry.

> I have drawn out the melody of my poems,
> With the help of sorrowful heart. (A)

Again:

> Do you know what is this flow of language
>   that you see?
> It is the blood of my heart that I drink and
>   bring out of my mouth. (B)

Abr-i-Goharbar is full of such verses:

> What use is poetry that is not the outcome of
>   heart-break:
> The tongue that cannot drip out blood should
>   be chopped off. (C)

> In the path which my imagination has
>   traversed,
> My sorrow has become the guide of my
>   poetry. (D)

> The sorrow that strikes my heart
> Adds to the greatness of my poetry. (E)

Stricken with grief on all side, as we have seen, Ghalib did not become either cynical or pessimistic. His poetry is not the poetry of despair and dejection, but of longing and wistfulness. Not that life ever lost its savour for him, but that it became all the more charming as his privations increased. His was a life of one prolonged and ever increasing yearning and regret and that is the central note of his poetry.

In a well-known verse, he has a tiff with God when the time of the punishment for his sins arrives and implores Him not to take stock of his sins, for that reminds him of the wistfulness for those uncommitted. *Khwāhish* (desire), *armān* (longing), *dāgh* (scar), *hasrat* (yearning) are his favourite words and his most frequent imagery is that of fire, flame, smoke—not so much the fire that warms, brightens and cheers, but that smoulders or burns, not the flame that is lit and shining, but that is extinguished and lifeless—*ātish-i-khāmosh, chirāgh-i-kushtah, soz-i-nātamām* or it is *sāz-i-besadā*

(instrument without melody), *vīrān bastī* (deserted village) and the rest; and imagery, more than anything else, shows the poet.

> I am the scar of the unfulfilled desires of a
>   burning heart,
> Like the candle which is prematurely
>   extinguished. (F)

> Thousands of strangled urges lurk in my
>   silence:
> I am the extinguished lamp of the grave of the
>   poor. (G)

That is pure Ghalib—the Ghalib of eternal aspirations and yearnings. There is no limit to his desires. He meets rebuff after rebuff, but is never crushed by it. The more he is denied, the more he desires. Along with the images of unfulfilled longings, occur also the images of buoyancy and movement, *valvalah* (enthusiasm), *shauq* (fondness), *mauj* (wave), *barq* (lightning), *bahir* (ocean), *harkat* (movement) and the rest.

> God, after bestowing both the worlds on me,
>   thought that I was content;
> On my side, I kept quiet, feeling too shy to
>   haggle. (H)

Look at a poet who is not satisfied even with a gift like that. In actual life, he had to beg and borrow for humbler gifts which were denied and he felt miserable. Rebuffed by the ugly present, he sought shelter in brooding over the memories of his comparatively happy past. That is his frequent theme. There is a whole poem on it with *kahāñ* (where) as *radif.*

> Where has vanished the glow of imagination,
> That used to spark off at the thought of the
>   beloved. (I)

Another poem with *kiye hue* (since doing that) as *radif* is equally pathetic. Even in his old days, he cherished the ardours of youth, though he had lost the capacity to enjoy them. My renunciation, he says, is not out of contentment, but out of infirmity (*zu'f sē hai nai Qinā't sē hai tark-i-ārzū*). He wanted the cup of wine to lie before him, for, though his hands were too weak to pick it up, his eyes still had the power to see. Wistfulness could go no further. In a Persian verse, he says that the more desires he has, the more rebuffs he meets, like the patient of dropsy whose thirst increases, but to whom water is forbidden.

Though at times Ghalib gave vent to despair in life, in his poetry he mostly sublimated it. In fact, poetry helped him to overcome his sorrow. It always does. The great end of poesy, said Keats.

The great end
Of poesy, that it should be a friend
To soothe the cares and lift the thoughts of
    men[7]

There is no doubt that Ghalib wrote from experience, but the poetry of experience does not mean that the emotions should gush out as they come. When Wordsworth said that poetry was 'the spontaneous overflow of powerful feelings', he at once qualified his statement by saying that it takes its origin from 'emotion recollected in tranquillity'.[8]

And here is Hebert Read: Poetry is "the culture of feelings, not the cultivation of feelings".[9]

Ghalib himself says that a poet should himself undergo suffering, but he should not let others suffer. The thorns are meant for the poet, the flowers for the reader. The poet should create beauty out of sorrow itself, garden out of fire, good out of evil. That, he claims, he has been doing.

In poetry, Ghalib generally got control over his grief and took it philosophically. In a well-known verse, he says that if beauty does not requite your love, why not enjoy its coquettish gait and winsome smile and if spring has no time to stay, why not enjoy the splendour of the garden and the delight of its breeze?

A friend who sent him a message of consolation got the reply: "My dear, what are you saying? He who considers himself wiser than a money–lender is mad. Patience and resignation, surrender and submission are the philosophy of the Sufis. Who understands it more than I do that you are instructing me?"[10]

Wine helped him too. In a Persian verse, he pleads with God in his characteristic waggish way. "What could I do? You gave me sorrows and made wine their remedy."(J)

Ghalib intellectualised his emotions like the English Metaphysical poets whom he resembled in many respects. His is the poetry of controlled passion, unlike Mir's, another poet of sorrow, as another man of sorrow like Ghalib. Both of them had to undergo extreme privation and torture after a comparatively happy childhood. Mir too was brought up in great cheer and respect on account of the holiness of his father, who was revered far and wide. Like Ghalib, he lost not only his father, but also his (spiritual) "uncle", Sayyid Amanullah, while still a child. He was discarded by his elder step-brother who not only deprived him of his share of property, but also pursued him with malice wherever he went because of a love-scandal that he is supposed to have created. This shock of desertion as well as disappointment in love stuck to him all his life. Like Ghalib, again, he was always in financial difficulties for which he had to depend on the charity of whoever was in a mood to help. Added to this was his sensitive temperament which made him

ego-centric, even arrogant. Unlike Ghalib, however, he was ill-tempered, proud, morbid and melancholy.

Ghalib was equally proud, but he had one saving grace which Mir lacked—his limitless fund of humour. He could have a laugh even in the most tragic circumstances, which not only kept up the sanity of his mind, but helped him to make fun even of his miseries. Mir was moody and maudlin, which not only made him lachrymose both in life and poetry, but ultimately led him to insanity.

Mir, like Ghalib, wrote from experience and was equally touching in the tragic note. It is said that he made sorrow poetry and poetry sorrow, but he did not exhibit Ghalib's self-possession. His poetry was not 'recollected in tranquillity'. He was soaked in sorrow and almost succumbed to it. He took pleasure in luxuriating in pain. It had become so much a part of his being that he felt uncomfortable without it.

mujhē kām ronē sē aksar hai nāsih
tu kab tak mērē munh kō dhōtā rahēgā

(O mentor, weeping is my second nature
How long will you keep on washing my face.)

har gil zamīn jahan kī rōnē kī hī jagah thī
mānind i-abr har jā main zār zār rōyā.

(Every spot on earth was a place of weeping;
I wept bitterly everywhere like a cloud.)

There is no end to such verses. He shrieks without control. Ghalib, on the whole, is tranquil. He does not grow lyrical or hysterical like Mir.

When my life has passed thus,
Shall I too think that I had God. (K)

How pathetic and how quiet! What immense grief there is, but it is suggested, not expressed. He only says *thus* and sublimates it with facetious reference to God. Here is another equally pathetic verse.

If there was so much grief in my lot,
You should have given me many hearts, O
    God! (L)

All that he says is *so much* and once again he has a tiff with God who gave him only one heart to bear it. If God gave him one heart, He gave him two eyes, but even two were inadequate.

The blood in my heart is boiling: I would
    have wept bitterly
If I had many blood-shedding eyes. (M)

What excuse he makes for not weeping! Even when he is in a Mirian mood and wants to commit suicide, he stops short, for he cannot find a wall in the wilderness (of Delhi!) to knock his head against. The fact is that whereas for Ghalib sorrow was only a part of life, for Mir it was his whole life. Ghalib knew sorrow, but did not luxuriate in it.

The difference between Mir and Ghalib is the difference between Shelley and Keats. Shelley shrieks:

> O lift me from the grass:
> I die, I faint, I fail.[11]

Again:

> O lift me as a wave, a leaf, a cloud!
> I fall upon the thorns of life! I bleed![12]

Keats, in one of the saddest poems in all literature, *Ode to a Nightingale,* begins with a quietly personal note, 'My heart aches and a drowsy numbness pains my sense', but immediately becomes impersonal and begins to mourn for the sorrows of the world—

> Where youth grows pale and spectre-thin and dies,
> Where but to think is to be full of sorrow,
> And leaden-eyed despair.

Ghalib does the same. He very often universalises his grief and mourns for the ills of humanity.

> What help was Khizar to Alexander?
> Whom should one have for a guide?
> Who is there that is not needy?
> Whose need can one satisfy? (N)

There is no morbidity about Ghalib. His attitude is of a normal, healthy man and his poetry is throughout enlivened with a zest for life and love. He believes in making the best even of his sorrow:

> naghmahāe gham kō bhī ai dil ghanīmat
>   jāniye
>
> (O heart, consider even the songs of sorrow
>   as a blessing.)

Quite often he welcomes grief. He feels sorry when his beloved stops being cruel, finding him enjoying his pain. He feels happy for the boils under his feet when the path becomes thorny.

Begging was the greatest curse of his life. At times it unnerved him completely, but when he came to write about it, he took it as a fun.

Putting on the garb of a beggar, he said, he enjoyed the fun of generosity.

> O Asad! I did not cease having fun even in begging!
> When I became a beggar, I fell in love with my patrons. (O)

Ghalib's poetry of sorrow is neither that of the escapist nor of the fatalist. There is neither superficial optimism nor oppressive gloom about him. He was a realist to the core and came to consider sorrow an essential part of life, even synonymous with it. In a well-known verse, he said, that the bonds of life and the noose of grief were one and the same thing. How could a man gain freedom before death? In another equally well-known verse, he said still more forcefully, that there was no remedy for the grief of life except death: the candle kept on burning till the dawn. There is therefore no use trying to escape the trials.

> What use is the fruitless effort to escape from struggles?
> The freedom of movement has fastened the water in the chain of waves. (P)

This struggle, in fact is essential for development. Life, without struggle, has no meaning. Here he is one with Browning and Iqbal.

Browning is the poet of eternal aspiration rather than of achievement. Life is one prolonged, continuous effort. It is the ideal, not fulfillment, that gives zest to life.

> What I aspired to be
> And was not, comforts me.[13]

He has been called the poet of 'triumphant failure'. No amount of rebuffs could discourage him. It is not the achievement, but the aim that determines the value of life. To achieve our aim may be good; not to be able to achieve it is better. It strengthens us and makes life worthwhile. Achievement indicates that our aim was low. "Try to be Shakespeare", he says, "and leave the rest to fate"[14], and so on endlessly. It is not what life gives you, but what it makes of you, that really matters and failure makes a better man of you than success. Success, by putting an end to struggle, puts an end to the zest for life itself.

Iqbal's message is the same.

> Do not measure it with the yard-stick of today and tomorrow,
> Life is eternal, ever running, ever young.[15]

Ask Farhad, he continues, and he will tell you that life is the hard stone and the adze and the stream of milk. Elsewhere he refers the reader to Khizar, of the sacred feet, who thought that life consisted in unsuccessful effort. The cup of life gets strong by constant rotation. The complicated path is more pleasant than the goal. The goal implies death. Constant action and struggle is the central theme of Iqbal's philosophy, as it is Browning's and Ghalib's.

Listen to Ghalib again. His greatest poetry of sorrow and failure, as of every other topic, is in Persian. There he says that rebuffs are essential for spiritual development and give a peep into reality. They separate the chaff from the grain and are the test of a man's worth. They sharpen the intellect. *sakhti-i-dahr shavad tegh marā sang fasān.* (The hardships of the world act like a whet-stone for my sword.)

Ghalib's courage is boundless. In this race of life he compares himself to the sun that moves on eternally. He is tired and his feet have been rubbed off up to the knees, but he is still running on. Sorrow is like a flame which, though it burns, also brightens. It is like the tying of the fractured foot that hurts as well as heals. It makes the path smooth and acts like a load on the horse which keeps it from going astray. Ghalib feels grateful to God not so much for the blessings as for the afflictions.

> It pleases my heart to see that the inundation
>   of grief.
> In my eyes and heart is from you (O God).
>   (Q)

Once when, in dejection, he asked Gabriel why he was condemned to eternal torture, he got the reply that he was a nightingale who had been imprisoned for music and not a crow or an eagle that should be let loose.

That buoys him up.

> zi yazdān gham āmad dil afrōz man,
>
> (God gave me sorrow to enlighten my heart.)

Such courage was characteristic of Ghalib in his letters too. This is what he wrote to a friend:

> I have learnt the art of living without livelihood, sir: You may rest assured on that account. The month of Ramzan I spent by eating fasts. For future I depend on God. If I get nothing else to eat, I can live on my grief.[16]

Again, in one of his most characteristic letters:

> Look at me. I am neither free nor bound, neither ill nor well, neither happy nor unhappy, neither alive nor dead. I go on living and talking. I eat every day and drink now and again. When death comes, I shall die. I am neither thankful nor querulous. Whatever I have said is a fact.[17]

In the same mood, he called this world child-play (*bāzīchah-i-itfāl*) where he enjoyed the fun day and night.

For Ghalib, the two severest afflictions were the sorrow of love (*gham-i-jānāñ*) and the sorrow of living (*gham-i-daurāñ*). The latter was the curse of life and he dreaded it. It forced him to supplicate and flatter, much against his innate nature. It was debasing. The sorrow of love, though he had not seen it the way Mir and Keats had, was, he knew, deeper and more intense and hence drove out the sorrow of living. The sorrow of love was welcome, as the sorrow of living was not. It appears to me sometimes that there is not a thing that can be said about sorrow but Ghalib has said it.

It may be interesting to compare Ghalib with Iqbal. I have already indicated how they think alike on the subject, but it is as poets of sorrow, not as thinkers, that I am interested in. Iqbal is not a poet of sorrow, as such, though he has written a great deal about it. Yes, that is the difference—whereas Iqbal gives his views, his philosophy of sorrow, Ghalib gives sorrow itself. Iqbal had a comparatively care-free life and passed from success to success. He never went through the furnace like Ghalib, and his great poetry lies elsewhere. His mother's death did touch him sorely and his poem in her memory (*vāldah marhāmah kī yād men*) can fitly rank with the greatest elegies of the world. But, on the whole, he had neither Ghalib's depth nor his vibration in his poetry of grief. He could write about the philosophy of grief: *Falsàfah-i-gham* (the Philosophy of Sorrow) is, in fact, one of his greatest poems, but it is about what sorrow does, not what sorrow is.

Talking of Wordsworth, Matthew Arnold said: "Nature not only gave the matter for his poem, but wrote his poem for him".[18] With even greater justification, it can be said that whereas sorrow gave the matter for Iqbal's poetry, it wrote his poem for Ghalib. Iqbal wrote poetry like a philosopher: Ghalib was a poet first and last, like Keats and Shakespeare. Here is what Iqbal says:

> Sorrow awakens youth from the luxury of
>   dream,
> Like the plucker that brings melody out of
>   the instrument.
> It provides wings for the heart to fly:
> Human heart is a mystery: sorrow unfolds it.
> Sorrow is not sorrow: it is the silent melody
>   of the spirit
> Which is in tune with the music of the
>   universe.[19]

Brilliant indeed both in content and imagery, but does it touch the heart? It is all thought translated into poetry. It is the philosophy of sorrow as the title of the poem indicates. As against this, here is Ghalib presenting to you the shattered pieces of his lascerated heart.

> I am not afraid that I shall be consigned to
> hell,
> But woe be it if my tomorrow is like today.
>   (R)

Iqbal was an optimist like Browning and hated the cultivated gloom of the oriental poets in general.

> There are childish tears in their cups,
> Sighs and sorrows are their possessions.
> They are miserable, unhappy and tortured
> And dead with the kicks of the rulers.[20]

Iqbal hated to luxuriate in pessimism, though he, like Ghalib, regarded sorrow as the gift of God meant for His favourites.

> We can buy the comforts of Parvez in the
> world,
> But the treasure of Farhad's sorrow is the gift
> of God.[21]

Iqbal talks about sorrow from a distance, from the pulpit, so to say.

> Do not settle down on the shore,
> Because the tempo of life there is soft.
> Jump into the river and struggle with the
> waves,
> For life eternal consists in strife.[22]

Yes, you do it, says Iqbal. I do it, says Ghalib.

> I have been fighting with my luck for a long
> time:
> I throw myself on the naked sword,
> I play with daggers,
> And kiss the saber and the rapier blade. (S)

To Iqbal, the optimist, even death is merely the regeneration of life.

> Death is the renewal of the taste of life:
> It is the message of waking under the garb
> of sleep.[23]

That is Iqbal's frequent theme. "If the law of life is that every evening should have a morning, he says, why should not the evening of a man's death end in the morning of his life", and so on. Splendid indeed again! But does it look like a felt and realised experience? Does one face death like that? It is, of course, splendid philosophy about sorrow.

Ghalib, who had seen the death of seven children, one after the other, and of a very dear brother and a still

dearer ward, knew better. How quietly deep and deeply pathetic his elegy on Arif is:

> While leaving you say that we shall meet on
> doomsday,
> As if doom were some day other than this,
> You are silly if you ask me why I am
> surviving,
> I am destined to long for death for some time
> more. (T)

Not that Ghalib is afraid of death: he prefers it to the life of misery that he is leading. He prefers it, not because, like Iqbal, he thinks that it will give him a fresh lease, but because it will release him from his sorrows. It is not the renewal, but the remedy for the ills, of life.

For once, Iqbal too becomes pathetic in the elegy on his mother's death.

> Alas! who will wait for me now in my native
> land?
> Who will feel restless for delay in my letter?
>
> Your love was at my service throughout my
> life,
> When I became fit to serve you, you
> departed.[24]

There is no match for Ghalib as a poet of sorrow in Urdu. For that, as mentioned above, one has to go to Keats, another man who passed through equally severe agonies and probed their depth as tenderly. Shelley wrote about him:

> The sweetest lyricist of her saddest wrong,
> And Love taught Grief to fall like music from
> his tongue.[25]

Having lost his father when he was only nine and his mother (who remarried with indecent haste, much to his shock) half a dozen years later, he was left to the mercy of an unsympathetic uncle who made no effort at all to understand him and, much against his taste and desire, put him as an apprentice to a surgeon. Nothing can be more sickening for a genius than an uncongenial profession. Luckily he gave it up, though thereby he lost whatever little help he could receive from his uncle. Like Ghalib, he was then left to the charity of whoever would help.

Ghalib had at least his mother to look after his education and a loving uncle who left him a subsidy for life. For Keats there was no subsidy, no king or Nawab to look to for pension, nor had he the taste or temperament to write *qasidahs* if his society would tolerate them. But, like Ghalib, he was lucky in friends who came to his rescue whenever he was in need. Like

Ghalib, again, he had to face unsympathetic critics. He was subjected to the most savage attacks, mixed with the most virulent and vindictive abuse. "It is a better and a wiser thing", wrote *The Blackwood's Magazine,* "to be a starved apothecary than a starved poet; so back to the shop, Mr. Keats, back to plasters, pills, and ointment boxes". This, I know, is nothing when compared to being called dog and donkey like Ghalib, but Keats had done nothing to deserve it except publishing his poems. His sister, Fanny, was a virtual prisoner with her guardian and was not even allowed to meet him, not to talk of extending any sympathy. Of his brothers of whom, like Ghalib, he was very fond, one left for America and the other died of consumption, in spite of his most assiduous nursing. Thus deprived of all love in life, as if to fill the void, he soon got into the grip of a hopeless and consuming passion for a girl who was incapable of deep emotion. Then followed a period of feverish unrest, of alternating moods of wild craving and torturing jealousy which left him utterly broken. As if this consuming passion were not enough, he was soon caught up with a still more consuming disease and a constantly haunting fear of death. Born a couple of years earlier than Ghalib, Keats composed some of the world's greatest poems and died at an age when Ghalib was still groping his way through the mazes of Bedil.

I have gone into a little detail, because there is so much affinity between the two, so far as their life or their poetry of sorrow is concerned. Keat's poems like Ghalib's are throughout permeated with melancholy. His Odes are his maturest work and the predominant note of almost all of them is melancholy and wistfulness.

Full of the love of life and its beauty, like Ghalib, Keats mourned its transience in a world,

Where Beauty cannot keep its lustrous eyes,
Or new Love pine at them beyond tomorrow.[26]

Like Ghalib, he was athrill with human as well as scenic beauty which he could not clutch. There is the nightingale before him, singing with 'full-throated ease', whereas he himself is subject to 'the weariness, the fever, and the fret' of this world. There is the scene of 'happy, happy love', depicted eternally on the Grecian Urn, whereas human passion, as he knows from experience,

Leaves a heart high-sorrowful and cloy'd,
A burning forehead, and a parching
  tongue.[27]

His saddest poems are *Ode to Melancholy* and the dirge of the Indian Maid in *Endymion.* For Ghalib, love is an immedicable torture (*dard la dawā*), for

Keats every glorious thing that makes life worth living—love, beauty, joy—is tinged with melancholy.

In her dirge of sorrow, the Indian Maid narrates how she tried to drown her grief in wine and music and followed Bacchus, but in vain. Ghalib did the same but was also disappointed. It added to his grief, instead of assuaging it, by adding to his debt.

People who regard wine and music as the
  antidote to grief
Are old fashioned: let them alone. (U)

Ghalib ultimately came to realise that sorrow itself was the remedy of sorrow. It healed, though it hurt, like the tying of a fractured foot. It brightened, though it burnt, like the flame. The Indian Maid, too, ultimately returned to the shelter of sorrow. 'Sweetest sorrow', she said:

now of all the world I love thee best.[28]

Notes

[1] Singing is sweet, but be sure of this,
Lips only sing when they cannot kiss. (James Thomson, *Sunday Up the River.*)

[2] *Shelley: Julian and Madello.* l. 545 He also says, "Our sweeter songs are those that tell of saddest thoughts" (*To a Skylark,* l. 90).

[3] *The Fall of Hyperian,* ll. 148-149.

In his famous Chambers letter, he wrote that it was essential for a poet to pass through the chamber of maiden thought, when the world was full of 'Misery and Heart break, Pain, Sickness and Oppression'. (*The Letters of John Keats. op. cit.,* p. 143.) "Thwarted passions", said Robert Grave, "stimulates poetic thought". (*Oxford Addresses on Poetry,* London, 1961-Foreword.) "If Plutarch's passion had been gratified", wrote Schopenhauer, "his song would have been silenced." (*The Story of Philosophy, op. cit.,* p. 241.)

[4] *Ramayana,* I, ii, 15.

[5] *Ibid.,* p. 41.

[6] *Bang-i-Dara, op. cit.,* p. 236.

[7] *Sleep and Poetry,* ll. 245-47.

[8] *English Critical Essays, op. cit.,* p. 22.

[9] *Wordsworth* (London, 1950), p. 31.

[10] *Urdu Mu'alla, op. cit.,* p. 168.

[11] *The Indian Serenade,* ll. 17-18.

[12] *Ode To The West Wind, ll.* 53-54.

[13] *Rabbi Ben Ezra,* ll. 30-31.

[14] *Bishop Blougram's Apology,* l. 493.

[15] *Bang-i-Dara, op. cit.,* p. 293.

[16] *Urdu Mu'alla, op. cit.,* p. 191.

[17] *Ibid.,* p. 60.

[18] *Essays in Criticism,* II Series, *op. cit.,* p. 92.

[19] *Bang-i-Dara, op. cit.,* pp., 168-169.

[20] *Asrar-o-Ramuz* (Delhi, 1971), p. 41.

[21] *Bal-i-Jibrail* (Lahore, 1954), p. 102.

[22] *Payam-i-Mashriq, op. cit.,* p. 41.

[23] *Bang-i-Dara, op. cit.,* p. 262.

[24] *Ibid.,* p. 256.

[25] *Adonais,* ll. 269-70.

[26] *Ode to a Nightingale,* ll. 29-30.

[27] *Ode on a Grecian Urn,* ll. 29-30.

[28] *Endymion,* IV, 1, 284.

Muhammed Sadiq (essay date 1984)

SOURCE: "The Age of Ghalib," in *A History of Urdu Literature,* Oxford University Press, 1984, pp. 228-88.

[*In the following excerpt, Sadiq stresses the less attractive side of Ghalib's character to bring to light those subconscious traits that largely determined his inner life and therefore his poetry.*]

5

Mirza Asadullah Khan, surnamed Ghalib, was born on 27 December 1797, in Āgra. His father, Mirza 'Abdullah, an officer in the Alvar army, dying during a punitive expedition, Ghalib, who was then hardly five, became the ward, first, of his uncle Nasrullah Khan, a cavalry officer in the British army, and on his death, four years later, that of his brother-in-law, Nawab Āhmad Bakhsh, recognized by the British government as the guardian of the former's family. Though nominally a ward of the Nawab, Ghalib passed his childhood and youth under the roof of his maternal grand-uncle in Āgra, in a state of sumptuous ease. As a result of this early freedom, he plunged into youthful excesses and low company, and had, by his own account, his fill of the fashionable vices of the day. These costly and extravagant habits weighed heavily on him in later life, when, in reduced circumstances, he had to fend for himself as best he could.

Ghalib's early escapades have lent colour to the view that his education must have been neglected. But this opinion does not seem to be correct. Poetry was then considered one of the necessary accomplishments of the gentry, and Ghalib, who is said to have begun writing in the difficult style of Bedil at twelve or so, must have gone through a course of regular training early in life. By his own account, the chief formative influence in his life, so far as education was concerned, was that of Hurmuz ('Abdus-Samad), a Zoroastrian convert, who stayed with him as his guest for some two years and introduced him to Persian literature, mythology and history. Later, Ghalib was wont to treat this teacher of his as an imaginary figure, invented to silence the critics who ascribed his literary oddities to the absence of a regular literary training.[7] This mild expression of vanity has been made into a serious ground for his moral arraignment by Dr 'Abdul Latīf.[8] Without going into the ethical implications of the case, it is enough to point out that Ghalib, as his correspondence shows, continued to revere the memory of his teacher; nor was he far wrong in appropriating some praise for his self-education. It is hard to believe that such competent scholarship as Ghalib's could have been acquired in a year or two of casual study at a time when, as we learn from his correspondence, he was more interested in chess, kite-flying, and other boyish sports than in books. Ghalib was essentially a self-taught man, and there is no escaping the idea that, at some stage in his youth, he must have employed himself diligently to the improvement of his mind.

The year 1826 came as a turning-point in his life. He had been for some time in straitened circumstances, and came to believe that the Nawab had all along withheld a part of the pension to which he was entitled as a member of his uncle's family. This led to a prolonged lawsuit, which being decided against him in 1831, left him almost a ruined man. He had acquired expensive habits which his meagre pension of Rs sixty-two or so per mensem did not enable him to support, and he was involved in serious financial difficulties. The shadow of the debtor's prison hung over him, and his peace of mind was gone for ever. Henceforth, we find him making desperate efforts to add to his emoluments by seeking preferment at court; but the Emperor who had taken a dislike to him for some political reasons (which we need not go into in this brief sketch), continued to look askance at him; and it was only in 1850, when he was already an old man, that he relented so far as to honour him with a title and appoint him as Royal Historiographer at Rs fifty per mensem. A few years before, in 1847, he had been made to taste the bitterness of life to the dregs on being imprisoned for gambling at the report of a police inspector.[9] He was released before he had served his term, at the intercession of some influential friends, but his heart was broken by the humiliation. In 1854, on Zauq's death, he was appointed poetic preceptor to the Emperor, but these small mercies disappeared with the Mutiny. His troubles now reached their climax. His pension was withdrawn and for some time he lived precariously by selling his household effects. Two years after the Mutiny, the Nawab of Rāmpur bestowed upon him a stipend of Rs 100 per mensem for life. A year after, his pension was restored, probably at the intercession of Sayyid Ahmad Khān, and he was able to pass his last days in comparative ease, dying on 15 February 1869.

6

I have reserved for separate discussion an event in Ghālib's life, namely, his visit to Calcutta in connection with the pension he used to get in return for the fief of his uncle. He stayed in that semi-Westernized city for about two years and was much impressed by the technological advance made by the British. Consequently, when Sayyid Ahmad Khān requested him to write a favourable review of his edition of Ā 'īn-e-Akbarī, he sent him a qita to the effect that the British had so much outstripped the Mughals in the art of civilization that it was a sheer waste of time to resurrect works which had had their day.

Influenced by this encomium on the British, Professor Ihtishām Husain had drawn the conclusion that Ghālib's visit to Calcutta was a turning-point in his life and gave him a new outlook on life. Discussing the impact this visit had on him, he writes:

> No conclusive evidence can be drawn, but noting the striking similarity that exists between the prose of Ghālib's Urdu letters and the style that was being consciously cultivated in the prose at Fort William College, it does appear conceivable that during his two years in Calcutta, Ghālib studied the new prose and benefited from the beauty and effect with which other Urdu writers were as yet unacquainted.[10]

This view is flatly contradicted by Ghālib's own account of why he discarded the old florid style in favour of the simple one he used in a part of his correspondence. He himself assigns two reasons for it: (1) he found the difficult style too exacting in old age and decided to give it up, and (2) his duties as Royal Historiographer left him little time for it. With Ghālib this change to the simple style was merely a matter of convenience, and he set no store by it. It was only on being complimented by his friends for it that he realized how unwittingly he had given a new direction to prose.

Professor Ihtishām Husain's viewpoint is untenable from the purely historical angle as well. According to him Ghālib studied the new prose during his stay in Calcutta in 1828 and was impressed by it, yet it was somewhere in 1845 that he began to use it in his correspondence. Surely this presupposes an inordinately long incubation period.

It is also noteworthy that Ghālib in his writings nowhere speaks of the Fort William College literature; he does not include it in his encomiums on the British. He writes of charming ladies and fine buildings and lawns and costly wines. But there is not the slightest reference to the College and the new prose. And if he broke away from the old prose style under the impact of the Fort William College literature, it is most surprising that he should have made no mention of it.

In fact, Ghālib attached no importance to the new style; he used it for correspondence with his friends and equals, but in his letters to the nobility he scrupulously stuck to the old florid style.

One might as well ask: was the Fort William College literature strictly confined to the bounds of Calcutta and not known outside that city? We have clear evidence that it was known in northern India, as is provided by Rajab 'Alī Surār's attack in Fasānā-e-'Ajāib on Mīr Amman's Bagh-o-Bahār which he ridicules as bald and savourless in style. Like so many others, Ghālib, in all probability, had heard of it but there is nothing to prove that he was even remotely interested in it.

7

The idealistic view of Ghālib the man, curiously enough, thought by some to be the necessary adjunct to his poetic achievement, and based on nothing better than an anecdote or two and a few of his verses, is not supported by facts. His letters to the Nawab of Rāmpur, published in 1937, are typically oriental and courtier-like in their fulsome adulation and are a bitter pill to swallow for his admirers. Reviewing the book, Dr 'Abdul Haq wrote:

> In some of these letters he has implored monetary help to meet his liabilities in such words as are incompatible with the dignity of a great poet, and it is possible that some readers should resent their publication and consider them to be a slur on their beloved poet. But intelligent admiration demands that we should study both sides of his character, good and bad, as truthfully and honestly as possible.[11]

Even a casual study of these letters would convince any disinterested person that the man who wrote: . . .

Even in adoration I am so intent on my
    self-respect
That I would retrace my footsteps if I did
    not find the door of the Ka'ba open,

seldom tried to follow this counsel of perfection in the
practical affairs of life.

The more carefully Ghālib's correspondence is studied, the more evident it becomes that he was essentially a man of the world. There was very little of the
hero or the hero-worshipper in him. An egoist by temperament, like most poets and artists, he was very little
endowed either with enthusiasm or loyalty. Of him it
may be said that he knew only one hero—Ghālib—and
he worshipped him with unremitting assiduity. That he
developed a sensitivity to the wrongs and sufferings of
his community after the Mutiny, his letters fully establish. But a few years before the Mutiny he had felt no
qualms in transferring his allegiance to the British on
learning that the East India Company had decided to
terminate the Mughal dynasty on Bahadur Shah's demise. He had no sooner come to know of this than he
decided to cement friendly relations with the British,
and composing a *qasīda* in praise of Queen Victoria,
forwarded it to Lord Canning with the request that, as
a leading poet, he might be honoured with 'title, robe
of honour, and pension'.[12] After the Mutiny, when he
was a political suspect and his pension had been withdrawn, he plied Lord Canning with a large number of
qasīdas, and did not desist until he was told in unequivocal terms 'not to send such things to him in future'.[13]

From the above it is possible to draw one inference
only—that Ghālib was an opportunist and was not
troubled with feelings and sentiments. He held that
ideals were for men and not men for ideals, and were
on the whole a pretty disagreeable thing if your object
was to get on in life. The desperate efforts he made
for the restoration of his pension, the pertinacity with
which he courted the officials, the rebuffs he encountered in his attempts to contact them—all show that
he was a practical man with an eye to his own interests. Ghālib had a genius for perseverance. He had set
his heart on being admitted to the Imperial court, and
undeterred by Bahādur Shāh's coldness, he plied him
with *qasīda* after *qasīda,* until he had gained his object. And the motive was self-love. It was not enough
for him to know that his genius as a poet had been
recognized by the leading men of the day. It must be
ratified by the Emperor; he must have his place by the
side of his hated rival Zauq, who, he believed, had
come between him and preferment at court. Ghālib's
self-esteem sometimes bordered on the comic. I wonder if there is any other poet of equal fame or merit
who strove so much to be in the limelight, or took
such a childish delight in titles, distinctions, robes of
honour, invitations to durbars, or plumed himself so
much on his contacts with the official world. He

smacks his lips over them in his correspondence and
recounts them to his friends with elaborate unction.
When he was bespattered with mud by a critic for his
attack on the author of *Burhān-e-Qāti',* what pained
him most was that he (the critic) had been wanting in
respect to a titled person who stood well with the
Government.

> All the abusive epithets that exist in the language
> have been showered by him on me. He should
> have realized that even if I am not a poet and scholar,
> I hold, at least, a distinguished position among the
> gentry and aristocracy. I am an honourable man,
> nobly descended, and on friendly terms with the
> Indian gentry, chiefs, and mahārājas. I have been
> recognized as *Raīs-Zāda* by the Government, awarded
> the title of *Najm-ud-Daula* by the Emperor, and
> addressed as *Khān Sāhib* and *Very Dear Friend*
> by the Government. Did he ever think: Why should
> I call him *insane, dog, ass,* when he is addressed
> as *Khān Sāhib* by the Government? In reality this
> is putting a slight on the Government, nobility,
> and gentry of India.[14]

We would be tempted to treat Ghālib as the injured
party in this controversy, if we did not know that he
himself was by no means a model of forbearance as
a controversialist.[15] As regards the merits of the controversy, Ghālib's position was untenable. His contention was that no one could say the last word on Persian lexicography except Persian scholars. So far he
was not far wrong. But being himself a Mughal and,
therefore, as much an outsider as any Indian scholar,
what grounds had he, one wonders, for posing as an
authority on the Persian language?

Interesting light is thrown on this aspect of his mind
by his attitude towards the masses. He disliked the
popular taste in poetry both as a scholar and an aristocrat. Yet what really gave point to his contempt for
the masses was that they had failed to recognize his
genius. His position was illogical. He deliberately cultivated a difficult style to rise above the rank and file
of poets; and when people failed or refused to respond
to his style, he was angry with them for not doing him
justice. No reprieve was to be given to them because
they had injured his ego.

His twin weakness was envy, which often degenerated
into a scathing contempt for his successful rival Zauq,
whose plebeian taste often provoked him into saying
very ungenerous things about him.[16] Ghālib was what
we would call a highbrow today, but I cannot withstand the
conclusion that his vehement dislike of the popular element in poetry was enormously strengthened by his dislike of Zauq—the most popular poet of the age.

In stressing the less attractive side of Ghālib's character my sole desire is to bring to light those subconscious traits which, as we shall see, largely determined

his inner life and therefore his poetry. He had his good points no less; he had all the virtues of the aristocracy. His treatment of the poor was full of aristocratic condescension. Generous to a fault, he continued to support his servants and dependents even in his darkest days, with his usual cheerfulness and liberality. His eminence as a poet made him friends, and his wit, generosity, and courtly manners enabled him to retain them. *Noblesse oblige* was not a cultivated attitude with him, it was an instinct. Such was the amiable side of his character; but the other, the less amiable side, too, was no less pronounced. Ghālib could forgive a thousand things, but if you hurt his self-esteem, he pursued you with ineradicable malignity. His range of vituperation was wide; the old sores continued to fester and were beyond time's healing touch. In his old age he came to contemplate life with some philosophic detachment; but he never forgave Zauq. As regards Qatīl,[17] he completely forgot himself at the barest mention of his name, and then nothing was too strong or too coarse for him. And why? Because he had been cited as an authority against him in a *mushā'ara* in Calcutta.

To conclude: Ghālib was a man of the world, endowed with a genius for poetry. Beyond this, neither in his virtues nor in his vices is there anything heroic. The only remarkable thing about him is his poetry. He was an accomplished courtier and had the virtues and defects peculiar to that class. As an astute man of the world he believed that he must get on in life and to this end he must stand well with those who could dispense patronage. He was always eager to make new contacts because they were useful.

8

Perhaps it will enable the reader to have a more indulgent view of Ghālib's idiosyncrasies in which his egoism involved him if we tried to explain their genesis by reference to his life and state of mind. We have already seen how life smiled on him in his childhood and youth. Brought up in the lap of luxury he had a grand and worshipful image of himself. With the sudden decline in his fortune, he should have faced reality, adjusted himself to altered circumstances, and given up his aristocratic pretensions. But he was not so made. He clung tenaciously to the old image, and the greater his financial difficulties the more assiduously he worshipped that image. And as that image grew fainter and fainter, he refurbished it with an arabasque of fantastic embroideries. Of these the first was the glorification of his ancestry; and the reader has only to go through his correspondence to know with relish he dwells on the greatness of his forbears and revels in the memories of his earlier happy days. His one effort was to forget the harrowing sense of his decline. And here, besides his ancestry, his most coveted possessions were the titles with which he had

been honoured by the Emperor and the titles and other conventional epithets used by the British government in their letters to him. He let his imagination run on them, magnified their worth and importance out of all proportion, and invested them with meanings which they were not meant to have. They soothed his wounded pride, assured him that all was not lost, and he recounted them with pride and joy to his friends and admirers. The pathetic part of it is that it was all make-believe. He thought all along that he was the model of dignity and self-respect and yet, in practice, he had to stoop to abject flattery to keep body and soul together. We have referred to this already; for further confirmation of the view take this extract from his letters:

> On Lord Canning taking over office as governor, I sent him a *qasīda*. The letter of acknowledgement from his secretary, hitherto unknown to me, contains an addition to my titles. So far I have been addressed as *Khān Sāhib, Bisyār Mihrbān Dostān*. This gentleman, *endowed with true discernment* [italics mine] by way of adding to my honour, has addressed me as *Sāhib Mushfiq Bisyār Mihrbān Mukh lisān*. Now tell me why shouldn't I deem him as my patron and benefactor? Am I a *kāfir* that I should not acknowledge his favour?[18]

9

The conventional character of the greater part of Urdu poetry often makes it difficult to know for certain the strictly personal element contained in it. In this respect, Ghālib is no exception to the general rule. His themes are the usual themes of Urdu poetry; and the fact that he made a deliberate departure from the style of his predecessors and contemporaries does not change the conventional nature of his poetry. At the same time, as in other poets, his *ghazals* are interspersed with intimately personal utterances; and it is in these alone that his inner life is to be sought. The rest is a masquerade; and the reader cannot be warned too often and too seriously against taking the greater part of his verse as a genuine expression of his mind.

It is equally important to remember that judged by the volume of his Persian verse and the just pride he took in it, Ghālib would be classed as a Persian poet. Urdu poetry was merely an accident in his career and forms a very small fraction of his works, having been written (barring his early poetry which terminated in 1821) during 1821-7, and 1847-57. His ripest years (1827-47) were given mainly to Persian. The post-Mutiny period is again one of Persian. He based his hope of poetic immortality on his Persian verse, as witness the gibe at Zauq— . . .

> Study my Persian poetry so that thou mayst find numerous many-coloured
>   pictures;
> Pass over my collection of Urdu verses because it is insipid and colourless.

I am pointing this out because I fear that by confining myself to his Urdu poetry, as I should and must, I shall be seriously delimiting my range of reference. His poetry, as the expression of his personality, is an indivisible whole, and an estimate based on a small part of it may not only be incomplete but even misleading. And yet on account of the exigencies of this work I must perforce make his Urdu poetry my chief guide, supplementing it by some citations from his Persian poetry.

10

Ghālib's outlook on life was essentially and overwhelmingly pagan. Salāh-ud-Dīn Khuda Bakhsh was right in comparing him with the German poet, Heine.[19] He, too, would have said with the latter:

> The fairer and happier generations . . . that will rise up and bloom in the atmosphere of a religion of pleasure, will smile sadly when they think of their poor ancestors, whose life was passed in melancholy abstinence from the joys of this beautiful earth, and who faded away into spectres, from the mortal compression which they put upon the warm and glowing emotions of the sense.[20]

Ghālib had no conscious theory of life to offer: he was more intent on living his life than on theorizing about it; but if there is one thing more than another that his life and poetry substantiate, and to which ample testimony is borne by those who knew him personally, it is that he yearned to have more and more of life and explore its possibilities for personal enjoyment. His attitute towards the hereafter, as is well known, was sceptical; and even if, occasionally, he was led to think of the rewards promised to the righteous, a class to which he emphatically did not belong, he decided to have the cash and let the credit go.

Yet the word 'pagan' as defined by Matthew Arnold (the ideal, cheerful, sensuous life[21]) is applicable to him only in a general way. The difference between a pagan strictly so called, and a modern pagan is this: the former led a life of the senses because he lived at a physical level; because neither by training nor by experience did he know of an attitude above or beyond it. He followed the senses, but there was nothing militant or revolutionary about his sense-worship; nor did it imply a conscious selection of an ideal from a tangle of conflicting motives. But between us and the old pagan world there lies, historically, the wide gulf of religious puritanism with its inhibitions and repressions, and a new set of values, ascetic or semi-ascetic. Paganism is in our blood; it is the voice of our deepest nature, but during the last two thousand years or so the native sensuous impulse has been overlaid with successive layers of a restrictive morality. Consequently, today, paganism implies a revolt or a conscious repudiation of religious ideals. And this revolt is quite evident in Ghālib. Not only was he uncomfortable in the religious framework; he broke through it proclaiming aloud that he owed no allegiance to it. Nor was there a particle of mysticism in his temperament. It implies, among other things, a disbelief in the reality and, very often, the goodness of the world; and Ghālib knew no other reality and no other good. The world was in perfect accord with his deepest impulses. The note of revolt is struck quite stridently in these Persian verses: . . .

> I have inherited the nature of Adam and am descended from him,
> I openly declare that I indulge in sins.
>
> Do not upbraid me, because I belong to the sect
> Which considers the stain of sin to be the beautiful mole on the cheek of
>   the beloved.
>
> Take delight in revelry, riotous passions, and luxurious living;
> Why dost thou die of thirst in the mirage of religion?
>
> Youth and piety—what a disparagement of the gift of life!
> It is a calamity for the youthful to be pious.
>
> If I am inclined towards wine I should not be censured; I am not a theologian
>   but a poet;
> Why should poetry be afraid of moral defilement?
>
> I do not know the ways of religion, and I should be held excusable,
> I am Persian by nature although my religion is that of the Arabs.

Ghālib's repudiation of orthodoxy, though temperamental, was also a reasoned creed and was, in one important respect, a reaction to the narrow-mindedness and hypocrisy of the orthodox. The following verses illustrate his viewpoint: . . .

> I am aware of the promised reward for worship and piety,
> But my heart is not inclined that way.
>
> In brief, my heart, too, is inclined towards piety,
> But disgusted by the shameful behaviour of the pious I have drifted into
>   heterodox ways.

A great deal of his verse is devoted to the criticism of religious ideals, especially the incentives to morality.

Ghālib is of the opinion that virtue should be its own reward. But the calculated morality, the morality that is motivated by the desire for reward in the hereafter, is really a species of selfishness, a profitable investment or a convenient barter.

He writes: . . .

> Awhile entertaining hopes of heaven, awhile
>   afraid of hell,
> Beshrew it even if it be God's worship, it is
>   in no way different from the
>   vexatious pursuit of worldly things.

The pious who aim at winning rewards in heaven, Ghālib argues, are for ever tossing between the hope of reward and the fear of punishment. They have no peace of mind and, as such, there is no difference between them and those who have set their heart on worldly things: . . .

> So that there should be no lure of wine and
>   honey (Joys of paradise) in God's
>   worship.
> Let heaven be flung into hell.

> My heart is bored by the narrowness of
>   Ka'ba;
> O for a wanderer who should traverse with
>   me the open spaces of the idol
>   houses of China and India!

Ka'ba here symbolizes the restrictive morality which condemns the senses, and the idol-houses stand for pagan joys, the healthy enjoyment of the senses.

Note the humorous juxtaposition of the tedium of the formal aspect of religion with the poet's joy in love, song, and music in: . . .

> I find food for joy in the insipid sermon of
>   the preacher;
> For though it has no music there is at least
>   a frequent mention of harp, wine,
>   and lute in it.

> The talk took a turn from the garden of
>   paradise to the beloved's lane;
> It was like the path that swerves from the
>   desert to the tulip-field.

Here is direct criticism of the abstinence that defeats its own end: . . .

> Man's gluttony increases with abstinence.
> The Ramazān has no attraction except the
>   eager preparation for fast-breaking.

And here is scepticism: . . .

> I know what paradise really is—
> A pleasing illusion to titillate the fancy.

I am aware that some critics have tried to bring Ghālib within the fold of orthodoxy on the strength of some of his utterances, mostly in prose, and a few others in poetry as well. There is no doubt that in his capacity as a Muslim he subscribed to the dogmas of Islam, and he was perfectly sincere in doing that. But, as we have stressed repeatedly, poetry like Ghālib's, at any rate, the one on which I have based the estimate of his mind, is the voice of his inner self. It reveals him as he really was, and it is at variance with what he said or felt in his capacity as the product of the social order in which he had been brought up and to the forms, convictions, and views of which he mechanically subscribed. He had a profound admiration for Hazrat Ālī and wrote in praise of the Prophet also. But this personal loyalty or admiration is compatible with his general sceptical attitude towards religion and its utilitarian morality.

And if, occasionally, he is found jeering at life and proclaiming its vanity, it is because he feels that there was so much in life that remained beyond his reach: . . .

> The period of joy was all too brief like the
>   dance (writhing in agony) of a
>   slaughtered bird;
> It was not commensurate with the extent of
>   my desires.

Ghālib had his tribulations, his moments of gloom and despondency, but it will be obvious to anyone who reads him with an open and critical mind that he never proclaimed life to be a vanity. He nowhere says that life cannot give us anything that is worth having. He holds that life is good and believes in making the best of it. A healthy, all-round responsiveness to life—such seems to be his general attitude towards life: . . .

> O Ghālib, the beauty of the flower sharpens
>   the power of perception in the
>   beholder;
> It is meet, therefore, that the eye remain
>   open under all circumstances.

Not only this. He believes that life is worth living even at its poorest. The very act of existence, shorn of all adventitious considerations, is a great privilege. Even in the fever and fret of life, in pain and sorrow, there is an excitement that is life. The worst is death, the darkness of the grave: . . .

> O my heart! Make the best even of the
>   strains of sorrow;
> It is not long before the harp of life will be
>   silenced for ever.

The life of my house depends on some sort
of commotion;
If it is not a song of joy then let it be a
dirge of sorrow.

O Asad, we should be grateful for this
sorrow and pain, because at the end
There are neither the morning tears nor the
midnight sighs.

He knew the pain of love, its heartaches and sorrow,
but he held that . . .

The stir of life is owing to the all-consuming
passion of love,
When the lightning does not fall on the
harvest of life, the assembly is without
a candle.

And is there not behind the self-commiseration of the
following a devouring passion for life? . . .

I bear on my heart the scar of longing for life.
I am like the extinguished candle which is no
longer fit for the assembly.

I am reminded of numerous unsatisfied
yearnings in the world,
O God! Do not ask me to furnish an account
of my transgressions!

It is not possible to get over the regret at the
lost opportunities of life,
Even if we have devoted the best part of
life to the worship of God.
A thousand desires, each most ardently
pursued;
No doubt, a large number of them were
satisfied, yet I feel that they were not
enough.

O God! If there be punishment for the sins
committed by me,
There should be compensation too, for
those that I planned, but failed to
commit.

Looking at the garden, we have the urge to
pluck flowers;
O Creator of Spring! we are guilty.

Says Ghālib, God has implanted strong instincts in us to
make the most of life, yet our eagerness to satisfy our
basic instincts is treated as sin. The verse is highly ironical and means that it is just and right that we should avail
ourselves of what the world has to give us: . . .

O Asad, complaint is sheer heresy, and
solicitation ingratitude,

We are in a strange dilemma because of the
intensity of desires.

I had the affliction of a hundred thousand
desires,
O God, whose unlucky star am I?

In silence there are a thousand stifled desires,
I, tongue-tied, am like the extinguished lamp
at a stranger's grave.

I, too, gaze at the magic show of desire;
I do not really mean that the desires should be
fulfilled.

According to Ghālib, to cherish or entertain desires is a sign
of life. Take them away and there would be no zest for life.

If this view of the mind of Ghālib is accepted, and a study
of his works leaves one no alternative, it is not a little
surprising to find him dubbed a pessimist. For a pessimist
is one who believes that life is not worth living even at its
best; and Ghālib was a confirmed believer in the goodness
and beauty of life. The pessimism theory of Ghālib, so far
as his poetry is concerned, is, in my opinion, based exclusively on his self-commiseration, generally misunderstood.
Hālī, who knew him personally, denies that he was tem-
peramentally or habitually gloomy, and ascribes his moodi-
ness and self-pity to the conventional tendency of our
poets to exaggerate their woes.[22] Ghālib, like most people,
obtained relief by airing his grievances, but considering his
general responses to life as revealed in his prose and poetry,
and taking into account, further, the unequivocal views
expressed about his heartiness by some of his contemporaries, it looks like wilful misrepresentation to take the
following as his real or final verdict on life. In all these I
see self-pity and no more: . . .

Sorrow ceases to be felt when one gets
used to it;
So numerous have been my trials that I can
now meet them with equanimity.

When such is the sort of life I have been
fated to live,
How painful would it be, then, to cherish
the thought that I had a benevolent
God to look after me!

There is no cure for the sorrow of life
except death. O Asad;
The lamp must continue burning till the
arrival of the dawn.

The imprisonment that is life and the chain of
sorrows are, in reality, one and the
same thing.
How can one be free from the sorrows of
life before the arrival of death?

It may be autumn, springtide or any other
season;
I am the same in all the seasons, mourning
my captivity and the loss of wings and
feathers.

The financial worries in which Ghālib was involved on account of his prolonged lawsuit, came as a watershed or dividing line in his life; on one side, memories of joy, wine, women, music, and good-fellowship, on the other, carking cares, poverty, and thwarted passions and desires. He now lingers wistfully on the past and yearns for the golden period of his life, the paradise from which he has been driven out: . . .

How importunately we ask the sky to
restore our lost pleasures to us,
We think this lost property to be a debt
due from a highwayman (sky).

Those reduced to poverty love to linger in
imagination on the wealth they have
lost,
I am the flower vendor of the lustre of my old
scars.

The artful Fancy is given to shifting the
scenes:
I am, thus, the turner of the leaves of a
fascinating picture-book.

I, too, knew how to arrange colourful festive
assemblies,
But they have become now the decoration
of the shelf of forgetfulness.

Gone is the intoxication of last night's
carousal,
Wake up now, for the sweet sleep of the
early hours of the dawn is gone.

You have been brought low by the hand of
time, O Asadullah Khān,
Whither have gone the early longings of
your heart and the youthful ardour of
your soul?

The above are all from *ghazals* composed after 1830 and embody memories of his youth, when not only was his ardour for life at its highest, but he possessed also the wherewithal to make the best of it. In this respect, the following, composed in 1831 when he was thirty-four years old, has a special autobiographical significance: . . .

Whither are gone those days of union and
separation!
Those nights and days, those months and
years!

No leisure have I now for the affairs of the
heart,
Whither is gone that keen desire for looking
at beauty!

Not only my heart but the entire temper of my
mind is changed,
Whither is fled that rapturous joy in the
loveliness of form and figure!

It was all due to the inspiration I received
from the love of a certain lady,
Where are those rare thoughts that once
visited me!

It is not easy to shed tears of blood,
My heart has lost its strength, my spirits
their buoyancy.

Reluctantly, I have retired from the gambling
house of love,
And even if I go there, there is no cash in my
pocket.

Vexed by the worries of life I eat out my
heart in grief—
I who am least fit to bear these vexations.

My faculties have fallen into a state of
decay, O Ghālib!
And gone is the balance of the elements
that composed my nature.

For the comfortable life to which Ghālib had been accustomed and which he longed to lead, three things were essential—youthful ardour, means, and leisure, i.e., freedom from worries. With his changed circumstances the last two had disappeared. The note of depression in the poem quoted above appears to have been deepened by the emotional crisis referred to in the fourth line, but the poem offers on the whole a true picture of the general state of his mind at the time, and of his temperament in general. The worries of life left him no leisure, and he must perforce relive in memory the days that were no more. It is significant that when this youthful mood revives in the *ghazal* beginning with the line . . .

It is long since I had my love as my guest,
And lit the festive assembly with the
shining cup of wine,

it is on this absence of leisure that he dwells: . . .

My heart is once more seeking those
carefree days,
So that I should sit lost in thoughts of the
sweet countenance of my beloved.

11

Ghālib's view of life, then, is that of a pagan. It is an extreme view, like that of the puritans, and leaves out so much that makes life significant and heroic. To quote Matthew Arnold:

> [Paganism] by the very intensity and unremittingness of its appeal to the senses and the understanding, by its stimulating a single side of us too absolutely, ends by fatiguing and revolting us; ends by leaving us with a sense of tightness, of oppression,—with a desire for an utter change, for clouds, storms, effusion, and relief.[23]

Ghālib escaped this narrowness, because in him the life of the senses, vigorous and full-blooded as it was, had been reinforced and supplemented by an equally keen intellect. So important, so apparent, is this aspect of his mind that there is an almost universal tendency to regard him as a philosopher. And yet a moment's reflection will show that this view is based on a misunderstanding of the word 'philosopher'. If by a philosopher we mean, as we should, one who presents a systematic and abstract system of thought or a consistent theory of life, as did, for example, Iqbāl, then Ghālib would be found to be anything but a philosopher, the distinguishing quality of his mind being a keen intellectual awareness, a tendency to question things, and offer fresh and often profound comments on them, or rediscovering old truths anew for himself. It is this objectivity, this capacity for being influenced by things as they are, without seeing them through the distorting medium of preconceived views and theories that has led to his being called a pessimist, optimist, believer, agnostic, mystic, sceptic, etc. In an open mind there is scope for all these moods or attitudes; but it is uncritical to regard these momentary reactions, even if they repeat themselves occasionally, as settled convictions.

The fact is that Ghālib had an open mind and did not permit any one aspect of life, however important, to blind him to its other sides. The world is too vast, too complex, too contradictory, to fit into any one scheme of things. Hence, a philosophy of life necessarily implies selection, omission, or at least, a belittlement, conscious or unconscious, or experiences not in accord with one's bias. All philosophies of life are based on experience and truth, but not on the whole truth, the totality of experience. Consequently, a predisposition towards any philosophy implies a certain amount of narrowness, if not blindness. The distinguishing trait of Ghālib's mind is a wide receptivity and not a predisposition towards any one theory of life.

Ghālib had an inquiring mind: as he lived his life, he no less thought about it. Hence, all his impressions are of the nature of a personal discovery, his vision of life as it appeared to him at a given moment. Some of these impressions tend to recur. Probably they have a greater relevance to the cast of his mind or the nature of his experience. But he does not surrender himself to them; they do not constitute his final verdict on life. Note, for example, the following: . . .

> Even in my construction there is implict an
>   element of disintegration;
> The warm blood in the veins of a farmer is
>   itself the bolt that is hurled on the
>   harvest of his life.

> How eagerly we plan ever new activities!
> Take away death and there would be left no
>   zest in life.

> The heedless person ascribes his achievements
>   to his own unaided efforts,
> As a matter of fact, there is not a blade of
>   grass but owes its gloss to the comb of the
>   morning breeze.

> The stir and bustle of life is all due to the
>   ravages of love,
> Without this lightning falling on the harvest
>   of life, the assembly remains
>   immersed in darkness.

> If your envy does not permit you to enjoy
>   life, go out of yourself and study life in
>   general,
> It is quite likely that your narrow outlook
>   may widen by a fuller knowledge of life.

> We are made restless by our eagerness to
>   satisfy our desires,
> Otherwise the absence of light is good for
>   the extinguished lamp.

> Life's leisure is no more than a single
>   glance.
> The ardour of the festive assembly is
>   momentary like the dance of a spark.

> What are idol-houses and the *Ka'ba* except
>   images of the persistence of desire,
> The unfulfilment of desire invents places of
>   refuge for itself.

Here *dair-o-haram* stands for religious systems in general. According to Ghālib, they have their origin in man's failure to obtain happiness in the world. Faced with unfulfilled desires, men seek refuge in imagination and invent a world of bliss in the form of pleasing dogmas which not only take away the sting of failure, but also promise happiness in one form or another. In a perfect world there would be no place for religion and its consolatory vision of a blissful world where all wrongs would be righted, and the believers rewarded for their faith. Note how the conquest of Nature and the evolution of a just order have weakened the hold of faith in the West: . . .

> The beauteous one has not yet done with
>   adornment,
> The looking-glass is still in front of the
>   beloved under the veil.

Here is something akin to the evolutionary conception of life presented in the imagery of the *ghazal.* The world is not a being but a becoming— . . .

> The world is full of the dust raised by the
>   madness of Majnān.
> How long can one beguile oneself with the
>   loveliness of the crest of Lailā!

Face to face with the confusion and disorder that figure so large in life, it is difficult to beguile ourselves with the belief that all is for the best in the best of possible worlds: . . .

> All the elements of creation are tending
>   towards decay.
> The sun in heaven is like a lamp set in the
>   path of a gale.

In Time eternal the sun may one day be snuffed out like a candle, says Ghālib.

These lines are not cold intellectual diagrams or platitudes; they are charged with emotion. The truths they embody may be as old as man himself; some of them actually are, but under the stress of emotions they come as revelations to us. Then we see them for the first time in a new light; and they are not a second-hand or tenth-hand reproduction of other people's experiences, but a palpitating and vital discovery as personal as Newton's or Galileo's.

It has been held by Hālī, and after him by Dr Ikrām, that Ghālib has enriched poetry with certain ideas unknown before. It is difficult to say how far this is true. But it would be generally conceded that a capacity for originating thought or discovering phases of experience unknown before, however praiseworthy, does not constitute poetic greatness. There is in the reasoning of these critics a confusion between scientific truth and poetic truth. The former lies in discovering some tendency in nature or man unknown before. But poetic truths are very old truths, and we feel them so intensely because they are so old.

It would not be out of place to point out that they have not been able to produce much evidence for this type of originality. . . .

I am not sure that it is a new idea, or being new it is true also. Besides, poetry is judged primarily by the beautiful work it makes with ideas. . . .

12

The high esteem in which Ghālib is held is mostly due to his excellence as a poet. His personality is much less attractive. One must admit, however reluctantly, that a careful study of his writings leaves one in no doubt that though there is much that is admirable in his temperament, there is also a great deal which, if not positively ugly, at least fails to inspire much love or enthusiasm.

Probably the least attractive side of his character comes out in his conception of love. 'Love in the highest type of poetry,' writes Priestly, 'is always a facing outward, and not a facing inward, a mere emotional barter; it is a life to be lived together by two in a divine companionship.'[24] For the most part, love with Ghālib is an appetite not a sentiment: it is a commodity that can be bought and sold. Ghālib, as I have pointed out in his character-sketch, was essentially possessive, egoistical, and there is no instance in his life, and there is none in his verse, to show that he ever felt love as an ideal passion calling forth self-surrender and self-sacrifice. His attitude towards it was that of a voluptuary: . . .

> He alone enjoys a good sleep, mental
>   composure and joyous nights,
> Whose arm carries over it thy dishevelled
>   locks.

With his usual frankness, he wrote to one of his friends on the death of his mistress:

> I am sixty-five now. I have tasted life for fifty years. In my early youth a perfect guide advised me thus: I do not approve of piety and righteousness, nor do I disapprove of a life of pleasure. Eat, drink, and be merry; but remember that in your pursuit of pleasure you must be a fly, not a bee. One who is himself a mortal should not deplore the death of another mortal. Why shed tears and raise a hue and cry? Be thankful for your freedom. And if you have set your heart on bondage, then one mistress is as good as another. . . . Come to your senses and give your heart to someone else.[25]

Harmless banter! says the admiring critic, thrown on the defensive by the cynicism of the confession. I shall let it go at that, for once. But what is there to say in defence of a poet who dismisses domestic life, after fifty years of companionship, with such shocking cynicism, as in the passage below:

> I pity Umrāo Singh and at the same time envy his lot. O, my God! There are some who have been freed twice from matrimonial bondage: and yet, so

far as I am concerned, it is now over fifty years since this noose of death was cast around my neck, yet neither the noose breaks nor do I die.[26]

Obviously this does not read like badinage. But Ghalib has taken the question out of the sphere of controversy by another utterance, still more outspoken, on his pet grievance.

> Married life is my death. I have never been happy in this imprisonment. There was disgrace and humiliation in going to Patiāla, but, at any rate, it would have brought me, the wealth of *singleness.* But, alas, what is the good of this *temporary singleness,* this borrowed celibacy![27]

In his straitened circumstances when his pension had been withdrawn, he did not think of his wife's privations and sufferings, but harping as usual on the strings of self, wrote:

> Had I been single, I could have lived a happy and carefree life on this small allowance. Heaven knows whether my pension will be granted or not. In my present circumstances however, the prospect of leading a comfortable life on my pension, as a *single man,* seems extremely remote.[28]

Ghalib's egoism is distressing. Nature had been bountiful to him in several ways, but she had not sown the seed of the ideal in him; and we cannot escape the conclusion that when he speaks of his unsatisfied desires and uncommitted sins, he is thinking of some unsuccessful intrigue like the one with the 'tantalizing *dūmnī*',[29] over which he used to smack his lips even in old age. I feel almost certain that it is the absence of devotion to a great ideal that explains the recurrent note of discontent and fidgetiness in his writings. His life lacked serenity. If he had been capable of true love he would have found in it a recompense for the comparative poverty and want of recognition of which he so often complained. Love, which is nature's greatest gift to man in this imperfect world, had been denied to him. What really makes life worth living is some ideal passion, a devotion to something outside us, be it the love of one's country, religion, humanity, a woman; or of nature, as with Wordsworth, who writes:

> . . . if in this time of dereliction,
> Of dereliction and dismay, I yet
> Despair not of our nature, but retain
> A more than Roman confidence, a faith
> That fails not, in all sorrow my support,
> The blessing of my life, the gift is yours
> Ye winds and sounding cataracts! 'tis yours,
> Ye mountains! thine, O Nature! Thou hast
>   fed
> My lofty speculations: and in thee,
> For this uneasy heart of ours I find

A never-failing principle of joy
And purest passion.

13

Ghalib's end was pathetic. In his youth he had defied the gods. But when the shadow of old age dimmed his intellect and weakened his body, he made a pathetic surrender to the powers he had all along challenged. His correspondence is full of quietistic utterances—now that he has lost the energy that had fed his revolt. The horrors of the Mutiny and his personal sufferings and bereavements shook his life to the foundations. He was a broken man, with little or no hold on life, and it was now, for the first time, that he came really to subscribe to the unreality of life and sought refuge in a weak and enervating mysticism. There is a similar change too in his strident faith in the goodness of life. All that he had admired, all that he had lived for, is now like dust and ashes in the mouth. The great achievements of man in poetry, philosophy, religion, what are they, he writes, but the quintessence of dust!

> You are cultivating the art of poetry and I am cultivating the art of immersion in the divine spirit. I consider the scholarship of Avicenna and the poetry of Nizāmī to be useless, unprofitable, and unreal. To live we require a little happiness: as for philosophy, kingship, poetry, magic—they are all absurd. If someone was an avatar among the Hindus, what then? If you make a name in the world, what then? or if you are unknown, what then? Some means of livelihood, a little health—these matter: all else is vain. No doubt, these also may be felt as vain, but I have not yet attained this stage. Who knows that in a little while the curtain may be rung up, and I may ignore the means of livelihood, health and comfort also. I may enter on the stage of non-existence. There is no sign of the world or both the worlds in the great silence on which I have now entered. . . . I consider all to be unreal. It is not a river but a mirage; it is not existence but an illusion. We are good poets, and may be as famous as Sa'dī and Hāfiz. What did they gain by their renown, and what shall we?[30]

And again:

> What did 'Urfi gain by the fame of his panegyrics that I should look forward to some good by the publication of my *qasīdas?* What did Sa'dī gain by his *Bostān?* Everything besides God is unreal and non-existent. There is neither poetry nor poets, nor *qasīda,* nor will. Nothing exists but God.[31]

This apathetic self-surrender and sense of futility, this disbelief in the greatness and achievement of man, in poetry, religion, and philosophy, this negation of life, of strenuousness and effort—here is the grim spectre of pessimism under whose shadow Ghalib appears to have passed his last days.

14

In one important respect the life of Ghālib was a tragedy. It was the tragedy of a highly original person, born in a conventional age, which gave him little or no scope for rising to the highest possibilities of his mind. At almost every point he was at odds with his society, and although he strove hard to find an outlet for his energies and rise above the pressure of the age, he was never completely successful. He was wont to speak of authority with a certain amount of irritability and vehemence, even braggadocio. In an age when the ancients were held in extreme veneration, he could say: 'Do not think that whatever the ancients have written is true. Were not foolish men born in those days?'[32] And criticizing a line of Hazīn, he wrote: 'Hazīn was a man. If this opening line were archangel Gabriel's I should refuse to take it as an authority and follow it.'[33]

And yet, despite this tilting at authority, Ghālib could not find his way to a constructive vision. His revolt against puritanism and conventional morality came very near bohemianism, while his passion for originality resulted in eccentricity and a feverish desire to be unlike others. The fact remains that he could not transcend his age.

The reason for this failure was that his age was too mediocre, too commonplace, and too incurious to supply the necessary stimulus for high original work. With this view not a few will disagree. In fact, those who maintain that Ghālib really fulfilled himself—and there are many—hold that he was a great poet because he was born in a creative period. On this point I have already expressed my views. I maintain that although there was a revival of peace and learning during the period—thanks to the advent of the British—and the old interests in literature and scholarship had to some extent been revived, yet of really active or living thought there was little or nothing in the age; and unless we allow our enthusiasm to blind us to facts, we shall see in the closing years of the Mughal rule in Delhi, the after-glow of a sunset rather than the promise of a sunrise. So much with regard to the revival of the old Muslim learning. As regards the religious revival of the period already hinted at, it did not even remotely touch him. His friends and contemporaries of whom we hear so much—Shāh Nasīr, Momin, Zauq, Maulvī Fazl Haq, Nawab Mustafā Khān Shefta—were intellectually commonplace, though models of good breeding and courtesy. Ghālib stood outside the ferment which gave us the Earlier Renaissance. He belonged to the past and had no affiliations with the forces, religious, educational, and scientific, which heralded the modern age.

Given a man with a passion for originality, born in a narrow and insular society, how will he react to his environment? He will affect singularity and condemn the ideal he cannot break through or demolish. Ghālib's attitude towards his contemporaries was superior and aristocratic. His vanity, which, as we have seen, was terribly hurt by the refusal of his age to take his oddities for genius, led him to decide that he would have no truck with it and eschew whatever was popular. He decided that he must be different from the masses in every way—'not only in poetry, but in his personal appearance, his dress, his food, his mode of life; nay, even in life and death'.[34] This contempt amounted to an obsession, and he studiously avoided in life and literature anything that could be traced to the vulgar herd. So far as poetry was concerned, he strove to be new in imagery, diction, thought, feeling, at all costs. Hence his conceits, his 'metaphysical' fancy, his love of the recondite, and his highly Persianized diction. All these had their root in an intense desire to be unlike others, especially the popular writers of the day, adored by the multitude. In all this, he forgot the great truth that great men are unlike others, not because they strive to be different from them but simply because they are. Again, although a great writer's genius may tower over the populace, yet the warp and woof of his art are the very thoughts and feelings he shares with them. A great writer has simply to be himself and go the way his genius leads, to rise above the rank and file. Let this become a conscious craze and he will become affected and artificial. Ghālib's failures as a poet are principally due to a passion for originality at all costs which often degenerated into a desire to be unlike other people. Priestley's analysis of Meredith's failure as a writer is so true of Ghālib that I cannot do better than quote him at some length.

> This is in part due to the fact that his pride forbade him to take any interest in the commonplaces, in what any Tom, Dick, or Harry could do fairly well. He was always too self-conscious on this score to be a really great artist, for the really great artist, forgetful of everything but the work in hand, does not wonder whether he is being original or merely commonplace and platitudinous, does not try to be different from other people, but merely does the work as well as it possibly can be done.

> A great many of his defects proceed from this self-consciousness. His later novels are almost ruined by the writer's obvious desire to avoid the commonplace. As he grew older he coddled himself and frankly abandoned himself to his pet mannerisms. His pride would not allow him to state a plain fact in a plain way. In much of his work he was compelled to appear somewhat obscure simply because he was trying to express really subtle and difficult impressions and states of mind. But by the time he came to write *One of Our Conquerors* . . . he had to give an appearance of subtlety and difficulty whether there happened to be anything subtle and difficult to express or not. His style had mastered him, and the reason why it was allowed to master him was that his genuine

artistic impulse was by this time weak, whereas his pride, his self-consciousness, his desire not merely to be 'different' but to be increasingly more 'different', to be more and more the Meredith whom the public had neglected and his friends had adored, were stronger than ever. It is generally supposed that these later novels of his are more subtle and complicated than the earlier ones, but actually they are nothing of the kind. . . . Either he was by this time the slave of his own mannerisms, or he deliberately covered up this interior simplicity with a surface complexity, determined that it should not be said that George Meredith was at last coming to terms with his hostile critics and the public.[35]

Similar as Ghalib's mind was to that of Meredith, we find at work in him a reverse process. He began where Meredith ended. His earliest poetry is hopelessly riddled with the defects associated with him. But as time passed, his good sense prevailed, though not without a sharp reminder from the public. And he is the poet that he is, because he grew less self-centred as time passed, and came to feel that originality was not the same thing as singularity.

Ghalib owed his salvation partly to his critics and friends and partly to his own common sense. He began by imitating Bedil, one of the most obscure and mannered of Persian poets. With this ideal before him, he wrote a poetry which is the most arid and impenetrable of its kind. In his old age, reviewing his youthful vagaries, he wrote: 'From the beginning my nature had been seeking rare and lofty thoughts, yet on account of my unconventionality, I mostly followed those poets who are unacquainted with the right path.'[36]

How long he would have continued to sow these literary wild oats, it is difficult to say; but it is clear that he set much store by his early poetry, and left to himself he would have stuck to it much longer than he did.

Out of these self-complacent dreams, Ghalib was rudely shaken by contemporary criticism, sharp, stinging, but just. For some time he stood his ground, replying attacks like— . . .

> If you alone understand your verses and no one else, you have not achieved
>   much;
> What is really praiseworthy is that others understand what you say.

> We have understood the poetry of Mīr and Mirza,
> But what you write can be understood by you or by God alone,

with— . . .

> I am neither hankering after praise, nor am I solicitous of reward,

> If there is no meaning in my verses, it does not matter much.

But this was no more than bravado. The laughter of his contemporaries made him think, and, when to the censure of his critics was added the persuasion of his friends, he decided to hold out no longer. He handed over his *dīvān* to his friends whose drastic excisions reduced it to nearly one-third of the original. Henceforth, as he tells us, his guides were to be 'Urfī, Nazīrī, and Tālib Āmulī—poets who without being extremists, represented the same ideal as Bedil.

From the above it would be evident that, even after this compromise, Ghalib's literary sympathies were predominantly with the Persian 'metaphysicals'. From first to last, excepting the brief interval when he wrote in the style of Mīr, Ghalib did not try to fall in line with the tradition of the Urdu *ghazal*. In his poetry one is struck more by the line of departure from this tradition than by the points of contact with it. A brief study of his diction, imagery, and obscurity will confirm this viewpoint.

15

Ghalib maintained that the language of poetry should not be the same as the spoken language of the day. Here was a radical departure from the practice of his predecessors and contemporaries. The poets before him had cultivated, especially in the *ghazal* (the reader will remember that *ghazal* means conversation with women), what has been called the neutral style; a style which differs from the best spoken language, as the language of feeling will naturally differ from the language of less exalted moods. Ghalib is in favour of a highly Persianized, learned, and elegant diction. 'Even now', writes Hālī, criticizing his excised *dīvān*, 'nearly one-third of his *dīvān* consists of verses to which the word Urdu can be applied with difficulty.'[37] Later on he adds: 'The thoughts are as strange as the language is unfamiliar. He made free use of the characteristic Persian infinitives, conjuctions, and adverbs . . . in his Urdu writings. Many of his Urdu verses could be easily converted into Persian by altering a single word.'[38]

This excessive predilection for Persianized diction may rightly be ascribed to his becoming immersed in Persian; but it is quite as much, and sometimes exclusively, due to his horror of the commonplace in expression, corresponding to his horror of the obvious in thought. This is also Hālī's view. 'He avoided the common modes of expression as far as possible and refused to negotiate the beaten path. Consequently, he preferred novelty and originality in thought and expression to simplicity.[39] This partiality for Persian, whatever its cause, is proved by the nonchalance with which he uses Persian idioms and expressions in Urdu. No doubt, in importing Persian vocabulary and idioms into Urdu he was following an old precedent; but what had been done with moderation by his predecessors was often carried to licence and abandon by him. . . .

Ghālib's obscurity is an indubitable fact, and during the past sixty years or so has provided the most extensive scope for guesswork and critical ingenuity. That he is difficult on account of fundamental brain work is one of those fictions by which the hagiologist has always tried to cover up the failures of his hero all over the world. As far as I can see, Ghālib's obscurity may be ascribed to three convergent causes: (1) his learned diction, far-fetched imagery and allusive style; (2) vagaries with regard to the use of Persian idioms and expressions; and (3) by and large, his compression, involving omission, sometimes, of vital links in the chain of thought. . . .

The avoidance of the familiar, or the instinctive desire for what is far-fetched, remote, and subtle, is abundantly proved by his imagery. Imagery in Urdu poetry is mostly simple and drawn from the world of familiar observation. Ghālib's imagery is far-fetched, ingenious, and intellectual. Even when it is familiar, he is generally arrested by its unfamiliar aspect. Except in his early poetry and a few other instances, where he may be said to be straining for effect, neither his bizarre imagery nor his learned diction can be ascribed exclusively to affectation. With him the style is the man; and the key to his grotesque imagery is provided by the fact that what is unfamiliar to the ordinary man is familiar to him. His was essentially a subtle, brooding, and introspective mind, looking at things from odd and unexpected angles, so that his imagery comes home to us with a shock of surprise, like some of his profound comments on life discussed in an earlier section. The subtlety of his imagery can be aptly illustrated by the following: . . .

> I am without the favour of a friendly breath,
> Otherwise there lies hidden in every bone of
> mine a cry of anguish, as in a reed.

> I do not know the real nature of the urge
> for quest which is ever driving us
> forward,
> Like the wave in the river I am an
> amputated tongue.

> The dissolution of the festive assembly is a
> source of pain,
> Every piece of a broken glass plate is sharp
> and painful like a lancet.

> The final outcome of love has never been
> other than disappointment,
> The two hearts bound together in love were
> like the lips compressed in sorrow
> and regret.

This is not the pictorial imagery of one who lives by preference in the objective world only; it is that of a self-communing mind at home in thought also.

When his ingenuity is carried to excess, he becomes bizarre, as in . . .

> The dead are lost in wonder at the
> thoughtlessness of the living,
> The verdure at the mouth of the grave is
> like the finger raised to the lips in a
> moment of surprise,

or strained as in the following: . . .

> Not even the smallest particle of the garden is
> without its verdure and flowers,
> The pathway is like the plug inserted into the
> wound of the poppy.

The abstract character of his imagery can be studied in these: . . .

> No one can fathom the mystery of another
> person,
> Each individual in the world is like an
> undeciphered manuscript.

> No one was adventurous enough to meet
> the challenge of love,
> The wilderness (in which lovers wander)
> was probably narrow like the eye of a
> jealous person.

> If this is the spring, it is no better than the
> henna applied to the feet of the autumn,
> All that we do in the world is a source of
> perpetual vexation.

His finest imagery has no touch of the bizarre: . . .

> Consign yourself to extinction if you are
> eager to know your true nature,
> A chip of wood leaps into a flame when it
> is cast into a furnace.

> The light of the sun imparts the lesson of
> annihilation to the dew,
> I also will endure till you bestow a
> favourable glance at me.

> Like unto the egg, this confinement in the
> cage of the body is a disgrace for
> your wings and feathers,
> Set your self free by obtaining a new life.

> Thy light is the source of all existence,
> The particle of dust shines by the light
> reflected from the sun.

16

Ghālib's theory of poetry was a part of his theory of life. With an aristocrat's sense of the futility and limitations of conventions, the goal of his endeavour was to discover new paths in poetry. So far so good. The refusal to tread the beaten path is a necessary condition for renovation and progress. Ghālib's instincts were sound; unluckily, in trying to be a reformer he was reckoning without the age he lived in; for it is not enough to be discontented with things as they are, or to refuse to follow the herd, as he did, to renovate literature. Every genius gives something positive to its age, although this positive something may in the last analysis be discovered to be no more than the contribution of the age itself. Ghālib knew his age to be a prison, but there were no cracks and fissures in its walls to enable him to have a vision of a different world. Hence, his iconoclasm, finding no constructive outlet, turned upon itself like a dammed stream. Eccentricity is originality without a conscious goal, a dynamic urge that is directionless; and since Ghālib felt thwarted, he became self-centred, eccentric, defiant, as his early poetry only too clearly shows. I believe it was the general aridity of his age which accounts for the feverishness and discontent that characterized his life. We can say of him what Matthew Arnold says of Gray: 'Born in the same year with Milton, Gray would have been another man; born in the same year with Burns, he would have been another man'.[40] All through his life he prided himself on the avoidance of plebeian contacts; but what was the net gain? Artificiality. The greater part of his poetry lacks passion; but to give it the appearance of freshness, he must bedizen it with useless scholarship and subtlety. Consequently his poetry looks most profound when it is least so. It is a hard nut to crack, but the reader gets little or no kernel for his pains.

We are now in a position to take our final stock of Ghālib's achievement as a poet. To begin with, as already explained and illustrated, he excelled in a certain capacity for thought. Here his pre-eminence is undeniable. It is no less true that being a confirmed egoist, he was deficient in feeling. He does not appear to have gone through any great emotional experience, and is wanting in pathos and feeling for others.

His poetry is said to be tough and the reason assigned is its depth. That his poetry is often tough is no doubt true; that it is due to the recondite nature of his thought, is incorrect. The best of his poetry in which he truly expresses himself, the poetry from which I have quoted, is transparent. In the poetry that strikes us as difficult and obscure he has nothing of his own to say; it is merely an exercise in ingenuity and no more. It consists of well-worn themes of the *ghazal* swathed in conceits and recondite learning and allusions. It makes an impressive show, but is found to be hollow on analysis. You laboriously remove the trappings and come upon a hyperbole or a violent distortion of some simple fact, in short a conceit.

Of late it has been fashionable to say that Ghālib stood at the parting of the ways and looked forward to the future. Having broken away from the past both in thought and style, he stands at the threshold of the modern world. It is needless to say, Ghālib is wholly a product of the past. He did break away from the traditions of poetry from Valī to Mīr, but it was only to find masters in the Persian decadents whose ingenuity, conceit-writing and obscurity he imported in Urdu.

17

Ghālib's letters which have given him a permanent place in the evolution of modern Urdu prose were begun about 1849. In writing them he was following no conscious theory of style. Indeed, so far was he from feeling sure of his ground that he felt his innovation required an explanation if not an apology. All this has been discussed in an earlier section. The view that he deliberately broke with the past showing the way to others is not supported by facts. The writers of the Aligarh school did not go to him for inspiration; they followed the Time Spirit. Ghālib's prime motive was convenience and it was quite inadvertently that he became the forerunner of modern prose.

Ghālib's letters, except those addressed to the nobility, where he crosses his t's and dots his i's with punctilious care, have all the directness, informality, and well-bred ease of polite conversation. I believe the secret of all successful letter-writing is the joy of communication or expression. One feels, as one reads these letters, that the writer has something to say, and he says it without stint or reserve. The contrast between his prose style and poetry is striking. In the latter, he is self-conscious, pithy, intellectual, and wrote in full panoply. He wrote his prose in lounge-suit and slippers. Essentially utilitarian in tone, it possesses an easy, familiar, leisurely movement, and has no intellectual interest, having been written, for the most part, at a plane of consciousness totally different from that of his poetry.

Most of these letters have little interest beyond their style. Their themes are the well-worn themes of correspondence—instructions to his pupils on versification; critical dicta; news, inquiries; information or directions about the publication of his books; relations with the British Government; the withdrawal and restoration of his pension; greetings; condolences; reminiscences; and other personal odds and ends. They reveal a temperament at once cultured, urbane, social, and egoistical, in which much that is polished and courteous alternates with savage and rasping moods. The fact is that Ghālib was self-centred, and only a true hero-worshipper would fail to note some of his limitations.

From this engrossing self-love Ghālib was, to some extent, awakened by the Indian Mutiny. Ghālib, who had brooded over his wrongs, was now suddenly made to see by that great catastrophe all the cruelty and brutality of life. Some of the letters of the period are the best of their kind. They are the works of a sensitive man who is also a humorist—the sensitive man whose heart goes out to suffering humanity, and the humorist who from the vantage ground of this new knowledge can smile at his own mishaps.

Ghālib has been acclaimed as a great humorist. His letters do not provide much evidence for this judgement. His gift of humour was at best intermittent, and is confined to half a dozen letters of the post-Mutiny period. But though the quantity is limited, the quality is high. On the other hand he is often witty; and those who praise his humour usually mistake the former for the latter.

Besides the light they throw on his life, interests, and character, these letters are valuable for their style. Strange as it may sound, the earliest of them are quite as mature as the latest. For sheer beauty of style, the best of them are only surpassed by Muhammad Husain Āzād at his very best. I mean Āzād the raconteur and not the letter-writer.

Notes

[7] See *Yādgār-e-Ghālib*, p. 13. A letter in which he speaks very highly of the training he received from Hurmuz is quoted in *Ghālib Nāma (Āsār-e-Ghālib)*, p. 18.

[8] 'Abdul Latif, *Ghālib* (Haidarābād, 1928).

[9] I have given Ghālib's own sentimental version of the mishap. According to 'Abul Kalām Azād, the events that led to his imprisonment are as follows:

Before the Indian Mutiny Ghālib's only source of income was the pension from the Government and the stipend of Rs 50/- from the Fort. At that time, the well-to-do young men of the city and some jewellers had selected gambling as a pastime and the Mirza was also fond of it. In the course of time, some of the jewellers from Chānd§ Chauk began to assemble at his house which led to regular gambling there. The usual practice with regard to gambling is that the proprietor of the gambling-house is entitled to a part of the winnings. Whoever wins gives a certain percentage of his winnings to the proprietor. With the commencement of gambling at his house, he also became a proprietor and began to earn a goodly sum without any effort on his part. . . . Gambling according to British law was a crime, but the houses of the well-to-do

were treated as an exception, and gambling was treated on the same footing as Bridge today. For a time the *kotvāl* and other officers were such persons as were on friendly terms with Ghīb. But in 1845 a new *kotvāl* was transferred to Delhi from Agra. On his arrival he began to enforce rules strictly and appointed spies. Some of the friends of the Mirza warned him and advised him to suspend the meetings. But he paid no heed to it, confident that no action could be taken against him. It so happened that on a certain day when the gambling was in full swing the *kotvāl* suddenly appeared at the scene and knocked at the door. The others made good their escape through the backdoor, but the Mirza was arrested. Some of his friends approached the Emperor on his behalf, but to no purpose. He was fined Rs 100/- and in default to undergo imprisonment for four months.

In 1847 he was again arrested for gambling. He was sentenced to six months' rigorous imprisonment in default and fined Rs 200/- which was to be converted into additional imprisonment for six months. However, if in addition to the fine he paid a sum of Rs 50/- the rigorous imprisonment was to be converted into simple imprisonment.

[10] Ihtishām Husain, *Tanqīd aur 'Amalī Tanqīd*, pp. 82-3.

[11] The *Urdu*, Jan. 1938, pp. 204-5.

[12] *Ghālib Nāma (Āsār-e-Ghālib)*, op. cit., p. 104.

[13] ibid., p. 122.

[14] ibid., pp. 145-6.

[15] Blockmann, Secretary, Asiatic Society, Calcutta, in his letter dated 18 September 1876 to Muhammad Husain Āzād wrote in a footnote about the controversy: 'I forgot to mention that I value Ghālib as a poet and as a writer, that as a *lughvī* I think very little of him. When Ahmad 'Alī brings reasons, Ghālib only abuses. But abuse is no argument.' The letter is in my possession.

[16] See *Khitāb-ba Zauq*, *Ghālib Nāma (Armughān-e-Ghālib)*, pp. 194-6.

[17] Mirza Qatīl is the poetical name of Mirza Muhammad Hasan. He was a native of Delhi and a Hindu of the tribe of Khatrī, but became a convert to Islam. He died in Lucknow in 1817. He is the author of several works which include: *Nahr-ul-Fasāhat, Chahār Sharbat,* and a *dīvān*.

[18] *Khutūt-e-Ghālib*, ed. Ghulām Rasāl Mihr, 1951, pp. 216-17.

[19] S. Khuda Bakhsh, 'Ghālib: An Appreciation', *Essays Indian and Islamik,* (London, 1912), pp. 127-39.

[20] Matthew Arnold, 'Religious Sentiments', *Essays Literary and Critical* (Everyman's Library), p. 141.

[21] ibid., p. 137.

[22] *Yādgār-e-Ghālib,* pp. 377-8.

[23] Arnold, op. cit., p. 137.

[24] J. A. Priestley, *George Meredith* (London, 1927), p. 130.

[25] Mahesh Parshād, *Khutūt-Ghālib,* 1st ed. (Allahābād, 1941), pp. 315-16.

[26] ibid., p. 60.

[27] ibid., p. 220.

[28] ibid., p. 221.

[29] ibid., p. 315.

[30] ibid., pp. 68-9.

[31] ibid., p. 78.

[32] *Yādgār-e-Ghālib,* op. cit., p. 78.

[33] ibid., p. 78.

[34] ibid., p. 105.

[35] Priestley, op. cit., pp. 169-70.

[36] *Yādgār-e-Ghālib,* op. cit., p. 182.

[37] ibid., p. 100.

[38] ibid., pp. 102-3.

[39] ibid., p. 103.

[40] Matthew Arnold, *Essays in Criticism,* II, p. 92.

C. M. Naim (essay date 1992)

SOURCE: "The Ghazal Itself: Translating Ghalib," in *The Yale Journal of Criticism,* Vol. 5, No. 3, 1992, pp. 219-32.

[In the following essay, Naim discusses five couplets belonging to a ghazal Ghalib wrote before he was nineteen, providing both the transcripted Urdu and free prose translation. The ghazal is considered a typical Ghalibean one and, in the earliest manuscript, an autograph.]

For centuries, the ghazal has been a major genre of poetry in Arabic, Persian, Turkish, and Urdu. A ghazal usually consists of five or more couplets, sharing meter and rhyme. The rhyme itself may be in two parts: the *qawāfi*[1] (sing., *qāfiya*), which are structurally similar words with rhyming final syllables, followed by the *radīf,* which form a fixed rhyme consisting of one or more words. Not every ghazal contains a *radīf,* but every ghazal must have a unifying set of *qawāfi.* The opening couplet has rhymes in both lines. Subsequent couplets rhyme only in the second line, hence the common rhyme scheme of a ghazal: *a a, b a, c a, d a, e a,* etc. The final couplet of a ghazal may contain the pen name of the poet. Fundamentally, each couplet in a ghazal is a distinct and organic unit of thought, not necessarily linked in any way to the other couplets except in meter and rhyme. In the ghazal discussed below, the *qawāfi* are *adā, hayā, hinā, kyā, wafā,* and *Xudā,* and the *radīf* is *hai.*

Mirza Asadullah Khan Ghalib was born in Agra in 1797, six years before the British took over Agra and Delhi. Son of a mercenary soldier, he was orphaned at a young age. Raised by an uncle, he received the usual instruction and care, and was married into a wealthier family in Delhi when he was thirteen (his bride was eleven). The rest of his life was spent mostly in Delhi, except for a short but significant stay in Calcutta, then the capital city. His source of income was mainly a small share in his uncle's pension from the British, supplemented by the irregular patronage that came to him from the last Mughal king of Delhi, and the Nawabs of Rampur and Oudh. He is believed to have completed a volume of Urdu ghazals by the time he was nineteen, but the collection, highly abridged by Ghalib himself, first appeared in 1841. Ghalib was also a noteworthy poet in Persian. In either language, his favorite genre was the ghazal. Contrary to the general practice in his day, Ghalib did not have a mentor (*ustād*) in the art of poetry, though he himself had a considerable number of disciples (*shāgird*).

Once Ghalib was asked if he made a list of rhymes or followed some earlier master's ghazal when he wrote his own. Ghalib replied, "You think I'm like other poets who add strings of words to rhymes? God forbid! A curse on me if ever I do that. I merely note the meter and the rhyme, then start writing whatever sort of verse I wish to write in that particular *zamīn* [meter and rhyme pattern]. . . . My friend, poetry doesn't mean chasing rhymes; poetry is the art of creating 'meanings.'"

It is also characteristic of Ghalib that when he was housebound in Delhi for fifteen months during the

Great Indian Mutiny of 1857, he arbitrarily chose to write his journal in archaic Persian, avoiding Arabic words. Then, being a true poet in the terms of his times, he published the journal himself and, together with a panegyric, sent a copy to Queen Victoria, expecting to be made her poet laureate. He received only a terse note of thanks from a secretary.

In 1969, the centenary year of Ghalib's death was observed in the United States, where the most interesting homage was a book, *Ghazals of Ghalib*. It was a collaboration between a Pakistani/Urdu poet—Aijaz Ahmad—and a number of American poets—W. S. Merwin, Adrienne Rich, William Stafford, David Ray, Thomas Fitzsimmons, Mark Strand and William Hunt. Ahmad selected thirty-seven ghazals out of the 237 in the common edition, and reduced them to five couplets each. He prepared prose translations and notes for his collaborators, and held detailed discussions with them. The American poets then produced their own poetic "versions." Not all the poets worked on all the ghazals, nor did they observe the same degree of fidelity to the originals. Ahmad chose to publish all the available versions: he aimed not to produce English translations but to bring about a creative encounter between Ghalib and contemporary American poets.

The five couplets I discuss below belong to a ghazal included in Ahmad's selection (Ghazal XXI). A typical Ghalibean ghazal, it also has an interesting history. Ghalib wrote it before he was nineteen. In the earliest manuscript, considered to be an autograph, it has seven couplets, with one more added in the margin. Much later, when Ghalib published his highly selective collection, this ghazal appeared with eleven couplets, four of which were new. Ghalib discarded one of the original couplets, kept the remaining seven with some changes, and added four new ones. That, for him, did not effect the integrity of his ghazal. Ghazal is an open-ended poem; it can be reduced or expanded by the poet at any time.

The five couplets will be presented here in a format adapted from Stanley Burnshaw's *The Poem Itself*. In each instance, first the Urdu couplet appears in a transcription. Next comes a somewhat free prose translation. To give the reader a more intimate sense of the original, the third section serially lists and translates individual words and phrases. Each line is also separately translated. The fourth section explains the more unusual conventions and points out certain rhetorical features—in other words, provides the kind of information an educated Urdu reader/listener would bring to the verse. Lastly, the transcripted Urdu verse is reprinted, with the expectation that the reader will now be in a position to get some pleasure from it directly. In two cases, a sixth section has been added to discuss Aijaz Ahmad's "versions" of those couplets.

I

The Couplet

> shabnam ba gul-e lāla na Xālī za adā hai
> dāG-e dil-e b'-dard nazargāh-e hayā hai

Prose Translation

The dew on the tulip is charming; it is also for a purpose. A cruel heart, when itself scarred, should be embarrassed to tears.

Lexicon

shabnam: dew.

ba gul-e lāla: on the tulip flower. In contemporary Urdu, *lāla* also refers to the common poppy flower. In either case, the flower is deep red, with a distinctive black center.

na Xālī za adā hai: is not devoid of *adā*.

adā: coquetry; charm; elegance; style. A word full of nuances, it implies self-awareness or design in any act.

First line: "The dewdrop on the tulip flower is not without *adā*."

dāG-e dil-e b'dard: literally, the scar on a pitiless heart.

nazargāh: lit., the place where a glance should fall. Object of perception: deserving notice and response.

hayāā: modesty; a sense of shame.

Second line: "The scar on the heart of a pitiless person must be touched by modesty and shame."

Explication

The first line makes a specific, descriptive statement; the second line interprets and universalizes.

The tulip conventionally represents both the beloved's beauty and lack of compassion or pity.

In Urdu idiom, one sign of acute shame is heavy perspiration. In English one says, "shamed to tears"; in Urdu, one "becomes water, perspires heavily." Hence the dew on the tulip expresses its shame. The charming dewdrop on the tulip is there for a reason: the flower has the color and the shape of a heart but cannot feel any emotion; hence, it is pitiless. Should it not then sometimes feel ashamed of itself?

In the second line, the focus is more on the "scar" (the dark center) than on the "heart" (the red flower). If the flower could not feel, it should have no scar. Therefore, the scar must have been forced upon it. How shameful!

The dew enhances the tulip's beauty, just as any display of modesty on the part of the beloved would only make her charms more devastating.

To summarize: the first line presents a concrete image; the second offers an explanation for something that ordinarily does not need one. The tightly constructed lines contain a number of words that form a network of associations. There are some ambiguities, also a parataxis that depends for its effect on our knowledge of the way in which classical Urdu ghazals are contextualized.

The Couplet Itself

> shabnam ba gul-e lāla na Xālī za adā hai
> dāG-e dil-e bʻ-dard nazargāh-e hayā hai

(Versions)

This couplet is included in Ahmad's selection. Here is his prose version:

> The dewdrop on the red poppy is not
> without
>   end/function/meaning:
> The spot on the heart of her who is cruel is
> a place
>   where shame has come (to
> pass).

In his explanatory notes, Ahmad adds:

> Lala: Red poppy, or tulip. The Indian poppy is smaller than the Western variety and, with the poetic license which is common in Urdu, one could imply that a dewdrop is sufficient to cover the black that lies at the heart of the flower. Matters are further complicated by the fact that, in the highly stylized language of nineteenth-century Urdu poetry, it is used as a metaphor for the heart, or for the eye. If the heart, it is a bleeding heart, like Shelley's. If the eye, always that of a woman who has been crying (eyes are therefore red). Thus, dewdrop on a red poppy could be tears in the bloodshot eyes of a woman.

Ahmad makes two mistakes. First, he transfers the contemporary meaning of a word to an earlier period, and to a poet who prided himself on his Central Asian heritage. *Lāla* in the classical tradition only means "tulip." Ahmad's second error takes him far in an interesting direction: he asserts that *lāla*

may be a metaphor for the eye—particularly that of a woman who has been crying. Nothing in the lexicons or the traditions of Urdu poetry justifies this interpretation. "Tulip-face" or "tulip-cheeks" are fairly common, but no "tulip-eyes." (For example, such a construction is not found in that fascinating book, *Mustalahāt alShuʻarā,* or *The Lexicon of Poets,* a great favorite of Ghalib's.)

But is this really a serious mistake? Where does it lead? In an additional note, Ahmad explains:

> The poppy is the heart, the function of the dew is to hide the blemish. However, dew is again a metaphor for tears. Where do these tears come from? We come to the other metaphorical meaning of the poppy: the eye. The meaning of the metaphor becomes clear. If the poppy is also the eye, and the dew is tears, then these are the tears the eyes shed in order to make up for, to wash away, to undo the blemish of cruelty. Thus the function of the dew is not only to hide the blemish, but also to make up for it: regaining, or becoming capable of, sympathies even after the denial of love.

The meaning Ahmad gives may be radical, but his method is not. He finds similarity between the eye and the poppy based on color, and though it remains unstated, on shape. The dewdrop and tears also share their physical shape and property. In other words, the logic that links the dewdrop to a tear of repentance is the same as that which links it to the perspiration of embarrassment. And so we find that the American poets' versions do not destroy the essential *strategy* of the couplet.

> Dewdrop on poppy petal
> there for a reason
>
> in that place the cruelty of her heart can be
>   concealed only by one of her own
>   tears
>
>   (W. S. Merwin)

> There's meaning in the teardrop that blurs
>   the red eye of
> the poppy:
> the heart that knows its flaw understands
>   the need for
> concealment.
>
>   (Adrienne Rich)

> Dew on a flower—tears, or something:
> hidden spots mark the heart of a cruel
>   woman.
>
>   (William Stafford)

II

The Couplet

> dil XūN-shuda-e kash-ma-kash-e hasrat-e
> dīdār
> ā'īna ba-dast-e but-e bad-mast hinā hai

Prose Translation

The heart strove to gain a vision of the beloved, but, unsuccessful, turned to blood. The beloved, mirror in hand, remained transfixed in her place, intoxicated with her own beauty.

Lexicon

dil: heart.

XūN-shuda: bloodied; become blood.

kash-ma-kash: struggle; dilemma; lit,. pull-not-pull.

hasrat: longing; unfulfilled desire.

dīdār: sight; vision; appearance.

First line: "The heart [has] become blood from the tussle caused by the longing for a sight [of the beloved]."

ā'īna: mirror.

ba-dast-e: in the hand of . . .

but: lit., idol; metaphorically, the beloved.

bad-mast: intoxicated, amorous.

but-e bad-mast: the beautiful, intoxicated beloved.

hinā: henna. Women use its paste to stain their hands and feet. Of course, one must remain immobile while the paste is drying.

hai: is.

Second line: "The mirror in the hand of the intoxicated beauty is (or acts like) henna."

Explication

I find this couplet fascinating, and difficult to analyze precisely. Its music attracts me. I also note the neat pattern in the two lines: the heart becomes blood, the mirror becomes henna. (Of course, the color similarity between blood and henna is obvious.) Finally, I recall that, for Sufis, the heart is a mirror, which must be kept unblemished so that it might reflect the Divine Beloved.

Next, I'm beguiled by the fact that the couplet contains only one verb: *hai,* "is." The first word we read is *dil,* a noun; we therefore expect the next word to be its predicative complement, but it turns into a long adjectival phrase. We then expect *ā'īna* to be the complement, but again our expectation is frustrated: what follows *ā'īna* is not a verb but another long adjectival phrase. That suggests a possible parallelism between the two lines until we come to the end and suddenly find a noun, *hinā,* followed by the verb "is," which forces us to reconsider the syntactic arrangement. First we think that "the heart is bloodied," but then it appears as if "the bloodied heart is the mirror." Proceeding further, we are surprised to discover that "mirror" itself is the subject of the verb: "the mirror is henna." And yet ambiguities remain. Consider the following two readings.

Reading A:

First line: "The heart . . . is bloodied."

Second line: "The mirror . . . is henna."

Reading B:

The two lines together: "The heart, bloodied, a mirror in the hand of the intoxicated beloved, is henna."

The rules of Urdu syntax may be unambiguous, but the language of poetry keeps creating ambiguities, and we are left with a struggle, or *kash-ma-kash,* of our own.

Ghalib's marvelous choice of a word, *kash-ma-kash,* both phonetically and graphically reflects what it connotes. Itself formed like a see-saw, it occurs in the exact center of the first line, balancing its two parts and asserting its own pivotal status. It is derived from *kashīdan,* a Persian verb with diverse meanings: to draw; attract; prolong; delineate; exhaust; carry; endure; support; experience. Its precise meaning depends on the context, in particular its grammatical object. Here, its object is *hasrat,* "longing"—the distress or struggle arising out of an unfulfilled desire. But *kash-ma-kash* is also related to almost all the key words in the couplet. *Dil,* or "heart," is, of course, where the struggle takes place. *XūN kashīdan* means "to draw blood out of something or someone." The link between *kashīdan* and *ā'īna,* "mirror," becomes obvious when we recall that mirors used to be made of metal and had to be "scrubbed" or "scraped" to remain reflecting. And let's not forget the Sufis, who burnish their heart/mirror by enduring hardships and "drawing" sighs of longing for their Beloved. Finally, *kash-ma-kash* may even be linked with "henna," for henna is made by grinding its leaves, and grinding in Urdu culture is like the word *kash-ma-kash,* back and forth.

Now consider this. The mirror is in the hand of the beloved; like henna, it keeps her transfixed, engrossed in her own beauty, away from the sight of the lover. However, the heart of the lover longs for the beloved, becomes blood, i.e., red, i.e., henna—and, idiomatically, where is the lover's heart except in the beloved's hands? In other words, the more the heart longs the more it causes the beloved to remain transfixed. Further, the beloved is very intoxicated, *bad-mast*. Intoxication implies wine, which in turn is associated (through the verb *kashīdan*, "to distill") with *kash-ma-kash*, "struggle," and (through its red color) with *Xūn*, "blood." Now heart becomes blood, becomes wine: the suffering that the lover endures becomes the source of the beloved's pleasure.

Why make the neglectful beloved also *bad-mast?* First, it helps generate the above described network of associations. (In their written forms, *ba-dast* and *bad-mast* are almost identical.) Second, it creates a stronger contrast between the two protagonists' states. And finally, its alliteration contributes to the music of the couplet: *ba-dast-e but-e bad-mast.*

The Couplet Itself

> dil XūN-shuda-e kash-ma-kash-e hasrat-e
> dīdār
> ā'īna ba-dast-e but-e bad-mast hinā hai

III

The Couplet

> qumrī kaf-e X~kistar-o bulbul qafas-e rang
> ai nāla, nishān-e jigar-e sÇXta kyā hai

Prose Translation

The turtledove is a handful of ashes, the nightingale, a cage of colors. But, o my cry, what sign is left of the heart that was consumed by fire?

Lexicon

qumrī: turtledove. According to poetic convention, it loves the cypress.

kaf: palm; handful.

Xākistar: ashes.

bulbul: nightingale. According to poetic convention, it loves the rose.

qafas: cage.

rang: color(s).

First line: "The turtledove, a handful of ashes; the nightingale, a cage of colors."

ai: O!

nāla: a cry or lament.

nishān: sign; mark; trace.

jigar: lit., liver. In medieval theory, the liver was considered the seat of the soul, whereas the heart was the seat of the life-force. But in poetry the distinction was not rigorously maintained. However, for Ghalib and for us, *jigar* stands for fortitude, courage and enthusiasm, as opposed to *dil*, which is identified with love and empathy.

sÇXta: burnt, consumed.

kyā hai: lit., what is . . . ?

Second line: "O cry, what is the sign of a consumed heart?"

Explication

The poet, the nightingale and the turtledove are all in love with someone, and their loves consume them. To the poet's mind, the nightingale and turtledove retain some visible trace, whereas he is nothing but an ephemeral cry of anguish. On the other hand, being so totally consumed, is he not superior to the nightingale and turtledove?

The words *qafas-e rang* create an alliterative effect with *kaf.* They also play upon a conventional phrase, *qafas-e 'unsurī*, "the elemental cage," that is, the human body (made of four elements—fire, water, air and dust) within which the soul is imprisoned until it is released in death. Properly, the body of the bird enamored of the colorful rose is called "a cage of colors."

Ghalib, asked to explain this couplet, replied: "read *juz* [except for] instead of *ai* [O!]; the meaning will become clear." If Ghalib had himself used *juz* instead of *ai*, the line would still be metrically sound: a good example of Ghalib's habit of eliding a few steps from a series, thereby creating suspense and surprise.

The Couplet Itself

> qumrī kaf-e Xākistar-o bulbul qafas-e rang
> ai nāla, nishān-e jigar-e sÇXta kyā hai

(Versions)

Here is Ahmad's prose version:

> The dove is merely a handful of ashes and
>   the nightingale a prison

of color;
O my cry, the scar of burnt heart is nothing
   (in comparison).

In his notes, Ahmad explains the image of *qafas-e rang* as "precisely that, a prison of color. *Not* prisoner. It is somewhat unusual to come across a line which stresses the color, rather than the sound, of the nightingale." As a general explanation, he adds, "In terms of sound, both the dove and the nightingale serve implicitly as metaphors for the poet's cry, or lament; both are singing birds. Visually, they both serve, particularly the dove, as images of the burnt heart."

"Prison of color" is indeed unusual, but Ghalib saw no need to explain the image to his perplexed friend. He felt the difficulty lay elsewhere. Ahmad is fascinated by the unusual image and makes sure that its contituents are clearly understood. Ghalib's interests go beyond it.

The first line consists only of nouns and nominal compounds: "The turtledove, a handful of ashes; the *bulbul,* a cage of colors." The words *kaf,* "handful," and *qafas,* "cage," create a balanced line: they occur as heads of nominal compounds in identical positions within the two halves of the line. They also create assonance. The two compounds' respective second elements further link them: "ashen" (*Xākistar*) is a particular "color" (*rang*).

Ghalib's primary aim was to find the *bulbul's* "measure" of color. If *qafas* seemed unusual, so much the better. But was it a radical departure? *Qafas* has a conventional association with the *bulbul:* the bird's fate is to be "encaged" by a nemesis, the *sayyād,* or "hunter." Further, a trite idiom portrays the human soul as a "bird" imprisoned in "the cage of the four elements."

The second line begins with a vocative: "O cry!" It poses a question: "What is the sign of the burnt heart?" Ahmad treats this as a rhetorical question that implies complete negation: there is no sign. Rich's and Stafford's versions concur.

> The turtle-dove is a heap of cinders, the
>   nightingale a
> vivid cage of sounds;
> O my cry, you are nothing to these.

>   (Adrienne Rich)

> The dove is a clutch of ashes, nightingale a
>   clench of
> color:
> a cry in a scarred, burnt heart, to that, is
>   nothing.

>   William Stafford)

But Merwin's version is novel in opposing the burnt-out heart and the cry. He also comes closer to Ghalib's intention by making the cry more substantial. Here is Merwin's version:

> The heart is burnt out
> but its sufferings were nothing to yours
>   oh my cry

> charred dove
> nightingale still burning

Ghalib's protocol required that the poet-lover's passion be supreme; it could in no way be inferior to any metaphor. The classical poet idolized and idealized Love, but simultaneously he idolized and idealized his own particular love. Ghalib could use unusual images but he could not breach the rules of hierarchy, or of his own sense of uniqueness.

Let's look more closely at what Ghalib has tried to do in this couplet. He mentions the two birds but totally suppresses the sound element, an essential part of the convention. Instead, Ghalib undersores their appearance. Only with regard to himself does he mention a sound, a cry. For Ghalib, colors are concrete; sounds are abstract. Given the dichotomy of spirit and body, abstract is superior to concrete. Also, in the tradition, hearing is superior to sight. With reference to the poetlover, Ghalib introduces two motifs: *nāla,* "the cry," and *jigar,* "the liver." The liver was believed to be the seat of the soul, and was associated with courage and fortitude. In other words, the motifs in the first line contrast with the motifs in the second and are implied to be inferior.

The second line is a question (rhetorical or otherwise): "O cry, what's the sign of the burnt-out heart?" In keeping with Ghalib's comment, it could easily have been a flat statement: "There is no sign . . . except for the cry." Evidently, Ghalib prefers ambiguity. On the other hand, he leaves the answer staring us in the face. The only trace of the lover's all-consumed heart is an anguished, vanishing cry, while the dove and the *bulbul,* mere metaphors, persist—tangible, colorful, inferior.

IV

The Couplet

> majbūrī-o dā'wā-e giraftārī-e ulfat
> dast-e tah-e sang-āmada paimān-e wafā hai

Prose Translation

We have no choice but to love, but we exclaim, "Love takes us prisoner." Our hand is caught under a rock, but we say, "We have made a pact of fidelity."

Lexicon

majbūrī: helplessness; the state of not having a free will; related to *jabr* (compulsion, force), which is used in opposition to *qadr* (will, authority).

-o: lit., and. Here, a device for juxtaposition.

dā'wā: claim; boast.

giraftārī: imprisonment.

ulfat: love.

First line: "Helpless—[yet we] claim to be imprisoned by love."

dast: hand.

tah-e sang: under the rock.

dast-e tah-e sang āmada: lit., a hand caught under a rock. Idiomatically, the state of having no choice and yet claiming to have one, making virtue out of a necessity.

paimān: pact.

wafā: fidelity, sincerity.

Second line: "The hand caught under a rock is [our] pact of fidelity."

Explication

In the first line, a single noun, *majbūrī,* is juxtaposed to a long noun phrase, *dā'wā-e giraftārī-e ulfat:* "We claim that love took us prisoners [otherwise we would have been free]. Nonsense! We had no choice [but to fall in love, for the beloved is overwhelmingly beautiful, and love is inherent to our nature, as the universal scheme of things exists due to Love]."

The second line contains a long noun phrase, *dast-e tah-e sang āmada,* followed by a short noun phrase, *paimān-e wafā.* This reversal of the order in the first line allows two neat patterns for interlinking the various substantives:

Substantive 1 + Substantive 2   (Order)
Substantive 1 + Substantive 2

Short Substantive + Long Substantive   (Quantity)
Long Substantive + Short Substantive

This is one of the eight couplets that Ghalib wrote before the age of nineteen, but its original version differs from what he later published. The changes are revealing. In the original second line, Ghalib had used *dāman,* "the hem or skirt of an upper garment," instead of *dast,* "hand"; and *ahrām,* "the simple robes required of Muslim pilgrims during the Hadj" instead of *paimān,* "a pact or solemn promise." The changes did not alter the basic relationship between the two lines: the first presents a state of mind, while the second offers an image and a comment. More significantly, whereas the original words, *dāman* and *ahrām,* shared only one general attribute (they were associated with clothes), the new words enmesh all of the elements in the couplet.

A formal avowal of sincerity usually required the symbolic gesture of putting one's hand in the hand of the other party. *Paimān* contains the word *pai,* "foot," and hands and feet go together in so many ways. *Paimān* also shares a quality with *dā'wā,* "a claim," in that both are verbal acts; that was not the case with *ahrām. Dast zīr-e sang āmadan,* "hand getting caught under a rock," is a well-known Persian idiom; the familiar nominal compound makes for a tighter and more fluid expression. *Dast,* "hand," is also associated with *giraftīrī,* "being caught," which is derived from *giraftan,* "to hold or grab."

The Couplet Itself

majbūrī-o dī'wī-e giraftīrī-e ulfat
dast-e tah-e sang-īmada paimān-e wafā hai

V

The Couplet

b'gāngī-e Xalq s' b'-dil na hǾ Gālib
kǾ'ī nahīN t'rā to merī jān Xudā hai

Prose Translation

Ghalib, don't let the alien world get you down. If no one stands by you, my dear, there is always God.

Lexicon

b'gāngī: foreignness; hostility; from *b'gāna:* alien; foreign.

Xalq: the created beings; the world; mankind.

b'-dil: disheartened; lit., without heart.

First line: "O Ghalib, don't be disheartened by the hostility of mankind . . ."

kǾ'ī nahīN t'rā: there is none belonging to you; there is none to side with you.

to: then; in that case.

merī jān: my dear.

Xudā: God.

Second line: "If there is none here to call your own, there is at least God."

Explication

As the last verse of the ghazal, it contains the poet's pen name. This convention allows the poet to disassociate himself from the persona of the poet-lover and to make wide-ranging ironic comments. The irony here is that God is as much the Creator of the Xalq as of Ghalib. An utterance that at first appears to express trust in God turns into a statement full of doubt.

The Couplet Itself

> b'gāngī-e Xalq s' b'-dil na hÇ Gālib
> kÇ'ī nahīN t'rā to merī jān Xudā hai

Ghalib seeks not merely a vivid or uncommon image to create poetry, but also a clustering of associations among as many elements in each couplet as possible. His ghazal as a whole remains a collection of heterogeneous ideas yoked together by the meter and rhyme pattern, but within each individual couplet he exerts tremendous effort to create a terse, compact poetic statement, closely linked in all its parts, and at once cerebral and sensuous.

Notes

[1] Urdu words are indicated in italic type in a normalized phonetic transcription. A macron over a vowel indicates length. *X* is "ch," as in German "nach"; *G,* its voiced counterpart, sounds something like "r" in the French *roi. N* indicates that the preceding vowel is nasalized; *H* indicates that the preceding consonant is aspirated. In Urdu, failure to pronounce a consonant exactly does not cause as much confusion or shame as the mispronunciation of a vowel.

FURTHER READING

Biography

Ram, Malik. *Mirza Ghalib.* New Delhi, India: National Book Trust, 1968, 93 p.
   A biography of Ghalib and an assessment of his poetry.

Rushaid, H. E. Yacoub A. "A Centenary Tribute." In *Ghalib's Passion Flower—Consuming, Flower-Fresh, Heady,* by Satya Deo Misra, pp. 71-79. New Delhi, India: S. D. Misra, 1969.

A tribute to Ghalib, with translations of his poetry, on the centenary of his death.

Varma, Pavan K. *Ghalib: The Man, the Times.* New Delhi, India: Viking, 1989, 224 p.
   Paints a portrait of Ghalib the man and, through him, of the Delhi in which he lived.

Criticism

Ahmad, Aijaz. "Ghalib: The Dew Drop on the Red Poppy." *Mahfil* V, No. 4 (1968-1969): 59-69.
   Comprehensive examination of Ghalib's "The Dew Drop on the Red Poppy," including an introduction, notes, and translations.

Hasan, Muhammad. "Some Important Critics of Ghalib." *Mahfil* V, No. 4 (1968-1969): 31-43.
   Discusses Ghalib's critics and their perceptions of his Urdu literature.

————. "Urdu: Ghalib Centenary Year." *Indian Literature* XIII, No. 4 (1970): 106-13.
   A brief overview and assessment of the literary output on Ghalib and other poets and writers in the centenary year of his death.

Khan, Shujaatullah. "Ghalib: The Monarch of Urdu Poetry." *Eastern Horizon* VI, No. 1 (January 1967): 49-52.
   Provides a brief overview of Ghalib's life, highlighting several ghazals.

Kumar, Ish. *Ghalib and Iqbal.* Chandigarh, India: Publication Bureau, Panjab University, 1988, 124 p.
   Compares the work of Ghalib with another Urdu poet, Iqbal, as well as with some English poets.

Narang, G. C. "Ghalib and the Rebellion of 1857." *Indian Literature* XV, No. 1 (1972): 5-20.
   Discusses Ghalib's thoughts and feelings about the Mutiny of 1857 as recorded in his letters and his Persian diary, *Dastambu.*

Qadir, Abdul. "Ghalib as a Poet." In his *Famous Urdu Poets and Writers,* pp. 17-46. Lahore: New Book Society, 1947.
   A lecture on the life and work of Ghalib.

Qadir, Abdul. "Ghalib as a Master of Urdu Prose." In his *Famous Urdu Poets and Writers,* pp. 47-70. Lahore: New Book Society, 1947.
   A lecture on the prose writing of Ghalib, particularly the letters collected in his *Urdu-I-Mualla.*

Rizvi, S. Ehtisham Husain. "The Elements of Ghalib's Thought." *Mahfil* V, No. 4 (1968-1969): 7-29.
   Attempts to understand Ghalib and his poetry by examining the milieu that both influenced him and was influenced by him.

Zaheer, Sajjad. "Ghalib and Progressive Urdu Literature." *Afro-Asian Writings* 1, No. 5 (April 1970): 171-79.

Discusses Ghalib's influence on Urdu literature and on poetry specifically.

Søren Kierkegaard

1813-1855

(Full name Søren Aabye Kierkegaard) Danish philosopher and theologian. For additional information on Kierkegaard, see *NCLC*, Vol. 34.

INTRODUCTION

Because of his rejection of the traditional approaches of philosophy to existence, reason, and faith, Kierkegaard is often referred to as an "anti-philosopher." Kierkegaard's opposition to the tradition of Western philosophy, represented by the rationalistic system of G. W. F. Hegel, is rooted in Kierkegaard's concern with the existence of the individual. Whereas Hegel and others focused on the search for universal truths, Kierkegaard emphasized that reason and universal truths are limited. Kierkegaard believed that only the individual, through faith and self-renunciation, could begin to perceive the Absolute, God. Kierkegaard's emphasis on the individual and personal responsibility in discerning appropriate courses of action has come to be viewed as a cornerstone of the twentieth-century Existential movement. Kierkegaard's prolific writings have a decidedly poetic, imaginative bent to them. He penned many of his works under a variety of pseudonyms and made much use of irony, subtlety, and paradox. For these reasons, one of the most controversial areas of modern debate is the issue of how one should read Kierkegaard and his pseudonymous works. Additionally, the themes of the nature of existence and faith recur repeatedly in Kierkegaard's authorship and continue to be scrutinized by modern critics.

Biographical Information

Kierkegaard was born in Copenhagen two months after his parents were married. His father, Michael, a deeply religious man, was a retired merchant, and his mother had formerly served in the Kierkegaard household as a maid to Michael Kierkegaard's first wife. After graduating in 1830 from a local school, Kierkegaard enrolled in the University of Copenhagen with plans to become a Lutheran minister. Kierkegaard's mother's death in 1834 was followed, four years later, by the death of his father. While Kierkegaard passed his theological examination with distinction in 1840, he decided not to enter the ministry. That same year, he proposed to Regine Olsen, who accepted his offer of engagement. During 1841, Kierkegaard finished his dissertation, *Om Begrebet Ironi med stadigt Hensyn til Socrates* (*On the Concept of Irony, with Special Reference to Socrates*), for the

Master of Arts degree from the Royal Pastoral Seminary. Shortly after his well-attended public dissertation defense, Kierkegaard broke off his engagement to Olsen and embarked on a trip to Berlin, where he began work on *Enten/Eller* (1843; *Either/Or*). He wrote prolifically during the next several years, publishing *Gjentagelsen* (1843; *Repetition*), *Frygt og Baeven* (1843; *Fear and Trembling* (1843), *Philosophiske Smuler* (1844; *Philosophical Fragments*), and *Stadier paa Livets Vej* (1845; *Stages on Life's Way*), among other works. The satirical journal *Corsair* began lampooning Kierkegaard in 1846 after Kierkegaard published a letter under the pseudonym Frater Taciturnus, in which he criticized the journal for what he viewed as unscrupulous tactics. The *Corsair* attacks on Kierkegaard continued for about six months and contributed to Kierkegaard's reputation as an eccentric. In 1854 and 1855, Kierkegaard, in a series of pamphlets, reacted to what he believed was an unmerited tribute to a church official by condemning the church's compromise with public and political interests as well as the hypocrisy and complacency of Christians. The pamphlets were republished in 1855 as

Hvad Christus dömmer om officiel Christendom (Kierkegaard's Attack on "Christendom") and were met with public scorn. Later that year, Kierkegaard suffered a stroke and died shortly thereafter.

Major Works

In several works, including *Either/Or, Fear and Trembling*, and *Stages on Life's Way*, Kierkegaard identified three modes, or "spheres," of living: the aesthetic, the ethical, and the religious. While these works focus on the presentation of these modes, the concept pervades Kierkegaard's other works as well. *Either/Or*, written under the pseudonym Victor Eremita, focuses on the choice between the aesthetic mode, in which novelty and pleasure are one's motivation, and the ethical mode, which is identified with marriage, responsibility, and self-appraisal. Within the ethical mode, the individual discerns a rational system of universal moral rules. Kierkegaard maintained that the foundation for this way of life is entirely subjective, as there exists no objective criterion for determining what is rational. Both *Fear and Trembling* (written under the pseudonym Johannes de Silentio) and *Stages on Life's Way* (written under the pseudonym Hilarius Bogbinder) are concerned with the religious mode. Kierkegaard stressed that the road to this way of life, which offers spiritual peace, involves a "leap" to faith. Universal ethical truths are to be disregarded, in favor of turning to God as the basis for resolving moral questions. In *Fear and Trembling*, the pseudonymous author de Silentio discussed the biblical story of Abraham, who is called on by God to sacrifice his son Isaac. De Silentio used the story as a way of conveying the necessity of subordinating rational, universal ethical truths to faith. Kierkegaard admitted that in this sense, Christianity is "irrational."

Kierkegaard's other most significant works include those written under the pseudonym Johannes Climacus, including *Philosophical Fragments* and *Afsluttende uvidenskabelig Efterskrift* (1846; *Concluding Unscientific Postscript to the Philosophical Fragments*). In these works, Climacus reacted against Hegel's abstract systematic philosophy and derided Hegel's glorification of reason. Through Climacus, Kierkegaard attacked the notion of objectivity, maintaining that an individual is not comprised of pure reason alone; history and heredity condition an individual's consciousness. Instead, Kierkegaard advocated the search for subjective truth and personal validation through choice.

Critical Reception

Kierkegaard's use of pseudonyms, irony, subtlety, and paradox, among other devices, make reading and analyzing his work especially challenging. Many critics have outlined various methods for Kierkegaard interpretation. Patrick Goold notes that Kierkegaard "writes so as to discourage the lazy reader and to perplex those with an unreflective cast of mind." Goold observes that many critics are often misled by taking Kierkegaard too literally, making his work seem self-refuting, while others mistakenly view his work as entirely ironic. A more appropriate approach, Goold argues, is to identify general themes in Kierkegaard's writings and to observe similarities in the treatments of such themes in order to discern those views that can be regarded as Kierkegaard's own. C. Stephen Evans also discusses three ways to read Kierkegaard: the philosophical approach (which ignores the significance of the pseudonyms); the literary approach (in which the ironic structure undermines the philosophical content); and a combination of the two approaches, which Evans favors. In this approach, Evans argues, the pseudonyms and literary structure are taken seriously. However, Kierkegaard's subversion of traditional philosophical arguments is viewed by Evans as an opportunity for the reader to more freely encounter the text philosophically.

Kierkegaard's views on the nature of existence are also an area of his work that receives much critical attention. Patrick Gardiner reviews Kierkegaard's aesthetic, ethical, and religious modes of existence, describing Kierkegaard's approach as poetic and creative. John D. Caputo analyzes another aspect of Kierkegaard's views on existence. Caputo explains that the traditional philosophical approach, beginning with Plato, takes the side of "thought" and "Being" over "existence" and "becoming." Caputo explains that this traditional view emphasizes a recovery or return to the realm of "primordial Being and pure presence." Kierkegaard, on the other hand, argues for "repetition," or *kinesis*, that is, forward motion. With repetition, Caputo maintains, eternity is not something lost, but rather, a goal to be attained. In examining Kierkegaard's views on fiction, Gabriel Josipovici reveals some of Kierkegaard's views on existence. Josipovici observes that to Kierkegaard, the world was one of gossip and rumor. When a writer writes, he implies that he has escaped the world of gossip and rumor to reach a transcendental source of authority. Kierkegaard claims that the authority on which most writers write is false; they have attained no such transcendence. Furthermore, Josipovici notes, Kierkegaard contended that an individual's life is "infinitely precious" as one's own and not as part of some larger pattern.

Kierkegaard's beliefs about the nature of existence are closely tied to faith issues. Several critics have analyzed the Kierkegaardian "self" and its relation to God. Sylvia I. Walsh, in her discussion of the "feminine" and "masculine" forms of conscious despair presented in *Sygdommen til Døden* (1849; *The Sickness unto Death*), demonstrates that both forms of despair result from an individual straying from the "pathway to selfhood," a path in which self-consciousness and self-analysis leads the way to a relationship with God. C. Stephen Evans studies the way Kierkegaard treated the unconscious in his works and notes in particular the way in which the development of the unconscious self affects one's relationship with God. Evans comments that to Kierkegaard, "all selfhood depends ontologically on God, and genuine selfhood depends on a conscious relation to God, for which individuals may substitute a relation to what is less than God. All of this presupposes a developing 'pre-self,' which is formed through relations with other persons and which is a significant element in the identity of a mature, healthy self." Similarly, Julia Watkin argues that to Kierkegaard, one's relationship to God is so significant that it requires total self-renunciation. Watkin explains that this belief influenced Kierkegaard, especially in his later years, to the point that he could not fully endorse marriage and procreation.

PRINCIPAL WORKS

Om Begrebet Ironi med stadigt Hensyn til Socrates (treatise) 1841
[On the Concept of Irony, with Special Reference to Socrates, 1966]

Enten/Eller. 2 vols. [as Victor Eremita] (treatise) 1843
[Either/Or: A Fragment of Life. 2 vols., 1944]

Frygt og Baeven [as Johannes de Silentio] (treatise) 1843
[Fear and Trembling: A Dialectical Lyric by Johannes de Silentio, 1939]

Gjentagelsen: Et Forsøg i den experimenterende Psychologi [as Constantin Constantius] (essay) 1843
[Repetition: An Essay in Experimental Psychology, 1941]

Opbyggelige Taler (essays) 1843-44
[Edifying Discourses, 1943-46]

Begrebet Angest [as Virgilius Haufniensis] (treatise) 1844
[The Concept of Anxiety, 1944]

Philosophiske Smuler [as Johannes Climacus] (essay) 1844
[Philosophical Fragments; or, A Fragment of Philosophy, 1936]

Stadier paa Livets Vej [as Hilarius Bogbinder] (treatise) 1845
[Stages on Life's Way, 1940]

Tre Taler ved taenkte Leiligheder (essays) 1845
[Thoughts on Crucial Situations in Human Life: Three Discourses on Imagined Occasions, 1941]

Afsluttende uvidenskabelig Efterskrift [as Johannes Climacus] (essay) 1846
[Concluding Unscientific Postscript to the Philosophical Fragments, 1941]

*En literair Anmeldelse. To Tidsaldre (criticism) 1846
[Two Ages: The Age of Revolution and the Present Age, a Literary Review, 1978]

†"Bogen om Adler" (criticism) 1846-47
[On Authority and Revelation: The Book on Adler, 1955]

Kjerlighedens Gjerninger (essays) 1847
[Works of Love, 1946]

Opbyggelige Taler i forskjellig Aand (essays) 1847
[Edifying Discourses in a Different Vein, 1938]

Christelige Taler (essays) 1848
[Christian Discourses, 1939]

Krisen og en Krise i en Skuespillerindes Liv [as Inter et Inter] (essays) 1848
[The Crisis and The Crisis in the Life of an Actress, 1967]

Sygdommen til Døden [as Anti-Climacus] (essay) 1849
[The Sickness unto Death, 1941]

Tre Taler ved Altergangen om Fredagen (essays) 1849
[Three Discourses at the Communion on Fridays, 1939]

Tvende ethisk-religieuse Smaa-Afhandlinger [as H. H. Moreover] (treatises) 1849
[Two Minor Ethico-Religious Treatises, 1940]

Indøvelse i Christendom [as Anti-Climacus] (essay) 1850
[Training in Christianity, 1941]

Om min Forfatter-Virksomhed (criticism) 1851
[On My Work as an Author, published in The Point of View for My Work as an Author: A Report to History, 1939]

Til Selvprøvelse (essay) 1851
[For Self-Examination, 1940]

‡Hvad Christus dömmer om officiel Christendom (criticism) 1855
[Kierkegaard's Attack upon "Christendom," 1854-1855, 1944]

§Synspunktet for min Forfatter-Virksomhed (criticism) 1859
[The Point of View for My Work as an Author: A Report to History, 1939]

Papirer. 20 vols. (collected journals, memoirs, note books, and letters) 1909-48
[Søren Kierkegaard's Journals and Papers. 7 vols., 1967-78]

Samlede Vaerker. 20 vols. (collected works) 1962-64

Kierkegaard's Writings. 26 vols. (collected works) 1985-88

*The Present Age, a partial translation of En literair Anmeldelse. To Tidsaldre, was published in 1940.
†Written in 1846-47; published in Papirer, vol. 7.
‡Originally published in 1854-55 as nine pamphlets entitled "Øjeblikket" ("The Moment").
§Written in 1848.

CRITICISM

Theodor W. Adorno (essay date 1962)

SOURCE: "Concept of Existence," in *Kierkegaard, Konstruktion des Asthetischen,* 1962, published as *Kierkegaard: Construction of the Aesthetic,* translated and edited by Robert Hullot-Kentor, University of Minnesota Press, 1989, pp. 68-85.

[*In the following essay, originally written in 1962, Adorno critiques Kierkegaard's doctrine of existence, focusing on the philosopher's concern with paradox, ambiguity, and subjectiveness.*]

Existence and Truth

Of all of Kierkegaard's concepts, that of existence is currently the most prominent. If his struggle with "official Christianity" has lost its urgency for a mentality in which the established church and individual life long ago left behind the dialectic in which Kierkegaard found them linked, however antagonistically; if the abstract transcendence of the idea of God—which dialectical theology extracts from **Fear and Trembling** and the **Philosophical Fragments**—appears all too bound to positive dogmatics and at the same time all too wanting in any binding content to become a significant epochal concern beyond the boundaries of the intra-Protestant controversy; then Kierkegaard's formulation of the problem of truth is most compelling when, without dogmatic thesis and without speculative antithesis, it is addressed to existence in the form in which it defines the circumference of his philosophical experience: when it is addressed, that is, to individual existence. The ontological question, as the question of the "meaning of existence," is today read out of Kierkegaard more than any other.[1] To be sure, the doctrine of "meaning" is equivocal from the beginning. In Kierkegaard existence is not to be understood as a "manner of being," not even if it were one "laid open" to itself.[2] He is not concerned with a "fundamental ontology" that "must be sought in the existential analytic of existence."[3] For Kierkegaard, the question of the "meaning" of existence is not that of what existence properly is, but rather what gives existence—meaningless in itself—a meaning. Philosophy's concern is not the "being of beings," but ideas insofar as they occur within the movement of existence without remaining in it. Existence does not interpret itself through "meaning"; rather, it separates itself from the meaningless, from contingency. This is acutely formulated not only by "aesthete A" but even more definitively by the "anonymous friend" in **Repetition:** "One sticks a finger into the ground to smell what country one is in; I stick my finger into existence—it has no smell. Where am I?

What does it mean to say: the world? What is the meaning of that word? Who tricked me into this whole thing and leaves me standing here? Who am I? How did I get into the world? Why was I not asked about it, why was I not informed of the rules and regulations but just thrust into the ranks as if I had been bought from a peddling shanghaier of human beings? How did I get involved in this big enterprise called reality? Why should I be involved? Isn't it a matter of choice? And if I am compelled to be involved, where is the manager—I have something to say about this. Is there no manager? To whom shall I make my complaint?"[4]—Kierkegaard himself used the term ontology only polemically, as equivalent to metaphysics. If it is applied to truth, the figure of which his philosophy wants to produce, then, according to his intention, existence could not be termed ontological. "Existence is ontically distinctive in that it is ontological:"[5] Heidegger's thesis is incompatible with Kierkegaard's intention. True, for Kierkegaard ontology is bound to creaturely existence, from which it must be inseparable if it is not to dissolve in the uncertainties of speculation: "All essential knowledge relates to existence, or only such knowledge as has an essential relationship to existence is essential knowledge. All knowledge that does not inwardly relate itself to existence, in the reflection of inwardness, is, essentially viewed, accidental knowledge; its degree and scope is essentially indifferent."[6] But since ontology is sought within the field of existence, it is not at the same time the answer to the ontological "question," and "meaning" is much more than simply the structure of the possibility of existence. This is Kierkegaard's point: "It is only momentarily that the particular individual is able to realize existentially a unity of the infinite and the finite that transcends existence."[7] Accordingly, "meaning" is not designated as the intention of interpretive ontological questioning, but as the unquestionable "infinity" that transcends existence. It is conjured up out of existence; transcendence is sought in immanence; and it is the movement of individual human consciousness—as engrossment—that offers the form of the conjuration. Kierkegaard's concept of existence does not coincide with mere existence, but with an existence that, dynamic in itself, obtains a transcendent meaning that is supposedly qualitatively different from existence. Accordingly, it does not pose the question of existence as that of simple existence, but as that of historical existence. For the paradox of a "meaning" that is not self-identically posited by the subject as a "unity of the finite and the infinite," yet all the same exclusively situated in the "reflexion of inwardness"—this paradox is none other than the law of Kierkegaard's objectless inwardness itself, which can be located historically. Unlike current existential philosophy, Kierkegaard's unrelenting polemic against Hegel and speculative metaphysics does not want to hold a transcendent meaning at a distance from the interpretation of existence, a meaning of which he felt more assured than Hegel ever did. On the contrary, Kierkegaard wants to preserve immanent consciousness as an arena of a manifest transcendent meaning, whereas in Hegel this meaning is to be immanent in transcendent being. What is real is rational. This makes possible the misrepresentation that, in its restriction to subjective existence, the interest of Kierkegaard's philosophy is "existential-ontological," whereas actually his dialectic of engrossment merely binds existence and ontology in order ultimately to divide them. The ontological question of interpretation is anathematized as "objective": "the way of objective reflection makes the subject accidental and thereby transforms existence into something indifferent, something vanishing. The way to objective truth leads away from the subject, and while the subject and his subjectivity become indifferent, the truth also becomes indifferent, and this indifference is precisely its objective validity; for all interest, like all decisiveness, is rooted in subjectivity. The way of objective reflection leads to abstract thought, to mathematics, to historical knowledge of different kinds; and always it leads away from the subject, whose being or non-being from the objective point of view quite rightly becomes infinitely indifferent. Quite rightly, since as Hamlet says, being and non-being have only subjective significance. In its perfection this way will arrive at a contradiction, and in so far as the subject does not become wholly indifferent to himself, this merely constitutes a sign that his objective striving is not objective enough. At its maximum this way leads to the contradiction that only the objective has come into being, while the subjective has gone out; that is to say, the existing subjectivity has vanished, in that it has made an attempt to become what in the abstract sense is called subjectivity, the mere abstract form of an abstract objectivity. And yet, the objectivity which has thus come into being is, from the subjective point of view in its perfection, either an hypothesis or an approximation, because all eternal decisiveness is rooted in subjectivity."[8] This is a critique not only of the scientific comprehension of the objective world, but equally of the "objectifying" interpretation of subjectivity and, therefore, *a priori,* of the possibility of an "existential analytic of existence." Fichte's "I am I" and Hegel's "subject-object" are for Kierkegaard hypostatizations under the sign of identity and are rejected precisely to the extent that they set up a pure being of existence in opposition to the existing "particular individual": "Speculative philosophy will immediately transport us into the fantastic realism of the I-am-I, which modern speculative thought has not hesitated to use without explaining how a particular individual is related to it; and God knows, no human being is more than such a particular individual. If an existing individual were really able to transcend himself, the truth would be for him something final and complete; but where is the point at which he is outside himself? The I-am-I is a mathematical point which does not exist, and to this extent there is nothing to prevent everyone from occupying this standpoint; the one will not be in the way of the other."[9] And similarly in opposition to Hegel: "Or is the existing spirit himself the identity of subject and object, the subject-object? In that case I must press the question of where such an existing human being is, when he is thus at the same time also a subject-object?"[10] Because the existing thus takes the place of existence, ontology is removed further from existence the more that the question of the existing is directed toward the existing particular person. Individual existence is for Kierkegaard the arena of ontology only because it itself is not ontological. Hence the existence of the person is for Kierkegaard a process that mocks any objectivation; hence, with regard to inner-philosophical constitution, absolute spirituality is held to be dynamic-dialectical. Spirituality is not being whose meaning is to be released ontologically, but a function that locks meaning within itself. As such, spirituality is not accidentally named by a word reminiscent of subjugation to nature, passion. Through passion the existing person should participate in truth, without being ontologized; and at the same time, without truth, hypostatized, being withdrawn from the person: "It is the passion of the infinite that is the decisive factor and not its content, for its content is precisely itself. In this manner subjectivity and the subjective 'how' constitute the truth";[11] that is, in Kierkegaard's opinion, insofar as passion is not the decisive factor, but becomes itself through infinite negation of itself. Under the category of negativity, of "uncertainty," truth is separated from any ontological project of the person, to whom ontology belongs only paradoxically: "An objective uncertainty held fast in an appropriation-process of the most passionate inwardness is the truth, the highest truth attainable for an existing individual."[12] Kierkegaard's idea of truth is distinguished from one that is merely subjectivistic by the postulate of "infinity," with which the finite self is simply incommensurable; and it is distinguished from objectivity of whatever sort by the rejection of any positive transsubjective criterion: "When the question of truth is raised in an objective manner, reflection is directed objectively to the truth, as an object to which the knower is related. Reflection is not focused upon the relationship, however, but upon the question of whether it is the truth to which the knower is related. If only the object to which he is related is the truth, the subject is accounted to be in the truth. When the question of the truth is raised subjectively, reflection is directed subjectively to the nature of the individual's relationship; if only the mode, the 'how,' of this relationship is in the truth, the individual is in the truth even if he should happen to be thus related to what is not true."[13] Immanent and transcendent truth are no longer "mediated" by the hypostatization of subjective and objective "participation" in truth. The predication of truth, just as any predication of content, would "objectivate" the idea of truth and is therefore, for Kierkegaard, not permissible. Truth's transcendence is produced instead through the negation of immanent subjectivity, through the infinite contradiction. Subjectivity and truth intersect in paradox: "Inwardness in an existing subject culminates in passion; corresponding to passion in the subject the truth becomes a paradox."[14] Thus Kierkegaard's idea of the paradox—conceived this side of all theological paradox of the symbol—has its philosophical genesis in the relationship of objectless inwardness and ontology. In Kierkegaard, paradoxy is raised to the highest power of conjuration; a power that renounces aesthetic semblance; a power, that is, without images. The critique of his concept of existence is concerned with this paradoxy, and not with the meaning of the being of existence.

Paradox and Ambiguity

The movement of existence is for Kierkegaard one that is to lead objectless inwardness out of its mythical entanglement in "freedom" to the presence of truth itself. Kierkegaard does not expressly conclude that this truth in paradox destroys semblance: for him, semblance is not bound to mythical content, but to the subjective mode of behavior, and is therefore unable to constitute the antithetical idea to that of existence. But the conception of paradoxical truth as imageless inheres in his terminology. For Kierkegaard, truth is "transparentness," and the profound gaze that without any resistance penetrates the transparent seems to be the complete opposite of what is embodied in the mythical images in which it satiates itself but at the same time encounters its own impenetrable border.—The centrality of the category of transparentness in Kierkegaard's doctrine of existence has been recognized by Guardini: "To be 'transparent' to oneself. For Kierkegaard the word has the greatest significance. It means ingenuous, free of all obscurity, manifestly authentic."[15] Clearly, Guardini's commentary is a Catholic interpretation of Kierkegaard's "transparentness": for him, nature has been atoned for by the sacrifice of Christ, whereas for the Protestant, Kierkegaard, a sinful-ambiguous nature stands ever again in need of rescue. Guardini takes transparentness as "simplicity" in the Christian sense: "There, where Kierkegaard looks back on his work, in **The Point of View of My Work as an Author,** he names 'simplicity' the highest value of Christian perfection, as Christ's said: 'Except ye become as little children, ye shall not enter into the kingdom of heaven.' Matthew 18:3—, simplicity and transparentness belong together."[16] This misses the dialectical character, which for Kierkegaard the idea of transparentness itself preserves. Simplicity, the concrete condition of transparentness, is for him not identical with simple-correct "ethical" life. As the goal of infinite and "negative" movement, simplicity remains virtual; it is the "highest value of Christian perfection" not so much in life as in perfect contradiction to it, i.e. in sacrifice. To understand this it is not enough to suppose "that Kierkegaard was perhaps the most complicated person who ever

wrote on religious matters."[17] For the dialectical conception of transparentness is not adequately grasped psychologically, but only in terms of the configuration of Kierkegaard's idea of truth. Transparentness is indeed conceived ontologically: "I could have called the good 'transparency.'"[18] But it is, according to the concept of knowledge, not so much an achieved level of being as dynamic in itself: "The ethical individual knows himself, but this knowledge is not a mere contemplation (for the individual would understand himself only as determined by necessity), it is a reflection upon himself that itself is an action, and therefore I have deliberately preferred to use the expression 'choose oneself' instead of know oneself."[19] But then transparentness is no longer paradoxical truth but ambiguous. Imageless truth, into which the movement of individual consciousness is to flow paradoxically, negating itself, is itself drawn into the movement without any possibility of differentiation: the ontological good is the ontical existence in the act of "choice," and ontology, previously wrenched away from subjective immanence by the strength of "infinity," threatens once again to sink back into itself as soon as the idea of truth itself—as "transparentness"—is subjected to the dialectic. This ambiguity of Kierkegaard's idea of truth is to be emphatically separated from the paradox. Truth appears paradoxical in the subjective—and not only subjective—dialectic that is extinguished in it; truth becomes ambiguous as the quintessence of dialectical movement without being its measure. It is easy to suppose, and it has been often enough asserted, that Kierkegaard's dialectic reaches its pinnacle when spirit emerges pure and undisguised from the dialectic in order to achieve transcendence as simplicity. Whether or not this is true of Kierkegaard's Christology, this schema does not hold good for the doctrine of truth and the corresponding dialectic of existence. For truth, metamorphosed as fear, does not absorb into itself the rising sap of the dialectic, instead it is conceded to the aimless growth of the tree.

The Abstract Self

For Kierkegaard, ontological "meaning" is not one in which a self-interpretive existence could know its own being; rather, existence must conjure meaning; conjure it without imagery in order to gain self-possession in pure, unmanifest spirituality. What spirituality conjures is granted to it ambiguously and entangled with mere existence; this throws the critique of Kierkegaard's idea of truth back onto the structure of his concept of existence as the origin of ambiguity.—To understand this concept, it will help to bring Kant's synthesis to mind, which prepared the way for Fichte's and Hegel's systems as much as for Kierkegaard's doctrine of existence. The critique of pure reason was a critique of rational ontology, specifically of Wolff's ontology. This ontology was subjected to its most severe test: that of the contingency of the categorically undeducible material of intuition. If ontology is not to be rescued as the content of experience, it may be conceived only as the form of experience. It shrinks to a synthetic *a priori* judgment to the extent that it is not relegated to the secure and powerless transcendence of the postulates. The gap between the inner and the contingent outer is still mastered in the system of principles: subjectively produced by means of the synthetic unity of apperception, they belong to the immanence of consciousness; as constitutive conditions of all objective knowledge, they are themselves objective. Ontology is preserved in their double meaning: it is protected from contingency through the systematic strength of the spontaneous center and protected from the deceptions of speculative thought through experiential validity. The cost of this security is abstractness: the principles are "necessary" only insofar as they are "universal." The idealist systems undertook once again to recover the lost content of ontology through the elimination of the contingency of the "material," which is itself derived from the synthetic unity of apperception, developed as "content" out of the subjective forms from which "ontology" can be deduced and through "development" posited as identical with subjectivity. This is the model of Kierkegaard's philosophico-historical effort. For Kierkegaard, just as for Hegel, Kant's subjective ontology is rendered powerless by its abstractness. At the same time, however, Kierkegaard recognizes the fraud of the material ontology of the late expositional sections of the Hegelian system—the Hegelian construction of the status quo as meaningful: the identity of the real and the reasonable volatilizes ontology by spreading it out over the whole of existence and thus forgoes any binding measure of exalted existence as of "meaning," a meaning whose ubiquity threatens to reverse into being nowhere at all. Kierkegaard's project is the precise antithesis of the Kantian thesis and the Hegelian synthesis. Against Kant, he pursues the plan of concrete ontology; against Hegel, he pursues the plan of an ontology that does not succumb to the existent by absorbing it into itself. He therefore revises the process of post-Kantian idealism: he surrenders the claim of identity. What remains is, however, not the Kantian landscape of a transcendental subject whose forms of intuition and concepts of order objectify the manifold of perceptual data as experience. Along with Hegelian identity, he sacrifices the Kantian transcendental objectivity. Whereas in Kant, "consciousness in general" persists—this side of the gap—as the guarantor of ontology, Kierkegaard renounces the scientific validity of "results" and contrasts the particular consciousness of the individual person, as concrete, with the contingency of external experience. The individual becomes, for Kierkegaard, the bearer of a material meaning that the philosophy of identity was unable to realize in contingent sensuous material, whereas the abstract Kantian "I think" did not suffice to confirm the existence it had mastered as meaningful. Hegel is turned inside out: world history is for Hegel what the individual is for

Kierkegaard. Yet Kierkegaard is not exempted from the obligation of paying the Kantian tribute to contingency. For the person's existence and quiddity, which cannot be understood on the basis of any "meaning," is as contingent as any perceptual data. To prevent the individual's contingency from losing its "meaning," the concrete individual is subjected to a procedure that indeed ensures him of concrete meaning—just as the Kantian "idea" ensures the coherence of the intellect (*Verstand*)—yet renders the individual abstract: the ontological determinations that are sought in him are hollowed out, be it that they—like the terms "meaning," "freedom," and "idea"—are in no way less abstract than the Kantian categories; be it that insofar as they remain concrete, they are overtaken—as determinations of mere facticity—by the same contingency from which the restriction to inwardness was supposed to give protection. This is made perfectly evident by the ambiguity of ontological meaning in Kierkegaard. The origin of this ambiguity is the abstract self. Its abstractness is the counterpole to the abstractness of the universal. It is the abstractness of the particular. This abstractness stands in contrast to the transparentness that is Kierkegaard's aim. True, this transparentness is imageless, yet what lies closest to it remains as impenetrable as are only those images that are seen at the most extreme distance. Kierkegaard gives evidence of this in a passage from *The Concept of Anxiety;* while the passage is concerned with an "egoist," no criterion distinguishes it from his positive presentation of existence: "For selfishness is precisely the particular, and what this signifies only the single individual can know as the single individual, because when it is viewed under universal categories it may signify everything in such a way that it signifies nothing at all. . . . 'Self,' however, signifies precisely the contradiction of positing the universal as the particular. Only when the concept of the particular is given can there be any talk of selfishness; however, although there have lived countless millions of such 'selves,' no science can say what the self is without again stating it quite generally."[20] The self, the hoard of all concretion, contracts in its singularity in such a fashion that nothing more can be predicated of it: it reverses into the most extreme abstractness; the claim that only the individual knows what the individual is amounts to no more than a circumlocution for its final unknowability. Thus the most determinate self remains the most indeterminate. Modern logic did not fail to perceive the indeterminateness of the pure substratum of any form of categorial determination. In Husserl's analysis of noematic "meaning" in the *Ideas,* there is a description that precisely sums up the situation of the Kierkegaardian "self": "There detaches itself as the central noematic phrase: the 'object,' the 'objective unity,' the 'self-same,' the 'determinable subject of its possible predicates'—the pure x in abstraction from all predicates."[21] Just as in Husserl's many synonymous expressions, the logical center of the Kierkegaardian self, the object of all possible predication, the inherently "concrete," becomes an indeterminate, indeterminable, abstraction. Its abstractness is the reflection of the abstractness of the highest universalities to which it is subordinated: the idea, decisiveness, and spirit. That, however, this abstractness characterizes not only the egoistic, "selfish" self, but the "existential" self as well, can be interpretively inferred from an excursus from the ***Concluding Unscientific Postscript:*** "What does it mean in general to explain anything? Does it consist in showing that the obscure something in question is not this but something else? This would be a strange sort of an explanation; I thought it was the function of an explanation to render it evident that the something in question was this definite thing, so that the explanation took the obscurity away but not the object. Otherwise the explanation would not be an explanation, but something quite different, namely, a correction."[22] The sort of "explanation" that Kierkegaard demands would be possible only in image and name, and precisely these are excluded by the demand for "transparentness." It is, in addition, generally blocked by Kierkegaard's subjectivistic-nominalistic theory of language, which grounds his doctrine of "communication." Transparentness, however, which helplessly perseveres in the face of its blind, unilluminable, and closed object, completely renounces knowledge in a different manner. The object resists all transparentness. This is evident in the relationship of the category of transparentness to the category of the paradox: "The explanation of the paradox makes it clear what the paradox is, removing any remaining obscurity."[23] If here transparentness, as the name for ontology, is the subordinating concept of the paradoxical, whose obscurity is to be "removed"—how should transparentness accomplish this, if the paradoxical itself remains obscure, indeterminate, and abstract? For indeed all illumination has its boundaries defined by the condition of determinate existence. True illumination will never gnostically volatilize existence into a system of "significations." Nor can illumination ever mean the mere constatation of obscurity; knowledge may be unable to solve its material, yet it may indeed construct its material in figures of the existing in which the material—however obscure and however impoverished of meaning it is for itself—all the same functionally contributes to illumination. The empty and blind "x" is set up as truth only by a pseudo-dialectic in which illumination is identical with categorization under universal concepts and which celebrates its triumphs there where such categorization is no longer possible because it takes the negation, the transcendence, and the explosion of the concept to be its material's highest accomplishment. All that this pseudo-dialectic really demonstrates is the inappropriateness of its categories to its philosophical-historical objects. Kierkegaard was able to deceive himself about this by the force of his opposition to Kant. He thought he had warded off its abstractness along with the transcendental subject, without, however, noticing that the abstractness returns in

the narrowing of concretion to the pure this-there. Where he recognized the danger, he defended himself by tearing concretion away from knowledge: "Certitude and inwardness are indeed subjectivity, but not in an entirely abstract sense. It really is the misfortune of the most recent knowledge that everything has become so terribly magnificent. Abstract subjectivity is just as uncertain and lacks inwardness to the same degree as abstract objectivity."[24] If concrete subjectivity were exclusively reserved for praxis, praxis itself would be without orientation and knowledge would have abdicated. For this reason Kierkegaard must unceasingly concern himself with the theoretical interpretation of concrete subjectivity, with the person as the bearer of "meaning." But this theoretical effort necessarily entangles itself in tautology: "The most concrete content that consciousness can have is consciousness of itself, of the individual himself—not the pure self-consciousness, but the self-consciousness that is so concrete that no author, not even the one with the greatest power of description, has even been able to describe a single such self-consciousness, although every single human being is such a one. This self-consciousness is not contemplation, for he who believes this has not understood himself, because he has not seen that he himself is in the process of becoming and consequently cannot be something completed for contemplation. This self-consciousness, therefore, is action."[25] Only the Fichtean turn toward "action," as the unity of theory and praxis, leads out of the tautology. Yet had Kierkegaard insisted on such unity, he would have been consigned to the philosophy of identity. Thus the doctrine of existence at every turn comes up against aporia. Sometimes its center, the "self," is abstract and only tautologically definable; sometimes the self falls to a praxis that would first have to receive its rule from the self; sometimes the conception of the self leads to nebulous positings of identification. In spite of the various constructions, the self becomes obviously fully abstract there where its content was to have been interpreted, in the "psychology": "I may lose my wealth, my honor in the eyes of others, my intellectual powers, and suffer no damage to my soul. I could gain it all and yet suffer damage. What then is my soul? What is this inmost being of mine which can remain unaffected by this loss and suffer damage by this gain? To the despairing man this apparently insubstantial abstraction proves to be 'something.'"[26] The discussion here is of an insubstantial abstraction; the "something," however, its corrective, remains equally abstract. If one wanted, by a questionable method, to search out the grounding nexus of Kierkegaard's concept of existence in praxis, i.e., in its moral theses, it would not gain adequate concreteness. For Kierkegaard, the instrument of moral "action" is the "earnestness" of decisiveness. Through earnestness the anthropological schemata of the self and of existence are to gain their content. But since earnestness may not draw its determinations from the objective world, it is defined by the same "inwardness" to which it is supposed to grant "meaning"; and hence, once again, the thought is tautological: "But this same thing to which earnestness is to return with the same earnestness can only be earnestness itself."[27] Just as earnestness remains tautological, the subject remains its own object: "The phrase 'What has made him earnest in life' must of course be understood, in a pregnant sense, as that from which the individuality in the deepest sense dates his earnestness. Having become truly earnest about that which is the object of earnestness, a person may very well, if he so wishes, treat various things 'earnestly,' but the question is whether he first became earnest about the object of earnestness. This object every human being has, because it is himself."[28] Ultimately the self, which as existence is the theoretical-anthropological category, and earnestness, the practical category, are directly identified: "Inwardness, i.e. certitude, is earnestness."[29] This prompts the contrary insight: "This seems a little paltry."[30] But this insight is immediately turned into self-righteous irony that intends to finish off transcendental idealism: "If at least I had said that it [earnestness] is subjectivity, the pure subjectivity, the encompassing subjectivity, I would have said something, something that no doubt would have made many earnest. However, I can also express earnestness in another way. Whenever inwardness is lacking, the spirit is finitized. Inwardness is therefore eternity or the constituent of the eternal in man."[31] Thus, when the "impoverishment" becomes evident, the abstractness of the past, of the general categories of eternity, spirit, and infinity, is substituted for the abstractness of the most minute, the abstractness of the self. This becomes drastically evident in the central definition of the self in the **Unscientific Postscript:** "The negativity that pervades existence, or rather, the negativity of the existing subject, which should be essentially reflected in his thinking in an adequate form, has its ground in the subject's synthesis: that he is an existing infinite spirit. The infinite and eternal is the only certainty, but as being in the subject it is in existence; and the first expression for this, is its elusiveness, and this tremendous contradiction, that the eternal becomes, that it comes into being."[32] Such concepts spin a web around the ethical substratum without opening it up. As a self, it remains indeterminate; as the intersection of conceptual projections, it is not grasped as *this* specific self. "This is the single fashion in which the ethical can manifest itself; in itself, in its positive meaning, it is concealed in the deepest layer of the soul,"[33] that is, it remains totally opaque.

Existence Mythical

Spirit, separated from nature, disdains imagery. This enmity manifests itself as abstractness in the concept of the self, and it is the origin of both the powerlessness of conjuration and the ambiguity of what is conjured. But this enmity is at the same time expression.

Abstractness, as opaqueness, bears witness to mere nature, into which Kierkegaard's spiritualism invariably reverses. Like the universal concepts, so the pure this-there remains abstract in Kierkegaard's doctrine of existence. In it the content of the concept of existence expresses itself. It may be said that abstractness is the seal of mythical thought. The ambiguity of the guilty natural context, in which everything undifferentiatedly communicates with everything else, knows no true concretion. Here the names of created things are confounded and blind material or the empty sign remains in its place. The commonplace attribution of the highest concreteness to mythical, archaic thought by virtue of the conceptually unmediated intuition of the this-there is misleading. Primitive speechless intuition is unable to give its objects lasting boundaries; although it bestows everything individual with its own word, the word rigidifies under its gaze as a fetish that locks itself even deeper in its own existence. The universal concepts, however, distilled from the intuited objects as abbreviations of their common characteristics, are, like these characteristics, dependent upon speechless intuition for their fulfillment. The concrete, already lost in the case of the universal concept and still obscure to pure intuition, is not the secure middle between the two. It is the spark that—in the name—shoots across from the most universal concept to the material of the this-there and ignites.—Material statements about existence that contain more than the proclamation of the factual there-ness of the self or the attempt at its localization through the combination of universal concepts, occur in Kierkegaard only rarely and with the greatest abridgement. Kierkegaard—as Johannes de Silentio and Frater Taciturnus—may have been able to justify his silence with the "concealedness" of the existential substrate, with the insufficiency of the *ratio,* to develop a "system of existence." The concept of existence is presented in positive form, without any supporting apparatus, only on the first several pages of **The Sickness unto Death;** and it receives a (qualifying) commentary exclusively in two passages in the **Training in Christianity,** which—without referring to **The Sickness unto Death**—unmistakably pursue the terminology of the earlier work. It is from these fragments that concrete criticism must start if it wants to do more than to understand existential thought banally in terms of its antithesis to systematic thought, as thought directed toward being, without troubling over the specific idea of being at which, beyond all mere relativity of existence, Kierkegaard's concept of existence aims.—**The Sickness unto Death** begins with the thesis of spiritualism, with the determination of existence as spirit. Guardini has trenchantly noted the danger in this: "Kierkegaard . . . pushes his thesis one-sidedly to an extreme; for this thesis should be weighty, weighty in such a fashion that it becomes catastrophic in that it becomes a functionally, meaningful impossibility. Thus he says: 'Spirit' is identical with the 'self'—a thesis whose destructive consequences cannot be presented here."[34] Creation is reduced to spirit in the self in order to rescue the self from its fallenness to guilt-laden nature. Since, however, man as creation—as "existing," which is precisely how Kierkegaard conceives him in opposition to speculative idealism—is not identical with spirit, nature overcomes him there where he thinks he has secured the supranatural for himself, i.e., in the self, precisely as in something absolutely spiritual. "Man is spirit. But what is spirit? Spirit is the self."[35] This is Kierkegaard's axiom. But is the self spirit? And does not spirit, identified with created being, become a mythical quality? Kierkegaard attempts to escape this implication through his ruling idea of the dialectic as one between "nature and spirit, mythical content and consciousness as qualitatively different, strictly contrary powers."[36] In *The Sickness unto Death* this idea is reduced to its basic formula and joined with the definition of the self as spirit: "But what is the self? The self is a relation which relates itself to its own self."[37] In that Kierkegaard interprets the self not as existing statically but, functionally, as spirit, it is to transcend the natural world to which its substratum necessarily belongs in its "opaqueness." The commentary in the *Training* makes the functional character of the doctrine of "relationship" evident: "What is it, then, to be a self? It is a duplication. Hence in the relation established here the phrase, 'truly draw to oneself,' has a double meaning. The magnet draws iron to itself, but iron is not a self: hence, in the relation established here, 'draw to itself' indicates a single and simple act. But a self is a duplication, it is freedom: hence in this case 'drawing truly to oneself' means to present a choice. In the case of iron which is drawn, there is not and cannot be any question of a choice. But a self can be truly drawn to another only through a choice, so that 'truly drawing to oneself' is a composite act."[38] This conception of the self as a "relation" reveals its mythical character. The "relation which relates itself to its own self" has no precise meaning if exactly that "x" is not accepted as the substratum of the relation. The definitions of *Sickness unto Death* want, however, in contradistinction to those of the *Unscientific Postscript* to exclude precisely the "opaque" substratum through the introduction of pure functions. The concept of relation, however, says nothing else than that its elements relate to one another; not that their relation relates to the "whole." The "relation which relates itself to its own self" can therefore, in the first place, not be reflectively comprehended without a "substratum." If, however, the relation which relates itself to its own self is neither the reference to a substratum nor the reflection of the relationship to itself, which would indeed already amount to objectivation, then nothing else could be meant by Kierkegaard's reflective diction than a structure of the relation itself that could then be reflected upon. It must be asked: what distinguishes a "relation" from a "relation which relates itself to its own self"? Only one answer is possible: the latter relation produces, as a unity, the self-relating elements out of itself, just as "life" for the

young Hegel is a unity that is self dividing; whereas the former, the mere "relation," posits divergent elements in regard to one another. The relation which relates itself to its own self is a metaphorical designation for the original, productive unity that at once "posits" and unifies the contradictions. Thus not only the Kantian transcendental synthesis but even the macrocosm of the Hegelian, infinitely productive "totality" is hidden in the microcosm of the Kierkegaardian self. Kierkegaard's self is the system, dimensionlessly concentrated in the "point." That in fact a "totality" sustains the plan of the self is betrayed by a passage from *The Concept of Anxiety,* Kierkegaard there demands of the "psychological observer" that "hence he ought also to have a poetic originality in his soul so as to be able at once to create both the totality and the invariable from what the individual always presents in fragmented and erratic form."[39] The transcendental synthesis in the configuration of totality and primordiality is easily sensed. This self, in its primordiality at once totally posited and positing, bears an unmistakable resemblance—as "un-fragmented"—to the organic, the simply natural self. For in that the creature, split between nature and the supranatural, as self, as "a relation which relates to its own self," as a primordial and productive unity spontaneously produces the duality of nature and the supranatural, it has raised itself unnoticed to the status of creator. Accordingly, however, the "spirit," to which the creature has laid claim, is pulled down to the level of the creature and is transformed back into nature. The creature remains mythically self-positing in the undifferentiated nexus of the natural and measures the highest concept of itself on that of organic life. It could only become transparent through transcendence. On its own, it remains self-opaque.—The absurdity of Kierkegaard's doctrine of the "self relating relationship" has its origin here. It attempts to rescue the dark, spontaneous, and self-positing "I" of transparentness by a postulate: "By relating itself to its own self and by willing to be itself the self is grounded transparently in the power which posited it."[40] As a "relation which relates to its own self," it is itself the "power which posited it," and hence its transparentness is a reflection, just as in the images of the *intérieur,* and as such it is indeed semblance. Kierkegaard's "self" remains mythically-ambiguously between autonomy as the immanent production of meaning and a reflection that perceives itself in the semblance of ontology. The reflective element is accentuated in the definition of despair: "Despair is the disrelation in the relation of a synthesis which relates itself to itself. But the synthesis is not the disrelation, it is merely the possibility, or, in other words, the possibility of the disrelation is latent in the synthesis. If the synthesis were the disrelation, there would be no such thing as despair, for despair would then be something inherent in human nature as such, that is, it would not be despair."[41] The disrelation with regard to the synthetic relation can occur as despair only in reflection; without reflection, there can be no "disrelation" in a relation, for a disrelation may only be measured by some further reflected relation. This corresponds to Kierkegaard's resistance to making despair a category of nature in the immediateness of the "relation." But Kierkegaard's portrayal of despair, if despair were identical with "synthesis" as mere immediacy, is to be literally applied to the definition of the self relating relation itself. It becomes "duplication" simply because, in contrast to reflective semblance, the contradiction between ontological transparentness and mythical self-positing could not be mollified. The unity that produces the relation pulls Kierkegaard's self back into the same nature that transparentness vis-à-vis the positing power was to have purged from it. The dialectic of nature and the supranatural proceeds from natural spirit as from their unity; the dialectic does not attain transparentness, and it must constantly begin anew. Therefore the domineering role of "duplication" and "repetition" not only provides the title of a work, but essentially constitutes the image of the *intérieur*. Caught in the circle of natural life, repetition remains mythic and invocational even when Kierkegaard lays claim to it as an "existential" form of correct life. Repetition turns in circles in the mythical center of his philosophy, in the "relation to relation," which is how he defines the self. If Kierkegaard communicates with Nietzsche anywhere more deeply than is vaguely supposed, it is here: the "image of eternity modeled on endless repetition,"[42] which Bloch has shown Nietzsche's eternal return to be, is also the image of what is eternal in the person around which the concepts of Kierkegaard's doctrine of existence collect themselves in vain.

Objective Despair

The mythical essence of existence breaks loose in Kierkegaard's doctrine of despair. The doctrine anticipates the criticism of the concept of existence: "In order to will in despair to be oneself there must be consciousness of the infinite self. This infinite self, however, is really only the abstractest form, the abstractest possibility of the self, and it is this self the individual despairingly wills to be by detaching the self from every relation to the power which posited it, or detaching it from the conception that there is such a power in existence. By the aid of this infinite form the self despairingly wills to preside freely over itself or to create itself."[43] For Kierkegaard, the central insight transforms itself into a delusion where it should become fruitful for the interpretation of the self; if the self sacrifices its claim to autonomy, in return it succumbs to blind devotion to its fateful essence that it itself earlier produced in blind defiance; in Kierkegaard only the despairing undertakes "to refashion the whole thing, in order to get out of it in this way a self such as he wants to have, produced by the aid of the infinite form of the negative self—and it is thus he wills to be himself."[44] Every escape from the entanglement

of the encircling concepts is blocked to "existence." All Kierkegaardian existence is in truth despair, and this is the single source of the power of the tenets of *The Sickness unto Death.* Hope has no place in "existence," and the Christian paradox is not bestowed as a miracle of faith on a universal, existential "religiosity A," but despairingly demanded of it. No theology has ever conceived the idea of hope for a "relation," or for the indeterminate substratum of the relation, but solely as hope for the mortal creature. Kierkegaard's explication of existence, however, fractures the creature by deceptively exalting it into transcendence as "spirit." Kierkegaard makes the apersonality of "existence" evident in despair. Indeed, despair is to serve as the counterconcept to existence. But the origin of the distinction is not for him the apersonality of despair but the refusal of the "relation" to be itself. Its apersonality is averted only by the indeterminate substratum of the self. If "reflection"—which as "transparentness" was to open the existential relation to "meaning"—was semblance, this semblance disappears in the doctrine of despair and nothing is able to prevent the fall from existence. For despair is objective for Kierkegaard and independent of all self-knowledge. Kierkegaard accepts as certain "that one form of despair is precisely this of not being in despair, that is, not being aware of it."[45] The self is thereby surrendered to nature; every illumination has lost its power over it; and nothing remains but an apersonal "relation" from which the comfort of the mirror—the "self which relates to itself"—has been withdrawn. The last word of the existential dialectic is death; and Heidegger had good reason to interpret Kierkegaardian existence as "being toward death," however Kierkegaard may have rejected such being as despair. "If in the strictest sense we are to speak of a sickness unto death, it must be one in which the last thing is death, and death the last thing. And this precisely is despair."[46] But it is also "existence." If death is the last word of imageless conjuration, it is also its exemplary image. In despair the primeval figures of existential repetition flash up demonically: Sisyphus and Tantalus as the bearers of the myths of repetition. In death a realm of imagery silently reveals itself: the image of timeless hopelessness in abject, endless, fallen nature. It is the inability to die as negative eternity: "On the contrary, the torment of despair is precisely this, not to be able to die. So it has much in common with the situation of the moribund when he lies and struggles with death, and cannot die. So to be sick unto death is, not to be able to die—yet not as though there were hope of life; no, the hopelessness in this case is that even the last hope, death, is not available. When death is the greatest danger, one hopes for life; but when one has become acquainted with an even more dreadful danger, one hopes for death."[47] In the most extreme depths of the existential dialectic, in the impersonality of despair in which the mere spirit of the existing individual finally sinks through the vortex of an ever-circling repetition,

Kierkegaard's subjectivism hits bottom. Certainly, it lands where he least expected: not in ontological meaning, but in eternal meaninglessness. Under a thin, deceptive covering Kierkegaard's doctrine of existence conceals the ontology of hell: "It is in this last sense that despair is the sickness unto death, this agonizing contradiction, this sickness in the self, everlastingly to die, to die and yet not to die, to die the death. For dying means that it is all over, but dying the death means to live to experience death; and if for a single instant this experience is possible, it is tantamount to experiencing it forever. If one might die of despair as one dies of a sickness, then the eternal in him, the self, must be capable of dying in the same sense that the body dies of sickness. But his is an impossibility; the dying of despair transforms itself constantly into a living. The despairing man cannot die; no more than 'the dagger can slay thoughts' can despair consume the eternal thing, the self, which is the ground of despair, whose worm dieth not, and whose fire is not quenched."[48] Thus the explicit description of the punishment of hell, of whose eternity he approvingly speaks,[49] is developed not from Christian dogmatics but directly from the philosophy of existence and its idealistic core. Only the image of hell, however, pulls the person out of the enchantment of his hopeless immanence; and it does so by shattering him.

Reversal of the Existential Dialectic

"But to reach truth one must pierce through every negativity. For there applies what the fairy-tale recounts about a certain enchantment: the piece of music must be played through backwards; otherwise the enchantment is not broken."[50] If the self, the productive unity of the "relation which relates itself to its own self," blocks transparentness in illusory reflection and circling repetition, its power dwindles in the face of the manifest images of the demonic. The demonic cancels the autonomy of the self along with its dynamic configuration. This is ultimately revealed as more than mere mythical obdurateness toward being transparent; it turns out to be the desperate resistance of nature to its dissolution and dismemberment. As "relation," the self is to be secure from the insanity that unrelentingly threatens its disparate elements. Thus the dialectical double meaning of the abstract choice of self: it demands that the immanently imprisoned individual not fall altogether to the mercy of mythical dissociation from which the autonomous act ultimately protects it: "Can you imagine a more horrible end than your nature actually being dissolved? that the potentialities in you with which you now toy might one day toy with you? that you . . . would become a play-ground for a legion of demons? and be deprived of the inmost and holiest thing of all in a man, the unifying power of personality."[51] This is how hell appears to the subject that has been pulled down into its depths; the subject may climb out of it to the extent that the semblance of its self-posited essence

is volatized before the actuality of that being that has its source in the collapse of the subject's false, immanent unity. The self that approaches such regions is still mythical. Its faith remains profoundly bound to the "will," as to the mythical figure of idealism. In Kierkegaard's characterization of the "Christian" and "Socratic," sinfulness and willfulness are bound together: "But where does the difficulty lie? It is to be ascribed to a fact of which the Socratic view itself was aware (though only to a certain degree) and sought to remedy, that it lacks a dialectical determinant for the transition from having understood something to the doing of it. In this transition Christianity makes its start; by proceeding along this path it proves that sin lies in the will thus attaining the concept of defiance; and then, in order to make the end thoroughly fast, it adjoins to this the dogma of original sin."[52] If, however, it is the will that incurred sin, it is not able to wipe it out: just as in the fairy tale, so in the transformation of myths; wishes do not permit themselves to be arbitrarily revoked. Sins originating in the autonomous will may not—according to Kierkegaard—be wished away by that same will: "To wish to have it that sin might never have come into the world"—and according to *The Sickness unto Death* sin is precisely despair—"reduces mankind to a more imperfect stage. Sin has entered in, but when the individuals have humbled themselves under it they stand higher than they stood before."[53] Whereas the self thus entrenches itself in its immanence through the freedom to sin in order to escape mythical collapse, it is driven precisely toward this: toward the state of despair, toward total sinfulness. Despair dissociates the self, and the ruins of the shattered self are the marks of hope. In Kierkegaard's work, this remains the innermost (and hence from Kierkegaard hidden) dialectical truth, which could only be disclosed in the posthumous history of his work. It justifies the puzzling phrase—nowhere explicated in his writings—found in the preface to *The Sickness unto Death,* that "in this whole book, as the title indeed says, despair is conceived as the sickness, not as the cure. So dialectical is despair,"[54] reversing into a remedy for the spiritual body as soon as it breaks through the "continuity of sin,"[55] the continuity of the autonomous will. In objective despair, in the ontology of hell, Kierkegaard's philosophy renders the true image of man: shattered, separated, and condemned; no longer in the twilight of freedom and nature but explicitly in the name of judgment and grace. In the idea of judgment, not in that of the autonomy of human spirit, Kierkegaard's concept of the individual is rescued, who—unjudged—would fall to mythology: "What, a judgment! Why, we men have learned, indeed experience teaches, that when there is a mutiny aboard ship or in an army, the guilty are so numerous that the punishment cannot be applied; and when it is a question of the public, 'the highly respected cultured public,' the people, then not only is there no crime, but, according to the newspapers, upon which one can rely as upon the Gospel or divine revelation, this is the will of God. Why is this? The reason for it is that the concept of judgment corresponds to the individual, one does not pronounce a judgment *en masse;* one can put the people to death *en masse,* play the hose on them *en masse,* flatter them *en masse,* in brief can treat the people in many ways like beasts, but to hold judgment over the people as beasts one cannot do, for one cannot hold judgment over beasts; even though ever so many are judged, if there is to be any seriousness and truth in the judgment, it is each individual who is judged. Lo, for this reason God is 'the Judge' because before him there is no crowd but only individuals. . . . Yes, doubtless they are secured if it was only in eternity they became individuals. But they were and are before God constantly individuals."[56] Kierkegaard's "transparentness" would have its time and place in the light of the final judgment. Nature, which as existing, despairing nature perishes, would here, after damnation and reconciliation, become pellucid. In the world of experience, however, that is concrete onto which a trace of this light once falls. To describe the course of concretion through Kierkegaard's mythical-abstract realm amounts to the surveyal of the extensive organization of a system that is intertwined in itself intensively as existence.

Notes

[1] Martin Heidegger, *Being and Time,* trans. John Macquarrie and Edward Robinson (New York: Harper and Row, 1962), 31. (On the translation of *Dasein* and *Existenz,* see the Foreword.)

[2] Ibid., 34.

[3] III, 200.

[4] Cf., 430-31.

[5] Heidegger, *Being and Time,* 32.

[6] VII, 176-77.

[7] Ibid., 176.

[8] Ibid., 173.

[9] Ibid., 176.

[10] Ibid., 172.

[11] Ibid., 181.

[12] Ibid., 182.

[13] Ibid., 178.

[14] Ibid., 177.

[15] Romano Guardini, "Der Ausgangspunkt der Denkbewegung Søren Kierkegaards." in *Hochland* 24 (1926/27) (no. 7; April 1927), 17.

[16] Ibid.

[17] Ibid.

[18] V, 127.

[19] II, 263.

[20] V, 77-78.

[21] Edmund Husserl, *Ideas,* trans. W. R. Boyce Gibbons (New York.: Collier, 1931), 337.

[22] VII, 196.

[23] Ibid.

[24] V, 141.

[25] Ibid., 143.

[26] II, 225.

[27] V, 149.

[28] Ibid., 150.

[29] Ibid., 151.

[30] Ibid.

[31] Ibid.

[32] VII, 75-76.

[33] II, 226.

[34] Guardini, "Der Ausgangspunkt der Denkbewegung Søren Kierkegaards," 23.

[35] VIII, 146.

[36] Cf. this volume, p. 58.

[37] VIII, 146.

[38] IX, 159-60.

[39] V, 55.

[40] VIII, 147.

[41] Ibid., 148.

[42] Ernst Bloch, *Durch die Wueste,* Kritische Essays (Berlin, 1923), 110.

[43] VIII, 201.

[44] Ibid., 202.

[45] Ibid., 156.

[46] Ibid., 150.

[47] Ibid., 150-51.

[48] Ibid., 151.

[49] Cf. ibid., 211, VI, 80.

[50] VIII, 177.

[51] II, 164.

[52] VIII, 224.

[53] II, 94.

[54] VIII, 143.

[55] Ibid., 236.

[56] Ibid., 253-55.

Jean-Paul Sartre (essay date 1972)

SOURCE: "Kierkegaard: The Singular Universal," in *Between Existentialism and Marxism,* 1972, reprinted in *Modern Critical Views: Søren Kierkegaard,* edited by Harold Bloom, Chelsea House, 1989, pp. 75-98.

[*In the following essay, Sartre appraises Kierkegaard's work, commenting in particular on Kierkegaard's views on history and subjectivity. Sartre also examines the way Kierkegaard was influenced by his environment and notes the relevance of Christian dogma to Kierkegaard's thought.*]

The title of our colloquium is "The Living Kierkegaard." It has the merit of plunging us to the very heart of *paradox,* and Søren himself would have appreciated this. For if we had gathered here today to discuss Heidegger, for example, no one would have dreamed of entitling our debate "The Living Heidegger." The living Kierkegaard, in other words, turns out to mean "the dead Kierkegaard." But not just this. It means that for us he exists, that he forms the object of our discussions, that he was an instrument of our thought. But, from this point of view, one could use the same expression to designate anyone who became part of our culture after he died. One could say, for example, "The Living Arcimboldo," since

surrealism has allowed us to reappropriate this painter and cast him in a new light; but this would amount to making an *object* of him within what Kierkegaard called the *world-historical.* But, precisely, if Søren is in our eyes a sort of radioactive object, of whatever potency and virulence, then he can no longer be this living being whose subjectivity necessarily appears—in so far as it is lived—as other than what we know of it. In short, he sinks into death. The abolition of the subjective in a subject of History—the reduction of one who was an agent to an object—is an explosive historical scandal in the case of all who disappear from amongst us. History is full of holes. But nowhere is this more obvious than in the case of the "knight of subjectivity." Kierkegaard was a man who set out to pose the problem of the historical absolute, who emphasized the scandalous paradox of the appearance and disappearance of this absolute in the course of History. If we cannot revive this martyr of interiority other than in the form of an object of knowledge, a determination of his *praxis* will forever escape us: his living effort to elude knowledge through reflective life, his claim to be, in his very singularity and at the heart of his finitude, the absolute subject, defined in interiority by his absolute relationship with being. In other words, if death is historically no more than the passage of an interior to exteriority, then the title "The Living Kierkegaard" cannot be justified.

If we retain something of this life which, in its time and place, removed all traces of itself, then Kierkegaard himself is the scandal and the paradox. Unable to be understood as anything other than this immanence which for forty years never stopped designating *itself* as such, either he eludes us forever and the world rid itself, in 1856, of *nothing;* or else the paradox exposed by this dead man is that a historical being, beyond his own abolition, can still communicate as a non-object, as an absolute subject, with succeeding generations. What will attract our attention then will not be the religious problem of Christ incarnate nor the metaphysical problem of death, but the strictly historical paradox of survival: we shall plumb our knowledge of Kierkegaard in order to locate what in a dead man eludes knowledge and survives *for us* beyond his destruction. We shall ask ourselves whether the presence, that is the subjectivity of someone else, always inaccessible to cognition in its strict sense, can nevertheless be given to us by some other means. Either History closes back over our knowledge of this death, or the historical survival of the subjective ought to change our conception of History. In other words either Kierkegaard today, 24 April 1964, is dissolved by the enzymes of knowledge or he persists in demonstrating to us the still virulent scandal of what one might call the transhistoricity of a historical man.

He posed the fundamental question in these terms: "Can History act as the point of departure for an eternal certitude? Can one find in such a point of departure anything other than an historical interest? Can one base eternal happiness on a merely historical knowledge?"

And of course what he has in mind here is the scandalous paradox of the birth and death of God, of the historicity of Jesus. But we must go further; for if the answer is yes, then this transhistoricity belongs to Søren, Jesus' witness, just as much as to Jesus himself; and to us as well, Søren's grand-nephews. As he says himself, we are all contemporaries. In a sense, this is to explode History. Yet History exists and it is man who makes it. Thus posteriority and contemporaneity mutually imply and contradict each other. For the moment we cannot proceed further. We must go back to Kierkegaard and question him as a privileged witness. Why privileged? I am thinking of the Cartesian proof of the existence of God through the fact that *I exist with the idea of God.* Kierkegaard is a singular witness—or, as he says, the Exception—by virtue of a *redoubling* in himself of the subjective attitude: in our eyes he is an object of knowledge in so far as he is a subjective witness of his own subjectivity, that is to say, in so far as he is an existent announcer of existence by virtue of his own existential attitude. Thus he becomes both object and subject of our study. We should take this subject-object in so far as it demonstrates a historical paradox that transcends it; we shall question its testimony in so far in its historicity—he said such-and-such on such-and-such a date—transcends itself and makes the paradox of the object-subject burst within History. By integrating *his* words into our language, in translating him with *our* words, will the limits of knowledge be revealed? And by virtue of a paradoxical reversal of meaning, will this knowledge point to the signifier as its silent foundation?

In principle everything about him can be *known (connu).* Doubtless he kept his secrets well. But one can press him hard and extract statements from him and interpret them. The problem can now be formulated: when everything is *known (su)* about the life of a man who refuses to be an object of knowledge and whose originality rests precisely in this refusal, is there an irreducible beyond this? How are we to seize it and think it? The question has two sides to it—prospective and retrospective. One can ask what it means to have lived when all the determinations of a life are *known.* But one can also ask what it means to live when the essential core of these determinations has been foreseen? For the singularity of the Kierkegaardian adventure is that, as it unfolded, it revealed itself to itself as known in advance. Thus it lived within and in spite of knowledge. It must be borne in mind that this opposition between foreseen and lived experience was made manifest around 1850 in the opposition between Hegel and Kierkegaard. Hegel had gone, but his system lived on. Søren, whatever he did, acted within the limits of what Hegel had called the unhappy consciousness—that is to say he could only realize the complex dialectic of the finite and the infinite. He would never be able to surpass it. Kierkegaard

knew that he already had his place within the system. He was familiar with Hegel's thought, and he was aware of the interpretation it conferred *in advance* on the movements of his life. He was trapped and held in the beam of the Hegelian projector; he either had to vanish into objective knowledge or demonstrate his irreducibility. But, precisely, Hegel was dead and this death pronounced his knowledge as dead knowledge, or as knowledge of death. While Kierkegaard showed by the simple fact of his life that all knowledge concerning the subjective is in a certain sense false knowledge. Foreseen by the system, he disqualified its legitimacy by not appearing *in it* as a moment to be surpassed and at the site assigned to him by the master, but on the contrary, emerging quite simply as a survivor of the system and its prophet, as one who, despite the dead determinations of an anterior prophecy, had to live this foreseen life as if it were indeterminate at the outset and as if its determinations had arisen of their own accord within free "non-knowledge."

The new aspect of the problematic that Kierkegaard reveals to us is the fact that in his personal life he did not contradict the content of knowledge but illegitimized knowledge of any content. By negating the concept through the very fashion in which he realized its prescriptions in another dimension, he was traversed through and through by the light of knowledge—for others and also for himself, as he was acquainted with Hegelianism—but at the same time remained utterly opaque. In other words, this pre-existent knowledge revealed a being at the heart of future existence. Thirty years ago, the contradictions of colonialism constituted, in the eyes of the generation of colonized born into it, a being of misery, anger, blood, revolt and struggle; a few amongst the best-informed of the oppressed and of the colonialists themselves were aware of this. Or to take a quite different example, a vacancy created high up or low down on the social scale creates a destiny, that is to say a future but foreseeable being for the person who will fill it, even though this destiny remains for each candidate, if there is more than one, no more than a *possible being.* Or, in the narrow particularity of private life, the structures of a specific family (seen as a local example of an institution produced by the movement of History) permit the psychoanalyst, in theory at least, to foresee the future destiny (to be lived and undergone) that will be a particular neurosis for a child born into this milieu. Kierkegaard *foreseen* by Hegel is but a privileged example of such ontological determinations which pre-date birth and allow themselves to be *conceptualized.*

Søren identified with the problem because he was conscious of it. He knew that Hegel, in pointing to him as a moment of universal History vainly posed for itself, attained him in the being which he suffered as a schema to be accomplished in the course of his life, and which he called his Untruth, or the error that he was at the start of his life, as a truncated determination. But this was the point: Hegel's designation attained him like the light from a dead star. The untruth *had to be lived;* it too belonged to his subjective subjectivity. And so he could write, in the **Fragments:** "My own Untruth is something I can discover only by myself, since it is only when I have discovered it that it is discovered, even if the whole world knew of it before." But when it is discovered, my Untruth becomes, at least in the immediate, my Truth. So subjective truth exists. It is not knowledge (*savoir*) but self-determination; it can be defined neither as an extrinsic relation of knowledge (*connaissance*) to being, nor as the internal imprint of a correspondence, nor as the indissoluble unity of a system. "Truth," he said, "is the act of freedom." I would not know how to *be* my own Truth even if its premises were given in me in advance: to reveal it means to produce it or to produce myself as I am; to be for myself what I have to be.

What Kierkegaard highlighted was the fact that the opposition between non-knowledge and knowledge is an opposition between two ontological structures. The subjective has to be what it is—a singular realization of each singularity. One would have to go to Freud for the most illuminating commentary on this remark. In fact psychoanalysis is not knowledge nor does it claim to be, save when it hazards hypotheses on the dead and thus allows death to make it a science of death. It is a movement, an internal labour, that at one and the same time uncovers a neurosis and gradually makes the subject capable of supporting it. With the result that at the term (actually an ideal) of this process, there is a correspondence between the being that has developed and the truth it once was. The truth in this case is the unity of the conquest and the object conquered. It transforms without teaching anything and does not appear until the end of a transformation. It is a non-knowledge, an effectivity, a placing in perspective that is present to itself in so far as it is realized. Kierkegaard would add that it is a decision of authenticity: the rejection of flight and the will to return to oneself. In this sense *knowledge* cannot register this obscure and inflexible *movement* by which scattered determinations are elevated to the status of being and are gathered together into a tension which confers on them not a signification but a synthetic meaning: what happens is that the ontological structure of subjectivity escapes to the extent that the subjective being is, as Heidegger has put it so well, in question in its being, to the extent that it never *is* except in the mode of having to be its being.

From this point of view, the moment of subjective truth is a temporalized but transhistorical absolute. And subjectivity is temporalization itself: it is *what happens to me,* what cannot be but in happening. It is myself in so far as I can only be a random birth—and, as Merleau-Ponty said, in so far as I must, no matter how short my life, *at least* experience the occurrence of death; but it is also myself in so far as I try to regain control of my own adventure by assuming—we shall come back to this point—its original contingency in order to establish it in necessity. In short, in so far as *I* happen to myself. Dealt with in advance by Hegel, subjectivity becomes a moment of the objective spirit, a determination of culture. But if nothing of lived experience can elude knowledge, its *reality* remains irreducible. In this sense, lived experience as concrete reality is posed as *non-knowledge.* But this negation of knowledge implies the affirmation of itself. Lived experience recognizes itself as a projection into the milieu of meaning, but at the same time it fails to recognize itself there since, in this milieu, an ensemble is constituted which aims randomly at objects and since, precisely, it is itself not an object. Doubtless, one of the principal concerns of the nineteenth century was to distinguish the being of an object from one's knowledge of it, in other words to reject idealism. Marx attacked Hegel not so much for his point of departure, as his reduction of being to knowledge. But for Kierkegaard, as for ourselves today when we consider the Kierkegaardian scandal, the question is one of a certain ontological region in which being claims at once to elude knowledge and to attain itself. Waelhens has rightly written: "With the advent of Kierkegaard, Nietzsche and Bergson, philosophy ceased to be *explanation at a distance,* and claimed to be henceforth *at one* with experience itself; it was no longer content to throw light on man and his life, but aspired to become this life in its full consciousness of itself. It seemed that for the philosopher this ambition involved an obligation to renounce the ideal of philosophy as a rigorous science, since the basis of this ideal was inseparable from the idea of a detached . . . spectator."

In short, the determinations of lived experience are not simply heterogeneous to knowledge, as the existence of thalers was heterogeneous for Kant to the concept of thaler and to the judgement that combined the two. It is the very way in which these determinations attain themselves in the redoubling of their presence to themselves that reduces knowledge to the pure abstraction of the concept and, in the first moment at least (the only one Kierkegaard described) turns an object-subjectivity into an objective *nothing* in relation to a subjective subjectivity. Knowledge (*savoir*) itself has a being; bodies of knowledge (*connaissances*) are realities. For Kierkegaard, even in his lifetime, the being of knowledge was obviously radically heterogeneous to that of the living subject. Thus we can designate the determinations of existence with words. But *either* this designation is nothing but a place-marker, a set of references without conceptualization, *or else* the ontological structure of the concept and of its links—i.e. objective being, being in exteriority—is such that these references, grasped as notions, cannot but yield a false knowledge when they present themselves as insights into being in interiority.

In his life, Kierkegaard lived this paradox in passion: he desperately wanted to designate himself as a transhistorical absolute. In humour and in irony, he revealed himself and concealed himself at the same time. He did not refuse to communicate, but simply held on to his *secrecy* in the act of communication. His mania for pseudonyms was a systematic disqualification of *proper names:* even to *assign* him as an individual before the tribunal of others, a welter of mutually contradictory appellations was necessary. The more he becomes Climacus or Virgelin Hufnensis, the less he is *Kierkegaard,* this Danish citizen, this entry in the registers of the civil authorities.

This was all very well so long as he was alive: by his life he gave the lie to a dead man's predictions which were a knowledge of death. That is to say he ceaselessly fabricated himself by writing. But on the 11th of November 1855 he died, and the paradox turned against him without ceasing to be scandalous *in our eyes.* The prophecy of a dead man condemning a living being to exist as an unhappy consciousness, and our knowledge of this living being once he has died, reveal their homogeneity. In fact in our own time Käte Nadler—to cite but one example—has applied to the late Kierkegaard the prediction of the late Hegel. A dialectical pair is formed, in which each term denounces the other: Hegel foresaw Kierkegaard in the past, as a superseded moment; Kierkegaard gave the lie to the internal organization of Hegel's system by showing that superseded moments are conserved, not only in the *Aufhebung* that maintains them as it transforms them, but in themselves, without any transformation whatever; and by proving that even if they arise anew, they create, merely through their appearance, an anti-dialectic. But, once Kierkegaard died, Hegel regained possession of him. Not *within the System,* which visibly crumbled in so far as it was a finished totality of Knowledge which, as a system, was subsequently totalized by the onward movement of History itself—but simply by virtue of the fact that the late Kierkegaard has become *in our eyes* homogeneous with the descriptions that Hegelian knowledge gives of him. The fact remains, of course, that he contested the whole system by appearing in a place that was not assigned to him: but since the system itself is an object of knowledge and as such is contested, this anachronism provides us with nothing really new. By contrast, the Knowledge that *we* have of him is knowledge of a dead man and thus knowledge of death; as such it rejoins the Hegelian intuition which produced and conceptualized a future death. In ontological terms, Kierkegaard's pre-natal being was homogeneous with his post-mortem being and his existence seemed merely to be a way of enriching the first so that it could equal the second: it was no more than a provisional *malaise,* an essential means of getting from one to the other, but, in itself, an inessential fever of being. The notion of the unhappy consciousness became Søren's insurpassable destiny as well as the generality enveloping our most

particularized items of knowledge concerning his dead life. Or if you like, to die meant to be restored to being and to become an object of knowledge. That at least is the recurrent lazy conception whose aim is to close a breach. Is it true? Should we say that death terminates the paradox by revealing that it is nothing more than a provisional appearance, or on the contrary, that it pushes it to the extreme and consequently, since we die, the whole of History becomes paradoxical—an insurmountable conflict between being and existence, between non-knowledge and knowledge? It was Kierkegaard's merit that he formulated this problem *in the very terms of his life.* Let us come back to him.

Let us note at the outset that between him and us, History has *taken place.* No doubt it is still going on. But its richness puts a distance, *an obscure density* between him and us. The unhappy consciousness will find other incarnations, and each of them will contest this consciousness by his life and confirm it by his death, but none of them will reproduce Kierkegaard by virtue of a kind of resurrection. Knowledge has its foundations in this instance in noncoincidence. The poet of faith left texts behind. These writings are dead unless we breathe our life into them; but if revived they bear the stamp of thoughts committed to paper long ago, somewhere else, with the means to hand—they only partially answer to our present requirements. Unbelievers will pronounce *the Kierkegaardian proof to be unconvincing.* Theologians, in the name of dogma itself, may declare themselves unsatisfied and find the attitude and declarations of the "poet of Christianity" insufficient and dangerous. They may reproach him in the name of his own admission, through the very title of *poet* that he gave himself, with not having got beyond what he himself called the "aesthetic stage." Atheists will *either*—a formula dear to him—reject any relationship with this absolute and opt firmly for a relativism, *or else* define the absolute in History *in other terms*—and regard Kierkegaard as the witness of a false absolute or a false witness of the absolute. Believers, on the other hand, will declare that the absolute Kierkegaard aimed at is certainly that which exists, but that the relation of historical man to transhistoricity which he tried to establish, was involuntarily deflected and lost by him in the night of atheism. In each case, his attempt is pronounced a *failure.*

There is more: the failure is *explained.* In different ways, it is true, but by convergent approximations. Mesnard, Bohlen, Chestov and Jean Wahl are all agreed in stressing the psychosomatic significance of the "thorn in the flesh." This means that, in the case of this dead man, lived experience itself is contested. Later conceptual judgement renders the life itself inauthentic. Kierkegaard lived out badly—in the sense of obscurely, disguisedly—determinations that we can perceive better than he. In short, in the eyes of historical knowledge, one lives to die. Existence is a mild surface ripple that is soon stilled in order to allow the dialectical development of concepts to appear; chronology dissolves into homogeneity and in the end, into timelessness. Every lived venture ends in failure for the simple reason that History continues.

But if life is a scandal, failure is even more scandalous. First we describe and denounce it by collections of words that aim at a certain object named Kierkegaard. In this sense the "poet of faith" is a signified—like this table, like a socio-economic process. And it is true that death first presents itself as the fall of the subject into the realm of absolute objectivity. But Kierkegaard in his writings—today inert or living with our life—proposes a usage of words that is the converse of this: what he seeks is a dialectical regression from signified and significations to signifier. He presents himself as a signifier, and at a stroke refers us back to our transhistoricity as signifiers. Should we reject this regression *a priori*? To do so is to constitute ourselves as relative—relative to History if we are unbelievers, relative to Dogmas and mediated by the Church if we believe. Now if such is the case, then everything should be relative, in us and in Kierkegaard himself, *except his failure.* For failure can be *explained* but not *resolved:* as non-being it possesses the absolute character of negation. In fact historical negation, even at the heart of a relativism, is an absolute. It would be a negative absolute to declare that at Waterloo *there were no* fighter planes. But this negative declaration remains a formality: as the two adversaries were equally without air power and were both incapable of missing it, this ineffectual absence is no more than a formal proposition devoid of interest, that merely registers the *temporal distance* from Waterloo to the present. There are, however, other negative absolutes and these are concrete: it is correct to state that Grouchy's army *did not* link up with the Emperor; and this negation is historical in the sense that it reflects the frustrated expectation of the head of an army, and the fear turned to satisfaction of the enemy. It is effective in the sense that Grouchy's delay in all probability *settled* the outcome of the battle. It is thus an absolute, an irreducible but a concrete absolute. Similarly in the case of the failure: the fact that an ambition is not realised in objectivity means that it returns to subjectivity. Or, more precisely, the interpretations of such a failure aim via moderate negations (he didn't consider . . . , he couldn't be aware at the time, etc.) to reduce it *to the positive,* to erase it before the affirmative reality of the Other's victory, whatever it may be.

But at once this relative positivity slips back and reveals what no knowledge could ever transmit directly (because no historical advance could recuperate it): failure lived in despair. Those who died of anguish, of hunger, of exhaustion, those defeated in the past by force of arms, are so many gaps in our knowledge in so far as they existed: subjectivity constitutes *nothing* for objective knowledge since it is a non-knowledge, and yet failure demonstrates that it has an absolute

existence. In this way Søren Kierkegaard, conquered by death and recuperated by historical knowledge, triumphs at the very moment he fails, by demonstrating that History cannot recover him. As a dead man, he remains the insurpassable scandal of subjectivity; though he may be known through and through, he eludes History by the very fact that it is History that constitutes his defeat and that he lived it in anticipation. In short, he eludes History because he is historical.

Can we go further? Or must we simply conclude that death irrevocably filches the agents of past History from the historian? Here it is necessary to question *what remains* of Kierkegaard, his verbal remnants. For he constituted himself in his historicity as an absolute contesting the historical knowledge that would penetrate him after his death. But the kind of interrogation with which we are concerned is of a particular type: it is a paradox itself. Kant situated himself in the realm of cognition in order to test the validity of our knowledges. We, the living, can approach him through the realm of cognition, question his words with words, and cross-examine him on concepts. But Kierkegaard stole language from knowledge in order to use it against knowledge. If we approach him, as we are compelled to do, through the realm of cognition, our words encounter his and are disqualified by disqualifying them. The fact is that his use of the Word and our own are heterogeneous. Thus the message of this dead man is scandalous through the very fact of its existence, since we are incapable of considering this residue of a life as a determination of knowledge. On the contrary, the paradox reappears since his thought expressed in words constitutes itself within knowledge as irreducible non-knowledge. Our interrogation must then either disappear without trace, or be transformed and itself become non-knowledge questioning non-knowledge. That is to say, the questioner is called into question in his very being by the questioned. Such is the fundamental virtue of the pseudo-object called the works of Kierkegaard. But let us push our examination to the very moment of this metamorphosis.

This philosopher was an anti-philosopher. Why did he reject the Hegelian system and, in a general way, the whole of philosophy? Because, he says, the philosopher seeks a first beginning. But why, one may ask, did he who rejected beginnings take as his point of departure the Christian dogmas? For to accept them *a priori* without even testing their validity is tantamount to making them the uncontested principles of thought. Is there not a contradiction here? Did not Kierkegaard, having failed to establish a solid beginning himself, take the beginning of others as the origin and foundation of his thought? And as he failed to test it through criticism, and as he neglected to doubt it to the point where it could no longer be doubted, did it not retain for him, even in his most intimate thought, its character of otherness?

This is, indeed, the unfair question that knowledge puts to existence. But, in Kierkegaard's pen, existence replies by rejecting knowledge's case. To deny dogma, it says, is to be mad and to proclaim the fact. But to prove dogma is to be an imbecile: while time is wasted proving that the soul is immortal, living belief in immortality withers away. At the absurd limit of this logic, the day would come when immortality was finally proved irrefutably—except that no one would believe in it any more. There is no way we could better understand that immortality, even if proven, could never be an object of knowledge: it is a particular absolute relationship between immanence and transcendence that can only be constituted in and through lived experience. And of course this is sufficient for believers. But for the non-believer that I am, what this means is that the real relation of man to his being can only be lived, in History, as a transhistorical relationship.

Kierkegaard replies to our question by rejecting philosophy or rather by radically changing its end and aims. To seek the beginning of knowledge is to affirm that the foundation of temporality is, precisely, timeless, and that the historical individual can wrench himself free of History, de-situate himself and relocate his fundamental timelessness by a direct vision of being. Temporality becomes the means of intemporality. Naturally Hegel was aware of the problem since he placed philosophy at the end of History, as truth-that-has-come-into-being and retrospective knowledge. But this is the point: History is never finished, so this atemporal reconstitution of temporality, understood as the unity of the logical and the tragic, becomes in turn an object of knowledge. From this point of view, there is no being at all at the beginning of Hegel's system, but only the person of Hegel, such as it had been fashioned, such as it had fashioned itself. This is the sort of ambiguous discovery that can lead, from the point of view of knowledge, only to scepticism.

To avoid this, Kierkegaard took as his point of departure the *person* envisaged as non-knowledge, that is to say in as much as he both produces and discovers, at a given moment in the temporal unfolding of his life, his relation to an absolute which is itself inserted in History. In short, far from denying the beginning, Kierkegaard testified to a beginning that is lived.

How is it possible that, in the context of History, this historical situation does not contest the claim of the thinker to have disclosed the absolute? How can a thought *that has appeared* testify on its own behalf after its *disappearance?* This is the problem Kierkegaard set himself in the **Philosophical Fragments.** Of course, this paradox was first and foremost a religious one. What was at stake was the appearance and disappearance of Jesus. Or equally, the transformation of one sin—Adam's—into original and hereditary sin. But it was just as much the personal problem of Kierkegaard the thinker: how could he establish the transhistorical

validity of a thought that had been produced within History and would disappear into it? The answer lay in "reduplication": the insurpassable cannot be knowledge, but must be the establishment in History of an absolute and non-contemplative relation with the absolute that has been realized in History. Rather than knowledge dissolving the thinker, it is the thinker who testifies on behalf of his own thought. But these ideas are obscure and can appear to be merely a verbal solution so long as one has not understood that they proceed from a novel conception of thought.

The beginning of the thinker's existence is analogous to a birth. This is not a rejection but a displacement of the beginning. Before birth there was non-being; then comes the leap, and the moment they are born to themselves, the child and the thinker find themselves immediately situated within a certain historical world that has produced them. They discover themselves as a particular adventure, whose point of departure is a set of socio-economic, cultural, moral, religious and other relations, which proceeds with whatever means are to hand, that is to say within the limits of these relations, and which gradually becomes inscribed in the same set. The beginning is reflective—I saw and touched the world, and so see and touch myself, this self who touches and sees the surrounding things; in this way I discover myself as a finite being, one that these same objects I touched and saw condition invisibly in my very sense of touch and sight. As against the constant and non-human beginning that Hegel postulated, Kierkegaard proposed a start that is in flux, that is conditioned and is conditioning, whose foundation approximates to what Merleau-Ponty called *envelopment.* We are enveloped: being is behind us and in front of us. He-who-sees is visible, and sees only by virtue of his visibility. "My body," said Merleau-Ponty, "is caught in the fabric of the world, but the world is made from the stuff of my body." Kierkegaard knew he was enveloped: he saw Christianity and in particular the Christian community in Denmark with the eyes that this community had given him. This is a new paradox: I see the being that fashioned me. I see it as it *is* or as it made me. "Overview thought" has an easy solution to this: having no qualities, the understanding grasps the objective essence without its own nature imposing particular deviations on it. Idealist relativism has an equally simple solution: the object fades away; what I see, being the effect of causes modifying my vision, contains no more than what these latter determine me to be. In each case, being is reduced to knowledge.

Kierkegaard rejects both solutions. The paradox, for him, is the fact that we discover the absolute in the relative. Kierkegaard was a Dane, born at the beginning of the last century into a Danish family, and conditioned by Danish history and culture. He came across other Danes as his contemporaries, people who were formed by the same History and cultural traditions. And at the same time, moreover, he could *think* the historical traditions and circumstances that had produced them all and produced himself. Was there either deviation or appropriation? Both. If objectivity has to be unconditioned knowledge, then there can be no true objectivity: to see one's surroundings, in this instance, would be to see without seeing, to touch without touching, to possess in oneself an *a priori* intuition of the other and, at the same time, to grasp him on the basis of common presuppositions that can never wholly be uncovered. Even in broad daylight my neighbour is dark and impenetrable, separated from me by his apparent resemblances; and yet I sense him in his underlying reality when I penetrate deeper into my own inner reality and attain its transcendental conditions. Later, much later, the presuppositions inscribed in things will be correctly deciphered by the historian. But at this level, the mutual comprehension that takes the existence of a communal envelopment for granted will have disappeared. In short, contemporaries understand each other without knowing each other, whereas the future historian will know them but his greatest difficulty—a difficulty bordering on the impossible—will be to understand them as they understood each other.

In fact—and Kierkegaard was aware of this—the experience which turns back upon itself, after the leap, comprehends itself more than it knows itself. In other words, it sustains itself in the milieu of the presuppositions that are its foundation, without succeeding in elucidating them. Hence a beginning that is a dogma. A particular religion produced Kierkegaard: he could not pretend to emancipate himself from it so that he could rise above it and see it as historically constituted. Note however that other Danes, from the same society, from the same class, became non-believers: but even they could do nothing to prevent their irreligion questioning or challenging *these* dogmas, this particular Christianity which had produced them—and hence their past, their religious childhood and finally themselves. Thus whatever they did, they remained wedded to their faith and their dogmas while vainly attempting to negate them by using other words to express their demand for an absolute. Their atheism was in fact a Christian *pseudo-atheism*. As it happens, one's envelopment determines the limits within which real modifications are possible. There are times when disbelief can only be verbal. Kierkegaard doubted as a youth, and hence was more consequential than these "free-thinkers": he recognized that his thought was not free and that whatever he might do or wherever he might go his religious determinations would follow him. If in spite of himself he saw Christian dogmas as irreducible, then it was perfectly legitimate for him to locate the beginning of his thought at the moment when it retraced its steps to them to get at its roots. Such a thought was doubly embedded in history: it grasped its envelopment as a conjuncture, and it defined itself as an identity between the beginning of thought and thought of the beginning.

If such was the case, what then was to become of the universality of historical determinations? Must we deny in absolute terms that there is any social sphere, with structures, pressures and developments of its own? Not at all. We shall see that Kierkegaard testified to a double universality. The revolution consisted in the fact that historical man, by his anchorage, turned this universality into a particular situation and this common necessity into an irreducible contingency. In other words, far from this particular attitude being, as in Hegel, a dialectical incarnation of the universal moment, the anchorage of the individual made this universal into an irreducible singularity. Did not Søren say to Levin one day: "How lucky you are to be a Jew: you escape Christianity. If I had been protected by your faith, I would have enjoyed a quite different life"? This was an ambiguous remark, for he often reproached Jews with being inaccessible to religious experience. There could be no doubt that dogma was truth, and the Christian who was not religious remained inauthentic, outside himself, lost. But there was a sort of humble birthright which meant, in the case of a Jew, a Moslem or a Buddhist, that the chance occurrence of their birth in one place rather than another was transformed into a statute. Conversely, Kierkegaard's deepest reality, the fabric of his being, his torment and his law appeared to him in the very heart of their necessity as the accidental outcome of his facticity. Again this contingency was common to all members of his society. He came across others which belonged only to him. In 1846 he wrote: "To believe is to lighten oneself by assuming a considerable weight; to be objective is to lighten oneself by casting off burdens . . . Lightness is an infinite weight, and its altitude the effect of an infinite weight." He was clearly alluding to what he called elsewhere the "thorn in the flesh." Here we are confronted with pure contingency, the singularity of his conditionings. Søren's unhappy consciousness was the product of random determinations which Hegelian rationalism did not take into account: a gloomy father who was convinced that he would be struck by a divine curse on his children; the mournings that seemed to bear out these expectations and ended by persuading Søren that he would die by the age of thirty-four; the mother, mistress and servant, whom he loved in so far as she was *his* mother and whom he reproved in so far as she was an intruder in the household of a widower and testified to the carnal lapses of his father, and so on. The origin of singularity is the random at its most radical: if I had had a different father . . . if my father had not blasphemed, etc. And this pre-natal accident reappears in the individual himself and in his determinations: the thorn in the flesh was a complex disposition whose inner secret has not yet been unearthed. But all authors are agreed in seeing a sexual anomaly as its kernel. A singularizing accident, this anomaly *was* Kierkegaard, it *made* him; it could not be cured, and hence could not be surpassed; it produced his most intimate self as a pure historical contingency, which might not have been and in itself meant nothing. Hegelian necessity was not negated, but it could not be embodied without becoming a singular and opaque contingency; in an individual the rationality of History is experienced irreducibly as madness, as an inner accident, expressive of random encounters. To our questioning, Kierkegaard replies by revealing another aspect of the paradox: there can be no historical absolute that is not rooted in chance; because of the necessity of anchorage, there can be no incarnation of the universal other than in the irreducible opacity of the singular. Is it Søren who *says* this? Yes and no: to tell the truth he *says nothing* if "to say" means the same as "to signify," but his work refers us back, without speaking, to his life.

But here the paradox has a twist to it, for to experience original contingency means to surpass it. Man, irremediable singularity, is the being through whom the universal comes into the world; once fundamental chance starts to be lived, it assumes the form of necessity. Lived experience, we discover in Kierkegaard, is made up of non-significant accidents of being in so far as they are surpassed towards a significance they did not possess at the beginning, and which I will call the singular universal.

To gain more insight into this message, let us come back to the notion of sin which lies at the centre of Kierkegaard's thought. As Jean Wahl has noted correctly, Adam exists in a pre-Adamite state of innocence, i.e. of ignorance. Nevertheless, although the Self does not yet exist, this being already envelops a contradiction. At this level, the spirit is a synthesis which unites and divides: it brings body and soul together and, in doing so, engenders the conflicts which oppose them. Dread makes its appearance as the interiorization of being, that is to say its contradiction. In other words, being has no interiority prior to the appearance of dread. But since the spirit can neither flee nor fulfil itself, since it is a dissonant unity of the finite and the infinite, the possibility of choosing *one* of the terms—the finite, the flesh, in other words the Self which does not yet exist—makes its appearance in the form of dread, at the moment when God's Thou Shalt Not resounds. But what is this prohibition? In actual fact, communication is not possible—no more than it was possible between Kafka's Emperor and the subject he wanted to touch but whom his message does not reach. But Kierkegaard gave his Shalt Not its full value when he deprived the Serpent of the power to tempt Adam. If the Devil is eliminated and Adam is not yet Adam, who can pronounce the prohibition and at the same time suggest to the pre-Adamite that he *turn himself* into Adam? God alone. A curious passage from the ***Journal*** explains why:

> Omnipotence . . . should make things dependent. But if we rightly consider omnipotence, then clearly it must have the quality of so taking itself back in the very manifestation of its all-powerfulness that the results of this act of the omnipotent can be independent. . . . For goodness means to give absolutely, yet in such a way that by taking oneself back one makes the recipient independent. . . . Omnipotence alone . . . can create something out of nothing which endures of itself, because omnipotence is always taking itself back. . . . If . . . man had even the least independent existence (in regard to *materia*) then God could not make him free.

The pre-Adamite state of innocence is the final moment of dependence. At any moment God will withdraw from his creature as the ebbing tide uncovers a piece of flotsam; and by this movement alone he creates dread—as the possibility of independence. In other words, God becomes at once the Prohibiter and the Tempter. Thus dread is the abandonment of being to the forbidden possibility of choosing finitude by a sudden retreat of the infinite. Dread is the internalization of this forsaken condition and it is completed by the free realization of the sole possible future of Adam abandoned—the choice of the finite. The moment of sin is defined by the restitution of original being as *meaning*. Being was the contradictory unity between the finite and the impalpable infinite, but this unity remained in the indistinction of ignorance. Sin as *re-exteriorization* makes the constituent contradiction reappear. It is the determination of it: the Self and God appear. God is infinite withdrawal but yet immediate presence, in so far as sin bars the way to any hope of return to Eden. The Self is chosen finitude, nothingness affirmed and delimited by an act; it is determination conquered by defiance; it is the singularity of extreme estrangement. Thus the terms of the contradiction are the same and yet the *state* of ignorance and sin are not homogeneous: the finite is now constituted as loss of the infinite, freedom as the *necessary* and irremediable foundation of the formation of the *Ego*. Good and Evil make their appearance as the meaning of this exteriorization of the interiority that is sinful freedom. Everything happens as though God *needed* sin in order that man might produce himself in front of him, as if he had solicited it in order to bring Adam out of his state of ignorance and *give* meaning to man.

But we are all Adam. Thus the pre-Adamite state is one with the contingency of our being. For Kierkegaard, what produces it is a disunited unity of accidents. In this sense, sin becomes the *establishment* of Kierkegaard as a surpassal of these scattered data *towards a meaning*. The contingency of our being is the beginning; our necessity only appears through the act which assumes this contingency in order to give it a *human meaning,* in other words to make of it a singular relationship to the Whole, a singular embodiment of the ongoing totalization which envelops and produces it. Kierkegaard was well aware of this: what he called sin is, as a whole, the supersession of the (pre-Adamite) *state* by the advent of freedom and the impossibility of retreat. Thus the web of subjective life—what he called passion, and Hegel called *pathos*—is nothing other than the freedom that institutes the finite and is lived in finitude as inflexible necessity.

If I wished to summarize what Kierkegaard's non-signifying testimony has to offer to me, a twentieth-century atheist who does not believe in sin, I would say that the state of ignorance represents, for the individual, being-in–exteriority. These exterior determinations are interiorized in order to be reexteriorized by a *praxis* which *institutes* them by objectifying them in the world.

This is what Merleau-Ponty was saying when he wrote that History is the milieu in which "a form burdened with contingency suddenly opens up a cycle of the future and commands it with the authority of the instituted." The cycle of the future is a *meaning:* in the case of Kierkegaard, it is the Self. Meaning can be defined as the future relation of the instituted to the totality of the world or, if you like, as the synthetic totalization of scattered chance occurrences by an objectifying negation, which inscribes them as necessity freely created in the very universe in which they were scattered, and as the presence of the totality—a totality of time and of the universe—in the determination which negates them by posing itself for itself. In other words, man is that being who transforms his being into *meaning,* and through whom *meaning* comes into the world.

The singular universal is this meaning: through his *Self*—the practical assumption and supersession of being as it is—man restores to the universe its enveloping unity, by engraving it as a finite determination and a mortgage on future History in the being which envelops him. Adam temporalizes himself by sin, the necessary free choice and radical transformation of what he is—he brings human temporality into the universe. This clearly means that the foundation of History is freedom in *each man*. For we are all Adam in so far as each of us commits on his own behalf and on behalf of all a singular sin: in other words finitude, for each person, is necessary and incomparable. By his finite action, the agent alters the course of things—but in conformity with what this course itself ought to be. Man, in fact, is a mediation between a transcendence behind and a transcendence in front, and this twofold transcendence is but one. Thus we can say that through man, the course of things is deviated in the direction of its own deviation. Kierkegaard here reveals to us the basis of his own paradox and of ours—and the two are the same. Each of us, in our very historicity, escapes History to the extent that we make it. I myself am historical to the extent that others also make history and make me, but I am a transhistorical absolute by virtue of what I make of what they make of me, have made of me and will make of me in the future—that is, by virtue of my historiality (*historialité*).

We still need to understand properly what the myth of sin holds for us: the *institution* of a man is his singularity become law for others and for himself. What is Kierkegaard's body of work but himself in so far as he is a universal? But on the other hand the content of this universality remains his contingency—even if elected and surpassed by his choice of it. In short, this universality has two sides to it: by virtue of its meaning it raises contingency to the level of concrete universality. This is its luminous and yet unknowable *recto* side—to the extent that knowledge refers to the "world-historical" by the mediation of an *anchorage*. Its *verso* side is in darkness, and refers back to the contingent set of analytical and social data which define Kierkegaard's being before his *institution*. Two errors in method are thereby denounced. The first of them, the world-historical, would define Kierkegaard's message in its abstract universality and as the pure expression of general structures; thus Hegelians would categorize it as the unhappy consciousness, incarnation of a necessary moment in universal History, or interpreters like Tisseau would view it as a radical definition of faith, an appeal by a true Christian addressed to all Christians.

The other error would be to deem his work a simple effect or translation of original chance occurrences: this is what I would call psychoanalytical scepticism. Such a scepticism is founded on the fact that the *whole* of Kierkegaard's *childhood* is present in his work and forms the basis of its singularity, and that in a sense, there is nothing more in the books he wrote than the life he instituted. Søren's works are rich in Freudian symbols, it is true, and a psycho-analytical *reading* of his texts is quite possible. The same holds good for what I would call sceptical Marxism, that is to say bad Marxism. Although its truth here is mediate, there is no doubt that Kierkegaard was radically conditioned by his historical environment: his disdain for the masses, and aristocratic demeanour, his attitude to money, leave no trace of doubt as to his social origins or his political position (for example his liking for absolute monarchy), which, though well concealed, surface time after time and obviously form the basis of his ethical and religious opinions.

But this is the point: Kierkegaard teaches us that the Self, action and creation, with their dark side and light side, are absolutely irreducible to the one or to the other. The shadow is wholly in the light because it is *instituted:* it is true that every act and every text expresses the whole of the Self, but this is because the Self-as-institution is homogeneous with action-as-legislator. It is impossible to make the general conditions *basis of it:* this would be to forget that they are general in a "world-historical" sense—for example the relations of production in Denmark in 1830—but that they are lived as nonsignificant chance by each individual, who is inserted in them fortuitously. By virtue of the fact that the individual expresses the universal in singular terms, he singularizes the whole of History which becomes at once *necessity,* through the very way in which objective situations take charge of themselves, and *adventure,* because History is forever the general experienced and instituted as a particularity which at first is non-signifying.

In this way the individual becomes a singular universal by virtue of the presence within himself of agents defined as universalizing singularities. But conversely, the side in shadow is already in light because the same individual is the moment of interiorization of exterior contingency. Without this preinstituting unity, the person could lapse into scattered disorder; too frequently psychoanalysis reduces meaning to non-meaning because it refuses to acknowledge that dialectical stages are irreducible. But Kierkegaard was perhaps the first to show that the universal enters History as a singular, in so far as the singular institutes itself in it as a universal. In this novel form of historiality we encounter paradox once again: here it acquires the insurpassable appearance of ambiguity.

But as we have seen, the *theoretical* aspect of his work, in the case of Kierkegaard, is pure illusion. When we *encounter* his words, they immediately invite us to another use of language, that is to say of our own words, since they are the same as his. Kierkegaard's terms refer to what are now called, in accordance with his precepts, the "categories" of existence. But these categories are neither principles nor concepts nor the elements of concepts: they appear as lived relationships to a totality, attainable by starting with the words and following their trajectory back from speech to speaker. This means that not a single one of these verbal alliances is *intelligible,* but that they constitute, by their very negation of any effort to know them, a reference back to the foundations of such an effort. Kierkegaard made use of irony, humour, myth and non-signifying sentences in order to communicate indirectly with us. This means that if one adopts the traditional attitude of a reader to his books, their words engender a series of pseudo-concepts which are organized under our eyes into false knowledge. But this false knowledge denounces itself as false at the very moment of its formation. Or rather it is constituted as knowledge of something which pretends to be an object but in fact cannot be other than a subject. Kierkegaard made *regressive* use of objective and objectifying ensembles in such a way that the self-destruction of the language necessarily unmasked he who employed it. In this way the surrealists were later to think that they could unmask being by lighting fires in language. But being was still, they believed, *in front of their eyes;* if the words—whatever they were—were burned, being would be unveiled to infinite desire as a surreality, something which was also ultimately a non-conceptual sur-objectivity. Kierkegaard by contrast constructed his language in such a way as to reveal within his false knowledge certain lines of force which allowed the possibility of a return from the pesudo-object to the subject. He invented

regressive enigmas. His verbal edifices were rigorously logical. But the very abuse of this logic always gave rise to contradictions or indeterminacies which implied a complete reversal of our own perspective. For example, as Jean Wahl has pointed out, even the title *The Concept of Dread* is a provocation. For in Kierkegaard's terms dread could never be the object of a concept. To a certain extent, in so far as dread is the source of a free and temporalizing choice of finitude, it is the non-conceptual foundation of all concepts. And each of us ought to be able to understand that the word "dread" is a universalization of the singular, and hence a false concept, since it awakens universality in us to the very extent that it refers to the Unique, its foundation.

It is by turning his words upside down that one can understand Kierkegaard in his lived and now vanished singularity, that is to say in his instituted contingency. His finitude, excluded, corrupted and ineffective, victim of the curse that he believed his father had brought on the whole family, could be described as impotence and as alterity. He is *other* than *all* others, other than himself, other than what he writes. He institutes his particularity by his free choice to be singular, that is to say he establishes himself at that ambiguous moment when interiorization, pregnant with future exteriorization, suppresses itself so that the latter may be born. Kierkegaard, who was afraid of being alienated by inscribing himself in the transcendence of the world, opted for identification with this dialectical stage, the perfect *locus of the secret.* Of course, he could not refrain from exteriorizing himself, as interiorization can only be objectification. Yet he did his best to prevent his objectification from defining him as an object of knowledge, in other words to ensure that the inscription of his person in the realm of reality, far from condensing him into the unity of ongoing History, should remain *as such* indecipherable, and refer back to the inaccessible secret of interiority. He performs brilliantly at a social function, laughing and making others laugh, and then notes in his journal that he wishes he could die. He could make people laugh because he wanted to die, and he wanted to die because he made people laugh. In this way his exteriority—a sparkling wit—was deprived of meaning, *unless* it is to be seen as the intentional contestation of every action reduced to its objective result, *unless* the *meaning* of any manifestation is not precisely incompletion, non-being, non-signification, forcing he who wishes to decipher it to return to its inaccessible source, interiority. Kierkegaard instituted his accidents by choosing to become the knight of subjectivity.

Now that he is dead, Søren takes his place in knowledge as a bourgeois who came to Denmark in the first half of the last century, and was conditioned by a specific family situation, itself an expression of the movement of history in its generality. But he takes his place in knowledge as unintelligible, as a disqualification of knowledge as a virulent lacuna, that eludes conceptualization and consequently death. We have now gone full circle and can reconsider our initial question. We asked what it was that prevented the late Kierkegaard from becoming the object of knowledge? The answer is that he was not such while he was alive. Kierkegaard reveals to us that death, which we took to be the metamorphosis of existence into knowledge, radically *abolishes* the subjective, but does not change it. If Kierkegaard, in the first instance, can appear to be an assemblage of items of knowledge, the reason is that the *known* is not contested in any immediate fashion by *lived experience*. But at the next moment it is knowledge which radically contests itself in the pseudo-object that this dead man is to us. It discovers its own limits as the object of study, impotent to become an autonomous determination of the exterior, escapes it.

The paradox, at this level, can be seen in a new light: can the contestation of knowledge by itself be surpassed? Can it be surpassed in the face of the living being who bears witness to his secret? Can it be surpassed when this living being has utterly disappeared? To these questions, Kierkegaard has but one reply, and it is always the same: the regression from signified to signifier cannot be the object of any act of intellection. Nevertheless, we can grasp the signifier in its real presence through what Kierkegaard calls *comprehension*. But the knight of subjectivity does not define comprehension, and does not conceive it as a new action. However, through his work, he offers his life to us *to be comprehended*. We encounter it in 1964, in History, fashioned as an *appeal to our comprehension*.

But is there anything left to be understood if death is utter abolition? Kierkegaard replied to this with his theory of "contemporaneity." In relation to the dead man Søren, there remains one thing to be understood, and that is ourselves. Søren, alive in his death, is a paradox for us: but Søren had already himself encountered the same paradox in relating to Jesus, in starting from Adam. And his first solution was to say that one comprehends what one becomes. To comprehend Adam is to become Adam. And certainly if an individual cannot become Christ, at least he can comprehend his unintelligible message without any temporal mediation by becoming the man to whom this message was destined—by becoming a Christian. Thus Kierkegaard lives on if it is possible for us to become Kierkegaard or if, conversely, this dead man is ceaselessly instituted by the living—borrowing their life, flowing into their life, and nourishing his singularity with our own. Or if, in other words, he appears at the heart of knowledge as the perpetual denouncer, in each of us, of non-knowledge, of the dialectical stage in which interiorization turns into exteriorization; in short, of existence.

Yes, says Kierkegaard; you may become myself because I may become Adam. Subjective thought is the reflective grasp of my being-an-event, of the adventure that I am and which necessarily ends in my becoming Adam—that is, in recommencing original sin in the very movement of my temporalization. Sin in this case is choice. Every man is at once himself and Adam renewed, precisely to the extent that Kierkegaard was at once himself and his father, the blasphemer whose blasphemy he took upon himself through his own sin. Every sin is singular in so far as it institutes, in particular conditions, a unique individual and, at the same time, it is sin in general in so far as it is the choice of finitude and blasphemous defiance of God. In this way the universality of sin is contained in the singularity of choice. By virtue of it, every man always becomes all man. Each individual moves History forward by recommencing it, as well as by prefiguring within himself new beginnings yet to come. From this point of view, if Kierkegaard could become Adam, it was because Adam was already at the heart of his sinful existence the premonition of a future Kierkegaard. If I can become Kierkegaard it is because Kierkegaard was in his being already a premonition of us all.

If we take up the question again in the initial terms in which we posed it, it comes to this: Kierkegaard's words are our words. To the extent that, within the framework of knowledge, they are changed into non-knowledge and are referred back via the paradox from the signified to the signifier, we are the signifier they regressively disclose. Reading Kierkegaard I reascend back to myself; I seek to grasp Kierkegaard and it is myself I hold; his nonconceptual work is an invitation to understand myself as the source of all concepts. Thus the knowledge of death, by discovering its own limits, does not issue into sheer absence, but comes back to Kierkegaard. I discover myself as an irreducible existent, that is to say as freedom that has become my necessity. I understand that the object of knowledge *is* his being in the peaceful mode of perennity and by the same token that I am a non-object because I have to be my being. In fact my being is a temporalizing and hence suffered choice—but the nature of this sufferance is to be *freely* suffered, and thus to be sustained as a choice.

Kierkegaard is restored as my adventure not in his unique meaning but at the level of my being-as-adventurer, in so far as I have to be the event that happens to me from outside. In so far as History, universalized by things—the bearers of the seal of our action—becomes, through each new birth of man, a singular adventure within which it enfolds its universality, Søren could continue to live after his death as my forerunner before birth, when I begin anew in different historical conditions. Curiously, this relationship of reciprocal interiority and immanence between Kierkegaard and each of us is established, not in the relativity of circumstances, but rather at the very level where each of us is an incomparable absolute. And what can demonstrate to us the reality that is common to all and yet in each case is singular, but words? Words are signs turned back on themselves, tools of indirect communication referring me to myself because they refer uniquely to him.

Kierkegaard lives on because, by rejecting knowledge, he reveals the transhistorical contemporaneity of the dead and the living. In other words, he unmasks the fact that every man is all man as a singular universal or, if you like, because he shows temporalization, in opposition to Hegel, to be a transhistorical dimension of History. Humanity loses its dead and begins them absolutely anew once more in its living. Kierkegaard is not myself, however—I am an atheist. Nor is he the Christian who will reproach him tomorrow for his negative theology. Let us say that he was, in his own time, a unique *subject.* Once dead he can be revived only by becoming a *multiple subject,* that is to say an inner bond linking our singularities. Each of us *is* Søren in our capacity as adventure. And each of our interpretations, contesting the others, nevertheless subsumes them as its negative depth. Just as each of them, conversely, is contested but subsumed by the others to the extent that, refusing to see in it a complete reality or knowledge concerning reality, they conceive of its possibility by referring to the susceptibility of Kierkegaard to several different interpretations: in fact, divergence, contradiction and ambiguity are precisely the determinate qualifications of existence. Thus it is today's Other, my real contemporary, who is the foundation of Kierkegaard's profundity, his way of remaining *other* within myself, without ceasing to be mine. Conversely he is, in each of us, the denunciation of ambiguity in himself and in others. Kierkegaard, comprehensible in the name of each ambiguity, is our link, a multiple and ambiguous existential relation between existent contemporaries, themselves lived ambivalences. He remains within History as a transhistorical relation between contemporaries grasped in their singular historiality. Within each of us he offers and refuses himself, as he did in his own lifetime; he is my adventure and remains, for others, Kierkegaard, the other—a figure on the horizon testifying to the Christian that faith is a future development forever imperilled, testifying to myself that the process of *becoming-an-atheist* is a long and difficult enterprise, an absolute relationship to these two infinites, man and the universe.

Every enterprise, even one brought to a triumphant conclusion, remains a *failure,* that is to say an incompletion to be completed. It lives on because it is open. The particular failure, in Kierkegaard's case, is clear. Kierkegaard demonstrated his historicity but failed to find History. Pitting himself against Hegel, he occupied himself over-exclusively with transmitting his instituted contingency to the human adventure and, because of this, he neglected *praxis,* which is rationality. At a stroke, he denatured *knowledge,* forgetting that the world we know is the world we make. Anchorage is a fortuitous event, but the possibility and rational meaning of this chance is given by general structures of envelopment

which found it and which are themselves the universalization of singular adventures by the materiality in which they are inscribed.

Kierkegaard is alive in his death in as much as he affirms the irreducible singularity of every man to the History which nevertheless conditions him rigorously. He is dead, within the very life that he continues to lead within ourselves, in as much as he remains an inert interrogation, an open circle that demands to be closed by us. Others, in his own time or shortly thereafter, went further than him and completed the circle by writing: "Men make history on the basis of prior circumstances." In these words there is and is not progress beyond Kierkegaard: for this circularity remains abstract and risks excluding the human singularity of the concrete universal, so long as it does not integrate Kierkegaardian immanence within the historical dialectic. Kierkegaard and Marx: these living-dead men condition our anchorage and institute themselves, now vanished, as our future, as the tasks that await us. How can we conceive of History and the transhistorical in such a way as to restore to the transcendent necessity of the historical process and to the free immanence of a historicization ceaselessly renewed, their full reality and reciprocal interiority, in theory and practice? In short, how can we discover the singularity of the universal and the universalization of the singular, in each conjuncture, as indissolubly linked to each other?

Sylvia I. Walsh (essay date 1987)

SOURCE: "On 'Feminine' and 'Masculine' Forms of Despair," in *International Kierkegaard Commentary: The Sickness unto Death,* edited by Robert L. Perkins, Mercer University Press, 1987, pp. 121-34.

[*In the following essay, Walsh reviews the two types of conscious despair as discussed by Kierkegaard (under the pseudonym Anti-Climacus) in* The Sickness unto Death. *Walsh analyzes Kierkegaard's views on feminine despair ("despair in weakness") and masculine despair ("despair in defiance"), and the relation of such despair to selfhood and to God.*]

Of the two forms of conscious despair, despair in weakness (not willing to be oneself) and despair in defiance (willing to be the self one wishes to be rather than the self one essentially is), the first is characterized by Kierkegaard as "feminine" despair, the second as "masculine" despair (*SUD,* 49). This distinction between the forms of despair in terms of sexual categories figures importantly in Kierkegaard's analysis of selfhood and despair in woman and man, but it has received little or no attention in studies of his thought.[1] For a generation grown skeptical of sexual stereotypes, such a distinction is quite questionable and calls for critical examination. Beginning with a brief account of what

Kierkegaard has to say about feminine and masculine despair, the following examination will focus on two areas of concern: 1) the congruence of his views with the general structure of selfhood and analysis of despair presented in his work; and 2) the compatibility of his perspective with recent findings on sexual differences and personality development. From a determination of these correlations we can more readily assess the significance and appropriateness of the sexual categories employed in Kierkegaard's analysis of despair.

As if anticipating objections to his classification of despair as feminine and masculine, Kierkegaard appends a lengthy note to the text that introduces this distinction, defending and commenting upon it in some detail. He claims that his classification is conceptually correct as well as true in actual life, although in exceptional cases masculine despair may occur in women, and conversely, feminine despair may appear in men (*SUD,* 49). The distinction is thus an ideal one that holds true largely, but not entirely, in actuality. It corresponds on the whole with the ways despair is generally experienced in human life. Women are more apt to manifest despair in weakness, while men are more prone to despair in defiance.

Kierkegaard goes on in this note to give a brief account of despair in weakness or feminine despair in women. Woman's nature, he says, is characterized by devotedness (*Hengivenhed*) or giving of herself in submission and abandonment to others (*Hengivelse*). Lacking a selfish concept of self and not possessing intellectuality in any decisive sense, woman is blessed by nature with an instinctive insight into that to which she ought to give herself. While she can be coy and particularly hard to please, her womanly nature first comes into existence through a metamorphosis or transfiguration of her boundless coyness into feminine devotedness (*SUD,* 49-50). Substantively, then, woman gains herself by losing herself; that is, she becomes a woman by giving herself in devotedness to others. Only when she gives herself thus is she herself, and only then is she happy.

Not intending to demean woman by this characterization, Kierkegaard lauds her sensitive instinctiveness, against which, he says, "the most eminently developed male reflection is as nothing," and he hails her devotedness as a "divine gift and treasure" (*SUD,* 49). Nevertheless, later on in the main text he states that femininity constitutes a "lower synthesis" than does masculinity, which alone falls within the qualification of spirit (*SUD,* 67). The reason for this, presumably, is that woman lacks the reflectiveness and internal orientation of man. As indicated in the note, she becomes herself instinctively, by giving herself to someone or something outside herself.

The crucial point in Kierkegaard's characterization of woman is that the devotedness (*Hengivenhed*) that is her nature also constitutes for her a mode of despair. If I read the Danish text correctly on this point, devotedness in itself is not despair, nor is the lack or loss of devotion, as is suggested by the new Princeton translation, which reads: " . . . woman, with genuine femininity, abandons herself, throws herself into that to which she devotes herself. Take this devotion away, then her self is also gone, and her despair is: not to will to be oneself" (*SUD,* 50). The word "devotion," however, does not appear in the Danish version of the second sentence quoted above; only the demonstrative pronoun "dette" or "this" is used, and grammatically it refers to the "det" or "that" to which woman devotes herself in the previous sentence, not to devotion.[2] The meaning of the text, therefore, is that in abandoning or throwing herself altogether into that to which she devotes herself, woman tends to have a sense of self only in and through the *object* of her devotion. When that object is taken away, her self is also lost. Her despair, consequently, lies in not willing to be herself, that is, in not having any separate or independent self-identity.

Kierkegaard further points out that man, like woman, gives himself (and "he is a poor kind of man who does not do so," Kierkegaard remarks), but his self, unlike hers, is not defined by devotion; rather, it is constituted by a "sober awareness" of his giving that remains behind when he gives (*SUD,* 50). Thus, he does not gain his substantive or sexual identity by giving himself, as she does, but already possesses and retains a sense of self apart from it. His despair, therefore, is quite different from hers, as it is characterized by an unwarranted self-assertion rather than by self-abandonment. In relation to God, however, sexual distinctions disappear, and it holds that for both woman and man selfhood is constituted by devotion to God, although Kierkegaard observes that "in most cases the woman actually relates to God only through the man" (*SUD,* 50).

I.

When these views are considered in relation to the general structure of selfhood and analysis of despair presented in *The Sickness unto Death,* a number of questions, problems, and issues arise. In the classic description of the self with which the work commences, a human being is viewed as becoming a self by relating itself to itself as a synthesis of the finite and the infinite, the temporal and the eternal, necessity (limitations) and freedom (possibility). Since the human self is established by a power other than itself, it becomes itself by relating itself not only to itself but also to that power which establishes it, that is, God. No distinction is made between man and woman in this description. Since the general term for human beings (*Mennesker*) is used, the basic structure of selfhood is presumably the same for both sexes. From Kierkegaard's note on feminine and masculine despair, however, it would appear that substantive differences nevertheless exist between woman and man within this general structure. Woman's being, we may recall, is centered in relatedness, in self-giving, while man's is characterized by a self-awareness sustained apart from relations to others. Although he gives to others, his self-identity is not constituted by giving.

It should be noted that giving or relating to others is not a constitutive factor in Kierkegaard's general description of a self either, as that includes relating to oneself and to God but says nothing about relations to others as forming an essential ingredient in the structure of the self. Kierkegaard's characterization of man's being thus corresponds more closely to the general description of a self than does that of woman, since it stresses self-consciousness or relating to oneself rather than relating to others.

The absence of a relation to others in Kierkegaard's general description of the self is rather puzzling inasmuch as only a year prior to the appearance of *The Sickness unto Death* he published *Works of Love* (1847), which focuses on relating to others through self-renouncing love and envisions a triadic structure (the lover, the beloved, and love or God as a third party) of existence in love (*WL,* 124). One must conclude either that there is a serious inconsistency in the authorship, or that Kierkegaard does not follow through with a systematic and integrated development of his thought, or that the insights of the earlier work are somehow implied in the later one. If the last alternative is accepted, it is possible to interpret the general description of a self in *The Sickness unto Death* as incorporating a social dimension in and through the relation to God or as a component in the self relation, under the rubric of giving the eternal concrete expression in love, faithfulness, and so forth.[3] Still, one wishes that Kierkegaard had addressed the matter of relatedness to others more directly in defining the structure of the self.

If self-renouncing love is included in the structure of the self, the resulting character of selfhood would correspond more to the feminine devotedness associated with woman than to the self-conscious masculinity of man.[4] That, however, would contradict Kierkegaard's contention that only the latter falls under the qualification of spirit; males, or at least those persons who are predominantly masculine in character, presumably have more spirit or self because they possess more self-consciousness ("the more consciousness, the more self" [*SUD,* 29]) than do most females.

Further problems appear in connection with Kierkegaard's claim that devotedness constitutes the proper mode of relating to God. Woman, as represented in the gospels by the woman who was a sinner (Luke 7:36-50), is presented by Kierkegaard in an edifying discourse as the model of religiousness because of her absolute submission to God.[5] Yet, as Sylviane Agacinski has perceptively pointed out, woman is not considered truly religious, or at least not as religious as man, because she abandons herself by nature, whereas man does not; ironically, therefore, it seems "as if the man were capable of being *more* and *better* a woman than the woman: that is to say, religious."[6] Since the self has its ground in the eternal, which consists essentially in love, and one's chief task in life is to actualize that quality, it would seem too that devotion to the eternal would properly be given expression in and through one's relations to others. That, in fact, is how he sees it commonly working in woman's existence, but not in man's, which sustains a separate, direct relation to God.

When Kierkegaard's distinction between feminine and masculine despair is considered in the context of his analysis of the two types of conscious despair, some incongruences can also be noted in relation to the despair in weakness. As delineated in the text, this form of despair occurs in two basic forms: despair over the earthly (the totality of worldly things) or over something earthly (the particular), and despair of the eternal or over oneself. The first of these is the most common form of despair, Kierkegaard says, and is immediate in nature, containing no (or only a measure of) reflection. In it there is no infinite consciousness of the self nor any awareness of despair as being despair. One seemingly suffers as a result of external circumstances, so that one's despair is not at all self-activated from within. With an increase in reflection, this form of despair becomes more internally motivated, and a greater distinction is made between oneself and the environment. As consciousness of the self increases, despair in weakness becomes despair *over* one's weakness, in which one shuts oneself off from the self (*Indesluttethed*) but becomes preoccupied with it, confessing in solitude one's weakness in willing to be that self.

Kierkegaard characterizes despair in weakness as feminine, but in his illustrations of it mostly male examples are used.[7] Indeed, if it is the most common form of despair, one would assume that it is more typical of males than is despair in defiance. Yet the latter is primarily associated with male experience, while despair in weakness is supposed to be representative of women. Kierkegaard's description of the first form of despair in weakness corresponds closely to his characterization of woman as instinctive, that is, immediate and unreflective, in contrast to man's self-consciousness and intellectuality. At the more conscious and intensive stage of despair in weakness, however, the introversion that arises in it concerns the masculine mode (one's relation to oneself) more than the feminine mode (one's relation to others). Thus his characterization of despair in weakness as feminine is not altogether consistent.

As Kierkegaard moves to an analysis of defiant despair, it is seen to presuppose a still higher level of self-consciousness and awareness of despair; but here the feminine mode is projected as the appropriate way to selfhood: "through the aid of the eternal the self has the courage to lose itself in order to win itself" (*SUD*, 67). Earlier this paradox was seen as characterizing woman's existence, but not man's. Now it is related to masculine or defiant despair in that the self "is unwilling to begin with losing itself but wills to be itself" (*SUD*, 67). Defiant despair thus results from an individual's unwillingness to adopt a feminine mode of selfhood.

In what sense the self is expected to lose itself is not stated in the text. Essentially, however, despair in defiance comes to expression when one seeks to become the self one wants to be instead of the self one is intended to be by God. Its distinctiveness lies in the fact that one will not recognize one's contingent or derived status as a self; rather, the self wishes to create itself, to be its own master. Fundamentally, then, this form of despair has to do with one's relation, or more precisely, misrelation to God and to oneself in the expression of an inappropriate form of self-assertion.

The pathway to selfhood thus includes both masculine and feminine modes of relating, and the possibility of going astray on this path arises in corresponding forms of despair. Feminine despair reflects a lack of self-consciousness (the masculine mode), while masculine despair indicates a need for the feminine mode (submission to that which is the ultimate source of life). While woman's self is lost or misplaced in a finite object of devotion outside herself, man's self is internally misplaced in himself. If being a self were only a matter of relating to oneself, and thus only a question of willing to be oneself, there would be only the possibility of despair in weakness. But since the self is constituted not only by its relation to itself but also to the divine power that establishes it, one can only become a true self through orienting oneself in (devoting or submitting oneself to) that power. Thus the feminine mode is inextricably involved in the process of becoming a self. How much that includes relatedness to other human beings in self-giving remains unclarified in *The Sickness unto Death.* Inasmuch as masculine self-consciousness provides individuality or a sense of separateness and consciousness of the eternal, it also plays an important and indispensable role. These modes and their corresponding forms of despair in woman and man are not altogether integrated in Kierkegaard's thought, but they indicate a complementary wholeness toward which he aims.

II.

Although the inclusion of both masculine and feminine categories in Kierkegaard's analysis of despair is preferable to defining selfhood in terms of one sex only, the appropriateness of the sexual distinction itself remains a matter of debate. While definite physiological differences obtain between men and women, it is now widely recognized that psychological characteristics distinguishing

them are often culturally rooted rather than biologically determined.[8] Indeed, many apparent differences turn out upon inspection to be mythical, the product of cultural stereotyping, rather than real. Thus far, psychological measurements devised for determining sex differences have shown only four such differences clearly to exist: males exhibit more aggression, better quantitative skill, and greater spatial visualization, while females excel in verbal ability.[9] There is no evidence supporting a gender difference in general intelligence, particularly the frequently held notion that women are less intelligent than men.

Kierkegaard's views on woman and man reflect traditional stereotypes of the sexes; and, to the extent that these continue to shape cultural perceptions and patterns of social development, his characterizations are compatible with popular viewpoints in contemporary society. Yet that does not necessarily make them valid or acceptable; indeed, his views on woman's intellectuality and spirituality, or lack of these, are highly questionable.

Insofar as woman's being is typically characterized by devotedness, as Kierkegaard claims, it may well not be an innate feature of her nature, but what she has been culturally conditioned to (generally at the expense of forming her own separate identity). Similarly, the egocentricity that Kierkegaard sees in males could be due to excessive encouragement of the individuation process in them, at the expense of developing a sense of relatedness to others.[10] Thus many social critics view the identification of woman and man in terms of conventional sex roles and characteristics as inhibiting their full blossoming as human beings, for these sex roles permit only a one-dimensional development of personality. Instead, they point to "psychological androgyny" or cultivation of both "feminine" and "masculine" characteristics in women and men as contributing to higher self-esteem and positive social adjustment.[11]

In substance, Kierkegaard's analysis of feminine and masculine despair is in line with that of proponents of androgyny inasmuch as he diagnoses woman's despair as a lack of masculine self-identity and man's despair as defiance against feminine devotedness and submission in relation to God. Ironically, however, his use of stereotyped characterizations of the sexes contributes to the perpetuation of cultural identifications of women and men in terms of those stereotypes and thus reinforces the very despair which his analysis is designed to counteract. Insofar as Kierkegaard's analysis is congruent with the views of contemporary advocates of androgyny, it offers a philosophical perspective that may be helpful in elucidating a common structure of selfhood in terms of the basic components of individuality (masculinity) and relatedness (femininity).[12] In at least two important respects, however, some contemporary social theorists differ from Kierkegaard. In contrast to his interpretation of despair as being essentially internally motivated or self-activated, they emphasize the need for, and impact of, change in the external structures of society so as to provide better opportunity for fuller personality development.[13] Second, whereas Kierkegaard analyzes masculine despair only in terms of man's relation to the divine, they point to man's need to develop more receptivity, intimacy, commitment, and giving in relatedness to other human beings, especially in relation to woman.[14]

It should be noted, too, that there is considerable disagreement among women concerning the notion of androgyny and its appropriateness for women's development. While some emphasize the need for women to be self-assertive and independent like men, others acknowledge and seek to preserve a distinctive character in woman. Labeling androgyny as a patriarchal construct that results in a pseudo-integrity in women, the radical feminist philosopher Mary Daly thinks woman can create a sense of selfhood that is not male-defined and that will manifest genuine differences from man, not those of traditionally defined femininity but of a kind yet to be determined, by spinning "threads of connectedness" with her sisters.[15]

Closer in line with Kierkegaard's association of femininity with devotion, psychologist Carol Gilligan identifies "a different voice" of women evident from the centrality of attachment and care for others in their lives and from the importance of relationships for the formation of their identity.[16] Claiming that "we know ourselves as separate only insofar as we live in connection with others," she finds in women's development a fusion of separation and attachment, identity and intimacy.[17] If that is true, Gilligan provides an important corrective to Kierkegaard in pointing to an interdependence of self-identity and relatedness in women.

Although Kierkegaard stresses devotion to others in woman's being, he views it as a potential mode of despair for her in that she tends to lose herself in the object of her devotion. Certainly that can and often does happen, but the possibility of despair does not negate the importance of relatedness in forming self-identity. It is the integral intertwining of these two components of selfhood that Kierkegaard does not sufficiently recognize and incorporate in his analysis. He rightly sees a need for both separateness and relatedness, but for him they appear to be separate categories, so that he fails to perceive the actual interconnection between them. Although Gilligan finds such an interconnection typifying women's development, this possibility can be extended to males, for with them also identity and relatedness are undoubtedly connected, even if perhaps in a somewhat different way. Thus, without negating sexual differences, one ultimately look beyond them to a common model of selfhood not defined by gender. Since Kierkegaard carries out much of his analysis of selfhood and despair without regard to the

sexes and in other works emphasizes our common humanity, the thrust of his analysis is in this direction.

How, then, shall we finally assess Kierkegaard's use of sexual categories in the analysis of human despair? While a distinction between the forms of despair can be made without them, they enable Kierkegaard to bring more concreteness and specificity into his analysis, as well as to account for what he perceives as differences between the sexes in the experience of despair.

Insofar as it is historically true that the lives of males and females have been characterized by patterns traditionally associated with masculinity and femininity, he provides an astute analysis of the connection between the forms of despair and these modes of sexual identity. In particular, his linking of despair with submissive self-abandonment on the part of women and defiant self-assertiveness by men illumines some of the dangers and limitations of traditional feminine and masculine modes. His pointing in the direction of androgyny within a common structure of selfhood for the sexes provides a conceptual basis for a fuller development of individuality and relatedness in both sexes. We can further appreciate the depth to which Kierkegaard's analysis goes in showing a fundamental connection of despair in woman and man with a misrelation to the divine. The idea of a relation to God coupling a high level of self-consciousness with devotion or self-giving establishes an ultimate matrix within which to affirm both individuality and relatedness in woman and man.

Despite these positive features, there are several aspects of Kierkegaard's analysis that remain unsatisfactory. First, it perpetuates stereotyped views of woman and man that are in some cases erroneous or unsubstantiated, in others perhaps historically accurate but largely the product of cultural conditioning unfavorable to the full development of both sexes. Second, it does not take sufficient account of the influence of external factors in occasioning and potentially overcoming despair. On a more theoretical level, his analysis fails to incorporate clearly or adequately relations to others besides God in the general description of a self and in particular as an essential dimension of male self-identity. Furthermore, it does not recognize the integral interdependence of individuality and relatedness to others in the formation of the self, particularly in female development. Finally, we may wonder whether feminine devotedness provides an appropriate model for the relation to God inasmuch as it traditionally involves a form of submissiveness that is often made the basis for male dominance over women. Indeed, Kierkegaard himself points to a less hierarchical model for the divine-human relation, and thus also for human relations, in *Philosophical Fragments,* where in the parable of a King and a Maiden (*PF,* 26-35), the two are made equal in love.

Notes

1 Recent studies of selfhood and despair in Kierkegaard's thought that do not treat the distinction between masculine and feminine despair include Mark Taylor, *Kierkegaard's Pseudonymous Authorship: A Study of Time and the Self* (Princeton: Princeton University Press, 1975) as well as his *Journeys to Selfhood: Hegel & Kierkegaard* (Berkeley: University of California Press, 1980); J. Preston Cole, *The Problematic Self in Kierkegaard and Freud* (New Haven: Yale University Press, 1971); essays in Joseph H. Smith, ed., *Kierkegaard's Truth: The Disclosure of the Self* (New Haven: Yale University Press, 1981); Kresten Nordentoft, *Kierkegaard's Psychology,* trans. Bruce H. Kirmmse (Pittsburgh: Duquesne University Press, 1978); Jann Holl, *Kierkegaards Konzeption des Selbst: Eine Untersuchung über die Voraussetzungen und Formen seines Denkens* (Meisenheim am Glan: Anton Hain, 1972); Vincent A. McCarthy, *The Phenomenology of Moods in Kierkegaard* (The Hague/Boston: Martinus Nijhoff, 1978); John Elrod, *Being and Existence in Kierkegaard's Pseudonymous Works* (Princeton: Princeton University Press, 1975); Alastair Hannay, *Kierkegaard* (London: Routledge & Kegan Paul, 1982). Libuse Lukas Miller, *In Search of the Self: The Individual in the Thought of Kierkegaard* (Philadelphia: Muhlenberg Press, 1962), notes the distinction between "manly" and "womanly" despair but does not explore it in her analysis. Several studies of Kierkegaard's view of woman and man touch on or are relevant to the discussion of this distinction: Howard P. Kainz, Jr., "The Relationship of Dread to Spirit in Man and Woman, According to Kierkegaard," *The Modern Schoolman* 47 (1969): 1-13; Christine Garside, "Can a Woman be Good in the Same Way as a Man?" *Dialogue* 10 (1971): 534-44; Gregor Malantschuk, "Kierkegaards Syn paa Mand og Kvinde," in *Den kontroversielle Kierkegaard* (Copenhagen: Vintens Forlag, 1976) 30-61; Birgit Bertung, "Har Søren Kierkegaard foregrebet Karen Blixens og Suzanne Brøggers kvindesyn?" *Kierkegaardiana* 13 (1984): 72-83; Peter Thielst, *Søren og Regine: Kierkegaard, Kærlighed og Kønspolitik* (Copenhagen: Gyldendal, 1980) 129-31. Sylviane Agacinski, *Aparté: Conceptions et morts de Søren Kierkegaard* (Paris: Aubier-Flammarion, 1977), also contains some pertinent reflections on Kierkegaard's view of woman and sexual differences (see especially 152-62).

2 The Danish text reads: " . . . Qvinden aegte qvindeligt styrter sig i, styrter sit Selv i Det, til hvilket hun hengiver sig. Tages nu Dette bort, saa er ogsaa hendes Selv borte, og hendes Fortvivlelse: ikke at ville være sig selv" (*Samlede Vaerker,* 3rd ed. A. B. Drachman, J. L. Heiberg and H. O. Lange, 20 vols. [Copenhagen: Gyldendal, 1962-64] 15: 106-07).

Emanuel Hirsch's German translation, *Die Krankheit zum Tode. Søren Kierkegaard/Gesammelte Werke,* 24-25 (Dusseldorf: Eugen Diederichs Verlag, 1957), interprets the text as I do: " . . . das Weib echt weiblich sich, ihr Selbst hineinstürzt in das, daran sie sich hingibt. Wird nun letzteres fortgenommen, so ist auch ihr Selbst fort, und ist es ihre Verzweiflung, dass sie nicht sie selbst sein will." The older German translation by Hermann Gottsched (Jena: Eugen Diederichs, 1911) interprets it similarly. Walter Lowrie's English translation, *Fear and Trembling and The Sickness unto Death* (Princeton: Princeton University Press, 1954), unfortunately omits the crucial second sentence of the text quoted above, as well as an earlier phrase identifying devotion as a mode of despair, so that on the basis of his translation it is impossible for the reader to determine wherein woman's despair lies.

3 John Elrod in "Kierkegaard on Self and Society," *Kierkegaardiana* 11 (1980): 178-96, also notes that Kierkegaard's pseudonymous works "pay no attention to the ontological and the epistemological roles played by the other in the development of a concept of the self." He sees *Works of Love* and all the later literature as being concerned with that deficiency, so that Kierkegaard discovers in them "a social conception of human beings based on the phenomenon of love" (181). Elrod makes a similar point in his book, *Kierkegaard and Christendom* (Princeton: Princeton University Press, 1981), treating *The Sickness unto Death* as part of the earlier pseudonymous literature even though it actually appears after *Works of Love* (131-32).

4 An important qualification should be noted here, however. Instead of devoting oneself exclusively to one other, as is the tendency in erotic love relations, in Christian self-renouncing love one is devoted to all, bestowing love equally on the basis of our common humanity. One must give up the type of devotion and boundless abandon that characterizes erotic love; such devotion, Kierkegaard maintains in *Works of Love,* is nothing more than a "devoted self-love" (cf. WL, 67-68, 78, 80).

5 See "The Woman That Was a Sinner," published in English with *Training in Christianity,* trans. Walter Lowrie (Princeton: Princeton University Press, 1941) 261-71.

6 Agacinski, 153-55. For a similar interpretation of Kierkegaard, see Garside.

7 See SUD, 53, 56, 59, 63-65. However, excellent examples of females who manifest despair in weakness as described in SUD can be found in *Either/Or,* vol. 1, in the characters of Marie Beaumarchais, Donna Elvira, and especially Margaret in Goethe's *Faust* (EO 1:175-213).

8 Janet T. Spence and Robert L. Helmreich, *Masculinity and Femininity: Their Psychological Dimensions, Correlates, and Antecedents* (Austin: University of Texas Press, 1978) 4-10, 121-22; Janet Shibley Hyde and B. G. Rosenberg, *Half the Human Experience*

(Lexington MA: D. C. Heath & Co., 1976) 7 (emphasizing an interaction of biological and environmental factors); Janet Saltzman Chafetz, *Masculine/Feminine or Human?: An Overview of the Sociology of Sex Roles* (Itasca IL: F. E. Peacock, Publishers, Inc., 1974) 4, 27.

[9] Eleanor Emmons Maccoby and Carol Nagy Jacklin, *The Psychology of Sex Differences* (Stanford: Stanford University Press, 1974), 349-55.

[10] This possibility is suggested also by David Bakan in *The Duality of Human Existence: Isolation and Communion in Western Man* (Boston: Beacon Press, 1966) 107-109.

[11] J. H. Block, "Conceptions of Sex Roles: Some Cross-cultural and Longitudinal Perspectives," *American Psychologist* 28: (1973) 512-26; June Singer, *Androgyny: Toward a New Theory of Sexuality* (Garden City NY: Anchor Press/Doubleday, 1977); Barbara Lusk Forisha, *Sex Roles and Personal Awareness* (Morristown NJ: General Learning Press, 1978) 30-36; 87-105; Spence and Helmreich, 109-110 (with references to others favoring an androgynous or dualistic approach); S. L. Bem, "The Measurement of Psychological Androgyny," *Journal of Consulting and Clinical Psychology* 42: (1974) 155-62; Judith M. Bardwick, *In Transition: How Feminism, Sexual Liberation, and the Search for Self-Fulfillment Have Altered Our Lives* (New York: Holt, Rinehart and Winston, 1979), 153-69, 177-78 (although retaining an appreciation of gender identity and differences).

[12] Although working primarily out of a Whiteheadian perspective, V. C. Saiving, "Androgynous Life: A Feminist Appropriation of Process Thought," in *Feminism and Process Thought,* ed. Sheila Greeve Davaney (New York: The Edwin Mellen Press, 1981) 11-31, seeks to develop a general model in which both individuality and relatedness are included. In an earlier, ground-breaking article, "The Human Situation: A Feminine View," published in *The Journal of Religion* (April, 1960) and repr. in Carol P. Christ and Judith Plaskow, eds. *Womanspirit Rising* (NY: Harper & Row, 1979) 25-42, Saiving analyzes masculine and feminine experience in a manner very similar to Kierkegaard, although without specific reference to his analysis of despair. Kierkegaard's analysis is explicitly discussed and appropriated in a feminist context in Wanda Warren Berry, "Images of Sin and Salvation in Feminist Theology," *Anglican Theological Review* 60 (1978): 25-54. See also my discussion of individuality and relatedness in "Women in Love," *Soundings* 65 (1982): 352-68.

[13] Hyde and Rosenberg, 275-78; Bardwick, 170-82. Critical of the dualistic origin of the term "androgyny" but endorsing the notion of wholeness associated with it, Rosemary Ruether, in *New Woman, New Earth: Sexist Ideologies and Human Liberation* (New York: Seabury Press, 1975), emphasizes the need for social,

economic, and political change (24-31, 204-211). See also Maccoby and Jacklin, 374; Dorothy Dinnerstein, *The Mermaid and the Minotaur: Sexual Arrangements and Human Malaise* (New York: Harper & Row, 1976).

[14] Bardwick, 97-99, 125-29; Eugene C. Bianchi and Rosemary R. Ruether, *From Machismo to Mutuality* (New York: Paulist Press, 1976) 84-85, 96, 120; Nancy Chodorow, *The Reproduction of Mothering* (Berkeley: University of California Press, 1978) 218.

[15] Mary Daly, *Gyn/Ecology: The Metaethics of Radical Feminism* (Boston: Beacon Press, 1978) xiii, 382, 387. To Daly androgyny conveys an image of "something like John Travolta and Farrah Fawcett-Majors scotch-taped together" (xi). Naomi Goldenberg, in *Changing of the Gods: Feminism and the End of Traditional Religions* (Boston: Beacon Press, 1979), finds some value in the figure of androgyny if it is used to inspire the imagining of a plurality of sexual styles, but she envisions a distinctly feminine form of religion and identity for women in the return to Goddess worship (78-81).

[16] Carol Gilligan, *In a Different Voice: Psychological Theory and Women's Development* (Cambridge MA: Harvard University Press, 1982). See also Saiving, "The Human Situation: A Feminine View."

[17] Gilligan, 63, 156, 159, 164. See also Christine Downing, *The Goddess: Mythological Images of the Feminine* (New York: Crossroad, 1981), which envisions for woman an "Aphroditic consciousness" that is a "loving consciousness" and a "being conscious in relationship" (202-207).

Abbreviations

EO: *Either/Or.* Volume 1. Trans. David F. Swenson and Lillian Marvin Swenson. Volume 2. Trans. Walter Lowrie. Second ed. rev. Howard A. Johnson. Princeton: Princeton University Press, 1971. (*Enten-Eller,* 1-2, ed. Victor Eremita, 1843.)

PF: *Philosophical Fragments* and *Johannes Climacus.* Trans. Howard V. and Edna H. Hong. Princeton: Princeton University Press, 1985. (*Philosophiske Smuler,* by Johannes Climacus, ed. S. Kierkegaard, 1844; "Johannes Climacus eller *De omnibus dubitandum est,*" written 1842-1843, unpubl., *Papirer* IV B 1.)

WL: *Works of Love.* Trans. Howard V. Hong and Edna H. Hong, New York: Harper & Row, 1962. (*Kjerlighedens Gjerninger,* by S. Kierkegaard, 1847.)

SUD: *The Sickness unto Death.* Trans. Howard V. Hong and Edna H. Hong, Princeton: Princeton University Press, 1980. (*Sygdommen til Doden,* by Anti-Climacus, ed. S. Kierkegaard, 1849.

Merold Westphal (essay date 1987)

SOURCE: "Kierkegaard and the Logic of Insanity," in *Kierkegaard's Critique of Reason and Society,* Mercer University Press, 1987, pp. 85-103.

[*In the following essay, Westphal explores the relationship between faith and insanity (or "divine madness") in Kierkegaard's writings, observing that faith appears to be opposed to reason, not merely beyond reason.*]

Feigned madness can be a valuable asset. King David once used it to escape from the Philistines (1 Sam. 21), and a twentieth-century king, Pirandello's Henry IV, used the same trick on a modern philistine culture. Thrown from his horse and struck on the head while on his way to a masquerade party dressed as the Henry of Canossa's chill repentance, he had for twenty years insanely identified himself with the eleventh-century monarch. At least this is what his family, and the court they provided for his humor, thought. As the play opens they are unaware that he has regained his sanity; he has continued to play Henry IV for the last eight of the twenty years, preferring the mad world in which he lived to the sane world to which he would have to return.

The scene in which Henry reveals his sanity to his privy counselors is one that poses some difficult philosophical questions about the logic of insanity.

> Words, words which anyone can interpret in his own manner! That's the way public opinion is formed! And it's a bad look out for a man who finds himself labelled one day with one of these words which everyone repeats: for example "madman" or "imbecile." . . . We're having a joke on those that think I am mad! . . . It's convenient for everybody to insist that certain people are mad, so they can be shut up. Do you know why? Because it's impossible to hear them speak. . . . Do you know what it means to find yourselves face to face with a madman—with one who shakes the foundations of all you have built up in yourselves, your logic, the logic of all your constructions? Madmen, lucky folk! construct without logic, or rather with a logic that flies like a feather. . . . One must see what seems true to these hundred thousand others who are not supposed to be mad! What a magnificent spectacle they afford when they reason! What flowers of logic they scatter![1]

Who is mad after all? What is the logic, the standard of reason by which a madman is judged mad? Is it sloganistic public opinion,[2] emotive words without fixed meaning? Is the foundation of our intellectual constructions itself a construction? Who is its maker?

What makes this logic or criterion of reasonableness better than the madman's? Is this question decided by majority vote? Is the truth "what seems true to these hundred thousand others who are not supposed to be mad"?

I

Socrates and Søren Kierkegaard would have to be reckoned among the most vigorous and dialectically skillful opponents of the idea that truth is a question of majority opinion. What brings them to mind together in this context is that both philosophers found it necessary to make their point with reference to madness, suggesting that public sanity is far from identical with the wisdom that is philosophy's object. The opening lines of Socrates' second speech in the *Phaedrus* set forth a theme to which Kierkegaard constantly recurs throughout his voluminous writings. "False is the tale that when a lover is at hand favor ought rather to be accorded to one who does not love, on the ground that the former is mad, and the latter sound of mind. That would be right if it were an invariable truth that madness is an evil, but in reality, the greatest blessings come by way of madness, indeed of madness which is heaven-sent."[3] Socrates concludes this opening statement with a reference to "the superiority of heaven-sent madness over man-made sanity."

As a Christian thinker Kierkegaard applies this idea to the problems of faith and reason. When the charge is made that Christianity is sheer madness and utter absurdity, he grants that from a certain point of view it surely is, and then goes on to ask for credentials of that point of view. When it is said that "modern man" finds the incarnation incredible, he acknowledges the sociological fact, but not without pausing to ask who "modern man" may be. He wants to know who is mad after all. Might it possibly be that the madness that is Christian faith is the higher, divine madness that actually possesses the truth that human sanity professes to love?

The roots of this motif in Kierkegaard's works are biblical. For example, his reflection on Abraham in *Fear and Trembling* reveals the standpoint of faith to be in such a radical and uncompromising either/or relationship with all other modes of thought[4] that the one must evidently appear madness to the others, and vice versa. The killing of Isaac (that he did not finally have to do it is irrelevant—he raised the knife) can only be viewed as murder by any secular ethic. Agamemnon, Jephtha, and Brutus may seek to justify their acts by viewing duty to their people (the state) as higher than duty to their children,[5] but no such public and possibly higher earthly duty is involved on Mount Moriah. Only the direct command from the God who is himself the ground of the ethical could justify this "suspension," or rather, trampling of the ethical. And such a God is sheer madness to any ethic within the limits of reason alone. It is equally true that such an ethic is insane *hubris* to a knight of faith like Abraham, irrespective of any appeals that may be made in the name of Reason, because he is committed to a "wisdom whose secret is foolishness," a "hope whose form is madness," to a faith that is "what the Greeks called the divine madness."[6] To appeal to Reason against the command of God would be, for Abraham and those who follow him in faith, to deny their fundamental insight that "as against God we are always in the wrong."[7]

The New Testament roots of this divine-madness motif are more frequently present in Kierkegaard's writings than this Old Testament paradigm. There are two: the concept of offense and the Pauline statements in the first two chapters of 1 Corinthians. The frequency with which the former appears in the Gospels, both directly and indirectly,[8] leads Kierkegaard to the conclusion that Jesus must be the sign of offense if he is to be the object of faith, and that "these words, 'blessed is he who shall not be offended in me,' belong *essentially* to the preaching about Christ."[9]

The most direct and sustained expression of the second (Pauline) source is a sermon that Kierkegaard preached in 1844 on 1 Corinthians 2:6-9 with special emphasis on the "hidden wisdom of God" and the announcement that "what never originated in the mind of man, God has prepared to those that love him"[10] But the basic ideas of the larger passage are everywhere present, even as far back as 1835, three years before his own conversion experience while he still spoke of Christians as "they." "Philosophy and Christianity cannot, however, be united," he writes. He knows how to confirm this "by describing how man as man, outside of Christianity, appears to the Christian. For this purpose it will suffice to recall how Christians regarded the pagans, considered their gods the inventions of devils, their virtues splendid vices . . . and how they themselves declared that their Gospel was to the pagans foolishness and to the Jews a stumbling block."[11] For himself it seemed that "in contrast to paganism—[Christians] are robbed of their manhood by Christianity and are now like the gelding compared to the stallion," and that due to preoccupation with a fixed idea, the Christian sees the world with vision so defective as to deserve the epithet "happy madness."[12]

The same Pauline idea, more sympathetically handled, is what the "acoustic illusion" of the *Philosophical Fragments* is all about. Unbelief is flying the flag of Reason, and in deference to this claim, Christianity presents itself for battle as the Paradox. Reason calls the Paradox absurd folly. The Paradox calls Reason absurd folly. And the point Kierkegaard seems to want to make is not simply that they are absolutely opposed, but that the Paradox has the honor of having started all the name calling. "When the Reason says that it cannot get the Paradox into its head, it was not the Reason that made the discovery but the Paradox, which is so paradoxical as to declare the Reason a blockhead and a dunce. . . . All that the offended consciousness has to say about the Paradox it has learned from the Paradox, though it would like

to pose as the discoverer, making use of an acoustic illusion," that is, mistaking its echo of the Paradox for the original statement.[13]

What is the point of vying for the honor of having fired the first shot? It is an attempt to shift the discussion to the real issue. There is no debate between Reason and Paradox about whether there is a great gulf fixed between them. What Reason affirms on this point Paradox affirmed long ago. It now says to Reason, "It is precisely as you say, and the only wonder is that you regard it as an objection."[14] Instead of overworking the obvious, radical difference between the incarnational *Weltanschauung* and all others (paganism, the natural man, human understanding), let's see whether the negative judgment about the former really follows from the reality of this difference.

It is obvious that Kierkegaard is not impressed by the banner of Reason, and this unwillingness to be intimidated by an appeal to Reason reflects a very definite view of what goes by that name. For him, as for Kant, it is *human reason* that is in question, and the adjective is not redundant. Human reason is a doubly contingent point of view regarding the world, before which the Christian paradoxes of revelation and incarnation, sin and atonement need not cower. Let them be madness from its point of view. It remains to be asked in all seriousness whether they possess "the superiority of the heaven-sent madness over man-made sanity."

To begin, there is the Kantian point; human reason fails through its essential finitude to be an absolute (perspectiveless) perspective of the world. If, as I have argued in another place,[15] the Kantian distinction between the noumenal and phenomenal worlds is that between the way in which one world appears to God and to us, then the Kantian dualism is fundamental to Kierkegaard's epistemology too. In the *Concluding Unscientific Postscript* the claim to absolute knowledge (philosophy as the divine's knowledge of itself as divine) is treated as one of the most comical of all philosophical howlers, the acme of professional absentmindedness in which, forgetting their names, philosophers identify themselves with the pure I-am-I, the divine self-knowledge. Humor is, of course, the highest mode in which the pseudonym who makes no Christian profession can operate. However, when this limit is no longer present, Kierkegaard is not reluctant to express his own offense at such a project. He calls it blasphemy again and again, thereby giving a theological twist to the Kantian finitism.[16]

Beyond the fact that reason is the broker of finiteness,[17] there is a second and even more important limitation, its openness to temporal conditioning (a Hegelian point turned against Hegel by Kierkegaard and the historical relativists). What goes under the name of reason are the fundamental assumptions of the established order. Reason is ideology, and ideologies are thoroughly historical productions. Because "the established order is the rational," the concept of Christ as madman and the concept of the established order are integrally related; in fact, they are introduced in the same paragraph[18] because one presupposes the other as a foreground requires a background. The clergyman is typical of the numerous representatives of the establishment (wise and prudent men, philosopher, statesman, solid citizen, mocker) who form a self-appointed jury that renders the unanimous verdict that this undeniably unusual fellow who claims to be God is mad. He argues, "But that it is God in his own person that should come is the expectation of no reasonable man. . . . The veritable Expected One will therefore appear totally different; he will come as the most glorious flower and the highest unfolding of the established order. . . . He will recognise the established order as an authority."[19]

Kierkegaard feels he has a right to be suspicious of this "reasonableness" that submits to the *authority* of the established order. That is why he is not bashful about calling modern philosophy nothing more than "traditional conceptions," describing Hegelianism as a "new wisdom which I already regard as outdated" (with a reference to the divine-madness theme of the Phaedrus). He even suggests that espousers of Hegel's views on time "must be regarded as mad."[20] When the established order presents itself as "the age" he respects its honesty, even if he cannot refrain from asking whether what the age demands is the same as what it needs. When it presents itself as Reason, he treats this as a confusion that is at best hilarious and at worst intellectually dishonest.

In the light of this account of Reason, it is both possible and necessary to take Kierkegaard's "irrationalism" seriously, precisely where he insists that faith is not merely beyond reason, but against it. It will not do simply to say that human reason is reason as such and in principle free from either or both of the limitations alleged above, for it is ambiguous whether such a view of human reason is not itself a familiar way in which historically conditioned establishments deify themselves. Further, it is possible to hope for a coherent account not only of faith, but also of "faith's capacity to understand"; not only of divine madness, but also of "the logic of insanity" (since this phrase, too, is Kierkegaard's own).[21] It may be that for Kierkegaard, as for Professor Findlay, if mysticism or radical theism is to survive the challenge of more familiar modes of thought that call themselves Reason, "it is not a question of being inconsistent or illogical, but of deciding what form one's consistency or logicality may take."[22] To express "faith's capacity to understand" is to do theology—to employ the language of faith with clarity and precision. To discuss "the logic of insanity" is to articulate the formal structures of this language, to do logic in the familiar, informal sense. Whereas the

philosophical logician tries to define "the logical features of ordinary discourse" (Strawson), the theological logician's task is to do the same for the extraordinary language of faith, though for Kierkegaard the boundary between these two tasks is not uncrossable. His work as logician is motivated by two questions. In response to the question whether Christianity can be proved true, he replies with a discussion of the problems of inference and evidence. In response to the question whether it can be proved false, he replies with a discussion of contradiction. We turn now to the first of these discussions.

II

"The man who journeyed from Jerusalem to Jericho and fell among thieves was not so badly off as Christianity; for the orthodox apologetic which had compassion upon it and took care of it treated it quite as badly as the thieves." Less picturesquely, Kierkegaard's point is "that orthodoxy and heterodoxy continue to be enemies who would extirpate one another, in spite of the fact that they want one and the same thing—to make Christianity plausible."[23]

Although Kierkegaard directs his antiapologetic polemic (e.g. "he who first invented the notion of defending Christianity in Christendom is *de facto* Judas No. 2"[24]) primarily at the notion that one can *prove* the reality of God, immortality, the incarnation, and so forth, he does so in such a way as to cut off the usual retreat of the apologist to the humbler claim that he merely seeks to show that Christianity is plausible or probable.[25] Since theological affirmations have to do with concrete existence, it is not surprising that he rejects the "incontrovertible *ergo*" and the "*direct* transition" that are suggested by the assimilation of theological inference to mathematical inference. But it comes as a surprise that he assimilates faith to the mode of belief proper to ordinary historical judgments; for the latter, while never proven in the strictest sense, are sometimes not only plausible, but also in some sense probable.

The difference between the two types of judgment can be understood only in terms of the "will to believe" motif that underlies Kierkegaard's account of their similarity and his rejection of the mathematical model. In the absence of the "incontrovertible ergo," the "direct transition," and the "promptly convinced," which would describe the quasi-mathematical entailment of theological conclusions from incorrigible premises, faith is possible "only by a choice," by "the most frightful act of decision."[26] Similarly, historical judgments possess an objective uncertainty that is negated in belief. The fear of error in such a context can lead to a thoroughgoing skepticism, but the suspension of judgment involved in such a skepticism, since it is a willed *epoche,* can only be overcome by an act of will. The "conclusion" is actually a "resolution." It involves a *decision* (a) to abandon what Hegel was fond of calling the I-won't-go-into-the-water-until-I'm-sure-I-can-swim attitude and (b) to accept a particular set of suggesting reasons as confirming reasons for the assertion that is made. The question about this *leap* that somehow bridges the gap between the *data* that are the initial premises of the inferences involved and the *conclusions* that they do not entail is the question of *warrants* in a voluntaristic context.

It is with Lessing's help that Kierkegaard formulates the question. He always sees the nonentailment just referred to as the "ugly, broad ditch" that, Lessing says, "I cannot get across, however often and however earnestly I have tried to make the leap."[27] Yet he realizes that the premises of the traditional apologetic, while not entailing the conclusions drawn from them, have stood in some relation to those conclusions. They have at least served as occasions. The question of warrants becomes the question of how this is possible. A transcendental deduction is required.

For Lessing the theological conclusions were "necessary truths of reason," this being understood in a Spinozistic-Leibnizian way. It is clear that empirical (contingent) propositions of any sort can stand in no evidential relation to such truths. So the warrant by which the data become an occasion is not a rule of inference that establishes such an evidential relationship. What then could it be? The data, as empirical and contingent, can neither support nor provide content for the conclusion that, on the contrary, stands as the criterion for the possibility and meaning of the former. In this particular case Lessing's Spinozistic view of God, taken as a necessary truth of reason, sets limits to the meaning of the historical life of Jesus and excludes the possibility of his life being an incarnation. The historical data can only serve as the occasion for recollection of the necessary truths that do not depend upon it, just as Socrates' questions and diagrams evoked geometrical truth from the slave boy. This assimilation of Lessing's view of theological propositions as necessary truths of reason with the Socratic affirmations that the Truth is within us and that knowledge is recollection expresses a distinctive answer to the question of warrants. The warrant and the conclusion are the same. They differ only as potentially or actually recollected. Lessing's formula is this:

> Data as occasion + the Truth within =
> knowledge as recollected Truth.

There is really no inference here, or, if you prefer, only a question begging one, since the conclusion is one of the premises.

Kierkegaard cannot accept this account. His thought moves toward bridging the gap in question by a leap that is more an act of will than of intellect, a resolution rather than a recollection. This voluntarism is a corollary of his view of reason as both finite and temporally conditioned. It leads him to see "necessary truths of reason" as necessary only within the context of an established order that defines a particular brand of reason, that is, only subsequent to the adoption (choice) of meaning postulates that are themselves contingent. Kierkegaard has no patience for attempts to cover this up by talking about Reason. The dogmatism that he complains against is not that of affirming something and then, consistently, rejecting the alternatives as false. Anyone who believes anything does this. His complaint is directed against the attempt to provide absolute guarantees that preclude even the possibility of being wrong. Lessing's a priori combined with his theory of it as a necessary truth of reason make it impossible for him to recognize an incarnation should it occur, since he knows in advance that it is not possible. Kierkegaard, on the other hand, agrees with William James that "a rule of thinking which would absolutely prevent me from acknowledging certain kinds of truth if those kinds of truth were really there, would be an irrational rule." And if James is inclined to describe such an approach as "an insane logic," Kierkegaard will agree and suggest that his logic of insanity is, among other things, a passionate protest against every insane logic. If James is inclined to view the absolute veto that such a logic issues as "the queerest idol ever manufactured in the philosophic cave," Kierkegaard also sees in the deification of the established order that underlies such a claim to absoluteness "the constant rebellion, the permanent revolt against God."[28]

So we are asked to consider the other possibility—that human reason is doubly defective, that the Truth is not within us, even that we not only lack it but stand in a polemical relation to it. (It is this last point that essentially distinguishes theological judgments from ordinary historical judgments.) The data, of course, still do not provide premises that entail the conclusion of faith, and it is one thing to be an eyewitness to the life of Jesus, quite another to be an eyewitness disciple. The historical data serve only as signs that point non-coercively in the direction of faith, signs whose true meaning can be missed through either misinterpretation or the failure to recognize even their function as signs. Since, on the present assumption, the Truth is not within us, and the function of these signs therefore cannot be to remind us of what we in some sense already know, it becomes a pressing question how they can ever be correctly interpreted, how they can ever function as the occasion for faith. The condition for interpreting them correctly must be given to us, who, if the Truth is not within us, do not have it; for to say that the Truth is within us is simply to say that we are able to recognize it as such when confronted with it. We need therefore, not only a Teacher who can confront us with the Truth, but also one who can implant within us the condition for recognizing it as such. This fundamental remaking is nothing short of an act of re-creation, and the one who performs it is not just a Teacher but a Savior.

Thus instead of Lessing's formula we have a very different formula:

> Data as occasion + the giving of the condition
> = faith as miracle.

That the end product is called both faith and miracle is appropriate since Kierkegaard emphasizes both the divine activity, the giving of the Truth and condition, and the human response, the act of obedience and trust that is a leap of faith, though he does not present a theory of how they are related.

The warrant here is very different from Lessing's. It is not the Truth within us but rather Truth given to us by the divine grace that grants the condition for recognizing it. Nothing here is introduced to free the situation from the objective uncertainty natural to the doubly limited human understanding. Neither sensible certainty nor rational self-evidence enters the scene to provide guarantees against the possibility of being mistaken or an absolute veto against alternatives. There is no easy retreat to probability or plausibility, for apart from the warrant that the condition provides, the data do not stand in *any* evidential relation to the conclusion of faith. The question is not so much whether there is enough evidence, but whether there is any at all. If there is any, there is more than enough.

This discussion with Lessing about the incarnation is illuminated by a comparison with comments about attempts to prove the existence of God. Would we prove the existence of God from the works of God, that is, those which only God could perform?

> Just so, but where then are the works of the God? The works from which I would deduce his existence are not directly and immediately given. The wisdom in nature, the goodness, the wisdom in the governance of the world—are all these manifest, perhaps, upon the very face of things? . . . From what works then do I propose to derive the proof? From the works as apprehended through an ideal interpretation, i.e. such as they do not immediately reveal themselves. But in that case it is not from the works that I make the proof; I merely develop the ideality I have presupposed. . . . In beginning my proof I presuppose the ideal interpretation, and also that I will be successful in carrying it through; but what else is this but to presuppose that God exists, so that I really begin by virtue of confidence in him?[29]

And so the conclusion of the argument emerges from it only by the leap in which one adopts (chooses) the interpretation (warrant) by which the works are seen to be the works of God. The question-begging character

of the process is evident. Kierkegaard's logic of the insanity of faith, far from denying this circular character of theological proofs, calls our attention to it in opposition to the insane logic of both the orthodox apologetics and their free-thinking opponents. It directs our attention to the necessity of choice and the inescapability of the leap. It reminds us that theological affirmation is grounded in presuppositions that are chosen, not proven.

III

Kierkegaard refers to Sextus Empiricus in his analysis of the question-begging character of theological proofs. It will be evident that his analysis of the proof for the existence of God from the works of God has the same formal structure as Sextus's critique of the syllogism, according to which the major premise can be known to be true only if the conclusion is also known to be true. Or, as Mill restated the same point, the major premise is the warrant that validates the inference from the minor premise to the conclusion, which therefore emerges from the proof as its conclusion only in virtue of the leap by which the major premise is adopted.

This raises the question whether Kierkegaard's position is another version of the nominalistic skepticism that runs from Sextus through Hume and Mill to many contemporary thinkers. Is Kierkegaard an empiricist in this sense of the word?

I believe not. To say this is not to underestimate the importance of his study of the ancient skeptics, but rather to recognize that he is always pushing beyond them, even if he finds it necessary to pass through their territory. His discussion of the skeptical epoche with regard to ordinary empirical (historical) judgments was directed at contrasting a will to believe with the skeptical will to suspend judgment, a fear of missed truth with the skeptical fear of error. The Jamesian character of this action reminds us that movement in Mill's direction is not the only alternative for one who is enough of an empiricist to deny the existence of "coercive evidence" for questions of fact.

Kierkegaard's argument as a whole fits more completely into a tradition other than the Sextus-Hume-Mill line. This is the voluntarist tradition where James corresponds to Mill, Fichte to Hume, and Augustine to Sextus Empiricus. Sufficient reference to James's position has already been made. Fichte's position is best expressed in his *Erste Einleitung in die Wissenschaftslehre*. After distinguishing idealism from dogmatism, he asks which is correct. "Reason provides no ground for a decision. . . . It is therefore a matter of choice [*durch Willkür*], and since even the resolution of free choice [*der Entschluss der Willkür*] needs some ground, it is determined through inclination and interest. . . . Thus what kind of philosophy one chooses depends on what kind of man he is."[30] It would be linguistically permissible to introduce the notion of arbitrariness in rendering the double reference to *Willkür,* but in the context it would obliterate one of the important aspects of Fichte's position. The decision may be arbitrary with respect to reason considered as the theoretical comprehension of the conditioned, since the question is about the unconditioned; but it is not entirely arbitrary. Fichte renders the question of decision an ethical question by making it a matter of inclination and interest. James had done this in a weak sense by speaking of the *right* to believe (under certain conditions) without coercive evidence, but Fichte seems to suggest that one has a *duty* in this matter. That would certainly be the implication in the Kantian context of introducing inclination and interest; how these affect our decisions and which inclinations and interests prevail is *the* ethical question. That Fichte is still a Kantian in this regard is clear because he continues, in the passage just cited, to list a number of vices that would automatically lead to the adoption of dogmatism rather than idealism.

That the question of faith is finally an ethical question is one of Kierkegaard's central themes, and thus he understands faith dialectically in terms of its opposites, which are not doubt, but rather despair, disobedience, offense, and resignation, all of which turn out to be forms of sin. Referring to ***Philosophical Fragments*** and ***The Sickness unto Death,*** Kierkegaard writes:

> It has been shown that in recent philosophy confusion has been wrought by talking about doubt where one ought to speak of despair. . . . Despair, on the other hand, at once indicates the right direction by bringing the relationship under the concept of personality (the individual) or under the rubric of ethics. But just as people have talked confusingly about "doubt" instead of talking about "despair," so also it has been customary to employ the category "doubt" where one ought to speak of "offence."

Because modern philosophy thus fails to see faith, through despair and offense as its opposites, as an "ethical," "religious," and "existential" question, it invites us "to be conceited because they doubt or have doubted."[31]

Similarly, in ***On Authority and Revelation,*** faith is viewed as a response to revelation, a relation of person to person. In terms of the authority inherent in divine revelation, the question of faith becomes an ethicoreligious question of obedience to God. "The question is quite simple: Will you obey? or will you not obey? Will you bow in faith before his divine authority? Or will you be offended? Or will you perhaps take no side? Beware! this also is offence."[32]

This ethicizing of the question of faith marks a distinctive difference between Kierkegaard, along with Fichte and James, and the tradition of Sextus, Hume, and Mill. Nevertheless, it could be argued that since the possibility of such a move presupposes a skepticism about objective and coercive methods for settling ultimate questions, the former group is able to "go beyond" the latter only by presupposing the nominalistic skepticism with which the latter were content to rest.

But not every skepticism is nominalistic. One of Kierkegaard's strongest statements about the personal and ethical dimensions of faith is a journal entry: "Therefore the *obedience* [his italics] of faith (i.e. Romans 1:5) is the apostolic expression; then faith is oriented toward will, personality, not toward intellectuality."[33] This is part of a complaint against Augustine for reducing the concept of faith to assent, thereby assimilating it to the Platonic problem of opinion and knowledge, and robbing it of its existential dimensions. While there are undeniable grounds for this complaint in Augustine's work, Kierkegaard's logic of insanity is in an important sense Augustinian, for it also operates in the mode of faith seeking understanding. This affinity is relevant to the question at hand.

No one would be tempted to call Augustine a nominalist. Yet he says the same things about proving the existence of God that Kierkegaard says. His famous "proof" from the reality of Truth, as it appears in *De Liberum Arbitrium,* is entirely within the framework of *credo ut intelligam.* It is given by a believer to a believer, both of whom confess their belief in God's existence before and during, as well as after the proof. They may believe that everyone should recognize the force of the proof, but they do not treat it as an objective and coercive weapon. Instead they talk as if the force of the proof depended upon their previous faith. To repeat, it is not belief but understanding that they seek. The belief rests upon an acceptance of the biblical revelation as authoritative. Reason, as it seeks to "prove" what faith believes, recognizes that it is "mutable, now struggling to arrive at truth, now ceasing to struggle, sometimes reaching it and sometimes not. . . . Reason discerns that it is inferior." Therefore the entire investigation of the treatise is undertaken, "depending on [God] and praying for his help" and in the confidence that "we shall find him when he himself shows us." If there is an appeal to "the truth within which teaches us," the power to find the answer through this "highest teacher of all" is something Augustine hopes God will give to Evodius.[34]

Talk like this would surely sound strange on the lips of Socrates or Lessing. We are reminded that the Augustinian doctrine of illumination is not simply a Platonic way of talking about knowledge, but a Platonic way of expressing a Christian epistemology. For the truth within, the highest teacher is Christ, who in his noetic function (John 1:9) is said to dwell in everyone, but whose noetic efficacy is dependent upon the moral condition of the individual and thus ultimately upon re-generation because the limitations of reason are primarily due to sin. Vice, not finitude, bars the door of truth.

In this context it is clear that the priority of faith to reason and the consequent question-begging character of proofs, if taken to be something other than faith seeking understanding, do not rest upon a nominalist account of the finitude of human reason, but upon a theological account of its limits. In the light of what Kierkegaard says about our polemical relation in sin to the truth and about the dichotomy of faith and sin, it is clear that his theory of the limits of human understanding is a theological theory like Augustine's. Not just Kantian finitude and Hegelian historicity, both of which could be built upon nominalist foundations but, above all, Augustinian sinfulness stands between human reason and the truth.

Joined to Kierkegaard's mention of Sextus Empiricus is a reference to Protagoras; this provides the opportunity for expanding our investigation of Kierkegaard's relation to empiricism, in particular to a couple of closely related Protagorean elements of twentieth-century empiricism: the conventionalist theory of necessary truth and the noncognitivist account of religious language. The theory of the *a priori* that Kierkegaard sets against Lessing's appears to have at least some affinities with these two elements of logical empiricism. It was, for example, quite natural to introduce the Carnapian notion of meaning postulates when speaking of Kierkegaard's theory of warrants.[35] In opposition to Lessing's treatment of necessary truths of reason, Kierkegaard, like Carnap, is willing to grant only a hypothetical and not a categorical necessity, the condition being the adoption of necessary presuppositions, whether these be called meaning postulates, ideal interpretations, or warrants. Both give theories of necessary truth *for me* or *for us,*—that is, for those who adopt the suitable framework of postulates—and both describe the adoption as a matter of choice.[36]

However, there is a crucial difference (other than the obvious fact that Kierkegaard is not giving a theory that explicitly applies to all necessary or a priori truth). When it comes to comparing alternative frameworks or postulate sets and deciding which one to adopt, Carnap leaves the question at the level of expediency, adopting a kind of pragmatic noncognitivism. Concerning the choice between the postulates of realism and those of phenomenalism, he writes, "If someone decides to accept the thing language, there is no objection against saying that he has accepted the world of things. But this must not be interpreted as if it meant his acceptance of a *belief* [his italics] in the reality of the thing world; there is no such belief or assertion or assumption, because it is not a theoretical question. To accept the thing world means nothing more than to accept a certain form of language." This means, among other things, to accept a certain set of inferences.[37]

Hare introduced the well-known concept of "bliks" for expressing this sort of noncognitivism and its application to theological statements. He suggested that certain fundamental theological statements, including "God exists," are neither true nor false, but are bliks. Like our "belief" in the uniformity of nature based on Hume's analysis and our "belief" in the reality of the external world based on Carnap's, such statements are the rules of inference or interpretation by which the truth or falsity of other statements is determined, and as such they are not true or false themselves. They may be sane or insane, and this introduction of the notion of insanity into the analysis of warrants, inference, and the a priori brings us right back to Kierkegaard. What is the relation of his analysis of Christian faith as divine madness to Hare's analysis of the insane blik of a poor fellow who was convinced that all the Oxford dons wanted to murder him?

Given the blik in question, our lunatic will accept no behavior of the dons as evidence that they are really friendly toward him. What appear to be signs of friendship he sees only as their "diabolical cunning." Of course, he may be right. He may be the victim of a diabolical conspiracy, and he may be in a better position to see through its camouflage than anyone else around. Nevertheless, he is judged insane, and the reason is quite clear: his blik differs from ours. This rephrases Kierkegaard's point that we consider those whose warrants differ radically from our own to be mad.

A further similarity is that Hare's lunatic, like Kierkegaard's believer, is no friend of Lessing and his insane logic. For while the lunatic will not accept anything presented to him as counting decisively against his conclusions, he does not have the courage (insanity) to say that nothing could ever come to count against it or even persuade him to abandon it.

There remains, however, one important difference. Kierkegaard does not share Hare's noncognitive interpretation of the bliks in question. While he denies that human understanding can have an objective certainty about the truth value of conflicting theological bliks, he never moves to make the question of choice a question of usefulness, a consequence that Carnap consistently draws from the noncognitive analysis. Kierkegaard affirms that reality is a system for God.[38] This means that there is a cognitive point of view that defines the truth values of conflicting bliks. God knows whether the Oxford dons are really in conspiracy against our poor friend. Although Kierkegaard insists that he cannot objectively settle the dispute between those whose theological a prioris differ radically, he never suggests that the issue between them is not one of truth or falsity. Only on the assumption that it is an issue of truth or falsity can the questions of our eternal happiness have the intensity of pathos that they achieve in Kierkegaard's writing and experience. The ease with which he speaks of God and immortality as possibilities to be taken seriously suggests that however problematic he may find theological truth claims, when it comes to questions of meaning, his affinities lie with the eschatological verificationists rather than with the noncognitivists.

IV

It is time to turn from questions about inference and evidence to the theory of judgment, for the serious objection remains that the whole preceding discussion is pointless inasmuch as Kierkegaard holds that the essential affirmations of Christian faith are self-contradictory, paradoxical, and absurd. Perhaps an open mind toward theism requires one to consider seriously the idea that the content of faith is a kind of madness, possibly divine, vis-á-vis ordinary human thinking. However, when the reason "against" which faith believes is not "what the age demands," but the simple requirement that one not simultaneously affirm "p" and "not-p," isn't that too much to swallow?

Granted, but is it so clear that this is what we are asked to swallow? The central contradiction (paradox, absurdity) of Christian faith is the incarnation, according to Kierkegaard, and the question is whether he holds its affirmation to be the simultaneous affirmation of some proposition and its denial. To begin with, the terms "absurd" and "paradox" do not suggest this. For example, "Faith therefore hopes for this life, but, be it noted, by virtue of the absurd, not by virtue of human understanding. . . . Faith is therefore what the Greeks called the divine madness."[39] As before, the contrast is not between formal consistency and formal inconsistency, but between the human understanding and the divine madness. This contrast has to do, not with logical consistency, but with real possibility. In *Fear and Trembling* the knight of faith gives up the beloved, saying, "I believe nevertheless that I shall get her, in virtue, that is, of the absurd, in virtue of the fact that with God all things are possible." The author's comment on this is that "at the moment when the knight made the act of resignation, he was convinced, humanly speaking, of the impossibility. This was the result reached by the understanding."[40] To believe by virtue of the absurd or, what is the same thing, to believe the absurd,[41] is to consider possible what is impossible, humanly speaking, because God has been left out of the account. "God can appear to man only in the miracle. . . . To see God or to see the miracle is by virtue of the absurd, for understanding must step aside. . . . But Christianity, which always turns the concepts of the natural man upside down and gets the opposite meaning out of them, relates $$Word$$ to the improbable. This concept of improbability, the absurd, ought, then, to be developed."[42] As the sign of the miraculous and the humanly improbable, the category of the absurd is "the negative criterion of the

divine or of relationship to the divine . . . of that which is higher than human understanding and knowledge."[43]

The situation is similar with the notion of paradox, which Kierkegaard treats as synonymous with the notion of the absurd. In the *Philosophical Fragments* it is presented in a strikingly Kantian context as equivalent to the unconditioned, which, so far from being self-contradictory, serves to reveal the internal contradictions in ordinary human thinking. In the *Postscript* paradoxical religiousness is that which must be believed "against the understanding," which in that context clearly means against the common human understanding and its "immanence thinking," not against formal consistency. Or again, in *On Authority and Revelation,* the paradox is found because the apostle, who is merely an individual, is superior to the established order (the universal). As in *Fear and Trembling* where a similarly paradoxical inversion of the normal relation involved the ethical rather than the epistemic, the paradoxical element is simply the tension between God's activity and the way things would be if he were not involved. The unique position of the apostle "can be explained only by the fact that it is God who makes use of him."[44] Nowhere is there a hint that the paradoxical is the formally self-contradictory.

But Kierkegaard is not content to describe Christian faith and its content as absurd and paradoxical. He constantly calls it self-contradictory. Is this simply another forceful way of expressing the divine madness theme, or is he saying that faith is no respecter of the law of contradiction? We dare not assume that Kierkegaard, speaking in a Hegelian context, must mean by "contradiction" what we mean by it in the context of the propositional calculus, since he may well have learned from Hegel how to use the term in a variety of nonformal senses to refer to otherness, conflict, tension, and so forth; but neither can we assume without evidence that he means the same by "contradictory" as "absurd" and "paradoxical." We must look at the way he uses the term to see whether it stays within the limits of what he elsewhere says about the logic of insanity, or whether it adds a new and more radical dimension. Such a look provides ample evidence that the former alternative is the case.

One of the strongest indications of this is the way in which the madness motif and the notion of the self-contradictory are used interchangeably in *Training in Christianity.*[45] Precisely where faith is described as madness one can expect to find it described as self-contradictory; and often this latter characteristic, like the former, is explicitly relative to the established order and human understanding. It is not only the incarnation that is described in this way, and the other definitions are very instructive. For example, "Humanly speaking, this is indeed the craziest contradiction, that he who literally 'has nowhere to lay his head,' that a person of whom (humanly) it was appropriately said, 'Behold the man!' that he says, 'Come hither to me, all ye that suffer—I will help!'"[46] Other "contradictions" are that a compassion so sublime, so divine as to be concerned for the sufferer alone and to make itself literally one with the most miserable in order to help them should become actual in daily life; that the Inviter of the poor, sick, and suffering really thought that sin is man's ruin and therefore offered them forgiveness; that the most frightful act of decision that was necessary for the contemporaries of Christ is no longer needed, since the truth of Christianity is now proved; that God, in becoming human, should become a lowly, poor, impotent, and suffering man; that the remedy offered by the Inviter appears worse than the disease; that the needy who respond to the Inviter's promise of help should thereby meet with persecution, and that those who oppose those who carry this word of invitation to the needy should think they are performing a divine service. It is in this context that the incarnation and the Christian message as a whole are said to be contradictions.[47]

The Journals of 1850 indicate beyond question that Kierkegaard personally affirmed the doctrine of the absurd and the paradoxical that appears in the works of his pseudonyms, Johannes de Silentio and Johannes Climacus. A similar unity of doctrine concerning the issue of contradiction is to be found between Kierkegaard's own views as expressed in *Training in Christianity*[48] and those of his pseudonym in the *Postscript.* There Johannes Climacus discovers the essence of the comical to be the contradictory. Thus he finds it comical (because it is contradictory) to think that walking on one's knees is a way of pleasing God; to do wrong knowingly, and then seek to erase the action by calling it unjustified; to swear, as Hamlet did, by the fire-tongs; to stake one's life on the value of a book's binding; or to offer to give one's life for one's country—for ten dollars.[49] In these and endless other examples of the comical that Kierkegaard gives, the contradiction that is their essence is not the affirmation of "p" and "not-p" together. Instead it lies in the conjunction of elements that are ordinarily incongruous.

Returning to the religious, Kierkegaard sees the same incongruity in the idea that an eternal happiness is based upon something historical; that, consequently, an infinite passion, faith, is directed toward that of which only imperfect knowledge (approximation) is possible; and that one who is already created becomes a Christian by the miracle of creation, by becoming a new creature. Therefore these too are "contradictions." Finally, there is the further dialectical contradiction that the historical fact in question is not an ordinary historical fact, but an incarnation. It "is constituted by that which only against its nature can become historical, hence by virtue of the absurd."[50]

As in *Training in Christianity,* the affirmation of the incarnation as a contradiction is embedded in a context that forbids us to take this in a formal sense. The only possible ground for another understanding of Kierkegaard here is that what becomes historical in the incarnation does so "against its nature." But when the iron axe head floated for Elisha and when Lazarus rose from the dead at the command of Jesus, they certainly did so against their nature, though I do not formally contradict myself if I affirm these events, nor utter a tautology if I deny them. The impossibility of things behaving contrary to their nature is not a logical impossibility. Kierkegaard confirms this understanding of his statement by reintroducing the category of the absurd, the sign of the miraculous.

So Kierkegaard leaves us with "the most frightful act of decision". The choice is between unbelief, which finds sheer madness in the affirmations of faith, and belief, which sees in that madness a divine wisdom. If Kierkegaard's analysis of inference and evidence robs belief of the security of objective proof, his analysis of the absurd, the paradoxical, and the contradictory robs unbelief of the security of an easy dismissal on the grounds that the content refutes itself. It is not the task of his logic of insanity to settle the substantial issue, though his personal stance is never in question.

At the end of his life, Ibsen's Brand hears a voice from heaven declare that man's redemption is by God's love. This message stands in stark opposition not only to the careless indifference of the common people, but also to his own rigoristic moralism. He learns this truth in the Ice Church on the peaks high above the scene in which his earlier life and those of his worldly opponents transpired. It is a genuinely Kierkegaardian inspiration that provides for Brand as his Beatrice in the realm of the Ice Church, the mad gypsy girl, Gerd.

Notes

[1] Luigi Pirandello, *Henry IV,* in *Naked Masks: Five Plays,* Eric Bentley, ed. (New York: Dutton, 1952).

[2] See Marcuse's critique of one-dimensional thinking in *One-Dimensional Man* (Boston: Beacon Press, 1964) esp. chs. 4 and 5, and the suggestion that slogans function hypnotically.

[3] 244a, Hackforth translation.

[4] Kierkegaard's favorite terms for non-Christian modes of thought are paganism, the natural man, and the human understanding or reason.

[5] This is a Hegelian view of the tragic hero. The priority of the state of the family is developed in his *Philosophy of Right,* and this conflict is given as the paradigm for tragedy in the *Phenomenology.*

[6] These phrases are found in *FT*, 16-17 and in a journal entry quoted in the translator's introduction to the older translation. See *Fear and Trembling and The Sickness unto Death*, Walter Lowrie, trans. (Garden City: Doubleday, 1954) 10. Cf. *FT*, 23.

[7] From the title of the sermon that concludes *Either/Or*. Cf. Psalm 143:2 (NEB): "Bring not thy servant to trial before thee; against thee no man on earth can be right."

[8] See *TC*, 86ff.

[9] *SUD*, 128.

[10] See the sermon included in *Johannes Climacus or, De Omnibus Dubitandum Est and A Sermon*, T. H. Croxall, trans. (Stanford: Stanford University Press, 1958) 159-73.

[11] *JP*, 3:3247.

[12] Ibid., 1:416.

[13] *PF*, 53.

[14] Ibid., 52.

[15] See "In Defense of the Thing in Itself," in *Kant-Studien* 59:1 (1968): 118-41.

[16] *TC*, 31-33.

[17] *FT*, 36. Cf. 47.

[18] *TC*, 42, 91.

[19] Ibid., 50, in the context of 45-55.

[20] The first and the third phrases come from *JC*, 127 and 142 n. 17. For the second see *Cl*, 13.

[21] *TC*, 81 and 58.

[22] See J. N. Findlay, "The Logic of Mysticism," in *Religious Studies* 2:2 (April 1967): 59.

[23] *OAR*, 60.

[24] *SUD*, 87.

[25] *PF*, 52, 94ff.; *OAR*, 59-60; *JP*, 1:7; *CUP*, 189.

[26] *TC*, 98-100; *PF*, 79ff.

[27] *Lessing's Theological Writings*, Henry Chadwick, trans. (Stanford: Stanford University Press, 1957) 55.

[28] *Essays on Faith and Morals* (New York: World Publishing Company, 1962) 56-61; and *TC*, 89.

[29] *PF*, 42.

[30] *Science of Knowledge with the First and Second Introductions*, Peter Heath and John Lachs, trans. (New York: Meredith Corporation, 1970) 14-16.

[31] *TC*, 83n.

[32] *OAR*, 26. Cf. liv and 116-17.

[33] *JP*, 1:180.

[34] *On the Free Choice of the Will*, Anna S. Benjamin and L. H. Hackstaff, trans. (Indianapolis: Bobbs-Merrill, 1964) 38, 49, 13, and 39.

[35] The relation between a theory of the analytic and a theory of inference is a very direct one. Thus meaning postulates can be described as rules that relate predicates in a language so that certain entailments take place, and entailment can in turn be defined in terms of analyticity ('P' entails 'Q'=df 'if P then Q' is analytic). Carnap proceeds in the first way, Strawson in the second.

[36] For Carnap's statements, see *Meaning and Necessity: A Study in Semantics and Modal Logic* (Chicago: University of Chicago Press, 1956) 207, 225.

[37] Ibid., 207.

[38] *CUP*, 107.

[39] *JP*, 1:5.

[40] *FT*, 46-47.

[41] *JP*, 1:11.

[42] Ibid., 1:7.

[43] Ibid., 1:10-11.

[44] *OAR*, 192-93.

[45] *TC*, 42, 62-66, 82, 100, 105, 112-13, 116-18, 121, 129.

[46] Ibid., 42.

[47] These "contradictions" are found in the passages listed in n. 45 above.

[48] Following Lowrie's argument, I take *Training in Christianity* to be a non-pseudonymous work.

[49] *CUP*, 413n and 458ff.

[50] Ibid., 508-12.

Abbreviations

CA: The Concept of Anxiety, vol. 8 of *Kierkegaard's Writings,* Reidar Thompte in collaboration with Albert B. Anderson, trans. (Princeton: Princeton University Press, 1980).

CI: The Concept of Irony, Lee Capel, trans. (New York: Harper & Row, 1965; Bloomington: Indiana University Press, 1968).

CUP: Concluding Unscientific Postscript, David F. Swenson and Walter Lowrie, trans. (Princeton: Princeton University Press, 1941).

EO: Either/Or, vol. 1: David F. Swenson and Lillian Marvin Swenson, trans.; vol. 2: Walter Lowrie, trans.; 2d ed.; rev. Howard A. Johnson (Princeton: Princeton University Press, 1971).

FSE: For Self Examination in *For Self Examination and Judge for Yourselves!,* Walter Lowrie, trans. (Princeton: Princeton University Press, 1941).

FT: Fear and Trembling in *Fear and Trembling/Repetition,* vol. 6 of *Kierkegaard's Writings,* Howard V. Hong and Edna H. Hong, eds. and trans. (Princeton: Princeton University Press, 1983).

JC: Johannes Climacus in *Philosophical Fragments / Johannes Climacus,* vol. 7 of *Kierkegaard's Writings,* Howard V. Hong and Edna H. Hong, eds. and trans. (Princeton: Princeton University Press, 1985).

JP: Søren Kierkegaard's Journals and Papers, 7 vols., Howard V. Hong and Edna H. Hong, assisted by Gregor Malantschuk, trans. (Bloomington: Indiana University Press, 1967-1978). Citations are by volume and *entry* number, not volume and page unless specifically noted.

OAR: On Authority and Revelation, The Book on Adler, Walter Lowrie, trans. (New York: Harper & Row, 1966).

PF: Philosophical Fragments in *Philosophical Fragments / Johannes Climacus.*

PV: The Point of View for My Work as an Author, including "The Individual: Two 'Notes' Concerning My Work as an Author" and "My Activity as a Writer," Walter Lowrie, trans. (New York: Harper & Row, 1962).

SUD: The Sickness unto Death, vol. 19 of *Kierkegaard's Writings,* Howard V. Hong and Edan H. Hong, eds. and trans. (Princeton: Princeton University Press, 1980).

SLW: Stages on Life's Way, Walter Lowrie, trans. (New York: Schocken, 1967).

TA: Two Ages, vol. 14 of *Kierkegaard's Writings,* Howard V. Hong and Edna H. Hong, eds. and trans. (Princeton: Princeton University Press, 1978).

TC: Training in Christianity, Walter Lowrie, trans. (London and New York: Oxford University Press, 1941; rpt., Princeton: Princeton University Press, 1944).

WL: Works of Love, Howard V. Hong and Edna H. Hong, trans. (New York: Harper & Row, 1964).

John D. Caputo (essay date 1987)

SOURCE: "Repetition and *Kinesis:* Kierkegaard on the Foundering of Metaphysics," in *Radical Hermeneutics: Repetition, Deconstruction, and the Hermeneutic Project,* Indiana University Press, 1987, pp. 11-35.

[*In the following essay, Caputo examines Kierkegaard's* Repetition *(written under the pseudonym Constantin Constantius), maintaining that Kierkegaard argued against philosophy and metaphysics in favor of the concept of "becoming" over "Being." In other words, according to Caputo, Kierkegaard defended movement or kinesis, which philosophy, since Plato' time, has denied.*]

For Kierkegaard, the question is whether movement in the existential sense is possible, whether it is possible for the existing individual to make progress. Taking his point of departure from the Eleatic denial of motion, which is for him the paradigmatic gesture of philosophical speculation, Kierkegaard argues on behalf of existence and actuality. He takes his stand against philosophy and metaphysics, for which movement is always a scandal, and argues the case for existential movement. Thus, Constantin Constantius—the immobilized one, the one suspended in Eleatic constancy—raises this serious philosophical question in the most whimsical terms.

> When the Eleatics denied motion, Diogenes, as everyone knows, came forward as an opponent. He literally did come forward, because he did not say a word but merely paced back and forth a few times, thereby assuming that he had sufficiently refuted them. When I was occupied for some time, at least on occasion, with the question of repetition—whether or not it is possible, what importance it has, whether something gains or loses in being repeated—I suddenly had the thought: You can, after all, take a trip to Berlin; you have been there once before, and now you can prove to yourself whether a repetition is possible and what importance it has. (*SV* III 173/*R* 131)

This hoary philosophical issue is thus to be posed in a farcical form, by way of the "jest of an analogous conception" (*SV* IV 290/*CA* 18n), by deciding whether Constantin can repeat his trip to Berlin. This is to be a parody of the real question, which is whether it is possible for the individual to move forward, to get off dead center and make existential progress. Repetition is an existential version of *kinesis,* the Aristotelian counterpoint to Eleaticism, a movement which occurs in the existing individual.

Kierkegaard thinks that philosophy—metaphysics—inevitably undermines movement. Philosophy, as Nietzsche says, is Egyptianism: "All that philosophers have handled for millennia has been conceptual mummies; nothing actual has escaped from their hands alive. . . . What *is,* does not *become; what becomes, is* not."[1] Philosophy is scandalized by motion and thus tries either to exclude movement outright from real being (Platonism) or, more subversively, to portray itself as a friend of movement and thus to lure it into the philosophical house of logical categories (Hegelianism). Kierkegaard objects to the mummifying work of philosophy, not because he thinks that eternity—the sphere of that which lies outside of time and movement—is an illusion, that the real world is a myth *(Fabel),* as does Nietzsche,[2] but because he thinks that philosophy makes things too easy for itself. It is ready to sneak out the back door of existence as soon as life begins. It does not have the courage for the flux, for the hard work of winning eternity in time, of pushing forward existentially for the prize which lies ahead. It is not eternity as such (Nietzsche's "real world") to which he objects but philosophy's effete manner of seeking it. He takes the side of becoming against Being, of existence against thought, of existential "interest" against metaphysics. For it is on the basis of interest that philosophy founders, that metaphysics comes to grief (*SV* III 189/*R* 149).[3]

Kierkegaardian repetition is the first "post-modern"[4] attempt to come to grips with the flux, the first try not at denying it or "reconciling" it, in the manner of metaphysics, but of staying with it, of having the "courage" for the flux. Kierkegaard wants resolutely to avoid turning the world into a frozen *eidos,* stilling its movement, arresting its play, and thereby allaying our fears. He wants to stay open to the *ébranler,* the wavering and fluctuating, and to keep ready for the fear and trembling, the anxiety by which the existing individual is shaken.

[In *Repetition and Kinesis: Kierkegaard on the Foundering of Metaphysics*], . . .I will show how the Kierkegaardian project of "repetition" enters into the heart of what Heidegger means by hermeneutics in *Being and Time.* Despite Heidegger's own failure to acknowledge his debt to Kierkegaard, and the tendency among Heidegger commentators to ignore Kierkegaard, the Kierkegaardian origin of what Heidegger calls *"Wiederholung"* (retrieval, repetition) cannot be denied.[5] When **Repetition (***Gjentagelse,* 1843) was translated into German in 1909 in the Diedrichs edition, it bore the title *Wiederholung.* And it was that early edition, which Heidegger certainly knew,[6] which fashions in an essential way what "hermeneutics" means in *Being and Time.* . . . For hermeneutics in the early sense

always involves inscribing the figure of the circle on the surface of the flux—like Zarathustra's eagle—and that circular movement is the circle of repetition. By virtue of repetition the individual is able to press forward, not toward a sheer novelty which is wholly discontinuous with the past, but into the being which he himself is. By repetition the individual becomes himself, circling back on the being which he has been all along. Repeating the Aristotelian *to ti en einai* (that which a thing was to be), repetition is that by which the existing individual becomes what he was to be, that by which he returns to himself (*Pap.* IV A 156/*R* 326).

I begin with the attempts of metaphysics to deny or subvert the flux, right at its inception in Plato (1) and in its consummation in Hegel (2). Then I turn to Constantin's psychological-phenomenological experiment (3). Finally, after surveying the three stages of repetition (4), I address the question of repetition and the "foundering" or overcoming of metaphysics (5).

Repetition and Recollection

For Constantin Constantius, to ask if repetition is possible amounts to asking whether movement is possible, whether there is such a thing as *kinesis,* after all, or whether it is just an illusion. What we get from the philosophers is either the outright denial of motion, as in the Eleatics, or some spurious theory which takes the teeth out of motion, even as it professes to be on its side. In philosophy, becoming is always getting subverted by being. That is why Constantin opens his "report" with a little philosophical prologue on the distinction between recollection and repetition (*SV* III 173-5/*R* 131-3). Among other things, this report gives the lie to Heidegger's complaint that Kierkegaard is a merely religious writer who does not appreciate the ontological dimension of the questions he asks.[7] For, by opposing the Greek denial of motion implicit in the doctrine of recollection to Christian becoming, to the movement *(kinesis)* of "existence," Kierkegaard takes his stand with Aristotle's defense of motion against all Eleatic tendencies.

For Kierkegaard, movement in any really serious sense ought to be movement *forward.* It ought to make some progress instead of simply retracing past steps. Moving backward, if it is movement at all, is a kind of antimovement which undoes the progress that has been made. There is a certain comic quality in one who boasts that he is "on the move" when what he means is that he is backing up. But that is what the theory of "recollection" is, and that is the sort of thing that philosophers, who distrust movement, are always giving us when they speak in the name of movement.

Philosophy—immanence, speculation—opened its doors with a theory of pseudomovement, meant to take the sting out of the flux. The Being of the soul, Plato maintained, is to return whence it came. Its coming into the world in the first place was a fall, and so the essential thing is to undo the fall as quickly as possible, to redress the wrong which has confined the soul to the realm of change. The essential destiny of the soul is to recover its origins in the sphere of primordial Being and pure presence. Knowledge, accordingly, is not a discovery which forges ahead—for that would be real movement—but a recovery, a recollection, which recoups a lost cognition. Learning means to reestablish contact with a cognition that we have always already possessed, which quells the seductive aporia about how we can acquire something new. The philosopher is no friend of movement, and the Platonic account of motion is in fact a theory of antimovement, of undoing what motion there has been. Movement is falling, and hence the only movement of which speculative thought approves is the unmovement which undoes the fall. In Plato therefore everything moves backward: from the fallen to the primordial, from the sensible to the supersensible, from the copy to the original, from loss to recovery, from forgetfulness to recollection. In short, movement is governed by a dynamics of nostalgia in which movement itself is something to be overcome.

In the place of this spurious movement Kierkegaard wants to put real movement, genuine *kinesis*. Thus he pits the Christian notion of "repetition," which forges ahead, covers new ground, against Greek recollection. To the paleness of Platonic retreat, Kierkegaard opposes the hardiness of Christian, existential advance:

> Say what you will, this question [whether repetition is possible] will play a very important role in modern philosophy, for *repetition* is a crucial expression for what "recollection" was to the Greeks. Just as they taught that all knowing is a recollecting, modern philosophy will teach that all life is a repetition. . . . Repetition and recollection are the same movement, except in opposite directions, for what is recollected has been, is repeated backward, whereas genuine repetition is recollected forward. Repetition, therefore, if it is possible, makes a person happy, whereas recollection makes him unhappy—assuming, of course, that he gives himself time to live and does not promptly at birth find an excuse to sneak back out of life again, for example, that he has forgotten something. (*SV* III 173-74/*R* 131)

Recollection and repetition alike undertake the transition from time to eternity. But the Greek wants to retreat back to an eternal preexistence. No sooner has life begun than speculative thought wants to sneak back out, like a philosophy professor claiming that he has forgotten his umbrella![8]

For the Greeks eternity always already has been; it is a presence which we always already possess but with which we have lost contact. Eternity is a lost actuality. Thus the point of philosophical speculation is to ease oneself out of time, as one would back out of a deadend, to steal back into eternity:

> When the Greeks said that all knowing is recollecting, they said that all existence, which is, has been; when one says that life is a repetition, one says: actuality, which has been, now comes into existence. (*SV* III 189/*R* 149)

Recollection begins at the end instead of at the beginning, with the "loss" instead of the task (*SV* III 178/*R* 136). In the *Postscript* Johannes Climacus calls Platonic recollection a "temptation" to recollect oneself out of existence, and he says that the greatness of Socrates was to have resisted this temptation (*CUP* 184-85).[9] As the movement opposite to recollection, repetition is movement indeed. It is the path from time to eternity which is cut by existence itself. It does not try to escape time but to immerse itself in it, to persevere in time. In repetition, eternity is not something lost but something to be attained, not a lost actuality but a possibility yet to be seized, not something passed (past) but something to come, not something to recover but something toward which we must press forward. For the Christian, eternity is the prize which awaits those who keep the faith.

In Christianity eternity has the essentially *futural* meaning of the *vita ventura,* the life which is to come (and in this "to come" we hear Heidegger's *"zu-kommen,"* *Zukunft*). It is the life which is promised to those who set their hands to the plow without looking back. It has to do with the possible, with effecting new life, not with reawakening one who slumbers. Repetition starts at the beginning, not at the end. It means to produce something, not to reproduce a prior presence. For the Christian, time (temporality) means an urgent task, a work to be done. Metaphysics wants to think its way out of time, while in Christianity every moment is literally momentous, an occasion for momentous choice. In the moments of time everything—all eternity—hangs in the balance. The Christian sees time in terms of futurity and decisiveness. But in metaphysics time and motion are an imperfection, an imitation. Nothing is decided in time; the point is to learn how to put time out of action. The love of repetition is happy, an exhilarating and earnest struggle, while the love of recollection is a nostalgic, melancholy longing for a lost paradise, a dreamy wistfulness.

For Kierkegaard the Greeks do not understand time, and they lack "the concept of temporality" (*SV* IV 358/*CA* 88). "Greek culture did not understand the moment" and "did not define it with a forward direction but with a backward direction" (*SV* IV 358/*CA* 88). The Greeks do not grasp the momentum—from *movere*—in the moment nor the Pauline "twinkling of the eye" in which the world may pass away (I Cor. 15:52; SW IV 358/ 88). For the Greeks, time signifies no more than a passing away which should be resisted in order to regain the permanence of the lost presence. They were innocent of the radical tension within man between spirit and flesh and of the fundamental tendency to evil, error, and sin. They thought that man belongs essentially to the truth (*CUP* 183-85) and that he presently suffers only a temporary fall. Time is the temporariness of the fall, a passing imperfection. They have no notion of the urgency and decisiveness of time. But for the Christian everything is different:

> The moment is that ambiguity in which time and eternity touch each other, and with this the concept of *temporality* is posited, whereby time constantly intersects eternity and eternity constantly pervades time. (*SV* IV 359/*CA* 89)

Every moment of the Christian conception of time is touched by the eternal, has the eternal at stake, is charged with the energy and momentousness of an eternal—and that means of a future—possibility *(vita futura, vita ventura.)* The future is the incognito of the eternal which is incommensurable with time (*SV* IV 359/*CA* 89). The Greeks see the moment not in terms of the primacy of the future but in terms of a past conceived merely as passing away. The authentic notion of time, of the temporality of time, is the contribution of Christianity (*SV* IV 359-60/*CA* 89-90).

A whole ontology underlies this opposition between recollection and repetition. One wonders how Heidegger can possibly have taken Kierkegaard to be only a "religious writer" with no ontological concerns. One wonders how he could have written the ontology of "temporality," which constitutes the meaning of the Being of Dasein in *Being and Time,* without so much as acknowledging Kierkegaard, when the whole analysis, in my view, derives in its main lines from Kierkegaard![10] Kierkegaard wants to undo the prestige of the metaphysics of presence embodied in Platonic recollection and to have us think instead in terms of temporality and movement (*kinesis*). Repetition is *kinesis,* the way the existing individual makes his way through time, the constancy with which he confronts the withering effects of time upon character and faith.

The old dispute between Heraclitus and the Eleatics thus has for Kierkegaard an ethico-religious significance. If Constantin's return trip to Berlin is a "parody" of existential repetition (*Pap.* IV B 111 269/294), the real question is whether existential movement is possible. Is it possible for the existing spirit to live in time without, on the one hand, being dissipated by the flux and losing his identity or, on the other hand, without retreating from time and existence into timeless speculation? His response to this question repeats the Aristotelian gesture of feeling around for the elusive reality of *kinesis* which "exists" in the interplay of potentiality and actuality, which is neither the

one nor the other, for it is that in-between land which alone describes the dynamics of freedom:

> In the sphere of freedom, however, [as opposed to that of logic] possibility remains and actuality emerges as a transcendence. Therefore, when Aristotle long ago said that the transition from possibility to actuality is a *kinesis* (motion, change), he was not speaking of logical possibility and actuality but of freedom's, and therefore he properly posits movement. (*Pap.* IV B117 290/*R* 309-310)

Like Heidegger, Kierkegaard regarded Aristotle as the supreme thinker of the ancient world. Both Kierkegaard and Heidegger were drawn to the Aristotelian critique of Platonic intellectualism, to Aristotle's taste for the dynamics of concrete existence. Contrary to Heidegger's view of matter, Kierkegaard pressed a strictly ontological issue or, better, he pressed against the limits of ontology, precisely in order to make room for existential movement which ontology tries systematically either to exclude or to make over in its own image.

Repetition and Mediation

The theory of recollection at least has the virtue of honesty. Recollection is an intelligible and frank attempt to undo the movement of time and becoming because it understands the sharp difference between eternity and time, logic and existence, Being and becoming. Kierkegaard thought there really were only two ways to address the question of movement: either to affirm it, with the category of repetition, or to negate it, with the category of recollection. Either way one makes sense of the flux.

> The dialectics of repetition is easy, for that which is repeated has been—otherwise it could not be repeated—but the very fact that it has been makes the repetition into something new. When the Greeks said that all knowing is recollecting, they said that all existence, which is, has been; when one says that life is a repetition, one says: actuality, which has been, now comes into existence. If one does not have the category of recollection nor of repetition, all life dissolves into an empty, meaningless noise. (*SV* III 189/*R* 149)

Without either recollection or repetition there is nothing but the flux, nothing but a meaningless turmoil. Recollection stills the turmoil; repetition finds a way to maintain one's head in the midst of it. Recollection says that everything important has already been. Repetition says that actuality must be continually produced, brought forth anew, again and again. Identity must be established, produced. Identity, as Derrida would say, is an effect of repetition.[11]

The worst muddle, however, would be to look for a way to reconcile movement, to try to mediate it, with

Being and eternity. Mediation, which attempts to find a third thing between recollection and repetition, is foolish chatter and a confusion:

> It is incredible how much flurry has been made in Hegelian philosophy over mediation and how much foolish talk has enjoyed honor and glory under this rubric. One should rather seek to think through mediation and then give a little credit to the Greeks. The Greek explanation of the theory of being and nothing, the explanation of "the moment," "non-being", etc., trumps Hegel. "Mediation" is a foreign word; "repetition" is a good Danish word, and I congratulate the Danish language on a philosophical term. There is no explanation in our age as to how mediation takes place, whether it results from the motion of the two factors and in what sense it is already contained in them, or whether it is something new that is added, and, if so, how. In this connection, the Greek view of the concept of *kinesis* corresponds to the modern category "transition" and should be given close attention. (*SV* III 189/*R* 148-49)

The Greeks either frankly denied motion (the Eleatic view) or produced an honest Aristotelian account of it (*kinesis,* which is taken over by the category of repetition). But mediation is a misguided attempt to accommodate motion to Being, which equivocates about whether there really is motion, about whether anything really new emerges, or whether motion is not kept all along under the constraints of necessity and timelessness.

Kierkegaard distrusted speculation, and he thought that metaphysics always ended up in a denial or subversion of time and motion. The project of "overcoming metaphysics," of the critique of the "metaphysics of presence," was launched by Kierkegaard, although he had to wait for philosophy professors like Heidegger and Derrida to give his project conceptual formulation and thematic development. (He did, however, as we have pointed out, speak of the "foundering of metaphysics.") Metaphysics cannot digest movement, becoming, temporality, genuine novelty, and the attempt to do so results in ludicrous logicizations. Plato understood clearly the incompatibility of time and movement with philosophical speculation and hence defined philosophy in terms of its capacity to remove itself from them. Platonism was more candid; it simply confessed the incommensurability of time and movement with philosophical thought and urged philosophy to learn to die to such shadowy realities. Hence while Kierkegaard criticized *anamnesis* because it was a direct attack on motion, he criticized Hegelian *Aufhebung* as a more insidious, subversive attack on motion, one which put up the front of being a friend of motion, the final effect of which was in fact comic.[12] To a great extent, I think, Derrida's readings of Hegel are a counterpart to Kierkegaard's, for they keep Hegel honest and make him stick to his guns about movement and difference instead of slipping quietly through the back door of metaphysics.

Hegel made a show of embracing time and *kinesis* even while subverting them to his own purposes. Hegelian time is not authentic, radical, Christian temporality, in which everything hinges on the "instant," the decision. It is a time which is not exposed to flux and contingency but precisely insulated from their effects. It is a time made safe by eternity, underwritten by reason, regulated by necessity. In Derrida's terms, Hegelian mediation wants to arrest the play even as it appears to affirm it. Hegelian time lacks what is truly proper to time: contingency, freedom, exposure to the future. It pays public homage to history and temporality while in private it subverts them, subordinating them to a rational teleology which monitors and controls their movements. Hegelian time is time reworked by metaphysics, made over into its image and likeness, and in which the groundlessness of radical freedom, which belongs to the essence of time and *kinesis,* is revoked.

Kierkegaard has a profoundly Protestant and voluntaristic conception of things.[13] The very Being of the world is contingent inasmuch as it originates in a free act of divine creation, and everything that happens in the world happens contingently. Not even the laws of nature give evidence of pure necessity since the phenomena which these laws govern might never have existed and since the laws themselves could be altered by the divine freedom. The Christian world is free; the Greek world is necessitarian.[14] When Kierkegaard speaks of the "transcendence" of movement, he means the absolute unpredictability of the next moment from the present, an Ockhamistic contingency in the successive moments of change, a Cartesian "conservation of the universe" from moment to moment thanks to the divine freedom. Aristotle alone among the Greeks recognized the contingency in things, although even he did not distinguish sharply enough between the necessary and the possible (*PF* 93).

Now whatever occurs in time occurs contingently, since at first it was not, and then at a later time it came to be. Coming to be "is *ipso facto* historical" (*PF* 93). Hence it is a sophistry to confuse the immutability of the past with any alleged necessity of the past. The past is the historical and as such contingent, i.e., it is something which has come into existence. Its contingency is not removed by the passage of time. The merely external fact that it is now a past event does not annul the truth that when it happened this event could have been otherwise. Indeed, to say that the past is necessary is equivalent to predicting the future, for if the contingency of the one is annulled, the contingency of the other must likewise be annulled.

Hegelianism is therefore fraudulent, for it arises from an intellectual illusion which is akin to an optical illusion.

> Distance in time tends to promote an intellectual illusion, just as distance in space provokes a sensory illusion. A contemporary does not perceive the

necessity of what comes into existence, but when centuries intervene between the event and the beholder he perceives the necessity, just as distance makes the square tower seem round. (*PF* 98)

Indeed Hegelianism is comic, for it attempts to wed logic and existence, necessity and freedom, thought and *kinesis*. Hegel wants to affirm the reality of time and becoming, but his affirmation is half-hearted, for he insists that there is a logical necessity inscribed in time, that time unfolds in accordance with the categories of reason, or contrariwise, that time is inscribed in logic, that the categories move, that they undergo becoming and *kinesis*. But time and contingency, the conditions of reality, forever resist the idealizing efforts of thought. Thought can flourish only in the element of necessity and essence, and it can appropriate becoming only at the expense of what is definitive for it, viz., its very contingency. Whence comes Climacus's account of "Lessing's Thesis" in the *Concluding Unscientific Postscript* (§4): it is possible for thought to construct a system, but the price it must pay is high, viz., such a system can lay no claim to reality. Conversely, any account which is faithful to existence must be prepared to face the worst, to founder on the paradox, for an existential account moves in an element which is hostile to thought, viz., time and *kinesis*.

We are now in a position to understand the claims of Constantin Constantius about the difference between Hegelian "mediation" and repetition. We are here indebted to a review of *Repetition* published by the Hegelian theologian J. L. Heiberg, the banality of which so outraged Kierkegaard that he was provoked to respond, again under the name of Constantin, with an illuminating commentary on *Repetition* which he did not, however, publish but which we are fortunate to have available in the new English edition of *Repetition.*

Heiberg accuses Constantin of naturalizing repetition by treating it in terms of movement. But Constantin's argument is that movement in its truest and most radical sense belongs above all to the individual spirit. For Heiberg movement in the realm of the spirit is at best the movement of world history, which is in fact governed by necessity and mediation, a movement whose dynamics are controlled by logic.

> In logic, transition is movement's silence, whereas in the sphere of freedom it becomes. Thus, in logic, when possibility, by means of the immanence of thought, has determined itself as actuality, one only disturbs the silent self-inclosure of the logical process by talking about movement and transition. (*Pap.* IV 117 290/*R* 309)

The movement of logic is an unreal, noiseless hush. It is nothing more than an unfolding of necessity, no more than a quiet rustle among concepts. There is talk about movement but no real movement. "In the sphere of freedom, however," Constantin continues, "possibility remains and actuality emerges as a transcendence" (*Pap.* IV 117 290/*R* 309-10). Here possibility is followed by an actuality genuinely transcendent to the possibility from which it emerges. Here—in freedom, which is movement in the preeminent sense—something new in fact appears. The actuality is transcendent to the possibility, not determined, enclosed, and precontained by it. The transition is alive with all of the noise and bustle of existence and genuine *kinesis*. Thus the whole question for Constantin is whether repetition is *possible*.

> But as soon as the individual is viewed in his freedom, the question becomes a different one: Can repetition be realized? It is repetition in this pregnant sense as a task for freedom and as freedom that gives the title to my little book and that in my little book has come into being depicted and made visible in the individuality and in the situation. . . . (*Pap.* IV B117 293/*R* 312-13)

Repetition means the task set for the individual to persevere in time, to stay with the flux, to produce his identity as an effect. And this ultimately is the religious task. The highest expression of repetition is the religious movement in which the individual passes from sin to atonement. Here is the most dramatic instance of a qualitative transition, of a transformation of the individual in which something new and transcendent is produced. Atonement, which is completely transcendent to the sin which it displaces, is repetition in the highest sense, *sensu eminentiore* (*Pap.* IV B117 302/*R* 320). Sin cannot be mediated but only forgiven. The transition is not lodged on the level of immanence but is a genuine passage, a genuine movement of transcendence, one indeed which is possible only in virtue of the absurd, that is, of faith in the power of God to intervene and to effect what logic and mediation can neither understand nor carry out (*SV* IV B117 293-94/*R*313). No such radical *kinesis* is possible in metaphysics, in Platonism or in Hegelianism. Such a repetition has nothing to do with world-historical progress or astronomy:

> In the individual, then, repetition appears as a task for freedom, in which the question becomes that of saving one's personality from being volatilized and, so to speak, a pawn to events. The moment it is apparent the individual can lose himself in events, fate, lose himself in such a way that he therefore by no means stops contemplating but loses himself in such a way that freedom is taken completely in life's fractions without leaving a remainder behind, then the issue becomes manifest, not to contemplation's aristocratic indolence, but to freedom's concerned passion. (*Pap.* IV B117 296/*R* 315)

Repetition is the power of the individual to forge his personality out of the chaos of events, in the midst of the flux, the power to create an identity in the face of the incessant "dispersal" of the self (*Pap.* IV B117 303/*R* 320), of the dissipating effects of the flux. There is always a "remainder" no matter how much is subtracted from the individual by the taxing business of everyday existence. Repetition is the exacting task of constituting the self as a self.

In sum, recollection retreats and repetition presses forward, but mediation makes a great show of movement, a grand but silent display of movement, like a mime who appears to be racing along while all the time he remains in place on the stage.

Letters To Constantin

It is in the context of this elaborate ontological preparation that Kierkegaard's **Repetition**—his "whimsical" treatise, his little joke—should be read. I have concentrated so far on the ontology which is written in the margins, in occasional excursions which interrupt the narrative, and in the unpublished papers. The text itself is meant to illustrate this abstract ontology with a concrete example, a psychological, phenomenological case study.[15] The first part, "Constantin's Report," is an account of a distraught young friend of Constantin's, caught in the throes of a difficult love affair. The second part, "Repetition," consists of a series of letters from the young man to Constantin. The second half of the text, which repeats the title, is the "serious" part (but are we to take that seriously?), where we really get to repetition, while the first half is a parody of genuine repetition.

This is not the place to undertake a detailed account of Kierkegaard's narrative but only to highlight certain features of the text. We are introduced to a young man who has fallen deeply but unhappily in love, for the girl he loves is no more than an occasion which has awakened the poetic nature in him. He is not so much in love with the girl, as in love with love itself and the occasion this affair provides him for poetizing. He is thus already in a stage of recollection which keeps leaping over life. He begins with the loss of the girl. He is not ready for the day-to-day work of making love last a lifetime. His love of this girl keeps getting transformed into "Eternal Love," the "Idea" of love, of which she is but the "visible form" (*SV* III 182/*R* 141). While her love for him is naturally directed toward the ethical relationship of marriage, his love for her keeps being diverted into the poetic. She moves in the sphere of ethical actuality, he in the sphere of poetic ideality. Constantin devises a scheme aimed at dissolving the relationship in which the young man would make himself out to be an unfaithful womanizer. This would provoke the girl to break off the relationship herself, leaving her with her honor intact and the feeling that she had saved herself from a bad marriage. She would be in the right, and the young man would look to be in the wrong (*SV* III 183/*R* 142). But the young man

lacks the nerve for the plan and simply absconds from Copenhagen to Stockholm.

The problem with the young man, Constantin conjectures, is that he may really be in love with the girl and not have the courage to follow the way of repetition out of his predicament (*SV* III 186/*R* 145). The young man faces the critical juncture between recollection and repetition. On the one hand, he may transform his concrete relationship with this girl into ideality and thus enter the poetic. On the other hand, he may press bravely ahead in the sphere of reality, making the real relationship work out with the hard work of a day-to-day faithfulness which would break with his poetizing, idealizing tendency. He may either retreat backward into poetic eternity or press forward to produce eternity in time, that is, a good marriage. In fact he just retreats, turning on his heels and fleeing.

At this point Constantin is driven to wonder whether repetition is possible at all, and so he undertakes the satiric experiment in repetition, whose seriousness is to be compared to Diogenes' attempt to refute the Eleatics merely by walking back and forth. He will undertake a return trip to Berlin, to see if he can repeat the pleasures of a previous holiday. The whole trip is a series of disasters, like the farce which he sees at the Königsberg Theatre, and proof positive that repetition is not possible. Constantin is humiliated. He who counsels the young man to repetition no longer believes in it himself (*SV* III 210/*R* 172).

Life is a swindle, Constantin complains. Instead of giving a repetition (*Gjentagelse,* literally: again-taking, re-taking, repetition), life simply takes everything back again (*tage Alt igjen*) (*R* 368, n. 79). Instead of providing us with a continuity, a repetition which enables us to move ahead, life just exposes us to the flux. The more we try to put life in order, the bigger the mess we create. We would be better off if we simply lived without care, like a child who is constantly being rescued from disaster by his nursemaid, and let things take their course.

The failure to achieve repetition throws us back into the flux, the Heraclitean stream. There are only two ways to come to grips with the flux: recollection and repetition. And Constantin is capable of neither.

> Do not all agree, both ecclesiastical and secular speakers, both poets and prose writers, both skippers and undertakers, both heroes and cowards—do they not all agree that life is a stream? How can one get such a foolish idea [repetition], and, still more foolishly, how can one want to make a principle of it? . . . Long live the stagecoach horn! It is the instrument for me for many reasons, and chiefly because one can never be certain of wheedling the same notes from this horn. A coach horn has infinite possibilities, and the person who puts it to his mouth

and puts wisdom into it can never be guilty of a repetition. . . . Praised be the coach horn. It is my symbol. Just as the ancient ascetics placed a skull on the table, the contemplation of which constituted their view of life, so the coach horn on my table always reminds me of the meaning of life. But the journey is not worth the trouble, for one need not stir from the spot to be convinced that there is no repetition. No, one sits calmly in one's living room; when all is vanity and passes away, one nevertheless speeds faster than on a train, even though sitting still. . . . Travel on you fugitive river. (*SV* III 212-13/*R* 174-76)

Constantin alludes not only to Heraclitus but also to Job. Like the Lord, life gives and takes away, and we would do better to live like a child—or the birds of the air, who sow not nor reap—ready to bless the name of the Lord, who will find a way to give-again *(gjen-tagelse)* what life takes away. The taking away and giving again, which defines repetition, is modeled after Job's famous declaration.

The story of Constantin's trip is a parody, a satire, of true repetition, which must be of a more inward, more religious character than was Constantin's effort to reconstruct a holiday in Berlin. Constantin's vacation is comically juxtaposed to the allusion to Heraclitus, Job, and religious repetition. We are thus to conclude not that repetition generally is impossible but only that "aesthetic" repetition, which is at the mercy of circumstances and accidental factors, is impossible. Constantin's journey proves that aesthetics, which is devoted solely to the interesting, should fear repetition and cultivate instead the art of variation, which always knows how to produce something interesting and hence to stave off boredom.

The question of the possibility of repetition has not been decided in the negative but raised up a notch, forcing us to discuss it in terms of the religious category. Thus the second half of the book—"Repetition"—repeats the title and repeats the question—whether repetition is possible—now by way of a series of letters to Constantin from the absconded young man. The question of repetition is repeated, not as a farce, not as a whimsical trip to Berlin, but on a higher level, as the drama of the ethico-religious fate of the nameless young man. For the young man is in a crisis; he has reached a crucial turning point, a fork in the road of life.

Constantin seems to have misjudged the young man. He thought him to possess only a dreamy, imaginative love which belongs to the category of recollection, but he finds him caught up in a real love, snared by actuality. The young man is left with no choice but to press forward—into marriage, love's ethical consummation—but being a poet, too, he is incapable of marriage. He must press forward, but he cannot—a dilemma whose only solution is religious.

He has now come to the borderline of the marvelous [faith]; consequently, if it [repetition] is to take place at all, it must take place by virtue of the absurd. (*SV* III 220/*R* 185)

But again Constantin cannot help suspecting that it is really not the girl herself who matters. Perhaps the girl is still an occasion, not now for the poetic but for the religious. In either case, then, the young man would make himself an exception and have no business with marriage, the ethical universal (*SV* III 220/*R* 185). The young man is in a crisis of repetition:

> The issue that brings him to a halt is nothing more nor less than repetition. He is right not to seek clarification in philosophy, either Greek or modern, for the Greeks make the opposite movement, and here a Greek would choose to recollect without tormenting his conscience. Modern philosophy [Hegel] makes no movement; as a rule it makes only a commotion, and if it makes any movement at all, it is always within immanence, whereas repetition is and remains a transcendence. It is fortunate that he does not seek any explanation from me, for I have abandoned my theory. I am adrift. Then, too, repetition is too transcendent for me. Fortunately, my friend is not looking for clarification from any world-famous philosopher or any *professor publicus ordinarius;* he turns to an unprofessional thinker who once possessed the world's glories but later withdrew from life—in other words, he falls back on Job. (*SV* III 221/*R* 186)

Then follow the young man's letters. The young man explains that Constantin's fraudulent scheme to deceive the girl was repugnant to his ethical instincts. He has found better counsel in Job who, driven to life's extreme, keeps repeating "the Lord gives and the Lord takes away; blessed be the name of the Lord." Job repeats the prayer of repetition, that is, of resoluteness in adversity, of the self-possession which knows how to press forward no matter what. In particular, Job resists the explanation that his suffering is a just punishment for his sins and insists upon his innocence. It is merely human wisdom, ethical rationality, which explains his situation in terms of guilt. Ethically, he is innocent. That is just the situation of the young man. Like Job he finds himself thrust into a situation not of his own making and then declared guilty. In a passage clearly anticipating Heidegger's notion of "thrownness" *(Geworfenheit)*, the young man laments:

> I am at the end of my rope. I am nauseated by life; it is insipid—without salt and meaning. . . . Where am I? What does it mean to say: the world? What is the meaning of that word? Who tricked me into this whole thing and leaves me standing here? Who am I? How did I get into the world? Why was I not asked about it, why was I not informed of the rules and regulations but just thrust into the ranks as if I had been bought from a peddling shanghaier of human beings? How did I get involved in this big

enterprise called actuality? And if I am compelled to be involved, where is the manager—I have something to say about this. Is there no manager? To whom shall I make my complaint? . . . How did it happen that I became guilty? Or am I not guilty? Why, then, am I called that in every language? . . .

Why should she be in the right and I in the wrong? If both of us are faithful, why then is this expressed in human language in such a way that she is faithful and I am a deceiver? (*SV* III 234-35/*R* 200-201)

If he marries her, that will destroy her—because of his poetic nature. If he does not marry her, he is guilty. If he marries her, he is indeed guilty; if he does not marry her, he is declared guilty by human language. Here is an either/or which no judge can resolve. And so he offers a reward to anyone who can invent a word for his state, who can find a category which names the condition of being innocent and seeming guilty. His condition is nameless, even as he himself is nameless. He is at a standstill, immobilized; he sees no way to press ahead.

Clearly all the possibilities of rational human discourse have been exhausted. The only way out is religious. And that is why he reads the book of Job with the eyes of his heart, which is the only way to deal with his "nameless anxiety about the world and life and men and everything" (*SV* III 239/*R* 205). The secret to repetition is in Job (*SV* III 241/*R* 207). Job was able to press forward, even though the whole world disagreed; he had the power to resist the ethical explanation. He knew the whole thing was not punishment for guilt but an "ordeal" in which God was putting his faith to the test. That is a category which does not exist in science; it is a strictly religious category which exists only for the individual. Because of faithfulness, Job's thunderstorm passes (*SV* III 247/*R* 214), and he is given back double everything that had been taken away from him. That is his repetition (*SV* III 245/*R* 212).

Job, however, is not a hero of faith, properly speaking, but of the region which lies just at the outskirts of faith. " . . . Job's significance is that the disputes at the boundaries of faith are fought out in him . . ." (*SV* III 243/*R* 210). An "ordeal" is a strictly religious category—it cannot be invoked on just any occasion, as when the oatmeal burns!—but it does not yet touch upon the extremities of Christian faith. The absurdity Job faces is not the absolute paradox of Christian belief. An ordeal is a temporary condition, which is rewarded at the end by a worldly repetition. Christian faith runs deeper than that.

But the application of Job's life to the young man is clear:

All I know is that I am standing and have been standing *suspenso gradu* [immobilized] for a whole month now, without moving a foot or making one single movement.

I am waiting for a thunderstorm—and for repetition.

What will be the effect of this thunderstorm? It will make me fit to be a husband. It will shatter my whole personality—I am prepared. It will render me almost unrecognizable to myself—I am unwavering even though I am standing on one foot. . . .

In other respects, I am doing my best to make myself into a husband. I sit and clip myself, take away everything that is incommensurable in order to become commensurable. (*SV* III 247-48/*R* 214)

Unable of his own strength to enter into marriage—everything rational in him tells him that marriage would destroy the girl and destroy himself—he awaits a transformation by God which will make him a fit husband and restore his honor, which will render his exceptional condition commensurable with the universal ethical measure. He cannot make progress, cannot take another step further, cannot make a movement—except in virtue of faith.[16]

Now Constantin inserts a word, in between the letters, like an aside from offstage: he distrusts the whole thing; he does not believe in thunderstorms. He is sure the whole thing will come to grief—as it does in the next letter:

She is married—to whom I do not know, for when I read it in the newspaper I was so stunned that I dropped the paper and have not had the patience since then to check in detail. I am myself again. Here I have repetition; I understand everything, and life seems more beautiful to me than ever. It did indeed come like a thunderstorm, although I am indebted to her generosity for its coming. . . . Let existence reward her as it has, let it give her what she loved more; it also gave me what I loved more—myself, and gave it to me through generosity. (*SV* III 253/*R* 220)

The repetition is that he is given himself back. But this is not religious repetition. His freedom is to be employed not in the service of God but in the service of the poetic idea. Despite the flirtation with the religious, the deeply religious tone of the thunderstorm, despite the invocation of Job, the young man becomes a poetic, not a religious exception to marriage (*SV* III 254-55/*R* 221-22).

But it is to Constantin that Kierkegaard gives the last word, and with good reason, for now Constantin confesses that the nameless young man does not exist, that he is an experiment devised by Constantin himself (*SV* III 262/*R* 228). Both parts of **Repetition** thus are a kind of farce, an imaginative construct, the end result of which is to show that repetition is nowhere to be found—not in Constantin, not in the young man, not in philosophy, not even, properly, in Job. Genuine religious repetition keeps deferring itself. It is nowhere to be found in this book, or in any book. It cannot be circumscribed by the margins of a book.[17] The young man was an analogue, a parody, of religious repetition (*SV* III 262/*R* 228).

The critical point the young man reached was the point of readiness for divine action, where he had completely surrendered his own sense of self-sufficiency and put himself at the disposal of God's action on him. He was ready to have his whole nature as a poetic exception destroyed and to be remade in God's image, according to God's plan for him. That is the point of religious repetition, when we are ready to let God make something new in us, effect a transcendence in us of which we are incapable ourselves. But when the thunderstorm came, he managed to break through, not to the religious, but to a poetic existence in which he is loosened from the universality of marriage and free to exist as a poetic exception, thanks to the girl. That is his repetition, which consists in "the raising of his consciousness to the second power" (*SV* III 263/*R* 229). But *that* repetition is but an imperfect analogue and transition stage to a higher repetition which he at times skirted but never attained (*SV* III 263/*R* 229). When the thunderstorm broke, he took the poetic way out, instead of weathering it out religiously (*SV* III 263/*R* 229-30).

The forward momentum of existence can be sustained only by the energy of faith. The passion of existence which remains faithful to the chosen way must be the passion of faith, which operates "with religious fear and trembling, but also with faith and trust" (*SV* III 263/*R* 230). In the end, repetition is possible neither for Constantin nor for the young man. The experiment undertaken in **Repetition** ends in failure, but this is meant, not to fill us with despair about the possibility of repetition, but rather to sharpen our sense of its illusive and self-deferring quality, of the demands it makes. It is meant to persuade us that repetition is not to be found within the margins of a book. It is a way of writing a book about repetition which arises from an understanding that we have reached the end of the book (cf. **CUP,** "A First and Last Declaration").

Repetition and the Stages of Existence

We can clarify what Kierkegaard means by repetition by differentiating the well-known "stages" or "spheres of existence"—the aesthetic, ethical, and religious. Clearly, aesthetic repetition has proven to be a disaster. Repetition spells the end of aesthetics and hence must be feared, for repetition "has a magic power to keep [aesthetic] freedom captive" (***Pap.*** IV B 117 281/*R* 301). It is the death of unqualified pleasure seeking. With each repetition the edge of aesthetic pleasure is dulled until it

becomes tedious and vanishes. The trip to Berlin is an exercise in naive aesthetic repetition, simple reduplication. Constantin is unwary, naive; he thinks a pleasure can just be reenacted, reproduced. Had he been a little more clever he would have had the sense to fear repetition, to see in it the enemy of freedom-as-pleasure seeking.

Hence the despair of straightforward pleasure seeking generates a higher form of aestheticism equipped with a "sagacity," a finite, worldly wisdom illustrated by the famous "Rotation Method" (in *Either/Or,* vol. 1) meant to fool repetition (*SV* IV B 117 281/*R* 301-302). If the repetition of a pleasure dulls it, then freedom must learn to be more cunning. On the aesthetic level, the question is not indeed whether repetition is possible—that was Constantin's mistake—but whether it is *avoidable*. The whole problem for the aesthete then is to acquire the art of variation and constant alteration. The rotation method is a shrewd and systematic attempt to offset the fatal effects of repetition upon aesthetic life, a way to keep it at bay and avoid it, always altering pleasure so as to keep pleasure alive. But this too breaks down in despair, to the extreme of the Seducer and his repugnant treatment of Cordelia. Aesthetically speaking, the Seducer is a higher type—more reflective, more careful, and premeditating—but ethically he is cruel and diabolical. Ethically repulsed, we are driven to seek higher ground.

Freedom becomes itself, becomes truly free, not when it seeks ways to evade repetition, but when it seeks repetition itself, when it asks the guiding question of **Repetition:**

> Now freedom's supreme interest is precisely to bring about repetition, and its only fear is that variation would have the power to disturb its eternal nature. Here emerges the issue: *Is repetition possible?* Freedom itself is now the repetition. . . . What freedom fears here is not repetition but variation; what it wants is not variation but repetition. (*SV* IV B 117 281-82/*R* 302)

Here repetition is looked upon not as a fatal affliction which kills off the life of freedom but as freedom itself. The rotation method has as little to do with real repetition as does an alehouse keeper who happens to look like the king. We ought to smile at Constantin's trip to Berlin as we would smile at such a man. True freedom and genuine repetition converge; repetition has become inward, a matter of freedom, of "the individuality's own repetition raised to a new power" (***Pap.*** IV B 111 270/*R* 294).

With that, the question of repetition enters the sphere of the ethical and religious. But it is important to distinguish the two. The ethical significance of repetition is embodied in marriage, whose aesthetic validity and higher ethical worth are defended by the Judge in the second volume of **Either/Or.** All of the books written just after the breach with Regine are addressed to her; they are explanations to her, and to Kierkegaard himself, of what he had done, of why he made of himself an exception and departed from the ethical-universal, whose Archimedean point is married life. The Judge, who represents conjugal fidelity, the paradigm case of ethical repetition, attacks the aesthete on the grounds that for him genuine love is impossible (*E/O* II 144).

The aesthete lacks substance and actuality. His relationship with the girl ends like a novel, at the point where the lovers are to get married, which is precisely the point where the ethical begins (*E/O* II 144). Marriage is eternity, not the moment; actuality, not flirtation; possession, not conquest. The aesthete is intoxicated with first love, by the charm of the first kiss, the first embrace, but the Judge knows that first love is unhistorical—it has not proved itself in time—whereas marriage is tested by time and ripened by development.[18] What the aesthete fears most about time is monotony (*E/O* II 128ff.)—boredom, it was noted in the "Rotation Method," is the *radix malorum*—for he cannot imagine love when it is not young and new. He dreads the repetition of marriage because of a defective understanding of time. He prefers the time which leads up to something and then is over and done with (*E/O* II 138). He knows nothing of ethical time, the toilsome process in which something is slowly built up and grows into the fullness of its being. The ethical individual has learned to do battle, not with dragons and lions, but with the most difficult enemy of all, time. He has learned to hold fast in time, both by finding constancy in the midst of the flux, and by finding novelty in the midst of the customary and everyday. Marriage and the ethical have a different conception of time and repetition, says the Judge, for where the aesthete finds monotony the ethical man finds preservation and increase.

Repetition is thus the centerpiece in Kierkegaard's "existential theory of the self." For the self is defined by choice, as something to be "won" (*E/O* II 167). This is an ethical, not a metaphysical, account of the self (which clearly anticipates §64 of *Being and Time),* which treats the self not as a substance, a permanent presence which endures beneath the changing fortunes of age and bodily change, but as a task to be achieved—not as presence but as possibility. Without choice, the individual lapses into the diversions of "half hour works" (*E/O* II 202). The aesthete lacks memory, not in the usual sense but in the sense of "memory of your own life, of what you have experienced in it" (*E/O* II 202). For the aesthete the past is simply over; it has lost all interest for him. But the ethical individual has long memory, stretching himself out toward his past, for which he assumes responsibility, even as he stretches himself out anticipatorily toward what is expected of him in the future, holding his entire life together in the unity and continuity of a self, thereby constituting himself as a self:

> Only when in his choice a man has assumed himself . . . has so totally penetrated himself that every moment is attended by the consciousness of a responsibility for himself, only then has he chosen himself ethically, only then has he repeated himself. . . . (*E/O* II 207-208)

To speak of choosing oneself is of course paradoxical, for the self does not exist until it is brought forth by choice, and yet the self must exist if it is to choose:

> . . . that which is chosen does not exist and comes into existence with the choice; that which is chosen exists, otherwise there would not be a choice. For in case what I chose did not exist but absolutely came into existence with the choice, I would not be choosing, I would be creating; but I do not create myself, I choose myself. (*E/O* II 219-20)

Kierkegaardian repetition, like Derrida's, is productive. It does not limp along after, trying to reproduce what is already present, but is productive of what it is repeating. The repeating is the producing—of the self. But not absolutely: One does not create *ex nihilo* but always beginning from a situated standpoint one gradually carves out an identity for oneself. The paradox is resolved, therefore, in a way which anticipates the hermeneutical paradoxes in §32 and §33 in *Being and Time:* by introducing a kind of existential circle, according to which the self by choosing the self comes to be the being which it all along has been:

> He becomes himself, quite the same self he was before, down to the last significant peculiarity, and yet he becomes another, for the choice permeates everything and transforms it. (*E/O* II 227)

He does not create something altogether new, but actualizes what he has been all along *(to ti en einai).*

Repetition thus is not an ethical gymnastics which thinks anything possible. It begins with the situatedness in which one finds oneself. It is not abstract freedom but the freedom to actualize possibilities. It does not depend upon the favor of world history to give it an opportunity, but it knows how to find the possible in any situation in which it is put. It knows how to transform necessity (facticity) into freedom. The individual knows himself:

> . . . as this definite individual, with these talents, these dispositions, these instincts, these passions, influenced by these definite surroundings, as this definite product of a definite environment. But being conscious of himself in this way, he assumes responsibility for all of this. (*E/O* II 255)

If necessity thrusts him into a certain place, freedom chooses this place. Freedom knows that it is not possible always to have good fortune but that the essential thing is "what one sees in every situation, with what energy he regards it" (*E/O* II 257). The ethical does not require one to be in the right place at the right time, for the essentials of ethical repetition are at hand in any time or place. The aesthete requires good fortune, but the ethical requires only one thing, "and that is . . . his self" (*E/O* II 257).

In sum, repetition on the ethical level is the constancy and continuity of choice by which the self constitutes itself as a self, by which it returns again and again to its own innermost resolution and establishes its moral identity. Ethical repetition means the steadiness of the unbroken vow, the enduring bond of the lasting marriage, the capacity to find ever new depths in the familiar and self-same. It means a recurrent cycle of growth and development by means of which the self becomes itself.

But eventually the bravado of ethical repetition must come to grief. In the ethical, one needs only oneself, and that is its illusion. The ethical sphere is predicated on the false assumption that everything in life is weighed on the scales of human justice, that it means everything to be innocent. But what if a man were entirely innocent and yet still suffered? Furthermore, what if a man attributes such innocence as he has to himself, as if there were something to him of himself, independently of his God-relationship? Ethical repetition maintains the illusion that a resolute will with good intention is enough to constitute the self, to keep a man whole, that a balance is possible between the ethical and the aesthetic factors in the personality. The Judge's argument against the aesthete is that the self cannot be dependent upon external factors, upon the vagaries of good fortune. But that argument finally skews because it leads in the end to the illusion of the self-sufficiency of the will. What if a man were ethically whole, a just man, and yet is struck down and deprived of all aesthetic immediacy, which, according to the Judge, is an integral complement to ethical righteousness, part of the balanced whole of the personality? Ethics suffers from the illusion that repetition lies within its power.

Relative to the idle caprice of the rotation method, ethical repetition presses forward resolutely, makes progress, effects transcendence. But inasmuch as it calls upon nothing more than human resources, upon resolve and firmness of will, ethical repetition pushes ahead within the sphere of immanence. Repetition in its deepest registers, therefore, has to do with the exception, with the breakdown of the human, the loss of human compensation, a transformation which shatters the categories of immanence. It concerns that most extreme inwardness which arises only from the shipwreck of ethical humanism.[19] Genuine repetition, which is absolutely transcendent and effected in virtue of the absurd, occurs only when the individual does not see how he can

go on, when every rational human resource is exhausted. Then the individual gives up everything and awaits the thunderstorm. The young man reached that point, but he had recourse to the poetic, not the religious, when the thunderstorm broke. The young man was caught in an ethical paradox; he was guilty but he had done no wrong. Here indeed was a stumbling block to confound the Judge's cheery moralism and ethical balancing act. That is the importance of Job, who saw his suffering not as punishment for a wrongdoing but as purposely visited upon him by God so as to accentuate the purely personal God-relationship and to diminish the juridical one.

Job and the young man reach the point of the breakdown of the ethical wisdom and sanguine rationality of the Judge. They enter a sphere not governed by the rule of credit and debit, investment and return, an economy of expenditure without reserve.[20] In this mad religious economy, if one gives up everything, everything is repeated, returned, even a hundredfold, in virtue of the absurd. Here there is not sound reason but a "play" in which the world, that is, the hand of God, is playing with man in order to humble his finite understanding and lead him into another and transcendent sphere. Repetition is reached not by achieving ethical steadfastness but by realizing that, from a human standpoint, everything is lost, that there is nowhere to turn (*SV* III 245-46/*R* 212). At that point we learn what we have all along heard in the sermons: that unless a man loses his soul he cannot have it back, that of himself a man can do nothing. These are the first laws of the dynamics of religious repetition, of the religious way through the flux.

Indeed, even Job and Abraham fall short of this demanding sense of repetition. The paradox they faced was not the absolute paradox, and the repetition they were granted retained an earthly sense: the restoration of Job's goods and honor and the restoration of Isaac. Thus, the repetition had not been sufficiently interiorized, had not yet been driven inward. Repetition cannot have to do with the restoration of outward goods. Repetition is a law of inwardness which moves ahead precisely in virtue of outward loss. The outer loss is an inner gain; the detachment from the finite is progress toward the infinite. The whole question of finitude becomes a matter of indifference (*SV* III 263/*R* 230). Repetition takes place only if the finite is crucified and the individual surrenders everything in order to enter the divine absence, the dark night, the fear and the trembling. The individual takes his stand in the abyss, endures the withdrawal of presence, lets himself be led by God, who is alone the true teacher of repetition. In the abyss of the God-relationship the individual is able to move ahead. True repetition is the radical transition from sin to atonement. Therefore, the only authentic *kinesis,* which is repetition, is set in motion by eternity.[21]

Repetition and the End of Metaphysics

Kierkegaard inaugurated the delimitation of the metaphysical tradition—which today is spoken of in terms of "the end of philosophy," "the end of metaphysics"—and it is a great mistake on the part of the Heideggerians to write him off as a merely religious or psychological thinker. Far from having only a passing significance for the more "existentialist" elements in the "existential analytic," Kierkegaard set in motion the "destruction of the history of ontology" and hence anticipated the central ontological argument of *Being and Time* and the whole gesture of "overcoming metaphysics" in the later Heidegger.

By opposing existential repetition to Platonic recollection and Hegelian mediation, the beginning and end of metaphysics, he mounted a sweeping attack upon the whole history of metaphysics. Platonism makes light of time while Hegelianism offers a fraudulent version of time. Hegelianism is but a variation of Platonism which undermines the contingency of temporal movement, even as Platonism undermines time itself. Together they completely subvert *kinesis* and becoming; they turn them over to the rule of essence and necessity, to pure thought and disengaged speculation. Metaphysics is an exercise in disinterested *nous* looking on at the spectacle of *eidos* or of a phenomenological "we" serenely observing the logical unfolding of the formations *(Gestaltungen)* of the spirit.

For Kierkegaard everything turns on our ability to take our stand in the flux, to press forward in the element of actuality and becoming rather than to seek some way around it. It is a matter of "interest" in the literal sense of *inter-esse,*[22] of being-between, of firmly placing oneself in and amidst the strife of temporal becoming:

> If one does not have the category of recollection or of repetition all life dissolves into an empty, meaningless noise. Recollection is the pagan *[ethniske]* view of life, repetition the modern; repetition is the *interest [Interesse]* of metaphysics, and also the interest upon which metaphysics comes to grief; repetition is the watchword *[Losnet]* in every ethical view; repetition is the *conditio sine qua non* [the indispensable condition] for every issue in dogmatics. (*SV* III 189/*R* 149)

Repetition displaces the disinterested posture of metaphysical thought and sets in motion the "foundering" of metaphysics, the way it "comes to grief." In this foundering the Heideggerian gestures of *Destruktion* and *Überwindung* are already anticipated. For Kierkegaard, metaphysics, ethics, and theology—in short, the length and breadth of "onto-theo-logic"—shatter against the rocks of "interest."

"As soon as interest steps forth, metaphysics steps aside," Kierkegaard explains. Repetition forces metaphysics to

the side in order to make room for the existing spirit. The existing spirit belongs to the sphere of actuality, for which the categories of logic are a bad fit. Metaphysics wants either to negate movement and make its way out the back door of time or to replace them with seductive logical counterfeits. Repetition cuts off all subterfuge, forcing the spirit to proceed without recourse to the fantastic constructions of *eidos* and *Geist.* Metaphysics puts becoming under the protective rule of essence so that nothing genuinely new can emerge. But religious repetition, which is the subjective passion that presses forward in virtue of faith, says with St. Paul, "Behold all things have become new" (II Cor 5:17).

Even ethics, which takes its stand in actuality and real choice, remains bound to the sphere of immanence and a logic of moral development. Hence even in the ethical sphere, nothing really new happens. Ethics functions within the range of law-governed change. Religious repetition, on the other hand, means a more radical transition—from fall to grace, from sin to at-one-ment—shattering all ethical continuity.

> Either all of existence comes to an end in the demand of ethics, or the condition [faith] is provided and the whole of life and existence begins anew, not through an immanent continuity with the former existence, which is a contradiction, but through a transcendence. (*SV* IV 289/*CA* 17n)

Religious repetition, as a discontinuous wrenching free from sin, does not arise immanently, from laws internal to moral development, but transcendently, from the intervention of God's saving act. Ethics does not make a single step forward out of the sphere of immanence. Here then is the end—the delimitation—of metaphysics and ethics, of ethical and metaphysical humanism, of any future metaphysics of morals:

> If repetition is not posited, ethics becomes a binding power. No doubt it is for this reason that the author states that repetition is the watchword in every ethical view. (*SV* IV 290/*CA* 18n)

Despite his talk of "subjectivity," what Kierkegaard has in mind is the foundering of all human categories, the shattering of the subjective and the anthropocentric. In the face of the fury of the flux, only faith can move forward. Faith intervenes just where everything human and rational, everything ethical and metaphysical, every form of humanism, comes to grief. And not only ethics and metaphysics but also theology ("dogmatics") too. For inasmuch as theology takes itself to be capable of making progress in sorting out the flux by means of its onto-theo-logical categories, it too is a kind of paganism:[23]

> If repetition is not posited, dogmatics cannot exist at all, for repetition begins in faith, and faith is the organ for issues of dogma. (*SV* IV 290/*CA* 18n)

The full range of onto-theo-logic—of metaphysics, ethics, and theology—is thereby delimited. There can be no mistaking the character of Kierkegaard's project. If it is "religious," as it certainly is, it proceeds by way of a religious delimitation of onto-theo-logic, a religous way out of philosophy and metaphysics, and hence belongs essentially to the project of the deconstruction or overcoming of metaphysics.

Without having this vocabulary at his disposal, Kierkegaard saw quite clearly into the shortcomings of the metaphysics of presence—the essential tendency of metaphysics to arrest the flux. He saw in the beginnings of metaphysics, in the doctrine of recollection, a philosophy of timeless presence which tells the story of the loss of presence and how presence lost can be restored. And he saw in its Hegelian completion the subordination of time and becoming to the immobility of logical necessity: In the beginning, an archeology of lost presence; at the end, a teleology of history rushing headlong into a historical *pleroma,* a *parousia,* a consummation of presence. In the one case, a nostalgia for a presence lost; in the other, a dreamy hope and rational optimism about presence promised. Metaphysics is essentially an archeo-teleological project.

Within the history of metaphysics, Kierkegaard saw only one alternative to its inveterate idealism, and that lay in the Aristotelian doctrine of *kinesis.* Against Plato and the Eleatics, Aristotle set his sights on movement and actuality, the real transition from the possible to the actual. But in fact Kierkegaard was pressing Aristotelianism, and philosophy generally, beyond its limits, putting demands upon it which it could not meet. That is why Kierkegaard always had to look for heroes *outside* metaphysics: Socrates, the great existing individual just before metaphysics who regarded the doctrine of recollection as a temptation to be resisted; Abraham and Job, on the outskirts of faith in the Old Testament; and finally the knight of faith himself, the Christian believer, St. Paul's "just man." The real, the concrete, the existing, the temporal, the free and contingent—these were matters for which the categories of metaphysics were in principle unprepared. Metaphysics always wants to keep a safe distance from the flux and to maintain its balance by means of an objectifying thinking. It maintains itself at a distance from the flux and thereby induces the optical illusion of stillness, even as from a distance the square tower looks round. It is always on the lookout for the stable essence, the law that constrains movement, the *eidos* and the *Begriff* which keeps the flux in check.

But as soon as metaphysics becomes interested, as soon as it is drawn into the flux and loses its protective barrier, it is forced to acknowledge the groundless play, the abyss, the absence inhabiting every claim to presence. What concerned Kierkegaard above all was the mysterious movement of faith, the midnight hour of faith, the abyss in which the existing individual, outside the protective shelter of the universal, takes his stand before God. What concerned Kierkegaard was the darkness of faith, not the light of reason, the abyss of freedom, not the reliability of logic. His thought takes place in the twilight zone between presence and absence, the point of intersection, of the interweaving of eternity and time.

Thus the deeply deconstructive element in Kierkegaard, which begins the work of dismantling the apparatus of metaphysics, belongs to a hermeneutic[24] attempt to restore the sphere of "actuality." Kierkegaard displaces the philosophy of Being and presence with *inter-esse,* with being-in-the-midst-of, with existence always already exposed to the flux. This deconstructive work leads us back to the human condition, not in the sense of the humanism which he rejected, but in the sense of a decentering of human willfulness which reveals the poverty of our circumstances. It leads us back to the original difficulty of life which metaphysics always wants to erase. In repetition we press ahead into what Derrida calls the *ébranler,* where the whole trembles *(sollicitare),* a region which is marked for Kierkegaard by "fear and trembling," from which, like the companion piece published on the same day, repetition cannot be separated.

Notes

1 Friedrich Nietzsche, *Twilight of the Idols and The Anti-Christ,* trans. R. J. Hollingdale (Baltimore: Penguin Classics, 1968), p. 35.

2 Nietzsche, *Twilight,* pp. 40-42.

3 "Founders," which appears in the old Lowrie translation (in Hong: "comes to grief"), is worth preserving. See Kierkegaard, *Repetition,* trans. W. Lowrie (Princeton: Princeton University Press, 1946), p. 34.

4 See the series edited by Mark Taylor, *Kierkegaard and Post-Modernism* (Florida State University Press).

5 Both Macquarrie and Robinson *(Being and Time)* and James Churchill *(Kant and the Problem of Metaphysics)* translate *Wiederholung* as "repetition" (without noting its Kierkegaardian origin), whereas Richardson uses "retrieve," rightly remarking that it is closer to the sense of *Wiederholung* in Heidegger himself. See Richardson, *Heidegger: Through Phenomenology to Thought* (The Hague: M. Nijhoff, 1962), p. 89, n. 181.

6 Kierkegaard, *Gesammelte Werke,* B. 3, *Wiederholung,* trans. H. Gottsched (Jena, 1909). Cf. Hans-Georg Gadamer, *Philosophical Hermeneutics,* trans. David Linge (Berkeley and Los Angeles: University of California Press, 1976), p. 214. See also Gadamer's remarks in his letter to Richard Bernstein in Bernstein, *Beyond Objectivism*

and Relativism (Philadelphia: University of Pennsylvania Press, 1983), p. 265.

[7] Heidegger's assessment of Kierkegaard is severe and precisely the one I contest. . .: "The comparison between Nietzsche and Kierkegaard that has become customary, but is no less questionable for that reason, fails to recognize, and indeed out of a misunderstanding of the essence of thinking, that Nietzsche as a metaphysical thinker preserves a closeness to Aristotle. Kierkegaard remains essentially remote from Aristotle, although he mentions him more often. For Kierkegaard is not a thinker but a religious writer, and indeed not just one among others, but the only one in accord with the destining belonging to his age. Therein lies his greatness, if to speak in this way is not already a misunderstanding." (GA 5, 249/QCT 9). Cf. WHD 129/ WCT 213. To what extent Kierkegaard had studied Aristotle directly is not clear. His reading of "to ti en einai" seems to have been based on G. Marbach, *Geschichte der Philosophie des Mittelalters* (Leipzig, 1841), par. 128, pp. 4-5, and of *kinesis* on W. G. Tennemann, *Geschichte der Philosophie* (Leipzig, 1798-1819), Ktl. 815-26, III, 125-28. I find Kierkegaard's interest in *kinesis* striking in the light of the work of Thomas Sheehan on Heidegger's interpretation of *kinesis*.

[8] This is, of course, the remark of Heidegger. *The Question of Being,* trans. W. Kluback and J. Wilde, with the German text (London: Vision Press, 1959), pp. 90-91, which Derrida relates to a random note found among Nietzsche's papers in *Spurs,* 140-43.

[9] On this passage from CUP, see J. Preston Cole, *The Problematic Self in Kierkegaard and Freud* (New Haven: Yale University Press, 1971), 150-55.

[10] Calvin Schrag has long alerted us to the Kierkegaardian resonances in Heidegger; see his *Existence and Freedom* (Athens: Ohio University Press, 1960); and "Heidegger on Repetition and Historical Understanding," *Philosophy East and West,* 20 (1970), 287-96. Michael Zimmerman, *Eclipse of the Self: The Development of Heidegger's Concept of Authenticity* (Athens: Ohio University Press, 1981) is also very good on the Kierkgaard connection. Recently the connection between Heideggerian hermeneutics and Kierkegaard has been made by William Spanos, "Heidegger, Kierkegaard and the Hermeneutic Circle: Towards a Post-Modern Theory of Interpretation as Dis-closure," *Boundary 2,* 4 (1976), 455-88. Among French scholars, Jean Wahl established the general relationship between the early Heidegger and Kierkegaard; see "Heidegger et Kierkegaard," *Rescherches philosophiques,* 2 (1932-33), 349-70, and *Etudes Kierkegaardiennes* (Paris: Aubier, 1938). Alphonse de Waelhens regarded the notion of repetition in Kierkegaard as too obscure to allow a fruitful comparison with Heidegger; see *La philosophie de Martin Heidegger,* 4th ed. (Louvain: Publications

universitaires, 1955), pp. 231, 352. I also think that Dan Magurshak has been doing a good job recently of settling the score between Kierkegaard and Heidegger; see his "*The Concept of Anxiety:* The Keystone of the Kierkegaard-Heidegger Relationship," forthcoming in *International Kierkegaard Commentary: The Concept of Anxiety.*

[11] I treat the notion of repetition in Derrida in chap. 5 [in "Repetition and *Kinesis*: Kierkegaard on the Foundering of Metaphysics"]. . . , when I examine Derrida's critique of Husserl.

[12] For an excellent study of repetition and mediation, see André Clar, "Médiation et Répétition: Le lieu de la dialectique Kierkegaardienne," *Revue des sciences philosophiques et théologiques,* 59 (1975), 38-78.

[13] See Richard Popkin, "Kierkegaard and Scepticism," in *Kierkegaard: A Collection of Critical Essays,* ed. Josiah Thompson (Garden City: Doubleday Anchor Books, 1972), pp. 289-323.

[14] Kierkaardian repetition is thus the opposite of a repetition compulsion. See George Stack, "Repetition in Kierkegaard and Freud," *The Personalist,* 58 (1977), 249-61. Jacques Lacan is also interested in the connection between Kierkegaard and the repetition compulsion; see "The Unconscious and Repetition," in *The Four Fundamental Concepts of Psycho-Analysis,* trans. Alan Sheridan (New York: Norton, 1978); see also André Clar, p. 74, n. 78.

[15] *Repetition* is subtitled "A Venture in Experimenting Psychology." See Hong's helpful explanation in R xxff.

[16] At this point the original manuscript which Kierkegaard drafted breaks off. What follows is a rewrite done after Kierkegaard hears the news that Regine has married. We know, of course, that Kierkegaard has all along been addressing his abandoned Regine, whom he had left in Copenhagen, taking flight to Berlin. Considering that Job got his possessions back, that Abraham got Isaac back, that the young man expected to be made a fit husband, and that there is a thinly disguised bitterness in the remark about "feminine generosity" in the text announcing the girl's marriage, one has the distinct sense that Kierkegaard thought that God would make him fit to be a husband, too. And we know that Kierkegaard, like the young man, once observed that had he more faith he would have married Regine.

[17] Here and elsewhere in this chapter I give Derridean formulations to Kierkegaardian themes. For a Derridean reading of *Repetition,* see Louis Mackie, "Once More with Feeling: Kierkegaard's *Repetition,*" in *Kierkegaard and Literature: Irony, Repetition and Criticism,* ed. R. Schleifer and R. Markley (Norman: University of Oklahoma Press, 1984), pp. 80-115; and Ronald Schleifer,

"Irony, Identity and Repetition," *Substance,* no. 25 (1980), 44-54. Mackie's "Slouching Toward Bethlehem: Deconstructive Strategies in Theology," *Anglican Theological Review,* 65 (1983), 255-72, is the best Derridean treatment of Kierkegaard I have seen. Mackie reads Kierkegaard's denial that there can be an "immediate contemporaneity with Christ" as the self-deferring of the divine. In a similar vein, see Patrick Bigelow, "Kierkegaard and the Hermeneutic Circle," *Man and World,* 15 (1982), 67-82. I use this notion of the self-deferral of the object of faith in this chapter. Also see Sylviane Agacinski, *Aparté: Conceptions et morts de Sören Kierkegaard* (Paris: Aubier-Flammarion, 1977). Mark Taylor is preparing a collection of studies on *Fear and Trembling* to which Derrida is contributing; Taylor contributes a piece on Abraham as "Outlaw."

[18] Both Kierkegaard and Derrida criticize the notion of the "first time" in the name of repetition: Kierkegaard, because he thinks it is aesthetically unrepeatable and ethically fragile and unproven; Derrida, perhaps more radically, because he thinks there never really is a first time. Derrida is speaking of Husserlian *Erstmaligkeit* (in "The Origin of Geometry"), which he treats as a transcendental illusion, a fiction which cannot be certified. See chap. 5 [in "Repetition and Kinesis: Kierkegaard on the Foundering of Metaphysics"]. . .

[19] Kierkegaard was already a critic of humanism, and on this point, his argument is more ontologically advanced than is Heidegger's in *Being and Time* (rather than ontologically naive, as Heidegger claimed), a point which Bultmann made against Heidegger as well. See Michael Zimmerman's discussion in *Eclipse of the Self,* pp. 144-45.

[20] I allude to chap. 9 of *Writing and Difference.* For a suggestive expansion of an unrestricted economy in religious terms, see Mark Taylor, *Erring: A Postmodern A/theology* (Chicago: University Press, 1984), pp. 140-48.

[21] For more on Kierkegaard's notion of repetition, see George E. and George R. Arbaugh, *Kierkegaard's Authorship* (London: George Allen and Unwin, 1968), pp. 94-105 (an illuminating commmentary); Robert P. Harrison, "Heresy and the Question of Repetition: Reading Kierkegaard's *Repetition,*" in *Textual Analysis: Some Readers Reading,* ed. Mary Ann Caws (New York: Modern Language Association, 1986), pp. 281-88; George Stack, *Kierkegaard's Existential Ethics* (University Park: University of Alabama Press, 1977). See also the entries under "repetition" in *Soren Kierkegaard's Journals and Papers,* 5 vols., vol. 3, *L-R,* ed. and trans. Howard and Edna Hong (Bloomington: Indiana University Press, 1975). Cf. also "Strengthened in the Inner Man," in *Edifying Discourses,* 4 vols., trans. D. Swenson and L. Swenson (Minneapolis: Augsburg Publishing House, 1943), vol. 1, pp. 93-119.

[22] See also *Johannes Climacus: or De omnibus dubitandum est, and a Sermon,* trans. T. H. Croxall (Stanford: Stanford University Press, 1958), pp. 151-52: "interest" means *inter-esse,* which has the twofold meaning of being-between and of being a matter of concern, clearly anticipating the notion that the Being of being-in-the-world *(in-der-Welt-sein)* is "care."

[23] It is just this Kierkegaardian and Barthian project of sorting out the categories of Greek ontology from Christian reflection which Joseph O'Leary undertakes in *Questioning Back: Overcoming Metaphysics in Christian Tradition* (Minneapolis: Winston-Seabury Press, 1985).

[24] It is precisely what I call here a hermeneutic—even if it be a cold and trembling hermeneutic—element in Kierkegaard which Gilles Deleuze opposes in the Kierkegaardian notion of repetition. Deleuze sees clearly that the central point of repetiton in Kierkegaard is to oppose the fraudulent "movement" defended by Hegel and that on this point Kierkegaard is to be compared with Nietzsche. Something new happens in both these thinkers. They operate in the medium of the theatrical, not pure reflection. They are interested not in a conceptualization of movement but in inducing it: in Kierkegaard, the movement of the leap of faith; in Nietzsche, the movement of the dance. But Deleuze thinks that in the end Kierkegaard is not willing to "pay the price" for a philosophy of movement. Kierkegaardian repetition is always inward, spiritual, and recuperative "once and for all" of God and self. But Nietzsche's thought of becoming and movement is one of pure dispersal, earthly and natural, and needs to be affirmed again and again. Atheistic repetiton is more radical than the repetition of faith. Cf. Gilles Deleuze, *Difference et Répetition* (Paris: PUF, 1981), pp. 12-20, especially 16-20, and 126-27, 377. Deleuze does indeed have more radical intentions than Kierkegaard. Deleuze wants to liberate difference, to defend a "pure" difference no longer subjected to identity, as it is in dialectics, where it is but a moment in the unfolding of identity. Liberated from identity, repetition means not the recurrence of the same but the occurrence of the new, always repeating with a difference. He defends profusion and "nomadic" dispersal which he somewhat misleadingly calls a new form of the "univocity" of Being (as opposed to that of Scotus and Spinoza). Being is not to be thought of as neatly differentiated and hierarchized into chains and categorial groups—which always manage to contain and constrict difference within the rule of identity—but rather as a pure acategorial profusion. Being thus is always, unremittingly, "univocally" different. Its difference keeps repeating itself; it is repeatedly different. It is always the same, viz., different. For a Kierkegaardian reaction, see André Clar, p. 77, n. 87. See Foucault's remarkable essay on Deleuze, "Theatricum philosophicum," *Language, Counter-memory, Practice,* trans. D. F.

Bouchard (Ithaca: Cornell University Press, 1977), 165-96, especially 182-87, 192-96. Deleuze's more radical intentions, however, still fall under the influence of what I call here a radical hermeneutics. I will test this claim in Part II [in "Repetition and Kinesis: kierkegaard on the Foundering of Metaphysics"] with another philosopher of difference and profusion, not Deleuze but Derrida. For a parallel treatment of Deleuze and Derrida as philosophers of difference, see Vincent Descombes, *Modern French Philosophy,* trans. L. Scott-Fox and J. M. Harding (Cambridge: Cambridge University Press, 1980), pp. 136-67.

List of Abbreviations

The following abbreviations are used in the body of the text to provide references to works in both the original language and, where available, the English translation; the latter is separated from the former by a slash. References to other works by these authors are to be found in the notes. . . .

Works of Heidegger

GA 5: *Gesamtausgabe,* vol. 5: *Holzwege* (Frankfurt: Klostermann, 1971). . . .

QCT: *The Question Concerning Technology and Other Essays,* trans. William Lovitt (New York: Harper and Row, 1977). . . .

WCT: *What Is Called Thinking?,* trans. J. Glenn Gray and Fred Wieck (New York: Harper and Row, 1968).

WHD: *Was Heisst Denken* (Tübingen: Niemeyer, 1961). . . .

Works of Kierkegaard

CA: *Kierkegaard's Writings,* vol. VIII: *The Concept of Anxiety,* ed. and trans. Reidar Thomte and Albert Anderson (Princeton: Princeton University Press, 1980).

CUP: *Concluding Unscientific Postscript to the Philosophical Fragments,* trans. David Swenson and Walter Lowrie (Princeton: Princeton University Press, 1941).

E/O: *Either/Or,* trans. Walter Lowrie and Howard Johnson, 2 vols. (Princeton: Princeton University Press, 1959).

Pap.: *Soren Kierkegaards Papirer* (Copenhagen: Gyldendal, 1909-48).

PF: *Philosophical Fragments,* trans. David Swenson and Howard Hong (Princeton: Princeton University Press, 1962).

R: *Kierkegaard's Writings,* vol. VI: *"Fear and Trembling" and "Repetition,"* ed. and trans. Howard Hong and Edna Hong (Princeton: Princeton University Press, 1983).

SV: *Soren Kierkegaards Samlede Vaerker* (Copenhagen: Gyldendal, 1901-06).

Patrick Gardiner (essay date 1988)

SOURCE: "Modes of Existence," in *Kierkegaard,* Oxford University Press, 1988, pp. 40-64.

[*In the following essay, Gardiner studies the three "modes," or "spheres," of existence identified by Kierkegaard (the aesthetic, ethical, and religious). Gardiner explains that in the works in which Kierkegaard discusses these modes, he takes an indirect approach in demonstrating the three perspectives.*]

There can certainly be no dispute that all the early 'aesthetic' works—***Either/Or, Repetition, Fear and Trembling,*** and ***Stages on Life's Way***—exemplify the 'indirect' approach to which Kierkegaard attached such importance. Not only do they set out to present opposed outlooks and styles of living; they do this in an imaginative or 'poetical' fashion which is designed to exhibit—from the inside—what it is like to envisage life within the perspectives identified. The reader is invited to participate vicariously in these contrasting visions, much as he might if he were entering into the minds of characters portrayed in a novel or a play. The fictional analogy is, indeed, apposite in more than one way, Kierkegaard never addressing the reader directly, as the author, but instead speaking to him through the medium of different pseudonyms under which the books were published; by adopting such masks and shifting disguises he appeared to distance himself, if sometimes rather disingenuously, from the positions to which his pseudonyms or invented personages variously subscribed. This served a dual purpose: it was designed to convey in an intimate manner the distinctive flavour and texture of disparate life-views; at the same time, it left the reader to draw his own practical conclusions from what was communicated to him—the various outlooks were allowed to 'speak for themselves', no external attempt being made to arbitrate or decide between them.

What form did they take? Kierkegaard distinguishes three basic modes or 'spheres' of existence: the aesthetic, the ethical, and the religious. Although allusions to all of them are to be found, in one shape or another, in each of the books mentioned, the contrast between the aesthetic and the ethical comes out most clearly in ***Either/Or*** and that between the ethical and the religious in ***Fear and Trembling;*** attention can therefore be focused on the latter works. Even so, the three categories Kierkegaard introduces are in certain respects deceptively wide-ranging, and what they cover is more autobiographical in content than his favoured method of presentation would suggest. In each case the attitudes comprised show considerable variations, reflecting not only his perception of contemporary cultural trends but also the complex patterns of his own history and development; indeed, some of the material was drawn directly from his journals. Thus traces of the psychological difficulties and dilemmas of his student years, including those connected with his ambivalent relationship with his father, are frequently discernible; so, too, are the traumatic repercussions of his broken engagement to Regine Olsen, Kierkegaard making oblique references to it which she was intended to read and understand. This lends to parts of the writing a rather contrived air which has evoked a sympathetic response from some of his modern votaries but which has produced a cooler reaction amongst more critically inclined commentators. In any event, it certainly informs a good deal of what he has to say about the relations between the different outlooks that are portrayed.

The aesthetic and the ethical

Either/Or is by any standards a remarkable book, and it is not surprising that it was greeted with a kind of bemused fascination when it first appeared. The aesthetic and ethical standpoints are presented in the form of edited sets of papers and letters. The papers are ascribed to a representative of the aesthetic position, referred to as 'A', and the letters to an older person, 'B': the latter, who is the protagonist of the ethical and whose communications are addressed to A, is said by the fictitious editor to have been by profession a judge. A's papers seem at first sight almost calculated to arouse puzzlement; they display a dazzling variety of styles and deal with assorted topics that often appear to be only loosely related to one another. Thus they range from scattered aphorisms and personal observations to reflective discussion of tragedy (the *Antigone*), opera and the erotic (Mozart's *Don Giovanni*), and Goethe's treatment of the Faust legend, and they conclude with a protracted account, in the form of a diary, of a minutely planned and cerebrally conceived seduction; the last (as Kierkegaard wryly noted later) may have been partly responsible for the book's initial success. The diffuseness and apparent lack of determinate direction of this section of the work, which were perhaps intended to mirror problems inherent in A's point of view, contrast sharply with the form taken by its second half. Here we are offered two, extremely lengthy, epistles by B. Written in a sober and deliberate prose, they give the impression of being designed to throw into relief the effervescent and rather self-conscious 'brilliance' of their supposed recipient. At the same time, they serve to illustrate—through the various criticisms which the Judge makes of A's position—what lies behind Kierkegaard's use of the terms 'aesthetic' and 'ethi-

cal' to identify opposed outlooks and modes of living. To some extent this emerges from the long disquisition on the significance of marriage which is the subject of the first letter; it is, however, in B's second communication, the well-known 'Equilibrium between the Aesthetic and the Ethical in the composition of the Personality', that what Kierkegaard has in mind receives general and comprehensive expression.

Some writers have interpreted the division in question in terms of more familiar theoretical contrasts: hedonism and conventional morality, for example, or the Kantian distinction between sensuous inclination and the imperative requirements of reason. Echoes of both are certainly present in a number of the Judge's remarks. None the less, 'Equilibrium' is a rich and involved piece of writing where a multitude of ideas are to be found densely, and at times confusingly, crowded together; consequently, such simple dichotomies as those proposed provide at best an inadequate guide. Although, early on in the Judge's letter, the main interest and object of the aesthetic mode of life is said to consist in enjoyment, it quickly becomes apparent that this is by no means a complete or exhaustive characterization. 'Aestheticism', as understood in Kierkegaard's generous and in some ways idiosyncratic sense, can take on different guises: it manifests itself at diverse levels of sophistication and self-consciousness and it ramifies in directions beyond those of a mere pursuit of pleasure for pleasure's sake; indeed, what he says about it is more frequently reminiscent of nineteenth-century Romantic attitudes than the rather mundane hedonism associated with much eighteenth-century philosophical literature. Similarly with the 'ethical'. Here there is undoubtedly talk of the importance of determinate duties and responsibilities; but we should misconstrue Kierkegaard's overall conception if we assumed that it could be reduced, either to a mere observance of socially recognized rules, or alternatively to a Kantian respect for the deliverances of pure practical reason. Not only is the truth more complex and less straightforward than these limited interpretations suggest; it also has significant points of contact with other, more far-reaching, implications of his position.

Let us then consider the matter in more detail, beginning with the case of the aesthetic individual. Despite Kierkegaard's explicit claim that there is 'no didacticism' in ***Either/Or*** (CUP 228), it is arguable that he does not really confine himself to presenting two rival viewpoints, leaving the question of which is finally to be preferred entirely to the reader. For one thing, the ethicist is given the second, and therefore the last, word. For another, we are given the impression that B has, in some fundamental sense, seen through A's attitude; he grasps its motivation and is thereby enabled to criticize it in a way that undermines it. Thus, as the Judge proceeds, it becomes clear that the condition of such a person is regarded by him as being in certain crucial respects a pathological one. Of these, two in particular stand out and can be seen to be connected.

In the first place, it is indicated that the man who lives aesthetically is not really in control, either of himself or his situation. He typically exists *ins Blaue hinein;* he tends to live 'for the moment', for whatever the passing instant will bring in the way of entertainment, excitement, interest. Committed to nothing permanent or definite, dispersed in sensuous 'immediacy', he may do or think one thing at a given time, the exact opposite at some other; his life is therefore without 'continuity', lacks stability or focus, changes course according to mood or circumstance, is 'like a witch's letter from which one sense can be got now and then another, depending on how one turns it'. Even so, it should not be inferred that such a man is always or necessarily governed by mere impulse; on the contrary, he may be reflective and calculating, like the seducer whose diary is included amongst A's papers. If, however, he does adopt long-term goals or decide to follow certain maxims, it is in a purely 'experimental' spirit: he will continue only for so long as the idea appeals to him, the alternative of giving up if he gets tired or bored, or if some more attractive prospect offers itself, remaining forever open; such 'gymnastic experimentation' in the practical sphere may be regarded, in fact, as the analogue of sophistry in the theoretical. For, whatever the variations, life is still envisaged in terms of possibilities that may be contemplated or savoured, not of projects to be realized or ideals to be furthered.

Such attitudes are held to be symptomatic of something which the Judge believes to be endemic to the aesthetic point of view, revealing its ultimate inadequacy. As he puts it, the aestheticist 'expects everything from without'; his approach to the world is basically a passive one, in that his satisfaction is finally subject to conditions whose presence or fulfilment is independent of his will. This submission to the contingent, the 'accidental', to what occurs in the course of events, may take a variety of shapes. Sometimes it is reliance upon 'external' factors, like possessions or power or even the prized affection of another human being; but it may also involve ones that are intrinsic to the individual himself, like health or physical beauty. The point is that, in all instances of this kind, the person is placed at the mercy of circumstances, of 'what may be or may not be'; his mode of life is tied to things that are necessarily uncertain or perishable, and no volition on his part can ever guarantee their attainment or preservation, or even his continued enjoyment of them if he has them. If they fail him—and that will in the end be a matter of chance—it may seem to him that the point of his existence has gone; he will feel, temporarily at least, that he has been deprived of what makes life worth living. As Kierkegaard expressed it elsewhere, in such a view the self is 'a dative, like the

"me" of a child . . . ; its concepts are: good luck, bad luck, fate' (*SD* 51). Hence it is the mark of the aesthetic individual that he does not seek to impose a coherent pattern on his life, having its source in some unitary notion of himself and of what he should be, but rather allows 'what happens' to act upon him and to govern his behaviour. Inward reflection can show this to be so, and when it occurs it is liable to produce a pervasive sense of despair in the person concerned; his entire life—in general, and not merely in particular respects—may be seen to rest upon an uncertain basis and thus appear drained of meaning. That, however, leads to a further, extremely important, aspect of the aesthetic outlook, and one about which the Judge has much to say.

For it is now claimed that such self-awareness may be repressed or ignored, or that at any rate its true implications may be subtly evaded. Despair about his life and its foundation is, in fact, a necessity if the aesthetic individual is to recognize that a 'higher' form of existence is an absolute requirement; yet it is precisely this crucial step in the direction of the ethical that he is unwilling to take. He remains too deeply rooted in his own mode of life and thought to attempt to liberate himself and seeks instead, by a variety of stratagems, to keep the truth from impinging upon him. This sometimes happens through a person's trying to overcome or obliterate his inner dissatisfaction by various kinds of activity: it may take a 'demonic' form, as in the Faustian case; but it can equally well find expression in the life of a 'respectable' man of affairs, going pertinaciously about his business. There is, however, a more insidious shape which it is apt to assume. For there exists what Kierkegaard once called a 'dialectical interplay of knowledge and will' which can make it hard to tell whether a person is consciously trying to distract himself from a predicament which he realizes (however obscurely) to be his or whether, on the other hand, he has so interpreted his condition as to make it appear to preclude the whole notion of fundamental choice and change. And the second of these possibilities may be actualized.

Hence, by a strange modification of the aesthetic position, a man may come to treat sorrow, not pleasure, as 'the meaning of his life', taking a perverse satisfaction in the thought that this at least is something of which he cannot be deprived. For he may regard it as a state to which he is doomed, fated; what he is and feels, how he stands—these all follow inexorably from the nature of things. Thus he may ascribe his unhappiness to something fixed and unalterable in his character or his environment: he has a 'sad disposition', or he has been treated badly by other people. Alternatively, it can be that he portrays himself under grandiloquent labels that somehow determine his place and destiny in the world: for example, the 'unfortunate individual', the 'tragic hero'. Again, and more generally, he may take refuge in a Romantic *Weltschmerz,* using a tone of disillusioned pessimism and treating questions of practical decision as if they could be of no final significance; whatever a man does he will end up regretting. In all such ideas it is possible to find a spurious tranquillity; one can even take a quiet pride in them. For their eventual issue is 'an out and out fatalism, which always has something seductive about it' (*EO* ii, 241); by accepting a fatalistic or necessitarian viewpoint, the individual tacitly absolves himself from accountability for his condition as well as from an obligation to do anything about it. It is implied, however, that this is never more than a pretence, a cover, behind which he conceals his unavowed determination to remain at a stage from which he could, if he chose, release himself.

All in all, Kierkegaard's analysis of aestheticism is conducted with a psychological subtlety and an elaborate attention to detail that defy brief summary, and it has been possible here only to pick out some of its leading themes. As I have already indicated, he employed his basic categories in an extremely elastic way. This allowed him to point up unexpected connections between apparently diverse phenomena in a manner that can be genuinely illuminating; even so, there are times when his extended use of them seems to put their determinate significance in jeopardy, and a reader of 'Equilibrium' may be excused if he occasionally wonders if there is anything that could not, with a little ingenuity, be interpreted as 'living aesthetically'. Nor is this the sole problem which it poses. For it is not always clear whether Kierkegaard is speaking of the aesthetic consciousness in quite general terms or whether, on the other hand, he is concerned with some specific manifestation of it that was of particular relevance to his own period and culture. There can, however, be no question that he supposed much of what he said to bear upon contemporary currents of thought and behaviour. At one point, for instance, it is explicitly stated that aesthetic 'melancholy', the failure 'to will deeply and sincerely', is a sickness under which 'all young Germany and France now sighs' (*EO* ii 193). And there are also discernible parallels between the Judge's account of certain typical aesthetic attitudes and Kierkegaard's later strictures, in *The Present Age* and elsewhere, on other tendencies implicit in the prevalent social ethos of his time: absorption in the 'outward', the external; absence of a clear sense of individual identity and responsibility; complacent acquiescence in deterministic myths as opposed to serious practical commitment; a pervasive cult of indifference presenting itself under the guise of sophisticated detachment. Nor, as we shall discover, are these imputations unconnected with his subsequent diagnosis of the contemporary appeal and influence of Hegel's metaphysics.

Nevertheless, it would be wrong to identify Kierkegaard's approach to Hegel at the time of writing *Ei-*

ther/Or too unreservedly with that manifested in some of his later polemics against the 'system'. Admittedly, and as the title itself implies, the book was partly conceived as a protest against the Hegelian notion that distinct forms of consciousness follow one another in a dialectically necessary sequence, mutually opposed standpoints being successively reconciled at higher stages in the progressive unfolding of universal mind or spirit. In Kierkegaard's eyes, the transition from one mode of existence to another conformed to a wholly different pattern. It could only be achieved through an unconstrained and irreducibly personal choice between alternatives; moreover, the alternatives themselves must be seen as being finally incompatible and not such that they could be ultimately harmonized or 'mediated' in the light of some over-arching theoretical insight. Yet, notwithstanding these considerations, the fact remains that the picture of the ethical sphere which actually emerges from 'Equilibrium' is not altogether free from Hegelian overtones. For one thing, the passage to it from the aesthetic is treated as a progressive spiritual movement. Crises occur in the aesthetic consciousness which at least 'call for' the adoption of a new form of life, even if this is not how the person involved himself undertakes to resolve them; as the Judge remarks in terms that have a markedly Hegelian ring, there 'comes a moment in a man's life when his immediacy is, as it were, ripened and the spirit demands a higher form in which it will apprehend itself as spirit' (*EO* ii 193). Further, we are also told that the ethical does not so much 'annihilate the aesthetical' as 'transfigure' it— a remark that consorts a little awkwardly with what Kierkegaard has to say in general about mediation. But it is in the Judge's treatment of the relation between the individual and the universal at the ethical level that one is most conscious of the Hegelian background.

In crucial respects the account provided of the ethical point of view appears to focus uncompromisingly upon the individual. Personality is the 'absolute', is 'its own end and purpose'; in describing the emergence and development of the ethical character, the Judge treats as basic the notion of 'choosing oneself', this in turn being closely associated with the ideas of self-knowledge, self-acceptance, self-realization. The ethical subject is portrayed as one who regards himself as a 'goal', a 'task set'. Unlike the aestheticist, who is continually preoccupied with externals, his attention is directed towards his own nature, his substantial reality as a human being with such and such talents, inclinations, and passions, this being something which it constantly lies within his power to order, control, and cultivate. There is thus a sense in which he can be said, consciously and deliberately, to take responsibility for himself; he does not, as the aestheticist is prone to do, treat his personal traits and dispositions as an unalterable fact of nature to which he must tamely submit, but regards them rather as a challenge—his self-knowledge is not 'a mere contemplation' but a 'reflection upon himself which itself is an action' (*EO* ii 263). Moreover, by such inward understanding and critical self-exploration a man comes to recognize, not only what he empirically is, but what he truly aspires to become; thus the Judge refers to an 'ideal self' which is 'the picture in likeness to which he has to form himself'. In other words, the ethical individual's life and behaviour must be thought of as infused and directed by a determinate conception of himself which is securely founded upon a realistic grasp of his own potentialities and which is immune to the vicissitudes of accident and fortune. He is not, as the aestheticist was shown to be, the prey of what happens or befalls, for he has not surrendered himself to the arbitrary governance of outside circumstances and incalculable contingencies. Nor, from the standpoint he adopts, can success or failure be measured by whether or not his projects in fact find fulfilment in the world. What finally matters is his total identification of himself with these projects; it is the spirit in which things are done, the energy and sincerity with which they are undertaken and pursued, that are relevant here—not the observable consequences of the actions performed.

There is much in all this that strikes a familiar chord, appearing in some ways as an extension of classical doctrines of self-determination that reach back to the Stoics and beyond. But it also has significant affinities to ideas more recently advanced by Kant. Kant, as we noticed earlier on, had stressed the freedom and independence of the moral consciousness, the individual being subject to requirements that derived from his nature as an autonomous, self-directing being. Moreover, it was central to the Kantian position that estimates of moral worth rested solely upon the quality of the agent's will; it was the intentions from which he acted, what he tried to do, that counted here, and not success or failure in actually accomplishing what was aimed at or envisaged. Both these features seem to be reflected, not to say magnified, by Kierkegaard's own account of the moral point of view. Yet that account— at least as so far presented—may strike the reader as inadequate, if only because it appears to interpret the ethical life in a fashion that pays no attention to its content. For it is arguable that a person who lives such a life must also be understood to acknowledge specific norms and values which he regards as holding for others as well as for himself and which justifiably command general agreement and acceptance. And this, indeed, is a point on which B himself seems anxious to insist. Thus the Judge certainly goes out of his way to deny that the 'higher form' embodied in the ethical outlook is something which each person is entitled to interpret according to his private tastes and sentiments: such a conception, savouring of 'experimentalism' and ascribable to some kinds of Romanticism, rightfully belongs to the aesthetic, not the ethical, domain. The fundamental categories of the ethical are 'good and evil' and 'duty', and they are referred to as if they had

a meaning necessarily shared by all who used them; with this in mind, it can legitimately be affirmed that the ethical individual 'expresses the universal in his life'. But if that is so, how far is it reconcilable with the uncompromisingly self-orientated theory propounded above? There it seemed to be implied that such a man's values ultimately had their source in himself alone: if, on the other hand, he accepts that there exist socially recognized duties which are binding upon him, is he not committed to renouncing his essential independence, being thereby placed once more in a position of subordination to the outward, the external?

To this apparent dilemma Kant's own doctrine of practical reason might have been invoked as offering a solution. According to that doctrine, the moral subject sought to conform to self-imposed principles that satisfied the test of consistency embodied in the Kantian 'categorical imperative'—namely, that the maxim of his action could be 'willed as a universal law'. Respect for such consistency was intrinsic to the 'rational nature' which was common to all human beings in their capacity as moral agents; hence it could be maintained that, for the ethical individual to express what B refers to as 'his inmost nature', it was sufficient that his actions should be governed by rules that met the requirement in question, the general acceptance of these rules being thereby guaranteed. It is far from clear, however, that the Judge wishes to endorse such an austerely formal account, and what is in fact said in 'Equilibrium' points towards an Hegelian rather than a Kantian approach to the problem. Amongst other things, Hegel had criticized the Kantian criterion of morality for being too abstract to offer determinate guidance and for appearing to justify any principle, even the most immoral, provided only that no contradiction was involved in willing its universal adoption. Instead, it should be recognized that moral duties were 'rooted in the soil of civil life'. In other words, it was from the practices and institutions embedded in actual societies that both the content and the authority of moral requirements derived, these practices and institutions constituting an intelligible framework whose rationale the ethical subject could appreciate and in terms of which he could fulfil his potentialities as a free and purposive being. There need be no conflict here between individual aspirations and the demands of communal existence; as an integral part of the society to which he belonged, the individual experienced the duties and responsibilities it imposed, not in the shape of alien constraints, but rather as giving objective form to values and interests that he inwardly acknowledged to be his own. In this way the claims of individual conscience (which Kant had rightly stressed) and the claims inherent in a socially based conception of the moral life were finally reconciled.

It must be admitted that Hegel's theory rested upon certain questionable assumptions about the rational structure of the kinds of society he envisaged; these were connected with his philosophy of history and raise issues that cannot be entered into at this point. None the less, many of the Judge's remarks imply that the ethical as he understood it accorded with the Hegelian notion of *Sittlichkeit* just outlined. He says, for instance, that the self which it is the task of the ethical individual to develop must not be thought of as existing 'in isolation', in the manner envisaged by certain 'mystical' doctrines; he stands in 'reciprocal relations' with his public surroundings and conditions of life, the self he seeks to realize being 'a social, a civic self', not an abstract one that 'fits everywhere and hence nowhere'. The Judge speaks, too, as if things such as marriage, having a job or useful occupation, undertaking civil and institutional responsibilities, are all essential from this point of view. It did not, however, follow that the duties that derived therefrom presented themselves to such an individual as external limitations, 'foreign to the personality' and restrictive of freedom. Unlike the aestheticist—the 'accidental man' for whom 'the adventitious plays a prodigious role'—he identified himself with the requirements to which he was subject as an active member of society, his character being permeated with the spirit that informed them. In this sense, the universal was not something 'outside the individual'; on the contrary, he was at one with it, giving it concrete expression in the unconstrained fulfilment of those obligations which he recognized to be specifically his. That, indeed, was 'the secret of conscience'—the individual life was conceived to be 'at the same time the universal, if not immediately, yet according to its possibility' (***EO*** ii 260). Thus the gap between the two, which at first sight threatened to undermine the unity and coherence of the ethical outlook, had apparently been closed.

Yet how comprehensive, in the end, does the position set out in 'Equilibrium' turn out to be? Does it provide the only alternative to the aesthetic mode of existence with which it is compared? More crucially, to what extent can it be said to resolve all the problems that may beset a person in the course of his life? The Judge himself seems at times to entertain doubts on the latter score: both here and later in ***Stages on Life's Way,*** where he makes a characteristic reappearance, it is possible to detect strains and tensions underlying the self-confident surface of his prose. As we have seen, there are passages where he appears to be primarily concerned with the subjective quality, the experienced texture, of the life of one who has committed himself to the moral standpoint; whatever efforts he has made elsewhere to accommodate the universal content of the ethical, the fact remains that in these contexts it is not the applicability of general or publicly shared standards which the Judge stresses but rather the ways in which the agent approaches what he does and the depth of conviction, of truth to himself, they involve. And it is hard to detach such concern from an implicit pre-

occupation with the idea that, in the last resort, each person has to find his own path through a process of inner understanding that does justice to his unique individuality and which may—however paradoxically—ultimately carry him beyond the boundaries of the ethical itself. Troublesome suspicions about the self-sufficiency of the ethical outlook and its basic categories emerge towards the end of the Judge's disquisitions in ***Either/Or*** and the ***Stages*** alike: in both cases, and particularly in the latter, he acknowledges the extreme difficulties certain 'exceptional' individuals may meet when trying to realize the ethical universal in their lives. There, though, the problems raised are only touched upon in a guarded fashion, with careful reservations and with a noticeable reluctance to arrive at a positive resolution. In ***Fear and Trembling,*** on the other hand, the doubts to which they give rise are given overt and eloquent expression, and in a setting that explicitly contrasts the claims of ethics with those of religion. The frontier that was hesitantly and somewhat obliquely approached in 'Equilibrium' has here been crossed.

Suspension of the ethical

The pseudonymous author of ***Fear and Trembling***—Johannes *de silentio*—disclaims any pretensions to be a philosopher, at least in the fashionable Hegelian sense. Nor, it seems clear, does he purport to be a committed Christian, speaking from the standpoint of religious belief. Even so, what he says is evidently intended to bear upon matters that would have been seen by his intended audience as having a philosophical as well as a religious significance. For, although he himself stands within the ethical, he shows himself to be acutely conscious of the apparent limitations of the sphere to which he belongs; more specifically, he is concerned with its inability to comprehend the phenomenon of faith. And his insistence upon the latter point can, of course, be taken as marking a fundamental divergence from approaches of the type initiated by Kant and Hegel. Both writers had, though in very different ways, sought to assimilate or subordinate the notion of religious faith to other categories of thought—Kant by treating its claims as postulates of practical or moral reason, Hegel by regarding it as prefiguring at a pictorial or imaginative level of consciousness ideas that achieved rational articulation within the framework of his own all-encompassing philosophical theory. In ***Fear and Trembling,*** by contrast, faith is represented as possessing a wholly independent status: it lies beyond the province of ethical thinking and it resists elucidation in universal or rational terms. This does not mean, however, that it should be viewed as something essentially primitive or unworthy of respect; it is not like 'a childhood disease one may wish to get over as soon as possible'. On the contrary, the book concludes with the observation that it constitutes 'the highest passion of a person'. Moreover, it is implied throughout that only an individual who is himself morally sensitive and mature is in a position to recognize the scale of its mysterious and exacting demands.

Kierkegaard's object was to bring home, in a vivid and compelling manner, the disconcerting character of these demands. By focusing attention on a particular instance and by revealing its salient features, he hoped to throw into sharp relief the significance of a concept to which most of his contemporaries paid lip-service but whose actual import had either been smothered by the comfortable words of clergyman or else spirited away by the rationalizations of philosophers. Nor, in doing so, had he any desire to conceal its practical implications. As he goes out of his way to emphasize, in the instance discussed they will inevitably appear shocking, even scandalous, when contemplated within an exclusively ethical perspective.

It can hardly be denied that the example selected was well chosen for the purposes he had in mind. It is drawn from the biblical account of Abraham, the 'father of faith'. Abraham is called upon by God to kill his son, Isaac, offering him as a sacrifice. Abraham follows this instruction, up to the point of drawing the fatal knife; at the last moment, however, his hand is stayed and a ram is provided for him to sacrifice instead. The whole incident is portrayed as a divinely appointed test or spiritual trial, one that he triumphantly passes.

How should one react to such a story? Its value in Kierkegaard's eyes lay, evidently enough, in its stark portrayal of the nature of the choice that confronted Abraham. He could only fulfil God's command by acting, not merely against his natural inclinations as a loving father, but in defiance of the deeply grounded moral principle that forbids the killing of an innocent person; furthermore, the moral enormity of the action was compounded by the fact that the person in question was his own son. Thus what he was required to do must have appeared to him, as it does to us, abhorrent on both human and ethical grounds. Yet—as Johannes de silentio points out—he is continually praised, from the pulpit and elsewhere, for his grandeur in setting out to accomplish the repulsive task assigned to him. And this raises the question of the extent to which those who indulge in such eulogies have a real grasp of what they are saying. One has merely to imagine how a pastor might address one of his flock who took seriously the possibility of following Abraham's example:

> If the preacher found out about it, he perhaps would go to the man, he would muster all his ecclesiastical dignity and shout, 'You despicable man, you scum of society, what devil has so possessed you that you want to murder your son?' (*FT* 28)

He might even take pride in his righteous eloquence. But with what justification? Had he not in his sermons extolled Abraham for the very thing he was now condemning? According to ethics, the answer could only be: yes. Simply stated, 'the ethical expression for what Abraham did is that he meant to murder Isaac'. This was something that had to be faced, clearly and without fudging, by anyone who wished to arrive at a proper comprehension of Abraham's case and of what his action involved. Kierkegaard's pseudonymous author does not claim to understand Abraham himself, in the sense of being able to enter into the content of his life and thought. He does, however, believe that he can lay bare the conditions that make it possible to speak of faith in such a context; he believes, too, that he can thereby illuminate (if only indirectly) the true relationship between the ethical and religious standpoints—a relationship which, in the intellectual climate of his time, has been persistently misconstrued.

One way of approaching what was at issue was to compare Abraham's predicament with that of the moral or 'tragic' hero. An individual of the latter sort also finds himself called upon to do something that is deeply offensive to him, whether on the ground of natural sentiment or because it involves infringing powerful moral constraints, or possibly on account of both. In the case of such a hero, though, the basis upon which he feels bound to act is itself a recognizably ethical one: an example Kierkegaard gives is Agamemnon's decision to sacrifice his daughter Iphigenia for the sake of the state. He is vindicated in his own eyes by the fact that in performing the terrible deed he still 'reposes' within the ethical universal; whatever the pain it causes him, however deep his feelings of personal loss and of compunction, he none the less has the assurance that he is conforming to the requirements of an acknowledged principle or general objective with which he can identify and which takes precedence over all other considerations. Hence, in the hard circumstances confronting him, he can legitimately expect the sympathy and respect of those around him—'the tragic hero gives up the certain for the even more certain, and the observer's eye views him with confidence' (*FT* 60). He is at least able to 'rejoice in the security of the universal', knowing that what he does can be defended in terms that all, including even its victims, are in a position to recognize and understand.

Things are quite otherwise with Abraham, the 'knight of faith'. The tragic hero, we are told, still treats the ethical as his 'telos' or goal, even if this entails subordinating particular duties to its attainment. Abraham, on the other hand, has transgressed the ethical altogether, having a higher telos outside it 'in relation to which he suspended it'. And this 'relinquishment of the universal' involves a degree of distress that surpasses any attributable to his moral counterpart. He stands isolated and alone, without the possibility of justifying to others an action which, at the level of rational thought and conduct, must necessarily appear outrageous, indeed absurd. As a particular individual he has placed himself in 'an absolute relation to the absolute'. If his action is justifiable, it can only be by reference to a divine command that is addressed to him alone and whose content is such that he cannot hope to render what he does intelligible by human standards; according to those, he must be deemed either to be mad or else simply hypocritical. Moreover, the very attempt to vindicate himself in humanly understandable terms would be tantamount to seeking to evade the conditions of the task assigned to him, a task that presupposes an absolute duty to God which transcends the domain of ethical discourse and which must be fulfilled in the face of all temptations to the contrary. It was by resisting these temptations—moral as well as natural—that Abraham withstood the trial to which his faith was subjected. He was prepared, in other words, to follow through to the end the frightening consequences of his paradoxical commitment; therein lay his true claim to the 'greatness' which is often, but largely unthinkingly, accorded him.

There is an undeniable poignancy about Kierkegaard's depiction of the plight of those who pursue in anguish their undisclosed missions and who in doing so 'walk without meeting one single traveller'. What he writes has the sharp flavour of personal experience and suggests that he partly had in mind his own sense of distraught isolation at the time of his broken engagement; it may also evoke the vertiginous feelings induced by practical dilemmas that seem to elude the grasp of general categories and where a person can come to view compliance with established norms as threatening his integrity as an individual. But, however impressive psychologically, such considerations do nothing in themselves to validate his central thesis. For this concerns the possibility of a 'teleological' suspension of the ethical by the religious, and it is one that has—perhaps not unnaturally—run into a good deal of criticism. Amongst other things, the contention that in certain circumstances all ethical requirements may be set aside has been stigmatized as amounting to the advocacy of a 'moral nihilism' which no rhetorical appeals of the kind he provides can conceivably excuse, let alone justify. To invoke beliefs which apparently entail an acquiescence in 'the absurd' in order to legitimize morally abhorrent deeds is scarcely to the purpose; if anything, its sole effect must be to undermine confidence in all our valuations, since it permits the rejection of even those about which we feel most assured. It may, of course, be replied that Abraham, considered as a 'knight of faith', was not acting *in vacuo* and without warrant: he was carrying out what he took to be the will of God. But what were the grounds for that assurance? As Kant drily noted, when discussing the very example Kierkegaard later took as his model, 'it is at least possible that in this instance a mistake has prevailed'. Where a supposedly divine command conflicts with a moral judgement that impresses us as being

intrinsically certain, we have the clear option of refusing to ascribe it to God. And in Kant's view—as presented in his *Religion within the Limits of Reason Alone*—that was the option which, in a case of the sort described, a 'conscientious' individual would naturally and correctly choose.

From what Kierkegaard says it would appear that there is a sense in which he had no wish to dissent from this. In so far as such an individual is defined as one who takes his stand upon ethics alone, moral judgements that seem self-evident to human reason must certainly, indeed necessarily, be decisive in his eyes. From the position in question the whole of human existence is seen as a 'perfect self-contained sphere' which ethics fills and completes, God himself being thereby reduced to 'an invisible vanishing point'. Here people may, to be sure, use religious language, speaking of the duty to love and obey the Deity; but in their employment of such expressions what they really mean comes down to no more than a truism. As it is put in one place:

> If in this connection I . . . say that it is my duty to love God, I am actually pronouncing only a tautology, inasmuch as 'God' in a totally abstract sense is here understood as the divine—that is, the universal, that is, duty. (*FT* 68)

In the discussion that follows this passage, Kierkegaard reverts to the point on which much of his essay can be said to turn. It was one thing to accord supremacy to the ethical; it was quite another to maintain that the religious could be reduced to this, its essential content being expressible in terms wholly acceptable to finite reason. From a religious point of view, ethics never possesses more than a 'relative' status; the denial that from *that* standpoint it could be envisaged as ultimate or supreme was something which his treatment of the Abraham story was expressly designed to bring into sharp focus. But to insist that it only had relative validity was not to assert that it had no validity at all: it did not follow from his account of the story that moral requirements were devoid of all foundation or that they could in a general way be dispensed with. What he did wish to argue was that within a religious perspective they took on an altered aspect, received a 'completely different expression'. And by this he seems partly to have meant that the obligation to conform to them finally rests upon a prior commitment to God, where the latter is conceived to be an infinite or absolute 'other' that transcends human reason and understanding: 'the single individual . . . determines his relation to the universal by his relation to the absolute, not his relation to the absolute by his relation to the universal' (*FT* 70).

In one sense it is possible to regard *Fear and Trembling* as simply making a point about the religious consciousness which contemporary theorists, and above all those of an Hegelian persuasion, chose to distort or else to reason away. Whatever they might protest to the contrary, on their view of the matter to act as Abraham did was to stand condemned. None the less, faith as he understood it and exemplified it in his life is presupposed by the religious consciousness, and any attempt to present the 'inner truth' of religion in a fashion that eliminates or emasculates what such faith involves must necessarily be misconceived. But the incapacity of current thought to come to terms with the religious outlook was by no means the sole object of Kierkegaard's concern; here, as in his other 'aesthetic' books, what he wrote was not intended to be a mere exercise in academic criticism. By throwing into the strongest relief the contrast between the standpoint of faith and one that made ethics supreme, he also sought to silhouette the limitations of the latter—limitations that emerged when proper account was taken of vital aspects of personal experience which were resistant to its sway and with which it seemed powerless to deal. As we have noticed, intimations of these appeared at certain moments in the Judge's presentation of the ethical position in *Either/Or* and *Stages on Life's Way.* There it was suggested that an individual may believe himself to be subject to the demands of a unique calling which cannot be accommodated within the framework of socially determined duties or universally accepted principles of conduct; yet the status of such an awareness must inevitably be problematic, and the Judge shows no inclination to play down the consequences incurred by trying to follow it:

> He must comprehend that no one can understand him, and must have the constancy to put up with it that human language has for him naught but curses and the human heart has for his sufferings only the one feeling that he is guilty. (*SLW* 175)

At the level of religious faith, which is the theme of *Fear and Trembling,* the significance of these intimations becomes at last fully manifest. While the importance of moral requirements is not as such denied, the absolute sovereignty of the ethical can no longer be assumed; rather, it is transcended by a perspective in which the self-sufficiency of morality, regarded as a socially established and universally acknowledged institution, is explicitly challenged. The notion that a person might be conscious of an 'exceptional' mission, to be fulfilled at whatever cost and in the face of ostensibly overwhelming objections, was not something that could be simply passed over or shrugged off, nor could it be relegated to 'the rather commonplace company of feelings, moods, idiosyncrasies, *vapeurs,* etc.' (*FT* 69). Abraham's conception of his assignment belied all this: in seeking to accomplish it he was not only prepared to resist the dictates of ordinary morality; he further believed—against every rational expectation—that he would in some fashion 'receive back' the son he had been commanded to sacrifice. To com-

plain that what he did was contrary to reason, that he ran a terrible risk and might be making a mistake, was in a way true enough; it merely served, however, to underline the distinctive character of the standpoint he occupied. Faith in the sense here in question lay outside the aegis of human standards of rationality, and the transition to what it involved was not susceptible to justification in those terms. On the contrary, it demanded a radical venture or 'leap', a spiritual movement requiring a commitment to something that was objectively uncertain and in the last analysis paradoxical.

In order to grasp the underlying tenor of such pronouncements regarding the true import of religious faith, it is necessary to turn to what Kierkegaard referred to as his 'philosophical works.' These will be the subject of the next chapter [in *Modes of Existence*]. But before taking leave of the 'aesthetic' literature, we must revert briefly to an issue alluded to at the close of the previous chapter.

That, it will be remembered, concerned Kierkegaard's later contention that his imaginative presentation of different modes of existence had been essentially directed towards leading his readers out of the illusion that they were Christians. As he put it in the *Point of View,* they lived in 'aesthetic, or, at the most, aesthetic-ethical categories' and hence were unable to appreciate the depth of the deception, or self-deception, in which they were immersed: by approaching such persons through their own characteristic ways of thinking and by appearing in the first instance to 'go along' with these, it might be possible to cause them to see for themselves the extent and the sources of their pervasive misunderstandings. Yet, whatever attractions this view of his overall intent held for Kierkegaard himself when he looked back on his career as an author, it may none the less strike one as being somewhat strained when the full content and range of the writings in question are taken into account. It is not merely that they often give the strong impression of having been to a considerable degree motivated by autobiographical preoccupations, including a compulsive fascination with the course taken by his abortive love-affair. It would also appear that, at least so far as the aesthetic outlook is concerned, the 'illusions' allegedly fostered are related to fatalistic or collectivist myths about the human condition rather than to anything specifically connected with the false consciousness ascribed to contemporary 'Christendom'; if there is supposed to be an association with the latter, it seems at best to be an indirect one. It may be, though, that Kierkegaard meant no more than that an aesthetically attuned individual is liable to view Christianity as something which—along with everything else—demands no serious commitment on his part; it is simply 'interesting', a subject that invites detached contemplation as opposed to decisive action and participation.

In any event, his retrospective claim may impress us as being more obviously applicable to what he had to say, in *Fear and Trembling,* about the invasion of the religious standpoint by categories of thought that belonged to the ethical rather than to the aesthetic sphere. Here it is easier to see what he might have had in mind.

Abbreviations

The following abbreviations are used in references to Kierkegaard's works: . . .

CUP: *Concluding Unscientific Postscript,* tr. D. F. Swenson and W. Lowrie (Princeton, Princeton University Press, 1941)

EO: *Either/Or,* 2 vols., tr. D. F. and L. M. Swenson and W. Lowrie (Princeton, Princeton University Press, 1959)

FT: *Fear and Trembling* and *Repetition,* tr. H. V. and E. H. Hong (Princeton, Princeton University Press, 1983) . . .

SD: *The Sickness unto Death,* tr. H. V. and E. H. Hong (Princeton, Princeton University Press, 1980)

SLW: *Stages on Life's Way,* tr. W. Lowrie (New York, Schocken Books, 1967)

C. Stephen Evans (essay date 1989)

SOURCE: "Kierkegaard's View of the Unconscious," in *Kierkegaard: Poet of Existence,* 1989, reprinted in *Kierkegaard in Post/Modernity,* edited by Martin J. Matuštík and Merold Westphal, Indiana University Press, 1995, pp. 76-97.

[*In the following essay, Evans studies the role of the unconscious in Kierkegaard's writings. In particular, Evans analyzes the way in which the unconscious informs Kierkegaard's "relational" view of the self.*]

No informed observer of the twentieth century world of letters could fail to notice the significance of the concept of the unconscious in psychology, psychiatry, literature, and even in philosophy. We live in the age of depth psychology, an age in which the notion of the unconscious has passed over into what is termed "common sense." Despite or because of the popularity of the concept it is by no means evident that the unconscious is clearly understood. Indeed, the very notion that there is such a thing as the concept of the unconscious is itself part of the confusion; a little reflection uncovers radically different concepts which are often confusedly rolled together.

Commentators have not been slow to notice the importance of the concept of the unconscious in Kierkegaard's thought as well. The unconscious plays a central role in *The Sickness unto Death* and *The Concept of Anxiety,* but is nearly as prominent in *Either/Or,* and plays a significant role in quite a few of Kierkegaard's published works. . . .I shall try to give a straightforward account of what I take to be Kierkegaard's view of the unconscious, focusing mainly on *The Sickness unto Death.*

It is of course impossible to discuss the unconscious without discussing a host of significant concepts which are intricately linked to it: self-deception, consciousness, and the nature of the self in general, to mention just a few. My account will of necessity treat these related notions, but will just as necessarily treat them briefly and schematically. My hope is that the sketchiness of my comments will be redeemed somewhat by the ways in which these notions are in turn illumined by closer attention to the unconscious.

I. Situating Kierkegaard's View of the Unconscious

In order to understand Kierkegaard's view, it will be helpful to situate it with respect to some other major views of the unconscious. Two views stand out as deserving special attention, that of Freud, because of its historical importance, and the view of the school of psychoanalysis known as object-relations theory, because of the interesting parallels between this view and Kierkegaard's. Before looking at these views, we must first look briefly at Kierkegaard's Christian faith, which is surely the most significant factor in his perspective.

A. Kierkegaard the Christian Clinician

Though Kierkegaard was not a clinical psychologist in the contemporary sense, his primary aims as a psychologist must decidedly be viewed as therapeutic. Like Freud he is interested in the unconscious primarily in a clinical context. This is made quite explicit in *SUD [The Sickness unto Death]* where the pseudonym Anti-Climacus grounds this therapeutic concern in Christianity: "Everything essentially Christian must have in its presentation a resemblance to the way a physician speaks at the sickbed; even if only medical experts understand it, it must never be forgotten that the situation is the bedside of a sick person" (*SUD* 5).[1]

It is hardly surprising, then, that Kierkegaard connects the unconscious with pathology. The ideal for human life is transparency. In part I of *SUD* this ideal is described simply like this: "In relating to itself and in willing to be itself, the self rests transparently in the power that established it" (*SUD* 14).

In putting forward this ideal of transparency, I do not think Kierkegaard is arguing that a person must constantly be aware of everything about himself. He certainly does not wish to claim that one must focus on one's own autonomic physical processes, and I see no reason to think that he wishes to deny that in a fully healthy person mental processes might occur which are not the focus of conscious attention. Hence Kierkegaard is not really denying that there are unconscious processes in the sense that the contemporary cognitive psychologist affirms, who thinks of the unconscious as "off-line information processing."[2]

The ideal of transparency is rather one of self-understanding, an ability to recognize and understand what needs to be understood about one's self. The unconscious which is relevant is not what I shall call the unnoticed unconscious, but the unconscious which I do not wish to notice, or have chosen to ignore, or perhaps have made myself unable to comprehend. That there are aspects of the self which are beyond one's conscious purview may be helpful in understanding how the development of the unconscious in Kierkegaard's sense is *possible,* but the unconscious in Kierkegaard's sense is clearly what Freud called the "dynamic unconscious," the part of myself which I actively resist confronting.

In linking his clinical analysis of the unconscious to Christianity, as Anti-Climacus does constantly in *SUD,* some might object that his view is thereby disqualified from comparison with genuinely scientific theories. If Kierkegaard's view of the unconscious is linked to his Christian faith, can it be genuinely scientific?

Anti-Climacus of course anticipates this objection to his work: "To many the form of this 'exposition' will seem strange; it will appear to them too rigorous to be edifying, and too edifying to be strictly scientific" (*SUD* 5, my translation). Though Anti-Climacus says he has "no opinion" as to the correctness of the latter opinion, this can hardly be because he accepts the assumption that scientific work must be completely objective and "value-free." Only a bit later he tells us that the kind of scientific learning which prides itself on being "indifferent," is from a Christian point of view "inhuman curiosity" rather than the "lofty heroism" it would like to make itself out to be (*SUD* 5).

Regardless of the merits of this view of Anti-Climacus in general with regard to science, it is eminently defensible with respect to theories of the dynamic unconscious. This unconscious is what I choose not to recognize, or intentionally fail to perceive. It is hardly possible for such an analysis not to impinge on our moral and religious concerns, since the motivation for such self-obscuring activity will surely relate to what we value and disvalue as persons, what we find admirable and noble, or base and ignoble. A theory of the dynamic unconscious which links the unconscious to pathology can hardly be a value-free affair, since the concept of pathology clearly presupposes a value-concept—that of mental health.

Some would argue that "mental health" is a value concern which can still be segregated from moral values. The therapist should deal with the former and leave the latter for the preacher and the moralist. But this distinction between mental health values and general moral values cannot withstand close scrutiny. It is true that people of different moral persuasions can agree on certain "minimal" characteristics of mentally healthy people. In general mentally healthy people are in touch with their environment, are not crippled by phobias, obsessions, or other neuroses, and so on. But though these characteristics may be generally desirable, there is certainly no agreement as to exactly what they are, and even less agreement that possession of such characteristics is enough to qualify someone as mentally healthy, or that their lack necessarily means someone is "sick." Most therapists would agree, in fact, that a facade of "normality" and being "well-adjusted" can hide a personality which is seriously damaged in a variety of ways.

It is true that in such matters it seems vain to hope for "objective proof" of a view, and if lack of such proof disqualifies a view from being scientific, Kierkegaard's view certainly is disqualified. But such a requirement presupposes a naive view of science and, in any case, its strict application would eliminate not only Kierkegaard's view, but those of such thinkers as Freud as well. Though Kierkegaard's view certainly is grounded in his Christian understanding, he has every right to present it in the marketplace of ideas and try to show its descriptive, explanatory, and therapeutic power. It may well be that the power of such a view will be opaque to non-Christians, though this is by no means certain, and in fact, the contrary is supported by the strong influence Kierkegaard has had on non-Christian psychologists. But the fact that one's ability to recognize the truth is conditioned by one's own subjectivity is hardly a thesis that Kierkegaard would want to shrink from.

I shall therefore take full account of the ways in which Kierkegaard's therapeutic analysis of the unconscious is rooted in his Christian vision. Both his analyses of sickness and health presuppose a Christian understanding of human beings as creatures of God who have rebelled against their creator.

B. The Freudian View

It is not possible to overestimate the significance of Freud's theory of the unconscious. Such Freudian concepts as repression and defense mechanisms have now penetrated deeply into ordinary modes of thought. Despite the influential character of Freud's view, and the centrality of the concept of the unconscious in his own thought, Freud's view of the unconscious is not altogether free of tension.

In Freud's original "topographical" theory of mind, the unconscious was one of three "systems": the unconscious (Ucs), conscious (Cs), and preconscious (Pcs).[3] The unconscious was closely associated with instinctual demands, which were blocked or repressed from consciousness. (Freud wavered back and forth between the view that the instincts themselves composed the unconscious, and the view that the unconscious was composed of "ideas" that represented the instincts.) The repression was attributed to a preconscious "censor."

The role of the censor in this theory is crucial. It is at this point that Sartre was later to concentrate his criticism of Freud in the famous section of *Being and Nothingness* which contains his critique of the unconscious.[4] Sartre argues that the person must in some way be aware of what he is repressing, since repression is a selective activity. (Note that I am here using the term "repression" as Sartre does, and as Freud himself sometimes does, to refer to the defense mechanisms in general, not to a specific mechanism.) Yet to be aware of the activity of repression would seem to make repression impossible, since a recognition that I am repressing X would seem to imply an awareness of X.

This problem is part of the motivation for Freud's revised "structural" theory of the mind, the well-known "id, ego, superego" view which he developed later in his career.[5] This theory emerged because Freud became aware that anxiety was not simply the result of the repression of instinctual material, but was often a signal or anticipation that instinctual material was not being adequately repressed. Anxiety here is not primarily a consequent of the damming up of instinctual material, but a consequence of the "leaking" of such material into consciousness. To deal with this phenomenon, Freud postulated the existence of unconscious elements in the ego, as well as in the superego, the moralistic element of the psyche which punishes the individual for forbidden instinctual desires.

The tension in Freud's view seems to me to be this: the unconscious appears to be both something primitive and something formed. On the one hand the unconscious is associated with biological instincts which are seen as givens in the psyche. On the other hand the unconscious is something which is formed as the individual confronts elements in the psyche which are unpalatable. This tension infects Freud's whole view of the self, even on the later "structural" model of the self. The id is the source of the psyche, the origin of all psychic energy. The ego and superego are simply aspects of the id which have developed special functions. It is this conviction that led Freud to borrow the term "Id" (it) from Groddeck, who had written, "We should not say 'I live' but 'I am lived by the It.'"[6] Such a view leads inevitably to seeing the self as a victim and the unconscious as a force which shapes the self.

Yet Freud also wants to see the unconscious as what is formed as a result of repression. Here the unconscious is not simply a force of which I am a victim; it is in some sense the result of my activity as my personality develops through interaction with others. This tension in Freud is part of his legacy, the reason that his successors include both biologically oriented thinkers such as Hartmann, as well as the object-relations theory, which we shall now discuss.

C. Object Relations Theory

Object relations theory is a form of psychoanalysis developed in England by W. D. Fairbairn and popularized by Harry Guntrip.[7] Recognizing the tension in Freud between the biological and distinctively psychological elements, which we alluded to above, object relations theory rejects the notion of the id altogether, and the theory of instincts closely associated with it. On this view, the infant is fundamentally an undifferentiated unity with "ego-potential." The unconscious is something which develops in the individual as a result of interaction with "objects," an odd choice of terminology since what is meant is primarily the significant persons in the infant's life.

The primary developmental task, in this view, is the passage from infantile dependence to the kind of mature dependence which is compatible with having an identity of one's own. This developmental task cannot be carried out properly unless the infant feels a strong sense of being loved unconditionally and an equally strong sense that the infant's love is accepted by the parent. The initial identity of the child is formed through "primary identification" with the care-giving parent. Without a basic sense of security, the child cannot develop an identity which is independent of this "internalized parent."

As Guntrip tells the story (relying heavily on Fairbairn), the unconscious is the product of interaction with this primary care-giver, which in most societies has historically been the mother. The mother is for the child both exciting and a source of frustration, since it is inevitable that not all of the infant's desires will be met. In the developing child a mental image of the mother is formed, which initially forms the core of the child's own identity. This introjected mother figure then is split or dissociated, as the child attempts to deal with the frustrating or "bad" mother by disowning those aspects.[8] The unconscious is formed as the child tries to deal with a part of himself which he wishes to regard as not really himself.

In people who are fortunate enough to have what Winnicott calls "good-enough mothering" the split or dissociation is not too severe, and people are able to function reasonably well despite the blow to their wholeness. In those who are not so fortunate, what Guntrip calls the "schizoid problem" descends with full force. All of us need what Guntrip terms a "basic security-giving relationship."[9] Those who lack this lose a sense of their true self. They become the victims of the "anti-libidinal ego," the internalized "saboteur" or "bad, sadistic mother," who does not allow them to discover who they are. Unless such withdrawn, dissociated people are able to find such a relationship later in life and repair the early damage, they have great difficulty in feeling or connecting with other people.

As we shall see, this object-relations theory of the unconscious is of great value in understanding Kierkegaard's own view. It consistently views the unconscious, however much power it may have over me and however difficult it may be for me to change it, as something I have formed, and therefore something for which I may be in some ways responsible. And it views the process of formation and the possibilities of transformation of the unconscious as closely linked to my relationships with others.

II. Kierkegaard's Relational View of the Self

It is not possible to describe Kierkegaard's view of the unconscious without briefly describing his view of selfhood. I believe that one of the best treatments of Kierkegaard's view of the self is found in Merold Westphal's paper, "Kierkegaard's Psychology and Unconscious Despair."[10] Westphal maintains that Kierkegaard's view of the self can be understood as involving Aristotelian, Cartesian, and Hegelian elements, in a creative, critical way, so that it is equally illuminating to understand his view as anti-Aristotelian, anti-Cartesian, and anti-Hegelian.[11]

Kierkegaard's view is broadly Aristotelian in that he wants to see the self as shaped by its activity, and the health of the self to be something which is dependent on what the self does, rather than what befalls it. It is anti-Aristotelian in that the health of the self is seen by Aristotle as happiness, and Kierkegaard insists that happiness is not an adequate understanding of the goal of human life once it is understood that human beings are spiritual creatures (*SUD* 25).

Kierkegaard's view can be understood as Cartesian in that it stresses the significance of the inner, self-conscious life of the individual, an emphasis which reflects the Cartesian focus on the interior life as the locus of selfhood. It is, however, anti-Cartesian in that the self is not merely seen by Kierkegaard as a mental substance, but as something to be achieved, a dynamic process rather than simply being a completed object.

Finally, Westphal characterizes the Kierkegaardian view of the self as Hegelian in that Kierkegaard, like Hegel, sees the self as fundamentally relational in character. (I shall postpone temporarily an account of how Kierkegaard's view is also anti-Hegelian.) The self-consciousness of the individual is not complete in itself but is mediated through the relationship to the other. Thus the "I" cannot be understood except in relationship.

This last characterization of Westphal's is controversial, yet it is of the utmost significance for an understanding of Kierkegaard's view of the unconscious. It is controversial because it seems to undermine the conception of Kierkegaard as a radical individualist, a conception firmly held by friend and foe alike. And it is controversial because many lovers of Kierkegaard have an inveterate dislike for admitting that Kierkegaard borrowed anything from his arch-foe, Hegel.

Even writers such as Sylvia Walsh and John Elrod, who would like to read Kierkegaard as putting forward a relational view of the self, have difficulty finding such a view there. Elrod, for example, says that Kierkegaard's pseudonymous works "pay no attention to the ontological and epistemological roles played by the other in the development of a concept of the self."[12] Elrod thinks this lack of a social perspective is remedied in Kierkegaard's later religious authorship, beginning with *Works of Love,* but oddly enough, he treats the crucial first section of *SUD* as belonging with the early, individualistic pseudonymous authorship.[13]

Sylvia Walsh (Perkins), in a fine paper, similarly bemoans the "absence of a relation to others in Kierkegaard's general description of the self" in the first part of *SUD,* especially given the clearly relational view in *Works of Love.*[14] Walsh says that one must either conclude that there is an inconsistency in the works or else one must interpret the social view of *Works of Love* as somehow implicit in *SUD.* She opts for the latter view, but still finds it distressing that Kierkegaard did not address more directly the relatedness of the self to others "in defining the structure of the self."[15]

These criticisms seem rather surprising in view of the explicit statement of Anti-Climacus that the human self is not an autonomous self whose being is self-contained: "The human self is such a derived, established relation, a relation that relates itself to itself and in relating itself to itself relates itself to another" (*SUD* 13-14). Elrod and Walsh are certainly familiar with this passage. Why then do they not think that part I of *SUD* contains a relational view of the self? The most plausible answer is that they interpret the "other" referred to in this passage as God, the "power" which "established" the relationship which constitutes the self. In claiming that Kierkegaard's view of the self here is not relational, they must mean that it does not include a relation to other human beings.

I find this objectionable. First, most obviously and most importantly, these critics seem to assume that God somehow doesn't count as a genuine "other person." But it is crucial for Kierkegaard's whole project of getting the individual to stand before God as an individual that God be construed as a genuine person to whom I can relate as an other. It is the fact that God can be the other to whom I relate, and must be that other if I am genuinely to be myself, that ultimately makes Kierkegaard's view anti-Hegelian.

Second, it is by no means clear that Kierkegaard thinks God is the only "other" who is significant in forming the self's identity. At this point we must take seriously the interesting differences between part I and part II of **SUD**. Although it has seemed obvious to most readers that the "power" in part I which constitutes the self must be God, several things make it necessary to go slowly in making such an identification, at least without qualification.

First, there is the fact that Anti-Climacus uses abstract, formal language. He talks about the "power" which established the self, and "another" to which the self is related. Given Anti-Climacus's strident Christianity and complete lack of reticence in using the name of God in other places, I think his choice of this abstract language is intentional and significant.

The second significant point is that Anti-Climacus describes the difference between parts I and II in a way that implies that the concept of God is somehow not fully operative in part I. In part II, the despair which was described in part I is redescribed as sin, and the difference is said to be this: sin is despair which is "before God" (**SUD** 77).

The odd thing about this is that the concept of God is by no means absent from part I. Those who wish to identify the "power" which established the self with God have abundant textual evidence to justify the equation, for Anti-Climacus frequently uses the word "God" in part I in ways which suggest that he is thinking of the other which forms the basis of the self (**SUD** 16, 27, 30, 32, 35, 38-42, 68-69, and 71).

To resolve this puzzle I believe we must recognize that Kierkegaard frequently intermixes ontological and ethical discourse in his descriptions of the self. He describes the self *both* as something I am *and* something I must become, *both* as a substance *and* as something

to be achieved. This is not confusion on his part, because to understand the self it is imperative to see the self in both of these dimensions. But it is easy to become confused about the relationship of the individual to God and the relationship of part I and II of **SUD** if we do not distinguish the two contexts.

In Kierkegaard's view a relation to God is in one sense inescapable; in another sense it is a task. In a similar manner, a self is on the one hand something I simply am, something I cannot help being; the torment of the despairer who wills not to be a self is precisely that he has no choice in the matter. On the other hand, a self is precisely what no individual simply is as a matter of course. It is something that one must become.

Ontologically, the "other" to which the self must relate and cannot help relating to is God, who is indeed the creator of the self. However, God has created human persons as free and responsible creatures. As Anti-Climacus says, "God, who constituted man a relation, releases it from his hand, as it were" (**SUD** 16). Notice that there is no true independence from God. God does not really let the relationship go out of his hand ontologically, but he endows humans with the ethical freedom to define their own identity.

If humans misuse their freedom, they do not cease to be relational beings; that is part of their ontological structure. Nor do they cease to have a relation to God. They may, however, cease to relate *consciously* to God, consciously forming their selves in relation to what is less than God. One might say that individuals in this case attempt to ground their selves in a God-substitute. Their conscious identities are rooted in "powers" or "others" which are less than God.

Actually there is a sense in which the identity of the self is formed through relationships with others independently of the misuse of freedom. For Kierkegaard, genuine selfhood is a never-completed task of maturity which requires a consciousness of God, or, as we have claimed, a God-substitute. However, this mature self does not spring from nothing; individuals begin to form their identity in infancy. Thus, when an individual begins to be a self in the most profound sense, he or she already has a self of sorts, what one might call a "pre-self." This pre-self is certainly formed through early relationships. In the developing child, therefore, there is nothing inherently pathological in the grounding of one's identity in those significant others who shape the child's emerging self. Nor is there anything pathological in the adult's identity being partly rooted in relationships to other finite selves. The problem comes into being when the adult lacks a God-relationship and thus gives to the relations with other human selves (and with what is less than human) a priority and ultimacy such relations do not deserve. I am not here talking merely about a case of "arrested development," a case in which an individual does not discover God and fails to grow, but the case in which the individual chooses not to grow by suppressing the knowledge of God.

So Kierkegaard, as I read him, is very far from a non-relational view of the self. All selfhood depends ontologically on God, and genuine selfhood depends on a conscious relation to God, for which the individual may substitute a relation to what is less than God. All of this presupposes a developing "pre-self," which is formed through relations with other persons and which is a significant element in the identity of a mature, healthy self. That the self is constituted by relations with others, including those "others" other than God, is portrayed very clearly:

> And what infinite reality the self· gains by being conscious of existing before God, by becoming a human self whose criterion is God! A cattleman who (if this were possible) is a self directly before his cattle is a very low self, and, similarly, a master who is a self directly before his slaves is actually no self— for in both cases a criterion is lacking. The child who previously has had only his parents as a criterion becomes a self as an adult by getting the state as a criterion, but what an infinite accent falls on the self by having God as the criterion! (*SUD* 79)

Here Anti-Climacus deepens our understanding of the relational character of the self by describing the self as a task. By a "criterion" he means that by which a self measures itself. To be a self is to be a being who is striving toward a certain ideal; that ideal provides the "measure" for the self. For human selves this measure is derived from the conscious relationships with others which have formed the self.

Human beings constantly define themselves through relations with others. A person who thinks of himself as a self through his superiority to the cattle he tends is actually not a self at all; one might say his standards are simply too low. Similarly, a person whose selfhood is grounded in his superiority to the slaves he owns fails to be a self. In this case it is not that he is not related to other selves; his slaves are persons. It is that in regarding the slaves as slaves, the owner does not regard them as genuine persons. Hence his measure is still a defective one, and this infects his own self-conception.

Kierkegaard therefore recognizes that actual human selves are formed relationally, but he thinks that a self which *only* has other human beings as its measure, even the "adult" who takes the "official" standards certified by the state as his measure, can never be secure. Genuine selfhood requires that the self stand consciously before God.

This means that though the ontological "power" which grounds the self is always God, insofar as the self is a

task it is shaped by "powers" that are less than God. In the infant and the child this is not pathological, and even in the healthy adult relations to others continue to form part of one's identity. This is proper so long as those relations have an appropriate priority. Unfortunately, human beings are sinners, and hence do not maintain "an absolute relation to the absolute and a relative relation to the relative," as Johannes Climacus describes the task in *Postscript* (CUP 414). Other humans (and what is sub-human) do function as "God-substitutes."

III. Self-Deception and the Divided Self

In understanding the self as an achievement, Kierkegaard fundamentally divorces his view from the Cartesian conception of the self as a unified, self-transparent consciousness. What Descartes sees as the essence of the self, Kierkegaard views as the goal. The actual self God creates includes within it diverse possibilities, and with these are given the possibility of forming a unified self. These possibilities are not bare possibilities, but concrete potentialities of an actual bodily being. The self is not purely a set of possibilities, since there must be an actual being to contain the possibilities, as it were, and this actual being must be or contain an agent which has the power of choice. Otherwise freedom and responsibility would not exist. However, there is no reason to think that this agency is a transparent, unified Cartesian self. Rather, the self contains within itself "obscure powers," to use the telling phrase of Judge William (*EO, [Either/Or]*, II, 164).

Such a claim by itself only brings us to what we have called the unnoticed unconscious, and does not explain the reality of the dynamic unconscious. For that, will and choice must be brought into the story. The dissociation of consciousness is, however, part of the explanation of the *possibility* of the dynamic unconscious.

Many philosophers have, under the influence of a Cartesian picture of the self, denied that self-deception is really possible. Analyzing self-deception as a lie to oneself, they have argued that such a lie is impossible, since the person would have to be both deceiver and deceived, both the liar and the one lied to, and this requires that the person both know the truth and not know the truth. If the self were a unified, Cartesian, transparent mind, this would indeed be impossible.

It is not, however, impossible for the same person to be both deceiver and deceived if there is duality in the self. If my consciousness is dissociated, then this is completely possible, and in fact occurs frequently. Nothing is more common, in a case of self-deception, for the person to see in retrospect that he knew the truth all along, and yet failed to admit it to himself.

One might object at this point that such a view compromises the unity of the self, and still does not solve the problem of how self-deception is possible. For self-deception requires that it be the same self that both knows and does not know the truth. If the self's knowledge of itself is dissociated, so that the consciousness of the truth is divorced from the consciousness which obscures the truth, then have we not divided the self into two selves, innocent victim and guilty deceiver?

To answer this objection, we must explore the process by which the divided self comes into being. While it is a dissociated consciousness that makes self-deception possible, self-deception is a special kind of division in the self. In such a case the division in the self can be traced to the will of the self. In cases of self-deception the dissociation in consciousness is not simply a natural fact, but is grounded in the choices the person has made.

As we have noted, self-deception appears paradoxical and some have alleged that it is literally impossible. To deceive myself I must know the truth and intentionally obscure the truth. But how can I convince myself that what I know is true is not true? Such a project seems as difficult as trying not to think of a pink elephant. It might seem that the harder one tries to do it, the more difficult the task becomes. Kierkegaard's answer to this problem rests on the fact that human beings are temporal creatures and that the process of self-deception is therefore a temporal process.

The problem is treated by Anti-Climacus in at least a couple of passages, most notably in the course of analyzing the Socratic principle that sin is ignorance. Anti-Climacus agrees that from a Christian perspective this is in a sense correct. Sin is a kind of ignorance, or preferably, stupidity (*SUD* 88). What the Socratic view does not recognize is that it is a willed ignorance, an ignorance for which the individual is culpable. Obviously, however, to say that the ignorance is willed is to say that it involves self-deception, for to will to be ignorant of something, I must in some way be aware of the knowledge which I will to suppress.

Anti-Climacus wishes to trace evil back ultimately then to the will. But he recognizes that it is rare if not impossible for the individual simply to will what he knows to be evil. The normal process is for the will to corrupt one's knowledge; sin goes hand in hand with self-deception.

This process of corruption is a temporal one. When the will does not want to do what a person knows to be right, the usual response is not for the individual consciously to do what he knows to be wrong, but simply to delay doing anything. "Willing allows some time to elapse, an interim called 'We shall look at it tomorrow'" (*SUD* 94). This period of time allows the indi-

vidual to carry out any number of strategies to subvert his understanding. "The lower nature's power lies in stretching things out" (*SUD* 94). Eventually, "little by little" (*SUD* 56), Anti-Climacus says, the understanding is changed so that knowing and willing can "understand each other," can "agree completely" (*SUD* 94).

What are some of these strategies? One is simply to *delay,* to wait for the knowledge to decay. Since we have seen that human beings are not Cartesian selves, and since they are temporal creatures, delay may result in some dissociation "naturally." As Anti-Climacus puts it, the knowledge simply "dims" or "becomes obscure." The fact that this is a natural process does not absolve the individual of responsibility, for it is the willed delay that makes this dimming possible, and the individual is guilty for the delay since it is motivated by the hope that just this dimming will occur. At particular moments the knowledge may come to consciousness, but over time these moments come more and more infrequently, and the consciousness involved becomes more and more dim.

A second strategy is distraction. Here the individual does not merely wait for nature to take its course, but actively intervenes. "He may try to keep himself in the dark about his state through diversions and in other ways, for example, through work and business as diversionary means, yet in such a way that he does not entirely realize why he is doing it, that it is to keep himself in the dark" (*SUD* 48).

Here Kierkegaard is helping us see that it *is* possible to intentionally avoid thinking of a pink elephant. Obviously one must think of a pink elephant at some time to have this intention, but the intention is nevertheless one that can be successfully carried out over time. Eventually one can put oneself into a state in which one is not thinking of a pink elephant. The trick is diversion. One must focus on something else. If the something else is engrossing enough for me to lose myself in it, I will eventually forget the elephant.

In the same way, if I plunge into various activities: useful work, committees, sports, games, or even religious work, I may eventually find that the disturbing insights into who I am no longer haunt my consciousness. The individual may even, Anti-Climacus says, do this with a certain shrewdness or insight into what is going on. That is, he may recognize in general terms that this process of diverting himself is a way of "sinking his soul in darkness" (*SUD* 48). This is psychologically possible so long as the individual does not clearly focus on the specific insights he wishes to avoid.

Such strategies could usefully be termed "defenses," to use Freudian language, since they are crucial not only in obscuring our self-knowledge originally, but also in keeping the troubling knowledge at bay.

Kierkegaard does not systematically catalogue the various defenses available to human beings, but he does give interesting and insightful analyses of a variety of such strategies.

One of the most common and dangerous of such defenses might be termed "intellectualizing." The self-knowledge in question is existential knowledge, knowledge about how life should be lived. It is tempting for the individual to substitute for such knowledge a kind of intellectual knowledge. I convince myself that I am ethical because I know a lot about ethical theory. I convince myself that I am a Christian because I know a lot of theology. It is this kind of defense that Kierkegaard thinks the educated intellectual, "the professor," is particularly prone to, and it is one on which he pours unwithering scorn.

Even Socrates had recognized that there was a difference between "understanding and understanding." What Socrates had failed to see was that the intellectual understanding which in the genuine sense is no understanding at all is not simply ignorance. There is a difference between "not *being able* to understand and not *willing* to understand" (*SUD* 95). Intellectual understanding can be a defense against genuine understanding.

IV. Self-Deception and Sin

The paradoxicalness of self-deception and the difficulty of understanding it underlie one of the central problems of *SUD,* namely the paradoxical attitude of Anti-Climacus toward unconscious despair and toward paganism, the "despairing unconsciousness of God." On the one hand Anti-Climacus clearly wants to say that there can be unconscious despair. "Not being in despair, not being conscious of being in despair, is precisely a form of despair" (*SUD* 23). On the other hand, unconscious despair does not quite seem to be despair in a full-blooded sense; such despair one is tempted, humanly speaking, to describe as a kind of innocence. "It is almost a dialectical issue whether it is justifiable to call such a state despair" (*SUD* 42).

This ambivalence about unconscious despair is even more pronounced with respect to unconscious sin, as well it might be, since sin for Anti-Climacus is an intensified form of conscious despair. Sin is a spiritual disorder, and a spiritless being would seem to be incapable of sin. On the one hand Anti-Climacus seems to view paganism as a kind of innocence: "The sin of paganism was essentially despairing ignorance of god, . . . Therefore, from another point of view, it is true that in the strictest sense the pagan did not sin, for he did not sin before God, and all sin is before God" (*SUD* 81). Yet in the final analysis Anti-Climacus is loathe to give the pagan a blanket dispensation, and recognizes the strangeness of a view that absolves

paganism of sin. "Christianity regards everything as under sin; we have tried to depict the Christian point of view as rigorously as possible—and then this strange outcome emerges, this strange conclusion that sin is not to be found at all in paganism but only in Judaism and Christendom, and there again very seldom" (*SUD* 101). So Anti-Climacus retreats from the general absolution of the pagan and insists that the lack of consciousness which forms the basis of the pagan's "innocence" is itself culpable, and must be seen therefore as grounded in self-deception. "Is it (being in a state of spiritlessness) something that happens to a person? No, it is his own fault. No one is born devoid of spirit, and no matter how many go to their death with this spiritlessness as the one and only outcome of their lives, it is not the fault of life" (*SUD* 102).

The problem is that this suggests that the ignorance cannot have been complete. One must have, or at least one must have had, spirit in order to have become spiritless. To be spiritless is to lack a consciousness of God. Kierkegaard's view here seems to lead to the conclusion that there is in all human beings an original knowledge of God, a knowledge which becomes obscured and repressed over time, but which is nonetheless enough to make the individual responsible.

V. Is There a Natural Awareness of God in All Humans?

This view that there is something like a universal, natural knowledge of God is puzzling and difficult to accept, but it seems implicit at many points in Kierkegaard's authorship and explicit at a few points. In the *Papirer,* in a draft version of *Philosophical Fragments,* it is said that there has never been a genuine atheist, only people who did not wish to "let what they knew, that God existed, get power over their minds" (*JP [Søren Kierkegaard's Journals and Papers]* 3:662). The hostility to the idea of proving God's existence in both *Postscript* and *Fragments* seems to be linked to the idea that such proofs are unnecessary because God is in some sense already present to human beings (*CUP [Concluding Unscientific Postscript to the Philosophical Fragments]* 545).

One may reasonably ask about such a universal knowledge of God, "In what does it consist?" On the surface many people do not seem to have any conscious awareness of God. This fact is quite compatible with Kierkegaard's view, of course, since the thesis is not that everyone is actually aware of God. The whole point of much of *SUD* is that this knowledge has become repressed, and that understanding this repression is the key to understanding the unconscious in humans. Still, in order to repress this knowledge, humans must once have had it, and one may reasonably ask whether such a view is in accord with what we know about human psychological development.

To make sense of Kierkegaard's position, I think we must distinguish between a conscious awareness of God, and a conscious awareness of God *as* God. It is implausible to claim that the latter kind of knowledge is universally present in human beings, even originally or as a kind of potential knowledge. It is not, however, absurd to maintain that human beings in fact have an awareness of God, even though they do not always understand that it is God whom they are aware of. Anti-Climacus explicitly claims that it is *conscience* which constitutes the relationship to God (*SUD* 124). This is consistent with the general Kierkegaardian view that the religious life, while never reducible to the ethical life, always arises out of a confrontation with ethical ideals.

Every child does not have a clear, explicit understanding of the nature of God. However, Kierkegaard thinks, every child does encounter ideals which are experienced as absolute in character, and in experiencing these ideals gains some sense of the "infinity" of the self. (A degree of cultural relativity in the content of the ideals does not matter, since it is their absolute form which is determinative.) In encountering such ideals I gain a sense of my self as more than a product of accidental circumstances. I am rather called to exercise responsible choice and become the ideal self I see it as my task to become. Whether the child understands this or not, such an encounter is an encounter with the ontological "other" which is the "power" which constitutes the self.

VI. Conscience and the Self

That conscience is decisive in the development of the self is not a thesis unique to Kierkegaard. In a way this is Freud's view as well, since for Freud, the resolution of the Oedipus conflict and the development of the superego are also decisive in becoming an adult.

The differences with Freud are, however, more significant than the similarities. For Freud, the superego is simply the internalized parent; there is no question of the superego as in any sense the voice of God. It does not represent absolute truth but cultural relativity. For Kierkegaard, conscience, while certainly reflecting cultural norms, also reflects the coming into being in a human person of a sense of his own freedom and responsibility through an encounter with ideals that have absolute validity.

This difference makes one suspect that the Freudian superego and the Kierkegaardian conscience are simply not identical. I think this suspicion is correct, and that its correctness can be seen by looking at the crucial time period when each is formed. For the superego the crucial age is clearly around three. However, this cannot be the crucial age for the development of conscience in the significant sense for Kierkegaard. Once

conscience is in place the capacity of the individual to despair and to sin is in place as well, but it is well known that Kierkegaard did not think children were capable of sin in any genuine sense. Anti-Climacus says plainly that children are not capable of despair, but only bad temper (*SUD* 49n.).

I think therefore that we must look to adolescence or at least pre-adolescence as the crucial period for the emergence of conscience in the Kierkegaardian sense. (The exact age surely differs from child to child.) It is in adolescence that the individual discovers that he or she must choose and affirm—or reject—what has been handed down to him or her by culture. Such a call to responsible choice is at the same time a discovery that choices matter—that one is called to choose responsibly. In Kierkegaard's language it is the discovery that human persons are spirit, and Kierkegaard interprets this encounter as God's call to individuals to become what God has created them to be.

One other significant difference between Freudian and Kierkegaardian views now comes into view, and that concerns the relation between conscience, pathology, and the unconscious. For Freud, the overactive superego is a source of pathology. It is the sadistic, internal saboteur which must be tamed and moderated for the sake of individual psychological health, even if we must retain it in some form for the sake of civilized society. Kierkegaard is hardly ignorant of the torments of the overly active conscience, but he is far from seeing this as the most significant source of human sickness.

Like Freud, he favors an approach to the child's development which avoids excessive guilt. The imposition of strict Christian concepts on the child is even characterized as a "rape, be it ever so well meant" (*CUP* 603). Children who are victims of such a rape have a struggle to go through, as they attempt to come to terms with the love and forgiveness of God.

Despite this apparent agreement with Freud and neo-Freudians who see the major problem of human life to be guilt-feelings caused by an overactive superego, Kierkegaard would by no means be enthusiastic about the banishment of guilt from contemporary life. The real problem is not that we have excessive guilt feelings, but that we avoid coming to terms with the fact that we are really guilty.

The development of the pathological unconscious must be seen in connection with just this point. The motivation for the development of the unconscious is our sensuousness, our failure to rise above the categories of what feels pleasant and unpleasant, for the experience of guilt is decidedly unpleasant. Most human beings do not have "the courage to venture out and to endure being spirit" (*SUD* 43).

When the call of conscience comes, humans therefore have a reason to ignore it. And once they have ignored it, they have a double reason for ignoring it, for to face conscience would be not only to face the unpleasantness of responsible decision-making, but the greater unpleasantness of having decided to shirk responsibility. Thus the dynamic unconscious emerges, the long process of deceiving oneself about oneself, employing the strategies outlined above, and a host of others.

Thus we see that Kierkegaard's view of the unconscious is as thoroughly relational as his view of the self. Object-relations theorists trace the emergence of the unconscious to the divided self which comes into being through relations with others. Kierkegaard recognizes the role of these relations in the formation of the self, especially with regard to what I have termed the pre-self, the identity the self already has when it becomes a self in a deeper sense. These early relations certainly will involve conflicts, and may lead to the development of dissociation and unconscious processes. So Kierkegaard does not have to reject the understanding of object-relations theorists about the significance of early relations.

Nevertheless Kierkegaard traces the emergence of the unconscious in the most significant sense to the divided self which emerges through a relation to *the* significant other which forms the basis for the true self. For Kierkegaard the really significant unconscious is the one that I form as an adolescent and as an adult, as I encounter God and deceive myself as I deal with the resultant moral failure and guilt. Of course this does not mean that Kierkegaard believes that the unconscious processes which result from early relations with others are unrelated to the deeper unconscious which is his primary concern. To the contrary, the psychological conflicts and predispositions which the child brings to adolescence are fraught with significance. I believe that these problems are understood by Kierkegaard as bound up with the nest of problems associated with original sin.

In *The Concept of Anxiety* Vigilius Haufniensis maintains that every individual "is both himself and the race" (*CA* 28). Original sin is not simply a physical, inherited malady. To the extent that I am a sinner, it is because I have chosen to be a sinner, just as Adam chose sin. Such a choice is scientifically inexplicable, but that simply shows that sin must be understood as the result of freedom (*CA* 32-33, 51, 92).

Qualitatively, therefore, the sin of every individual is the same. This does not mean, however, that sin does not have real consequences for the individual and for the race. The individual who is born to a sinful race does not begin life with a blank slate, but as possessing sinful inclinations, which he or she did not choose him or herself and which quantitatively differ from the innocence of Adamic Eden.

I believe that this provides the context for understanding early relations with others and the foundation of the personality for Kierkegaard. Though he will not hear of a "universal excuse," since individuals must recognize that they have become what they have chosen to become and take responsibility for what they are, it is nevertheless true that the child who is the product of a sinful race and a sinful upbringing bears heavy burdens. The self such a child will choose to be is a self "already bungled," a self already seriously distorted and misshapen by bad parental relationships and relations with others.

VII. Healing the Unconscious

To summarize, Kierkegaard's view of the unconscious is basically that the unconscious is something which I develop as I deceive myself about who and what I am. The process of forming and disguising my identity is in turn a process of relating to others, with God as the ultimate and intended other, but other persons playing a role in shaping what I have termed the pre-self and (later) playing the role of God-substitutes in the formation and maintenance of one's sinful identity. This view implies, as we have seen, some remarkable claims: that everyone has an unconscious relation to God and that every person has to some degree obscured this relation and thus divided the self.

On the surface such views may seem implausible, but we must recognize that if we are indeed self-deceivers, then such self-deception will not be obvious to us. Ultimately, I think Kierkegaard's view stands or falls with the Christianity to which it is so intimately linked, and it is well-known that Kierkegaard thought it crucial to maintain that Christianity could not be rationally demonstrated to be true. Rather, the possibility of offense must be safeguarded, and we must therefore safeguard this possibility in his view of the unconscious as well. Kierkegaard's view of the unconscious contains an analysis of the condition of the "natural man" which that person can only hope to recognize as true with the help of divine revelation.

Nevertheless, it is important to see how Kierkegaard's views can be used to interpret contemporary psychological findings. Those findings cannot be demonstrative evidence of the correctness of Kierkegaard's views, but if Kierkegaard's perspective gives us no interpretive power, no ability to illuminate our situation, then the understanding it claims to offer must be illusory.

To this end I should like to draw attention to some interesting parallels between Kierkegaard's view and the object-relations theory which is, as we have seen, his closest neighbor on the contemporary psychological scene. The parallels are especially interesting with respect to possible cures for the problem of the divided self.

Kierkegaard's claim that the self-deception associated with sin and despair is a universal phenomenon closely parallels the claim of the object-relations theorist that the "schizoid self" is universal. W. D. Fairbairn, in his important paper, "Schizoid Factors in the Personality," recognizes that the universality of his claims will be disturbing to many. "The criticism for which I must now prepare myself is that, according to my way of thinking, everybody without exception must be regarded as schizoid."[16] Fairbairn's response to this criticism is simply that it is true that everyone is at bottom schizoid, and thus that the criticism is not a criticism. "The fundamental schizoid phenomenon is the presence of splits in the ego; and it would take a bold man to claim that his ego was so perfectly integrated as to be incapable of revealing any evidence of splitting at the deepest levels."[17]

If this is correct, Kierkegaard might well take this universal "splitting" to be confirmation of his claims about the universality of sin and despair. The object-relations theorist also agrees with Kierkegaard that this dissociation of the self from itself is fundamentally the result of faulty relationships with others. Of course the psychoanalytic thinker sees the faulty relationships to be primarily with the initial care-giver, while, as we have seen, Kierkegaard focuses attention on the relation to God. Once we recognize, however, that different ages are of concern here, there is no real contradiction between the two views. Object-relations theory is attempting to understand the initial formation of the psyche, and the focus is therefore on early childhood. Kierkegaard is analyzing the becoming of a self in the decisive sense, and thus his views center on adolescence and the early adult years. We have seen that Kierkegaard does not deny that significant psychological developments may occur in early childhood, developments that may, under the impact of original sin, predispose the self towards brokenness. Also, the psychoanalytic perspective of such thinkers as Guntrip and Fairbairn presupposes the possibility of a genuine self, which can continue to develop and assume responsibility for itself. So there is no objection from the psychological side toward seeing decisions later than early childhood as decisive in the formation of the self.

The significance of such later decisions and later relationships comes through clearly if we look at the views of Guntrip and Fairbairn on the healing of the broken self. Though Guntrip wants to affirm a genuinely "personal self," which can assume responsibility for itself and cannot see itself as the helpless victim of biological forces, he affirms in an equally emphatic way the need of the self for a healing relationship to become truly whole.

Guntrip sees the therapist as attempting to provide the client who was not fortunate enough to have had "good-enough mothering" a sense of identity and security which his parents failed to provide him originally. "At the deepest level, psychotherapy is replacement therapy, providing for the patient what the mother failed to provide at the beginning of life."[18] The therapist does not really use "techniques," but must simply be a real person for the client, a person who is accepting and non-judgmental, which allows the divided ego to accept all of itself.

From Kierkegaard's point of view, there is wisdom in Guntrip's view, but it fails to capture the depths of the self's situation in several ways. First, Guntrip, with his talk of "good-enough mothering," ignores the universality of the problem. If the divided self is as universal as he and Fairbairn maintain, one may well ask as to whether any parenting can be "good-enough" to produce the whole self being held forward as an ideal.

Even more significantly, Kierkegaard would, I think, while affirming the need for a "basic security giving personal relationship," question the adequacy of the therapist to play this role. However much the therapist may try to be a "real person" to the client, one must recognize that the therapeutic relationship is in the end an artificial one. The client and the therapist are engaged in a commercial transaction; the non-judgmental acceptance of the therapist can hardly be anything other than a therapeutic technique. Client and therapist do not interact outside the therapeutic session, and if by chance they do, one would hardly expect the therapist always to maintain an accepting attitude. Suppose, for example, that the client is having an affair with the spouse of the therapist?

But even if the therapist is a model of love and acceptance, the fundamental problem, from Kierkegaard's perspective, is that such a therapist would still provide an inadequate "criterion" of the self. The therapist would still be an inadequate substitute for the person whose love and acceptance can genuinely form the basis of selfhood.

This is not to say that therapy cannot be helpful for individuals who are psychologically crippled. Though I am not sure Kierkegaard has room for this idea, the therapist may indeed help a troubled individual move toward wholeness, much as a relationship with a good friend may help an individual. It may even be in some cases that therapy is part of what makes faith possible, since for some people the pre-self may be so broken that the idea of a loving, accepting God is literally unbelievable. "Perhaps there are times when the sick are too weak for the surgery that would cure them."[19]

In the final analysis, however, the ultimate cure is not human therapy but faith in God, at least as Kierkegaard sees it. My identity or non-identity cannot be rooted in the acceptance or non-acceptance of another self struggling towards wholeness. Only the absolute love of God can provide the security which allows the self to accept itself completely as it is, while recognizing the possibility and responsibility for becoming what it may fully be. The cure for the human condition is simply faith: "Faith is: that the self in being itself and in willing to be itself rests transparently in God" (*SUD* 82). Such a faith would mean that the unconscious as that part of myself which I cannot and will not recognize has been blotted out. I would know myself, even as I am known.

Notes

[1] Though I cite the Hongs' pagination (SUD), where noted in the text I have preferred my own translation.

[2] The typical cognitive psychologist views mental activity as information processing in the brain. The part of this activity that "gets noticed" is consciousness. See [Jonathan] Winson, *Brain and Psyche,* [New York: Random House, 1986] for a lucid account of this perspective, which relates this view to Freudian theory.

[3] This early account can be found in several of Freud's writings; for example, see his *An Outline of Psycho-Analysis* [trans. James Strachey. New York: Norton, 1949].

[4] See chapter 2 of Sartre's *Being and Nothingness* [trans. Hazel E. Barnes. New York: Philosophical Library, 1956].

[5] See Freud's *The Ego and the Id* [London: Woolf, 1935].

[6] This account of Freud's relation to Groddeck is found in [Harry] Guntrip, *Psychoanalytic Theory, Therapy, and the Self* [New York: Basic, 1971]. p. 105.

[7] See the previous note for Guntrip. [W.D.] Fairbairn's most significant work is *Psychoanalytic Studies of the Personality* [London: Tavistock, 1952].

[8] Guntrip credits Melanie Klein for the first account of how this takes place. See chapter 3 in Guntrip, *Psychoanalytic Theory.*

[9] See Guntrip, *Psychoanalytic Theory,* p. 191.

[10] [Merold] Westphal, "Kierkegaard's Psychology and Unconscious Despair," in *International Kierkegaard Commentary: The Sickness unto Death* (henceforth IKC-SUD), ed. Perkins [vol. 19, Macon: Mercer University Press, 1987], pp. 39-66.

[11] Westphal, "Kierkegaard's Psychology" in IKC-SUD, p. 49.

[12] [John] Elrod, "Kierkegaard on Self and Society," in *Kierkegaardiana* XI, pp. 178-96.

[13] Elrod, *Kierkegaard and Christendom* [Princeton: Princeton University Press, 1981], pp. 131-32.

[14] [Sylvia (Perkins)] Walsh, "On 'Feminine' and 'Masculine' Forms of Despair," in IKC-SUD, p. 125.

[15] Walsh, "On 'Feminine'" in IKC-SUD, pp. 126-27.

[16] Fairbairn, *Psychoanalytic Studies,* p. 7.

[17] Fairbairn, *Psychoanalytic Studies,* p. 8.

[18] Guntrip, *Psychoanalytic Theory,* p. 191.

[19] This sentence comes from some comments by Merold Westphal on an earlier draft of this chapter. I am deeply in Westphal's debt for his suggestions.

Patrick Goold (essay date 1990)

SOURCE: "Reading Kierkegaard: Two Pitfalls and a Strategy for Avoiding Them," in *Faith and Philosophy,* Vol. 7, No. 3, July, 1990, pp. 304-15.

[*In the following essay, Goold argues that many critics of Kierkegaard's writing read him in a manner that is either overly literal or overly ironic. Goold notes the error of such readings and suggests a more suitable method of approaching Kierkegaard's authorship—that is, searching out general themes and conclusions in the philosopher's works in an effort to gain "views both true and profound."*]

Kierkegaard has much to teach us. On the nature of religious faith, for example, there is no author since Paul who is more profound or more enlightening. Deciphering his message, however, is very difficult. For various reasons he writes so as to discourage the lazy reader and to perplex those with an unreflective cast of mind. Pseudonymity is only the most obvious way among many in which he has sought to foil the collectors of conclusions. But the deviousness of these devices and the difficulties they present to an honest and reflective reader have been greatly exaggerated by interpreters of Kierkegaard, often to the point of making nonsense of his work. Some see his writings as entirely poetic (ironic) and as unconcerned with the sort of truth that preoccupies science or philosophy. Others find it patently self-refuting. Both readings made Kierkegaard unworthy of rational criticism, the latter because he never gets off the ground, the former because he never touches down. Both views rest on a failure to read carefully and to make needed distinctions, and both are mistaken.

Every interpretation that makes Kierkegaard's writings opaque to rational analysis is based, it seems to me, upon a failure to make an obvious and elementary distinction between levels of discourse. Every such interpretation fails to distinguish between those passages in which Kierkegaard is 'existentializing' or 'doing existential philosophy' from those in which he is writing about the nature, content, structure, etc. of his existentializing. This familiar and useful distinction between discourse *within* a realm of discourse and discourse *about* that realm is important here not because it allows us "to make inwardness academically respectable" or "to give human existence the dubious prestige of professorial sanction,"[1] but because it allows us to avoid making nonsense of Kierkegaard. The inanation of Kierkegaard resulting from failure to observe this distinction takes two forms. The form most commonly in evidence among philosophers might be called 'over-literalization,' the alternative 'over-poeticization.' Both approaches have the logical (if not always consciously intended) result of making Kierkegaard either self-refuting or vacuous.

Over-Literalization

Examples of the pitfalls of over-literalization abound. Climacus is the most prolific provocateur of interpretative failures of this sort, and of all the things he says none is more thoroughly misunderstood by literal-minded philosophers than the 'doctrine' that truth is subjectivity. A. E. Murphy, Paul Edwards, and Brand Blanshard, for example, all make the same sort of attack on subjective truth, a sort of attack that sensitivity to Climacus' therapeutic use of language would obviate. Murphy writes:

> While it ostensibly turns away from the issue of objective truth, Kierkegaard's procedure presupposes such truth at every step in its retreat into recessive inwardness. His subjectivity is parasitic for its 'existential' significance on the assumed objective truth of a doctrine about man and God whose right to claim such truth it strives at every point to discredit.[2]

Edwards contends that "Kierkegaard reverts and must revert from the new sense of 'true' in which to say that a belief is true means no more than that it is held sincerely and without reservations, to the old sense in which it means that it is in accordance with the facts or with reality."[3] And Blanshard thinks that the author of "truth is subjectivity," because of this ambiguity in his position, faces the following dilemma:

> His philosophy terminates in a rejection of those very principles of logic on which he proceeded as a philosopher. . . . If the logic he assumes in his philosophy is valid, then the faith ('truth' would work equally well here) which stands at the summit of 'the stages on life's way' is meaningless. If that

irrational faith is accepted, the principles on which reflection conducts itself are everywhere impugned. In that case, Kierkegaard . . . should remain silent.[4]

Murphy starts out on the right track here. The man who is "in the truth" in the Climacean sense does indeed "turn away" from the issue of objective truth, not merely ostensibly but in fact, and with total decisiveness. And the procedure by means of which he accomplishes this is precisely "to presuppose such truth at every step." For example, finding God objectively, i.e. proving his existence, is not a concern of the subjective thinker because he seizes his certainty directly, before the proof can ever begin. He is satisfied to have at once a "militant certainty,"[5] rather than wait for the completion of proofs to satisfy him. He does not, however, do this because he feels what he believes must be objectively false, but because he knows that the objective truth of what he believes cannot come to light in time. The distinction is large, and this is where the second part of Murphy's statement goes astray. He sees Climacus as attempting to discredit, for example, the believer's right to claim that God has in fact existed. Climacus does not deny that the believer holds his beliefs to be objectively true, this is not what his "turning away from the question to objective truth" amounts to at all. Rather he is denying that the believer can claim to know that his beliefs are true, indeed he takes it to be a requirement for faith that one understand the necessity of uncertainty in this manner.

All this is in the text, but obscure and difficult to grasp if one takes the point of "truth is subjectivity" to be a new conceptual determination of the property people have traditionally tried to get at with the notion of objective truth. This is not what is going on here. Climacus is using the term 'truth' in his definition in the sense in which it was commonly used by his contemporaries. He has Hegel in mind, and the Hegelian distinction between truth and correctness, truth being the according of a thing with its concept. Climacus employs this notion to define a very small subspecies of truth, the truth of an existing individual human being. Instead of redefining 'truth' Climacus is laying out what the truth (as commonly understood) of the individual consists in. The result is not a new 'truth' which is to usurp the role of the old one, but an explication of the 'old truth' applied to a new object, i.e. the single existing individual. It is called by the name 'subjective truth' because ultimately the 'objective' truth of the existing individual consists in his entire identification with his own subjectivity.

Of course, "truth is subjectivity" is not the most perspicuous formulation of such an insight. If one is preoccupied with a different problematic, one that takes propositions to be the proper objects of belief and truth to be a property solely of propositions, then it is not surprising that one comes to the wrong conclusion.

This less than perfectly perspicuous rendering, however, can be accounted for as more edifying than more patent ones.

The point of real existentializing is to open the eyes of one's readers to new ways of living and to move them to reshape their lives. The first step toward this goal is moving them to a passionate interest in the question. Climacus uses the verbal identity to emphasize the contextual difference between the truth of human existence and the truth of propositions. People alive to his edificatory purpose would not mistake him here. To ignore this purpose and to proceed as if Climacus were choosing his words for a disinterested academic audience is Murphy's downfall. It is also the misdirection in the accounts of Edwards and Blanshard.[6]

Misled by the literal (immanent) sense of "truth is subjectivity" into assuming that subjective truth is put forward as a REPLACEMENT for objective truth, Blanshard concludes that the search for subjective truth requires "a rejection of logic." And with this conclusion before his eyes he is blind to the genuine meta-position that justifies the edificatory rhetoric. Blanshard's picture could not be more misleading. Climacus gives an account of the necessary and (presumably) sufficient conditions for an individual human being to be true, or "in the truth." One of these conditions is dialectical insight into the impossibility in principle of attaining objective certainty concerning what is believed. Thus the subject who would be "in the truth" rather than being required to reject logic is obligated to reach a dialectically very sophisticated position with respect to his beliefs. "With all the strength of his mind, to the last thought, he must try to understand . . . and then despair of the understanding" [*CUP,* p. 201]. It is the attempt to understand that entitles him to despair, the latter without the former is unjustified, or more accurately, impossible.

Reason, in the Climacean scheme, provides an important service for faith. "The highest principles for all thought can be demonstrated only indirectly (negatively)" [*CUP,* p. 197]. The last three words are an important qualification of "demonstrated" but they by no means nullify it. The role of an indirect demonstration might still be very important indeed, as Climacus points out in the following: "For dialectics is in its truth a benevolent helper, which discovers and assists in finding where the absolute object of faith and worship is. . . . Dialectics[7] itself does not see the absolute, but it leads, as it were, the individual up to it, and says: 'Here it must be, that I guarantee; when you worship here, you worship God'" [*CUP,* p. 438f.]. It accomplishes all this "only indirectly," of course, i.e. it makes clear what the absolute is not. So, for example, it tells one that neither God nor an eternal happiness is such that it can be pointed out, pictured, imagined, described poetically, and so forth. It reveals that true religiousness is not such that any outward show is demanded. It proves that the object of belief is not an object of speculation as well, and that it is not something subject to confirmation or disconfirmation by the results of historical inquiry. Thus the picture Climacus draws of the relationship between faith and reason is this: reason's task is carefully and deeply to ponder the matters of infinite importance to us, and diligently to apply the standard of consistency[8] to our conception of the matter and to the existential expression we have given it. If we adduce a conception and an expression for it which stands unfalsified by the dialectical scrutiny, then we are at a point where it is appropriate to believe our conception to be the right one.

This is not to say that our belief has been rationally justified, because all these dialectical labors take place within the framework of our belief, i.e. our belief constitutes the unargued-for presupposition of the search for consistency. It is passion alone which motivates one initially to embrace a given framework. One might, for example, believe that pleasure is the ultimate goal of human existence and with this belief as datum dialectics might lead him to see that really to hold this one must become a 'solipsist of the present moment.' But if one were motivated by an infinite passion, such a solipsism would not be satisfying, and so one's passion would drive one to leap beyond it, into (say) the comfort of the ethical and its universality. At each stage dialectic, the critical use of our understanding, reveals to us the consistent formulation of an expression for what we believe, but this in no way justifies our adoption of that belief. This is a task, as Anti-Climacus will argue in *Sickness Unto Death,* for the passion itself. For these reasons the Hegelians are damned on two counts: they are dialectically inconsistent and completely lacking in passion; while Zeno is praised for the consistency of his life and doctrine, but ultimately rejected because a way of deeper passion is possible.

Ultimately, this search for the deepest possible passion is justified by appeal to an ethics of virtue, coupled with a definite theory about human nature, something Alasdair MacIntyre does not seem to recognize when he phrases the objection to Climacus in these terms:

> If I hold that truth is subjectivity, what status am I to give to the denial of the proposition that truth is subjectivity? If I produce arguments to refute this denial I appear committed to the view that there are criteria by appeal to which the truth about truth can be vindicated. If I refuse to produce arguments, on the ground that there can be neither argument nor criteria in such a case, then I appear committed to the view that any view embraced with sufficient subjective passion is as warranted as any other in respect of truth, including the view that truth is not subjectivity. This inescapable dilemma is never faced by Kierkegaard and consequently he remains trapped by it.[9]

There is one fact, however, that is true at every stage on life's way and in every possible existential attitude: the person who occupies that stage is an existing individual. And if Climacus, who is at one stage, grasps what it means to be an existing human being in truth (and this is what the definition of truth is intended to describe), then he possesses a notion that is at least implicitly contained in all others. And if he can show that the truth of, e.g. the metaphysical sphere consistently followed contradicts this human truth, then he can show (since the metaphysician is himself human) that eo ipso the metaphysician contradicts himself existentially. Climacus has in this fact of existence an objective (in the sense that it is necessarily and universally applicable) criterion by which the validity of any existential stage may be evaluated. In Aristotelian terms, man's specific ergon, to do well at what is his virtue or specific excellence (and in one sense, his truth), is to maximize his own subjectivity. And Climacus can assert this as objectively true without thereby contradicting himself, and without committing himself to the equipollence of all objective assertions.

Climacus is not satisfied simply to state this imperative to maximize one's subjectivity. He also undertakes the therapeutic task of producing this state in his readers. One of the tools he uses in doing this is compressed and pseudo-paradoxical language like "truth is subjectivity," in which familiar terms are purposely imported into new and unanticipated contexts to reveal new facets of the concepts they refer to. To make his doctrine clear, one might distinguish between truth in the sense of correctness, a sense in which only sentences and propositions are true, and truth in the sense of soundness in which any entity whatsoever may be true. Then the Climacean doctrine might be formulated as "The following is a correct assertion: 'A human being is sound when he or she maximizes his or her own subjectivity.'" But if one wishes to go beyond the mere statement of doctrine, and to proceed to the edification of one's readers, the original formulation might well be preferable. Forgetting that Climacus wants to go beyond mere statement in this way is the source of the mistakes of Murphy and company.

Over-literalization, of course, can take other forms. Many authors, thinking of one or another of the pseudonyms, take Kierkegaard to task for his one-sided and extreme view of Christianity. But to ignore the poetic indirection of the pseudonyms is to miss much of the point of the pseudonymous books and to turn Kierkegaard into a schizophrenic. Humor and irony are other means he uses to protect himself from being given a position of authority, and from being merely informative rather than edifying. I chose to focus on the trick of paradoxical word-choice only because it has led to a particularly pervasive and egregious misunderstanding.

Over-Poeticization

In *Kierkegaard: A Kind of Poet,* Louis Mackey established himself as the over-poeticizer laureate. Emphasizing the edificatory function of the pseudonyms at the expense of the meta-theoretical ideas that inform the edificatory project, Mackey unintentionally volatilizes Kierkegaard. Kierkegaard's books are reduced to rhetorical smoke, the substance of his discourse dispersed. "Kierkegaard's poetic is at once a rhetoric designed to coerce its reader to freedom," and in so doing it "deprives him of any warrant for action except his own freedom." Is there no warrant whatsoever? Then all the argument of the pseudonyms is sham. "The Kierkegaardian corpus can neither be 'believed' nor 'followed': it is and was meant to be—poetically—the impetus, the occasion, and the demand for the reader's own advance to selfhood and to a solitary meeting with the divine."[10] For the most part this is an eloquent statement of the edifying purpose of Kierkegaard's authorship. In the denial of "any warrant" for acting in a certain way, however, it goes too far, making Kierkegaard's position self-undermining in much the same way that Blanshard's over-literal reading does.

For what is Mackey's evidence that so single-minded a focus on inwardness was Kierkegaard's intention? He quotes Johannes Climacus. But why is this to the point? Because Climacus has a meta-theory about subjective truth that shows WHY it cannot be communicated directly, and why the pseudonyms, the humor and irony, the paradoxical language, etc., are necessary. This, however, is to the point only if at least some of what Climacus says can itself be believed to be objectively true. But this is precisely what Mackey denies, hence his over-emphasis of the poetic undermines his own argument for that emphasis. Josiah Thompson is more consistent when he labels even the doctrine of indirect communication part of the pseudonymous charade.[11]

The schizophrenia of Mackey's position is compactly expressed in his statements about Kierkegaard's intentions. He speaks of "the impropriety of presuming to read Kierkegaard's mind" and maintains that "taken as instruments of his intent, his works add up to a magnificent nonsense."[12] But I have already quoted a passage in which Mackey claims to know the purpose for which Kierkegaard's poetic is designed, and of course, telling us what Kierkegaard intended by this profusion of ink is precisely what every commentator, including Mackey, has as his central task. Mackey knows this. The final paragraph of his book makes reference to "Kierkegaard's thought," "the mind of Kierkegaard," and even what it is "to understand Kierkegaard." What he doesn't see is that this is impossible if nothing in the authorship can be taken to be intended as literal truth, or can be mapped onto the literally true.

It might be objected that although Mackey has made a tactical blunder here, the damage can be easily repaired. Frequently, instead of quoting Climacus or another pseudonym to support his views, Mackey quotes *The Point of View, Journals and Papers,* or some other non-pseudonymous work. And were he consistent about this, so the counter runs, he would have a stable meta-position, the "real" Kierkegaard, to argue from. Stephen Evans argues for a view like this. After correctly noting that to say Kierkegaard's views are independent of those of his pseudonyms is not to say that Kierkegaard's views are in every case opposed to those of his pseudonyms, he continues:[13]

> As a matter of fact, it is not hard to show that a good many of the opinions expressed by the pseudonyms were held by Kierkegaard himself. The method whereby this can be done is simply to compare the pseudonymous works with works that Kierkegaard wrote under his own name and with his opinions as expressed in his *Journals and Papers.*

Although I have at one time found this position attractive, I believe it now to be unsafe. The occasion of this change was Henning Fenger's *Kierkegaard: The Myths and Their Origins.* Fenger argues plausibly that Kierkegaard was a poet even in his putatively private writings, that he falsified, poeticized, tidied and 'corrected' historical facts throughout his letters and journals, and that even in these writings Kierkegaard was engaged in a literary production. Where literal truth is our goal, we are no better off looking in the letters and journals, and by extension, the other non-pseudonymous works, than in the pseudonymous ones.[14] To put it the other way round, there is no *a priori* ground for rejecting the meta-theoretical material contained in the pseudonymous works. The remaining problem is to establish a criterion by means of which one can decide when and how to take a given pseudonym seriously.

The Correct Approach

When he is not trying to convince us that Kierkegaard is "only poetry," Mackey is aware that sometimes the pseudonyms must be taken at their word. He admits that "there is some truth to be found in the mouth of each of the pseudonyms." He is even willing to admit that "in a sense the whole truth, as Kierkegaard understood it, is found in each of the works."[15] It is, however, distorted by partiality. Mackey suggests the following methodological principle for those who would sort the chaff of partiality from the kernel of truth: "whatever truth and reality is imagined in the Kierkegaardian corpus must be sought in the internal organization of the several works and in the reciprocal limitation and reinforcement they offer each other."[16] This, I think is sound as far as it goes and it

is the main source of my confidence in my reading of Kierkegaard. I am convinced, for example, that the notion of obedience is central to Kierkegaard's understanding of faith, because pseudonyms as different from one another as De Silentio, Climacus, and Anti-Climacus, characters who are described as being at different stages of intellectual and ethical insight, take up this theme again and again and develop it in similar ways. Moreover, the theme of 'obedience as the heart of religious faith' runs through the *Journals and Papers,* and many of the non-pseudonymous published works such as *On Authority and Revelation, Of The Difference Between a Genuis and an Apostle,* and several of the *Edifying Discourses.* That sources so dissimilar in other ways offer "reciprocal reinforcement" to each other in specifying the relationship between obedience and faith indicates that this relationship is part of the literal, meta-theoretical kernel of Kierkegaard's thought. The focus on obedience shows clearly through the partiality of the various pseudonyms.

If this is correct, then there is an interpretative principle that readers of Kierkegaard can rely on: the more generally a theme is found in Kierkegaard's writings, and the greater the similarity in the conclusions of the various treatments of this theme, the more likely it is that something like the view one can derive from these treatments was actually held by Kierkegaard. This principle gives us a means of justifying the claim that, Mackey and Thompson to the contrary notwithstanding, genuinely substantive conclusions can be drawn from the Kierkegaardian corpus.

A second justification for reading Kierkegaard with philosophical seriousness can be drawn from an application of the reciprocal reinforcement principle to his writings. To the objection that an approach so 'didactic' cannot lay hold of a 'subjective' author, i.e. one who communicates 'indirectly,' it is enlightening to examine the evidence that Kierkegaard and his pseudonyms have left us in the form of their actual practice on this score. This practice is observable in diverse parts of the authorship, it is sufficiently uniform as fairly to be called the same practice, and it is clearly at variance with the volatilizing approach of, for example, Thompson. To cite some of the clearer examples: (1) Kierkegaard frequently interprets the work of the pseudonyms in *Journals and Papers,* and comes to definite conclusions about what they meant. See, for example, *Journals and Papers 11,*[17] in which Kierkegaard sorts out the difference between "the absurd" in *Fear and Trembling* and "the paradox" in *CUP.* His technique implies that this is a close reading by a third party, but it does not suggest that there is nothing clear to be gotten from these books. In fact, it suggests precisely the reverse, it suggests that they will stand up to very close critical scrutiny. (2) Anti-Climacus refers to the work of Johannes Climacus, and not to turn him into poetry, but to cite him as an authority with whom Anti-Climacus is in clear agreement.[18] Moreover, this agreement is with respect to the very doctrine that the poeticizers would use to evaporate the pseudonyms, indirect communication. (3) Climacus [in *CUP,* pp. 225-66] surveys much of the previous pseudonymous literature, and even a book by "Magister Kierkegaard" himself. And he does not suggest that what is written there is something that can have no literal sense for him. In fact, he opens by saying that in *Either/Or* "was realized precisely what I had proposed to myself to do" [CUP, p. 225]. He allows that there is room for interpretation. Nevertheless, the "misused" in the following quotation gives evidence that he thinks it is possible to determine what is right in it.

> Every time I read through such a pseudonymous work, it became clearer to me what I had intended to do. In this manner I became a tragicomically interested witness of the productions of Victor Eremita and the other pseudonyms. Whether my interpretation is the same as that of the authors, I can of course not know with certainty, since I am only a reader; on the other hand, it gives me pleasure to see that the pseudonyms, presumably aware of the relation subsisting between the method of indirect communication and the truth as inwardness, have themselves said nothing, nor misused a preface to assume an official attitude toward the production, as if an author were in a purely legal sense the best interpreter of his own words. . . . [*CUP,* p. 225]

The quotation also contains, I think, a description of the major fault which it is the function of pseudonymity to avoid: the assumption of "an official attitude toward the production," i.e. putting it forward as if one had the authority to proclaim it objectively. If it is correct to see this as the main function of the device of pseudonymity, then probably much too much has been made of this device and the notion of indirect communication by the poeticizing school.

(4) Perhaps the most striking example of the proper way of approaching a "subjective" author is Climacus' reading of Lessing in the second book of *CUP* [pp. 67-114]. Its conclusions are the same: one should be grateful to Lessing because he maintains his distance and does not directly proclaim his insights into the religious. Why is this something to be grateful for? Because it preserves and strengthens the edifying, rather than the merely informative, function of Lessing's writing. We are to be grateful to him because the literal truths to which he has worked his way are framed in such a way that we are forced to think our way to them, and through them, for ourselves. And this is a benefit to us because the truths are about the proper mode of existing as a human being, something we should not only wish to know, but to do. In short, we should be grateful to Lessing for writing as he did for reasons much different from the ones that oblige us to admire Rimbaud.

Of course, if all the texts have a pseudonymous taint (including *Journals and Papers* and the letters), and if it is largely on the "reciprocal reinforcement" of the pseudonyms that one must rely, then it will never be possible to say that one's interpretation is the one correct description of Kierkegaard's intentions. Every interpreter of Kierkegaard will need to keep in mind a caveat similar to the one with which Climacus prefaces his discussion of Lessing in *CUP:*

> Without presuming to appeal to Lessing or daring to cite him definitely as my authority, without pledging anyone because of Lessing's fame dutifully to understand or profess to understand that which brings him into embarrassing connection with my obscurity . . . I now propose to set forth what, in spite of all, I refer to Lessing, although uncertain whether he would acknowledge it.

But one ought not to make too much of this necessary humility.

That all our ascriptions must to some extent be tentative is finally of little consequence. First of all, it is a sufficient ground for invoking Kierkegaard's name that one's account is a possible interpretation of his work, that one has arguments in its favor, and that it explains certain aspects of the texts that are not otherwise well understood. Secondly, and more importantly, the goal of the philosophical reader is enlightenment, and to the project of understanding, for example, the actual structure of religious faith, meticulous scholarly questions about the correct attribution of views to Kierkegaard are irrelevant. The philosophical reader simply need not address them. Evans states the case well when he says:

> Biographers and intellectual historians have a right to examine the pseudonymous literature and use it as best they can to fulfill their goals of understanding Kierkegaard's life and thought. (Though in view of Kierkegaard's warnings they should employ extreme caution in doing so.) But if our purposes are essentially personal and philosophical—if we are interested in the truth of the views presented, in understanding more profoundly some basic existential concepts, and thereby understanding ourselves and our existence more deeply—then it really does not matter very much whether Kierkegaard personally held these views. For from the fact that he held a view nothing follows as to the truth, profundity, or value of the view.[19]

This said, however, it does not follow that Kierkegaard disappears from the scene. If by reading and reflecting on his work we are lead to views both true and profound, then we owe him grateful acknowledgement whether or not we can say with certainty that these are precisely the views he intended us to find there. Such acknowledgement is entirely consistent with the 'doctrines' of indirect communication and the subjectivity of truth.

Notes

1 Louis Mackey, *Kierkegaard: A Kind of Poet* (Philadelphia: University of Pennsylvania Press, 1971), p. 292.

2 A. E. Murphy, "On Kierkegaard's Claim That 'Truth Is Subjectivity,'" in *Reason and the Common Good* (Englewood Cliffs, NJ: Prentice-Hall, 1963), p. 178.

3 Paul Edwards, "Kierkegaard and the 'Truth' of Christianity," *Philosophy 46* (1971):97.

4 Brand Blanshard, "Kierkegaard on Faith," *Personalist 49* (1968):p. 15.

5 *Concluding Unscientific Postscript,* trans. D. Swenson and W. Lowrie (Princeton, NJ: Princeton University Press, 1941), p. 199. Hereafter referred to as CUP.

6 Climacus' procedure of using language in this way is perhaps the same procedure Cavell describes as the "dialectical examination of a concept." See Stanley Cavell, "Kierkegaard's *On Authority and Revelation*" in *Must We Mean What We Say?* (New York: Cambridge University Press, 1976), p. 169f. Such an examination shows, says Cavell, "how the subject of which it is the concept changes, as the context in which it is used changes: the dialectical meaning is the history or confrontation of these differences." The point is the same; the telos of the dialectical procedure is not to be more accurate, but to connect with, and to change, the reader.

7 The relation between Kierkegaardian dialectics and the Kantian procedure for detecting the necessary illusions of reason is an interesting topic for speculation.

8 For a good discussion of Kierkegaard's use of the concept of consistency as a philosophic tool see Gregor Malantschuk, *Kierkegaard's Thought* (Princeton, NJ: Princeton University Press, 1974), chapter II.

9 Alasdair MacIntyre, "Existentialism," in *Sartre,* (ed.) M. Warnock (New York: Doubleday Anchor, 1971), p. 8. See also AFTER VIRTUE (1984). Esp. 39-43.

10 All of the above quotations are from Louis Mackey, *Kierkegaard: A Kind of Poet* (Philadelphia: University of Pennsylvania Press, 1971), p. 294.

11 Josiah Thompson, *Kierkegaard* (New York: Knopf, 1973), p. 185.

12 Mackey, pp. 292 and 290, respectively.

13 C. Stephen Evans, *Kierkegaard's "Fragments" and "Postscripts": The Religious Philosophy of Johannes Climacus* (Atlantic Highlands, NJ: Humanities Press, 1983), p. 8.

14 Henning Fenger, *Kierkegaard: The Myths and Their Origin,* trans. G. C. Schoolfield (New Haven: Yale University Press, 1980).

15 Mackey, p. 261.

16 *Ibid.*

17 The number refers to the entry number in the edition of *Soren Kierkegaard's Journals and Papers* edited and translated by Howard and Edna Hong and published by Indiana University Press in 1967-78.

18 *Training in Christianity,* trans. Walter Lowrie (Princeton, NJ: Princeton University Press, 1975), pp. 132-33.

19 Evans, pp. 8-9.

M. Jamie Ferreira (essay date 1991)

SOURCE: "Surrender and Paradox: Imagination in the Leap," in *Transforming Vision: Imagination and Will in Kierkegaardian Faith,* Oxford at the Clarendon Press, 1991, pp. 85-113.

[*In the following essay, Ferreira explores the relationship between faith and imagination in the writing Kierkegaard produced under the pseudonym Johannes Climacus, arguing that the imagination allows for the suspension of standard ethical judgment, a suspension necessary for one to make the "leap" to faith.*]

'Faith', Climacus tells us, 'has in fact two tasks: to take care in every moment to discover the improbable, the paradox; and then to hold it fast with the passion of inwardness.'[1] Kierkegaard reinforces and extends this understanding when in his journals he connects faith, passion, and possibility: 'Faith is essentially this—to hold fast to possibility'.[2] These descriptions not only point to the active and passionate character of the act of faith; they also imply the importance of imagination to it, for it is imagination which appropriates paradox and which envisions or gives us access to 'possibility'. . . . I want to explore a formulation of the transition to faith in which imaginative activity comes into its own. In particular, I want to explore ways in which imagination can be said to work to give us access to Christian possibility, and to argue that the Climacus account of the transition to faith is best understood on the model of an imaginative *surrender* composed of moments or aspects of imaginative *suspension* and imaginative *engagement*.

The model of surrender suggests itself in the following way. What occurs in a 'leap', as Climacus describes it in the ***Fragments,*** is a 'letting go'.[3] The parallel movement in faith occurs 'when the understanding steps aside' or 'is discharged', and these two claims are treated by Climacus as interchangeable with his claim that in faith the 'understanding surrender[s] itself'.[4] The notion of surrender is particularly suggestive because even at a common-sense level it embodies an inherent tension between active and passive which is similar to that revealed in our earlier consideration (Chapter 1 [of *Transforming Vision*]) of the dual character of 'passion'. The maintenance of such tension . . . requires imagination.

The role of imagination, however, in the 'happy passion' called 'faith' is even more central, I shall argue, for imagination is at work in the surrender not only in holding elements in tension but also in the engagement or involvement normally associated with passion. That is, the transition or transformation or transfiguring move is composed of moments of both suspension and engagement. The suspension and engagement are not separable in practice, but as two aspects of the unitary act of surrender they can be distinguished. . . .I will explore the imaginative suspension at work, including its relation to the imaginative achievement of unity (by way of comparison with a Coleridgean view of imagination) and the kind of suspension involved in imaginative revisioning (as expressed in various accounts of conversion).

Surrender as Imaginative Suspension

In *Christian Ethics and Imagination*, Philip S. Keane writes that 'One of the main functions of moral imagination is to help us suspend our standard moral judgments so that we can entertain and play with new images which might be more appropriate in a changed social context'.[5] In my preceding consideration of the structure of the task of subjectivity in various Kierkegaardian accounts, I emphasized how the need to hold elements in tension which is central to that task necessarily involves imaginative activity; the activity of holding elements in tension is, I suggest, precisely the suspension to which Keane calls our attention. Moreover, I suggest in what follows that the 'stepping aside' or 'letting go' or 'surrender' which, on Climacus's account, is what the understanding is said to do in the moment of faith can be seen as just such suspension. The tension between active and passive, which I will highlight in the transition to faith and which introduces the relevance of imagination, is particularly apparent in the notion of suspension, and I propose that a model of imaginative surrender, constituted in part by imaginative suspension, can usefully illuminate the 'stepping aside' and 'letting go' which constitute the leap of faith.

Captivity and Surrender

Climacus makes clear that the purely active dimension does not do justice to the character of the stepping aside in faith when he writes in the **Fragments** that just as in erotic love, self-love is 'not annihilated but is taken captive' and 'can come to life again', so too in faith the understanding is not annihilated but is taken captive.[6] This description suggests a state of suspension or, alternatively, of holding elements in tension. Although, on the one hand, the notion of being 'taken captive' implies passivity, on the other hand, this non-annihilation is connected later by him with the notion of activity and contrasted with an event which just happens (p. 50). The implication is that the understanding remains active and free—for without its active presence there could be no recognition of paradox, nothing in opposition to the understanding—yet its letting go is an experience of being 'taken captive'.

The relation between active and passive is explicitly recognized by Climacus as a complex one in his discussion of 'offence'. It is, as I noted in Chapter 1 [of *Transforming Vision*], always a case of saying active *yet* passive; they are not separable, although we can 'distinguish' between them. All offence is, he says, 'suffering', being 'wounded', yet we can 'distinguish between suffering offense and active offense'; we can distinguish them, yet suffering offence is always to some extent active and active offence is always to some extent weak or passively wounded (pp. 49-50). The notion of 'offence' is such that it can be spoken of both in terms of being offended and of taking offence (p. 50); the offence 'takes affront, therefore passively, even though so actively that it itself takes affront' (p. 50 n.). Calling attention as he does to this Janus-faced character of offence reveals his recognition that even though aspects of activity and passivity can be 'distinguished', some activities either hold them in tension or maintain them in such a way as to transcend a dichotomy between them. Surrender is, for Climacus, just such an activity—a surrender at the same time implies the passivity of being 'taken captive' (the aspect of being 'taken captive', which is included in 'surrender', suggests what goes on in being 'captivated', and 'captivation' is not something achievable by direct wilful decision) and the active character of something we do (an action rather than an event that just happens to us). In virtue of the captivity involved, surrender is a suspending of what 'can come to life again'. Suspension is, I think, exactly what is pointed to in this description of the tension in a state in which something is neither straightforwardly expressed nor annihilated.

Such surrender (letting go, stepping aside), which cannot be neatly put under either rubric of active or passive, could be seen as the obverse of offence. If 'offence' is the name for the 'unhappy' lack of 'mutual understanding' of the difference between the paradox and the understanding, and the 'happy passion' of faith is the transition achieved in the 'happy', 'mutual understanding', then what is true of offence is true of the converse letting go which constitutes embrace: 'The more deeply the expression of offense is couched in passion (acting or suffering), the more manifest is the extent to which the offense is indebted to the paradox' (p. 51). The letting go is an activity in which the dualism between active and passive is transcended, and both are held in tension; it is *not* to be understood on the model, then, of a one-sidedly active 'will-power' kind of 'leap'.

Suspension of the Understanding

This interpretation of the understanding's stepping aside or letting go in terms of captivity or suspension can be made clearer by reconsidering for a moment the presentation by Climacus of the relation between reason and faith. The paradox provides the occasion for the understanding to step aside, and it provides the condition which allows it do so.[7] In the *Postscript* Climacus elaborates the idea of willing the downfall of the understanding, its stepping aside or letting go, by his constant references to believing 'against the understanding' and the need to 'give up' the understanding or reason or 'break with' the understanding.[8] But what precisely is it for the understanding to do these things? There seem to be two possibilities, corresponding roughly to the claims that faith is against reason or that faith is beyond reason. The understanding can say that: (1) this is against my judgement, and it is in my legitimate domain of judgement, but I will accept it anyway (faith against reason), or (2) in so far as I am judge this is not understandable, but there may be more than I can judge of, so I accept what is not understandable (faith above or beyond reason).

The first option—that faith is *against* reason's legitimate judgement—is the only one which makes it plausible to speak of the 'absurd' in connection with faith,[9] but it seems difficult to call it a case in which the understanding sets itself aside. To claim that a given domain is its legitimate domain is to claim that it is the supreme arbiter in that domain, and that effectively precludes an acceptance of what contradicts its judgement in that domain. To accept what contradicts its judgement in that domain is to deny its supremacy in that domain (i.e., to give up the claim that it is in fact reason's legitimate domain). It is difficult to see what it would mean for the understanding to deny *itself* in what it continues to claim as its legitimate domain.

The second option, on the other hand, is a version of the Jamesian view that it is sometimes reasonable to accept what is not understandable. Indeed Climacus speaks of reason coming to its limits (the unknown). But this option seems to emphasize the reasonableness of affirming the paradox and thus to render vacuous or at least dilute the references to the 'crucifixion of the understanding'. 'Crucifixion' does not, for Climacus, mean 'annihilation'; nevertheless, it is not clear that

the second option does justice to his intentions when he speaks of the 'absurd' or of 'madness'.[10]

This way of phrasing the options assumes, however, that the only alternatives are acceptance or denial by the understanding, and I want to suggest that this does not do justice to Climacus's presentation. The situation he describes in the *Fragments* is rather one in which a tension is maintained: 'the understanding has strong objections to it [the double paradox of the God-Man]; and yet, on the other hand, in its paradoxical passion the understanding does indeed will its own downfall' (p. 47). Climacus likewise writes that one 'must have it [understanding] in order to believe against understanding'.[11] I suggest that the notion of 'suspension' expresses this tension (as well as the idea of captivity) more than either the notion of acceptance or that of denial. The understanding must be at the same time abandoned and maintained— it must be active enough to continue to perceive a paradox and yet not so active as to reject it automatically as an offence to its standards.[12] That is, the understanding must both maintain its traditional associations (or it faces no paradox) and yet will their downfall (or it cannot step aside)—the condition is one of neither acceptance nor annihilation, but one of suspension.

The understanding must remain discriminating enough to face a genuine paradox, 'the' absurd. Kierkegaard writes in his journals that he tried to explain in the *Postscript* that 'not every absurdity is the absurd or the paradox. The activity of reason is to distinguish the paradox negatively—but no more.'[13] To know it negatively, however, requires the active presence in some form of the traditional associations or standards of the understanding. But in order that rejection not be inevitable, in order, that is, that embrace of the paradox be possible, the traditional associations or standards cannot be operative as usual.[14] In other words, only if the understanding is 'supreme' can it face a paradox, and yet if it is 'supreme' it can only reject the paradox. What is called for is not denial (or acceptance), but suspension; suspension seems to provide a way to understand the requisite ability 'to care and not to care', to maintain and not maintain at the same time.

The letting go or holding opposites in tension which I have analysed as suspension occurs in the face of paradox—more specifically, it occurs both in the perception and in the embrace of paradox. It takes imagination to *perceive* a paradox—a statement of two elements which, at least apparently, contradict each other—because it takes imagination to *perceive* elements in tension, to put 'differences together'.[15] But the paradox is not limited to what is propositionally formulatable; rather, the passion is itself paradoxical,[16] a practical rather than theoretical paradox, for embracing the paradox is at the same time a letting go and a maintaining of the standards of the understanding. That too is an exercise of imagination. To perceive a paradox, therefore, is one use of imagination, but to embrace it is another use. That is, the perception of paradox can occur even when the understanding is not set aside (i.e., even when one rejects the paradox), so the setting aside of the understanding which occurs when a paradox is embraced employs the imagination in still another way.

Suspension and Union

What occurs in the letting go of the understanding is therefore a holding of opposites in tension, a maintaining and not maintaining at the same time, a *suspension* of, traditional standards; such a holding of opposites in tension is precisely the work of imagination, and it is precisely when passion is generated. Such holding of opposites in tension, however, is also spoken of by Climacus in terms of *union:* the Paradox, he writes, cannot be an object of knowledge precisely because it 'unites contradictories'[17]—any appropriation of it is then in some sense a unifying activity. In this respect it is like the realization of 'a unity of the infinite and the finite which transcends existence'[18]—both are realizations of unity which can only occur in the moment of passion, and both involve uniting opposites. It is important, then, to see how the role of imagination in holding opposites in tension is to be understood in terms of the union involved: what is the character of such union; how do the opposites relate? One way of becoming clearer about Climacus's understanding of opposites and unity is to compare it with a similar-sounding one proposed a generation before Kierkegaard by a well-known defender of imagination, namely, the romantic poet and critic, Samuel Taylor Coleridge (1772-1834).

Like others in the philosophical tradition before him, Coleridge considered imagination an 'intermediate' or 'mediating' or 'synthetic' faculty. Such mediation or synthesis, moreover, is in the service of the search for unity, for the 'manifold *One*',[19] and addresses itself to 'opposite or discordant qualities'. Consider some of his descriptions in detail.

Imagination, he writes, is the 'idealising Power, of symbols mediating between the Reason and Understanding'.[20] It is the 'reconciling and mediatory power, which incorporating the Reason in Images of the Sense, and organizing (as it were) the flux of the Senses by the permanence and self-circling energies of the Reason, gives birth to a system of symbols, harmonious in themselves, and consubstantial with the truths, of which they are the *conductors*'.[21] That reconciling power is also the 'synthetic and magical power' which 'blends, and (as it were) *fuses* [our faculties], each into each', and

reveals itself in the balance or reconcilement of opposite or discordant qualities: of sameness, with difference; of the general with the concrete; the idea with the image; the individual with the representative; the sense of novelty and freshness with old and familiar objects; a more than usual state of emotion with more than usual order; judgement ever awake and steady self-possession with enthusiasm and feeling profound or vehement; and while it blends and harmonizes the natural and the artificial, still subordinates art to nature. . . .[22]

Coleridge also provides a characterization of imagination with an eye to its philosophical definition when, as a *not* 'unapt emblem of the mind's self-experience in the act of thinking', he suggests the 'pulses of active and passive motion' by which a water insect resists the current and then yields to obtain a fulcrum for further propulsion. He explains: 'There are evidently two powers at work, which relatively to each other are active and passive; and this is not possible without an intermediate faculty, which is at once both active and passive. In philosophical language, we must denominate this intermediate faculty in all its degrees and determinations, the IMAGINATION.'[23] Interestingly, this description of imagination occurs in the conclusion of a consideration of 'what we do when we leap'. I shall return shortly to this intriguing Coleridgean association between imagination and leap.

The 'synthetic' power of imagination, for Coleridge, seeks unity through mediation, fusion, blending, and balance, and does so in a manner 'at once both active and passive'. In such varied descriptions and definitions, however, we find significantly different emphases and implications. In what follows I will explore these, suggesting how Climacus's view of the role of imagination in maintaining tension in unity is illuminated by comparison and contrast with Coleridge's views.

One kind of emphasis in the Coleridge view of imagination is illustrated in the references to it as a faculty which is 'at once both active and passive', and to the role of 'balance' of opposite qualities. This sounds at first hearing like a reference to the role of imagination in maintaining elements in tension which I have described as 'suspension' and found to be an important role for imagination in the Climacus account. These descriptions, then, indicate a way in which imagination is understood to transcend a dichotomy between active and passive and to sustain a genuine tension. At other times, however, a quite different emphasis can be detected in Coleridge's thought—namely, an emphasis on imagination as that faculty which 'fuses' and 'blends'. In fact, Coleridge echoes a Hegelian notion of synthesis when he writes of the reconciliation of opposites as achieved when 'the two component counterpowers actually interpenetrate each other, and generate a higher third including both the former, *"ita tamen ut sit alia et major"*.[24]

That the goal is unity or synthesis in both of these kinds of Coleridgean description is unquestionable— but the implications of the two contrasting ways of understanding the achievement of unity are remarkably different. In so far as Coleridge's thought on the imagination emphasizes the 'balance' of elements in unity, it expresses the role of imagination in maintaining a genuine tension or suspension between 'opposite or discordant qualities', and an activity which is 'at once both active and passive'. On the other hand, in so far as it assumes the second emphasis—on fusion and blending and the generation of a 'higher third'—it belies the descriptions which suggest a genuine 'balance'. An interpenetration to 'generate a higher third', through fusion and blending, suggests a unifying understood as resolution of tension in a higher synthesis—fusion or blending does not reflect a maintained tension, but rather a resolved tension, which on that account ceases to be a tension.

The suggestion that the 'higher third' *includes* the former two components might be thought to be sufficient to maintain their integrity in tension, but that integrity is rendered problematical by an example of synthesis— namely, the compound H2O—which Coleridge uses repeatedly. He contrasts the 'mere juxta-position of Corpuscles' with 'Synthesis', for 'Water is neither Oxygen nor Hydrogen, nor yet is it a commixture of both; but the Synthesis or Indifference of the Two'.[25] Such an example of the sought-after union is clearly at odds with any genuine notion of balance or tension between elements in their integrity.

Climacus's view of the paradox parallels his view of the task of subjectivity, for the task, we saw, consists of 'uniting opposites in existence'. This involves, as much as does Coleridge's philosophy, a prescriptive quest for unity. The locus of disagreement and/or agreement between the Climacus and Coleridge views of the synthetic role of imagination can be brought out more clearly by focusing on Climacus's rejection of Hegelian synthesis and 'mediation' and distinguishing between two meanings of 'both-and' which are part of his account. One of these meanings comes up when Climacus explicitly argues against a Hegelian notion of synthesis and 'the both-and of the principle of mediation'.[26] In general his diatribes against Hegelian 'mediation' and synthesis issue in the counterproposal of an 'either/or'.[27] Yet in the context of the Climacus account it is clear that he nevertheless does actually require a 'both-and' of a certain sort: that is, his account of existence in which discordant elements are 'put together', lived together, exhibits a 'both-and' character. Although it is not a Hegelian kind of 'both-and' (and is certainly incapable of resolution into a higher unity) it is still not a case of

alternatives of 'either/or', for there is no choice required between the contradictory elements that constitute existence: the task is to 'remain' in the 'tremendous contradiction'.[28] We cannot choose one element or the other, we must hold them in tension: *both* finite *and* infinite, *both* positive *and* negative, *both* comic *and* tragic. We must strive to understand, perceive, see, and think 'the greatest oppositions together';[29] the task, for example, is 'to think one [thought] and simultaneously have the opposite in mind, uniting these opposites in existence'.[30] But the meaning of 'uniting these opposites in existence' is that we understand them 'together', as 'both-and'—not in a higher synthesis, but not as an 'either/or'. The alternative to the Hegelian 'both-and' is not here an 'either/or' but rather the 'both-and' which constitutes paradox.

Although they share much in their appreciation of imagination in its role of 'uniting opposites in existence', Climacus's understanding of the unifying function of imagination is thus quite different from that strand in Coleridge which emphasizes fusion and blending and which calls to mind Hegelian synthesis and 'mediation'. The unity of contradictories which I have described in the Paradox as well as in the constitution of 'existence' is clearly not simply two elements side by side, or one contained in the other, but it is just as clearly not the kind of fusion exemplified in the synthesis of the compound water. That fusion is one which precludes the kind of integrity of elements which is necessary for a genuine tension or 'balance'—in so far as they fail to maintain their integrity they cease to be in tension. Such a version of the romantic quest for unity would seem to Kierkegaard just as existentially inadequate as Hegel's strategy of *Aufheben:* on the one hand, Climacus's quest for unity seeks more (for it does not simply reconcile in thought) and, on the other hand, less (for it does not preclude the mutual integrity which allows for genuine tension). One could, then, argue that by emphasizing the maintenance of a genuine tension Climacus's account actually does more justice to Coleridge's insight that imagination, 'at once both active and passive', exhibits and achieves 'balance' than does much of Coleridge's own discussion.[31]

One could, however, equally well turn the matter on its head and argue that Climacus's account of maintaining elements in tension sheds light on the resources within Coleridge's own account to avoid the criticism levelled at Hegelian 'mediation' and thus to bring the two accounts of unity and imagination closer. Climacus's account can do this by encouraging us to look again, long and hard, at Coleridge's thought for an account of 'interpenetration' (fusion or blending) generating a 'higher third' which does not empty of content the suggestions of balance and genuine tension. One possible account is found in the *Biographia Literaria,* chapter 13, in the discussion which precedes the famous definitions of primary and secondary imagination and fancy. This discussion is taken up with an attempt to relate the Kantian insight about 'real' opposites to the *'tertium aliquid'* achieved in the generation of 'an inter-penetration of the counteracting powrs, partaking of both'.[32] His initial example of 'real' opposites is that of the 'motory force of a body in one direction, and an equal force of the same body in an opposite direction', for these are 'not incompatible, and the result, namely, rest, is real and representable'.[33] In the 'process of our own self-consciousness', likewise, 'two inherent indestructible yet counteracting forces' operate in 'one power'.[34] The reference to two equally indestructible forces in one power suggests the polarity exhibited in the phenomenon of magnetism—and this is explicitly affirmed in the concluding Chapter 24, when he speaks of how the 'two poles of the magnet manifest the being and unity of the one power by relative opposites'.[35] Such an appreciation of polarity invokes a notion of genuine tension which dispels the crude notion of fusion and blending sometimes found in Coleridge's account, and allows a *rapprochement* of the existentialist and romantic understandings of imaginative synthesis and tension.

Letting Go, Conversion, and Imaginative Revisioning

The 'letting go' in faith in terms of the suspension involved in embracing opposites (a paradox, 'the absurd') is one expression of the 'leap', but another expression for it is suggested by those journal entries, noted earlier, where Kierkegaard repeatedly refers to 'the leap of inference in induction and analogy', claiming that in such cases 'the conclusion can be reached only by a LEAP' and 'all other conclusions are essentially tautological'.[36] This leap is a letting go in the face of what is not logically or demonstrably compelling, and the surrender in such a case focuses on the generic gap between non-compelling evidence and a conclusion. This way of considering a letting go or a leap also implies imaginative activity, although here it is not a case of the imaginative suspension of *opposites*. Rather, it is a case of the suspension (or holding in tension) involved in imaginative revisioning, and the suspension implied in the imaginative synthesis and extension through which we achieve the unity of a new seeing.

Such imaginative revisioning is another name for what I have already been considering as the shift in perspective which constitutes the transition to faith. The role of imagination in embracing the Paradox—in appropriating a uniting of contradictories, in holding elements in tension—also informs this revisioning because there is a relation between embracing the Paradox and embracing a new way of looking at the world (and self). That relation can be seen as follows. Climacus makes it clear in the *Fragments* that to accept the Paradox is not to accept a set of teachings or propositions: it is to accept a person, the 'Teacher'.[37] There is

a message, nevertheless, which is thereby embraced, for the 'Teacher' exemplifies or embodies a paradoxical message (the message of unlikeness and likeness, of 'absolute difference' and 'absolute equality'[38]) and embracing the 'Teacher' is effectively embracing a new self-understanding and a concomitant new way of looking at the world. The uniting of contradictories in the 'Teacher' is echoed back into the new paradoxical self-understanding—in ways which recall the paradoxical self-understanding achieved in striving for subjectivity. In fact, the deeper subjectivity (subjectivity thrust back into itself in the face of the Paradox) is precisely what sin-consciousness is supposed to consist in, and it is significant that this new self-understanding is termed by Kierkegaard, we saw earlier, 'the leap of sin-consciousness'.[39]

The notion of imaginative revisioning which I am introducing is one of synthetic activity, yet one in which tension is not eliminated—what we see and embrace is a world (and self) in which tension is maintained. The new seeing is not a resolution of the tension, but the affirmation or active recognition of it; the imaginative synthesis which achieves revisioning will involve suspension. It will no more result in a resolution or elimination of tension than did the suspension considered earlier. What is achieved is a kind of unified vision, inclusive of tension.

That new understanding, as we saw with Coleridge, is a form of unity in which we imaginatively, creatively put things together. But we learn something else from Coleridge about this imaginative revisioning, for, as I noted in passing, he speaks of the activity of imagination in the course of considering 'what we do when we leap'. A brief exploration of this suggestive connection between imagination and leap will be a useful preliminary to the examination of autobiographical accounts of conversion. . .

Coleridge and James: Leaps and Volitions

In chapter 7 of his *Biographia Literaria* Coleridge considers 'what we do when we leap' in a non-religious context. He begins by addressing the question of 'voluntary' movement: 'In every voluntary movement we first counteract gravitation, in order to avail ourselves of it. It must exist, that there may be a something to be counteracted, and which, by its re-action, may aid the force that is exerted to resist it.'[40] He then refers to the particular movement of interest to us:

> Let us consider what we do when we leap. We first resist the gravitating power by an act purely voluntary, and then by another act, voluntary in part, we yield to it in order to alight on the spot, which we had previously proposed to ourselves. Now let a man watch his mind . . . while he is trying to recollect a name; and he will find the process completely analogous.

Coleridge's indication that the character of a leap is illuminated by reference to the process of trying to recollect a name suggests that it will be useful to turn for a moment to his own description, elsewhere, of that frustrating activity. We go through the alphabet 'in vain', he writes, then the name all 'at once' starts up, 'perfectly insulated, without any the dimmest antecedent connection, as far as my consciousness extended'; the recollection occurs suddenly, 'by-act-of-will-unaided'.[41] The explanation, Coleridge continues, depends on a 'full sharp distinction of Mind from Consciousness—the Consciousness being the narrow *Neck* of the Bottle':

> The name, Daniel, must have been a living *Atom*-thought in my mind, whose uneasy motions were the craving to recollect it—but the very craving led the mind to a reach where each successive disappointment (= a tiny pain) tended to contract the orifice or *outlet* into Consciousness. Well—it is given up—and all is quiet—the Nerves are asleep, or off their guard—and then the Name pops up, makes its way, and there it is!—not assisted by an association, but the very contrary—by the suspension and *sedation* of all associations.

This activity, remember, he claims is 'analogous' to what occurs in a 'leap'.

In the conclusion of his consideration of 'what we do when we leap' he elaborates the dual aspect of the leap and ties it to imagination. He describes how an animal, in parallel fashion to 'what we do when we leap', 'wins its way up against the stream, by alternate pulses of active and passive motion, now resisting the current, and now yielding to it in order to gather strength and a momentary *fulcrum* for a further propulsion'.[42] This description, he immediately continues, is 'no unapt emblem of the mind's self-experience in the act of thinking', and his explanation of this is striking:

> There are evidently two powers at work, which relatively to each other are active and passive; and this is not possible without an intermediate faculty, which is at once both active and passive. In philosophical language, we must denominate this intermediate faculty in all its degrees and determinations, the IMAGINATION.

We can glean from these passages the following interesting suggestions about 'what we do when we leap'. First, the leap is said to be a single 'voluntary movement' composed of 'an act purely voluntary' and then 'another act, voluntary in part'. The former is later referred to an 'active' power, the latter to a 'passive' power—hence even the expression of the 'passive' power (or yielding) is, at least in part, a 'voluntary' exercise. Second, the combination of 'two powers at work' is exercised through 'an intermediate faculty', 'the IMAGINATION'. 'which is at once both active and passive'. Third, the passive, yielding act (which itself is 'voluntary in part') is paralleled with the frustrating recollection of a name, which recollection is, he says, 'by act-of-will-unaided'. Fourth, that yielding only occurs in virtue of the 'suspension and *sedation* of all associations'. In sum, then, Coleridge views the leap as (1) a 'voluntary movement', of which one act is a 'voluntary in part' yet 'by-act-of-will-unaided' activity. That is, the discrete moment of the 'recollection' is considered to be preceded by straightforwardly voluntary activity, to be itself 'voluntary in part' and yet 'by act-of-will-unaided'. The transition, then, is not simply involuntary, though it is not intentional or 'on purpose'. Moreover, the leap (2) requires the exercise of a faculty—Imagination—'which is at once both active and passive', and (3) is constituted as much by a yielding as by an exercise of active power—a yielding illuminated by reference to the 'suspension and sedation of associations'.

The element of yielding in the leap and the idea of the suspension and sedation of associations are particularly intriguing in that they call to mind some considerations put forth by a thinker very different from Coleridge—namely, the American psychologist and pragmatist philosopher, William James (1842-1910). In particular, they call to mind aspects of James's discussion of 'volition'. The parallel between the two accounts can be instructive. In his *Principles of Psychology* James describes a case—an account of a decision to get out of bed on a cold morning—which seems to him 'to contain in miniature form the data for an entire psychology of volition'.[43] Consider someone saying 'I *must* get up' but not doing it—the 'resolution faints away and postpones itself again and again just as it seemed on the verge of bursting the resistance and passing over into the decisive act' (p. 524). How, then, does one get up? His answer:

> If I may generalize from my own experience, we more often than not get up without any struggle or decision at all. We suddenly find that we *have* got up. A fortunate lapse of consciousness occurs; we forget both the warmth and the cold; we fall into some revery connected with the day's life, in the course of which the idea flashes across us, 'Hollo, I must lie here no longer'—an idea which at that lucky instant awakens no contradictory or paralyzing suggestions, and consequently produces immediately its appropriate motor effects. It was our acute consciousness of both the warmth and the cold during the period of struggle which paralyzed our activity then and kept our idea of rising in the condition of *wish* and not of *will*. (pp. 524-5)

In all of this James is wanting to argue, he explains, against the 'common prejudice that voluntary action without "exertion of will-power" is Hamlet with the prince's part left out' (p. 526). Here he echoes Coleridge's claim that 'voluntary' action may yet be 'by-act-of-will-unaided'.[44]

For James, it is not a question of 'will-power'—rather, we 'find that we *have* got up'. It is not a 'decision', he says, but rather 'a fortunate lapse of consciousness' which accounts for our getting out of bed; what is responsible is not the idea 'I must lie here no longer', but rather (what Coleridge calls) the suspension and sedation of those associations which could provide 'contradictory or paralyzing suggestions'. Admittedly, James's observations are addressed to the question of the 'mechanism of production' of 'voluntary [bodily] movements', which are the 'only *direct* outward effects of our will'; his topic is whether movement requires an 'express fiat' preceding it. But his discussion ultimately includes various types of decision-making in relation to such a 'fiat', because 'our higher thought is full' of the parallel phenomenon of 'blocking and its release' which is found in cases of bodily movement (p. 527). His example, therefore, has wider implications.

Examining 'voluntary action', James writes that an 'express fiat, or act of mental consent to the movement, comes in when the neutralization of the antagonistic and inhibitory idea is required', but is not needed 'when the conditions are simple'—in such cases voluntary action can occur 'with no fiat or express resolve' (p. 526). We are less likely to think that 'exertion of will-power' is required in all cases if we realize that 'consciousness is *in its very nature impulsive*. (Is this perhaps parallel to the impulse to will its own downfall which Climacus sees as the very nature of thought?) Presumably, what is required in such cases is simply a lapse or suspension, not a positive effort of will.

The 'popular notion' that activity 'must result from some superadded "will-force" ' is, he writes, 'a very natural inference from those special cases in which we think of an act for an indefinite length of time without the action taking place'. Such cases, however,

> are not the norm; they are cases of inhibition by antagonistic thoughts. When the blocking is released we feel as if an inward spring were let loose, and this is the additional impulse or *fiat* upon which the act effectively succeeds. We shall study anon the blocking and its release. Our higher thought is full of it. But where there is no blocking, there is naturally no hiatus between the thought-process and the motor discharge. (pp. 526-7)

Even this 'additional impulse or *fiat*' achieved by 're-lease' is not to be understood as 'some superadded "will-force," ' however, for when we examine what James argues we do when 'we are said to *decide*' we can see that the appeal is not to decision as directly constituted by will-power. The category of 'deliberate

action' or 'action after deliberation' is explained by him in terms of cases in which an extremely complex set of 'motives and their conflict', ideas in antagonistic or reinforcing relations, is present to our consciousness—'when finally the original suggestion either prevails and makes the movement take place, or gets definitively quenched by its antagonists, we are said to *decide,* or to *utter our voluntary fiat* in favor of one or the other course' (p. 528). That prevailing or quenching occurs against a background in which, while we realize 'the totality' of the ideas 'more or less dimly all the while, certain parts stand out more or less sharply at one moment in the foreground, and at another moment other parts, in consequence of the oscillations of our attention, and of the "associative" flow of our ideas' (pp. 528-9). What we call 'decision' occurs, that is, 'in consequence of the oscillations of our attention'. It is for this reason that James's elaboration of his initial claim that 'will consists in nothing but a manner of attending to certain objects, or consenting to their stable presence before the mind' (p. 320) later yields the crucial suggestion that '*effort of attention is thus the essential phenomenon of will*' (p. 562). In particular, and all the emphases remain James's, '*The essential achievement of the will, in short, when it is most "voluntary", is to* ATTEND *to a difficult object and hold it fast before the mind*' (p. 561).

Two points need to be made here. First, such 'effort of attention' is not the 'superadded "will-force" ' whose universal relevance James is concerned to argue against. The 'decision' to focus my attention is not the 'decision' whose origin is being sought. The decision (or decisive movement) which occurs in virtue of the oscillations of our attention is not subject to 'will-force' in the way in which the effort of attention preliminary to that decision may be. We cannot will to recognize something in the same way that we can will to focus on what may help us to recognize it.

But second, James's reference to the phenomenon of attention fits in with Coleridge's reference to imagination for the following reason. Imagination is not only the paradigmatic synthesizing ability—it is also required for the 'effort of attention' or focusing to which James points. To focus ourselves, to 'attend', is an activity of imagination because it requires a separating off, a creative and hypothetical restructuring. James's understanding of 'attention' reminds us how indispensable such focusing (or hypothetical restructuring) is, given the constant flux before us; the way in which imagination allows us to 'attend' is parallel, I suggest, to the way imagination, for Coleridge, is the power 'that *fixing* unfixes'.[45]

In order to illustrate the lack of 'will-power' in most fiats, James discusses 'four chief types' of decision or ways of ending deliberation. In what he calls a 'reasonable' type of decision the arguments before us leave 'a clear balance in favour of one alternative, which alternative we then adopt without effort or constraint' (p. 531). In such a case we have 'a perfect sense of being *free,* in that we are devoid of any feeling of coercion' even though 'the reasons which decide us' appear to 'owe nothing to our will'. In cases where no 'paramount or authoritative reason for either course' is apparent, however, 'our feeling is to a certain extent that of letting ourselves drift' in a direction 'accidentally determined' either from without or from within; these determinations constitute the second and third type of decision.

The fourth form of decision is described in ways which seem especially relevant to our concern with conversion, for they are 'changes of heart, awakenings of conscience, etc., which make new men of so many of us' (p. 533). They come, James says,

> when, in consequence of some outer experience or some inexplicable inward change, *we suddenly pass from the easy and careless to the sober and strenuous mood,* or possibly the other way. The whole scale of values of our motives and impulses then undergoes a change like that which a change of the observer's level produces on a view. . . . The character abruptly rises to another 'level', and deliberation comes to an immediate end. (p. 533)

In some cases, then, decision is constituted by something like a 'change of the observer's level' or an abrupt rise 'to another "level"'. These phrases call to mind the phenomenon of a *Gestalt* shift in perspective and James's claim is that deliberation ends in virtue of such a shift.

What distinctively characterizes a fifth type of decision and separates it subjectively or phenomenally from the others is the 'slow dead heave of the will that is felt', the *'feeling of effort'*, 'the sense of *inward effort*' (p. 534). In this case, whether 'reason has balanced the books' or not, James writes:

> We feel, in deciding, as if we ourselves by our own wilful act inclined the beam; in the former case by adding our living effort to the weight of the logical reason which, taken alone, seems powerless to make the act discharge; in the latter by a kind of creative contribution of something instead of a reason which does a reason's work. (p. 534)

What misleads us into thinking such effort usually accompanies decision is 'the fact that *during deliberation* we so often have a feeling of how great an effort it would take to make a decision *now*. Later, after the decision has made itself with ease, we recollect this and erroneously suppose the effort also to have been made then' (p. 535). But in contrast to this 'peculiar sort of mental phenomenon', he concludes, 'the immense majority of human decisions are decisions without effort'.

Now, although James does not, like Coleridge, explicitly refer to imagination in the processes he describes, in so far as his account of decision attempts, as it does, to disabuse us of the notion that a 'superadded "will-force"' is necessary to cause movement or end deliberation, it leaves room for the activity of imagination. It has been argued, as I noted earlier, that the *suspension* of traditional associations is precisely the task of imagination,[46] and the role of 'lapse' and 'release' in James's account suggest the element of suspension involved, an element which is reinforced by his own very Coleridgean reference, in his own discussion of 'conversion', to 'how it is when you try to recollect a forgotten name' (namely, how you need to 'give up the effort entirely').[47] In this respect we can see James's account as implying a role for imagination.[48] Moreover, there is a (Kierkegaardian-sounding) explicit reference to imagination in his discussion of 'self-surrender' conversion (as opposed to 'volitional' conversion), for one of the 'two things in the mind of the candidate for conversion' is the (albeit dim) 'imagination of . . . [a] positive ideal we can aim at'; in this 'ripening' process of 'rearrangement' it is not the 'exercise of personal will' at work, but rather an 'act of yielding', and 'it is more probably the better self *in posse* which directs the operation'.[49] James also, as we have seen above, provides some specification of this locus of imaginative activity when, qualifying a crude notion of the effort of will involved in decisions, he highlights the importance: (a) of a shift in perspective, (b) of 'finding' ourselves in the situation of having *already* made the decisive transition, and (c) of the phenomenon of 'attention'.

Independently of the question of the adequacy of these accounts by Coleridge and James of leap and volition, both accounts are suggestive and provide what, I think, can be a fruitful vantage-point for assessing accounts of religious conversion. At the very least, their emphasis on notions of yielding, suspension, sedation, and of action which is active and passive at the same time, counteracts a one-sidedly active account of leaping or volition. Second, they suggest (Coleridge directly and James indirectly) an important role for imagination in their enriched notion of the activity of leaping or volition.

Faith, Unfaith, and Transforming Vision

I turn now to some accounts of conversion, or paradigmatic 'leaps' of faith, to see what these accounts might look like, both from the vantage-point of the suggestions by Coleridge and James as well as from the perspective of one sensitized by Kierkegaard. . .to the phenomenon of paradoxical change, transparency, and transforming transitions. I suggest that we will discover in them, even in those specifically addressed to Christian faith, warrant for reading the leap or decision in terms of an imaginative revisioning.

Consider the following self-description given by someone who, after serious inquiry into Christianity, judged herself to have 'done it', to have made a 'leap' of faith. She wrote:

> Today, crossing from one side of the room to the other, I lumped together all I am, all I fear, hate, love, hope, and well, DID it. I committed all my ways to God in Christ.[50]

It is easy to see why the idiom of will or decision sounds appropriate—namely, to emphasize the active, free, and qualitative character of the transition. In light of the preceding, however, we can now ask how this account relates to those given by Coleridge and James: in what way might this be seen as an activity exercised through imagination; does this activity exhibit a 'yielding' dimension; is it voluntary yet without exertion of 'will-power'; does anything in the account correspond to 'attention' and to the 'suspension and sedation of association'?

The following interpretation of this account of conversion along those lines suggests itself: namely, that the lumping together of hopes and fears and loves and hates is an imaginative activity—an imaginative gathering, a synthesis and extension by imagination—which effects a reorienting shift of perspective. What the agent *did,* that is, could be understood as an imaginative gathering together of her self in which a decisive reorientation is accomplished. What she *did* was to experience a change in her 'observer's level', to see something new come into focus. The act of committing herself could be understood, not as a decision which followed upon the lumping together of her hopes and fears and loves, but rather as an active recognition or affirmation of the attraction and alignment which she saw in her newly gathered self.

In Coleridge's terms, what she did was an imaginative gathering, an active and free lumping things together in a new way which came after disciplined, desiring inquiry (propulsion)—lumping them together in such as way as to *see* it differently (yielding) and be changed by it.[51] In both Coleridge's and James's terms, what she did just *was* a letting go of hitherto accepted associations—a shift in perspective, an abrupt rise to another level of observation, a transition which is not achievable by fiat, but rather by imaginative synthesis and extension. The synthesis and extension which constitute a revisioning of life are activities of imagination and can be read, not as prolegomena to a change, but as constituting the change which alters her whole life. In other words, the description of her 'leap' could be explained as the achievement of a new imaginative revisioning: it is a recognition of what is implied in the perception of the self as gathered together in this way, a reorienting shift in perspective.

On such a reading the coming to faith is the surrender of an old vision in the activity of seeing a new way in which things can be together. Such a seeing things together in a new way is an imaginative suspension because it assumes an imaginative positing of counterfactuals and hypotheticals—for example, it involves assuming a hypothetical place (or many such places) from which to assess what stands before us. It is not a simple cumulative endeavour, putting together a mosaic of things already there, the whole of which is equal to the sum of its parts. Neither, however, is it the resolution into a higher unity, the fusion, or reduction of multitude into unity, which, as we noted earlier, is sometimes suggested by Coleridge's examples of imaginative synthesis. The reorganization which takes place is a re-creation, a creative perception, which brings to mind Coleridge's other remarks on this 'shaping spirit'.[52] For example, while it is not a synthesis into a higher unity, it is a re-creation, a 'shaping', which assumes the kind of suspension alluded to in Coleridge's description of 'secondary Imagination' as a power which actively 'dissolves, diffuses, dissipates, in order to re-create'.[53] This description re-emphasizes the role of imagination in suspending associations—sedating associations and yielding—which we saw earlier in his description of imagination as the intermediate faculty which is 'at once both active and passive'.

The letting go or surrender assumes an imaginative suspension because it is a paradoxical seeing of what is both not yet there and already there, for sometimes it is only by putting-together imaginatively what could be there that we are able to recognize what is in some sense already there. The synthesis it achieves is not the discovering of a unity which underlies all, or a reduction of multitude into unity, or a resolution of tension in a 'higher third'—but rather a putting-together-imaginatively. Moreover, such a shift in perspective arising from imaginative activity—a seeing things together differently—would be a free, qualitative transition or leap as much as any deliberate, self-conscious decision would.

The plausibility of this kind of interpretation of a description of a 'leap of faith' is supported by other autobiographical accounts of conversion. Writing movingly of his decision to leave the Anglican Church for that of Rome, one author tells how, having been 'on the brink' for a year and a half, he responds to a friend's question by a realization:

> Then it came to me that perhaps I could go on drifting, but, if I faced up to decision, I could not *reject* Holy Mother Church—just as, long years before, I had realized that I could not reject Jesus. . . . if I *cannot* reject the Church—if only one way is possible—I *have* decided, haven't I?[54]

The suggestion is that the moment of choice is, as James suggested, really one of coming to see that we have already decided—that is, we *realize* that we have already become engaged with a possibility in a reorienting, hence 'decisive', way. What one calls the 'decision' is the *realization* of our decisive engagement with a possibility, the realization of how real it is for us. That we can stifle or undermine its impact on us, its power to engage us, does not show that we can or must deliberately decide to feel that power.

A similar appeal to the non-volitionalist dimension of such change is found in the various accounts of conversion experiences recorded by a very well-known convert, C. S. Lewis. In his autobiography, *Surprised by Joy,* Lewis describes a succession of 'conversions' of differing kinds. His description of one early transition is clearly in terms of a shift in perspective, a new seeing of old-yet-new: he writes that what was now seen was in some sense exactly like the old, yet 'all was changed'.[55] Moreover, his was a sense that something was 'out of reach not because of something I could not do but because of something I could not stop doing'—more precisely, 'If I could only leave off, let go, unmake myself, it would be there'.[56] Such an affirmation of the role of letting go or yielding informs his conclusion that 'all this was given to me without asking, even without consent'.[57]

Although Lewis's account of his later and distinctively religious conversion is framed in the idiom of 'choice', his actual explication of the character of the choice reinforces the sense of it as a realization or new seeing or a shift in perspective. For example, when he writes that 'I felt myself being, there and then, given a free choice', he qualifies this significantly—'I say, "I chose", yet it did not really seem possible to do the opposite'.[58] He continues to explain: 'People talk about "man's search for God". To me, as I then was, they might as well have talked about the mouse's search for the cat.'[59] Even more dramatically, he suggests that 'it was more like when a man, after long sleep, still lying motionless in bed, becomes aware that he is now awake.'[60]

Lewis's own retrospective look, in a later interview, at his earlier descriptions also repeatedly qualifies the ordinary sense of 'decision'. To the interviewer's question, 'Do you feel that you made a decision at the time of your conversion?' Lewis responds

> I would not put it that way. What I wrote in *Surprised by Joy* was that 'before God closed in on me, I was in fact offered what now appears a moment of wholly free choice'. But I feel my decision was not so important. I was the object rather than the subject in this affair. I was decided upon.[61]

The interviewer's rejoinder—'That sounds to me as if you came to a very definite point of decision'—is met by Lewis's explanation:

> Well, I would say that the most deeply compelled action is also the freest action. By that I mean, no part of you is outside the action. It is a paradox. I expressed it in *Surprised by Joy* by saying that I chose, yet it really did not seem possible to do the opposite.[62]

Lewis obviously wants to preclude an understanding of the conversion as a purely passive happening, and his reference to the exercise of an activity which is at the same time compelled yet free, hence passive yet active, recalls Coleridge's view of imagination. What occurs in 'the choice' is imaginative because it is an admittedly paradoxical holding together of opposites. 'The choice' is, in sum, an abrupt shift in the 'observer's level', in and through a yielding which is voluntary and free, yet without a 'superadded "will-force." '

The conviction, expressed in the second account of conversion noted earlier, that 'only one way is possible' is surely not meant to deny the undeniable—namely, that other ways are in some sense also possible, for they are actually exemplified in the lives of others we know; it is not an expression of a compulsion which renders us unfree, but rather an expression of the way in which one possibility has decisively become 'real' for us. We cannot immediately effect that engagement by a decision by fiat. Flannery O'Connor makes the same point indirectly when she writes to a correspondent: 'I hope you'll find the experience you need to make the leap toward Christianity seem the only one to you'.[63] But a leap which 'seem[s] the only one' is surely an imaginative crystallization, a decisive engagement, rather than a selection among perceived alternatives; its seeming to be 'the only one' is thus not a denial of the possibility of other ways or of our freedom, but rather an indication of the constraint compatible with a free recognition. This, I take it, is what C. S. Lewis meant when he wrote that 'I say, "I chose" ', yet it did not really seem possible to do the opposite', and commenting on that, explained that 'the most deeply compelled action is also the freest action'.[64] It is also what I take Judge William to mean when he writes that if, driven by the recognition of the contradiction in the aesthetic, we 'contemplate existence under ethical categories', we 'will see that *only* then does existence become beautiful, that *only* in this way can a man succeed in saving his soul and gaining the whole world . . . '.[65]

The model of *Gestalt* shift is relevant here because in such a case the shift in perspective occurs only when a 'critical threshold' has been reached. Initially we perceive only one option, only one is 'real' to us. Although we can be told of and admit the possibility of another option, at the critical moment of transition there is no set of equally real alternatives which we recognize from among which to choose—the moment of transition is rather the point at which what has been an abstract possibility (one we have been assured is there) suddenly comes into focus for us, the point at which it is so real that it seems to be the only way to see it (though, of course, we can try to revive the earlier picture by an effort of refocusing). The examples I have considered suggest that this point or 'critical threshold' is what in the description of faith is often called 'the decision'.

Such a shift in perspective is, I suggest, what Iris Murdoch (attempting in ethics to replace a model of will by a model of vision) describes as a 'piecemeal' effort working up to moments where 'most of the business of choosing is already over', rather than a leap of will at a crucial moment.[66] Stanley Hauerwas, following Murdoch in affirming 'the significance of vision for the moral life', suggests that the free activity integral to moral development is neither a 'sudden leap the isolated will makes' nor an 'efficacious' assertion of will.[67] He explains his alternative in terms of a 'disciplined overcoming of the self that allows for the clarification of our vision'—he emphasizes not an act of will, but 'attention' and 'reorientation' of vision.[68] Appropriating the theme of 'attention', Hauerwas notes Murdoch's direct indebtedness to Simone Weil's thought on 'attention', but, as we noted earlier, William James too saw *'effort of attention'* as *'the essential phenomenon of will'.*[69]

Murdoch's suggestion of a 'piecemeal' effort is not contrary to the qualitative *Gestalt* shift I have been using as an analogy—this shift in perspective occurs only when a 'critical threshold' has been reached, but it cannot occur unless preliminary material is registered or processed. In this sense the shift is able to be spoken of as both continuous and discontinuous. The decision which seems necessary turns out to be the recognition or realization that we have already decided. On the one hand, it is the result of a 'piecemeal' effort without being the cumulative issue of a quantitative process and, on the other hand, the qualitatively different character of the realization is achieved without being the direct result of a momentary act of will.

A variety of ordinary intentional decisions may be necessary to the final realization of faith (disciplined inquiry may need to be deliberately undertaken, deliberate decisions may be necessary to put oneself in a place conducive to the shift in perspective, to focus on this rather than that), but the shift itself is an activity of imaginative revisioning. It is not a case of seeing before you leap, or leaping before you see—the new seeing *is* the leap in understanding. On such a reading the new seeing would constitute the letting go of an old seeing. I repeat, some deliberate decisions may be a necessary preliminary to the new seeing, or seem appropriate as a response to the new seeing, but it is the new seeing itself which is effectively the leap or qualitative transition. In sum, such a qualitative shift

in perspective is an example of a qualitative transition which is distinguishable from a quantitative process as well as from a momentary, separable, act of will which fills a gap. In particular, the category of a 'critical threshold' seems especially suited to illuminate this kind of transition (which is not reached by degrees, yet cannot occur unless preliminary material is registered and processed) and to show why one wants to say of it both that it is continuous and discontinuous.[70]

An understanding of willing in these terms is consonant with and reinforced by the non-deliberate character of the leap found in accounts of a converse 'leap of unfaith'. One of the most famous is Tolstoy's description of a man's loss of faith. It was *not,* he insists,

> because he had resolved something in his heart, but simply because this comment of his brother ['Do you still do that?' in response to his kneeling to pray] was like a finger being pushed against a wall that was on the verge of collapsing from its own weight. *These words indicated that the place where he had thought faith to be had long been empty* and that the words he spoke, the signs of the cross and genuflections he made in prayer, were essentially meaningless actions. *Having recognized their meaninglessness he could no longer continue doing them.*[71]

Similarly, in a contemporary autobiography the author not only tells us how, after reading some Catholic literature, he first 'saw the world in a new way, saw explanations where there had been frustrating mysteries and alluring mysteries where there had been unsatisfying explanations'[72] (and these, unfortunately, one cannot simply choose to do), but also details the non-volitional process of the decay of that faith. Working with metaphors of faith's slipping away and dissolving, he writes of the process in which his earlier stance 'started to seem irrelevant':

> Particular beliefs became obscure, grew faint and at last vanished; urgencies melted and crumbled; attachments loosened and became undone. The world I had been inhabiting shifted and rearranged itself along a new axis.[73]

We cannot deliberately choose to make something seem irrelevant, or to make an urgency melt. Such accounts suggest, then, that in either direction, coming to or turning from faith, the qualitative transition is a new, active, and free *seeing* rather than the direct achievement of an intentional, self-conscious decision.

These accounts of conversion and these contemporary suggestions reinterpreting decision in terms of attention and reorientation illustrate the reading I have been developing of the transition to faith in the Climacus account. The discussion in Chapter 3 [of *Transforming Vision*] of choice and transparency as paradoxical transition assumed that his presentation of the qualitative difference or leap to the ethical or subjectivity can bear illuminatingly on the character of the other qualitative transitions of which he speaks, including the transition to Christian faith. The warrant there for reading his radical emphasis on choice in terms of imaginative vision is at the same time prima-facie warrant for reading his notion of the transition to faith in the same way. As I noted earlier, Climacus himself speaks of a transition to the religious in terms of both 'attention' and vision: 'only in the inwardness of self-activity, does he have his attention aroused, and is enabled to see God'.[74] Moreover, this applies to religiousness B, for the emphasis on seeing is found as well in the **Fragments**'s description of the thought experiment of Christianity and its 'condition': 'if the learner could envision the god by himself, then he himself would possess the condition', and 'the god gave the follower the condition to see it and opened for him the eyes of faith', for 'without the condition he would have seen nothing'.[75] On such a reading the surrender in faith is the surrender of an old vision in the activity of seeing a new way in which things can be together; the qualitative transition would likewise be a clarification of our vision through the disciplined effort of 'attention', a qualitative shift in perspective arising from imaginative activity.

I have tried to show how the correlative attribution of 'passion' to the concept of faith highlights the role of imagination in the 'decision' and coincides with independent suggestions about the necessity of imagination for subjectivity; it also reminds us that the 'leap' need not be seen as a deliberate decision in order to guarantee its character as a free and qualitative transition. Kierkegaard's concept of a 'leap' or 'decision' can be understood in terms of at least two expressions of imaginative activity: it is both (1) a letting go in the sense of captivity or suspension of the understanding through imaginatively holding opposites in tension, and (2) a shift in perspective through the imaginative synthesis and extension (presupposing suspension) which constitutes the imaginative revisioning. A letting go can be a surrender embodying a tension between active and passive; it can be a 'recognition' that something is the case, a qualitative shift in perspective effected through an imaginative suspension in which opposites are held in tension or an imaginative suspension in which a synthesis and extension issues in a revisioning of the self and world.

Notes

[1] *Postscript,* 209.

[2] *Journals,* ii. IX A 311, n.d. [1848], 13; he puts it more strongly: it is 'the fight of *faith,* which fights madly (if one would so express it) for possibility' (*Sickness unto Death,* 171-2).

[3] *Fragments,* 43.

[4] Ibid. 59, 64, 54.

[5] *Christian Ethics and Imagination* (New York, 1984), 118. In a discussion of the role of imagination in the Ignatian spiritual exercises, Antonio T. De Nicolas likewise suggests that the exercise of imagining will 'desensitize subjects to their original unities and attachments while sensitizing them to fresh and new sensations' (*Powers of Imagining: Ignatius of Loyola* (Albany, NY, 1986), 43).

[6] *Fragments,* 48. Further parenthetical page references will be to the *Fragments* as introduced in the text.

[7] Refer to my discussion of the sufficiency of 'the condition' in relation to faith, in 'Kierkegaardian Faith: "the Condition" and the Response', in the *International Journal for Philosophy of Religion,* 28 (Oct. 1990), 63-70.

[8] *Postscript,* 208-9, 384, 502-5; 159, 337, 502; 505.

[9] John Wisdom, for example, suggests that the 'absurd' (as opposed to 'nonsense') cannot be beyond the scope of reason. He writes that a statement is absurd if it is 'against all reason'; a statement may have meaning and yet be 'absurd and *against* all reason and therefore *not* beyond the scope of reason' ('The Logic of God' (1950) in *Paradox and Discovery* (Berkeley, CA, 1970), 20).

[10] *Postscript,* 159, 381.

[11] Ibid. 503. C. Stephen Evans is especially sensitive to this, noting that submergence is not the same as suicide of the understanding, but the character of such submergence is left unexplained (*Subjectivity and Religious Belief,* 120).

[12] In *Sickness Unto Death* Kierkegaard distinguishes three kinds of offence: indifference, negative/passive, negative/active (pp. 260-2).

[13] *Journals,* i. X² A 354, n.d. [1850], 4. Similarly, he writes: 'The absurd is not the absurd or absurdities without any distinction. . . . The absurd is a category, and the most developed thought is required to define the Christian absurd accurately and with conceptual correctness.' (i. X⁶ B 79, n.d. [1850], 7.)

[14] I use the word 'embrace' deliberately since if the understanding is set aside it cannot strictly speaking be said that we either affirm or deny the paradox. The embrace or 'mutual understanding' may be simply a stand-off—not denying or rejecting a proposition but acting as if the proposition expressing the paradox were true (although one still needs to ask what it is to act according to a contradiction).

[15] *Postscript,* 449; see 473 where he refers to the 'requirement of existence: to *put things together*'.

[16] *Fragments,* 44, 47.

[17] *Fragments,* 61.

[18] *Postscript,* 176.

[19] October 1805, # 2705, *The Notebooks of Samuel Taylor Coleridge* (1804-1808), ii, ed. Kathleen Coburn (Princeton, NJ, 1961). See James S. Cutsinger's useful and detailed discussion of Coleridge's complex notion of 'unity' or varied senses of 'one' (*The Form of Transformed Vision: Coleridge and the Knowledge of God* (Macon, GA, 1987), esp. Part II.

[20] *Coleridge's Miscellaneous Criticism,* ed. Thomas Middleton Raysor (Cambridge, Mass., 1936, reprint edn., Folcroft, Pa., 1969), 286.

[21] *Statesman's Manual* (1816), in *Lay Sermons, The Collected Works of Samuel Taylor Coleridge,* vi, ed. R. J. White (Princeton, NJ, 1972), 29.

[22] *Biographia Literaria,* Everyman's Library (London, 1906), 151-2. Reference to Imagination as 'the fusing power' is made in #4066, April 1811, in *The Notebooks,* iii.

[23] *Biographia Literaria,* ch. 7, 60.

[24] MS note printed by A. D. Snyder, 'Coleridge's "Theory of Life" ', *Modern Language Notes,* 47 (1932), 301, cited in James V. Baker, *The Sacred River: Coleridge's Theory of Imagination* (Baton Rouge, La., 1957), 200.

[25] Essay 13, *The Friend, The Collected Works of Samuel Taylor Coleridge,* i, ed. Barbara E. Rooke (London, 1969), 94 n. Basil Willey illustrates the contrast between Coleridgean 'Fancy' and 'Imagination' with examples which make my point: 'mechanical mixtures (as of salt with iron filings)' as opposed to 'chemical compounds (say, of sodium and chlorine)' (*Nineteenth Century Studies: Coleridge to Matthew Arnold* (New York, 1949), 16).

[26] *Postscript,* 358-9.

[27] Ibid. 270-1; the either/or of subjectivity/objectivity, 23, and the either/or expressed in both volumes of *Either/Or.*

[28] *Postscript,* 313.

[29] Ibid. 316.

[30] Ibid. 317.

[31] Baker in the *Sacred River* argues that 'Coleridge's whole theory of imagination, then, rests on a sharp distinction between active and passive powers' which Coleridge sometimes confusingly expresses by the contrast between 'imagination' and 'fancy' (pp. 128-9). Baker's own discussion is confusing, however, because he goes on to claim that Coleridge expresses a 'supreme insight into the alliance of active and passive in the creative act' (p. 228) and an appreciation of the 'collaboration' and 'coalition' of both powers (pp. 179, 191), but nevertheless concludes that Coleridge was right 'to sharply oppose' active and passive powers (p. 248); moreover, quoting on p. 135 the passage from the *Biographia Literaria* he leaves out (without providing ellipses!) the very sentence in which Coleridge claims that imagination is 'at once both active and passive'.

[32] Coleridge, *Biographia Literaria,* 143.

[33] Ibid. 142.

[34] Ibid.

[35] Ibid. 297. John Coulson's discussion of Coleridge focuses exclusively on this strand of his thought on unity and tension, ignoring those elements less congenial to his thesis about polarity (*Religion and Imagination: 'in aid of a grammar of assent',* 135; also 113-14, 132).

[36] *Journals,* iii. V C 7, n.d. [1844]; V A 74, n.d. [1844], 19 and 16.

[37] *Fragments,* 62.

[38] Ibid. 47.

[39] *Journals,* iii. V C 7, n.d. [1844], 19.

[40] *Biographia Literaria,* 60.

[41] *Inquiring Spirit: A Coleridge Reader,* ed. Kathleen Coburn (Minerva Press, 1951), 30-1. My attention was called to this passage by James S. Cutsinger's study, *The Form of Transformed Vision: Coleridge and the Knowledge of God,* 23.

[42] *Biographia Literaria,* 60.

[43] ii. 525. Further parenthetical references in this section will be to this work unless otherwise noted.

[44] Gilbert Ryle likewise distinguishes between 'voluntary' and 'intentional' in *The Concept of Mind,* 70 ff.

[45] April 1811, #4066, emphasis mine, *The Notebooks of Samuel Taylor Coleridge* (1808-1819), iii, ed. Kathleen Coburn (Princeton, 1973).

[46] See n. 5 above.

[47] *The Varieties of Religious Experience* (New York, 1982), 205.

[48] Rollo May argues that, although James succeeds in showing the bankruptcy of the Victorian notion of 'will-power', he nevertheless fails to do justice to the category of willing because he ignores the element of 'imaginative participation' which constitutes the positive movement which is effective within the context of a suspension of contradictory associations (*Love and Will*, 220). I suggest that James leaves room for that 'imaginative participation'.

[49] *The Varieties of Religious Experience*, 209-10.

[50] Jean Davis Vanauken, as cited by Sheldon Vanauken in *A Severe Mercy* (San Francisco, 1977), pp. 95-6.

[51] Note that the model of vision invoked here need not imply the passive and confrontational ocular model of knowing which contemporary philosophers (Richard Rorty and others) criticize; reference to 'vision' need not, as Iris Murdoch notes, imply reference to (rightly discredited) 'inner or private psychological phenomena, open to inspection' ('Vision and Choice in Morality', in *Christian Ethics and Contemporary Philosophy*, ed. Ian T. Ramsey (New York, 1966), 200).

[52] *Biographia Literaria*, ch. 10, 76 (esemplastic: 'shape into one'); 'Dejection: An Ode' (1802): 'My shaping spirit of Imagination'.

[53] *Biographia Literaria*, ch. 13, 146.

[54] Sheldon Vanauken, *Under the Mercy* (Nashville, Tenn., 1985), 238.

[55] *Surprised by Joy* (London, 1955), 145.

[56] Ibid.

[57] Ibid. 146.

[58] Ibid. 179.

[59] Ibid. 182. Note the striking similarity of this thought to Simone Weil's suggestion that 'We do not have to search for him, we only have to change the direction in which we are looking. It is for him to search for us' (*Waiting for God*, 216).

[60] Ibid. 189.

[61] Interview 7 May, 1963, in *The Grand Miracle and Other Essays*, ed. Walter Hooper (New York, 1970), 154.

[62] Ibid.

[63] Flannery O'Connor, 25 July 1962, in *The Habit of Being*, letters ed. Sally Fitzgerald (New York, 1979), 485.

[64] *Surprised by Joy*, 179; *The Grand Miracle*, 154.

[65] *Either/Or*, ii. 182, emphasis mine.

[66] 'The Idea of Perfection' (1964), in *The Sovereignty of Good* (New York, 1971), 37.

[67] 'The Significance of Vision: Towards an Aesthetic Ethic', in *Vision and Virtue: Essays in Christian Theological Reflection* (Notre Dame, Ind., 1974), 36, 41.

[68] Ibid. 42.

[69] *Principles of Psychology*, ii. 562. Simone Weil's treatment of the relevant 'act of attention' is often in terms of 'looking' or changing 'the direction in which we are looking'; 'religion', she concludes, 'is nothing else but a looking' and 'looking is what saves us' (*Waiting for God*, 193, 212, 216, 199, 192).

[70] I take my position to be an elaboration which is consonant with the suggestion of both continuity and discontinuity in faith put forth by John W. Elrod in *Being and Existence in Kierkegaard's Pseudonymous Works* (Princeton, NJ, 1975), esp. 232-4. I suggest that it is also compatible with the position espoused by C. Stephen Evans in *Subjectivity and Religious Belief*, especially the conclusions on 116, 120, 123.

[71] 'A Confession' (1879), from *A Confession and Other Religious Writings*, trans. Jane Kentish (New York, 1987), 20-1, emphasis mine.

[72] Richard Gilman, *Faith, Sex, Mystery: A Memoir* (New York, 1986), 56.

[73] Gilman, *Faith, Sex, Mystery*, 228, 227.

[74] *Postscript*, 218.

[75] *Fragments*, 63, 65.

C. Stephen Evans (essay date 1992)

SOURCE: "On Reading Kierkegaard and Johannes Climacus," in *Passionate Reason: Making Sense of Kierkegaard's Philosophical Fragments*, Indiana University Press, 1992, pp. 1-12.

[*In the following excerpt, Evans uses Kierkegaard's Philosophical Fragments, written under the Johannes Climacus pseudonym, to demonstrate that of the three basic approaches to Kierkegaard's writings (a straight, philosophical approach; a literary approach; and a literary-philosophical approach), the literary-philosophical approach provides the best means for making sense of Kierkegaard's indirect discourse.*]

Philosophical Fragments is generally agreed to be one of Kierkegaard's most significant works. There is, however, no general agreement about the nature of the book's significance. It is a short book, only a little over a hundred pages in length, attributed to a pseudonym, one Johannes Climacus. It is in one sense a simple book. Though Climacus himself says that it is not a book which every divinity school student could write,[1] this is, I think, due more to a lack of "dialectical fearlessness" on the part of the seminarian than to a lack of knowledge on the part of the student, since the content of the book is for the most part "nothing but old-fashioned orthodoxy with a suitable degree of severity."[2] But in a deeper sense it is a book which is far from easy to understand, one full of irony and satire, with a literary form whose relation to the content is deeply puzzling.

As if the book itself did not present enough difficulties, it is impossible to decide how the book should be approached without seeing it in the larger context of Kierkegaard's authorship. One must decide whether Kierkegaard's authorship does have, as he claimed, a unifying purpose, and if so, what that purpose is. The nature and purpose of the pseudonyms must be decided, as well as the relation between the pseudonymous section of the authorship and that which Kierkegaard published under his own name. Having done that, one must then decide the specific character and purposes of the Johannes Climacus pseudonym and its role in Kierkegaard's overall literature.

I have no illusions that I can answer these questions to the satisfaction of all Kierkegaard interpreters. Nevertheless, I owe my readers some account of the assumptions with which I shall approach the work, and the thinking which lies behind those assumptions. The richness of Kierkegaard's authorship makes the quest for anything like a final, definitive interpretation a hopeless one, and there are approaches to Kierkegaard's literature which differ radically from my own, and yet have shown themselves to be interesting and fruitful. I claim only that my approach is one that is faithful to the text and that it provides an illuminating way of approaching a host of significant problems.

Three Types of Kierkegaard Literature

I find it useful to divide recent literature on Kierkegaard into three broad types. First, there are books which more or less ignore the pseudonyms and read Kierkegaard as a straight philosopher, drawing on Kierkegaard's literature as a whole.[3] I would place in this group philosophers such as Stephen Dunning, Louis Pojman, John Elrod, and the early writings of Mark C. Taylor. Though obviously the philosophical approaches of these authors differ greatly, ranging from the analytic perspective of Pojman to the structuralist, dialectical reading of Dunning, they have in common an approach which emphasizes Kierkegaard as a philosopher and makes the particular character of the pseudonyms unimportant. We might call this the philosophical approach.

The second way of reading Kierkegaard could be called the literary approach, since to some degree it stems from Louis Mackey's important book, *Kierkegaard: A Kind of Poet.*[4] However, the term "literary approach" is not completely satisfactory, since I have in mind here the later writings of Mark C. Taylor and others associated with the series *Kierkegaard and Postmodernism,* of which Taylor is editor. These authors wish to bring Kierkegaard into relation with deconstructionism and other contemporary movements in literary criticism.[5] The term "literary approach" is suggestive, since for these authors the literary form of Kierkegaard's work is decisive. Kierkegaard is fundamentally a poet or literary artist, and in Mackey's words, "Whatever philosophy or theology there is in Kierkegaard is sacramentally transmitted 'in, with, and under' the poetry."[6]

However, the term "literary approach" fails to express the distinctive way the Kierkegaardian texts are approached as literature here. Following Derrida, these authors see Kierkegaard's work as fundamentally subverting its apparent content. The search for any overall "point of view" in Kierkegaard is therefore regarded as hopeless. The pseudonyms must be read on their own terms, and their work is more ironical and destructive than directed toward establishing—or even undermining—traditional philosophical positions through straightforward arguments, dialectical analyses, and so on. Hence I think the best description of this second perspective may be "the ironical approach."[7]

A third category of work is best seen as a synthesis of the first two; I would term it literary-philosophical. Recent books on **Philosophical Fragments** by H. A. Nielsen and Robert Roberts would be excellent illustrations of what I have in mind.[8] Like the second group, Nielsen and Roberts take the pseudonyms seriously, and this leads them to take the literary structure of the books seriously. Also, as is the case with the ironical interpreters, they see much of Kierkegaard's intent as negative, humorous, and ironical subversion of the philosophical and theological status quo. However, unlike the ironical group they do not see this approach as blocking any consideration of the text as primarily philosophical, but, on the contrary, as freeing the reader up for an encounter with the text which will be philosophical in what might be termed a Socratic sense. Though I have learned much from representatives of all three approaches, it is this third approach that I shall attempt to follow most closely in the present work.

The assumption that underlies my approach is that though Kierkegaard does subvert the epistemological tradition of classical foundationalism, he is no friend of historicism and relativism either. Kierkegaard reminds us forcefully of our finitude, and he wants us to recognize the relativity and historicity of our situation, even with respect to what philosophers like to call Reason and Evidence. There is no risk-free method of grasping the truth. Nevertheless, there is truth to be grasped, and what Kierkegaard wants us to see is that our subjectivity is not just a screen that distorts the truth, but may be or become a medium that, when controlled by the right kind of passion, opens us up to an encounter with truth. This encounter cannot produce "the system"; it cannot eliminate the risk that we are mistaken. However, it can allow us to participate in a truth that, provisionally and partially at least, can transform our lives.

A Point of View On the Authorship

I begin by affirming that I agree with Kierkegaard himself that his literature has an overall religious purpose and that Kierkegaard was, as he put it in *The Point of View for My Work as an Author,* "from beginning to end a religious author." In this review of his literature, Kierkegaard views his whole authorship as consisting of two streams, one aesthetic and one religious. The apparently aesthetic writings have, however, as their purpose leading the aesthetic reader to the place where he can seriously confront the religious works. This claim of Kierkegaard has often been attacked on the grounds that it is by no means clear that Kierkegaard understood his purposes at the beginning of his authorship as he did at the end, when he wrote *The Point of View.* Louis Mackey has recently argued that there can be no such "point of view" for Kierkegaard's writings, only points of view.[9] This charge goes in hand with a view of Kierkegaard as deeply confused and even radically self-deceived about his own life and authorship.[10]

I have no wish to endow Kierkegaard with superhuman self-insight or clarity about his life. Like the rest of us, he surely struggled in these areas, though I do think he probably struggled more energetically and successfully than most of us. The readings of his works and life given us by Josiah Thompson,[11] Henning Fenger, and in the later writings of Louis Mackey seem unjustifiably cynical to me; certainly they fall short of the standard of love discussed by Kierkegaard himself in *Works of Love,* where he argues that the lover "believes all things" in the sense of always seeking to discover the most charitable interpretation of another's life.[12] However, for my purposes, it is not necessary to decide the truth of Kierkegaard's account of his own life. For in the final analysis, as Kierkegaard himself would be the first to affirm, the meaning of a body of literature cannot be determined by the intentions of the author, but by what the author realized.

In other words, my justification for seeing a religious purpose as providing a unity to Kierkegaard's literature is not that he affirms that he intended such a unity, but that looking at the literature in this way illuminates it in a powerful manner. Kierkegaard himself admits that he did not have a clear understanding of the plan of the literature at the outset.[13] His own understanding of what he was about changed as he personally developed. He attributed the unity of the authorship to providence,[14] an explanation which many will doubtless discount, but which certainly involves a recognition on his part that the whole thing was not planned out in advance. Whether Kierkegaard intended it or not, the unity is there in the text, in the sense that an honest reading of the authorship beginning with *Either/Or* and continuing through the later explicitly Christian writings can discern a consistent *telos.* Arguments and literary forms work together in an amazing way to draw the reader toward religious issues.

In a sense what I am offering on behalf of this thesis is testimony; I can truly affirm that the literature has taken on a power for me when read in this manner. But I also hope to show my readers how the literature is clarified and illuminated when read in this way, and, ultimately, challenge them to test my claims by going back to Kierkegaard.

Taking Johannes Climacus Seriously

No area of Kierkegaard interpretation has given rise to more controversy than the pseudonyms. Some have taken as literal fact Kierkegaard's remark at the end of *Concluding Unscientific Postscript,* in which he affirms that though he is the legally responsible author of the pseudonymous books, "not a single word" of the pseudonymous authors belongs to Kierkegaard himself.[15] Indeed, Louis Mackey has even suggested that the books Kierkegaard authored under his own name are simply from another pseudonym, so that "Søren Kierkegaard" is just one more literary *persona.*[16] At the other extreme, some authors have simply ignored the pseudonyms altogether, and have developed an overview of "Kierkegaard's" views by drawing from all the pseudonymous works.[17]

The Johannes Climacus pseudonym has given rise to as much controversy as any. There has been a tendency to view the Climacus pseudonym as a mask for Kierkegaard, even on the part of those who take other Kierkegaardian pseudonyms quite seriously. Niels Thulstrup, for example, argues that because of the similarities between *Fragments* and other works Kierkegaard published at the time, and because there is documentary evidence that the work was originally written under Kierkegaard's own name, with only minor changes when the pseudonym was added, "the work is both thought and written in Kierkegaard's own name and therefore cannot be considered a truly pseudonymous work."[18] Consistent with this claim, Thulstrup's own commentary takes the *Fragments* as a straightforward philosophical work. Thulstrup locates its historical antecedents, tries to discern main theses and arguments, looks at objections, and so on, under the guiding assumption that the text is Kierkegaard's own.

In contrast, H. A. Nielsen's *Where the Passion Is: A Reading of Kierkegaard's* Philosophical Fragments takes the Johannes Climacus pseudonym with great seriousness, or with as much seriousness as one can give to a professedly playful author. Nielsen takes deliberate account of the non-Christian point of view from which Climacus writes in interpreting and assessing the book. For example, at the end of chapter 1, Climacus puts forward what he describes as a "proof" of the truth of the hypothesis he has "invented," a hypothesis which bears a striking resemblance to the Christian story of the incarnation as God's plan to provide salvation for human beings. Since Climacus professes not to be a Christian, Nielsen argues that there must be a difference between accepting the truth of this hypothesis and genuine Christian faith.[19] In a similar manner, Robert Roberts, who also takes the pseudonym seriously, tentatively suggests that some of the arguments in the "Interlude" section of the book are bad arguments which are to be read ironically as parodies of genuine arguments, a conjecture which Roberts partially bases on the humoristic character of the pseudonym.[20]

. . . I intend to follow the policy of Roberts and Nielsen and the precedent of my own *Kierkegaard's* Fragments *and* Postscript, by taking the Johannes Climacus pseudonym as a genuine pseudonym. Thulstrup is undoubtedly right in claiming that *Fragments* was originally written under Kierkegaard's own name, but that fact does not have the decisive importance that Thulstrup gives it. First, as Thulstrup himself points out, there were revisions to the book after the pseudonym was added, notably to the preface. One cannot say in an a priori manner that these changes, however small, may not be significant in altering the thrust of the book as a whole. Taking the pseudonym seriously, for example, allows one to consider the possibility that the tone of the preface alters the sense of the book as a whole.

Even more significantly, taking the pseudonym as a genuine *persona* leaves open the possibility that the transition to a pseudonym was the result of a discovery on Kierkegaard's part about the character of the book. Any creative author, and Kierkegaard was nothing if not creative, makes discoveries about his own work in the process of writing and rewriting. It may well be that the humoristic, non-Christian Climacus pseudonym embodies the standpoint that Kierkegaard found himself to have taken in the composition of the book. In fact, the mere affixing of the pseudonym,

even if no other changes in the book had been made, can be seen as a significant act of rewriting on Kierkegaard's part, one which potentially alters every sentence by altering the perspective of the author.

Finally, taking the pseudonym seriously is a strategy which offers little risk. In reading the book as written by Johannes Climacus, I make no a priori assumptions about the character of the pseudonym or its relation to Kierkegaard himself. If the book presents us with serious and sober philosophy, as Thulstrup asserts (and I think it does indeed do this in some sections), we will not be barred from learning things simply because we choose to play along with Kierkegaard and regard ourselves as learning from Climacus. And if Climacus does present views which are substantially in agreement with Kierkegaard's own at the time the book was written, there is nothing to prevent our recognizing that fact. In summary, taking the pseudonym seriously safeguards several significant possibilities for the reader while foreclosing none. At least this will be true for the philosophical reader. If our purpose in reading *Philosophical Fragments* is to construct a history of the development of Kierkegaard's own views, then some potential for loss may be present in attributing the book to the pseudonym. If, however, we read the book, as I wish to do, as forcing us to grapple with a set of significant philosophical questions, then we do well to grapple with Johannes Climacus.

Getting To Know Johannes Climacus

If we are to grapple with Johannes Climacus, we need to get to know him, of course. That task turns out not to be an easy one. Climacus is a somewhat elusive, as well as ethereal, character. We have no real biographical facts to work with, and this is no accident. Climacus wants readers to focus on the issues he discusses; he does not want nosy, curious readers who speculate on his own personal standpoints. Such readers are frustrated by being given nothing to work with.

This is said most clearly in the preface, where Climacus does his best to fend off the reader's curiosity: "But what is my opinion? . . . Let no one ask me about that, for next to knowing whether I have an opinion, nothing could be more insignificant to another person than knowing what my opinion is."[21] Climacus goes on to say that it is possible that he may find some personal benefit from his work, but if so, it is his business. "Do I get any reward for this, am I like those who, serving by the altar, themselves eat of what is laid on the altar? . . Leave that to me."[22] The same reasons that lead me to take the Johannes Climacus pseudonym seriously lead me to respect this request for privacy, and I shall try to follow this policy, though at times the literary form of the book will force us to think about the perspective from which the book was written.

Still, one can, without a nosy desire to know Johannes Climacus' opinions, want to know more about what kind of an author he is and what kind of literature he is offering us. The literature is evidently philosophy of a sort, which presumably makes Johannes Climacus a philosopher of a sort. It is equally evident from the content of the book that Climacus has a great interest in what some might call religious issues, but which I would prefer to term spiritual issues, since there are a host of issues which come up in what is today termed "religious studies" which do not interest Climacus at all.

Some insight here is provided by the name. Johannes Climacus means "John the Climber." The name is that of a monk from the monastery on Sinai, who is well known for having written *The Ladder of Divine Ascent,* a book which purports to give step- by-step instructions for attaining spiritual perfection. Our Johannes Climacus is obviously a different person, and he shows no interest in or knowledge of the original Johannes Climacus. However, like the monk, he is interested in the question as to how an individual attains spiritual wholeness. Perhaps a remark about Hegel in Kierkegaard's *Journals and Papers* gives us the right clue here. "Hegel is a Johannes *Climacus* who does not storm the heavens as do the giants, by setting mountain upon mountain—but enters them by means of his syllogisms."[23] As a philosopher Johannes Climacus is interested in the question as to the value of thought in attaining spiritual perfection. What role can philosophy, or thought in general, play in becoming what I should become?

Many commentators have explored an early, unfinished work of Kierkegaard's, unpublished during his lifetime, *Johannes Climacus, Or De Omnibus Dubitandum Est,*[24] in order to gain more knowledge about Johannes. In this work Kierkegaard sketches a biography of a young man, Johannes Climacus, who tries seriously to realize the philosophical program of universal doubt. The subject of this biography raises a number of acute questions about the nature of doubt and its relation to philosophy. Kierkegaard evidently intended the book as an indirect critique of contemporary philosophers who wrote as if doubt were an easily attained and easily transcended standpoint. The plan of the book was evidently to have young Johannes enmesh himself in doubt and then discover no way of resolving his doubts, even his doubts about doubt.

While *Johannes Climacus* is a work that is well worth studying for its own sake, I shall not employ it as an intellectual biography of the author of *Philosophical Fragments.* There are several reasons for this. First, we must remember that *Johannes Climacus* is an unfinished work that Kierkegaard decided not to publish. Secondly, we have no real basis for assuming that the subject of the book is identical with the author of *Philo-*

sophical Fragments. Thirdly, *Johannes Climacus* is a book authored by Kierkegaard. Even if we made the unwarranted assumption that the subject of the book is identical with the author of *Fragments,* we would have only the third-person testimony of Kierkegaard about Climacus. Furthermore, the picture given of Climacus is of a young innocent who seems far removed from the mature, self-confident, if somewhat enigmatic, author of *Philosophical Fragments.*

We are not limited to the text of *Fragments* for our knowledge of Climacus, however, for he is the author of *Concluding Unscientific Postscript to the Philosophical Fragments,* a work which is obviously tied to *Fragments* in a number of ways. The *Postscript* is a sequel to *Fragments* which is half-promised at the end of the first book, and the sequel discusses *Fragments* in a number of places. We have every right therefore to look at *Fragments* in light of that latter work, with the proviso of course that the text of *Fragments* itself remains our primary concern. And we have every right to understand Climacus as the author of *Postscript* as well. With respect to both works, however, we shall keep in mind the fact that Climacus turns out to be an elusive, if not downright devious author, who perhaps cannot always be trusted to say what he means or thinks in a straightforward manner.

In the *Postscript* Climacus describes himself as a *humorist.* This suggests of course that his writings will be funny, and the reader who looks for wit and humor in Climacus' writings will not be disappointed. However, the concept of humor for Climacus is a rich one, which involves much more than just wit. This is not the place for a full account of the concept of humor in Climacus' writings (and Kierkegaard generally).[25] Here I will merely try to sketch a few significant aspects of the concept which shed light on Climacus as an author and character.

Humor for Climacus is not merely amusement, a relief from the important business of life. It involves insight into the human predicament. We find humor in what Climacus calls contradictions, perhaps better termed incongruities. A caricature is comical because of the contradiction between likeness and unlikeness it contains. A comedian who takes a pratfall by falling into a hole while gazing up at the sky is funny because of the incongruity between the upward gaze and the downward ascent.[26]

Of course not every incongruity or contradiction is humorous; often such incongruities are tragic. To qualify as humorous, a contradiction must have the sting removed. We must somehow find the situation painless, by gaining a detached perspective on the contradiction, by having what Climacus calls "a way out."[27]

Everyone is in this situation some of the time; everyone laughs at some things. The person Climacus describes as a humorist is someone who has somehow been able to take this humoristic perspective on life as a whole. The whole of human existence is seen as deeply incongruous. We human beings have the grandest plans and yet are frustrated by the most trivial of circumstances. Nevertheless, the final word on human life is not tragedy. The existential humorist has somehow found "the way out" which allows him to smile at the contradiction between human aspirations and what life has to offer.

As to what this "way out" is, Climacus is coy, and perhaps it will be different things for different humorists. However, it seems to involve something like a religious perspective for Climacus. The humorist sees a contradiction between our busy striving for meaning and significance and the fact that in the end, "we all get equally far;"[28] we all in fact seem to get nowhere. Nevertheless the humorist finds this funny and not tragic, and in so doing reveals a conviction, however obscure, that what we human beings are seeking is something we possess, at least in the end. The assumption seems to be that what various religions have called "salvation," "eternal life," or "eternal consciousness" is present within us. This allows the humorist to relax a bit, to take an attitude not far removed from that of the speculative philosopher, whom William James described as taking a "moral holiday" from the seriousness of the ethical life. A humorist, says Climacus, has "no seriousness of purpose." Though he may be active, in the end he always "revokes" his action, regards it as having no fundamental importance.[29]

Climacus is careful to distinguish this humoristic religious perspective from Christianity. The religious perspective of the humorist may have come about through an encounter with Christianity; in at least one place Climacus suggests that a humorist is someone who has gained a kind of intellectual knowledge of Christianity that has not been existentially realized.[30] Still, the humorist is far from being a Christian. The religious perspective of the humorist leads, not to the commitment and passion of Christian faith, but to a kind of detached perspective, one which is conducive to philosophical reflection and what Climacus calls psychological experimentation (more on the latter will follow). It is true that Climacus also says that humor can be the outward disguise, the incognito, of a true Christian, and in reading **Fragments,** it is tempting at times to speculate that Climacus may be just such a Christian, who has adopted humor as his outer cloak. This is possible, but we are still better off in such a case respecting the disguise, unless we find Climacus himself taking it off to reveal himself. (There are some passages in **Fragments** that can be read as doing this, as we shall see.) I shall therefore, at least initially, take Climacus at his word when he says he is not a Christian.

Philosophical Fragments, among other things, is a book about the relation of Christianity to philosophy. One can easily see, from the preceding description of the humorist, that someone like Johannes Climacus is an ideal author for such a book. As a humorist, Climacus can be knowledgeable about Christianity and interested in Christianity, as well as other religious perspectives. He can, however, maintain the philosophical detachment necessary to look at the issues fairly. His thinking as a humorist has what one might call an experimental quality to it. By "experiment" Climacus does not mean anything one does in a laboratory of course. Rather, he experiments by thinking hypothetically. The Hongs have chosen to translate the Danish *experiment* by "imaginative construction," and the translation certainly captures an essential aspect of what is meant. The experimenter is a thinker who thinks under the guise of "suppose this were so." **Philosophical Fragments** is just such an experiment, as we shall see, a grand attempt to think out the consequences of a certain assumption, one which is never asserted as true but only entertained hypothetically. . . .

Notes

[1] *Concluding Unscientific Postscript,* translated by David F. Swenson and Walter Lowrie (Princeton: Princeton University Press, 1968), p. 14 (*Samlede Værker,* 1st ed., 14 vols. [Copenhagen: Gyldendals, 1901-1906] vol. VII, 2). In future references to the *Postscript,* the first number will refer to the pagination of the old Swenson-Lowrie translation. All references to Kierkegaard's published writings will also include, as a second number in parentheses, the pagination of the first edition of the Danish *Samlede Værker* (volume number will appear first, followed by the page number). The new Hong translation of *Postscript,* as well as the other volumes in the *Kierkegaard's Writings* series, includes the pagination of this edition in the margins. Throughout this book I have freely modified translations or used my own, but I always supply an English page reference for the benefit of the reader.

[2] *Postscript,* p. 245n (VII, 234n).

[3] See, for example, Louis Pojman, *The Logic of Subjectivity: Kierkegaard's Philosophy of Religion* (University, Alabama: University of Alabama Press, 1984); Steve Dunning, *Kierkegaard's Dialectic of Inwardness: A Structural Analysis of the Theory of Stages* (Princeton: Princeton University Press, 1985); John Elrod, *Being and Existence in Kierkegaard's Pseudonymous Works* (Princeton: Princeton University Press, 1975); and Mark Taylor, *Kierkegaard's Pseudonymous Authorship: A Study of Time and the Self* (Princeton: Princeton University Press, 1975).

[4] Louis Mackey, *Kierkegaard: A Kind of Poet* (Philadelphia: University of Pennsylvania Press, 1971).

[5] This approach is well illustrated in discussions of Kierkegaard in two of Mark Taylor's recent works, though neither work is devoted solely to Kierkegaard. See his *Tears* (Albany: State University of New York Press, 1990), and also *Erring: A Postmodern A/Theology* (Chicago: University of Chicago Press, 1984).

[6] Louis Mackey, *Kierkegaard: A Kind of Poet,* p. xi.

[7] Besides Taylor's own work, the following books from the *Kierkegaard and Postmodernism* series illustrate the kinds of tendencies I have in mind: Louis Mackey, *Points of View: Readings of Kierkegaard* (Tallahassee: Florida State University Press, 1986); Sylviane Agacinski, *Aparté: Conceptions and Deaths of Søren Kierkegaard* (Tallahassee: Florida State University Press, 1988); and John Vignaux Smyth, *A Question of Eros: Irony in Sterne, Kierkegaard, and Barthes* (Tallahassee: Florida State University Press, 1986). A writer who differs from the above in some important respects but still situates Kierkegaard in the radical milieu of Derrida is John Caputo, *Radical Hermeneutics: Repetition, Deconstruction, and the Hermeneutic Project* (Bloomington: Indiana University Press, 1987).

[8] See H. A. Nielsen, *Where the Passion Is: A Reading of Kierkegaard's* Philosophical Fragments (Tallahassee: Florida State University Press, 1983); and Robert Roberts, *Faith, Reason, and History: Rethinking Kierkegaard's* Philosophical Fragments (Macon, Georgia: Mercer University Press, 1986).

[9] Mackey, *Points of View,* p. 190.

[10] See Henning Fenger, *Kierkegaard: The Myths and Their Origins* (New Haven: Yale University Press, 1980). P. 147 and p. 214 contain particularly good examples of this kind of debunking.

[11] See Josiah Thompson, *Kierkegaard* (New York: Alfred Knopf, 1973).

[12] *Works of Love,* translated by Howard and Edna Hong (New York: Harper and Row, 1962), pp. 213-30 (IX, 216-34).

[13] *The Point of View for My Work as an Author: A Report to History,* translated by Walter Lowrie (New York: Harper and Row, 1962), p. 72 (XIII, 561-62).

[14] See again *The Point of View,* pp. 64-92 (XIII, 556-75).

[15] "A First and Last Declaration," in *Postscript,* p. 551 (VII, 546).

[16] See Mackey, *Points of View,* p. 187.

[17] Many books could be cited as illustrating this procedure, for example John Elrod, *Being and Existence in Kierkegaard's Pseudonymous Works,* and James Collins, *The Mind of Kierkegaard* (Chicago: Regnery, 1953).

[18] Niels Thulstrup, "Commentator's Introduction," in *Philosophical Fragments,* translated by David Swenson, revised by Howard V. Hong (Princeton: Princeton University Press, 1962), p. lxxxv.

[19] See Nielsen, *Where the Passion Is,* pp. 22-23.

[20] See Robert Roberts, *Faith, Reason, and History,* p. 7.

[21] *Philosophical Fragments,* p. 7; (IV, 177). This quote and all future quotations and references from *Philosophical Fragments* will be referenced to the new Princeton edition, *Philosophical Fragments* (with *Johannes Climacus*) edited and translated by Howard V. Hong and Edna H. Hong (Princeton: Princeton University Press, 1985). The first number given is to this edition; the number in parentheses is to the pagination of the first edition of *Samlede Værker,* volume IV. The translations are usually my own; the English reference given is for the convenience of the reader. If no book is cited in a note, the reference is to *Fragments.*

[22] P. 7 (178).

[23] *Søren Kierkegaard's Journals and Papers,* 7 vols., edited and translated by Howard V. Hong and Edna H. Hong (Bloomington: Indiana University Press, 1967-78), entry #1575. (Subsequent references to the *Journals and Papers* will give only the entry number for the Hong edition.)

[24] Published in English with the new Hong translation of *Philosophical Fragments.*

[25] For a fuller account see my article "Kierkegaard's View of Humor: Must Christians Always Be Solemn?" *Faith and Philosophy* 4, 2 (1987), 176-86, and chapter 10 of my book *Kierkegaard's* Fragments *and* Postscript (Atlantic Highlands, N.J.: Humanities Press, 1983).

[26] *Postscript,* pp. 459-62n (VII, 447-52n).

[27] *Postscript,* p. 462 (VII, 451).

[28] *Postscript,* p. 403 (VII, 391).

[29] *Postscript,* p. 402 (VII, 391).

[30] *Postscript,* p. 243 (VII, 231).

Howard A. Slaatté (essay date 1995)

SOURCE: "The Problems of Reason," in *A Re-Appraisal of Kierkegaard,* University Press of America, 1995, pp. 27-38.

[In the following essay, Slaatté argues that contrary to what some rationalists have charged, Kierkegaard did not "scorn" reason. Rather, Slaatté maintains, Kierkegaard's writings suggest that reason does make up one part of human existence, but it does not reflect the entirety of one's selfhood.]

1. Reason and the Reasoner

Existentialist thinkers have been influenced by Kierkegaard, directly or indirectly, upon recognizing that "existence precedes essence." This implies that it is erroneous to speak of man as a rationally objectified concept or an abstraction called human nature or mankind. We begin and end our theorizing with the self, who can say "me."

In Western philosophy it was Parmenides and Plato who reversed this perspective placing essence before existence. The rational conceptualization of man was an objectification of a subjective existence. Aristotle accepted this precedent in his realism. However, these Greek philosophers overlooked the fact that a man exists concretely before he theorizes abstractly; he is subject before he is object. "I am" has priority to "man is." Thus an existence-related reason must take precedence over a theoretical reason. Similarly Kant's *Verstand* is prior to *Vernunft;* a practical reason or understanding is more basic than a pure reason.

One's genuine existence involves a self-transcendence upon seeking his true selfhood. Choice or acts of commitment are made before reason presents its idealistic blueprints. Kierkegaard saw this shrewdly in relation to what he called the three "stages of life," the aesthetic, the ethical and the religious.[1] The aesthetic stage is one of neutrality or non-commitment; the ethical involves decisions relative to personal life; the religious moves to a kind of moral idealism but is mature only through "the Moment," referred to above, in "the leap of faith" yielding an encounter with the Eternal in the present moment of existence. This is what enabled S. K. to say, "I am Transcended." Only a self-transcending subject-self could experience this encounter in which infinitude becomes meaningful to a despairing finitude. No self-sufficient reason could realize this or arrange for it.

In his way Kierkegaard could see that reason cannot account for itself. In this respect, between the lines he concurred with Kant's practical reason based on a priori categories of reason mixed with sense perceptions, and with Pascal's underlying intuitions basic to logic and mathematics. Relating this to concrete existence, Pascal said, "We know truth not only by reason but also by the heart, and it is by this last way that we know first principles." Pascal had in mind the awareness of number, motion, space and time and added, "And reason must trust these intuitions of the heart."[2] He said, "The heart has its reasons which reason does not know."[3]

Kant's a priori categories of reason[4] were not unlike Pascal's intuitions, but, unlike Pascal and Kierkegaard he separated the theoretical or pure reason from the practical. In doing this he bi-furcated the self. This violated or destroyed the holistic existentiality of man and his reason. In doing so he invited Hegel to run wild with pure reason as he projected it into a cosmic, monistic inflation thereof, a hypostasized cosmic Being of Reason lacking individuality while synthesizing all opposites dialectically. Thus the individual mind basic to Kierkegaard's philosophy was reduced by Hegel to a mere speck of a universal Reason.[5] It was this losing sight of the individual in favor of the universal that was revolting to S. K. Existence was lost track of in a cosmic essence. Kierkegaard saw that weakness also in Hans Martensen's rationalized theology linked with Hegelian metaphysics.[6] Kierkegaard saw that concrete existence cannot escape the clash of opposites and be reduced to a neat synthesis of reason. Reason has no grounds for erecting a remote pedestal removed from life's tensions. Reason itself cannot adequately account for its own implicit tensions between logic and its underlying intuitions. Nor can reason resolve the tension between the concrete knowing self with its involvements in nature and society while simultaneously transcending them. Reason must cope with paradox and not by-pass it.

Impatient critics have labeled Kierkegaard as "pathological," but perhaps these observations put the matter in a truer light. Kierkegaard neither bi-furcated man as did Kant nor projected him ontologically into a cosmic process with Hegel, let alone de-man him with the materialist, behaviorist and positivist. This is because S. K. contended that man was an individual or concrete subject-self, who must be viewed as a whole self or none at all. This even suggests a latent or presupposed existential element in Descartes' *cogito ergo sum,* when not pressed rationally. Thus reason's own paradox is apparent. One can affirm, doubt or even negate the self with David Hume, only as he presupposes the self existentially. This, in fact, was Descartes' basic weakness upon doubting himself and, thereby, rationally "proving" himself. Such thinking neglects the primacy of the thinker in favor of his objectified thought. Yet Descartes was sensitive to the prejudices and finitude within one's reasoning, another pre-existential factor in his favor.[7]

The German philosopher Richard Kroner speaks to the main issue here when he says, "It is not important to conclude from the fact that I think, as Descartes did, that I exist; but it is important to conclude that I exist in distinction from whatever is the content of my thought."[8] The matter is especially important when the self is seen to be characterized by a freedom to assert itself and to choose—even to choose to reason away the very capacity to choose! While many of the contradictory elements in human experience, including S. K.'s either/or ethical tensions, are due to moral freedom under the constraints of natural and social necessities, together with the moral imperative to choose, reason cannot legitimately project itself away from the concrete reasoning self. The existing thinker precedes what he thinks. Thus Kierkegaard was correct in stressing the primacy of the thinking subject over all objectifications whether rationalistic or scientific. The subject can know the object, but the object cannot know the subject. Subject and object (even objective concepts) are interrelated, but precisely because the existing knower has priority over what he knows. Here we see how the either/or is related to the both/and. The paradox of moral choice is really within the paradox of reason per se, though Berdyaev surpassed Kierkegaard in clarifying this.

2. Reason and Human Existence

Rationalists are inclined to attack Kierkegaard for scorning reason.[9] This is misleading. Kierkegaard acknowledges that reason is an implicit aspect of concrete human existence but by no means the whole of the self nor able to do full justice to the holistic individual in his concrete existence. Kierkegaard did not scorn reason but detested rationalism's idolatry of reason. To attack rationalism as having the last word on reality is not to dismiss the role of reason but to keep it in its rightful place. It is a tool, not a tribunal. Human existence is also irrational and transrational in various ways. In such contexts reason must be kept instrumental, not authoritative with finality. It is akin to Kant's practical reason with skepticism about pure reason. It cannot know *das Ding an sich* or the essence of things. As Nicholas Berdyaev put it in his *Slavery and Freedom,* "A thinker engaged in epistemology seldom arrives at ontology."

Kierkegaard did not deny the objectivity of the object. He approached a phenomenalism akin to Kant's skepticism that implies that we only know the appearance of the object; it is an interpretation wherein consciousness interrelates sense perceptions with intuitive mental insights. To be significant the object has to be relevant in this way to the knowing subject, which is conscious. The primacy of this conscious subject brings existentialism close to Husserl's phenomenology.

Reason has no self-contained answer to the meaning of a holistic, concrete existence, for reason must always function from within existence. It is enmeshed with the very existence it seeks to understand. This undergirds Kierkegaard's emphasis upon inwardness. Reason's objective theories are refracted by existence, and its ontological objectifications are idolatrous. This reflects the paradox of reason per se. It also suggests

the priority of the existential perspective, for, as already stated, existence precedes or is more basic than a theoretical essence. A man thinks in a variety of ways before he speculates rationally.

The self-transcending and thing-transcending self is fundamental. It alone can ask "Why?" after all the empirical explanations and rationalistic speculations are posed. In fact, each person sees the world in his way or from his perspective not always amenable to objective theories. He sees things through his particular glasses, as it were, and he has no assurance that such a perspective is rendered with fairness by a rational objectification or scientific explanation. There is no guarantee that each self sees the world the·same as another, let alone as it is, realistically "out there." My color-blind friend does not know what he is missing, and my dog and cat suggest that I don't either! This inconstancy of our sense perceptions is accentuated all the more when we put drab-looking stones under an ultraviolet ray lamp. The accommodation of light rays to our limited eye sight all the more reveals how limited our daily knowledge really is when we behold the breath-taking beauty of the stones. Similarly, there is no assurance that the *Begrifflichkeit* or thought forms, precepts and concepts of any two persons are the same. Much the same epistemological relativism applies to the human will, which Kierkegaard regarded as more basic to existence than reason. His emphasis upon either/or accentuates the decisiveness of existence. Decisions or choices are fundamental to daily life, S. K. stressed. To find yourself you "must choose." The will is basic. As Karl Heim put it in behalf of S. K., "My will is a particular form of the existence of my ego."[10] Yet the will cannot be localized directly with the body, brain or heart. Paradoxically, reason cannot objectify the will but must presuppose it in the holistic, concrete "I" who even wills to reason. The cognitive and volitional self are interrelated, if not the same. Yet the rationalists among the Greeks, notably Socrates and Plato, failed to see this.

A molten imagination often takes over where a solidifying reason leaves off. Upon seeing the need of something less direct and at the same time more penetrating than a cold reason by which to communicate with other selves, Kierkegaard astutely turned to what is called "indirect communication," a more poetic to mythical type of expression.[11] Instead of one's being constrained by logic to see a point, he is persuaded from within to see it pictorially. It helps one to see himself. Often S. K. used a provocative incident, parable, metaphor or simile that speaks to the whole self when reason cannot. Where reason is coldly and remotely direct, this method of communication is warmly and winsomely indirect. It is the difference between being told something and discovering it for oneself. It is a method that proves most provocative to the self when a rational theory or empirical account proves limited if not repulsive. But, then, once recognized, even reason is influenced by such thought. Thus, human understanding involves an impertinent paradox that proves pertinent to reason itself, existentially.

It was in this context that S. K. found the meaning of existence *for him,* which it must be. He found it where most rationalists and empiricists are too reluctant or proud to look, viz from within the darkness of a close-to-home despairing finitude. It was in that Moment when the Eternal absolute flashed like a lightning bolt into his anxiety-laden, but faith-conditioned, consciousness, giving his finite existence a new dimension of a qualitative meaning. Kierkegaard in this respect proved to be the first thinker to see the qualitative difference between the finite and the infinite. He saw this contrast as the Abyss, which is healed only by the either/or decision within the "leap of faith" associated with "the Moment." Whereas the opposite poles remain pronounced for Kierkegaard and are interrelated only through a faith-subsumed reason, Hegel mediated them too readily in his rational monism.[12] Thus S. K. was truer to the existing self.

As partially an existentialist, Friedrich Nietzsche failed to find a meaning in existence.[13] Though he joined Kierkegaard in the rejection of rationalistic ontologies, he failed to find the Absolute and found no answer to the question of life's meaning. However, critically it can be said that Kierkegaard did not clarify sufficiently the relation of reason to faith so as to show the difference between a responsible and irresponsible decision.[14] But this criticism is a rationalistic one which fails to understand the transrational nature of faith as an important aspect of a holistic existence. Many things, including ethical issues come alive with relevance to the subject self on a faith-conditioned basis, not the least of which is the meaning and role of an expendable *agape* love. No rational theory can do it justice nor account for it. The moral idealisms of rationalists are too abstract and "unparticular" to be truly relevant to the "me" of existence, but a Christly love is not.

3. Reason and Philosophical Issues

A criticism sometimes hurled at the existentialist is that he reduces man to nothing or to something meaningless. This is an attempt to make the existentialist appear to be a nihilist. While Nietzsche's pessimism, Sartre's ethical relativism and Heidegger's doctrine of "nothingness" seem to invite the accusation, actually it cannot fully apply even to these thinkers. Each takes man very seriously, keeping him responsible for his existence and refuting every intellectual attempt to reduce a man to a mere concept, brute or thing.

Though every existentialist accentuates man as a problem to himself, he sees that the individual is not yet what he really is, can become or ought to be. As S. K.

suggested, a man is seen yearning to be what he is not, while he senses that what he is not is really what he is! This profound paradox is fundamental to the existence of the self. It implies, as Karl Jaspers recognizes, that a person's real self is, so to speak, ahead or above himself, though not removed from his concrete self-in-existence.[15] Until this is recognized in some way a person fails to live wholesomely, i.e. he is uncommitted to what he yearns for or sees to be his real self. To exist, as Heidegger suggests, is to be able to "stand apart" from oneself (ex-sistere) in an inward manner so as to appraise oneself.[16] This is not a projected removal from the concrete self but a kind of psychological introspection or intrinsic capacity of the self to turn upon itself from within in the interest of seeking, finding and fulfilling true selfhood. In this light, Socrates' "Know thyself" and Kierkegaard's: "Choose thyself," become exceedingly important admonitions. Only selves can choose themselves, or even care who they are.

We must assert that a thinker like Friedrich Nietzsche sometimes sounds like a nihilist in his repudiation of moral and spiritual values or meanings in favor of new ones based on the natural search for power. But his kind of nihilism is really more of a warning than a recommendation. Nietzsche is sensitive to the hypocracies in European culture and, therefore, thinks the Christian ethic is defeated internally by the "mendaciousness of all Christian interpretations of the world and of history."[17] Moral skepticism, he believes, is a product of idealistic moral interpretations no longer acceptable. But the lack of sanction, we reply, is not the falsity of that to which it gives reference. Though Kierkegaard would not deny the common mendacities of social life, he would not concede that they are necessary. Men are free to live on a higher level. There may be an Unconditioned source of moral truth, which men do not sanction but which sanctions them. This Kierkegaard saw so clearly in his encounter with the Absolute that transcended him as well as all rationalistic universals. It is unfortunate that Nietzsche and Sartre did not come to understand this. Kierkegaard received his clue from the Bible. Not making him a nihilist, it pointed him to values and ideals identified with the divine Absolute revealed especially through Christ. It is this which offsets for him the relativism of existence giving him a new outlook, meaning and hope as well as love ethic.[18]

Man is not simply involved in his problems; he is a problem, even to himself. To assert this is not to be a nihilist, however, and certainly not an escapist, but quite the contrary. Man is a self, and a self-in-the-making at that. If a man is said to amount to "nothing" it is only in the sense that, unless his concrete self acts, wills, chooses or takes sides, he is nothing. To be a self is to assert oneself, and this includes the matter of relating oneself to himself and others. Thus, to a great extent a person is not just what he thinks and does but what he decides, chooses, acts upon and commits himself to. Hence, he is no bigger than that to which he is committed. To discover this is the prelude to self-discovery, self-fulfillment and authentic existence. S. K. found that in facing up to despair the Absolute breaks through to his consciousness giving him a re-orientation of life, which yields his true self.

But does a person exist even if he does not act or choose? This question is legitimate, we believe, but apt to be a "leading question" of a kind that is misleading. It is apt to be "loaded" rationally so that its presuppositions constrain the answer. We must realize that man is not an ontological substance, even if he yearns to know his being or what it means. To exist is to be a particular conscious being, who is aware of his being. Yet, right here existentialists may differ greatly. Nicolas Berdyaev, for instance, has seen shrewdly that not only is freedom, creativity and act fundamental to man's personal existence but intrinsic to the *pneuma* or spirit that he is.[19] We cannot rationally ontologize this, however, for it falls outside the pall of reason. To do so with the Scholastics, modern idealists and others is to be much in error. Not a rational concept, only the spirit-self can *exist* and be a free or responsible self, hence, a possibly fallen or enslaved self, too. *Ontos* and *nous* are immune to both freedom and *pneuma*. Though *pneuma* can embrace the functions of *soma* and *psyche,* it moves beyond them, incorporating man as a total spirit-subject-self, as Berdyaev stressed it. Only such a self can question or yearn for himself, his true identity, vocation and destiny. Whereas the atheistic-to-agnostic existential thinker sees the self's identity and vocation strictly within his own grasp, if at all, the theistic existential thinker sees the need of the Kierkegaardian "leap of faith," since one's *true* identity and vocation transcend him as he now is in his concrete actuality. Not irrational, this rather respects the prerational or transrational dimension of the rational, even as it concedes the limitations of the rational.

Kierkegaard provocatively suggests that there are three moral alternatives on the sea of personal existence; either to sink, swim or be saved; a hopeless despair with no self-contained guidance available; a meaningless foundering with no shore in sight; or a meaningful hope from beyond oneself. The latter is linked with the faith-conditioned encounter with the eternal Absolute, the Unconditioned beyond all that is conditioned, relative or finite. Looking beyond reason's limitations it may be more imperative and more tenable, too, than atheistic existentialists like Jean Paul Sartre dare to admit. For a person to be caught in an oceanic whirlpool of meaningless existence is to toy with a psychosis, not to mention a hell-on-earth. It is not to find but to lose one's real self; it is to be trapped in a state of artificial existence, which makes no headway. To settle for just that is to surrender either by frustration, inertia or suicide to nothingness.[20] Dunked in existence men may need a firmer footing provided from beyond a fallen, finite selfhood, if they are to know their real meaning. Dare men admit it today? Kierkegaard did when he saw himself transcended in the Absolute, the meaning-giving locus of one's true Existenz. Sartre has failed to see it, perhaps because he has not looked beyond himself, from within himself. Likewise Nietzsche. They settled only for what their finitude could supply. S. K. looked to the infinite or the Absolute.

While one cannot live without assertion and resolve, it takes more than sheer self-assertion or Stoical resolve to exist authentically in this world. It demands the self-seizure of oneself, a facing up to one's existence as-it-is. Thus, the man who comes to despair of his quasi-private life can begin to exist genuinely. He sees that he has questions, which he cannot answer of himself. In the face of this paradox of selfhood, he must assert himself from within himself to realize himself. But how? Only when his *angst,* the inner despair at failing to be himself, becomes a form of self-transcendence does he cross the threshold of self-disclosure. But this occurs, Kierkegaard maintains, only as one's self-transcending consciousness comes to the point of being able to concede: "I am Transcended." This is based on a faith commitment and opens up a faith-subsumed reason that can grasp existentially the issues that make theology possible, relevant and meaningful. Whereas Nietzsche viewed self-transcendence mainly in the search for power, an idea which influenced Adler's psychoanalysis, Kierkegaard viewed it through the *Credo quia absurdum* of the faith referred to above, which is "the highest immediacy" and makes for nonconformity to social precedents and pressures. Since both thinkers reacted against the Greek rationalistic ontologies and believed in the primacy of the self, ethical decision was to them basic to existence and self-realization. Every person must think for himself. As S. K. said, universals and systems fail to do the self justice. Nietzsche agreed. Both thinkers rebelled against all hypocrisy and a state which coddled the Church with a soft idealism. Both rejected the view of the idealists that what you must think by reason must *be.*[21]

For Kierkegaard the self is a paradox in which the finite and infinite meet. Self-transcendence in the form of faith yields a final truth to give oneself to—in "the Moment" which transcends temporal existence. S. K. thus can say, "With God's help, I shall be myself."[22] Faith accepts the paradox of Christianity and finds the new focal point that supercedes a despairing finitude as rationalism cannot. Reason counts the paradox of Christ as "absurd." For a long while Heidegger seemed to be of this persuasion by not addressing the question of God, but eventually he came to respect "the Holy." This was his later-found respect for the awesomeness of Being in the Being of his existence.[23] As Richard Kroner has pointed out, Heidegger wanted to retain the biblical truth but only by stripping it of its transcendent and mythical elements.[24] In a sense Jean-Paul Sartre followed Kierkegaard to the precipice of despair but left a person "to make himself" or find his self-made meaning.[25] What both Nietzsche and Sartre have failed to understand is that God transcends all the rational speculations which can be rejected by the same kind of reasoning. Kierkegaard saw this and viewed God as the Unconditioned Absolute that supercedes all finite speculative projections. Commitment to this makes for the true self-transcendence. No institutionalized religion can be a substitute for such a "total-self commitment," he said,—not that all religious institutions must be abrogated, for they are responsible for a witness to God. Nietzsche, in contrast, rejected both religious substance and form. He denounced all the values of life based on faith as though faith had no room for reason in existence. This he did upon stressing his cynical version of "the transvaluation of all values" in favor of whatever makes for power over others and a super-race based thereupon.[26]

Karl Jaspers said with some justification that both Nietzsche and Kierkegaard have doctrines of transcendence, which few can follow. Admittedly, each sees the struggling man of existence, but the one version is of an idolator; the other a worshipper; the one settles for a new nihilism, the other for a faith-conditioned meaningfulness. Jaspers is much closer to Kierkegaard. Not only does he reject rationalistic objectifications in favor of concrete existence but sees truth linked with das Ümgreitende or the "The Encompassing" much like William James' view of "the More." This is an awareness of Transcendent Being and is essential to one's true being as the *unconditioned ground* of the self.[27] Neither reason nor science can explain it. It is akin to Tillich's pro-Kierkegaardian "Ultimate concern" and "ground of being," while the basis of a higher freedom. Jaspers sees that to be true to the self reason must function in relation to this paradoxical condition of existence, quite as S. K. does. Jaspers states provocatively, "Since all existential strivings for Transcendence are dialectical, a definitive (rational) statement of their direct contents is always prone to be false."[28] For him Transcendence is the real, eternal Being that is man's source of self-fulfillment, the Deity "as it appears to us in this world."[29] Not fully identical with S. K.'s view, Jasper's view is closer to deism than to theism, since his deity concept is not clearly identified with the biblical "I Am," being closer to one's own self-transcendent being. Jaspers contends that reason "has suffered shipwreck," and sees with S. K. that this is where one's philosophy must begin existentially, while it helps prepare one for an acquiescence to "Eternity inside Time" or to an "ascent to Transcendence."[30] Unlike Nietzsche, who said "God is dead," Jaspers says philosophy cannot fight off religion but must relate itself to this polarity of existence, which centers about the finite self's awareness of the infinite or Transcendent.

What Jaspers tried to assert from a psychoanalytical perspective was that the self-transcending self really finds meaning in the divinely Transcendent.[31] In this respect he was pro-Kierkegaardian. Much the same could be said in behalf of Karl Gustave Jung after many years of stressing divine immanence in relation to man. A holistic, existential subjectivity was finally recognized as basic to "the subjective variety of an individual life." Also, Jung eventually conceded that man needs "a wisdom greater than his own," an illumination from a transcendent source.[32] Karl Menniger as another psychoanalist came to see that people are persons, not just organisms.[33] Each of these psychiatrists saw that persons lack meaning without reference to the transcendent. Yet, what to Jung was long accepted as religiously immanental may be likened to the psychological aspects of existence, which allowed for what Kierkegaard viewed as subjective "apprehension" giving rise to religious "relevance," also to what the theologian Emil Brunner claimed was das Anknüpfungspunkt or "point-of-contact" between man and the divine. . . These psychological factors are immanental seats of religious relevance but not seats of religious authority.

Notes

[1] S. K., *Stages On Life's Way,* pp. 399-403 and *Concluding Unscientific Postscript,* pp. 309-350, 440, 498 nt, 499-502. The former book elaborates what the latter brings forth.

[2] *Pensees,* 282, p. 96.

[3] *Ibid,* 277, p. 95.

[4] Kant, *Critique of Pure Reason,* Book I, Chap. I.

[5] Hegel, *The Phenomenology of Mind,* p. 798. cf. my work, *The Pertinence of the Paradox,* pp. 121, 136.

[6] See the second chapter of this book [*A Re-Appraisal of Kierkegaard*].

[7] "I think, therefore I am," a presumed proof beginning with doubt. Rene Descartes, "The Principles of Philosophy," Pt. I, *A Discourse On Method,* Everyman's Library, p. 165 ff. cf., Pt. I.I.XXXVI, LXXL, LXXIL.

[8] Kroner, "Heidegger's Private Religion," *Union Seminary Quarterly Review,* Vol. XI, no. 9, May, 1956, p. 31, Cf. pp. 46-48.

[9] Cf. L. H. DeWolf, *The Religious Revolt Against Reason,* Chap. III.

[10] Heim, *Christian Faith and Natural Science,* p. 64.

[11] S. K. *Training in Christianity,* pp. 46, 132, 141.

[12] Cf. Croxall, *Kierkegaard Commentary,* p. 32.

[13] Heim, *op cit,* p. 17.

[14] Cf. Kaufmann, *Existentialism from Dostoevsky to Sartre,* p. 17.

[15] *Reason and Existenz,* pp. 18, 141, 25, 132.

[16] *Existence and Being,* pp. 334, 346.

[17] *The Will to Power,* Book One, II, ed. Kaufmann, p. 110.

[18] For the latter see S. K.'s work *Purity of Heart,* which, I believe, he would have expanded had he lived longer.

[19] *Spirit And Reality,* pp. 13, 15ff, 32ff.

[20] Upon dismissing God, Sartre also dismissed all ideals in favor of "an absurd world." As for the latter point, see Viktor Frankl's works including *Man's Search For Meaning* which emphasizes that the new form of neurosis in the West today is due to various types of meaninglessness. Cf. his *Doctor and the Soul. . .*

[21] S. K. *Concluding Unscientific Postscript,* 1941 ed., pp. 107, 297, 176, 178, 273, 275, 278, 319, 350, 437.

[22] S. K. *The Journals,* p. 138.

[23] Cf. Slaatte and Sendaydiego, *The Philosophy of Martin Heidegger,* Chapter III.

[24] Kroner, *op cit,* pp. 5, 25, 28f.

[25] Sartre, *Existentialism,* trans. B. Frechman, Philosophical Library, 1941, pp. 16-20.

[26] Nietzsche, *Thus Spake Zarathustra,* pp. 6, 104, 106 (and) "The Gay Science," *Existentialism* . . . ed. Kaufmann, p. 105f.

[27] Jaspers, *Reason and Existenz,* pp. 25, 52f, 141, 189, Cf. Jaspers, *Der Philosophische Glaube,* pp. 131, 134.

[28] *Der Philosophische Glaube,* p. 130.

[29] Jaspers, "On My Philosophy," *Existentialism* . . . ed. by Kaufmann, pp. 112, 136, 138.

[30] *Ibid,* pp. 139, 145, 154. Cf. pp. 152-155.

[31] Jaspers, *Reason and Existenz,* pp. 131, 135.

[32] Jung, *The Undiscovered Self,* p. 110. Cf. Chaps. iv, vi.

[33] Menninger, *Theory of Psychoanalytic Technique,* p. 94.

Julia Watkin (essay date 1997)

SOURCE: "The Logic of Søren Kierkegaard's Misogyny, 1854-1855," in *Feminist Interpretations of Søren Kierkegaard,* edited by Céline Léon and Sylvia Walsh, Pennsylvania State University Press, 1997, pp. 69-82.

[*In the following essay, Watkin contends that despite the negative remarks Kierkegaard makes about women in his* Journals, *remarks which seem to contradict his earlier, more favorable views on marriage and sexuality, the later writings are not aimed solely at women and are not, in fact, inconsistent with his earlier statements. Watkin further explains that Kierkegaard's beliefs regarding the relationship of the self to God made it nearly impossible for him to square marriage and procreation with the need for self-renunciation.*]

When one reads the ***Journals*** of the last two years of Kierkegaard's life, one cannot help being struck by the negative expressions about women. We read that "woman is personified egoism. Her burning, hot devotion to man is neither more nor less than her egoism," whereas man "is not originally an egoist," he does not become that until "he is lucky enough to be united to a woman," when he becomes the thorough egoist in the union "commonly known as marriage . . . the proper enterprise of egoism."[1] We learn that woman's characteristic fault is "cunning, subtlety and lies," she is "the weaker sex," expected to "wail and scream."[2] Man "was structured for eternity" but woman "leads him into a digression." Woman in her relation to the religious "explains nothing," her devotedness "is essentially related to interjections, and it is unfeminine if it is more than that."[3] For she relates to things directly, "breathes the air of directness"; she "participates in religion at second hand, through the man."[4] So "at the greatest distance from the ideal is: mother, madam. The real fury against the ideal comes from family life, from the lioness, or, to say it another way . . . from the suckling sow."[5] Parallel to these statements are Kierkegaard's many comments (often invoking the authority of Saint Paul)[6] praising celibacy and rejecting the sexual drive with its begetting of children as something anti-Christian, as in the piece headed **"Propagation of the Species, Christianity wants to bar the way."**[7]

Several reasons have been given as to why Kierkegaard in his last years seems to make a violent attack on women, sex, and marriage—an attack that seems all the more strange when one considers his positive attitude earlier toward marriage.[8] Most obvious is a psychological-pathological explanation. One can suggest that Kierkegaard could not fulfill his engagement in the reality of marriage to Regine Olsen;[9] over the years he developed a vicious "sour grapes" attitude concerning women and sex. Eduard Geismar considers that Kierkegaard's struggle with his "thorn in the flesh" is an element in the situation when he develops his view that the philosophy of Schopenhauer is to blame. Kierkegaard, who was already leaning in a similar direction, developed "an asceticism hostile to life" because he was influenced by Schopenhauer's cynical disgust with life. Schopenhauer's thought encouraged Kierkegaard to relieve his feelings in the *Journals* from 1854 and in several numbers of **"The Instant."**[10]

Yet another possibility is that advanced by Birgit Bertung, who sees in Kierkegaard's statements about women a "poetical provocation or repulsion." By using such negative language Kierkegaard aims at a dialectical attack on, not women, but on the mixing up of a temporal relationship to the husband with the spiritual relationship to God, something that they are in risk of doing, since woman as the child-bearer is in danger of falling into the role of existing only as "being for others," of becoming a victim to the animal-temporal side of human nature and thus moving away from spirit and the command of her own personality. On this view, Kierkegaard is not an ascetic, but is ironizing over the domination of women by men to which women give their assent. By using such language he hopes to provoke Society, and especially women, into an insight into the situation and to movement toward the proper preservation (in this world) of the equality of men and women before God through the relation to God.[11]

From the above it can be seen that an important consideration must influence an assessment of Kierkegaard's final statements about women. It has to be decided whether or not he means his attack to be taken at face value. Linked to this question is the problem of Kierkegaard's description of women. Is it meant to apply to women only in the cultural situation of his time, or does he regard it as a true account of women in every age? Is it the case, as Sylvia Walsh suggests in her article "On 'Feminine' and 'Masculine' forms of Despair," that in his use of "stereotyped characterizations of the sexes" he reflects and helps perpetuate such characterizations, even though his analysis of the self rests on a common structure of selfhood for both sexes?[12]

With respect to the second question, I am inclined to think that even in his last years, Kierkegaard was describing Society the way he observed it around him, and that he probably never considered the question of cultural conditioning on personality the way we understand that question today, even though he realized that each individual starts out from an historically conditioned situation. Although he respects and idealizes

women and asserts a fundamental equality of the sexes before God, Kierkegaard, like many other authors of his generation and later, also perceived fundamental external and natural differences between the sexes, seeing woman as frail, as needing the support of the man, and as instinctive and intuitive in intellectual matters. Thus one must try as far as possible to distinguish between Kierkegaard's nineteenth-century view of women—a view that includes the above-mentioned and very modern emphasis on fundamental equality—and the extreme polemic of his final years.[13]

Regarding the first and main question, I here develop the view that Kierkegaard's attack is to be taken directly at face value, but that it is not aimed exclusively at women and that it makes sense in terms of the structure of his authorship as well as of the cultural situation of the time. The extreme statements of the last years are in agreement with the logic of basic metaphysical assumptions in the authorship.[14] In this connection I shall be taking a look at Kierkegaard's view of God, the world, and humankind, with special reference to the significance of marriage, before finally turning to his cultural situation.

Kierkegaard makes it clear many times in his authorship that he presupposes the existence of the personal God of Christianity, a God who is pure personhood, "pure subjectivity," and who "creates out of nothing."[15] As Kierkegaard explains in a *Journal* entry from 1846, in the act of creating from nothing God withdraws himself so that creation may come into being. He withdraws himself in order to give himself, because it is by so doing that he "makes the recipient independent." That is, in finite relationships, the recipient of a gift is not independent because he is obligated to the giver, who, in turn, lacks the power to give without creating obligation. Although God omnipotently creates human beings "out of nothing" in that humankind is not already in independent existence prior to creation, he renounces the obligation established through humanity's factual total dependence on him in order that human beings may truly be free.[16] Kierkegaard's thought here is very like Simone Weil's "creative renunciation of God."[17] and already comes to expression in the early years in his criticism of Solger in the comment that "in that God sacrifices himself, he creates."[18]

God's self-giving, self-sacrificing creativity has two expressions. On the one hand, the divine ominipotence is "able to create the most fragile of all things—a being independent of that very omnipotence"; on the other, it is also able to create "the most impressive of all things—the whole visible world."[19] This latter is directly dependent on God; it is the realm of nature, of the aesthetic, where life in its immediate state unconsciously fulfills its development according to God's design.[20] The former, since the individual is independent while partaking of the substance of visible creation, is a synthesis, not only of psyche and body, but also of the temporal and the eternal. The individual is animal, but also spirit.[21] God has created humankind in his own image and since the eternal God is spirit, to be spirit is a person's "invisible glory."[22] Yet, as Judge William points out in *Either-Or,* the individual is "finite spirit" assigned to temporality, which latter is the possibility of that spirit's glorification.[23] Within the realm of temporality each person is as yet only finitely "like God" and must use the period allotted to him to fulfill and make real his God-given potentiality or possibility.

For Kierkegaard, then, there are two realms, temporality and eternity, with eternity transcending all time—past, present, and future.[24] These two realms stand in an inverse relation to each other, and "God is always the inverse of man" because of the character of the nature of God and of eternity. For Kierkegaard, God's realm is the realm of the intensive, whereas temporality is the realm of the extensive.[25] In the temporal world, it is the nature of all existence to extend and assert itself. Creation is Being, opposite God, as it were, and humankind in its self-consciousness is actively ego opposite God in freedom and not passively so like animals and the rest of nature, which follow instinct according to God's will. To the world of temporality belong progression and assertion of self-hood, quantity, expansion; to the realm of eternity belong self-denial, quality, renunciatory withdrawal. The opposite of the extensive life of the world is the intensive life of the spirit.[26]

Such a life can be lived in the world and is expounded by Judge William to the young man in *Either-Or.* For Judge William temporality "exists for the sake of humankind and is the greatest of all the gifts of grace," because in it each member of the community can relate to the Christian God, "the eternal Power who omnipresently pervades the whole of existence." Authentic community is formed by each individual living unselfishly in relation to God and neighbor. The aesthetic world-order of human nature in the raw is brought under control of the ethical-religious.[27] This thought is expanded in the *Journals* where Kierkegaard regards the individual in his relation to God as being "decisive as the presupposition for forming community," true neighbor love being "self-denial, rooted in the relationship to God."[28] "Earthly love . . . at its highest is love only for one single human being in the whole world," "spiritual love . . . loves more and more people, has its truth in loving all." "Erotic love and friendship are preferential," but in authentic love to the neighbor there is an equality belonging to eternity.[29]

In this way, the individual can live the life of eternity now, within the context of human relationships. Instead of living the competitive life of the temporal world in the manner of the animal kingdom, he dies to self-centeredness and lives the life of fellowship with God and the transcendent kingdom of heaven, something that is everlasting in that at death the individual enters into full membership of that realm.[30]

Yet just because the realm of eternity is the end and aim of existence, marriage and physical continuity of the race are treated ambiguously in Kierkegaard's writings. For Judge William, if the temporal is the realm where the individual is placed by God, then, as we have seen, the individual's duty is to aim at the highest within the finite sphere by living a self-denying and hence eternally orientated life within finite relationships. Marriage must be the highest and a duty in the finite sphere because otherwise the physical and spiritual structure in which individuals make up families and the social whole would disappear. In this sense marriage unites the spiritual and the physical, providing the spiritual and physical continuity of the race. Yet the Judge's outlook is not to be confused with that of one for whom this life is all. Marriage does not exist merely for the sake of continuing the race, but as the necessary presupposition for the possibility of ethical-religious life in temporality. The temporal world remains the sphere of humankind's unavoidable self-orientation as the individual extends himself in space and time, and even the Judge can see that this is what gives marriage—"the deepest form of life's revelation" and "the beautiful mid-point of life and existence"—a natural egocentricity from which it cannot be freed by the most unselfish love.[31]

For what hampers the God-like self-renouncing life in the temporal order is the unavoidable fact of natural preference. In concrete terms, a man or woman who neglects partner and children in order to give the appropriate love and care to others is hardly the paragon of love. There is a sense in which individuals must put the selfhood of the family unit first, however unselfishly they live. Similarly, even where a nation has an idealistic democratic constitution, it is impossible to escape conflict of interest, not only within the state but between nations where a government must put the interest of the nation before that of other nations.[32] Viewed in that light, the state, as Kierkegaard points out, functions as a "higher egoism" with the task of controlling personal egoisms[33] and cannot be regarded as Christian. Instead, the best government aims at the greatest happiness of the greatest number as best it can, with emphasis on protecting posterity.

This fact of natural preference is thus the reason why Johannes Climacus in *Philosophical Fragments* points out that "self-love" is "the ground in all love," the basic starting-point of all human relationships before they are transformed into something higher, while Judge William in *Stages on Life's Way* says that "from the essentially religious point of view . . . it makes no difference whether or not a person has been married" and that not marrying is "higher" than marrying, the Judge's revision of his earlier statement being a necessary consequence of a standpoint that has the transcendent realm of God as the ultimate goal. This is seen clearly in Climacus's discussion of "Religiousness A" in *Concluding Unscientific Postscript,* where the individual is shown as directing his attention more profoundly toward the transcendent. Here, "self-annihilation is the essential form of the God-relationship." The individual concentrates on his God-relationship with greater detachment from human relationships, though paradoxically participating in them more effectively because of aiming to do so on a totally non-self-regarding basis.[34] The movement of the authorship is away from any form of self-orientation to a God-centeredness that requires an ever-increasing self-denial and self-renunciation.

At this point, it is useful to take a look at Kierkegaard's view of human-kind's place in creation in connection with the Christian doctrine of the Fall. For the factor of unavoidable natural self-concern must be taken into consideration when looking at Kierkegaard's later statements that treat procreation as a fall into sin. The "ideality" preceding the Fall is for Kierkegaard here the God-intended ideal state in which humankind is like God through a totally self-denying God-relationship. The Fall itself is the human race "lost" or separated from God, this state of affairs seen as occurring when self-conscious man first failed to be willing to renounce everything for God and thus consciously asserted himself. In that sense, procreation is particularly "the Fall" as the assertion of the human ego in physical existence. From this standpoint, every child and generation is lost and fallen through being born, the child sharing in the parental egoism insofar as it is a part of it.[35] As early as 1844 we learn from Vigilius Haufniensis in *The Concept of Anxiety* that if Adam had not sinned—that is, by his disobedience stressed mankind's opposite relation *to* God as opposition to God—he would have become eternal immediately, "would in the same moment have passed over into eternity."[36] Instead of which, the emphasis on man as separate ego means that the sexual, because of sin, becomes "the centre of human egoism," a propensity to carry humanity further away from God. In a *Journal* note from the draft of *The Concept of Anxiety,* Kierkegaard's pseudonym even goes as far as to state that "first with sin time actually comes into being," implying that temporality originates through sin, a thought that occurs in the *Journal* entries of the final years. Adam asserts himself, and expands his ego self-assertively on the horizontal plane of history, instead of relating in total self-denial to God on the vertical plane of eternity. Sexuality leads to the fact of human history, and with the advent of human self-consciousness, procreation becomes a purposive instead of an instinctive activity. Viewed in that light, existence can be described by

Kierkegaard as "crime" and "punishment" in that humankind, having defied the divine purpose, willfully continues in a situation that tends to isolation from God.[37]

God can therefore be seen as self-denyingly creating nature so that man in freedom can choose between two ways of being like God or having "kinship with the Deity." The individual can either be a physical creator in giving life or he can surrender himself to an existence of total self-denial: he can propagate the species as "animal creature" or as "man of spirit"—choose to be naturally self-asserting in creation to a greater or lesser extent, or, in utter self-denial can be an example encouraging others to follow the pattern of God's nature, Jesus, incarnate God and suffering, atoning servant, who gives up everything, even life itself.[38]

Humankind, however, interprets God's omnipotence as self-assertive monarchic power. The individual wishes to be the independent lord of creation. Hence his first idea is to propagate his kind. He expresses his egoism through reproduction: "Man wants to dabble in the creator's activity, if not by creating man, at least by giving life," says Kierkegaard, but "to create is reserved for God . . . the giving of life is a weak analogy to this . . . human egoism culminates at this point." In humankind, "the instinct for the propagation of the race" is in fact as strong as "the instinct of self-preservation," because through the strength of numbers it is part of self-preservation, while family life centered round the mother with her children becomes, as in the animal kingdom, a species of egoism, in which "woman most certainly does not love herself foremost but through (egoistically) loving her own she loves herself."[39]

For this reason, Kierkegaard points out that "the way marriage is regarded is decisive for every religious view of life" and that "propagation of the race is a substitute for immortality."[40] All life-views—even religions that presuppose a personal God and advocate individual self-denial for the sake of others—are rejected by Kierkegaard if they postulate a false "unity of the divine and this life." Humankind in defiance of God wishes to remain within the realm of temporality. It establishes family life as "a form of godliness," centering its hopes on this world in terms of extension of the human ego in the form of race, relationships, and goods. There is a tendency to identify the natural order of existence with the religious, nationality with religion, and to recast God in the image of man.[41] Not willing himself to be a real Christian, the individual turns Christianity into "Christendom" when he "undertakes to beget children who shall become Christians and these children in their turn behave in the same way" thus turning Christianity into enjoyment of life in "the ordinary human sense."[42]

It can thus be seen that Kierkegaard does not become distorted in his later writings about marriage and sexuality. It is his metaphysical assumptions about God and creation, the eternal and the temporal, that make it difficult, if not impossible, for him to reconcile marriage and procreation with an ideal likeness to God that demands total self-renunciation. Thus his attitude to marriage shifts when he moves from discussing how the Christian individual relates to God in and through the temporal world to how he relates to God from the temporal world in the light of the demand of Christian ideality. In the writings of the Judge, marriage is the important relationship sanctifying the temporal under God, though he is careful to emphasize it as a relationship rather than in its aspect of continuing the race. Later though, when Kierkegaard begins to speak of the exception and of self-annihilation before God, marriage becomes viewed not just as something one may give up under certain circumstances, or as something one has no time for if one intends to serve the Absolute absolutely, but as something one must normally give up in order to fulfill the divine command totally, especially where the human emphasis on marriage is on having children and on the continuation of the race. If the true spiritual path consists of dying to selfishness, denying the natural self, expansion of the ego in space and time in one's descendants can be seen as a form of the assertion of selfhood difficult to reconcile with self-denial when absolute ideality is demanded.[43]

The ideality of the renunciation of marriage is in a sense implied at the beginning of Kierkegaard's authorship because Kierkegaard does not have a closed definition of Christianity. Judge William does not set up his ethical-religious way as ultimate perfection, but puts it forward as the path of development, after which the situation is seen as being between God and the individual.[44] Even toward the end of the authorship, however, when Kierkegaard as the "corrective" scornfully rejects the thought that "everyone is duty-bound to marry and that marriage is the genuinely ennobling life," he still allows the permissibility of marriage, in "the Moral" in *Training in Christianity.* In the last years, side by side with demands for a "stop" to procreation and a rejection of Christian "epicureanism," he points out that there are exceptional dialectical situations where the ideal of total renunciation may in fact require the individual to marry, as in the case of Luther. There are times when to keep "the things of the world does not signify that one wants to keep them—no, but that one wants to do something still higher than to give them away."[45] Also, although Kierkegaard regards the Christian injunction to hate one's life in this world as a principle logically "so asocial that it cannot constitute community" and says that he is "unable to comprehend how it can occur to any man to unite being a Christian with being married," he points out that he is "not thinking of the case of a man who was already married and had a family, and then at that age became

a Christian" but of the one who "is unmarried and says he has become a Christian."[46] In retrospect he believes that his own desire to marry was a mistake, and it is surely his own situation he is describing when he speaks of letting the loved one go "in order to love God."[47] The New Testament's "hatred of men" thus does not mean "conceitedly and arrogantly" wanting to "despise man and love God," but is a rejection of temporality whenever and wherever it becomes divorced from God.[48]

We can now return to the statements about women with which we started, having ascertained that Kierkegaard's misogyny is rather a "misogamy" or attack on marriage in which both male and female roles are sharply criticized. Here, it should be noted that the bulk of the negative statements, and especially those dealing mainly with women, appear in the *Journals* and not in the *Works,* and that there is nothing to suggest that the *Journal* entries in question were sketches for a proposed special "attack" on women only, dialectical or otherwise.[49] We should therefore see Kierkegaard as dealing here, not with the relationship between men and women, but with the attitude toward marriage current in the society of his day in the light of his view of Christian ideality. Certainly one can regard Kierkegaard's published "anti-marriage" statements of the last years as shock tactics, as a part of his attack on "Christendom," but these and the *Journal* entries on marriage and women ought also to be viewed in the light of other *Journal* entries that tell us not a little about attitudes in society toward married and single persons.

We learn from a number of *Journal* entries that, whereas celibacy was regarded as belonging to holiness in the Middle Ages, after the Reformation the reverse has become the case: "Fasting, celibacy, etc. is ridiculous extremism, madness, unreasonable worship of God. But marriage is the true and reasonable worship of God." Under the influence of Protestantism, marriage has not only come to be "well-pleasing to God," it now also "constitutes the meaning of life." This has affected attitudes toward the unmarried. We thus also learn that "the unmarried girl who is not lucky enough to marry . . . is overlooked and minimized." Whereas the married are regarded as the only "genuine citizens in this world," the single person "is an alien," "ridiculous." Married people regard such a person as "selfish," and just as families prefer their doctor to be married because "they are afraid that an unmarried man will be lecherous," so the congregation "will have no confidence in someone as a spiritual adviser etc. if he is not married." Even Kierkegaard's brother, Peter Christian, has, by 1848, come to believe that "the blessing of God does not rest upon an unmarried person."[50]

Even if we must consider Kierkegaard's harsh comments about women and marriage as having reference only to the situation of his time, can they say anything to us today in our cultural situation where both men and women concentrate their energies on career and family? I think they probably can. To the extent that we live in a time of overemphasis on the pursuit of sexuality in various forms, Kierkegaard's statements ought to give us pause for thought, for the "abstainer" is still regarded with suspicion as selfish and as a deviant from the "norm,"[51] while various forms of self-denial and self-renunciation tend to be understood only in relation to this-worldly goals, for example, fasting as a political protest in China. As we have seen, Kierkegaard's statements are to be understood as being linked to the basic point that he is making in his authorship, his definition of Christianity and Christian ideality, with final emphasis on asceticism in relation to the traditional hope of eternal life. It can be argued that this is still something that we can take into consideration as a possibility, instead of taking it for granted that it is "ridiculous extremism" about something untrue because it goes against our natural inclinations and our current assumptions about the nature of existence.

Notes

References are to the following works:

Kierkegaard's Collected Works: Søren Kierkegaards Samlede Vaerker, 14 vols., 1st ed., ed. A. B. Drachmann, J. L. Heiberg, and H. O. Lange (Copenhagen: Gyldendal, 1901-6); here cited as SV.

Søren Kierkegaards Papirer, vols. 1-13, 2d ed., ed. P. A. Heiberg, V. Kuhr, E. Torsting, and N. Thulstrup (Copenhagen: Gyldendal, 1968-70); index, vols. 14-16, ed. N. J. Cappelørn, 1975-78; here cited as Pap.

Søren Kierkegaard, *Kierkegaard's Writings,* ed. and tr. Howard and Edna Hong et al., general editor Howard V. Hong (Princeton: Princeton University Press, 1978-); here cited as KW. Other translations are named in the appropriate notes.

Søren Kierkegaard, *Søren Kierkegaard's Journals and Papers,* vols. 1-7, ed. and tr. Howard and Edna Hong (Bloomington: Indiana University Press, 1967-68); here cited as JP.

[1] Pap. XI, 1 A 226 cf. 281 1854 (JP IV 5000, 5003).

[2] Pap. XI, 1 A 228, 233 1854 (JP III 3175, IV 5002).

[3] Pap. XI, 1 A 426 1854, XI, 2 A 70 1854 (JP IV 5005, 5006).

[4] Pap. XI, 2 A 192 1854 pp. 207-9, cf. SV XI 163 ft. (JP IV 5007, cf. KW XIX *The Sickness unto Death* SUD 50 n).

[5] Pap. XI, 2 A 271 1855 (JP II 1823 p. 306).

[6] I Cor. 7:7-9; cf. e.g. Pap. XI, 1 A 157, 169, 313, 1854, SV XIV 199, 254, 261 (JP III 2908, 2618, 2621 p. 138, Søren Kierkegaard, *Kierkegaard's Attack Upon "Christendom"* 1854-1855, tr. Walter Lowrie (Princeton: Princeton University Press, 1968 ed.) AX 165, 213, 220).

[7] Pap. XI, 2 A 150 1854, cf. XI, 1 A 129, 150, 169, 253, 295, 313, 1854, XI, 2 A 153, 154, 160, 172, 176, 231, 238, 241, 1854, 372, 1854-55 (JP III 2622, cf. 2616-2621, 2623-2631).

[8] See Pap. XI, 1 A 210 n.d., SV II 5-140, VI 85-74, V 204-25 (JP VI 6882, KW IV EO II 5-154, KW XI *Stages on Life's Way* SLW 87-184, Søren Kierkegaard, *Thoughts on Crucial Situations in Human Life,* Three Discourses on Imagined Occasions, tr. David F. Swenson (Minneapolis: Augsburg Publishing House, 1941) TDIO 43-74, "On the Occasion of a Wedding," where Kierkegaard refers to, for example, "the sacred vocation of marriage," SV V 219, TDIO 65 (*Ægteskabets hellige Kald*).

[9] In a paper to the Søren Kierkegaard Society Denmark (Vartov, Copenhagen, 24.3.1988) psychiatrist Dr. Thorkil Vanggard suggests that Kierkegaard was very scared of a close relationship with a woman and could not cope with the physical side of marriage.

[10] Eduard Geismar, *Søren Kierkegaard,* I-II (Copenhagen: G. E. C. Gads, 1927) II, section VI 40-45. For the references to comments involving women in "The Instant" see SV XIV 175, 197, 252-56, 260, 265 (AX 145, 163, 212-16, 219-20, 223).

[11] Birgit Bertung in her paper "Yes, a Woman *Can* Exist," in *Kierkegaard Conferences I "Kierkegaard Poet of Existence."* (Copenhagen: C. A. Reitzels, 1989). See also her book, *Om Kierkegaard, Kvinder og Kærlighed* en studie i Søren Kierkegaards kvindesyn (Copenhagen: C. A. Reitzels, 1987).

[12] *International Kierkegaard Commentary: The Sickness unto Death,* ed. Robert L. Perkins, (Macon: Mercer University Press, 1987), IKC 19: 121-35.

[13] On the individual's historical context see, for example, SV I 123, II 193-94, 231, IV 301 (KW III EO I 145, KW IV EO II 216, 258, KW VIII *The Concept of Anxiety* CA 28-29). On the assertion of spiritual equality of men and women before God mentioned with their external and psycho-physical differences, see, for example, SV IX 133-34, Pap. III A 234 1842, V B 53:25 1844, XI, 1 A 231 1854, XI, 2 A 192, 193 1854 (Søren Kierkegaard, *Works of Love,* tr. Howard and Edna Hong [New York: Harper and Row, 1962] WL 139-40, JP I 95, IV 4989, 5001, 5007, 5008). In the

last two *Journal* entries women are depicted as relating directly to things, as unable to "endure a dialectic." It is interesting to compare Kierkegaard's entries here with a statement by J. L. Heiberg in 1833, when he went as far as to invite women as well as men to attend his philosophy lectures. He observed that "although men usually have a sharper and more consistent reason, a greater capacity for dialectic, women usually have a surer, more infallible feeling for immediately grasping truth." J. L. Heiberg, lecture programme: *Om Philosophiens Betydning for den nuværende Tid* (Copenhagen: 1833), 53.

[14] In this I shall be following up the thought of Gregor Malantschuk in his essay, "Kierkegaard's View of Man and Woman" in his *Controversial Kierkegaard,* tr. Howard and Edna Hong, The Kierkegaard Monography Series, ed. Alastair McKinnon (Waterloo, Ontario: Wilfred Laurier Press, 1980), 37-61. Malantschuk sees Kierkegaard in the last years as looking at everything from an "extreme Christian point of view, consequently as one who in his thinking and in his life earnestly tried to break with this world." From such a viewpoint, "the whole earthly enterprise looks different than when one feels altogether bound to it." Kierkegaard now looks at woman from the "plane of the solitary hermit." See esp. pp. 58-59.

[15] Pap. XI, 2 A 54 cf. 97 1854, II A 359, 758 1838, VII, 1 A 181 1846, X, 2 A 563 1850, XI, 1 A 491 1854, XI, 2 A 3 1854, SV I 210, IV 352 ft. VI 118, VII 220 (JP III 2570, IV 4571, 4412, II 1310, 1251, 1299, 2099, 1224, KW III EO I 236, KW VIII CA 83 ft., KW XI SLW 122, Søren Kierkegaard, *Kierkegaard's Concluding Unscientific Postscript,* tr. David F. Swenson and Walter Lowrie (Princeton: Princeton University Press, 1941) CUP 232-33. See also on God as creator out of nothing in the church fathers, Anselm, Aquinas, Augustine, references in e.g. F. C. Copleston, *Aquinas* (Great Britain: Penguin Books, 1955) 70-71, 141-48, and Copleston, *A History of Philosophy* I-VIII (London: Burns Oates and Washbourne, 1946-66), II:74-77.

[16] Pap. VII, 1 A 181 1846 (JP II 1251).

[17] Simone Weil, *Waiting on God—The Essence of Her Thought* (England: Collins, Fontana, 1959), 113-14, 102.

[18] SV XIII 382, Søren Kierkegaard, *The Concept of Irony,* tr. Lee M. Capel (London: Collins, 1966), CI 329.

[19] Pap. VII, 1 A 181 1846 (JP II 1251).

[20] See e.g. Søren Kierkegaard, *Edifying Discourses in Different Key,* "What we Learn from the Lilies of the Field and the Birds of the Air," SV VIII 245-96, esp. 269, cf. SV II 201, 161, 172 (Søren Kierkegaard, *The*

Gospel of Suffering and the Lilies of the Field, tr. David F. and Lillian M. Swenson [Minneapolis: Augsburg Publishing House, 1948], GS 165-236, esp. 197, cf. KW IV EO II 225, 178, 191).

[21] SV II 38, IV 355, 358, VII 258, XI 127-31, II 224 cf. 238, Pap. XI, 1 A 408 1854 (KW IV EO II 41, KW VIII CA 85, 88, CUP 267, KW XIX SUD 13-17, KW IV EO II 250 cf. 265, JP I 87).

[22] SV VIII 278-79 (GS 210-11).

[23] SV II 224 (KW IV EO II 250).

[24] SV IV 360 (KW VIII CA 90).

[25] Pap. XI, 2 A 123 1854, XI, 1 A 402 1854 (JP IV 4814, II 1807). Thought about opposition of the intensive and the extensive is repeated a number of times in Kierkegaard's authorship: Pap. IX A 126 1848, X, 4 A 219, 392, 1851, X, 4A 541 1849, X, 5 A 26 1852, XI, 1 A 189, 402, 414, 468, 500, 1854, XI, 2 A 64, 76, 123, 146, 1854 (JP III 2640, II 2100, 2101, 1852, 2102, 2056, 1807, III 2448, IV 4810, II 2103, 2104, IV 4813, 4814, III 2994).

[26] Pap. XI, 2 A 123, 51, 53-55 1854 (JP IV 4814, III 3099, II 1444, III 2570-71).

[27] SV II 224, 152, 133, 229, 235, cf. 18 (KW IV EO II 250, 167, 147, 255-56, 262-63, cf. 19).

[28] Pap. X, 2 A 390 1850, VIII, 1 A 196 1847, X, 2 A 351 1850, VII, 1 A 20 1846, cf. SV IX esp. 58-60 (JP III 2952, 2410, IV 4170, 4110, WL esp. 68-70).

[29] SV II 57, IX 54, 59-60 (KW IV EO II 62, WL 65, 70).

[30] On Kierkegaard's view of death see my article: "Kierkegaard's View of Death," in *Journal of the History of European Ideas* II, no. 1 (1990).

[31] SV II, 56-57, 224, 270, VI 97-98, 162-63, VII 214, Pap. IV A 234, SV VI 44-45, 112-14 (KW IV EO II 60-61, 250, 302, KW XI SLW 101-2, 171, CUP 227, KW XI SLW p. 42-43, 117).

[32] As, for example, in the "cod war" between Britain and Iceland in the seventies.

[33] Pap. XI, 2 A 108, cf. 111 (JP IV 4238, cf. 4501).

[34] SV IV 206, 215, VI 104, 161, 164, VII 401, 335-484, IX 135 (KW VII PF 39, 48, KW XI SLW 107, 169, 172, CUP 412, 347-493, WL 141).

[35] Pap. XI, 2 A 154, 201 1854, SV XIV 267, Pap. XI, 1 A 289 1854, XI, 2 A 150 1854, XI, 2 A 439, 434,

420, 1855 (JP III 2624, II 1818, AX 226, JP III 3643, 2622, VI 6969, II 1940, Søren Kierkegaard, *The Last Years Journals, 1853-55,* ed. and tr. Ronald Gregor Smith [London: Collins, Fontana, 1968] JRGS 346-47). In following up Kierkegaard's thought about Fall-doctrine, I will also be following up a comment by Eduard Geismar, *Søren Kierkegaard* II, section VI, 45, "that if one believes that most people are eternally lost, fallen, it is difficult to look positively at procreation."

[36] SV IV 363, 348, 319 (KW VIII CA 93, 79, 49).

[37] Pap. XI. 2 A 154, 150 1854, V B 55:12 1844, XI, 2 A 176, 202 1854, XI, 1 A 289 1854, XI, 2 A 439 1854, SV XIV 265, 267, Pap. XI, 2 A 434 1855 (JP III 2624, 2622, cf. KW VIII CA 198, JP III 2627, IV 3970, 3643, VI 6969, AX 223, 226, JP II 1940).

[38] SV XIV 330, cf. 256, Pap. XI, 2 A 150 1854, XI, 1 A 194 1854, X, 3 A 150 1850, XI, 1 A 158, 22, 358, 115, 1854 (AX 265 cf. 215, JP III 2622, II 1803, I 1061, II 1929, 1925, I 83, IV 4980).

[39] Pap. XI, 2 A 154 1854, XI, 2 A 439 1855, SV XIV 199, Pap. XI, 1 A 141 1854 p. 99 (JP III 2624, VI 6969, AX 165, JP IV 4998).

[40] Pap. XI, 1 A 150 1854, XI, 2 A 154, 176 1854, SV XIV 262 (JP III 2617, 2624, 2627, AX 221).

[41] Pap. IX A 424 1848, X, 3 A 293, 139 1850, XI, 1 A 139, 151, 184, 1854, X, 3 A 426 1849, X, 3 A 157 1850 SV VII 38-9, 349, Pap. XI, 2 A 183 1854, SV XI 209-10, 226-38, Pap. XI, 1 A 168 1854, XI, 2 A 164 1854, XI, 1 A 552, 524, 1854 (JP II 2217, 2221, 2218, 2224, 2225, 2227, I 843, II 2219, CUP 49, 360, JP II 1766, KW XIX SUD 99, 117-29, JP II 2054, I 370, III 3209, IV 4352).

[42] SV XIV 255-56, 53, 252, Pap. XI, 1 A 259 1854, XI, 2 A 222 1854, XI, 1 A 295 1854 (AX 215-16, 38, 212, JP IV 3969, III 2337, 2620).

[43] SV XIII 359 ft., SV XIV 252-56, 259-63, Pap. X, 2 A 181 1849, XI, 2 A 231, 226, 1854 (CI 305 ft., AX 212-16, 219-22, JP III 2608, 2628, IV 5000).

[44] See e.g. SV II 306-18, VII 100, Pap. X, 3 A 509 1850 (KW IV EO II 341-54, CUP 110, JP II 1789).

[45] Pap. X, 4 A 15 1851, XI, 1 A 226 1854, SV XII 64-65, Pap. XI, 1 A 295, 313, 1854, XI, 2 A 150, 153, 1854, XI, 1 A 552, 546, 1854, XI, 2 A 301 1853-54 (JP I 708, IV 5000, Søren Kierkegaard, *Training in Christianity,* tr. Walter Lowrie [Princeton: Princeton University Press, 1941] TX 71, JP III 2620-23, 3209, I 602, III 2543). On the duty of marriage it is interesting to note a fairy story recorded by Carl Ewald in his

Eventyrskrinet Gamle Danske Sagn og Eventyr I-V (Copenhagen and Kristiania: Gyldendalske Boghandel Nordisk, 1906-7) IV p. 35-45. "Præstekonens Synd" (The pastor's wife's sin), where because the wife deliberately marries when she is too old to have children she is regarded by the heavenly powers as having murdered her unborn children.

[46] Pap. XI, 1 A 190 n.d., 313 1854, SV XIV 253-54 (JP II 2057, III 2621, AX 213). On hating and forsaking the temporal in the New Testament see Matt. 10:37, 19:19, and 29, Mk. 10:29, 13:12, Lk. 12:52-53, 14:26, 21:16-17, Jn. 15:18.

[47] Pap. XI, 1 A 226 1854, SV XIV 197 (JP IV 5000, AX 163).

[48] Pap. XI, 1 A 279 1854 (JP III 2443).

[49] See notes 1-2 and 11 above.

[50] Pap. XI, 1 A 129 1854, XI, 2 A 154, 238 1854, XI, 1 A 169 1854, VIII, 1 A 190 1847, X, 1 A 440 1849, IX A 245 1848, X, 3 A 293 1850 (JP III 2616, 2624, 2629, 2618, 2569, 2605, 2601, II 2221).

[51] I have encountered this outlook as late as autumn 1988 in Copenhagen, where a married man with a university education described Mother Teresa of India as "selfish" for not marrying. The reason given was that she had "run away" from the responsibilities and difficulties of marriage.

Abbreviations

AN: Armed Neutrality and *An Open Letter.* Edited and translated by Howard V. Hong and Edna H. Hong. Bloomington: Indiana University Press, 1968. (*Den bevæbnede Neutralitet,* written 1848-49, published 1965; "Foranlediget ved en Yttring af Dr. Rudelbach mig betræffende," *Fædrelandet,* no. 26, 31 January 1851.)

C: The Crisis [and a Crisis] in the Life of an Actress. Translated by Stephen Crites. New York: Harper and Row, 1967. (*Krisen og en Krise i en Skuespillerindes Liv,* by Inter et Inter. *Fædrelandet,* nos. 188-91, 24-27 July 1848.)

CA: The Concept of Anxiety. Edited and translated by Reidar Thomte in collaboration with Albert B. Anderson. Princeton: Princeton University Press, 1980. (*Begrebet Angest* by Vigilius Haufniensis, edited by S. Kierkegaard, 1844.)

CD: Christian Discourses and *The Lilies of the Field and the Birds of the Air* and *Three Discourses at the Communion on Fridays.* Translated by Walter Lowrie. London: Oxford University Press, 1940.

Christelige Taler, 1848; *Lilien paa Marken og Fuglen under Himlen,* 1849; *Tre Taler ved Altergangen om Fredagen,* 1849.)

CI: The Concept of Irony with Continual Reference to Socrates, together with "Notes on Schelling's Berlin Lectures." Edited and translated by Howard V. Hong and Edna H. Hong. Princeton: Princeton University Press, 1989. (*Om Begrebet Ironi,* 1841.)

COR: The Corsair Affair. Translated by Howard V. Hong and Edna H. Hong. Princeton: Princeton University Press, 1982. (Articles by Kierkegaard and others relating to the *Corsair* affair.)

CUP: Concluding Unscientific Postscript, 2 vols. Edited and translated by Howard V. Hong and Edna H. Hong. Princeton: Princeton University Press, 1992. (*Afsluttende uvidenskabelig Efterskrift,* by Johannes Climacus, edited by S. Kierkegaard, 1846.)

EO: Either/Or, 2 vols. Edited and translated by Howard V. Hong and Edna H. Hong. Princeton: Princeton University Press, 1987. (*Enten/Eller* I-II, edited by Victor Eremita, 1843.)

EPW: Early Polemical Writings. Edited and translated by Julia Watkin. Princeton University Press, 1990. (*Af en endnu Levendes Papirer,* 1838, and early writings from before the "authorship.")

EUD: Eighteen Upbuilding Discourses. Translated by Howard V. Hong and Edna H. Hong. Princeton: Princeton University Press, 1990. (*Opbyggelige Taler,* 1843, 1844.)

FSE: For Self-Examination (published with *Judge for Yourself!*). Edited and translated by Howard V. Hong and Edna H. Hong. Princeton: Princeton University Press, 1990. (*Til Selvprøvelse,* 1851; *Dømmer Selv!* 1852.)

FT: Fear and Trembling (published with *Repetition*). Edited and translated by Howard V. Hong and Edna H. Hong. Princeton: Princeton University Press, 1983. (*Frygt og Bæven,* by Johannes de Silentio, 1843; *Gjentagelsen,* by Constantin Constantius, 1843.)

JC: Johannes Climacus. See *PF.*

JFY: Judge for Yourself! See *FSE.*

JP: Søren Kierkegaard's Journals and Papers, 7 vols. Edited and translated by Howard V. Hong and Edna H. Hong, assisted by Gregor Malantschuk. Bloomington: Indiana University Press, vol. 1, 1967; vol. 2, 1970; vols. 3 and 4, 1975; vols. 5-7, 1978. (From *Papirer* I-XIII; and *Breve og Akstykker vedrørende*

Søren Kierkegaard, 2 vols., edited by Niels Thulstrup [København: Munksgaard], 1953-54.)

KAUC: Kierkegaard's Attack upon "Christendom." Translated by Walter Lowrie. Princeton: Princeton University Press, 1944. (*Bladartikler* 1-21, *Fædrelandet,* 1854-55; *Dette skal siges; saa være det da sagt,* 1855; *Øieblikket* 1-10, 1855; *Hvad Christus dømmer om officiel Christendom,* 1855.)

LD: Kierkegaard: Letters and Documents. Translated by Henrik Rosenmeier. Princeton: Princeton University Press, 1978. (*Breve og Aktstykker vedrøende Søren Kierkegaard,* vol. 1, edited by Niels Thulstrup.)

LY: The Last Years. Translated by Ronald C. Smith. New York: Harper and Row, 1965. (From *Papirer* XI^1-XI^2.)

OAR: On Authority and Revelation: The Book on Adler, or a Cycle of Ethico-Religious Essays. Translated and edited by Walter Lowrie. Princeton: Princeton University Press, 1955. (*Bogen om Adler,* written and twice rewritten, 1846-47; unpublished except for one section, "Om Forskjellen mellem et Genie og en Apostel" ["On the Difference between a Genius and an Apostle"], *Tvende Ethisk-Religieuse Smaa-Afhandlinger,* by H. H., 1849.)

P: Prefaces: Light Reading for Certain Classes as the Occasion May Require. Translated by William McDonald. Tallahassee: Florida State University Press, 1989. (*Forord. Morskabslæsning for Enkelte Stænder efter Tid og Leilighed,* by Nicolaus Notabene, 1844.)

PAP: Søren Kierkegaards Papirer, 2d enlarged ed. 16 vols. Edited by Niels Thulstrup, with index, vols. 14-16 by N. J. Cappelørn. Copenhagen: Gyldendal, 1968-78.

PC: Practice in Christianity. Translated by Howard V. Hong and Edna H. Hong. Princeton: Princeton University Press, 1991. (*Indøvelse i Christendom,* by Anti-Climacus, edited by S. Kierkegaard, 1850.)

PF: Philosophical Fragments (published with *Johannes Climacus*). Edited and translated by Howard V. Hong and Edna H. Hong. Princeton: Princeton University Press, 1985. (*Philosophiske Smuler* by Johannes Climacus, edited by S. Kierkegaard, 1844; "Johannes Climacus eller de omnibus dubitandum est," written 1842-43, unpublished, *Papirer* IV C I.)

PV: The Point of View for My Work as an Author: A Report to History and Related Writings, including "'The Individual': Two 'Notes' Concerning My Work as an Author" and "My Activity as a Writer." Translated by Walter Lowrie. London: Oxford University Press, 1939. Reprint edited by Benjamin Nelson. New York: Harper and Row, 1962. (*Synspunktet for min*

Forfatter-Virksomhed, posthumously published 1859; *Om min Forfatter-Virksomhed,* 1851.)

R: Repetition. See *FT.*

SLW: Stages on Life's Way. Edited and translated by Howard V. Hong and Edna H. Hong. Princeton: Princeton University Press, 1988. (*Stadier paa Livets Vej,* edited by Hilarius Bogbinder, 1845.)

SUD: The Sickness unto Death. Edited and translated by Howard V. Hong and Edna H. Hong. Princeton: Princeton University Press, 1980. (*Sygdommen til Døden,* by Anti-Climacus, edited by S. Kierkegaard, 1849.)

SV: Søren Kierkegaards Samlede Værker. 1st ed. 14 vols. Edited by A. B. Drachmann, J. L. Heiberg, and H. O. Lange. Copenhagen: Gyldendalske Boghandels Forlag, 1901-6.

TA: Two Ages: The Age of Revolution and the Present Age: A Literary Review. Edited and translated by Howard V. Hong and Edna H. Hong. Princeton: Princeton University Press, 1978. (*En literair Anmeldelse: To Tidsaldre,* 1846.)

TDIO: Three Discourses on Imagined Occasions. Translated by Howard V. Hong and Edna H. Hong. Princeton: Princeton University Press, 1993. (*Tre Taler ved tænkte Leiligheder,* 1845.)

UDVS: Upbuilding Discourses in Various Spirits. Translated by Howard V. Hong and Edna H. Hong. Princeton: Princeton University Press, 1993. (*Opbyggelige Taler i forskjellig Aand,* 1847.)

WL: Works of Love. Translated by Howard V. Hong and Edna H. Hong. Princeton: Princeton University Press, 1995. (*Kjerlighedens Gjerninger,* 1847.)

Roger Poole (essay date 1998)

SOURCE: "The Unknown Kierkegaard: Twentieth-Century Receptions," in *The Cambridge Companion to Kierkegaard,* edited by Alastair Hannay and Gordon D. Marino, Cambridge University Press, 1998, pp. 48-75.

[*In the following essay, Poole surveys the treatment Kierkegaard has received at the hands of contemporary and modern critics. Additionally, Poole outlines the characteristics of Kierkegaard's "indirect communication" and comments on how this indirect approach has contributed to misreadings of the philosopher.*]

Søren Kierkegaard wrote his books for "that *individual,* whom with joy and gratitude, I call *my* reader." He opposed the ruling philosophical system of his day, despised lecturers and professors almost as much as paid churchmen, entered into dispute with his entire home town, and regarded having a disciple as the worst fate that could ever befall him. His books were written in an ironic, sophisticated, parodic style that allowed of no clear position for the reader and allowed of no definite result either.

It cannot be a matter of surprise, then, that the history of the reception of his work must be an account of the ways that individuals have reacted to his work. Time and time again, it is noticeable that, at a key point of their own thinking, philosophers, theologians, and writers have been influenced by the almost "random" encounter with Kierkegaard, both by his passionate and ambiguous private journal, which he kept throughout his lifetime, and the rich and ambivalent work he published between 1843 and 1855.

There can be no attempt, that is, to "fit" Kierkegaard into some overarching scheme, such as the history of German Romanticism, or of idealism, or even of the history of existentialism. However he is "placed" in any such history, Kierkegaard remains inassimilable to it. His irony and his many-voiced-ness, his *heteroglossia,* distance him from any position that could be asserted to be finally "his" position. In the last twenty years or so, much more attention has been paid than before to his actual manner of writing, his sheer literary virtuosity, which consists of playing just within, and yet just outside of, the conventions of the ruling "Romantic Irony" of his time, such that he has made any final "closure" on the matter of "his" meaning impossible. With this new "literary" perception of his work he has taken on a new status as a postmodernist, someone who, in a certain sense, is writing "after Derrida" in what Harold Bloom would call an *apophrades.*

Kierkegaard wrote for "that individual," and through time he has in fact been read by "that individual," and remains important for those making an individual, dissonant, or even subversive, contribution to their own subject. Official, academic philosophy does not have much use for him, is given to denying him philosophical status, and quite often raises the question as to whether he is even of any philosophical interest. And all this is exactly the way Kierkegaard would have wanted it.

After a tempestuous life, he died amidst recrimination, odium, and scandal. When he died in 1855, the Danish public, exhausted by the demands he had made on it, consigned the man and his works to oblivion, hoping never to hear his name again. This attitude was encouraged by his brother, Bishop Peter Christian Kierkegaard, who had done his best to subvert Søren's cause while he was alive and included in his funeral oration some remarks that were little short of excuses for a brother who had become unhinged. Two assiduous scholars, H. P. Barfod and H. Gottsched, collected editions of Kierkegaard's papers, which appeared between 1869 and 1881. The bishop kept many of the papers back for himself, and, as they arranged their entries, Barfod threw away the originals, thus creating a problem that has bedeviled Kierkegaard scholarship ever since.

I. The Danish, German, and French Reception

Danish philosophy never took Kierkegaard up at a serious level. The first monograph about him (1877) was by the positivist philosopher Georg Brandes, and it is on record that Brandes himself said that, just as he had attacked German Romanticism in order to hit indirectly at the Danish Romantics, so he wrote about Kierkegaard to free the Danes from his influence. Brandes may not have had to try very hard, for the Danes were never in danger of being seriously under Kierkegaard's influence in the first place. Nevertheless, Brandes' book certainly gave the seal of philosophical disapproval that has kept Kierkegaard's writings unread and unpopular until very recent times.

Brandes must have had second thoughts, however, for ten years after his book came out, he wrote to Friedrich Nietzsche telling him that he must read Kierkegaard. Nietzsche replied that, on his next visit to Germany, he intended to work upon "the psychological problem" of Kierkegaard. That Nietzsche was interested enough to want to do so is interesting. Here is a major intellectual confrontation of the nineteenth century that never took place.

Subsequent Danish philosophical accounts of Kierkegaard were equally dismissive. Harald Høffding, another philosopher of a positivist persuasion, gave Kierkegaard very low marks for philosophical acumen in his *Søren Kierkegaard as a Philosopher* (1919). The noted historian Troels Frederik Troels-Lund, who was related to Kierkegaard, and a man of considerable influence in the literary circles of his day, opined, in his two autobiographical essays of 1922 and 1924, that Kierkegaard was little better than an eccentric, though obviously one of genius—a typically Danish evasion of the problem. Troels-Lund remembers the wandering philosopher with affection and admiration, admits that he was personally influenced by him in a way that changed the course of his entire life, and yet could not find it in his heart to say that Kierkegaard's existential thinking would or could have any lasting importance.

It was abroad that Kierkegaard's "indirect communication" began to fascinate individuals here and there. Kierkegaard's influence can only be decisive within a personal problematic that exists already. He modifies a worldview, in a suggestive and insidious way. Franz Kafka is a perfect example:

> Today I got Kierkegaard's **Buch des Richters.** As I suspected, his case, despite essential differences, is very similar to mine, at least he is on the same side of the world. He bears me out like a friend.[1]

This is how the reading of Kierkegaard usually goes: a sudden self-identification with the thought of the man, which has a compelling existential significance, and which causes a reformulation of all existing personal thought-structures. Kafka continued to meditate on Kierkegaard, as a diary entry for 27 August 1916 shows:

> Give up too those nonsensical comparisons you like to make between yourself and a Flaubert, a Kierkegaard, a Grillparzer. That is simply infantile . . . Flaubert and Kierkegaard knew very clearly how matters stood with them, were men of decision, did not calculate but acted. But in your case—a perpetual succession of calculations, a monstrous four years' up and down.[2]

There is a certain irony in considering Flaubert and Kierkegaard as men of decision, as men of action. This may be an indication of the extent to which Kafka needed to impose a strong misreading on the text of his own life. But it is typical of the way that the oblique effect of Kierkegaard's indirect communication has the power to generate new directions of thought.

It was the same in the case of the philosopher Karl Jaspers, who was at the time (1913) working in a psychiatric hospital in Heidelberg. The "treatments" were based upon the principles of Kraepelin. Kraepelin believed that mental illnesses were diseases of the brain, and so the patients were kept strapped down or immersed for hours in hot baths. Jaspers was appalled at the sheer philosophical primitiveness of this model of mental illness. It was in reading Kierkegaard that Jaspers became convinced that "mental illness" is most often nothing but an important event in the structure and development of the *Existenz* of the patient. The discovery of the concept of *Existenz* itself, and the emphasis and importance Jaspers attributed to it throughout an entire writing life, cannot but be derived from an attentive reading of Kierkegaard, where the concept of existence is foregrounded in so many works. Jaspers, in his work in psychiatry, began to wonder if some mental states did not actually allow us "fleeting glimpses of the ultimate source of *Existenz*." In the case of a Van Gogh, for instance, or Strindberg or Hölderlin or Swedenborg, could we actually speak of any of these as being "mad"? It was doubtless also due to an attentive reading of Kierkegaard's "indirect communication," that Jaspers came to regard the "will to total communication" as the basis of all true philosophical method. This doctrine he set out in his 1935 lectures, published as *Reason and Existence*.[3] The importance of fully personal, authentic communication emerges again as late as the 1947 lecture at the university of Basel published as *Der philosophische Glaube.*[4] Kierkegaard's communication, which he insisted upon calling "indirect," has most often been indirect in its effect and, quite often too, only indirectly alluded to, even by those who have fallen heavily under its influence. In the case of Heidegger, the affliction Harold Bloom calls "The Anxiety of Influence" is particularly marked. Heidegger, struggling with Husserl for the effective leadership of the phenomenological enterprise, remorselessly ransacks Kierkegaard in his magisterial *Sein und Zeit* (1927). Although there are the minimal footnote acknowledgments demanded by academic custom, the extent to which Kierkegaard has supplied Heidegger with many if not most of his main poetical *trouvailles* is something Heidegger spends a great deal of art trying to hide.

Angest is one of the most striking ones, of course. It was Kierkegaard who, writing under the pseudonym Vigilius Haufniensis in 1844, had elevated *Angest* (dread) to the dignity of a concept. "If then we ask further what is the object of dread," writes Vigilius, "the answer as usual must be that it is nothing. Dread and nothing regularly correspond to one another."[5] The sheer audaciousness of this inspired Heidegger to his own flight of fancy:

> That in the face of which one has anxiety is characterised by the fact that what threatens it is *nowhere.* Anxiety "does not know" what that, in the face of which it is anxious, is . . . it is already "there" and yet nowhere; it is so close that it is oppressive and stifles one's breath, and yet it is nowhere.[6]

The linguistic categories, too, are derived from Kierkegaard. Kierkegaard had written, in that passionate outpouring of bile he called "The Present Age" in *A Literary Review,* of "The Public" as "a monstrous Nothing."[7] The nature of public speech was itself "a monstrous Nothing." The linguistic categories of modernity are "talkativeness," "formlessness," "superficiality," "flirtation," and what is called "reasoning."[8]

The closeness of Heidegger's imitations should be a matter for a little embarrassment, perhaps. Heidegger writes out his own linguistic categories of modernity as "Idle Talk," "Curiosity," "Ambiguity," and "Falling and Thrownness."[9] All of these are uttered by that abstraction called *"Das Man,"* usually translated as "the 'They.'"[10] Kierkegaard had inveighed against loose public speech, comparing it to a masterless dog, which is free to bite all and sundry, but for which no one is responsible.[11] Heidegger's "Idle Talk" (*Gerede*) is defined as "*gossiping* and *passing the word along.*" "Idle talk is the possibility of understanding everything without previously making the thing one's own."[12] It is impossible to reproduce Kierkegaard's meaning more closely than this, without actually quoting directly from the text. But this Heidegger will not do. *Dasein* itself, that master-trope of the Heideggerian discourse, is, in its various modalities of "Care," drawn directly from the Kierkegaardian analysis of *dread.* "*Dasein's* being reveals itself as *care.*"[13] Vigilius Haufniensis describes the "vertigo" (*Svimmel*) before choice, which leads to the Fall. The relation of Heidegger's "Falling" and "Thrownness" to Kierkegaard's ironic treatment of "The Fall" in ***The Concept of Dread*** needs some properly ironic exposure.

Of course, Heidegger's philosophical purpose in borrowing thus shamelessly from Kierkegaard was his own. Concerned not to existentialize but to phenomenologize and ontologize his concepts, he shrank from suggesting that individuals were ethically responsible in any real political or practical world. Patricia J. Huntington, in a recent essay, has described the results of this decision on Heidegger's part.[14] In a section of her essay called "Heidegger's De-Ethicization of Kierkegaard," she observes that "Heidegger's deliberate efforts to sever psychological matters from epistemology led him to underplay the role of interiority in how I engage, assume complicity with, or position myself in relation to reigning world-views. . . . Heidegger's tendency to attribute blame for his participation in National Socialism to destiny seems consistent with his de-ethicization of Kierkegaard's concept of guilt."[15]

Every thinker who falls under Kierkegaard's sway does so for his own reasons. Kierkegaard's effect on theologians has usually been because of the existential nature of his own theological thinking. The Paradox, the God in Time, the Moment, contemporaneous discipleship, these themes, so strongly stated in the Kierkegaardian oeuvre, have had a great attractiveness to theologians trying to make sense of the literal and historical claims of Christianity in a modern skeptical world. One important theologian, whose life was brutally cut short by the Nazis in 1945, was Dietrich Bonhoeffer, whose *Letters and Papers from Prison* introduced to the world the idea of "religionless Christianity."[16]

Early influenced as an academic theologian by Kierkegaard, Bonhoeffer later had reason to come to understand the existential or lived nature of Christianity when he was imprisoned in 1943 for his resistance to Hitler and for his involvement in a plot on his life. During the two years he wrote his *Letters and Papers* in Tegel prison, he was forced to conceive of a Christianity that would become entirely a matter of the individual conscience, a faith shorn of all the trappings of "religion" and one that might very well have to become an "arcane discipline" and go underground for a thousand years. In "a world come of age," there was no longer any place for religion as form, for religion as organized practice. In the Third Reich things had become too serious for that. In prison, Bonhoeffer was recognized, by fellow inmates and by warders alike, to be living out a form of the Imitatio Christi, and he had a copy of Thomas à Kempis' masterwork in the cell with him. His taking on of the secular authorities of his time, his deliberate entry into the political events of his own Germany, unheard of for a Lutheran pastor, was deeply indebted to that Kierkegaard who had found it his duty in his own time to enter into conflict with the whole established Danish Church.

If Heidegger had phenomenologized Kierkegaard, it was Jean-Paul Sartre who existentialized him. Sartre, however, as a Marxist could not accede to the Christianity of Kierkegaard and like Heidegger had to occlude the extent of his debt to him. Thus the reading of, say, *l'Être et le Néant* (1943) is an uncanny experience, in which Kierkegaard's influence is everywhere though his name is unspoken. The central idea, however, of personal authenticity, of the avoidance of *mauvaise foi,* indeed the entire scope of the existentialist notion of a free and responsible human life in a world of "bourgeois" hypocrisy and mediocrity, is in fact Kierkegaardian, however little it may be acknowledged. The phenomenological descriptions of the body, the debate with Kierkegaard on "vertigo" and "anguish" in the section called "The Origin of Nothingness," the concept of freedom laid upon us as an unavoidable fate, all these are derived from an anxious reading of the early pseudonymous works of Kierkegaard.[17] In his novel *l'Âge de Raison* (1945) for example:

> All around him things were gathered in a circle, expectant, impassive, and indicative of nothing. He was alone, enveloped in this monstrous silence, free and alone, without assistance and without excuse, condemned to decide without support from any quarter, condemned for ever to be free.[18]

It is the world exactly as Kierkegaard described it, and by an act of magical fictional transformation Sartre has transformed it into an existentialist vision of the modern world. Nevertheless, Sartre never ceased trying to evade the issue of his debt to Kierkegaard; and as late as 1964, when UNESCO held a conference on Kierkegaard in Paris, of which the proceedings were published as *Kierkegaard Vivant,*[19] Sartre insisted blindly that he was free of debt to Kierkegaard. It will hardly do. One has only to reread the Sartrean "empathetic" reconstructions of the lived worlds of Baudelaire, of Genet, of Flaubert to realize the extent to which Sartre derived from Kierkegaard the doctrine that "freedom alone can account for a person in his totality."[20]

Paradoxically enough, however, it was Hegelianism that was the most influential philosophical tendency during the Occupation of Paris by the Nazis. Alexandre Kojève's lectures on Hegel in the late 1930s had chimed in exactly with the mood of the moment. Just as Kierkegaard has been Hegelianized in the last twenty years, so in the Paris of the 1930s Hegel was being Kierkegaardianized. Sartre attended Kojève's lectures, as did Jean Wahl, Maurice Merleau-Ponty, Simone de Beauvoir, and Jean Hyppolite. All fell under the influence of Kojève's "Hegel" to a greater or less degree. But the political strain of reading Hegel while Paris was occupied proved too great for Simone de Beauvoir, who writes in her autobiography:

> I went on reading Hegel, and was now beginning to understand him rather better. His amplitude of detail dazzled me, and his System as a whole made me feel giddy. It was indeed tempting to abolish one's individual self and merge with Universal Being, to observe one's own life in the perspective of Historical Necessity. . . . But the least flutter of my heart gave such speculations the lie. Hate, anger, expectation or misery would assert themselves against all my efforts to by-pass them, and this "flight into the Universal" merely formed one further episode in my private development. I turned back to Kierkegaard, and began to read him with passionate interest. . . . Neither History, nor the Hegelian System could, any more than the Devil in person, upset the living certainty of "I am, I exist, here and now, I am myself."[21]

In the mid-1940s, then, out of this conflict between Kierkegaard and Hegel, emerged the existentialism of the Left Bank, of the cafés and the Caves. The philosophical and political situation was experienced as one of diremption, of bad faith, of unwilling complicity. Simone de Beauvoir's *Pour une Morale de l'Ambiguité* (1947) gives the tone exactly. It is not surprising that the Kierkegaardian category of "The Absurd" was reconceived and projected into this modern moment. Sartre had used the idea in *La Nausée* (1938) in his brilliant cadenza on the "superfluousness" of the external world, and in particular the root of a chestnut tree. But the absurdity of the external world was a result of its being unnecessary. No God had created it, no force required its presence, it has no meaning.

It was doubtless this aspect of the Absurd, that everything existed without God, and in spite of there being no God, that led the young Albert Camus to give lapidary expression to the concept of the Absurd in *Le Mythe de Sisyphe* (1942). Kierkegaard's frank acceptance of the logical unthinkability of the central doctrine of Christianity, and his relegation of this problem to the Absurd, had allowed in turn, a hundred years later, of a translation into the secular world, in the form of a secular Absurd. Camus' text is, as it were, ***Philosophical Fragments,*** with all its premises, and yet taking its conclusion literally. The Absurd in Kierkegaard might best be seen as a category introduced to make livable something that is unthinkable. "The Absurd is sin without God" is Camus's answering proposal. Camus found in Kierkegaard an ideal model for an existentialism without God. The absence of God being so painful, the Absurd is the only way out. Camus, of course, is a militant atheist, but it is often to atheists, as Graham Greene suggests again and again in his novels, that powerful theological arguments most appeal.

In *Le Mythe de Sisyphe,* Camus sums it up in a question:

> Kierkegaard can cry out, and warn: "If man did not have an eternal spirit, if, at the bottom of things, there were nothing but a wild and tempestuous power producing everything, the great as well as the mean in the whirlwind of obscure passions, if the bottomless emptiness which nothing can fill were hidden beneath everything, what would life be, if not despair?" This cry has nothing in it which could bring Absurd man to a halt. To look for that which is true must be distinguished from looking for that which would be desirable. If, in order to escape Kierkegaard's anguished question "What would life be?" it is necessary to feed, like the poor ass, on the roses of illusion rather than to resign itself to a lie, the Absurd spirit prefers to adopt Kierkegaard's answer: "despair." Everything considered, the resolute soul will manage to get along with that.[22]

II. The British and American Reception

The German period of phenomenology and the French period of existentialism had, of course, no corresponding movements in England. Postidealist philosophy in England, under the influence of Bertrand Russell, G. E. Moore, Ludwig Wittgenstein, and eventually, after A. J. Ayer's *Language, Truth and Logic* of 1936, what came to be known as "Oxford" philosophy, was resolutely opposed to the "woolly abstractions" of "Continental philosophy," and developed along a parallel and entirely independent path. Indeed, sadly, even the most superficial connections between these two traditions of philosophy were hardly maintained. Edmund Husserl came to give four lectures in German at University College in 1922. His major work "The Crisis of European Sciences," Parts I and II of which were published in the Belgrade review *Philosophia* in 1936, went unnoticed. As the thirties darkened with the threat of war, only one spark of interest in Kierkegaard's work could have been observed in England, and that was the editorial effort of Charles Williams at the Oxford University Press.

Charles Williams was one of that group of Oxford intellectuals known as "The Inklings," a group that included J. R. Tolkien, C. S. Lewis and Owen Barfield. Charles Williams had come to perceive some prophetic quality in the writings of the Danish master and set out on a one-man crusade to get as much of it as possible into translation and into print as fast as he could. He

entered into communication with Alexander Dru and invited him to translate a selection from the then unknown *Journals and Papers.* Dru responded with the magnificent *The Journals of Kierkegaard 1834—1854,* which appeared in 1938. It made Kierkegaard's inner thought-world available in English for the first time in any completeness and set the standard for Kierkegaard research for a generation.

But Charles Williams was also in contact with the retired American pastor Walter Lowrie, whose enthusiasm for Kierkegaard was just as great as Williams's own. Lowrie's great biography *Kierkegaard,* which also appeared in 1938, had the same trailblazing quality for the American reading public as Dru's translation of the *Journals* had for the British. It is typical of the pure and ascetic quality of Charles Williams's mind that he should have elected just these two men to act as translators for the Oxford University Press. They both understood Kierkegaard inwardly and translated him as a labor of love. Their translations seize the linguistic appropriateness and the accurate tonality every time, even when (as happens quite often in Lowrie's translations) there are errors at the level of the literal sense.

Thus it was that, from the New York office of the Oxford University Press, Walter Lowrie's translations appeared in a regular flow: *Christian Discourses* (1939); *The Point of View for My Work as an Author* (1939); (in collaboration with Alexander Dru) *The Present Age* and *Two Minor Ethico-Religious Treatises* (1940); *Training in Christianity* (1941); *For Self-Examination* and *Judge for Yourselves!* (1941); and, in a collaborative enterprise between Oxford University Press and Princeton University Press, appeared *Stages on Life's Way* (1940); *Repetition, Fear and Trembling, The Sickness unto Death* and the completion of David Swenson's monumental *Concluding Unscientific Postscript,* all in 1941; with *The Concept of Dread,* the completion of the second volume of *Either/Or* (again left unfinished by David Swenson), and *Attack upon "Christendom" 1854—1855,* all in 1944.[23]

Walter Lowrie's remarkably rapid productivity meshed in with a much more slowly paced, but nevertheless meticulous, activity of translation, that of David F. Swenson of Minnesota. As he tells it himself, Swenson's first encounter with Kierkegaard was a kind of conversion, and he spent the rest of his life trying, through his teaching and translating, to express a debt to Kierkegaard that he thought of as unpayable.[24] Thus it was that his early translation of *Philosophical Fragments* (1936) was followed by the translations of the two most extensive works in the *oeuvre, Concluding Unscientific Postscript* (1941) and *Either/Or* (1944). But his death in February 1940 meant that he left both of these vast works uncompleted, and it fell to Walter Lowrie to complete *Postscript* and the second volume of *Either/*

Or. In a collaborative effort with his wife, Lillian Marvin Swenson, David Swenson also posthumously made available the "edifying" stream of the authorship. The four volumes of *Edifying Discourses* appeared between 1943 and 1946 from the Augsburg Publishing House in Minneapolis. *Works of Love* appeared in 1946, and *The Gospel of Suffering* and *The Lilies of the Field* in 1948.

III. Blunt Reading

The fact that the original translators were theologians or philosophers of religion has had a decisive effect upon the way that Kierkegaard has been received in the United States and indeed throughout the English-speaking world. There was from the first a remarkably impoverished awareness of Kierkegaard as a writer, as a stylist, and as a rhetorician.

Lowrie had spent his life as an ordained minister before he began to translate Kierkegaard in retirement. Swenson was a professor of religion at the University of Minnesota from 1898 until 1939. This emplacement within theology is the reason why Kierkegaard was translated as he was, to a very great extent translated as an orthodox Christian believer, and also translated in a manner that paid extraordinarily little attention to the contours of what Kierkegaard obsessively used to refer to as his "indirect communication."

Kierkegaard put a great deal of thought and reflection into the construction of his "indirect communication." It was his belief that what he had to say could not be proposed in some direct, blunt manner, like the "paragraph communication" of the Hegelian professors. His indirection consisted, then, partly in the use of pseudonyms for many of his works; partly in the use of an unremitting irony that did not allow of the reader's "placing" him as author within his own thought-process; partly in the fact that he issued a stream of "edifying discourses" to "accompany" the works that he called "aesthetic"; and partly in the fact that the indirection of the communication consisted very largely in setting up a "lived presence" in Copenhagen, the streets and squares of the town, that would "counteract" or "work against" (*modarbejde*) or in some other way dialectically inflect or subvert the expectations about him personally that had been set up by his works, both edifying and aesthetic. The "indirect communication," then, consisted of at least four elements from the start and was cunningly woven together in terms of a known cultural space. It was made even more complex than this four-part intention would allow for, when in early 1846 Kierkegaard found himself attacked and lampooned in the pages of a popular magazine called *The Corsair.* The effect upon his sensibility of the crude cartoons by P. Klaestrup, as well as the hurtful and spiteful articles, forced him to abandon his walks in the town and to modify in a dramatic way the structure

of the fourth part of the "indirect communication." Thus, the "indirect communication" expanded from being a four-part to a five-part intention, and the demands made upon the reader became of an advanced degree of subtlety.[25]

Most of this subtlety was lost on the plain, honest mind of Walter Lowrie. In his footnotes and prefaces, Lowrie consistently diminished the importance of the first three elements in the "indirect communication": he virtually disregarded the use of pseudonyms; very largely missed the irony; and he believed that the entire "aesthetic" stream was simply there to drive the reader into reading the "edifying" stream, thus, so to speak, "getting the point" of the whole enterprise. Thus, in his translator's preface to *The Concept of Dread,* for instance, probably the most ironic and certainly the most parodic of all the aesthetic works, Lowrie can quite seriously opine: "We need not therefore apply to this book S K's emphatic admonition not to attribute to him anything that is said by his pseudonyms. This was his first completely serious book, and everything we find in it may safely be regarded as his own way of thinking."[26] Why, then, one might ask, did Kierkegaard bother to write the work under a pseudonym at all? Why would he have been so "emphatic" in his "admonition" if he had intended Walter Lowrie to disregard it completely?

Lowrie's method of reading, however, spread widely, due to the prestige of his translations, and it might perhaps best be called "blunt reading." Blunt reading is that kind of reading that refuses, as a matter of principle, to accord a literary status to the text; that refuses the implications of the pseudonymous technique; that misses the irony; that is ignorant of the reigning Romantic ironic conditions obtaining when Kierkegaard wrote; and that will not acknowledge, on religious grounds, that an "indirect communication" is at least partly bound in with the *pathos* of the lived life.

The Lowrie translations were often carried out in haste, and Lowrie often made blunders at the literal level. Plainly a new and scholarly edition was necessary. It fell to the two dedicated Kierkegaard scholars and translators Howard V. Hong and Edna H. Hong to provide the learned world with what was required. First, they translated the *Journals and Papers,* which appeared from the Indiana University Press from 1967 to 1978. Then, in a major effort beginning in 1980 and which is nearing completion, they undertook the translation of all the works, which have appeared from the Princeton University Press under the title *Kierkegaard's Writings.*

It goes without saying that this major edition, especially with its massive annotation and addenda of relevant journal entries for each work, has changed the climate for Kierkegaard studies and made available an edition that can be used internationally. If there is a drawback, it consists in the fact that the translation of key terms, which Kierkegaard uses again and again in different contexts, has been decided upon by an editorial committee, and that these terms have always to be translated the same way, irrespective of context. The existential, humorous, continuously self-referring nature of Kierkegaard's syntax is expunged from the translation. In effect, what the Princeton translations do, is constantly to imply that Kierkegaard is laying down the law or proposing truth or telling us something, whereas, sufficiently understood, the Kierkegaardian text does not tell us something, it asks us something.

And Kierkegaard is, first and foremost, a writer. The parallel is surely with Plato. Plato used the dialogue form, so as to achieve a certain degree of "indirect communication" in his dialogues, that precluded the reader from deciding, once and for all, what his, Plato's, "own view" was. Plato also uses Socrates as a figure of irony, within the dialogues, such that the literal, final, "Hegelian" meaning is forever impossible quite to grasp hold of. He also uses mistakes and traps and apparent forgetfulnesses to achieve a dramatic structure. Above all, it has been necessary to distinguish, in Plato's work, the "written" and the "unwritten" doctrines.

In spite of the dramatic and dialectical structure of Kierkegaard's texts, though, the tradition of "blunt reading" insists on interpreting him as a "serious" writer who is didactic, soluble and at bottom, "edifying." His puzzles are only seemingly so. His meaning is, by assiduous effort, capable of final solution. Thus the tradition of scholarship represented by C. Stephen Evans, for instance, attempts to "solve" the mystery of *Philosophical Fragments,* first in a book of 1983, *Kierkegaard's Fragments and Postscript: The Religious Philosophy of Johannes Climacus,* and then, a decade later, in *Passionate Reason: Making Sense of Kierkegaard's Philosophical Fragments.*[27] It is this determined effort to "make sense" of something that is taken as being in a state of disarray, or confusion, from which it has to be rescued by the efforts of the academic philosopher, that provides the risible side of the tradition of "blunt reading." Would it be possible to entitle a book *Making Sense of Plato's Theaetetus?*

The efforts of the "blunt reader" are ultimately doomed to failure, though, because the direction of attention is 180 degrees in the wrong direction. Kierkegaard's text does not offer itself to be the object of the question "What does it mean?" It offers itself as the proponent of the question "What do you think?"

It goes without saying that, given these literalist and fundamentalist assumptions, given this kind of readerly intentionality, the entire dialectical structure of the Kierkegaardian text will be simply invisible. Kierkegaard will go on and on saying what the critics expect him to say, because they are always asking him the same question. Unless the critic is unusually candid and open, unless he or she is unusually aware that what you derive from a text will be very much what you put into it in the first place, the hermeneutic adventure will never begin.

It should by now have emerged clearly enough that the major problem in the reception of Kierkegaard has been the hermeneutic one: how, in what way, adequately to read Kierkegaard? Derrida could write, at the beginning of *Glas,*

> Quoi du reste aujourd'hui, pour nous, ici, maintenant, d'un Hegel?

We might well then ask

> What, after all, today, for us, here, now, about Kierkegaard?

The reason that so little satisfaction has been achieved is due largely to the refusal to take seriously the nature of the "indirect communication," the refusal to pay it more than lip service. Yet, an "authorship" so consciously crafted refuses to give up its secrets to those who choose to disregard the author's intentions. "My wish, my prayer," writes Kierkegaard in his own name, at the end of the *Postscript,* "is, that if it might occur to anyone to quote a particular saying from the books, he would do me the favour to cite the name of the respective pseudonymous author."[28] Since the learned world has refused him the fulfillment of his prayer, it is not surprising if his work resists all attempts at forcible entry.

Theologians, as well as philosophers of religion, have made heavy weather of his work. An early work by Paul Sponheim, *Kierkegaard and Christian Coherence* (1968), so far from facing the problems raised by the pseudonyms, subsumes them all under its overarching theme. His aim is to demonstrate the underlying harmony in the works, a harmony that would be based upon the figure, nature, and reality of Christ himself in Kierkegaard's thought. While of course, you *can* achieve such a reading by ignoring the fact that Climacus and Anti-Climacus disagree profoundly about the nature of Christ, you can only do so against the grain of the texts, and your result will be spurious. John Elrod, in his *Being and Existence in Kierkegaard's Pseudonymous Works* (1975), commits this error consciously and as a matter of policy. Refusing heterogeneity to the pseudonyms, Elrod mediates the distinctions set up by them and reads them as mere developments on the way to a conception of a unified "self," which would be, ultimately, consistent with the Christian doctrine, the Christian hope, of a self no longer at odds with itself. A harmonious and pleasing thought, though far from a

Kierkegaardian one. Continuing this tradition of deliberate misreading, George Connell, as late as 1985, in his *To Be One Thing: Personal Unity in Kierkegaard's Thought,* makes the same resolute gesture of refusal to Kierkegaard's "wish and prayer." He refuses autonomy to the pseudonyms and insists that the works move through "varieties of turbulence" and "the negative oneness of the ironist" toward the unity of the religious self. Excellent, except that the Kierkegaardian originals work hard against any such easy assumption. By the constant use of "difference" between the views of the pseudonyms, Kierkegaard has made any such serendipitous "oneness of the Christian self" impossible. He insists on diremption to the last, and only the determinedly "theological" reading can manage to "unify" so many jarringly different accounts of what it is to be a "Christian self."

The same problem, the refusal of autonomy to the pseudonyms, is at the root of the unhappiness in expositions of Kierkegaard that concentrate on his "aesthetics." In the footsteps of Mark Taylor, George Pattison, in *Kierkegaard: The Aesthetic and the Religious* (1992), and Sylvia Walsh, in *Living Poetically, Kierkegaard's Existential Aesthetics* (1994), manage, by reducing the specificity and the sheer incompatibility of the pseudonyms' views, to impose a Hegelian pattern upon them, in which they become mere *Gestalten* in a kind of phenomenology of the aesthetic. Sylvia Walsh reads the pseudonyms as "moments" of a coming-to-comprehension-of-itself of a "Kierkegaardian" view of the aesthetic. She assumes that Kierkegaard was a philosopher of an aquiline and transcendental kind, staring down upon his creations from the height of a fixed, single "philosophy" of how the "aesthetic" relates to the "ethical" and the "religious." Like the translating committee of the Princeton edition of *Kierkegaard's Works,* she assumes that Kierkegaard was in perfect control of his work, whereas it is evident that Kierkegaard struggled with each and every work, at the limits of his endurance, aiming to *survive,* writing, as the poet Lorca says of Goya, "with his fists and his elbows."

Neither, ultimately, can the "indirect communication" and the devices of pseudonymity be simply, in the last analysis, abandoned, in order to come, as George Pattison believes that the theologian can come at last, once all the games are over, to a pure and uncontaminated *gnosis.* It is part of the convention of Kierkegaardian writing, as it is of Platonic writing, that the artistic devices of dialogue and displacement play their role until the very end, forbidding any withdrawal to "higher" conceptual ground.

Some philosophers have refused to take account of the "indirect communication" and the principle of pseudonymity, simply because they *will* not deal with it and are determined to talk "philosophy" with "Kierkegaard,"

whichever one of the strange many-colored costumes he may choose to turn up in. Stephen N. Dunning's *Kierkegaard's Dialectic of Inwardness: A Structural Analysis of the Theory of Stages* (1985), for instance, is one of the most brilliant pieces of straight philosophical reconstruction in the literature. But, as its title indicates, it moves straight through the aesthetic works and, as it goes, departs further and further from any possible verisimilitude. Hegel may well have thought like this, in "Stages" across "works," but Kierkegaard had made it a matter of principle to make sure that pseudonymity builds contradiction into the discourse and makes all linear or "structural" progress impossible.

There have been philosophers however, who have recognized the heterogeneity of the pseudonyms and chosen to argue strictly philosophically *within* those constraints, and this is going a very long way toward reading Kierkegaard as he desired to be read. H. A. Nielsen's *Where the Passion Is: A Reading of Kierkegaard's Philosophical Fragments* (1983) takes the pseudonymity of Climacus seriously and acknowledges straight away that he occupies a position *outside* Christianity. "Climacus offers himself as a sort of lens-grinder, a sharpener of perceptions. . . . Through his art the reader may be helped to discern sameness, and where there is not, to discern difference."[29] A refreshing change of emphasis. Robert C. Roberts's *Faith, Reason and History: Rethinking Kierkegaard's Philosophical Fragments* (1986) is another such breakthrough study. "I am proposing to read Kierkegaard as he intended to be read . . . he does not want to be read as *Kierkegaard.* He wants, instead, to be a dispensable vehicle for his reader's coming to understand *other* things. . . . The present book is an experiment in honouring Kierkegaard's desire to be read in a more primitive way . . . I shall treat Climacus with experimental tentativeness and personal independence that befits reading such an ironic author." Roberts dismisses Niels Thulstrup's view (that **Fragments** represents Kierkegaard's "own views") with contempt. "Nowhere in Kierkegaard's writings is the irony as unwearied, incessant, dark and masterful as it is in this book."[30]

This shows that things, within philosophy as such, are on the move. Jeremy Walker, too, in his *The Descent into God* (1985) has a crisp, no-nonsense attitude toward reading the text that constitutes a very timely recall to priorities: "This situation should not continue. It is in the interests of scholarship in its widest sense, that we (*a*) pay Kierkegaard the elementary compliment of using his own chosen titles: (*b*) recall that he wrote and thought in Danish—just as Plato wrote in Greek, Aquinas in Latin, and Kant in German—and begin to read him in his own language; and (*c*) refrain from using English titles which cut English-language scholarship partially off from concurrent scholarly work in, say, French and German."[31]

Alastair Hannay, too, may be counted as one of those who take the pseudonymity seriously, and yet manage to argue consequently and rigorously within those constraints at a philosophical level. His *Kierkegaard* (1982, rev. ed. 1991) is a study determined to come to grips with what is living and what is dead in Kierkegaard's philosophy. In order to give Kierkegaard just that wider context that Jeremy Walker desiderates, Hannay discusses his thought in the context of Hegel, Kant, Feurbach, Marx, and Wittgenstein. "I found that the most effective way of bringing out the latent structure and logical content of Kierkegaard's writings was to compare and contrast his views with those of accredited philosophers whose thought is better known and more accessible."[32] Hannay translated that most contemporary of Kierkegaard's texts, *Fear and Trembling,* for the Penguin Classics in 1985, and it is significant that, as a result of that activity, he has almost entirely rewritten Chapter 3 in his new edition of 1991, in order to point up the debts to Kant in that work. Hannay wants, by this means, to make a serious philosophical claim about the importance of *Fear and Trembling* in the context of today. Like Ronald Green, whose work on Kierkegaard and Kant over the last fifteen years has been one of the ticking bombs in Kierkegaard scholarship,[33] Alastair Hannay believes that Kierkegaard's debts to Kant are at least as great as those to Hegel, and he cites Alasdair MacIntyre as the origin of that insight. After translating *Fear and Trembling* in 1985, Alastair Hannay translated, for the Penguin Classics series, *The Sickness unto Death* (1989), *Either/Or* (1995), and a selection from the *Journals* (1996). Hannay has restored much of the colloquial life and local semantic color to these works, which is a welcome move toward establishing the individual "tonality" of each aesthetic text, each one of which has quite a different "voice" behind it.

IV. The Deconstructive Turn

A reaction to "blunt reading" set in eventually. In 1971, a pioneering book by Louis Mackey entitled *Kierkegaard: A Kind of Poet* appeared. The title is subtle, both making the claim and immediately modifying it in an important way, "a kind" of poet. What "kind" of poet, then, is Kierkegaard?

> The thesis of this book is neither difficult nor novel. Quite simply, it argues that Søren Kierkegaard is not, in the usual acceptation of these words, a philosopher or a theologian, but a poet. . . . Old and obvious as it is, the thesis still needs to be defended. For though the interpreters of Kierkegaard have conceded it in principle—they could scarcely do otherwise in view of his own abundant declarations—they have almost all abused it in fact.[34]

The thesis he advances in that book, however, certainly was, for its time, novel, and has been, for many,

difficult. Mackey opens up the old Platonic distrust of the poets. Philosophers had for too long disregarded the literary nature of the books and attempted to secure univocal meaning. But Mackie argues sensitively and with detailed attention to the ambiguous and deceptive nature of Kierkegaard's texts, and proposes that considerable care has been taken to avoid univocal meaning, and that this was an authorial intention:

> The fact is, that if Kierkegaard is to be understood *as Kierkegaard,* he must be studied not merely or principally with the instruments of philosophic or theological analysis, but also and chiefly with the tools of literary criticism. That is what this book tries to do.[35]

Louis Mackey followed his book with two major essays, "The View from Pisgah: A Reading of *Fear and Trembling*" and "The Loss of the World in Kierkegaard's Ethics," in a breakthrough collection of critical essays edited by Josiah Thompson, *Kierkegaard: A Collection of Critical Essays,* in 1972. In retrospect, this Thompson collection had a much greater importance in opening up a more "modern" phase of Kierkegaardian scholarship than was obvious at the time. After these two essays, Louis Mackey fell silent for a decade while he thought the matter through again, falling under the influence, as he did so, of contemporary deconstructive patterns of thought. When he finally issued his *Points of View: Readings of Kierkegaard* in 1986, he republished the two old essays, but accompanied them with two important essays of 1981 and 1984, as well as two spanking new essays in which the full draught of the Derridean wisdom had been drunk. "Starting from Scratch: Kierkegaard Unfair to Hegel," a brilliant transumption of Donald Barthelme's short story "Kierkegaard Unfair to Schlegel," insists that the entire job of reading Kierkegaard has to be started again. In the preface to his 1986 book Mackey writes:

> Once it is recognised that Kierkegaard's writings are not to be arrayed under the rubrics of philosophy and theology, it is not sufficient (as some of us used to think) to call them "literary." . . . To double business bound, their tone is just as ambivalent as their purpose is devious and their method duplicitous. . . . By virtue of his authorial self-restraint, his texts exhibit an almost complete abstention from determinate meaning and an almost perfect recalcitrance to interpretation. Like poetry, they "resist the intelligence almost successfully" (Stevens, *Opus Posthumous,* 171).[36]

It is very much to Mackey's credit that he lays out so plainly both the necessity for a literary approach and the inevitability of its falling short. That insight has not been profitably absorbed by others who have also wanted to "apply" Derridean method. Some have decided that, in the face of the impossibility of establishing "determinate meaning," there is no reason why one should not play fast and loose with the Kierkegaardian text and make it mean anything that the fantast wishes to make it say. This was the path chosen by Mark C. Taylor.

Mark C. Taylor's opening book was a careful accounting for the literary reality of the Kierkegaardian technique. *Kierkegaard's Pseudonymous Authorship* (1975) is an admirable piece of scholarly work, laying out the principles according to which the pseudonymous authors have to be read. But at some point shortly thereafter he fell more profoundly under the influence of Hegel than he had previously been under that of the Danish master, and his *Journeys to Selfhood: Hegel and Kierkegaard* inaugurates a period of Hegelianization of the Kierkegaardian texts that has become both widespread and fashionable in his wake:

> Unity *within* plurality; being *within* becoming; constancy *within* change; peace *within* flux; identity *within* difference; the union of union and non-union—reconciliation *in the midst* of estrangement. The end of the journey to selfhood.[37]

In a string of subsequent books, Taylor sketched out, in ever more detail, a postmodern "A/theology" that uses Hegel as master both of thought and of method. In *Altarity* (1987) Taylor creates an intertextual palimpsest, in which the work of Hegel, Heidegger, Merleau-Ponty, Lacan, Bataille, Kristeva, Levinas, Blanchot, Derrida, and . . . Kierkegaard are interrelated and interwoven in a huge nihilistic tapestry. It is that last name that so ill fits its frame, for its own "altarity" from the others is so striking.

Mark Taylor's deconstructive approach to the Kierkegaardian text was helpful, then, while it restricted itself to exegesis but becomes distinctly unhelpful when a condition of textual "free play" is set loose across the page, and a kind of acoustic play, of punning jokiness, is substituted for the effort to explain some original meaning in the Kierkegaardian text. Occasionally the acoustic play becomes absurd, as when it simply hops over from one language to another. Commenting upon the fact that Kierkegaard's mother is never once named in the works or in the ***Journals,*** Taylor can write:

> The silence of the mother repeatedly interrupts the *é*-cri-*ture* of the son with the incessant *cri:* *"Mor, Mor, Mor,"* To hear the echoes of this cry, it is important to note that *"Mor,"* the Danish word for mother, sounds much like the English word "more." The child's cry for *"Mor"* is the cry for an impossible "more." Neither the mother nor any of her substitutes can ever still this cry. The endless cry of *"Mor"* bespeaks a certain absence.[38]

Mark Taylor has come to interpret philosophical writing as a kind of "free play" of the subjective fantasy, an art form in which passing insights can be jotted down in the service of describing an ever greater nihilism of vision. He takes a licence to follow any line of assonance or consonance, whether or not the text permits this. This is clear already in *Erring: A Postmodern A/theology* (1984) and it descends through his work in the eighties, culminating in a four-part dialogue, *Theology at the End of the Century,* with Thomas Altizer, Charles E. Winquist, and Robert P. Scharlemann (1990).

This collection throws into relief the way in which A/theology has shrunk to a mere recitation of vatic names. "Nothing Ending Nothing," Mark Taylor's contribution, is a series of meditations upon canvases by Yves Klein and Lucio Fontana, upon which nothing, or very little, is painted. It is a discussion of the minimalist conditions of theological discourse, ending with a sculpture by Enrique Espinosa called "The Silence of Jesus." A/theological discourse has wound down to a Beckettian nihilism, where nothing can be asserted anymore. "In the aftermath of the death of God, religion no longer heals wounds by binding together the opposites that tear apart. To the contrary, religion exposes wounds that can never be cured."[39]

On the other hand, to his credit, Mark Taylor launched, in the mid 1980s, a series of books from the Florida State University Press at Tallahassee under the general title *Kierkegaard and Post/Modernism.* Four volumes appeared between 1986 and 1988, and all of them make strong advances in the hermeneutic problem of how to read the Kierkegaardian text. Louis Mackey's *Points of View: Readings of Kierkegaard* (1986), I have already commented upon. John Vignaux Smyth, with *A Question of Eros: Irony in Sterne, Kierkegaard and Barthes* (1986), expands the field of reference in a most refreshing way, putting the Kierkegaardian irony into a wider modern context. His book shows the influence of Paul de Man and has much of the subtlety of reading which that implies. Pat Bigelow's *Kierkegaard and the Problem of Writing* (1987) makes an important conceptual leap by starting from a thorough knowledge of Husserl and of modern phenomenology generally, and thus manages to treat the problems of meaning, reference, text, and language far more accurately than was possible heretofore. Pat Bigelow's book is also a Kierkegaardian "text" in its own right, using all the forms of self-reference and self-reflection of ***Either/Or*** in order to achieve "The Poetic Poaching of Silence." Pat Bigelow is also the only thinker I know of who has integrated the acoustic world of James Joyce, particularly that of *Finnegans Wake,* into his analysis. With Husserl, Heidegger, and James Joyce as guides, it is not surprising that this book does actually produce some information that is both new and valuable. I instance, merely as an example, the interesting, responsible, and—yes—discussable conclusions at page 161. Pat Bigelow has made it possible to discuss Kierkegaard's "meaning" by the use of his phenomenological-acoustic method, and this is a genuine hermeneutic advance in the struggle against "blunt reading."

Aparté: Conceptions and Deaths of Søren Kierkegaard by Sylviane Agacinski (1988) is the fourth in the Tallahassee series and originally appeared in French in 1977. Agacinski starts from a fundamentally Freudian basis but thinks, and indeed often lays out her argument also, on Derridean lines. By following the "traces" and "supplements" across the works, she manages to pick up continuities at the level of sense, which lead her to some quite exciting and insightful hypotheses. These hypotheses are, of course, always offered "under erasure," but her reading of the events that lie behind "Solomon's Dream," for instance (240-55), achieve their verisimilitude precisely because the attention to the rhetorical-unconscious nature of the text itself is so sure.

Although not part of the *Kierkegaard and Post-Modernism* series, nor indeed from the same press, Roger Poole's *Kierkegaard: The Indirect Communication* (1993) should be mentioned in this context, for it too attempts to construct and reconstruct "meanings" in the texts by an attentive study of the rhetoric and of the "traces" and "supplements" through which, and only through which, Kierkegaard's intentions can be descried. The first half of the book examines certain key aesthetic texts in the authorship deconstructively, while the second half of the book, starting out from a detailed discussion of Derrida on Husserl, attempts to show how the indirect communication became "lived" after the attack of *The Corsair* in 1846.

It is in the field of ethics, indeed, that Kierkegaard has emerged recently as a major figure in contemporary American philosophy. In a philosophical climate brought to a conceptual standstill by the naive consumerism of Richard Rorty, Kierkegaard's little parable in *Fear and Trembling* has provoked new life in the debate about ethics. If Richard Rorty's aim is to make the idea of ethical obligation "as quaint and as old-fashioned as the divine right of kings," the emergence of Jacques Derrida's *The Gift of Death* in 1992 reinstated it as one of the most urgent of modern discussions:

> *The Gift of Death* starts from an analysis of an essay by the Czech philosopher Jan Pato...ka, who, along with Vaclav Havel and Jiri Hajek, was one of the three spokesmen for the Charta 77 human rights declaration of 1977. He died of a brain hemorrhage after eleven hours of police interrogation on 13 March 1977.[40]

So runs the translator's preface in the 1995 American translation. Derrida has divided his essay into four parts, of which the first deals with the notion of responsibility in the Platonic and Christian traditions and begins with the provocative "Secrets of European Responsibility." The fourth section is directly about economic and political reality in a recognizably twentieth-century world. In winding together the theme of responsibility for others and the theme of sacrifice, Derrida manages to arbitrate between Kierkegaard and Levinas, on whom he had written a major essay as early as *l'Ecriture et la différence* in 1967. But Derrida, animated by the spirit of Pato...ka, and those who are prepared to die for their belief in liberty, is in his most serious mood; and the third section, "Whom to give to," contains the essence of what Derrida has to say about *Fear and Trembling*. The argument is expertly summarized by John D. Caputo in *Kierkegaard in Post/Modernity*.[41]

Derrida's book appeared when John D. Caputo's *Against Ethics* (1993) was still in preparation. Caputo had taken **Fear and Trembling** seriously as a philosophical parable for our time, and his distinction between "ethics" (which is backed up by a "reassuring" philosophical discourse) and "obligation" (which affects the way we have to treat our neighbor here and now "in fact") is an attempt to mediate **Fear and Trembling** in a way that a modern philosophical community could engage with. In taking his distances from Levinas, who "weaves a fabulous, poetic story about absolute alterity," which is in the end unbelievable, and in examining the difference between "ethics" and "obligation" "close up" in the case of **Fear and Trembling,** Caputo manages to free Kierkegaard into contemporary debate.[42]

The debate has been attempted recently by Martin J. Matuštík in a detailed analysis in which Habermas, Charles Taylor, and two versions of "Derrida" are run against Kierkegaard, in an attempt to disentangle the substantive issues between them. The critique of both versions of "Derrida" is particularly accurate and well defined, and yet the Kierkegaardian "individual" remains intact as a working and workable hypothesis. Once again, the theme of justice emerges as central. Caputo's remarkable fourth chapter in *Against Ethics* is reinforced by Matuštík. A dialogue with Kierkegaard, he concludes, would involve presenting "multiculturally positioned individuals with questions on how to become more responsible for a more just world."[43]

Kierkegaard then, is emerging after Rorty, after Habermas, after Taylor, after both versions of "Derrida," as a thinker who would enable us to reopen the question of justice in a mood of new optimism. He has evaded all the critiques that have been leveled against him and emerged as a powerful thinker who could continue the line of thought expressed so magisterially, for instance, in Edmund Husserl's *The Crisis of European Sciences,* a meditation in which science and philosophy would rejoin in a common concern for the *telos* of our civilization, and in a common concern for what Husserl called the *Lebenswelt*.[44] It is hardly too much to say that, in a philosophical world reduced to impotence by a naive and uncritical acceptance of the consumer society as a good in itself, Kierkegaard remains the best hope for renewal of philosophical conversation that we have.

All we have now to do, is to learn, at last, *how* to read his texts.

Notes

[1] *The Diaries of Franz Kafka,* ed. Max Brod (Harmondsworth: Penguin Press, 1972), p. 230. The entry is for 21 August 1913.

[2] *The Diaries of Franz Kafka,* pp. 369-70.

[3] Karl Jaspers, *Reason and Existenz,* five lectures, trans. William Earle (New York: The Noonday Press), 1955. See especially the third lecture, "Truth as Communicability."

[4] Karl Jaspers *Der philosophische Glaube* (München: R. Piper and Co. Verlag, 1963). See especially part 3 of the second lecture, "Vernunft und Kommunikation." "Vernunft fordert grenzenlose *Kommunikation,* sie ist selbst der totale Kommunikationswille" (p. 45).

[5] Kierkegaard, *The Concept of Dread,* trans. Walter Lowrie (Princeton: Princeton University Press, 1957), p. 86.

[6] Martin Heidegger, *Being and Time,* trans. John Macquarrie and Edward Robinson (London: SCM Press, 1962), p. 231.

[7] Kierkegaard, *The Present Age,* trans. Alexander Dru (London: Collins, 1962), pp. 66-76 on "The Public."

[8] *The Present Age,* pp. 76-90.

[9] Heidegger, *Being and Time,* pp. 211-24.

[10] Ibid., pp. 163-8.

[11] *The Present Age,* pp. 73-5.

[12] Heidegger, *Being and Time,* pp. 212-3.

[13] Ibid., §6, "Care as the Being of Dasein," esp. pp. 227-35. Heidegger must have felt that his debts to Kierkegaard here were too flagrant to go without at least a formal acknowledgment, which he makes in a note at p. 492. ("The man who has gone farthest in analysing the phenomenon of anxiety . . . is Soren Kierkegaard.")

[14] Patricia J. Huntington, "Heidegger's Reading of Kierkegaard Revisited: From Ontological Abstraction to Ethical Concretion," in *Kierkegaard in Post/Modernity,* ed. Martin J. Matuštík and Merold Westphal (Bloomington and Indianapolis: Indiana University Press, 1995), pp. 43-65.

[15] Huntington, "Heidegger's Reading of Kierkegaard Revisited," pp. 47, 55.

[16] Dietrich Bonhoeffer, *Letters and Papers from Prison,* ed. Eberhard Bethge (London: SCM Press, 1953); 2nd ed., enl., 1971. Kierkegaard's influence on Bonhoeffer is perhaps most marked in his book *The Cost of Discipleship.*

[17] Jean-Paul Sartre, *Being and Nothingness,* trans. Hazel E. Barnes (London: Methuen, 1957). In that section of chap. I called "The Origin of Nothingness," pp. 21-45, it is difficult to say whether Sartre is more indebted to Kierkegaard or to Heidegger's reading of Kierkegaard: "In anguish freedom is anguished before itself inasmuch as it is instigated and bound by nothing" (35). Whatever the case, Sartre is no more prepared than Heidegger is to acknowledge the extent to which his early work is quarried out of *The Concept of Dread.*

[18] Jean-Paul Sartre, *The Age of Reason,* trans. Eric Sutton (Harmondsworth: Penguin Press, 1961), pp. 242-3.

[19] *Kierkegaard Vivant,* ed. Rene Maheu for UNESCO (Paris: Gallimard, Collection Idées, 1966). An account of the proceedings, and of Sartre's unwilling and half-hearted participation, is provided by William L. McBride in his essay "Sartre's Debts to Kierkegaard: A Partial Reckoning," in *Kierkegaard and Post/Modernity,* ed. Matuštík and Westphal, pp. 18-42. Sartre's desire to evade the question of the "anxiety of influence" extended even to absenting himself from the discussions, "much to the annoyance of some of the others" (p. 39)!

[20] Jean-Paul Sartre, *Saint Genet, Actor and Martyr,* trans. Bernard Frechtman (New York: George Braziller, Inc., 1964), p. 628. In a postface entitled "Please Use Genet Properly," Sartre writes: "I have tried to do the following: to indicate the limit of psychoanalytical interpretation and Marxist explanation and to demonstrate that freedom alone can account for a person in his totality . . . to prove that genius is not a gift but the way out that one invents in desperate cases."

[21] Simone de Beauvoir, *The Prime of Life,* trans. Peter Green (Harmondsworth: Penguin Press, 1965), pp. 468-9.

[22] Albert Camus, *Le Mythe de Sisyphe* (Paris: Gallimard, Collection Idées, 1962), p. 61, my translation.

[23] A useful summary of translations and critical studies of Kierkegaard can be found in the bibliographical note,

bibliographical supplement, and bibliographical note (1983) in the revised edition of James Collin's *The Mind of Kierkegaard* (Princeton: Princeton University Press, 1983).

[24] David F. Swenson, *Something about Kierkegaard* (Minneapolis: Augsburg Publishing House, 1941; rev. ed. 1945).

[25] On the way that the "indirect communication" moved from being a purely literary construct to one that involved the signifying activity of the "lived body," see Roger Poole, *Kierkegaard: The Indirect Communication* (Charlottesville: The University Press of Virginia, 1993).

[26] *The Concept of Dread,* p. x. The whole translator's preface is of great interest in what it shows us of the presuppositions in Lowrie's mind as he translated.

[27] C. Stephen Evans, *Passionate Reason: Making Sense of Kierkegaard's Philosophical Fragments* (Bloomington and Indianapolis: Indiana University Press, 1992). Evans's division of recent writing on Kierkegaard into "three broad types" (pp. 2-4) and his general methical reflections in chap. I, are useful insights into the structure of the problem as he perceives it.

[28] Kierkegaard, *Concluding Unscientific Postscript,* trans. David Swenson and Walter Lowrie (Princeton: Princeton University Press, 1941), p. 552. The passage is of vital importance for a responsible hermeneutic approach to Kierkegaard.

[29] H. A. Nielsen, *Where the Passion Is: A Reading of Kierkegaard's* Philosophical Fragments (Tallahassee: Florida State University Press, 1983), p. 3.

[30] Robert C. Roberts, *Faith, Reason and History: Rethinking Kierkegaard's* Philosophical Fragments (Macon, Ga.: Mercer University Press, 1986), pp. 1-3, 10.

[31] Jeremy Walker, *The Descent into God* (Kingston and Montreal: McGill-Queens University Press, 1985), p. 3.

[32] Alastair Hannay, *Kierkegaard* (London: Routledge and Kegan Paul, 1982; rev. ed. 1991), p. xiv.

[33] Ronald M. Green, *Kierkegaard and Kant: The Hidden Debt* (Albany: State University of New York Press, 1992).

[34] Louis Mackey, *Kierkegaard: A Kind of Poet* (Philadelphia: University of Pennsylvania Press, 1971), p. ix.

[35] Ibid., p. x.

[36] Louis Mackey, *Points of View: Readings of Kierkegaard* (Tallahassee: Florida State University Press, 1986), p. xxii-xxiii.

[37] Mark C. Taylor, *Journeys to Selfhood: Hegel and Kierkegaard* (Berkeley and Los Angeles: University of California Press, 1980), p. 276.

[38] Mark C. Taylor, *Altarity* (Chicago: University of Chicago Press, 1987), p. 156. This passage is set inside the chapter called "Woman," which is on Julia Kristeva.

[39] Robert P. Scharlemann, ed., *Theology at the End of the Century: A Dialogue on the Postmodern with Thomas J. J. Altizer, Mark C. Taylor, Charles E. Winquist, and Robert P. Scharlemann* (Charlottesville: The University Press of Virginia, 1990), p. 69.

[40] Jacques Derrida, *The Gift of Death,* trans. David Wills (Chicago: University of Chicago Press, 1995), p. vii.

[41] John D. Caputo, "Instants, Secrets, and Singularities: Dealing Death in Kierkegaard and Derrida," in *Kierkegaard in Post/Modernity,* ed. Matuštík and Westphal, pp. 216-38.

[42] John D. Caputo, *Against Ethics* (Bloomington and Indianapolis: Indiana University Press, 1993). See especially chaps. 4 and 10.

[43] Martin J. Matuštík, "Kierkegaard's Radical Existential Praxis, or Why the Individual Defies Liberal, Communitarian, and Postmodern Categories," in *Kierkegaard in Post/Modernity,* ed. Matuštík and Westphal, pp. 259-60.

[44] Edmund Husserl, *The Crisis of European Sciences and Transcendental Phenomenology,* trans. David Carr (Evanston: Northwestern University Press, 1970). This massively documented and virtually unknown work is the context in which a reread Kierkegaard could make sense in our current philosophical vacuum. It offers hope for an intelligible future.

Gabriel Josipovici (essay date 1998)

SOURCE: "Kierkegaard and the Novel," in *Kierkegaard: A Critical Reader,* edited by Jonathan Rée and Jane Chamberlain, Blackwell Publishers, 1998, pp. 114-28.

[*In the following essay, Josipovici discusses Kierkegaard's views of fiction and fiction writers, illuminating the parallels between these views and Kierkegaard's doctrine of existence.*]

My intention is not to write here about Kierkegaard as novelist, though that would be an interesting subject. After all, each of his pseudonymous works is in a sense an attempt to extend the range of fiction, and I can see no good reason why they should be dumped in a box marked 'Philosophy', while Sterne's *Tristram Shandy,* for example, or Dostoevsky's *Notes from Underground* are dumped in one marked 'Literature'.

However, to write about Kierkegaard as novelist implies that we know what a novel is, and what is really interesting about Kierkegaard is that he raises questions about that very issue, and does so by reminding us that we cannot begin to understand what novels are, what fiction is, until we recognize that how we think about fiction depends on how we think about ourselves. In other words, if the concept of fiction cannot be taken for granted, it is because story-telling is intimately bound up with what we are, not in any absolute sense but in our concrete social and historical reality. Kierkegaard's critique of his time ('the present age'), his struggles to understand himself and his experiments with form are part of one single enterprise, and there is no easy way to separate the different strands from each other. But if that makes matters difficult it also ensures that the investigation will at least be dealing with serious, not to say fundamental matters.

A good place to start is Kierkegaard's Introduction to *The Book on Adler.*[1] The book turns on the question of authority: what authority do I have for what I say and write? What authority do authors have in general and in the present age in particular? Artists are fond of referring to their 'calling', but in what sense have they been called? In the same sense as the Apostles were called by Jesus? And, if not, are they justified in using such a term?

Kierkegaard begins his Introduction in a typically offhand way with a reference to the world of the barber-shop, where rumours and gossip fly and which acts in small communities as a kind of informal newspaper. Then with no apparent change of gear, he plunges into the heart of the matter: 'It is not improbable that the lives of many men go on in such a way that they have indeed premises for living but reach no conclusions. . . . For it is one thing that a life is over and a different thing that a life is finished by reaching its conclusion.' The ordinary man, he goes on, the one whose life has no conclusion, may, if he finds he has talent, decide to become an author. But, says Kierkegaard, though

> he may have extraordinary talents and remarkable learning . . . an author he is not, in spite of the fact that he produces books. [. . .] No, in spite of the fact that the man writes, he is not essentially an author; he will be capable of writing the first . . . and also the second part, but he cannot write the third part—the last part he cannot write. If he goes ahead naïvely (led astray by the reflection that every book must have a last part) and so writes the last part, he will make it thoroughly clear by writing the last part that he makes a written renunciation to all claim to be an author. For though it is indeed by writing that one justifies the claim to be an author, it is also, strangely enough, by writing that one virtually renounces

this claim. If he had been thoroughly aware of the inappropriateness of the third part—well, one may say, *si tacuisset, philosophus mansisset* [If he had kept quiet he would have remained a philosopher!].

And he concludes with a pregnant aphorism: 'To find the conclusion it is necessary first of all to observe that it is lacking, and then in turn to feel quite vividly the lack of it.'[2]

It is not too much to say that those who have felt the full force of Kierkegaard's argument here will be forever separated from those—the bulk of writers, readers and reviewers of fiction in Kierkegaard's day and our own—who have not. And I hasten to add that one does not need to have read Kierkegaard to feel it, only to be aware of the possibilities of art in the post-Romantic age. For Kierkegaard is merely articulating, with great humour but also great power and acumen, what has been felt and struggled with by Hölderlin and Mallarmé, Kafka and Proust, Rilke, Eliot and Wallace Stevens: that since the writer has no authority for what he is saying, to go on writing as if he had is the greatest sin, for it falsifies the way things are instead of helping to clarify it.

The argument turns on the question of the difference between endings and conclusions: 'For it is one thing that a life is over and a different thing that a life is finished by reaching its conclusion.' In the first case a man goes through life and then dies. His life has not had any meaning, it has simply consisted of a series of actions and reactions, and his death does not have any meaning either. It is like a line which goes along the page for a while and then stops. To say that line goes from A to B implies that there is a shape to it, a certain kind of progression. But the line does not 'go' anywhere. It exists for a while and then stops. Clov and Hamm, in Beckett's *Endgame,* wind up an alarm clock and then listen to it ringing. When it stops Clov says: 'The end is terrific!' 'I prefer the middle', replies Hamm.[3] This is both funny and disturbing. Funny because Hamm and Clov, by treating, or pretending to treat the undifferentiated sound of an alarm clock as they would a piece of music, make fun of concert-goers. Disturbing, because behind the concert-goer stands the critic of art in general, and its practitioners, and we ourselves, who insist on seeing meaning and value in our lives when we know full well that in the end there is none. As Kierkegaard puts it: all we ever have in life are gossip and rumours; our world is the world of the newspaper and the barber-shop, it is not the world of Jesus and his Apostles. A person seduced by our culture's admiration for art into becoming a writer embarks on a more dangerous enterprise than they may realize. If they embark on a work of fiction they imply that they have escaped the world of rumour, that instead of living horizontally, as it were, they live vertically, in touch with some transcendental source of authority. And we who read them do so because we feel that this must indeed be the case. But the closer they get to the end the clearer it becomes that there is no vertical connection. And should they try to bring their work to a close the contradiction between what the novel implies and the truth of the matter will become quite obvious. The only way for some semblance of truth and clarity to emerge is for the author to recognize that the conclusion, that which would finally give authority to the book, is lacking, to feel this quite vividly and make us feel it as well.

I have been moving indiscriminately between the terms 'fiction', 'the novel' and 'the story-teller', but it is time to try to distinguish them. Kierkegaard himself does not do so explicitly, but it is clear that in the passage above he is thinking of novels, and elsewhere he makes it clear that there is a historical dimension to the problem, that earlier writers, such as the authors of fairy-tales and the ancient Greek tragedians, were not faced with the same problems as those who write in the age of the barber-shop and the newspaper. It may be helpful, though, to turn first to a writer who, our of the same concerns as Kierkegaard, *has* attempted to define the difference between the story-teller and the novelist. That writer is Walter Benjamin.

In one of his finest essays, 'The Storyteller', Benjamin notes that

> the earliest symptom of a process whose end is the decline of storytelling is the rise of the novel at the beginning of modern times. [. . .] What differentiates the novel from all other forms of prose literature—the fairy-tale, the legend, even the novella—is that it neither comes from oral tradition nor goes into it. [. . .] The storyteller takes what he tells from experience—his own or that reported by others. And he in turn makes it the experience of those who are listening to his tale. The novelist has isolated himself. The birthplace of the novel is the solitary individual, who is no longer able to express himself by giving examples of his most important concerns, is himself uncounseled, and cannot counsel others.[4]

And Benjamin finds the authority of the story-teller to rest in death: 'Dying was once a public process in the life of the individual and a most exemplary one. . . . In the course of modern times dying has been pushed further and further out of the perceptual world of the living.' As we live isolated and alone, so we die, 'stowed away in sanatoria or hospitals.' But 'not only a man's knowledge or wisdom, but above all his real life—and this is the stuff that stories are made of—first assumes transmissible form at the moment of death.' A public death surrounded by traditional customs is what once gave 'authority which even the poorest wretch in dying possesses for the living around him.' 'This authority', concludes Benjamin, 'is at the very source of the story.'[5]

There may be something romantic and mystical in Benjamin's formulation, but it is easy to see that he is on to something serious and substantial. The story-teller is part of a tradition: he acquires his wisdom from others and in turn passes it on to others. The novelist, by contrast, is isolated, 'is himself uncounseled and cannot counsel others'.

Kierkegaard, unfortunately, did not write about story-telling as opposed to novel writing, but he did touch on the issue in a diary entry from 1837, before, that is, he had published any of his works. He is meditating on the telling of stories to children, and he puts forward the view that there are

> two recommended ways of telling children stories, but there is also a multitude of false paths in between. The *first* is the way unconsciously adopted by the nanny, and whoever can be included in that category. Here a whole fantasy world dawns for the child and the nannies themselves are deeply convinced the stories are true . . . which, however fantastic the content, can't help bestowing a beneficial calm on the child. Only when the child gets a hint of the fact that the person doesn't believe her own stories are there ill-effects—not from the content but because of the narrator's insincerity—from the lack of confidence and suspicion that gradually develops in the child.

The second way, he goes on, 'is possible only for someone who with full transparency reproduces the life of childhood, knows what it demands, what is good for it, and from his higher standpoint offers the children a spiritual sustenance that is good for them—who knows how to be a child, whereas the nannies themselves are basically children.' And he concludes that '*false paths* crop up by coming beyond the nanny position but not staying the whole course and stopping half-way.'[6]

The movement here is typical of Kierkegaard's method. First we have an original, 'natural', situation; then a series of false intermediary positions, positions which fail to take account of the new situation; and, finally, a radical solution which does take the new situation fully into account. The story-teller in Benjamin's argument, we could say, is like the nanny, who, deeply convinced of the truth of what she is saying, bestows a beneficial calm on the child. The novelist is like the nanny who can no longer quite believe what she is saying, and thus leaves the child uneasy and suspicious. The 'essential writer', the one who senses that a conclusion is lacking, feels quite vividly that lack and makes the reader feel it too; by so doing he 'from his higher standpoint offers the children a spiritual sustenance that is good for them.' The 'essential writer' thus in a sense 'knows how to be a child, whereas the nannies themselves are basically children'.

The same pattern is to be found in an essay in the first part of *Either/Or,* **'The Tragic in Ancient Drama**

Reflected in the Tragic in Modern Drama'. Here it is drama, not fiction, that Kierkegaard is concerned with, but the parallels with Benjamin's essay are striking. In ancient Greek culture, says Kierkegaard, 'even if the individual moved freely, he nevertheless rested in substantial determinants in the state, the family, in fate.' Modern man, on the other hand, is alone, and takes all decisions for himself. Thus tragedy is alien to him, for by throwing 'his whole life upon his shoulders as his own deed,' he turns tragic guilt into ethical guilt.[7] The tragic hero becomes merely bad, and badness and goodness have no aesthetic interest. Thus writers who persist in trying to write tragedy merely produce banality and confuse instead of clarifying our relation to the world. There is, however, he goes on, a truly modern kind of tragedy, but it cannot form the subject of drama because it does not belong to the realm of the aesthetic at all. This is a totally inward kind of tragedy, and its paradigm is Christ, who lived a life of absolute obedience without any outward evidence that he was doing so. The modern writer who wishes to write tragedy must do so then in a roundabout way, by showing us that tragedy is no longer possible and making us intuit what cannot be said. In other words, he must force us to recognize that the conclusion, that which would finally give authority to his play, is lacking, and make us feel vividly the lack of it.

That of course is what Beckett does in *Endgame.* 'What's happening? What's happening?' Hamm asks at one point. 'Something is taking its course,' replies Clov.[8] Something, somewhere, is taking its course, which is quite a different thing from the ringing of the alarm clock having a beginning, middle and end. But the sense of lack, of modern story-telling as false coinage, pseudo-nutrition, is to be found in all the great modernists, and notably in Kafka, where it reaches its clearest expression in one of his last stories, *A Hunger Artist,* in which the fasting showman confesses, as he is dying, that he only fasted 'because I couldn't find the food I liked. If I had found it, believe me, I should have made no fuss and stuffed myself like you or anyone else.'[9] It is already there in Kafka's outburst, in an early letter to his friend Oskar Pollack:

> I think we ought to read only the kind of books that wound and stab us. If the book we're reading doesn't wake us up with a blow on the head, what are we reading it for? So that it will make us happy, as you write? Good Lord, we would be happy precisely if we had no books, and the kind of books that make us happy are the kind we could write ourselves if we had to. But we need the books that affect us like a disaster, that grieve us deeply, like the death of someone we loved more than ourselves, like being banished into forests far from everyone, like a suicide. A book must be the axe for the frozen sea inside us. That is my belief.[10]

For Kierkegaard, trained as a theologian and a philosopher, however, the quarry was only incidentally the novel. He simply wanted to bring out the striking similarity between the false aura of authority that surrounds the novel and all the other fraudulent assertions of authority with which 'the present age' bombards us. Chief among these is the fraudulent authority of Hegel and the Hegelians. 'I nurture what is for me at times a puzzling respect for Hegel', he writes in his journal in 1845, for all the world like Nietzsche trying to come to terms with his own terribly mixed feelings towards Wagner. 'I have learned much from him, and I know very well that I can still learn much more when I return to him again. [. . .] His philosophical knowledge, his amazing learning, the insight of his genius, and everything else good that can be said of a philosopher, I am willing to acknowledge. [. . .] But nevertheless, it is no less true that someone who is really tested in life, who in his need resorts to thought, will find Hegel comical despite all his greatness.'[11]

What is it that is so comic about Hegel? It is that he forgets the one essential thing: that each of us has a single, unique life and each of us must die, and that this is not a mere contingent fact about us, but the most important thing. 'Now, all in all, there are two ways for an existing individual', he says in the *Postscript,* that massive work he thought would cap his pseudonymous production and lay the ghost of Hegel once and for all:

> Either he can do everything to forget that he is existing and thereby manage to become comic . . . because existence possesses the remarkable quality that an existing person exists whether he wants to or not; or he can direct all his attention to his existing. It is from this side that an objection must first be made to modern speculative thought, that it has not a false presupposition but a comic presupposition, occasioned by its having forgotten in a kind of world-historical absentmindedness what it means to be a human being, not what it means to be human in general, for even speculators might be swayed to consider that sort of thing, but what it means that we, you and I and he, are human beings, each one on his own.[12]

What Kierkegaard objects to in Hegel's system (leaving aside the question of how right his critique of Hegel may be and how far he is simply attacking Hegelianism, the dominant philosophy of the age) is this: that in asking us to think of history and of individual lives from the end, backwards, it misses what is central to life: that it is lived forwards.[13] As far as history is concerned this means that it will always be an account of the winners, never of the losers, since in world-historical terms it was necessary for the losers to lose. As far as the individual is concerned it leaves out of account the fact that we live our lives forward, that for us there is no pattern, only the moment with its choices. For Kierkegaard, Hegel's System and the bland Hegelian Christianity trumpeted from pulpits every Sunday are not simply wrong on that score: in their insistence that a pattern is known to the speaker (that Abraham sacrificed his son as a prefiguration of Christ's sacrifice for us, for example) it falsifies both the past (it ignores Abraham's anguish as he went to Mount Moriah) and the present (since it treats its audience as though they were already dead and in heaven).

Sartre, perhaps influenced by his reading of Kierkegaard, makes the same point about the novel in his *Nausea*. We start a novel, he says, and read about a man walking down a road. The man seems free, the future open before him. At once we identify with him, for that is how our existence seems to us. We too are walking down the road of life, unsure of what is to come. But the pleasure of reading the novel lies in the fact that we know that the man is in fact the subject of an adventure that is about to befall him. How do we know this? Because he is there at the start of the novel and he would not be there if nothing were going to happen to him. 'But the end is there. For us, the fellow is already the hero of the story.'[14] The extraordinary power of the traditional novel lies in this fact, that it makes us feel that our lives are both free *and* meaningful. It does not say this, for it neither needs to nor is fully aware of it, but nevertheless that is its essence, the secret of its power.

How to wake people up? How to bring them back to a sense that their own lives are infinitely precious as their own and not as part of some large pattern? Not, at any rate, by presenting them with another system, for the whole point is that

> a system of existence cannot be given. Is there, then, not such a system? That is not at all the case. Neither is this implied in what has been said. Existence itself is a system—for God, but it cannot be a system for any existing spirit. System and conclusiveness correspond to each other, but existence is the very opposite. . . . In order to think existence, systematic thought must think it as annulled and consequently not as existing. Existence is the spacing that holds apart; the systematic is the conclusiveness that brings together.[15]

Kierkegaard has a model for his method, which depends not on what is said but on the tension between what is said and the person speaking, and that model is Socrates. In his earliest book, *The Concept of Irony,* he contrasts the irony of Socrates with the System of Hegel, and shows how little Hegel understands Socrates. Hegel does not understand, says Kierkegaard, that the 'self' of Socrates is not a plenum, but only the sense the 'I know nothing.' Hegel sees Socrates as a part of his System, as the triumph of the individual and subjectivity over the Gods and external authority, whereas, says Kierkegaard in a wonderful image, Socrates 'placed individuals under his dialectical

vacuum pump, pumped away the atmospheric air they were accustomed to breathing, and left them standing there'.[16] The discourse of Socrates, he says, 'does not have the powerful pathos of enthusiasm; his bearing does not have the absolute authority of personality; his indifference is not a blissful relaxation in his own repletion. [. . .] What bears him up is the negativity that still has engendered no positivity.'[17] And if the contrast drawn here between Socrates and his opponents strikes us as more like that between, say, Kierkegaard himself and Goethe, or Kierkegaard and Beethoven, rather than anything in the Greek world, that would not be the first time a philosopher has dramatized his own relation to his age in his portrait of an earlier thinker.

Kierkegaard comes back to this point about negativity in the *Postscript.* As ever, he is aware of the traps that lie in wait for even the most rigorous thinker: 'The subjective existing thinker who has the infinite in his soul has it always, and therefore his form is continually negative,' he says. 'When this is the case, when he, actually existing, renders the form of existence in his own existence, he, existing, is continually just as negative as positive, for his positivity consists in the continued inward deepening in which he is cognizant of the negative.' He goes on to say that,

> among the so-called negative thinkers, however, there are a few who, after gaining an inkling of the negative, succumb to the positive and go roaring out into the world in order to recommend, urge, and offer their beatifying negative wisdom for sale. These hawkers are scarcely more sagacious than the positive thinkers, but it is rather inconsistent of the positive thinkers to become angry with them, for they are essentially positive. The hawkers are not existing thinkers. Perhaps they were so once, until they found a result; from that moment they no longer exist as thinkers, but as hawkers and auctioneers.[18]

We have seen many such in modern times. Indeed, the entire movement known as Postmodernism can be seen as a prime example of Kierkegaard's dictum. Instead of a struggle to 'hold apart', came a new system, which 'brings together', even if it was a system based on some theory of apartness. Kierkegaard, by contrast, remains aware that 'the genuine subjective existing thinker is always just as negative as he is positive', and that 'he is always that as long as he exists, not once and for all in a chimerical mediation.' Such a thinker, he says, is conscious of 'the negativity of the infinite in existence; he always keeps open the wound of negativity, which at times is a saving factor.'[19] The others let the wound heal over and become positive; they cease to be learners and become teachers.

How to stop oneself becoming a teacher? How to think against thinking? For that is what it amounts to, since thinking, even thinking that existence is always more and other than thinking, is still always thinking. That is Kierkegaard's central insight and his central preoccupation, as the **Journals** show, from the beginning to the end of his writing life. Thus, in a series of diary entries from 1837 (before, that is, he had written any of his books), he notes that 'the humorist' can never become 'a Systematizer', since 'the systematizer believes he can say everything, and that whatever cannot be said is wrong and unimportant,' whereas the humorist 'lives in life's fullness and so feels how much is always left over, even if he has expressed himself in the most felicitous manner possible (hence his disinclination to write).' This leads him into a powerful meditation on the difference between the indicative and the subjunctive, between, that is, the mode of existence and the mode of possibility: 'The indicative thinks something as actual (the identity of thinking and the actual). The subjunctive thinks something as thinkable.' The writer sensitive to the difference between thinking and living will reflect this distinction by choosing the subjunctive, the mode of possibility, not the indicative, the mode of actuality: 'One should be able to write a whole novel in which the present tense subjunctive was the invisible soul, as light is for painting.' The true writer, conscious of the precious nature of the actual, will use the subjunctive precisely because the indicative means so much to him: 'That is why one can truthfully say that the subjunctive, which enters as a glimpse of the individuality of the person in question, is a dramatic line whereby the narrator steps aside and makes the remark as being true of the character (poetically), not as factual, not even as if it might be fact; it is presented under the illumination of subjectivity.'[20]

This is why Kierkegaard uses pseudonyms: not to confuse his readers, nor to play games with them, but to bring out the subjunctive nature of what is being said. It is not Kierkegaard saying this but Johannes de Silentio or Johannes Climacus; saying that which Kierkegaard *imagines* them to say, were they to speak, to write. And that is why so many modern novelists emphasize, in their writing, that their novels are novels. Not to play games on their readers and not to trick them (though of course some do this for these banal reasons), but to bring out the gap that will always exist between lived life and written-about life.

Kierkegaard is still struggling with the problem in 1850, five years after the publication of the **Postscript,** which was supposed to have settled it once and for all. ' "Actuality" cannot be conceived,' he writes in his journal for that year:

> Johannes Climacus (in the **Postscript**) has already shown this correctly and very simply. To conceive something is to dissolve actuality into *possibility*—

but then it is impossible to conceive it, because conceiving something is transforming it into possibility and so not holding on to its actuality. As far as actuality is concerned, conception is retrogressive, a step backward, not a progress. Not that 'actuality' contains no concepts, by no means; no, the concept which is come by through conceptually dissolving it into possibility is also inside actuality, but there is still something more—that is actuality. To go from possibility to actuality is a step forward . . . to go from actuality to possibility is a step backward. But there's this deplorable confusion in that modern times have incorporated 'actuality' into logic and then, in distraction, forgotten that 'actuality' in logic is still only a 'thought actuality', i.e. it is possibility.[21]

Everything would be fine if works like Hegel's *Phenomenology* presented their ideas as hypotheses, not as actuality, but does this happen? No. And it is the same with history:

> But isn't history actual? Certainly. But what history? No doubt the six thousand years of the world's history are actuality, but one that is put behind us; it is and can exist for me only as thought actuality, i.e. as possibility. Whether or not the dead have actually realised existentially the tasks which were put before them in actuality has now been decided, has been concluded; there is no more existential actuality for them except in what has been put behind them, which again, for me, exists only as ideal actuality, as thought actuality, as possibility.[22]

In other words, I can think of history as actuality, but the very thinking of it robs it of its actuality.

This is so difficult to grasp precisely because 'to grasp' means to understand and Kierkegaard is arguing that there will always be a gap between understanding and lived actuality. We can get a purchase on his argument by turning to one of Beckett's finest stories, *Dante and the Lobster*. There the protagonist, Belaqua Shua, a Dublin intellectual and layabout, having bought a lobster for dinner with his aunt, is appalled when he discovers that the creature is alive and that the aunt is about to cook it by dropping it alive into boiling water. He tries to placate his feelings of guilt and horror with the cliché: 'It's a quick death, God help us all.' But the narrative will not let him get away with this: 'It is not', the story ends.[23] Here the distinction between the subjunctive and the indicative is a gulf which divides those—the aunt, Belaqua, the reader—who are only asked to *imagine* what it is like to die by being plunged alive into boiling water, and the lobster, for whom this is actuality. Of course 'It is not' is still part of the story, and even the reader's recognition that 'it is not' a quick death is still only an imaginative recognition, still, for us, a possibility among others. So Beckett will have to start again and, as he says elsewhere, fail again, fail better, if he is to get at the truth.[24]

We can now begin to see why Kierkegaard said that the more an inessential writer writes the more they reveal that they are no writer. For they write as though system and existence were one, and, not noticing that anything is amiss with their method, they therefore merely perpetuate confusion and misunderstanding. In *Fear and Trembling,* on the other hand, Kierkegaard brings out powerfully how impossible it is for narrative and even for language ever to convey what the individual is going through as he faces the choices life puts before him. For both narrative and language generalize and so lose what is unique to the individual. All the narrator, Johannes de Silentio, can say is: I understand only that I do not understand Abraham. Thus he can bring us to the point where we too understand that we do not understand, and then leave us there.

In *Either/Or* Kierkegaard set two life-views against each other by means of collage, forcing us to make our choice between them and then to recognize that both are right and neither is, so that we go round and round, warming to the young man of the first part, with his wit and his melancholy and his vulnerability, then recognizing that the older man is right when, in the second half, he criticizes the young Aesthete for wallowing in his condition, for wanting to have all women, all lives, instead of committing himself to one. Yet we also come to see that the older man is a complacent and self-satisfied bore who has no inkling of the impossibility of choice for one who has begun to question the values of a bourgeois existence of marriage and children and getting on in life. Still, tiresome as he is, is the older man not perhaps right? Would things not perhaps change decisively for the young man were he to take the plunge and commit himself? Perhaps the older man has been through the same thing and simply found it in himself to make his choice.

In *Fear and Trembling* the question is no longer to set two life-views against each other, but to ask how it is possible to become a Knight of Faith, like Abraham. The narrator can make us feel vividly that he—and we—cannot really understand Abraham, but the implication remains that so long as he goes on writing about Abraham he himself will never be a Knight of Faith. This is Kierkegaard's problem. He cannot remain simply ironical, like his beloved Socrates. Times have changed. Christianity, with its new imperatives, has come into the world and, besides, there is no Plato to write down his words. He is committed to writing in order to make people see the lies they are telling themselves, but so long as he goes on writing he remains in the subjunctive mode and so cuts him-

self off from the life he most desires. He feels that if only he could make the leap he would himself become a Knight of Faith, quietly going about his tasks in the world, unknown to men but in a meaningful relationship to God and to himself. But what does it mean to make the leap? To stop writing? To take Holy Orders? He has in a sense already made the leap by devoting himself to his vocation. But what is this vocation? Has God in fact called him? Is this what God really wanted of him? Did he not perhaps rather want him to marry Regine and lead a quiet, unadventurous life, far from the temptations of authorship? There is, of course, no answer to these questions, yet they will not go away. If only, he thinks, he could quiet his intellect, put to sleep his febrile imagination, then perhaps he would, finally, *be* a kind of Abraham. But he cannot. This is the sort of person he is and the sort of person his upbringing has made him, and all he can do is go on writing about the difficulty, the impossibility, the desirability, of that leap.

The trouble is that Abraham does not need to make a leap. He just is—Abraham. Kierkegaard understood this well, and seeks to explain the difference by arguing that since Christ's Incarnation matters have changed totally. To be natural is no longer enough, for what Christ teaches is that nature must be redeemed by faith:

> Voltaire is said to have remarked somewhere that he would refuse to believe in the hereditary nobility until there was historical proof of a child being born with spurs. Similarly I would say: I propose for the time being to keep to the old view that the Christian and the human, the humane, are qualitative opposites; I propose keeping to that until we are informed that a naturally, in other words innately self-denying child has been born.[25]

As no child is born with spurs, so no child is born a Christian. And baptism is of course merely the Church's way of fitting spurs on to the child and pretending they are now a natural part of him. For Kierkegaard, for this radical Protestant, the logic of his position is simply this: 'To love God is . . . impossible without hating what is human.'[26]

At other times though he is less certain of his ground. Perhaps this Manichean view is not the truth but only his own biased perspective on things: 'If I look at my personal life, am I a Christian or isn't this personal existence of mine a pure poetic existence with a dash of the demonic? . . . Is there not an element of despair in all this, starting a fire in a kind of betrayal, just to throw oneself into God's arms? Maybe, since it might turn out that I didn't become a Christian.'[27]

Such torments can be replicated in the letters and diaries of Kafka and in the utterances of many of the great modernist writers. They, however, seem to have been able to develop and grow through an innate trust in the act of writing itself as a way out of the impasse, in their willingness to embrace confusion and uncertainty and find a new voice in the process. But a very narrow line divides such trust from the bad faith of becoming a 'hawker' and so failing to keep 'the wound of negativity' open. One could say that Kierkegaard's personal tragedy lay in the fact that he was not enough of a writer to take pleasure in the writing process itself, but too much of one ever to be a Knight of Faith. But then that too could perhaps be seen as the best way of defining all those modern writers whom, like Kierkegaard, we may call 'essential writers' to distinguish them from the scribblers, even the highly talented scribblers, who will always be with us.

Notes

[1] Søren Kierkegaard, *Fear and Trembling and The Book on Adler,* translated by Walter Lowrie (David Campbell, London, 1994).

[2] *Fear and Trembling and The Book on Alder,* pp. 113-14.

[3] Samuel Beckett, *Endgame* (Faber and Faber, London, 1964), p. 34.

[4] Walter Benjamin, 'The Storyteller', in his *Illuminations,* edited by Hannah Arendt and translated by Harry Zohn (Jonathan Cape, London, 1970), p. 87.

[5] 'The Storyteller', pp. 93-4.

[6] II A 12; *Papers and Journals: A. Selection,* translated by Alastair Hannay (Penguin Books, London 1996), pp. 73-7; or, for the standard translation, see *Søren Kierkegaard's Journals and Papers,* translated by Howard V. Hong and Edna H. Hong (7 vols, Indiana University Press, Bloomington, 1967–78), 265, vol. 1, pp. 113-19.

[7] Søren Kierkegaard, *Either/Or,* translated by Howard V. Hong and Edna H. Hong (2 vols, Princeton University Press, Princeton, 1987), vol. 1, pp. 143-4.

[8] Samuel Beckett, *Endgame,* p. 17.

[9] Franz Kafka, 'A Hunger Artist', translated by Willa and Edwin Muir, in *The Complete Short Stories of Franz Kafka,* edited by Nahum N. Glatzer (Reed International, London, 1992), p. 277.

[10] Franz Kafka, *Letters to Friends, Family, and Editors,* translated by Richard Winston and Clare Winston (John Calder, London, 1978), p. 16.

[11] VI B 54 12; *Papers and Journals: A Selection,* p. 195; cf. *Journals and Papers* 1608, vol. 2, p. 221.

[12] *Concluding Unscientific Postscript,* p. 120.

[13] [See IV A 164: 'It is quite true what philosophy says: that life must be understood backwards. But then one forgets the other principle: that it must be lived forwards. Which principle, the more one thinks it through, ends exactly with the thought that temporal life can never properly be understood precisely because I can at no instant find complete rest in which to adopt the position: backwards.' (*Papers and Journals: A Selection,* p. 161; cf. *Journals and Papers,* 1030, vol. 1, p. 450.)]

[14] Jean-Paul Sartre, *Nausea,* translated by Robert Baldick (Penguin Books, Harmondsworth, 1965), p. 62.

[15] *Concluding Unscientific Postscript,* vol. 1, p. 118 [translation altered].

[16] Søren Kierkegaard, *The Concept of Irony,* translated by Howard V. Hong and Edna H. Hong (Princeton University Press, Princeton, 1989), p. 178.

[17] *The Concept of Irony,* p. 196.

[18] *Concluding Unscientific Postscript,* pp. 84-5.

[19] Ibid., p. 85.

[20] II A 140, 156, 160, 161; *Papers and Journals: A Selection,* pp. 90-1; cf. *Journals and Papers,* 1702, vol. 2, p. 259 and 2310, 2314, 2315, vol. 3, pp. 4, 5.

[21] X 2 A 439; *Papers and Journals: A Selection,* p. 470; cf. *Journals and Papers,* 1059, vol. 1, p. 461.

[22] X 2 A 439; *Papers and Journals: A Selection,* p. 470. Cf. *Journals and Papers,* 1059, vol. 1, p. 461.

[23] 'Dante and the Lobster', in Samuel Beckett, *More Pricks than Kicks* (Calder, London, 1993), p. 21.

[24] That is why all his work could bear the title of one of his fragments, 'Imagination Dead Imagine', just as Wallace Stevens's remark that 'Yet the absence of the imagination had / Itself to be imagined' is merely the articulation of the imperative he had always set himself (Wallace Stevens, 'The Plain Sense of Things', in *Collected Poems* (Faber and Faber, London, 1955), pp. 502-3).

[25] X 4 A 258; *Papers and Journals: A Selection,* p. 525; cf. *Journals and Papers,* 3647, vol. 3, p. 689.

[26] XI 1 A 445; *Papers and Journals: A Selection,* p. 606; cf. *Journals and Papers,* 6902, vol. 6, pp. 526-7.

[27] X 1 A 510; *Papers and Journals: A Selection,* p. 392; cf. *Journals and Papers,* 6431, vol. 6, pp. 172-3.

FURTHER READING

Beabout, Gregory R. *Freedom and Its Misuses: Kierkegaard on Anxiety and Despair*. Milwaukee, Wisc.: Marquette University Press, 1996, 192 p.

In seven chapters, discusses Kierkegaard's views on anxiety, despair, and freedom, based on a reading of Kierkegaard's *The Concept of Anxiety* and *The Sickness unto Death*.

Bové, Paul A. "The Penitentiary of Reflection: Søren Kierkegaard and Critical Activity." In *Kierkegaard and Literature: Irony, Repetition, and Criticism*, edited by Ronald Schleifer and Robert Markley, pp. 25-57. Norman: University of Oklahoma Press, 1984.

After examining how Kierkegaard is regarded by literary scholars as a literary critic, Bové reviews *Two Ages* and argues that to Kierkegaard, critical activity must examine its own origins, assumptions, and effects in order to regulate its participation and influence on social institutions.

Connell, George B. and C. Stephen Evans, eds. *Foundations of Kierkegaard's Vision of Community: Religion, Ethics, and Politics in Kierkegaard*. New Jersey: Humanities Press, 1992, 245 p.

Collection of essays focusing on Kierkegaard's views on faith and religion, the ethical life, subjectivity, the individual's role in society, and political and feminist issues.

Fenves, Peter. *"Chatter": Language and History in Kierkegaard*. Stanford, Calif.: Stanford University Press, 1993, 312 p.

A book-length study, covering a number of Kierkegaard's works, which analyzes Kierkegaard's attitude toward the function of speech as well as written language.

Gellman, Jerome I. "The Fear and the Trembling." In *The Fear, the Trembling, and the Fire: Kierkegaard and Hasidic Masters on the Binding of Isaac*, pp. 1-21. Lanham, Md.: University Press of America, 1994.

Maintains that the standard reading of Kierkegaard's account of the biblical Abraham story "is not the best reading." Gellman demonstrates that reading the story as Abraham's defiance of ethical norms in order to "heed a higher voice" leaves Kierkegaard open to several major criticisms. Additionally, Gellman offers another interpretation which focuses less on Abraham's choice between universal ethics and faith and more on Abraham's choice to define himself.

Kirmmse, Bruce H., ed. *Encounters with Kierkegaard: A Life as Seen by His Contemporaries*, collected, edited, and annotated by Bruce H. Kirmmse and translated by Bruce H. Kirmmse and Virginia R. Laursen. Princeton, N.J.: Princeton University Press, 1996, 358 p.

A collection of anecdotes and letters by contemporaries of Kierkegaard, including Hans Christian Anderson, Andrew Hamilton, and Georg Brandes, among others, which discusses Kierkegaard's reputation, works, and personality.

Mackey, Louis. "Starting from Scratch: Kierkegaard Unfair to Hegel." In *Points of View: Readings of Kierkegaard*, pp. 1-22. Tallahassee: Florida State University Press, 1986.

Focuses on Kierkegaard's master's thesis, *On the Concept of Irony*, and discusses the ways in which Kierkegaard employed irony to attack Hegel.

Mooney, Edward F. *Selves in Discord and Resolve: Kierke-gaard's Moral-Religious Psychology from* Either/Or *to* Sickness unto Death. New York: Routledge, 1996, 140 p.

Examines the relationship between poetry and philosophy in Kierkegaard; the concepts of self-acquisition and responsibility; Kierkegaard's discussions of Job and Abraham; and Kierkegaard's views on subjectivity and the "relational" self.

Pattison, George, ed. *Kierkegaard on Art and Communication*. New York: St. Martin's Press, 1992, 189 p.

Collection of essays exploring the form and content of Kierkegaard's works as a poet, philosopher, and theologian.

Perkins, Robert L. *International Kierkegaard Commentary:* Two Ages. Macon, Ga.: Mercer University Press, 1984, 265 p.

Collection of essays designed, states Perkins in the introduction to the volume, to destroy the myth that "Kierkegaard presents his concept of the individual in a social and political vacuum, that Kierkegaardian inwardness and subjectivity is so pervasive and unqualified that for the Kierkegaardian individual . . . there is no social and historical context, that society and history stop and cease to have effect on the individual who chooses himself before God."

Walsh, Sylvia I. "Forming the Heart: The Role of Love in Kierkegaard's Thought." In *The Grammar of the Heart: New Essays in Moral Philosophy and Theology*, edited by Richard H. Bell, pp. 234-56. San Francisco: Harper & Row, Publishers, 1988.

Studies the "role of love in forming the heart" as Kierkegaard discusses the matter in the Christian discourses found in *Works of Love*.

"The Tell-Tale Heart"

Edgar Allan Poe

The following entry presents criticism of Poe's short story "The Tell-Tale Heart" (1843). For information on Poe's complete career, see *NCLC*, Volume 1; for information on Poe's short stories, see *NCLC*, Volume 16; for information on Poe's essays, see *NCLC*, Volume 55.

INTRODUCTION

Among the many strange and complex short stories of Poe, "The Tell-Tale Heart" has come to be known as one of the most mysterious and psychologically intriguing. Poe's preoccupations with death, with madness, and with troubled human relationships all find their culmination in this brief narrative. The murder of the old man and its aftermath, which form the center of the story, are told with dazzling clarity, a clarity that itself obscures the meaning of the act and calls into question the emotional stability of the unnamed narrator. The subjectivism of this story, the confusion of the line between reader and character within the narrative, and the use of language support the claim that Poe prefigures and indeed develops many of the tropes usually associated with more recent fiction.

Biographical Information

"The Tell-Tale Heart" was written and published during the most furiously productive phase of Poe's life, when he lived in Philadelphia with his young wife Virginia (a cousin) and her mother. During this period he was also editing the literary journal *Burton's Gentleman's Magazine,* and in 1840 he had collected his previously published tales into *Tales of the Grotesque and Arabesque,* including the popular "The Fall of the House of Usher" and the grim "King Pest." Now in his forties, Poe had become a well-known writer of short fiction, even though his education was uneven (he left the University of Virginia during his first year) and he experienced constant financial struggles. Early works of poetry had been largely neglected by the literary scene, but five stories were published in the *Philadelphia Sunday Courier* in 1832. From that point onward, Poe's stories appeared in journals throughout the United States. Yet periodic setbacks in his fortunes (his wife's illness, continuing alienation from his uncle John Allen, who had raised him, and his inability to secure a stable source of income) triggered fits of depression, which Poe tended to aggravate by turning to alcohol. In the stories of this period, the mood of Poe's

works varies considerably, between the fantastic narrative of a sleep-walker in "Mesmeric Revelation," the strangely wrought "Life in Death" a study of the relationship between art and life, and the horrific portrayal of murder in "The Black Cat." The last story is one that is often linked to "The Tell-Tale Heart," as both have the form of a narrated confession of violence and murder without directly addressing the reason for the crime. These two stories mark Poe's increasing interest in and ability to portray the psychologically gruesome and the supernatural, as well as his return to poetry.

Plot and Major Characters

The sparse plot of "The Tell-Tale Heart" concerns the "murder aforethought" of an old man, who is never named nor described fully, by the narrator, who is also never identified. Its narration is clearly retrospective but otherwise unlocated; the circumstances of the confession of this crime are never described, and so it seems that the narrator is speaking directly and passionately to the reader. The sequence of events is simple enough: the narrator is disturbed by the eye of an old man; he complains that "one of his eyes resembled that of a vulture—a pale blue eye, with a film over it." The narrator decides to rid himself of this eye by killing the old man. This is accomplished after seven painstaking nights of creeping into the man's room in order to see if the offending eye is open. It is only on the eighth night that the old man opens his eyes, and the crime is committed. How the man is actually killed is not described in detail: the narrator merely says that he pulls "the heavy bed over him." This same night, he dismembers the body and hides it beneath the floorboards of the man's room. Soon after, three police officers, who also remain anonymous and characterless, arrive (presumably to investigate the terrified shriek of the old man). Although the narrator takes pride in his calm comportment toward the officers as they sit directly above the hiding-place of the old man's body, he discerns a noise, "a low, dull, quick sound" that he identifies as the heartbeat of the old man. In rage and desperation, convinced that the police officers also hear this noise and have detected his guilt, he confesses to the crime. At this point the narrative abruptly ends.

Major Themes

The slow and apparently reasonable beginning of the narrative gradually quickens toward its feverish conclusion; the language of the story, particularly the use of dashes to express the obscure connections of the tale and the repetitions that mark the emphatic denial of insanity, is one of its most striking features. The nineteenth-century concern with death and madness appear in many of Poe's stories, but in "The Tell-Tale Heart" these themes seem to have been distilled into an unparalleled intensity. The strange vacillation between bare narration (the reader is given no setting beyond the walls of the house, no history beyond the events of the plot, and no characterization at all beyond what may be gleaned from the narrator's excited tale) and the magnification of critical moments (the narrator's patient vigil at the door of the old man's room and the repetition of the heartbeat that provokes the narrator's confession). Indeed, as in dreams, the sense of time in the story is a distorted reflection of "ordinary" time; it is this strangeness, along with the terrible clarity of the narration and the vociferous protestations of sanity, that lead the reader to suspect the emotional health of the narrator. The confession is not an explanation, although it superficially appears to be one: the eye of the old man, which becomes an obsessive object of the narrator's attention. The internal tension of the narrator, which leads him to understand the terror of the old man and to anticipate the responses of his listener/reader, dramatically underscores the uncertain status of the narrative: as real-

ity or hallucination, involving two persons or a single split subject, and the audience to which it is directed.

Critical Reception

One of Poe's most popular and anthologized stories, "The Tell-Tale Heart" is considered a stunning example of the deep connections between the Gothic tale and modern fiction, especially in its innovative use of the subjective narrative and its psychologically rich portrayal of a human situation that remains simultaneously strange and familiar in its intimacy. Poe's popularity in Europe, exemplified by Jacques Lacan's celebrated study of "The Purloined Letter", reflects his works' affinities with psychoanalytic tropes, such as the unconscious, repression, and the significance of the gaze. Many critics claim that the madness or dreamlike quality of the narrative is unambiguous, and have gone so far as to diagnose the narrator with paranoid schizophrenia, a medical definition unknown in Poe's age. The frequently cited obsession with time and mortality that inhabits Poe's writing is evident in "The Tell-Tale Heart" as well. This has led some recent scholars to argue that the narrator is struggling against his own death and in James W. Gargano's words "the tyranny of time," which he has projected onto the figure of the old man. The narrative has suggested to others, particularly Christopher Benfey, an internalized conflict between the need for interpersonal contact and the desire to protect oneself from the vulnerability that arises with such contact. The style of writing draws the reader into the narrative by appearing to transcribe directly the passionate confession of a fascinating if ultimately repulsive character. The combination of surrealism and immediacy that constitutes the peculiarity of the narrative disrupts simple or conventional interpretations. The psychological complexity of both the content and the form of "The Tell-Tale Heart" has continued to grip both the critical and popular imagination, and anticipates more recent fictional explorations into the concealed intricacy of the human condition.

CRITICISM

E. Arthur Robinson (essay date 1965)

SOURCE: "Poe's 'The Tell-Tale Heart,'" *Nineteenth-Century Fiction,* Vol. 19, No. 4, March, 1965, pp. 369-78.

[*In the following essay, Robinson provides a general overview of major themes in the story and focuses upon its dramatization of "self-destruction through extreme subjectivity."*]

Poe's **"The Tell-Tale Heart"** consists of a monologue in which an accused murderer protests his sanity rather than his innocence. The point of view is the criminal's, but the tone is ironic in that his protestation of sanity produces an opposite effect upon the reader. From these two premises stem multiple levels of action in the story. The criminal, for example, appears obsessed with defending his psychic self at whatever cost, but actually his drive is self-destructive since successful defense upon either implied charge—of murder or of criminal insanity—automatically involves admission of guilt upon the other.

Specifically, the narrator bases his plea upon the assumption that madness is incompatible with systematic action, and as evidence of his capacity for the latter he relates how he has executed a horrible crime with rational precision. He reiterates this argument until it falls into a pattern: "If still you think me mad, you will think so no longer when I describe the wise precautions I took for concealment of the body."[1] At the same time he discloses a deep psychological confusion. Almost casually he admits lack of normal motivation: "Object there was none. Passion there was none. I loved the old man." Yet in spite of this affection he says that the idea of murder "haunted me day and night." Since such processes of reasoning tend to convict the speaker of madness, it does not seem out of keeping that he is driven to confession by "hearing" reverberations of the still-beating heart in the corpse he has dismembered, nor that he appears unaware of the irrationalities in his defense of rationality.

At first reading, the elements of **"The Tell-Tale Heart"** appear simple: the story itself is one of Poe's shortest; it contains only two main characters, both unnamed, and three indistinguishable police officers; even the setting of the narration is left unspecified. In the present study my object is to show that beneath its narrative flow the story illustrates the elaboration of design which Poe customarily sought, and also that it contains two of the major psychological themes dramatized in his longer works.

It is important to note that Poe's theory of art emphasizes development almost equally with unity of effect. There must be, he insists, "a repetition of purpose," a "dropping of the water upon the rock;"[2] thus he calls heavily upon the artist's craftsmanship to devise thematic modifications of the "preconceived effect." A favorite image in his stories is that of arabesque ornamentation with repetitive design. In **"The Tell-Tale Heart"** one can distinguish several such recurring devices filling out the "design" of the tale, the most evident being what the narrator calls his "over acuteness of the senses." He incorporates this physical keenness into his plea of sanity: ". . . . why *will* you say that I am mad? The disease had sharpened my senses—not destroyed, not dulled them. Above all was the sense of hearing acute." He likens the sound of the old man's heart to the ticking of a watch "enveloped in cotton"

and then fancies that its terrified beating may arouse the neighbors. His sensitivity to sight is equally disturbing, for it is the old man's eye, "a pale blue eye, with a film over it," which first vexed him and which he seeks to destroy. Similar though less extreme powers are ascribed to the old man. For example, the murderer congratulates himself that not even his victim could have detected anything wrong with the floor which has been replaced over the body, and earlier he imagines the old man, awakened by "the first slight noise," listening to determine whether the sound has come from an intruder or "the wind in the chimney." Variations such as these give the sensory details a thematic significance similar to that of the "morbid acuteness of the senses" of Roderick Usher in **"The Fall of the House of Usher"** or the intensity with which the victim of the Inquisition hears, sees, and smells his approaching doom in **"The Pit and the Pendulum."**

These sensory data provide the foundation for an interesting psychological phenomenon in the story. As the characters listen in the darkness, intervals of strained attention are prolonged until the effect resembles that of slow motion. Thus for seven nights the madman enters the room so "very, very slowly" that it takes him an hour to get his head through the doorway; as he says, "a watch's minute-hand moves more quickly than did mine." When on the eighth night the old man is alarmed, "for a whole hour I did not move a muscle." Later he is roused to fury by the man's terror, but "even yet," he declares, "I refrained and kept still. I scarcely breathed." On different nights both men sit paralyzed in bed, listening for terrors real or imagined. After the murder is completed, "I placed my hand upon the heart and held it there many minutes." In the end it seems to his overstrained nerves that the police officers linger inordinately in the house, chatting and smiling, until he is driven frantic by their cheerful persistence.

This psychological process is important to **"The Tell-Tale Heart"** in two ways. First, reduplication of the device gives the story structural power. Poe here repeats a dominating impression at least seven times in a brief story. Several of the instances mentioned pertain to plot, but others function to emphasize the former and to provide aesthetic satisfaction. To use Poe's words, "by such means, with such care and skill, a picture is at length painted which leaves in the mind of him who contemplates it with a kindred art, a sense of the fullest satisfaction. The idea of the tale, its thesis, has been presented unblemished. . . . "[3] Here Poe is speaking specifically of "skilfully-constructed tales," and the complementary aspects of technique described are first to omit extraneous material and second to combine incidents, tone, and style to develop the "pre-established design." In this manner, form and "idea" become one. The thematic repetition and variation of incident in

"The Tell-Tale Heart" offer one of the clearest examples of this architectural principle of Poe's at work.

Second, this slow-motion technique intensifies the subjectivity of **"The Tell-Tale Heart"** beyond that attained by mere use of a narrator. In the psychological triad of stimulus, internal response, and action, the first and third elements are slighted and the middle stage is given exaggerated attention.[4] In **"The Tell-Tale Heart,"** stimulus in an objective sense scarcely exists at all. Only the man's eye motivates the murderer, and that almost wholly through his internal reaction to it. The action too, though decisive, is quickly over: "In an instant I dragged him to the floor, and pulled the heavy bed over him." In contrast, the intermediate, subjective experience is prolonged to a point where psychologically it is beyond objective measurement. At first the intervals receive conventional description—an "hour," or "many minutes"—but eventually such designations become meaningless and duration can be presented only in terms of the experience itself. Thus, in the conclusion of the story, the ringing in the madman's ears first is "fancied," then later becomes "distinct," then is discovered to be so "definite" that it is erroneously accorded external actuality, and finally grows to such obsessive proportions that it drives the criminal into an emotional and physical frenzy. Of the objective duration of these stages no information is given; the experience simply "continued" until "at length" the narrator "found" that its quality had changed.

Through such psychological handling of time Poe achieves in several of his most effective stories, including **"The Tell-Tale Heart,"** two levels of chronological development which are at work simultaneously throughout the story. Typically, the action reaches its most intense point when the relation between the objective and subjective time sense falters or fails. At this point too the mental world of the subject is at its greatest danger of collapse. Thus we have the mental agony of the bound prisoner who loses all count of time as he alternately swoons and lives intensified existence while he observes the slowly descending pendulum. The narrator in **"The Pit and the Pendulum"** specifically refuses to accept responsibility for objective time-correlations: "There was another interval of insensibility; it was brief; for, upon again lapsing into life, there had been no perceptible descent in the pendulum. But it might have been long; for I knew there were demons who took note of my swoon, and who could have arrested the vibration at pleasure."[5] These demons are his Inquisitional persecutors, but more subjective "demons" are at work in the timeless terror and fascination of the mariner whirled around the abyss in **"The Descent into the Maelström,"** or the powerless waiting of Usher for days after he first hears his sister stirring within the tomb. In each instance the objective world has been reduced to the microcosm

of an individual's experience; his time sense fades under the pressure of emotional stress and physical paralysis.

Even when not literally present, paralysis often may be regarded as symbolic in Poe's stories. In *The Narrative of Arthur Gordon Pym* (1838), Pym's terrifying dreams in the hold of the ship represent physical and mental paralysis: "Had a thousand lives hung upon the movement of a limb or the utterance of a syllable, I could have neither stirred nor spoken. . . . I felt that my powers of body and mind were fast leaving me."[6] Other examples are the "convolutions" of bonds about the narrator in **"The Pit and the Pendulum,"** the death-grasp on the ring-bolt in **"The Descent into the Maelström,"** the inaction of Roderick and (more literally) the catalepsy of Madeline Usher, and in part the supposed rationality of the madman in **"The Tell-Tale Heart,"** which turns out to be subservience of his mental to his emotional nature. In most applications of the slow-motion technique in **"The Tell-Tale Heart,"** three states of being are present concurrently: emotional tension, loss of mental grasp upon the actualities of the situation, and inability to act or to act deliberately. Often these conditions both invite and postpone catastrophe, with the effect of focusing attention upon the intervening experience.

In the two years following publication of **"The Tell-Tale Heart,"** Poe extended this timeless paralysis to fantasies of hypnosis lasting beyond death. **"Mesmeric Revelation"** (1844) contains speculations about the relation between sensory experience and eternity. In **"The Facts in the Case of M. Valdemar"** (1845) the hypnotized subject is maintained for nearly seven months in a state of suspended "death" and undergoes instant dissolution when revived. His pleading for either life or death suggests that his internal condition had included awareness and suffering. Similarly the narrator in **"The Tell-Tale Heart"** records: "Oh God! what *could* I do? I foamed—I raved—I swore!"—while all the time the police officers notice no foaming nor raving, for still they "chatted pleasantly, and smiled." His reaction is still essentially subjective, although he paces the room and grates his chair upon the boards above the beating heart. All these experiences move toward ultimate collapse, which is reached in **"The Tell-Tale Heart"** as it is for Usher and the hypnotized victims, while a last-moment reprieve is granted in **"The Pit and the Pendulum"** and **"The Descent into the Maelström."**

A second major theme in **"The Tell-Tale Heart"** is the murderer's psychological identification with the man he kills. Similar sensory details connect the two men. The vulture eye which the subject casts upon the narrator is duplicated in the "single dim ray" of the lantern that falls upon his own eye; like the unshuttered lantern, it is always one eye that is mentioned, never two. One man hears the creaking of the lantern hinge, the other the slipping of a finger upon the fastening. Both lie awake at midnight "hearkening to the death-watches in the wall." The loud yell of the murderer is echoed in the old man's shriek, which the narrator, as though with increasing clairvoyance, later tells the police was his own. Most of all the identity is implied in the key psychological occurrence in the story—the madman's mistaking his own heartbeat for that of his victim, both before and after the murder.

These two psychological themes—the indefinite extension of subjective time and the psychic merging of killer and killed—are linked closely together in the story. This is illustrated in the narrator's commentary after he has awakened the old man by an incautious sound and each waits for the other to move:

> Presently I heard a slight groan, and I knew it was the groan of mortal terror. It was not a groan of pain or of grief—oh, no!—it was the low stifled sound that arises from the bottom of the soul when overcharged with awe. I knew the sound well. Many a night, just at midnight, when all the world slept, it has welled up from my own bosom, deepening, with its dreadful echo, the terrors that distracted me. I say I knew it well. I knew that he had been lying awake ever since the first slight noise, when he had turned in the bed. His fears had been ever since growing upon him. He had been trying to fancy them causeless, but could not. He had been saying to himself—"It is nothing but the wind in the chimney—it is only a mouse crossing the floor," or "it is merely a cricket which has made a single chirp." Yes, he had been trying to comfort himself with these suppositions: but he had found all in vain.

Here the slow-motion technique is applied to both characters, with emphasis upon first their subjective experience and second the essential identity of that experience. The madman feels compelled to delay the murder until his subject is overcome by the same nameless fears that have possessed his own soul. The groan is an "echo" of these terrors within. The speaker has attempted a kind of catharsis by forcing his own inner horror to arise in his companion and then feeding his self-pity upon it. This pity cannot prevent the murder, which is a further attempt at exorcism. The final two sentences of the paragraph quoted explain why he believes that destruction is inevitable:

> *All in vain;* because Death, in approaching him, had stalked with his black shadow before him, and enveloped the victim. And it was the mournful influence of the unperceived shadow that caused him to feel—although he neither saw nor heard—to *feel* the presence of my head within the room.

The significance of these sentences becomes clearer when we consider how strikingly the over-all effect of time-extension in **"The Tell-Tale Heart"** resembles that produced in Poe's **"The Colloquy of Monos and Una,"** published two years earlier. In Monos's account of dying and passing into eternity, he prefaces his final experience with a sensory acuteness similar to that experienced by the narrator in **"The Tell-Tale Heart."** "The senses were unusually active," Monos reports, "though eccentrically so. . . . " As the five senses fade in death, they are not utterly lost but merge into a sixth—of simple duration:

> Motion in the animal frame had fully ceased. No muscle quivered; no nerve thrilled; no artery throbbed. But there seems to have sprung up in the brain . . . a mental pendulous pulsation. . . . By its aid I measured the irregularities of the clock upon the mantel, and of the watches of the attendants. . . . And this—this keen, perfect, self-existing sentiment of *duration* . . . this sixth sense, upspringing from the ashes of the rest, was the first obvious and certain step of the intemporal soul upon the threshold of the temporal Eternity.[7]

Likewise the old man in **"The Tell-Tale Heart"** listens as though paralyzed, unable either to move or to hear anything that will dissolve his fears. This resembles Monos' sensory intensity and the cessation of "motion in the animal frame." Also subjective time is prolonged, becomes partially divorced from objective measurement, and dominates it. The most significant similarity comes in the conclusion of the experience. The old man does not know it but he is undergoing the same dissolution as Monos. He waits in vain for his fear to subside because actually it is "Death" whose shadow is approaching him, and "it was the mournful influence of that shadow that caused him to feel" his destroyer within the room. Like Monos, beyond his normal senses he has arrived at a "sixth sense," which is at first duration and then death.

But if the old man is nearing death so too must be the narrator, who has felt the same "mortal terror" in his own bosom. This similarity serves to unify the story. In Poe's tales, extreme sensitivity of the senses usually signalizes approaching death, as in the case of Monos and of Roderick Usher. This "over acuteness" in **"The Tell-Tale Heart,"** however, pertains chiefly to the murderer, while death comes to the man with the "vulture eye." By making the narrator dramatize his feelings in the old man, Poe draws these two motifs together. We must remember, writes one commentator upon the story, "that the criminal sought his own death in that of his victim, and that he had in effect become the man who now lies dead."[8] Symbolically this is true. The resurgence of the beating heart shows that the horrors within himself, which the criminal attempted to identify with the old man and thus destroy, still live. In the death of the old man he sought to kill a part of himself, but his "demons" could not be exorcised through murder, for he himself is their destined victim.

From this point of view, the theme of **"The Tell-Tale Heart"** is self-destruction through extreme subjectivity marked paradoxically by both an excess of sensitivity and temporal solipsism. How seriously Poe could take this relativity of time and experience is evident in the poetic philosophy of his *Eureka* (1849). There time is extended almost infinitely into the life-cycle of the universe, but that cycle itself is only one heartbeat of God, who is the ultimate subjectivity. Romantically, indeed, Poe goes even further in the conclusion to *Eureka* and sees individual man becoming God, enclosing reality within himself, and acting as his own creative agent. In this state, distinction between subjective and objective fades: "the sense of individual identity will be gradually merged in the general consciousness."[9] Destruction then becomes self-destruction, the madman and his victim being aspects of the same universal identity. Death not only is self-willed but takes on some of the sanctity of creative and hence destructive Deity. The heartbeat of the red slayer and the slain merge in Poe's metaphysical speculations as well as in the denouement of a horror story.

This extreme subjectivity, moreover, leaves the ethical problem of **"The Tell-Tale Heart"** unresolved. In the opening paragraph of the story is foreshadowed an issue of good and evil connected with the speaker's madness: "I heard all things in the heaven and in the earth. I heard many things in hell. How, then, am I mad?" To be dramatically functional such an issue must be related to the murder. The only outward motivation for the murder is irritation at the "vulture eye." It is the evil of the eye, not the old man (whom he "loved"), that the murderer can no longer live with, and to make sure that it is destroyed he will not kill the man while he is sleeping. What the "Evil Eye" represents that it so arouses the madman we do not know, but since he sees himself in his companion the result is self-knowledge. Vision becomes insight, the "Evil Eye" an evil "I," and the murdered man a victim sacrificed to a self-constituted deity. In this story, we have undeveloped hints of the self-abhorrence uncovered in **"William Wilson"** and **"The Imp of the Perverse."**

Poe also has left unresolved the story's ultimate degree of subjectivity. No objective setting is provided; so completely subjective is the narration that few or no points of alignment with the external world remain. From internal evidence, we assume the speaker to be mad, but whether his words constitute a defense before some criminal tribunal or the complete fantasy of a madman there is no way of ascertaining.[10] The difference, however, is not material, for the subjective experience, however come by, *is* the story. Psychologically, the lengthening concentration upon internal states of being has divorced the murderer first from normal chronology and finally from relationship with the "actual" world. The result, in Beach's words, is "disinte-

gration of the psychological complex." The victim images himself as another and recoils from the vision. Seeing and seen eye become identical and must be destroyed.

Notes

1 "The Tell-Tale Heart," *Works,* ed. Clarence Edmund Stedman and George Edward Woodberry (New York, 1914), II, 70. Unless otherwise specified, all quotations from Poe are from this edition.

2 "Hawthorne's 'Tales'," *Works,* VII, 37.

3 "Twice-Told Tales," *Selected Writings of Edgar Allan Poe,* ed. Edward H. Davidson (Boston, 1956), p. 448.

4 Joseph Warren Beach in *The Twentieth-Century Novel* (New York, 1932), p. 407, describes a similar effect in stream-of-consciousness writing: "The subjective element becomes noticeable in fiction, as in everyday psychology, when an interval occurs between the stimulus to action and the resulting act." In extreme application of this technique, he declares, "there is a tendency to exhaust the content of the moment presented, there is *an infinite expansion of the moment,*" and he adds that the danger is that "there may come to pass a disintegration of the psychological complex, a divorce between motive and conduct" (p. 409). This is close to the state of Poe's narrator and murderer.

5 *Works,* I, 241-242.

6 *Works,* V, 38.

7 *Works,* I, 120-121.

8 Patrick F. Quinn, *The French Face of Edgar Poe* (Carbondale, Illinois, 1957), p. 236. Quinn makes this identity the theme of the story, without describing the full sensory patterns upon which it is based.

9 *Works,* IX, 164-169.

10 Despite lack of objective evidence, "The Tell-Tale Heart" bears much resemblance to a dream. The narrator acknowledges that the murdered man's shriek was such as occurs in dreams, and his memory of approaching the old man's bed upon eight successive midnights has the quality of a recurring nightmare. Poe frequently couples madness and dreaming, often with the variant "opium dreams," as in "Ligeia" and "The Fall of the House of Usher." "The Black Cat," a companion piece published the same year as "The Tell-Tale Heart" (1843), opens with an explicit denial of both madness and dreaming. The introductory paragraph of "Eleonora" (1842) runs the complete course of madness—dreams—death—good and evil: "Men have called me mad; but the question is not yet

settled, whether madness is or is not the loftiest intelligence: whether much that is glorious, whether all that is profound, does not spring from disease of thought—from *moods* of mind exalted at the expense of the general intellect. They who dream by day are cognizant of many things which escape those who dream only by night. In their gray visions they obtain glimpses of eternity, and thrill, in awaking, to find that they have been upon the verge of the great secret. In snatches, they learn something of the wisdom which is of good, and more of the mere knowledge which is of evil" (*Works,* I, 96).

James W. Gargano (essay date 1968)

SOURCE: "The Theme of Time in 'The Tell-Tale Heart,'" *Studies in Short Fiction,* Vol. V, No. 4, Summer, 1968, pp. 378-82.

[*In the essay that follows, Gargano argues that the primary conflict of the narrator in "The Tell-Tale Heart" involves "the tyranny of time."*]

The critic who wishes to read Edgar Allan Poe's "**The Tell-Tale Heart**" as a mere horror story may be content to accept its incidents as unmotivated and mysterious. How, the critic may argue, can the story be rationally explained when the narrator himself is at a loss to account for the frenzy inspired in him by his victim's "evil eye?" The critic may further maintain that Poe deliberately establishes and enhances the mystery of his tale by having the murderer eschew all explanations for his deed: "Object there was none. Passion there was none. I loved the old man." The critic may conclude that Poe waives logical and realistic considerations and simply sets out to make his reader feel the terror that comes from observing the unfolding of an inexplicable crime.[1]

Yet, there are two irresistible reasons for believing that Poe's purpose in "**The Tell-Tale Heart**" goes beyond the concoction of horror and mystification. First of all, he has artfully complicated his tale by making the narrator's description of himself and his actions appear unreliable. Ironically, the protagonist attempts to prove in language that is wild and disordered that he is methodical, calm, and sane. In addition, though he persuades himself that he felt no "passion" against the old man, he talks frequently of his "fury," "anxiety," and "uncontrollable terror." Secondly, Poe has built into his tale a set of internally consistent symbols that are charged with meaning. The structure of the story contains so much arrangement that it becomes almost impossible to view the pattern and accumulated force of the symbols as accidental.

If we approach "**The Tell-Tale Heart**" without traditional blinders, I am convinced that it will reveal itself to be a well-organized and thoughtful work of art with a striking economy of images and symbols. I believe, however, that any serious analysis of the story must recognize a basic irony: that the narrator, though he does not understand his own character or actions, unconsciously provides all the clues necessary to a comprehension of them. Obviously, for all his acuteness and the "fine art" of his crime, Poe's protagonist increasingly demonstrates, with every vain denial, that he is mad. Moreover, in ascribing strangely revolting powers to someone outside himself, he reveals that his revulsion is a symptom of his own internal disorder. Finally, in focusing his violence against one man, he makes known that he is rebelling against the very terms on which life is granted to all men. In his rage against the nature of things, he resembles Prince Prospero, who immures himself in a castle fortified against death, and William Wilson, who tries one of the most amazing (and perhaps common) of all experiments—to repudiate a part of his own being.

An analysis of the symbolism of "**The Tell-Tale Heart**" will, I hope, identify the narrator's ultimate antagonist as the force that will inevitably cause him to resemble the old man with the appalling "eye of a vulture." His quarrel, then, is not with a ravaged individual but with Time, which on one level is symbolized by the omnipresent "watches" and on another by the "tell-tale" heart. The revelatory moments in the tale, thus, occur when both sets of symbols merge and when the old man, after death, becomes inseparable from his murderer.

As many of his works show, Poe was infatuated with puzzles, hoaxes, and ironies. It seems a bit incongruous, then, to insist that his horror tales be taken as straightforward and artless examples of American Gothicism. For Poe, human thought and motive were often the tricky means of leading men into self-created labyrinths. Such men devise their own confusions and intellectually refine them into a crooked but convincing rationale. But the unperceived logic of their well-thought-out schemes coerces them into self-exposure and destruction because fundamentally their inner turmoil cannot be resolved through the specious "organization" of their actions. Indeed, the planned actions themselves not only fail to be curative but betray the original delusions which inspired them. In a real sense, Poe's characters often trap themselves in the most elaborate of fine-spun hoaxes.

"**The Tell-Tale Heart**" is, technically speaking, a ruse perpetrated by the protagonist against himself. His ingenious concealment and ritualized rehearsal of his deed, apparently directed against the old man, are practiced upon himself. His cherished plot is an escape from self-knowledge into an absorbing and distracting action; yet, in his careful stalking of his enemy, he suggests the basis of his psychological insecurity. His "structured" violence draws him on to talk of his compulsive obsession with images and sounds that evoke the rhythm of time. Finally, he completes his own entrapment when his irrational preoccupation with these images and sounds breaks down the impressive order he has imposed upon his machinations.

Poe's major strategy in working out his design is to have the narrator attribute his own anguished feelings to his victim. Therefore, because of their "common" emotions, the murderer and the old man appear to be not only related but identical. The barrier between their individual beings begins to break down when the old man, hearing someone at his chamber door, springs up in bed and cries out. At that moment, the narrator offers a remarkably precise interpretation of his intended victim's state of mind: he declares that the old man "was still sitting up in bed listening—*just as I have done, night after night,* hearkening to the death watches in the wall." (My italics.) Poe effectively implies that the only emotions experienced by the old man are sensations that have afflicted the protagonist night after night. In short, the narrator may be said to feel for both men; he has, even before murdering the old man, entered into and completely preëmpted his life. What he does not see, however, is that in possessing another man's being, he is in turn assimilated and consumed by it.

Poe devotes a large part of his short tale to the narrator's analysis of the old man's agony as death approaches; ironically, however, the brilliant schemer unconsciously characterizes his own long-standing derangement: "Many a night, just at midnight, when all the world slept, it [a groan like the old man's] has welled up, from my own bosom, deepening, with its dreadful echo, the terrors that distracted me." Clearly, he can trace the gradual intensification of the old man's dread because he, too, has been subject to it. He, like the old man, has tried to dismiss this dread as "causeless," only to find it invading and filling his mind until he acknowledged all resistance to it as "vain." He knows, because he has already uttered them, the very words with which the suffering man tries to comfort himself in his extremity: "He had been saying to himself—'It is nothing but the wind in the chimney—it is only a mouse crossing the floor,' or 'it is merely a cricket which has made a single chirp.'"

It is significant, then, that the narrator sees the old man's responses to the menaces of the night as identical to his own. Indeed, the intended victim becomes a kind of surrogate for his persecutor, a projection of his most ingrained terrors. All his irrational hates and fears are embodied in the man he wishes to destroy. He wildly assumes that by ridding himself of the external symbol of his dementia he will be able to free himself from his psychic troubles.

But, as I have stated, the narrator's dream of freedom is illusory because the pervasive villain of **"The Tell-Tale Heart"** is Time itself. Heard from the "death watches" in the wall and seen in the waiting and expectant "eye of a vulture," it subtly undermines the narrator's self-assurance. Indeed, he has become so obsessed by the sound of time that he hears it everywhere and in all things. There is a great deal of psychological meaning to be found in his feverish declaration: "Above all was the sense of hearing acute. I heard all things in the heaven and in the earth. I heard many things in hell." Listening to the old man's groan, he even hears in it "the low stifled sound that arises from the bottom of the soul." For the narrator, all the sounds are inter-related and one; moreover, they have their source in a haunted and bewildered imagination.

Poe allows the main character's concern with the tyranny of time to betray itself through the nature and organization of his fictional details. First, the object of the narrator's crime is not so much an individual man, but an old man made revolting by time. In addition, the watches, which are obviously symbols of time, have become part of the narrator's consciousness and even lurk within the walls of his house. Climactically, the incessant beating of the old man's heart locates the cadence of time within the center of man's being. As if to leave no doubt about the primary connection between the heart and the watches, Poe has the protagonist speak of them as if they gave forth the same sounds: "there came to my ears a low, dull, quick sound, such as a watch makes when enveloped in cotton. I knew *that* sound well, too. It was the beating of the old man's heart." It requires no imaginative daring, then, to conclude that the "low stifled sound that arises from the bottom of the soul" is also intimately related to the low, muffled sound of the cotton-enveloped watch. In short, when the narrator is betrayed by the still-beating heart of his dead victim, he is really betrayed by the triumphant din of time, which is the sum of all sounds, within and outside of man.

Expertly as Poe manages the "sound images" in **"The Tell-Tale Heart,"** he displays equal skill in making the old man's "evil eye" the external counterpart of the hidden watches and the beating heart. To begin with, the eye's similarity to a vulture's suggests the predatoriness of "Father Time." Moreover, the relation of the eye to the theme of time is further shown by the sequence of events leading up to the murder. On the fateful night, the protagonist cannot go ahead with his crime until he has trained the rays of his lamp upon the eye; "Chilled [to] the very marrow in my bones" by the sight of "the damned spot," he becomes preternaturally sensitive to sound. In the still moment before he leaps upon and kills the old man, he tries to "maintain the ray upon the eye." It is then that the "hellish tattoo of the heart increased." The inextricable association of the eye and the heart (and by extension of the watches) is most effectively established once the old man is dead; the criminal now places his hand over the heart and, feeling no "pulsation," calmly asserts, "His eye would trouble me no more."

Of course, the narrator's intellectually flawless plot cannot overcome the subtle and radical forces that pursue him, for reason used for a foolish end is essentially unreasonable. Action, no matter how decisive and organized, dissipates into futility when it expends itself against eternal obstacles. The narrator naively persists in thinking that his foe is external and mortal when, in fact, he represents an immutable law of life. Consequently, no amount of intellectualized cunning will stop the old man's heart because, as the dénouement of the story proves, the old man's heart beats within the protagonist himself as well as in the walls and beneath the planks of the floor.

The major irony of **"The Tell-Tale Heart"** is that the narrator, like William Wilson, is crushed by, but never understands the meaning of, his experience. He does not know that his disgust at the old man's eye is merely a symptom of a more serious disease. Clearly revealed in his hallucinations, which are more "real" than his reasoning, this disease can be diagnosed as his refusal to accept himself as a creature caught in the temporal net. He cannot acknowledge the limitations that bind him to the earth and time, the limitations that wither, corrupt, and destroy. Like so many of his confrères in Poe's other tales, he wishes, essentially, to transcend his human limitations: one can almost imagine him echoing Ligeia's hope that "Man does not yield him to the angels, *nor unto death utterly, save only through the weakness of his feeble will.*" Yet, perversely, the only means he can employ to attain his ends inevitably act as agents of doom.

His misguided intellect and the ingenious schemes it hatches set him more firmly on the path he strives to avoid. For a brief interval after he has committed his crime, he mistakenly imagines that he has gained security and inward peace by the "wise precautions" he has taken in disposing of the old man's corpse. It is not long, however, before his solid assurance disintegrates. Once again, the fantastic sound to which all sounds attune themselves begins its heart-like, watch-like rhythm: "the sound increased—what could I do? It was *a low, dull, quick sound—much such a sound as a watch makes when enveloped in cotton.*" (Poe's italics.) The narrator's reliance on his spurious and concocted order collapses as he shrieks out his confession to the police and helplessly and ignorantly submits to the ceaseless and measured flow of time.

Notes

[1] There have been very few extended or illuminating critical analyses of "The Tell-Tale Heart." Most critics sum it up in a phrase or two, or, like William

Bittner, *Poe: A Biography* (Boston, 1962) and Edward Wagenknecht, *Edgar Allan Poe: The Man Behind the Mask* (New York, 1963) seem to assume that the story is self-explanatory. One of Poe's best early critics, George Woodberry, formulistically refers to "The Tell-Tale Heart" as a "tale of conscience," *Edgar Allan Poe* (Boston, 1885), p. 186. In a fuller treatment of the story, Arthur Hobson Quinn mentions the "clock imagery" and the evil eye; he even declares that the effect of Poe's tale is heightened by the fact that the narrator "has himself suffered causeless terrors in the night," *Edgar Allan Poe: A Critical Biography* (New York, 1941), p. 394. Quinn, however, concerns himself with the "effect" rather than the meaning of Poe's work. Edward H. Davidson's insights into "The Tell-Tale Heart" are invariably interesting and perceptive. In *Poe: A Critical Study* (Cambridge, 1957), he sees the narrator as someone who "commits a crime because of the excess of emotion over intelligence; [someone who] is impelled to give himself up and pay the death penalty because he may thereby return to selfhood or primal being" (p. 203). I agree with Davidson that the narrator is deluded and invites his own destruction, but I feel, finally, that Davidson does not consider the nuances of Poe's story in arriving at his statement of the theme (pp. 188-189). By far the best intensive study of Poe's tale is E. Arther Robinson's "Poe's 'The Tell-Tale Heart,'" *Nineteenth-Century Fiction,* XIX (March, 1965), 369-378. Although Robinson dwells on the "murderer's psychological identification with the man he kills," he does not significantly relate the Evil Eye and the omnipresent watches. Essentially, Robinson's brilliant essay is preoccupied with Poe's "slow-motion technique" and not with theme.

John W. Canario (essay date 1970)

SOURCE: "The Dream in 'The Tell-Tale Heart,'" *English Language Notes,* Vol. VII, No. 3, March, 1970, pp. 194-97.

[*In the following essay, Canario discusses "The Tell-Tale Heart" as the narration of a dream, with its sense of intermingled clarity and obscurity, along with its increasing implausibility.*]

> All that we see or seem
> Is but a dream within a dream.
>
> —E. A. Poe

Hervey Allen observed in a footnote to *Israfel* that the logic of Poe's stories is "the mad rationalization of a dream."[1] This observation is especially applicable to **"The Tell-Tale Heart,"** which becomes fully understandable only when the narrator is recognized as the deranged victim of an hallucinatory nightmare.

Most commentators on the story have praised it either for its powerful evocation of terror or its artistically skillful revelation by degrees of the narrator as a ho-micidal maniac. Arthur Hobson Quinn's description of the story as "a study of terror" and "a companion piece to '**The Pit and the Pendulum**'" exemplifies the first view.[2] E. Arthur Robinson's close analysis of Poe's handling of two psychological themes in the story— "the indefinite extension of subjective time" and "the murderer's psychological identification with the man he kills"—illustrates the second view.[3] Without deny-ing the value of either of these widely held perspec-tives, I would like to suggest that Poe, on the most subtle level of his artistic aims, intended the tale of the narrator to be recognized finally as a madman's con-fession of a nightmare about death.

To understand the story as the relation of a dream, one must respond to suggestions of parallel situations and symbolic meanings in the action and imagery. That the narrator is reporting the events of a nightmare rather than actual happenings is not immediately discernible because the narrator himself is unable to separate fact from fancy. However, the hallucinatory nature of the events he relates becomes steadily clearer as he de-scribes his victim and the circumstances of the sup-posed murder.

From the beginning of the story, the narrator's de-scription of his relationship with the old man gradu-ally gives rise to the suspicion that the old man is really an alter ego representing a side of the narrator toward which he feels ambivalent emotions of love and hate. This possibility is initially suggested by the narrator's statement that he loves the old man and by the fact that he lives in intimate association with him, but it is soon thereafter given more support by other developments. The narrator admits, for example, that he has experienced the same mortal terror as the old man, that he has groaned in the identical manner, and that he has undergone this experience again and again just at midnight, the time which he has chosen for his observations of the old man. Finally, the suspicion that the narrator and the old man are doubles be-comes a certainty when the narrator complains of the loudness with which the old man's heart is beating. It is the increasing loudness of this beating heart, ex-pressive of mounting emotion, that precipitates the narrator's leap upon his victim. Significantly, at this instant the murderer and the old man cry out simul-taneously.

The discovery that the two characters are doubles raises the question as to what the narrator's desire to kill his alter ego means. The narrator announces very early in his confession that it is not the old man he wishes to do away with, but one of his eyes: "the eye of a vulture—a pale blue eye, with a film over it."[4] The narrator's obsession with this eye soon makes it apparent that he fears it not simply because it is ugly, but because he sees it as an emblem of his own

mortality. That the eye is a symbol of death is sug-gested by its resemblance to the eyes of a corpse, by the fact that it belongs to an old man, and by the narrator's association of it with a vulture.

The identification of the narrator and the old man as doubles establishes that the narrator's account of the manner in which he killed the old man must be the report of a dream: "In an instant I dragged him to the floor, and pulled the heavy bed over him. I then smiled gaily, to find the deed so far done. But, for many minutes, the heart beat on with a muffled sound." In the symbolism of this dream, the old man can be seen to stand for the physical body of the dreamer, and the narrator to represent the mind and will of that body. Thus, the dream, which is hardly plausible as the description of a real murder, really objectifies the speaker's belief that he has destroyed his body and thereby escaped from death.

The narrator's elaborate preparations for the crime also establish that he is obsessed by a fear of death. His excessive concern with time ("it took me an hour," "seven long nights—every night just at midnight," "just at twelve," "a watch's minute hand moves more quickly than did mine," etc.) and his nightly visits to the room of the old man, during each of which he permitted only a single ray of light from his darkened lantern to shine upon his victim's face, are soon recognized as assist-ing in no practical way the accomplishment of the murder. On the other hand, these preparations, which are proudly held up by the narrator as evidences of his sanity, are really symbolic expressions of his insane conviction that he has indeed escaped from time and mortality through his own cunning.

The story ends with the narrator's anguished discov-ery that the old man's heart has resumed beating in thunderously loud pulsations, even after his body has been dismembered and stuffed under the floor. What is actually revealed is the narrator's sudden, horrified discovery, at the very moment when his exultation over his fantasy conquest of death is most intense, that he is still mortal. The narrator terminates his confession in mad ravings to three police officers who, having been attracted to the house by its occupant's scream in the night, are only waiting for conclusive evidence of the man's insanity before taking him into custody.

Notes

[1] Hervey Allen, *Israfel* (New York, 1927), II, 567.

[2] Arthur Hobson Quinn, *Edgar Allan Poe, a Critical Biography* (New York, 1941), p. 394.

[3] E. Arthur Robinson, "Poe's 'The Tell-Tale Heart,' " *Nineteenth-Century Fiction,* XIX (March, 1965), 374.

[4] Quotations from the story are from the text of the *Broadway Journal,* August 23, 1845, as reprinted in Eric W. Carlson, ed., *Introduction to Poe, A Thematic Reader* (Glenview, Ill., 1967).

Paul Witherington (essay date 1985)

SOURCE: "The Accomplice in 'The Tell-Tale Heart,'" *Studies in Short Fiction,* Vol. 22, No. 4, Fall, 1985, pp. 471-75.

[*In the essay that follows, Witherington contests the apparently self-evident diagnosis of madness often applied to the narrator of the short story by taking into account Poe's more subtle engagement of the reader's assumptions and expectations.*]

"Poe's narrator tells a plain and simple story, which leaves no doubt that he is mad," T. O. Mabbott says in his preface to **"The Tell-Tale Heart."**[1] Most readers would agree, not only because the murder of an old man seems motiveless, but also because the narrator's confession comes across as calculated and heartless. Whereas **"The Cask of Amontillado"** offers witty dialogue and a romantic setting, inviting us into the story and thus eliciting our sympathy for the narrator in spite of our antipathy to the murder, **"The Tell-Tale Heart"** entombs us with the narrator's stark obsessions to which we react by shrouding ourselves with moral indignation and psychic detachment.

The story's plainness and simplicity, in fact, seem the means by which the narrator's madness is rendered transparent. Undistracted by context or extenuating circumstances, we focus our attention on his protestations of sanity, which of course fall apart with every "reason" he gives the listener, the "you" of the story who hears the confession. "Why *will* you say that I am mad?" the narrator asks (p. 792), explaining that his senses were not dulled but heightened during the horror; mania can't be madness, he argues unconvincingly. "Observe how healthily—how calmly I can tell you the whole story," he says, proceeding to undercut both calmness and wholeness by his agitated and incomplete rendition. And his emphasis on murder as a rational process only underscores the barbarity of the act itself. Faced with these attractive ironies, Poe critics have institutionalized the narrator's madness and gone on to concentrate on either the dynamics of that mental state (how the narrator becomes both murderer and victim)[2] or Poe's use of it to illustrate such ideas as passage to original Unity, or the frustrating of demon Time.[3]

This verdict of madness, however, comes less from the story itself than from our commonly held assumptions that all obsessive murderers are mad and that their madness is easily recognizable. If, on the other hand, we begin by assuming that anyone canny enough to carry out such a crime might be canny enough to disguise his own motives, and if we further assume that the narrator knows his listener's moral and rational position and thus makes his claims of mental health so absurd that they must fail to convince his audience, then we have a different story, though one quite faithful to Poe's other works where characters show no end to their duplicity, and where the lines between sanity and insanity blur in a nightmare atmosphere. To activate this reading, our attention must shift from the red herring of madness to the more subtle designs of the confession and the language by which the reader is induced, like one of M. Dupin's dupes, to select "odd" when he should have selected "even."

Pretending to share with the listener a universal concern for reason, the narrator seduces the listener by getting him to participate vicariously in the crime, an accomplice after the fact. He accomplishes this quickly and subtly in the third paragraph through the sense of sight: "You should have seen *me,*" the narrator says and immediately repeats it: "You should have seen how wisely I proceeded—and with what caution—with what foresight—with what dissimulation I went to work!" (p. 792). Later in that same paragraph, he takes further advantage of the listener by assuming his sympathetic reaction to the scene where the murderer pokes his head into the old man's room: "Oh, you would have laughed to see how cunningly I thrust it in!" (p. 793). By these suggestive nudges, the auditor is transformed into an active voyeur. The narrator concludes that long third paragraph with another subtlety: "So you see he would have been a very profound old man, indeed, to suspect that every night, just at twelve, I looked in upon him while he slept" (p. 793). In this sentence, "see" takes on the sense of understanding, though it does so without entirely relinquishing its primary meaning which is returned to by the narrator's claim to have "looked in." Meanwhile, the listener has been maneuvered from thoughts of missed opportunity ("You should have seen") to the thoughts that he and the narrator presumably share ("So you see").

After the third paragraph, the listener, now assumed to be a silent accomplice, comes across as being somewhat timid but anxious for the deed to be done: "Now you may think that I drew back—but no" (p. 793). He is put in the position not only of encouraging the narrator's story but also of egging on the murderer. The listener is also chided for his deficiency in imagination while the narrator exhibits his own powers of metaphor: "So I opened it [the lantern]—you cannot imagine how stealthily, stealthily—until, at length, a single dim ray, like the thread of the spider, shot from out the crevice and fell upon the vulture eye." (p. 794). This technique of attempting to limit the listener's access to the story and then tantalizing him with its details resembles in its psychological awareness and ultimate effect the game Montresor plays with Fortunato, enticing him to go more deeply into the wine cellar by telling him he should leave.

Final references to the listener return to the innocuousness of the opening remarks: "Have I not told you?" and "Do you mark me well? I have told you." (p. 795). The narrator may be chiding the "you" for his inattentiveness. But by this stage of the story his intent seems more gloating than goading, a kind of "I told you so," for we suspect that the listener is deeply and emotionally involved in the tale. The narrator has in fact assumed this involvement, for the "you" references disappear after paragraph thirteen (though the listener resurfaces at the end, as we shall see). The "you" of **"The Cask of Amontillado"** appears only once, in the first paragraph, perhaps to show that the narrator is speaking to a close friend. But Poe's narrator in **"The Tell-Tale Heart"** needs a continuing listener, somewhat less than a character but somewhat more than a device, to prove his point that if anyone can be seduced by narrative, then it becomes difficult to separate those who take pleasure in committing and confessing crime from those who take pleasure in hearing about it.

The motif of the listener becoming an accomplice comes directly from late eighteenth-century and early nineteenth-century Gothic literature. The confession of a villain often blasts the innocent listener out of composure and security, as in Coleridge's "The Rime of the Ancient Mariner" and William Godwin's *Caleb Williams*. Borrowed effectively for American literature by Brockden Brown and Hawthorne, this technique features a diabolical contract in which the two figures become collaborators moving away from the extremes of their original positions.

Poe himself uses demonic collaboration variously in earlier stories. The narrator's outfitting of a pentagonal room appropriate for Ligeia's return, and his attempt to invoke her by calling her name at Rowena's deathbed indicate that he may be in league with the occultish Ligeia who herself "used" him earlier to read the poem which seems to have precipitated her death. And the narrator in **"The Fall of the House of Usher"** reads to Roderick the very story most calculated to excite him to the imagination (or reality) of the bizarre ending. The influential opinion of Jungian critics that Ligeia dramatizes the narrator's anima and Roderick the narrator's shadow, in fact supports this collaboration theory, all being one in the psyche. But by making the listener in **"The Tell-Tale Heart"** a voiceless yet clear presence, Poe effects some last minute twists which are not typical of Gothic literature, and which point instead toward a much more sophisticated esthetic.

Toward the end of the story the police arrive and the narrator gives himself away to them while sitting over the dismembered body of his victim. Conscience wins out, or the "narrator's compulsion to unmask and destroy himself by finally admitting the crime," as Edward H. Davidson puts it.[4] In this mainstream interpretation, the police may be thought of as the murderer's super-ego, and the entire inner story a psychodrama of compulsions and counter compulsions.

Although the narrator may not have been in conscious control of the actual events, however, he seems to know exactly what he is doing in retelling them to the listener. By ignoring the listener toward the story's end, he encourages the listener to become more actively involved in the ending and thus to identify with the police officers who listened to the murderer's original confession. This reaction seems reasonable for the listener because after becoming involved symbolically as accomplice, he must feel the need to shuck off guilt by identifying with the accusers rather than the accused. He can imagine himself sitting with the officers around the murderer, awaiting the final outburst with considerable pleasure since he is already familiar with the details. He has been allowed a margin of safety, to eat his cake and then have it returned to him whole.

Here of course the narrator springs another trap, telling the listener that at the climax of his confession to the police, he cried out, calling them "Villains!" (p. 797). Though this counterattack is anticipated a few lines earlier by his reference to the "hypocritical smiles" of the officers, its intensity (the narrator's accusation of the police is the only part of the story rendered in quotation marks) must come as a shock to the listener who has put himself in their shoes. What may well have been simple projection in the inner story now becomes a more calculated and loaded indictment of the listener, as he is made to feel the full guilt of his vicarious fantasies. He's a villain for wanting to listen to the recreation of a tale of horror, and he's a naive hypocrite for imagining that he can do so with impunity.

The cry of "Villains!" remains also to haunt the perceptive reader who has also presumably played the game of accomplice and accuser, whose desire for a good story has kept him reading and whose conscience has brought him up short—provided of course he is capable of this kind of response. Poe's contemporaries may not have been, we assume from our experience with reflexive literature and our cultivated self-consciousness as readers. In Alain Robbe-Grillet's "The Secret Room," for example, an implied narrator views a painting of the aftermath of a vicious murder and then, apparently by his curiosity, causes the scene to run backward as if it were movie film so that the murder itself is reenacted. Thus the reader, who shares this desire to know what has happened, becomes accomplice to both the viewer and the murderer. But Poe too envisioned this kind of reader response. In his 1847 review of Hawthorne's tales for *Godey's Lady's Book,* Poe speaks of the reader's engagement as co-creator: "He feels and intensely enjoys the seeming novelty of the thought, enjoys it as really novel, as absolutely original with the writer—*and himself.* They two, he fancies, have, alone of all men, thought thus. They two have, together, created this thing."[5]

Poe did not share Hawthorne's overly scrupulous concerns for the artist as one who observes life from a self-indulgent distance. But Poe certainly understood the demands audiences make on art: how the poet may be forced to write short stories in order to make a living, and how the gothic interests of readers often force writers to perversions of their craft. The relationship between murderer and victim is a two-way pull, as is the relationship between writer and reader. We are all accomplices, though some, by virtue of experience, are more aware of it.

Notes

1 Thomas Olive Mabbott (ed.), *Collected Works of Edgar Allan Poe* (Cambridge, Mass.: Harvard University, Belknap Press, 1978), III, 789. All following quotations from this work will be indicated in the body of the text.

2 See for example Edward H. Davidson, *Poe: A Critical Study* (Cambridge, Mass.: Harvard University, Belknap Press, 1966), pp. 189-190, and David Halliburton, *Edgar Allan Poe: A Phenomenological View* (Princeton, New Jersey: Princeton University Press, 1973), pp. 333-338.

3 See for example Joseph J. Moldenhauer, "Murder as a Fine Art: Basic Connections Between Poe's Aesthetics, Psychology, and Moral Vision," *Publications of the Modern Language Association,* 83 (May 1968), 292-293, and E. Arthur Robinson, "Poe's 'The Tell-Tale Heart.' " *Nineteenth-Century Fiction.* 19 (March, 1965), 369-378.

4 Davidson, p. 190.

5 James T. Harrison (ed.), *The Complete Works of Edgar Allan Poe* (New York: AMS Press, 1965), XIII, 146.

Gita Rajan (essay date 1988)

SOURCE: "A Feminist Rereading of Poe's 'The Tell-Tale Heart,'" *Papers on Language and Literature,* Vol. 24, No. 3, Summer, 1988, pp. 283-300.

[*In the following essay, Rajan contends that by using analytic tropes developed by Jacques Lacan and Helene Cixous, the narrator of "The Tell-Tale Heart" can be identified as female.*]

1

Some contemporary feminists and theorists argue that there is a difference between masculinist and feminist discourse in literary texts. French theorists like Julia Kristeva, Luce Irigaray, and Hélène Cixous follow Jacques Lacan and psychoanalytic theory and trace the unconscious drives exhibited in the discourse of the text as repressed male/female desires. Even though these desires may be contradictory and conflicting, they reveal the position of the speaking subject (male or female) within the discourse of the text. The French scholars, in seeking the overlapping or androgynous places of discourse in the text, assert that males and females engage in differently gendered readings. Kristeva and Cixous argue that sexual identity (male or female) is a metaphysical construct outside the boundaries of the text, while gender identity is based upon cultural notions of maleness and femaleness evidenced in the text. Gender identity is more fluid than the former and makes room for the crucial concept of androgyny that is central to feminist readings in demolishing the rigid patriarchal notion of what is male/female. Androgyny deconstructs crippling binary oppositions of masculinity and femininity by allowing the speaking subject to occupy either or both positions.

While sexual identity, and, consequently, discrimination, feature prominently in masculinist readings, French theorists are radically shifting the very nature of the struggle of the sexes by focusing on gender-governed identity. Hence, a feminist reinterpretation of a narrative typically could argue that an unmarked narrator can be seen as female. Such a reading would displace a whole series of masculinist assumptions. In accordance with this approach, I will focus on Poe's **"The Tell-Tale Heart,"** especially its narrator, and argue that the narrator is indeed female. Poe himself never indicates that the narrator is male; in fact, his text offers no gender markings. Readers have assumed that the narrator is male because a neutralized and unmarked term *is* generally granted to be male. This is a trap that the language of the tale innocuously lays before the reader. By positing a female narrator, I propose to dislodge the earlier, patriarchal notion of a male narrator for the story. I argue, instead, that a gender-marked *rereading* of this tale reveals the narrator's exploration of her female situation in a particular feminist discourse. My feminist reading of **"The Tell-Tale Heart"** profiles the identity of the narrator as filtered through Freud's, Lacan's, and Cixous's theories of narrativity.

2

Psychoanalysis partially bridges the gap between conscious and unconscious thought and language through dream theory. Freud argues that instinctual forces—eros and thanatos—manifest themselves through dreams, and that these forces coexist and continually contradict each other, being intertwined in pairs like love/hate, life/death, and passivity/aggression. However, Freud maintains that people manage to lead ordered lives because they sublimate these forces as desires in dreams through at least two specific mechanisms, "condensation" and "displacement." Freud builds his psychoanalytic theory on human sexuality and desire, seeing the male as superior, in possession of the phallus, i.e., power. A female is inferior for Freud because of her lack of the sexual organ to signify the phallus and the power it symbolizes. In short, Freud's definition of the male and female, locked into this privative power equation, automatically privileges the male and marginalizes the female.

Lacan, in his revision of Freudian theory, fastens upon three principles: desire (the phallus as power), condensation/displacement (the dream as a system of signs), and hierarchy (the male as superior, or possessing power through the penis: the female as inferior, or lacking power).[1] Relying on Roman Jakobson's structural linguistics, he combines these three principles to establish a relationship between language *per se* and conscious/unconscious thought. Jakobson uses language as a model of *signs* to explain human thought and consequent behavior. A sign, for Jakobson, is a representation through language of the relationship between signifier (the physical sound of speech or the written mark on the page) and the signified (the invisible concept that this sound or mark represents). Jakobson's linguistic formulations reveal the doubleness of the sign and the fragility of the signifier (word) and signified (concept) relationship. In effect, he sees meaning emerging in discourse not through the relationship between signifier and signified but through the interaction of one signifier with another.

Jakobson maintains that language is constructed along two axes—the vertical/metaphoric and the horizontal/metonymic. Lacan's matches Jakobson's theory of language with Freud's theory of dreams, positing that dreams are structured along metaphoric and metonymic lines.[2] Lac[a]n claims that the "rhetoric of the unconscious" is constructed on two main tropes—metaphor and metonymy. He equates condensation with metaphor because it is a process of selection, substituting one signifier/word *for* another. Displacement he sees as metonymy because it combines one signifier/word *with* another. For Lacan, unconscious desire, like language, is structured as a system of signs, articulated metaphorically and metonymically in dreamwork and considered as discourse. While in Freudian analysis the focus is on the excavation of the subject's behavior, in Lacan it shifts to language, tracing the path of

desire as a sequential power transaction in the discourse of the text. Thus, Lacan reconstructs Freud's behavioral model into a *seemingly* less prejudiced linguistic one by emphasizing the arbitrariness and precariousness of language itself.

Further, according to Lacan, the metaphoric register represents the masculine through the "transcendental phallus," embodying the ultimate power of the signifier as a linguistic mark whose meaning is forever repressed (in the unconscious or the "text") and never attainable. Hence, every subject must engage in a constant metaphoric game of substitution in the attempt to grasp this final desire. In contrast, the metonymic is temporal and sequential; it propels the signifier forward in an attempt to recover the (unconscious) signified through narration. Significantly, Lacan claims that this reaching forward to achieve completeness is a mark of femininity, a feminine marker in discourse. Finally, Lacan concludes that even though language itself is symbolic, the symptom that prompts discourse is metonymic. Thus, the metonymic, feminine, "imaginary" register is the force that propels narrative.[3]

It is at this point that Lacan differs radically from Freud. While Freud assumes that language can completely appropriate and express thought, granting closure in the text, Lacan posits an inherent gap in this relationship, arguing for never-ending narrativity. For Lacan, the sign can never be complete or made whole because a signifier can only point to another signifier, resulting in an unending chain of signifiers we *forever attempt* to bridge through language and thought. Lacan connects language to thought as expressions of patterns of desire, motivated and propelled towards possessing the ultimate sign of power—the "transcendental signified," or phallus. Thus, the transcendental signified belongs in the metaphoric register, and the desire to possess it creates narrativity, which belongs to the metonymic register. Lacan strategically argues that the desire to possess the "transcendental phallus" is universal, both in males and females, and *appears* to collapse sexual difference. But this apparent egalitarianism, I argue, does not in fact work.

A masculinist reading of Poe's tale using Lacan's theory still supports the Freudian notion of the Oedipal myth. However, the Lacanian approach emphasizes sexual difference less than the Freudian approach does. Robert Con Davis analyzes Poe's **"The Tell-Tale Heart"** using Lacanian principles in "Lacan, Poe and Narrative Repression." He focuses on the latent and repressed levels of the text as a method of locating the nexus of power. Davis argues the act of gazing, whether the old man's or the narrator's, is a metaphoric power transaction between the subject and the object of the gaze. Using Freud's "Instincts and Their Vicissititudes," with its traditional patriarchal dichotomies of "subject/object, active/passive," Davis matches Freud's theme of the "gaze" with Lacan's theory of voyeurism to interpret Poe's tale.[4] Davis highlights the "Evil Eye" as a predominant metaphor in Poe's tale that functions primarily through its power of the Gaze. Building on the theme of the gaze and voyeurism, Davis validates his masculinist reading by arguing that the old man and the narrator are indeed doubles, always already connected by the gaze. He sees both characters as having similar, almost paranoically sensitive hearing and sight, insomnia, and a preoccupation with death. The "eye" of the old man represents the Symbolic Law of the Father, or Lacan's version of Freud's Oedipal complex. Davis argues that in an attempt to escape paternal subjugation, the narrator engages in his own vindictive game of voyeurism. Davis sees the murder of the old man as a cruelly symbolic act of Oedipal mastery: "in choosing to heighten the old man's fear of death and kill him, the narrator controls—just as a voyeur sadistically controls—a situation *like his own,* as if the subject and object could be merged in a mirror phase of complete identification" (255). Davis even argues for a third voyeur in the figure of Death: "Death . . . had stalked with his black shadow . . . and enveloped the victim."[5] This allows him to posit a typical Lacanian triangle, consisting of the old man, the narrator, and Death, and create a constant shift in the power of the gaze through the triple itinerary of the signifier.

Because Davis places the narrator and the old man in the "double" positions connected by the gaze, he sees the gaps in the gaze between the subject and object *and* the gazer and voyeur as forces that produce the narrative, propel the tale forward, and alternately manifest and repress the text. Based on a primarily metaphoric interpretation—the eye as the Symbolic Gaze of the Father—Davis argues for a male narrator who acts as voyeur and exhibitionist alternately. Davis neatly sums up the final scene of Poe's tale as clearly metaphoric by saying: "His [the narrator's] resistance to being seen points to a desire to escape subjugation absolutely and to choose death rather than to become passive while alive" (254). Significantly, Lacan's suggestion that the metonymic dimension of the text is female is absent in Davis's reading. Thus, even though Lacanian readings *seem* to open the door to feminist perspectives, they ultimately only nudge the door ajar.

3

Cixous's feminist approach to psychoanalytic interpretation and her notion of feminine writing provide a fruitful way of sabotaging the masculinist-biased reading of texts. Hence a rereading of Poe's **"The Tell-Tale Heart"** with Cixous's paradigm offers an alternate gender-marked interpretation. She systematically interrogates existing critical presuppositions, deconstructs them, and advocates a three-step reinscription procedure.[6] First, according to Cixous, one must recognize a latent masculinist prejudice in society, a hidden

privileging of the male and marginalizing of the female. Next, one must consciously undo the basic slanting in favor of the male term over the female term at the very nodes of these *seemingly logical* oppositions, such as male/female, reason/feeling, culture/nature, etc. Patriarchy, by creating these oppositions, privileges the first term and lowers the status of the second, forcing the textual subject to occupy either of these positions and accept the power (or lack thereof) that goes along with it. This logic divides each term against itself and makes the whole system of binary (Western) thought rigidly prescriptive. The male, according to this system of thought, can have an identity and value only in juxtaposition to an inferior female signifier and vice versa. Also, in privileging one term over another, the first term sets the norm for the second. More important, oppositional thinking, which is characteristic of patriarchy, forbids a wholeness or a shared existence for any term, focusing on maleness or on femaleness instead of the androgyny that Cixous and other French feminists advocate.

Consequently, Cixous's final step is to combat this problem of division by embracing these oppositions and erasing their differences. This is the "pretext," or background, for the process of *jouissance* that Cixous advocates. The strategy behind jouissance is to discredit the notion of difference by going beyond the idea of constraining divisions, to explore instead the freedom of excess, a utopian vision that subverts the male definition of desire. Patriarchy is based on a system of libidinal economy (a repression of desire both conscious and unconscious that creates meaning in a text). Cixous's jouissance demands a libidinal excess—additions of unconscious meanings through consciously constructed texts. The practical method behind this political feminist position is to create a multiplicity of meanings. In linguistic terms, jouissance creates an excess of signifiers, the freeplay of which will build several levels of meanings, all of which can be validated by the text. These meanings do not depend upon a series of repressed previous ones; they do not impoverish the meanings that come before them through a process of substitution but, instead, enhance each other through a process of addition. An example of this is the notion of androgyny which is central to some feminist readings. Instead of focusing on either male or female voice in the text, androgyny allows the same voice to be male and/or female in various parts of the text, allowing for numerous complementary interpretations.

Kristeva, in *Desire and Language,* and Cixous, in *La Juene Née,* argue that the concept of androgyny belongs to the realm of the "Imaginary," which, in Lacanian theory, is pre-Symbolic, or pre-Oedipal, and thus, is before the Law of the Father. While Cixous is explicit in calling this jouissance in the sense of the purely pleasurable state of excess, Kristeva connects jouissance to reproduction. However, they share this vision of utopia, with no boundaries or barriers of any kind, a vision that is based on unlimited joy.[7]

The inherent danger in Kristeva's and Cixous's vision of utopia is their marked privileging of the imaginative/poetic over the analytical/theoretical in feminist writing. Because of their emphasis on emotions rather than reason as the feminine mode, some patriarchal theorists do not treat feminist discourse seriously. Sentimentality is precisely the club that patriarchy holds over the woman to control and deem her inferior. However, there *is* a definite value in adopting Cixous's position of abundance in an effort to invalidate the rigid male parameters and explore the text with an expectation of plentitude and multiple meanings. It is essential to point out that Cixous's notion of jouissance as a pleasure principle is different from Lacan's notion of free space with an abundance of signifiers (or even Barthes's version of the "pleasures of the text"). The latter suggests a chasm with an abundance of repressed, free floating signifiers, while the former gathers up this abundance of signifiers to nourish and cherish separate multiple readings.

Cixous begins by questioning the validity of categories like male/female in both writing and reading texts. She sees these as gaps created by ideological differences propagated by a phallogocentric (phallus- and logos-oriented) interpretive community. Further, she argues that this kind of oppositional thinking is itself aggressive (very much like the male logic and body behind it), because one term in the couple comes into existence through the "death of the other." Cixous, in *La Jeune Née* asks, "Where is she?" (115) in a patriarchal binary thought system that creates divisions like "Activity/Passivity, Culture/Nature, Father/Mother, Head/Emotions, Logos/Pathos" (116) which is structured primarily on the male/female opposition. An effective way to allow both terms to exist is to ask for a gendered position that both males and females can occupy either jointly or individually within the texts, as speaking subjects. This is made possible through the notion of jouissance, which focuses on the speaking subject with a gendered (hence mobile) identity. Also, this deliberate exploration of multiple meanings would ceaselessly expose the hidden male agenda which is created to silence women.

4

I preface my rereading of Poe's tale with a Freudian analysis, much like that in Marie Bonaparte's *Life of Poe*.[8] However, while Bonaparte's emphasizes the element of primal-scene voyeurism, mine sees the male narrator's retelling of his story/dream as a narration of

a rite of passage. "**The Tell-Tale Heart**" begins by describing the narrator's feelings about taking care of an old man. The old man's disturbing stare upsets the narrator, who decides on an impulse to kill him. The rest of the tale focuses on the narrator's elaborate plan to murder him, and ends with the narrator's confession of the crime. The story has Poe's typical macabre atmosphere and deliberately contradictory syntactical style. By killing the old man, the narrator symbolically castrates him, eliminating him from the text, and hopes to escape subjugation. This allows him to step into the old man's position of unchallenged power. The act of murder reveals the condensed expression of his desire to usurp the old man's place and authority. Similarly, his swing between neurotic and hysteric utterances, repeatedly assuring the reader of his sanity, is an effort to displace the sense of fear that is incumbent upon possessing such authority. At the beginning of the tale, the narrator shelters the old man (love), but ends up murdering him (hate). The narrator's contradictory actions, in an effort to possess ultimate power, are the result of the intertwining of eros and thanatos. The narrator's final confession to the policemen (the substitute father figures) is a combination and sublimation of his desire for power and fear of castration as a challenge to his new power.

The standard Oedipal interpretation is explicit in the climactic bedroom scene that graphically reveals the simultaneous condensed and displaced desires of the narrator. The bed serves to feed the contradictory instinctual urges of eros and thanatos, satisfying the young man's passion while smothering him to death, granting the young man power while nullifying it in the old man. The narrator's imbalanced emotional utterances about being "driven" by the old man's "eye" are symptoms of the condensed desire that make him conceive his elaborate plan of shutting the old man's "Evil eye forever" (303). It is his attempt to usurp that very authority of the old man's surveillance. And the narrator's own deafening "heartbeat" prods him on, leading him from one event to the next in the narrative, revealing his efforts to escape the displaced sense of fear in letting this desire get out of control. While the eye (condensation) represents the narrator's problem through a sense of abstract desire, the heartbeat (displacement) serves as the significant, concrete sense of fear in dealing with this problem. This enables the tale to maintain its ambivalence between myth and reality, dream and nightmare, due to a co-existing tension between metaphor/condensation and metonymy/displacement throughout the narration. In this traditional Freudian analysis, the identity of narrator remains fixedly male.

However, my rereading of the tale includes both a masculinist and feminist approach to the narrator. Using Lacanian principles, I profile the narrator as "speaking subject," presenting the narrator first as male, then as female. Unlike Davis's reading, my masculinist re-reading focuses on both the metaphoric and metonymic aspects of the text, moving away from an exclusive "Gaze"-oriented interpretation of manifest and repressed levels of discourse. I treat the eye as a metaphor of patriarchal scrutiny and social control, and the heart as metonymic device to subvert such control. The narrator admits his obsession in saying, "when it [the eye] fell upon me, my blood ran cold; and so by degrees—very gradually—I made up my mind to take the life of the old man, and thus rid myself of the eye forever" (305). The narrator explicitly reveals his anger at the old man's symbolic method of subjugation and expresses his consequent desire to annihilate the old man, thereby negating and usurping his power. Davis too, points this out by showing how the narrator first isolates the gaze, then inverts it, so that he can gaze at and subjugate the old man. The narrator retaliates against the "Evil Eye" by voyeuristically gazing at the sleeping man. Thus, the gaze moves from the old man to the narrator, symbolizing the shift of power between them. Lacan calls this mobility the "itinerary of the signifier" (171) to indicate the constant substitution maneuvers that the metaphoric register undertakes in its attempt to possess the ultimate object of desire—the transcendental signifier.[9] Within Poe's tale, the "itinerary of the signifier" can be graphically traced along the "single thin ray" of light from the narrator's lantern that falls upon the "vulture eye . . . directed as if by instinct, precisely upon the damned spot" (306). Gaining new power through his reversal of the gaze makes the narrator heady, and he cries exultantly that the old man "was stone dead. His eye would trouble me no more" (306).

However, the "itinerary of the signifier," due to its constant process of substitution, does not allow power to rest with one gazer for a long period. The very nature of the gaze, as posited by both Freud and Lacan, is extremely volatile, temporary, and unpredictable. Consequently, in Poe's story the power of the gaze destabilizes the narrator, and it is for this reason that he breaks down and confesses to the mildly suspecting policemen. The police in Poe's tale are the literal representations of societal power, but they are also a metaphor for the Law of the Father in the unconscious. The policemen's gaze, thus, both literally and metaphorically represents the sanctioned authority that the narrator had just usurped from the old man. When they gaze at the narrator, they reverse the path of the gaze, once again throwing him back into the passive object position that is revealed by his hysterical and humiliating confession.

Equally crucial in a Lacanian analysis is the metonymic register, marked by the "heart" in Poe's tale. It exhibits a complicated displacement process working simultaneously on two manifest levels. At one level it rep-

resents the narrator's confused emotions, such that the narrator's passions and fears combine and clash, spurring the tale forward. The tale unfolds through the narrator's hysterical utterances, extreme passion (even though the narrator explicitly denies this at the beginning of his tale), obsessive desire, neurotic fears, and pathetic confession. At another level, it represents the physical pounding of the narrator's heart, giving him the energy to kill the old man. On the night of the assault, the narrator remarks: "Never, before that night, had I *felt* the extent of my own powers" (306). Notably, it is the narrator's fear of the imagined sound of the old man's heart, that overwhelming roar, that ultimately betrays him into confessing to the policemen. These two aspects of displacement embodied metonymically in the heart are fused in a strange manner, alternating between hearing and feeling throughout the tale, such that they keep plummeting the narrative onwards. Thus, the sounds in the tale moves rapidly from heartbeat to creaking doors, to muffled smothering sounds, to loud ticking watches, and finally pounds as unbearable noise in the narrator's head till he articulates his fear through the confused discourse of a hysterical confession.

There is also a third kind of displacement at the repressed level of the text. This is evidenced in the metonymic shift not only between one aspect of the heart to the other, but in a total shift from sound to sight at crucial points in the text. Thus, the metonymic register displaces the narrator's feelings throughout the text in various ways. A good example is the elaborate precautions that the narrator takes to direct a single ray of light in a darkened room on the old man's eye (sight). When the narrative has been raised to a fever pitch on the night of the murder, the narrator suddenly fumbles with the catch on the lantern and goes into a detailed description of sounds of "death watches," and crickets in "chimneys," effectively displacing reader attention. The displacement and metonymic tactics repressed in the narrative itself act as a marker for signaling the manifest displacement of the narrator's fears regarding his uncontrolled and unsanctioned actions. It is here that Lacan's notion of the "itinerary of signifiers" in the metonymic register serves him well. Metonymy, as both agent and trope, by constantly shifting, mediates between thought and language, showing both the instability of this relationship, and its inability to bridge the gap. At the textual level, it highlights the constant forward movement in an attempt to narrate through the rapid and confusing chain of events. It reveals the obsessively fragmented discourse of the narrator, in a painful effort to make meaning, and to make whole this relationship between thought and language. Thus, in my masculinist reading, by using the Lacanian paradigm of a male speaking subject, I reveal the problematic nature of language itself. When the narrator fails, one glimpses—with a strange pathos—the failure of language, too.

In contrast, my Lacanian feminist rereading of Poe's tale, identifying a female narrator, yields an interpretation that is the reverse of the Oedipal myth. Instead of a young man desiring the power symbolized by the Father, *she* is the daughter desiring her father. I will show that Lacan's innovativeness lies in the way he volatilizes the metaphoric and metonymic registers through his theory of the "itinerary of the signifier." Lacan suggests that sex roles as represented by linguistic tropes can be made less rigid. Hence sexual difference can be erased by energizing and mobilizing these linguistic tropes. Metaphor as a trope represents a pattern of desiring and desired where the object of desire is the transcendental, signified, or phallus. Metonymy would be the act of seeking and transacting this power through narrative. Thus, Lacan's strategy is to dislocate the fixity of sexual identity, or what he claims is gender identity, through the use of tropes as agents of desire. This would allow both men and women to possess the transcendental phallus, or its metaphoric power; but because of the temporary nature of this power, the very act of possession would be continually deferred and drawn out metonymically in narrative for both masculine and feminine subjects.

Within this framework, the narrator in Poe's tale can be posited as a female rather than a male who desires power. She stalks the old man and father figure for "seven long nights" and kills him in an attempt to escape the surveillance of his Evil Eye. The female narrator begins in the traditional feminine position of a *nurturer*. She takes him into her house and even remarks with dark irony after terrifying him with her nightly ritualistic voyeurism: "I went boldly into his chamber, and spoke courageously to him, calling him by his name in a hearty tone, and inquiring how he had passed the night" (306). But she deeply resents the scrutiny of his eye, feeling abused and objectified by his paternal surveillance. Angered and humiliated by his gaze, she goes through the same maneuver that the male narrator does in reversing the path of this gaze. Unlike the male narrator, her primary desire is to rid herself of the male gaze, or domination. However, in traveling through the gaze's path, she substitutes the first desire for her need physically to possess the old man. In this context, the climactic scene in the bedroom, with its implied sexual overtones, supports a Lacanian feminist reading better than a Oedipal one. In that one moment of possession, she becomes the aggressor; she even assumes a male sexual posture, forcing the old man to receive her, almost raping him, so that "he shrieked once—once only" (305). The scene culminates with her smirk: "There was nothing to wash out—no stain of any kind—no blood spot whatsoever. . . . A tub caught it all" (305). In this one act, the female narrator captures both the masculine gaze and masculine role. Thus, in appropriating the male posture, she even refers to herself in explicitly masculine terms, claiming repeatedly, that her actions are not those of a "madman."

Yet, ironically, the very authority of her newfound power makes her more vulnerable, more of an object of desire by others. Metaphorically, she moves from the position of actively desiring that Lacan allows to both the male and female to the position of being passively desired, one that is traditionally only the female's. It is here that the Lacanian "itinerary of the signifier" betrays her. The movement between male/female roles is ultimately restrictive to the female. Unlike the male narrator who confesses for fear of castration, the female narrator is denied this option. Acknowledging her femininity, she stands before the policemen, stripped of her power in her traditional posture as female, passive, subservient, and accountable to the male gaze—and exposed in the eyes of the Law through the return of the repressed (murdered) father. She begins and ends in a stereotypically feminine posture, the nurturer who has returned to her quintessentially repressed object position.

My feminist rereading with metonymy as focal point again reveals the confined position of the female narrator. The heart as an allegory of metonymy displaces the narrator's fears and desires, working on the two levels already examined, making her obey the dictates of her confused emotions. Further, Poe's text, if reread as narrated by a female speaking subject, indicates that this desire and fear is more frequently associated with a female "voice" than it is with the male's. The female narrator of **"The Tell-Tale Heart"** focuses on evocations of space and emptiness, which are typical expressions of female consciousness. The narrator claims her fear was engulfing, making her feel as if "enveloped in cotton" (305), just like her "terrors" which "welled" up in her bosom, "deepening, with its dreadful echo" (304). Interestingly, Lacan's theory of metonymy as the motor of language supports the psychoanalytic view that links the female phobia of emptiness (as a primal corollary to lacking the phallus) with gaps in narrativity that make this tale seem discontinuous and disjointed.[10] Thus, the narrator's confused recounting of her tale is a method of compensating for this emptiness, from the initial display of desire in her heart to the culminating betrayal of that desire, resulting in her agonizing confession.

This feminist investigation into the speaking subject, both male and female, unmasks the hidden male agenda; it also shows that a feminist rereading using only the Lacanian principles of psychoanalysis is problematic. As already shown, the female narrator's voluntary confession to the mildly suspecting policemen reveals her restricted position. As woman, she reoccupies her traditional role as a submissive, victimized object, offering herself up to be scrutinized once more by the male gaze. She can, finally, never aspire to usurp this power or be outside/above the Law of the Father. Ironically, even though a feminist rereading grants the female narrator a temporary masculine, active, subject posture, it undercuts this interpretation in returning her to a traditionally female position by superimposing a judicial and patriarchal closure. Such a feminist reading shows how clearly the female is boxed into a role, making both her sexual and gender identity rigid. A feminist rereading must go beyond the unmasking of such oppression; it must seek alternate positions for the female speaking subject.

Although Lacanian psychoanalysis first creates a division between male/female and then erases it under the guise of gender equalization, it seems to suggest that certain codes of behavior and discourse are allowable *only* to a male. Should a female dare to transgress, she will be punished by the Law of the Father. Consequently, the female narrator is permitted to desire the "metaphoric" phallus as power, but she can never aspire to possess it. And if she chooses to disobey this basic patriarchal dictum, not only will she fail but she must bear the moral consequences. In a feminist rereading of the ending of the tale, the female narrator's marginalization becomes explicit. What was successfully interpreted as a dramatization of the Oedipal *myth* for the male narrator turns to the harsh *reality* of oppression for the female narrator.

A feminist theorist must suspect that this development reveals Lacan's bias in adapting Freud's notion of manifest and repressed texts. At the manifest level, Lacan explicitly advocates sexual egalitarianism, but at the repressed (more influential) level he implicitly subverts it. My feminist rereading of the manifest text is as presented in the above analyses. Yet if one were to reread the repressed text, the Lacanian prejudice against the female would become obvious. I submit that the unconscious, or repressed text, through the pressure it exerts on the conscious or manifest text, shows that patriarchal morality condemns a woman for being aggressive, for desiring power, and ultimately punishes her for achieving this power even temporarily. Both male and female readers of Poe's story have tended to accept the Law of the Father, together with all its arbitrary presuppositions, and grant power only to the male. Thus, the status of the male narrator in Poe's **"The Tell-Tale Heart"** has remained stable. But if one wishes to transcend this phallogocentric prejudice, one must look elsewhere than Freud and Lacan.

To experience what Cixous explains as jouissance within Poe's text, we must erase the rigidity of metaphor (eye) and metonymy (heart) as separate categories. Instead, a gendered reading of Poe's tale would make the "eye" and the "heart" serve as metaphors and metonymies simultaneously, intermingling and creating multiple meanings. Quite accurately, Cixous's use of tropes can be called gendered, as they have greater maneuverability than Lacan's sexual tropes, which are clearly marked as *metaphor/symbolic/male*, and *metonymy/imaginary/female*. This strategy is Cixous's way of combating Lacan's notion of gender dissemination, which is actually based on a sexual paradigm. Lacan's position is invested with patriarchal biases such that the female term is violated and abused either at the conscious (manifest text) or unconscious (repressed text) level. The "eye" as metaphor has yielded meaning to Poe's text, but reading it metonymically enriches the tale further. The "eye" is the virtual symptom of the female narrator's desire to gain power in a male dominated society. In this context, it energizes the sequence of events in the tale to climax in the narrator's confession. Since killing the old man does not grant her lasting power, she confesses to the policemen and, thus, recirculates her power. Paradoxically, in the confessional scene "she" adroitly forces the male gaze to expose the controlled violence of the patriarchy. Her aggression against the old man is an explicit assault on male domination. Her confession becomes her implicit critique of domination. For a feminist reader, this is gratifying, an expression of solidarity through her exposure of ideology. For a masculinist reader, it is one more reminder of rebellion against patriarchal oppression. Her confession reveals the latent fetters of bondage in a patriarchal ideology, and she *re*reverses the gaze of the policemen by letting it bounce off her objectified body by using the eye as a metonymic instrument. Here the gaze is just one more part in her plan to expose the system. She exchanges the virtual prison bars of the Father's Law for the actual ones of the penal system. Henceforth, she will covertly make her point on discrimination against women through the underlying irony of her tale.

Writhing under the policemen's scrutiny, she protests: "they were making a mockery of my horror! . . . But any thing was better than this agony . . . more tolerable than this derision" (306). This indicates that her first plan to usurp power from the old man had failed, and now she must adopt another, creating a new perspective for the final scene. Her confession, now read ironically and not as evidence of guilt, directs the gaze back into the metaphoric register. It activates her plan for the exposé. For a moment, between her first plan and the second one, the gaze falls on the metaphoric spectre of the Law. In this sense, the interweaving of metaphor and metonymy, as a slippage of tropes, allows for multiple readings that build on one another instead of repressing one meaning to manifest another. This is an example of the jouissance that Cixous advocates as a method of accretion.

Similarly, luxuriating in the jouissance of multiplicity, the "heart" can be moved from the metonymic to the metaphoric register. As a metaphor, it serves to foreground the tale as belonging to the romance genre, with all its associations of passion and fantasy. It also allows the tale to be read as wish fulfillment, a dream in which the narrator as melodramatic heroine becomes the cynosure in a male arena, the active speaking subject, instead of the fetishized object. She proudly declares: "I foamed—I raved—I swore" (307), as a way of explaining her frantic attempts to remain on center stage. This is an enactment of the stereotypical feminine posture. By obeying the dictates of her heart in committing the passionate crime (exaggerated, no doubt), she dramatizes her execrated position as woman. Now the female narrator emerges as the martyr through her confession, also a typical position for the female.

But when examining the text under the light of jouissance, the first step in reading is to expose such a patriarchal stereotyping. Yet the interweaving of the metaphoric and metonymic registers gives diverse readings. According to the metonymic register (eye), the female narrator is an active speaking subject who assumes a male gendered identity, but the metaphoric register (heart) forces her back into the archetypical female position of martyr. This slip between the metaphoric and metonymic registers is crucial to feminist writing because it reveals the androgyny created by jouissance. Moreover, gendered identity sheds a different light on the other characters in the tale, too. In the crucial, confessional scene, all the characters can be read androgynously. The literal keepers of the Law of the Father, the police*men* observe *passively* while the *female* narrator is explosively *active*. She is the speaking subject, frantically pacing, vigorously thumping the furniture, and energetically talking. She is catapulted into her final ironic, yet male and active posture by "the beating of *his* heart!" (307, italics added). It is the old man's heart, dramatized like a damsel in distress, that vocalizes the narrator's confession. In the ironic conclusion of the tale, both the policemen and the old man remain static, while the female narrator adopts the dynamic and aggressive role, deliberately calling attention to the subservient status of all women. What needs to be emphasized here is the active androgynous narrator who can be contrasted to the passive males; her actions should not be mistaken for the actions for a stereotypical "hysterical" female. This erroneous stereotyping will, no doubt, create a neat niche for the female, but leave the male position in the discourse vacant. Thus, Cixous's brand of androgyny and multiple readings cancel out stereotypical sexual markings of the text.

Poe's "**The Tell-Tale Heart**" can indeed be read as the female narrator's own cry from "the soul when overcharged with awe" (304), a tale of escape, but escape into deliberate captivity so that she can articulate a female discourse. She experiments and functions in both the active and passive registers as a speaking subject and passive object. In this venture, her discourse becomes a painful tool of signifying and defin-

ing herself within the confines of patriarchy. Through jouissance, interweaving metaphors and metonymies, constantly slipping between the tropes, defying libidinal economy, and creating an excess of signifiers, she inscribes an "other" discourse. This rewriting becomes possible through the complex pattern of gendered tropes that are occupied by both male and female characters in the tale. It is this embracing, this gathering together, not only of the tropes, but also of the characters occupying these gendered tropes, that makes this tale a revelation of feminist rewriting as well as rereading.

Notes

[1] Jacques Lacan, "L'Instance de la lettre dans l'inconscient," *Ecrits I,* trans. Alan Sheridan (New York: Norton, 1977). Lacan argues that metonymy is the "derailment of instinct . . . externally extended towards the desire of something else" (278).

[2] Roman Jakobson, "Two Aspects of Language and Two Types of Aphasic Disturbances," in *Fundamentals of Language* (The Hague: Mouton, 1956) 55-82. Lacan matches Saussure's linguistic model with Jakobson's to formulate the signifier/signified and metaphor/metonymy relationship (274).

[3] See Jerry Ann Flieger, "The Purloined Punchline: Joke as Textual Paradigm," *Contemporary Literary Criticism,* ed. Robert Con Davis (New York: Longman, 1986) 277-94, who claims that a text through its intersubjectivity acts as a feminine symptom of inexhaustible desire. Toril Moi, in her introduction to *Sexual/Textual Politics,* discusses Lacan's theory of the "symbolic/metaphoric" and male vector as always coexisting with the "imaginary/metonymic" and female vector in any discourse in an attempt to make meaning within the text. See Anthony Wilden, *The Language of the Self* (New York: Dell, 1975) 249-70, for a discussion of Lacan's symbolic/imaginary registers.

[4] Robert Con Davis, "Lacan, Poe, and Narrative Repression," in *Lacan and Narration: The Psychoanalytic Difference In Narrative Theory* (Baltimore: Johns Hopkins UP, 1984). Davis argues that, according to Freud, the act of gazing represents the gazer's status as subject actively engaged in a pleasurable power game with the receiver of the gaze. In the object position, the receiver passively submits to the painful humiliation of the gazer's oppressive surveillance. By incorporating Lacan into Freud's theory, Davis shows that the "Gaze" is composed of three shifting positions of the subject's desire for the Other. Beginning with the gazer in a voyeuristic subject position, scrutinizing an exhibitionist as object, we move to a second, mirror-like stage, where the subject/object of the gaze are replicas of each other. In the final moment, positions are reversed when the (former subject and current) object returns the gaze. Like the ever-shifting signifiers in

language, the gaze is also a never-ending game. Davis's Lacanian interpretation sees the gaze as a mark of desire for the Other that is revealed in the text through intersubjectivity and reciprocal looking. Thus the looker, by looking, loses some of his power through the gaze itself.

5 Edgar Allan Poe, *The Complete Tales and Poems of Edgar Allan Poe* (New York: Modern Library, 1965) 303; cited hereafter in the text.

6 Hélène Cixous, "An Imaginary Utopia," *Sexual/Textual Politics,* ed. Toril Moi (New York: Methuen, 1985) 102-27. Cixous's theoretical paradigm is based on Derrida's deconstructive poetics. This particular three-step reinscription is my synthesis of Cixous's position as expressed in "The Laugh of the Medusa," in *New French Feminisms,* ed. Elaine Marks and Isabelle de Courtivron (Amherst: U of Massachusetts P, 1980) 245-64, and in "Castration or Decapitation?" *Signs* 7 (1981):41-55.

7 For a more detailed discussion on the nature of patriarchal thought, the concept of sexual difference, and *écriture feminine* see Hélène Cixous and Catherine Clément, *La Jeune Née* (Paris: Union General d'Editions, 1975) 147; Julia Kristeva, *Desire in Language: A Semiotic Approach to Literature and Art,* ed. Leon S. Roudiez, trans. Thomas Gora, Alice Jardine, and Roudiez (New York: Columbia UP, 1980) 239-40; both cited hereafter in the text.

8 Marie Bonaparte, *The Life and Works of Edgar Allan Poe* (1949; London: Hogarth P, 1971).

9 Lacan, "L'Instance" 171.

10 Jacques Lacan, "Seminar XX" in *Feminine Sexuality,* ed. Juliet Mitchell and Jaqueline Rose (New York: Norton, 1982). For Lacan's discussion of women, see 48.

Brett Zimmerman (essay date 1992)

SOURCE: "'Moral Insanity' or Paranoid Schizophrenia: Poe's 'The Tell-Tale Heart,'" *Mosaic,* Vol. 25, No. 2, Spring, 1992, pp. 39-48.

[*In the essay that follows, Zimmerman analyzes the ways in which "The Tell-Tale Heart" anticipates the psychological concept of paranoid schizophrenia, and concludes that Poe belongs to that group of "modern artists who find in science not a threat but an ally."*]

In our time, creative writers are expected to do their "homework," and consequently to find "modern" scientific accuracy in a literary text comes as no surprise.

To discover similar scientific accuracy in a text from an early period is a different matter—one which involves not only questions about the sophistication of the artist but also about the sophistication of the science of his/her time. A case in point is Poe's short story of 1843, **"The Tell-Tale Heart."** Narrated in retrospect, Poe's confessional tale features a "mad" protagonist who recalls his grisly murder of an old man, his living companion, and who tries to explain the reasons for both this abominable act and his ultimate confession. My purpose in the following essay is to demonstrate the extent to which Poe's characterization of this narrator corresponds with current psychoanalytic profiles of the "paranoid schizophrenic" personality. Subsequently, my purpose is to consider the "science" of Poe's time in order to show how it "anticipates" current thinking and so provides the context for Poe's own acute insights into the nature, cause and consequences of this kind of mental illness.

. . . . .

According to current psychological theory, the "active" phase of paranoid schizophrenia is preceded by a "prodromal" phase during which premonitory symptoms occur, one of which is "superstitiousness" (*DSM* 195).[1] In Poe's tale, what precipitated the narrator's insanity and the subsequent murder was his irrational obsession with the old man's so-called "Evil Eye." The narrator freely admits to his auditors that this was his *primum mobile:* "yes, it was this! He had the eye of a vulture— a pale blue eye, with a film over it. Whenever it fell upon me, my blood ran cold; and so by degrees—very gradually—I made up my mind to take the life of the old man, and thus rid myself of the eye forever" (88). Although it might be argued that the madman's comments about the "Evil Eye" constitute his rationalization about his decision to murder, the way he describes the object suggests that the "Eye" was indeed the thing which drove him to commit his atrocities. Although mad, he is not *entirely* an unreliable narrator, for what we should consider is the way his *idée fixe,* his superstition concerning the "Evil Eye," generated a kind of anxiety or "overwhelming stress" which, according to current theories, can lead to a full schizophrenic breakdown (Sue 441-42).

A major symptom of the active phase of schizophrenia involves hallucinations, and it is here that Poe critics have come closest to identifying the specific nature of the narrator's mental condition. For example, before she abandons herself to a Freudian interpretation, Marie Bonaparte refers to "auditory hallucinations of paranoia" (498). Similarly, in their anthology of short fiction, *The Abnormal Personality Through Literature,* Alan Stone and Sue Smart Stone include **"The Tell-Tale Heart"** in a chapter on psychotic symptoms— specifically, hallucinations. Closest to a more precise identification of the narrator's condition is John E. Reilly, who indeed describes the protagonist as a paranoid schizophrenic (5-6). To Reilly, the key index to the narrator's condition is his "hyperacusis," but it is at this point that his analysis falls short and the directions from current research become important.

According to modern researchers, paranoid schizophrenics often experience sensory perceptions that are not directly attributable to environmental stimuli. They also note that 74% of schizophrenics suffer from *auditory* hallucinations: they hear sounds that are not real to others (Sue 428). Usually these sensorial illusions involve voices which the victim perceives as originating outside his/her head, but occasionally "the auditory hallucinations are of sounds rather than voices" (*DSM* 189).

Poe's narrator insists that his "disease had sharpened [his] senses—not destroyed—not dulled them," and that "Above all was the sense of hearing acute." Yet when he goes on to add "I heard all things in the heaven and in the earth. I heard many things in hell" (88), his absurdly grandiose claim encourages us to suspect related claims he makes regarding his auditory capacity. He explains, for example, that "there came to my ears a low, dull, quick sound, such as a watch makes when enveloped in cotton" (91). He interprets this sound as the beating of the old man's heart, but it would have been impossible for him to hear such a noise unless his ear were against the old man's chest. Some scholars argue, in turn, that the narrator was in fact hearing his *own* heart (Shelden 77; Hoffman 232; Howarth 11). While such an interpretation is possible, the narrator's claim to hear things in heaven, hell and the earth makes it more logical to conclude that the sound he heard was not the beating of his own heart, but rather was an auditory hallucination.

To Reilly, the cause of the sound was actually an insect called the "lesser death-watch," but he also admits that there are certain discrepancies in his theory: "Whereas the narrator heard the sound on two occasions during the night of the murder, the ticking of the lesser death-watch is said to continue for hours. Moreover, the narrator reports that the sound he heard increased in tempo just before the murder and grew in volume on both occasions, whereas the ticking of the lesser death-watch is uniformly faint" (5). Reilly then tries to account for the discrepancies by saying that the narrator's "subjective sense of time accelerated the regular ticking of the lesser death-watch" and its volume (7). Such a convoluted explanation is, however, entirely unnecessary if we view the protagonist as a paranoid schizophrenic. If we see him as suffering from auditory hallucinations, then we do not need to suggest any material source, whether insect or heart, for the sounds he claims to have heard—they originated inside his head.

The narrator, of course, insists that "the noise was *not* within my ears" (94), but such a disclaimer simply highlights another, the most common, symptom of schizophrenia—a lack of insight: "during the active phase of their disorder, schizophrenics are unable to recognize that their thinking is disturbed" (Sue 426). Although Poe's narrator admits to having some kind of sensorial disease, he is obviously unaware that it is in fact a *mental* aberration: "why *will* you say that I am mad?"; "You fancy me mad. Madmen know nothing. But you should have seen *me*"; "have I not told you that what you mistake for madness is but over acuteness of the senses?"; "If still you think me mad, you will think so no longer when I describe the wise precautions I took for the concealment of the body" (88, 91, 92). One of the greatest sources of irony—and perhaps pathos—in the tale is the narrator's vehement insistence that he is sane, rather than insane.

The protagonist's inflated opinion of himself is also in keeping with the current view that a "common delusion among paranoid schizophrenics involves exaggerated grandiosity and self-importance" (Sue 439). Poe's narrator brags and boasts specifically of his brilliant circumspection in preparing to murder the old man: "You should have seen how wisely I proceeded—with what caution—with what foresight—with what dissimulation I went to work! . . . Never before that night, had I *felt* the extent of my own powers—of my sagacity. I could scarcely contain my feelings of triumph" (88-89). The narrator believes that he has engaged in what Thomas de Quincy thinks of as "the fine art of murder." He would agree with the facetious de Quincy that a murder can be a very meritorious performance—when committed by a man of superior powers.

Not only was the murder performed with circumspection and with finesse, but so was the disposal of the corpse; Poe's narrator believes that in hiding the evidence of his crime he had considered every possible contingency:

> If still you think me mad, you will think so no longer when I describe the wise precautions I took for the concealment of the body. . . .
>
> I then took up three planks from the flooring of the chamber, and deposited all between the scantlings. I then replaced the boards so cleverly, so cunningly, that no human eye—not even *his*—could have detected any thing wrong. There was nothing to wash out—no stain of any kind—no blood-spot whatever. I had been too wary for that. A tub had caught all—ha! ha!
>
> (92-93)

Then this narrator *gloriosus* boasts of the "enthusiasm of my confidence" and of "my perfect triumph."

Other symptoms of paranoid schizophrenia include shifts of mood (Sue 433-34), and Poe's madman exhibits these in a number of ways. When he begins his recall, he boasts of "how calmly I can tell you the whole story" (88), and indeed his recollection starts calmly enough. As soon as he begins to recall the alleged beating of the old man's heart, however, he becomes frenetic and he loses his composure: "The old man's terror *must* have been extreme! It grew louder, I say, louder every moment! . . . Yet, for some minutes longer I refrained and stood still. But the beating grew louder, louder! I thought the heart must burst. And now a new anxiety seized me—the sound would be heard by a neighbour! The old man's hour had come!" (92). As James W. Gargano has demonstrated, "there is often an aesthetic compatibility between [Poe's] narrators' hypertrophic language and their psychic derangement . . ." (166). In **"The Tell-Tale Heart"** Poe dramatizes the madman's shift from calmness to hysteria by the increased use of such rhetorical devices as repetition (diacope, epizeuxis, ploce), exclamations, emphatic utterances (italics), and the dash. After he confesses how he murdered the old man, Poe's narrator calms down again—until he relates how the police entered his house and the sound of the "heartbeat" recommenced, at which point he becomes one of the most hysterical, most frenzied narrators in all of Poe's fiction.

Associated with the narrator's mood alterations are other symptoms of schizophrenia, including the display of emotions that are at variance with the normal reaction to a given situation: "Schizophrenic patients may exhibit wild laughter or uncontrollable weeping that bears little relationship to current circumstances. . . . Schizophrenics may express the wrong emotions or may express them inappropriately" (Sue 433-34). Evidencing this trait, Poe's protagonist recalls with delight the artful way he performed the most hideous of crimes. He assumes, as well, that his audience shares similar emotions; relating his stealth and patience while putting his head into the old man's chamber, he explains: "Oh, you would have laughed to see how cunningly I thrust it in! . . . To think that there I was, opening the door, little by little, and he not even to dream of my secret deeds or thoughts. I fairly chuckled at the idea . . ." (89-90). Although he pitied his intended victim, he nevertheless "chuckled at heart." In addition, the care he displayed in avoiding blood stains is for him a great source of complacency and humor: "A tub had caught all—ha! ha!" (93).

Complications of schizophrenia include "violent acts" (*DSM* 191), and, of course, the murder of the old man is clearly the ultimate manifestation of such a tendency. Not all paranoid schizophrenics are homicidal maniacs, however; often if they are violent at all the violence is turned against themselves rather than others.

Clearly, though, Poe's schizophrenic is the most dangerous kind: his violence is turned outward, and he originally had no intention of coming to harm himself.

Features of paranoid schizophrenia associated with violence include anxiety, anger and argumentativeness (*DSM* 197). The anxiety of Poe's narrator is something he admits to and, indeed, stresses at the outset: "True!—nervous—very, very dreadfully nervous I had been and am . . ." (88). Anger and argumentativeness are also evidenced in his response to the police: "I arose and argued about trifles, in a high key and with violent gesticulations. . . . I foamed—I raved—I swore!" (94). Such symptoms constitute what is currently labeled "dysphoric mood" (*DSM* 190).

Unfortunately for Poe's paranoid schizophrenic, what finally proved his undoing is yet another symptom of his disease—delusions of persecution. Psychologists note that "deluded individuals believe that others are plotting against them, are talking about them, or are out to harm them in some way. They are constantly suspicious, and their interpretations of the behavior and motives of others are distorted" (Sue 438-39). When Poe's narrator invited the three officers in, he was at first certain that they suspected nothing; then his auditory hallucination began again, and eventually he became convinced that they could not fail to hear the sound which was tormenting him:

> It grew louder—louder—*louder!* And still the men chatted pleasantly, and smiled. Was it possible they heard not? Almighty God!—no, no! They heard!—they suspected!—they *knew!*—they were making a mockery of my horror!—this I thought, and this I think. But anything was better than this agony! Anything was more tolerable than this derision! I could bear those hypocritical smiles no longer! I felt that I must scream or die! and now—again!—hark! louder! louder! louder! louder! *louder!*
>
> (94)

Just as current researchers note the way paranoid schizophrenics might see a "friendly, smiling bus driver . . . as someone who is laughing at them derisively" (Sue 439), so the smiles of the police served only to convince Poe's narrator that they were conspiring against him—with the end result being his confession: " 'Villains!' I shrieked, 'dissemble no more! I admit the deed!' "

What especially recommends a view of the narrator as a paranoid schizophrenic is that it uncovers the most plausible reason *why* he confessed. Contrary to the explanations usually given, I would argue that Poe's madman revealed his crime not because of a guilty conscience, not because some "imp of the perverse" goaded him into confessing, not because he hates himself and really wanted to be caught—not because he has self-destructive tendencies, in other words—but because he suffers from delusions of persecution. He believed that the officers had discovered his crime, and he could not bear the thought that they were mocking him. As Reilly notes, "the narrator purged his rage by exposing what be believed was the hypocrisy of the police," and thus "self-incrimination" was merely the by-product (7).

The time span of "**The Tell-Tale Heart**"—from the time Poe's narrator began looking in on the old man every night at midnight, until the consummation of the murder, and even while he is confessing and insisting upon his sanity—corresponds nicely with the active phase of paranoid schizophrenia. According to psychiatrists, the active phase is of at least a week's duration and is characterized by the manifestation of psychotic symptoms (*DSM* 194). Poe's narrator had been suffering such symptoms for this same time period: he speaks of "the whole week before I killed him" (89), and when he mentions the "low, dull, quick sound" which he attributes to the old man's heart, he says that he "knew *that* sound well" (91). In other words, he had been experiencing his auditory hallucinations during the week before the murder, not just on the night of the crime.

It is one thing to apply twentieth-century psychology to Poe's tales, but it is quite another to account for the fact that Poe has given us a paranoid schizophrenic in the *absence* of twentieth-century psychology. In Poe's day the field of scientific psychology was relatively young, and schizophrenia did not even have a specific name; it was not until 1898 that Emil Kraepelin labeled the disease "Dementia Praecox," and it was given its modern name by Eugen Bleuler only in 1911. Thus, Poe portrayed a paranoid schizophrenic decades before nosologists labeled and separated that disease from other mental abnormalities.

Several explanations for this situation are possible. One is that Poe himself had experienced symptoms of paranoid schizophrenia, and used these as the basis for his narrator in "**The Tell-Tale Heart**." Another hypothesis is that Poe's portrait is purely a product of his imagination (and it is therefore a matter of coincidence that he portrayed what twentieth-century psychology calls a paranoid schizophrenic). The explanation I would like to advance and support, however, is that Poe acquired his knowledge of the symptoms by familiarizing himself with the scientific theories of his time.

The allusion to the phrenologist Spurzheim in "**The Imp of the Perverse**"; the references to the "moral treatment" of the insane in "**Dr. Tarr and Prof. Fether**"; the review of Mrs. L. Miles's *Phrenology* in the *Southern Literary Messenger*—these and other references to coeval theories of psychology in Poe's works show that he was very much a student of mental diseases. He

may have learned a great deal from his discussions with medical men like his acquaintance Pliny Earle (a physician who dealt extensively with the insane at asylums in both Pennsylvania and New York), but probably he gleaned information from literary sources as well.

I. M. Walker is only one of several scholars (Elizabeth Phillips, Allan Gardner Smith, Robert D. Jacobs) who insist that Poe was familiar with the works of the psychologists of his day: "With his passion for scientific fact and his interest in abnormal mental states, Poe would have been likely to turn to systems of contemporary psychology in the same way that modern writers have turned to Freud and Jung. Moreover, in Poe's day . . . information regarding both mental and physical diseases was readily available to the intelligent layman, not only in the original works of the scientists, but also in popular journals and encyclopaedias" (588). A specialized publication, the *American Journal of Insanity,* began appearing in 1844 (only a matter of months before the final publication of "**The Tell-Tale Heart**" in the *Broadway Journal* on 23 August 1845). As for books, Paige Matthey Bynum notes that "Between 1825 and 1838, the Philadelphia publishing house of Carey and Lea published almost twice as many medical books as those in any other category except fiction, and mental health was a staple concern in these works" (150). In the bibliography to *The Analysis of Motives* Smith lists many works on psychology which were extant in Poe's America—books in English that describe the various symptoms which characterize the abnormal mental state of his narrator in "**The Tell-Tale Heart**."

Such descriptions are scattered, however. Because the science of psychology was in its infancy, there was much confusion and disagreement between medical men on how to classify and relate the symptoms of insanity. While twentieth-century students can find entire chapters devoted solely to schizophrenia in various manuals and textbooks, it is more difficult to find specific chapters which group *only* the features of this disease in the books by Poe's contemporaries—their categories were very broad and often vague.

Occasionally, however, we *can* find three or more of the symptoms listed together. One of the earlier texts available to Poe was John Haslam's *Observations on Madness and Melancholy* (1809). In a general chapter on insanity—"Symptoms of the Disease"—Haslam refers to suspiciousness (42) and later to auditory hallucinations and violence (69). In the next chapter he provides particular case studies. One of these. "Case XVI," concerns a man whose "temper was naturally violent, and he was easily provoked. . . . He would often appear to be holding conversations: but these conferences always terminated in a violent quarrel between the imaginary being and himself. He constantly supposed unfriendly people were placed in different parts of the house to torment and annoy him" (118-19). Here we have not only violence and argumentativeness, but also the two *essential* features of paranoid schizophrenia that modern psychologists have identified (*DSM* 197): delusions (of persecution) and the most common kind of auditory hallucination—that which involves voices.

Haslam's "Case XX" involves a woman who, like the male patient, evinced violent tendencies and delusions of persecution, in addition to mood shifts and optical and olfactory hallucinations: "At the first attack she was violent, but she soon became more calm. She conceived that the overseers of the parish, to which she belonged, meditated her destruction. . . . She fancied that a young man, for whom she had formerly entertained a partiality, but who had been dead some years, appeared frequently at her bed-side, in a state of putrefaction, which left an abominable stench in her room" (126-27). Haslam also notes that the woman began to suffer her mental affliction "shortly after the death of her husband." The likelihood that the demise of her spouse created the extreme stress which triggered her breakdown corresponds with the current view that a "psychosocial stressor" may trigger the active phase of schizophrenia (*DSM* 190).

In his Introduction to a recent edition of Haslam's work, Roy Porter observes that "Historians of psychiatry have credited Haslam with giving the first precise clinical accounts of . . . schizophrenia" (xxvii). Prior to the publication of "**The Tell-Tale Heart**," however, there were also other works which described the illness. In his *Treatise on Insanity and Other Disorders Affecting the Mind* (1837), for example, the American physician James Cowles Prichard records the case of a young man who suffered from what he calls "moral insanity":

> He frequently changed his residence, but soon began to fancy himself the object of dislike to every person in the house of which he became the inmate. . . . On being questioned narrowly as to the ground of the persuasion expressed by him, that he was disliked by the family with which he then resided, he replied that he heard whispers uttered in distant apartments of the house indicative of malevolence and abhorrence. An observation was made to him that it was impossible for sounds so uttered to be heard by him. He then asked if the sense of hearing could not, by some physical change in the organ, be occasionally so increased in intensity as to become capable of affording distinct perception at an unusual distance. . . . This was the only instance of what might be termed hallucination discovered in the case after a minute scrutiny [by physicians].
>
> (38)

Apparent in this case are delusions of persecution and voice hallucinations. The young man's query about the possibility of hearing sounds at great distances, furthermore, certainly recalls Poe's insane narrator. Finally, the patient's hypothesis that his disorder is physiological rather than mental also indicates that he too lacks insight into his true psychical condition—another symptom of paranoid schizophrenia.

Other works on abnormal mental states written during Poe's day that describe symptoms of schizophrenia include Isaac Ray's *A Treatise on the Medical Jurisprudence of Insanity* (1838), in which he cites Joseph Mason Cox's *Practical Observations on Insanity* (1804). In a chapter on "General Moral Mania" Ray quotes Cox's report of a certain variety of "maniacs" who

> take violent antipathies, harbor unjust suspicions . . . are proud, conceited and ostentatious; easily excited . . . obstinately riveted to the most absurd opinions; prone to controversy . . . always the hero of their own tale, using . . . unnatural gesticulation, inordinate action. . . . On some occasions they suspect sinister intentions on the most trivial grounds; on others are a prey to fear and dread from the most ridiculous and imaginary sources. . . . If subjected to moral restraint, or a medical regimen, they yield with reluctance to the means proposed, and generally refuse and resist, on the ground that such means are unnecessary where no disease exists. . . .
>
> (172-73)

The symptoms Cox describes correspond very closely to those current psychologists associate with paranoid schizophrenia, just as they also closely match those evinced by the narrator of "**The Tell-Tale Heart**": violence, delusions of persecution and of grandeur, mood shifts, nervousness, and a lack of insight into his own psychopathy.

Clearly, then, Poe and his contemporaries were describing paranoid schizophrenia, even if its symptoms were classified under the broad heading "Moral Insanity," which, as Norman Dain observes, "served as a catch-all for many forms of mental illness" in the early nineteenth century (73)—and which, as Bynum confirms, would indeed have been the way Poe's contemporaries would have diagnosed the condition of his narrator. Accordingly, although romanticists may like to see Poe as a tormented artist who wrote "**The Tell-Tale Heart**" to explore or to purge himself of his own psychotic or self-destructive tendencies, it seems better to regard him as a sophisticated writer who consulted scientific books and journals in an attempt to achieve accuracy and verisimilitude in his own works—the same Poe who familiarized himself with, for instance, the writings of Sir John Herschel, Thomas Dick and John P. Nichol for the astronomy in *Eureka;* and whose reviews of Washington Irving's *Astoria* and J. N. Reynolds's "South Sea Expedition" informed *Pym*. For Poe to consult psychology texts for the sake of scientific precision in "**The Tell-Tale Heart**" would have been typical of his standard practice.

In many ways, therefore, Poe is a precursor of modern artists who find in science not a threat but an ally, and the sophistication of his insights might encourage us to be more humble about our own sophistication. His insights might make us wonder whether the major contribution of twentieth-century psychology has taken the form of new knowledge or whether it consists instead in naming and classification, for it appears that Poe and his contemporaries knew a good deal about paranoid schizophrenia—even if they did not use this terminology.

Notes

¹ The abbreviation refers to the standard reference work in the field of psychology—*Diagnostic and Statistical Manual of Mental Disorders* (see my first entry in Works Cited).

Works Cited

American Psychiatric Association. "Schizophrenia." *Diagnostic and Statistical Manual of Mental Disorders*. 3rd ed, rev. Washington, D.C.: American Psychiatric Association, 1987. 187-98.

Bonaparte, Marie. "The Tell-Tale Heart." *The Life and Works of Edgar Allan Poe: A Psycho-Analytic Interpretation*. Trans. John Rodker. 1949. New York: Humanities, 1971. 491-504.

Bynum, Paige Matthey. " 'Observe How Healthily—How Calmly I Can Tell You the Whole Story': Moral Insanity and Edgar Allan Poe's 'The Tell-Tale Heart'." *Literature and Science as Modes of Expression*. Ed. Frederick Amrine. Boston Studies in the Philosophy of Science 115. Boston: Kluwer, 1989. 141-52.

Dain, Norman. *Concepts of Insanity in the United States, 1789-1865*. New Brunswick, NJ: Rutgers UP, 1964.

Gargano, James W. "The Question of Poe's Narrators." *Poe: A Collection of Critical Essays*. Ed. Robert Regan. Englewood Cliffs: Prentice, 1967. 164-71.

Haslam, John. *Observations on Madness and Melancholy*. 2nd ed. London, 1809.

Hoffman, Daniel. "Grotesques and Arabesques." *Poe Poe Poe Poe Poe Poe Poe*. Garden City: Doubleday. 1972. 226-32.

Howarth, William L. Introduction. *Twentieth-Century Interpretations of Poe's Tales: A Collection of Critical Essays*. Englewood Cliffs: Prentice, 1971. 1-22.

Jacobs, Robert D. "The Matrix." *Poe: Journalist & Critic*. Baton Rouge: Louisiana State UP, 1969. 3-34.

Phillips, Elizabeth. "Mere Household Events: The Metaphysics of Mania." *Edgar Allan Poe: An American Imagination*. Port Washington: Kennikat, 1979. 97-137.

Poe, Edgar Allan. "The Tell-Tale Heart." In vol. 5 of *The Complete Works of Edgar Allan Poe*. Ed. James A. Harrison. 1902. New York: AMS, 1965. 88-94.

Porter, Roy. Introduction. *Illustrations of Madness*. By John Haslam. New York: Routledge, 1988. xi-lxiv.

Prichard, James Cowles. *A Treatise on Insanity and Other Disorders Affecting the Mind*. Philadelphia, 1837.

Ray, Isaac. *A Treatise on the Medical Jurisprudence of Insanity*. Boston, 1838.

Reilly, John E. "The Lesser Death-Watch and 'The Tell-Tale Heart'." *American Transcendental Quarterly* 2 (1969): 3-9.

Shelden, Pamela J. " 'True Originality': Poe's Manipulation of the Gothic Tradition." *American Transcendental Quarterly* 29.1 (1976): 75-80.

Smith, Allan Gardner. "Chapter Two: Edgar Allan Poe." *The Analysis of Motives: Early American Psychology and Fiction*. Amsterdam: Rodopi, 1980. 38-75.

———. "The Psychological Context of Three Tales by Poe." *Journal of American Studies* 7.3 (1973): 279-92.

Stone, Alan A., and Sue Smart Stone. "Psychotic Symptoms." *The Abnormal Personality Through Literature*. Englewood Cliffs: Prentice, 1966. 126-31.

Sue, David, Derald Sue, and Stanley Sue. *Understanding Abnormal Behavior*. 2nd ed. Boston: Houghton, 1986. 425-45.

Walker, I. M. "The 'Legitimate Sources' of Terror in 'The Fall of the House of Usher'." *Modern Language Review* 61 (1966): 585-92.

Christopher Benfey (essay date 1993)

SOURCE: "Poe and the Unreadable: 'The Black Cat' and 'The Tell-Tale Heart,'" in *New Essays on Poe's Major Tales*, edited by Kenneth Silverman, Cambridge University Press, 1993, pp. 27-44.

[*In the following essay, Benfey studies Poe's exploration of "the unreadable in human relations," the opacity that separates one person from another, in the short stories "The Black Cat" and "The Tell-Tale Heart".*]

Two fears should follow us through life. There is the fear that we shan't prove worthy in the eyes of someone who knows us at least as well as we know ourselves. That is the fear of God. And there is the fear of Man—the fear that men won't understand us and we shall be cut off from them.

—Robert Frost[1]

Poe aimed to puzzle his readers. Tale after tale begins or ends with an invitation to decode or decipher a peculiar sequence of events. Some of Poe's most memorable characters are themselves solvers of riddles—amateur scientists, private detectives, armchair philosophers who glorify in what Poe calls "that moral activity which *disentangles.*"[2] The modern-day Oedipus, according to Poe, "is fond of enigmas, of conundrums, of hieroglyphics; exhibiting in his solutions of each a degree of *acumen* which appears to the ordinary apprehension praeternatural" (528).

Poe's critics have tended to divide into two camps: on the one hand, those who claim to have keys to the puzzles, and on the other, those who find the puzzles impossible or unworthy of solution. In the first group one finds a wealth of extraordinary psychoanalytic readings of Poe—surely no other writer other than Freud himself has so engaged the psychoanalytic literary community, from Marie Bonaparte's pioneering reading of Poe to Lacan's famous interpretation of "**The Purloined Letter**" and the further commentary it inspired. In the first group one also finds psychologically astute—though not explicitly psychoanalytic—readers like the poet Richard Wilbur, who finds in Poe's tales representations of the ordinary phases of falling asleep.[3]

In the second group—the resistant readers—belong such dismissive critics as Harold Bloom, who claims to find Poe's prose literally unreadable. "Translation even into his own language," Bloom acidly remarks, "always benefits Poe."[4] To this group also belong such historically minded critics as David Reynolds, for whom Poe's puzzles are interesting primarily as literary conventions, the sort of lure for the masses that Poe, writing at mid-nineteenth century for a magazine-reading public, had no choice but to employ.[5]

I do not propose to steer a middle course between these two camps, even if it were easy to say what such a course might be. My aim instead is to show how one kind of puzzle—perhaps not the most obvious or "crackable" kind—is at the heart of some of Poe's best known tales. This sort of puzzle concerns the ways in which people are themselves enigmas to one another: people (that is characters) both within the stories and on either side, so to speak (the author and the reader). Poe was an early student of the ways in which human beings have access, or are denied access, to the minds of other people. Twentieth-century philosophers such as Ludwig Wittgenstein and J. L. Aus-

tin have devoted a good deal of attention to what has come to be called "the problem of other minds," trying to answer the arguments of skeptics who claim, for example, that we cannot know for certain that another person is in pain. Poe's tales, it seems to me, address such questions from oblique and unexpected angles. If figures from as divergent cultural and historical milieux as Poe and Freud can be invited into useful dialogue, the same could be said for Poe and Wittgenstein. (The latter, by the way, came of age in precisely the same turn-of-the-century Viennese culture as did Freud.)

Poe was fascinated by mind readers and unreadable faces, the twin fantasies of utter exposure and complete secrecy. His private eye Auguste Dupin is the preeminent example of the former. In a scene from "**The Murders in the Rue Morgue**," Dupin astonishes the narrator by reading his mind, having boasted that "most men, in respect to himself, wore windows in their bosoms" (533). Dupin pulls off this feat by being extraordinarily attentive to psychological association, a process Poe relates to the solving of puzzling crimes. In "**The Purloined Letter**," Dupin retrieves the hidden letter by reproducing the mental calculations of the deceitful minister D. The devil, in the less familiar story "**Bon-Bon**," has kindred powers—he can even read the mind of a pet cat (a subject to which we will return).

Poe was equally interested, however, in the opposite phenomenon of the unknowable mind, the mind that remains, despite all attempts at access, ultimately mysterious. One of his best known tales, "**The Man of the Crowd**"—it drew commentary from Baudelaire as well as from the great modern critic Walter Benjamin—begins and ends by comparing certain people to the sort of book that "does not permit itself to be read":

> Men die nightly in their beds, wringing the hands of ghostly confessors, and looking them piteously in the eyes—die with despair of heart and convulsion of throat, on account of the hideousness of mysteries which will not *suffer themselves* to be revealed. (506-7)

It is to this theme of the unreadable in human relations that my subtitle refers. It is not by accident that Poe should invite us to compare reading minds with reading books, or that his stories should involve both activities. He saw the most intimate relation between these two acts of reading, constantly drawing analogies between them. We will now turn to two such tales: "**The Tell-Tale Heart**" and "**The Black Cat**." We will also give some attention to a third text, a sort of hybrid of essay and tale entitled "**The Imp of the Perverse.**"

These tales are not whodunits—we know right from the start who the murderer is. They are closer to the genre now called thrillers, where the crime itself and the psychology of the killer are more the focus than the question of who committed the crime. If there is a mystery in these tales, it is the mystery of motive: not who did it but why. Poe's fascination with the idea of a crime without a clear motive has proved to be one of his richest bequests to later writers, informing such works as Dostoevsky's *Crime and Punishment,* André Gide's *Lafcadio's Adventures (Les Caves du Vatican),* and Camus's *The Stranger,* all three of which test the idea that human freedom is most convincingly exhibited in an extreme and gratuitous act, specifically an act of murder with no obvious advantage to the murderer. Poe's interest in motiveless crime, however, had less to do with human freedom than with human knowledge. He was drawn to two ideas connected with it: one, the ways in which the murderer is a mystery to himself (a dominant idea in **"The Black Cat"**), and two, the related ways in which the murder results from some barrier to the killer's knowledge of other people (a major theme in **"The Tell-Tale Heart"**).

"The Tell-Tale Heart" begins *in medias res,* in the midst of things. We seem to be overhearing a conversation—one that began before our arrival on the scene—between a murderer and his interlocutor. The identity of the latter is never specified; it could be a prison warden, a doctor in a madhouse, a newspaper reporter, a judge. The very indefiniteness makes it easy for the reader to imagine that the killer is speaking directly to him or her.

> True!—nervous—very, very dreadfully nervous I had been and am; but why *will* you say that I am mad? The disease had sharpened my senses—not destroyed—not dulled them. Above all was the sense of hearing acute. I heard all things in the heaven and in the earth. I heard many things in hell. How, then, am I mad? Hearken! and observe how healthily—how calmly I can tell you the whole story. (792)

The first word is a concession—this speaker wants to communicate, to persuade. He thinks that by giving some ground ("granted I'm nervous"), he can win the battle ("but I'm not crazy").

Like other characters in Poe's tales (and to some degree, apparently, Poe himself), the narrator believes that certain diseases of the mind can actually sharpen mental acuity. In "Eleonora," for example, another half mad speaker tries to persuade us that he is sane: "Men have called me mad," he says, "but the question is not yet settled . . . whether all that is profound—does not spring from disease of thought—from *moods* of mind exalted at the expense of the general intellect" (638). And when the narrator of **"The Murders in the Rue Morgue"** tries to explain Dupin's extraordinary powers, he remarks: "What I have described in the Frenchman was merely the result of an excited, or perhaps of

a diseased intelligence" (533). If the speaker in **"The Tell-Tale Heart"** is willing to admit that he's the victim of a disease, madness he will not concede. Like much else in the tale, the nature of the disease remains unspecified, unless it is the general nervousness that he mentions.

He does make perfectly clear what madness is. It is the inability to communicate. His proof of his sanity will therefore be his ability to "*tell* . . . the whole story" [my emphasis]—the verb is crucial—"healthily" and "calmly." Sanity is equated in this character's mind with telling tales. He invites us to gauge how healthily and calmly he can recount the story of the murder.

It is an extraordinary opening, with its mad dashes and nervous, halting delivery. Among his "Marginalia" Poe has preserved a miniature essay on the expressive powers of the dash. Always attentive to punctuation, he was especially fond of the dash, with its suggestion of mental leaps and quick associations. "It represents," he wrote, "a second thought—an emendation."[6] As our speaker begins his "calm" narrative, turning first to the question of motive, we are attuned to the contrasting rhythms of the dash, and we await its recurrence throughout the tale as a sort of trademark of this speaker's style.

> It is impossible to say how first the idea entered my brain; but, once conceived, it haunted me day and night. Object there was none. Passion there was none. I loved the old man. He had never wronged me. He had never given me insult. For his gold I had no desire. I think it was his eye! yes, it was this! One of his eyes resembled that of a vulture—a pale blue eye, with a film over it. Whenever it fell upon me, my blood ran cold; and so by degrees—very gradually—I made up my mind to take the life of the old man, and thus rid myself of the eye forever. (792)

Note how casually the speaker arrives at the eye as cause, as though he is casting about for the motive, and has just now thought of it—"I *think* it was his eye! yes, it was this!" [my emphasis] This is no ordinary eye, of course, but what exactly is so troubling about it? For one thing, it has "a film over it." There is something unseeing about it. When we look at someone "eye to eye" we feel in touch with the person, but this eye is blocked, filmed over. Richard Wilbur links this vulture eye with the vulture in Poe's early sonnet **"To Science,"** in which Poe addresses the anti-imaginative spirit of science that changes "all things with the peering eyes":

> Why preyest thou thus upon the poet's heart,
> Vulture, whose wings are dull realities?[7]

Wilbur wants to nudge us toward an allegorical reading of the tale, with the speaker-killer representing the imaginative faculty of the mind and the old man representing the scientific, rational side.

But let us stay within the terms of the story a bit longer, before trying to arrive at its "larger meaning." We are never told the exact relationship between the old man and his killer. We never learn their names, their jobs, what town they live in, or anything much else about them. We simply know that they live together in the same house.

For all the concision with which our speaker tells his tale, eliminating almost every detail that would help us place him in time and space, he goes on at elaborate length about things that might seem peripheral to the main plot of the story. Nearly a quarter of the narrative, for example, is devoted to the seven nights in which the narrator watches the old man sleep. Why such sustained attention to such *undramatic* behavior?

According to the narrator, this patient observation is meant to provide further and conclusive proof of his sanity. All his preparations—the opened door, closed lantern, and so on—are so *deliberate* (a key word in both **"The Black Cat"** and **"The Tell-Tale Heart"**) that no madman could have accomplished them.

> Now this is the point. You fancy me mad. Madmen know nothing. But you should have seen *me*. You should have seen how wisely I proceeded—with what caution—with what foresight—with what dissimulation I went to work! (792)

It is only in his account of the eighth and crucial night that Poe hints at the significance of this long rigmarole of door, lantern, and eye.

> Never, before that night, had I *felt* the extent of my own powers—of my sagacity. I could scarcely contain my feelings of triumph. To think that there I was, opening the door, little by little, and he not even to dream of my secret deeds or thoughts. I fairly chuckled at the idea; and perhaps he heard me; for he moved on the bed suddenly, as if startled. Now you may think that I drew back—but no. (793)

This is a crucial moment in the story. It shows how much the speaker's motivation has to do with secrecy, with keeping his thoughts hidden. (There is a remarkably similar moment of mute triumph in **"The Black Cat"**: "The glee at my heart was too strong to be restrained. I burned to say if but one word, by way of triumph" [858].) He enters the old man's room night after night as a sort of ritual to establish this secrecy, this fact of human separateness.

And yet, for all his secrecy, our speaker claims to have access to the mind of the old man. His very privacy, his enclosedness, seem to allow him to see into the minds of other people.

> Presently I heard a slight groan, and I knew it was the groan of mortal terror. It was not a groan of pain or of grief—oh, no!—it was the low stifled sound that arises from the bottom of the soul when overcharged with awe. (794)

We may wonder how the speaker claims to know this. The answer, he tells us, is by analogy with his own experience and its expression:

> I knew the sound well. Many a night, just at midnight, when all the world slept, it has welled up from my own bosom, deepening with its dreadful echo, the terrors that distracted me. I say I knew it well. I knew what the old man felt, and pitied him, although I chuckled at heart. I knew that he had been lying awake ever since the first slight noise. (794)

This scene of mind reading continues a bit longer, as the killer claims to know the very words the victim is thinking:

> His fears had been ever since growing upon him. He had been trying to fancy them causeless, but could not. He had been saying to himself—"It is nothing but the wind in the chimney—it is only a mouse crossing the floor," or "it is merely a cricket which has made a single chirp." Yes, he has been trying to comfort himself with these suppositions: but he had found all in vain. (794)

It is only after this sustained scene of mind reading versus secrecy that the old man's eye opens, and the murder is accomplished. It is precisely the breach of secrecy, the penetrating-yet-veiled eye, that seems to motivate the murder.

Poe puts unmistakable emphasis on this claim to *knowledge*: "I say I *knew* it well. I *knew* what the old man felt. . . . I *knew* that he had been lying awake" [my emphasis]. It is precisely this claim to knowledge of another's mind, especially knowledge of another's feelings of pain, that has given rise to some of the most challenging philosophical reflections in our century. Wittgenstein, in a couple of classic passages in his *Philosophical Investigations,* defines the issues succinctly:

> 246. In what sense are my sensations *private?*—Well, only I can know whether I am really in pain: another person can only surmise it.—In one way this is wrong, and in another nonsense. If we are using the word "to know" as it is normally used (and how else are we to use it?), then other people very often know when I am in pain.—Yes, but all the same not with the certainty with which I know it myself!—It can't be said of me at all (except perhaps as a joke) that I *know* I am in pain. What is it supposed to mean—except perhaps that I *am* in pain?[8]

Wittgenstein, in his characteristically dialogical style, is challenging the skeptic's claim that we cannot "know" another's pain. Wittgenstein appeals to our ordinary use of language—"and how else are we to use it?"—as opposed to some special philosophical use, and argues that it's ridiculous to claim that we never can know that another is in pain. We know this—under ordinary circumstances (the stubbed toe, the woman in labor, the burst blister)—all the time. Wittgenstein, here and elsewhere, wants to cure us of our tendency to step outside our ordinary ways of living our lives, and our tendency to demand, for example, kinds of certainty that are inappropriate to our dealings with other people. (Poe seems to have something similar in mind when he insists that the events in **"The Black Cat"** are "ordinary.")

Poe's killers claim to have the very certainty challenged by Wittgenstein. They are always insisting on their special knowledge of others' minds, as though we had been challenging their knowledge: "I say I knew it well. I knew what the old man felt." The killer's claim, in **"The Tell-Tale Heart,"** that he knows the man's feelings by analogy with his own—"I know that he feels *x* when he cries *y* because when I cry *y* I feel *x*"—is another of Wittgenstein's subjects:

> 302. If one has to imagine someone else's pain on the model of one's own, this is none too easy a thing to do: for I have to imagine pain which I *do not feel* on the model of the pain which I *do feel*. That is, what I have to do is not simply to make a transition in imagination from one place of pain to another. As, from pain in the hand to pain in the arm. For I am not to imagine that I feel pain in some region of his body. (Which would also be possible.)

> Pain-behaviour can point to a painful place—but the subject of pain is the person who gives it expression.

Poe's killer makes oddly parallel claims: "I knew the sound well. Many a night, just at midnight, when all the world slept, it has welled up from my own bosom. . . . I say I knew it well. I knew what the old man felt." It does seem as though he is "imagining someone else's pain on the model of [his] own."

The skeptical view of ultimate human separateness ("We can never know for certain what another person is thinking or feeling") is intolerable to Poe's killers; their response is simply to deny it, even to the point of killing in order to prove their certainty. Rather than push the parallels between Poe and Wittgenstein further (perhaps we have already pushed them quite far enough), let us turn to another tale of murder and concealment, namely **"The Black Cat."** In comparing the two tales, especially their endings,

we might find more to say about the two fears—of total exposure and total isolation—that Poe keeps giving voice to.

"The Black Cat" was first published later the same year, 1843, as **"The Tell-Tale Heart."** It resembles the earlier story in several obvious ways, as though Poe were digging deeper in a familiar vein. It too purports to be a killer's confession, and the murder victim is again a member of the killer's household. This killer is also eager to assure us of his sanity: "Yet, mad am I not—and very surely do I not dream." In both stories, furthermore, the police seem almost reluctant to pursue their investigations. The killers must insist on their guilt, even offer proof of it. In each case the discovery of the concealed body is the result of the killer's own obsessive need to reveal its hiding place.

The ways in which the two stories are told are quite distinct, however. One begins at the beginning ("From my infancy . . . I married early . . .") while the other begins in the midst of things. **"The Tell-Tale Heart"** purports to be a spoken narrative and much of its effect is achieved through the illusion of oral delivery. **"The Black Cat,"** by contrast, presents itself from its opening sentence as a written narrative: "For the most wild, yet most homely narrative which I am about to pen, I neither expect nor solicit belief." What is more, the first of the narrator's series of crimes is explicitly linked to this writing instrument:

> I took from my waistcoat-pocket a *pen*-knife, opened it, grasped the poor beast by the throat, and deliberately cut one of its eyes from the socket! I blush, I burn, I shudder, while I *pen* the damnable atrocity. [my emphasis] (851)

The pen may be mightier than the sword, but in this passage Poe skillfully conflates the two. The weapon here is a pen-knife, which was used to sharpen a quill pen. Poe wants us to divine a connection between violence and the act of writing. (Similarly in **"The Imp of the Perverse"** the murder instrument is a poisoned candle used for *reading*.) Significantly, the murderer doesn't blush, burn, and shudder while committing the crime, but while writing about it later.

The link of pens and pen-knives points to a larger contrast in these tales. For the more we read and reread them, the more we see that Poe is less interested in the *commission* of crimes than in the *confession* to them. These are not so much stories of crime and detection as of crime and confession. For Poe, crime itself is not intellectually compelling. The actual business of murder is hurried through in both tales under discussion. In Poe's fullest exploration of the motiveless crime, **"The Imp of the Perverse,"** the crime takes up almost no space at all. We don't know till we are two-thirds of the way through the largely essayistic text that we're reading a crime story at all.

Poe's murderers are not so much obsessive killers as obsessive *talkers*. Afflicted with what Poe calls in "**The Black Cat**" "the spirit of PERVERSENESS," their perversity lies not in their need to kill but in their need to tell. Thus, "**The Imp of the Perverse**" ends with the murderer's sense of safety: He's safe, he tells himself, "if I be not fool enough to make open confession" (1225). This thought is his undoing. "I well, too well understood that, to *think,* in my situation, was to be lost" (1225-6).

Concealment is ultimately unbearable for these killers, for whom secrets are like bodies buried alive, imprisoned souls seeking freedom. Thus, in "**The Imp of the Perverse**":

> For a moment, I experienced all the pangs of suffocation; I became blind, and deaf, and giddy; and then, some invisible fiend, I thought, struck me with his broad palm upon the back. The long-imprisoned secret burst forth from my soul.

Poe gives minute attention to the style of the released confession: "They say that I spoke with a distinct enunciation, but with marked emphasis and passionate hurry, as if in dread of interruption" (1226). Interruption would restore human separateness; these killers long for human transparency.

We have to consider other factors in making sense of the odd balance of crime and confession in these tales. Surely Poe had aesthetic reasons for minimizing the gore in his stories; as David Reynolds has pointed out, he wished to distance himself from popular practitioners of crime journalism, who relied on explicit horror to shock and titillate their readers.[9] It is Poe's corresponding emphasis on the act of confession that needs explanation. "**The Tell-Tale Heart**," "**The Black Cat**," and "**The Imp**" all record a confession—a *perverse* confession since the crimes would otherwise have been undetected. All three tales purport to be first-person narratives; they represent confessions within confessions—confessions to the second degree. These killers need to confess to the perverse act of having confessed. The fear of the criminals is not the fear of being caught, it is the fear of being *cut off,* of being misunderstood. Thus the narrator of "**The Imp of the Perverse**": "Had I not been thus prolix, you might either have misunderstood me altogether, or, with the rabble, have fancied me mad." Here, as in the other two tales, the claim to sanity is a response to the fear of being cut off from other people, of being "misunderstood altogether."

The speaker of "**The Tell-Tale Heart**," as we noted earlier, tells his story to convince his audience that he is not mad, not cut off from other people. The tale-telling heart is finally the narrator's own, for this is a tale about the need to communicate, the fear of being cut off, of becoming incommunicado. The narrator of "**The Black Cat**" writes: "Yet, mad am I not. . . . But to-morrow I die, and today I would unburthen my soul. My immediate purpose is to place before the world, plainly, succinctly . . . a series of mere household events." Communication, for these speakers, is itself a kind of salvation.

With this fear of isolation in mind, we can begin to make sense of what drives these killers crazy. The features these men can't stand are uncannily inexpressive: the eye with the hideous "film" or "veil" over it; the missing eye of the cats; the black fur. Similarly, the meaning of the ever-present walls in these stories is easily decoded. They represent the fantasy of being immured in one's own body, with the voice suffocated inside, the tale-telling heart silenced. Poe is quite explicit in "**The Black Cat**" when he says that the wall "fell bodily."

What of the beds that recur in so many of Poe's tales? We see immediately the attraction of beds as the site of many interrelated activities: sleep and dreaming; making love and conceiving children; dying. It is astonishing how many of Poe's stories centrally involve beds and bedrooms. In "**The Imp**" the victim is murdered by a poisoned candle while reading in bed; a bed is the means of escape in the Rue Morgue murders; and there are many tales—"**Ligeia**" especially—in which a woman lies on her deathbed.

Beds figure more prominently still in "**The Tell-Tale Heart**" and "**The Black Cat**." In the earlier story the killer, after a week of watching the old man asleep in bed, uses the bed itself as a murder weapon. It is not clear exactly how this is done, and this very lack of clarity makes Poe's choice of the bed more emphatic; he's willing to sacrifice verisimilitude—why not a knife or a noose?—in order to stress the meanings associated with the bed. Here is the description of the murder:

> He shrieked once—once only. In an instant I dragged him to the floor, and pulled the heavy bed over him. I then smiled gaily, to find the deed so far done. But, for many minutes, the heart beat on with a muffled sound. This, however, did not vex me; it would not be heard through the wall. At length it ceased. The old man was dead. I removed the bed and examined the corpse. Yes, he was stone, stone dead. I placed my hand upon the heart and held it there many minutes. There was no pulsation. He was stone dead. His eye would trouble me no more. (795-6)

Again the wall is clearly enough a stand-in for the body: "it would not be heard through the wall." But the bed also seems closely related to the body—Poe even appears to be playing on the similar sounds of the two words. The link of bed and dead body is clear enough in the sentence: "I removed the bed and examined the corpse."

Why should the bed be the murder weapon? Why not something more keyed to the filmed and infuriating eye? The answer, I think, is that whereas the bed resumes meanings associated with the body and its dissolution, it also draws on meanings linked to sexuality. The relationship between killer and victim in **"The Tell-Tale Heart"** is never specified, but we are told that the killer "loved the old man." The relation between killer and victim is similarly oblique in **"The Imp of the Perverse,"** though we learn, in passing, that the killer inherits the victim's money.

Only in **"The Black Cat"** are these themes of intimacy and violence explored. We find ourselves amid walls and beds again after the killer's perverse act of hanging his cat—after he has "hung it *because* I knew that it had loved me, and *because* I felt it had given me no reason of offense." The following night the killer awakes to find "The curtains of my bed were in flames." When he returns to the ruins of the house he finds the following scene:

> The walls, with one exception, had fallen in. This exception was found in a compartment wall, not very thick, which stood about the middle of the house, and against which had rested the head of my bed. (853)

A crowd has assembled around this wall: "I approached and saw, as if graven in *bas relief* upon the white surface, the figure of a gigantic *cat*." The word "graven" is a brilliant stroke, for this is the cat's grave as well as his engraved monument. Poe is again—as with the pen/pen-knife and the poisoned reading candle—associating the violence of writing with the violence he is describing. Similarly, the "head of the bed" reminds us of the relation between bed and body.

Many critics have seen in this tale a close link between the cat and the wife, but this seems to me to place too much emphasis on marriage for at least two reasons. First, Poe is interested more in the issue of access to other minds—"hung it because *I knew* that it had loved me, and because *I felt* it had given me no reason of offense" [my emphasis]—and second, Poe is as interested in our access to the minds of cats as to the minds of people. (This is as good a place as any to acknowledge that I am leaving out two aspects of the narrative that are of obvious importance to a full reading of **"The Black Cat"** but are tangential to the themes of this essay: the issue of alcohol abuse and the issue of violence against women.)

The evidence for the second point lies in such essays as "Instinct vs Reason—A Black Cat," in which Poe speculates about the inner life of cats. After describing in some detail how his cat has mastered the art of opening the complicated latch of a door, he concludes that "The line which demarcates the instinct of the brute creation from the boasted reason of man, is, beyond doubt, of the most shadowy and unsatisfactory character" (477). Poe's meditations bear a surprising similarity to some of Wittgenstein's regarding the difference between animal thinking and that of humans. "Why can't a dog simulate pain?" asks Wittgenstein. "Is he too honest?" (250) Both writers speculate on how animals regard the future; Wittgenstein asks why we have difficulty imagining a hopeful animal ("And why not?" [174]), whereas Poe claims that the way his cat negotiates, step by step, the act of opening the latch demonstrates almost prophetic powers.

We are more interested, however, in the other focus of Poe's concern: our access to other (human) minds. "Unmotivated treachery, for the mere intent of injury, and self violence are," according to Allen Tate, "Poe's obsessive subjects."[10] This seems to me partly an oversimplification and partly wrong. Poe's killers do have motives, but these motives remain concealed from the killers. In the space remaining in this essay, I want to specify the link in Poe's tales between the profession of love and the need to confess. Both arise from what Frost, in our epigraph, called "the fear of Man—the fear that men won't understand us and we shall be cut off from them."

We need to understand what the teller/killer of **"The Tell-Tale Heart"** is really telling us when he claims that "Object there was none. Passion there was none. I loved the old man." He is, despite himself, providing both object (or motive) and passion. It is precisely his love for the old man that makes him kill, just as the man's love for the cat—"hung it *because* I knew that it had loved me"—prompts the murder of the cat and, presumably, the wife as well. At this point I must acknowledge the work of the philosopher Stanley Cavell in relation to the nature of Shakespearean tragedy. In plays like *Othello* and *King Lear* Cavell finds a repeated pattern of what he calls "the avoidance of love." Tragedy results from the burden that Lear and Othello find imposed by the love of others. In some sketchy and speculative remarks about Poe's **"The Black Cat"** and **"The Imp of the Perverse,"** Cavell invites us to look for "some relation between the wish to be loved and the fear of it."[11]

The man we encounter in **"The Black Cat"** seems (and I am not claiming this is necessarily Cavell's view) to find the devotion of others repulsive. When the second cat follows the narrator home, he finds that "its evident fondness for myself rather disgusted and annoyed."

> With my aversion to this cat, however, its partiality for myself seemed to increase. It followed my

footsteps with a pertinacity which it would be difficult to make the reader comprehend. Whenever I sat, it would crouch beneath my chair, or spring upon my knees, covering me with its loathsome caresses. (855)

Even in his dreams he finds the cat with him, and awakens "to find the hot breath of the thing upon my face, and its vast weight . . . incumbent eternally upon my heart!" Our suspicion that Poe wishes, with the word "incumbent," to remind us of the sexual attentions of the mythical *incubus* and its counterpart the *succubus* is confirmed in the sentence immediately following: "Beneath the pressure of torments such as these, the feeble remnant of the good within me *succumbed.*"

It is another act of unbearable intimacy—when cat and wife insist on "accompanying" him into the cellar, and the cat follows him down "the steep stairs" so closely that it "exasperated me to madness" (856)—that incites the man to kill his two closest companions. We don't need Freud to point out the erotic connotations of steep stairs in dreams to feel that this man finds intimacy intolerable.

What Poe is giving voice to in these murders is the second fear Frost names: "the fear that we shan't prove worthy in the eyes of someone who knows us at least as well as we know ourselves." Frost calls this the fear of God, but it could as well be called the fear of Love. Here I am reminded of the German poet Rainer Maria Rilke's extraordinary reading of the parable of the Prodigal Son. Rilke interprets this tale of another once-tender man who flees into intemperance as "the legend of a man who didn't want to be loved." The picture Rilke paints is remarkably like the speaker in **"The Black Cat."** Here is Poe:

> From my infancy I was noted for the docility and humanity of my disposition. My tenderness of heart was even so conspicuous as to make me the jest of my companions. I was especially fond of animals. (850)

And here is Rilke:

> When he was a child, everyone in the house loved him. He grew up not knowing it could be any other way and got used to their tenderness, when he was a child.[12]

Both Poe's narrator and Rilke's prodigal come to find this intimacy unbearable. Rilke:

> He wouldn't have been able to say it, but when he spent the whole day roaming around outside and didn't even want to have the dogs with him, it was because they too loved him; because in their eyes he could see observation and sympathy, expectation, concern; because in their presence too he couldn't do anything without giving pleasure or pain.

The son's flight is from what he perceives as the prison of love—the way it defines and confines us.

> The dogs, in whom expectation had been growing all day long, ran through the hedges and drove you together into the one they recognized. And the house did the rest. Once you walked in to its full smell, most matters were already decided. A few details might still be changed; but on the whole you were already the person they thought you were; the person for whom they had long ago fashioned a life, out of his small past and their own desires; the creature belonging to them all, who stood day and night under the influence of their love.

Both Poe and Rilke (who would have known Poe's works through Baudelaire's essays and translations if through no more direct way) find in the very walls of the house and the eyes of pets the confining nature of domestic life, of what Poe calls "mere household events."

If there is salvation for Rilke's prodigal in learning to love, and in accepting, eventually, God's love, there is none for Poe's murderers. As Allen Tate remarked, "He has neither Purgatory nor Heaven."[13] Poe's narratives can be read as cautionary tales—"Go thou and do otherwise"—but rightly read their warning is more complex. Poe seems, like Frost, to be saying: These fears are always with us—the fear of love and the fear of isolation. Taken to extremes, they both lead to disaster: One cat avoids us and is blinded, another cat follows us and is killed. To live life is to steer a dangerous course between these extremes and there is no point at which the current widens. To declare onself safe—as the imp of the perverse tempts us to do—is to be lost.

Notes

[1] Robert Frost, "Introduction" to Edwin Arlington Robinson, *King Jasper* (New York: Scribner's, 1935), p. vi.

[2] *Collected Works of Edgar Allan Poe,* ed. Thomas Ollive Mabbott (Cambridge: Harvard University Press, 1978), p. 528. All future page references to this edition are indicated in parentheses in the text.

[3] Richard Wilbur, "The House of Poe," in *Edgar Allan Poe: Modern Critical Views,* ed. Harold Bloom (New York: Chelsea House, 1985), pp. 51-69.

[4] Harold Bloom, "Introduction," in *Edgar Allan Poe,* p. 8.

[5] David S. Reynolds, *Beneath the American Renaissance: The Subversive Imagination in the Age of Emerson and Melville* (New York: Knopf, 1988), pp. 225-48.

[6] Poe, *Essays and Reviews,* ed. G. R. Thompson (New York: Library of America, 1984), p. 1426.

[7] Richard Wilbur, "Poe and the Art of Suggestion," in *Critical Essays on Edgar Allan Poe,* ed. Eric W. Carlson (Boston: G. K. Hall, 1987), p. 166.

[8] Ludwig Wittgenstein, *Philosophical Investigations,* trans. G. E. M. Anscombe (New York: Macmillan, 1958). The numbers attached to this and later references to Wittgenstein refer not to pages but to numbered sections of the *Investigations.*

[9] Reynolds remarks that "Poe . . . avoids repulsive accounts of violence or blood, shifting his attention to the crazed mind of the obsessed narrator. By removing us from the realm of horrid gore to that of diseased psychology, he rises above . . . tawdry sensationalism" (*Beneath the American Renaissance,* p. 232).

[10] Allen Tate, "Our Cousin, Mr. Poe," in *Poe: A Collection of Critical Essays,* ed. Robert Regan (Englewood Cliffs, N.J.: Prentice-Hall, 1967), p. 46.

[11] Stanley Cavell, *In Quest of the Ordinary* (Chicago: University of Chicago Press, 1990), p. 137. See also Cavell, *The Claim of Reason: Wittgenstein, Skepticism, Morality, and Tragedy* (Oxford: Oxford University Press, 1979), pp. 481-96.

[12] Rainer Maria Rilke, *The Notebooks of Malte Laurids Brigge,* trans. Stephen Mitchell (New York: Random House, 1983), pp. 251-60.

[13] Tate, "Our Cousin," p. 46.

Johann Pillai (essay date 1997)

SOURCE: "Death and Its Moments: The End of the Reader in History," *Modern Language Notes,* Vol. 112, No. 5, December, 1997, pp. 836-75.

[*In the following essay, Pillai considers "The Tell-Tale Heart" as a text that expresses a complicity between the fictional narrator and the reader of the narrative, and a breach in the conventional border between literature and criticism; this breach results in what Pillai calls a narrative's "afterlife."*]

> On its own account, historiography takes for granted the fact that it has become impossible to believe in this presence of the dead that has organized (or organizes) the experience of entire civilizations; and the fact too that it is nonetheless impossible "to get over it," to accept the loss of a living solidarity with what is gone, or to confirm an irreducible limit.
>
> —Michel de Certeau[1]

> All history, moreover, must more or less blindly encounter the problem of a transferential relation to the past whereby the processes at work in the object of study acquire their displaced analogues in the historian's account.
>
> —Dominick LaCapra[2]

A historiographical paradox leads me, in what follows, to perform a reading of a "tale," a narrative which declares as such its fictiveness, in its relation to history, which it purports to transcend or slide past.[3] It is not my intention here simply to identify or reconstruct the historical conditions under which the tale was produced, nor to relate it to the various times of its reception, nor again to describe its putative extratextual referents.[4] My concern is rather with the temporal mode of "modernity"—by which I mean the *contemporary readability,* the presentness—of a text which has left its moment of origin and floats before a reader in any age, apparently with no strings attached; that is, with the historiographical relation between the narration of a fictional tale and the critical performance of reading it.[5]

This relation, in its most general terms, has two fundamental aspects. First, the understanding that a tale is a narration of events—real, ideal or imagined—and hence establishes, within its own temporality, logical, causal, figurative, and other kinds of relations between signs of objects, subjects, and events. The tale thus functions in itself as a story or history of "what it is about."[6] A second aspect concerns the act of reading the tale, an act which simultaneously constitutes the tale as a history, and (in doing so) establishes itself in a metahistorical relation to the tale. The performance of reading thus takes as its point of origination the text of the tale which it has itself constituted as origin. The circularity of this relationship is the abyssal ground of what is commonly articulated as a battle between literary theory and literary history, or simply as *crisis.*[7]

To read the tale critically is to read in the mode of crisis, to participate in a hearing without a sentence being pronounced: for the tale demands that its reader recognize from the outset its status as fiction—and accordingly *suspend,* while reading, the arbitrarily established conventions by which we are accustomed to distinguish between the conventions of reference, the levels of understanding termed "literal" and "figurative." It is precisely this elision of difference which enables both the mythopoeic distancing of the events referred to in the tale from a past "historical reality" and the historical realization of these events in the experiential time of the reader. The historical conditions of the tale, in short, are located in the present of its being told and heard—in its lived presentness to a reader in any age.[8] And it is the hermeneutic relation of the narrative voice of the tale to the narrative voice of criticism that determines this paradoxical temporality; its articulation requires the reading, not only of a tale—Poe's **"The Tell-Tale Heart"** will serve as example—but also, in the space before and after the tale, the full and expressive silence which precedes the beginning and succeeds the end, of reading.

I

"The Tell-Tale Heart"—the title—is first of all, and by convention, an index, pointing to what the tale will be about. Simultaneously, however—it is here initially that the literal/figurative distinction must be suspended—it labels or names, confers an identity on the text it signifies[9], and thus this text which confronts the reader can be, *is,* nothing but the heart itself, palpable and red—not read as a representation of a heart, but the very bodily organ responsible for circulation, the seat of emotion, of passion, of the affections. It is the organ which sustains life—and yet, paradoxically, a heart on its own seems to imply its own extraction from a body; it may produce no circulation, may or may not beat. Beyond what it *is,* too, lies the question of what it *does,* for this is a heart which tells a tale—a "tell-tale" heart; and by the same token an informing heart, a give-away, a tattler; a warning, betrayer, traitor. The tale it will tell is also—for such is also the function of a title to indicate—*about* the tell-tale heart; it is an organ which tells the story of itself. The narrative voice which tells the tale is no less the voice *of* the tale, both the subject and the object of its own narration.

This circular, abyssal self-mirroring—by which the tale names itself as an organ without a body,[10] a fragment which tells a tale about a fragment which tells a tale—might appear on the surface to close it off from any attempt to situate it within an external historicity. The first word of the text, however—"True!"—indicates otherwise; it situates what follows within the factual context of a (granted) past history:[11]

> nervous—very, very dreadfully nervous I had been and am; but why *will* you say that I am mad? The disease had sharpened my senses—not destroyed—not dulled them. Above all was the sense of hearing acute. I heard all things in the heaven and in the earth. I heard many things in hell. How, then, am I mad?[12]

The apostrophe—and certainly the entire narration is an extended apostrophe—prosopopoeically gives face to its addressee, locates the time of narration in the present of the reader. Or rather, in the present of an implied reader, an invisible addressee who might, or who has already, diagnosed the narrator—"why *will* you say . . . ?" The dread and anxiety of the narrator reflect his (her?) being ill at ease, the victim of a dis-ease.[13] But the question is taken up again: "How,

then, am I mad?" How, indeed, are we to read this question? What reader could conclude at this point that the narrator is mad? These apostrophic questions, their implicit answers, serve to close the text off from the actual reader in another sense by insisting, counter-productively, that the narrator is not mad but has been, or will be, categorized as such regardless; the narrator's rationalizations attempt to breach—while simultaneously his denials reinforce—the virtual barrier of the disciplinary separation[14] by which the *reader* maintains a sense of security (sane, empirical) in relation to the text, is able to demarcate the limits of the text as fiction. Thus, paradoxically, the typical reader of this text on the one hand takes the narrator at his word, believes that the tale describes the commission of a murder; while on the other hand is convinced of the insanity of the narrator, refusing to believe the latter's arguments in his own defense.[15] To consider the narrative as *"true!"* in both respects—the rationalizations and the denials—would be to breach the demarcation between the perceived criminality and insanity of the events related in the fictional text, and the culturally constructed sanity and morality of the historical reality which the reader is living.

This typical, automatic response—which believes the narrator's description of events, but refuses to believe his evaluation of them—not only reflects a culturally determined delimitation of a madness/sanity boundary but also indicates a confusion of fiction and reality on the part of a reader who, missing altogether the nature of the tale's fictionality—which necessitates a suspension of these differences—arbitrarily reads some parts of the text literally, and treats others as metaphorical.[16] To read the tale *as* a tale means to take its internal logic as simultaneously, and at all times, both literal and figurative, historical (in the sense of the perceptual, experiential reality it provides in the present of the reader) and fictional. Thus, for example, in reply to his own apostrophe, and as if to refute the purported diagnosis of madness, the narrator claims that the dis-ease "had sharpened my senses . . . not dulled them." By *senses,* initially, one assumes a reference to wits, *mental* faculties: he is mentally alert (sharp) and hence not mad. But the further qualification regarding his sense of hearing suggests that the narrator's claim to sanity is based on a certain *sensory* acuteness; a moment later, this is carried to the point of being *supersensory:* he hears all things in heaven and earth, and many in hell. There are no grounds for privileging these qualifications one over the other in terms of credibility; taken together in the *res gestae* they show state of mind, while simultaneously warning the reader not to mistake an extraordinary sense of hearing for madness—that is, not to misjudge the narrator.

For this is also a judicial or diagnostic hearing, at which the narrator makes his apology, and where the reader is instructed to hear fairly, to "*Hearken!* and observe how healthily—how calmly I can tell you the whole story." The reader is invited to sharpen his or her senses, to hear what the narrator hears in heaven, earth and hell; in short, to become like the narrator on levels mental, sensory and supersensory, cross the boundary between history and fiction.[17]

In what follows, the nature of this boundary begins to be defined. The narrator establishes initially that the events under consideration have no identifiable motive—no cause or origin:

> It is impossible to say how first the idea entered my brain; but once conceived, it haunted me day and night. Object there was none. Passion there was none. I loved the old man. He had never wronged me. He had never given me insult. For his gold I had no desire.

The "idea," which arises spontaneously, is ghostly and persistent, and of obscure purpose ("object") as well as origin. At its heart there is not passion, but love—the two assertions cancel each other out. Neither revenge nor desire is the motive, and yet there is one consistent characterization of the narrator's state of mind: he is "very, very *dreadfully* nervous." The fear, the dread of the narrator is projected, embodied, finds its expression, and is figured forth, in the image of the old man's eye:

> I think it was his eye! yes, it was this! One of his eyes resembled that of a vulture—a pale blue eye, with a film over it. Whenever it fell upon me, my blood ran cold; and so by degrees—very gradually— I made up my mind to take the life of the old man, and thus rid myself of the eye for ever.

These two consecutive passages reveal the predicament of presentness, the temporal mode of modernity which characterizes the tale, in that they stage the twofold and paradigmatic founding gesture of historiography— *and then its negation:* first, the positing of an (absence of) origin for the narrative which will follow, and the figuration of that archic absence as an alterity—"*his* eye," the eye of the other—which legitimates the narrated events; secondly, the eschatological projection, into the future, of the figured origin as the end and purpose of the narration, as an *eschaton* which legitimates it in retrospect; and finally, the proposed negation of this twofold gesture by the elimination of the eye, the very figure which defines and determines the historiographical operation of the narrator. **"The Tell-Tale Heart"** thus both affirms and denies its status as a narrative of historical events, and in this gesture establishes its modernity as a textual space both within and without history.[18]

The consequences of such a temporal paradox can only be unsettling for the act of reading, if we hearken to the complex relation betokened by the homophonic and homonymic play on *eye/I,* between the narrative I and the eye/I of the other, the old man.[19] It is this singular eye/I which is simultaneously the narrating subject, the object of the narrative, and the origin and telic end of the narration. At stake in the death which is to come— on the level of sound, on the crucial level of *hearing*— is the (self-)elimination of the very "I" which speaks, of the narrative voice itself—and, by extension, since the reader is implicated in this eye/I persona in the act of reading and writing which retells the tale, in the act of hearing which replicates the narrator's disease: what is at stake is precisely the critical relation between fiction and history—the *end* of the reader.

The narrator's dread is hypostatized prosopopoeically in the eye: its resemblance to the eye of a carrion-eating bird suggests that death is imminent; its association with the gaze of the old man, that the death awaited is that of the narrative voice. Here too, perhaps, we have the first sign of the absent body of which the tell-tale heart posits itself as an organ and a metonymy—and yet, curiously, is not—that film which veils the pale blue eye of the old man: is it not the very film of death, the dimming vision of dying eyes? The narrator's blood runs cold, in a turn of phrase which both expresses his fear and dread, and foreshadows a killing in cold blood. It also suggests the cold temperature of a corpse and hence the consanguinity of the narrator and the old man. The narrative I decides "to rid *myself*" of the eye of the other, for paronomastically that eye/I is his own; we shall see (for we are not only to "hearken," but to "observe") that the stakes are indeed high in exchanging glances with his, for it is our own eye/I which is implicated in the narrator's apostrophe:

> Now this is the point. You fancy me mad. Madmen know nothing. But you should have *seen* me. You should have seen how wisely I proceeded—with what caution—with what foresight—with what dissimulation I went to work! I was never kinder to the old man than during the whole week before I killed him.

In the first place, the narrator's initial apostrophe— "why *will* you say . . ."—is now qualified: "You fancy me mad." If this fancy is deluded, then the contemptuous "madmen know nothing" is a thrust at the reader ("you") as well as the narrator ("I"), for determining the limits of madness depends on the gaze of the reader, on *our* ability to see; twice we are told: "you should have *seen*. . . ." The reader's judicial gaze becomes a critical factor in the middle term of the convoluted enthymeme which governs the tale, and of which the major premise is that madmen know nothing. What will dispel the fancy of madness is our seeing now not only "how healthily—how calmly" the tale is told, but "how wisely" its events take place, and with what *fore-sight*—the ability to provide for, but also *see* into, the future. Indeed, the very nature of the event described as the murder of the old man by the narrator (" . . . I killed him") is thrown into question by the playful linguistic exchange between eye and I which establishes a scopic reciprocity between the two: the narrator's phrase "to take the life of the old man" suggests not simply killing, but substitution and resemblance—*taking on* his life.

It is this exchange which is revealed in the thanatoptic premeditation that follows:

> And every night, about midnight, I turned the latch of his door and opened it—oh, so gently! And then, when I had made an opening sufficient for my head, I put in a dark lantern, all closed, closed, so that no light shone out, and then I thrust in my head. Oh, you would have laughed to see how cunningly I thrust it in! I moved it slowly, very slowly, so that I might not disturb the old man's sleep. It took me an hour to place my whole head within the opening so far that I could see him as he lay upon his bed. Ha!—would a madman have been so wise as this? And then, when my head was well in the room, I undid the lantern cautiously—oh, so cautiously—cautiously (for the hinges creaked)—I undid it just so much that a single thin ray fell upon the vulture eye. And this I did for seven long nights—every night, just at midnight—but I found the eye always closed; and so it was impossible to do the work; for it was not the old man who vexed me, but his Evil Eye. And every morning, when the day broke, I went boldly into the chamber, and spoke courageously to him, calling him by name in a hearty tone, and inquiring how he had passed the night. So you see, he would have been a very profound old man, indeed, to suspect that every night, just at twelve, I looked in upon him while he slept.

Here several structures of repetition combine. There is, first, a temporal movement, which becomes increasingly more precise, and also more measured: "every night, about midnight . . . every night, just at midnight . . . every night, just at twelve. . . . " The duration of events staged in the narrator's description of his movements—"oh, so gently! . . . slowly—very, very slowly . . . cautiously—oh, so cautiously . . ."—takes up the pace of his decision to kill the old man "by degrees—very gradually," his proceeding "with what caution." The metrical style of the narration is itself an indication of "how healthily—how calmly" the narrator can tell the whole story.

But there is another kind of repetition here, to which this temporal movement lends its measure. The narrator "opened" the door, "made an opening," put in a lantern "all closed, closed." He placed his head within the opening, and then "undid the lantern"—that is, *opened* it. For seven days, he could proceed no further, because he found "the eye always *closed*." There is also a contrapuntal movement of physical penetration and withdrawal here which echoes the mental penetration of the narrator when "the idea entered my brain";[20] as the idea haunts the narrator, so he, by day and night, haunts the old man: "I put *in* a dark lantern . . . no light shone *out* . . . I thrust *in* my head . . . I thrust it *in*. . . ." What, then, is the nature of the space—of the inside and outside—of these events? What is implied by the measure of the narrator's words, by the opening and closing they describe?

These characterizations establish, first, the interchangeability of head, lantern and chamber—even the apparently insignificant reference to creaking hinges connotes, by association, both the panel of the lantern and the door of the chamber—since knowledge of and in each is determined by optical perception; it is light which enables the narrator to see. The events described take place in a chamber, but the space of the chamber is coextensive with the space of the narrator's head, for these events are recounted in the light of his memory—perhaps his hallucination, perhaps his dream. This space is also coeval with the space of the text of the narration, and the physical space of the pages into which we, as readers, are looking—both through the narrator's eyes and as critical observers of the narrator. The optical thresholds—the door, the panel of the lantern—which mark the difference between inside and outside mark, no less, the separation between the eye/I of the reader and the eye/I of the narrator.

"His door," "the room," "the chamber," are architectural commonplaces, but a "chamber" is also the cameral seat of a judge conducting a hearing out of court. And chambers define the brain, the eye—and the heart: the upper cavities, or auricles, derive their name from the Latin word *auris,* or ear. We return, then, to the narrator's—and the judicious reader's—extraordinary sense of hearing: in the opening and closing, the in/out movement of the narrator's actions there must be heard a pulsing, systolic and diastolic: the textual heartbeat of a system of circulation.

The nature of this circulation does not appear to be bodily; indeed luxation from all physical contexts, or the positing of the body as absent, appears to be the very premise of the tale's title, and apart from a few *disjecta membra*—the narrator's hand which opens the door, his thumb which in a moment will slip on the metal fastening of the lantern—no physical features are given in the tale which would permit the identification of its narrator or characters. The two organs whose senses circumfuse the economy of the text are the ear (the sense of hearing) and the eye (the sense of sight). What circulates in the economy of the tell-tale heart and its reading—through the valvular opening and closing of doors and panels, through the ebb and flow of the narrator's movement and vision—is *light,* which enables the scopic exchange of the gaze, the eye; and conterminously—through the caesurae and hiatuses of the narrative voice, through the space between narrator and reader—its homologue, *sound:* the specular exchange of the subject, the I.

Thus are implicated, in the thin ray of light released by the narrator to enable vision, three gazes: not only the narrator's, and that of the old man,[21] but the apostrophized reader's as well: "So *you see,* he would have been a very profound old man, indeed, to *suspect* that every night, just at twelve, *I looked* in upon him while he slept."[22] It is in following the injunction to *"Hearken! and observe,"* in the critical acts of hearing and seeing, that the reciprocal nature of the relation between narrator and reader is realized; indeed, the very laugh he attributes to the *reader*—"you would have laughed . . ."—is expressed by the narrator himself in a singular exclamation: "Ha!" And when he asks, not altogether rhetorically, "would a madman have been so wise as this?" it must be remembered that one of the measures of wisdom is fore*sight.*

Now presumably, taking the life of the old man, if we assume the traditional interpretation of this event as a murder, could be achieved easily enough while the old man is unconscious: we are told of the "old man's sleep:" that "he lay upon his bed," that the narrator "found the eye always closed," that "I looked in upon him while he slept." But the act which the narrator contemplates is not, *cannot* be murder, and it is precisely for this reason that when the eye is closed he finds it "impossible to do the work"—which will "rid myself of the *eye/[I]* for ever"—which entails a blinding and self-negating act of narrative and historiographical suicide.

What is in fact required for the narrator to proceed is the penetration by light of the old man's eye: it is necessary, for "death" to occur, that the *old man's* eye be open, able to see. It is this eye which vexes the narrator, afflicts him like a disease; for it is indeed a dis-ease, ultimately, by which the narrator is vexed: not a sickness as such, but the dread of a specular subject which refuses to die, an EVIL EYE/I, which, mirrored back in the gaze of the narrator, always declares: "I/EYE LIVE!"

These observations are all prefatory to the night of the central event of the tale, when the narrator makes his move:

> Upon the eighth night I was more than usually cautious in opening the door. A watch's minute hand moves more quickly than did mine. Never before that night had I *felt* the extent of my own powers—of my sagacity. I could scarcely contain my feelings of triumph. To think that there I was, opening the door, little by little, and he not even to dream of my secret deeds or thoughts. I fairly chuckled at the

idea; and perhaps he heard me; for he moved on the bed suddenly, as if startled. Now you may think that I drew back—but no. His room was as black as pitch with the thick darkness (for the shutters were close fastened, through fear of robbers), and so I knew that he could not see the opening of the door, and I kept pushing it on steadily, steadily.

> I had my head in, and was about to open the lantern, when my thumb slipped upon the tin fastening, and the old man sprang up in the bed, crying out—"Who's there?"

In this controlled slowness of movement[23] the narrator feels his powers, his *sagacity*—the wisdom of foresight—but his estimation of the old man is thrown into question when he assumes the latter will "not even . . . dream of my secret deeds or thoughts." Like a suspicion, a dream is—if not an intangible thought—a vision, a sight, a *seeing* during sleep; and at this very moment, the old man "moved on the bed suddenly, as if—"—as if, indeed, he is aware of the other's thoughts. Although the narrator tries to explain this in terms of his chuckle—"perhaps he *heard* me" (and let us not forget the narrator's own extraordinary sense of hearing)—he is able to know, remarkably, what the old man is dreaming. And whence that attribution of fear to the old man—"as if startled"? No sound, in fact, is made by the narrator; he merely chuckles "at heart," "fairly." Similarly, in a room with shutters "close fastened" like his lantern,[24] the narrator is able to attribute "fear of robbers" to the old man, a fear which recalls his own dreadful nervousness. He also *knows* what the old man can see: "I knew that he could not see the opening of the door." As the "idea" enters the narrator's brain and he the room, as he knows the mind of the old man, so, now, his own "secret deeds or thoughts" appear to enter the old man's. The relation between the two is indeed puzzling, and the pressing question, the central problematic of the text, is that of the narrator's identity, which is posed suddenly, fearfully, by the old man: "Who's there?"

To this critical question the narrator makes no reply, but in what follows, the relation between narrator and old man is elaborated with surprising sympathy:

> I kept quite still and said nothing. For a whole hour I did not move a muscle, and in the meantime I did not hear him lie down. He was still sitting up in the bed listening;—just as I have done, night after night, hearkening to the death watches in the wall.

> Presently I heard a slight groan, and I knew it was the groan of mortal terror. It was not a groan of pain or of grief—oh, no!—it was the low stifled sound that arises from the bottom of the soul when overcharged with awe. I knew the sound well. Many a night, just at midnight, when all the world slept, it has welled up from my own bosom, deepening,

with its dreadful echo, the terrors that distracted me. I say I knew it well. I knew what the old man felt, and pitied him, although I chuckled at heart. I knew that he had been lying awake ever since the first slight noise, when he had turned in the bed. His fears had been ever since growing upon him. He had been trying to fancy them causeless, but could not. He had been saying to himself—"It is nothing but the wind in the chimney—it is only a mouse crossing the floor," or "it is merely a cricket which has made a single chirp." Yes, he has been trying to comfort himself with these suppositions; but he had found all in vain.

The narrator keeps silent; and so must the old man, for despite the former's acute sense of hearing, he does not hear him lie down. And he *knows* that the old man is still sitting up, doing what he himself is best at: *listening,* "just as I have done." In this dreadful silence, punctuated by the ticking of death watches,[25] a sound is heard; and the narrator identifies it with absolute certainty: "I knew it was the groan . . . I knew the sound well . . . I knew what the old man felt." And the reason (dreadfully nervous) he is able to identify this sound of "mortal terror" and "awe" is that at the same time that it emanates from the old man, *just at midnight,* it wells up "from my own bosom." The voice of the old man is thus doubled, in a "dreadful echo," in the narrator's own voice.[26]

The groan is "stifled"; it is no longer clear from which soul it emanates. The effect of this loss of breath, this unspeakable suffocation, is to increase "the terrors that distracted me"—and here the narrator's *dis-traction* suggests not merely lack of concentration, but a pulling asunder, a physical dismemberment; it also characterizes a mind torn in different directions, whence mental derangement, madness.[27] Since as readers we too—even though no sound is actually uttered—have been privy to the singular laugh ("Ha!") of the narrator, we must take this matter under advisement; if and indeed the old man hears the narrator chuckle "at heart," then must his own hearing be likewise extraordinary.

We are told that, like the narrator's, the old man's fears have been "growing upon him." Like the narrator, the old man has been "trying to fancy them causeless . . ."[28] and, simultaneously, in a repetition of the narrator's figuration of origin, fancying their causes: the wind, a mouse, a cricket. These fancies are not altogether aleatory—the "wind" carries in its connotations the breath of the narrator and of life; "mouse" is etymologically related to the "muscle" which the narrator does not move;[29] and the sound made by the hinges of the lantern, that *creak,* not only means, in an archaic sense, to utter a vulturine croak, but also describes the strident sound of insects, the creak of crickets and refers, by extension, to a death watch—but, we are told, futile to indulge:

All in vain; because Death, in approaching him, had stalked with his black shadow before him, and enveloped the victim. And it was the mournful influence of the unperceived shadow that caused him to feel—although he neither saw nor heard—to *feel* the presence of my head within the room.

When I had waited a long time, very patiently, without hearing him lie down, I resolved to open a little—a very, very little crevice in the lantern. So I opened it—you cannot imagine how stealthily, stealthily—until, at length, a single, dim ray like the thread of the spider, shot from out the crevice and full upon the vulture eye.

The old man's attempts—to "fancy [his fears] causeless," and then to name and figure the origin of his fears—are to no avail because of the impending moment which will, in theory, negate cause and origin—the moment of Death. This is a moment neither seen nor heard, only felt—for Death stands without the narrative economy of light and sound marked by eye and ear, as its legitimating ground, as its origin and end; and within that economy, as an enveloping influence, a *shadow* which—unlike an optical shadow, a visible figure cast by the form of a body, interrupting light—must therefore appear *unperceived,* a figure personified. Death is thus behind and foregrounds every move of the narrative voice: as the narrator stalks the old man, so Death; as the narrator is preceded by a dark lantern, so Death, "his black shadow before him."

In the confusion of this approach, the antecedents of "his," "him" and the "victim" cannot be differentiated—for whose is the shadow? To whom does it appear? And who the victim? Indeed, as Death, old man and narrator become for a moment indistinguishable, the focus of the narration shifts—from the narrator's feelings to those of the old man as they are known and felt by the narrator. The Old Testament psalmist's dauntlessness in the valley of the shadow of death[30] is ironically both gainsaid—in the awe and fear shadowing both narrator and old man—and affirmed, for if, as they dreadfully echo each other's voices, old man and narrator shadow each other, then Death is both the subject and object of the narrative action, both slayer and victim. The outcome of such a self-negation of death can only be a new subject within and without history, a subject which, in spite of itself—and terrifyingly to the reader whose commentary must in its execution echo and shadow the voice of the tale—declares, "I live!"

The narrator waits, "without hearing" and unable to see—as the old man, "neither saw nor heard"—and a crack is opened in the lantern. The crevice releases light; the narrator's eye opens; by this light he will see. His furtiveness—"stealthily, stealthily"—is transparent, for *stealth* refers to the practice of stealing, and the chamber is in darkness, the shutters drawn, *through fear of robbers:* as the narrator's fears are figured in the eye/I of the old man, so the latter's are answered in the eye/I of the narrator. As the lantern opens, enabling the narrator's vision, a ray of light is released like a spider's thread—the thread of Arachne, by which suicide is aborted into life.[31] The gaze is a predatory act, light the medium of predation; and the vision of the gazing I is reciprocated by the sudden sight of the vulture eye:

> It was open—wide, wide open—and I grew furious as I gazed upon it. I saw it with perfect distinctness— all a dull blue, with a hideous veil over it that chilled the very marrow in my bones; but I could see nothing else of the old man's face or person: for I had directed the ray as if by instinct precisely upon the damned spot.

Light enters the eye of the old man, but it is the *narrator's* gaze which is described. By neither madness nor passion is he seized, but dread of the veil *videlicet,* that hideous surface which marks the coincidence and refraction of his and the old man's gaze.[32] The old man's "face or person" is invisible, for the focus, instinctive and inevitable, is on the subjectivity represented by the eye/I, the damned spot[33] which marks the state and position—moral, mental, topographical, temporal—of the narrative I/eye relative to (across the disciplinary boundaries between the historical and the fictional, the literal and the figurative) the listener and observer; marks, in short, the beginning and the end of the tale, the critical state of the eye/I which is the very *subject* of the tale.

Two gazes hang in suspense on a thread of light; now, and in this long moment, the narrator becomes conscious of a sound, a rhythmic beat which has hitherto remained subliminal:

> And now have I not told you that what you mistake for madness is but overacuteness of the senses?— now, I say, there came to my ears, a low, dull, quick sound such as a watch makes when enveloped in cotton. I knew *that* sound well too. It was the beating of the old man's heart. It increased my fury, as the beating of a drum stimulates the soldier into courage.

As eye confronts eye, the tell-tale heart is heard *within* **"The Tell-Tale Heart"**: it is a sound described and figured within—as an abyssal echo of—the sound of the narrator's own voice. And indeed, the narrator "knew *that* sound well too;" he admits a familiarity with the old man's heartbeat which one would have only with one's own.[34]

The effect of "the beating of the old man's heart" is thus that it—eliding the differences between the narrator's self and the other's—"increased *my* fury";

the heartbeat can only be compared to "the beating of a drum,"[35] for what increases the narrator's fury is the resonance of the extraordinarily sensitive barrier responsible for his acuteness of hearing: a tympanic membrane stretched across the abyss between the voice of the tell-tale heart and its echo; an *eardrum* which reverberates in time to the measure of the heart's low/ dull/quick sound.[36] As the narrator's fury increases, the measure of tale-telling builds: less calm, more repetitive; less healthy, more strident.

> But even yet I refrained and kept still. I scarcely breathed. I tried how steadily I could maintain the ray upon the eye. Meantime the hellish tattoo of the heart increased. It grew quicker and quicker, and louder and louder every instant. The old man's terror *must* have been extreme! It grew louder, I say, louder every moment!—do you mark me well? I have told you that I am nervous: so I am. And now at the dead hour of the night, amid the dreadful silence of that old house, so strange a noise as this excited me to uncontrollable terror. Yet, for some minutes longer I refrained and stood still. But the beating grew louder, louder! I thought the heart must burst. And now a new anxiety seized me—the sound would be heard by a neighbour!

The narrator *refrains,*[37] both movement and breath stifled. His gaze wavers; he attempts to keep the light steady; the palpitations increase. The ominous beating sound—one of many the narrator hears "in hell"—is also audible to the reader[38]—as the rhythmic repetition, "quicker and quicker, and louder and louder," of the tell-tale heart. And now, at the moment when their identities appear to have merged, a subtle distance is introduced in the reciprocal vision of the narrator and old man. Rather than declare his knowledge that "the old man's terror" *was* extreme, the narrator conjectures—the italics stress this—that it "*must* have been extreme." As the sound grows louder, he demands, "do you mark me well?"[39] To mark is to hear, to hearken; it is also to delimit a boundary, *differentiate:* we are asked, in short, to recognize the "me" which speaks, to answer the old man's question, "Who's there?" And indeed, the "dreadful silence" recalls the "dreadful echo" of the shared groan—but the heartbeat, which the narrator "knew . . . well" a moment ago, has now become *so strange.* This sound, which but an instant past was likened to the soldier's stimulus to courage, now ironically causes "uncontrollable terror"; there is an emphatic shift from the old man's terror to the narrator's own, and a "new anxiety" seizes the narrator ("me").

Not that he may be heard by the old man, but that his preternatural sense of hearing may be shared by a neighbor. It is the possibility of a social intrusion, the intrusion of a third party in the narrator's private and specular vision[40] that precipitates him into action:

The old man's hour had come! With a loud yell, I threw open the lantern and leaped into the room. He shrieked once—once only. In an instant I dragged him to the floor, and pulled the heavy bed over him. I then smiled gaily, to find the deed so far done. But, for many minutes, the heart beat on with a muffled sound. This, however, did not vex me; it would not be heard through the wall. At length it ceased. The old man was dead. I removed the bed and examined the corpse. Yes, he was stone, stone dead. I placed my hand upon the heart and held it there many minutes. There was no pulsation. He was stone dead. His eye would trouble me no more.

What occurs here has a striking symmetry: both narrator and old man utter a cry—there is a *yell,* and also a *shriek.* The narrator underscores the singularity of the old man's shriek by doubling it in his repetition: "once—once only." And instead of throwing open the door, he throws open the *lantern:* coinciding with the yell and the shriek is a flash of light, a blinding moment of sight. There is, however, no detailed description of a murder, no sudden moment of death[41]—the crucial act of physical violence is glaringly and conspicuously omitted.

Eventually, as the narrator becomes calmer, the danger of the heart's being audible to a neighbor of extraordinary hearing decreases—until finally, after "many minutes," the heartbeat stops. The heavy bed—burden of sleep and dreams—is "removed" with no apparent effort, its plane a plane of reflection between the narrator and the old man—or metempsychosis—whose thoughts, dreams, and even pulses, seem to synchronize. The old man, we are told no less than thrice, is dead;[42] the owner of the vulture eye has himself become carrion. Or so it would appear. For in the uncanny light of resemblance between narrator and old man, what certainty is there that "the heart" upon which he places his hand is not the narrator's own? that the "muffled sound" has not been the subsiding of his own heartbeat quickened by "uncontrollable terror"? And if from the narrator's own heart "no pulsation" can be felt, then who has died? whose voice speaks? what dread voice narrates the tale?

For if the narrator has, as he claims, rid himself of the eye/I forever—"His eye/[I] would trouble me no more"—one would expect the narrative to end here. Yet (for reasons which will soon become clear) it does not, proceeding immediately to an explicit scene of physical dismemberment:

> If you still think me mad, you will think so no longer when I describe the wise precautions I took for the concealment of the body. The night waned, and I worked hastily, but in silence. First of all I dismembered the corpse. I cut off the head and the arms and the legs.
>
> I then took up three planks from the flooring of the chamber, and deposited all between the scantlings.

> I then replaced the boards so cleverly, so cunningly, that no human eye—not even *his*—could have detected anything wrong. There was nothing to wash out—no stain of any kind—no bloodspot whatever. I had been too wary for that. A tub had caught all—ha! ha!

The narrator has built part of his defense against the accusation of madness on his sagacity, and one of its measures is his ability to dissimulate. The body—a disarticulated head, arms and legs—is introduced briefly as *corpus delicti* before being concealed from human detection.[43] No mention is made of the heart or its beat; and there is "no stain . . . no bloodspot," for suddenly humanized in death, the damned spot of the vulture eye can no longer be seen; the subjectivity represented by the old man's I has been incarnated, killed, dismembered and interred. It would seem that the narrator has put an end to "the terrors that distracted me"—and yet an acute sensibility might notice, *sotto voce,* an ominous doubling of that singular chuckle we heard earlier into almost an ironic laugh: "ha! ha!"

Some four hours have passed in dissimulation—"the night [has] waned"[44]—since midnight, when the groan of mortal terror was heard, and a knock at the door signals the neighbor's intrusion that the narrator had anxiously and fearfully anticipated:

> When I had made an end of these labors, it was four o'clock—still dark as midnight. As the bell sounded the hour, there came a knocking at the street door. I went down to open it with a light heart,—for what had I *now* to fear?

> There entered three men, who introduced themselves, with perfect suavity, as officers of the police. A shriek had been heard by a neighbour during the night; suspicion of foul play had been aroused; information had been lodged at the police office, and they (the officers) had been deputed to search the premises.

The appearance of the three policemen—identical in number, significantly, to the "three planks" under which the corpse is concealed—marks a sudden expansion of the events described by the narrator into a volume of social space. The focus on the old man's chamber has broadened to place it in perspective in "that old house"; the possibility of a neighbor, and now the "street door" and "police office," suggest encounters and sights in an organized world beyond darkness and closed shutters.[45] The reason for this societal intervention in the narrator's world is that a sound has been overheard by a neighbor: not the hearbeat the narrator feared, but "a shriek"—and thus, curiously, not the voice of the narrator, who gave a "loud yell," but the voice of the old man:

I smiled,—for *what* had I to fear? I bade the gentlemen welcome. The shriek, I said, was my own in a dream. The old man, I mentioned, was absent in the country. I took my visitors all over the house. I bade them search—search *well.* I led them, at length, to *his* chamber. I showed them his treasures, secure, undisturbed. In the enthusiasm of my confidence, I brought chairs into the room, and desired them *here* to rest from their fatigues, while I myself, in the wild audacity of my perfect triumph, placed my own seat upon the very spot beneath which reposed the corpse of the victim.

The narrator welcomes and disarms the officers with comparable suavity: with the old man absent in the country, only he himself could have been overheard.[46] Confirming our suspicious, he claims the old man's shriek as his own; in the same breath he suggests that all that has occurred has occurred in a dream—a text produced in his own sleep. He then displays a surprising familiarity with the old man's treasures, confidently inviting the policemen to rest in the latter's own chamber, where his corpse is encrypted.[47] And now, in an extraordinary moment, the narrator faces his inquisitors upon the very spot below which the body has been concealed, a scene which brings together simultaneously the entire series of reflections and refractions which have structured the text: narrator | old man; narrator | reader; eye | eye; I | I; self | other; sleep | waking; yell | shriek; inside | outside; presence | absence; dissimulation | truth; fiction | fact; figurative | literal; sanity | insanity; nervous | mad.

The bar ("|") which here represents the fold between these possibilities is in some cases a physical barrier—as when it stands for the heavy bed, with the narrator on top and the old man pressed below; or for the three planks of the floor, with the narrator seated above, and the old man dismembered below. It may be architectural or mechanical: the chamber or street door between inside and outside space, the window shutters or lantern panel on the hesitant threshold of darkness and light; physiological: the veil over the eye, the tympanum of the ear; psychological or philosophical: the line between dreams and consciousness, or truth and falsehood, fact and fiction, self and other. It may stand for rhetorical difference, such as that between a shriek and a yell; for an ideological or societal barrier between legitimate action and crime, or what is accepted as truth and what as metaphor; for historical distance, such as the hermeneutic space between the reader and the text; or for a limit of systematic thought, as in the case of disciplinary barriers drawn by the clinical or legal professions to separate health from sickness, or sanity from madness.

The number of policemen corresponds to the number of floor-boards below the narrator because they have the same function: although they are portrayed sitting and talking with the narrator, the three men are not physical characters; rather, they are figures of society, of the *internalized law which separates the narrator from himself,* separates what is superficial from what is latent, what exists within the limits of systematic thought from what is unthought, the social and historical self from absolute alterity. The three floorboards and the three men thus do not react; they simply mark a limit, social and psychological, the bar ("*") between self and other:

> The officers were satisfied. My *manner* had convinced them. I was singularly at ease. They sat, and while I answered cheerily, they chatted familiar things. But, ere long, I felt myself getting pale and wished them gone. My head ached, and I fancied a ringing in my ears: but still they sat and still they chatted. The ringing became more distinct:—it continued and became more distinct: I talked more freely to get rid of the feeling: but it continued and gained definitiveness—until, at length, I found that the noise was *not* within my ears.

The narrator's *singularity* continues to draw attention to the absence of the old man, and his paleness and headache reveal his internal tension,[48] which manifests itself psychologically and physiologically as a fancied "ringing in my ears." The sound becomes more distinct and yet more distant, as it is casually, almost accidentally, revealed to be a *feeling* whose source is, in fact, *outside* his ears; the effect of this tympanic tension between inside and outside is to stimulate the narrator to speak:

> No doubt I now grew *very* pale;—but I talked more fluently, and with a heightened voice. Yet the sound increased—and what could I do? It was *a low, dull, quick sound—much such a sound as a watch makes when enveloped in cotton.* I gasped for breath—and yet the officers heard it not. I talked more quickly—more vehemently; but the noise steadily increased. I arose and argued about trifles, in a high key and with violent gesticulations, but the noise steadily increased. Why *would* they not be gone? I paced the floor to and fro with heavy strides, as if excited to fury by the observation of the men—but the noise steadily increased. Oh God! what *could* I do? I foamed—I raved—I swore! I swung the chair upon which I had been sitting, and grated it upon the boards, but the noise arose over all and continually increased.

As the sound from within and without the narrator's ears increases, it is echoed and reflected in the increasing fluency, pitch, speed and intensity of his own narration. This voice—the voice of **"The Tell-Tale Heart"**—now describes its own collapse as the narrator is rapidly disarticulated into three uncontrollable, twitching fragments: first, his speech, which proceeds from his *head:* fluent, heightened, quick, vehement, high-pitched, foaming, raving, swearing. Second, his *arms:* gesticulating violently, swinging the chair. Finally, his *legs:* arising, furiously and excitedly "pac[ing] the floor to and fro with heavy strides." This disarticulation, this dis-traction (preceded by a gasp for breath), is an experience on the level of narrative voice, of what has been described by that voice and enacted as the physical dismemberment of the old man: "First of all I dismembered the corpse. I cut off the head and the arms and the legs."

Previously at pains to establish that it was not the voice of madness, the narrator's voice is now *vehement*,[49] and the "I" paces the floor, foaming and raving. All that separates the dissevered parts of the narrative voice from the severed limbs of the old man is the thin bar ("*") of three floorboards—the bar which marks the limit between speech and silence; the bar at which the narrator must be heard:

> It grew louder—louder—*louder!* And still the men chatted pleasantly, and smiled. Was it possible they heard not? Almighty God!—no, no! They heard!—they suspected—they *knew!* they were making a mockery of my horror!—this I thought, and this I think. But any thing was better than this agony! Any thing was more tolerable than this derision! I could bear those hypocritical smiles no longer! I felt that I must scream or die!—and now—again!—hark! louder! louder! louder! *louder!*—

The three men smile, as the narrator smiled a moment ago, and their smiles are *hypocritical*—grinning thespian masks.[50] The narrator's despair—"Oh God! . . . Almighty God!—no, no!"—and agony come from the fear that what is concealed may be made known, that the three men's demeanor re-presents and mirrors, mocking and deriding, his own dissimulation. It is his suppression of knowledge of the old man which threatens to burst through; and silence would seem to be the wisest course. Yet, paradoxically, the narrator feels that there are only two options: "I must scream or die." This feeling seems inexplicable—the narrator has confessed no guilt, no remorse has been admitted, and the entire narration has been based on a justification of the sanity of his actions—until one recalls the moment of "death," when the narrator leaped into the room and confronted the old man. The reason for the policemen's visit soon afterwards was that "[a] shriek had been heard by a neighbour during the night"; there no mention is made of the narrator's "loud yell," and here no conclusion can be drawn but this: that the yell and the shriek sound as one voice. And that the narrator is closer to the truth than he admits when he claims that the shriek was his own in a dream.

The moment when the narrator must "scream or die" is now suspended on the brink of identity or difference: it is a moment of uncertainty suspended on the bar between narrator and old man, a wavering between the presence and absence of the old man's voice within the narrator's voice. The moment is resolved dramatically in the crisis of the narrator's final words, where a complex network of relationships is suddenly unravelled: the narrator ironically accuses the policemen of his own act of dissimulation, confesses his own commission of the deed, and calls for an unveiling or unmasking—a removal of the floorboards which will reveal the old man's presence. In the same punning breath, he calls on his listeners to hearken—"hear, hear!"—and distances himself from his own narration, from the voice of the **"Tell-Tale Heart,"** by referring to it in the third person—"his heart." All of this happens without warning, in a sudden, bone-chilling, singular *shriek*—by which the yell of the narrative voice becomes possessed by its other, comes to its end in the I of the old man:

> "Villains!" I shrieked, "dissemble no more! I admit the deed!—tear up the planks!—here, here!—it is the beating of his hideous heart!"

II

Forgiven be the reader whose reason is stretched, whose blood runs cold, on hearing these last words. The end of the tale, the climactic shriek, plunges and recedes in a sudden void before the critical eye. A murder is committed; the killer possessed; a dead voice speaks through a living mouth. A death has occurred—a suicide; a disembodied voice speaks from beyond the grave. No murder may have taken place, no death—or else it may be a corpse's voice which shrieks at the end of the tale. The narrator has taken the old man's life; the narrator has disappeared; only the old man remains. Narrator and old man are the same—or are not the same at all. There neither is, nor ever was, an old man. Nothing has happened in the tale; or if it has, it was only a dream, the old man's or the narrator's. A second reading must recognize the voice of the narrator as that of the old man. What judgment can be passed, now that it is no longer clear that a crime has been committed, that any event within the space of narration has not been a hallucination, and no longer certain from the close of the tale what can be said of it when it began? What has happened in the tale, and what, in its reading, must be the end?

The narrator's shriek confronts the reader with a synesthetic image in light and sound. Striking our eye, impinging on our eardrums, is the homophonic imperative to "hear, hear!"—which is also a deixis, a pointing out in space—both *here* and *here!*—of the hideous site of the tell-tale heart. Visually, unspeakably, the image is the sight of a heart cut out from a body, and sole: beating, living, palpitating, red. The space of the end unfolds before us in mingled horror and vertiginous fascination, a moment not adequated by speech.[51] Here, and in this space, reader and narrator share a present, for the latter's cries have brought the events of the narrative's past into the time of its reading: *"and now—again!—hark! louder! louder! louder! louder!"* The tale thus ends in the past of its narration and simultaneously in the present of its reading: now the reader must construct the sequel to the tale; now its consequences must by implication follow. These events, projecting forward beyond the end—on a literal level the charge of madness; arrest, questioning and confinement, perhaps—must then become the past, *precede the tale's beginning,* for the end of the tale has placed the reader in its narration's past, facing a future which is already a figment of the narrator's memory.

As the critical "I" stands on the brink of this temporal vortex, drawn inexorably down into the maelstrom's eye of narrative time, ghostly echoes and fleeting associations suggest a momentary diversion, a respite, in two of Poe's other tales. The narrator of "**The Black Cat**" speaks from a "felon's cell . . . for tomorrow I die and today I would unburden my soul"; it is in order to provide "a cause for my wearing these fetters and for tenanting this cell of the condemned" that the speaker in "The Imp of the Perverse" narrates.[52] The incarceration of the "**Tell-Tale Heart**"'s narrator is implicit in the denials of his own madness and in his final confession to officers of the law. In all three cases, the narration is an act of speech—suspended on the threshold between life and its radical other. Thus the "**Cat**" narrator is "consigned . . . to the hangman"; the "**Imp**" ends with a rhetorical question: "To-day I wear these chains, and am *here!* To-morrow I shall be fetterless!—*but where!*" Between the here of today and the where of tomorrow—when presumably the narrator will be damned, executed, or found to be mad— the difference is both spatial and temporal, marked by the physical and conceptual boundaries of the cell which both contains and compels the act of narration.

The "I" of "**The Black Cat**" confronts its other in the eye of a black cat: "I took from my waistcoat-pocket a penknife, opened it, grasped the poor beast by the throat, and deliberately cut one of its eyes from the socket. I blush, I burn, I shudder, while I pen the damnable atrocity. . . . " Here two acts conjoin as one— the act of telling or penning the tale and the act of penknifing the eye/I of the other, (self-)mutilation or *ommacide*—in the atrocious performative of narration. The deed is consummated in a "death scene" where the cat is hanged, executed by the suspension of breath and speech; damnation physical and symbolic is then visited upon the narrator, in the form of flames which consume his worldly wealth and leave, at the head of his bed, a gigantic image in bas-relief of a hanged cat. A second, identical, one-eyed cat appears thereafter to vex him, marked in white fur upon its chest the gallows, a symbol of death and resurrection.[53] When the narrator finally strikes, the blow of his axe is displaced from the cat (which vanishes) to his wife, whose corpse

he walls up in the cellar. He is calm when the law arrives—"I scarcely knew what I uttered at all"—but as the officers are about to leave, the narrator raps on the wall with a cane, precisely on the spot where his wife is immured:

> I was answered by a voice from within the tomb!— by a cry, at first muffled and broken, like the sobbing of a child, and then quickly swelling into one long, loud, and continuous scream, utterly anomalous and inhuman—a howl, a wailing shriek, half of horror and half of triumph, such as might have arisen only out of hell, conjointly from the throats of the damned in their agony and of the demons that exult in the damnation. . . . Swooning, I staggered to the opposite wall. . . . In the next [instant] a dozen stout arms were toiling at the wall. It fell bodily. The corpse, already greatly decayed and clotted with gore, stood erect before the eyes of the spectators. Upon its head, with red extended mouth and solitary eye of fire, sat the hideous beast whose craft had seduced me into murder, and whose informing voice had consigned me to the hangman.

The tale ends with the shriek of the narrator's alter ego— figured as the black cat and represented metonymically by a single I/eye and a mouth whose words are red and read. The voice which finally betrays the narrator of "The Black Cat" is his own, but in it a difference, a strangeness, has been introduced, "anomalous and inhuman," and in which the narrator cannot recognize himself. It is for this reason that the voice of the cat is described as at the same time the voice of the damned and the voice which exults in damning. Just as the "**Tell-Tale Heart**" ends in the old man's shriek, here the narrator will become the other, take on the life of the hanged black cat and in his turn be hanged.

In the premeditated murder of "**The Imp of the Perverse**," the relation of stalker to stalked is explicit, and not simply a relation of perpetrator to victim—"I am one of the many uncounted victims of the Imp of the Perverse," the narrator declares—but a complex of exchanges involved in the act of reading. Both the narrator and his victim read, prefiguring and implicating— "I need not vex you with impertinent details"—our own narrative. The brief "murder scene" thus describes not an act of violence, but the substitution of the narrator's light for the reader's, a pharmaceutical replacement of the air in the victim's ill-ventilated apartment by air of the narrator's own making:[54]

> At length, in reading some French memoirs, I found an account of a nearly fatal illness that occurred to Madame Pilau, through the agency of a candle accidentally poisoned. I knew my victim's habit of reading in bed. I knew, too, that his apartment was narrow and ill-ventilated. But I need not vex you with impertinent details. I need not describe the easy artifices by which I substituted, in his bed-room

candle-stand, a wax-light of my own making for the one which I there found. The next morning he was discovered dead in his bed. . . .

Unsuspected, the narrator inherits his victim's estate and enjoys years of "absolute security"—until, at length, he comes to be haunted by a thought "like the ringing in our ears," a temptation to confess: "And now my own casual self-suggestion, that I might possibly be fool enough to confess the murder of which I had been guilty, confronted me, as if the very ghost of him whom I had murdered—and beckoned me on to death." The narration ends with the narrator's betrayal by his *own* voice, which breaks into social space out of a confinement here revealed to be psychological. The limits of containment are breached, and a shortage of breath, a gasp, a swoon, preludes the end:

I walked vigorously—faster—still faster—at length I ran. I felt a maddening desire to shriek aloud. . . . I still quickened my pace. I bounded like a madman. . . . At length the populace took the alarm, and pursued me. I felt *then* the consummation of my fate. Could I have torn out my tongue, I would have done it—but a rough voice resounded in my ears—a rougher grasp seized me by the shoulder. I turned—I gasped for breath. For a moment I experienced all the pangs of suffocation; I became blind, and deaf, and giddy; and then some invisible fiend, I thought, struck me with his broad palm upon the back. The long-imprisoned secret burst forth from my soul. They say I spoke with a distinct enunciation, but with marked emphasis and passionate hurry, as if in dread of interruption. . . . Having related all that was necessary for the fullest judicial conviction, I fell prostrate in a swoon. . . .

The three tales taken together, "**Imp**," "**Cat**" and "**Heart**," present a composite narrative pattern in its several dimensions. On the simplest level, each tale is told by an unnamed narrator ("I"), and features a second character who is the narrator's figurative double or alter ego: the old man, the black cat, the victim who reads. The narrator's voice speaks to an implied reader (or engages in an internal monologue) initially in a self-justifying mode of confession, and describes a "murder" of the narrator's other. The dead other is then interred—under floorboards, behind a wall, as a "long-imprisoned secret" in the narrator's mind. Eventually, in a social space—policemen, the crowd in the street—the narrator is driven by an irrepressible urge to betray himself, and does so by a second narration within the tale, the other's voice: the cry of the black cat, the shriek and heartbeat of the old man, the narrator's own voice unknown to him—"they say I spoke with a distinct enunciation . . ."—in confession.[55]

Each narrative places in relief its own voice, as a radical alterity within this compelling moment of speech;

the moment staged as a death scene is thus revealed to be a scene of recognition in which the subject and object of narration confront each other, exchange identities, and yield to difference. The relation enacted in each tale—between subject and object, or the act of narration and the acts described by narration—is grounded, strangely and irreducibly, in a quality, tendency, feeling or character, which the "Cat" narrator identifies as "the spirit of PERVERSENESS," and the "Imp" as "a paradoxical something:"

. . . one of the primitive impulses of the human heart—one of the indivisible primary faculties or sentiments, which give direction to the character of Man[;] . . . a perpetual inclination, in the teeth of our best judgment, to violate that which is *Law,* merely because we understand it to be such[;] . . . [an] unfathomable longing of the soul *to vex itself*—to offer violence to its own nature. . . . ("**Cat**," 225)

. . . an innate and primitive principle of human action, . . . a *mobile* without motive, a motive not *motiviert.* Through its promptings we act without comprehensible object; . . . through its promptings we act, for the reason that we should *not.* . . . ("**Imp**," 281)

These characterizations locate perversity, in its role as the founding and self-undermining ground of the tales' telling, within the compass of the fundamental trope of irony:[56] the relation between narrator and old man appears in this context as a doubling within the sign "I" of the narrating subject—I = (self * other)—where the bar or veil separating self from other is a plane of infinite reflection between the subject and its self-perception as object, a crevice or space marking the disjunction between an I and an I which do not altogether see eye to eye.

This relation finds its paradigmatic moment in death; it is the play of irony in the narration of death which is staged in these three tales. The "death scene" in the "**Tell-Tale Heart**" should be the end of the narration, a moment where difference is erased and beyond which there is no further possibility of language. The moment appears, however, as a staging *within* the language of narration, of the end of narration—a staging in language of the impossibility of language. An irreducible difference is thus introduced—the veil which prevents recognition, the fine line between a shriek and a yell—even in Death, which becomes a sign. Death—where the bar of difference must disappear, and self and other become one—is prevented at the moment it occurs from being itself; it is recovered, absorbed, circumscribed by language and folded back on itself in the ironic doubling—(shriek * yell)—of the narrative voice.

The dissolution of language which must follow the moment of death is then enacted both *in* and *as* the language of narration: *within* the narration as a description of the dismemberment of the old man, and—doubling and repeating this dismemberment—*as* the narrator's voice, which itself becomes disarticulated in the act of narration. Even as it asserts its singularity, the narrator's voice doubles and folds in upon itself: the "corpse," the "body" described *in* the text is at the same time doubled as the body *of* the text; it coincides physically with the textual space of its narration. What confronts the reader is the *corpus* of the old man: a textual avatar or embodiment of the old man's (dead, absent) voice as a presence in the narrator's, the sound of the tell-tale heart in the sound of "**The Tell-Tale Heart**."

It is a sound always *stifled,* like the beat of a watch muffled in cotton, because the temporality of the narrative voice—its yell—is caught on the threshold of an absolute moment of language, between screaming and dying, between narration and its impossibility. The space of the narrative, its duration, is doubled back upon itself and negated as the narrating subject collapses into its own object; as the "I" falls back from death into the abyssal voice of the other. The return of the dead occurs as a necessary event, of and in the language of the tale, for Death cannot signify itself without being other than itself, and it is this—the appearance of the end of language in the middle of language—which is reflected—"I live!"—in the gaze of the old man's evil eye.

This apparition, like a burst of dark laughter, confronts the reader across the chasm which falls between literature and criticism. The act of reading abolishes chance, for it draws the reader into an inevitable hermeneutic relation with alterity within the sign of Death: the recognition scene of narrator and old man is ultimately enacted between the I/eye of the narrator and the I/eye of the reader, as the transferential relation of the narrative voice of the tale to the narrative voice of criticism. The narrative I's gestures are doubled—perversely, allegorically[57]—by the critical I: in our act of quotation, which foregrounds the voice of the narrator; in the cutting, pasting and articulation of the "**Tell-Tale Heart**" within a narrative of criticism, which echoes the narrator's dismemberment of the old man; in the (deictic, exemplary) introduction of evidence to sustain the argument of criticism, which repeats the narrator's gesture of "hear, here!" Death—its sign—envelops the act of reading, wherein narrative I and critical I exchange glances across a bar which now appears as the space—linguistic, cultural, historical—between reader and text.

Between the text and the reader's eye, this space is physical: semiotically, it also represents a temporal distance within the sign of Death: the natural belatedness of criticism with respect to literature. The narrator of the "**Tell-Tale Heart**" decides to rid "[him]self" of the eye/I of the old man, which is figured as the origin and eschatological end of the narrative: thus Death—the confrontation/recognition/murder/suicide of the narrator's other's I/eye—becomes present in the middle of narrative time as a sign whose full meaning would be the end of narrative time. The sign of Death is then ironically emptied of its meaning and folded back on itself in a fell resurrection, betraying itself in the duplicitous shriek of the old man. This fold, eliminating origin and end, precludes the possibility of narrative time, of plot and of the narrative's functioning as a history of what it is about. The text of the tale thus appears without history and floats before the reader in history—hermetic, masqued, closed in on itself; a disembodied voice, a veiled I. That it is cast adrift from its time of origin and present to a reader in any age accords it the temporal status of myth;[58] the tale is paradigmatically modern, for it shares a present with any and every reader. As "primary text" the tale becomes the mythic point of origin which legitimates the historiographical operation of "secondary literature"—the figure of origin for the critical I.

The eye of the reader must then inevitably take up the gaze of the narrative I, perversely continue the life of the narrative in the strange voice of criticism, its afterlife.[59] The act of reading "**The Tell-Tale Heart**" stages a doubling of the reading subject across the bar of history—I (literature * criticism). Not because it describes the horror of historical events is it a tale of dread, but because it threatens the reader from across the chasm—threatens to breach the boundary between the I of fiction and the I of criticism. For if the text is an internal monologue, the critical eye penetrates into the mind of the narrator when reading; the act of reading is also a process by which the narrator's secret deeds or thoughts enter the mind of the reader.[60] And if, again, the voice of the tale speaks from beyond the grave, its address throws into question the spatial and temporal location of the reader in relation to the "here!" from which it can be heard. What case can now be made for reading—betrayed, indicted, arraigned by its own voice?

Two lines of argument appear for the critical subject. The first is a "historicization" of the tale, where the frames of reference would be its conditions of production and reception. A recognition that the conditions of a text's production in the past, even as they shape the present of its reading, are reconstructed and themselves shaped by that reading, compels an understanding of the tale's present conditions of reception as prejudicial in reconstructing its past.[61] From this perspective, the relation of the tale to the present centers not on its author or implied author, but on the occasional identities of the narrative I and its implied reader as they are determined for the space of a reading by the social and ideological contexts imposed by the actual reader on the subject positions they represent:

homosexual, heterosexual, oedipal, biographical, feminist, marxist, postcolonial, etc.[62] Armed with contemporary social and linguistic codes, preconceptions about madness, conventions of interpretation; and imposing and intruding ideologically on the tale, the reader—in the role of policeman or arbiter of social law—patrols its neighborhood, marking the borders or limits of its closure. Thus both the tale and its criticism are tethered to the specificity of the historical moment of reading: localized, politicized, historicized, *explained.*

The alternative critical path—precarious, partaking of the tale's paradoxical temporality—affirms the modernity of criticism as the mode of being of the tale in its afterlife. Here, in this dread undertaking, the imperative of criticism is to extend the life of literature beyond its natural end by sharing its present and generalizing it beyond the specificity of its own historical moment. A criticism founded on the primary myth of literature as its object must itself be granted the temporality of myth: the critical I takes the life of the narrative I, becomes both the subject and the object of its own narration. The primary mythopoeic gesture of modernity is thus given by the "death of the author" and the "disappearance of the subject"; a *modern* criticism acquires the ontological status of literature,[63] and the reader—agent of history and historical agent—two apparently incompatible roles: critically demythologizing the tale by demonstrating the relevance of its myth to the present, and at the same time preserving the myth in the afterlife of the tale by refusing the present of criticism. This double gesture of literary theory, perverse in the extreme, is fundamental to history and its writing; it does not oppose itself to anything that would properly be called "literary history." The I of criticism, indeed, has no choice but to speak, gazing unblinkingly from a tale of history condemned always to be present, to be *here*—literature.

Notes

[1] de Certeau, *The Writing of History,* 5.

[2] LaCapra, *History & Criticism,* 11.

[3] The tale, by its very formulation in a formal, fictional genre, appears to sidestep the epistemological question of what "reality" it refers to. I consider the determination of the tale's frame of reference to be a function of the performance of reading, following Jan Mukarovsky: "The change which the material relationship of the work—the sign—has undergone is thus simultaneously its weakening and strengthening. It is weakened in the sense that the work does not refer to the reality which it directly depicts, and strengthened in that the work of art as a sign acquires an indirect (figurative) tie with realities which are vitally important to the perceiver" (Mukarovsky, 74-90; Newton, 36). From this perspec-

tive, the language of the tale constructs and refers to a fictional world which assumes a certain reality for the reader in the present; the "realness" this fictional world appears to have will depend on the various factors which constitute the hermeneutic space between reader and text: social, cultural, linguistic, psychological, and so on.

[4] On the internal and heuristic coherence of fictions, see Vaihinger, *The Philosophy of As If.* Necessary heuristic fictions, critical or readerly, include the assumptions that a text reflects the life of an author, a psychological state, or a social reality at the time it was written. These approaches tacitly imply that fiction in a pure state is impossible, since it requires the mediation of non-fiction; or that the language of fiction can only be understood if it is grounded in the (supposedly extratextual) ordinary language of non-fiction; in short, that fiction is always contaminated by something to which it is radically different, and yet on which it depends, and which appears in various formulations as "non-fiction," "ordinary language," "common sense," "truth," or "reality." More explicitly constructed are approaches to literature which read into a text from the past the moral or sociological concerns of "today," and which claim therefore to have demonstrated its universal, eternal, intrinsic or literary value—when what has in fact been demonstrated is its susceptibility to critical appropriation and ideological manipulation.

[5] I use "modernity" here in the very specific sense that "[i]t designates more generally the problematical possibility of all literature's existing in the present, of being considered, or read, from a point of view that claims to share with it its own sense of a temporal present" (de Man, "Lyric and Modernity," 166). LaCapra's formulation of a "transferential relation to the past," which appears in the epigraph to this paper, is essentially a re-articulation in Freudian terms of one of the paradigmatic gestures of deconstruction: the repetition and continuation, within criticism, of the mode of being of its object, literature. LaCapra's sense of "displaced analogues" appears to correspond to de Man's concept of "allegories of reading." (See the latter's "Semiology and Rhetoric" and "Literary History and Literary Modernity.")

[6] This is a broad interpretation of what M. H. Abrams terms the *universe* of a work of art: " . . . the work is taken to have a subject which, directly or deviously, is derived from existing things—to be about, or signify, or reflect something which either is, or bears some relation to, an objective state of affairs" (Abrams, 6). The notion that a text can be history or the converse trivializes neither term; the factors which establish a text's status as a narration of fact or fiction are not intrinsic to it; rather, they are the ideological, conventional limits placed on its possibilities of interpretation

by the community of its interpreters. For a selection of views on the ethical and pragmatic necessities and consequences of limiting interpretive possibilities, see Levinson and Mailloux, *Interpreting Law and Literature.*

[7] For broad-ranging studies of the constitutive aspects of metahistorical discourses, see de Certeau, *The Writing of History,* LaCapra, *History & Criticism,* Rancière, *The Names of History,* and White, *Metahistory.* Suggestive engagements in the long tradition of the theory-history debate are Jauss, "Literary History as a Challenge . . ." and de Man, "The Resistance to Theory." A detailed study of the concept of crisis can be found in de Man's "Criticism and Crisis," where he argues that "all true criticism occurs in the mode of crisis" (8).

[8] Thus de Certeau: "On the one hand, writing plays the role of a burial rite, in the ethnological and quasi-religious meaning of the term; it exorcises death by inserting it into discourse. On the other hand, it possesses a symbolizing function; it allows a society to situate itself by giving itself a past through language, and it thus opens to the present a space of its own" (*The Writing of History,* 100).

[9] See Valdes and Miller, *Identity of the Literary Text,* for a collection of diverse and thoughtful essays on the nature of textual identity. An overview of some of the assumptions involved in relatively broad definitions of textuality is provided by various authors in Veeser, *The New Historicism,* and the editor's closing essay in *Reader-Response Criticism* (Tompkins, 201-32).

[10] On the need to "imaginatively construct the body," see Ortega y Gasset, "The Difficulty of Reading." The social implications of the organ without a body are explored in Deleuze and Guattari's *Anti-Oedipus.*

[11] Our identification of the genre of the text has already constituted a judgment of its truth-value; this prejudice must be bracketed momentarily, for the space of our reading, if we are to reserve judgment on the narrator and examine the narration on its own terms.

[12] The story is quoted in its entirety in this essay from Poe, *Collected Works.*

[13] This is an archaic sense of the word, etymologically derived from Latin *dis-*(privative) + *esse,* to be. (The derivations here and throughout this paper are taken from *The Compact Oxford English Dictionary* and *Webster's Deluxe Unabridged Dictionary,* hereafter denoted *OED/WUD.*) My use of etymology here and elsewhere in this essay calls for some comment. The question of whether or not the author, Poe, intended the meanings which I attribute to his words is bracketed in this reading because my focus is on the rela-

tionship between the text and the reader in the present. This philological approach neither affirms nor denies the author's intention; it concerns itself rather with opening and enriching the possibilities of interpretation in the tale by following the echoes and resonances of its language. The role of the reader becomes more complex in consequence: the narrator's apostrophe may address a character who does not appear in the tale; or he may be talking to himself—in which case the reader overhears a mental conversation or internal monologue. To encompass these and other possibilities, I use the term "the reader" to refer to the subject position occupied by the narrator's listener, the position with which the actual reader enters into a (negative, positive or neutral) relation.

[14] The modes of classification and principles of exclusion by which systematic thought—legal/penal, medical, and psychiatric—marks its own limit of separation from what it cannot think, are explored "archeologically" in Michel Foucault's *Discipline & Punish, The Birth of the Clinic,* and *Madness and Civilization.*

[15] Most readers of this tale assume that the narrator describes an actual murder; see, for instance, Frank, on the Gothic "I" in "Neighbourhood Gothic . . ."; Witherington on the reader as voyeur in "The Accomplice . . ."; and the various readings derived from psychoanalytic theory: Davis, "Lacan, Poe, and Narrative Repression"; Rajan, "A Feminist Rereading . . ."; Sussman, "A Note on the Public and the Private. . . . "

[16] I use the word "arbitrary" here in Saussure's sense, to suggest not randomness or anarchy, but determination by (social) convention (*Course in General Linguistics,* 68-69, 73.) Most readers of "The Tell-Tale Heart," for example, assume that the narrative voice is male, although the narrator's gender is never specifically identified (see note 62 below). This assumption may be conditioned by a number of factors: knowledge of the author's sex, or of that of typical narrators in his oeuvre; the traditional, patriarchal treatment of narrators as male; or the attribution of an active role to a masculine protagonist. A recognition that such prejudices are conventions of reading reveals the strategies of closure employed by past generations of readers of the tale.

[17] Here it is not simply a matter of empathizing with the narrator; listening to the voice of the text on its own terms involves a self-consciously critical act, the recognition that, as Hayden White remarks in a commentary on New Historicism, "one's philosophy of history is a function as much of the way one construes one's own special object of scholarly interest as it is of one's knowledge of 'history' itself" (White, "New Historicism," 302).

[18] For still classic surveys of eschatological models of history, see Bultmann, *History and Eschatology;* Kermode, *The Sense of an Ending;* and Löwith, *Meaning in History.*

[19] The I/eye homophony is discussed in terms of its relationship to intersubjectivity and the concept of the double in Halliburton's excellent book, *Edgar Allan Poe. A Phenomenological View.* Other related studies can be found in Hamel, "Un texte à deux voix"; and Williams, *A World of Words.* A detailed treatment of the I/eye subject in general can be found in Lombardo's *Edgar Poe et la Modernité* (esp. 7-69).

[20] Joan Dayan, in two passing references to this tale, acknowledges that the heart which will beat under the floorboards "is of course the narrator's own" (144), and recognizes the "language of penetration" used here. She fails, however, to reconcile this with her assertion that "Poe turns the protracted attempt to look into the old man's bedroom in order to kill him into a most secret and transgressive act of love" (*Fables of Mind,* 225).

[21] Etymologically, "suspicion" connotes mistrust, the act of looking askance; Latin *suspicere: sub,* up from under, + *spicere,* to look at (*OED/WUD*).

[22] In similar fashion, the narrator's voice at daybreak becomes indistinguishable from the sound of the tell-tale heart—with its "hearty" tone and "courageousness" (Latin *cor,* heart [*OED/WUD*])—which speaks first to the old man, but ultimately to the reader.

[23] The comparison of the narrator's hand to the minute hand of a watch does not merely or simply convey inordinate slowness of movement; it suggests, as well, the personification of time in and as the figure of the narrator. In this comparison converge, too, the ticking of the watch and the beating of the tell-tale heart with the temporality of the events described in the text and of the voice of narration, for metaleptically the "hand" is both that which writes and, by extension, the voice in which that hand narrates. The echo of a familiar expression also resonates in the text's title: a *tell-tale* is a mechanical device used for recording or indicating temporal measure; the *tell-tale clock,* for example, is a clock "with an attachment of some kind requiring attention at certain intervals, by which the vigilance of a watchman may be checked" (*OED/WUD*).

[24] The narrator's "thin ray" of light cuts through the "thick darkness," evoking traditional metaphorical associations: optical perception (to *see* meaning to *perceive* or to understand) set against blindness or obscurity (incomprehension); or a transition from ignorance to knowledge.

[25] The "death watches in the wall" point, on the one (minute) hand, to the narrator's association with time; and, on the other hand, to the relation of this temporality to death, a relation to ending which will find its articulation in the end of the tale. A death watch is also, however, a vigil kept by the dead or the dying or those who attend them; and both narrator and old man, by their wakefulness "night after night," are implicated in this act of seeing. On a third level—the most immediate sense of the word—a death watch is an insect which makes a sound like the ticking of a watch, and is considered superstitiously to be an omen of death.

[26] Similarly, both narrator and old man share their vigil—"I knew that he had been lying awake"—and echo each other's dissimulation—"lying." And since a wake is a vigil or a death watch, it may be, in this dissimultation, that no death will occur—nor has, in the past which the tale describes.

[27] Latin *distrahere,* to pull apart (*OED/WUD*).

[28] The shifting tenses here—"Yes, he *has* been trying to comfort himself with these suppositions; but he *had* found all in vain"—indicate the temporal dilemma of the narrative voice, fluctuating between the past of the old man and the present of the narration, in which a third voice—the I/eye of the reader—is implicated, and where the old man yet lives.

[29] The word "muscle" is derived from the Latin *musculus,* "little mouse," from the shape of certain muscles (*OED/WUD*).

[30] The reference is to *Psalms* 23:4. The "shadow" may also be seen here as a Jungian, archetypal projection of the unknown self.

[31] According to classical mythological accounts, the Lydian princess Arachne competed with the goddess Athena in a weaving contest, and proved herself superior. Made to feel guilt and shame for her pride, Arachne attempted to hang herself, but Athena prevented the suicide by turning her into a spider and the rope into a cobweb. Thus the moment when Arachne should cease to weave is transformed into a textual eternity where arachnids unceasingly (and to our knowledge, unknowingly) fabricate webs which are allegorical narrations of the original myth. For various versions of this myth, see Bulfinch, 91-93, and Graves, 98-99. Ovid's account is presented in prose and poetry respectively in *Metamorphoses,* trans. Innes, 134-38; and *The Metamorphoses,* trans. Gregory, VI. v. I. 145, 163-167.

[32] Certainly the narrator grows "furious," a characterization which—ironizing his earlier denials—seems to indicate passion, madness, and the raging of a disease whose symptom is a fearful chill; but these indications are occasional rather than causal at this moment; and

even the vexatious "dull blue" of the old man's eye serves here only to throw into relief the "sharpened" senses resulting from the narrator's disease.

[33] This "spot," medically speaking, suggests a speck on the eye symptomatic of a disease; its damning implies judicial condemnation as well as, theologically, a consignment to hell—where the narrator hears many things. But telling, too, is the evocation of a moment when the somnambulous Lady Macbeth is able "to receive at once the benefit of sleep and do the effects of watching"—symptomatic, Shakespeare's Doctor of Physic admits, of a "disease beyond my practice." Indeed, the narrator's sympathy with the old man suggests the entire narration may be a somniloquy. That the narrative assumes the textuality of a dream envisioned by the narrator and pleads conversely, reciprocally—since the old man may indeed be dreaming of his secret deeds and thoughts—that the narrator himself is figured in the cycle of the old man's dream. In this context, it is doubtful whether knowledge—of secret deeds and thoughts, disclosed to the reader in the confidence of reading—can remain material in calling the narrator's power to account. Nor is it simply a matter of extenuating circumstances or diminished responsibility, for the "damned spot" here is not merely a physical object or location but a conceptual, alephic mark which signifies bloodstain, consanguinity, moral stain, state of mind, self-consciousness of guilt or fear—in short, the entire shifting network of relationships which surrounds and informs the eye/I.

Curiously, the intertextual relationship between "The Tell-Tale Heart" and *Macbeth* has not received any critical attention, although each text sheds some light on the other: thus, Poe's allusion to Act V, Scene I of the play suggests, among other things, a female protagonist, sleepwalking, accountability and guilt, the blood of a murder victim ("the old man") which spreads metaphorically into a stain on the conscience, and a complex relation between power and knowledge; or again, taking structural elements as an example, Lady Macbeth's taper is transformed into the "Heart" narrator's lantern, and the knocking she hears at the gate into the knocking he hears at the door when the policemen arrive (Shakespeare, *The Tragedy of Macbeth,* 115-18).

[34] The narrator's refutation of his reader's judgment is here more pointed, having progressed from "you say . . ." to "you fancy . . ." to "you mistake . . ."; and while in the same glossing breath his sensibility is subtly characterized as *over*acute, this admission of excess also has a different ironic effect: to indicate that what is sensed and heard is of the order of the supersensory. The sound, both familiar and unfamiliar, which comes to the narrator's ears is *dull,* like the color of the old man's eye; and also *quick,* in contrast to the slowness of the narrator's actions. It is akin to the *low stifled sound* heard earlier—the groan of terror which arises from both the old man's and the narrator's bosom. Death has indeed "enveloped the victim," and here it is the *watch*—which figures not only the heartbeat, the life of the old man, but also the very temporality of the narrative voice, the historical life of the narrator whose hand moves slower than a minute hand—which is enveloped, stifled. The narrator's relation to the old man, simultaneously close and murderously distant, may be considered from a variety of perspectives, the most obvious being the homoerotic and the Oedipal.

[35] The soldier's "courage" here recalls the bold and hearty tone in which the narrator addresses the old man at daybreak (cf. n.22).

[36] Some depths of the eardrum are sounded in Jacques Derrida's "Tympan." Derridean "difference" and its variations suggest numerous critical frames within which the relation between narrator and old man may be situated. One such frame, which is not discussed here except by implication, is that which circumscribes the relation between an author—in this case, Poe—and his or her literary persona (the narrative "I"); some explorations of this frame are provided in Derrida, *The Ear of the Other.*

[37] Etymologically, to "refrain" connotes the reining in of a (soldier's) horse: Latin *refrenare,* to bridle, from *frenum,* bridle (*OED/WUD*). This is one of several latent allusions to soldiering (cf. n.35, n.39, n.48; for their possible significance, see n.45).

[38] The "tattoo" must be understood here not simply as a beat; it is also a stained inscription marking the surface, or outer limits of the (still absent) body.

[39] This question also inserts itself into a continuing chain of associations: in addition to drawing attention to the "me" of the voice, *mark* evokes both "spot" and "tattoo"—as well as the quotidian connotation of marking the time, and the soldier's of marking time.

[40] For a discussion of the broader implications of this intrusion, see Sussman, "A Note on the Public and the Private. . . . "

[41] It is, in fact, only by implication, by the suggestiveness of the word "heavy," that the critical tradition has assumed the old man is being pressed or held down by the bed. The narrator, in fact, smiles (as he earlier chuckled, and as we would have laughed to see), that the deed is *so far done;* it is not yet completed, and the heart actually continues to beat "for many minutes." Its sound is muffled, like that of the "watch . . . enveloped in cotton" and the "stifled sound" of the shared groan, suggesting—but only *suggesting*—that what is taking place is a suffocation, a pressing of the old man

(so that, like the narrator, he can scarcely breathe) to death. For both narrator and old man have been likened to a timepiece: the former's hand to a minute-hand, the latter's heartbeat to a watch.

[42] The narrator's turn of phrase—"I examined the corpse"—is clinical and unemotional in its detachment, reminding us for a moment of how lucidly, "how healthily—how calmly" he can tell his story.

[43] Latin *de* (privative) + *tegere;* uncover (*OED/WUD*). Thus a "detective" is one who uncovers.

[44] The narrator remarks that "the night waned," but there is no indication of any more light in the chamber than is provided by the lantern, for the shutters are, as always, "close fastened." Even at four in the morning it is as *dark* as at midnight—but when the narrator opens the door a few moments from now, he will do so with a "light" heart. The playful, contrasting juxtaposition of light and dark in this passage suggests that "darkness" and "night" can be understood in context not simply as physical phenomena, but as metaphors of truth (against the *light*heartedness of the narrator's dissimulation) or of the burden of conscience (made light of by his concealment of the corpse). On another level, the narrator's "light" heart ironically reflects the heaviness of the bed which he pulled over the old man.

[45] The three men at the door are suave—their urbanity suggests a breadth of social experience—and as *police* they represent the force of order in the *polis* or city, a trinity of civil law. This legal intervention indicates one of many subtexts in the tale: its underlying interrogation of the efficacy of law. As the reference to the Old Testament (n.30), and later, the narrator's exclamations—"Oh God! [. . .] Almighty God!"—refer obliquely to divine law, so the scattered references to soldiers (see n.37) point to the possibility of martial law, one alternative when civil law has broken down.

[46] The old man's absence "in the country" implies the narrator's presence in the city or *polis*.

[47] The narrator's characterizations of his state of mind, however, seem to belie his confidence: *enthusiasm,* connoting daemonic possession; *triumph,* evoking Bacchic frenzy; and *wild audacity*—passion uncontrollable, madness, and distraction. Similarly, he projects his own tiredness onto the officers, inviting them to "rest from their fatigues," when in fact it is he who has been engaged in "labors" through the night.

[48] The narrator is "at ease," a phrase which at first suggests relaxation, but then recalls his dis-ease—and the military drill command which describes a state less relaxed than standing "easy." His *singularity* continues

to draw attention to the absence of the old man, and his pallor evokes the latter's "pale blue eye." He *fancies* hearing a sound (as we fancied him mad, and as the old man tried to fancy his fears causeless), a reminder of that "dreadful echo" resonating through the tale, and of the bell which "sounded the hour," coinciding with the policemen's knocking on the door and a hint that what the narrator is hearing may be imaginary.

[49] The word *vehement* today means intense or severe, but derives from roots (Latin *vehere,* to carry, + *mens,* mind) meaning "carried out of one's mind" (*OED/WUD*).

[50] Greek *hupokrites,* actor; from *hupokrinein,* to play a part (*OED/WUD*).

[51] The narrative's play on the auditory imperative "hear" and the visual deixis "here" may be seen as the staging of a hiatus or disjunction between the mediation of representation and the immediacy of experience, or the sign and its referent. This moment marks an apocalyptic transition from the end of narrative time to the time of the reader, and finds its rhetorical and psychoanalytic analogues in the idea of the "sublime" and "ekphrasis." For expositions of these concepts, see Fry, "Longinus at Colonus"; Weiskel, "The Logic of Terror"; and Mitchell, "Ekphrasis and the Other."

[52] Passages quoted here of "The Black Cat" and "The Imp of the Perverse" are taken from Poe, *The Complete Illustrated Stories and Poems,* 235-43 and 439-45, respectively.

[53] The word "gallows" is derived from the Middle English *galwe,* cross or apparatus for hanging, from the Old English *gealga* (*OED/WUD*).

[54] This substitution may be seen as a narrative parricide which constitutes and supplements the "structurality" of the narration. The various permutations and configurations of narrative pharmacology are explored in minute detail in Derrida's *Dissemination.*

[55] The relation suggested here between the individual and society perhaps calls for a socio-historical analysis of the narrator in terms of what Michel Foucault calls the *soul*—"which, unlike the soul represented by Christian theology, is not born in sin and subject to punishment, but is born rather out of the methods of punishment, supervision and constraint. This real, non-corporal soul is not a substance; it is the element in which are articulated the effects of a certain type of power and the reference of a certain type of knowledge, the machinery by which the power relations give rise to a possible corpus of knowledge, and knowledge extends and reinforces the effects of this power" (*Discipline and Punish,* 29).

[56] Hayden White characterizes the dialectical dilemma of historiographical irony as follows: "In Irony, figurative language folds back on itself and brings its own potentialities for distorting perception under question. . . . The trope of Irony . . . provides a linguistic paradigm of a mode of thought which is radically self-critical with respect not only to a given characterization of the world of experience but also to the very effort to capture adequately the truth of things in language. It is, in short, a model of the linguistic protocol in which skepticism in thought and relativism in ethics are conventionally expressed" (*Metahistory,* 37-38). In a similar vein, Paul de Man, following Friedrich Schlegel, comments: "Irony divides the flow of temporal existence into a past that is pure mystification and a future that remains harassed forever by a relapse within the inauthentic. It can know this inauthenticity but can never overcome it. It can only restate and repeat it on an increasingly conscious level, but it remains endlessly caught in the impossibility of making this knowledge applicable to the empirical world. It dissolves in the narrowing spiral of a linguistic sign that becomes more and more remote from its meaning, and it can find no escape from this spiral" ("The Rhetoric of Temporality," 222).

[57] I use "allegory" here in de Man's sense: "The meaning constituted by the allegorical sign can . . . consist only in the *repetition* (in the Kierkegaardian sense of the term) of a previous sign with which it can never coincide, since it is of the essence of this previous sign to be pure anteriority. . . . [A]llegory designates primarily a distance in relation to its own origin, and, renouncing the nostalgia and the desire to coincide, it establishes its language in the void of this temporal difference. In so doing, it prevents the self from an illusory identification with the non-self, which is now fully, though painfully, recognized as a non-self" ("The Rhetoric of Temporality," 207).

[58] Here I am referring to Lévi-Strauss's general characterization of the time-frame of myth: " . . . a myth always refers to events alleged to have taken place in time. . . . But what gives the myth an operative value is that the specific pattern described is everlasting: it explains the present and the past as well as the future [. . .] Whatever our ignorance of the language and the culture of the people where it originated, a myth is still felt as a myth by any reader throughout the world" ("The Structural Study of Myth," 84-86).

[59] I take the supplementary relation between literature and criticism to be analogous to that quality of a text which Walter Benjamin calls "translatability"—by which the original text calls for translation as its mode of being in its afterlife. Thus "the language of a translation can—in fact, must—let itself go, so that it gives voice to the *intentio* of the original not as reproduction but as harmony, as a supplement to the language in which it expresses itself, as its own kind of *intentio*" ("The Task of the Translator," 79).

[60] A general paradigm for a phenomenological approach to this relation between reader and text is outlined in Georges Poulet's analysis of "interior objects": "I am someone who happens to have as objects of his own thought, thoughts which are part of a book I am reading, and which are therefore the cogitations of another. They are the thoughts of another, and yet it is I who am their subject . . . Whenever I read, I mentally pronounce an *I,* and yet the *I* which I pronounce is not myself. This is true even when the hero of a novel is presented in the third person, and even when there is no hero and nothing but reflections or propositions: for as soon as something is presented as *thought,* there has to be a thinking subject with whom, at least for the time being, I identify, forgetting myself, alienated from myself . . . Reading, then, is the act in which the subjective principle which I call *I,* is modified in such a way that I no longer have the right, strictly speaking, to consider it as my *I.* I am on loan to another, and this other thinks, feels, suffers, and acts within me" ("Criticism and the Experience of Interiority," 59-60).

[61] This would be a pragmatic approach to criticism, prioritizing either the past or the present as the determining field of meaning and ignoring or refusing to engage the hermeneutical situation. Against this, Hans-Georg Gadamer suggests that "[t]he real meaning of a text as it addresses the interpreter does not just depend on the occasional factors which characterize the author and his original public. For it is also always co-determined by the historical situation of the interpreter and thus by the whole of the objective course of history. . . . The meaning of a text surpasses its author not occasionally, but always. Thus understanding is not a reproductive procedure, but rather always a productive one. . . . It suffices to say that one understands *differently when one understands at all*" (280). Similarly the present can only afford occasional closures, because it too is only a moment in the flow of history: "Indeed, it is even a question whether the special contemporaneity of the work of art does not consist precisely in this: that it stands open in a limitless way for ever new integrations. It may be that the creator of a work intends the particular public of his time, but the real being of a work is what it is able to say, and that stretches fundamentally out beyond every historical limitation" (*Warheit und Methode,* 96, translated and quoted in the "Editor's Introduction" to Gadamer, *Philosophical Hermeneutics,* xxv and xxvi, respectively).

[62] I regretfully employ these terms here in their most general (and perhaps unfashionable) senses and usages,

acknowledging that each implies a wealth of diverse "isms" and approaches to texts which are outside the limited framework of this essay. Gita Rajan has remarked, to take one example, that the narrator's gender is never explicitly identified in the text; this could, of course, be the case even when the narrator asks, "would a mad*man* have been so wise as this?" She then goes on to declare, in the absence of gender markings, "that the narrator is indeed female . . . I propose to dislodge the earlier, patriarchal notion of a male narrator for the story. I argue, instead, that a gender-marked *rereading* of this tale reveals the narrator's exploration of her female situation in a particular feminist discourse" (Rajan, "A Feminist Rereading . . . ," 284). Predictably, Rajan, now occupying the subject position of the narrator, prepares to "take the life of the old man"—in this case, a "masculinist" reading of the tale by Robert Con Davis; and her reading of the tale becomes a somewhat formulaic allegory of the relation between her own feminist criticism and the tradition of masculinist criticism—an allegory which regretfully does not question its own status as such, or the tale as its own myth of origin.

[63] This is a point of departure for studying the implications of Paul de Man's question: "Could we conceive of a literary history that would not truncate literature by putting us misleadingly *into* or *outside* it, that would be able to maintain the literary aporia throughout, account at the same time for the truth and the falsehood of the knowledge literature conveys about itself, distinguish rigorously between metaphorical and historical language, and account for literary modernity as well as for its historicity? Clearly, such a conception would imply a revision of the notion of history and, beyond that, of the notion of time on which our idea of history is based" ("Literary History and Literary Modernity," 164).

Works Cited

Abrams, M. H. *The Mirror and the Lamp*. New York: Oxford University Press, 1953.

Benjamin, Walter. "The Task of the Translator," *Illuminations*. Trans. Harry Zohn. Ed. Hannah Arendt. New York: Schocken Books, 1969, pp. 69-82.

Bulfinch, Thomas. *Mythology. A Modern Abridgment by Edmund Fuller*. New York: Dell Publishing, 1959, reprint 1979.

Bultmann, Rudolf. *History and Eschatology: The Presence of Eternity*. New York: Harper Torchbooks, 1962.

The Compact Oxford English Dictionary, Second Edition. Oxford: Clarendon Press, 1992.

Davis, Robert Con. "Lacan, Poe, and Narrative Repression," *Lacan and Narration: The Psychoanalytic Difference in Narrative Theory*. Baltimore: The Johns Hopkins University Press, 1984.

Dayan, Joan. *Fables of Mind: An Inquiry into Poe's Fiction*. New York: Oxford University Press, 1987.

de Certeau, Michel. *The Writing of History*. Trans. Tom Conley. New York: Columbia University Press, 1988.

Deleuze, Gilles and Felix Guattari. *Anti-Oedipus*. Trans. Robert Hurley et al. Minneapolis: University of Minnesota Press, 1983.

de Man, Paul. *Blindness and Insight*. Minneapolis: University of Minnesota Press, 1983.

———. "Criticism and Crisis," *Blindness and Insight*, pp. 3-19.

———. "Literary History and Literary Modernity," *Blindness and Insight*, pp. 142-65.

———. "Lyric and Modernity," *Blindness and Insight*, pp. 166-86.

———. "The Resistance to Theory," *The Resistance to Theory*. Minneapolis: University of Minnesota Press, 1986, pp. 3-20.

———. "The Rhetoric of Temporality," *Blindness and Insight*, pp. 187-228.

———. "Semiology and Rhetoric," *Allegories of Reading*. New Haven: Yale University Press, 1979, pp. 3-19.

Derrida, Jacques. *Dissemination*. Trans. Barbara Johnson. Chicago: University of Chicago Press, 1981.

———. *The Ear of the Other: Otobiography, Transference, Translation*. Ed. Christie McDonald. Lincoln: University of Nebraska Press [Schocken Books], 1985.

———. "Tympan," *Margins of Philosophy*. Trans. Alan Bass. Chicago: University of Chicago Press, 1982, pp. ix-xxix.

Foucault, Michel. *Discipline & Punish*. Trans. Alan Sheridan. New York: Vintage Books/Random House, 1977.

———. *The Birth of the Clinic*. Trans. A. M. Sheridan Smith. New York: Pantheon Books/Random House, 1973.

———. *Madness and Civilization*. Trans. Richard Howard. New York: Vintage Books/Random House, 1965.

Frank, F. S. "Neighbourhood Gothic: Poe's Tell-Tale Heart," *The Sphinx* 1981 v.3[4]: 53-60.

Fry, Paul H. "Longinus at Colonus." *The Reach of Criticism: Method and Perception in Literary Theory.* New Haven: Yale University Press, 1983, pp. 47-86.

Gadamer, Hans-Georg. *Warheit und Methode: Grundzüge einer philosophischen Hermeneutik.* Tübingen: Mohr, 1960. Excerpts translated and quoted in "Editor's Introduction," *Philosophical Hermeneutics.* Trans. and Ed. David E. Linge. Berkeley: University of California Press, 1976, pp. xi-lviii.

Graves, Robert. *The Greek Myths: 1.* Middlesex, England: Penguin, 1960.

Halliburton, David. *Edgar Allan Poe. A Phenomenological View.* Princeton: Princeton University Press, 1973.

Hamel, Bernard. "Un texte à deux voix." *Textes et Langages* 5 (1982): 6-18.

Jauss, Hans Robert. "Literary History as a Challenge to Literary Theory," *Toward an Aesthetic of Reception.* Minneapolis: University of Minnesota Press, 1982, pp. 3-45.

Kermode, Frank. *The Sense of an Ending: Studies in the Theory of Fiction.* New York: Oxford University Press, 1967.

LaCapra, Dominick. *History & Criticism.* Ithaca: Cornell University Press, 1985.

Levinson, Sanford and Steven Mailloux, eds. *Interpreting Law and Literature: A Hermeneutic Reader.* Evanston: Northwestern University Press, 1988.

Lévi-Strauss, Claude. "The Structural Study of Myth," *Myth: a Symposium.* Ed. Thomas A. Sebeok. Bloomington: Indiana University Press, 1965, pp. 81-106.

Lombardo, Patrizia. *Edgar Poe et la Modernité: Breton, Barthes, Derrida, Blanchot.* Birmingham, Alabama: Summa, 1985.

Löwith, Karl. *Meaning in History.* Chicago: University of Chicago Press, 1949.

Macksey, Richard. and Eugenio Donato. *The Structuralist Controversy: The Languages of Criticism & the Sciences of Man.* Baltimore: The Johns Hopkins University Press, 1972.

Mitchell, W. J. T. "Ekphrasis and the Other," *Picture Theory: Essays on Verbal and Visual Representation.* Chicago: University of Chicago Press, 1994, pp. 151-81.

Mukarovsky, Jan. *Aesthetic Function, Norm, and Value as Social Facts.* Trans. M. E. Suino. Ann Arbor, 1979. Reprinted in *Twentieth-Century Literary Theory: A Reader.* Ed. K. M. Newton. New York: St. Martin's Press, 1988.

Newton, K. M., ed. *Twentieth-Century Literary Theory: A Reader.* New York: St. Martin's Press, 1988.

Ortega y Gasset, Jose. "The Difficulty of Reading." Trans. Clarence E. Parmenter. *Diogenes* 28 (Winter, 1959): 1-17.

Ovid. *Metamorphoses.* Trans. Mary M. Innes. Middlesex, England: Penguin, 1955.

————. *The Metamorphoses.* Trans. Horace Gregory. New York: Viking Press [New American Library 5th reprint], 1958.

Poe, Edgar Allan. *Collected Works of Edgar Allan Poe: Tales and Sketches, 1843-1848.* Ed. Thomas Ollive Mabbott. Cambridge, Mass.: Harvard University Press, 1978, pp. 792-97.

————. "The Black Cat," *The Complete Illustrated Stories and Poems of Edgar Allan Poe.* Great Britain: Chancellor Press/Octopus Books, 1988, pp. 235-43.

————. "The Imp of the Perverse," *The Complete Illustrated Stories and Poems of Edgar Allan Poe.* Great Britain: Chancellor Press/Octopus Books, 1988, pp. 439-45.

Poulet, Georges. "Criticism and the Experience of Interiority," in Macksey, *The Structuralist Controversy,* pp. 56-72.

Rajan, Gita. "A Feminist Rereading of Poe's 'The Tell-Tale Heart'," *Papers on Language and Literature* 24 (3) [Summer 1988]: 283-300.

Rancière, Jacques. *The Names of History.* Trans. Hassan Melehy. Minnesota: University of Minnesota Press, 1994.

de Saussure, Ferdinand. *Course in General Linguistics.* Trans. Wade Baskin. New York: McGraw-Hill, 1959, reprinted 1966.

Shakespeare, William. *The Tragedy of Macbeth.* Ed. Sylvan Barnet. New York: New American Library/Signet Classics, 1963.

Sussman, Henry. "A Note on the Public and the Private in Literature: The Literature of 'Acting Out'." *MLN* 104 (3) [April 1989]: 597-611.

Tompkins, Jane P., ed. *Reader-Response Criticism.* Baltimore: The Johns Hopkins University Press, 1980.

Vaihinger, Hans. *The Philosophy of "As If": A System of the Theoretical, Practical, and Religious Fictions of Mankind.* Trans. C. K. Ogden. New York: Harcourt, Brace, & Co., 1924.

Valdes, Mario J. and Owen Miller, eds. *Identity of the Literary Text.* Toronto: University of Toronto Press, 1985.

Veeser, H. Aram, ed. *The New Historicism.* New York: Routledge, 1989.

Webster's Deluxe Unabridged Dictionary, Second Edition. New York: Dorset and Baber/Simon & Schuster, 1979.

Weiskel, Thomas. "The Logic of Terror," *The Romantic Sublime: Studies in the Structure and Psychology of Transcendence.* Baltimore: The Johns Hopkins University Press, 1976, pp. 83-106.

White, Hayden. *Metahistory.* Baltimore: The Johns Hopkins University Press, 1973.

————. "New Historicism: A Comment," *The New Historicism.* Ed. H. Aram Veeser. New York: Routledge, 1989, pp. 293-302.

Williams, Michael J. S. *A World of Words: Language and Displacement in the Fiction of Edgar Allan Poe.* Durham: Duke University Press, 1988, pp. 36-38.

Witherington, Paul. "The Accomplice in 'The Tell-Tale Heart'," *Studies in Short Fiction* 22 (4) [Fall 1985]: 471-75.

FURTHER READING

Davis, Robert Con. "Lacan, Poe, and Narrative Repression." *Modern Language Notes* 98, No. 5 (December 1983): 983-1005.

    Interprets "The Tell-Tale Heart" through Jacques Lacan's analysis of the gaze and the structure of repression.

McIlvaine, Robert. "A Shakespearean Echo in 'The Tell-Tale Heart.' " *American Notes and Queries* 15, No. 3 (November 1976): 38-40.

    Examines the connection between the narrator's description of his victim's eye as "the damned spot" and Lady Macbeth's exclamation following the murder of Duncan.

Pitcher, Edward W. "The Physiognomical Meaning of Poe's 'The Tell-Tale Heart.' " *Studies in Short Fiction* 16, No. 3 (Summer 1979): 231-33.

    Argues that Poe's narrative enacts the splitting of one subject into two roles, and that the meaning of this drama can be interpreted according to the principles of physiognomical theory.

Reilly, John E. "The Lesser Death-Watch and 'The Tell-Tale Heart.' " *American Transcendental Quarterly* No. 2 (1969): 3-9.

    Discusses the possibility that the lesser death-watch—an insect that makes a sound resembling the muffled ticking of a watch—is the source of the sound that drives the narrator to confess his crime.

Tucker, B. D. " 'The Tell-Tale Heart' and the 'Evil Eye.' " *The Southern Literary Journal* 13, No. 2 (Spring 1981): 92-98.

    Studies the narrator's obsession with the eye of his victim, particularly as that obsession relates to the common superstition of a malignant and all-seeing power.

Additional coverage of Poe's life and career is contained in the following sources published by The Gale Group: *Poetry Criticism,* **Vol. 1,** *Short Story Criticism,* **Vols. 1, 22, and 34,** *World Literature Criticism, 1500 to the Present,* **and** *Dictionary of Literary Biography,* **Vols. 3, 59, 73, and 74.**

Our Nig; or, Sketches from the Life of a Free Black

Harriet E. Wilson

INTRODUCTION

Considered the first novel in English published by a black American woman, *Our Nig; or, Sketches from the Life of a Free Black in a Two-Story White House, North. Showing that Slavery's Shadows Fall Even There* (1859) fuses elements from several genres, including the sentimental novel, the slave narrative, the gothic romance, and the satire, to portray the life of a mulatto indentured servant in the antebellum North. The book was relatively unknown until it was discovered by Henry Louis Gates, Jr., and published under his editorship in 1983. Since then the novel has forced critics to reevaluate the history of African American literature and to reconceive the development of the fictional narrative form in the United States.

Biographical Information

Most of what is known about Harriet E. Wilson's life has been pieced together by literary historians following the rediscovery of *Our Nig;* accordingly, reconstructions of Wilson's biography are incomplete and contain many contradictions. According to the 1860 Boston federal census, Harriet E. Adams was born in 1807 or 1808 in Fredericksburg, Virginia; however, the 1850 New Hampshire federal census claims she was born in 1827 or 1828 in New Hampshire. The 1850 census lists Adams as a resident of Milford, New Hampshire, in the home of a white family, the Boyleses, who served as the model for the Bellmonts in *Our Nig,* according to Henry Louis Gates, Jr. Recent work by Barbara A. White, though, shows Adams to have resided with the Boyleses for a brief period following her indentured servitude to a family named Hayward, the more likely model for the Bellmonts.

In the fall of 1851 Adams married Thomas Wilson, whom she may have met through the abolitionist movement. Abandoned by her husband nine months after their marriage, Harriet Wilson delivered a son, George Mason Wilson, in 1852; mother and son lived together in poverty and poor health. In an effort to secure a more comfortable life for her son, Wilson left George with a couple in New Hampshire and traveled to Boston, where she remained from 1856 until 1863. There, hoping to become self sufficient and to regain her son, she registered the copyright for *Our Nig* in 1859, paying for the novel's publication with money she had earned as a seamstress. The book received little attention, however, and George's death is recorded in an obituary in the *Farmer's Cabinet* of February 29, 1860. There is no record of Wilson's life after 1863, although some sources list her death date as 1870.

Plot and Major Characters

In *Our Nig* a white orphan, Mag Smith, is seduced by a wealthy gentleman, who then abandons her. Later Mag bears a child, who dies within weeks of its birth, and she is ostracized from the community. She lives in virtual isolation until an African named Jim befriends her and proposes. Overcoming her initial shock at an interracial marriage, Mag marries Jim and later bears two children. When Jim dies of consumption shortly afterward, Mag, together with Jim's partner Seth Shipley, leaves her six-year-old daughter Frado at the home of a middle-class white family, the Bellmonts, and flees town.

When Frado reaches the age of seven, she becomes the Bellmonts' indentured servant and is beaten regularly by Mrs. Bellmont. For years Frado suffers at the hands of Mrs. Bellmont and her daughter Mary; her only respite comes from her relationships with the family's male members, particularly the oldest son James, who plans to take Frado to Baltimore as his servant. However, illness forces James to return to his parents' home, where both his and Frado's health decline. As she grows older, Frado prevents further beatings from Mrs. Bellmont by threatening not to work. Feeling "the stirring of free and independent thoughts," Frado turns to books for comfort and, when she is eighteen, is freed.

Having very little with which to support herself, Frado is employed in a number of different professions, but her failing health forces her to accept public charity intermittently. However, she gradually perfects her needlework skills and sews straw hats with a white woman, who teaches Frado more about sewing and shares her library with her. This brief period of Frado's life is interrupted when a black man named Samuel comes to town on the fugitive slave lecture circuit. Frado and Samuel marry, but Samuel often leaves his wife to lecture, and eventually runs away to sea. When Frado bears their son, Samuel returns for a short time, only to abandon them again and die of fever in New Orleans. The novel closes with an abbreviated account of Frado's adventures fleeing slave-catchers and "kidnappers" and being abused by professed abolitionists who "didn't want slaves at the South, nor niggers in their houses, North." Appended to the text is Harriet

Wilson's direct appeal to her audience, imploring them to purchase her book and provide her with the means to retrieve her son George.

Major Themes

In his introduction to the 1983 edition of the novel, Gates claims that "*Our Nig* is a major example of generic fusion in which a woman writer appropriated black male (the slave narrative) and white female (the sentimental novel) forms and revised these into a synthesis at once peculiarly black and female." In many ways Frado does typify the sentimental heroine—parentless, poor, friendless and abused, relying on her own strength of character—but she also diverges from that tradition in her rejection of religion and her inability to establish a stable domestic life. Julia Stern (1995) contends that such differences mark Wilson's synthesis of sentimental and gothic traditions, particularly in the portrayal of Frado's suffering. And, while the novel itself is not literally a slave narrative, some critics have conjectured that the slave-narrative conventions used in *Our Nig* were intended to demonstrate the parallels between the treatments of blacks in the North and the South, including the similar economic motivations that structure relations within both systems.

Critical Reception

Our Nig was largely forgotten soon after its publication in 1859, possibly due to its criticism of abolitionists and the controversial portrayal of an interracial marriage. Although the novel was mentioned in Herbert Ross Brown's *The Sentimental Novel in America* (1940) and Joseph Kinney's "The Theme of Miscegenation in the American Novel to World War II" (1972), *Our Nig* was virtually unknown among literary scholars until 1983, when Henry Louis Gates, Jr., reintroduced it to the public. Subsequently many critics have addressed Wilson's manipulation of genres and her representation of African Americans and of Northern abolitionists, and have compared the novel with Harriet A. Jacobs' *Incidents in the Life of a Slave Girl,* Frances Ellen Watkins Harper's *Iola Leroy,* and William Wells Brown's *Clotel.* While, in the words of reviewer Francis Browne (1987), *Our Nig* "hardly ranks with the masterpieces of the genre," its historical importance as a "forerunner of the Afro-American literary tradition" is unmatched nonetheless.

CRITICISM

Elizabeth Breau (essay date 1993)

SOURCE: "Identifying Satire: *Our Nig,*" *Callaloo,* Vol. 16, No. 2, Spring, 1993, pp. 455-65.

[*In the following essay, Breau contends that* Our Nig *is meant to satirize the slavery and indentured servitude that were allowed to exist in the antebellum North.*]

In his introduction to Harriet Wilson's novel, *Our Nig,* Henry Louis Gates argues that the book is both a sentimental novel and an autobiography.[1] Establishing the autobiographical nature of the text is his first concern; he begins his essay by referring to the historical data—publishing records, census information, and the death certificate of Wilson's son—that helped him establish Wilson's historical identity and authorship. He supports his argument by comparing the plot details of *Our Nig* with the information contained in the three appendices that follow the text.

A reader guided by this interpretation of *Our Nig* reads it as a serious text, written by one who "preferred the pious, direct appeal to the subtle or ambiguous."[2] The image of Harriet Wilson as a desperate mother "forced to some experiment which shall aid me in maintaining myself and child without extinguishing this feeble life" hovers over *Our Nig* as we read, underscoring the similarities between the author's claims in the preface and the suffering of her heroine, Frado.[3] Gates claims that Wilson would have produced an inferior product had she strayed from her lived experience and attempted to write fiction:

> the 'autobiographical' consistencies between the fragments of Harriet Wilson's life and the depiction of the calamities of Frado, the heroine of *Our Nig,* would suggest that Mrs. Wilson was able to gain control over her materials more readily than her fellow black novelists of that decade precisely by adhering closely to the painful details of suffering that were part of her experience.[4]

Gates also implicitly disparages Wilson's creativity in his discussion of the ways in which her narrative compares with what Nina Baym has called the "overplot" of the sentimental fiction produced by Wilson's white female contemporaries. Although Gates credits Wilson with the creation of a new form of fiction, "the black woman's novel . . . because she *invented* her own plot structure through which to narrate the saga of her orphaned mulatto heroine," he implies that Wilson mimicked that literature with which she was most familiar, altering it only when it did not conform to her real life experience.[5] The picture drawn of Wilson in Gates' introduction is therefore not that of a creative writer comfortably in control of her material, but instead that of a nearly illiterate woman who stumbled onto originality because her life story—the only story she was equipped to tell—did not conform entirely to contemporary literary convention.

Gates' definition of *Our Nig* as largely autobiographical convinces us that we must ignore indications that

Wilson's meaning is not always straightforward and that textual inconsistencies or "inversions" may not be due to lack of authorial skill. Once *Our Nig* is perceived as a true life story, similar to the slave narratives written by Wilson's contemporaries, it becomes difficult to read the text's satiric or ironic moments as more than the angry aberrations of an unskilled writer. A detailed examination of Wilson's prose, however, suggests that large portions of *Our Nig* are satiric and that Wilson's indictment of antebellum Northern racism derives most of its power from that satire.

Michael Seidel writes that one of the first hints that a text may be satiric is "the claim to truth as a narrative privilege."[6] Although this is most notably true in those satires that are patently false, such as *Don Quixote, Candide,* or *Gulliver's Travels,* a satire that disguises itself as truth need not be obviously fantastical. *Our Nig* purports to be truthful in several ways. Its full title is *Our Nig; or, Sketches from the Life of a Free Black, In A Two-Story White House, North. Showing that Slavery's Shadows Fall Even There. By 'Our Nig.'* Gates comments that "the boldness and cleverness in the ironic use of 'Nig' as title and pseudonym is, to say the least, impressive, standing certainly as one of the black tradition's earliest recorded usages."[7] Wilson's "pseudonym" functions to convince her readers that the author and protagonist of her tale are the same. The pseudonym also suggests that, as a true narrative, *Our Nig* will conform to the generic model of the slave narratives that themselves mimicked the sentimental fiction written by white women. The allegorical phrase, "Two-Story White House, North," further suggests a serious, non-satiric text because it also conforms to the generic expectations of both abolitionist literature and sentimental fiction.

In contrast, the juxtaposition of "Our Nig" and "Free Black" does not conform to such generic expectations but instead implies that the narrative concerns itself with an aberration from the status quo. This part of the title supports Wilson's satiric pseudonym, challenging beliefs in Northern equality and suggesting social depravity. As a satirist, Wilson is outraged that slavery, or its partner, indentured servitude, can exist among those who congratulate themselves on their moral superiority to Southern slaveholders. Significantly, Frado is not even legally indentured; she is bound by default as it becomes increasingly clear that her mother is never going to return for her. The Bellmonts, at whose home she is abandoned, never consider that Frado might do something besides work for them; by the time she becomes an adolescent, she knows she is compelled to remain with them until her eighteenth birthday.

Wilson's preface invites inspection. Beginning with the usual demurrals regarding her literary talents and a seemingly straightforward statement about her financial desperation, she disguises her purpose with a disclaimer that conforms to the satirist's tendency "to deny what they are doing at the same time that they are doing it, and this presents the satirist as something of a hypocrite (her)self."[8] Wilson tells us that she "would not . . . palliate slavery at the South by disclosures of its appurtenances North."[9] By accepting this statement, innocently placed after a description of how her poverty has induced her to write, the reader is lulled into accepting the assertion (surprising for Wilson's time) that the injustices commonly said to belong only to the South also exist in the North. Although Wilson hastens to reassure us that "my mistress was wholly imbued with *southern* principles," the text contains no other indications that Mrs. Bellmont is a southerner, and none of the book's other characters are so excused. Wilson continues:

> I do not pretend to divulge every transaction in my own life, which the unprejudiced would declare unfavorable in comparison with treatment of legal bondmen; I have purposely omitted what would most provoke shame in our good anti-slavery friends at home.

Wilson could, in other words, make the North seem even crueler and more inhumane than the South, had she the desire to do so. And, in telling us that she has omitted the worst of her tale, the real cruelty, she has ironically informed us that the free North is crueler to its black residents than the slaveholding South. As the events of Frado's life make clear, "our good anti-slavery friends at home" have every reason to feel ashamed.

Before beginning my analysis of the text proper, I would like to say a few words about the three letters appended to it. Gates relies heavily on these to support his claim that *Our Nig* is autobiographical, even going so far as to suggest that Wilson's style reveals that she felt less anxiety about those portions of the text that are historically verifiable than she did about those sections for which we have no supporting documentation.[10] Wilson could not have known, however, that those reading her work in the twentieth century would have access only to certain historical records—we have her marriage certificate, for example, but do not know either the exact date of her birth or who her parents were. Moreover, Gates does not remark on the ways in which the appended letters are inconsistent with the careful authentication that usually accompanies nineteenth-century African-American autobiographical texts. Wilson's text lacks, for example, prefatory letters by distinguished white friends of the author vouching for her honesty and integrity. This lack of white approval sets *Our Nig* apart from other antebellum African-American texts and indicates that it may not be restrained by the author's deference to her white patrons. Wilson further indicates the extent to which her text rejects white assistance by ending it with three letters that supposedly verify the events it depicts. The placement of the letters at the end of the text, rather than at its beginning, inverts the form of antebellum African-American literature and suggests that Wilson may be parodying generic requirements.

The authorship of the three appended letters is dubious. The second letter, written by "Margaretta Thorn," "is the source of the little that we know about the author's childhood . . . she was hired out to a family 'calling themselves Christians' . . . [who] put her to work . . . allegedly ruining her health by unduly difficult work."[11] Although this account corresponds with Frado's servitude in the Bellmont household, it seems odd that Gates should suddenly forget his meticulous concern with verifying every detail of Wilson's life with historical documentation enough to be silent on the identity of Margaretta Thorn, the author of this crucial letter. Even her name, "Thorn," is strange, underscoring the ways in which her anonymity prickles at the reader seeking reassurance that Wilson is a reliable black storyteller and not one who takes advantage of white sympathies and credulity.

The first and third letters are even less convincing as authenticating documentation. The first letter is signed "Allida," with no surname. Although Gates declares Allida's letter conclusive in establishing the autobiographical nature of *Our Nig*, he gives no more thought to the identity of Allida than he does to that of Thorn. He is a little more concerned with the author of the third letter, who has simply signed with the initials, C. D. S. Since these initials were a "*legal* abbreviation for 'Colored Indentured Servant,'" Gates concludes that C. D. S. was either an indentured mulatto or a white friend who chose not to sign his or her name.[12]

Rather than suggesting that Gates overlooked essential information that holds the key to *Our Nig*'s authenticity, I would like to propose that the three appended letters function as a deceptive claim to truth, masking the novel's satiric intent by parodying the form of slave narratives. If parody, as Linda Hutcheon writes, "is a form of imitation, but imitation characterized by ironic inversion, *not always at the expense of the parodied text*," and if Wilson was writing a satiric tale of slavery in the ostensibly free North, it seems logical that she would mimic, without insulting, the genuinely autobiographical slave narratives that were also written to advance the position of African-Americans.[13] Wilson could, in other words, have written all three letters herself. The placement of the letters at the end, rather than the beginning of the text, constitutes one parodic inversion; that they are signed in two cases with incomplete names (either female or neuter), rather than with the names of respectable, well-known (male) citizens is another.

It is no trivial matter, given the ongoing pressure felt by African-American scholars to verify the claims made by slave narratives, to suggest that Wilson's narrative is not an authentic autobiography. A false or fictional autobiography impugns the claims of black abolitionists to be truthful and undermines assertions about the horrific nature of slavery. As I suggest above, however, the expectation that nineteenth-century black-authored first-person narratives contain only unaltered truth restricts our ability to see the authors of such texts as creative artists and confines them to the limiting role of political advocates who did their inadequate best with the existing white literary tradition.

Wilson recognized the trespass her fiction constituted and addressed it by including a portrait of a dishonest African-American who misrepresents his suffering under slavery within her text. Frado's husband, Samuel, "left her to her fate—embarked at sea, with the disclosure that he had never seen the South, and that his illiterate harangues were humbugs for hungry abolitionists."[14] In a genuine slave narrative, this disclosure of Samuel's fraudulence would be accompanied with moralizing, the author's lament about how the degradations of unequal treatment had bestialized the man so that he could no longer comprehend the damage his imposture did to his race. Wilson, in contrast, merely has Samuel die, less than a page later, "of yellow fever, in New Orleans." His death serves as a satiric punishment: *yellow* fever signifies his cowardice and dishonesty. It is also fitting that he, a pretended runaway slave, should die in the deep South, captured, as it were, by his own falsehood.

The text proper of *Our Nig* is rife with inconsistencies that, to the reader who interprets all statements at face value, suggest authorial incompetence or error. The story begins with a discrepancy that should alert the wary reader that this text may contain more than it appears to at first glance. Although Wilson uses only third-person narration, the first three chapter headings are all in the first person: "Mag Smith, My Mother," "My Father's Death," and "A New Home for Me."[15] The titles of the remaining chapters conform to the third-person narration, leaving Gates to suggest that Wilson's anxiety over her credibility led to a psychological spillover.[16] Even if this were true, however, it seems doubtful that the error would have gone unnoticed during the lengthy, meticulous processes of editing, typesetting, and printing. Given the unlikeliness of such a glaring oversight, we must search for another explanation.

The first three chapters concern the downfall, degradation, and ultimate descent into heartlessness of Frado's mother, Mag Smith. Frado only enters the story in the middle of chapter two and does not become a prominent character until after her mother abandons her in chapter three. The chapter headings inform the reader that Mag Smith is not the protagonist and that her adventures are only the impetus behind the sufferings of her daughter.

In addition to stressing yet again that the author and the protagonist are the same person, the first-person chapter headings remind us that this individual is not white, but "our Nig." This recollection is crucial; without it, one would be tempted to read important lines of Wilson's prose as though they were written by one who agreed with white racist ideology. When, for example, the "kind-hearted African," Jim, resolves to propose marriage to the destitute, *white* Mag, he reasons that "she'd be as much of a prize to me as she'd fall short of coming up to the mark with white folks. I do n't [sic] care for past things. I've done things 'fore now I's ashamed of. She's good enough for me, any how [sic]."[17]

If one accepts the literal meaning of these words, Jim's acceptance of white superiority and his conviction that a "white wife" is a "treasure" is disturbing in a black-authored, ostensibly non-racist text. The reader's discomfort increases with Jim's proposal speech:

> You's had trial of white folks, anyhow. They run off and left ye, and now none of 'em come near ye to see if you's dead or alive. I's black outside, I know, but I's got a white heart inside. Which you rather have, a black heart in a white skin, or a white heart in a black one?[18]

Jim's conflation of skin tone with morality identifies him as entirely coopted by a white supremacist ideology that insists on a correlation between criminal or immoral behavior and a non-white skin. The reader can, however, still hope for authorial condemnation of Jim's ignorance, at least until the next page when the narrator, "our Nig," exclaims that Mag's marriage to Jim "has sundered another bond which held her to her fellows. She has descended another step down the ladder of infamy."

Both Jim's proposal and the narrator's lament become less problematic, however, if interpreted as irony. Wayne Booth explains that when interpreting ironic writing, the reader compares the literal meaning of the words with his or her knowledge of the author, the context, and the intentions of the text.[19] Wilson's content and delivery appear at odds with her supposed belief that racial inequality is wrong. Assuming, as Booth does when considering a potential ironist, that Wilson was neither crazy nor stupid and that she further did not believe in white racial superiority, her words must be interpreted ironically as meaning the opposite of what they say.

Wilson's depiction of Mag's sexual downfall is also satirically motivated, geared as it is toward discrediting white northerners. Mag's moral decline begins not, as we might expect, with the loss of her "priceless gem" to a deceitful lover, but with her "pious" thankfulness at the death of her illegitimate child. Her grateful prayer is an inversion of normal parental grief: "God be thanked," ejaculated Mag, as she saw its breathing cease; "no one can taunt *her* with my ruin."[20] Although Mag's words could indicate a conviction that life tainted with a moral stain is not worth living—a commonplace of sentimental fiction—her later abandonment of Frado suggests that her relief at the child's death is motivated more by selfishness than by religious sentiment.

Mag's "ruin" is not a private affair. Even among strangers, she is beset with "foul tongues" that "jest of her shame, and averted looks and cold greetings disheartened her."[21] The narrative voice sermonizes on the condemnation that haunts Mag as the plot reveals how "disdaining to ask favor or friendship from a sneering world," she vows to "die neglected and forgotten before she would be dependent on any."[22] The cruelty experienced by Mag, Frado's white mother, prepares the reader for a society in which the vulnerable are persecuted as a matter of course; "our good anti-slavery friends at home" have even more on their consciences than the victimization of African-Americans.

Mag is not merely characterized as a victim, however. As an unchaste, degraded woman who is unmotherly enough to abandon her daughter to Mrs. Bellmont, a woman she herself describes as a "she-devil," she also introduces Wilson's portrayal of white women as cruel, lustful, and unmotherly—the opposite of the nineteenth-century ideal of women as nurturing, gentle, kind, and chaste. Wilson's attack on this image also works along racial lines. Not only were black women believed to be more lustful than white women, but slave-owning ideology denied that family bonds were operative within the African-American community, insisting instead that black women felt no love for their children. Rather than attempting to prove that black women are as pure and motherly as their white counterparts, Wilson attacks images of white women as angels in the house through both Mag and Mrs. Bellmont, a woman devoid of any of the lofty, "feminine" sentiments for which her sex was so praised by Wilson's white contemporaries.

Gates includes Mrs. Bellmont in his description of Wilson's "thinly veiled fictional account of her life in which *she* transforms her tormentors into objects, the stock, stereotypical objects of the sentimental novel,"[23] implying that Wilson was inept at character development. However, satire frequently subordinates the character development normally expected of the novel to a two-dimensional portrayal of vice; Frances Burney's Madame Duval and Captain Mirvan, for example, are thoroughly incapable of reform. Mrs. Bellmont is similarly two-dimensional and vice-ridden.

Mrs. Bellmont's primary sins are racism and cruelty, recalling Juvenal's description of bloodthirsty female slave

owners.[24] She believes that Frado needs no more nour-
ishment than "skimmed milk, with brown bread crusts,"
and that she needs neither shoes in the winter nor an
education: "Mrs. Bellmont was in doubt about the utility of attempting to educate people of color, who were
incapable of elevation."[25] Here, Wilson satirizes people
of Mrs. Bellmont's ilk merely by reporting their beliefs
in her dryest, most sophisticated prose, underscoring that
her verbal and intellectual capabilities far exceed theirs.

Additionally, Mrs. Bellmont's cruelty toward the
helpless, patiently enduring Frado flatly contradicts
the portrait of women as angels of mercy and kindness. The enjoyment she derives from frequently
beating Frado is probably the text's most recurrent
theme, and if there is one image, usually "fantastic"
and violent, at the heart of every satire, then in *Our
Nig* it is surely the picture of Frado imprisoned in a
closet with a piece of wood inserted by Mrs. Bellmont
"propping" her mouth open.[26] This image, compelling because of the immediacy of the pain it conveys, is also a powerful satiric inversion—Frado
cannot speak because her mouth is *open*. The piece
of wood is both an unusually painful gag and a
parodic one, depriving Frado of the speech that should
emerge from her open mouth. The "norm" concealed
behind this violently imposed speechlessness is the
white-abolitionist-assisted liberation of black speech.
Although many slave narratives begin with the author's
thanks to his or her white benefactors, Wilson, notably, does not thank anyone. Frado's silencing by such
a white "benefactor" indicates Wilson's disgust with
the self-congratulatory tendencies of the abolitionist
movement that ignored the ongoing abuses around them.

The Bellmont family is a microcosmic reproduction of
white abusiveness and hypocrisy, with the better-natured
of the Bellmonts either helpless or unwilling to prevent
the cruelty of Mrs. Bellmont and her daughter, Mary.
Although Mr. Bellmont, Jack, Jane, Aunt Abby, and
James all oppose Frado's abuse, they are only able to
help her sporadically and cannot prevent her starvation
or severe beatings for any prolonged time. The power
dynamics by which the majority continually succumbs
to the evil authority of Mrs. Bellmont and Mary are
complicated, including an inversion of traditional sexual
politics, a satire against women modelled on male-
authored misogynist satire, the satiric depiction of men
as weak, effeminate, and hypocritical, and an exclusively
female power struggle in which the evil women invariably defeat the good. The apostolic names given to the
members of the Bellmont family indicate the extent to
which Wilson believes Christianity is implicated in the
brutality of slavery: Mary could not be less like her
gentle namesake, and James is almost completely unable to inspire Frado with Christian devotion.

Mrs. Bellmont rules the Bellmont household. Her husband, when asked by the kindly Aunt Abby why he

does not assert himself on Frado's behalf, replies, "How
am I to help it? Women rule the earth, and all in it."[27]
The narrator has explained earlier that opposing Mrs.
Bellmont's wishes is "like encountering a whirlwind
charged with fire, daggers and spikes," indicating Mr.
Bellmont's helplessness in the face of his wife's wrath.[28]
A silenced, unwilling witness to Frado's daily torture,
Mr. Bellmont is "feminized" to the extent that he can
only shed silent tears in sympathy with her misery.[29]
Having acquired a power never meant for her gender,
both Mrs. Bellmont's femininity and her humanity have
become completely distorted, and only her feminine
flaws remain: she is irrational, tyrannical, manipula-
tive, and given to crocodile tears when thwarted.

Jack and James, the Bellmont sons, are more effective
at helping Frado than their father—when they try. Jack
buys Frado a dog, and James teaches her Christian
doctrine and compels his mother to permit her to eat at
the table. As the narrative continues, however, their
help becomes both less frequent and less effective.
James' influence is weakened as he lies dying of a
lingering sickness while his attempts to teach Frado to
love God and Jesus lead her to love him instead. Here,
James' illness and his ineptitude as a religious instruc-
tor indicate the powerlessness of the abolitionist movement. Jack, representing another kind of abolitionist,
becomes progressively less sensitive to Frado's suffering. On one visit home he remarks, "Same old story, is
it; knocks and bumps? Better times coming; never fear,
Nig."[30] Here, the reader hardly needs the narrator's
lament about Jack's new callousness; we recall that he
is responsible for coining Frado's degrading nickname.[31]

Jack's loss of interest in Frado's well-being is a satiric depiction of the hypocritical abolitionists who
sustain interest in their cause only as long as it remains interesting and present. When Jack sees that
Frado continues to live and suffer within his mother's
household, she becomes merely a fixture: familiarity
leads to complacency. Wilson's disgust with "professed abolitionists, who didn't [sic] want slaves at
the South, nor niggers in their own houses, North.
Faugh! to lodge one; to eat with one; to admit one
through the front door; to sit next one; awful!" underlies her characterization of those who claim to feel
sympathy but take no concrete action: although Frado
begs both Jack and James to take her with them to
their new homes, neither does, preferring to leave her
a prisoner in their mother's household.[32] Helping Frado
would involve not only defying their vicious, repulsive mother but would also entail accepting moral
responsibility for Frado's well-being. If they allow
her to serve them as she does their mother, they would
be implicated in Mrs. Bellmont's crimes, whereas
granting Frado freedom (or simply paying her) would
require making an independent moral decision. Like
the insincere abolitionists against whom Wilson in-
veighs, Jack and James find it more convenient to

observe the status quo while mouthing words of opposition to it. That Mrs. Bellmont is the *mother* of these professed philanthropists indicts all white Americans for the oppression of African-Americans; their deeply ingrained prejudices and ongoing complicity with a slavery system from which they benefit belie all claims of opposition to black suffering.

The dynamics between Mrs. Bellmont (and Mary, who supports her in every way) and the good women who reside in her household differ from those between Mrs. Bellmont and the men because both Aunt Abby and Jane are dependent on Mrs. Bellmont for economic support, whereas her sons and husband are not. Although Jane and Aunt Abby are not subject to the physical abuse Frado endures, their attempts to defy Mrs. Bellmont are often thwarted. In fact, we suspect that Jane's efforts to assert independence have been frustrated so often that she can no longer muster even the most passive resistance: she never defends Frado and needs the help of both her father and Aunt Abby to marry the man of her choice. Aunt Abby, whose moral guilt is perhaps lessened by her lack of a blood tie to Mrs. Bellmont (she is Mr. Bellmont's sister), does help Frado, but is threatened with explusion from the household and denied entry into James' sickroom as a result. Aunt Abby and James are also partners in their attempt to instruct Frado in the tenets of Christianity; here, their good intentions are foiled when Mrs. Bellmont convinces Frado that only white people are admitted to heaven.

The most sustained conflict takes place between Mrs. Bellmont and Frado, whose defiance takes several forms. Not only does the girl survive, despite Mrs. Bellmont's best attempts to the contrary, but she manages to charm all those who know her with her persistent cheerfulness, sense of humor, and predilection for playing practical jokes (another possible sign that Wilson herself is joking). Frado's patience and ability to endure do not endear her to those around her, however, since their native selfishness permits only an interest in that which amuses them. Thus, the hired farm hands cheer Frado's antics on the barn roof, but do not help her with her work. Even Frado's popularity suffices to enrage Mrs. Bellmont, however, prompting her endeavor to spoil the child's looks.

Mrs. Bellmont keeps Frado's hair shorn as close to her head as possible, never gives her anything but rags to wear, and forbids her any protection from the sun so that her fair, almost white, complexion will darken. These particular persecutions are *Our Nig*'s only indications of the sexually motivated conflicts that usually predominate in nineteenth-century narratives about female mulattos. *Our Nig* is unusual because its interracial heroine, Frado, is not an object of white men's lust, but is sexually oppressed only by the jealousy of Mrs. Bellmont, who sees her beauty (a hallmark of the female mulatto story) as a threat to the desirability of white women. Frado's freedom from sexual harassment is significant, stressing both the passivity and weakness of the male characters and the female nature of the conflict. In other words, if Mrs. Bellmont is derived from traditional, male misogynist satire such as that of Juvenal and is a wrongful holder of male power, the ability of the male characters to molest Frado would signify incomplete emasculinization. The power they would acquire over Frado from forced sexual relations with her would undermine Mrs. Bellmont's tyrannical hold over her. By not permitting any threats to Mrs. Bellmont's power, and by removing the danger of rape, Wilson completes the sexual inversion of *Our Nig* and forces her readers to concentrate on the racially- and class-derived oppressions that marked most black-white relations.

Whereas the sexual harassment that usually faces female mulattos in nineteenth- (and twentieth-) century fiction adds awareness of gendered power imbalances, it also permits readers to focus on the titillating details of sexual pursuit and conquest while ignoring the social criticism embedded within the plot. By desexualizing her plot, in other words, and therefore rendering it less arousing, Wilson forces her readers to maintain their awareness of her exposure of social evil. Frado's mixed racial heritage is less important to the plot of *Our Nig* than is usual for a book of this type; here, Wilson's deviation from the norms of sentimental fiction furthers her satire by not permitting her readers to coast through a familiar plot line.

Frado's one overt act of defiance occurs when Mr. Bellmont, concerned for her ongoing ill health, advises, "you are looking sick . . . you cannot endure beating as you once could."[33] Frado responds to this generous counsel by verbally defying Mrs. Bellmont for the first and only time in the book:

> "Stop!" shouted Frado, "strike me, and I'll never work a mite more for you;" and throwing down what she had gathered, stood like one who feels the stirring of free and independent thoughts.[34]

Mrs. Bellmont backs down, as does the overseer in the scene from the *Narrative of the Life of Frederick Douglass* in which Douglass defeats his oppressor in a fight. However, unlike Douglass, whose victory began his journey toward freedom, Frado is content to know that her one disobedience has lessened her beatings, although she still works just as hard, continues to be physically unwell, and receives as many "scoldings" as before. Here, Wilson satirizes the lofty goals supposedly held by those who flee captivity; in a world where no one is heroic, the persecuted are content merely to lessen their suffering. Frado, unlike Douglass, does not *feel* "the stirring of free and independent thoughts," but simply *stands "like"* one who does. She is appearance rather than content and this, if anything, is her fatal flaw. Because Frado is satisfied to endure and suffer, her health is destroyed. Although adulthood brings her freedom from Mrs. Bellmont, she is able to work only for short periods. Dependent on the charity of those who house the poor for money, she is shunted about, becoming weaker and more helpless all the time. As *Our Nig* ends, merging with the "biographical" data that follows it, Frado's fate as a perpetual victim once again inverts the plots of slave narratives and sentimental fiction, both of which reward the suffering of their protagonists with self-sufficiency and happiness.

Satire's endings must mete out justice. Just as Frado's fate reflects and punishes her passivity, Mrs. Bellmont becomes so "irritable" that even her family shuns her, and she finally dies "after an agony in death unspeakable." Mary also dies a painful death, Aunt Abby "enters heaven," and James dies from his lingering sickness. These judgments on the worth of each character enable Wilson to condemn the world she depicts without ever making explicit the alternative she considers acceptable. Such moralizing is unnecessary, however, because Wilson's satire paints such a bleak picture of northern antebellum society that her criticism of it cannot be missed. *Our Nig* was thus doomed to failure: a poor, black woman, Wilson had no right, in the eyes of the community in which she lived, to censure any aspect of white society. White contemporary readers almost certainly saw her as ungrateful and inpudent; black abolitionists who were dependent on the patronage of white allies probably viewed her book as one that could potentially alienate that support.

Wilson's satire targeted her for what may be the worst punishment any author, satirist or otherwise, can receive—her book was ignored. Her particular vulnerabilities of race, class, and gender made it possible to disregard what would otherwise have been hailed as a significant literary event: the publication of the first novel by a black woman in the United States. That novel's content, however, compelled both the white abolitionist movement, normally supportive of black literary endeavors, and the budding African-American male literary community to ignore this unpleasant text published by an outsider. The text's survival, due mainly to the efforts of Henry Louis Gates, forces us to reassess our notions about the literary capabilities of nineteenth-century African-Americans and reminds us that aspiring genres are capable of great creativity and innovation. Wilson's titular phrase, "Two-Story White House, North," intimates her innovations to us; her story is in fact two stories, a multi-layered text that combines aspects of two genres with a satire that undercuts many of the conventions of both. Our recognition of her abilities requires that we replace our image of the desperate, awkward writer with that of an intelligent woman who was capable of both conceiving and executing a groundbreaking work of literature.

Notes

[1] Henry Louis Gates, Jr., "Introduction," in *Our Nig; or, Sketches from the Life of a Free Black* (New York: Random House, 1983).

[2] Gates, xl.

[3] Gates, xii.

[4] Gates, xxiii.

[5] Gates, xlvi.

[6] Michael Seidel, *Satiric Inheritance: Rabelais to Sterne* (Princeton: Princeton University Press, 1979), 61.

[7] Gates, xxvii.

[8] Seidel, 25.

[9] Harriet E. Wilson, *Our Nig; or, Sketches from the Life of a Free Black* (New York: Random House, 1983), 3.

[10] Gates, xxxvii.

[11] Gates, xviii.

[12] Gates, xix-xx.

[13] Linda Hutcheon, *A Theory of Parody: The Teachings of Twentieth-Century Art Forms* (New York: Methuen, 1985), 6. Emphasis mine.

[14] Wilson, 127-28.

[15] Wilson, 5, 14, and 24.

[16] Gates, xxxvii.

[17] Wilson, 9, 11.

[18] Wilson, 12.

[19] Wayne C. Booth, *A Rhetoric of Irony* (Chicago: University of Chicago Press, 1974), 11.

[20] Wilson, 6.

[21] Wilson, 21.

[22] Wilson, 7-8.

[23] Gates, li.

[24] Rolfe Humphries, *The Satires of Juvenal* (Bloomington: Indiana University Press, 1958), 71.

[25] Wilson, 30.

26 Ronald Paulson, *The Fictions of Satire* (Baltimore: The Johns Hopkins Press, 1967), 9.

27 Wilson, 44.

28 Wilson, 25.

29 Wilson, 36.

30 Wilson, 70.

31 Wilson, 26.

32 Wilson, 129.

33 Wilson, 104.

34 Wilson, 105.

Cynthia J. Davis (essay date 1993)

SOURCE: "Speaking the Body's Pain: Harriet Wilson's *Our Nig*," *African American Review*, Vol. 27, No. 3, Fall, 1993, pp. 391-404.

[*In the* following *essay, Davis reads* Our Nig *as a challenge to the sexualization of the black body, contending that the novel humanizes blacks by testifying to their capacity for pain.*]

> "I know
> That care has iron crowns for many brows;
> That Calvaries are everywhere, whereon
> Virtue is crucified, and nails and spears
> Draw guiltless blood; that sorrow sits and
>   drinks
> At sweetest hearts, till all their life is dry;
> That gentle spirits on the rack of pain
> Grow faint or fierce, and pray and curse by
>   turns;
> That hell's temptations, clad in heavenly guise
> And armed with might, lie evermore in wait
> Along life's path, giving assault to all."
>
> —Holland (Epigraph to *Our Nig*)

With these images of blood, sorrow, suffering, and crucifixion, Harriet Wilson introduces and frames *Our Nig; or, Sketches from the Life of a Free Black*. Wilson's choice of this particular epigraph foregrounds a central preoccupation of *Our Nig*: pain. As Henry Louis Gates, Jr., concludes in his introduction to the novel, " . . . Mrs. Wilson was able to gain control over her materials more readily than her fellow black novelists of that decade precisely by adhering closely to the *painful* details of suffering that were part of her experience" (xxiii; emphasis added). Over the course

of Wilson's narrative, we watch in horror as Frado's once healthy body is tortured, maimed, beaten, and broken; before our eyes, Frado's body is transformed from her strongest asset to her greatest liability.

In Wilson's narrative it is pain, not sexuality, which explicitly determines Frado's physical experiences, which makes her body visible, and which marks this body as worthy of note. I say "not sexuality" because, at the time of *Our Nig*'s writing, not only was racial difference inscribed on the body through skin color, hair texture, and facial features; it was also policed and predicated upon an assumption of an essential sexual difference, especially between black and white women.[1] In order to make distinctions between persons who shared the same gender assignment, the dominant ideology, which defined the ideal white woman as pure and chaste, created the mythic "loose black woman" as her necessary correlate. Since the ideal white woman was virtually (and virtuously) bodiless, her black counterpart came to be defined as "body" and little else.[2] As Barbara Christian maintains, "If the southern lady was to be chaste, except for producing heirs, it would be necessary to have another woman who could become the object of men's sexual needs and desires" (190). This "necessary object" was the black woman.

In *Essentially Speaking*, Diana Fuss discusses the implications inherent in the sexualization of black bodies: "It is not merely that to be a 'Negro' . . . is to possess a particular genetic or biological make-up; it is, rather, to *be* the biological" (75). She reminds us that, in *Black Skin, White Masks*, Franz Fanon refers to this mythicized black other as "the biological-sexual-sensual-genital-nigger" (qtd. in Fuss 75). While both Fuss and Fanon emphasize that this "nigger" is a fabrication of the powerful, they also recognize that *its* power derives from a widespread cultural belief in the essential "truth" of this construction.

In light of this preoccupation with black sexuality, Harriet Wilson's *Our Nig* becomes all the more conspicuous in that, while its protagonist, Frado, is largely defined by and through her body, it is explicitly pain, not sexuality, which delineates her body; pain, not sexuality, which threatens to ruin her; and pain, not sexuality, which eventually compels her to speak out on her own behalf.[3]

Further, in contrast to her silence about sexualization, Wilson vividly represents Frado as raced and vehemently condemns the racism that induces whites to abuse black bodies.[4] It is precisely because the racializing of bodies goes unchallenged—is posited as a given—in *Our Nig* that I focus on sexualizing discourses in what follows. It is my belief that many nineteenth-century black American writers contested the imposition of a sexualized narrative on their bodies, while never contesting racializing narratives; that is, they accepted that they were innately black but vehemently denied that they were inherently (overly) sexual. As I read these nineteenth-century narratives, the "truth" of a raced bodily narrative was by and large accepted; it is the sexualized narrative that produced a number of reverse discourses, seeking to challenge the simplified, monological representation of black bodies as truly and innately lascivious.

I believe that we can read Wilson's description of the black body in pain as one such challenge, although, interestingly, it intervenes in the racist attempt to classify blacks as bestial not by taking on the sexualizing narrative but by testifying to a black subject's ability to feel pain and condemn torture. Of course, Wilson's narrative was not the only one to describe black (wo)men being beaten or experiencing pain. Slave narratives and antislavery tracts provide us with ample evidence of the cruel and unusual types of punishment blacks were made to suffer. In "American Slavery As It Is: Testimony of a Thousand Witnesses," Sarah M. Grimké recounts the sufferings of

> a handsome mulatto woman, about 18 or 20 years of age, whose independent spirit could not brook the degradation of slavery. . . . she had been repeatedly sent by her master and mistress to be whipped. . . . This had been done with such inhuman severity, as to lacerate her back in a most shocking manner; a finger could not be laid between the cuts. But the love of liberty was too strong to be annihilated by torture; and, as a last resort, she was whipped at several different times, and kept a close prisoner. A heavy iron collar, with three prongs projecting from it, was placed round her neck, and a strong and sound front tooth was extracted, to serve as a mark to describe her, in case of escape. (Lerner 18)

Surely, this is as dire an indictment of the cruelties inflicted in the South as is Wilson's testimonial to the cruelties inflicted in the North, "showing that slavery's shadows fall even there" (title-page). And yet, notice that this unnamed mulatto does not speak for herself; it is another (white) woman who feels compelled to describe this black woman's bodily pain. Grimké's testimony provides an excellent example of the way racial difference between women is reinscribed through descriptions of pain: here a disembodied white voice can speak for the abused black woman who cannot speak. As I go on to demonstrate, however, *Our Nig* uses descriptions of pain not to reinscribe racial difference but to transcend it.

Few were the black women who lived to tell of such beatings, and many of those that did survive were often silenced in the process. Solomon Northup's *Twelve Years a Slave* (1853) includes the story of "Patsey," "a joyous creature, a laughing, light-hearted girl, rejoicing in the mere sense of existence," despite the frequent beatings she received from a jealous mistress. One particularly severe whipping, however, left Patsey less than "what she had been. . . . The bounding vigor, the sprightly . . . spirit of her youth was gone. . . . She became *more silent* than she was, toiling all day in our midst, *not uttering a word*" (Lerner 50-51; emphasis added).

Our Nig differs from these narratives of physical suffering in that, rather than allowing pain to silence her, it is precisely her pain which compels Wilson/Frado to speak. Before delving further into how pain functions in *Our Nig,* however, I would like to take a brief detour through some of the images of black women in nineteenth-century writings in order to pave the way for an examination of *Our Nig,* its images, its possibilities.

Bodies . . .

In the period during which *Our Nig* was written, the focus—when and if black women's bodies were addressed in literature—was usually upon either their sexual exploitation or their sexual appetites. Whether the writer believed black women to be exploited objects or promiscuous sluts, the discourses describing black women were predominantly sexual(ized) ones.

In the white-authored and -authorized racist scripts, black women were cast as the seducers, (white) men rendered helpless in the face of their exaggerated animal sexuality. In *White Over Black,* Winthrop D. Jordan explains the logic behind this myth: "If she was *that* lascivious—well a man could scarcely be blamed for succumbing against overwhelming odds" (151). As Gerda Lerner contends,

> By assuming a different level of sexuality for all blacks than that of whites and mythifying their greater sexual potency, the black woman could be made to personify sexual freedom and abandon. A myth was created that all black women were eager for sexual exploits, voluntarily "loose" in their morals, and, therefore, deserved none of the consideration and respect granted to white women. Every black woman was, by definition, a slut according to this racist mythology. . . . (163)

Although it was primarily white men and their wives who constructed this myth as a justification for their own actions, "the bad black woman" (to use Lerner's phrase) made her way into the writings of blacks as well. In *Clotel,* William Wells Brown, writing for a predominantly white audience, aligns himself with the myth-makers by observing,

> Reader, when you take into consideration the fact, that amongst the slave population no safeguard is thrown around virtue, and no inducement held out to slave women to be chaste, you will not be surprised when we tell you that immorality and vice pervade the cities of the Southern States. . . . Indeed most of the slave women have no higher aspiration than that of becoming the finely-dressed mistress of some white man. (118-19)

As if to contradict his own thesis, Brown goes on to introduce us to his heroine, Clotel, who certainly would be considered exempt from such aspirations: Like Frances Harper's Iola Leroy, Brown's protagonist is that allegedly *rara avis*—a "pure and chaste" black woman.

But are Clotel and Iola merely exceptions that prove the rule? Is their virtue supposed to be read as all the more estimable when compared to their baser sisters? On the contrary, there is plenty of evidence to indicate that Brown miscalculated. For many black women, becoming a white man's mistress was their greatest fear, not, as Brown maintained, their greatest aspiration. When black women took up their pens to address the image of themselves as sexually promiscuous, their strategy was often to attack this construction from within: By testifying to the reality of their sexual exploitation, many black women wrote to counter the myth of their exaggerated sexuality. The essentially lascivious black body was, according to these writers, not born but made.

Gerda Lerner insists that "the sexual exploitation of black women by white men was so widespread as to be general. Some black women made the best of an inescapable necessity; others tried to strike an advantageous bargain" (46). The actions of Linda Brent, the protagonist of Harriet Jacobs's *Incidents in the Life of a Slave Girl,* could be regarded as an example of Lerner's first alternative. Instead of resigning herself to Dr. Flint's lecherous advances, Brent/Jacobs chooses to "make the best of an inescapable necessity," proclaiming that, if she must surrender to a (white) man, it will be one of her own choosing: "It seems less degrading to give one's self, than to submit to compulsion. There is something akin to freedom in having a lover who has no control over you, except that which he gains by kindness and attachment" (55). Thus, while Jacobs/Brent sees no way out of her prescribed role as a sexual being, by asserting herself as a sexual subject rather than an object, she gains some power *within* this "inescapable" sexualization.

There were some women, however, who opted for neither of Lerner's two responses—women who neither resigned themselves nor capitalized upon their own sexual exploitation but managed to defy the dominant sexualized construction of the black woman as well as the sexual advances of the very men responsible for this construction. There were women like Fannie, a slave of the Jennings of Nashville, who told her daughter, "'I'll kill you, gal, if you don't stand up for yourself. . . . Fight, and if you can't fight, kick; if you can't kick, then bite'" (Lerner 35). There was also the anonymous slave woman who "lost [her] place because [she] refused to let the madam's husband kiss" her (Lerner 155).

I make this point not to valorize these women's resistance over the course(s) settled upon by Brent/Jacobs and other women, many of whom, despite such protests, were still raped and raped repeatedly by white men. For whether she resisted or acquiesced, each of these women was forced at some point to see herself as (many) others saw her—as almost completely defined and bound by her always already (lasciviously) sexed body. One marker of the way in which ***Our Nig*** "signifies"[5] on dominant representations is the fact that, in light of the extreme sexualization of *black* women's bodies, it is a *white* woman whom Wilson represents as sexual—Frado's mother Mag, but not Frado herself. Through this twist, Wilson challenges the widespread racist notion that black women, and only black women, were innately promiscuous.

. . . And Souls

Accused of an essential lasciviousness, there were a few black women writers in the nineteenth century who opted not to defend themselves by merely reversing the genders of seducer and seduced. Instead, these writers chose to dispel the myth of "the bad black woman" by substituting another image (myth?) of the black woman in its place: Many women (both black and white) saw an escape from their physical sufferings on this earth by (re)defining and (re)presenting themselves not as physical but as spiritual beings, not as bodies but as souls.

Certainly Brown's Clotel typifies this (re)definition, but she is by no means the only fictional prototype of the spiritual black woman. Ann Plato, a young schoolteacher from Hartford, Connecticut, reassures her readers in her poem "Advice to Young Ladies" (1841) that

> Religion is most needful for
> To make in us a friend.
> At thirteen years I found a hope,
> and did embrace the Lord;
> And since, I've found a blessing great,
> Within his holy word. (qtd. in
>   Shockley 29)

While Plato uses the somewhat sexual metaphor of "embrace" in association with black women, here the embrace is a spiritual one—the Lord's—quite different from the more physical and more fleeting embrace of an earthly master.

In "The Two Offers," the first known short story to be published by an African-American woman, Frances Harper introduces us to the saintly Janette Alston, who closely resembles her fictional and spiritual sister, Harper's famed Iola Leroy. Not satisfied with simply chronicling Janette's pious life and sacrifices as exemplary, Harper makes her revisionist aims explicit by interrupting her narrative to preach to/about her ideal black woman:

> But woman—the true woman—if you would render her happy, it needs more than the mere development of her affectional nature. . . . The true aim of female education should be, not a development of one or two, but all the faculties of the human soul, because no perfect womanhood is developed by imperfect culture. (qtd. in Shockley 65)

Here Harper redefines the "true (black) woman" not as perpetually unfulfilled body but as temporarily unfulfilled soul. Her definition of the perfect black woman as desiring soul strongly contradicts the trope of the black woman as desiring body, but in order to put forth this definition, Harper must elide the lived reality of many black women's physical sense of themselves as bodies.

In addition to countering the dominant image of the profoundly sexual black woman, this spiritual redefinition occasioned other consequences for the women who embraced it: For many black women, finding religion was synonymous with finding a voice. Abused, degraded, discriminated against, silenced, it was only *after* they discovered that all were one in Christ that these women dared to speak up and out. When they did speak, however, it was usually not to rehash oppressive pasts but to foretell glorious futures, not to give voice to their wounded bodies but to harken to the summons of their uplifted souls. Thus Maria Stewart, the first black women known to have spoken in public in the U.S., introduced an 1833 lecture in Boston with the following preamble:

> On my arrival here, not finding scarce an individual who felt interested in these subjects, . . . my soul became fired with a holy zeal for your cause; every nerve and muscle in me was engaged in your behalf. I felt that I had a great work to perform, and was in haste to make a profession of my faith in Christ that I might be about my Father's business. Soon after I made this profession the Spirit of God came before me, and I spake before many. When going home, reflecting on what I had said, I felt ashamed, and knew not where I should hide myself. A something said within my breast, "press forward, I will be with thee."

And my heart made this reply: "Lord, if thou wilt be with me, then will I speak for thee so long as I live." (Lerner 563-64)

Maria Stewart claims that she is able to speak only with God's help and with God's voice. Of course, given societal strictures against women—let alone black women—speaking in public, she may have felt it necessary to attribute her gumption to God's inspiration. And yet, for my purposes here, it is still worth noting that, upon finding her voice, it is not of herself but of God and *His* doings that she speaks.

In striking contrast to women like Maria Stewart, Harriet Wilson and her Frado are "saved" not through religion but through speech itself. By speaking up, Frado in effect saves her own life, and Wilson ultimately achieves a certain immortality. Both protagonist and author speak of themselves and their own agony—not of God and His glory. What's more, rather than negate the image of the black woman as sexual animal with an image of the black woman as spiritual aesthete, Frado refuses to supplant her definition of herself as a body in pain with the more conventional one of a soul in glory.[6]

Perhaps Wilson was aware that the odds of a black woman escaping bodily oppression through spirituality were indeed slim: Not all black women were as fortunate as Janette Alston or Maria Stewart. For instance, in *In Search of Our Mother's Gardens,* Alice Walker describes Jean Toomer's encounter with

> black women whose spirituality was so intense, so deep, so *unconscious,* they were themselves unaware of the richness they held. They stumbled blindly through their lives: creatures so abused and mutilated in body, so dimmed and confused by pain, that they considered themselves unworthy even of hope. In the selfless abstractions their bodies became to the men who used them, they became more than "sexual objects," more even than mere women: they became "Saints." Instead of being perceived as whole persons, their bodies became shrines: what was thought to be their minds became temples suitable for worship. These crazy Saints stared out at the world, wildly, like lunatics— or quietly, like suicides; and the "God" that was in their gaze was as mute as a great stone. (231-32)

Rather than achieve sainthood by transcending the flesh, Toomer's "Saints," tragically, get sainthood bestowed upon them as a direct result of the most severe bodily suffering. What's more, although others might have seen in these women a certain perverse yet "intense spirituality," the women themselves neither heard God's voice nor used their own.

As if heeding the warning embodied in these women, Wilson allows freedom and reward to come not through praying for one's soul to rise in the next world, but through speaking up on behalf of one's embodied self, in all its complex materiality, in this world.[7]

Our Nig

In light of these other nineteenth-century black women's attempts to either defuse or deny the black woman's sexualized body, *Our Nig*'s detailed descriptions of the physical body appear all the more striking. What we are forced to witness throughout Wilson's tale (even more, perhaps, than we might wish) is a body whose primary and delineating experience is not sexuality, but pain. Frado's dominant bodily experience is of pain; the dominant motif in *Our Nig* not rape but torture. Pain defines both voice and body, the speaker and the spoken.

When we first begin reading *Our Nig,* it is difficult to envision how pain will ever figure as anything but a brutally silencing force. From the moment Frado enters the Bellmont's "Two-Story White House, North," we are confronted with scene after scene depicting her brutal torture at the hands of Mrs. Bellmont. As Wilson informs us,

> . . . Mrs. Bellmont felt that [Frado's] time and person belonged solely to her. . . . What an opportunity to indulge her vixen nature! No matter what occurred to ruffle her, or from what source provocation came, real or fancied, a few blows on Nig seemed to relieve her of a portion of her ill-will. (41)

Frado is repeatedly beaten (34-35, 110), kicked (43-44), whipped with the ubiquitous rawhide (30, 77, 101), forced to go shoeless even after the frost has set in (66), and made to eat and work standing, even when faint with illness (29, 81-82). A wedge of wood is twice inserted between Frado's teeth, causing "her face [to become] swollen, and full of pain" (36, 93). Again and again in *Our Nig,* we are forced to read about and encouraged to empathize with experiences like the following:

> Angry that [Frado] should venture a reply to her command, [Mrs. Bellmont] suddenly inflicted a blow which lay the tottering girl prostrate on the floor. Excited by so much indulgence of a dangerous passion, she seemed left to unrestrained malice; and snatching a towel, stuffed the mouth of the sufferer, and beat her cruelly.
>
> Frado hoped she would end her misery by whipping her to death. (82)

This passage and others like it in *Our Nig,* as many will have noted, bear chilling similarities to classic depictions of rape. As such they speak, if to nothing

else, to the close parallels between rape and beatings in the lives of black women. Both are forms of violence—both attempts to exert control, to assert dominance over the black woman's body by marking that body as the master's (rapist's, torturer's) personal property to do with as s/he will. We might even want to read such brutalizing scenes as further evidence for the hypothesis that Wilson employs pain in her narrative as a metonym for sexual exploitation. Through these passages, she is able to talk about black women's frequent bodily oppression while displacing the reductive notion of black women's bodily experiences as always and only sexual.

But why does Wilson feel compelled to revisit these painful experiences, to relive them through a narrative which constantly bombards us with image after image of her own pain? If, as Wilson claims in her preface, it is true that she does not "divulge every transaction in [her] own life," why divulge these pain-filled ones? If she has "purposely omitted what would most provoke shame in our good anti-slavery friends at home" (rape?), what emotion does she hope to provoke by *not* omitting her experiences of torture?

It would, of course, be naïve to suggest that Wilson consciously intended to substitute a body in pain for a sexualized body, just as it would be misguided to assume that pain and sexuality form some sort of disjunctive binary. But since it is specifically pain and not sexuality through which Frado's body becomes present to us in *Our Nig,* it is worth exploring the possible signifying *effects* of a body in pain and how it might differ from a sexualized body. If Wilson does indeed omit the sexual but retain the painful, what does a pain-filled presence open up that a sexualized body might close down?

A case could surely be made that the sexualized body— overdetermined, reified, essentialized, always already gendered (female), and hence often othered ("That's not *my* body!")—might have evoked less empathy in a reader, more of a tendency to "blame the victim" than the rarely spoken, potentially universalizable, contingent and temporal body in pain. A body experiencing pain might indeed engender a more responsive audience, not only because we all (across genders, races, classes, ages, etc.) might feasibly identify with such an experience but also, crucially, because we each could feel capable of doing something to ease that pain.

Pain, unlike sexuality, is rarely essentialized as atemporal and innate to the body. Instead, it is more frequently conceived as having an external source, a clear beginning and, importantly, a possible end.[8] Although the veritable absence, at least until recently, of any reader response to *Our Nig* makes this case difficult to dis/ prove, we can at least surmise that the prevalence of the sexually (over)determined black body led many writers to avoid writing/speaking of bodies (any body) at all in their writings. By speaking the black female body as it was rarely spoken, by speaking of her own bodily pain, Wilson manages to address black women's experience of themselves as bodies without risking perpetuating the definition of black women as sexualized body and nothing else.

It is my conviction, then, that Wilson's "body in pain" should not be read as oppositional to the sexualized black body but instead as metonymically displaced from yet still connected to it. *Our Nig* signifies on that overdetermined sexualized body, displacing its more negative implications while still retaining the body as experiential referent and strategic vehicle. The pain-filled body in *Our Nig,* with its potentially universal sympathetic appeal, provides a sort of insurance that cries for help on its behalf have a better chance of being heard, of being answered.

But does this mean that pain is somehow easier, even less painful, to articulate than is sexual exploitation? A brief digression should shed further light on the nexus between pain and language.

Deborah McDowell has astutely noted the scant critical attention afforded the whipping scenes in Frederick Douglass's autobiographical narratives. In these passages, Douglass struggles to express what it feels like to be a helpless witness of another's (usually a woman's) pain. For instance, having stood by as a slave woman named Esther was lashed repeatedly by her master, Douglass exclaims:

> The whole scene, with all its attendants, was revolting and shocking, to the last degree; and when the motives of this brutal castigation are considered, *language has no power to convey a just sense of its awful criminality.* . . . From my heart I pitied her, and—child though I was—the outrage kindled in me a feeling far from peaceful; *but I was hushed, terrified, stunned, and could do nothing, as the fate of Esther might be mine next.* (88; emphasis added)

In the face of this brutality, both Douglass and language are stripped of power. Moreover, for Douglass, lack of language is closely related to lack of action: He "was hushed . . . and could do nothing." Watching a black woman suffer, it would seem, leads to impotency in both word and deed.

In *The Body in Pain,* Elaine Scarry underscores the antithetical nature of pain and language.[9] She claims that "resistance to language" is essential to pain: "Intense pain is . . . language-destroying: as the content of one's world disintegrates, so the content of one's language disintegrates; as the self disintegrates, so that which would express and project the self is robbed of

its source and subject" (35). Similarly, Douglass suggests pain's language-destroying potential; but he claims that the sufferer is not the only one deprived of (her) voice. As McDowell argues, in Douglass's narrative, slave women operate as mute physical bodies, while black men are cast as impotent onlookers, condemned to watch abuse in silence for fear that they will be the next in line.

And yet, to put it rather crudely, "impotency" here does not preclude arousal (even orgasm?). For in addition to his powerlessness, McDowell points to the pleasure Douglass derives as "both witness [to] and participant" in those whipping scenarios. She contends that the erotic nature of such whippings, while offending Douglass morally, simultaneously offers up to him the pornographic pleasures of the voyeur. Through the very act of looking, Douglass is able to derive not only pleasure but power from his identification with the (over)seer.

McDowell's account of how narrating/observing another's torture can result in a complex blend of impotence and erotic pleasure returns us to the question of what Wilson herself achieves by recounting her persona's sufferings.[10] Is "our nig," as both seer and seen, narrator and narrated, a masochist, deriving pleasure from her narrative compulsion to repeat her own pain? As observer/narrator of her own experience under the lash, does Wilson, as did Douglass, find herself impotent? And what about the reader's role as onlooker: Do we, as voyeurs, "get off" on Frado's pain? And/or are we, like Douglass's childhood self, left powerless, too afraid to get involved?

If Douglass gains a certain power through the pleasure of narrating/watching such scenarios, I want to argue that, if Wilson does gain any pleasure in her narrative, it comes from the power she attains through the very act of narrating.[11] That is to say, by documenting, by testifying again and again to her pain, Wilson effectively takes control of that pain, wresting power from her torturer and appropriating it for herself—this from a woman who, after meeting her future husband, does not ask him of his enslavement, for " . . . she felt that, like her own oppression, it was painful to disturb oftener than was needful" (127). In writing *Our Nig,* Wilson was willing to disturb this pain because it was "needful"; and this time around, she uses pain rather than allowing it to use her.

In order for "our nig" to use her pain effectively, however, she must first claim the right to use her voice, by no means an easy task. For it was not only through their bodies that black women (and men) were oppressed and "othered." If language does indeed equal power, it was the power of language—of the written and ("properly") spoken word—that was kept from blacks in order to keep them illiterate, silent, impotent. Pain and black women's bodies can be read, in a way, as strangely similar: Both have been framed as the converse of language (and, consequently, of power). While one's own pain, as Scarry maintains, is nearly impossible to articulate, black women's bodies came to symbolize the spoken, the voiced without a voice (remember Grimké's testimony).

As a pain-filled black woman's body could appear the quintessence of mute powerlessness, we might never expect a suffering black woman to speak of her own experience as a body in pain. The fact that a black woman like Wilson does manage to speak of her own pain, then, means that she has quite literally mapped out uncharted territory, in which both pain and the black female body are redefined via powerful language as capable of both power and language. Language in *Our Nig* is no longer antithetical to pain; instead, language serves to make pain and even "our nig" herself intelligible.

By speaking the unspeakable, by narrating her pain, her body, her body's pain, "our nig" transforms herself from mute, pain-filled object to speaking, pain-filled subject. Scarry argues that pain is essentially objectless: While we fear snakes, hunger for food, thirst for water, etc., pain is the one state that does not require an object (5). However, pain does have a *subject*. By defining herself as the subject in/of pain, Wilson/Frado assumes the position of authoritative speaking subject. As Gates contends, " . . . Frado's awakened speaking voice signifies her consciousness of herself as a subject. With the act of speaking alone, Frado assumes a large measure of control over the choices she can possibly make each day" ("Introduction," liv).

Just as the act of narration in *Our Nig* ultimately functions to subvert the muting effects of pain, it also functions to undermine the dehumanizing effects of torture. In order to torture another human being, the torturer must first redefine that other being as "other," as less than human, even as beast. What's more, it is generally easier to "other" the already silent (silenced). The assumption is that, because they don't speak, they can't think or feel. When Mrs. Bellmont scoffs," . . . you know, these niggers are just like black snakes; you *can't* kill them" (88), we see this pernicious logic in action: Mrs. Bellmont justifies her own *inhuman* actions by declaring "our nig" *subhuman.*

One could say, then, that the project of *Our Nig* is essentially a humanist one, designed to clear a space in which "our nig" can assert her essential humanity. For when she does eventually speak, she turns torture's human-beast dichotomy on its head. By speaking, she effectively protests Mrs. Bellmont's definition of her as beast and asserts instead—though protesting torture, not sexualization—that she is a thinking, feeling *hu-*

man being, and that it is the white woman who, because of her cruel actions, is inhuman(e).

If, through an inversion of the power structure, the "beast" becomes "human," Mrs. Bellmont herself becomes "the beast," tortured through narration. While Wilson is certainly not so relentless and sadistic a torturer as Mrs. Bellmont had been, we do sense a certain vindictive pleasure in her ability to wound her former mistress with words. As Minrose Gwin argues, narratives like *Our Nig* convey the black woman writer's

> impulse to control and dominate, in language, those who controlled and dominated her. . . . At long last the slave woman controls the plantation mistress, and the vehicle of that domination, language, becomes infinitely more powerful and more resonant than the lash or the chain could ever be. (48)

By narrating their fictional personae's experience of pain, writers like Wilson transform themselves from powerless objects to potentially powerful subjects. The pen for these writers may not really be mightier than the sword, but it does offer its own brand of power, of pleasure.

Scarry argues that during torture " . . . the body is its pain, a shrill sentience that hurts and is hugely alarmed by its hurt; and the body is its scars, thick and forgetful, unmindful of its hurt, unmindful of anything, mute and insensate" (31). For at least the first two-thirds of the narrative, Scarry's description of muteness aptly summarizes Frado's relation to her own body, a body which speaks loudly in its muteness, but only of its muteness in the face of such agonizing pain. However, at a crucial moment in the text, Frado decides that she will no longer allow pain to silence her. Instead of hating her flesh as the enemy, then, Frado ultimately speaks up on behalf of her physical self: " 'Stop!' shouted Frado, 'strike me, and I'll never work a mite more for you'; and throwing down what she had gathered, stood like one who feels the stirring of free and independent thoughts" (105). "Our nig's" rebellious speech works here not only to articulate but to ease her pain. It may not erase her wounds, but it is a first step toward healing, towards a (talking) cure.

When Frado "talks back" to Mrs. Bellmont, she is in effect (re)constructing herself, moving beyond Scarry's description of the "mute and insensate" body which is only acted upon to her description of the speaking body which acts. As Scarry contends, healing begins when the torture victim re(dis)covers his or her voice:" . . . the voice becomes a final source of self-extension; so long as one is speaking, the self extends out beyond the boundaries of the body, occupies a space much larger than the body" (33). Unlike Ralph Ellison's "invisible man," represented as all voice and no body, or

Richard Wright's Bigger, a body which is nonetheless voiceless and powerless,[12] Wilson's protagonist represents the presence of both body and voice simultaneously. The body in pain becomes more-than-body, more-than-pain by finding a voice at last.

In addition, in contrast to Mary Stewart and other black women who discovered their voices concomitant with their discovery of religion, when Frado speaks it is self- and not God-inspired. Realizing that it might be possible for Mrs. Bellmont to go to heaven, Frado ultimately resolves "to give over all thought of the future world, and strove daily to put her anxiety far from her" (104). Significantly, it is in the very next paragraph that Frado "talks back" to Mrs. Bellmont: Unlike Mary Stewart, it is only after renouncing, not entertaining, thoughts of heaven that Frado gains her voice. And when she does, she realizes that she must not look to higher powers for aid but must speak for and of herself.

This pivotal instance of self-defense within the text may also serve as representative of Wilson's corresponding decision at the narrative level to give voice to her pain. Just as, in this textual moment, Frado defends herself in order to ward off future pain, by writing her story Wilson speaks up for herself in hopes of receiving "patronage" from her "colored brethren," sustenance which could help ease not only her own but her son's pain.

As Scarry speculates, "The human being who creates on behalf of the pain originating in her own body may remake herself to be one who creates on behalf of the pain originating in another's body" (324). Although *Our Nig* is the story of her own pain, it might never have been told had not another's pain—her son's—rendered it necessary. Wilson, through Frado, describes her own unbearable pain and isolation in order to reach out to a community on behalf of another. In her self-translation from torture's object to pain's subject, she becomes a subject whose intention in expressing her pain is to share it with others, to compel others to respond to her pain, to find their *own* voices in order to respond. She leaves it to her audience to decide whether, like Wilson, they, too, will speak and act, or whether, like Douglass, they will remain mute and impotent in the fact of such manifest suffering.

In thus predicating itself upon reader response, *Our Nig* remains an ultimately open-ended text. In his introduction, Gates claims that

> *Our Nig*'s tale ends ambiguously, if it ends at all. . . . the protagonist's status remains indeterminate, precisely because she has placed the conclusion of her "story," the burden of closure, upon her readers, who must purchase her book if the author-protagonist is to become self-sufficient. (xlvii)

In Rachel Blau DuPlessis's sense, then, Wilson "writes beyond the ending" of her novel, postponing closure pending help from her audience for her ailing son.

But if this help came, it came too late. George Wilson died, and the novel all but faded into obscurity until Gates published the 1983 edition. However, as Gates points out, it is George's death which actually rescues Wilson from anonymity and restores his mother to life:

> Ironically, George's death certificate helped to rescue his mother from literary oblivion. His mother wrote a sentimental novel, of all things, so that she might become self-sufficient and regain the right to care for her only son; six months later, her son died of that standard disease, "fever"; the *record* of his death, *alone,* proved sufficient to demonstrate his mother's racial identity and authorship of *Our Nig.* (xiii)

As I have argued, Gates's resurrection of *Our Nig* from its untimely grave has had significant signifying consequences. To my mind, *Our Nig* provides an alternative to representations of nineteenth-century Afro-American women as either disembodied saints or wanton bodies. One might say, then, as Barbara Christian does of Frances Ellen Watkins Harper's *Iola Leroy,* that *Our Nig* is "an important novel . . . because it so clearly delineates the relationship between the images of black women held at large in society and the novelist's struggle to refute these images" (183). But, unlike Harper's, Wilson's struggle to refute dominant images of the black woman does not involve an erasure of black women's bodies and bodily experiences. Instead, in *Our Nig,* Frado's body serves as both her prison and her escape, the source of both her pain and her inspiration. Pain not only motivates Wilson to write her story, it *is* her story. Wilson finds her voice in her pain, in her ability to survive torture and her desire to see the suffering of yet another body (her son's) come to an end.

As Gates has clearly documented, for over 100 years this audience was not only less then heartfelt, it was virtually nonexistent: *Our Nig* and its author have long been conspicuously absent from the pages of literary history. Contemporary criticism has noted the lack of response to *Our Nig,* its ultimate "failure" to be heard, claiming the text and its history as paradigmatic of a larger societal silence (silencing) of black women's lives and writings. Such readings are correct in underscoring that, if any flaw exists, it is not in *Our Nig* itself. The flaw, I believe, exists in a cultural inability or unwillingness to listen, in the way we decide certain texts and certain topics are more deserving of a hearing than others. For ultimately, if Wilson's narrative was not heard, it was most certainly *not* because she did not speak.

Notes

[1] Here the operating, differentiating dichotomy is not *homo-* versus *hetero-,* but *human* versus *bestial.*

[2] Black women's bodies were valued for production (labor) and reproduction (as suppliers of labor), not just as sexual objects, a valuing Wilson discusses in representing Frado's servitude. But since Wilson resembles other writers in addressing Frado's "value" as both worker and mother, yet is unusually silent when it comes to representing her protagonist in explicitly sexual(ized) terms, I have chosen to narrow my focus to the sexual construction of black women's bodies in order to tease out the significance of Wilson's silence— or, rather, her decision to speak the body elsewise.

[3] Of course, the sexual life of black women was by no means devoid of pain; in many cases, sex and pain were coextensive, as exemplified in accounts of rape and sex-related beatings. Although I am *not* trying to set up a binary in which sex and pain act as opposing terms, it intrigues me that the pain Frado suffers in *Our Nig* is not explicitly related to sexuality; instead, it seems she is tortured solely for the sadistic (but arguably still tinged with sexual) pleasure Mrs. Bellmont derives from the act of torture. More importantly, we are only afforded glimpses of Frado's body when it is being tortured.

[4] In fact, Frado is a mulatto, the daughter of a black father and white mother. It is not her "white blood," however, upon which Frado bases her appeals for better treatment; instead, she bases them on the premise that no human being, regardless of color, should be made to suffer what she has suffered.

[5] See Henry Louis Gates, Jr., "Figures of Signification," in his *The Signifying Monkey,* for further discussion of "Signifyin(g)" as a frequently employed trope in Afro-American discourse.

[6] It is true that Frado does come near to a "conversion" at one point in the narrative, and that the letters appended to the text suggest that Wilson herself was a "good Christian." However, religious conversion is not *essential* to Frado/Wilson's "recovery," nor is it even instrumental in her/their "salvation." Indeed, recovery and salvation are "signified" upon and secularized in *Our Nig.*

[7] Despite Wilson's attempt to speak of and through her body, however, even the friends who write letters on Wilson's behalf misread her mission and reinscribe it in sentimental, religious terms. For instance, after reframing *Our Nig* as a sentimental novel and tragic romance, "Allida" pens a poem to offer Wilson solace. In this poem, God addresses Wilson, saying, "What though thy wounded bosom bleed, / Pierced by affliction's dart; / Do I not all thy sorrows heed, / And bear thee on my heart?" *Our Nig* could be read as an emphatic "no" to Allida's poetic question. The narrative argues that the bleeding and wounded bosom cannot be healed by God's presence alone. Wilson demands help in this world, not just in the next.

[8] This is especially true of the kind of pain experienced and described by Wilson/Frado.

[9] While I have found Scarry's work on pain and language extremely helpful in my struggle to understand the role of pain in Wilson's narrative, I did not feel I could fairly apply her analysis of torture to *Our Nig* directly, for *The Body in Pain* represents the torture of raceless male bodies as generic and generalizable to every body's experience under torture, regardless of race, class, gender, generational (etc.) differences across those bodies.

[10] Of course, it is her protagonist, Frado, that undergoes the torture in *Our Nig,* not Wilson herself. In one sense, inventing this surrogate may have helped distance Wilson from her own experience, perhaps making the telling of her own abuse somewhat easier; and yet, *Our Nig* is authored by "our nig," and the occasional slips from "she" to "I," "her" to "my" within the text suggest that the narrative is more an autobiography than a fictional account. I will be using the term *our nig* to refer to this blurred persona in what follows.

[11] Douglass, too, attains power through this act, but in regard to the incident just described, the power he attains feels much more like the power of the voyeur than does Wilson's.

[12] See Gates, "Figures of Signification," for a more detailed analysis of how the body figures in Ellison's and Wright's discourse.

Works Cited

Brown, William Wells. *Clotel; or, The President's Daughter. Three Classic African-American Novels.* Ed. William L. Andrews. New York: Mentor, 1990. 71-283.

Christian, Barbara. "Shadows Uplifted." *Feminist Criticism and Social Change.* Ed. Judith Newton and Deborah Rosenfelt. London: Methuen, 1985. 181-215.

Douglass, Frederick. *My Bondage and My Freedom.* Ed. William L. Andrews. Urbana: U of Illinois P, 1987.

DuPlessis, Rachel Blau. *Writing Beyond the Ending: Narrative Strategies of Twentieth-Century Women Writers.* Bloomington: Indiana UP, 1985.

Felman, Shoshona. "Woman and Madness: The Critical Phallacy." *Diacritics* 5 (1975): 2-10.

Fuss, Diana. *Essentially Speaking.* London: Routledge, 1989.

Jacobs, Harriet. *Incidents in the Life of a Slave Girl.* Ed. Jean Fagan Yellin. Cambridge: Harvard UP, 1987.

Jordan, Winthrop D. *White Over Black.* Chapel Hill: U of North Carolina P, 1968.

Gates, Henry Louis, Jr. "Introduction." Wilson xi-iv.

———. *The Signifying Monkey: A Theory of Afro-American Literary Criticism.* New York: Oxford UP, 1988.

Genovese, Eugene D. *Roll, Jordan, Roll: The World the Slaves Made.* Rev. ed. New York: Vintage, 1974.

Gwin, Minrose C. "Green-eyed Monsters of the Slavocracy: Jealous Mistresses in Two Slave Narratives." *Conjuring: Black Women, Fiction, and Literary Tradition.* Ed. Marjorie Pryse and Hortense J. Spillers. Bloomington: Indiana UP, 1985. 39-52.

Lerner, Gerda, ed. *Black Women in White America: A Documentary History.* New York: Pantheon, 1972.

McDowell, Deborah. "In the First Place: Making Frederick Douglass and the African-American Narrative Tradition." Lecture, Duke U, 20 Apr. 1990.

Scarry, Elaine. *The Body in Pain.* New York: Oxford UP, 1985.

Shockley, Ann Allen, ed. *Afro-American Women Writers, 1746-1933.* New York: Meridian, 1988.

Walker, Alice. *In Search of Our Mothers' Gardens: Womanist Prose.* San Diego: Harcourt, 1983.

Wilson, Harriet. *Our Nig; or, Sketches from the Life of A Free Black.* New York: Vintage, 1983.

John Ernest (essay date 1994)

SOURCE: "Economies of Identity: Harriet E. Wilson's *Our Nig,*" *PMLA,* Vol. 109, No. 3, May, 1994, pp. 424-38.

[*In this essay, Ernest explores the paradox of Wilson's attempt to seek patronage from her readers: To be successful, such an effort would depend on the good will of Northern white readers, yet her story exposes Northern racism and criticizes abolitionists, thereby alienating the very audience she needed to cultivate.*]

Over one hundred years after Harriet E. Wilson's ***Our Nig; or, Sketches from the Life of a Free Black*** (1859) appeared and disappeared, the book can be bought and read again.[1] Purchasers of the 1983 reprinting fulfill, belatedly, the terms of the work's existence. For inextricably bound to Wilson's commentary on gender, class, and race in the nineteenth-century northern states is her insistence on the book's status as a product for consumption in the marketplace. As Allida testifies in the appendix, Wilson, having met with some success in selling a formula "for restoring gray hair to its former color," was forced by failing health to "resort to another method of procuring her bread—that of writing an Autobiography" (137). Wilson herself, in the preface, calls the book an "experiment which shall aid me in maintaining myself and child without extinguishing this feeble life" (3).[2]

An appeal for patronage was characteristic of many African American publications in the nineteenth century, but Wilson's stands out as something of an anomaly. In a study of pre-1860 African American autobiographies, William L. Andrews notes that "more than a few slave autobiographies were published as fund-raisers for their narrators, and most were labeled so." But Andrews says as well that "in a society as hostile to blacks as the North was in the 1840s [and later], an ex-slave [or, I would add, a northern "free" black] who hoped for a good sale of his narrative was not likely to embarrass his white sponsors or contradict his audience's expectations" by presenting the work's subject "in an unsanctioned manner" (108-09). As Henry Louis Gates, Jr., speculates, ***Our Nig*** might well have been ignored because it offers an aggressively unsanctioned story that not only focuses on northern racism but also criticizes abolitionists (*Figures* 137).

A blend of autobiography and fiction, ***Our Nig*** tells the story of Frado, the child of a mixed-race marriage. The narrative begins with Mag Smith, a white woman who is the victim of an upper-class seducer. As the news of her seduction spreads, Mag becomes increasingly desperate, and she eventually crosses racial lines to marry "a kind-hearted African," Jim (9). After Jim dies, Mag lives with another black man, Seth Shipley; and when they can no longer care for the children she had with Jim, Mag and Seth abandon one, Frado, at the home of a white New Hampshire family, the Bellmonts, who take her in and claim her as "our nig," a domestic servant. Abused, primarily by Mrs. Bellmont and her daughter Mary, befriended mainly by a dog, Fido, Frado leaves the family at the end of her term of service.[3] In the closing chapter, Frado's problems are augmented by her troubled marriage to a black sailor who claims to be a fugitive slave and who eventually dies of yellow fever in New Orleans, leaving her with a child. After problems with both health and employment, Frado draws from the limited education she received during her term with the Bellmonts—an education continued under the tutelage of "a plain, poor, simple woman, who could see merit beneath a dark skin" (124). In the final chapter, as Gates notes, *Our Nig*'s third-person narrator shifts to the first person as "the protagonist, the author, and the novel's narrator all merge explicitly into one voice to launch the text's advertisement for itself" (Introduction xlvii).

Depicting the life of a "free" black woman, showing that "slavery's shadows fall" even in the North (title p.), and covering the experiences not only of the black laboring class but also of the white laboring and lower middle classes, Wilson conflates in a single ethical study racial, gender, and economic enslavement. The book's status as product for sale is significant, for Wilson counters the proslavery accounts of the evils of capitalism with an appeal for salvation by way of the marketplace. Indeed, Wilson reminds her readers that judgment on Frado's life is solely the province of God, and she frames her call for patronage as a "demand" for "sympathy and aid" (130), by extending which black and white readers alike can endorse and enact a system capable of converting into human transactions what Martin R. Delany would later call "God's economy" (26). In other words, Wilson's self-advertisements are directed not merely toward her own elevation from poverty but also toward a program of mutual elevation in a marketplace that is deconstructed and reenvisioned in the narrative. Wilson does not, however, propose the possibility of harmony and trust between blacks and whites in the United States. Rather, she pictures a system that recognizes and *capitalizes* on racial tensions and mutual distrust, a new system of exchange and balanced conflict—a new economy of identity— that readers support by purchasing the book and participate in by reading it.

"Silent Sympathy" and Cultural Understanding

To speak of this project raises questions about Wilson's intended audience, and they can be answered only with speculations. The subject is more complicated than her opening appeal to her "colored brethren" suggests (3). In a painstaking reconstruction of Wilson's biography, Barbara A. White identifies the "predicament" Wilson faced as she prepared to publish *Our Nig:* "although it was necessary to receive the support of at least some 'good antislavery friends' to sell her narrative, she could not distribute it very widely without alerting" those good antislavery friends who had caused many of her misfortunes. Wilson must have known that her story "could be received only by a small group, her 'colored brethren'" (40, 45).[4] Similarly, Hazel Carby asserts that "Wilson sought her patronage not from a white Northern audience but from her 'colored brethren.' Wilson attempted to gain authority for her public voice through a narrative that shared its experience with a black community which she addressed as if it were autonomous from the white community in which it was situated" (43).[5]

Certainly Wilson's "direct appeal to the black community marginalized a white readership" (Carby 44), but I think that her experience had taught her well that the black community was not autonomous from the white. Her task was to transform their dominant-subordinate relation to mutual dependence. The full title of the work itself signals Wilson's awareness of her white audience, for her "colored brethren" would need no reminders that "slavery's shadows fall" even in the North. Moreover, any marginalization of the white readership in the preface is at least complicated by Wilson's handling of the first chapter, "Mag Smith, My Mother." Presenting Frado's story as the sequel of a tale of love and seduction and postponing the identification of Mag Smith as white, Wilson undermines any assumption that the relationship between narrator and reader can be defined according to the conventions of racial affiliation. Both in the preface and throughout the narrative, Wilson signals her awareness that this text might be read and misread by those anxious to defend slavery (by comparing the conditions of southern slaves and northern blacks) and to dismiss African Americans (by defining them as slaves, in effect, to their "inferior" racial features).[6]

Wilson's concern, I believe, is not to reach an identifiable community of "colored brethren" but rather to help create a reconfigured community of understanding. One can say of Wilson what Andrews says of Henry Bibb, that he "dismisses the fictive reader as unreasonable and implicitly calls for a reader who can interpret his actions according to the standards that emerge dramatically and pragmatically in the narrative itself." As Andrews argues, "[T]he act of reading autobiographies like Bibb's involves the reader in a decision about his own identity and his own position vis-à-vis the black and white categories of any socio-moral system of thought" (30). Similarly, Wilson appeals to an understanding "colored" by the reading of *Our Nig,* generated by a confrontation with complex relations that have been reduced to a simplistic dichotomy of white and black supported only by an ever more contrived and corrupt ideological system. The legal and social codification of cultural simplifications is always complex, and *Our Nig*— which starts with an appeal to colored brethren and then begins again with a story of a white woman— leads its readers to recognize that complexity.

By tracing Frado's identity to her white mother's experiences, Wilson establishes Frado as a product of northern United States culture. That is, Mag Smith's story highlights structures of cultural identity that later confine Frado even more tightly than they did her mother. As Mag successively crosses what one might call the concentric borders of infamy, accumulating increasingly inflexible and restrictive labels along the way, the system of values that distinguishes between acceptable and notorious identity, between cultural insiders and outsiders, becomes clear. Mag begins as a woman with a "loving, trusting heart" who has the democratic simplicity to believe that she can "ascend" to the social level of her duplicitous seducer and "become an equal" (5-6). The result is a bad reputation that follows her wherever she goes, leaving her with a "home . . . contaminated by the publicity of her fall" and with "a feeling of degradation," yet also with the hope that "circumspect" behavior might still enable her to "regain in a measure what she had lost" (7). Forced to remain in her assigned sphere of immorality, her prospects diminished further by the immigrant labor that altered significantly women's opportunities for employment in the Jackson era, Mag is soon left "hugging her wrongs, but making no effort to escape" (8). "[T]he climax of repulsion," according to the narrator (15), is Mag's interracial marriage to Jim—by which Mag "sunder[s] another bond which held her to her fellows" and "descend[s] another step down the ladder of infamy" (13). Her final step, into "the darkness of perpetual infamy," is the result of having "lived an outcast for years" (16): her extramarital relationship with a second black man after Jim dies. Had Mag set out deliberately to transgress the implicit boundaries of the dominant culture's standards, she could not have done a better job. The point here, though, is that her acts are not deliberate and that in learning of the consequences of seduction, *Our Nig*'s readers witness the process by which collective cultural identity is maintained at the expense of individual moral character. Although Mag repents, she must remain an outsider. Frado is an outcome of these transgressions, and her identity as cultural product, defined before birth, is finalized when on the title page of the book she becomes "Our Nig."

In identifying Frado as a cultural product, I refer to Clifford Geertz's conception of culture as "not so much the empirical commonalities in [human] behavior, from place to place and time to time, but rather the mechanisms by whose agency the breadth and indeterminateness of [one's] inherent capacities are reduced to the narrowness and specificity of [one's] actual accomplishments" (45). Wilson would amend this conception of individuation by viewing the process morally and would thereby judge it. As Anna Julia Cooper would later put it in *A Voice from the South by a Black Woman of the South* (1892),

> Our money, our schools, our governments, our free institutions, our systems of religion and forms of creeds are all first and last to be judged by this standard: what sort of men and women do they grow? How are men and women being shaped and molded by this system of training, under this or that form of government, by this or that standard of moral action?
>
> (282)

Arguing that "all other values are merely relative" to the "value" of the individual, Cooper maintains that the United States—"divinely ordered as we dream it to be"—will be divinely judged by its ability, in relation to nations with other forms of government, to "give us a sounder, healthier, more reliable product from this great factory of *men*" (282-83). Beginning the narrative with the story of Frado's birth and her eventual (and seemingly inevitable) creation as "Our Nig," Wilson takes her readers on a tour of the United States *factory* and then centers the action and the grounds for judgment on this remarkable *product*.

It is Wilson's attention to the common cultural factory—one incapable of producing stable, uniform grounds for trust—that complicates attempts to imagine that she wrote solely for a community of black readers. Prevailing prejudices created the appearance of commonality by setting blacks apart and grouping them together as ideologically marked sites for political action in the form of charity. By such logic, blacks were either physical or ideological fugitives in need of white protection. The resulting dangers for the artificially delineated black community become clear in the ultimate chapter, "The Winding Up of the Matter." Again Wilson enters into delicate cultural territory, for she begins by alluding to "*professed* fugitives from slavery, who recounted their personal experience in homely phrase, and awakened the indignation of non-slaveholders against brother Pro" (126; my emphasis). False professions were an issue in both the North and the South. In newspapers and books, antiabolitionists warned potential fugitives that self-proclaimed representatives of the Underground Railroad could not be trusted; similarly, northern abolitionists and members of antislavery societies warned against free blacks who pretended to be fugitives to procure money and clothing from Underground Railroad sympathizers.[7] Wilson presents her protagonist as a victim of this kind of impostor:

> Such a one appeared in the new home of Frado; and as people of color were rare there, was it strange she should attract her dark brother; that he should inquire her out; succeed in seeing her; feel a strange sensation in his heart towards her; that he should toy with her shining curls, feel proud to provoke her to smile and expose the ivory concealed by thin, ruby lips; that her sparkling eyes should fascinate; that he should propose; that they should marry?
>
> (126)

Telling a familiar story of courtship, love, and marriage in a single sentence, Wilson joins the sentimental associations readers would bring to the tale with the cultural divisions that make it seem like a series of nearly inevitable steps. This conflation of the sentimental destinies of love and the limited destinies of cultural identity undermines the romance of it all, revealing how innocent, unworldly love can entail trust in deceptive appearances. This story echoes that of Frado's mother. But whereas Mag's love led her to the hope of transcending class divisions, Frado's *extends from* what proves to be an equally naive belief in the inherent community of race.[8] It is this belief—the product of "her own oppression"—that enables Frado to view his silence about his enslavement, when they are alone, as evidence that they share an experience "painful to disturb oftener than was needful." "There was a silent sympathy," the narrator emphasizes, "which Frado felt attracted her, and she opened her heart to the presence of love—that arbitrary and inexorable tyrant." In the end, the tyrant shows his face, for Frado's husband leaves "her to her fate . . . with the disclosure that he had never seen the South, and that his illiterate harangues were humbugs for hungry abolitionists" (127-28). Frado is the victim not merely of an oppressive culture but also of her experience as a victim. The culture, against which she has begun to develop strategic defenses, reveals a further level of power. The sense of a community of silent sympathy among the oppressed becomes another dimension of oppression, another layer of identity defined by others.

Unable to control the terms of her own cultural identity or to trust others similarly defined, Wilson speaks both to and against those—black or white, male or female—who see her as a cultural type, a familiar product. That is, as almost all critics of this narrative note, Wilson signifies on her own culturally determined identity in her use of "Our Nig" as the title of both the book and its author. I think, though, that critics are sometimes led by their retrospective readings of an African American literary tradition to a narrow understanding of the nature and terms of this signifying. Gates, for example, argues cogently that **Our Nig** "manifests" "the transformation of the black-as-object into the black-as-subject" (Introduction lv), and certainly he is right. But as Wilson makes painfully clear, this "black-as-subject" still must face a culture capable of transforming her into woman-as-object and, within yet another concentric circle of identification, worker-as-object. In other words, it is important to remember that Frado begins as a product not only of racist formulations but also of ethical, gender, and economic formulations. Troping one's way into black subjecthood affects only the color of the corner one has been backed into; one is still faced with the adjoining walls of social and economic objectification. To escape this corner and save her son, Wilson would need to transform her economic as well as her racial identities.

"Slavery's Shadows" and the Politics of Labor

Wilson knew that she ran risks in telling a story both unsanctioned by northern abolitionists and sanctionable by northern and southern racists. Specifically, she risked undermining what Houston A. Baker, Jr., calls "the New England ideal so frequently appearing in Afro-American narratives," that of "free, dignified, and individualistic labor" (49). For example, one of the many proslavery responses to *Uncle Tom's Cabin,* W. L. G. Smith's *Life at the South; or, "Uncle Tom's Cabin" As It Is. Being Narratives, Scenes, and Incidents in the Real "Life of the Lowly"* (1852), published in the North, tells the story of an escaped slave who experiences unbearable hardships in the North and who, by the end of the novel, willingly returns to the plantation, having recognized the value of the economic system and of his "natural" place in it. This is but a strikingly direct representative of the many attempts to counter Stowe's portrayal of slavery by justifying the system as a paternal one designed to prepare those of African origins for their destiny in "God's own good time" (Smith vi). Indeed, in the mid-nineteenth century, southern defenses of slavery often incorporated attacks on northern capitalism, transforming the (northern) capitalist laborer into worker-as-object and the (southern) black slave into worker-as-subject, a formulation aimed at making the reified southern economic system a national (and even universal) model.[9] Such arguments, like many nineteenth-century writings on slavery and labor, were complicated by the advocates' free borrowing from a number of ideologies and discourses—those of religion, science, politics, sociology, and economics—to dress up fundamental assumptions in new clothing. As Augustine St. Clare says about slavery in *Uncle Tom's Cabin,* "Planters, who have money to make by it,—clergymen, who have planters to please,—politicians, who want to rule by it,—may warp and bend language and ethics to a degree that shall astonish the world at their ingenuity; they can press nature and the Bible, and nobody knows what else, into the service . . ." (Stowe 261). The historian Laurence Shore calls this veiling of assumptions "the process by which 'elastic' men shaped and reshaped Southern ideology" (194). The pervasive influence of the elastic proslavery-anticapitalist arguments is indicated by the number of antislavery authors who felt the need to respond to them.[10]

Proslavery commentators seized on the writings of social theorists like Auguste Comte and Thomas Carlyle to present the slave system as not only effective but also entirely just and humane. Two of the first American authors to use Comte's term "sociology" were slavery advocates: George Fitzhugh, in *Sociology for the South; or, The Failure of Free Society,* and Henry Hughes, in *A Treatise on Sociology, Theoretical and Practical,* both published in 1854. Hughes argues for "warranteeism"—a system that "warrant[s] the existence and progress of all." He bases the concept of warranteeism on his assertion that for the "healthy existence of all" in a society, "three warranted or ordered systems are necessary"—"the Political, the Economic, and the Hygienic" (52). By this logic, slavery becomes simply

"WARRANTEEISM WITH THE ETHNICAL QUALIFICATION." Another name for warranteeism, one learns, is "liberty-labor," and as a call for universal adoption of a form of government modeled after the American southern slave system, Hughes presents the slogan "LIBERTY-LABOR MUST BE THE SUBSTITUTE OF FREE-LABOR" (55). Whereas in warranteeism "necessary association, adaptation and regulation are . . . not accidental: they are essential," in "the Free-labor form of societary organization" these necessities of social order "are not essential; they are accidental" (53-54). Slavery thus may be seen as both the manifestation and the guarantor of social order, health, and justice.

Arguably the most forceful proponent of this view was Fitzhugh, who draws from Carlyle often and insistently in his second book, *Cannibals All! or, Slaves without Masters,* published in 1857, two years before *Our Nig.* With characteristically aggressive confidence, Fitzhugh asserts:

> [W]e not only boast that the White Slave Trade is more exacting and fraudulent (in fact, though not in intention) than Black Slavery; but we also boast that it is more cruel, in leaving the laborer to take care of himself and family out of the pittance which skill or capital have allowed him to retain.

(15)

Arguing that the precepts of Christianity and those of capitalism are mutually exclusive, Fitzhugh concludes that "it is impossible to place labor and capital in harmonious or friendly relations, except by the means of slavery, which identifies their interests" (31).

Fitzhugh is most effective in suggesting that debates on the ethics of economic systems should extend beyond southern slavery to the broader field of labor. *Cannibals All!* quotes extensively from American and European socialist and anticapitalist writings, some arguing that slavery is the solution to the oppression of the poor, regardless of race. For example, in an essay Fitzhugh reprints in its entirety, one self-professed English "Philanthropist" contends that

> *slavery and content, and liberty and discontent, are natural results of each other.* Applying this, then, to the toil-worn, half-fed, pauperized population of England, I found that the only way to permanently and efficiently remedy the complicated evils, would be to ENSLAVE *the whole of the people of England who have not property.*

(155)

Similarly, the southern scientific agriculturist Edmund Ruffin states in *The Political Economy of Slavery* (1853) that "in their main doctrines, the socialists are

right" and that the slavery system is the most effective means of securing the benefits of "the *association of labor"* (83, 82).

The consideration of slavery as a mode of organized labor provided not only convenient proslavery defenses against abolitionists but also powerful rhetorical tools for mobilizing labor within the developing capitalist economy. David R. Roediger demonstrates that slavery in the United States shaped the formation of the antebellum labor movement, which was "exceptional in its rhetoric" and "exceptionally militant as it critiqued evolving capitalist social relations as a kind of slavery" (66). By use of the vague and inclusive phrase *white slavery,* "[a]bolitionists, free Blacks, bankers, factory owners and prison labor could, in sundry combinations, be cast as villains in a loose plot to enslave white workers" (73). But though the comparison between the white hireling and the black slave could encourage analyses of wage labor as bondage, the emphasis on visible social contrasts "also could reassure wage workers that they belonged to the ranks of 'free white labor' " (47) and highlight the need for and progress toward improved labor conditions for white workers. In short, Roediger argues, "the growing popular sense of whiteness represented a hesitantly emerging consensus holding together a very diverse white working class" by enabling white antebellum workers to shift their anxieties onto blacks (97, 100).[11] As Frederick Douglass put it in 1855, "The impression is cunningly made, that slavery is the only power that can prevent the laboring white man from falling to the level of the slave's poverty and degradation" (*My Bondage* 310-11).

Wilson signals in her preface her awareness of the flexible logic of proslavery activists, noting her decision to omit "what would most provoke shame in our good anti-slavery friends at home," carefully identifying Mrs. Bellmont with *"southern* principles," and asserting, "I would not . . . palliate slavery at the South, by disclosures of its appurtenances North" (3). Throughout *Our Nig,* which begins with a white woman displaced in the job market by "foreigners who cheapened toil and clamored for a livelihood" (8), Wilson deliberately and forcefully conflates the economic situations of working-class whites and culturally enslaved "free" blacks. Wilson's task was to transform herself from an object of charity to a laboring subject in an economy apparently designed to exclude or delegitimize her labor. Increasingly, her only material for this transformation—the only material with which she could perform as laborer—was the life that the culture had produced, and the only product she could offer was the narrative of that life.[12]

Human Transactions and "God's Economy"

As Baker writes of Douglass's 1845 *Narrative,* in *Our Nig* "[t]he tones of a Providentially oriented moral suasion eventually compete with the cadences of a secularly oriented economic voice." Like Douglass, Wilson works to combine "literacy, Christianity, and revolutionary zeal in an individual and economically profitable job of work" (Baker 43, 49). However, Wilson's experiences had not offered her the kind of hope that Douglass's revolutionary self-creation seemingly had provided him in 1845, nor was she writing under the auspices of an antislavery organization that would have made it advisable to *represent* hope in the northern states. Rather, Wilson grounds her goal of an "economically profitable job of work" in an eschatological vision of the existing economic system, in a consideration of the market economy as the vehicle God provided to regulate and improve human affairs. In 1879, Wilson's contemporary Martin R. Delany would speak of race as "a means in the providence of God's economy, to the accomplishment of his ends in the progress of civilization" (26). A similar notion of "God's economy" led Anna Julia Cooper to argue in 1892 that "you need not formulate and establish the credibility and authenticity of Christian Evidences, when you can demonstrate and prove the present value of CHRISTIAN MEN." To judge a culture by its "productions," Cooper suggests, is to evaluate its adherence to moral law:

> And this test for systems of belief, for schools of thought, and for theories of conduct, is also the ultimate and inevitable test of nations, of races and of individuals. What sort of men do you turn out? *How* are you supplying the great demands of the world's market?

> (284)

In 1859, Wilson hoped to produce something that would enable her to enjoy the profits of God's economy.[13]

In this vision of economy, wealth and poverty are moral concepts, measured not by economic status but by character. Poverty, Gates argues, is "the great evil in this book," "both the desperation it inflicts as well as the evils it implicitly sanctions" (Introduction xlvi); but I suggest that the great evil is rather the will to dominate, which feeds on cultural and personal vulnerability. After all, the only character who views poverty as a disgrace and a dishonor is one of the narrative's most visible villains, Mrs. Bellmont. She is unable to see that her son's chosen wife (and Frado's favorite) is, as Jack Bellmont puts it to his mother, "*worth a million dollars . . . though not a cent of it is in money*" (112). It is also Mrs. Bellmont who insists that her daughter Jane marry Henry Reed, for the mother has "counted the acres which were to be transmitted to" him and "knew there was silver in the purse" (56). In each case, Mrs. Bellmont displays, though circumspectly, the same will to dominate that inspires her verbal and physical abuse of Frado, distorting perceptions in her effort to control or destroy those who threaten her ambitions.

Once Jack is away and his wife is "more in [Mrs. Bellmont's] power," the narrator says, the mother "wished to make [Jenny] feel her inferiority" and watches for acts "which might be construed into conjugal unfaithfulness" (113). This project, like Mrs. Bellmont's response to Frado's attempts to understand and experience Christianity, demonstrates that nothing is sacred in the struggle for power, as the discourse of morality itself becomes a tool of domination.

Mrs. Bellmont dramatizes the corruption of cultural discourse, its deliberate misuse—but what the narrator takes the discourse to signify remains untainted. The narrator's disapproval of Mrs. Bellmont's motives for interfering with these relationships does not suggest disapproval of wealth. The narrator celebrates the marriage of Jack's brother James to a wealthy woman, while observing that James "did not marry her wealth" but that "he loved *her,* sincerely" (55). Similarly, when Mr. Bellmont insists that Jane not be "compelled to violate her free choice in so important a transaction" (60), her preference for George Means over Henry Reed is a choice of love over the accumulation of wealth for its own sake. Although Mrs. Bellmont tries to make George Means's name signify that he is, in fact, mean, Wilson shows that proper motivations inform the power of the cultural system, for this couple find *means* enough to maintain their "early love" beyond the end of the narrative (130).[14] The lesson is emphasized later, in what seems like a pun on the other suitor's name, when the narrator notes that Mr. Bellmont "bowed like a 'bruised reed,' under the loss of his beloved son." No longer the "reed" he once was, Mr. Bellmont begins to worry about his past actions—about the relation between his professions and his practices and about the preparation of his soul for "the celestial city" (102).

Mr. Bellmont's subsequent attempt to reinvest discourse with meaning leads to the most striking turning point of the narrative, Frado's first direct act of resistance against Mrs. Bellmont's violence. Fearing for his own soul, Mr. Bellmont allows Frado to return to religious meetings; Mrs. Bellmont, afraid that word will get out about her beating Frado, tells Frado to "stop trying to be religious," threatening to "whip her to death." Mr. Bellmont then acknowledges to Frado that "he had seen her many times punished undeservedly" and advises her "to avoid it if she could" "when she was *sure* she did not deserve whipping" (104). "It was not long," the narrator notes pointedly, "before an opportunity offered of profiting by his advice" (105). In this confrontation, Frado—"the only moving power in the house" (62)—recognizes the power of her position as laborer and essentially threatens to go on strike: " 'Stop!' shouted Frado, 'strike me, and I'll never work a mite more for you;' and throwing down what she had gathered, stood like one who feels the stirring of free and independent thoughts." This act of resistance is

Frado's most successful one, for the "affair never met with an 'after clap,' like many others" (105). The lesson is that, rightly perceived, the system works: moral self-government supports American political ideals. The principles of liberty and independence ingrained in nineteenth-century national mythology but often corrupted by practice are renewed, reenacted, in a natural chain of events that begins with Mr. Bellmont's attempt to align his professions and his practice.

Indeed, all Frado's economic opportunities are associated with providential guidance over the marketplace. When Frado hears that "in some towns in Massachusetts, girls make straw bonnets" and that the work is "easy and profitable," she wonders how "*she,* black, feeble and poor," could "find any one to teach her" to do it. The answer is that "God prepares the way, when human agencies see no path." The way, in this case, is a woman who, guided by faith, is capable of seeing "merit beneath a dark skin" and who teaches Frado not only the art of the needle but also "the value of useful books." This lesson leads to a project of "self-improvement," as Frado comes to feel "that this book information supplied an undefined dissatisfaction she had long felt, but could not express" (124-25). Similarly, when she finds herself abandoned toward the end of the narrative, "watched by kidnappers" and "maltreated by professed abolitionists," Frado again gains help from a guiding hand: "In one of her tours, Providence favored her with a friend who, pitying her cheerless lot, kindly provided her with a valuable recipe, from which she might herself manufacture a useful article for her maintenance" (129). Episodes such as these inform her final claim that "[r]eposing on God, she has thus far journeyed securely." Her reliance on God has been a progressive self-reliance; the rewards she received for fulfilling her duty—her "steadfast purpose of elevating herself"—are the material means that make self-reliance possible (130).

But far from promoting naive acceptance of "the New England ideal" of "free, dignified, and individualistic labor" (Baker 49), Wilson presents a complex perspective on the workings of God's economy in her depiction of the "courtship" of Mag Smith and Jim. Critics have focused on the signifying conclusion of Jim's appeal to Mag: "Which you rather have, a black heart in a white skin, or a white heart in a black one?" (12).[15] Equally important, however, is the process that leads to the conclusion, for Wilson highlights the economic contingencies and marketplace logic that enable Jim to act on his original inspiration to marry Mag. Knowing that Mag is out of wood, Jim asks, "How's the wood, Mag?" When she admits it is gone, he says, "Too bad!" The narrator notes that "his truthful reply would have been, I'm glad." When Jim asks Mag about food and she says that she has none, he replies, "Too bad!"—but "with the same *inward* gratualtion as before." His marriage proposal does not even pretend to be romantic; Mag is desperate, and Jim, having forced her hand with good marketplace technique, simply presents himself as the last available source of supply: " 'Well, Mag,' said Jim, after a short pause, 'you's down low enough. I do n't see but I've got to take care of ye. 'Sposin' we marry!' " (12).

The significance of this episode lies not merely in the victory of a pure heart over a culturally derogated black skin but also and more fundamentally in the process by which the victory is achieved and in the economic system that enables the cross-racial exchange. After all, Wilson's final reason for Mag's acceptance is that "want is a . . . powerful philosopher and preacher" (13). But the sermon preached by want is about more than the virtues of economic gain. In a book that calls for the readers' "sympathy and aid" (130) but dramatizes—through Frado's husband and the Bellmonts—the possibility that sympathy can be used as a mask for self-interest, it is important to remember that Jim's efforts to help Mag (and himself) begin with pity. This pity leads to genuine reciprocity, however, for Mag surrenders her hope to reenter the circle of cultural respectability, and Jim not only gets what he wants but also commits himself to give what he can. No simple act of charity, no simple attempt to purchase ideological self-definition, pity here becomes part of a system of sentiments, the initial point of exchange that provides entrance into God's economy and thereby promotes the development of finer feelings. For "pity and love," the narrator summarizes, "know little severance. One attends the other. Jim acknowledged the presence of the former, and his efforts in Mag's behalf told also of a finer principle" (10).

Wilson carefully contrasts this genuine reciprocity, the motive force of God's economy, with charity in narrating the experiences Frado has after being reduced by circumstances and poor health to a situation similar to that of her mother many years earlier. With "one only resource," public support, Frado is left to two elderly maidens, who, the narrator notes with sarcasm, have "principle enough to be willing to earn the money a charitable public disburses." When Frado falls ill, she is turned over to the appropriately named Mrs. Hoggs, "a lover of gold and silver" who asks "the favor of filling her coffers by caring for the sick" (122). This move aggravates yet more Frado's decline; and when her health gradually begins to improve and she starts to feel "hope that she might yet help herself," Mrs. Hoggs reports her to the authorities (123). Charity diverts the motive power in their relationship from the principal parties to a third party and instead of mutual exchange establishes a chain of funds from the community to Mrs. Hoggs to Frado, a linear connection in which Frado must be dependent so that Mrs. Hoggs's position as a self-aggrandizing benefactor can be secure. In other words, the relationship must remain stagnant, with clearly defined and delimited roles.

Our Nig is designed to initiate a more active system of exchange, based on mutual dependence and devoted to communal development. In Wilson's vision of Christianity, as presented in this work, redemptive faith requires that one redeem one's resources in an economic management of selfhood. When James Bellmont finds "his *Saviour*," he wishes that Frado might find hers because the discovery would enable her to manage the "elements in her heart which . . . would make her worthy [of] the esteem and friendship of the world." This esteem has practical significance, as well as social:

> A kind, affectionate heart, native wit, and common sense, and the pertness she sometimes exhibited, he felt if restrained properly, might become useful in originating a self-reliance which would be of service to her in after years.

However, such self-reliance can operate successfully only in a community of others who are similarly "transformed and purified by the gospel" and attuned to the directives of Providence (69). One can receive only as others offer, and one can offer only as others are disposed to receive. And as Jim tried to expose Mag's need, so Wilson works to expose the deprivation, the utter want, of her world, thereby indicating the still unacknowledged demand for what only she and others like her can supply: the products of experience and the profits of a fully realized and hard-earned Christian perspective.

Wilson's strategy of exposure and exchange is neatly summarized in two episodes. In the first, Frado deals with one of the sheep she tends, a "willful leader, who always persisted in being first served," often throwing Frado down in his zeal. She locates herself at "the highest point of land nearest the stream" and entices the sheep with a dish, calling "the flock to their mock repast." As she expects, the willful leader comes "furiously leaping and bounding far in advance of the flock," and as he leaps for the dish, Frado steps aside, causing him to tumble down into the river, on the other side of which he has to remain until the night, a sheepish victim of his own greed (54-55). Frado refers to this incident later, when she half-seriously wishes for the death of Mary Bellmont, another willful leader: "I'd like to try my hand at curing *her* too" (80). The sheep episode echoes an earlier experience, when Mary tries to force Frado into a stream and, in the struggle, loses her footing and falls in herself. The eschatological implications of these stories of willful leaders and just deserts are underscored when Mary dies, inspiring Frado to say, "She's got into the *river* again" (107).

In the second exemplary episode, Frado is forced to eat from a plate Mrs. Bellmont has used. Annoyed at being "commanded to do what was disagreeable . . . *because* it was disagreeable," Frado has her dog, Fido,

lick the plate clean, a job he does "to the best of his ability," and afterward she eats from it (71). What makes this image a fitting one for Wilson's own strategies is that Frado not only enjoys a symbolic victory over Mrs. Bellmont but also receives a silver half-dollar from Mrs. Bellmont's son, who is pleased at seeing his mother exposed and defeated. As James explains to his mother, "You have not treated her, mother, so as to gain her love; she is only exhibiting your remissness in this matter" (72). Mrs. Bellmont never learns the lesson, but it remains for others, an education that begins when one pays the price of this narrative. Wilson's message is that the exposure of "remissness" must be recognized as a valuable service if the nation is to maintain its moral foundations. The unmasking of willful leaders and tyrannical employers returns economic relations to their moral grounds, there to be evaluated.

The value of a marketplace economy, then—and what makes it a practical entrance into "God's economy"—is that it depends not on hopeful cooperation but rather on inevitable conflict. In this, Wilson anticipates Anna Julia Cooper, who views the "race problem" as a vital part of God's mode of governance, by which "eternal harmony and symmetry" are "the unvarying result of the equilibrium of opposing forces" (150). As Cooper argues, noting her preference for the troubled present over Edward Bellamy's utopian "grandmotherly government" in *Looking Backward,* "Progressive peace in a nation is the result of conflict; and conflict, such as is healthy, stimulating, and progressive, is produced through the co-existence of radically opposing or racially different elements" (151). Closer to Wilson's time, in an essay of 1844 titled "On the Moral and Political Effect of the Relation between the Caucasian Master and the African Slave," a slavery advocate contends that the emancipation of female slaves would force them to rely on "cold charities," replacing "a *community* of interests" with "a *conflict* of interests" (339). Distrusting the community of interests, Wilson supports a renewed understanding of the dynamic exchanges between conflicting interests, for the interests that she knew were sure to conflict. But the conflicts, she suggests, may contain the terms of mutual dependence, the demands of collective survival—the initial and fundamental elements of a genuine and morally secure community of interests.

Throughout this narrative, Wilson maintains implicitly that community can come only from the recognition of conflict and that the nation can progress only by way of ongoing negotiations among antagonists who acknowledge that each has something another needs to survive, in a world governed by God. Baker's brilliant examination of the economic argument in Douglass's *Narrative* illustrates how Douglass presents his life as a process by which he "eventually converts property, through property, into humanity" (Baker 48). Addressing slavery's northern shadows, Wilson certainly hopes to do the same. But as Douglass himself realized after his initial optimistic vision of the New England economic system, the self-purchase necessary to African American survival in the growing capitalist environment of the North required communal self-purchase by all citizens. The ostensibly empowered had to recognize that, like the physically enslaved, they too had been converted to property by the economic and political network that both supported and depended on the slave system. Ultimately, *Our Nig* argues that communal self-purchase begins with this book; the story of the life produced by this culture serves as the catalyst for new productions in the ongoing quest to convert disparate cultural property into a common humanity.[16]

Notes

[1] On the critical and cultural implications of the reprint and its format, distribution, and reception, see Dearborn 31-33; Gardner; White 20, 46n.

[2] The final tragedy of this book is that Wilson's young son died shortly after it was published.

[3] White's essay on *Our Nig* is a model of careful research, and her documentary evidence supports her speculation that Wilson was "bound out" to the Hayward family—the model for the Bellmonts—under the "vendue system," or "New England method," of disposing of the poor, "in which the poor were auctioned off or bound out" (46n).

[4] Among White's numerous valuable findings is the resounding evidence that the Haywards had "strong abolitionist connections" (34). Gardner speculates that "abolitionists knew about the book but . . . may have consciously chosen *not* to publicize it" (227).

[5] On Wilson's intended audience, see also Doriani; Fox-Genovese. Addressing a racially mixed audience, Frederick Douglass was also sharply critical of northern prejudice and of abolitionists after the late 1840s, pointedly in his revisionist 1855 autobiography, *My Bondage and My Freedom.*

Gardner's recent research into the publishing history of *Our Nig* is valuable here, though his discoveries concerning Wilson's actual audience only emphasize the problem of determining her intended audience. Gardner argues that "ownership patterns . . . sustain the theory that Wilson was responsible for distributing the book herself—and that the distribution was limited to personal acquaintance with the author or her friends and agents" (240). Gardner notes as well that Wilson apparently was not able to market her book in Boston, where she would have found a large black community, perhaps because her son's death took her back to

Milford before she could do so. Many purchasers, Gardner suggests, "either interpreted or deployed *Our Nig* as a book geared toward the moral improvement of young readers" (228).

See also Tate, who rightly distinguishes between Wilson's intended audience and "those readers who live outside the historical exigencies of Wilson's epoch, namely ourselves" (32). Focusing on Wilson's attempt to "re-create herself in a novelized form" (38), Tate implies that Wilson's first audience was both herself and the world that had constructed a restrictive selfhood for her. See especially 36-42.

[6] I am thinking in particular of "scientific" racialism of the type in Nott and Gliddon and in Cartwright.

[7] That false fugitives were a fact of antebellum life is suggested by the casualness with which Douglass, in discussing the character of the enslaved, remarks, "So uniformly are good manners enforced among slaves, that I can easily detect a 'bogus' fugitive by his manners" (*My Bondage* 70). On the complex deceptions and legends accompanying the pro- and antislavery movements generally and the Underground Railroad specifically, see Gara.

[8] On Mag's and Frado's similar situations and different responses, see Tate 37-38.

[9] The economic arguments surrounding slavery are as complex as nineteenth-century religious, scientific, and legal justifications of it. Temperly provides a useful entrance into the issues, as does Shore. See also Tise; Genovese; Frederickson; Takaki; and Bender.

[10] In Jacobs's *Incidents in the Life of a Slave Girl,* see ch. 37; in W. Brown's *Clotel,* see ch. 15; see also ch. 19 of *Uncle Tom's Cabin.*

[11] G. Brown's comments on abolition as "the reformation of labor" and on Stowe's comparisons of Irish and black domestic servants seem relevant here (54-59). On labor issues related to gender, race, or national origins, see Litwack; Turbin; Bennett; Foner; and Lown.

According to Roediger, examination of "the labor and radical Democratic press of the 1840s shows that *white slavery* was the most common phrasing of metaphors regarding white workers' oppression with *slavery of wages* second and *wage slavery* a very distant third. . . . [T]he term *white slavery* was at times used even in articles speculating about the fate of free *Blacks* if abolition prevailed" (72). See also Douglass's 1855 discussion of white southern laborers, which includes the point that "[t]he difference between the white slave, and the black slave, is this: the latter belongs to *one* slaveholder, and the former belongs to *all* the slaveholders, collectively" (*My Bondage* 310).

[12] White emphasizes "the extent to which economic motives predominate in Wilson's narrative" (33). White documents Wilson's struggle to support herself and, later, her son after her years with the Hayward family. Often dependent on the town of Milford, New Hampshire, and at times forced to leave her young son either to the mercies of the county poor farm, which had "terrible conditions" (24), or to the publicly financed care of a local family, Wilson knew intimately the complex cultural labyrinth assigned to "free" black northern laborers.

For a reading of the nature and significance of Wilson's economic enterprise that differs from the one I present here, see Holloway.

[13] Gates, as well as others, argues that Frado's conversion to Christianity is not real, that "Frado never truly undergoes a religious transformation, merely the *appearance* of one" (Introduction xlix). I agree with Tate, however, that Wilson offers her own version of the familiar African American distinction between profession and practice—or, as Douglass puts it, "between the Christianity of this land, and the Christianity of Christ" (*Narrative* 153). Tate argues, "Although the appendix clearly characterizes Wilson as a pious Christian . . . her faith is not without doubt and it mounts a sustained interrogation of the conventional practice of Christianity throughout the text" (47). The fact that Frado struggles to understand and accept Christianity should not be taken as evidence that she does not finally consider herself a Christian.

[14] It should be noted, however, that while Jane certainly never confuses the two rivals, Wilson apparently does, referring in the final pages to Jane's happiness with "Henry."

[15] See, for example, Bell 49; for a more recent analysis, see Tate 33. Critics sometimes treat this play on color-coded standards as if it were innovative. However, in 1846 Douglass, in a letter he included in *My Bondage and My Freedom*, sharply attacked standards that allowed African Americans to be ridiculed and oppressed "with impunity by any one, (no matter how black his heart,) so he has a white skin" (371).

[16] I presented an early version of this study at " 'Other Voices': American Women Writers of Color," a conference sponsored by Salisbury State University and the Maryland Humanities Council. I am grateful to the codirectors of that conference, Connie L. Richards and Thomas L. Erskine, and to members of the audience for their encouragement. This essay benefited also from my friend and colleague Adele Newson's careful reading of an early draft.

Works Cited

Andrews, William L. *To Tell a Free Story: The First Century of Afro-American Autobiography, 1760-1865*. Urbana: U of Illinois P, 1986.

Baker, Houston A., Jr. *Blues, Ideology, and Afro-American Literature: A Vernacular Theory*. Chicago: U of Chicago P, 1984.

Bell, Bernard W. *The Afro-American Novel and Its Tradition*. Amherst: U of Massachusetts P, 1987.

Bender, Thomas, ed. *The Antislavery Debate: Capitalism and Abolitionism as a Problem in Historical Interpretation*. Berkeley: U of California P, 1992.

Bennett, David H. "Women and the Nativist Movement." *"Remember the Ladies": New Perspectives on Women in American History. Essays in Honor of Nelson Manfred Blake*. Ed. Carol V. R. George. Syracuse: Syracuse UP, 1975. 71-89.

Brown, Gillian. *Domestic Individualism: Imagining Self in Nineteenth-Century America*. Berkeley: U of California P, 1990.

Brown, William Wells. *Clotel; or, The President's Daughter*. New York: Carol, 1989.

Carby, Hazel V. *Reconstructing Womanhood: The Emergence of the Afro-American Woman Novelist*. New York: Oxford UP, 1987.

Cartwright, Samuel A. *Essays, being inductions drawn from the Baconian philosophy proving the truth of the Bible and the justice and benevolence of the decree dooming Canaan to be a servant of servants. . . .* Natchez, 1843.

Cooper, Anna Julia. *A voice from the South by a Black Woman of the South*. New York: Oxford UP, 1988.

Dearborn, Mary V. *Pocahantas's Daughters: Gender and Ethnicity in American Culture*. New York: Oxford UP, 1986.

Delany, Martin R. *The Origin of Races and Color*. 1879. Baltimore: Black Classic, 1991.

Doriani, Beth Maclay. "Black Womanhood in Nineteenth-Century America: Subversion and Self-Construction in Two Women's Autobiographies." *American Quarterly* 43 (1991): 199-222.

Douglass, Frederick. *My Bondage and My Freedom*. New York: Dover, 1969.

————. *Narrative of the Life of Frederick Douglass, an American Slave. Written by Himself.* Penguin Classics. New York: Penguin, 1986.

Fitzhugh, George. *Cannibals All! or, Slaves without Masters.* Cambridge: Belknap-Harvard UP, 1960.

————. *Sociology for the South; or, The Failure of Free Society.* Richmond, 1854.

Foner, Philip S. *Women and the American Labor Movement: From Colonial Times to the Eve of World War I.* New York: Free, 1979.

Fox-Genovese, Elizabeth. "My Statue, My Self: Autobiographical Writings of Afro-American Women." *Reading Black, Reading Feminist: A Critical Anthology.* Ed. Henry Louis Gates, Jr. New York: Meridian, 1990. 176-203.

Frederickson, George M. *The Black Image in the White Mind: The Debate on Afro-American Character and Destiny, 1817-1914.* New York: Harper, 1971.

Gara, Larry. *The Liberty Line: The Legend of the Underground Railroad.* Lexington: U of Kentucky P, 1961.

Gardner, Eric. " 'This Attempt of Their Sister': Harriet Wilson's *Our Nig* from Printer to Readers." *New England Quarterly* 66 (1993): 226-46.

Gates, Henry Louis, Jr. *Figures in Black: Words, Signs, and the "Racial" Self.* New York: Oxford UP, 1987.

————. Introduction. Wilson xi-lv.

Geertz, Clifford. *The Interpretation of Cultures: Selected Essays.* New York: Basic, 1973.

Genovese, Eugene D. *The World the Slaveholders Made: Two Essays in Interpretation.* New York: Random, 1969.

Holloway, Karla F. C. "Economies of Space: Markets and Marketability in *Our Nig* and *Iola Leroy*." *The (Other) American Traditions: Nineteenth-Century Women Writers.* Ed. Joyce W. Warren. New Brunswick: Rutgers UP, 1993. 126-40.

Hughes, Henry. "A Treatise on Sociology." *Slavery Defended: The Views of the Old South.* Ed. Eric L. McKitrick. Englewood Cliffs: Prentice, 1963. 51-56.

Jacobs, Harriet. *Incidents in the Life of a Slave Girl.* New York: Oxford UP, 1988.

Litwack, Leon F. *North of Slavery: The Negro in the Free States, 1790-1860.* Chicago: U of Chicago P, 1961.

Lown, Judy. *Women and Industrialization: Gender and Work in the Nineteenth Century.* Minneapolis: U of Minnesota P, 1990.

Nott, J. C., and Geo. R. Gliddon. *Types of Mankind; or, Ethnological Researches, Based upon the Ancient Monuments, Paintings, Sculptures, and Crania of Races, and upon Their Natural, Geographical, Philological, and Biblical History. . . .* Philadelphia, 1854.

"On the Moral and Political Effect of the Relation between the Caucasian Master and the African Slave." *Southern Literary Messenger* June 1844: 329-39.

Roediger, David R. *The Wages of Whiteness: Race and the Making of the American Working Class.* London: Verso, 1991.

Ruffin, Edmund. "The Political Economy of Slavery." *Slavery Defended: The Views of the Old South.* Ed. Eric L. McKitrick. Englewood Cliffs: Prentice, 1963. 69-85.

Shore, Laurence. *Southern Capitalists: The Ideological Leadership of an Elite, 1832-1885.* Chapel Hill: U of North Carolina P, 1986.

Smith, W. L. G. *Life at the South; or, "Uncle Tom's Cabin" As It Is. Being Narratives, Scenes, and Incidents in the Real "Life of the Lowly."* Buffalo, 1852.

Stowe, Harriet Beecher. *Uncle Tom's Cabin; or, Life among the Lowly.* Library of America. New York: Vintage, 1991.

Takaki, Ronald. *Iron Cages: Race and Culture in Nineteenth-Century America.* New York: Oxford UP, 1990.

Tate, Claudia. *Domestic Allegories of Political Desire: The Black Heroine's Text at the Turn of the Century.* New York: Oxford UP, 1992.

Temperly, Howard. "Capitalism, Slavery and Ideology." *Past and Present* 75 (1977): 94-118.

Tise, Larry E. *Proslavery: A History of the Defense of Slavery in America, 1701-1840.* Athens: U of Georgia P, 1987.

Turbin, Carole. "Beyond Dichotomies: Interdependence in Mid-Nineteenth Century Working Class Families in the United States." *Gender and History* 1 (1989): 293-308.

White, Barbara A. "*Our Nig* and the She-Devil: New Information about Harriet Wilson and the 'Bellmont' Family." *American Literature* 65 (1993): 19-52.

Wilson, Harriet E. *Our Nig; or, Sketches from the Life of a Free Black, in a Two-Story White House, North. Showing That Slavery's Shadows Fall Even There. By "Our Nig."* New York: Vintage, 1983.

Jill Jones (essay date 1996)

SOURCE: "The Disappearing 'I' in *Our Nig*," *Legacy*, Vol. 13, No. 1, 1996, pp. 38-53.

[*In the following essay, Jones discusses the linguistic methods Wilson uses in* Our Nig *in order to create an authoritative voice against her disempowerment by race, class, and gender discrimination.*]

In "Song of Myself," Walt Whitman pledges himself to speak for the many voices that cannot be heard without him:

> Through me many long dumb voices,
> Voices of the interminable generations of
>   slaves,
> Voices of prostitutes and of deformed
>   persons,
> Voices of the diseased and despairing, and
>   of thieves and dwarfs.

Whitman acknowledges a reality of nineteenth-century United States society and letters: the difficulty for the disenfranchised—those who do not have access to power within the established structures of society—to be heard.[1] Issues of authority are particularly problematic in a first-person text. Because of the general perception that "the first-person narrator is by definition an 'unreliable narrator' " the disenfranchised speaker can almost never be heard without a mediating voice, like Whitman's, that is explicitly empowered (Stanzel 89).[2] In Harriet Wilson's *Our Nig* (1859), presently believed to be the first novel published by an African-American woman, the difficulties of "speaking" are exacerbated by the virtually complete powerlessness of the author/protagonist—a black woman in antebellum America.

This article will examine the narrative feints by which Wilson creates an authoritative voice for a novel in which the protagonist, narrator, and author (who at times are indistinguishable) are disempowered by race, class, and gender. Because she has no access to personal authority, Wilson's primary strategy is to tap into the authority that is inherent in certain literary traditions. I will argue that to authorize, that is to lend authority and the right of authorship, this text Wilson draws on the advantages of two different genres and two different voices. By slipping and sliding between the first- and third-person voice, by tapping into the inherent and particular authority of both the slave narrative *and* the sentimental novel, Wilson constructs the necessary illusion of authority for most of *Our Nig*.

Once she has initiated an empowered narrative voice, Wilson faces a second obstacle: the problems of authorizing the text exist in substance as well as form, in the plot as well as in the narrative. Wilson must not only deal with the difficulty of sustaining a voice, but must struggle to maintain her protagonist. Wilson's Frado is so completely powerless that she is always in danger of paralysis, a state, I will argue, that is absolutely incompatible with the nineteenth-century novel.[3] Wilson must empower her protagonist as well as her narrator; she must give her either enough freedom of movement, or the appearance of enough freedom, to propel a plot.

Remarkably, Wilson successfully creates, first, an authorized voice and, then, a protagonist who is capable of propelling a plot. After establishing the veracity of her story in the first person, she constructs a fictional third-person narrator who can project the illusion of authority. She then uses this authority to empower the protagonist, giving her the appearance of autonomy by emphasizing the choices that she can make, and even implying that Frado has choices when she does not. These strategies successfully authorize both narrator and protagonist until the last ten pages of the novel when, finally, Frado is unable to move and the narrator is unable to sustain a voice. The limits of the protagonist/author create problems with closure, and the end of the novel breaks down: the third-person narrator disappears and the plot rushes to an abrupt and unsatisfactory finish.[4] The conclusion of *Our Nig* is all too successful in revealing the inadequacy of traditional forms—either novel or slave narrative—to deal with the complexity of Wilson's plight.

Many critics have examined the difficulties inherent in authorizing a first-person voice. Jonathan Auerbach argues that "first-person narration in particular exposes the provisional nature of its authority" (17). Because of the additional difficulty of giving voice to the disenfranchised, the autobiography in both fiction and non-fiction has been the medium of winners—of the success story. In a recent article, Jill Johnston notes that "the traditional autobiography has hardly ever been a medium for victims" (30). The multiple difficulties of having a protagonist and an author who is, for all intents and purposes, a slave, seem insurmountable. As Myra Jehlen states, "The special problem novelists who are slaves confront has to do . . . with their own authorship and authority. . . . A slave author is a contradiction in terms" (384).

That Wilson faces this particular paradox becomes clear as early as the title's announcement that the novel was written "by Our Nig." Once she ties the implied author to the disenfranchised protagonist, Wilson has many of the authorship and authority problems of the "slave author." So, in a sense, it is not surprising that the work begins with the earmarks of the slave narrative.

Although the genre was largely dominated by men, it was virtually the only available African-American tradition.[5] However, despite Margaretta Thorn's testament in her appended letter that "the writer of this book . . . was indeed a slave" (139), in fact, she was not. The format of the slave narrative does not conform to Wilson's story, and, as a "Free Black," she has no authorized access to the genre.

Perhaps for this reason, although *Our Nig* begins with a title, preface, and chapter heading that appear to lay claim to the tradition of the slave narrative, the first page of the chapter places it in the realm of fiction, more specifically, in the unmistakable form of the sentimental novel. While the preface introduces the non-fiction "I" of the slave narrative then, putting forth both the familiar abolitionist agenda and confessing that the events of *Our Nig* are indeed the events of "my own life," the first page introduces not only a cliché-ridden third-person narrator, but a protagonist who is a white woman. Metaphorical and melodramatic, the opening of the novel is more reminiscent of Hannah Webster Foster than of Harriet Jacobs, and redefines *Our Nig,* this time as a sentimental novel, an established and popular literature both accessible to the woman writer, and complete with an omniscient, third-person narrator.

However, neither the slave narrative nor the sentimental novel quite fits Wilson's needs: while the slave narrative is an African-American tradition, it specifically involves the flight from slavery to freedom; and while the sentimental novel is a female tradition, until Wilson it is an exclusively *white* female tradition. In an attempt to construct an authorized voice, Wilson draws on both genres, maneuvering between the authenticity of first-person non-fiction[6] and the sentimental third-person voice that is so conventionalized that it carries its own authorization.[7] Although the use of the sentimental voice is not uncommon in (particularly female) slave narratives and direct address is not uncommon in (particularly abolitionist) sentimental novels, the two voices seem unusually distinct in *Our Nig.* The novel introduces, then re-introduces itself, telling us first that the author and the narrator are one and the same, enslaved and disempowered, only to later launch the story in the stylized omniscient voice of the sentimental storyteller. Bobbing and weaving between the first and third person, resonating here with echoes of the slave narrative and there with the sound of the sentimental novel, Wilson exploits both genres to lend her narrator authority.

From the preface to the conclusion, Wilson does a kind of narrative switch-hitting, using the voice most useful to her immediate needs. As though she doubts the power of her "I" to carry a narrative, Wilson writes the bulk of *Our Nig* in a third-person voice, a voice that is stripped of the personal by its use of melodramatic language, pat phrases ("gentle reader"), and traditional formats (the apology). The narrator's language is extremely conventional, reading more like a handbook for the generic sentimental novel than an autobiographical account. While Wilson announces her position as "Our Nig" on the novel's cover, in the preface she addresses the reader in the first person, identifying the following "fiction" as autobiography, noting that she does not divulge "every transaction in my own life" but has "purposely omitted" the more shameful acts of the northern racists. Yet she abandons the first person quickly. Even in the preface, her claim to authenticity is introduced in the third person. The title does not announce its author until the final three words, "By 'Our Nig,' " and the preface begins with a fairly standard third-person voice:

> In offering to the public the following pages, the writer confesses her inability to minister to the refined and cultivated, the pleasure supplied by abler pens. It is not for such these crude narrations appear.

Only after she has given the conventional apology for her own lack of skill, and simultaneously (paradoxically) demonstrated her ability to write by writing about her inability to write, does Wilson slide into the first person and explain her purpose: "Deserted by kindred, disabled by failing health, I am forced to some experiment which shall aid me in maintaining myself and child without extinguishing this feeble life."

These first three sentences of the preface showcase Wilson's dexterity in moving from one voice to another. She begins in the third person, the least "provisional" position of authority, referring to herself as "the writer." The conventional "apologia" places her in good literary company, from Sir Philip Sidney and Anne Bradstreet to Olauduh Equiano. The third sentence, which introduces the "I," identifies Wilson as a mother, "forced" to write to support herself and her child, an authorizing strategy milked by both sentimental novelists and abolitionists. This voice remains throughout the preface. Employing the political discourse of many slave narratives, Wilson contrasts the immorality of the Southern, slaveholding states to the (usually) better ethics of Northern ones, both appeasing the abolitionists and identifying herself with legal slaves by noting that her mistress was "wholly imbued with *southern* principles." Thus, even within the "succinct and straightforward 'Preface'," Harriet Wilson manipulates both the third-person voice that opens the preface, and the autobiographical first person (Braxton, 49).

Although Wilson opens her novel, like Harriet Jacobs, telling us that "this narrative is no fiction" (Jacobs xiii), when the actual novel begins, she shifts from the slave narrative's non-fictional premise. The body of *Our Nig* is not simply in the third person, but is *so* steeped in the conventions of the sentimental novel that it seems to belie any claim to autobiography. For instance, although the title of the first chapter is "Mag Smith, My Mother," the opening lines invoke the omniscient voice of the sentimental narrator, not the autobiographer: "Lonely Mag Smith! See her as she walks with downcast eyes and heavy heart. It was not always thus" (1). The melodrama, the appeal to the sentiments of the reader, is typical of sentimental fiction. Although ultimately it has little to do with the novel's plot, the very patness of this opening reinvests the narrative voice with the authority of omniscience.

Wilson further entrenches herself in the legitimacy of the sentimental text by introducing *Our Nig* with events that she is distanced from and can squeeze into conventional patterns—the woman betrayed, the woman fallen, the woman abandoned. Mag Smith is a fallen woman, like Foster's Eliza Wharton or Rowson's Charlotte Temple, and Wilson's language is as melodramatic as theirs, and as distanced. Although it becomes apparent quickly that Mag Smith is neither a likely nor a sympathetic heroine, she gives the narrator the opportunity to establish a voice that is relatively objective and quite conventional, and that gives no indication that the author is a black woman. Although the chapter ends with a direct address to the reader, it resembles less Harriet Jacobs's personal form of that address, "Pity me, and pardon me, O virtuous reader!" (56), than Harriet Beecher Stowe's didactic second- and third-person addresses: "Perhaps you laugh too, dear reader; but you know humanity comes out in a variety of strange forms now-a-days, and there is no end to the odd things that humane people will say and do" (8). Wilson concludes her chapter with this more general approach—as in Stowe's address we know who the reader is, but we are not quite so sure of the narrator's identity:

> You can philosophize, gentle reader, upon the impropriety of such unions, and preach dozens of sermons on the evils of amalgamation. Want is a more powerful philosopher and preacher. Poor Mag. She has sundered another bond which held her to her fellows. She has descended another step down the ladder of infamy. (13)

Although Mag disappears from the novel by the end of the second chapter, her dilemma allows the narrator to move away from the personal voice to establish a safer, more traditional narrator.

Once the authorized narrative voice has been established, *Our Nig* begins to tell the story of Frado's life. As the material grows increasingly personal, the narrative distances itself even further from any autobiographical implications. Whereas the first three chapters of *Our Nig* have first-person headings ("Mag Smith, My

Mother," "My Father's Death," and "A New Home For Me"), as the protagonist becomes the center of the text, and the extent of her *de facto* enslavement is revealed, even the chapter titles either refer to the protagonist as "Nig" ("A Friend For Nig," "Spiritual Condition of Nig"), or are generic ("Departures," "Varieties"). The mid-section of the novel is narrated in the third-person.

This anonymous narrator makes judgments about events and characters that an autobiographical voice would have trouble authorizing, praising Frado and criticizing Mrs. Bellmont. In the middle chapters of the novel, Wilson carefully constructs a distanced and sentimentalizing narrator. Here, sentimental conventions facilitate authorial editorializing. The narrator portrays Nig as a Cinderella-like heroine, at one point referring to her as "a frail child, driven from shelter by the cruelty of [James's] mother" (50), and noting that "from early dawn until after all were retired, was she toiling, overworked, disheartened, longing for relief" (65).

Similarly, the narrator paints Mrs. Bellmont as an evil stepmother. In the first reference to Mrs. Bellmont, Mag calls her a "she-devil" (17), and the omniscient narrator confirms this description, claiming that "she was self-willed, haughty, undisciplined, arbitrary and severe. In common parlance, she was a *scold,* a thorough one" (25). Such stereotypical characters serve, as Jane Tompkins states, "as a cultural shorthand" (xvi). Wilson's use of sentimental conventions is more efficient and effective than a first-hand account of Mrs. Bellmont's wrongs, and the third-person voice does not raise the question of the speaker's judgment. In this familiar sentimental setting, the reader may forget that a black author is criticizing a Northern white woman and accept Mrs. Bellmont as a clearly drawn "type."

However, as the novel nears its conclusion, the narrative voice begins to slip. As P. Gabrielle Foreman points out, Wilson's "autobiographical voice continually interrupts her fictional fabric" (314). In the last few chapters, the autobiographical voice is implicit, but powerful: the events coincide with those that the letter writers discuss, and at the end of the last chapter, the narrator repeats the entreaties that the author made in the preface. The distanced voice of the sentimental narrator is interrupted by a personal, passionate one, from the angry description of Samuel's "illiterate harangues" and "humbugs" (128) to her exclamation of disgust about "professed abolitionists . . . Faugh!" (129). The illusion of distance between the narrator, the author, and Frado begins to collapse, and with it, the illusion of an enfranchised speaker.

As the first-person and the third-person voices run together, Wilson cannot maintain the balance of authority and authenticity that she has hitherto managed so well, and the final chapters of *Our Nig* fragment. The sentimental novel yields to the immediate and desperate autobiography, and the pace changes drastically. The last two chapters cover Frado's marriage, her desertion by her husband, her child's and her own sickness, and her attempts to make a living. Characters are abruptly introduced and, as abruptly, disappear. Frado's marriage and subsequent abandonment are covered in two pages. Harriet Wilson was compelled to rush her ending, indeed, her entire novel because (as she tells the reader in the preface, in the body of the narrative, and through the writers of her letters) she desperately needs the money she hopes this book will bring. The eruption of the first person destroys the distance and the conventionality of the third-person narrator; the autobiography careens frantically forward, and *Our Nig* reaches its unsatisfactory ending. The slave narrative consumes the sentimental novel and its authorized omniscient narrator with it.

The distance between them now collapsed, Frado/Wilson writes this book in an attempt to escape from public charity—in part because the public has not been particularly charitable. *Our Nig* is, in the beginning and the end, a cry for help and support. In the preface, Wilson appeals "for patronage"; at the end she demands it:

> And thus, to the present time, may you see her busily employed in preparing her merchandise; then sallying forth to encounter many frowns, but some kind friends and purchasers. Nothing turns her from her steadfast purpose of elevating herself. Reposing on God, she has thus far journeyed securely. Still an invalid, she asks your sympathy, gentle reader. Refuse not, because some part of her history is unknown, save by the Omniscient God. Enough has been unrolled to demand your sympathy and aid. (129-30)

This paragraph, her final but for the parting history of the Bellmonts, is a fascinating interplay of begging and ordering, implied first-person and explicit third-person, admission of weakness and insistence on independence. The narrative voice remains in the third person, but the movement into the present tense, the similarity of this paragraph to the first-person preface, and the merging of the plot with the letters that she includes at the end all reveal the narrator to be the author and protagonist as well, and so, equally disenfranchised.

It is perhaps this reality that drives the author to abandon hope of wielding authority even through a constructed voice, and to fall back on a convention of the slave narrative: third-party letters of reference. *Our Nig* does not end in Wilson's words or with Wilson's voice, first- or third-person, but with an appendix, consisting of three letters, allegedly written by friends of the author. William L. Andrews points out that

> the framing of a slave's narrative with endorsements of his or her character (usually written by whites) had been standard procedure in the black autobiographical tradition for decades. But when Wilson, a black novelist, solicits such authentication to buttress the status of her voice, one might wonder if she is not still writing a kind of enslaved narrative, in which the privilege of authority is implicitly yielded to the natural discourse of white literary overseers. (27)

Andrews's choice of the words "solicits" and "yielded" suggests that Wilson's "enslavement" is psychological, but, in fact, as Andrews himself notes, for the African-American writer at this time, authority and authenticity are inextricably tangled. If, in the end, her use of techniques from the slave narrative detracts from Wilson's authority, it is important to remember that in the beginning she manipulates those techniques to authenticate herself as a black writer.

Wilson's society ultimately limits her possibilities for taking control of her life. At the end of the novel she runs out of options, as does her protagonist. A number of factors contribute to the collapse of the ending: the untidy and inconsistent re-emergence of the autobiographical voice, the change of pace, and finally, Frado's unresolved status. While twentieth-century readers may applaud the end of *Our Nig* for exposing the inadequacy of traditional structures to resolve issues as complex as race in America, the end also reveals the very real difficulties the author faces, both in maintaining a narrative voice and in sustaining a protagonist who is so extremely powerless. Frado's ultimate inability to move forward helps bring the novel crashing to a finish, with neither the tidy closure that virtually defined the popular women's novel in nineteenth-century America, nor the sense of achievement inherent in the form of the slave narrative (despite a certain common protest against closure by writers like Douglass and Jacobs).

Only Wilson's successful exploitation of dual traditions gives the narrator the ability to keep Frado afloat for as long as she does. Although many protagonist/narrators in any literature are without power within their society, Frado is *so* disenfranchised that she has virtually no agency. (If Huck Finn had not escaped from Pap, but had remained locked in the cabin with him for 229 pages, he would have been in a similar situation.) Since the very definition of the novel and its protagonist involves movement, growth, and change, Wilson uses the narrator (now authorized) to create enough freedom for Frado to maintain her position as protagonist. Wilson's strategy is twofold: the narrator stresses the choices that Frado *can* make, and she creates the illusion of choice, even when Frado essentially has none.

In "The Family Militant: Domesticity Versus Slavery in *Uncle Tom's Cabin,*" Myra Jehlen compares the novel to a republic, noting that a protagonist must be a character whose social position enables him or her to possess himself or herself and to make choices. She notes that slavery and the nineteenth-century novel thus involve "a fatal contradiction, between the terms that engender modern characters and plots and those that authorize modern slavery." She goes on to compare the novel to society, noting that the novel's

> *primum mobile* is precisely its characters' capacity, born of self-possession, for self-direction. This capacity is often thwarted, it is true, and the failure of characters to control their lives generates more plots than their successes. But just as republican theory after Rousseau and Hobbes cannot encompass a social category of slaves, for the same reason the novel after Richardson cannot envision a being lacking potential autonomy and incapable of choice. Modern republic and novel alike depend on the assumption that it is in the nature of individuals to be able to at least try to govern themselves. (383)

Freedom of choice and the ability to grow, socially and personally, are prerequisites for a novel's protagonist. For this reason, Jehlen states, a slave cannot be a protagonist. Politically, the slave "is deprived of his birthright to become himself; in novelistic terms, he is denied his own plot" (387)

Certainly, Jehlen's argument applies to Frado. Despite the fact that Frado, or "Nig," is a "Free Black" legally, in practice, she is a slave. In order to assure her of enough "self-possession" to carry her own plot, the narrator repeatedly stresses her rebellious and independent character. Frado will not be given much room to *act* freely or rebelliously in her life (or in the novel) but by emphasizing these characteristics, the narrator insists that Frado has choices, creating the appearance of autonomy narratively even when the plot cannot substantiate it.

Our introduction to Frado comes as her mother and her mother's lover are discussing her abandonment, an incident of victimization over which the six-year-old Frado can have no control:

> "It's no use," said Seth one day; "we must give the children away, and try to get work in some other place."
>
> "Who'll take the black devils?" snarled Mag. . . . "Nobody will want any thing of mine."
>
> "Frado's six years old, and pretty if she is yours, and white folks'll say so. She'd be a prize somewhere." (16-17)

Even as the decision to abandon Frado is being reached, a decision in which she has no choice, no control, no

voice, the narrator describes Frado in a manner that implies a certain independence: "Frado, as they called one of Mag's children, was a beautiful mulatto, with long, curly black hair, and handsome roguish eyes, sparkling with an exuberance of spirit almost beyond restraint" (17). This emphasis on Frado's unbreakable spirit is almost immediately reinforced by her mother's claim that "Frado is such a wild, frolicky thing, and means to do jest as she's a mind to; she won't go if she don't want to" (18). Her mother insists, in effect, that Frado has control, that she cannot be controlled or enslaved. As though to prove her mother's (and the narrator's) point, the child takes independent action at the end of this conversation and runs away. Although Frado is returned, the narrator uses the incident to call attention to her leadership, independence, and lack of fear. It is the novel's relentless insistence on a spiritual independence and rebellious temperament that allows the narrator to sustain Frado as the protagonist for much of the text, despite her position as virtual slave.

At the end of the first chapter, Mag abandons Frado at the Bellmonts', telling them that she is just leaving the child there for a moment. When Mag knocks on the door, and sends Frado inside, the narrator says "Why the impetuous child entered the house, we cannot tell" (23), again creating an illusion of choice. Further, while the Bellmonts argue about Frado's usefulness, and whether to "keep her," Wilson calls attention to Frado's status as a person who is capable of making choices:

> While this conversation was passing below, Frado lay, revolving in her little mind whether she would remain or not until her mother's return. She was of wilful, (sic) determined nature, a stranger to fear, and would not hesitate to wander away should she decide to. . . . She thought she should, by remaining, be in some relation to white people she was never favored with before. So she resolved to tarry, with the hope that mother would come and get her some time. (28)

Wilson emphasizes Frado's free will, the idea that she *chooses* to stay with the Bellmonts, by using the word "resolve" twice, and again noting Frado's "wilful, determined nature." Frado's pondering "whether" or not to remain preserves the idea that Frado is as capable as Hamlet of choosing her fate. Frado is not an adult prince of Denmark, but a six-year-old who has been deserted by her mother. As we see at the end of the novel, there is not much opportunity for a black female to support herself in the North. Even as an adult, Frado will be unable to survive without charity. Here, her choices are created and implied wholly by the narrator.

Although Wilson's narrator can occasionally move the plot simply by suggesting Frado's potential for autonomy—her ability to choose if only she had the opportunity—to sustain her role as protagonist Frado must make actual decisions rather than simply think about them. The problem, as Bakhtin has stated, is that "the hero should not be portrayed as an already completed and unchanging person but as one who is evolving and developing, a person who learns from life" (10). A protagonist must have the ability to grow, to improve herself, in order to sustain a plot. Thus, within the text, Mrs. Bellmont's continued attempts to keep Frado subservient are, in effect, an attempt to keep her from being a protagonist.[8] Because of her limited freedom, Frado's choices must be internal, changes within herself. Thus, *Our Nig* devotes much time to Frado's self-improvement, emphasizing her intellectual and religious education. While many nineteenth-century protagonists have a single goal for self-improvement—to "be better," to be more educated, to be more religious, or to be more "spectable"[9]—Frado has a number, none of which she is able to achieve. The point of each is simply to keep Frado evolving, and to keep the plot moving.

Frado's first phase of self-improvement begins with her education. When she is seven years old, Mr. Bellmont, his sister, and his children decide to send her to school, against the wishes of Mrs. Bellmont, who "was in doubt about the utility of attempting to educate people of color, who were incapable of elevation" (30). When Frado is nine years old Mrs. Bellmont terminates Frado's education and her attempt to "elevate" herself, proclaiming that the child's "time and person [belong] solely to her" (41). The narrator then attempts to move the plot by focusing on a number of "Nig's" pranks, but while Frado's antics give the narrator the opportunity to remind us of her often repressed "fire" and "exuberance," they are not substantive enough to drive a plot. Without a battle to fight or a goal to strive for, Frado cannot play the role of protagonist. Chapter 5 begins with Frado's pranks, but the chapter is then turned over to Jane, the Bellmont's invalid daughter. Because she has nowhere to go or grow, Frado cannot conclude her own chapter.

The story of Jane highlights Frado's lack of options. Although Jane is an invalid, female, and ruled by an overbearing mother, compared to Frado, even Jane has the power to make real choices. She is courted by two men: each wants "to love and possess her as his own" (58). Mrs. Bellmont would force her to marry the man of property rather than the man she loves, but for his own daughter, at least, Mr. Bellmont puts his foot down. Mr. Bellmont tells Jane,

> that he would see that she was not compelled to violate her free choice in so important a transaction. . . . He could not as a father see his child compelled to an uncongenial union; a free, voluntary choice was of such importance to one of her health. She must be left free to her own choice. (60)

Mr. Bellmont gives Jane the necessary ingredient for her to complete her own story—free choice.[10] Jane gets the happy ending that appears to be impossible for Frado.

Wilson's momentary abandonment of the protagonist for another points to some of the problems that she encounters in her attempt to sustain Frado as a protagonist. The chapter that begins with Frado's education and the marks of her own personality, ends with the conclusion of Jane's plot. There is nowhere to go with Frado, so Wilson temporarily shifts the plot to a protagonist who is capable of movement.

Frado's struggle for religion becomes central to the story in *Our Nig,* as it is in many nineteenth-century American novels. But in *Our Nig,* religion is a means rather than an end. In order to maintain her protagonist, the narrator must create a struggle for Frado, a purpose through which the character can define herself. As we have seen, her options are very limited. Religion is both available and conventional. It is perhaps the only authorized struggle—the only battle that Frado might win.

Like education, religion provides an area of growth and individual choice. It also provides another area for rebellion. Here Frado defines herself in opposition to Mrs. Bellmont, who insists that "religion was not meant for niggers" (68), a natural extension of the logic that school is not meant for "people of color, who were incapable of elevation" (30). Like the battle over Frado's education, Mrs. Bellmont's denial of Frado's humanity presents an opportunity for the other characters to legitimize it. Aunt Abby takes Frado to evening meetings with her, recognizing that Frado has "a soul to save" (69). James encourages Frado's conversion because

> he felt sure there were elements in her heart which, transformed and purified by the gospel, would make her worthy the esteem and friendship of the world. A kind, affectionate heart, native wit, and common sense, and the pertness she sometimes exhibited, he felt if restrained properly, might become useful in originating a self-reliance which would be of service to her in after years. (69)

James not only recognizes Frado's existence as an individual, but as a particularly worthy and unique individual capable of the "self-reliance" that Emerson put forth as particularly valuable in the American citizen.

While James and Aunt Abby reinforce Frado's position as protagonist in the plot, the narrator reinforces her role as protagonist in the text by repeatedly articulating Frado's religious doubts in terms of a classic inward struggle, reminding us that an inner struggle requires an inner self—a soul. The narrator calls attention to Frado's spiritual struggle by noting that Frado's "anxiety increased; her countenance bore marks of solicitude unseen before; and though she said nothing of her inward contest, they all observed a change" (85). Again, the good Bellmonts and the bad Bellmonts are divided in their interpretation of Frado's actions. James and Aunt Abby hope that it's a sign of Frado's conversion; Mrs. Bellmont "saw no appearance of change for the better. She did not feel responsible for her spiritual culture, and hardly believed she had a soul." Wilson passes directly from Mrs. Bellmont's belief to the omniscient voice of Truth. The narrator states: "Nig was in truth suffering much." As the phrase "in truth" indicates, the narrator is contradicting a previous statement. Nig's ability to suffer, the fact that "her feelings were very intense on any subject when once aroused," contradicts Mrs. Bellmont's attempt to make her less than human, to render her soulless (86).

While Frado's struggle initially seems clearly defined in terms of Mrs. Bellmont, the first time that Frado seems to triumph over Mrs. Bellmont the narrative begins to falter: what Frado is striving for becomes as murky as what she is struggling against. Novelistically, the point is merely to continue the struggle itself, and thus the always deferred possibility for growth and attainment. In other words, the narrator has more interest in keeping Frado struggling than in resolving her struggles. Thus, even when the issue seems resolved, the narrator keeps circling back to Mrs. Bellmont, and defining Frado's religious doubts in opposition to her.[11] Because of the extent of her disenfranchisement, Frado defines herself (and is defined by the narrator), in effect, against Mrs. Bellmont. While this is obviously a problem—she's defining herself negatively, by what she is not (*not* incapable of elevation, *not* a possession of Mrs. Bellmont)—it is a useful device for defining Frado in terms of the novel. She has so little freedom that even a negative definition is better than none at all.[12]

Frado's religious battle is never resolved. After pages of searching and striving, Frado simply renounces God:

> Frado pondered; her mistress was a professor of religion; was *she* going to heaven? then she did not wish to go.[13] If she should be near James, even, she could not be happy with those fiery eyes watching her ascending path. She resolved to give over all thought of the future world, and strove daily to put her anxiety far from her. (104)

And, until the mandatory mention of God in the last two pages, Frado and Wilson leave the question of God aside. Frado's striving for religion ends as abruptly as her education. Frado does not seem to have moved towards anything; the entire long struggle ends where

it began, with no apparent change or growth in the protagonist. However, the narrator was able to keep the plot moving for more than thirty pages on the *question* of the "spiritual condition of Nig" (73). The act of searching and questioning kept Frado alive as protagonist; it allowed her a place to act independent of, and in opposition to, Mrs. Bellmont. For "our nig," the religious battle is more important than its outcome.

Frado's penultimate development is very brief and signals the collapse that will take place at the end of the novel. In a scene that was probably inspired by Frederick Douglass's narrative, Frado defies and triumphs over Mrs. Bellmont. However, although the drama and the language place it as a climactic moment, the event has no significant effect on Frado or the plot. Painted as the most triumphant moment of all Frado's phases of development, her "power" ends as abruptly as her education or her struggle for religion, and is even more completely dropped.

When Mrs. Bellmont picks up a stick to hit Frado, Frado takes a stand:

> "Stop!" shouted Frado, "strike me, and I'll never work a mite more for you;" and throwing down what she had gathered, stood like one who feels the stirring of free and independent thoughts. . . . Her mistress, in amazement, dropped her weapon, desisting from her purpose of chastisement. Frado . . . did not know, before, that she had a power to ward off assaults. Her triumph in seeing her enter the door with *her* burden, repaid her for much of her former suffering. (105)

This scene has all the earmarks of a classic turning point; however, this potentially pivotal moment in Frado's development, like all of the other moments and phases of development in this novel, exists in a vacuum rather than a continuum. Frado's momentary triumph is just that:

> A few weeks revived the former tempests, and . . . Frado felt them to be unbearable. She determined to flee. But where? Who would take her? . . . She might have to return, and then she would be more in her mistress' power than ever. (107, 108)

Although the narrator notes that Frado's outburst at the woodpile "never met with an 'after clap' " (105), and insists "she had learned how to conquer" (108), there is no subsequent shift in power or independence. The actions that follow Frado's outburst are very much the same as before: Mrs. Bellmont oppresses, Frado considers her limited options (poisoning Mrs. Bellmont, running away) and comes to the "determination previously formed, to remain until she should be eighteen" (109). Frado's courage and humanity are again highlighted, but again they cannot enfranchise her.

Up to this point, *Our Nig* has followed conventional patterns. Gates states that *Our Nig* "shares the tripartite structure of other women's novels, including an unhappy childhood, a seemingly endless period of indenture, and the conclusion" (xliii, xliv). However, there is one very revealing difference in *Our Nig*'s plot. *Our Nig* lacks one-third of that three part structure—the conclusion. The happy ending.

The moment of Frado's departure and freedom *should be* the climax of the novel. Typically the crucial moment in both the sentimental tradition and the slave narrative, Frado's impending independence has been foreshadowed throughout the novel. However, because of her health, because she is black, because she is abandoned by her husband, Frado will not be able to succeed on her own, and once again, she will not get the happy ending to which Jane Bellmont is entitled. As the narrator finally admits, "So much toil as was necessary to sustain Frado, was more than she could endure" (129). Ultimately, her lack of privilege and her poverty—her inability to support herself—make it impossible for Frado to evolve any further and cause the novel's collapse.

In writing *Our Nig,* Harriet Wilson has taken control and authority over the events of her own life. But at the end of the novel the narrator can no longer sustain a voice; the protagonist can no longer move a plot forward. As the protagonist, the narrator, and the author begin to meld into one indistinguishable persona, it is all too clear (in the author's plea for help and support) that this novel, in a sense, is the last ditch effort by an author/protagonist to remain capable of being an author/protagonist. When the fiction runs into the present, Wilson's last act of self-improvement is coming to a close—the act of writing *Our Nig.*

Notes

[1] In using the words "speak" and "hear" I am participating in the illusion that there is a speaker and a listener rather than a writer and (potential) readers. As Jacques Derrida has pointed out, Western civilization from Aristotle to Saussure has privileged the spoken over the written word, defining the written word as simply a substitute for the spoken word.

I am further assuming that writers who publish write in order to be taken seriously, to be able to wield some influence. In *The Art of Telling,* Kermode notes repeatedly that most authors aspire to be "taken seriously" (37), and states that those who cannot have popular success aspire to write "narratives capable of interesting competent readers" (73).

[2] Many critics have pointed out that in a first-person text, issues of authority are particularly problematic. The individualized speaker is deprived of

the third-person narrator's "god-like view" (Scholes 53), and must confront the politics of speaking directly. Because the first-person voice exposes the "provisional nature" of its authority (Auerbach 17), the autobiographical narrative calls upon the speaker to prove that s/he is always already authorized.

[3] Traditional and contemporary critics agree that movement is essential to the protagonist of the traditional novel. Norman Friedman defines the protagonist as "the one who undergoes the major change" (154), Mikhail Bakhtin argues that "the hero should not be portrayed as an already completed and unchanging person but as one who is evolving and developing, a person who learns from life" (10), and Myra Jehlen, who I quote at length in this article, believes that the novel's "*primum mobile* is precisely its characters' capacity . . . for self-direction" (383).

[4] Recent criticism would point out that a satisfactory closure is a fiction. However, so is *Our Nig,* and among the fictions that nineteenth-century United States novels sought to perpetuate was the idea of neat closure, as is indicated by all the criticism on the "flawed" ending of *Adventures of Huckleberry Finn.* D. A. Miller points out that "both Sartre and Barthes have maintained that the end-orientation of the traditional novel serves the repressive order of the nineteenth-century bourgeoisie" (281). I would argue that disenfranchised narrators in particular need to tap into the authority of traditional structures, particularly endings. Given both traditions that Wilson is working with, it seems clear that she was striving for a more traditionally successful closure than she achieved.

[5] In "Spirit Matters: Re-Possessing the African-American Women's Literary Tradition," Anne Dalke argues that we should "explore an alternative beginning to the [African-American Women's] tradition" in the form of the spiritual autobiography. However, while spiritual autobiography was clearly a powerful tradition, and as Dalke points out, often a liberating one, it may not have been an established African-American *literary* tradition. Dalke's own focus, Rebecca Jackson's journal, was first published in 1981. One thinks also of Sojourner Truth, whose autobiography *was* published in 1850, but was dictated to and published through a white woman.

[6] On the subject of authenticity, William L. Andrews states: "During the antebellum era, when black narrative in the United States developed into a highly self-conscious and rhetorically sophisticated tradition, black writers who aimed at a serious hearing knew that the authority they aspired to was predicated on the authenticity that they could project into and through a text." Black writers' authority existed only in the arena of non-fiction, and the black narrative voice must at least "sound truthful" (23). Andrews's main point is to dis-

cuss the "fictionalizing" of the black narrative whereas I'm discussing the "narrativizing" of black fiction, but I think the issues of authenticity and authority are the same.

[7] Scholes and Kellogg discuss the idea of a genre having its own authority, noting, "In mythic or traditional narrative . . . the tradition itself carries its own authority" (242). And, of course, an omniscient narrator is . . . omniscient. In the case of *Our Nig* the very anonymity of placing the narrative voice within a tradition is useful.

[8] Mrs. Bellmont's actions also seem to be an attempt to keep her from being a narrator/author. Elizabeth Ammons points out that Mrs. Bellmont's favorite way to punish Frado is "propping the child's mouth open with a block of wood while she whips her, an act designed to render the child literally speechless: without voice" (184).

[9] The protagonists of *Little Women, The Wide, Wide World,* and *Ragged Dick* strive for at least one of these goals, which, though they sometimes overlap, remain constant. For example, to be "better" involves keeping her temper for Jo March, following her religion for Ellen Montgomery, and educating himself (and thus becoming "spectable") for Ragged Dick, and they strive for these goals from the beginning to the end (where they usually have had *some* success). None simply change to a new goal without having reached the first, as Frado does.

[10] Although it might be argued that Jane will now be "possessed" by her husband, she at least chooses to whom to give herself. Jehlen notes that "a woman must possess herself to give herself away and, in becoming what her fond husband may call his most precious possession, she proves she was first her own" (395).

[11] First, the narrator tells us Frado's concern, raised by Mrs. Bellmont's words: "*is* there a heaven for the black? She knew there was one for James, and Aunt Abby, and all good white people; but was there any for blacks?" (84). The phrasing here makes this sound like the central problem. But this problem is resolved almost as soon as it's defined; Frado's minister resolves it:

> "Come to Christ," he urged, "all young or old, white or black, bond or free, come all to Christ for pardon; repent, believe."
>
> This was the message she longed to hear; it seemed to be spoken for her.

Frado has been given the "message she longed to hear," that Christ welcomes all people, "white or black." However, a true conversion would end Frado's struggle

for self-improvement, so the narrator keeps positing new problems. In the sentence following the "message [Frado] longed to hear," the narrator staves off a resolution to Frado's confusion:

> But he had told them to repent; "what was that?" she asked. She knew she was unfit for any heaven, made for whites or blacks. She would gladly repent, or do anything which would admit her to share the abode of James. (85)

When the first issue (whether blacks can go to heaven) appears to be approaching resolution, the narrator raises the apparently critical issue of Frado's wanting to follow James rather than Jesus. However, this new problem disappears almost immediately. Despite the minister's words, the narrator continues to focus on the struggle in terms of Mrs. Bellmont, even though that particular battle appears to have been won repeatedly and definitively by the union of Frado, the "good Bellmonts," and the minister. Frado needs something to fight *against* as well as something to struggle for.

[12] It's interesting to note that even at the end of the novel Wilson/Frado is struggling to prove that Mrs. Bellmont was wrong. At the end of chapter 11 (the penultimate), the narrator states that "she felt herself capable of elevation" (124), and again at the end of chapter 12, and the very end of the novel, she says, "Nothing turns her from her steadfast purpose of elevating herself" (130). She is still defining herself in opposition to Mrs. Bellmont.

[13] Twain's *Huckleberry Finn* will make an almost identical statement in 1885, when the finicky Miss Watson stops picking at him long enough to say that she plans to go to "the good place." Huck tells us, "Well, I couldn't see no advantage in going where she was going, so I made up my mind I wouldn't try for it. But I never said so, because it would only make trouble, and wouldn't do no good" (8).

Although Frado and Huck come to nearly identical conclusions, the context and the implications are quite different. Huckleberry is a boy, the hero of a boy's book, complete with the implicit understanding that "boys will be boys." Frado is a girl, and thus, willingly or not, bound to a certain level of piety and goodness.

Also, Huck's profession comes at the beginning of the novel, and the purpose it serves is entirely comic. By the time Frado makes her statement, the reader has read pages of her suffering, anxiety, and concern over the subject of religion and understands that in some essential way she has been beaten. Something has been taken from her. Huck's understated "I couldn't see no advantage" is amusing whereas Frado's nightmarish vision of Mrs. Bellmont following her, even to heaven, is not.

Works Cited

Ammons, Elizabeth. "Stowe's Dream of the Mother-Saviour: *Uncle Tom's Cabin* and American Women Writers before the 1920s." *New Essays on Uncle Tom's Cabin.* Ed. Eric Sundquist. Cambridge: Cambridge UP, 1986.

Andrews, William L. "The Novelization of Voice in Early African American Narrative." *PMLA* 105 (1990): 23-34.

Auerbach, Jonathan. *The Romance of Failure: First-Person Fictions of Poe, Hawthorne, and James.* New York: Oxford UP, 1989.

Bakhtin, M. M. *The Dialogic Imagination.* Ed. Michael Holquist. Trans. Caryl Emerson and Michael Holquist. Austin: U of Texas P, 1981.

Braxton, Joanne M., and Andree Nicola McLaughlin, eds. *Wild Women in the Whirlwind: Afra-American Culture and the Contemporary Literary Renaissance.* New Brunswick: Rutgers UP, 1990.

Dalke, Anne. "Spirit Matters: Re-Possessing the African-American Women's Literary Tradition." *Legacy* 12 (1995): 1-16.

Derrida, Jacques. *Of Grammatology.* Trans. Gayatri C. Spivak. Baltimore: Johns Hopkins UP, 1976.

Foreman, P. Gabrielle. "The Spoken and the Silenced in *Incidents in the Life of a Slave Girl* and *Our Nig.*" *Callaloo* 13 (1990): 313-24.

Friedman, Norman. "Forms of the Plot." *The Theory of the Novel.* Ed. Philip Stevick. New York: Free P, 1967. 145-66.

Gates, Henry Louis, Jr. "Editor's Introduction: Writing 'Race' and the Difference it Makes." *Critical Inquiry* 12 (1985): 1-20.

Jacobs, Harriet. *Incidents in the Life of a Slave Girl.* 1861. Ed. Jean Fagan Yellin. Cambridge: Harvard UP, 1987.

Jehlen, Myra. "The Family Militant: Domesticity versus Slavery in *Uncle Tom's Cabin.*" *Criticism* 31 (1989): 383-400.

Johnston, Jill. "Fictions of the Self in the Making." *New York Times Book Review.* 25 April, 1993. 1+.

Kermode, Frank. *The Art of Telling.* Cambridge: Harvard UP, 1983.

Miller, D. A. *Narrative and its Discontents: Problems of Closure in the Traditional Novel.* Princeton: Princeton UP, 1981.

Scholes, Robert, and Robert Kellogg. *The Nature of Narrative.* New York: Oxford UP, 1966.

Stanzel, Franz K. *A Theory of Narrative.* Trans. C. Godsche. Cambridge: Cambridge UP, 1984.

Stowe, Harriet Beecher. *Uncle Tom's Cabin.* 1851-52. New York: Bantam, 1981.

Tompkins, Jane. *Sensational Designs: The Cultural Work of American Fiction, 1790-1860.* New York: Oxford UP, 1985.

Wilson, Harriet. *Our Nig; or, Sketches from the Life of a Free Black.* 1859. Introd. Henry Louis Gates, Jr. New York: Vintage, 1983.

Elizabeth Fox-Genovese (essay date 1997)

SOURCE: "'To Weave It into the Literature of the Country': Epic and the Fictions of African American Women," in *Poetics of the Americas: Race, Founding, and Textuality,* edited by Bainard Cowan and Jefferson Humphries, Louisiana State University Press, 1997, pp. 31-45.

[*In the following essay, Fox-Genovese argues that* Our Nig *reverses the conventions of domestic fiction in an attempt to describe the obstacles facing the integration of the stories of African-American women into the American literary landscape.*]

Toward the end of Frances Ellen Watkins Harper's novel, *Iola Leroy,* Dr. Frank Latimer asks Iola Leroy (to whom he will shortly propose marriage), who is seeking to do "something of lasting service" for her people, why she does not write a "good, strong book that would be helpful to them?" More than willing, she reminds him that the writing of a successful book requires leisure and money and, even more, "needs patience, perseverance, courage, and the hand of an artist to weave it into the literature of the country."[1]

By the time that Harper published *Iola Leroy; or, Shadows Uplifted* in 1892, she had been a successful and admired writer for almost forty years, as well as an indefatigable worker for the advancement of her people, but she had never previously published a novel. With empathetic hindsight, it should be possible to understand why she had not. Leisure and money had their say for her and, even more, for other African American women writers, but may not alone have accounted for the apparent difficulty of telling the story of African American women or even for the difficulty of African American women's telling the story of their people.

Consider the special qualities that Harper thought such a telling required: "patience, perseverance, courage, and the hand of an artist." She believed that those qualities were necessitated by what must be the object of such a telling: "to weave it into the literature of the country." Today, it has become a commonplace among many critics, especially those interested in the writing of women and African Americans, that the literature of the country was not noticeably receptive to dissident points of view. Many, indeed, would hold that those to whom the dominant culture has been less than receptive have no call to respect its sensibilities and, yes, prejudices. How, such critics ask, can you be expected to write yourself into a culture that trivializes or stereotypes, when it does not blatantly ignore, your experience?

The prospect appears all the more daunting when we acknowledge that African American women knew that their experience turned the expectations and assumptions of the dominant culture topsy-turvy. Harriet Wilson, the first African American woman (so far as we know) to try her hand at novel writing, saw her only effort, *Our Nig,* sink into oblivion.[2] On reflection, the fate of *Our Nig* should not occasion undue surprise. It was, if ever there was one, a countertext and an almost unbearably angry one at that. Harriet Wilson had no truck with the sentimental domestic pieties of mid-nineteenth-century American culture, and from its opening pages *Our Nig* reverses all of them.

Within two brief chapters, Wilson sketches the spiraling "degradation" of Mag Smith, white mother of her mulatto protagonist, Frado. Abandoned after having succumbed to the seduction of a man who considerably outranks her in social station, Mag bears an "unwelcomed" child, who almost immediately dies. Mag welcomes the death, which Wilson suggests her readers should acknowledge as a "blessed release." What, she ponders, could have been the fate of such a child? "How many pure, innocent children not only inherit a wicked heart of their own, claiming life-long scrutiny and restraint, but are heirs also of parental disgrace and calumny, from which only long years of patient endurance in paths of rectitude can disencumber them" (6-7). Wilson has thus identified her text with the seduction and abandonment of what, at this point in the novel, appears to be her main female character, the birth and death of her illegitimate child, and the passing assertion that many of those who are formulaically called "pure, innocent" children inherit wicked hearts of their own.

In defying the conventions of womanhood and the prescribed feelings of motherhood, Mag has embraced a fate from which she can no longer escape. When a move to another town fails to free her from her past or to improve her material circumstances, she returns to the scene of her disgrace, eking out a meager living from the few odd jobs that immigrant laborers disdain. The black man, Jim, who supplies her with wood, offers the only human fellowship she experiences, and when he asks her to marry him, she listlessly acquiesces. Viewing his white wife as a "treasure," Jim does his best to provide well for her. Together, they have two children, including the girl Frado. But after Jim dies of consumption, Mag spirals even lower, living, unmarried, with his black business partner, Seth Shipley.

Wilson explains that Mag, having lived for years as an outcast, had stifled the feelings of penitence and the agonies of conscience. "She had no longings for a purer heart, a better life. . . . She entered the darkness of perpetual infamy. She asked not the rite of civilization or Christianity. Her will made her the wife of Seth" (16). And, when circumstances again worsen, Seth persuades her to give the children away. The main story begins with Mag's leaving Frado at the house of the affluent, white Bellmont family. Throughout the first day, "Frado waited for the close of day, which was to bring back her mother. Alas! it never came. It was the last time she ever saw or heard of her mother" (23). Yet in comparison with Mrs. Bellmont, an acknowledged "she-devil," whose viciousness dominates Frado's experience throughout the remainder of the novel, Mag ranks as the good mother.

These opening chapters stand alone among the writings of nineteenth-century American women, perhaps alone among all nineteenth-century American literature. And they introduce what probably qualifies as the angriest and least compliant novel by a nineteenth-century woman writer. The willful noncompliance with cultural conventions and fierce determination to tell a story that few were eager to hear do much to account for the oblivion to which *Our Nig* was relegated. On the face of it, nothing could seem further from Harper's determination to write her story into the literature of the country. The simple lesson to be drawn from *Our Nig* is that the attempt to write the story of African American women into the literature of the country runs into what may well be insuperable obstacles. Wilson seems to suggest that if you tell the truth, no one will read you, which is tantamount to saying that you cannot both tell the truth and meet prevailing literary expectations. Conversely, if you do meet prevailing literary expectations, you will not be telling the truth, which may make it very difficult for you to write with power and conviction.

It would be easy, but not entirely accurate, to attribute the long disappearance of *Our Nig* to racial and sexual prejudice.[3] In publishing the novel, Wilson clearly understood the risk she ran of alienating even those most likely to be sympathetic. In the preface, she attempts to anticipate and disarm hostility. First, she mobilizes the conventions of her own lack of talent and the distressing circumstances that have nonetheless driven her to write. Even the most pressing misfortunes would not, however, lead her to "palliate slavery at the South, by disclosures of its appurtenances North" (3). Her mistress's principles were wholly *"southern."* And had she recounted every misery of her life, as she has not because of her reluctance to provoke shame in her antislavery friends, "the unprejudiced would declare [her treatment] unfavorable in comparison with treatment of legal bondmen" (3). Like other authors before and since, Wilson dares to hope that her candid confession will disarm the severest criticism. And finally, she appeals to all of her "colored brethren" for "patronage, hoping they will not condemn this attempt of their sister to be erudite" (3).

In essential respects, as Wilson may have known or at least suspected, *Our Nig* has more in common with antebellum southern women's writing than with northern women's. I know of no southern woman writer who had the audacity to claim that the brutal neglect of white working women in the North drove them into the arms of free black men, but many claimed that it drove them to death. Wilson's portrait of Mrs. Bellmont's cruelty, bad faith, and lack of manners should have warmed the heart of Caroline Lee Hentz, Mary Eastman, or Louisa McCord.[4] *Our Nig* offers little or nothing to flatter the sensibilities of antislavery northerners. To the contrary, it forcefully suggests that the curse of racism has so infected the United States as to make the choice between sections, and even the choice between slavery and freedom, virtually meaningless. To drive the point home, Wilson introduces into her own antislavery text a final ironic gloss by having her protagonist, Frado, marry a black man who was working for abolition and who falsely claimed to be a former slave. Thus Wilson, admittedly against the odds, was trying to make her readers understand that even the righteous work of antislavery may not be what it seems. This was not a story that many readers would have found useful to pass on.

If Wilson could lay any claim to having written her story into the literature of the country, it could only be by a series of reversals that bordered on insults none were willing to accept. Yet if one gets beyond what we might call the overt political "message" of her story, the ways in which she was trying to weave it into the literature of the country command attention. Unlike Harriet Jacobs, Wilson did not drop so much as a passing curtsy to prevailing views about the purity of women or the devotion of mothers. Whereas Jacobs goes to great lengths to establish the respectability of her mother and her own devotion to her, Wilson represents her mother as abandoning her as the logical and unemotional consequence of a degraded life. Where Jacobs represents her fair-skinned, literate black mother as having enjoyed a loving and respectable marriage to a man who had all the feelings of a free man, Wilson represents her white mother as having had a bastard before marrying a black man simply to put bread on the table.

Henry Louis Gates sees *Our Nig* as essentially autobiographical with Frado as Wilson's persona, and he calls attention to the ways in which Wilson slipped into the use of personal pronouns to refer to relations that properly adhere to Frado. Similarly, Jacobs used the persona of Linda Brent to disguise her own identity and, presumably, to conceal aspects of her experience. Jacobs' greatest disguise, however, lies in the language in which she wrote and represented Linda Brent as speaking and in the middle-class sensibilities that she represented Linda Brent as embodying. Notwithstanding Linda Brent's profuse apologies for having had her children by a man to whom she was not married, there is nothing about *Incidents in the Life of a Slave Girl* that would not have passed muster in any respectable northern, middle-class home.

Our Nig is another matter entirely. Wilson made virtually no concessions to middle-class sensibilities. Not only did she represent white folks in a harsh light but she unambiguously represented the debilitating cost of their behavior for black folks. Being abandoned and abused does not transform Frado into a long-suffering saint. Wilson represents Frado as openly hating her mistress and as taking her revenge any way she can. Tellingly, Wilson forthrightly acknowledges that children may inherit a wicked heart that is all their own and that requires restraint. Throughout *Our Nig,* in other words, Wilson frontally attacks the comfortable pieties that might have made her novel palatable to white readers. Suffering, abuse, and discrimination, she insists throughout, do not necessarily—and perhaps do not ever—transform fallible human beings into saints.

Wilson's uncompromising insistence on disrobing the most cherished white, middle-class icons indirectly confirms that she knew that which she was attacking. Her request that her colored brethren not condemn their sister's attempt to be erudite was probably no casual figure of speech. A comparison of her and Jacobs' texts strongly suggests that she was, if anything, the more learned of the two. Like so many African American writers, Wilson manifests considerable knowledge of American and British elite culture. She borrowed many of the epigraphs at the head of each chapter from highly appreciated white poets, primarily of the first half of the nineteenth century: Shelley, Byron, Thomas Moore, Martin Tupper, Eliza Cook, and, for the final chapter, the book of Ecclesiastes.

Notwithstanding dramatic differences in tone and diction between the epigraphs and the chapters, the ways in which they complement and gloss each other are clear. Thus, the verse from Thomas Moore that introduces the first chapter about Mag Smith speaks of the grief beyond all others that

> First leaves the young heart lone and desolate
> In the wide world, without that only tie

For which it loved to live or feared to die;
Lorn as the hung-up lute, that ne'er hath
  spoken
Since the sad day its master-chord was
  broken!

And, immediately following the verse, the chapter begins, "Lonely Mag Smith! See her as she walks with downcast eyes and heavy heart. It was not always thus. She *had* a loving, trusting heart" (5). But Mag, like her daughter after her, had lost her parents early and been left to develop into womanhood, "unprotected, uncherished, uncared for" (5). Wilson does not specify whether the loss that cripples Mag's ability to feel is her loss of her parents, especially her mother, or her loss of the well-born lover to whom she transferred that most basic love "for which she loved to live and feared to die."

The fourth chapter, "A Friend for Nig," in which James Bellmont first appears, is preceded by a verse from Byron on the blessings of friendship. The verse emphasizes the unique place of friendship in youth, "When every artless bosom throbs with truth, / Untaught by worldly wisdom how to feign." Youth, it concludes, is the time

  When all we feel our honest souls disclose—
  In love to friends, in open hate to foes;
  No varnished tales the lips of youth repeat,
  No dear-bought knowledge purchased by
    deceit.

The chapter that follows contains two references to Frado's loss of her mother. In the first, she tells the friendly Aunt Abby, " 'I've got to stay out here and die. I ha'n't got no mother, no home. I wish I was dead' " (46). In the second, she responds to James's assurance that she will not be whipped because she ran away and his injunction that she must try to be a good girl. " 'If I do, I get whipped. . . . They won't believe what I say. Oh, I wish I had my mother back; then I should not be kicked and whipped so. Who made me so?' " (51).

When James responds to her query that God made her so, just as He made James, and Aunt Abby, and her mother, she asks if the same God made her as made her mother. And when James assures her that He did, she responds that then she does not like that God, " 'Because he made her white, and me black. Why didn't he make us *both* white?' " (51). James, at a loss to answer her "knotty questions," encourages her to go to sleep, promising that she will feel better in the morning. It took, Wilson informs us, "a number of days before James felt in a mood to visit and entertain old associates and friends" (51).

In these instances, as in innumerable others throughout the novel, Wilson demonstrates a remarkable literary skill that is all the more difficult to appreciate because it is so very much her own. Her striking mixture of voices combines the spare, almost modernist, narrative of the early chapters about Mag Smith; the direct and unvarnished conversations, including Frado's dialect; and occasional interventions of an omniscient narrator in a rather studied neoclassical voice. The various voices tend to be divided between the specific situations and general reflections. Thus the chapter that follows the passage from Byron and introduces James begins, "With what differing emotions have the denizens of earth awaited the approach of to-day" (40).

In some ways, the alternation between the specific and the general resembles the alternation between the use of the personal pronouns that identify Mag Smith as "my mother" and the use of Frado to identify the protagonist who, by the logic of Mag Smith as "my mother," should be I. The novel never pretends to resolve these apparent contradictions. It does not even explicitly acknowledge them. Throughout, the voice of Harriet Wilson remains somewhat confused and divided among Frado and the various narrative voices. Unlike Harriet Jacobs, she does not try to fit the voice of her protagonist into the rhetoric of domestic fiction. And unlike Harriet Jacobs, she does not restrict her judgments about human nature and the order of the universe to the formulas of domestic fiction. *Our Nig* never attains the unity of tone that characterizes *Incidents in the Life of a Slave Girl*. To put it differently, *Incidents* attempts to placate its readers; *Our Nig* does not.

Jacobs, it appears, believed that to write the story of African American women into the literature of the country, the story would, at least in some measure, have to be tailored to the expectations of its prospective readers. Wilson was no less interested in having readers appreciate and, especially, buy her book, which she claimed to have written out of a desperate need for money, but she proved less able or willing than Jacobs to force either her story or her language into the prevailing mode of domestic fiction.

Even the cautious Jacobs hinted that the conventions of domestic fiction did not perfectly capture her own experience, but she steadfastly persevered in shaping that experience to fit the conventions as closely as possible. She especially exploited the dictum of the leading domestic sentimentalists, notably Harriet Beecher Stowe, that slavery represented the absolute contradiction of domestic norms. Adherence to this dictum permitted her to present her own lapses from domestic virtue as the consequence of slavery, not of her character or breeding. To represent her mother as the model of domesticity, she emphasized the ways in which her mother's experience had resembled that of a free woman.

Freedom, in Jacobs' pages, emerges as the condition of and proxy for female virtue. This assumption perfectly mirrored the most cherished claims to moral superiority advanced by white northeastern women writers. It further linked virtuous female behavior to the ideology of male individualism that was, increasingly, condemning slavery as the antithesis of freedom.[5] For the majority of the northeastern domestic sentimentalists, the natural corollary to their belief in the complementarity of female domestic virtue and male individualism was human perfectibility. In their view, children, who were born innocent, confirmed the innate goodness of human nature which, with proper nurturing, could continue to perfect itself throughout life.

The assumptions and goals of the domestic sentimentalists left little place for tragedy. As a rule, occurrences that presumably contradicted their commitment to perfectionism—losses, reversals of fortune, deaths, evil deeds, the breaking up of families—resulted from specific character failings or corrupt social institutions or bad mothering. By attributing these failings to specific causes, rather than to the inherent tragedy of the human condition or the innate possibilities for evil in human nature, the domestic sentimentalists successfully presented evil as correctable and tragedy as avoidable. Thus they rarely distinguished between the evils inherent in slavery and those which must attend any social system. And they thereby dramatically narrowed the variety of human experience. Clinging firmly to the belief that their values embodied the highest aspirations of humanity, they blithely assumed that those values should be acknowledged as moral norms. In any event, nineteenth-century American politics increasingly confirmed their view of their values as normative. The triumph of bourgeois individualism in politics proceeded in tandem with and ensured its triumph in literature.

It is safe to assume that Harriet Wilson sensed what was coming and that *Our Nig* embodies her rejection of it. Northeastern, middle-class complacency did not, in her view, exhaust either the complexities of human nature or the possibilities of literature. After the Civil War, at an accelerating rate, others would come to criticize what they perceived as the self-satisfied narrowness of middle-class American culture. In general, their criticisms did not overturn the paradigmatic narratives of individualism, although at their best they began to insist on the varieties of individualism. Many recent critics have called attention to the ways in which women writers began to wrestle with the inherently masculine assumptions of the master plots of American culture, but their primary mission has been to reclaim individualism for women.[6] The same, with appropriate qualifications, can be said for African American male writers, who from slavery days have focused on their own exclusion from individualism's promises of male authority and autonomy.

Thus following the Civil War, as before it, the political and literary premises of individualism dominated what Harper called "the literature of the country." These premises, which explicitly emphasized individual autonomy and responsibility as universal attributes, implicitly harbored sexual and racial assumptions that restricted access to an authoritative literary voice. Perhaps more important, they intertwined with a vision of the history of the country that continued to feature slavery as the antithesis of freedom. The persistence of slavery as the sign of national sin proved wonderfully compatible with the commitment to perfectionism. Northerners enthusiastically embraced anti-slavery as the sign of their own transcendence of sin. Southerners never accepted the equation of slavery with sin, but they also faced serious obstacles in writing their distinct views into the literature of the country. Before the war, their defense of slavery as the foundation of a more humane social order met with irate resistance from the antislavery North. After the war, defeat stripped southerners of the will to defend slavery as an alternate vision of social order, and they settled upon a racism that had disfigured but by no means overwhelmed their antebellum worldview.

Harriet Wilson shared the northern opposition to slavery but not white northerners' righteous conviction that they had put slavery behind them. As she suggested in the preface to *Our Nig,* she believed that the most insidious forms of slavery did persist in the North. Her fictional illustration of this persistence resulted in a comprehensive and angry indictment of the many insidious forms that slavery can take. Obviously, Mrs. Bellmont's abuse of and disregard for the humanity of Frado top the list and constitute the primary focus of the novel. But the early chapters on Mag Smith add an important dimension that links Wilson's work to a distinct tradition of African American women's writing.

Wilson depicts the free white Mag Smith as eerily similar to unfortunate black slave mothers. Mag is drawn, by overwhelming circumstances, into bearing and abandoning mulatto children. As she tumbles toward the nadir of her misfortunes, she enters into a marriage sanctified only by her own will. On the face of it, the use of Mag to introduce Frado's story seems puzzling. Many domestic novelists chose to make their heroines orphans, but normally paid little attention to their mothers, who were invariably presented as having died. To the extent that white domestic novelists, notably Harriet Beecher Stowe, considered the circumstances of slave mothers, they wrote them directly into the conventions of maternal devotion and attributed their possible failures to fulfill those conventions to the brutality of slavery. In *Incidents,* Harriet Jacobs hewed closely to this model, with respect both to her own mother and to her attitudes toward her own children.

In *Our Nig,* Wilson implicitly asserts that prevailing domestic conventions cannot be stretched to fit the story she wants to tell. But, in so doing, she confronts the intractable problem of how it is possible to tell the story, especially the woman's story, of slavery. As a free white woman whose life resembles that of a black slave woman, Mag Smith represents a double inversion: the inversion of the conventional story of free white women by behaving like a slave; the inversion of the story of black slave women by being white. Her life confuses the neat boundaries favored by the narrative of individualism. It is no wonder that *Our Nig* did not attract a large readership. And because it fell into such a long neglect, it is difficult to argue that Wilson's concerns directly influenced subsequent African American women writers. Yet I am prepared to argue that the themes of *Our Nig* continued to engage the imaginations of African American women who struggled, with mixed success, to write their own story into the literature of the country. Above all, however, *Our Nig* suggests the magnitude of the obstacles African American women writers confronted.

Many African American writers tried to solve some of the problems by selecting mulatto heroines. Such heroines, of whom Clotel, Iola Leroy, Sappho Clark, and Hagar Ellis are but the better known, offered the perfect compromise between the virtues of freedom and the degradation of slavery. The compromise worked especially well with fair-skinned female protagonists who could plausibly be described as innately virtuous and innocent victims. (Victimization posed problems for the representation of men, as the figure of Uncle Tom confirms.) Such heroines could plausibly be represented as beautiful by white standards, as speaking in perfect English, and, frequently, as having been raised in the belief that they were white, which means having been raised to observe the conventions of bourgeois domesticity.

Such a sketch of the mulatto heroine should clarify the problems that confronted any African American woman writer who attempted to write of a woman's experience of slavery from the subjective perspective. The main requirement for the high yaller heroine was that she have internalized none of the abuses of slavery. She must be a victim, but only in her external circumstances. Her scars must never be those of character. The formula of the mulatto heroine contains a significant measure of racism, especially in its assumption that white standards of female beauty are normative. More important, however, the formula betrays the hold of the individualist narrative on the literary imagination. For the individualist narrative, in emphasizing women's difference from men, effectively cast all women as victims and claimed that they willingly embraced their victimization. White women had a point, albeit a more limited one than they admitted, in comparing the condition of women to the condition of slaves. But then, free white women and black slave women shared an unwillingness to speak openly of the most scarring pains of their situation.

Normally the critics who write about mulatto heroines do not include Frado. Yet Frado was a mulatto. She differed from her literary sisters in having a white mother and a black father, in her appearance, and, above all, in the anger with which she responded to the indignities of her situation. In essential respects, Frado represents the inversion of the "tragic" mulatto of convention. Where the tragic mulatto is patient and long-suffering, Frado is angry and rebellious. Unlike the conventional mulatto heroine, Frado exposes the internal scars that her experience has traced in her mind. In many ways, she more closely resembles a heroine in an ancient Greek tragedy than the heroine of a domestic novel. No comforting domestic pieties can encompass the experience of the child who has been born into an interracial union based on economic dependence and who has been abandoned, again for economic reasons, by the mother she loves but whom she also resents for not having made her white. Wilson's evocation of Frado carries an especially bitter and biting irony because enslavement did follow the condition of the mother.

Frado's conflicted feelings about her mother begin to hint at what may have been the conflicted feelings of slave girls toward their mothers. Such conflicts are, indeed, the stuff of tragedy. But the domestic tradition did not allow for tragedy in the sense of inherent and irreconcilable conflicts. The orphan heroines of domestic fiction do not admit to having hated the mothers who abandoned them, if only through a death that was no fault of their own, and whom they also loved. Harriet Jacobs firmly assures us that Linda Brent's daughter felt no resentment toward her mother. And as African American women began to write their story into the literature of the country, they were understandably tempted to sustain the silence.

It is safe to assume that the oral culture of slaves, most of whom were not literate, found a way of preserving some of the conflicts and tensions. The sources abound with examples of slave mothers who beat their own children out of the panicky determination to teach them that the world was a dangerous place. The same mothers frequently risked their own safety to provide their children with tokens of love. And, yes, occasionally a slave mother, who could take no more, ran off, abandoning her children. Now and then a slave mother even killed one of her children to put it out of the reach of conditions she finally judged intolerable. But these were not stories that could easily be woven into the literature of the country. In *Beloved,* Toni Morrison breaks the silence, but until recently this was truly, in her words, "not a story to pass on."[7]

Following emancipation, African American women were primarily concerned with establishing families and communities and beginning to enjoy the prerogatives of freedom. Even when their hopes were most sorely deceived, many remained committed to the ideal of comfortable respectability. And then, for those who could write of their experience, there was the problem of shame. The literature of the country did not invite women's public confessions of sexual abuse, much less confessions of extramarital sexual pleasure or conflicted feelings toward children. In the end, the real cost and horror of slavery did not lend themselves to the narratives of bourgeois individualism, if only because whoever told the story would have to admit that this was done to me. And admitting that this was done to me amounted to writing oneself out of the story entirely.

In trying to write themselves into the literature of the country, African American women were, if for understandable reasons, also tempted to write themselves out of the oral culture of their people and into the "proper-speaking" English that signaled middle-class respectability. More dangerous yet, they were tempted to deny or bury the truth about the real suffering of their mothers and grandmothers. The conventions of domestic fiction offered them no way to write of that experience, primarily because the conventions remained so closely tied to individualist premises. And, pretenses to universality notwithstanding, the individualism of American culture trailed innumerable assumptions about the specific ways in which women, slaves, and blacks related to the free white male embodiment of individualism. Individualism thus confronted African American women writers with a wall of denial. If they wrote as women, they had to write themselves white—and passive. If they wrote as blacks, they had to write themselves male. In retrospect, it appears that this overdetermined denial of African American women's experience may account for the extraordinary vitality of their writing in our own time.

To break the stranglehold of silence, African American women writers have had to find ways to tell stories that fundamentally challenged the most unyielding assumptions of the literature of the country. More than has commonly been recognized, Harriet Wilson pointed the way. However significant *Our Nig* remains for having been the first novel written by an African American woman, it deserves special attention for throwing down the gauntlet to received conventions, even as it proclaimed its author's conversance with high literary tradition.

Recall, if you will, that Wilson prefaced each of her chapters with a passage of verse. She apparently wrote some herself; others she borrowed from the most appreciated literature of her day. In general, her choices were excellent, especially because, on first reading, they serve to assimilate her story to the prevailing

sensibilities of her epoch. The verses apparently confirm that Mag and Frado's emotional travails echo those that preoccupied established poets. The borrowed verses thus suggest that Mag and Frado's pain merges with a universal experience. But look again. When Wilson quotes Byron on the ways in which youth honestly discloses the soul and disdains deceit, does she really mean that school boys are honest with each other in a way that adults are not? Or is she subtly mocking the claim of honesty and casting her readers, by implication the American public, as the foes who deserve open hate? To choose one reading or another would miss the complexity of her intent. She wanted both.

Wilson, by her use of those verses, was proudly writing herself into the literature of the country. By the double entendre with which her text endowed them, she was also serving notice that to accommodate her story the literature would have to change. Her strategy unmistakably implied that the literature of the country would have to allow for conflicted readings and multiple perspectives. In this respect, Wilson bequeathed an important legacy to her most talented successors who, even if they had never read her, drew something of her sensibility from the experience that they shared with her.

African American women's experience of slavery indelibly colored their relation to the literature of the country, because the pieties of that literature could not encompass their experience. Gradually and unevenly, African American women writers have created an alternative literature that features collective rather than individual subjects. The point is not, as some like to claim, that they repudiated the dominant (white male) literary tradition. They did not. From Wilson's evocation of Byron and Shelley to Hurston's love of Shakespeare and Milton to Morrison's admiration for the ancient Greek dramatists, their continuing engagement with the high Western literary tradition resonates throughout their work. But as they have increasingly felt freer to try to tell the hard, unvarnished truth of their mothers' and grandmothers' lives, they have been led to conjoin the oral tradition of their people with the literary tradition of their aspirations.

The most compelling work of African American women writers draws its peculiar vitality from its attempt to fuse disparate oral and literate traditions and from its determination to make the literary tradition apply. Like Harriet Wilson, they are implicitly posing the question, If this is beautiful and moving, then what is it about? And they are answering that if it is indeed about you, must it not also be about me? Their insistence is helping to move the literature of the country away from the narrow assumptions of individualism toward a properly epic vision. The story of African American slavery is, ultimately, an epic that implicates all of us.

The abolitionists' attempt to cast it as a Manichaean struggle between the forces of good and evil rested on an individualist vision of the good that denied the slaves' experience. Today, the descendants of slaves are forcefully reminding us that their experience has been and may yet be ours. In this spirit, Harriet Wilson chose, for the last chapter of **Our Nig,** an epigraph that ironically invoked a biblical favorite of the slaveholders—as if, once again, to demonstrate the strange and conflicted close connection between the two variants of southern culture. She chose the words of the biblical preacher, "Nothing new under the sun."

Notes

[1] Frances Ellen Watkins Harper, *Iola Leroy; or, Shadows Uplifted* (New York, 1988), 262.

[2] Harriet E. Wilson, *Our Nig; or, Sketches from the Life of a Free Black, in a Two-Story White House, North, Showing that Slavery's Shadows Fall Even There, by "Our Nig,"* ed. Henry Louis Gates, Jr. (1859; New York, 1983), hereinafter cited parenthetically by page number in the text. For the history of the novel and a discussion of its relation to the culture of the period, see Gates's Introduction.

[3] See *ibid.,* xxxi-xxxiv, on the paucity of references to it.

[4] Caroline Lee Hentz, *The Planter's Northern Bride* (Chapel Hill, 1970); Mary Eastman, *Aunt Phyllis's Cabin* (Philadelphia, 1852); Louisa S. McCord, Review of *Uncle Tom's Cabin, Southern Quarterly Review,* XXIII (n.s. VII) (January, 1853), 81-120.

[5] See Elizabeth Fox-Genovese, *Feminism Without Illusions: A Critique of Individualism* (Chapel Hill, 1991), for a discussion of the ideology of bourgeois individualism and its implications for women.

[6] See, among many, Jane Tompkins, *Sensational Designs: The Cultural Work of American Fiction, 1790-1860* (New York, 1985). Many feminist critics argue that women's literature embodied different values from those of men, but in my judgment even when the purported female values appear most harshly to criticize (male) competitive self-assertion, they remained tied to the fundamental premises and worldview of individualism, which was responsible for a specific vision of female nature and values. For a fuller development of the argument, see Fox-Genovese, *Feminism Without Illusions.*

[7] Toni Morrison, *Beloved* (New York, 1987). For references to such events in the lives of slave women, see also Elizabeth Fox-Genovese, *Within the Plantation Household: Black and White Women of the Old South* (Chapel Hill, 1988).

Ronna C. Johnson (essay date 1997)

SOURCE: "Said But Not Spoken: Elision and the Representation of Rape, Race, and Gender in Harriet E. Wilson's *Our Nig,*" in *Speaking the Other Self: American Women Writers,* edited by Jea Campbell Reesman, University of Georgia Press, 1997, pp. 96-116.

[*In the following essay, Johnson claims that the narrative structures and lacunae in* Our Nig *encode the sexual violence committed against the author.*]

Many critics and historians have established the idea that rape and its threat, as well as struggles to meet dictates of the code of "true womanhood," placed intertwined burdens on the narrative self-representation of antebellum black women. In Harriet E. Wilson's **Our Nig: or, Sketches from the Life of a Free Black,** white male sexual abuse is a powerful if unspoken threat to the protagonist, Frado, though a threat suggested only indirectly, by means of the author's and the narrator's interventions and narrative elisions. Wilson's representation of Frado's vulnerability to sexual abuse fits into her promise of a narrative that discloses southern slavery's "appurtenances North" but one that does not "divulge every transaction" constituting the life of the "Free Black" subject.[1] Nevertheless, to date commentators have sought primarily to situate **Our Nig** within the historical and literary discourse of related period texts, such as those by Harriet Beecher Stowe, Frederick Douglass, Harriet Jacobs, and Elizabeth Keckley, focusing on Wilson's use of the received structures of the sentimental novel and the slave narrative.[2] Though many commentators have noted what Henry Louis Gates Jr. has termed the text's "silences and lacunae," these have not been examined in connection with a sustained and powerful, albeit oblique, representation of sexual abuse.[3] Yet these lacunae and other narrative discontinuities allusively divulge a history of abuse of the indentured Frado that is elided in the tale.

Our Nig's representation of Frado's indenture follows codes for true womanhood by inscribing elisions in the narrative. This discursive activity produces and preserves a surface of narrative modesty that attests to authorial "concern for discursive respectability."[4] But by coding sexual abuse of the protagonist in narrative irregularities that point to its elisions, the text subverts its avowed reticence to suggest the full implications for gender and sexuality of a northern indenture that replicates southern slavery. That is, **Our Nig** says figuratively through narrative structure what cannot be confessed in speech: the sexual transgression against the black female. Constituting what Claudia Tate correctly characterizes as the text's "deliberately constructed double-voiced representations," narrative irregularities replicate structurally the double silences of sexual exploitation and its socially and formally co-erced denial.[5] Further, *Our Nig*'s assertions of omissions match lacunae in representations of the Bellmont men, and their trespasses, once recognized, provide conjunctions that unify the otherwise disjunctive narrative of the tale.

We are invited to trace a coded subtext by *Our Nig* itself. The text both announces its narrative inhibition and hints at the causes. Statements made in the preface by Wilson and in the conclusion by the omniscient narrator alert us to confessional constraints on the text that prompt its inscription of an enigma. Assertions in the preface that "every transaction" of Wilson's and Frado's often conflated stories is not "divulged," that Wilson has "purposely omitted what would provoke most shame" in white abolitionists, and the warning in the text's closing that "some part of [Frado's] history is unknown save by the Omniscient God" all imply narrative inhibitions and elisions that challenge assumptions about the tale as told. These admonitions resonate with sexual implications that cannot be stated directly; indeed, from *Clarissa* to *The Color Purple*, confidences entrusted by women in narrative to "the Omniscient God" have signified sexual violation. In this, *Our Nig*'s claims to narrative silence ominously remind us that for black women, the southern slavery to which Frado's northern indenture is compared meant rape. And the egregiousness of this common trauma was doubled by patriarchal ideologies of racism and of slavery as an institution, both of which made it virtually impossible to declare the occurrence of rape without inculpating the (black female) victim and exculpating the (white male) perpetrator.[6]

Thus *Our Nig* reserves a subtextual discursive space in which is inscribed what antebellum dominative discourse forbids, assertions of white male exploitation of black female sexuality. Or, the narrative expresses subtextually experiences that, in Wilson's words in the preface, she "do[es] not pretend to divulge"; this labored phrase itself typifies the text's "double-voiced representations" because it suggests that textual reticence "pretends" to keep secret something that is nevertheless said. The allusive subtext of *Our Nig* signifies through disruptive signifiers, destabilizing tropes, and effaced analogies that constitute a second, encoded narrative voice, which may be called that of the signatory "Our Nig," who mediates between author Wilson and protagonist Frado. The subtext signifies structurally in correspondences between avowed lacunae in the narrative and discrepancies and discontinuities in storytelling that the surface tale reveals but denies are there. Exemplifying this double-voiced textuality, the preface offers oblique, coded explanations for narrative inhibition that contextualize the story's elisions. In Wilson's usage in the preface, slavery itself is a veiled reference to or code for rape, for the word "slavery" occurs in conjunction with a shame that she wants to avoid by censoring disclosure. Wilson claims that she would not "palliate slavery at the South, by disclosures of its appurtenances North" and that she has "purposely omitted what would most provoke shame in our good anti-slavery friends." Her insistence on omissions effects a complicated double move that practices what Elizabeth Fox-Genovese calls "discursive respectability" but simultaneously inscribes the incidence of something shameful, and discursively binds it to slavery.

Moreover, establishing the coded relationship with the narrative that characterizes the subtext, this avowal of an unnamed shame associated with slavery flags, and is correlated with, a marked omission in the text's account of Frado's indenture. The narrative explicitly recounts Frado's endurance of virtually every form of psychic and physical violence associated with slavery, except the shame often imposed on the black female subject, rape. The relentless account of abuses Frado suffers calls into question Wilson's claim of omissions and, because it is so graphic, the account uneasily points to sexuality. This reading foregrounds gender, which is first displaced by Wilson in the preface onto political discourses via abolition, and then underplayed in the narrative's account of Frado's indenture. Foregrounding gender clarifies that Wilson's concern for discursive modesty expressly limits narrative self-representation with regard to sexual experience. Just so, sexual exploitation is the one "shame" specific to black women's experience of slavery that is conspicuously missing from the narrative's list of abuses. This absence works with other irregularities to evoke allusively the full implications of slavery for the black female body in Frado's northern indenture. Tropes, eccentric signifiers, and narrative discontinuities palpably signify the repressed material of the subtext and permit us to identify and name as a presence an absence that is said to be omitted.

This dimension of Wilson's narrative and the subtext's detectable referent of sexual abuse are elucidated by a textual reading cast from feminist, historicist, and Freudian perspectives. Because women are objects, not subjects, of dominative discourses of sexuality, Wilson's inability to state directly aspects of Frado's experience reflects power hierarchies that forbid black women from representing their sexuality. To contend with these environmental constraints on women's self-representation, Hortense Spillers has argued that it is incumbent on feminist critics to "supply the missing words" of female sexual experience by "actively imagin[ing] women in their living . . . confrontations with experience (at least, the way they report it)."[7] The subtext of *Our Nig* must be "actively imagine[d]" in order to bring into view what Wilson warns has been "purposely omitted" but what, as Freud notes of repressed material, returns to be detected. Attention to the manner of *Our Nig* resorts to inscribing crucial aspects of Frado's life aslant, in enigmatic allusions; as Barbara Christian aptly characterizes its contingent expressions, "scenes of attempted or covert seduction . . . might be implied in scenes in *Our Nig*'s transgressive subtext, which resists black female disempowerment in gender- and race-coded antebellum discourses by saying without speaking its confession to 'the Omniscient God.' "[8]

Our Nig's coded, subversive expressions take the form of textual elisions and narrative inconsistencies, such as those inhering in representations of the Bellmont men, as well as charged rhetorical figures, such as the eye rhyme Frado/Fido (the name of a dog) and the repeating signifier of a silver half-dollar. Anomalous fictive material in the text's opening chapters, which recount the life of Frado's mother Mag Smith, provides for a displaced representation of aspects of Frado's experience that are effaced in the tale. And in the tale's closing, an encoded biblical metaphor connects sexual impropriety with slavery and with Frado's indenture. These elements constitute the obscured subtext wherein the revelations alluded to by the text find discursive expression, where otherwise unspoken instances of Frado's experience are inscribed in tropic figures, textual reticences, and narrative discrepancies and allusions. A speaker of the unspoken is named on the title page, where it is said that *Our Nig* is "By 'Our Nig.' " The Signatory "Our Nig" is neither the historical personage Harriet E. Wilson nor the fictive protagonist Frado, but a disembodied figure that mediates between these two textual positions. A signifier for the subtext and a discursive product of the mystified aspects of the narrative, "Our Nig" is resonantly manifest in the encoded biblical metaphor with which the tale ends.

The symbolically supercharged sentence that concludes the tale mirrors and elaborates Wilson's assertions that parts of Frado's story remain untold. The text concludes with Chapter 12, subtitled "The Winding Up of the Matter," which recounts Frado's marriage to Samuel, a black man posing as a runaway slave, his abandonment of Frado after the birth of their son, and Samuel's untimely death from yellow fever. The final paragraph of the chapter acts as a coda to the tale's account of Frado's life; it summarizes the fate of members of the Bellmont family. This survey of the Bellmonts and the tale itself ends with this sentence: "Frado has passed from [the Bellmonts'] memories, as Joseph from the butler's, but she will never cease to track them till beyond mortal vision" (131). This magisterial pronouncement intoned by "Our Nig" suggests a motive of revenge in the preceding narrative, which, as a text that may survive its time, is a vehicle for tracking its objects beyond the living sight of its enunciator. The revenge of "Our Nig" is effected in the subtext of *Our Nig*, which is likewise a vehicle for surpassing narrative limits into an ineradicable, continuous present; the subtext is ineradicable because, like "Our Nig," it is not directly inscribed and thus is not vulnerable to expurgation. Although the subject Frado is the forgotten object of the Bellmont family memory, their perfidy is unforgotten, preserved subtextually in the biblical allusion that posits a metaphoric equivalence between Frado and the Bellmonts and Joseph and the butler.

The metaphor alludes to Genesis 39-42, which recounts the tale of Joseph, a Hebrew slave, and the Egyptian butler, both confined to Pharoah's prison. Joseph correctly interprets a dream the butler has about fertility and charges the butler to intercede with Pharoah on his behalf. The butler forgets Joseph until Pharoah has an enigmatic dream; then he recalls the clever interpreter still in prison. Joseph is summoned and correctly interprets Pharoah's dream of seven years of feast and seven years of famine. He is pardoned and rewarded with a high position in Pharoah's service, a happy ending to the ungrateful butler's lapse of memory. On its surface the analogy likens the Bellmonts to the butler as self-absorbed forgetters of their debt to a "slave," Frado. But the story of how Joseph came to be in Pharoah's prison, as well as his talent for renarrating or interpreting dreams, are significant buried elements of the biblical allusion, and they point to a similarly obscured sexual discourse in *Our Nig*.

The story of how Joseph came to be in prison might be said to be a slave narrative, while the last line of *Our Nig* suggests that it is an allegory of or analogous to Joseph's slave narrative. Before his imprisonment, Joseph is overseer of his master's house. He is recognized because he is "handsome and goodlooking" (Gen. 39:7), in the same way that Frado is initially valued by Jack for being "real handsome and bright, and not very black either" (25). Joseph becomes an object of sexual interest to his master's opposite, Potiphar's wife, who "cast her eyes upon" him and behind Potiphar's back repeatedly begs Joseph to "lie with her," an invitation Joseph steadfastly refuses (Gen. 39: 8-13). The analogy to Frado locates her as an object of sexual interest to her mistress's opposites, the Bellmont men, and indeed the story of their activities behind Mrs. Bellmont's back forms the subject of the tale's subtext. The gender bias of the dominative mode is evident in the sexual politics played out in the continued parallels between the biblical tale and the antebellum one. Frado's seduction is elided in the text because black women's discursive disempowerment assures that it would be read as implicating her. And this is precisely the same reason that Joseph's seduction by Potiphar's wife *can* be disclosed: it implicates the female. In both cases men are exonerated of desirousness or desirability; both are ascribed to women.

In the biblical story, Potiphar's wife, the spurned sexual aggressor enraged by her defeat, steals Joseph's garment to prove her false accusation that Joseph "came in to lie with" her (Gen. 39:8). Occupying the social position that ensures her version will prevail, Potiphar's wife reverses the facts with her lie and causes Potiphar to send Joseph to prison for refusing her; she mobilizes patriarchal power to effect her revenge. Still, like the antebellum tale that survives the Bellmonts and proves (their) northern white racism, the biblical tale that survives Potiphar's wife testifies to her perfidy. In the biblical tale, the victim of sexual aggression (the "slave" Joseph) is discursively rendered the predator by false testimony. Just so, on the plantation white male sexual violence was falsely ascribed to black female carnality, for prevailing essentialist ideologies of race assigned lasciviousness to the black female and masked white male culpability and sexual agency. In *Our Nig,* the Bellmont men are likewise invisible to their exercise of patriarchal "law." Joseph is never cleared of the charges of Potiphar's wife, even though they are shown to be fabricated; the stain of sexual transgression is never bleached from his person. But when Joseph interprets Pharoah's dream, when he retells a narrative to foreground its hidden meaning, he is freed and promoted to power. Similarly, the signatory "Our Nig" is never cleared of Frado's humiliating experience, but nevertheless achieves power and subjectivity by conveying hidden aspects of Frado's indenture in a metaphoric subtext of the narrative.

Thus the metaphor likening Frado and the Bellmonts to Joseph and the butler provides an allusive entry to the subtext or effaced sexual discourse of *Our Nig.* The subtext preserves yet subverts discursive modesty; it asserts black female subjectivity by alluding to white male sexual abuse without implicating Frado. Its double-voiced, indirect inscriptions are the means by which, in Gates's terms, the black-as-object may transform herself into the black-as-subject (1983, lv), eluding inculpation (here, the charges of sexual impropriety from which Joseph is never exonerated) by effacing the sexual discourse of the biblical slave narrative to which Frado's life is likened.[9] "Enough," the omniscient narrator insists at the tale's close, "has been unrolled to demand your sympathy" (130); enough, that is, has been provided to effect Frado's discursive status as a subject who renders her oppressors the objects of her discourse. The biblical metaphor represents Frado's shift from object to subject by drawing a connection between one common occasion for narrative, the restoration of (the Bellmonts') "forgotten" memories, and a part of Frado's experience that remains undivulged, (the Bellmonts') sexual predation. The text's unnameable "shame" is thus figured slantwise, as it were, and figured as the Bellmonts' transgression, in the metaphor's repressed allusion to Potiphar's wife. Matching this allusive manner of inscription and reiterating its claims, the text's opening chapters provide an account of Frado's mother that offers further correspondences to its avowed omissions and likewise points to a repressed discourse of sexual experience.

The question of Wilson's autobiographical relation to *Our Nig* has been of strong interest to scholars wishing to authenticate the text. The outline of Frado's experience has been matched to known facts of Wilson's life, permitting a general identification of author and protagonist. The exception to these equivalences is *Our Nig*'s account of Mag Smith, which occupies the first two chapters. Claudia Tate concludes that "all the events in the first two chapters must be presumed fictional inasmuch as their factual construction is beyond the competence of a young child's memory and understanding." Similarly, Henry Louis Gates maintains that "these early chapters describe events far removed from the author's experiences . . . [which] she cannot claim to recollect clearly and some which she cannot recollect at all, such as the courtship and marriage of her mother." Gates suggests that disparities in the text's opening chapters, where first-person chapter titles head third-person narration, evince Wilson's "anxiety about identifying with events in the text which she cannot claim to recollect," whereas later in the text, when Wilson treats events within her living memory, (auto)biographical and fictional points neatly overlap. It is salient that the events with which *Our Nig* begins, events Gates terms a source of authorial anxiety because they eclipse Wilson's experience, represent transgressions of female sexuality and respectability. Specifically, as Tate notes, these events are "elaborately constructed mitigations of what Mag's white culture regards as numerous transgressions of feminine virtue." They represent unfortunate sexual experiences that have befallen a *white* woman. The racial distinction is a determinative element of the subtextual allusions encoded in the parallels between Mag's story and Frado's.[10]

The first two chapters of *Our Nig* recount events of Mag Smith's life that Wilson could not have witnessed in her own mother's life. The authorial anxiety they reveal coincides with their content of female sexual experience, material that antebellum black female authors were unable to treat directly in their narrative self-representations. Differences in narrative candor with regard to Mag's and Frado's sexual experiences and conjugal histories measure inequities in discursive and experiential possibilities and privileges that derive from racial caste disparities. Mag is white, her daughter Frado, though half-white, is designated black. The limits in the antebellum era (as today) of what might be said of (and by) white women and of (and by) black women about their sexual experiences diverge significantly at the point at which the female is blamed for male desire. The lapses of white women like Mag Smith, as *Our Nig* shows, may be charitably adduced to misfortune and poverty; for black women who like Frado are conscripted into virtual slavery because of the social meaning given to their color, no charitable explanations obtain. In racialized antebellum codes for the feminine, black women are either virtuous or fallen.

Any account of Frado's sexuality that might compromise her virtuous status must be repressed or told by indirection. Let us then consider the fictive story of Mag Smith's life as a displaced representation of parts of Frado's story, as the first-person chapter titles imply. And as the third-person narration of these chapters intimate, this story of Mag Smith cannot be ascribed to Frado/Wilson, a strategy that preserves their good repute. Read as an allusive inscription of parts of Frado's story that are prohibited from the narrative of **Our Nig** because of its era's "social requirement for female sexual reticence," the story of Mag Smith correlates to Wilson's claims of omissions.[11]

Key parallels between Frado's narrated life and Mag's place them in a discursive, rather than solely familial, relation, and the narrative's directness in recounting Mag's life allows us to perceive what is veiled in its account of Frado's. Both Mag and Frado are "early deprived of parental guardianship, far removed from relatives" (5); Mag is said to have "merged into womanhood, unprotected, uncherished, uncared for" (5), a phrase repeated when Frado enters maturity (115). Both women marry black men in hopes of improving their economic lot: Mag can either "beg my living, or get it from" Jim (13), while Frado's marriage to Samuel promises her "the relief of looking to another for comfortable support" (127). Both mother and daughter are rendered destitute by the unexpected deaths of their black husbands; both are left to maintain children, and each in desperation sends a child out to foster care. Mag's relinquishment of Frado begins the story that constitutes the tale proper, while Frado's relinquishment of her son is one of the events with which this same tale closes. This reversed parallel calls attention to the opening and the closing of the narrative.

Further differences in structural correspondences between Mag's and Frado's stories point to lacunae in the narrative. In another reversed parallel, Mag's destitution and desperate marriage to a black man form the near beginning of the account of her life, while Frado's parallel destitution and marriage to a black man end the account of hers. Mag's story begins before her marriage, with her seduction and subsequent abandonment by an unseen, unnamed, implicitly white man who deceives her. This event, which precedes marriage to a black man, has no explicit parallel in the account of Frado's life before *her* marriage to a black man. The story told about Mag's seduction before her marriage suggests an effaced correspondence in the story of Frado's indenture: the elision of sexual experience preceding her marriage. Frado's metaphoric equivalence to the sexually wronged Joseph of Genesis in the text's last line and the repression of Joseph's sexual history in the metaphor point to a repressed story that is conveyed subtextually in structural juxtapositions and parallels between Frado's life and Mag's.

Turning from structural to figural inscriptions of Frado's sexual exploitation, we turn to **Our Nig**'s indictment of northern white racism. This discourse encompasses the text's apparent origin in maternal economic necessity and its allusions to slavery and connects them to an effaced discourse of sexuality. Because Frado is the child Mag must leave with another family to ensure her own economic survival, Frado becomes the abused "nig" whose experiences provide the narrative. Because she is later a mother who must herself put her son in foster care to ensure his survival, Frado is provided the occasion of telling her story. Because Wilson must provide maintenance for son and self, she produces **Our Nig** as a commercial "experiment," as she says in the preface. Only the signatory "Our Nig" lacks an economic motive for narrative; the biblical metaphor suggests a wish to revenge the Bellmonts' ingratitude, or their racism. As a discursive figure mediating the textual positions of Wilson and Frado, "Our Nig" also mediates economic motives and those of revenge, connecting and subordinating maternal economic necessity to northern white racism. Alluding to slavery's exploitation of the black female body by showing that racist assumptions underlie Frado's northern indenture, disruptive tropes and signifiers suggest that the narrative's economic motive is a screen. These narrative figures expose the sexual aspect of the antebellum economic exploitation of the black female body by conveying subtextually Frado's carnal commodity value for the Bellmonts.

Our Nig undertakes to represent and thus to expose the way race overdetermines northern indenture as a replication of slavery for the black female subject. Evelyn Brooks Higginbotham notes that "race came to life primarily as the signifier of the master/slave relation and thus emerged superimposed upon class and property relations."[12] Just so, Frado is conscripted to virtual slavery in the white Bellmont household because "the nigger in the child" (26), as Mrs. Bellmont puts it, signifies that her "time and person belonged solely to" the family (41). Her "shade" (39) means Frado may be "train[ed] up . . . from a child" (26) to do Mrs. Bellmont's work; for Mrs. Bellmont as for the plantation owner, a "dozen" children so complected would be "better than one" (26). Thus the Bellmonts' "Two-story White House, North" is conflated with the white-pillared southern plantation, where pigmentation differentiates master from slave. Yet even this apparent, if provocative, equation of northern indenture with southern slavery is complicated by figural inscriptions or transgressions denied *both* north and south. Frado's indenture is amplified in **Our Nig**'s subtext as a racialized condition that implicates her body beyond compulsory labor and corporal punishment. Disruptive tropes and signifiers effect the text's embedded social critique by suggesting that Frado's body is available to satisfy not only Mrs. Bellmont's avarice and sadistic impulses, but also (white male) carnal desires suppressed in the text.[13] For example, the disconcerting eye rhyme Frado/Fido constitutes a trope for Frado's commodification and conveys otherwise unspoken aspects of her status. Forged in the slippage between the names Frado and Fido, the rhyme problematizes signification by playing the terms against each other and thus destabilizing apparently innocuous narrative contexts. This figural play insists that the text's allegory of slavery represents the black female body in ways not directly expressible.

First, the narrative posits Frado's equivalence to a dog in the eyes of the Bellmont men when the son Jack remarks, "'Father is a sensible man . . . He would not wrong a dog. Where *is* Frado?'" (35-36, emphasis Wilson's). Jack's association to Frado from the dog his father would not wrong conflates the two and fixes the child in an animal register of discourse. Jack's remark occurs when his sister Mary has accused Frado of lying about an event in which Mary is to blame for her misfortune. The full context of his remark links the child's discursive equivalence to an animal with racialized privileges of speech and with representations of violence that have sexual connotations.

> "It is very strange you will believe what others say against your sister," retorted his mother, with flashing eye. "I think it is time your father subdued you."

> "Father is a sensible man," argued Jack. "He would not wrong a dog. Where *is* Frado?" he continued. (35-36)

Pointing to the fictive and intentional nature of this discourse, pointing to the hand of "Our Nig," Frado is not present for this exchange; she is in another part of the house, "her mouth wedged apart, her face swollen, and full of pain" (36). That is, she is being tortured and silenced for providing testimony that contravenes (Mary's) privileged white control of representation. Moreover, the threat Frado's speech poses to white hegemony is also ascribed to Jack, who ought to be "subdued" for his imputed preference for Frado over his white kin. This preference circularly implies an incestuous connection (he should prefer his sister to Frado, according to Mrs. Bellmont), a taint that is underscored by the suggestion of bestiality in Jack's elliptical association of Frado to a dog. Earlier, Mary herself wishes "to use physical force 'to subdue [Frado],' to 'keep her down'" (33); the repetition of "subdue" with regard to Jack's behavior discursively links him to Frado: both commit offenses to his sister and his mother. Jack's preferences should be "subdued" by an intervening father, but the Bellmont father "would not wrong a dog." This curious, eccentric figure of speech calls further attention to a transgressive subtext, for what can it mean to say that a person is so

"sensible" that "he would not wrong a dog." The referent of the metaphor is Jack; he is the dog in question. But it is Frado who occasions the metaphor, Frado to whom Jack's thoughts turn, so the metaphor becomes a discursive turn by which a carnal link is established between Jack and Frado in the animal register of discourse. Furthermore, because his father is too "sensible" to "subdue" Jack, the alliance or link between Jack and Frado contravenes only Mrs. Bellmont's privilege. For it is Frado, the racial other, and her "jollity" (a racialized code word) whom Mrs. Bellmont would differentiate through the exercise of her power to subdue or "quench by whipping or scolding" (38); it is this racially differentiated Frado whom Jack prefers, defends, and conflates with a dog. As Jack's remark implies, it is Frado whom the Bellmonts treat like a dog.

Then a real dog, Fido, enters the narrative in another curious inscription: Jack "resolved to do what he could to protect [Frado] from Mary and his mother. He bought her a dog, which became a favorite with both" (37). The juxtaposition of Jack's resolve to protect Frado with his procurement of a dog both he and Frado enjoy forms an unsettling non sequitur that suggests something is elided between resolution and procurement. It enigmatically aligns the dog's purchase with Frado's physical vulnerability, which is earlier specifically linked to her testimony, the very act of discursive subjectivity that challenges and contravenes white control of representation. Further, the cryptic phrase "do what he could" flags a variance between Jack's real power as a white male to protect Frado and his procurement of a pet for her, a token more suggestive of an exchange than an act in her defense. The subtle irregularity of this passage recounting Jack's purchase of the dog typifies the narrative's encoded subtextual discourse of "transactions" not "divulged," in Wilson's words.

In the same indirect and asymmetrical way, the eye rhyme Frado/Fido is charged with commodity and carnal associations. These associations are part of the discourse of slavery and serve to define Frado's indenture as an enslavement. The rhyme posits what Jack's remark conflating Frado with a dog implies, that a dog is Frado's discursive equivalent. The slippage between the names Frado/Fido inscribes Frado's status as the Bellmont's pet, a status borne out by the amusement of the Bellmont males and their hired men at her capering and prank-playing. Not only an extension of the child, the dog is a projection of a self split off from Frado in the narrative; he embodies her commodity value. Fido is bought by Jack, sold by Mrs. Bellmont, and "obtained" again by Mr. Bellmont (61-62). Like the people traded on plantations, Fido possesses exchange value: in him, Frado's debased chattel status is inscribed; through him, her indenture is equated with slavery. Moreover, Jack's purchase of the dog suggests the protection bribed sexual exploitation may have afforded female slaves, as does his subsequent gratification because the "gift" of Fido to Frado "answer[ed] his intentions" (42). Like the silver half-dollar he later gives the child, Fido may answer his intention to reward or bribe Frado for services that the dog's animal representation of her enslaved self suggests are carnal. Commenting on Fido's "dog-agility" in learning tricks—itself a phrase containing the potential for sexual double entendre about positions and dexterousness in intercourse—Jack "pronounced him very knowing" (42). This anthropomorphic phrase alerts us to a discontinuity between subject and rhetoric that suggests a premature knowing or expertise in the child for whom Fido represents a split-off self. This knowing is discontinuous with what the narrative represents overtly, but it correlates with the text's warnings of omissions. In one of many phrases that establish the eye rhyme, it is said that "Fido was the entire confidant of Frado" (41); he is the repository and embodiment of secrets suppressed in this narrative said to contain omissions.

Thus the eye rhyme Frado/Fido indicates the narrative's encoded subtext, and Fido marks discursive space signifying the unspeakable in Frado's life among the Bellmonts. Wilson observes in the preface that her life would be "declare[d] unfavorable in comparison with treatment of legal bondmen." So too Frado's treatment by the Bellmonts is unfavorable in comparison to Fido's. Thus, parting with Fido at the end of her indenture, Frado leaves behind her status as pet, her degrading obligation to entertain in order to survive, her life that is worse than the life of her dog. Fido signifies the child Frado was and simultaneously evokes the one she was never permitted to be. *Our Nig* represents de facto slavery in the North in its depiction of Frado's treatment as property acquired and nurtured for the purpose of whites' economic gain and comfort. Although the economic motives and exploitive racist views that render Frado's northern indenture the image of southern slavery are overtly depicted, undertones of sexuality complicate the process of signification. Racial differentiation, profit, and violence are discursively interrelated in unsettling, transgressive figures, as in the following exchange between the senior Bellmonts:

> "Why, according to you and James, we should very soon have her in the parlor, as smart as our own girls. It's of no use talking to you or James. If you should go on as you would like, it would not be six months before she would be leaving me; and that won't do. Just think of how much profit she was to us last summer. We had no work hired out; she did the work of two girls—"

> "And got the whippings for two with it!" remarked Mr. Bellmont.

> "I'll beat the money out of her, if I can't get her worth any other way," retorted Mrs. B. sharply. (89-90)

The Bellmont men would like to "go on" with Frado in a way that ostensibly threatens categories of racial differentiation and Mrs. Bellmont's power, her "right" to "beat the money out of" Frado, a phrase linking profit to violence. But the men's imputed wish to have Frado in the parlor marks discursive space for another kind of transgression, one that does not destabilize hierarchies of racial difference. Barbara Omolade observes of slavery's binary racial ethos that "the category 'white' would also mean that the people designated 'black' could be held in perpetual slavery."[14] The converse also holds true, that the category "black" means that those designated "white" would embody and enjoy hegemonic power and freedom. These are race-coded privileges Mrs. Bellmont retains by preserving distinctions between Frado and her daughters that define Frado as an economic asset and proof of white power, to which the stripes that scar her body attest. But, and this is to the point, these distinctions may be securely preserved even if the men's wish to have Frado in the parlor is realized. For their desire to "go on" with Frado evokes another register of profit made at her expense, that of sexual exploitation, a kind of profit authorized by empowered categories of racial differentiation and which nevertheless infuriates Mrs. Bellmont.[15] The allusion to an unrepresented desire of the Bellmont men points to the text's declared silences and the subtext that voices them, to aspects of the female slave narrative that are repressed in *Our Nig.*

The narrative of *Our Nig* plainly describes the protagonist's endurance of starvation, torture, beating, overwork, exposure to natural elements, sadistic psychological conditioning, and spiritual deprivation. Which is to say that the unexpurgated narrative plainly describes acts committed by Mrs. Bellmont, an admitted "right she-devil" (17). Because they are recounted, these acts cannot correspond to the text's avowed reticences. Let me say here that I appreciate and in no way intend to diminish or mitigate the text's depiction of white middle-class female brutality in the abuse meted out to Frado by Mrs. Bellmont and Mary. *Our Nig*'s representation of white female agency and responsibility for racial exploitation constitutes a fundamental indictment. Settling for this indictment at face value, however, risks a reading that underestimates its complex sophistication of expression. Such a reading also in effect repeats the silencing of women which sexual violence at least in part aims to achieve, and it preserves the immunity of white male sexual privilege, the privilege to trespass without penalty. Thus it is important to note that while Mrs. Bellmont is emphatically visible in her cruel displays of "vixen nature" (41), the men who are Frado's reputed allies are curiously invisible in their practice of sympathy, which is not to say that they do not intervene, only that their intervention is unrepresented in the narrative. Discrepancies and discontinuities in representations of the Bellmont men create a narrative vacuum that is inscribed as elision. These elisions reserve discursive space for the only abuse that is not explicitly represented in the narrative: sexual exploitation.

The Bellmont men are said to be, in the person of the father, the "law" whose "word once spoken admitted of no appeal" (31), yet they present themselves as Mrs. Bellmont's subordinates. The father claims he cannot stop his wife's abuse of Frado because "women rule the earth, and all in it," and his intervention would consign him to "live in hell meantime" (44). This claim blatantly contradicts what the tale repeatedly dramatizes, that his word *is* "law"; that he is an intercessor in domestic affairs "who could not be denied" (83). Mr. Bellmont is the patriarch of "determined eye" and "decisive manner" whose direct order " 'not [to] strike, or scald, or skin' " Frado (47) in fact does stop his wife's abuse, with no apparent cost to himself. His claim to the contrary suggests a cover-up, especially considering its distortion of white women's worldly power, which, even in the nineteenth-century middle-class home, was far inferior to that of white males, as indeed Mr. Bellmont's infrequent but always successful interventions demonstrate. His claim of inferiority to Mrs. Bellmont is further contradicted by its textualization as direct discourse, which reifies his subjectivity and power of self-representation. Moreover, although the men represent themselves as powerless before a sadistic Mrs. Bellmont, she is said to be "always foiled" (87) when she complains to them of Frado. And the men who alone possess the absolute power to intervene do so mostly in one way: they repeatedly take Frado to her room, or to theirs, to comfort her. For example, after one terrible scene, Jack, who "pitie[s]" Frado, "comforted her as well as he knew how, sat by her till she fell asleep, and then left for the sitting room" (36). That is, the men express their alleged discomfort with Mrs. Bellmont's violence by closeting themselves with Frado in a bedroom away from her, a response that vitiates their supposed beneficence. Evincing patriarchal privilege, what goes on in those closeted bedrooms is unseen, undramatized, elided; it is an exercise of patriarchal "law" that correlates to the text's claim of ommissions.

The "deleted sexuality" Claudia Tate feels "looming in these episodes" may also provide a deleted explanation for Mrs. Bellmont's violence.[16] Harriet Jacobs, Frederick Douglass, and numerous historians document that, rather than identify with black female victims of rape, white mistresses often brutally punished black women for the sexual transgressions of their white men.[17] Thus Mrs. Bellmont's violence may also register rage at trespasses her men commit; it may

express more without explicitly disclosing anything other than her well-known "vixen nature" (41). The men's prerogative of "law" above all ensures their sexual freedom, which they possess exclusively and whose exercise is not explicitly represented but may be felt to reverberate in Mrs. Bellmont's violence. Her violence is so excessive that it suggests a displacement that masks a shame even she is not empowered to speak. This interpretation is advanced by the narrative's manipulation of a silver half-dollar, a signifier for sexual transgression that inculpates the son Jack by its repetition in a later scene involving Mrs. Bellmont. The textualization of the coin provides an example of what Tate calls the text's tendency to "unsettling narrative repetitions"; it is one of those fraught "textual disruptions," because in both instances that Frado receives a silver half-dollar (from Jack and from Mrs. Bellmont), Fido is dramatically or discursively invoked, infusing the half-dollar signifier with carnal associations established in the dog.[18]

The coin first appears in a scene of Frado's resistance to Mrs. Bellmont's tyrannical regime. In this scene, Frado is commanded by Mrs. Bellmont to eat from her used dinner plate instead of a clean one.[19] Frado resists this humiliation with a gesture of contempt for Mrs. Bellmont: she bids Fido to lick the plate clean, "then, wiping her knife and fork on the cloth, she proceeded to eat her dinner" (71); predictably, Mrs. Bellmont explodes. Her comeuppance especially amuses her son Jack. "Boiling over with laughter" (72), he recounts the scene to James in Frado's presence and, "pulling a bright, silver half-dollar from his pocket, he threw it at Nig, saying 'There, take that; 'twas worth paying for' " (72). The half-dollar is an ambiguous signifier of payment to Frado for Jack's satisfaction because of the male-coded sexual innuendo in the phrase "boiling over." Jack ostensibly rewards Frado for her comic performance, which recalls literary and historical accounts of slaves rewarded for providing their masters' entertainment.[20] But Frado's humiliation of Jack's mother inscribes a darker association to chattel slavery, for slaves were surely not rewarded for mocking their masters. In this, the coin evokes payment often made to female slaves, as bell hooks notes, to encourage their entry into prostitution or to reward their submission to white male sexual demand.[21] Demonstrating his approval of Frado's humiliation of his mother, Jack is linked to Frado in a transgressive behavior that is represented with sexual overtones and which is offered in his ambiguous, sexualized way as an explanation of his mother's rage and violence.

Historians note both that a female slave's acquiescence to white male sexual advances might offer a modicum of protection for herself or her family and that sexual exploitation was "used as a punishment or demanded in exchange for leniency."[22] *Our Nig* depicts the Bellmont men as sources of such protection for Frado. James provides Frado "shelter" from "mal-treatment" (67) and "shield[s] her from many beat-ings" (76). Jack "resolves to do what he could to pro-tect her from . . . his mother" (37); "with Jack near [Frado] did not fear her" (71). What Frado pays for this shelter may be inferred from an exchange that precedes Mrs. Bellmont's humiliation at the dinner table:

> "Where are your curls, Fra?" asked Jack, after the usual salutation.

> "Your mother cut them off."

> "Thought you were getting handsome, did she? Same old story, is it; knocks and bumps? Better times coming; never fear, Nig."

> How different this appelative sounded from him; he said it in such a tone, with such a rogueish look!

> She laughed, and replied that he had better take her West for a housekeeper. (70)

Jack's persistent attention to Frado's "glossy ring-lets" (68) recalls his first comment about her, which sets an ominous tone for her indenture: " 'Keep her,' said Jack. 'She's real handsome and bright, and not very black, either' " (25). She is black enough to define white but not so black as to repel whites. In Jack's eyes, Frado is an attractive object, "that pretty little Nig" (47) he writes of to his brother James. All this intrusive attention to Frado's body resounds in Jack's question, "Where are your curls, Fra?" (70) and challenges its apparently innocuous jocoseness. The narrative's acquiescence to the hated "appelative" "Nig" implies the conditions of his protection: a co-erced, sexualized familiarity or intimacy or posses-sion. Frado's rejoinder that he should take her away for his housekeeper is understood as a wish to es-cape Mrs. Bellmont, although in this context it sounds coy. However, it is reported in indirect discourse, which discursively demonstrates Frado's submission to Jack's terms of interest, but in a disembodied way that precludes her subjectivity. The phrase implies Frado's acquiescence in her abused object status, but in fact it also shows Frado's objectification, which is manifest in the text but not spoken (and therefore not agreed upon) by her; she is stripped of subjec-tivity in the phrases that imply her cooperation. And that is the point: Jack's interest in Frado, signified by his trivializing attention to her shorn hair and beaten body ("knocks and bumps") is the sign of her objectification, not its antidote. Thus *Our Nig* shows that Bellmont male protection against maternal vio-lence is sexualized and is itself a source of Frado's objectification.[23] This is one reason the narrative comes into being: so that the signatory "Our Nig," who mediates between Wilson and Frado and reigns

in the subtext that neither author nor protagonist can own may condemn and subvert the hated "appelative" "Nig."

The sexualized associations of the silver half-dollar are intensified with its repetition. Frado's inden-ture finally ends in her eighteenth year, and we are told that "Mrs. Bellmont dismissed her with the assurance that she would soon wish herself back again, and a present of a silver half-dollar" (117). The outrageous idea that Frado will regret her lib-erty calls attention to and taints this silver half-dollar, which, echoing the earlier scene of Mrs. Bellmont's humiliation, evokes Jack and links him to his mother's abuse.[24] The appearance of Mrs. Bellmont's unprecedented gift of a silver half-dollar in a context devoid of her customary violence en-courages the inference that a customary violence is also elided in Jack's earlier such payment to Frado for his satisfaction. The repeated signifier linking son to mother connects the unseen to the seen, stain-ing the son's reputed beneficence with the mother's violence. The repetition of the silver half-dollar disrupts the surface tales's gender asymmetry of good sons/bad mother, white male benignity/white female malevolence, and shows that sons and mother, white males and white females occupy the same discourse, the same subtext of omissions: a northern exploita-tion of Frado equivalent to that of the plantation and the sexual significance of that equivalence for the black female.

The silver half-dollar that subverts claims of white male beneficence by linking it to white female vio-lence suggests that Mrs. Bellmont may provide a safe narrative site for expressing what cannot be said about the Bellmont men without connecting discourses that exonerate white male aggression with discourses that figure the "black woman as chronically promiscuous," in Angela Davis's words.[25] The transgressive subtext of *Our Nig* suggests that the Bellmont men do not view Frado in any significantly different way than does Mrs. Bellmont, but to name their violence would un-roll a mobius strip of racist, patriarchal antebellum inversions that revise accounts of material reality to protect white men and to indict black women—indict Frado. Thus *Our Nig*'s subtext of omissions, its ma-nipulation of signifiers, as well as its textual elisions and discrepancies in story-telling suggest that the Bellmont men also partake of the "opportunity" Frado signifies to Mrs. Bellmont "to indulge her vixen na-ture" (41); they too partake of what is described as Mrs. Bellmont's "manifest enjoyment" in abusing Frado (66), her "excite[ment] by so much indulgence of a dangerous passion" (82). Indeed, such representations of Mrs. Bellmont's sadistic pleasure may signify sites of displacement for an indulgence the men practice unseen and that cannot be named except in the en-coded subtextual discourse of the signatory "Our Nig."[26]

By coding white male sexual violence against the black female protagonist in the narrative's structures and figures rather than directly in the narration itself, *Our Nig* figures at once both the silence to which the female victim of sexual exploitation is enjoined and the invisibility enjoyed by the white male perpetrators. As a text coded for sexual transgression in its announced reticence, in its erasure of sexual violence and its effacement of perpetrators, *Our Nig* provides an account of its era's race and gender conventions. It is axiomatic that, above all, dictates of true womanhood oblige Wilson's indirection with regard to sexuality, the one part of Frado's story that is "unknown save by the Omniscient God" and prohibited from expression. Or from direct expression. *Our Nig* endeavors to say without speaking them the unnameable aspects of Frado's experience. In this, it conforms to true womanhood's prescriptions for female chastity and modesty, but it also indicates the fall of "slavery's shadows" on the indentured body of a "Free Black" woman, and by allusively inscribing her sexual exploitation, attests that the rule of the plantation and its masters also holds sway "In a Two-story White House, North."

Notes

1 These quotations are taken from Harriet E. Wilson, *Our Nig: or, Sketches from the Life of a Free Black* (1859; New York: Vintage, 1984). Subsequent references will be given parenthetically in the text.

2 Hazel V. Carby, *Reconstructing Womanhood: The Emergence of the Afro-American Woman Novelist* (New York: Oxford University Press, 1987); Henry Louis Gates Jr., introduction to *Our Nig;* and Claudia Tate, *Domestic Allegories of Political Desire: The Black Heroine's Text at the Turn of the Century* (New York: Oxford University Press, 1992). The focus common to all three writers is succinctly summarized by Tate when she calls *Our Nig* a "complex variation on the intersection of the conventions of sentimental fiction and the slave narrative" (39). See also Gates, "Parallel Discursive Universes: Fictions of Self in Harriet E. Wilson's *Our Nig*," in *Figures in Black: Words, Signs, and the "Racial" Self* (New York: Oxford University Press, 1987), 125-63.

3 Gates, "Introduction," xxxv. Carby pronounces *Our Nig* "an allegory of a slave narrative, a 'slave' narrative set in the 'free' North" (43), focusing her argument on the violence of the white mistress, but she does not pursue possible sexual transgressions of the white masters, which would complete the slave narrative allegory as it particularly pertains to black women. Tate identifies a "reticent sexual discourse in the novel" (35) but confines her discussion to the protagonist's relationship late in the tale with her husband Samuel. Gates finds in Frado's "complex

relationship" to the Bellmont son James "a curious blend of religion and displaced sexual desire," but he approaches the "dormant passion" as if it is Frado's repressed wish ("Introduction," xlix). Thus these critics and others imply and even recognize a repressed but pervasive sexual element in the narrative of *Our Nig,* yet they each follow the text's own protocol and account for the mysterious element in ways that preserve its indirection or obfuscating displacement.

4 Elizabeth Fox-Genovese, "My Statue, My Self: Autobiographical Writings of Afro-American Women," in *Reading Black, Reading Feminist,* ed. Henry Louis Gates Jr. (New York: Meridian, 1990), 198.

5 Tate goes on to identify "deliberately constructed double-voiced representations" in *Our Nig* (39), a formulation that also describes the narrative's practice of inscription by elision through a transgressive subtext that conveys material left out of the surface narrative of *Our Nig.*

6 Wilson's contemporaries Harriet Jacobs and Elizabeth Keckley address their sexual exploitation in slavery but, endeavoring to maintain decorum, they resort to telling it slant. Rennie Simson, in "The Afro-American Female: The Historical Context of the Construction of Sexual Identity," in *Powers of Desire: The Politics of Sexuality,* ed. Ann Snitow, Christine Stansell, and Sharon Thompson (New York: Monthly Review Press, 1983), 229-35, calls attention to Elizabeth Keckley's elided and indirect locations for the narration of sexual coercion in *Behind the Scenes,* pointing to Keckley's statement, "I do not care to dwell upon this subject [of being the object of sexual lust of the second of two white men who pursue and ravish her] for it is one that is fraught with pain. Suffice it to say, that he persecuted me for four years, and I—I became a mother" (Simson, 231; Elizabeth Keckley, *Behind the Scenes: Or, Thirty Years a Slave and Four Years in the White House* [1868; New York: Basic Books, 1985], 33). Keckley's text was published in 1868, within the same period as that of *Our Nig* (1859) and Harriet Jacobs's *Incidents in the Life of a Slave Girl* (1861; Cambridge: Harvard University Press, 1987). In Keckley's account, as in Wilson's, modesty and indirection prevail (she will not "dwell" on "this subject" "fraught with pain"); omission is indicated by the phrase "suffice it to say"; and elision is graphically inscribed by the dash between the two *Is* required for her to confess sexual exploitation, gestured to in the appositely demure figure of achieved motherhood. As in Jacobs's and Wilson's accounts, the verb "persecuted," a charged word used somewhat eccentrically becomes in this context a trope for sexual violation or penetration, while the phrase "for four years" indicates duration and suggests the repeated trauma that is too "fraught."

[7] Spillers cautions against the disabling effects of face-value assessments of black female self-expression with regard to sexuality and insists that "in order to supply the missing words in the discourse of sexuality, we would try to encounter agent, agency, act, scene, and purpose in ways that the dominative mode forbids. . . . To dissipate its energies requires that the feminist critic/historian actively imagine women in their living and pluralistic confrontations with experience (at least, the way they report it), and perhaps the best guarantee of such commitment is the critic's heightened self-consciousness with regard to the conceptual tools with which we operate" ("Interstices: A Small Drama of Words," in *Sexuality,* ed. Hortense Spillers [Boston: Routledge, 1984], 94).

[8] See Barbara Christian, Introduction to Mrs. A. E. Johnson, *The Hazeley Family* (1894; New York: Oxford, 1990).

[9] See Gates, "Introduction," iv.

[10] Tate, 35; Gates, "Introduction," xxxv-xxxvii.

[11] Tate, 38.

[12] Evelyn Brooks Higginbotham, "African-American Women's History and the Metalanguage of Race," *Signs* 17.2 (Winter 1992): 256.

[13] See Tate, 44.

[14] Barbara Omolade asserts that in U.S. race relations, the (black) "body could not be separated from its color" ("Hearts of Darkness," in Snitow, 353-55). So, too, in *Our Nig,* the conspicuously designated black body of Frado signifies that the Bellmont men do not view her any differently than does Mrs. Bellmont, though their sex implicates them in a further level of exploitation they would have been able to regard—and to take—as their racial due within the reigning racial discourses of the day: sexual transgression of black female subjectivity. Or as Angela Davis puts it, the white male "license to rape emanated from and facilitated the ruthless economic domination that was the gruesome hallmark of slavery" (*Women, Race and Class* [New York: Random House, 1981], 175). As slavery is the "gruesome hallmark" of Frado's indenture, so too is an undisclosed but subtextually inscribed sexual exploitation.

[15] Harriet Jacobs and Frederick Douglass both depict the fury of white women at white male sexual transgression. Both authors show that this transgression does not destabilize categories of racial difference but in fact preserves them and foregrounds gender as a central determinative of white (male) race privilege, the chief entitlement enacted in the sexual exploitation of black female slaves, or, in *Our Nig,* of Frado. See

Jacobs and Frederick Douglass, *Narrative of the Life of Frederick Douglass, An American Slave* (1845; Garden City, N.Y.: Doubleday, Anchor Books, 1973).

[16] Tate, 243.

[17] My reading of the Bellmont men's transgression against Frado as a further and deleted explanation of Mrs. Bellmont's violence is supported not only by the work of Barbara Omolade, but also by bell hooks. See hooks, *Ain't I A Woman: Black Women and Feminism* (Boston: South End Press, 1981), 15-49. See also Jacqueline Jones, *Labor of Love, Labor of Sorrow: Black Women, Work and the Family, from Slavery to the Present* (New York: Basic Books, 1985), and Eugene D. Genovese, *Roll, Jordan, Roll: The World the Slaves Made* (New York: Random House, 1974), among others, which substantiate the claim that that sexual exploitation of black female slaves by white masters was further exacerbated by the white mistresses' violence against the women for the males' transgressions. Omolade asserts that "most white women sadistically and viciously punished the black woman . . . for the [sexual] transgressions of their white men" (356-57); she also notes that white women competed for white male favor in "the social relationship of supervisor of black women's domestic labor" (351, 357), and, thus, "ultimately, white men were politically empowered to dominate all women and all black men and women: this was their sexual freedom" (352).

[18] Tate, 44.

[19] James exercises his male word of "law" when he "calmly, but imperatively" insists that Frado dine with the family and "eat such food as we eat" (68) instead of her usual way, "standing, by the kitchen table" eating scraps, forbidden to "be over ten minutes about it" (29). That is, his word of "law" sets the scene that will result in the transgression of Mrs. Bellmont's word of law; white women's power is inferior and subsidiary to white men's. Indeed, without James's agency, Frado would not be in a position to administer Mrs. Bellmont's comeuppance.

[20] This aspect of the scene recalls one from *Uncle Tom's Cabin* that captures the patronizing expectation of slavers to be amused by their slaves. Eliza's young son Harry is bidden to dance, sing, and perform imitations for the entertainment of Mr. Shelby and the trader Haley and is rewarded for his cleverness with raisins, a piece of orange, and Haley's disastrous desire to take the boy in acquittal of Shelby's debt. Topsy is similarly bidden to entertain Augustine St. Claire and his sister Ophelia on the day when St. Claire "gives" Topsy to Ophelia.

[21] Hooks, 24, 27.

[22] Jacquelyn Dowd Hall, " 'The Mind That Burns in Each Body': Women, Rape, and Racial Violence," in

Snitow, 332. See also Jones, 37; Melton A. McLaurin, *Celia, A Slave* (Athens: University of Georgia Press, 1991).

[23] The omniscient narrator—"Our Nig"—observes that the image of a "frail child, driven from shelter by the cruelty of his mother, was an object of interest to James" (50): read through the subtext that subverts the cover story of Bellmont male beneficence, this sentence suggests that James's "interest" is what makes Frado an "object."

[24] Indeed, in the sentence before, rather incongruously, we are told that Frado must leave Fido behind. This information evokes the Frado/Fido eye rhyme, the identification of pet and child, the dog's provision as gift to bribe or placate or reward the child, and the dog's narrative value as signifier for a split off part of the protagonist. Fido is not only Frado's "entire confidant" (41), the embodiment and repository of what may not be told directly in the narrative, he is Frado's accomplice in the humiliation of Mrs. Bellmont, which provides the occasion of her first gift of a silver half-dollar.

[25] Davis, 182.

[26] It cannot be named because it "would most provoke shame in our good anti-slavery friends," as Wilson says in the preface. That is, it cannot be named because it would cause shame for Wilson as well as for Frado. It cannot be named without inculpating its victim, for discourses, institutions, and laws in Harriet Wilson's time as well as in our own conspire to protect white male patriarchal privilege with invisibility, in this case by associating black women with carnality (Hall, 333) and, as the historian Richard Hofstadter explains, by blaming white male interest in black women (and the access to them permitted by their privilege) on myths of the women's lasciviousness (see Omolade, 365).

FURTHER READING

Curtis, David Ames, and Henry Louis Gates, Jr. "Establishing the Identity of the Author of *Our Nig*." In *Wild Women in the Whirlwind: Afra-American Culture and the Contemporary Literary Renaissance,* edited by Joanne M. Braxton and Andrée Nicola McLaughlin, pp. 48-69. New Brunswick, N.J.: Rutgers University Press, 1990.

> Compares the fictionalized autobiography of Harriet Wilson with the historical facts of her life.

Davis, Cynthia J. "Harriet E. Wilson (1827?-1863?)." In *Nineteenth-Century American Women Writers: A Bio-Bibliographical Critical Sourcebook,* edited by Denise D. Knight, pp. 484-89. Westport, Conn.: Greenwood Press, 1997.

> Reconstructs Wilson's life, explores the themes of *Our Nig* and its critical reception, and gives a short bibliography of secondary sources.

Doriani, Beth Maclay. "Black Womanhood in Nineteenth-Century America: Subversion and Self-Construction in Two Women's Autobiographies." *American Quarterly* 43, No. 2 (June 1991): 199-222.

> Identifies the rhetorical strategies used by Wilson and Harriet Jacobs in order to "defy the social constraints on the writers' identities as women and as blacks, as well as the reproduction of those constraints in the genre conventions that the writers manipulate."

Foreman, P. Gabrielle. "The Spoken and the Silenced in *Incidents in the Life of a Slave Girl* and *Our Nig*." *Callaloo* 13, No. 2 (Spring 1990): 313-24.

> Compares the ways in which Wilson and Harriet Jacobs "subvert and invert the authority of audience" and "negotiate the assertion of their voices."

Lindgren, Margaret. "Harriet Jacobs, Harriet Wilson and the Redoubled Voice in Black Autobiography." *Obsidian* 8, No. 1 (Spring-Summer 1993): 18-38.

> Explores the ways in which Jacobs and Wilson construct their autobiographies given that their mostly white audience did not share their social and cultural backgrounds.

Lovell, Thomas B. "By Dint of Labor and Economy: Harriet Jacobs, Harriet Wilson, and the Salutary View of Wage Labor." *Arizona Quarterly* 52, No. 3 (Autumn 1996): 1-32.

> Claims that, within the tradition of the sentimental novel, Wilson and Jacobs critique the relationship between the wage system and sentimental moral principles.

Mitchell, Angelyn. "Her Side of His Story: A Feminist Analysis of Two Nineteenth-Century Antebellum Novels William Wells Brown's *Clotel* and Harriet E. Wilson's *Our Nig*." *American Literary Realism 1870-1910* 24, No. 3 (Spring 1992): 7-21.

> Contends that, despite the fact that Brown and Wilson both discuss female slaves' quest for freedom, they characterize women very differently within their different choices of genre.

Stern, Julia. "Excavating Genre in *Our Nig*." *American Literature* 67, No. 3 (Sept. 1995): 439-66.

> Discusses the interplay between gothic conventions and the form of the sentimental novel in *Our Nig*.

Tate, Claudia. "Maternal Discourse as Antebellum Social Protest." In her *Domestic Allegories of Political Desire: The Black Heroine's Text at the Turn of the Century,* pp. 23-50. New York: Oxford University Press, 1992.

Relates *Our Nig* to Harriet A. Jacobs' *Incidents in the Life of a Slave Girl,* claiming that the novels typify attempts to equate "the nurturing household and a morally productive national polity" in an effort to protest the institution of slavery.

White, Barbara A. " 'Our Nig' and the She-Devil: New Information about Harriet Wilson and the 'Bellmont' Family." *American Literature* 65, No. 1 (March 1993): 19-52.

Historical study of the lives of Harriet Wilson and the family for whom she worked as an indentured servant.

Nineteenth-Century
Literature Criticism

Cumulative Indexes
Volumes 1-78

How to Use This Index

Literary Criticism Series
Cumulative Author Index

Bentley, E(dmund) C(lerihew) 1875-1956
TCLC 12
See also CA 108; DLB 70
Bentley, Eric (Russell) 1916- .... **CLC 24**
See also CA 5-8R; CANR 6, 67; INT CANR-6
Beranger, Pierre Jean de 1780-1857NCLC 34
Berdyaev, Nicolas
See Berdyaev, Nikolai (Aleksandrovich)
Berdyaev, Nikolai (Aleksandrovich) 1874-1948
TCLC 67
See also CA 120; 157
Berdyayev, Nikolai (Aleksandrovich)
See Berdyaev, Nikolai (Aleksandrovich)
Berendt, John (Lawrence) 1939- ..... **CLC 86**
See also CA 146; CANR 75; MTCW 1
Beresford, J(ohn) D(avys) 1873-1947 . T C L C
81
See also CA 112; 155; DLB 162, 178, 197
Bergelson, David 1884-1952 .... **TCLC 81**
Berger, Colonel
See Malraux, (Georges-)Andre
Berger, John (Peter) 1926- .... **CLC 2, 19**
See also CA 81-84; CANR 51, 78; DLB 14, 207
Berger, Melvin H. 1927- .... **CLC 12**
See also CA 5-8R; CANR 4; CLR 32; SAAS 2;
SATA 5, 88
Berger, Thomas (Louis) 1924-CLC 3, 5, 8, 11,
18, 38; DAM NOV
See also CA 1-4R; CANR 5, 28, 51; DLB 2;
DLBY 80; INT CANR-28; MTCW 1, 2
Bergman, (Ernst) Ingmar 1918- CLC 16, 72
See also CA 81-84; CANR 33, 70; MTCW 2
Bergson, Henri(-Louis) 1859-1941 TCLC 32
See also CA 164
Bergstein, Eleanor 1938- .... **CLC 4**
See also CA 53-56; CANR 5
Berkoff, Steven 1937- .... **CLC 56**
See also CA 104; CANR 72
Bermant, Chaim (Icyk) 1929- .... **CLC 40**
See also CA 57-60; CANR 6, 31, 57
Bern, Victoria
See Fisher, M(ary) F(rances) K(ennedy)
Bernanos, (Paul Louis) Georges 1888-1948
TCLC 3
See also CA 104; 130; DLB 72
Bernard, April 1956-........................ **CLC 59**
See also CA 131
Berne, Victoria
See Fisher, M(ary) F(rances) K(ennedy)
Bernhard, Thomas 1931-1989 CLC 3, 32, 61
See also CA 85-88; 127; CANR 32, 57; DLB
85, 124; MTCW 1
Bernhardt, Sarah (Henriette Rosine) 1844-1923
TCLC 75
See also CA 157
Berriault, Gina 1926-. CLC 54, 109; SSC 30
See also CA 116; 129; CANR 66; DLB 130
Berrigan, Daniel 1921- ....**CLC 4**
See also CA 33-36R; CAAS 1; CANR 11, 43,
78; DLB 5
Berrigan, Edmund Joseph Michael, Jr. 1934-
1983
See Berrigan, Ted
See also CA 61-64; 110; CANR 14
Berrigan, Ted .... **CLC 37**
See also Berrigan, Edmund Joseph Michael, Jr.
See also DLB 5, 169
Berry, Charles Edward Anderson 1931-
See Berry, Chuck
See also CA 115
Berry, Chuck .... **CLC 17**
See also Berry, Charles Edward Anderson
Berry, Jonas

See Ashbery, John (Lawrence)
Berry, Wendell (Erdman) 1934- CLC 4, 6, 8,
27, 46; DAM POET
See also AITN 1; CA 73-76; CANR 50, 73; DLB
5, 6; MTCW 1
Berryman, John 1914-1972CLC 1, 2, 3, 4, 6, 8,
10, 13, 25, 62; DAM POET
See also CA 13-16; 33-36R; CABS 2; CANR
35; CAP 1; CDALB 1941-1968; DLB 48;
MTCW 1, 2
Bertolucci, Bernardo 1940- .... **CLC 16**
See also CA 106
Berton, Pierre (Francis Demarigny) 1920-
CLC 104
See also CA 1-4R; CANR 2, 56; DLB 68; SATA
99
Bertrand, Aloysius 1807-1841 .... **NCLC 31**
Bertran de Born c. 1140-1215 .... **CMLC 5**
Besant, Annie (Wood) 1847-1933 .... **TCLC 9**
See also CA 105
Bessie, Alvah 1904-1985 .... **CLC 23**
See also CA 5-8R; 116; CANR 2, 80; DLB 26
Bethlen, T. D.
See Silverberg, Robert
Beti, Mongo ... CLC 27; BLC 1; DAM MULT
See Biyidi, Alexandre
See also CANR 79
Betjeman, John 1906-1984 CLC 2, 6, 10, 34,
43; DAB; DAM MST, POET
See also CA 9-12R; 112; CANR 33, 56; CDBLB
1945-1960; DLB 20; DLBY 84; MTCW 1,
2
Bettelheim, Bruno 1903-1990 .... **CLC 79**
See also CA 81-84; 131; CANR 23, 61; MTCW
1, 2
Betti, Ugo 1892-1953 .... **TCLC 5**
See also CA 104; 155
Betts, Doris (Waugh) 1932- ...... **CLC 3, 6, 28**
See also CA 13-16R; CANR 9, 66, 77; DLBY
82; INT CANR-9
Bevan, Alistair
See Roberts, Keith (John Kingston)
Bey, Pilaff
See Douglas, (George) Norman
Bialik, Chaim Nachman 1873-1934TCLC 25
See also CA 170
Bickerstaff, Isaac
See Swift, Jonathan
Bidart, Frank 1939- ....**CLC 33**
See also CA 140
Bienek, Horst 1930-........................**CLC 7, 11**
See also CA 73-76; DLB 75
Bierce, Ambrose (Gwinett) 1842-1914(?)
TCLC 1, 7, 44; DA; DAC; DAM MST; SSC
9; WLC
See also CA 104; 139; CANR 78; CDALB
1865-1917; DLB 11, 12, 23, 71, 74, 186
Biggers, Earl Derr 1884-1933 .... **TCLC 65**
See also CA 108; 153
Billings, Josh
See Shaw, Henry Wheeler
Billington, (Lady) Rachel (Mary) 1942-C L C
43
See also AITN 2; CA 33-36R; CANR 44
Binyon, T(imothy) J(ohn) 1936- ....**CLC 34**
See also CA 111; CANR 28
Bioy Casares, Adolfo 1914-1999CLC 4, 8, 13,
88; DAM MULT; HLC; SSC 17
See also CA 29-32R; 177; CANR 19, 43, 66;
DLB 113; HW 1, 2; MTCW 1, 2
Bird, Cordwainer
See Ellison, Harlan (Jay)
Bird, Robert Montgomery 1806-1854NCLC 1

See also DLB 202
Birkerts, Sven 1951- .... **CLC 116**
See also CA 128; 133; 176; CAAS 29; INT 133
Birney, (Alfred) Earle 1904-1995CLC 1, 4, 6,
11; DAC; DAM MST, POET
See also CA 1-4R; CANR 5, 20; DLB 88;
MTCW 1
Biruni, al 973-1048(?) .... **CMLC 28**
Bishop, Elizabeth 1911-1979 CLC 1, 4, 9, 13,
15, 32; DA; DAC; DAM MST, POET; PC
3
See also CA 5-8R; 89-92; CABS 2; CANR 26,
61; CDALB 1968-1988; DLB 5, 169;
MTCW 1, 2; SATA-Obit 24
Bishop, John 1935- ....**CLC 10**
See also CA 105
Bissett, Bill 1939- .... **CLC 18; PC 14**
See also CA 69-72; CAAS 19; CANR 15; DLB
53; MTCW 1
Bissoondath, Neil (Devindra) 1955-CLC 120;
DAC
See also CA 136
Bitov, Andrei (Georgievich) 1937- ....**CLC 57**
See also CA 142
Biyidi, Alexandre 1932-
See Beti, Mongo
See also BW 1, 3; CA 114; 124; CANR 81;
MTCW 1, 2
Bjarme, Brynjolf
See Ibsen, Henrik (Johan)
Bjoernson, Bjoernstjerne (Martinius) 1832-
1910 .... **TCLC 7, 37**
See also CA 104
Black, Robert
See Holdstock, Robert P.
Blackburn, Paul 1926-1971 .... **CLC 9, 43**
See also CA 81-84; 33-36R; CANR 34; DLB
16; DLBY 81
Black Elk 1863-1950TCLC 33; DAM MULT
See also CA 144; MTCW 1; NNAL
Black Hobart
See Sanders, (James) Ed(ward)
Blacklin, Malcolm
See Chambers, Aidan
Blackmore, R(ichard) D(oddridge) 1825-1900
TCLC 27
See also CA 120; DLB 18
Blackmur, R(ichard) P(almer) 1904-1965
CLC 2, 24
See also CA 11-12; 25-28R; CANR 71; CAP 1;
DLB 63
Black Tarantula
See Acker, Kathy
Blackwood, Algernon (Henry) 1869-1951
TCLC 5
See also CA 105; 150; DLB 153, 156, 178
Blackwood, Caroline 1931-1996CLC 6, 9, 100
See also CA 85-88; 151; CANR 32, 61, 65; DLB
14, 207; MTCW 1
Blade, Alexander
See Hamilton, Edmond; Silverberg, Robert
Blaga, Lucian 1895-1961 ....**CLC 75**
See also CA 157
Blair, Eric (Arthur) 1903-1950
See Orwell, George
See also CA 104; 132; DA; DAB; DAC; DAM
MST, NOV; MTCW 1, 2; SATA 29
Blair, Hugh 1718-1800 .... **NCLC 75**
Blais, Marie-Claire 1939-CLC 2, 4, 6, 13, 22;
DAC; DAM MST
See also CA 21-24R; CAAS 4; CANR 38, 75;
DLB 53; MTCW 1, 2
Blaise, Clark 1940- ....**CLC 29**

See also AITN 2; CA 53-56; CAAS 3; CANR
5, 66; DLB 53

Blake, Fairley
See De Voto, Bernard (Augustine)

Blake, Nicholas
See Day Lewis, C(ecil)
See also DLB 77

Blake, William 1757-1827. **NCLC 13, 37, 57;
DA; DAB; DAC; DAM MST, POET; PC
12; WLC**
See also CDBLB 1789-1832; CLR 52; DLB 93,
163; MAICYA; SATA 30

Blasco Ibanez, Vicente 1867-1928 **TCLC 12;
DAM NOV**
See also CA 110; 131; CANR 81; HW 1, 2;
MTCW 1

Blatty, William Peter 1928-**CLC 2; DAM POP**
See also CA 5-8R; CANR 9

Bleeck, Oliver
See Thomas, Ross (Elmore)

Blessing, Lee 1949- .... **CLC 54**

Blish, James (Benjamin) 1921-1975 **CLC 14**
See also CA 1-4R; 57-60; CANR 3; DLB 8;
MTCW 1; SATA 66

Bliss, Reginald
See Wells, H(erbert) G(eorge)

Blixen, Karen (Christentze Dinesen) 1885-1962
See Dinesen, Isak
See also CA 25-28; CANR 22, 50; CAP 2;
MTCW 1, 2; SATA 44

Bloch, Robert (Albert) 1917-1994 ... **CLC 33**
See also AAYA 29; CA 5-8R; 146; CAAS 20;
CANR 5, 78; DLB 44; INT CANR-5; MTCW
1; SATA 12; SATA-Obit 82

Blok, Alexander (Alexandrovich) 1880-1921
TCLC 5; PC 21
See also CA 104

Blom, Jan
See Breytenbach, Breyten

Bloom, Harold 1930- .... **CLC 24, 103**
See also CA 13-16R; CANR 39, 75; DLB 67;
MTCW 1

Bloomfield, Aurelius
See Bourne, Randolph S(illiman)

Blount, Roy (Alton), Jr. 1941- .... **CLC 38**
See also CA 53-56; CANR 10, 28, 61; INT
CANR-28; MTCW 1, 2

Bloy, Leon 1846-1917 .... **TCLC 22**
See also CA 121; DLB 123

Blume, Judy (Sussman) 1938- ... **CLC 12, 30;
DAM NOV, POP**
See also AAYA 3, 26; CA 29-32R; CANR 13,
37, 66; CLR 2, 15; DLB 52; JRDA;
MAICYA; MTCW 1, 2; SATA 2, 31, 79

Blunden, Edmund (Charles) 1896-1974 **C L C
2, 56**
See also CA 17-18; 45-48; CANR 54; CAP 2;
DLB 20, 100, 155; MTCW 1

Bly, Robert (Elwood) 1926-**CLC 1, 2, 5, 10, 15,
38; DAM POET**
See also CA 5-8R; CANR 41, 73; DLB 5;
MTCW 1, 2

Boas, Franz 1858-1942 .... **TCLC 56**
See also CA 115

Bobette
See Simenon, Georges (Jacques Christian)

Boccaccio, Giovanni 1313-1375 .. **CMLC 13;
SSC 10**

Bochco, Steven 1943- .... **CLC 35**
See also AAYA 11; CA 124; 138

Bodel, Jean 1167(?)-1210 .... **CMLC 28**

Bodenheim, Maxwell 1892-1954 .... **TCLC 44**
See also CA 110; DLB 9, 45

Bodker, Cecil 1927- .... **CLC 21**
See also CA 73-76; CANR 13, 44; CLR 23;
MAICYA; SATA 14

Boell, Heinrich (Theodor) 1917-1985 **CLC 2,
3, 6, 9, 11, 15, 27, 32, 72; DA; DAB; DAC;
DAM MST, NOV; SSC 23; WLC**
See also CA 21-24R; 116; CANR 24; DLB 69;
DLBY 85; MTCW 1, 2

Boerne, Alfred
See Doeblin, Alfred

Boethius 480(?)-524(?) .... **CMLC 15**
See also DLB 115

Bogan, Louise 1897-1970 .**CLC 4, 39, 46, 93;
DAM POET; PC 12**
See also CA 73-76; 25-28R; CANR 33; DLB
45, 169; MTCW 1, 2

Bogarde, Dirk ....**CLC 19**
See also Van Den Bogarde, Derek Jules Gaspard
Ulric Niven
See also DLB 14

Bogosian, Eric 1953- .... **CLC 45**
See also CA 138

Bograd, Larry 1953- .... **CLC 35**
See also CA 93-96; CANR 57; SAAS 21; SATA
33, 89

Boiardo, Matteo Maria 1441-1494 .... **LC 6**

Boileau-Despreaux, Nicolas 1636-1711 **LC 3**

Bojer, Johan 1872-1959 .... **TCLC 64**

Boland, Eavan (Aisling) 1944- .. **CLC 40, 67,
113; DAM POET**
See also CA 143; CANR 61; DLB 40; MTCW
2

Boll, Heinrich
See Boell, Heinrich (Theodor)
<indeBolt, Lee
See Faust, Frederick (Schiller)

Bolt, Robert (Oxton) 1924-1995 ..... **CLC 14;
DAM DRAM**
See also CA 17-20R; 147; CANR 35, 67; DLB
13; MTCW 1

Bombet, Louis-Alexandre-Cesar
See Stendhal

Bomkauf
See Kaufman, Bob (Garnell)

Bonaventura .... **NCLC 35**
See also DLB 90

Bond, Edward 1934- **CLC 4, 6, 13, 23; DAM
DRAM**
See also CA 25-28R; CANR 38, 67; DLB 13;
MTCW 1

Bonham, Frank 1914-1989 .... **CLC 12**
See also AAYA 1; CA 9-12R; CANR 4, 36;
JRDA; MAICYA; SAAS 3; SATA 1, 49;
SATA-Obit 62

Bonnefoy, Yves 1923- .. **CLC 9, 15, 58; DAM
MST, POET**
See also CA 85-88; CANR 33, 75; MTCW 1, 2

Bontemps, Arna(ud Wendell) 1902-1973**C L C
1, 18; BLC 1; DAM MULT, NOV, POET**
See also BW 1; CA 1-4R; 41-44R; CANR 4,
35; CLR 6; DLB 48, 51; JRDA; MAICYA;
MTCW 1, 2; SATA 2, 44; SATA-Obit 24

Booth, Martin 1944-........................... **CLC 13**
See also CA 93-96; CAAS 2

Booth, Philip 1925-............................ **CLC 23**
See also CA 5-8R; CANR 5; DLBY 82

Booth, Wayne C(layson) 1921- .... **CLC 24**
See also CA 1-4R; CAAS 5; CANR 3, 43; DLB
67

Borchert, Wolfgang 1921-1947 .... **TCLC 5**
See also CA 104; DLB 69, 124

Borel, Petrus 1809-1859 .... **NCLC 41**

Borges, Jorge Luis 1899-1986**CLC 1, 2, 3, 4, 6,
8, 9, 10, 13, 19, 44, 48, 83; DA; DAB; DAC;
DAM MST, MULT; HLC; PC 22; SSC 4;
WLC**
See also AAYA 26; CA 21-24R; CANR 19, 33,
75; DLB 113; DLBY 86; HW 1, 2; MTCW
1, 2

Borowski, Tadeusz 1922-1951 .... **TCLC 9**
See also CA 106; 154

Borrow, George (Henry) 1803-1881 **NCLC 9**
See also DLB 21, 55, 166

Bosman, Herman Charles 1905-1951 . **T C L C
49**
See also Malan, Herman
See also CA 160

Bosschere, Jean de 1878(?)-1953 ... **TCLC 19**
See also CA 115

Boswell, James 1740-1795**LC 4, 50; DA; DAB;
DAC; DAM MST; WLC**
See also CDBLB 1660-1789; DLB 104, 142

Bottoms, David 1949-......................... **CLC 53**
See also CA 105; CANR 22; DLB 120; DLBY
83

Boucicault, Dion 1820-1890 .... **NCLC 41**

Boucolon, Maryse 1937(?)-
See Conde, Maryse
See also BW 3; CA 110; CANR 30, 53, 76

Bourget, Paul (Charles Joseph) 1852-1935
TCLC 12
See also CA 107; DLB 123

Bourjaily, Vance (Nye) 1922- .... **CLC 8, 62**
See also CA 1-4R; CAAS 1; CANR 2, 72; DLB
2, 143

Bourne, Randolph S(illiman) 1886-1918
TCLC 16
See also CA 117; 155; DLB 63

Bova, Ben(jamin William) 1932- ..... **CLC 45**
See also AAYA 16; CA 5-8R; CAAS 18; CANR
11, 56; CLR 3; DLBY 81; INT CANR-11;
MAICYA; MTCW 1; SATA 6, 68

Bowen, Elizabeth (Dorothea Cole) 1899-1973
**CLC 1, 3, 6, 11, 15, 22, 118; DAM NOV;
SSC 3, 28**
See also CA 17-18; 41-44R; CANR 35; CAP 2;
CDBLB 1945-1960; DLB 15, 162; MTCW
1, 2

Bowering, George 1935- .... **CLC 15, 47**
See also CA 21-24R; CAAS 16; CANR 10; DLB
53

Bowering, Marilyn R(uthe) 1949- ... **CLC 32**
See also CA 101; CANR 49

Bowers, Edgar 1924-........................... **CLC 9**
See also CA 5-8R; CANR 24; DLB 5

Bowie, David .... **CLC 17**
See also Jones, David Robert

Bowles, Jane (Sydney) 1917-1973 **CLC 3, 68**
See also CA 19-20; 41-44R; CAP 2

Bowles, Paul (Frederick) 1910- **CLC 1, 2, 19,
53; SSC 3**
See also CA 1-4R; CAAS 1; CANR 1, 19, 50,
75; DLB 5, 6; MTCW 1, 2

Box, Edgar
See Vidal, Gore

Boyd, Nancy
See Millay, Edna St. Vincent

Boyd, William 1952-.............. **CLC 28, 53, 70**
See also CA 114; 120; CANR 51, 71

Boyle, Kay 1902-1992 **CLC 1, 5, 19, 58, 121;
SSC 5**
See also CA 13-16R; 140; CAAS 1; CANR 29,
61; DLB 4, 9, 48, 86; DLBY 93; MTCW 1,
2

Boyle, Mark
See Kienzle, William X(avier)

Boyle, Patrick 1905-1982 .... **CLC 19**
See also CA 127
Boyle, T. C. 1948-
See Boyle, T(homas) Coraghessan
Boyle, T(homas) Coraghessan 1948-**CLC 36,
55, 90; DAM POP; SSC 16**
See also BEST 90:4; CA 120; CANR 44, 76;
DLBY 86; MTCW 2
Boz
See Dickens, Charles (John Huffam)
Brackenridge, Hugh Henry 1748-1816**N C L C
7**
See also DLB 11, 37
Bradbury, Edward P.
See Moorcock, Michael (John)
See also MTCW 2
Bradbury, Malcolm (Stanley) 1932-**CLC 32,
61; DAM NOV**
See also CA 1-4R; CANR 1, 33; DLB 14, 207;
MTCW 1, 2
Bradbury, Ray (Douglas) 1920-**CLC 1, 3, 10,
15, 42, 98; DA; DAB; DAC; DAM MST,
NOV, POP; SSC 29; WLC**
See also AAYA 15; AITN 1, 2; CA 1-4R; CANR
2, 30, 75; CDALB 1968-1988; DLB 2, 8;
MTCW 1, 2; SATA 11, 64
Bradford, Gamaliel 1863-1932 ...... **TCLC 36**
See also CA 160; DLB 17
Bradley, David (Henry), Jr. 1950- .. **CLC 23,
118; BLC 1; DAM MULT**
See also BW 1, 3; CA 104; CANR 26, 81; DLB
33
Bradley, John Ed(mund, Jr.) 1958- . **CLC 55**
See also CA 139
Bradley, Marion Zimmer 1930-**CLC 30; DAM
POP**
See also AAYA 9; CA 57-60; CAAS 10; CANR
7, 31, 51, 75; DLB 8; MTCW 1, 2; SATA 90
Bradstreet, Anne 1612(?)-1672**LC 4, 30; DA;
DAC; DAM MST, POET; PC 10**
See also CDALB 1640-1865; DLB 24
Brady, Joan 1939- .... **CLC 86**
See also CA 141
Bragg, Melvyn 1939-........................ **CLC 10**
See also BEST 89:3; CA 57-60; CANR 10, 48;
DLB 14
Brahe, Tycho 1546-1601 .... **LC 45**
Braine, John (Gerard) 1922-1986**CLC 1, 3, 41**
See also CA 1-4R; 120; CANR 1, 33; CDBLB
1945-1960; DLB 15; DLBY 86; MTCW 1
Bramah, Ernest 1868-1942 .... **TCLC 72**
See also CA 156; DLB 70
Brammer, William 1930(?)-1978 ...... **CLC 31**
See also CA 77-80
Brancati, Vitaliano 1907-1954 .... **TCLC 12**
See also CA 109
Brancato, Robin F(idler) 1936- .... **CLC 35**
See also AAYA 9; CA 69-72; CANR 11, 45;
CLR 32; JRDA; SAAS 9; SATA 97
Brand, Max
See Faust, Frederick (Schiller)
Brand, Millen 1906-1980 .... **CLC 7**
See also CA 21-24R; 97-100; CANR 72
Branden, Barbara .... **CLC 44**
See also CA 148
Brandes, Georg (Morris Cohen) 1842-1927
TCLC 10
See also CA 105
Brandys, Kazimierz 1916- .... **CLC 62**
Branley, Franklyn M(ansfield) 1915-**CLC 21**
See also CA 33-36R; CANR 14, 39; CLR 13;
MAICYA; SAAS 16; SATA 4, 68
Brathwaite, Edward (Kamau) 1930-**CLC 11;**

BLCS; DAM POET
See also BW 2, 3; CA 25-28R; CANR 11, 26,
47; DLB 125
Brautigan, Richard (Gary) 1935-1984**CLC 1,
3, 5, 9, 12, 34, 42; DAM NOV**
See also CA 53-56; 113; CANR 34; DLB 2, 5,
206; DLBY 80, 84; MTCW 1; SATA 56
Brave Bird, Mary 1953-
See Crow Dog, Mary (Ellen)
See also NNAL
Braverman, Kate 1950- .... **CLC 67**
See also CA 89-92
Brecht, (Eugen) Bertolt (Friedrich) 1898-1956
**TCLC 1, 6, 13, 35; DA; DAB; DAC; DAM
DRAM, MST; DC 3; WLC**
See also CA 104; 133; CANR 62; DLB 56, 124;
MTCW 1, 2
Brecht, Eugen Berthold Friedrich
See Brecht, (Eugen) Bertolt (Friedrich)
Bremer, Fredrika 1801-1865 .... **NCLC 11**
Brennan, Christopher John 1870-1932**T C L C
17**
See also CA 117
Brennan, Maeve 1917-1993 .... **CLC 5**
See also CA 81-84; CANR 72
Brent, Linda
See Jacobs, Harriet A(nn)
Brentano, Clemens (Maria) 1778-1842**N C L C
1**
See also DLB 90
Brent of Bin Bin
See Franklin, (Stella Maria Sarah) Miles
(Lampe)
Brenton, Howard 1942- .... **CLC 31**
See also CA 69-72; CANR 33, 67; DLB 13;
MTCW 1
Breslin, James 1930-1996
See Breslin, Jimmy
See also CA 73-76; CANR 31, 75; DAM NOV;
MTCW 1, 2
Breslin, Jimmy .... **CLC 4, 43**
See also Breslin, James
See also AITN 1; DLB 185; MTCW 2
Bresson, Robert 1901- .... **CLC 16**
See also CA 110; CANR 49
Breton, Andre 1896-1966**CLC 2, 9, 15, 54; PC
15**
See also CA 19-20; 25-28R; CANR 40, 60; CAP
2; DLB 65; MTCW 1, 2
Breytenbach, Breyten 1939(?)- . **CLC 23, 37;
DAM POET**
See also CA 113; 129; CANR 61
Bridgers, Sue Ellen 1942- .... **CLC 26**
See also AAYA 8; CA 65-68; CANR 11, 36;
CLR 18; DLB 52; JRDA; MAICYA; SAAS
1; SATA 22, 90; SATA-Essay 109
Bridges, Robert (Seymour) 1844-1930**T C L C
1; DAM POET**
See also CA 104; 152; CDBLB 1890-1914;
DLB 19, 98
Bridie, James .... **TCLC 3**
See also Mavor, Osborne Henry
See also DLB 10
Brin, David 1950- .... **CLC 34**
See also AAYA 21; CA 102; CANR 24, 70; INT
CANR-24; SATA 65
Brink, Andre (Philippus) 1935- **CLC 18, 36,
106**
See also CA 104; CANR 39, 62; INT 103;
MTCW 1, 2
Brinsmead, H(esba) F(ay) 1922- .... **CLC 21**
See also CA 21-24R; CANR 10; CLR 47;
MAICYA; SAAS 5; SATA 18, 78

Brittain, Vera (Mary) 1893(?)-1970 . **CLC 23**
See also CA 13-16; 25-28R; CANR 58; CAP 1;
DLB 191; MTCW 1, 2
Broch, Hermann 1886-1951 .... **TCLC 20**
See also CA 117; DLB 85, 124
Brock, Rose
See Hansen, Joseph
Brodkey, Harold (Roy) 1930-1996 .... **CLC 56**
See also CA 111; 151; CANR 71; DLB 130
Brodskii, Iosif
See Brodsky, Joseph
Brodsky, Iosif Alexandrovich 1940-1996
See Brodsky, Joseph
See also AITN 1; CA 41-44R; 151; CANR 37;
DAM POET; MTCW 1, 2
Brodsky, Joseph 1940-1996 **CLC 4, 6, 13, 36,
100; PC 9**
See also Brodskii, Iosif; Brodsky, Iosif
Alexandrovich
See also MTCW 1
Brodsky, Michael (Mark) 1948- .... **CLC 19**
See also CA 102; CANR 18, 41, 58
Bromell, Henry 1947- .... **CLC 5**
See also CA 53-56; CANR 9
Bromfield, Louis (Brucker) 1896-1956**T C L C
11**
See also CA 107; 155; DLB 4, 9, 86
Broner, E(sther) M(asserman) 1930- **CLC 19**
See also CA 17-20R; CANR 8, 25, 72; DLB 28
Bronk, William (M.) 1918-1999 .... **CLC 10**
See also CA 89-92; 177; CANR 23; DLB 165
Bronstein, Lev Davidovich
See Trotsky, Leon
Bronte, Anne 1820-1849 .... **NCLC 71**
See also DLB 21, 199
Bronte, Charlotte 1816-1855 **NCLC 3, 8, 33,
58; DA; DAB; DAC; DAM MST, NOV;
WLC**
See also AAYA 17; CDBLB 1832-1890; DLB
21, 159, 199
Bronte, Emily (Jane) 1818-1848**NCLC 16, 35;
DA; DAB; DAC; DAM MST, NOV, POET;
PC 8; WLC**
See also AAYA 17; CDBLB 1832-1890; DLB
21, 32, 199
Brooke, Frances 1724-1789 .... **LC 6, 48**
See also DLB 39, 99
Brooke, Henry 1703(?)-1783 .... **LC 1**
See also DLB 39
Brooke, Rupert (Chawner) 1887-1915 **T C L C
2, 7; DA; DAB; DAC; DAM MST, POET;
PC 24; WLC**
See also CA 104; 132; CANR 61; CDBLB
1914-1945; DLB 19; MTCW 1, 2
Brooke-Haven, P.
See Wodehouse, P(elham) G(renville)
Brooke-Rose, Christine 1926(?)- .... **CLC 40**
See also CA 13-16R; CANR 58; DLB 14
Brookner, Anita 1928-**CLC 32, 34, 51; DAB;
DAM POP**
See also CA 114; 120; CANR 37, 56; DLB 194;
DLBY 87; MTCW 1, 2
Brooks, Cleanth 1906-1994 **CLC 24, 86, 110**
See also CA 17-20R; 145; CANR 33, 35; DLB
63; DLBY 94; INT CANR-35; MTCW 1, 2
Brooks, George
See Baum, L(yman) Frank
Brooks, Gwendolyn 1917- **CLC 1, 2, 4, 5, 15,
49; BLC 1; DA; DAC; DAM MST, MULT,
POET; PC 7; WLC**
See also AAYA 20; AITN 1; BW 2, 3; CA 1-
4R; CANR 1, 27, 52, 75; CDALB 1941-
1968; CLR 27; DLB 5, 76, 165; MTCW 1,

Burns, Tex
See L'Amour, Louis (Dearborn)
Burnshaw, Stanley 1906- .... **CLC 3, 13, 44**
See also CA 9-12R; DLB 48; DLBY 97
Burr, Anne 1937- .... **CLC 6**
See also CA 25-28R
Burroughs, Edgar Rice 1875-1950 . **TCLC 2, 32; DAM NOV**
See also AAYA 11; CA 104; 132; DLB 8; MTCW 1, 2; SATA 41
Burroughs, William S(eward) 1914-1997 **CLC 1, 2, 5, 15, 22, 42, 75, 109; DA; DAB; DAC; DAM MST, NOV, POP; WLC**
See also AITN 2; CA 9-12R; 160; CANR 20, 52; DLB 2, 8, 16, 152; DLBY 81, 97; MTCW 1, 2
Burton, SirRichard F(rancis) 1821-1890 **NCLC 42**
See also DLB 55, 166, 184
Busch, Frederick 1941- ..... **CLC 7, 10, 18, 47**
See also CA 33-36R; CAAS 1; CANR 45, 73; DLB 6
Bush, Ronald 1946- .... **CLC 34**
See also CA 136
Bustos, F(rancisco)
See Borges, Jorge Luis
Bustos Domecq, H(onorio)
See Bioy Casares, Adolfo; Borges, Jorge Luis
Butler, Octavia E(stelle) 1947- **CLC 38, 121; BLCS; DAM MULT, POP**
See also AAYA 18; BW 2, 3; CA 73-76; CANR 12, 24, 38, 73; DLB 33; MTCW 1, 2; SATA 84
Butler, Robert Olen (Jr.) 1945- **CLC 81; DAM POP**
See also CA 112; CANR 66; DLB 173; INT 112; MTCW 1
Butler, Samuel 1612-1680 .... **LC 16, 43**
See also DLB 101, 126
Butler, Samuel 1835-1902 . **TCLC 1, 33; DA; DAB; DAC; DAM MST, NOV; WLC**
See also CA 143; CDBLB 1890-1914; DLB 18, 57, 174
Butler, Walter C.
See Faust, Frederick (Schiller)
Butor, Michel (Marie Francois) 1926- **CLC 1, 3, 8, 11, 15**
See also CA 9-12R; CANR 33, 66; DLB 83; MTCW 1, 2
Butts, Mary 1892(?)-1937 .... **TCLC 77**
See also CA 148
Buzo, Alexander (John) 1944- .... **CLC 61**
See also CA 97-100; CANR 17, 39, 69
Buzzati, Dino 1906-1972 .... **CLC 36**
See also CA 160; 33-36R; DLB 177
Byars, Betsy (Cromer) 1928- .... **CLC 35**
See also AAYA 19; CA 33-36R; CANR 18, 36, 57; CLR 1, 16; DLB 52; INT CANR-18; JRDA; MAICYA; MTCW 1; SAAS 1; SATA 4, 46, 80; SATA-Essay 108
Byatt, A(ntonia) S(usan Drabble) 1936- **CLC 19, 65; DAM NOV, POP**
See also CA 13-16R; CANR 13, 33, 50, 75; DLB 14, 194; MTCW 1, 2
Byrne, David 1952- .... **CLC 26**
See also CA 127
Byrne, John Keyes 1926-
See Leonard, Hugh
See also CA 102; CANR 78; INT 102
Byron, George Gordon (Noel) 1788-1824 **NCLC 2, 12; DA; DAB; DAC; DAM MST, POET; PC 16; WLC**
See also CDBLB 1789-1832; DLB 96, 110

Byron, Robert 1905-1941 .... **TCLC 67**
See also CA 160; DLB 195
C. 3. 3.
See Wilde, Oscar
Caballero, Fernan 1796-1877 .... **NCLC 10**
Cabell, Branch
See Cabell, James Branch
Cabell, James Branch 1879-1958 .... **TCLC 6**
See also CA 105; 152; DLB 9, 78; MTCW 1
Cable, George Washington 1844-1925 **T C L C 4; SSC 4**
See also CA 104; 155; DLB 12, 74; DLBD 13
Cabral de Melo Neto, Joao 1920- ... **CLC 76; DAM MULT**
See also CA 151
Cabrera Infante, G(uillermo) 1929- **CLC 5, 25, 45, 120; DAM MULT; HLC**
See also CA 85-88; CANR 29, 65; DLB 113; HW 1, 2; MTCW 1, 2
Cade, Toni
See Bambara, Toni Cade
Cadmus and Harmonia
See Buchan, John
Caedmon fl. 658-680 .... **CMLC 7**
See also DLB 146
Caeiro, Alberto
See Pessoa, Fernando (Antonio Nogueira)
Cage, John (Milton, Jr.) 1912-1992 .. **CLC 41**
See also CA 13-16R; 169; CANR 9, 78; DLB 193; INT CANR-9
Cahan, Abraham 1860-1951 .... **TCLC 71**
See also CA 108; 154; DLB 9, 25, 28
Cain, G.
See Cabrera Infante, G(uillermo)
Cain, Guillermo
See Cabrera Infante, G(uillermo)
Cain, James M(allahan) 1892-1977 **CLC 3, 11, 28**
See also AITN 1; CA 17-20R; 73-76; CANR 8, 34, 61; MTCW 1
Caine, Mark
See Raphael, Frederic (Michael)
Calasso, Roberto 1941- .... **CLC 81**
See also CA 143
Calderon de la Barca, Pedro 1600-1681 .. **L C 23; DC 3; HLCS 1**
Caldwell, Erskine (Preston) 1903-1987 **CLC 1, 8, 14, 50, 60; DAM NOV; SSC 19**
See also AITN 1; CA 1-4R; 121; CAAS 1; CANR 2, 33; DLB 9, 86; MTCW 1, 2
Caldwell, (Janet Miriam) Taylor (Holland) 1900-1985 **CLC 2, 28, 39; DAM NOV, POP**
See also CA 5-8R; 116; CANR 5; DLBD 17
Calhoun, John Caldwell 1782-1850 **NCLC 15**
See also DLB 3
Calisher, Hortense 1911- **CLC 2, 4, 8, 38; DAM NOV; SSC 15**
See also CA 1-4R; CANR 1, 22, 67; DLB 2; INT CANR-22; MTCW 1, 2
Callaghan, Morley Edward 1903-1990 **CLC 3, 14, 41, 65; DAC; DAM MST**
See also CA 9-12R; 132; CANR 33, 73; DLB 68; MTCW 1, 2
Callimachus c. 305B.C.-c. 240B.C. **CMLC 18**
See also DLB 176
Calvin, John 1509-1564 .... **LC 37**
Calvino, Italo 1923-1985 **CLC 5, 8, 11, 22, 33, 39, 73; DAM NOV; SSC 3**
See also CA 85-88; 116; CANR 23, 61; DLB 196; MTCW 1, 2
Cameron, Carey 1952- .... **CLC 59**
See also CA 135
Cameron, Peter 1959- .... **CLC 44**

See also CA 125; CANR 50
Campana, Dino 1885-1932 .... **TCLC 20**
See also CA 117; DLB 114
Campanella, Tommaso 1568-1639 ...... **LC 32**
Campbell, John W(ood, Jr.) 1910-1971 **C L C 32**
See also CA 21-22; 29-32R; CANR 34; CAP 2; DLB 8; MTCW 1
Campbell, Joseph 1904-1987 .... **CLC 69**
See also AAYA 3; BEST 89:2; CA 1-4R; 124; CANR 3, 28, 61; MTCW 1, 2
Campbell, Maria 1940- .... **CLC 85; DAC**
See also CA 102; CANR 54; NNAL
Campbell, (John) Ramsey 1946- **CLC 42; SSC 19**
See also CA 57-60; CANR 7; INT CANR-7
Campbell, (Ignatius) Roy (Dunnachie) 1901-1957 .... **TCLC 5**
See also CA 104; 155; DLB 20; MTCW 2
Campbell, Thomas 1777-1844 .... **NCLC 19**
See also DLB 93; 144
Campbell, Wilfred .... **TCLC 9**
See also Campbell, William
Campbell, William 1858(?)-1918
See Campbell, Wilfred
See also CA 106; DLB 92
Campion, Jane .... **CLC 95**
See also CA 138
Campos, Alvaro de
See Pessoa, Fernando (Antonio Nogueira)
Camus, Albert 1913-1960 **CLC 1, 2, 4, 9, 11, 14, 32, 63, 69; DA; DAB; DAC; DAM DRAM, MST, NOV; DC 2; SSC 9; WLC**
See also CA 89-92; DLB 72; MTCW 1, 2
Canby, Vincent 1924- .... **CLC 13**
See also CA 81-84
Cancale
See Desnos, Robert
Canetti, Elias 1905-1994 **CLC 3, 14, 25, 75, 86**
See also CA 21-24R; 146; CANR 23, 61, 79; DLB 85, 124; MTCW 1, 2
Canfield, Dorothea F.
See Fisher, Dorothy (Frances) Canfield
Canfield, Dorothea Frances
See Fisher, Dorothy (Frances) Canfield
Canfield, Dorothy
See Fisher, Dorothy (Frances) Canfield
Canin, Ethan 1960- .... **CLC 55**
See also CA 131; 135
Cannon, Curt
See Hunter, Evan
Cao, Lan 1961- .... **CLC 109**
See also CA 165
Cape, Judith
See Page, P(atricia) K(athleen)
Capek, Karel 1890-1938 ... **TCLC 6, 37; DA; DAB; DAC; DAM DRAM, MST, NOV; DC 1; WLC**
See also CA 104; 140; MTCW 1
Capote, Truman 1924-1984 **CLC 1, 3, 8, 13, 19, 34, 38, 58; DA; DAB; DAC; DAM MST, NOV, POP; SSC 2; WLC**
See also CA 5-8R; 113; CANR 18, 62; CDALB 1941-1968; DLB 2, 185; DLBY 80, 84; MTCW 1, 2; SATA 91
Capra, Frank 1897-1991 ...?.............. **CLC 16**
See also CA 61-64; 135
Caputo, Philip 1941- .... **CLC 32**
See also CA 73-76; CANR 40
Caragiale, Ion Luca 1852-1912 ...... **TCLC 76**
See also CA 157
Card, Orson Scott 1951- **CLC 44, 47, 50; DAM POP**

See also CA 110

Challans, Mary 1905-1983
See Renault, Mary
See also CA 81-84; 111; CANR 74; MTCW 2;
SATA 23; SATA-Obit 36

Challis, George
See Faust, Frederick (Schiller)

Chambers, Aidan 1934- .... **CLC 35**
See also AAYA 27; CA 25-28R; CANR 12, 31,
58; JRDA; MAICYA; SAAS 12; SATA 1, 69,
108

Chambers, James 1948-
See Cliff, Jimmy
See also CA 124

Chambers, Jessie
See Lawrence, D(avid) H(erbert Richards)

Chambers, Robert W(illiam) 1865-1933
TCLC 41
See also CA 165; DLB 202; SATA 107

Chandler, Raymond (Thornton) 1888-1959
TCLC 1, 7; SSC 23
See also AAYA 25; CA 104; 129; CANR 60;
CDALB 1929-1941; DLBD 6; MTCW 1, 2

Chang, Eileen 1920-1995 .... **SSC 28**
See also CA 166

Chang, Jung 1952- .... **CLC 71**
See also CA 142

Chang Ai-Ling
See Chang, Eileen

Channing, William Ellery 1780-1842 . **N C L C
17**
See also DLB 1, 59

Chao, Patricia 1955- .... **CLC 119**
See also CA 163

Chaplin, Charles Spencer 1889-1977 **CLC 16**
See also Chaplin, Charlie
See also CA 81-84; 73-76

Chaplin, Charlie
See Chaplin, Charles Spencer
See also DLB 44

Chapman, George 1559(?)-1634 **LC 22; DAM
DRAM**
See also DLB 62, 121

Chapman, Graham 1941-1989 .... **CLC 21**
See also Monty Python
See also CA 116; 129; CANR 35

Chapman, John Jay 1862-1933 .... **TCLC 7**
See also CA 104

Chapman, Lee
See Bradley, Marion Zimmer

Chapman, Walker
See Silverberg, Robert

Chappell, Fred (Davis) 1936- ..... **CLC 40, 78**
See also CA 5-8R; CAAS 4; CANR 8, 33, 67;
DLB 6, 105

Char, Rene(-Emile) 1907-1988 **CLC 9, 11, 14,
55; DAM POET**
See also CA 13-16R; 124; CANR 32; MTCW
1, 2

Charby, Jay
See Ellison, Harlan (Jay)

Chardin, Pierre Teilhard de
See Teilhard de Chardin, (Marie Joseph) Pierre

Charles I 1600-1649 .... **LC 13**

Charriere, Isabelle de 1740-1805 ..**NCLC 66**

Charyn, Jerome 1937- .... **CLC 5, 8, 18**
See also CA 5-8R; CAAS 1; CANR 7, 61;
DLBY 83; MTCW 1

Chase, Mary (Coyle) 1907-1981 .... **DC 1**
See also CA 77-80; 105; SATA 17; SATA-Obit
29

Chase, Mary Ellen 1887-1973 .... **CLC 2**
See also CA 13-16; 41-44R; CAP 1; SATA 10

Chase, Nicholas
See Hyde, Anthony

Chateaubriand, Francois Rene de 1768-1848
NCLC 3
See also DLB 119

Chatterje, Sarat Chandra 1876-1936(?)
See Chatterji, Saratchandra
See also CA 109

Chatterji, Bankim Chandra 1838-1894 **NCLC
19**

Chatterji, Saratchandra .... **TCLC 13**
See also Chatterje, Sarat Chandra

Chatterton, Thomas 1752-1770 . **LC 3; DAM
POET**
See also DLB 109

Chatwin, (Charles) Bruce 1940-1989 **CLC 28,
57, 59; DAM POP**
See also AAYA 4; BEST 90:1; CA 85-88; 127;
DLB 194, 204

Chaucer, Daniel
See Ford, Ford Madox

Chaucer, Geoffrey 1340(?)-1400 **LC 17; DA;
DAB; DAC; DAM MST, POET; PC 19;
WLCS**
See also CDBLB Before 1660; DLB 146

Chaviaras, Strates 1935-
See Haviaras, Stratis
See also CA 105

Chayefsky, Paddy .... **CLC 23**
See also Chayefsky, Sidney
See also DLB 7, 44; DLBY 81

Chayefsky, Sidney 1923-1981
See Chayefsky, Paddy
See also CA 9-12R; 104; CANR 18; DAM
DRAM

Chedid, Andree 1920- .... **CLC 47**
See also CA 145

Cheever, John 1912-1982 **CLC 3, 7, 8, 11, 15,
25, 64; DA; DAB; DAC; DAM MST, NOV,
POP; SSC 1; WLC**
See also CA 5-8R; 106; CABS 1; CANR 5, 27,
76; CDALB 1941-1968; DLB 2, 102; DLBY
80, 82; INT CANR-5; MTCW 1, 2

Cheever, Susan 1943- .... **CLC 18, 48**
See also CA 103; CANR 27, 51; DLBY 82; INT
CANR-27

Chekhonte, Antosha
See Chekhov, Anton (Pavlovich)

Chekhov, Anton (Pavlovich) 1860-1904 **TCLC
3, 10, 31, 55; DA; DAB; DAC; DAM
DRAM, MST; DC 9; SSC 2, 28; WLC**
See also CA 104; 124; SATA 90

Chernyshevsky, Nikolay Gavrilovich 1828-1889
NCLC 1

Cherry, Carolyn Janice 1942-
See Cherryh, C. J.
See also CA 65-68; CANR 10

Cherryh, C. J. .... **CLC 35**
See also Cherry, Carolyn Janice
See also AAYA 24; DLBY 80; SATA 93

Chesnutt, Charles W(addell) 1858-1932
TCLC 5, 39; BLC 1; DAM MULT; SSC 7
See also BW 1, 3; CA 106; 125; CANR 76; DLB
12, 50, 78; MTCW 1, 2

Chester, Alfred 1929(?)-1971 .... **CLC 49**
See also CA 33-36R; DLB 130

Chesterton, G(ilbert) K(eith) 1874-1936
TCLC 1, 6, 64; DAM NOV, POET; SSC 1
See also CA 104; 132; CANR 73; CDBLB
1914-1945; DLB 10, 19, 34, 70, 98, 149,
178; MTCW 1, 2; SATA 27

Chiang, Pin-chin 1904-1986
See Ding Ling

Ch'ien Chung-shu 1910- .... **CLC 22**
See also CA 130; CANR 73; MTCW 1, 2

Child, L. Maria
See Child, Lydia Maria

Child, Lydia Maria 1802-1880 ...**NCLC 6, 73**
See also DLB 1, 74; SATA 67

Child, Mrs.
See Child, Lydia Maria

Child, Philip 1898-1978 .... **CLC 19, 68**
See also CA 13-14; CAP 1; SATA 47

Childers, (Robert) Erskine 1870-1922 **T C L C
65**
See also CA 113; 153; DLB 70

Childress, Alice 1920-1994 **CLC 12, 15, 86, 96;
BLC 1; DAM DRAM, MULT, NOV; DC 4**
See also AAYA 8; BW 2, 3; CA 45-48; 146;
CANR 3, 27, 50, 74; CLR 14; DLB 7, 38;
JRDA; MAICYA; MTCW 1, 2; SATA 7, 48,
81

Chin, Frank (Chew, Jr.) 1940- .... **DC 7**
See also CA 33-36R; CANR 71; DAM MULT;
DLB 206

Chislett, (Margaret) Anne 1943- ......**CLC 34**
See also CA 151

Chitty, Thomas Willes 1926- .... **CLC 11**
See also Hinde, Thomas
See also CA 5-8R

Chivers, Thomas Holley 1809-1858 **NCLC 49**
See also DLB 3

Choi, Susan .... **CLC 119**

Chomette, Rene Lucien 1898-1981
See Clair, Rene
See also CA 103

Chopin, Kate **TCLC 5, 14; DA; DAB; SSC 8;
WLCS**
See also Chopin, Katherine
See also CDALB 1865-1917; DLB 12, 78

Chopin, Katherine 1851-1904
See Chopin, Kate
See also CA 104; 122; DAC; DAM MST, NOV

Chretien de Troyes c. 12th cent. - ..**CMLC 10**
See also DLB 208

Christie
See Ichikawa, Kon

Christie, Agatha (Mary Clarissa) 1890-1976
**CLC 1, 6, 8, 12, 39, 48, 110; DAB; DAC;
DAM NOV**
See also AAYA 9; AITN 1, 2; CA 17-20R; 61-
64; CANR 10, 37; CDBLB 1914-1945; DLB
13, 77; MTCW 1, 2; SATA 36

Christie, (Ann) Philippa
See Pearce, Philippa
See also CA 5-8R; CANR 4

Christine de Pizan 1365(?)-1431(?) ...... **LC 9**
See also DLB 208

Chubb, Elmer
See Masters, Edgar Lee

Chulkov, Mikhail Dmitrievich 1743-1792 **LC 2**
See also DLB 150

Churchill, Caryl 1938- ..... **CLC 31, 55; DC 5**
See also CA 102; CANR 22, 46; DLB 13;
MTCW 1

Churchill, Charles 1731-1764 .... **LC 3**
See also DLB 109

Chute, Carolyn 1947- .... **CLC 39**
See also CA 123

Ciardi, John (Anthony) 1916-1986 . **CLC 10,
40, 44; DAM POET**
See also CA 5-8R; 118; CAAS 2; CANR 5, 33;
CLR 19; DLB 5; DLBY 86; INT CANR-5;
MAICYA; MTCW 1, 2; SAAS 26; SATA 1,
65; SATA-Obit 46

11, 15, 18, 37, 44, 65, 113; DAM NOV, POP
See also AAYA 22; AITN 2; BEST 89:3; CA
45-48; CANR 2, 33, 51, 76; CDALB 1968-
1988; DLB 2, 28, 173; DLBY 80; MTCW 1,
2

Dodgson, Charles Lutwidge 1832-1898
See Carroll, Lewis
See also CLR 2; DA; DAB; DAC; DAM MST,
NOV, POET; MAICYA; SATA 100; YABC 2

Dodson, Owen (Vincent) 1914-1983 **CLC 79;
BLC 1; DAM MULT**
See also BW 1; CA 65-68; 110; CANR 24; DLB
76

Doeblin, Alfred 1878-1957 .... **TCLC 13**
See also Doblin, Alfred
See also CA 110; 141; DLB 66

Doerr, Harriet 1910- .... **CLC 34**
See also CA 117; 122; CANR 47; INT 122

Domecq, H(onorio Bustos)
See Bioy Casares, Adolfo

Domecq, H(onorio) Bustos
See Bioy Casares, Adolfo; Borges, Jorge Luis

Domini, Rey
See Lorde, Audre (Geraldine)

Dominique
See Proust, (Valentin-Louis-George-Eugene-)
Marcel

Don, A
See Stephen, Sir Leslie

Donaldson, Stephen R. 1947- **CLC 46; DAM
POP**
See also CA 89-92; CANR 13, 55; INT CANR-
13

Donleavy, J(ames) P(atrick) 1926-**CLC 1, 4, 6,
10, 45**
See also AITN 2; CA 9-12R; CANR 24, 49, 62,
80; DLB 6, 173; INT CANR-24; MTCW 1,
2

Donne, John 1572-1631**LC 10, 24; DA; DAB;
DAC; DAM MST, POET; PC 1; WLC**
See also CDBLB Before 1660; DLB 121, 151

Donnell, David 1939(?)- .... **CLC 34**

Donoghue, P. S.
See Hunt, E(verette) Howard, (Jr.)

Donoso (Yanez), Jose 1924-1996**CLC 4, 8, 11,
32, 99; DAM MULT; HLC; SSC 34**
See also CA 81-84; 155; CANR 32, 73; DLB
113; HW 1, 2; MTCW 1, 2

Donovan, John 1928-1992 .... **CLC 35**
See also AAYA 20; CA 97-100; 137; CLR 3;
MAICYA; SATA 72; SATA-Brief 29

Don Roberto
See Cunninghame Graham, R(obert) B(ontine)

Doolittle, Hilda 1886-1961**CLC 3, 8, 14, 31, 34,
73; DA; DAC; DAM MST, POET; PC 5;
WLC**
See also H. D.
See also CA 97-100; CANR 35; DLB 4, 45;
MTCW 1, 2

Dorfman, Ariel 1942- ...... **CLC 48, 77; DAM
MULT; HLC**
See also CA 124; 130; CANR 67, 70; HW 1, 2;
INT 130

Dorn, Edward (Merton) 1929- ... **CLC 10, 18**
See also CA 93-96; CANR 42, 79; DLB 5; INT
93-96

Dorris, Michael (Anthony) 1945-1997 .. **C L C
109; DAM MULT, NOV**
See also AAYA 20; BEST 90:1; CA 102; 157;
CANR 19, 46, 75; CLR 58; DLB 175;
MTCW 2; NNAL; SATA 75; SATA-Obit 94

Dorris, Michael A.
See Dorris, Michael (Anthony)

Dorsan, Luc
See Simenon, Georges (Jacques Christian)

Dorsange, Jean
See Simenon, Georges (Jacques Christian)

Dos Passos, John (Roderigo) 1896-1970 **C L C
1, 4, 8, 11, 15, 25, 34, 82; DA; DAB; DAC;
DAM MST, NOV; WLC**
See also CA 1-4R; 29-32R; CANR 3; CDALB
1929-1941; DLB 4, 9; DLBD 1, 15; DLBY
96; MTCW 1, 2

Dossage, Jean
See Simenon, Georges (Jacques Christian)

Dostoevsky, Fedor Mikhailovich 1821-1881
**NCLC 2, 7, 21, 33, 43; DA; DAB; DAC;
DAM MST, NOV; SSC 2, 33; WLC**

Doughty, Charles M(ontagu) 1843-1926
TCLC 27
See also CA 115; DLB 19, 57, 174

Douglas, Ellen .... **CLC 73**
See also Haxton, Josephine Ayres; Williamson,
Ellen Douglas

Douglas, Gavin 1475(?)-1522 .... **LC 20**
See also DLB 132

Douglas, George
See Brown, George Douglas

Douglas, Keith (Castellain) 1920-1944**T C L C
40**
See also CA 160; DLB 27

Douglas, Leonard
See Bradbury, Ray (Douglas)

Douglas, Michael
See Crichton, (John) Michael

Douglas, (George) Norman 1868-1952**T C L C
68**
See also CA 119; 157; DLB 34, 195

Douglas, William
See Brown, George Douglas

Douglass, Frederick 1817(?)-1895**NCLC 7, 55;
BLC 1; DA; DAC; DAM MST, MULT;
WLC**
See also CDALB 1640-1865; DLB 1, 43, 50,
79; SATA 29

Dourado, (Waldomiro Freitas) Autran 1926-
CLC 23, 60
See also CA 25-28R; CANR 34, 81; DLB 145;
HW 2

Dourado, Waldomiro Autran
See Dourado, (Waldomiro Freitas) Autran

Dove, Rita (Frances) 1952-**CLC 50, 81; BLCS;
DAM MULT, POET; PC 6**
See also BW 2; CA 109; CAAS 19; CANR 27,
42, 68, 76; CDALBS; DLB 120; MTCW 1

Doveglion
See Villa, Jose Garcia

Dowell, Coleman 1925-1985 .... **CLC 60**
See also CA 25-28R; 117; CANR 10; DLB 130

Dowson, Ernest (Christopher) 1867-1900
TCLC 4
See also CA 105; 150; DLB 19, 135

Doyle, A. Conan
See Doyle, Arthur Conan

Doyle, Arthur Conan 1859-1930**TCLC 7; DA;
DAB; DAC; DAM MST, NOV; SSC 12;
WLC**
See also AAYA 14; CA 104; 122; CDBLB 1890-
1914; DLB 18, 70, 156, 178; MTCW 1, 2;
SATA 24

Doyle, Conan
See Doyle, Arthur Conan

Doyle, John
See Graves, Robert (von Ranke)

Doyle, Roddy 1958(?)- .... **CLC 81**
See also AAYA 14; CA 143; CANR 73; DLB

194

Doyle, Sir A. Conan
See Doyle, Arthur Conan

Doyle, Sir Arthur Conan
See Doyle, Arthur Conan

Dr. A
See Asimov, Isaac; Silverstein, Alvin

Drabble, Margaret 1939-**CLC 2, 3, 5, 8, 10, 22,
53; DAB; DAC; DAM MST, NOV, POP**
See also CA 13-16R; CANR 18, 35, 63; CDBLB
1960 to Present; DLB 14, 155; MTCW 1, 2;
SATA 48

Drapier, M. B.
See Swift, Jonathan

Drayham, James
See Mencken, H(enry) L(ouis)

Drayton, Michael 1563-1631 ...... **LC 8; DAM
POET**
See also DLB 121

Dreadstone, Carl
See Campbell, (John) Ramsey

Dreiser, Theodore (Herman Albert) 1871-1945
**TCLC 10, 18, 35, 83; DA; DAC; DAM
MST, NOV; SSC 30; WLC**
See also CA 106; 132; CDALB 1865-1917;
DLB 9, 12, 102, 137; DLBD 1; MTCW 1, 2

Drexler, Rosalyn 1926- .... **CLC 2, 6**
See also CA 81-84; CANR 68

Dreyer, Carl Theodor 1889-1968 ...... **CLC 16**
See also CA 116

Drieu la Rochelle, Pierre(-Eugene) 1893-1945
TCLC 21
See also CA 117; DLB 72

Drinkwater, John 1882-1937 .... **TCLC 57**
See also CA 109; 149; DLB 10, 19, 149

Drop Shot
See Cable, George Washington

Droste-Hulshoff, Annette Freiin von 1797-1848
NCLC 3
See also DLB 133

Drummond, Walter
See Silverberg, Robert

Drummond, William Henry 1854-1907**T C L C
25**
See also CA 160; DLB 92

Drummond de Andrade, Carlos 1902-1987
CLC 18
See also Andrade, Carlos Drummond de
See also CA 132; 123

Drury, Allen (Stuart) 1918-1998 .... **CLC 37**
See also CA 57-60; 170; CANR 18, 52; INT
CANR-18

Dryden, John 1631-1700**LC 3, 21; DA; DAB;
DAC; DAM DRAM, MST, POET; DC 3;
PC 25; WLC**
See also CDBLB 1660-1789; DLB 80, 101, 131

Duberman, Martin (Bauml) 1930- ...... **CLC 8**
See also CA 1-4R; CANR 2, 63

Dubie, Norman (Evans) 1945- .... **CLC 36**
See also CA 69-72; CANR 12; DLB 120

Du Bois, W(illiam) E(dward) B(urghardt) 1868-
1963 .. **CLC 1, 2, 13, 64, 96; BLC 1; DA;
DAC; DAM MST, MULT, NOV; WLC**
See also BW 1, 3; CA 85-88; CANR 34;
CDALB 1865-1917; DLB 47, 50, 91; MTCW
1, 2; SATA 42

Dubus, Andre 1936-1999**CLC 13, 36, 97; SSC
15**
See also CA 21-24R; 177; CANR 17; DLB 130;
INT CANR-17

Duca Minimo
See D'Annunzio, Gabriele

Ducharme, Rejean 1941- .... **CLC 74**

MAICYA; SATA 4, 68

Gallico, Paul (William) 1897-1976 ..... **CLC 2**
  See also AITN 1; CA 5-8R; 69-72; CANR 23;
    DLB 9, 171; MAICYA; SATA 13

Gallo, Max Louis 1932- .... **CLC 95**
  See also CA 85-88

Gallois, Lucien
  See Desnos, Robert

Gallup, Ralph
  See Whitemore, Hugh (John)

Galsworthy, John 1867-1933**TCLC 1, 45; DA;
  DAB; DAC; DAM DRAM, MST, NOV;
  SSC 22; WLC**
  See also CA 104; 141; CANR 75; CDBLB
    1890-1914; DLB 10, 34, 98, 162; DLBD 16;
    MTCW 1

Galt, John 1779-1839 .... **NCLC 1**
  See also DLB 99, 116, 159

Galvin, James 1951- .... **CLC 38**
  See also CA 108; CANR 26

Gamboa, Federico 1864-1939 .... **TCLC 36**
  See also CA 167; HW 2

Gandhi, M. K.
  See Gandhi, Mohandas Karamchand

Gandhi, Mahatma
  See Gandhi, Mohandas Karamchand

Gandhi, Mohandas Karamchand 1869-1948
  TCLC 59; DAM MULT
  See also CA 121; 132; MTCW 1, 2

Gann, Ernest Kellogg 1910-1991 ..... **CLC 23**
  See also AITN 1; CA 1-4R; 136; CANR 1

Garcia, Cristina 1958- .... **CLC 76**
  See also CA 141; CANR 73; HW 2

Garcia Lorca, Federico 1898-1936**TCLC 1, 7,
  49; DA; DAB; DAC; DAM DRAM, MST,
  MULT, POET; DC 2; HLC; PC 3; WLC**
  See also CA 104; 131; CANR 81; DLB 108;
    HW 1, 2; MTCW 1, 2

Garcia Marquez, Gabriel (Jose) 1928-**CLC 2,
  3, 8, 10, 15, 27, 47, 55, 68; DA; DAB; DAC;
  DAM MST, MULT, NOV, POP; HLC; SSC
  8; WLC**
  See also AAYA 3; BEST 89:1, 90:4; CA 33-
    36R; CANR 10, 28, 50, 75; DLB 113; HW
    1, 2; MTCW 1, 2

Gard, Janice
  See Latham, Jean Lee

Gard, Roger Martin du
  See Martin du Gard, Roger

Gardam, Jane 1928- .... **CLC 43**
  See also CA 49-52; CANR 2, 18, 33, 54; CLR
    12; DLB 14, 161; MAICYA; MTCW 1;
    SAAS 9; SATA 39, 76; SATA-Brief 28

Gardner, Herb(ert) 1934- .... **CLC 44**
  See also CA 149

Gardner, John (Champlin), Jr. 1933-1982
  **CLC 2, 3, 5, 7, 8, 10, 18, 28, 34; DAM NOV,
  POP; SSC 7**
  See also AITN 1; CA 65-68; 107; CANR 33,
    73; CDALBS; DLB 2; DLBY 82; MTCW 1;
    SATA 40; SATA-Obit 31

Gardner, John (Edmund) 1926-**CLC 30; DAM
  POP**
  See also CA 103; CANR 15, 69; MTCW 1

Gardner, Miriam
  See Bradley, Marion Zimmer

Gardner, Noel
  See Kuttner, Henry

Gardons, S. S.
  See Snodgrass, W(illiam) D(e Witt)

Garfield, Leon 1921-1996 .... **CLC 12**
  See also AAYA 8; CA 17-20R; 152; CANR 38,
    41, 78; CLR 21; DLB 161; JRDA; MAICYA;

SATA 1, 32, 76; SATA-Obit 90

Garland, (Hannibal) Hamlin 1860-1940
  TCLC 3; SSC 18
  See also CA 104; DLB 12, 71, 78, 186

Garneau, (Hector de) Saint-Denys 1912-1943
  TCLC 13
  See also CA 111; DLB 88

Garner, Alan 1934-**CLC 17; DAB; DAM POP**
  See also AAYA 18; CA 73-76; CANR 15, 64;
    CLR 20; DLB 161; MAICYA; MTCW 1, 2;
    SATA 18, 69; SATA-Essay 108

Garner, Hugh 1913-1979 .... **CLC 13**
  See also CA 69-72; CANR 31; DLB 68

Garnett, David 1892-1981 .... **CLC 3**
  See also CA 5-8R; 103; CANR 17, 79; DLB
    34; MTCW 2

Garos, Stephanie
  See Katz, Steve

Garrett, George (Palmer) 1929-**CLC 3, 11, 51;
  SSC 30**
  See also CA 1-4R; CAAS 5; CANR 1, 42, 67;
    DLB 2, 5, 130, 152; DLBY 83

Garrick, David 1717-1779 ....**LC 15; DAM
  DRAM**
  See also DLB 84

Garrigue, Jean 1914-1972 .... **CLC 2, 8**
  See also CA 5-8R; 37-40R; CANR 20

Garrison, Frederick
  See Sinclair, Upton (Beall)

Garth, Will
  See Hamilton, Edmond; Kuttner, Henry

Garvey, Marcus (Moziah, Jr.) 1887-1940
  TCLC 41; BLC 2; DAM MULT
  See also BW 1; CA 120; 124; CANR 79

Gary, Romain .... **CLC 25**
  See also Kacew, Romain
  See also DLB 83

Gascar, Pierre .... **CLC 11**
  See also Fournier, Pierre

Gascoyne, David (Emery) 1916- .... **CLC 45**
  See also CA 65-68; CANR 10, 28, 54; DLB 20;
    MTCW 1

Gaskell, Elizabeth Cleghorn 1810-1865**NCLC
  70; DAB; DAM MST; SSC 25**
  See also CDBLB 1832-1890; DLB 21, 144, 159

Gass, William H(oward) 1924-**CLC 1, 2, 8, 11,
  15, 39; SSC 12**
  See also CA 17-20R; CANR 30, 71; DLB 2;
    MTCW 1, 2

Gasset, Jose Ortega y
  See Ortega y Gasset, Jose

Gates, Henry Louis, Jr. 1950-**CLC 65; BLCS;
  DAM MULT**
  See also BW 2, 3; CA 109; CANR 25, 53, 75;
    DLB 67; MTCW 1

Gautier, Theophile 1811-1872 .. **NCLC 1, 59;
  DAM POET; PC 18; SSC 20**
  See also DLB 119

Gawsworth, John
  See Bates, H(erbert) E(rnest)

Gay, John 1685-1732 ... **LC 49; DAM DRAM**
  See also DLB 84, 95

Gay, Oliver
  See Gogarty, Oliver St. John

Gaye, Marvin (Penze) 1939-1984 ..... **CLC 26**
  See also CA 112

Gebler, Carlo (Ernest) 1954- .... **CLC 39**
  See also CA 119; 133

Gee, Maggie (Mary) 1948- .... **CLC 57**
  See also CA 130; DLB 207

Gee, Maurice (Gough) 1931- .... **CLC 29**
  See also CA 97-100; CANR 67; CLR 56; SATA
    46, 101

Gelbart, Larry (Simon) 1923- .... **CLC 21, 61**
  See also CA 73-76; CANR 45

Gelber, Jack 1932- .... **CLC 1, 6, 14, 79**
  See also CA 1-4R; CANR 2; DLB 7

Gellhorn, Martha (Ellis) 1908-1998 **CLC 14,
  60**
  See also CA 77-80; 164; CANR 44; DLBY 82,
    98

Genet, Jean 1910-1986**CLC 1, 2, 5, 10, 14, 44,
  46; DAM DRAM**
  See also CA 13-16R; CANR 18; DLB 72;
    DLBY 86; MTCW 1, 2

Gent, Peter 1942- .... **CLC 29**
  See also AITN 1; CA 89-92; DLBY 82

Gentlewoman in New England, A
  See Bradstreet, Anne

Gentlewoman in Those Parts, A
  See Bradstreet, Anne

George, Jean Craighead 1919- .... **CLC 35**
  See also AAYA 8; CA 5-8R; CANR 25; CLR 1;
    DLB 52; JRDA; MAICYA; SATA 2, 68

George, Stefan (Anton) 1868-1933**TCLC 2, 14**
  See also CA 104

Georges, Georges Martin
  See Simenon, Georges (Jacques Christian)

Gerhardi, William Alexander
  See Gerhardie, William Alexander

Gerhardie, William Alexander 1895-1977
  CLC 5
  See also CA 25-28R; 73-76; CANR 18; DLB
    36

Gerstler, Amy 1956- .... **CLC 70**
  See also CA 146

Gertler, T. .... **CLC 34**
  See also CA 116; 121; INT 121

Ghalib .... **NCLC 39, 78**
  See also Ghalib, Hsadullah Khan

Ghalib, Hsadullah Khan 1797-1869
  See Ghalib
  See also DAM POET

Ghelderode, Michel de 1898-1962**CLC 6, 11;
  DAM DRAM**
  See also CA 85-88; CANR 40, 77

Ghiselin, Brewster 1903- .... **CLC 23**
  See also CA 13-16R; CAAS 10; CANR 13

Ghose, Aurabinda 1872-1950 .... **TCLC 63**
  See also CA 163

Ghose, Zulfikar 1935- .... **CLC 42**
  See also CA 65-68; CANR 67

Ghosh, Amitav 1956- .... **CLC 44**
  See also CA 147; CANR 80

Giacosa, Giuseppe 1847-1906 .... **TCLC 7**
  See also CA 104

Gibb, Lee
  See Waterhouse, Keith (Spencer)

Gibbon, Lewis Grassic .... **TCLC 4**
  See also Mitchell, James Leslie

Gibbons, Kaye 1960-**CLC 50, 88; DAM POP**
  See also CA 151; CANR 75; MTCW 1

Gibran, Kahlil 1883-1931 . **TCLC 1, 9; DAM
  POET, POP; PC 9**
  See also CA 104; 150; MTCW 2

Gibran, Khalil
  See Gibran, Kahlil

Gibson, William 1914- .. **CLC 23; DA; DAB;
  DAC; DAM DRAM, MST**
  See also CA 9-12R; CANR 9, 42, 75; DLB 7;
    MTCW 1; SATA 66

Gibson, William (Ford) 1948- ... **CLC 39, 63;
  DAM POP**
  See also AAYA 12; CA 126; 133; CANR 52;
    MTCW 1

Gide, Andre (Paul Guillaume) 1869-1951

Gordon, Mary (Catherine) 1949-**CLC 13, 22**
See also CA 102; CANR 44; DLB 6; DLBY 81; INT 102; MTCW 1

Gordon, N. J.
See Bosman, Herman Charles

Gordon, Sol 1923- .... **CLC 26**
See also CA 53-56; CANR 4; SATA 11

Gordone, Charles 1925-1995**CLC 1, 4; DAM DRAM; DC 8**
See also BW 1, 3; CA 93-96; 150; CANR 55; DLB 7; INT 93-96; MTCW 1

Gore, Catherine 1800-1861 .... **NCLC 65**
See also DLB 116

Gorenko, Anna Andreevna
See Akhmatova, Anna

Gorky, Maxim 1868-1936**TCLC 8; DAB; SSC 28; WLC**
See also Peshkov, Alexei Maximovich
See also MTCW 2

Goryan, Sirak
See Saroyan, William

Gosse, Edmund (William) 1849-1928**TCLC 28**
See also CA 117; DLB 57, 144, 184

Gotlieb, Phyllis Fay (Bloom) 1926- . **CLC 18**
See also CA 13-16R; CANR 7; DLB 88

Gottesman, S. D.
See Kornbluth, C(yril) M.; Pohl, Frederik

Gottfried von Strassburg fl. c. 1210- . **C M L C 10**
See also DLB 138

Gould, Lois .... **CLC 4, 10**
See also CA 77-80; CANR 29; MTCW 1

Gourmont, Remy (-Marie-Charles) de 1858-1915 .... **TCLC 17**
See also CA 109; 150; MTCW 2

Govier, Katherine 1948- .... **CLC 51**
See also CA 101; CANR 18, 40

Goyen, (Charles) William 1915-1983**CLC 5, 8, 14, 40**
See also AITN 2; CA 5-8R; 110; CANR 6, 71; DLB 2; DLBY 83; INT CANR-6

Goytisolo, Juan 1931- . **CLC 5, 10, 23; DAM MULT; HLC**
See also CA 85-88; CANR 32, 61; HW 1, 2; MTCW 1, 2

Gozzano, Guido 1883-1916 .... **PC 10**
See also CA 154; DLB 114

Gozzi, (Conte) Carlo 1720-1806 .... **NCLC 23**

Grabbe, Christian Dietrich 1801-1836**N C L C 2**
See also DLB 133

Grace, Patricia Frances 1937- .... **CLC 56**
See also CA 176

Gracian y Morales, Baltasar 1601-1658**LC 15**

Gracq, Julien ....**CLC 11, 48**
See also Poirier, Louis
See also DLB 83

Grade, Chaim 1910-1982 .... **CLC 10**
See also CA 93-96; 107

Graduate of Oxford, A
See Ruskin, John

Grafton, Garth
See Duncan, Sara Jeannette

Graham, John
See Phillips, David Graham

Graham, Jorie 1951- .... **CLC 48, 118**
See also CA 111; CANR 63; DLB 120

Graham, R(obert) B(ontine) Cunninghame
See Cunninghame Graham, R(obert) B(ontine)
See also DLB 98, 135, 174

Graham, Robert
See Haldeman, Joe (William)

Graham, Tom

See Lewis, (Harry) Sinclair

Graham, W(illiam) S(ydney) 1918-1986**C L C 29**
See also CA 73-76; 118; DLB 20

Graham, Winston (Mawdsley) 1910- **CLC 23**
See also CA 49-52; CANR 2, 22, 45, 66; DLB 77

Grahame, Kenneth 1859-1932**TCLC 64; DAB**
See also CA 108; 136; CANR 80; CLR 5; DLB 34, 141, 178; MAICYA; MTCW 2; SATA 100; YABC 1

Granovsky, Timofei Nikolaevich 1813-1855 **NCLC 75**
See also DLB 198

Grant, Skeeter
See Spiegelman, Art

Granville-Barker, Harley 1877-1946**TCLC 2; DAM DRAM**
See also Barker, Harley Granville
See also CA 104

Grass, Guenter (Wilhelm) 1927-**CLC 1, 2, 4, 6, 11, 15, 22, 32, 49, 88; DA; DAB; DAC; DAM MST, NOV; WLC**
See also CA 13-16R; CANR 20, 75; DLB 75, 124; MTCW 1, 2

Gratton, Thomas
See Hulme, T(homas) E(rnest)

Grau, Shirley Ann 1929- ..**CLC 4, 9; SSC 15**
See also CA 89-92; CANR 22, 69; DLB 2; INT CANR-22; MTCW 1

Gravel, Fern
See Hall, James Norman

Graver, Elizabeth 1964- .... **CLC 70**
See also CA 135; CANR 71

Graves, Richard Perceval 1945- .... **CLC 44**
See also CA 65-68; CANR 9, 26, 51

Graves, Robert (von Ranke) 1895-1985 **C L C 1, 2, 6, 11, 39, 44, 45; DAB; DAC; DAM MST, POET; PC 6**
See also CA 5-8R; 117; CANR 5, 36; CDBLB 1914-1945; DLB 20, 100, 191; DLBD 18; DLBY 85; MTCW 1, 2; SATA 45

Graves, Valerie
See Bradley, Marion Zimmer

Gray, Alasdair (James) 1934- .... **CLC 41**
See also CA 126; CANR 47, 69; DLB 194; INT 126; MTCW 1, 2

Gray, Amlin 1946- .... **CLC 29**
See also CA 138

Gray, Francine du Plessix 1930- ..... **CLC 22; DAM NOV**
See also BEST 90:3; CA 61-64; CAAS 2; CANR 11, 33, 75, 81; INT CANR-11; MTCW 1, 2

Gray, John (Henry) 1866-1934 ...... **TCLC 19**
See also CA 119; 162

Gray, Simon (James Holliday) 1936- **CLC 9, 14, 36**
See also AITN 1; CA 21-24R; CAAS 3; CANR 32, 69; DLB 13; MTCW 1

Gray, Spalding 1941-**CLC 49, 112; DAM POP; DC 7**
See also CA 128; CANR 74; MTCW 2

Gray, Thomas 1716-1771**LC 4, 40; DA; DAB; DAC; DAM MST; PC 2; WLC**
See also CDBLB 1660-1789; DLB 109

Grayson, David
See Baker, Ray Stannard

Grayson, Richard (A.) 1951- .... **CLC 38**
See also CA 85-88; CANR 14, 31, 57

Greeley, Andrew M(oran) 1928- ..... **CLC 28; DAM POP**
See also CA 5-8R; CAAS 7; CANR 7, 43, 69;

MTCW 1, 2

Green, Anna Katharine 1846-1935 **TCLC 63**
See also CA 112; 159; DLB 202

Green, Brian
See Card, Orson Scott

Green, Hannah
See Greenberg, Joanne (Goldenberg)

Green, Hannah 1927(?)-1996 .... **CLC 3**
See also CA 73-76; CANR 59

Green, Henry 1905-1973 .... **CLC 2, 13, 97**
See also Yorke, Henry Vincent
See also CA 175; DLB 15

Green, Julian (Hartridge) 1900-1998
See Green, Julien
See also CA 21-24R; 169; CANR 33; DLB 4, 72; MTCW 1

Green, Julien .... **CLC 3, 11, 77**
See also Green, Julian (Hartridge)
See also MTCW 2

Green, Paul (Eliot) 1894-1981**CLC 25; DAM DRAM**
See also AITN 1; CA 5-8R; 103; CANR 3; DLB 7, 9; DLBY 81

Greenberg, Ivan 1908-1973
See Rahv, Philip
See also CA 85-88

Greenberg, Joanne (Goldenberg) 1932- **C L C 7, 30**
See also AAYA 12; CA 5-8R; CANR 14, 32, 69; SATA 25

Greenberg, Richard 1959(?)- .... **CLC 57**
See also CA 138

Greene, Bette 1934- .... **CLC 30**
See also AAYA 7; CA 53-56; CANR 4; CLR 2; JRDA; MAICYA; SAAS 16; SATA 8, 102

Greene, Gael .... **CLC 8**
See also CA 13-16R; CANR 10

Greene, Graham (Henry) 1904-1991**CLC 1, 3, 6, 9, 14, 18, 27, 37, 70, 72; DA; DAB; DAC; DAM MST, NOV; SSC 29; WLC**
See also AITN 2; CA 13-16R; 133; CANR 35, 61; CDBLB 1945-1960; DLB 13, 15, 77, 100, 162, 201, 204; DLBY 91; MTCW 1, 2; SATA 20

Greene, Robert 1558-1592 .... **LC 41**
See also DLB 62, 167

Greer, Richard
See Silverberg, Robert

Gregor, Arthur 1923- .... **CLC 9**
See also CA 25-28R; CAAS 10; CANR 11; SATA 36

Gregor, Lee
See Pohl, Frederik

Gregory, Isabella Augusta (Persse) 1852-1932 **TCLC 1**
See also CA 104; DLB 10

Gregory, J. Dennis
See Williams, John A(lfred)

Grendon, Stephen
See Derleth, August (William)

Grenville, Kate 1950- .... **CLC 61**
See also CA 118; CANR 53

Grenville, Pelham
See Wodehouse, P(elham) G(renville)

Greve, Felix Paul (Berthold Friedrich) 1879-1948
See Grove, Frederick Philip
See also CA 104; 141; 175; CANR 79; DAC; DAM MST

Grey, Zane 1872-1939 .. **TCLC 6; DAM POP**
See also CA 104; 132; DLB 212; MTCW 1, 2

Grieg, (Johan) Nordahl (Brun) 1902-1943 **TCLC 10**

See also CDBLB Before 1660; DLB 126

Herbert, Zbigniew 1924-1998 ..... **CLC 9, 43;
DAM POET**
See also CA 89-92; 169; CANR 36, 74; MTCW
1

Herbst, Josephine (Frey) 1897-1969 **CLC 34**
See also CA 5-8R; 25-28R; DLB 9

Hergesheimer, Joseph 1880-1954 .. **TCLC 11**
See also CA 109; DLB 102, 9

Herlihy, James Leo 1927-1993 .... **CLC 6**
See also CA 1-4R; 143; CANR 2

Hermogenes fl. c. 175- .... **CMLC 6**

Hernandez, Jose 1834-1886 .... **NCLC 17**

Herodotus c. 484B.C.-429B.C. ...... **CMLC 17**
See also DLB 176

Herrick, Robert 1591-1674 **LC 13; DA; DAB;
DAC; DAM MST, POP; PC 9**
See also DLB 126

Herring, Guilles
See Somerville, Edith

Herriot, James 1916-1995 **CLC 12; DAM POP**
See also Wight, James Alfred
See also AAYA 1; CA 148; CANR 40; MTCW
2; SATA 86

Herrmann, Dorothy 1941- .... **CLC 44**
See also CA 107

Herrmann, Taffy
See Herrmann, Dorothy

Hersey, John (Richard) 1914-1993 **CLC 1, 2, 7,
9, 40, 81, 97; DAM POP**
See also AAYA 29; CA 17-20R; 140; CANR
33; CDALBS; DLB 6, 185; MTCW 1, 2;
SATA 25; SATA-Obit 76

Herzen, Aleksandr Ivanovich 1812-1870
NCLC 10, 61

Herzl, Theodor 1860-1904 .... **TCLC 36**
See also CA 168

Herzog, Werner 1942- .... **CLC 16**
See also CA 89-92

Hesiod c. 8th cent. B.C.- .... **CMLC 5**
See also DLB 176

Hesse, Hermann 1877-1962 **CLC 1, 2, 3, 6, 11,
17, 25, 69; DA; DAB; DAC; DAM MST,
NOV; SSC 9; WLC**
See also CA 17-18; CAP 2; DLB 66; MTCW 1,
2; SATA 50

Hewes, Cady
See De Voto, Bernard (Augustine)

Heyen, William 1940- .... **CLC 13, 18**
See also CA 33-36R; CAAS 9; DLB 5

Heyerdahl, Thor 1914- .... **CLC 26**
See also CA 5-8R; CANR 5, 22, 66, 73; MTCW
1, 2; SATA 2, 52

Heym, Georg (Theodor Franz Arthur) 1887-
1912 .... **TCLC 9**
See also CA 106

Heym, Stefan 1913- .... **CLC 41**
See also CA 9-12R; CANR 4; DLB 69

Heyse, Paul (Johann Ludwig von) 1830-1914
TCLC 8
See also CA 104; DLB 129

Heyward, (Edwin) DuBose 1885-1940 **T C L C
59**
See also CA 108; 157; DLB 7, 9, 45; SATA 21

Hibbert, Eleanor Alice Burford 1906-1993
CLC 7; DAM POP
See also BEST 90:4; CA 17-20R; 140; CANR
9, 28, 59; MTCW 2; SATA 2; SATA-Obit 74

Hichens, Robert (Smythe) 1864-1950 . **T C L C
64**
See also CA 162; DLB 153

Higgins, George V(incent) 1939- **CLC 4, 7, 10,
18**

See also CA 77-80; CAAS 5; CANR 17, 51;
DLB 2; DLBY 81, 98; INT CANR-17;
MTCW 1

Higginson, Thomas Wentworth 1823-1911
TCLC 36
See also CA 162; DLB 1, 64

Highet, Helen
See MacInnes, Helen (Clark)

Highsmith, (Mary) Patricia 1921-1995 **CLC 2,
4, 14, 42, 102; DAM NOV, POP**
See also CA 1-4R; 147; CANR 1, 20, 48, 62;
MTCW 1, 2

Highwater, Jamake (Mamake) 1942(?)- **C L C
12**
See also AAYA 7; CA 65-68; CAAS 7; CANR
10, 34; CLR 17; DLB 52; DLBY 85; JRDA;
MAICYA; SATA 32, 69; SATA-Brief 30

Highway, Tomson 1951- **CLC 92; DAC; DAM
MULT**
See also CA 151; CANR 75; MTCW 2; NNAL

Higuchi, Ichiyo 1872-1896 .... **NCLC 49**

Hijuelos, Oscar 1951- **CLC 65; DAM MULT,
POP; HLC**
See also AAYA 25; BEST 90:1; CA 123; CANR
50, 75; DLB 145; HW 1, 2; MTCW 2

Hikmet, Nazim 1902(?)-1963 .... **CLC 40**
See also CA 141; 93-96

Hildegard von Bingen 1098-1179 . **CMLC 20**
See also DLB 148

Hildesheimer, Wolfgang 1916-1991 .. **CLC 49**
See also CA 101; 135; DLB 69, 124

Hill, Geoffrey (William) 1932- **CLC 5, 8, 18,
45; DAM POET**
See also CA 81-84; CANR 21; CDBLB 1960
to Present; DLB 40; MTCW 1

Hill, George Roy 1921- .... **CLC 26**
See also CA 110; 122

Hill, John
See Koontz, Dean R(ay)

Hill, Susan (Elizabeth) 1942- .... **CLC 4, 113;
DAB; DAM MST, NOV**
See also CA 33-36R; CANR 29, 69; DLB 14,
139; MTCW 1

Hillerman, Tony 1925- .. **CLC 62; DAM POP**
See also AAYA 6; BEST 89:1; CA 29-32R;
CANR 21, 42, 65; DLB 206; SATA 6

Hillesum, Etty 1914-1943 .... **TCLC 49**
See also CA 137

Hilliard, Noel (Harvey) 1929- .... **CLC 15**
See also CA 9-12R; CANR 7, 69

Hillis, Rick 1956- .... **CLC 66**
See also CA 134

Hilton, James 1900-1954 .... **TCLC 21**
See also CA 108; 169; DLB 34, 77; SATA 34

Himes, Chester (Bomar) 1909-1984 **CLC 2, 4,
7, 18, 58, 108; BLC 2; DAM MULT**
See also BW 2; CA 25-28R; 114; CANR 22;
DLB 2, 76, 143; MTCW 1, 2

Hinde, Thomas .... **CLC 6, 11**
See also Chitty, Thomas Willes

Hindin, Nathan
See Bloch, Robert (Albert)

Hine, (William) Daryl 1936- .... **CLC 15**
See also CA 1-4R; CAAS 15; CANR 1, 20; DLB
60

Hinkson, Katharine Tynan
See Tynan, Katharine

Hinton, S(usan) E(loise) 1950- **CLC 30, 111;
DA; DAB; DAC; DAM MST, NOV**
See also AAYA 2; CA 81-84; CANR 32, 62;
CDALBS; CLR 3, 23; JRDA; MAICYA;
MTCW 1, 2; SATA 19, 58

Hippius, Zinaida .... **TCLC 9**

See also Gippius, Zinaida (Nikolayevna)

Hiraoka, Kimitake 1925-1970
See Mishima, Yukio
See also CA 97-100; 29-32R; DAM DRAM;
MTCW 1, 2

Hirsch, E(ric) D(onald), Jr. 1928- ..... **CLC 79**
See also CA 25-28R; CANR 27, 51; DLB 67;
INT CANR-27; MTCW 1

Hirsch, Edward 1950- .... **CLC 31, 50**
See also CA 104; CANR 20, 42; DLB 120

Hitchcock, Alfred (Joseph) 1899-1980 **CLC 16**
See also AAYA 22; CA 159; 97-100; SATA 27;
SATA-Obit 24

Hitler, Adolf 1889-1945 .... **TCLC 53**
See also CA 117; 147

Hoagland, Edward 1932- .... **CLC 28**
See also CA 1-4R; CANR 2, 31, 57; DLB 6;
SATA 51

Hoban, Russell (Conwell) 1925- . **CLC 7, 25;
DAM NOV**
See also CA 5-8R; CANR 23, 37, 66; CLR 3;
DLB 52; MAICYA; MTCW 1, 2; SATA 1,
40, 78

Hobbes, Thomas 1588-1679 .... **LC 36**
See also DLB 151

Hobbs, Perry
See Blackmur, R(ichard) P(almer)

Hobson, Laura Z(ametkin) 1900-1986 **CLC 7,
25**
See also CA 17-20R; 118; CANR 55; DLB 28;
SATA 52

Hochhuth, Rolf 1931- ... **CLC 4, 11, 18; DAM
DRAM**
See also CA 5-8R; CANR 33, 75; DLB 124;
MTCW 1, 2

Hochman, Sandra 1936- .... **CLC 3, 8**
See also CA 5-8R; DLB 5

Hochwaelder, Fritz 1911-1986 **CLC 36; DAM
DRAM**
See also CA 29-32R; 120; CANR 42; MTCW 1

Hochwalder, Fritz
See Hochwaelder, Fritz

Hocking, Mary (Eunice) 1921- .... **CLC 13**
See also CA 101; CANR 18, 40

Hodgins, Jack 1938- .... **CLC 23**
See also CA 93-96; DLB 60

Hodgson, William Hope 1877(?)-1918 **T C L C
13**
See also CA 111; 164; DLB 70, 153, 156, 178;
MTCW 2

Hoeg, Peter 1957- .... **CLC 95**
See also CA 151; CANR 75; MTCW 2

Hoffman, Alice 1952- ... **CLC 51; DAM NOV**
See also CA 77-80; CANR 34, 66; MTCW 1, 2

Hoffman, Daniel (Gerard) 1923- **CLC 6, 13, 23**
See also CA 1-4R; CANR 4; DLB 5

Hoffman, Stanley 1944- .... **CLC 5**
See also CA 77-80

Hoffman, William M(oses) 1939- ...... **CLC 40**
See also CA 57-60; CANR 11, 71

Hoffmann, E(rnst) T(heodor) A(madeus) 1776-
1822 .... **NCLC 2; SSC 13**
See also DLB 90; SATA 27

Hofmann, Gert 1931- .... **CLC 54**
See also CA 128

Hofmannsthal, Hugo von 1874-1929 **TCLC 11;
DAM DRAM; DC 4**
See also CA 106; 153; DLB 81, 118

Hogan, Linda 1947- ... **CLC 73; DAM MULT**
See also CA 120; CANR 45, 73; DLB 175;
NNAL

Hogarth, Charles
See Creasey, John

See also CA 85-88; DLB 14
Jolley, (Monica) Elizabeth 1923-**CLC 46; SSC 19**
　See also CA 127; CAAS 13; CANR 59
Jones, Arthur Llewellyn 1863-1947
　See Machen, Arthur
　See also CA 104
Jones, D(ouglas) G(ordon) 1929- ..... **CLC 10**
　See also CA 29-32R; CANR 13; DLB 53
Jones, David (Michael) 1895-1974 **CLC 2, 4, 7, 13, 42**
　See also CA 9-12R; 53-56; CANR 28; CDBLB 1945-1960; DLB 20, 100; MTCW 1
Jones, David Robert 1947-
　See Bowie, David
　See also CA 103
Jones, Diana Wynne 1934- .... **CLC 26**
　See also AAYA 12; CA 49-52; CANR 4, 26, 56; CLR 23; DLB 161; JRDA; MAICYA; SAAS 7; SATA 9, 70, 108
Jones, Edward P. 1950-..................... **CLC 76**
　See also BW 2, 3; CA 142; CANR 79
Jones, Gayl 1949- ... **CLC 6, 9; BLC 2; DAM MULT**
　See also BW 2, 3; CA 77-80; CANR 27, 66; DLB 33; MTCW 1, 2
Jones, James 1921-1977 ...... **CLC 1, 3, 10, 39**
　See also AITN 1, 2; CA 1-4R; 69-72; CANR 6; DLB 2, 143; DLBD 17; DLBY 98; MTCW 1
Jones, John J.
　See Lovecraft, H(oward) P(hillips)
Jones, LeRoi .... **CLC 1, 2, 3, 5, 10, 14**
　See also Baraka, Amiri
　See also MTCW 2
Jones, Louis B. 1953- .... **CLC 65**
　See also CA 141; CANR 73
Jones, Madison (Percy, Jr.) 1925- ....**CLC 4**
　See also CA 13-16R; CAAS 11; CANR 7, 54; DLB 152
Jones, Mervyn 1922- .... **CLC 10, 52**
　See also CA 45-48; CAAS 5; CANR 1; MTCW 1
Jones, Mick 1956(?)- .... **CLC 30**
Jones, Nettie (Pearl) 1941- .... **CLC 34**
　See also BW 2; CA 137; CAAS 20
Jones, Preston 1936-1979 .... **CLC 10**
　See also CA 73-76; 89-92; DLB 7
Jones, Robert F(rancis) 1934- .... **CLC 7**
　See also CA 49-52; CANR 2, 61
Jones, Rod 1953-................................. **CLC 50**
　See also CA 128
Jones, Terence Graham Parry 1942- **CLC 21**
　See also Jones, Terry; Monty Python
　See also CA 112; 116; CANR 35; INT 116
Jones, Terry
　See Jones, Terence Graham Parry
　See also SATA 67; SATA-Brief 51
Jones, Thom 1945(?)- .... **CLC 81**
　See also CA 157
Jong, Erica 1942- **CLC 4, 6, 8, 18, 83; DAM NOV, POP**
　See also AITN 1; BEST 90:2; CA 73-76; CANR 26, 52, 75; DLB 2, 5, 28, 152; INT CANR-26; MTCW 1, 2
Jonson, Ben(jamin) 1572(?)-1637 .. **LC 6, 33; DA; DAB; DAC; DAM DRAM, MST, POET; DC 4; PC 17; WLC**
　See also CDBLB Before 1660; DLB 62, 121
Jordan, June 1936-**CLC 5, 11, 23, 114; BLCS; DAM MULT, POET**
　See also AAYA 2; BW 2, 3; CA 33-36R; CANR 25, 70; CLR 10; DLB 38; MAICYA; MTCW 1; SATA 4

Jordan, Neil (Patrick) 1950- .... **CLC 110**
　See also CA 124; 130; CANR 54; INT 130
Jordan, Pat(rick M.) 1941- .... **CLC 37**
　See also CA 33-36R
Jorgensen, Ivar
　See Ellison, Harlan (Jay)
Jorgenson, Ivar
　See Silverberg, Robert
Josephus, Flavius c. 37-100 .... **CMLC 13**
Josipovici, Gabriel 1940- .... **CLC 6, 43**
　See also CA 37-40R; CAAS 8; CANR 47; DLB 14
Joubert, Joseph 1754-1824 .... **NCLC 9**
Jouve, Pierre Jean 1887-1976 .... **CLC 47**
　See also CA 65-68
Jovine, Francesco 1902-1950 .... **TCLC 79**
Joyce, James (Augustine Aloysius) 1882-1941 **TCLC 3, 8, 16, 35, 52; DA; DAB; DAC; DAM MST, NOV, POET; PC 22; SSC 3, 26; WLC**
　See also CA 104; 126; CDBLB 1914-1945; DLB 10, 19, 36, 162; MTCW 1, 2
Jozsef, Attila 1905-1937 .... **TCLC 22**
　See also CA 116
Juana Ines de la Cruz 1651(?)-1695 .... **LC 5; HLCS 1; PC 24**
Judd, Cyril
　See Kornbluth, C(yril) M.; Pohl, Frederik
Julian of Norwich 1342(?)-1416(?) .... **LC 6**
　See also DLB 146
Junger, Sebastian 1962- .... **CLC 109**
　See also AAYA 28; CA 165
Juniper, Alex
　See Hospital, Janette Turner
Junius
　See Luxemburg, Rosa
Just, Ward (Swift) 1935-............... **CLC 4, 27**
　See also CA 25-28R; CANR 32; INT CANR-32
Justice, Donald (Rodney) 1925- .. **CLC 6, 19, 102; DAM POET**
　See also CA 5-8R; CANR 26, 54, 74; DLBY 83; INT CANR-26; MTCW 2
Juvenal c. 60-c. 13 .... **CMLC 8**
　See also Juvenalis, Decimus Junius
　See also DLB 211
Juvenalis, Decimus Junius 55(?)-c. 127(?)
　See Juvenal
Juvenis
　See Bourne, Randolph S(illiman)
Kacew, Romain 1914-1980
　See Gary, Romain
　See also CA 108; 102
Kadare, Ismail 1936-.......................... **CLC 52**
　See also CA 161
Kadohata, Cynthia .... **CLC 59**
　See also CA 140
Kafka, Franz 1883-1924 **TCLC 2, 6, 13, 29, 47, 53; DA; DAB; DAC; DAM MST, NOV; SSC 5, 29, 35; WLC**
　See also CA 105; 126; DLB 81; MTCW 1, 2
Kahanovitsch, Pinkhes
　See Der Nister
Kahn, Roger 1927- .... **CLC 30**
　See also CA 25-28R; CANR 44, 69; DLB 171; SATA 37
Kain, Saul
　See Sassoon, Siegfried (Lorraine)
Kaiser, Georg 1878-1945 .... **TCLC 9**
　See also CA 106; DLB 124
Kaletski, Alexander 1946- .... **CLC 39**
　See also CA 118; 143
Kalidasa fl. c. 400- .... **CMLC 9; PC 22**

Kallman, Chester (Simon) 1921-1975 **CLC 2**
　See also CA 45-48; 53-56; CANR 3
Kaminsky, Melvin 1926-
　See Brooks, Mel
　See also CA 65-68; CANR 16
Kaminsky, Stuart M(elvin) 1934- ..... **CLC 59**
　See also CA 73-76; CANR 29, 53
Kandinsky, Wassily 1866-1944 ...... **TCLC 92**
　See also CA 118; 155
Kane, Francis
　See Robbins, Harold
Kane, Paul
　See Simon, Paul (Frederick)
Kane, Wilson
　See Bloch, Robert (Albert)
Kanin, Garson 1912-1999 ....**CLC 22**
　See also AITN 1; CA 5-8R; 177; CANR 7, 78; DLB 7
Kaniuk, Yoram 1930- .... **CLC 19**
　See also CA 134
Kant, Immanuel 1724-1804 ..... **NCLC 27, 67**
　See also DLB 94
Kantor, MacKinlay 1904-1977 ....**CLC 7**
　See also CA 61-64; 73-76; CANR 60, 63; DLB 9, 102; MTCW 2
Kaplan, David Michael 1946- ....**CLC 50**
Kaplan, James 1951- .... **CLC 59**
　See also CA 135
Karageorge, Michael
　See Anderson, Poul (William)
Karamzin, Nikolai Mikhailovich 1766-1826 **NCLC 3**
　See also DLB 150
Karapanou, Margarita 1946- .... **CLC 13**
　See also CA 101
Karinthy, Frigyes 1887-1938 .... **TCLC 47**
　See also CA 170
Karl, Frederick R(obert) 1927-...........**CLC 34**
　See also CA 5-8R; CANR 3, 44
Kastel, Warren
　See Silverberg, Robert
Kataev, Evgeny Petrovich 1903-1942
　See Petrov, Evgeny
　See also CA 120
Kataphusin
　See Ruskin, John
Katz, Steve 1935-................................ **CLC 47**
　See also CA 25-28R; CAAS 14, 64; CANR 12; DLBY 83
Kauffman, Janet 1945- .... **CLC 42**
　See also CA 117; CANR 43; DLBY 86
Kaufman, Bob (Garnell) 1925-1986 . **CLC 49**
　See also BW 1; CA 41-44R; 118; CANR 22; DLB 16, 41
Kaufman, George S. 1889-1961 **CLC 38; DAM DRAM**
　See also CA 108; 93-96; DLB 7; INT 108; MTCW 2
Kaufman, Sue .... **CLC 3, 8**
　See also Barondess, Sue K(aufman)
Kavafis, Konstantinos Petrou 1863-1933
　See Cavafy, C(onstantine) P(eter)
　See also CA 104
Kavan, Anna 1901-1968 .... **CLC 5, 13, 82**
　See also CA 5-8R; CANR 6, 57; MTCW 1
Kavanagh, Dan
　See Barnes, Julian (Patrick)
Kavanagh, Julie 1952- .... **CLC 119**
　See also CA 163
Kavanagh, Patrick (Joseph) 1904-1967 **C L C 22**
　See also CA 123; 25-28R; DLB 15, 20; MTCW 1

CLC 12, 19, 58, 121; DAM MULT, NOV; WLCS
See also AAYA 8; CA 69-72; CANR 13, 38, 74; CDALBS; DLB 173, 212; DLBY 80; INT CANR-13; MTCW 1, 2; SATA 53

Kinnell, Galway 1927-**CLC 1, 2, 3, 5, 13, 29; PC 26**
See also CA 9-12R; CANR 10, 34, 66; DLB 5; DLBY 87; INT CANR-34; MTCW 1, 2

Kinsella, Thomas 1928- .... **CLC 4, 19**
See also CA 17-20R; CANR 15; DLB 27; MTCW 1, 2

Kinsella, W(illiam) P(atrick) 1935- **CLC 27, 43; DAC; DAM NOV, POP**
See also AAYA 7; CA 97-100; CAAS 7; CANR 21, 35, 66, 75; INT CANR-21; MTCW 1, 2

Kinsey, Alfred C(harles) 1894-1956**TCLC 91**
See also CA 115; 170; MTCW 2

Kipling, (Joseph) Rudyard 1865-1936 **T C L C 8, 17; DA; DAB; DAC; DAM MST, POET; PC 3; SSC 5; WLC**
See also CA 105; 120; CANR 33; CDBLB 1890-1914; CLR 39; DLB 19, 34, 141, 156; MAICYA; MTCW 1, 2; SATA 100; YABC 2

Kirkup, James 1918- .... **CLC 1**
See also CA 1-4R; CAAS 4; CANR 2; DLB 27; SATA 12

Kirkwood, James 1930(?)-1989 .... **CLC 9**
See also AITN 2; CA 1-4R; 128; CANR 6, 40

Kirshner, Sidney
See Kingsley, Sidney

Kis, Danilo 1935-1989 .... **CLC 57**
See also CA 109; 118; 129; CANR 61; DLB 181; MTCW 1

Kivi, Aleksis 1834-1872 .... **NCLC 30**

Kizer, Carolyn (Ashley) 1925-**CLC 15, 39, 80; DAM POET**
See also CA 65-68; CAAS 5; CANR 24, 70; DLB 5, 169; MTCW 2

Klabund 1890-1928 .... **TCLC 44**
See also CA 162; DLB 66

Klappert, Peter 1942- .... **CLC 57**
See also CA 33-36R; DLB 5

Klein, A(braham) M(oses) 1909-1972**CLC 19; DAB; DAC; DAM MST**
See also CA 101; 37-40R; DLB 68

Klein, Norma 1938-1989 .... **CLC 30**
See also AAYA 2; CA 41-44R; 128; CANR 15, 37; CLR 2, 19; INT CANR-15; JRDA; MAICYA; SAAS 1; SATA 7, 57

Klein, T(heodore) E(ibon) D(onald) 1947- **CLC 34**
See also CA 119; CANR 44, 75

Kleist, Heinrich von 1777-1811 **NCLC 2, 37; DAM DRAM; SSC 22**
See also DLB 90

Klima, Ivan 1931- .... **CLC 56; DAM NOV**
See also CA 25-28R; CANR 17, 50

Klimentov, Andrei Platonovich 1899-1951
See Platonov, Andrei
See also CA 108

Klinger, Friedrich Maximilian von 1752-1831 **NCLC 1**
See also DLB 94

Klingsor the Magician
See Hartmann, Sadakichi

Klopstock, Friedrich Gottlieb 1724-1803 **NCLC 11**
See also DLB 97

Knapp, Caroline 1959- .... **CLC 99**
See also CA 154

Knebel, Fletcher 1911-1993 .... **CLC 14**
See also AITN 1; CA 1-4R; 140; CAAS 3;

CANR 1, 36; SATA 36; SATA-Obit 75

Knickerbocker, Diedrich
See Irving, Washington

Knight, Etheridge 1931-1991**CLC 40; BLC 2; DAM POET; PC 14**
See also BW 1, 3; CA 21-24R; 133; CANR 23; DLB 41; MTCW 2

Knight, Sarah Kemble 1666-1727 .... **LC 7**
See also DLB 24, 200

Knister, Raymond 1899-1932 .... **TCLC 56**
See also DLB 68

Knowles, John 1926- ..**CLC 1, 4, 10, 26; DA; DAC; DAM MST, NOV**
See also AAYA 10; CA 17-20R; CANR 40, 74, 76; CDALB 1968-1988; DLB 6; MTCW 1, 2; SATA 8, 89

Knox, Calvin M.
See Silverberg, Robert

Knox, John c. 1505-1572 .... **LC 37**
See also DLB 132

Knye, Cassandra
See Disch, Thomas M(ichael)

Koch, C(hristopher) J(ohn) 1932- ....**CLC 42**
See also CA 127

Koch, Christopher
See Koch, C(hristopher) J(ohn)

Koch, Kenneth 1925- .... **CLC 5, 8, 44; DAM POET**
See also CA 1-4R; CANR 6, 36, 57; DLB 5; INT CANR-36; MTCW 2; SATA 65

Kochanowski, Jan 1530-1584 .... **LC 10**

Kock, Charles Paul de 1794-1871 ..**NCLC 16**

Koda Shigeyuki 1867-1947
See Rohan, Koda
See also CA 121

Koestler, Arthur 1905-1983**CLC 1, 3, 6, 8, 15, 33**
See also CA 1-4R; 109; CANR 1, 33; CDBLB 1945-1960; DLBY 83; MTCW 1, 2

Kogawa, Joy Nozomi 1935- ..**CLC 78; DAC; DAM MST, MULT**
See also CA 101; CANR 19, 62; MTCW 2; SATA 99

Kohout, Pavel 1928- .... **CLC 13**
See also CA 45-48; CANR 3

Koizumi, Yakumo
See Hearn, (Patricio) Lafcadio (Tessima Carlos)

Kolmar, Gertrud 1894-1943 .... **TCLC 40**
See also CA 167

Komunyakaa, Yusef 1947-**CLC 86, 94; BLCS**
See also CA 147; DLB 120

Konrad, George
See Konrad, Gyoergy

Konrad, Gyoergy 1933- .... **CLC 4, 10, 73**
See also CA 85-88

Konwicki, Tadeusz 1926- **CLC 8, 28, 54, 117**
See also CA 101; CAAS 9; CANR 39, 59; MTCW 1

Koontz, Dean R(ay) 1945- ..... **CLC 78; DAM NOV, POP**
See also AAYA 9; BEST 89:3, 90:2; CA 108; CANR 19, 36, 52; MTCW 1; SATA 92

Kopernik, Mikolaj
See Copernicus, Nicolaus

Kopit, Arthur (Lee) 1937-**CLC 1, 18, 33; DAM DRAM**
See also AITN 1; CA 81-84; CABS 3; DLB 7; MTCW 1

Kops, Bernard 1926- .... **CLC 4**
See also CA 5-8R; DLB 13

Kornbluth, C(yril) M. 1923-1958 .... **TCLC 8**
See also CA 105; 160; DLB 8

Korolenko, V. G.

See Korolenko, Vladimir Galaktionovich

Korolenko, Vladimir
See Korolenko, Vladimir Galaktionovich

Korolenko, Vladimir G.
See Korolenko, Vladimir Galaktionovich

Korolenko, Vladimir Galaktionovich 1853-1921 .... **TCLC 22**
See also CA 121

Korzybski, Alfred (Habdank Skarbek) 1879-1950 .... **TCLC 61**
See also CA 123; 160

Kosinski, Jerzy (Nikodem) 1933-1991**CLC 1, 2, 3, 6, 10, 15, 53, 70; DAM NOV**
See also CA 17-20R; 134; CANR 9, 46; DLB 2; DLBY 82; MTCW 1, 2

Kostelanetz, Richard (Cory) 1940- ..**CLC 28**
See also CA 13-16R; CAAS 8; CANR 38, 77

Kostrowitzki, Wilhelm Apollinaris de 1880-1918
See Apollinaire, Guillaume
See also CA 104

Kotlowitz, Robert 1924- .... **CLC 4**
See also CA 33-36R; CANR 36

Kotzebue, August (Friedrich Ferdinand) von 1761-1819 .... **NCLC 25**
See also DLB 94

Kotzwinkle, William 1938- ..... **CLC 5, 14, 35**
See also CA 45-48; CANR 3, 44; CLR 6; DLB 173; MAICYA; SATA 24, 70

Kowna, Stancy
See Szymborska, Wislawa

Kozol, Jonathan 1936- .... **CLC 17**
See also CA 61-64; CANR 16, 45

Kozoll, Michael 1940(?)- .... **CLC 35**

Kramer, Kathryn 19(?)- .... **CLC 34**

Kramer, Larry 1935-**CLC 42; DAM POP; DC 8**
See also CA 124; 126; CANR 60

Krasicki, Ignacy 1735-1801 .... **NCLC 8**

Krasinski, Zygmunt 1812-1859 .... **NCLC 4**

Kraus, Karl 1874-1936 .... **TCLC 5**
See also CA 104; DLB 118

Kreve (Mickevicius), Vincas 1882-1954**TCLC 27**
See also CA 170

Kristeva, Julia 1941- .... **CLC 77**
See also CA 154

Kristofferson, Kris 1936- ....**CLC 26**
See also CA 104

Krizanc, John 1956- ....**CLC 57**

Krleza, Miroslav 1893-1981 .... **CLC 8, 114**
See also CA 97-100; 105; CANR 50; DLB 147

Kroetsch, Robert 1927-**CLC 5, 23, 57; DAC; DAM POET**
See also CA 17-20R; CANR 8, 38; DLB 53; MTCW 1

Kroetz, Franz
See Kroetz, Franz Xaver

Kroetz, Franz Xaver 1946- ....**CLC 41**
See also CA 130

Kroker, Arthur (W.) 1945- ....**CLC 77**
See also CA 161

Kropotkin, Peter (Aleksieevich) 1842-1921 **TCLC 36**
See also CA 119

Krotkov, Yuri 1917- ....**CLC 19**
See also CA 102

Krumb
See Crumb, R(obert)

Krumgold, Joseph (Quincy) 1908-1980 **C L C 12**
See also CA 9-12R; 101; CANR 7; MAICYA; SATA 1, 48; SATA-Obit 23

Lathrop, Francis
　　See Leiber, Fritz (Reuter, Jr.)
Latsis, Mary J(ane) 1927(?)-1997
　　See Lathen, Emma
　　See also CA 85-88; 162
Lattimore, Richmond (Alexander) 1906-1984
　　CLC 3
　　See also CA 1-4R; 112; CANR 1
Laughlin, James 1914-1997 .... **CLC 49**
　　See also CA 21-24R; 162; CAAS 22; CANR 9,
　　47; DLB 48; DLBY 96, 97
Laurence, (Jean) Margaret (Wemyss) 1926-
　　1987 .. **CLC 3, 6, 13, 50, 62; DAC; DAM
　　MST; SSC 7**
　　See also CA 5-8R; 121; CANR 33; DLB 53;
　　MTCW 1, 2; SATA-Obit 50
Laurent, Antoine 1952-..................... **CLC 50**
Lauscher, Hermann
　　See Hesse, Hermann
Lautreamont, Comte de 1846-1870**NCLC 12;
　　SSC 14**
Laverty, Donald
　　See Blish, James (Benjamin)
Lavin, Mary 1912-1996**CLC 4, 18, 99; SSC 4**
　　See also CA 9-12R; 151; CANR 33; DLB 15;
　　MTCW 1
Lavond, Paul Dennis
　　See Kornbluth, C(yril) M.; Pohl, Frederik
Lawler, Raymond Evenor 1922- ...... **CLC 58**
　　See also CA 103
Lawrence, D(avid) H(erbert Richards) 1885-
　　1930 **TCLC 2, 9, 16, 33, 48, 61, 93; DA;
　　DAB; DAC; DAM MST, NOV, POET; SSC
　　4, 19; WLC**
　　See also CA 104; 121; CDBLB 1914-1945;
　　DLB 10, 19, 36, 98, 162, 195; MTCW 1, 2
Lawrence, T(homas) E(dward) 1888-1935
　　TCLC 18
　　See also Dale, Colin
　　See also CA 115; 167; DLB 195
Lawrence of Arabia
　　See Lawrence, T(homas) E(dward)
Lawson, Henry (Archibald Hertzberg) 1867-
　　1922 .... **TCLC 27; SSC 18**
　　See also CA 120
Lawton, Dennis
　　See Faust, Frederick (Schiller)
Laxness, Halldor .... **CLC 25**
　　See also Gudjonsson, Halldor Kiljan
Layamon fl. c. 1200-...................... **CMLC 10**
　　See also DLB 146
Laye, Camara 1928-1980 **CLC 4, 38; BLC 2;
　　DAM MULT**
　　See also BW 1; CA 85-88; 97-100; CANR 25;
　　MTCW 1, 2
Layton, Irving (Peter) 1912-**CLC 2, 15; DAC;
　　DAM MST, POET**
　　See also CA 1-4R; CANR 2, 33, 43, 66; DLB
　　88; MTCW 1, 2
Lazarus, Emma 1849-1887 .... **NCLC 8**
Lazarus, Felix
　　See Cable, George Washington
Lazarus, Henry
　　See Slavitt, David R(ytman)
Lea, Joan
　　See Neufeld, John (Arthur)
Leacock, Stephen (Butler) 1869-1944**TCLC 2;
　　DAC; DAM MST**
　　See also CA 104; 141; CANR 80; DLB 92;
　　MTCW 2
Lear, Edward 1812-1888 .... **NCLC 3**
　　See also CLR 1; DLB 32, 163, 166; MAICYA;
　　SATA 18, 100

Lear, Norman (Milton) 1922- .... **CLC 12**
　　See also CA 73-76
Leautaud, Paul 1872-1956 .... **TCLC 83**
　　See also DLB 65
Leavis, F(rank) R(aymond) 1895-1978**CLC 24**
　　See also CA 21-24R; 77-80; CANR 44; MTCW
　　1, 2
Leavitt, David 1961- ...... **CLC 34; DAM POP**
　　See also CA 116; 122; CANR 50, 62; DLB 130;
　　INT 122; MTCW 2
Leblanc, Maurice (Marie Emile) 1864-1941
　　TCLC 49
　　See also CA 110
Lebowitz, Fran(ces Ann) 1951(?)-**CLC 11, 36**
　　See also CA 81-84; CANR 14, 60, 70; INT
　　CANR-14; MTCW 1
Lebrecht, Peter
　　See Tieck, (Johann) Ludwig
le Carre, John .... **CLC 3, 5, 9, 15, 28**
　　See also Cornwell, David (John Moore)
　　See also BEST 89:4; CDBLB 1960 to Present;
　　DLB 87; MTCW 2
Le Clezio, J(ean) M(arie) G(ustave) 1940-
　　CLC 31
　　See also CA 116; 128; DLB 83
Leconte de Lisle, Charles-Marie-Rene 1818-
　　1894 .... **NCLC 29**
Le Coq, Monsieur
　　See Simenon, Georges (Jacques Christian)
Leduc, Violette 1907-1972 .... **CLC 22**
　　See also CA 13-14; 33-36R; CANR 69; CAP 1
Ledwidge, Francis 1887(?)-1917 .... **TCLC 23**
　　See also CA 123; DLB 20
Lee, Andrea 1953- .... **CLC 36; BLC 2; DAM
　　MULT**
　　See also BW 1, 3; CA 125
Lee, Andrew
　　See Auchincloss, Louis (Stanton)
Lee, Chang-rae 1965-......................... **CLC 91**
　　See also CA 148
Lee, Don L. .... **CLC 2**
　　See also Madhubuti, Haki R.
Lee, George W(ashington) 1894-1976**CLC 52;
　　BLC 2; DAM MULT**
　　See also BW 1; CA 125; DLB 51
Lee, (Nelle) Harper 1926- .. **CLC 12, 60; DA;
　　DAB; DAC; DAM MST, NOV; WLC**
　　See also AAYA 13; CA 13-16R; CANR 51;
　　CDALB 1941-1968; DLB 6; MTCW 1, 2;
　　SATA 11
Lee, Helen Elaine 1959(?)- .... **CLC 86**
　　See also CA 148
Lee, Julian
　　See Latham, Jean Lee
Lee, Larry
　　See Lee, Lawrence
Lee, Laurie 1914-1997 **CLC 90; DAB; DAM
　　POP**
　　See also CA 77-80; 158; CANR 33, 73; DLB
　　27; MTCW 1
Lee, Lawrence 1941-1990 .... **CLC 34**
　　See also CA 131; CANR 43
Lee, Li-Young 1957-............................. **PC 24**
　　See also CA 153; DLB 165
Lee, Manfred B(ennington) 1905-1971**CLC 11**
　　See also Queen, Ellery
　　See also CA 1-4R; 29-32R; CANR 2; DLB 137
Lee, Shelton Jackson 1957(?)- .... **CLC 105;
　　BLCS; DAM MULT**
　　See also Lee, Spike
　　See also BW 2, 3; CA 125; CANR 42
Lee, Spike
　　See Lee, Shelton Jackson

See also AAYA 4, 29
Lee, Stan 1922- .... **CLC 17**
　　See also AAYA 5; CA 108; 111; INT 111
Lee, Tanith 1947-................................ **CLC 46**
　　See also AAYA 15; CA 37-40R; CANR 53;
　　SATA 8, 88
Lee, Vernon .... **TCLC 5; SSC 33**
　　See also Paget, Violet
　　See also DLB 57, 153, 156, 174, 178
Lee, William
　　See Burroughs, William S(eward)
Lee, Willy
　　See Burroughs, William S(eward)
Lee-Hamilton, Eugene (Jacob) 1845-1907
　　TCLC 22
　　See also CA 117
Leet, Judith 1935- .... **CLC 11**
Le Fanu, Joseph Sheridan 1814-1873**NCLC 9,
　　58; DAM POP; SSC 14**
　　See also DLB 21, 70, 159, 178
Leffland, Ella 1931- .... **CLC 19**
　　See also CA 29-32R; CANR 35, 78; DLBY 84;
　　INT CANR-35; SATA 65
Leger, Alexis
　　See Leger, (Marie-Rene Auguste) Alexis Saint-
　　Leger
**Leger, (Marie-Rene Auguste) Alexis Saint-
　　Leger** 1887-1975 ..**CLC 4, 11, 46; DAM
　　POET; PC 23**
　　See also CA 13-16R; 61-64; CANR 43; MTCW
　　1
Leger, Saintleger
　　See Leger, (Marie-Rene Auguste) Alexis Saint-
　　Leger
Le Guin, Ursula K(roeber) 1929- **CLC 8, 13,
　　22, 45, 71; DAB; DAC; DAM MST, POP;
　　SSC 12**
　　See also AAYA 9, 27; AITN 1; CA 21-24R;
　　CANR 9, 32, 52, 74; CDALB 1968-1988;
　　CLR 3, 28; DLB 8, 52; INT CANR-32;
　　JRDA; MAICYA; MTCW 1, 2; SATA 4, 52,
　　99
Lehmann, Rosamond (Nina) 1901-1990**CLC 5**
　　See also CA 77-80; 131; CANR 8, 73; DLB 15;
　　MTCW 2
Leiber, Fritz (Reuter, Jr.) 1910-1992 **CLC 25**
　　See also CA 45-48; 139; CANR 2, 40; DLB 8;
　　MTCW 1, 2; SATA 45; SATA-Obit 73
Leibniz, Gottfried Wilhelm von 1646-1716**LC
　　35**
　　See also DLB 168
Leimbach, Martha 1963-
　　See Leimbach, Marti
　　See also CA 130
Leimbach, Marti .... **CLC 65**
　　See also Leimbach, Martha
Leino, Eino .... **TCLC 24**
　　See also Loennbohm, Armas Eino Leopold
Leiris, Michel (Julien) 1901-1990 ..... **CLC 61**
　　See also CA 119; 128; 132
Leithauser, Brad 1953- .... **CLC 27**
　　See also CA 107; CANR 27, 81; DLB 120
Lelchuk, Alan 1938- .... **CLC 5**
　　See also CA 45-48; CAAS 20; CANR 1, 70
Lem, Stanislaw 1921- .... **CLC 8, 15, 40**
　　See also CA 105; CAAS 1; CANR 32; MTCW
　　1
Lemann, Nancy 1956- .... **CLC 39**
　　See also CA 118; 136
Lemonnier, (Antoine Louis) Camille 1844-1913
　　TCLC 22
　　See also CA 121
Lenau, Nikolaus 1802-1850 .... **NCLC 16**

See also CA 115

Martinez Sierra, Maria (de la O'LeJarraga) 1874-1974 .... **TCLC 6**
See also CA 115

Martinsen, Martin
See Follett, Ken(neth Martin)

Martinson, Harry (Edmund) 1904-1978 **C L C 14**
See also CA 77-80; CANR 34

Marut, Ret
See Traven, B.

Marut, Robert
See Traven, B.

Marvell, Andrew 1621-1678 ... **LC 4, 43; DA; DAB; DAC; DAM MST, POET; PC 10; WLC**
See also CDBLB 1660-1789; DLB 131

Marx, Karl (Heinrich) 1818-1883 . **NCLC 17**
See also DLB 129

Masaoka Shiki .... **TCLC 18**
See also Masaoka Tsunenori

Masaoka Tsunenori 1867-1902
See Masaoka Shiki
See also CA 117

Masefield, John (Edward) 1878-1967 **CLC 11, 47; DAM POET**
See also CA 19-20; 25-28R; CANR 33; CAP 2; CDBLB 1890-1914; DLB 10, 19, 153, 160; MTCW 1, 2; SATA 19

Maso, Carole 19(?)- .... **CLC 44**
See also CA 170

Mason, Bobbie Ann 1940- **CLC 28, 43, 82; SSC 4**
See also AAYA 5; CA 53-56; CANR 11, 31, 58; CDALBS; DLB 173; DLBY 87; INT CANR-31; MTCW 1, 2

Mason, Ernst
See Pohl, Frederik

Mason, Lee W.
See Malzberg, Barry N(athaniel)

Mason, Nick 1945- .... **CLC 35**

Mason, Tally
See Derleth, August (William)

Mass, William
See Gibson, William

Master Lao
See Lao Tzu

Masters, Edgar Lee 1868-1950 **TCLC 2, 25; DA; DAC; DAM MST, POET; PC 1; WLCS**
See also CA 104; 133; CDALB 1865-1917; DLB 54; MTCW 1, 2

Masters, Hilary 1928- .... **CLC 48**
See also CA 25-28R; CANR 13, 47

Mastrosimone, William 19(?)- .... **CLC 36**

Mathe, Albert
See Camus, Albert

Mather, Cotton 1663-1728 .... **LC 38**
See also CDALB 1640-1865; DLB 24, 30, 140

Mather, Increase 1639-1723 .... **LC 38**
See also DLB 24

Matheson, Richard Burton 1926- .... **CLC 37**
See also CA 97-100; DLB 8, 44; INT 97-100

Mathews, Harry 1930- .... **CLC 6, 52**
See also CA 21-24R; CAAS 6; CANR 18, 40

Mathews, John Joseph 1894-1979 .. **CLC 84; DAM MULT**
See also CA 19-20; 142; CANR 45; CAP 2; DLB 175; NNAL

Mathias, Roland (Glyn) 1915- .... **CLC 45**
See also CA 97-100; CANR 19, 41; DLB 27

Matsuo Basho 1644-1694 .... **PC 3**
See also DAM POET

Mattheson, Rodney
See Creasey, John

Matthews, Brander 1852-1929 .... **TCLC 95**
See also DLB 71, 78; DLBD 13

Matthews, Greg 1949- .... **CLC 45**
See also CA 135

Matthews, William (Procter, III) 1942-1997 **CLC 40**
See also CA 29-32R; 162; CAAS 18; CANR 12, 57; DLB 5

Matthias, John (Edward) 1941- .... **CLC 9**
See also CA 33-36R; CANR 56

Matthiessen, Peter 1927- **CLC 5, 7, 11, 32, 64; DAM NOV**
See also AAYA 6; BEST 90:4; CA 9-12R; CANR 21, 50, 73; DLB 6, 173; MTCW 1, 2; SATA 27

Maturin, Charles Robert 1780(?)-1824 **N C L C 6**
See also DLB 178

Matute (Ausejo), Ana Maria 1925- ..**CLC 11**
See also CA 89-92; MTCW 1

Maugham, W. S.
See Maugham, W(illiam) Somerset

Maugham, W(illiam) Somerset 1874-1965 **CLC 1, 11, 15, 67, 93; DA; DAB; DAC; DAM DRAM, MST, NOV; SSC 8; WLC**
See also CA 5-8R; 25-28R; CANR 40; CDBLB 1914-1945; DLB 10, 36, 77, 100, 162, 195; MTCW 1, 2; SATA 54

Maugham, William Somerset
See Maugham, W(illiam) Somerset

Maupassant, (Henri Rene Albert) Guy de 1850-1893 **NCLC 1, 42; DA; DAB; DAC; DAM MST; SSC 1; WLC**
See also DLB 123

Maupin, Armistead 1944- **CLC 95; DAM POP**
See also CA 125; 130; CANR 58; INT 130; MTCW 2

Maurhut, Richard
See Traven, B.

Mauriac, Claude 1914-1996 .... **CLC 9**
See also CA 89-92; 152; DLB 83

Mauriac, Francois (Charles) 1885-1970 **C L C 4, 9, 56; SSC 24**
See also CA 25-28; CAP 2; DLB 65; MTCW 1, 2

Mavor, Osborne Henry 1888-1951
See Bridie, James
See also CA 104

Maxwell, William (Keepers, Jr.) 1908- **CLC 19**
See also CA 93-96; CANR 54; DLBY 80; INT 93-96

May, Elaine 1932- .... **CLC 16**
See also CA 124; 142; DLB 44

Mayakovski, Vladimir (Vladimirovich) 1893-1930 .... **TCLC 4, 18**
See also CA 104; 158; MTCW 2

Mayhew, Henry 1812-1887 .... **NCLC 31**
See also DLB 18, 55, 190

Mayle, Peter 1939(?)- .... **CLC 89**
See also CA 139; CANR 64

Maynard, Joyce 1953- .... **CLC 23**
See also CA 111; 129; CANR 64

Mayne, William (James Carter) 1928- **CLC 12**
See also AAYA 20; CA 9-12R; CANR 37, 80; CLR 25; JRDA; MAICYA; SAAS 11; SATA 6, 68

Mayo, Jim
See L'Amour, Louis (Dearborn)

Maysles, Albert 1926- .... **CLC 16**
See also CA 29-32R

Maysles, David 1932- .... **CLC 16**

Mazer, Norma Fox 1931- .... **CLC 26**
See also AAYA 5; CA 69-72; CANR 12, 32, 66; CLR 23; JRDA; MAICYA; SAAS 1; SATA 24, 67, 105

Mazzini, Guiseppe 1805-1872 .... **NCLC 34**

McAuley, James Phillip 1917-1976 . **CLC 45**
See also CA 97-100

McBain, Ed
See Hunter, Evan

McBrien, William Augustine 1930- . **CLC 44**
See also CA 107

McCaffrey, Anne (Inez) 1926- **CLC 17; DAM NOV, POP**
See also AAYA 6; AITN 2; BEST 89:2; CA 25-28R; CANR 15, 35, 55; CLR 49; DLB 8; JRDA; MAICYA; MTCW 1, 2; SAAS 11; SATA 8, 70

McCall, Nathan 1955(?)- .... **CLC 86**
See also BW 3; CA 146

McCann, Arthur
See Campbell, John W(ood, Jr.)

McCann, Edson
See Pohl, Frederik

McCarthy, Charles, Jr. 1933-
See McCarthy, Cormac
See also CANR 42, 69; DAM POP; MTCW 2

McCarthy, Cormac 1933- **CLC 4, 57, 59, 101**
See also McCarthy, Charles, Jr.
See also DLB 6, 143; MTCW 2

McCarthy, Mary (Therese) 1912-1989 **CLC 1, 3, 5, 14, 24, 39, 59; SSC 24**
See also CA 5-8R; 129; CANR 16, 50, 64; DLB 2; DLBY 81; INT CANR-16; MTCW 1, 2

McCartney, (James) Paul 1942- . **CLC 12, 35**
See also CA 146

McCauley, Stephen (D.) 1955- .... **CLC 50**
See also CA 141

McClure, Michael (Thomas) 1932- **CLC 6, 10**
See also CA 21-24R; CANR 17, 46, 77; DLB 16

McCorkle, Jill (Collins) 1958- .... **CLC 51**
See also CA 121; DLBY 87

McCourt, Frank 1930- .... **CLC 109**
See also CA 157

McCourt, James 1941- .... **CLC 5**
See also CA 57-60

McCourt, Malachy 1932- .... **CLC 119**

McCoy, Horace (Stanley) 1897-1955 **TCLC 28**
See also CA 108; 155; DLB 9

McCrae, John 1872-1918 .... **TCLC 12**
See also CA 109; DLB 92

McCreigh, James
See Pohl, Frederik

McCullers, (Lula) Carson (Smith) 1917-1967 **CLC 1, 4, 10, 12, 48, 100; DA; DAB; DAC; DAM MST, NOV; SSC 9, 24; WLC**
See also AAYA 21; CA 5-8R; 25-28R; CABS 1, 3; CANR 18; CDALB 1941-1968; DLB 2, 7, 173; MTCW 1, 2; SATA 27

McCulloch, John Tyler
See Burroughs, Edgar Rice

McCullough, Colleen 1938(?)- **CLC 27, 107; DAM NOV, POP**
See also CA 81-84; CANR 17, 46, 67; MTCW 1, 2

McDermott, Alice 1953- .... **CLC 90**
See also CA 109; CANR 40

McElroy, Joseph 1930- .... **CLC 5, 47**
See also CA 17-20R

McEwan, Ian (Russell) 1948- .... **CLC 13, 66; DAM NOV**
See also BEST 90:4; CA 61-64; CANR 14, 41, 69; DLB 14, 194; MTCW 1, 2

CLC 8, 19; DAM DRAM
See also CA 85-88; 37-40R; DLB 72; MTCW
1

Monty Python
See Chapman, Graham; Cleese, John
(Marwood); Gilliam, Terry (Vance); Idle,
Eric; Jones, Terence Graham Parry; Palin,
Michael (Edward)
See also AAYA 7

Moodie, Susanna (Strickland) 1803-1885
NCLC 14
See also DLB 99

Mooney, Edward 1951-
See Mooney, Ted
See also CA 130

Mooney, Ted .... **CLC 25**
See also Mooney, Edward

Moorcock, Michael (John) 1939-**CLC 5, 27, 58**
See also Bradbury, Edward P.
See also AAYA 26; CA 45-48; CAAS 5; CANR
2, 17, 38, 64; DLB 14; MTCW 1, 2; SATA
93

Moore, Brian 1921-1999**CLC 1, 3, 5, 7, 8, 19,
32, 90; DAB; DAC; DAM MST**
See also CA 1-4R; 174; CANR 1, 25, 42, 63;
MTCW 1, 2

Moore, Edward
See Muir, Edwin

Moore, G. E. 1873-1958 .... **TCLC 89**

Moore, George Augustus 1852-1933**TCLC 7;
SSC 19**
See also CA 104; 177; DLB 10, 18, 57, 135

Moore, Lorrie .... **CLC 39, 45, 68**
See also Moore, Marie Lorena

Moore, Marianne (Craig) 1887-1972**CLC 1, 2,
4, 8, 10, 13, 19, 47; DA; DAB; DAC; DAM
MST, POET; PC 4; WLCS**
See also CA 1-4R; 33-36R; CANR 3, 61;
CDALB 1929-1941; DLB 45; DLBD 7;
MTCW 1, 2; SATA 20

Moore, Marie Lorena 1957-
See Moore, Lorrie
See also CA 116; CANR 39

Moore, Thomas 1779-1852 .... **NCLC 6**
See also DLB 96, 144

Morand, Paul 1888-1976 .... **CLC 41; SSC 22**
See also CA 69-72; DLB 65

Morante, Elsa 1918-1985 .... **CLC 8, 47**
See also CA 85-88; 117; CANR 35; DLB 177;
MTCW 1, 2

Moravia, Alberto 1907-1990**CLC 2, 7, 11, 27,
46; SSC 26**
See also Pincherle, Alberto
See also DLB 177; MTCW 2

More, Hannah 1745-1833 .... **NCLC 27**
See also DLB 107, 109, 116, 158

More, Henry 1614-1687 .... **LC 9**
See also DLB 126

More, Sir Thomas 1478-1535 .... **LC 10, 32**

Moreas, Jean .... **TCLC 18**
See also Papadiamantopoulos, Johannes

Morgan, Berry 1919- .... **CLC 6**
See also CA 49-52; DLB 6

Morgan, Claire
See Highsmith, (Mary) Patricia

Morgan, Edwin (George) 1920- .... **CLC 31**
See also CA 5-8R; CANR 3, 43; DLB 27

Morgan, (George) Frederick 1922- . **CLC 23**
See also CA 17-20R; CANR 21

Morgan, Harriet
See Mencken, H(enry) L(ouis)

Morgan, Jane
See Cooper, James Fenimore

Morgan, Janet 1945- .... **CLC 39**
See also CA 65-68

Morgan, Lady 1776(?)-1859 .... **NCLC 29**
See also DLB 116, 158

Morgan, Robin (Evonne) 1941- .... **CLC 2**
See also CA 69-72; CANR 29, 68; MTCW 1;
SATA 80

Morgan, Scott
See Kuttner, Henry

Morgan, Seth 1949(?)-1990 .... **CLC 65**
See also CA 132

Morgenstern, Christian 1871-1914 . **TCLC 8**
See also CA 105

Morgenstern, S.
See Goldman, William (W.)

Moricz, Zsigmond 1879-1942 .... **TCLC 33**
See also CA 165

Morike, Eduard (Friedrich) 1804-1875**NCLC
10**
See also DLB 133

Moritz, Karl Philipp 1756-1793 .... **LC 2**
See also DLB 94

Morland, Peter Henry
See Faust, Frederick (Schiller)

Morley, Christopher (Darlington) 1890-1957
TCLC 87
See also CA 112; DLB 9

Morren, Theophil
See Hofmannsthal, Hugo von

Morris, Bill 1952- .... **CLC 76**

Morris, Julian
See West, Morris L(anglo)

Morris, Steveland Judkins 1950(?)-
See Wonder, Stevie
See also CA 111

Morris, William 1834-1896 .... **NCLC 4**
See also CDBLB 1832-1890; DLB 18, 35, 57,
156, 178, 184

Morris, Wright 1910-1998**CLC 1, 3, 7, 18, 37**
See also CA 9-12R; 167; CANR 21, 81; DLB
2, 206; DLBY 81; MTCW 1, 2

Morrison, Arthur 1863-1945 .... **TCLC 72**
See also CA 120; 157; DLB 70, 135, 197

Morrison, Chloe Anthony Wofford
See Morrison, Toni

Morrison, James Douglas 1943-1971
See Morrison, Jim
See also CA 73-76; CANR 40

Morrison, Jim .... **CLC 17**
See also Morrison, James Douglas

Morrison, Toni 1931-**CLC 4, 10, 22, 55, 81, 87;
BLC 3; DA; DAB; DAC; DAM MST,
MULT, NOV, POP**
See also AAYA 1, 22; BW 2, 3; CA 29-32R;
CANR 27, 42, 67; CDALB 1968-1988; DLB
6, 33, 143; DLBY 81; MTCW 1, 2; SATA 57

Morrison, Van 1945- .... **CLC 21**
See also CA 116; 168

Morrissy, Mary 1958- .... **CLC 99**

Mortimer, John (Clifford) 1923-**CLC 28, 43;
DAM DRAM, POP**
See also CA 13-16R; CANR 21, 69; CDBLB
1960 to Present; DLB 13; INT CANR-21;
MTCW 1, 2

Mortimer, Penelope (Ruth) 1918- .... **CLC 5**
See also CA 57-60; CANR 45

Morton, Anthony
See Creasey, John

Mosca, Gaetano 1858-1941 .... **TCLC 75**

Mosher, Howard Frank 1943- .... **CLC 62**
See also CA 139; CANR 65

Mosley, Nicholas 1923- .... **CLC 43, 70**
See also CA 69-72; CANR 41, 60; DLB 14, 207

Mosley, Walter 1952- **CLC 97; BLCS; DAM
MULT, POP**
See also AAYA 17; BW 2; CA 142; CANR 57;
MTCW 2

Moss, Howard 1922-1987 **CLC 7, 14, 45, 50;
DAM POET**
See also CA 1-4R; 123; CANR 1, 44; DLB 5

Mossgiel, Rab
See Burns, Robert

Motion, Andrew (Peter) 1952- .... **CLC 47**
See also CA 146; DLB 40

Motley, Willard (Francis) 1909-1965**CLC 18**
See also BW 1; CA 117; 106; DLB 76, 143

Motoori, Norinaga 1730-1801 .... **NCLC 45**

Mott, Michael (Charles Alston) 1930-**CLC 15,
34**
See also CA 5-8R; CAAS 7; CANR 7, 29

Mountain Wolf Woman 1884-1960 ... **CLC 92**
See also CA 144; NNAL

Moure, Erin 1955- .... **CLC 88**
See also CA 113; DLB 60

Mowat, Farley (McGill) 1921-**CLC 26; DAC;
DAM MST**
See also AAYA 1; CA 1-4R; CANR 4, 24, 42,
68; CLR 20; DLB 68; INT CANR-24; JRDA;
MAICYA; MTCW 1, 2; SATA 3, 55

Mowatt, Anna Cora 1819-1870 ...... **NCLC 74**

Moyers, Bill 1934- .... **CLC 74**
See also AITN 2; CA 61-64; CANR 31, 52

Mphahlele, Es'kia
See Mphahlele, Ezekiel
See also DLB 125

Mphahlele, Ezekiel 1919- .. **CLC 25; BLC 3;
DAM MULT**
See also Mphahlele, Es'kia
See also BW 2, 3; CA 81-84; CANR 26, 76;
MTCW 2

Mqhayi, S(amuel) E(dward) K(rune Loliwe)
1875-1945**TCLC 25; BLC 3; DAM MULT**
See also CA 153

Mrozek, Slawomir 1930- .... **CLC 3, 13**
See also CA 13-16R; CAAS 10; CANR 29;
MTCW 1

Mrs. Belloc-Lowndes
See Lowndes, Marie Adelaide (Belloc)

Mtwa, Percy (?)- .... **CLC 47**

Mueller, Lisel 1924- .... **CLC 13, 51**
See also CA 93-96; DLB 105

Muir, Edwin 1887-1959 .... **TCLC 2, 87**
See also CA 104; DLB 20, 100, 191

Muir, John 1838-1914 .... **TCLC 28**
See also CA 165; DLB 186

Mujica Lainez, Manuel 1910-1984 ... **CLC 31**
See also Lainez, Manuel Mujica
See also CA 81-84; 112; CANR 32; HW 1

Mukherjee, Bharati 1940-**CLC 53, 115; DAM
NOV**
See also BEST 89:2; CA 107; CANR 45, 72;
DLB 60; MTCW 1, 2

Muldoon, Paul 1951-**CLC 32, 72; DAM POET**
See also CA 113; 129; CANR 52; DLB 40; INT
129

Mulisch, Harry 1927- .... **CLC 42**
See also CA 9-12R; CANR 6, 26, 56

Mull, Martin 1943- .... **CLC 17**
See also CA 105

Muller, Wilhelm .... **NCLC 73**

Mulock, Dinah Maria
See Craik, Dinah Maria (Mulock)

Munford, Robert 1737(?)-1783 .... **LC 5**
See also DLB 31

Mungo, Raymond 1946- .... **CLC 72**
See also CA 49-52; CANR 2

Park, Jordan
  See Kornbluth, C(yril) M.; Pohl, Frederik
Park, Robert E(zra) 1864-1944 ...... **TCLC 73**
  See also CA 122; 165
Parker, Bert
  See Ellison, Harlan (Jay)
Parker, Dorothy (Rothschild) 1893-1967**C L C
  15, 68; DAM POET; SSC 2**
  See also CA 19-20; 25-28R; CAP 2; DLB 11,
  45, 86; MTCW 1, 2
Parker, Robert B(rown) 1932-**CLC 27; DAM
  NOV, POP**
  See also AAYA 28; BEST 89:4; CA 49-52;
  CANR 1, 26, 52; INT CANR-26; MTCW 1
Parkin, Frank 1940- .... **CLC 43**
  See also CA 147
Parkman, Francis, Jr. 1823-1893 ... **NCLC 12**
  See also DLB 1, 30, 186
Parks, Gordon (Alexander Buchanan) 1912-
  CLC 1, 16; BLC 3; DAM MULT
  See also AITN 2; BW 2, 3; CA 41-44R; CANR
  26, 66; DLB 33; MTCW 2; SATA 8, 108
Parmenides c. 515B.C.-c. 450B.C. **CMLC 22**
  See also DLB 176
Parnell, Thomas 1679-1718 .... **LC 3**
  See also DLB 94
Parra, Nicanor 1914- ...... **CLC 2, 102; DAM
  MULT; HLC**
  See also CA 85-88; CANR 32; HW 1; MTCW
  1
Parrish, Mary Frances
  See Fisher, M(ary) F(rances) K(ennedy)
Parson
  See Coleridge, Samuel Taylor
Parson Lot
  See Kingsley, Charles
Partridge, Anthony
  See Oppenheim, E(dward) Phillips
Pascal, Blaise 1623-1662 .... **LC 35**
Pascoli, Giovanni 1855-1912 .... **TCLC 45**
  See also CA 170
Pasolini, Pier Paolo 1922-1975 . **CLC 20, 37,
  106; PC 17**
  See also CA 93-96; 61-64; CANR 63; DLB 128,
  177; MTCW 1
Pasquini
  See Silone, Ignazio
Pastan, Linda (Olenik) 1932- **CLC 27; DAM
  POET**
  See also CA 61-64; CANR 18, 40, 61; DLB 5
Pasternak, Boris (Leonidovich) 1890-1960
  **CLC 7, 10, 18, 63; DA; DAB; DAC; DAM
  MST, NOV, POET; PC 6; SSC 31; WLC**
  See also CA 127; 116; MTCW 1, 2
Patchen, Kenneth 1911-1972 ... **CLC 1, 2, 18;
  DAM POET**
  See also CA 1-4R; 33-36R; CANR 3, 35; DLB
  16, 48; MTCW 1
Pater, Walter (Horatio) 1839-1894 .. **NCLC 7**
  See also CDBLB 1832-1890; DLB 57, 156
Paterson, A(ndrew) B(arton) 1864-1941
  TCLC 32
  See also CA 155; SATA 97
Paterson, Katherine (Womeldorf) 1932-**C L C
  12, 30**
  See also AAYA 1; CA 21-24R; CANR 28, 59;
  CLR 7, 50; DLB 52; JRDA; MAICYA;
  MTCW 1; SATA 13, 53, 92
Patmore, Coventry Kersey Dighton 1823-1896
  NCLC 9
  See also DLB 35, 98
Paton, Alan (Stewart) 1903-1988 **CLC 4, 10,
  25, 55, 106; DA; DAB; DAC; DAM MST,**

NOV; WLC
  See also AAYA 26; CA 13-16; 125; CANR 22;
  CAP 1; DLBD 17; MTCW 1, 2; SATA 11;
  SATA-Obit 56
Paton Walsh, Gillian 1937-
  See Walsh, Jill Paton
  See also CANR 38; JRDA; MAICYA; SAAS 3;
  SATA 4, 72, 109
Patton, George S. 1885-1945 .... **TCLC 79**
Paulding, James Kirke 1778-1860 ... **NCLC 2**
  See also DLB 3, 59, 74
Paulin, Thomas Neilson 1949-
  See Paulin, Tom
  See also CA 123; 128
Paulin, Tom ....**CLC 37**
  See also Paulin, Thomas Neilson
  See also DLB 40
Paustovsky, Konstantin (Georgievich) 1892-
  1968 ....**CLC 40**
  See also CA 93-96; 25-28R
Pavese, Cesare 1908-1950 ... **TCLC 3; PC 13;
  SSC 19**
  See also CA 104; 169; DLB 128, 177
Pavic, Milorad 1929- .... **CLC 60**
  See also CA 136; DLB 181
Pavlov, Ivan Petrovich 1849-1936 . **TCLC 91**
  See also CA 118
Payne, Alan
  See Jakes, John (William)
Paz, Gil
  See Lugones, Leopoldo
Paz, Octavio 1914-1998**CLC 3, 4, 6, 10, 19, 51,
  65, 119; DA; DAB; DAC; DAM MST,
  MULT, POET; HLC; PC 1; WLC**
  See also CA 73-76; 165; CANR 32, 65; DLBY
  90, 98; HW 1, 2; MTCW 1, 2
p'Bitek, Okot 1931-1982 .... **CLC 96; BLC 3;
  DAM MULT**
  See also BW 2, 3; CA 124; 107; DLB 125;
  MTCW 1, 2
Peacock, Molly 1947- .... **CLC 60**
  See also CA 103; CAAS 21; CANR 52; DLB
  120
Peacock, Thomas Love 1785-1866 . **NCLC 22**
  See also DLB 96, 116
Peake, Mervyn 1911-1968 .... **CLC 7, 54**
  See also CA 5-8R; 25-28R; CANR 3; DLB 15,
  160; MTCW 1; SATA 23
Pearce, Philippa ....**CLC 21**
  See also Christie, (Ann) Philippa
  See also CLR 9; DLB 161; MAICYA; SATA 1,
  67
Pearl, Eric
  See Elman, Richard (Martin)
Pearson, T(homas) R(eid) 1956- .... **CLC 39**
  See also CA 120; 130; INT 130
Peck, Dale 1967- .... **CLC 81**
  See also CA 146; CANR 72
Peck, John 1941- ....**CLC 3**
  See also CA 49-52; CANR 3
Peck, Richard (Wayne) 1934- .... **CLC 21**
  See also AAYA 1, 24; CA 85-88; CANR 19,
  38; CLR 15; INT CANR-19; JRDA;
  MAICYA; SAAS 2; SATA 18, 55, 97
Peck, Robert Newton 1928- ..... **CLC 17; DA;
  DAC; DAM MST**
  See also AAYA 3; CA 81-84; CANR 31, 63;
  CLR 45; JRDA; MAICYA; SAAS 1; SATA
  21, 62; SATA-Essay 108
Peckinpah, (David) Sam(uel) 1925-1984**C L C
  20**
  See also CA 109; 114
Pedersen, Knut 1859-1952

  See Hamsun, Knut
  See also CA 104; 119; CANR 63; MTCW 1, 2
Peeslake, Gaffer
  See Durrell, Lawrence (George)
Peguy, Charles Pierre 1873-1914 ... **TCLC 10**
  See also CA 107
Peirce, Charles Sanders 1839-1914 **TCLC 81**
Pena, Ramon del Valle y
  See Valle-Inclan, Ramon (Maria) del
Pendennis, Arthur Esquir
  See Thackeray, William Makepeace
Penn, William 1644-1718 .... **LC 25**
  See also DLB 24
PEPECE
  See Prado (Calvo), Pedro
Pepys, Samuel 1633-1703 **LC 11; DA; DAB;
  DAC; DAM MST; WLC**
  See also CDBLB 1660-1789; DLB 101
Percy, Walker 1916-1990**CLC 2, 3, 6, 8, 14, 18,
  47, 65; DAM NOV, POP**
  See also CA 1-4R; 131; CANR 1, 23, 64; DLB
  2; DLBY 80, 90; MTCW 1, 2
Percy, William Alexander 1885-1942**TCLC 84**
  See also CA 163; MTCW 2
Perec, Georges 1936-1982 .... **CLC 56, 116**
  See also CA 141; DLB 83
Pereda (y Sanchez de Porrua), Jose Maria de
  1833-1906 .... **TCLC 16**
  See also CA 117
Pereda y Porrua, Jose Maria de
  See Pereda (y Sanchez de Porrua), Jose Maria
  de
Peregoy, George Weems
  See Mencken, H(enry) L(ouis)
Perelman, S(idney) J(oseph) 1904-1979 **C L C
  3, 5, 9, 15, 23, 44, 49; DAM DRAM; SSC
  32**
  See also AITN 1, 2; CA 73-76; 89-92; CANR
  18; DLB 11, 44; MTCW 1, 2
Peret, Benjamin 1899-1959 .... **TCLC 20**
  See also CA 117
Peretz, Isaac Loeb 1851(?)-1915 .. **TCLC 16;
  SSC 26**
  See also CA 109
Peretz, Yitzhok Leibush
  See Peretz, Isaac Loeb
Perez Galdos, Benito 1843-1920 .. **TCLC 27;
  HLCS 2**
  See also CA 125; 153; HW 1
Perrault, Charles 1628-1703 .... **LC 2**
  See also MAICYA; SATA 25
Perry, Brighton
  See Sherwood, Robert E(mmet)
Perse, St.-John
  See Leger, (Marie-Rene Auguste) Alexis Saint-
  Leger
Perutz, Leo(pold) 1882-1957 .... **TCLC 60**
  See also CA 147; DLB 81
Peseenz, Tulio F.
  See Lopez y Fuentes, Gregorio
Pesetsky, Bette 1932- .... **CLC 28**
  See also CA 133; DLB 130
Peshkov, Alexei Maximovich 1868-1936
  See Gorky, Maxim
  See also CA 105; 141; DA; DAC; DAM DRAM,
  MST, NOV; MTCW 2
Pessoa, Fernando (Antonio Nogueira) 1888-
  1935**TCLC 27; DAM MULT; HLC; PC 20**
  See also CA 125
Peterkin, Julia Mood 1880-1961 .... **CLC 31**
  See also CA 102; DLB 9
Peters, Joan K(aren) 1945- .... **CLC 39**
  See also CA 158

See also AAYA 26; CA 126; SATA 109

Robinson, Lloyd
  See Silverberg, Robert

Robinson, Marilynne 1944- .... **CLC 25**
  See also CA 116; CANR 80; DLB 206

Robinson, Smokey .... **CLC 21**
  See also Robinson, William, Jr.

Robinson, William, Jr. 1940-
  See Robinson, Smokey
  See also CA 116

Robison, Mary 1949- .... **CLC 42, 98**
  See also CA 113; 116; DLB 130; INT 116

Rod, Edouard 1857-1910 .... **TCLC 52**

Roddenberry, Eugene Wesley 1921-1991
  See Roddenberry, Gene
  See also CA 110; 135; CANR 37; SATA 45;
  SATA-Obit 69

Roddenberry, Gene .... **CLC 17**
  See also Roddenberry, Eugene Wesley
  See also AAYA 5; SATA-Obit 69

Rodgers, Mary 1931- .... **CLC 12**
  See also CA 49-52; CANR 8, 55; CLR 20; INT
  CANR-8; JRDA; MAICYA; SATA 8

Rodgers, W(illiam) R(obert) 1909-1969**CLC 7**
  See also CA 85-88; DLB 20

Rodman, Eric
  See Silverberg, Robert

Rodman, Howard 1920(?)-1985 .... **CLC 65**
  See also CA 118

Rodman, Maia
  See Wojciechowska, Maia (Teresa)

Rodriguez, Claudio 1934- .... **CLC 10**
  See also DLB 134

Roelvaag, O(le) E(dvart) 1876-1931**TCLC 17**
  See also CA 117; 171; DLB 9

Roethke, Theodore (Huebner) 1908-1963**CLC
  1, 3, 8, 11, 19, 46, 101; DAM POET; PC 15**
  See also CA 81-84; CABS 2, CDALB 1941-
  1968; DLB 5, 206; MTCW 1, 2

Rogers, Samuel 1763-1855 .... **NCLC 69**
  See also DLB 93

Rogers, Thomas Hunton 1927- .... **CLC 57**
  See also CA 89-92; INT 89-92

Rogers, Will(iam Penn Adair) 1879-1935
  TCLC 8, 71; DAM MULT
  See also CA 105; 144; DLB 11; MTCW 2;
  NNAL

Rogin, Gilbert 1929- .... **CLC 18**
  See also CA 65-68; CANR 15

Rohan, Koda .... **TCLC 22**
  See also Koda Shigeyuki

Rohlfs, Anna Katharine Green
  See Green, Anna Katharine

Rohmer, Eric .... **CLC 16**
  See also Scherer, Jean-Marie Maurice

Rohmer, Sax ....**TCLC 28**
  See also Ward, Arthur Henry Sarsfield
  See also DLB 70

Roiphe, Anne (Richardson) 1935- . **CLC 3, 9**
  See also CA 89-92; CANR 45, 73; DLBY 80;
  INT 89-92

Rojas, Fernando de 1465-1541**LC 23; HLCS 1**

**Rolfe, Frederick (William Serafino Austin
  Lewis Mary)** 1860-1913 .... **TCLC 12**
  See also CA 107; DLB 34, 156

Rolland, Romain 1866-1944 .... **TCLC 23**
  See also CA 118; DLB 65

Rolle, Richard c. 1300-c. 1349 ...... **CMLC 21**
  See also DLB 146

Rolvaag, O(le) E(dvart)
  See Roelvaag, O(le) E(dvart)

Romain Arnaud, Saint
  See Aragon, Louis

Romains, Jules 1885-1972 .... **CLC 7**
  See also CA 85-88; CANR 34; DLB 65; MTCW
  1

Romero, Jose Ruben 1890-1952 ..... **TCLC 14**
  See also CA 114; 131; HW 1

Ronsard, Pierre de 1524-1585 ... **LC 6; PC 11**

Rooke, Leon 1934- .. **CLC 25, 34; DAM POP**
  See also CA 25-28R; CANR 23, 53

Roosevelt, Franklin Delano 1882-1945**T C L C
  93**
  See also CA 116; 173

Roosevelt, Theodore 1858-1919 ..... **TCLC 69**
  See also CA 115; 170; DLB 47, 186

Roper, William 1498-1578 .... **LC 10**

Roquelaure, A. N.
  See Rice, Anne

Rosa, Joao Guimaraes 1908-1967 .. **CLC 23;
  HLCS 1**
  See also CA 89-92; DLB 113

Rose, Wendy 1948-**CLC 85; DAM MULT; PC
  13**
  See also CA 53-56; CANR 5, 51; DLB 175;
  NNAL; SATA 12

Rosen, R. D.
  See Rosen, Richard (Dean)

Rosen, Richard (Dean) 1949- .... **CLC 39**
  See also CA 77-80; CANR 62; INT CANR-30

Rosenberg, Isaac 1890-1918 .... **TCLC 12**
  See also CA 107; DLB 20

Rosenblatt, Joe ....**CLC 15**
  See also Rosenblatt, Joseph

Rosenblatt, Joseph 1933-
  See Rosenblatt, Joe
  See also CA 89-92; INT 89-92

Rosenfeld, Samuel
  See Tzara, Tristan

Rosenstock, Sami
  See Tzara, Tristan

Rosenstock, Samuel
  See Tzara, Tristan

Rosenthal, M(acha) L(ouis) 1917-1996 . **C L C
  28**
  See also CA 1-4R; 152; CAAS 6; CANR 4, 51;
  DLB 5; SATA 59

Ross, Barnaby
  See Dannay, Frederic

Ross, Bernard L.
  See Follett, Ken(neth Martin)

Ross, J. H.
  See Lawrence, T(homas) E(dward)

Ross, John Hume
  See Lawrence, T(homas) E(dward)

Ross, Martin
  See Martin, Violet Florence
  See also DLB 135

Ross, (James) Sinclair 1908-1996 ... **CLC 13;
  DAC; DAM MST; SSC 24**
  See also CA 73-76; CANR 81; DLB 88

Rossetti, Christina (Georgina) 1830-1894
  **NCLC 2, 50, 66; DA; DAB; DAC; DAM
  MST, POET; PC 7; WLC**
  See also DLB 35, 163; MAICYA; SATA 20

Rossetti, Dante Gabriel 1828-1882 .**NCLC 4,
  77; DA; DAB; DAC; DAM MST, POET;
  WLC**
  See also CDBLB 1832-1890; DLB 35

Rossner, Judith (Perelman) 1935-**CLC 6, 9, 29**
  See also AITN 2; BEST 90:3; CA 17-20R;
  CANR 18, 51, 73; DLB 6; INT CANR-18;
  MTCW 1, 2

Rostand, Edmond (Eugene Alexis) 1868-1918
  **TCLC 6, 37; DA; DAB; DAC; DAM
  DRAM, MST; DC 10**

See also CA 104; 126; DLB 192; MTCW 1

Roth, Henry 1906-1995 ..... **CLC 2, 6, 11, 104**
  See also CA 11-12; 149; CANR 38, 63; CAP 1;
  DLB 28; MTCW 1, 2

Roth, Philip (Milton) 1933-**CLC 1, 2, 3, 4, 6, 9,
  15, 22, 31, 47, 66, 86, 119; DA; DAB; DAC;
  DAM MST, NOV, POP; SSC 26; WLC**
  See also BEST 90:3; CA 1-4R; CANR 1, 22,
  36, 55; CDALB 1968-1988; DLB 2, 28, 173;
  DLBY 82; MTCW 1, 2

Rothenberg, Jerome 1931- .... **CLC 6, 57**
  See also CA 45-48; CANR 1; DLB 5, 193

Roumain, Jacques (Jean Baptiste) 1907-1944
  TCLC 19; BLC 3; DAM MULT
  See also BW 1; CA 117; 125

Rourke, Constance (Mayfield) 1885-1941
  TCLC 12
  See also CA 107; YABC 1

Rousseau, Jean-Baptiste 1671-1741 ..... **LC 9**

Rousseau, Jean-Jacques 1712-1778**LC 14, 36;
  DA; DAB; DAC; DAM MST; WLC**

Roussel, Raymond 1877-1933 .... **TCLC 20**
  See also CA 117

Rovit, Earl (Herbert) 1927- .... **CLC 7**
  See also CA 5-8R; CANR 12

Rowe, Elizabeth Singer 1674-1737 ..... **LC 44**
  See also DLB 39, 95

Rowe, Nicholas 1674-1718 .... **LC 8**
  See also DLB 84

Rowley, Ames Dorrance
  See Lovecraft, H(oward) P(hillips)

Rowson, Susanna Haswell 1762(?)-1824
  NCLC 5, 69
  See also DLB 37, 200

Roy, Arundhati 1960(?)- .... **CLC 109**
  See also CA 163; DLBY 97

Roy, Gabrielle 1909-1983 **CLC 10, 14; DAB;
  DAC; DAM MST**
  See also CA 53-56; 110; CANR 5, 61; DLB 68;
  MTCW 1; SATA 104

Royko, Mike 1932-1997 .... **CLC 109**
  See also CA 89-92; 157; CANR 26

Rozewicz, Tadeusz 1921- ... **CLC 9, 23; DAM
  POET**
  See also CA 108; CANR 36, 66; MTCW 1, 2

Ruark, Gibbons 1941- ....**CLC 3**
  See also CA 33-36R; CAAS 23; CANR 14, 31,
  57; DLB 120

Rubens, Bernice (Ruth) 1923- .... **CLC 19, 31**
  See also CA 25-28R; CANR 33, 65; DLB 14,
  207; MTCW 1

Rubin, Harold
  See Robbins, Harold

Rudkin, (James) David 1936- .... **CLC 14**
  See also CA 89-92; DLB 13

Rudnik, Raphael 1933- ....**CLC 7**
  See also CA 29-32R

Ruffian, M.
  See Hasek, Jaroslav (Matej Frantisek)

Ruiz, Jose Martinez .... **CLC 11**
  See also Martinez Ruiz, Jose

Rukeyser, Muriel 1913-1980**CLC 6, 10, 15, 27;
  DAM POET; PC 12**
  See also CA 5-8R; 93-96; CANR 26, 60; DLB
  48; MTCW 1, 2; SATA-Obit 22

Rule, Jane (Vance) 1931- .... **CLC 27**
  See also CA 25-28R; CAAS 18; CANR 12; DLB
  60

Rulfo, Juan 1918-1986 ....**CLC 8, 80; DAM
  MULT; HLC; SSC 25**
  See also CA 85-88; 118; CANR 26; DLB 113;
  HW 1, 2; MTCW 1, 2

Rumi, Jalal al-Din 1297-1373 .... **CMLC 20**

Skelton, Robin 1925-1997 .... **CLC 13**
  See also AITN 2; CA 5-8R; 160; CAAS 5;
    CANR 28; DLB 27, 53
Skolimowski, Jerzy 1938- .... **CLC 20**
  See also CA 128
Skram, Amalie (Bertha) 1847-1905 **TCLC 25**
  See also CA 165
Skvorecky, Josef (Vaclav) 1924- **CLC 15, 39,
  69; DAC; DAM NOV**
  See also CA 61-64; CAAS 1; CANR 10, 34,
    63; MTCW 1, 2
Slade, Bernard .... **CLC 11, 46**
  See also Newbound, Bernard Slade
  See also CAAS 9; DLB 53
Slaughter, Carolyn 1946- .... **CLC 56**
  See also CA 85-88
Slaughter, Frank G(ill) 1908- .... **CLC 29**
  See also AITN 2; CA 5-8R; CANR 5; INT
    CANR-5
Slavitt, David R(ytman) 1935- ..... **CLC 5, 14**
  <indexhaSee also CA 21-24R; CAAS 3; CANR
    41; DLB 5, 6
Slesinger, Tess 1905-1945 .... **TCLC 10**
  See also CA 107; DLB 102
Slessor, Kenneth 1901-1971 .... **CLC 14**
  See also CA 102; 89-92
Slowacki, Juliusz 1809-1849 .... **NCLC 15**
Smart, Christopher 1722-1771 .. **LC 3; DAM
  POET; PC 13**
  See also DLB 109
Smart, Elizabeth 1913-1986 .... **CLC 54**
  See also CA 81-84; 118; DLB 88
Smiley, Jane (Graves) 1949- **CLC 53, 76; DAM
  POP**
  See also CA 104; CANR 30, 50, 74; INT CANR-
    30
Smith, A(rthur) J(ames) M(arshall) 1902-1980
  CLC 15; DAC
  See also CA 1-4R; 102; CANR 4; DLB 88
Smith, Adam 1723-1790 .... **LC 36**
  See also DLB 104
Smith, Alexander 1829-1867 .... **NCLC 59**
  See also DLB 32, 55
Smith, Anna Deavere 1950- .... **CLC 86**
  See also CA 133
Smith, Betty (Wehner) 1896-1972 ... **CLC 19**
  See also CA 5-8R; 33-36R; DLBY 82; SATA 6
Smith, Charlotte (Turner) 1749-1806 **N C L C
  23**
  See also DLB 39, 109
Smith, Clark Ashton 1893-1961 .... **CLC 43**
  See also CA 143; CANR 81; MTCW 2
Smith, Dave .... **CLC 22, 42**
  See also Smith, David (Jeddie)
  See also CAAS 7; DLB 5
Smith, David (Jeddie) 1942-
  See Smith, Dave
  See also CA 49-52; CANR 1, 59; DAM POET
Smith, Florence Margaret 1902-1971
  See Smith, Stevie
  See also CA 17-18; 29-32R; CANR 35; CAP 2;
    DAM POET; MTCW 1, 2
Smith, Iain Crichton 1928-1998 ...... **CLC 64**
  See also CA 21-24R; 171; DLB 40, 139
Smith, John 1580(?)-1631 .... **LC 9**
  See also DLB 24, 30
Smith, Johnston
  See Crane, Stephen (Townley)
Smith, Joseph, Jr. 1805-1844 .... **NCLC 53**
Smith, Lee 1944- .... **CLC 25, 73**
  See also CA 114; 119; CANR 46; DLB 143;
    DLBY 83; INT 119
Smith, Martin

See Smith, Martin Cruz
Smith, Martin Cruz 1942- ..... **CLC 25; DAM
  MULT, POP**
  See also BEST 89:4; CA 85-88; CANR 6, 23,
    43, 65; INT CANR-23; MTCW 2; NNAL
Smith, Mary-Ann Tirone 1944- .... **CLC 39**
  See also CA 118; 136
Smith, Patti 1946- .... **CLC 12**
  See also CA 93-96; CANR 63
Smith, Pauline (Urmson) 1882-1959 **TCLC 25**
Smith, Rosamond
  See Oates, Joyce Carol
Smith, Sheila Kaye
  See Kaye-Smith, Sheila
Smith, Stevie .... **CLC 3, 8, 25, 44; PC 12**
  See also Smith, Florence Margaret
  See also DLB 20; MTCW 2
Smith, Wilbur (Addison) 1933- .... **CLC 33**
  See also CA 13-16R; CANR 7, 46, 66; MTCW
    1, 2
Smith, William Jay 1918- .... **CLC 6**
  See also CA 5-8R; CANR 44; DLB 5; MAICYA;
    SAAS 22; SATA 2, 68
Smith, Woodrow Wilson
  See Kuttner, Henry
Smolenskin, Peretz 1842-1885 .... **NCLC 30**
Smollett, Tobias (George) 1721-1771 **LC 2, 46**
  See also CDBLB 1660-1789; DLB 39, 104
Snodgrass, W(illiam) D(e Witt) 1926- **CLC 2,
  6, 10, 18, 68; DAM POET**
  See also CA 1-4R; CANR 6, 36, 65; DLB 5;
    MTCW 1, 2
Snow, C(harles) P(ercy) 1905-1980 **CLC 1, 4,
  6, 9, 13, 19; DAM NOV**
  See also CA 5-8R; 101; CANR 28; CDBLB
    1945-1960; DLB 15, 77; DLBD 17; MTCW
    1, 2
Snow, Frances Compton
  See Adams, Henry (Brooks)
Snyder, Gary (Sherman) 1930- **CLC 1, 2, 5, 9,
  32, 120; DAM POET; PC 21**
  See also CA 17-20R; CANR 30, 60; DLB 5,
    16, 165, 212; MTCW 2
Snyder, Zilpha Keatley 1927- .... **CLC 17**
  See also AAYA 15; CA 9-12R; CANR 38; CLR
    31; JRDA; MAICYA; SAAS 2; SATA 1, 28,
    75
Soares, Bernardo
  See Pessoa, Fernando (Antonio Nogueira)
Sobh, A.
  See Shamlu, Ahmad
Sobol, Joshua .... **CLC 60**
Socrates 469B.C.-399B.C. .... **CMLC 27**
Soderberg, Hjalmar 1869-1941 ..... **TCLC 39**
Sodergran, Edith (Irene)
  See Soedergran, Edith (Irene)
Soedergran, Edith (Irene) 1892-1923 . **T C L C
  31**
Softly, Edgar
  See Lovecraft, H(oward) P(hillips)
Softly, Edward
  See Lovecraft, H(oward) P(hillips)
Sokolov, Raymond 1941- .... **CLC 7**
  See also CA 85-88
Solo, Jay
  See Ellison, Harlan (Jay)
Sologub, Fyodor .... **TCLC 9**
  See also Teternikov, Fyodor Kuzmich
Solomons, Ikey Esquir
  See Thackeray, William Makepeace
Solomos, Dionysios 1798-1857 .... **NCLC 15**
Solwoska, Mara
  See French, Marilyn

Solzhenitsyn, Aleksandr I(sayevich) 1918-
  **CLC 1, 2, 4, 7, 9, 10, 18, 26, 34, 78; DA;
  DAB; DAC; DAM MST, NOV; SSC 32;
  WLC**
  See also AITN 1; CA 69-72; CANR 40, 65;
    MTCW 1, 2
Somers, Jane
  See Lessing, Doris (May)
Somerville, Edith 1858-1949 .... **TCLC 51**
  See also DLB 135
Somerville & Ross
  See Martin, Violet Florence; Somerville, Edith
Sommer, Scott 1951- .... **CLC 25**
  See also CA 106
Sondheim, Stephen (Joshua) 1930- **CLC 30,
  39; DAM DRAM**
  See also AAYA 11; CA 103; CANR 47, 68
Song, Cathy 1955- .... **PC 21**
  See also CA 154; DLB 169
Sontag, Susan 1933- **CLC 1, 2, 10, 13, 31, 105;
  DAM POP**
  See also CA 17-20R; CANR 25, 51, 74; DLB
    2, 67; MTCW 1, 2
Sophocles 496(?)B.C.-406(?)B.C. .. **CMLC 2;
  DA; DAB; DAC; DAM DRAM, MST; DC
  1; WLCS**
  See also DLB 176
Sordello 1189-1269 .... **CMLC 15**
Sorel, Georges 1847-1922 .... **TCLC 91**
  See also CA 118
Sorel, Julia
  See Drexler, Rosalyn
Sorrentino, Gilbert 1929- **CLC 3, 7, 14, 22, 40**
  See also CA 77-80; CANR 14, 33; DLB 5, 173;
    DLBY 80; INT CANR-14
Soto, Gary 1952- . **CLC 32, 80; DAM MULT;
  HLC**
  See also AAYA 10; CA 119; 125; CANR 50,
    74; CLR 38; DLB 82; HW 1, 2; INT 125;
    JRDA; MTCW 2; SATA 80
Soupault, Philippe 1897-1990 .... **CLC 68**
  See also CA 116; 147; 131
Souster, (Holmes) Raymond 1921- **CLC 5, 14;
  DAC; DAM POET**
  See also CA 13-16R; CAAS 14; CANR 13, 29,
    53; DLB 88; SATA 63
Southern, Terry 1924(?)-1995 .... **CLC 7**
  See also CA 1-4R; 150; CANR 1, 55; DLB 2
Southey, Robert 1774-1843 .... **NCLC 8**
  See also DLB 93, 107, 142; SATA 54
Southworth, Emma Dorothy Eliza Nevitte
  1819-1899 .... **NCLC 26**
Souza, Ernest
  See Scott, Evelyn
Soyinka, Wole 1934- **CLC 3, 5, 14, 36, 44; BLC
  3; DA; DAB; DAC; DAM DRAM, MST,
  MULT; DC 2; WLC**
  See also BW 2, 3; CA 13-16R; CANR 27, 39;
    DLB 125; MTCW 1, 2
Spackman, W(illiam) M(ode) 1905-1990 **C L C
  46**
  See also CA 81-84; 132
Spacks, Barry (Bernard) 1931- .... **CLC 14**
  See also CA 154; CANR 33; DLB 105
Spanidou, Irini 1946- .... **CLC 44**
Spark, Muriel (Sarah) 1918- **CLC 2, 3, 5, 8, 13,
  18, 40, 94; DAB; DAC; DAM MST, NOV;
  SSC 10**
  See also CA 5-8R; CANR 12, 36, 76; CDBLB
    1945-1960; DLB 15, 139; INT CANR-12;
    MTCW 1, 2
Spaulding, Douglas
  See Bradbury, Ray (Douglas)

See also CA 9-12R; CANR 7, 38, 60; DLB 5
Van Dyne, Edith
  See Baum, L(yman) Frank
van Itallie, Jean-Claude 1936- .... **CLC 3**
  See also CA 45-48; CAAS 2; CANR 1, 48; DLB 7
van Ostaijen, Paul 1896-1928 .... **TCLC 33**
  See also CA 163
Van Peebles, Melvin 1932-. **CLC 2, 20; DAM MULT**
  See also BW 2, 3; CA 85-88; CANR 27, 67
Vansittart, Peter 1920- .... **CLC 42**
  See also CA 1-4R; CANR 3, 49
Van Vechten, Carl 1880-1964 .... **CLC 33**
  See also CA 89-92; DLB 4, 9, 51
Van Vogt, A(lfred) E(lton) 1912-......... **CLC 1**
  See also CA 21-24R; CANR 28; DLB 8; SATA 14
Varda, Agnes 1928- .... **CLC 16**
  See also CA 116; 122
Vargas Llosa, (Jorge) Mario (Pedro) 1936-
  CLC 3, 6, 9, 10, 15, 31, 42, 85; DA; DAB; DAC; DAM MST, MULT, NOV; HLC
  See also CA 73-76; CANR 18, 32, 42, 67; DLB 145; HW 1, 2; MTCW 1, 2
Vasiliu, Gheorghe 1881-1957
  See Bacovia, George
  See also CA 123
Vassa, Gustavus
  See Equiano, Olaudah
Vassilikos, Vassilis 1933- .... **CLC 4, 8**
  See also CA 81-84; CANR 75
Vaughan, Henry 1621-1695 .... **LC 27**
  See also DLB 131
Vaughn, Stephanie .... **CLC 62**
Vazov, Ivan (Minchov) 1850-1921 . **TCLC 25**
  See also CA 121; 167; DLB 147
Veblen, Thorstein B(unde) 1857-1929 **T C L C 31**
  See also CA 115; 165
Vega, Lope de 1562-1635 ..... **LC 23; HLCS 2**
Venison, Alfred
  See Pound, Ezra (Weston Loomis)
Verdi, Marie de
  See Mencken, H(enry) L(ouis)
Verdu, Matilde
  See Cela, Camilo Jose
Verga, Giovanni (Carmelo) 1840-1922 **T C L C 3; SSC 21**
  See also CA 104; 123
Vergil 70B.C.-19B.C. .... **CMLC 9; DA; DAB; DAC; DAM MST, POET; PC 12; WLCS**
  See also Virgil
Verhaeren, Emile (Adolphe Gustave) 1855-1916 **TCLC 12**
  See also CA 109
Verlaine, Paul (Marie) 1844-1896**NCLC 2, 51; DAM POET; PC 2**
Verne, Jules (Gabriel) 1828-1905 **TCLC 6, 52**
  See also AAYA 16; CA 110; 131; DLB 123; JRDA; MAICYA; SATA 21
Very, Jones 1813-1880 .... **NCLC 9**
  See also DLB 1
Vesaas, Tarjei 1897-1970 .... **CLC 48**
  See also CA 29-32R
Vialis, Gaston
  See Simenon, Georges (Jacques Christian)
Vian, Boris 1920-1959 .... **TCLC 9**
  See also CA 106; 164; DLB 72; MTCW 2
Viaud, (Louis Marie) Julien 1850-1923
  See Loti, Pierre
  See also CA 107
  <indVicar, Henry

See Felsen, Henry Gregor
Vicker, Angus
  See Felsen, Henry Gregor
Vidal, Gore 1925-**CLC 2, 4, 6, 8, 10, 22, 33, 72; DAM NOV, POP**
  See also AITN 1; BEST 90:2; CA 5-8R; CANR 13, 45, 65; CDALBS; DLB 6, 152; INT CANR-13; MTCW 1, 2
Viereck, Peter (Robert Edwin) 1916- **CLC 4; PC 27**
  See also CA 1-4R; CANR 1, 47; DLB 5
Vigny, Alfred (Victor) de 1797-1863**NCLC 7; DAM POET; PC 26**
  See also DLB 119, 192
Vilakazi, Benedict Wallet 1906-1947**TCLC 37**
  See also CA 168
Villa, Jose Garcia 1904-1997 .... **PC 22**
  See also CA 25-28R; CANR 12
Villaurrutia, Xavier 1903-1950 ...... **TCLC 80**
  See also HW 1
Villiers de l'Isle Adam, Jean Marie Mathias Philippe Auguste, Comte de 1838-1889 **NCLC 3; SSC 14**
  See also DLB 123
Villon, Francois 1431-1463(?) .... **PC 13**
  See also DLB 208
Vinci, Leonardo da 1452-1519 .... **LC 12**
Vine, Barbara .... **CLC 50**
  See also Rendell, Ruth (Barbara)
  See also BEST 90:4
Vinge, Joan (Carol) D(ennison) 1948-**CLC 30; SSC 24**
  See also CA 93-96; CANR 72; SATA 36
Violis, G.
  See Simenon, Georges (Jacques Christian)
Virgil 70B.C.-19B.C.
  See Vergil
  See also DLB 211
Visconti, Luchino 1906-1976 .... **CLC 16**
  See also CA 81-84; 65-68; CANR 39
Vittorini, Elio 1908-1966 .... **CLC 6, 9, 14**
  See also CA 133; 25-28R
Vivekananda, Swami 1863-1902 .... **TCLC 88**
Vizenor, Gerald Robert 1934-**CLC 103; DAM MULT**
  See also CA 13-16R; CAAS 22; CANR 5, 21, 44, 67; DLB 175; MTCW 2; NNAL
Vizinczey, Stephen 1933- .... **CLC 40**
  See also CA 128; INT 128
Vliet, R(ussell) G(ordon) 1929-1984 . **CLC 22**
  See also CA 37-40R; 112; CANR 18
Vogau, Boris Andreyevich 1894-1937(?)
  See Pilnyak, Boris
  See also CA 123
Vogel, Paula A(nne) 1951- .... **CLC 76**
  See also CA 108
Voigt, Cynthia 1942- .... **CLC 30**
  See also AAYA 3, 30; CA 106; CANR 18, 37, 40; CLR 13, 48; INT CANR-18; JRDA; MAICYA; SATA 48, 79; SATA-Brief 33
Voigt, Ellen Bryant 1943- .... **CLC 54**
  See also CA 69-72; CANR 11, 29, 55; DLB 120
Voinovich, Vladimir (Nikolaevich) 1932-**CLC 10, 49**
  See also CA 81-84; CAAS 12; CANR 33, 67; MTCW 1
Vollmann, William T. 1959- .. **CLC 89; DAM NOV, POP**
  See also CA 134; CANR 67; MTCW 2
Voloshinov, V. N.
  See Bakhtin, Mikhail Mikhailovich
Voltaire 1694-1778 **LC 14; DA; DAB; DAC; DAM DRAM, MST; SSC 12; WLC**

von Aschendrof, BaronIgnatz
  See Ford, Ford Madox
von Daeniken, Erich 1935- .... **CLC 30**
  See also AITN 1; CA 37-40R; CANR 17, 44
von Daniken, Erich
  See von Daeniken, Erich
von Heidenstam, (Carl Gustaf) Verner
  See Heidenstam, (Carl Gustaf) Verner von
von Heyse, Paul (Johann Ludwig)
  See Heyse, Paul (Johann Ludwig von)
von Hofmannsthal, Hugo
  See Hofmannsthal, Hugo von
von Horvath, Odon
  See Horvath, Oedoen von
von Horvath, Oedoen
  See Horvath, Oedoen von
von Liliencron, (Friedrich Adolf Axel) Detlev
  See Liliencron, (Friedrich Adolf Axel) Detlev von
Vonnegut, Kurt, Jr. 1922-**CLC 1, 2, 3, 4, 5, 8, 12, 22, 40, 60, 111; DA; DAB; DAC; DAM MST, NOV, POP; SSC 8; WLC**
  See also AAYA 6; AITN 1; BEST 90:4; CA 1-4R; CANR 1, 25, 49, 75; CDALB 1968-1988; DLB 2, 8, 152; DLBD 3; DLBY 80; MTCW 1, 2
Von Rachen, Kurt
  See Hubbard, L(afayette) Ron(ald)
von Rezzori (d'Arezzo), Gregor
  See Rezzori (d'Arezzo), Gregor von
von Sternberg, Josef
  See Sternberg, Josef von
Vorster, Gordon 1924- .... **CLC 34**
  See also CA 133
Vosce, Trudie
  See Ozick, Cynthia
Voznesensky, Andrei (Andreievich) 1933-
  CLC 1, 15, 57; DAM POET
  See also CA 89-92; CANR 37; MTCW 1
Waddington, Miriam 1917- .... **CLC 28**
  See also CA 21-24R; CANR 12, 30; DLB 68
Wagman, Fredrica 1937- .... **CLC 7**
  See also CA 97-100; INT 97-100
Wagner, Linda W.
  See Wagner-Martin, Linda (C.)
Wagner, Linda Welshimer
  See Wagner-Martin, Linda (C.)
Wagner, Richard 1813-1883 .... **NCLC 9**
  See also DLB 129
Wagner-Martin, Linda (C.) 1936- .... **CLC 50**
  See also CA 159
Wagoner, David (Russell) 1926- **CLC 3, 5, 15**
  See also CA 1-4R; CAAS 3; CANR 2, 71; DLB 5; SATA 14
Wah, Fred(erick James) 1939- .... **CLC 44**
  See also CA 107; 141; DLB 60
Wahloo, Per 1926-1975 .... **CLC 7**
  See also CA 61-64; CANR 73
Wahloo, Peter
  See Wahloo, Per
Wain, John (Barrington) 1925-1994 . **CLC 2, 11, 15, 46**
  See also CA 5-8R; 145; CAAS 4; CANR 23, 54; CDBLB 1960 to Present; DLB 15, 27, 139, 155; MTCW 1, 2
Wajda, Andrzej 1926- .... **CLC 16**
  See also CA 102
Wakefield, Dan 1932- .... **CLC 7**
  See also CA 21-24R; CAAS 7
Wakoski, Diane 1937-. **CLC 2, 4, 7, 9, 11, 40; DAM POET; PC 15**
  See also CA 13-16R; CAAS 1; CANR 9, 60; DLB 5; INT CANR-9; MTCW 2

Weinstein, Nathan
See West, Nathanael
Weinstein, Nathan von Wallenstein
See West, Nathanael
Weir, Peter (Lindsay) 1944- .... **CLC 20**
See also CA 113; 123
Weiss, Peter (Ulrich) 1916-1982**CLC 3, 15, 51;
DAM DRAM**
See also CA 45-48; 106; CANR 3; DLB 69, 124
Weiss, Theodore (Russell) 1916-**CLC 3, 8, 14**
See also CA 9-12R; CAAS 2; CANR 46; DLB 5
Welch, (Maurice) Denton 1915-1948**TCLC 22**
See also CA 121; 148
Welch, James 1940- ..... **CLC 6, 14, 52; DAM MULT, POP**
See also CA 85-88; CANR 42, 66; DLB 175; NNAL
Weldon, Fay 1931-..**CLC 6, 9, 11, 19, 36, 59; DAM POP**
See also CA 21-24R; CANR 16, 46, 63; CDBLB 1960 to Present; DLB 14, 194; INT CANR-16; MTCW 1, 2
Wellek, Rene 1903-1995 .... **CLC 28**
See also CA 5-8R; 150; CAAS 7; CANR 8; DLB 63; INT CANR-8
Weller, Michael 1942- .... **CLC 10, 53**
See also CA 85-88
Weller, Paul 1958- .... **CLC 26**
Wellershoff, Dieter 1925- .... **CLC 46**
See also CA 89-92; CANR 16, 37
Welles, (George) Orson 1915-1985**CLC 20, 80**
See also CA 93-96; 117
Wellman, John McDowell 1945-
See Wellman, Mac
See also CA 166
Wellman, Mac 1945- .... **CLC 65**
See also Wellman, John McDowell; Wellman, John McDowell
Wellman, Manly Wade 1903-1986 ... **CLC 49**
See also CA 1-4R; 118; CANR 6, 16, 44; SATA 6; SATA-Obit 47
Wells, Carolyn 1869(?)-1942 .... **TCLC 35**
See also CA 113; DLB 11
Wells, H(erbert) G(eorge) 1866-1946**TCLC 6, 12, 19; DA; DAB; DAC; DAM MST, NOV; SSC 6; WLC**
See also AAYA 18; CA 110; 121; CDBLB 1914-1945; DLB 34, 70, 156, 178; MTCW 1, 2; SATA 20
Wells, Rosemary 1943-...................... **CLC 12**
See also AAYA 13; CA 85-88; CANR 48; CLR 16; MAICYA; SAAS 1; SATA 18, 69
Welty, Eudora 1909- **CLC 1, 2, 5, 14, 22, 33, 105; DA; DAB; DAC; DAM MST, NOV; SSC 1, 27; WLC**
See also CA 9-12R; CABS 1; CANR 32, 65; CDALB 1941-1968; DLB 2, 102, 143; DLBD 12; DLBY 87; MTCW 1, 2
Wen I-to 1899-1946 .... **TCLC 28**
Wentworth, Robert
See Hamilton, Edmond
Werfel, Franz (Viktor) 1890-1945 ... **TCLC 8**
See also CA 104; 161; DLB 81, 124
Wergeland, Henrik Arnold 1808-1845**N C L C 5**
Wersba, Barbara 1932-..................... **CLC 30**
See also AAYA 2, 30; CA 29-32R; CANR 16, 38; CLR 3; DLB 52; JRDA; MAICYA; SAAS 2; SATA 1, 58; SATA-Essay 103
Wertmueller, Lina 1928- .... **CLC 16**
See also CA 97-100; CANR 39, 78
Wescott, Glenway 1901-1987**CLC 13; SSC 35**

See also CA 13-16R; 121; CANR 23, 70; DLB 4, 9, 102
Wesker, Arnold 1932-.... **CLC 3, 5, 42; DAB; DAM DRAM**
See also CA 1-4R; CAAS 7; CANR 1, 33; CDBLB 1960 to Present; DLB 13; MTCW 1
Wesley, Richard (Errol) 1945- .... **CLC 7**
See also BW 1; CA 57-60; CANR 27; DLB 38
Wessel, Johan Herman 1742-1785 .... **LC 7**
West, Anthony (Panther) 1914-1987 **CLC 50**
See also CA 45-48; 124; CANR 3, 19; DLB 15
West, C. P.
See Wodehouse, P(elham) G(renville)
West, (Mary) Jessamyn 1902-1984**CLC 7, 17**
See also CA 9-12R; 112; CANR 27; DLB 6; DLBY 84; MTCW 1, 2; SATA-Obit 37
West, Morris L(anglo) 1916- .... **CLC 6, 33**
See also CA 5-8R; CANR 24, 49, 64; MTCW 1, 2
West, Nathanael 1903-1940 **TCLC 1, 14, 44; SSC 16**
See also CA 104; 125; CDALB 1929-1941; DLB 4, 9, 28; MTCW 1, 2
West, Owen
See Koontz, Dean R(ay)
West, Paul 1930- .... **CLC 7, 14, 96**
See also CA 13-16R; CAAS 7; CANR 22, 53, 76; DLB 14; INT CANR-22; MTCW 2
West, Rebecca 1892-1983 ... **CLC 7, 9, 31, 50**
See also CA 5-8R; 109; CANR 19; DLB 36; DLBY 83; MTCW 1, 2
Westall, Robert (Atkinson) 1929-1993**CLC 17**
See also AAYA 12; CA 69-72; 141; CANR 18, 68; CLR 13; JRDA; MAICYA; SAAS 2; SATA 23, 69; SATA-Obit 75
Westermarck, Edward 1862-1939 . **TCLC 87**
Westlake, Donald E(dwin) 1933- **CLC 7, 33; DAM POP**
See also CA 17-20R; CAAS 13; CANR 16, 44, 65; INT CANR-16; MTCW 2
Westmacott, Mary
See Christie, Agatha (Mary Clarissa)
Weston, Allen
See Norton, Andre
Wetcheek, J. L.
See Feuchtwanger, Lion
Wetering, Janwillem van de
See van de Wetering, Janwillem
Wetherald, Agnes Ethelwyn 1857-1940**T C L C 81**
See also DLB 99
Wetherell, Elizabeth
See Warner, Susan (Bogert)
Whale, James 1889-1957 .... **TCLC 63**
Whalen, Philip 1923-..................... **CLC 6, 29**
See also CA 9-12R; CANR 5, 39; DLB 16
Wharton, Edith (Newbold Jones) 1862-1937 **TCLC 3, 9, 27, 53; DA; DAB; DAC; DAM MST, NOV; SSC 6; WLC**
See also AAYA 25; CA 104; 132; CDALB 1865-1917; DLB 4, 9, 12, 78, 189; DLBD 13; MTCW 1, 2
Wharton, James
See Mencken, H(enry) L(ouis)
Wharton, William (a pseudonym)CLC 18, 37
See also CA 93-96; DLBY 80; INT 93-96
Wheatley (Peters), Phillis 1754(?)-1784**LC 3, 50; BLC 3; DA; DAC; DAM MST, MULT, POET; PC 3; WLC**
See also CDALB 1640-1865; DLB 31, 50
Wheelock, John Hall 1886-1978 .... **CLC 14**
See also CA 13-16R; 77-80; CANR 14; DLB 45

White, E(lwyn) B(rooks) 1899-1985 **CLC 10, 34, 39; DAM POP**
See also AITN 2; CA 13-16R; 116; CANR 16, 37; CDALBS; CLR 1, 21; DLB 11, 22; MAICYA; MTCW 1, 2; SATA 2, 29, 100; SATA-Obit 44
White, Edmund (Valentine III) 1940-**CLC 27, 110; DAM POP**
See also AAYA 7; CA 45-48; CANR 3, 19, 36, 62; MTCW 1, 2
White, Patrick (Victor Martindale) 1912-1990 **CLC 3, 4, 5, 7, 9, 18, 65, 69**
See also CA 81-84; 132; CANR 43; MTCW 1
White, Phyllis Dorothy James 1920-
See James, P. D.
See also CA 21-24R; CANR 17, 43, 65; DAM POP; MTCW 1, 2
White, T(erence) H(anbury) 1906-1964 **C L C 30**
See also AAYA 22; CA 73-76; CANR 37; DLB 160; JRDA; MAICYA; SATA 12
White, Terence de Vere 1912-1994 ...**CLC 49**
See also CA 49-52; 145; CANR 3
White, Walter
See White, Walter F(rancis)
See also BLC; DAM MULT
White, Walter F(rancis) 1893-1955 **TCLC 15**
See also White, Walter
See also BW 1; CA 115; 124; DLB 51
White, William Hale 1831-1913
See Rutherford, Mark
See also CA 121
Whitehead, E(dward) A(nthony) 1933-**CLC 5**
See also CA 65-68; CANR 58
Whitemore, Hugh (John) 1936- ....**CLC 37**
See also CA 132; CANR 77; INT 132
Whitman, Sarah Helen (Power) 1803-1878 **NCLC 19**
See also DLB 1
Whitman, Walt(er) 1819-1892 . **NCLC 4, 31; DA; DAB; DAC; DAM MST, POET; PC 3; WLC**
See also CDALB 1640-1865; DLB 3, 64; SATA 20
Whitney, Phyllis A(yame) 1903- ..... **CLC 42; DAM POP**
See also AITN 2; BEST 90:3; CA 1-4R; CANR 3, 25, 38, 60; CLR 59; JRDA; MAICYA; MTCW 2; SATA 1, 30
Whittemore, (Edward) Reed (Jr.) 1919-**CLC 4**
See also CA 9-12R; CAAS 8; CANR 4; DLB 5
Whittier, John Greenleaf 1807-1892**NCLC 8, 59**
See also DLB 1
Whittlebot, Hernia
See Coward, Noel (Peirce)
Wicker, Thomas Grey 1926-
See Wicker, Tom
See also CA 65-68; CANR 21, 46
Wicker, Tom ....CLC 7
See also Wicker, Thomas Grey
Wideman, John Edgar 1941- **CLC 5, 34, 36, 67; BLC 3; DAM MULT**
See also BW 2, 3; CA 85-88; CANR 14, 42, 67; DLB 33, 143; MTCW 2
Wiebe, Rudy (Henry) 1934- .. **CLC 6, 11, 14; DAC; DAM MST**
See also CA 37-40R; CANR 42, 67; DLB 60
Wieland, Christoph Martin 1733-1813**N C L C 17**
See also DLB 97
Wiene, Robert 1881-1938 .... **TCLC 56**
Wieners, John 1934-............................**CLC 7**

Wodehouse, P(elham) G(renville) 1881-1975
**CLC 1, 2, 5, 10, 22; DAB; DAC; DAM
NOV; SSC 2**
See also AITN 2; CA 45-48; 57-60; CANR 3,
33; CDBLB 1914-1945; DLB 34, 162;
MTCW 1, 2; SATA 22

Woiwode, L.
See Woiwode, Larry (Alfred)

Woiwode, Larry (Alfred) 1941- ... **CLC 6, 10**
See also CA 73-76; CANR 16; DLB 6; INT
CANR-16

Wojciechowska, Maia (Teresa) 1927-**CLC 26**
See also AAYA 8; CA 9-12R; CANR 4, 41; CLR
1; JRDA; MAICYA; SAAS 1; SATA 1, 28,
83; SATA-Essay 104

Wolf, Christa 1929- .... **CLC 14, 29, 58**
<indeSee also CA 85-88; CANR 45; DLB 75;
MTCW 1

Wolfe, Gene (Rodman) 1931- **CLC 25; DAM
POP**
See also CA 57-60; CAAS 9; CANR 6, 32, 60;
DLB 8; MTCW 2

Wolfe, George C. 1954- .... **CLC 49; BLCS**
See also CA 149

Wolfe, Thomas (Clayton) 1900-1938**TCLC 4,
13, 29, 61; DA; DAB; DAC; DAM MST,
NOV; SSC 33; WLC**
See also CA 104; 132; CDALB 1929-1941;
DLB 9, 102; DLBD 2, 16; DLBY 85, 97;
MTCW 1, 2

Wolfe, Thomas Kennerly, Jr. 1930-
See Wolfe, Tom
See also CA 13-16R; CANR 9, 33, 70; DAM
POP; DLB 185; INT CANR-9; MTCW 1, 2

Wolfe, Tom .... **CLC 1, 2, 9, 15, 35, 51**
See also Wolfe, Thomas Kennerly, Jr.
See also AAYA 8; AITN 2; BEST 89:1; DLB
152

Wolff, Geoffrey (Ansell) 1937- .... **CLC 41**
See also CA 29-32R; CANR 29, 43, 78

Wolff, Sonia
See Levitin, Sonia (Wolff)

Wolff, Tobias (Jonathan Ansell) 1945- .. **C L C
39, 64**
See also AAYA 16; BEST 90:2; CA 114; 117;
CAAS 22; CANR 54, 76; DLB 130; INT 117;
MTCW 2

Wolfram von Eschenbach c. 1170-c. 1220
CMLC 5
See also DLB 138

Wolitzer, Hilma 1930- .... **CLC 17**
See also CA 65-68; CANR 18, 40; INT CANR-
18; SATA 31

Wollstonecraft, Mary 1759-1797 .... **LC 5, 50**
See also CDBLB 1789-1832; DLB 39, 104, 158

Wonder, Stevie .... **CLC 12**
See also Morris, Steveland Judkins

Wong, Jade Snow 1922- .... **CLC 17**
See also CA 109

Woodberry, George Edward 1855-1930
TCLC 73
See also CA 165; DLB 71, 103

Woodcott, Keith
See Brunner, John (Kilian Houston)

Woodruff, Robert W.
See Mencken, H(enry) L(ouis)

Woolf, (Adeline) Virginia 1882-1941**TCLC 1,
5, 20, 43, 56; DA; DAB; DAC; DAM MST,
NOV; SSC 7; WLC**
See also Woolf, Virginia Adeline
See also CA 104; 130; CANR 64; CDBLB
1914-1945; DLB 36, 100, 162; DLBD 10;
MTCW 1

Woolf, Virginia Adeline
See Woolf, (Adeline) Virginia
See also MTCW 2

Woollcott, Alexander (Humphreys) 1887-1943
TCLC 5
See also CA 105; 161; DLB 29

Woolrich, Cornell 1903-1968 .... **CLC 77**
See also Hopley-Woolrich, Cornell George

Wordsworth, Dorothy 1771-1855 .. **NCLC 25**
See also DLB 107

Wordsworth, William 1770-1850 .. **NCLC 12,
38; DA; DAB; DAC; DAM MST, POET;
PC 4; WLC**
See also CDBLB 1789-1832; DLB 93, 107

Wouk, Herman 1915-**CLC 1, 9, 38; DAM NOV,
POP**
See also CA 5-8R; CANR 6, 33, 67; CDALBS;
DLBY 82; INT CANR-6; MTCW 1, 2

Wright, Charles (Penzel, Jr.) 1935-**CLC 6, 13,
28, 119**
See also CA 29-32R; CAAS 7; CANR 23, 36,
62; DLB 165; DLBY 82; MTCW 1, 2

Wright, Charles Stevenson 1932- ... **CLC 49;
BLC 3; DAM MULT, POET**
See also BW 1; CA 9-12R; CANR 26; DLB 33

Wright, Frances 1795-1852 .... **NCLC 74**
See also DLB 73

Wright, Frank Lloyd 1867-1959 .... **TCLC 95**
See also CA 174

Wright, Jack R.
See Harris, Mark

Wright, James (Arlington) 1927-1980**CLC 3,
5, 10, 28; DAM POET**
See also AITN 2; CA 49-52; 97-100; CANR 4,
34, 64; CDALBS; DLB 5, 169; MTCW 1, 2

Wright, Judith (Arandell) 1915- **CLC 11, 53;
PC 14**
See also CA 13-16R; CANR 31, 76; MTCW 1,
2; SATA 14

Wright, L(aurali) R. 1939- .... **CLC 44**
See also CA 138

Wright, Richard (Nathaniel) 1908-1960 **C L C
1, 3, 4, 9, 14, 21, 48, 74; BLC 3; DA; DAB;
DAC; DAM MST, MULT, NOV; SSC 2;
WLC**
See also AAYA 5; BW 1; CA 108; CANR 64;
CDALB 1929-1941; DLB 76, 102; DLBD
2; MTCW 1, 2

Wright, Richard B(ruce) 1937- .... **CLC 6**
See also CA 85-88; DLB 53

Wright, Rick 1945- .... **CLC 35**

Wright, Rowland
See Wells, Carolyn

Wright, Stephen 1946- .... **CLC 33**

Wright, Willard Huntington 1888-1939
See Van Dine, S. S.
See also CA 115; DLBD 16

Wright, William 1930- .... **CLC 44**
See also CA 53-56; CANR 7, 23

Wroth, LadyMary 1587-1653(?) .... **LC 30**
See also DLB 121

Wu Ch'eng-en 1500(?)-1582(?) .... **LC 7**

Wu Ching-tzu 1701-1754 .... **LC 2**

Wurlitzer, Rudolph 1938(?)- .... **CLC 2, 4, 15**
See also CA 85-88; DLB 173

Wyatt, Thomas c. 1503-1542 .... **PC 27**
See also DLB 132

Wycherley, William 1641-1715**LC 8, 21; DAM
DRAM**
See also CDBLB 1660-1789; DLB 80

Wylie, Elinor (Morton Hoyt) 1885-1928
TCLC 8; PC 23
See also CA 105; 162; DLB 9, 45

Wylie, Philip (Gordon) 1902-1971 .... **CLC 43**
See also CA 21-22; 33-36R; CAP 2; DLB 9

Wyndham, John .... **CLC 19**
See also Harris, John (Wyndham Parkes Lucas)
Beynon

Wyss, Johann David Von 1743-1818**NCLC 10**
See also JRDA; MAICYA; SATA 29; SATA-
Brief 27

Xenophon c. 430B.C.-c. 354B.C. ... **CMLC 17**
See also DLB 176

Yakumo Koizumi
See Hearn, (Patricio) Lafcadio (Tessima Carlos)

Yamamoto, Hisaye 1921-**SSC 34; DAM MULT**

Yanez, Jose Donoso
See Donoso (Yanez), Jose

Yanovsky, Basile S.
See Yanovsky, V(assily) S(emenovich)

Yanovsky, V(assily) S(emenovich) 1906-1989
CLC 2, 18
See also CA 97-100; 129

Yates, Richard 1926-1992 .... **CLC 7, 8, 23**
See also CA 5-8R; 139; CANR 10, 43; DLB 2;
DLBY 81, 92; INT CANR-10

Yeats, W. B.
See Yeats, William Butler

Yeats, William Butler 1865-1939**TCLC 1, 11,
18, 31, 93; DA; DAB; DAC; DAM DRAM,
MST, POET; PC 20; WLC**
See also CA 104; 127; CANR 45; CDBLB
1890-1914; DLB 10, 19, 98, 156; MTCW 1,
2

Yehoshua, A(braham) B. 1936- .. **CLC 13, 31**
See also CA 33-36R; CANR 43

Yep, Laurence Michael 1948- .... **CLC 35**
See also AAYA 5; CA 49-52; CANR 1, 46; CLR
3, 17, 54; DLB 52; JRDA; MAICYA; SATA
7, 69

Yerby, Frank G(arvin) 1916-1991 **CLC 1, 7,
22; BLC 3; DAM MULT**
See also BW 1, 3; CA 9-12R; 136; CANR 16,
52; DLB 76; INT CANR-16; MTCW 1

Yesenin, Sergei Alexandrovich
See Esenin, Sergei (Alexandrovich)

Yevtushenko, Yevgeny (Alexandrovich) 1933-
CLC 1, 3, 13, 26, 51; DAM POET
See also CA 81-84; CANR 33, 54; MTCW 1

Yezierska, Anzia 1885(?)-1970 .... **CLC 46**
See also CA 126; 89-92; DLB 28; MTCW 1

Yglesias, Helen 1915- .... **CLC 7, 22**
See also CA 37-40R; CAAS 20; CANR 15, 65;
INT CANR-15; MTCW 1

Yokomitsu Riichi 1898-1947 .... **TCLC 47**
See also CA 170

Yonge, Charlotte (Mary) 1823-1901**TCLC 48**
See also CA 109; 163; DLB 18, 163; SATA 17

York, Jeremy
See Creasey, John

York, Simon
See Heinlein, Robert A(nson)

Yorke, Henry Vincent 1905-1974 ...... **CLC 13**
See also Green, Henry
See also CA 85-88; 49-52

Yosano Akiko 1878-1942 .... **TCLC 59; PC 11**
See also CA 161

Yoshimoto, Banana .... **CLC 84**
See also Yoshimoto, Mahoko

Yoshimoto, Mahoko 1964-
See Yoshimoto, Banana
See also CA 144

Young, Al(bert James) 1939-**CLC 19; BLC 3;
DAM MULT**
See also BW 2, 3; CA 29-32R; CANR 26, 65;
DLB 33

Young, Andrew (John) 1885-1971 ...... **CLC 5**
 See also CA 5-8R; CANR 7, 29
Young, Collier
 See Bloch, Robert (Albert)
Young, Edward 1683-1765 .... **LC 3, 40**
 See also DLB 95
Young, Marguerite (Vivian) 1909-1995 **C L C 82**
 See also CA 13-16; 150; CAP 1
Young, Neil 1945- .... **CLC 17**
 See also CA 110
Young Bear, Ray A. 1950- ..... **CLC 94; DAM MULT**
 See also CA 146; DLB 175; NNAL
Yourcenar, Marguerite 1903-1987**CLC 19, 38, 50, 87; DAM NOV**
 See also CA 69-72; CANR 23, 60; DLB 72; DLBY 88; MTCW 1, 2
Yurick, Sol 1925- ....**CLC 6**
 See also CA 13-16R; CANR 25
Zabolotsky, Nikolai Alekseevich 1903-1958 **TCLC 52**
 See also CA 116; 164
Zamiatin, Yevgenii
 See Zamyatin, Evgeny Ivanovich
Zamora, Bernice (B. Ortiz) 1938- .. **CLC 89; DAM MULT; HLC**
 See also CA 151; CANR 80; DLB 82; HW 1, 2
Zamyatin, Evgeny Ivanovich 1884-1937 **TCLC 8, 37**
 See also CA 105; 166
Zangwill, Israel 1864-1926 .... **TCLC 16**
 See also CA 109; 167; DLB 10, 135, 197
Zappa, Francis Vincent, Jr. 1940-1993
 See Zappa, Frank
 See also CA 108; 143; CANR 57
Zappa, Frank .... **CLC 17**
 See also Zappa, Francis Vincent, Jr.
Zaturenska, Marya 1902-1982 ...... **CLC 6, 11**
 See also CA 13-16R; 105; CANR 22
Zeami 1363-1443 .... **DC 7**
Zelazny, Roger (Joseph) 1937-1995 **CLC 21**
 See also AAYA 7; CA 21-24R; 148; CANR 26, 60; DLB 8; MTCW 1, 2; SATA 57; SATA-Brief 39
Zhdanov, Andrei Alexandrovich 1896-1948 **TCLC 18**
 See also CA 117; 167
Zhukovsky, Vasily (Andreevich) 1783-1852 **NCLC 35**
 See also DLB 205
Ziegenhagen, Eric .... **CLC 55**
Zimmer, Jill Schary
 See Robinson, Jill
Zimmerman, Robert
 See Dylan, Bob
Zindel, Paul 1936-**CLC 6, 26; DA; DAB; DAC; DAM DRAM, MST, NOV; DC 5**
 See also AAYA 2; CA 73-76; CANR 31, 65; CDALBS; CLR 3, 45; DLB 7, 52; JRDA; MAICYA; MTCW 1, 2; SATA 16, 58, 102
Zinov'Ev, A. A.
 See Zinoviev, Alexander (Aleksandrovich)
Zinoviev, Alexander (Aleksandrovich) 1922- **CLC 19**
 See also CA 116; 133; CAAS 10
Zoilus
 See Lovecraft, H(oward) P(hillips)
Zola, Emile (Edouard Charles Antoine) 1840-1902**TCLC 1, 6, 21, 41; DA; DAB; DAC; DAM MST, NOV; WLC**
 See also CA 104; 138; DLB 123
Zoline, Pamela 1941- .... **CLC 62**

 See also CA 161
Zorrilla y Moral, Jose 1817-1893 .... **NCLC 6**
Zoshchenko, Mikhail (Mikhailovich) 1895-1958 **TCLC 15; SSC 15**
 See also CA 115; 160
Zuckmayer, Carl 1896-1977 .... **CLC 18**
 See also CA 69-72; DLB 56, 124
Zuk, Georges
 See Skelton, Robin
Zukofsky, Louis 1904-1978**CLC 1, 2, 4, 7, 11, 18; DAM POET; PC 11**
 See also CA 9-12R; 77-80; CANR 39; DLB 5, 165; MTCW 1
Zweig, Paul 1935-1984 .... **CLC 34, 42**
 See also CA 85-88; 113
Zweig, Stefan 1881-1942 .... **TCLC 17**
 See also CA 112; 170; DLB 81, 118
Zwingli, Huldreich 1484-1531 .... **LC 37**
 See also DLB 179

Literary Criticism Series
Cumulative Topic Index

This index lists all topic entries in Gale's *Classical and Medieval Literature Criticism, Contemporary Literary Criticism, Literature Criticism from 1400 to 1800, Nineteenth-Century Literature Criticism,* and *Twentieth-Century Literary Criticism.*

Topic Index

Topic Index

NCLC Cumulative Nationality Index

Nationality Index